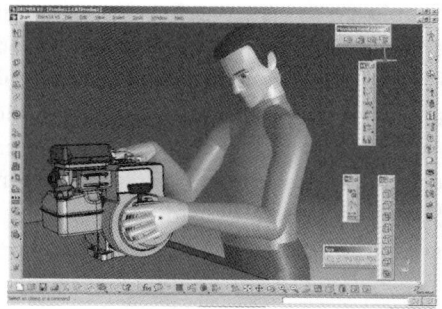

2006 edition

Profiles of Engineering
& Engineering Technology **Colleges**

Published 2007 by the American Society for Engineering Education (ASEE)

Address all inquiries concerning this book to:

Publications Department
1818 N Street, NW
Suite 600
Washington, DC 20036
USA
Telephone: (202) 331-3500

ISBN# 0-87823-192-7

Data Compiled by Michael T. Gibbons; Director of Data Research, The American Society for Engineering Education

Printed in the United States of America

Methodology

Using the Directory

Engineering Education By the Numbers

Statistical Tables

College Profiles

Indexes

The American Society for Engineering Education is a non-profit association of more than 12,000 engineering faculty members, U.S. and Canadian colleges of engineering and engineering technology, corporations, and other organizations dedicated to promoting excellence in engineering and engineering technology education. ASEE, which celebrated its centennial in 1993, plays a key role in developing and promoting policies that will enable engineering education to work with allied branches of science and technology to meet the new challenges of global competition and changing demographics.

Mission Statement

The American Society for Engineering Education is committed to furthering education in engineering and engineering technology. This mission is accomplished by promoting excellence in instruction, research, public service, and practice; exercising worldwide leadership; fostering the technological education of society; and providing quality products and services to members.

The Society seeks to encourage local, national, and international communication and collaboaration; influence corporate and government policies and involvement; promote professional interaction and lifelong learning; utilize effectively the Society's human and other resources; recognize outstanding contributions of individuals and organizations; encourage youth to pursue studies and careers in engineering and engineering technology; and influence the recruitment and retention of young faculty and underrepresented groups.

Vision Statement

ASEE will serve as the premier multidisciplinary society for individuals and organizations committed to advancing excellence in all aspects of engineering and engineering technology education.

ASEE Goals

To realize its vision, ASEE will:

- Enhance services to its members
- Work with educational institutions to improve engineering education and promote faculty development
- Facilitate productive collaborations among industry, academe, professional societies, and government
- Enhance the participation and success of underrepresented groups in the engineering enterprise
- Promote the value of the engineering profession to society
- Increase membership in ASEE in order to more completely serve the engineering and engineering technology enterprise

ASEE Board of Directors, 2006-07

David N. Wormley (2007), President
Pennsylvania State University

James L. Mesa (2007), President Elect
Iowa State University

Ronald E. Barr (2007) , Immediate Past President
University of Texas–Austin

Joseph T. O'Brien (2007), Vice President, Finance
Hewlett-Packard Company

J.P. Mohsen (2008), Vice President, Member Affairs
University of Louisville

ALbert L. McHenry (2007), Vice President, Public Affairs
Arizona State University East

Ray E. Morrison (2007), Chair, Corporate Member Council
Lockheed Martin Aeronautics Company

Paul S. Peercy (2007), Chair, Engineering Deans Council
University of Wisconsin - Madison

David M. Woodall (2007), Chair, Engineering Research Council
Oregon Institute of Technology

Walter W. Buchanan (2008), Chair, Engineering Technology Council
Texas A&M University

John S. Lamancusa (2008), Chair, Professional Interest Council I
Pennsylvania State University

Gary R. Crossman (2007), Chair, Professional Interest Council II
Old Dominion University

Shirley B. Pomeranz (2007), Chair, Professional Interest Council III
University of Tulsa

Mary R. Anderson-Rowland (2008), Chair, Professional Interest Council IV
Arizona State University

David H. Quick (2008) Chair, Professional Interest Council V
Rolls–Royce

Nelson A. Macken (2007), Chair, Council of Sections, Zone I
Swarthmore College

John J. Uhran, Jr. (2008), Chair, Council of Sections, Zone II
University of Notre Dame

Amir Karimi (2007), Chair, Council of Sections, Zone III
University of Texas at San Antonio

Jane M. Fraser (2008), Chair, Council of Sections, Zone IV
Colorado State University - Pueblo

Frank L. Huband, Executive Director
American Society for Engineering Education

ASEE's data collection process for the 2006 Edition of *Profiles of Engineering and Engineering Technology Colleges* began on September 18, 2006 and concluded on February 28, 2007. The five- month process was conducted in three phases. Between September 18, 2006 and December 31, 2007, participating institutions entered their data on ASEE's Web-based survey. During the second phase, January 2, 2007 through January 31, 2007, ASEE instituted quality control procedures, which included comparing data to that entered in previous years and contacting schools about questionable data. During the third, overlapping phase, January 22 through February 28, participating institutions were asked to verify their data using ASEE's Web-based data verification procedure. Although ASEE has made every effort to ensure that the information is correct, each institution is ultimately responsible for the accuracy of its data.

ASEE collected data from two academic years for this publication. Degrees awarded were collected for the July 1, 2005 to June 30, 2006 academic year. Research expenditures were collected for the fiscal year ending in 2006. All other information was collected for Fall 2006.

Totals are compiled based on discipline rather than department or degree program. This method allows us to track broader trends. For more exact views of each school's department and degree data, please refer to the individual web profiles located at www.asee.org/publications/colleges. Thirteen universities with ABET-accredited programs did not participate in the ASEE survey. The non-participating institutions are as follows:

The American University in Cario
Baker College
California Maritime Academy
Central State University
Dordt College
Geneva College
Hampton University
Hope College
University of Houston, Clear Lake
University of Missouri, St. Louis
Murray State University

Olivet Nazarene University
Philadelphia University

ASEE was unable to gather current data from the following 39 schools. In these cases, data from previous years was substituted to provide a more complete data set. These 39 schools totaled 2,091 bachelor's degrees. This allows us to provide more accurate comparative data for 1999-2006.

University of Alaska, Anchorage
California Maritime Academy
California State University, Fresno
California State University, Sacramento
Calvin College
Carroll College
Christopher Newport University
Colorado Technical University
University of Denver
University of the District of Columbia
Fairfield University
Fairleigh Dickinson University
Harvey Mudd College
Henry Cogswell College
Howard University
University of Louisiana at Lafayette
Loyola College in Maryland
Loyola Marymount University
Maine Maritime Academy
Massachusetts Maritime Academy
Merrimack College
University of Missouri - Kansas City
New Mexico Institute of Mining & Technology
State University of New York, Maritime College
City University of New York, College of Staten Island
SUNY, New Paltz
Oral Roberts University
Pennsylvania State Univerity Harrisburg
Rutgers, The State University of New Jersey
Saint Ambrose University
Saint Martin's College
Saint Mary's University
University of Saint Thomas
San Fransico State University
Texas A&M University, Galveston

Trinity University
U.S. Coast Guard Academy
Webb Institute
Wilkes University
Youngstown State University

Thirty-six institutions with four-year, ABET-accredited Engineering Technology programs did not participate in the ASEE survey. The non-participating institutions are as follows:

Ball State University
Bluefield State College
California University of Pennsylvania
Central Connecticut State University
Central Washington University
University of Cincinnati, OMI College of Applied Science
Cleveland State University
Colorado Technical University
University of Delaware
DeVry Istitute of Technology, Long Island City
DeVry University, Chicago
DeVry University, Columbus
DeVry University, Decatur & Alpharetta
DeVry University, DuPage
DeVry University, Federal Way
DeVry University, Fremont
DeVry University, Irving
DeVry University, Kansas City
DeVry University, North Brunswick
DeVry University, Orlando
DeVry University, Phoenix
DeVry University, Southern California
Devry University, West Hills
East Tennessee State University
Fairleigh Dickinson University (Teaneck Campus)
Fairmont State College
Florida A&M University
Fort Valley State University
Georgia Southern University
Grambling State University
Maine Maritime Academy
Middle Tennssee State University
Midwestern State University

Missouri Western State College
Montana State University, Northern
Murray State University
New England Institute of Technology
University of New Hampshire
State University of New York, Farmingdale
New York City College of Technology
State University of New York College at Buffalo
SUNY Institute of New York College at Utica/Rome
Northern Kentucky University
Northwestern State University of Louisiana
Paul Smith's College
Pennsylvania College of Technology
Pennsylvania State University, Altoona Campus
Pennsylvania State Univeristy, Berks Campus
Pennsylvania State University, New Kensington
Pennsylvania State University, Wilkes-Barre
University of Pittsburgh at Johnstown
Point Park College
Purdue University, Kokomo
Purdue University, North Central
Savannah State University
South Carolina State University
Univeristy of Southern Indiana
University of Southern Mississippi

Introduction

This directory provides a detailed profile of U.S. and Canadian schools offering undergraduate and graduate engineering and engineering technology programs. The descriptions of institutions represented in this directory allow students to compare schools using a range of characteristics from location and degrees offered to student expenses and enrollment information.

Information was furnished by institutions that responded to ASEE's annual survey. Before deciding upon an institution for study, students should contact the appropriate offices and consult the degree program catalogs for each institution to verify information. Questions about information provided should be addressed to the respective institutions.

Description of Data

Each institution's entry will vary according to the completeness of the information provided to ASEE. In instances in which a question was not applicable or information was not available, entire sections or subsections, including headings, may have been omitted for that institution.

Institutions appear alphabetically, according to the key words in their names (excluding terms such as "University," "The," etc.). Each profile is divided into three parts: Institutional Information, Undergraduate Information, and Graduate Information.

Engineering Colleges

Engineering Institutional Information

Institutional Information includes the address of the institution as well as the address, phone and fax numbers and the e-mail address of the head of the institution (usually the president or chancellor).

General Information provides enrollment figures (including those students not enrolled in engineering programs).

Engineering College Information includes contact information for the head of engineering, usually the dean.

Types of Engineering Degrees lists the bachelor's, master's, and doctoral degrees offered by the institution.

Undergraduate Engineering Information

Admission Inquiries includes the address, phone and fax numbers, and e-mail address for requesting admission information and application materials.

Student Expenses & Financial Aid includes student expenses and financial aid information for the 2006-07, nine-month academic year based upon an average undergraduate course load. The expenses are listed for a nine-month period so that schools on different calendars (semesters, quarters, etc.) can be compared based upon a standard-length school year, excluding summer terms. Expenses are itemized as tuition and required fees, college room and board (based on a seven-day meal plan, if available), books and supplies, and other costs (excluding transportation to and from school each term or during holidays and other personal expenditures, but including the cost of a computer if it is required or strongly recommended. If expenses differ for state residents and nonresidents, two sets of figures are given.

Engineering Student Information provides information on the number of undergraduate applicants, the number of applicants offered admission, and the number of students who matriculated.

Graduate Engineering Information

Admission Inquiries provides the address, phone and fax numbers, and e-mail address for requesting admission information and application materials.

Student Expenses & Financial Aid includes student expenses and other financial aid information for the 2006-07, nine-month academic year based on an average first-year graduate engineering course load. Expenses are listed for a nine-month period so that figures for schools on different calendars (semesters, quarters, etc.) may be compared based upon a standard-length school year, excluding summer terms. Estimated expenses are itemized as tuition and required fees, college room and board (based on a seven-day meal plan, if available), books and supplies, and other costs (excluding transportation to and from school each term or during holidays and other personal expenditures, but including the cost of a computer if it is required or strongly recommended). If expenses differ for state residents and nonresidents, two sets of figures are given.

New Applicants/Newly Enrolled Students provides information on the number of graduate applicants to the college of engineering, the number of applicants offered admission, and the number of students who matriculated.

Engineering Discipline Categories

Aerospace Engineering
Agricultural Engineering
Architectural Engineering
Biomedical Engineering
Chemical Engineering
Civil Engineering
Computer Engineering
Computer Science (inside engineering)
Computer Science (outside engineering)
Electrical/Computer Engineering
Electrical Engineering
Engineering (General)
Engineering Management
Engineering Science and Engineering Physics
Environmental Engineering
Industrial/Manufacturing Engineering
Mechanical Engineering
Metallurgical and Materials Engineering
Mining Engineering
Nuclear Engineering
Petroleum Engineering
Other Engineering Disciplines

Engineering Technology Discipline Categories

Aerospace Engineering Technology
Architectural Engineering Technology
Civil Engineering Technology
Computer Engineering Technology
Construction Engineering Technology
Electrical Engineering Technology
Engineering Technology (General)
Industrial/Manufacturing Engineering Technology
Mechanical Engineering Technology
Other Engineering Technology Disciplines

Changes to the 2006 Survey

In 2005, we improved the ASEE survey of engineering and engineering technology colleges by doing two things. First, we collected degree and enrollment data with greater demographic specificity. In the past, we collected degrees awarded by ethnicity on one page of the survey and degrees awarded by gender on another. In effect, we never knew how many African-American females or Caucausian males received degrees. We expanded this approach to the collection of enrollments, which were previously without any demographic information. Second, we now collect enrollment data for each degree program, which enables us to track this data more accurately. Prior to 2005, enrollment data was collected for each department. Since departments often award degrees in different diciplines, some enrollment data was grouped together into a single discipline. A common situation was the reporting of some aerospace students with mechanical students since departments of aerospace and mechanical engineering are typical. With this resolved, there is now some discontinuity in the enrollment data between 1999-2004 and 2005-2006. We believe that the current accounting is the most accurate.

The following text was offered to each school as a guideline for the calculation of externally-funded research expenditures for Fiscal Year 2006:

Include all expenditures associated with grants and contracts specifically budgeted for externally sponsored research and associated programs and expenditures associated with all gifts auditably used for research. Include expended funds provided by the following external sources:

1. Federal
2. State
3. Foreign
4. Industry
5. Non-profit organizations (e.g. foundations)
6. Individuals
7. Local

Notes:

- The expenditures reported should only be those funds provided by organizations, agencies, and individuals external to the institution. Cost sharing/matching funds should be included only if provided from sources external to the institution.

- Only State government funds that were obtained competitively or as matching funds associated with other externally funded programs should be included. State funds that are part of the normal operating budget should not be included regardless of purpose.

- For all joint or contracted projects or sub-projects, only the portion of the center research performed by faculty, staff, and students of the affiliated engineering school should be credited to that school. Expenditures for capital costs of research laboratory building construction should not be included.

- Expenditures for research laboratory renovations should not be included unless the renovation funds expended came from grants and contracts expressly intended for the direct support of engineering research.

- Any portion of academic year and/or summer salary for any researcher that is not derived from external research grants or contracts should not be counted.

- Research centers listed as "WITHIN an engineering department" on the Research Centers page of the College of Engineering Profile, will not have their expenditures added to the school's total research expenditures. Such expenditures can be included in the department total, while still being listed for the appropriate center. This allows users to list the expenditures in two areas without double-counting.

Total #: Report total number of individual grants, not the total dollar amount of the expenditures.

Expenditures: Report actual expenditures (as opposed to authorization amounts) in U.S. dollars.

Time frame for expenditures: Report expenditures for your 2006 fiscal year (the fiscal year that ended in 2006).

Empty fields: If you do not have expenditures for a category, leave the field empty; do not put N/A or other text.

The following text was offered to each school as a guideline for collecting faculty data by race and ethnicity for Fall semester, 2006:

Standards for Maintaining, Collecting, and Presenting
Federal Data on Race and Ethnicity

(Excerpt from Federal Register, October 30, 1997)

This classification provides a minimum standard for maintaining, collecting, and presenting data on race and ethnicity for all Federal reporting purposes. The categories in this classification are social-political constructs and should not be interpreted as being scientific or anthropological in nature. They are not to be used as determinants of eligibility for participation in any Federal program. The standards have been developed to provide a common language for uniformity and comparability in the collection and use of data on race and ethnicity by Federal agencies.

The standards have five categories for data on race: American Indian or Alaska Native, Asian, Black or African American, Native Hawaiian or Other Pacific Islander, and White. There are two categories for data on ethnicity: "Hispanic or Latino," and "Not Hispanic or Latino."

Categories and Definitions

The minimum categories for data on race and ethnicity for Federal statistics, program administrative reporting, and civil rights compliance reporting are defined as follows:

-- **American Indian or Alaska Native:** A person having origins in any of the original peoples of North and South America (including Central America), and who maintains tribal affiliation or community attachment.

-- **Asian:** A person having origins in any of the original peoples of the Far East, Southeast Asia, or the Indian subcontinent including, for example, Cambodia, China, India, Japan, Korea, Malaysia, Pakistan, the Philippine Islands, Thailand, and Vietnam.

-- **Black or African American:** A person having origins in any of the black racial groups of Africa. Terms such as "Haitian" or "Negro" can be used in addition to "Black or African American."

-- **Hispanic or Latino:** A person of Cuban, Mexican, Puerto Rican, South or Central American, or other Spanish culture or origin, regardless of race. The term, "Spanish origin," can be used in addition to "Hispanic or Latino."

-- **Native Hawaiian or Other Pacific Islander:** A person having origins in any of the original peoples of Hawaii, Guam, Samoa, or other Pacific Islands.

-- **Caucasian:** A person having origins in any of the original peoples of Europe, the Middle East, or North Africa.

The provisions of these standards are effective immediately for all new and revised record keeping or reporting requirements that include racial and/or ethnic information. All existing record keeping or reporting requirements shall be made consistent with these standards at the time they are submitted for extension, or not later than January 1, 2003.

U.S. Department of the Interior
1849 C. Street N.W.
Washington, DC 20240
(202) 208-3100

ENGINEERING

BY THE NUMBERS

By Michael T. Gibbons

Bachelor's degrees awarded in engineering increased slightly for the seventh consecutive year. The 2005-2006 academic year saw 74,186 new graduates from engineering colleges at this level. While bachelor's degrees increased by more than 20 percent since 1999, the past two years have seen annual growth less than one percent. A portion of this reduced growth is due to the 20 percent decrease in computer science degrees awarded by engineering colleges since 2004. Excluding computer science, engineering degrees have fared well, rising by 16.5 percent since 1999 and 4.9 percent since 2004.

Undergraduate enrollment rebounded slightly after two years of decline. The concern was that enrollment had peaked and that bachelor's degrees would soon dip. As of this year, that does not appear to be the case. The 373,074 undergraduates enrolled in engineering colleges in fall 2006 was 1.9 percent greater than the previous fall. Although this recent total is still lower than either 2003 or 2004, the growth of freshman to 101,291 is encouraging.

Master's degrees fell for the first time since 1999, dropping 3 percent to 39,015. This trend will continue for the near term following the recent drop in master's enrollment. Although master's engineering enrollment decreased by 9 percent from 2003 to 2005, it remained virtually unchanged from last year with a total of 83,515. Similar to the undergraduate level, computer science master's degrees and enrollments within engineering are declining after several robust years of growth.

Engineering doctorates continued their strong run, rising to a new high of 8,351. This total is more than 44 percent greater than the 5,772 doctoral degrees awarded in 2001. Enrollment at this rank has also grown by almost 40 percent since 2001. As with the master's level, doctoral students enrolled at almost the same rate as last year. Overall, enrollment increased by less than 1 percent to 57,561.

Foreign nationals once again increased their share of doctoral degrees for the seventh consecutive year. In 2005-2006, 61.7 percent of engineering doctorates went to foreign nationals. Although 1,018 more doctorates were awarded by engineering colleges this year, U.S. citizens received only 221 more than last year. Master' programs experienced the opposite trend as the percentage of U.S. graduates grew steadily for the past four years from 54 percent to 60.2 percent.

Several engineering disciplines continued their steady growth this year. Most notably, bachelor's degrees in aerospace engineering and biomedical engineering have increased by 132 percent and 187 percent, respectively, since 1999. While the largest discipline of electrical/computer engineering grew by 24.7 percent from 1999 to 2003, the 19,641 bachelor's degrees conferred in this field in 2006 represented a 4.3 percent decrease from 2003. The next largest field, mechanical engineering grew 13 percent over the past two years to 16,063 bachelor's degrees. Degree trends for graduate students have followed suit in these areas, with the notable exception that doctoral growth in aerospace has been much smaller, while electrical/computer engineering doctorates continue to proliferate.

The engineering faculty ranks are slowly becoming more diversified by gender, if less so for underrepresented minorities. The overall representation of women at the tenured and tenure-track level is 11.3 percent. This is up from 8.9 percent as recently as 2001. Almost 20 percent of assistant professors are women. Underrepresented minorities still comprise only 4.8 percent of the more than 23,000 faculty members nationwide. Both African-American and Hispanic engineering professors have equal shares at 2.4 percent. However, one-quarter of the African-American faculty members are located at just 7 of the country's Historically Black Colleges and Universities. Asian professors represent 22.2 percent of the total.

The engineering student population has seen fewer women at the undergraduate level in recent years. The 19.3 percent of bachelor's degrees awarded to women in 2005-2006 was the lowest representation since 1998. This pales in comparison to the larger pool, where women make up 56 percent of the undergraduate college population. Women are faring better at the graduate level. More than 22 percent of all enrolled graduate engineering students are women, which is a step up from the 17.4 percent of women enrolled at the undergraduate level. Despite the disparity in the overall percentages, women are well-represented in select engineering disciplines. Women account for over one-third of undergraduate engineering degrees in the agricultural, biomedical, chemical, industrial/manufacturing, and environmental disciplines. However, these disciplines comprise only 16 percent of all engineering bachelor's degrees. The largest fields of civil engineering, computer science (within engineering), electrical/computer engineering, and mechanical engineering make up 70 percent of all engineering bachelor's degrees, yet the proportion of women is only 14.8 percent.

The share of African-American and Hispanic students has remained low and virtually unchanged for the past decade. Despite comprising almost 25 percent of the U.S. population, these two groups earn just 11 percent of bachelor's degrees awarded to U.S. students combined. At the master's level, African-Americans receive 4.4 percent of degrees, while Hispanics receive 4.7 percent. Doctoral representation was lower for each population with African-Americans receiving 3.7 percent and Hispanic students receiving 3 percent of degrees at the highest level.

More detailed data for 338 U.S. and eight Canadian engineering colleges can be found in the following 500 pages of our 2006 Profiles of Engineering and Engineering Technology Colleges book or online at www.asee.org/colleges.

Michael T. Gibbons is director of data research for the American Society for Engineering Education. He can be contacted at m.gibbons@asee.org.

BACHELOR'S DEGREES BY ENGINEERING DISCIPLINE: 74,186

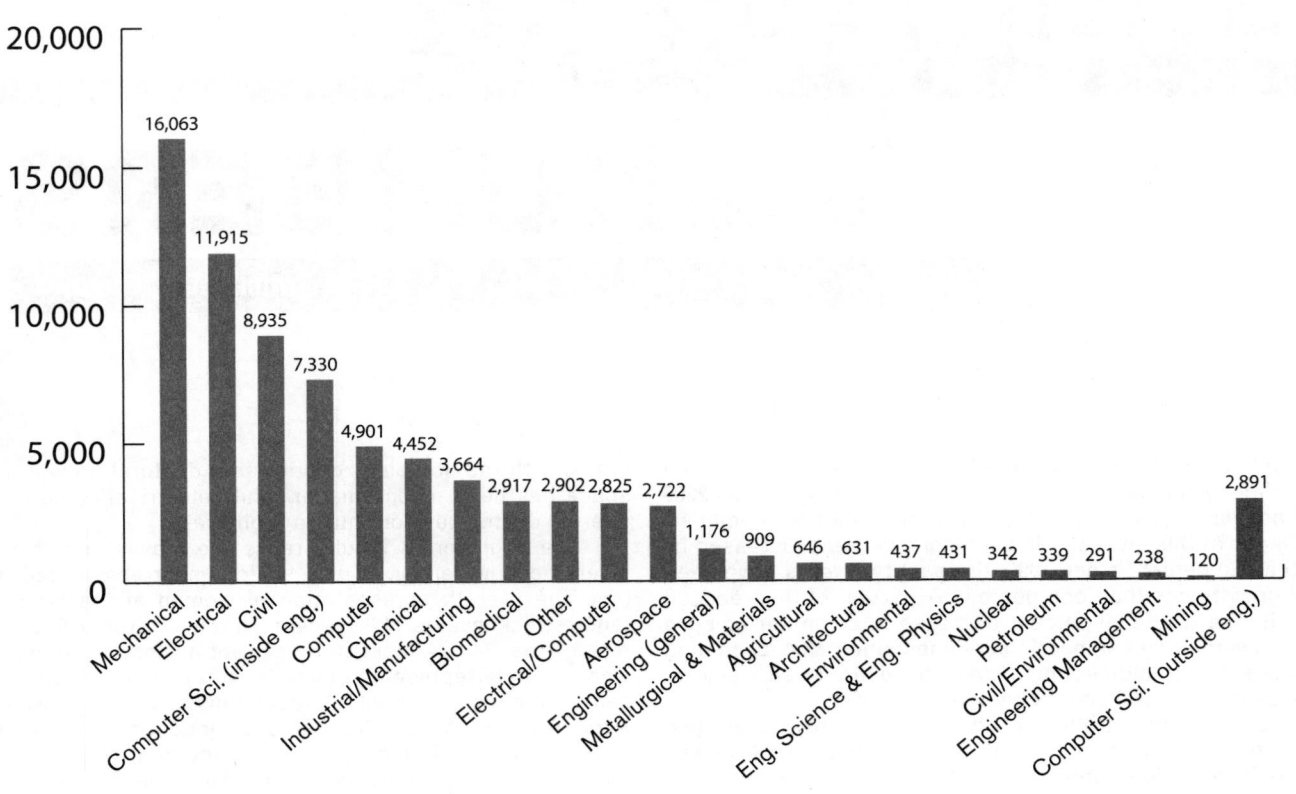

PERCENTAGE OF BACHELOR'S DEGREES AWARDED TO WOMEN BY DISCIPLINE: 19.3%

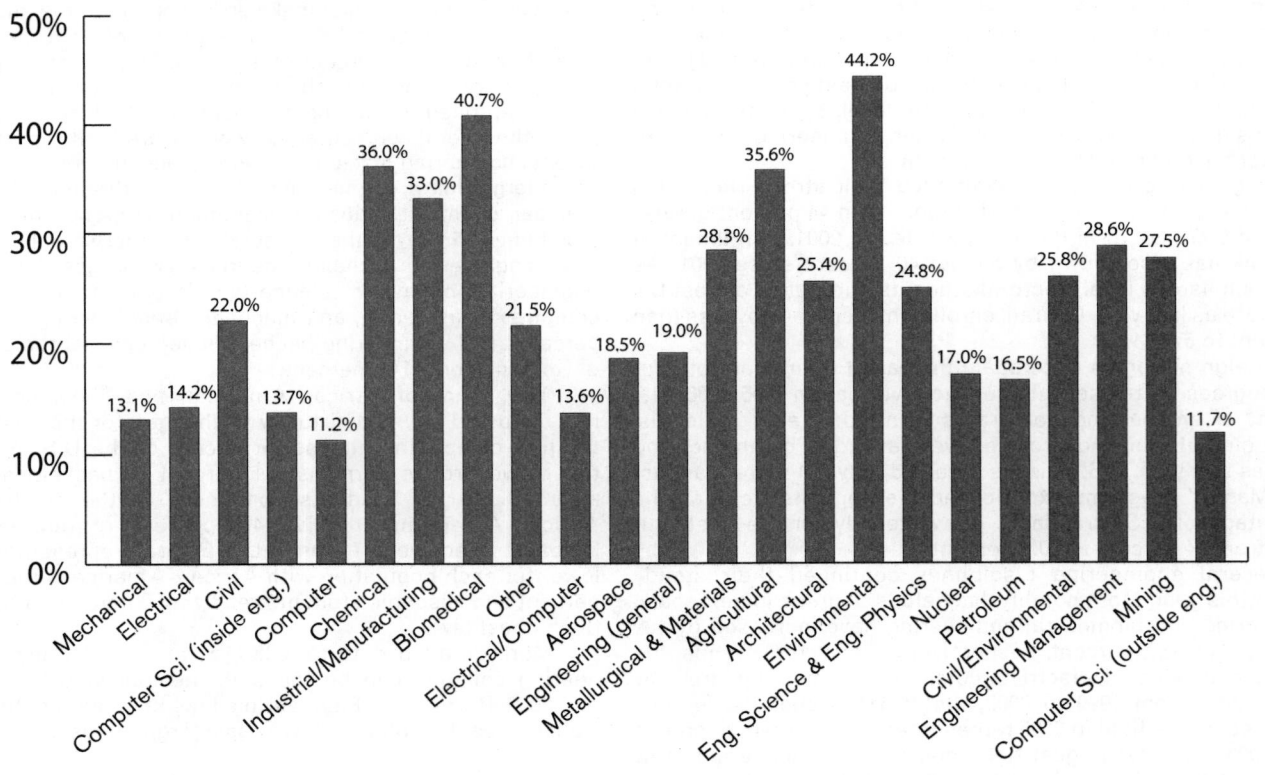

ENGINEERING BACHELOR'S DEGREES AWARDED BY SCHOOL

1. Georgia Institute of Technology — 1,391
2. Pennsylvania State University — 1,319
3. Purdue University — 1,238
4. Univ. of Illinois, Urbana-Champaign — 1,237
5. Virginia Tech — 1,187
6. Texas A&M University — 1,066
7. University of Michigan — 1,050
8. North Carolina State University — 1,040
9. University of Texas, Austin — 980
10. California Poly. State Univ., SLO — 974
11. University of California, San Diego — 955
12. Iowa State University — 932
13. University of California, Berkeley — 882
14. University of Florida — 867
15. Ohio State University — 848
16. University of Minnesota, Twin Cities — 738
17. University of Washington — 731
18. Cornell University — 704
19. Arizona State University — 673
20. Univ. of Maryland, College Park — 657
21. University of Wisconsin, Madison — 641
22. University of Central Florida — 640
23. Michigan Technological University — 616
24. Univ. of Puerto Rico, Mayaguez — 606
25. Oregon State University — 592
26. Michigan State University — 590
27. Massachusetts Inst. of Technology — 578
28. University of California, Davis — 573
29. Rensselaer Polytechnic Institute — 550
30. University of Colorado, Boulder — 544
31. Univ. of California, Los Angeles — 534
32. Colorado School of Mines — 527
33. Clemson University — 523
34. California State Poly. Univ., Pomona — 513
35. Drexel University — 509
36. University of Missouri, Rolla — 504
37. SUNY, Buffalo — 500
38. University of California, Irvine — 466
39. Florida International University — 464
40. Auburn University — 463
41. Stony Brook University — 454
42. University of Arizona — 448
43. George Mason University — 438
44. Brigham Young University — 437
45. San Jose State University — 432
46. Kansas State University — 421
47. Rutgers University — 415
48. University of Virginia — 410
49. Worcester Polytechnic Institute — 400
50. Louisiana State University — 398

336 total schools reported.

BACHELOR'S DEGREES BY ETHNICITY*

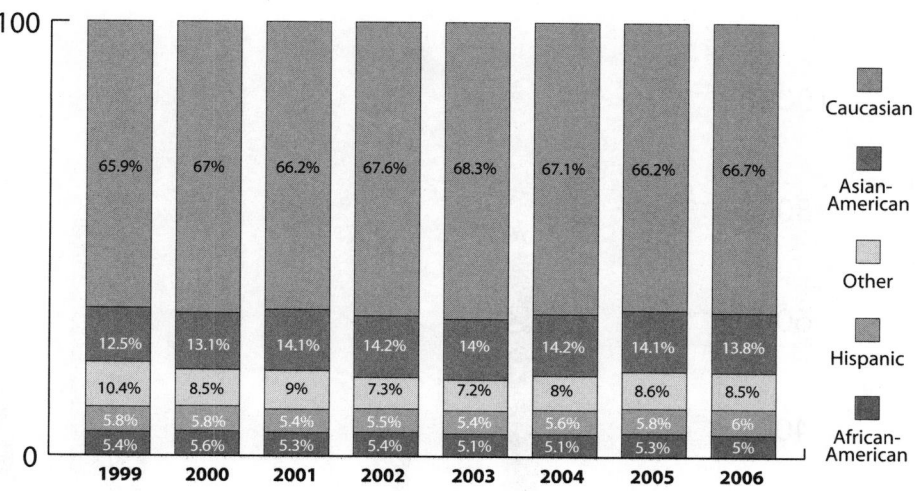

* Data on ethnicity does not include schools from Puerto Rico or foreign nationals.

BACHELOR'S DEGREES BY RESIDENCY

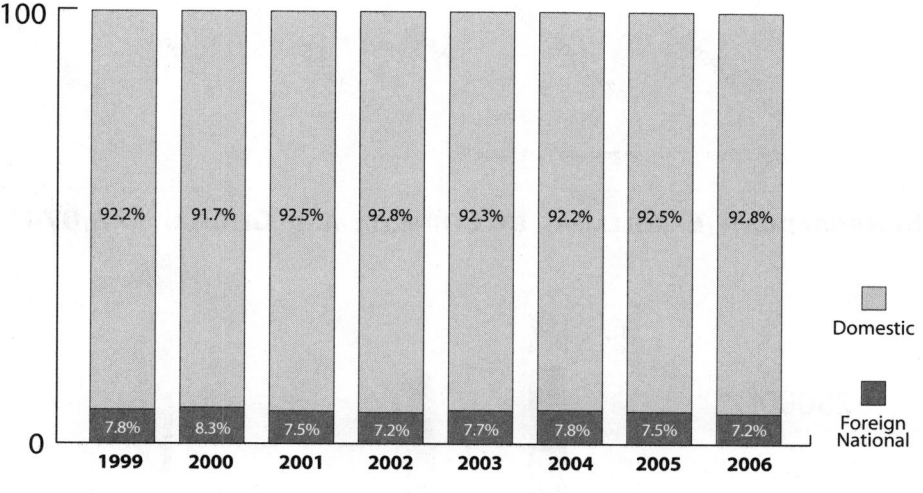

BACHELOR'S DEGREES BY GENDER

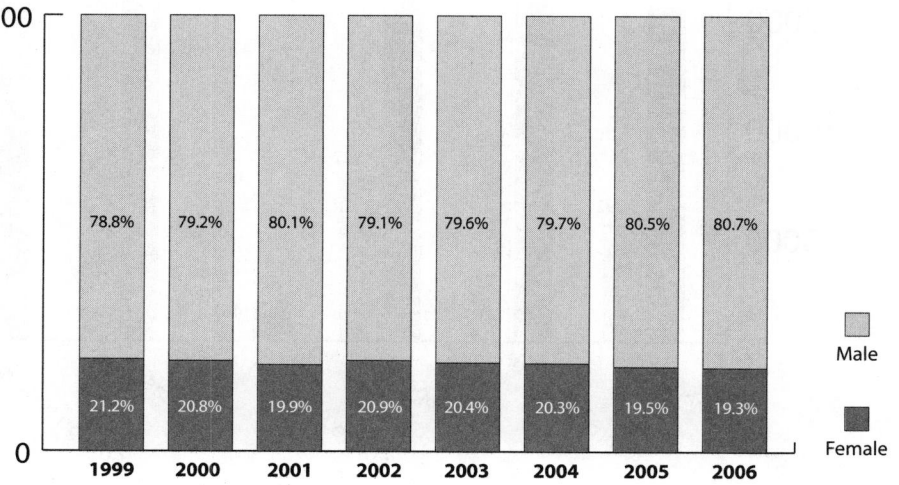

BACHELOR'S DEGREES BY ETHNICITY AND GENDER: 74,186*

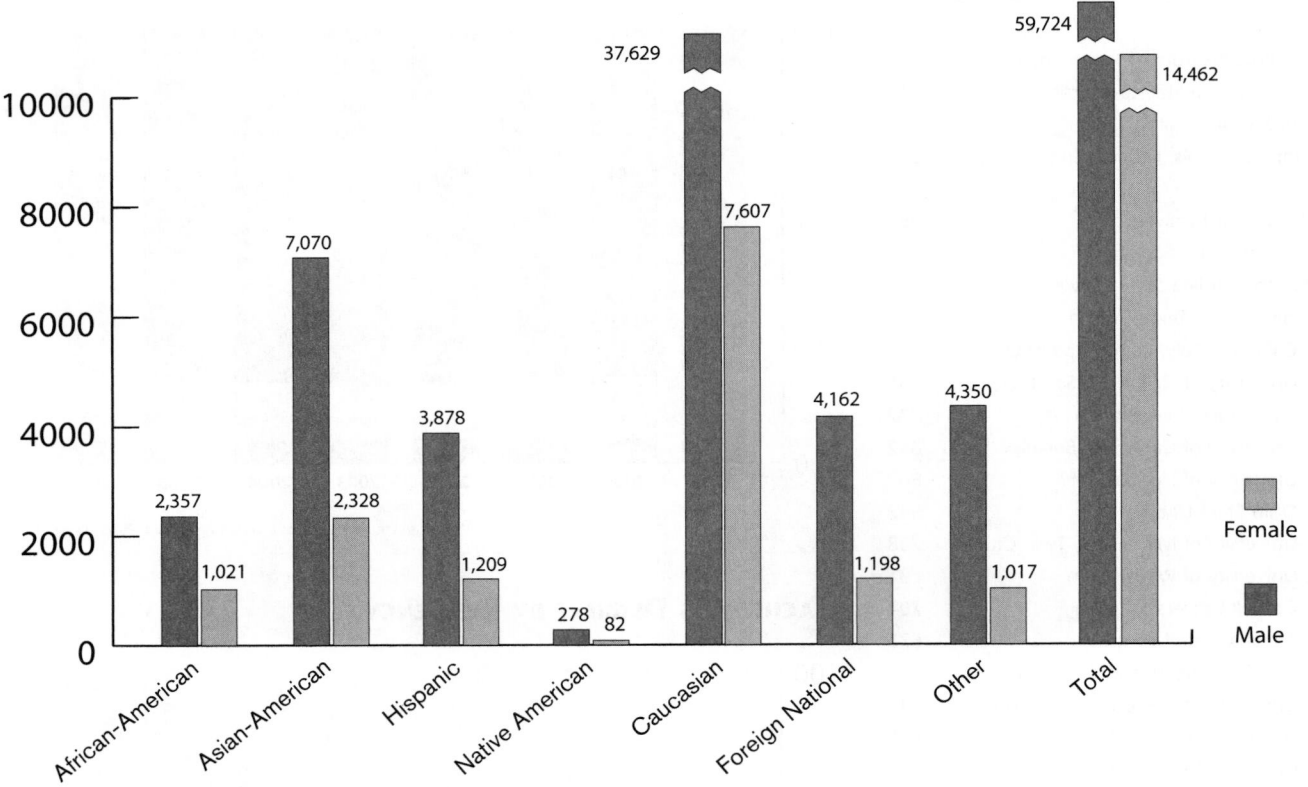

* Includes 664 male and 329 female graduates from schools in Puerto Rico.

UNDERGRADUATE ENROLLMENT BY ETHNICITY AND GENDER: 373,074*

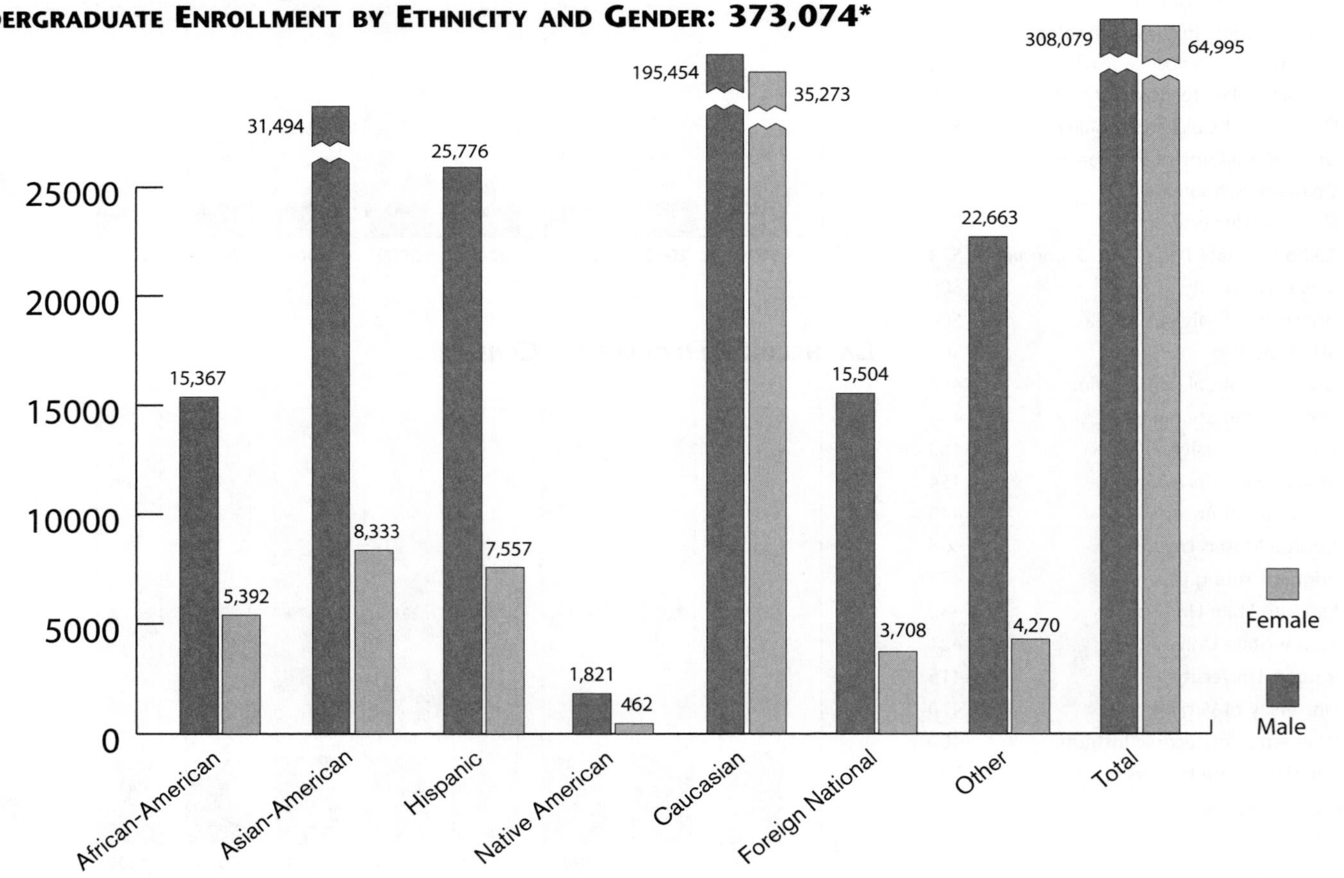

* Includes 5,866 male and 2,632 female enrolled students from schools in Puerto Rico. Enrollment is for full-time students.

ENGINEERING BACHELOR'S DEGREES AWARDED TO WOMEN BY SCHOOL

1.	Georgia Institute of Technology	306
2.	University of Michigan	295
3.	Univ. of Puerto Rico, Mayaguez	236
4.	Purdue University	234
5.	Texas A&M University	231
6.	Univ. of Illinois, Urbana-Champaign	218
7.	University of California, Berkeley	216
8.	University of Texas, Austin	214
9.	Pennsylvania State University	209
10.	Virginia Tech	200
11.	University of California, San Diego	192
12.	Cornell University	183
13.	Massachusetts Inst. of Technology	179
14.	North Carolina State University	168
15.	California Poly. State U., SLO	164
16.	University of Florida	161
17.	Iowa State University	144
18.	Arizona State University	139
18.	University of Washington	139
20.	Ohio State University	137
21.	Rensselaer Polytechnic Institute	126
22.	University of Wisconsin, Madison	125
23.	Univ. of Maryland, College Park	122
23.	Michigan State University	122
25.	University of California, Davis	121
26.	Michigan Technological University	113
27.	Univ. of California, Los Angeles	111
28.	Clemson University	110
28.	Colorado School of Mines	110
30.	University of Central Florida	104
30.	Stanford University	104
32.	Florida International University	103
33.	Lehigh University	102
34.	University of California, Irvine	100
34.	University of Southern California	100
34.	University of Virginia	100
37.	Northwestern University	99
38.	Worcester Polytechnic Institute	98
39.	Drexel University	97
40.	Auburn University	95
40.	Univ. of Minnesota, Twin Cities	95
42.	Polytechnic Univ. of Puerto Rico	93
42.	Vanderbilt University	93
44.	George Mason University	92
44.	Louisiana State University	92
46.	San Jose State University	91
47.	Rutgers University	90
48.	University of Arizona	89
49.	Stony Brook University	88
50.	University of Missouri, Rolla	87
50.	University of Pennsylvania	87
50.	University of Pittsburgh	87

336 schools reported.

PERCENTAGE OF BACHELOR'S DEGREES AWARDED TO WOMEN BY SCHOOL*

1.	Tennessee State University	45.5%
2.	Univ. of Puerto Rico, Mayaguez	38.9%
3.	Mercer University	36.6%
4.	Alabama A&M University	36.1%
5.	Tufts University	36.0%
5.	Tuskegee University	36.0%
7.	University of Miami	35.0%
8.	Brown University	34.8%
9.	Southern Methodist University	33.3%
10.	Saint Louis University	31.2%
11.	Massachusetts Inst. of Technology	31.0%
12.	Northwestern University	30.6%
13.	George Washington University	30.5%
14.	Washington University	29.3%
15.	Princeton University	29.2%
16.	Marquette University	29.1%
16.	Stevens Institute of Technology	29.1%
18.	William Marsh Rice University	29.0%
19.	Vanderbilt University	28.9%
20.	Morgan State University	28.4%

*Minimum of 50 BS degrees awarded.
261 schools fit this criterion*

ENGINEERING BACHELOR'S DEGREES AWARDED TO AFRICAN-AMERICANS BY SCHOOL

1.	North Carolina A & T State Univ.	138
2.	Georgia Institute of Technology	120
3.	FAMU-FSU College of Eng.	114
4.	Howard University	106
5.	Alabama A&M University	70
6.	University of Michigan	65
7.	North Carolina State University	64
8.	Univ. of Maryland, College Park	62
9.	Tuskegee University	61
10.	Prairie View A&M University	60
10.	Tennessee State University	60
12.	Southern Univ. and A&M College	53
13.	Morgan State University	51
14.	Virginia Tech	47
15.	Florida International University	45
16.	Clemson University	41
17.	University of Central Florida	40
18.	Drexel University	38
18.	Stanford University	38
20.	Auburn University	36

336 schools reported

ENGINEERING BACHELOR'S DEGREES AWARDED TO ASIAN-AMERICANS BY SCHOOL

1.	University of California, Berkeley	472
2.	University of California, San Diego	454
3.	University of California, Davis	298
4.	University of Texas, Austin	260
5.	Univ. of Illinois, Urbana-Champaign	246
6.	San Jose State University	235
7.	California State Polytech. U., Pomona	224
7.	University of California, Los Angeles	224
9.	Georgia Institute of Technology	215
10.	Cornell University	201
10.	University of Washington	201
12.	California Polytechnic State U., SLO	194
13.	Stony Brook University	190
14.	University of Michigan	168
15.	Massachusetts Inst. of Technology	152
16.	University of Maryland, College Park	135
17.	Rutgers University	126
18.	Virginia Tech	125
19.	Columbia University	116
20.	Stanford University	115

336 schools reported

ENGINEERING BACHELOR'S DEGREES AWARDED TO HISPANICS BY SCHOOL

1.	Univ. of Puerto Rico, Mayaguez	606
2.	Polytechnic Univ. of Puerto Rico	387
3.	Florida International University	248
4.	University of Texas, El Paso	177
5.	University of Florida	138
6.	Texas A&M University	111
7.	University of Texas, Austin	106
8.	California State Poly. Univ., Pomona	99
9.	Texas A&M University, Kingsville	96
10.	University of Texas, San Antonio	85
11.	California Polytechnic State Univ., SLO	84
12.	University of Central Florida	78
13.	University of Texas, Pan American	71
14.	California State University, Northridge	69
15.	Arizona State University	65
15.	New Mexico State University	65
17.	Massachusetts Inst. of Technology	59
18.	University of New Mexico	57
19.	University of Arizona	54
19.	Georgia Institute of Technology	54

336 schools reported

AEROSPACE ENGINEERING DEGREES AWARDED BY SCHOOL

1. Embry Riddle Aero. U., Daytona Beach	202
2. Georgia Institute of Technology	136
3. Purdue University	130
4. Virginia Tech	101
5. U.S. Air Force Academy	95
6. University of Michigan	88
7. Pennsylvania State University	83
8. University of Maryland College Park	80
9. University of Texas, Austin	75
10. Embry Riddle Aero. U., Prescott	73
11. Univ. of Illinois, Urbana-Champaign	72
11. Iowa State University	72
13. University of Colorado, Boulder	67
13. Massachusetts Inst. of Technology	67
15. U.S. Naval Academy	65
16. California Poly. State Univ., SLO	56
16. University of California San Diego	56
18. University of Minnesota, Twin Cities	55
18. University of Washington	55
20. Texas A&M University	48

63 schools reported

BIOMEDICAL ENGINEERING DEGREES AWARDED BY SCHOOL

1. University of California, San Diego	165
2. Duke University	122
3. Johns Hopkins University	114
4. Case Western Reserve University	94
5. University of Pennsylvania	88
6. University of California Berkeley	85
7. Northwestern University	84
8. Vanderbilt University	79
9. Arizona State University	77
9. Georgia Institute of Technology	77
11. University of Texas, Austin	75
12. Washington University	72
13. Boston University	70
14. Columbia University	67
15. University of California, Irvine	57
16. Marquette University	56
17. Rutgers University	55
18. University of Southern California	53
19. Rensselaer Polytechnic Institute	50
19. Texas A&M University	50

77 schools reported

CHEMICAL ENGINEERING DEGREES AWARDED BY SCHOOL

1. Univ. of Puerto Rico, Mayaguez	119
2. Pennsylvania State University	105
3. University of Texas, Austin	96
4. Purdue University	91
4. Texas A&M University	91
6. Ohio State University	80
7. University of Wisconsin Madison	78
8. Georgia Institute of Technology	73
9. Univ. of Minnesota, Twin Cities	71
9. University of Washington	71
11. University of Michigan	65
12. North Carolina State University	61
13. University of California Berkeley	59
14. Cornell University	58
15. Massachusetts Inst. of Technology	57
16. Louisiana State University	54
17. University of California Los Angeles	53
17. Univ. of Illinois, Urbana-Champaign	53
19. University of Delaware	52
19. Iowa State University	52
21. University of California Davis	50
22. University of Houston	47
22. Oregon State University	47
24. Carnegie Mellon University	45
24. Colorado School of Mines	45
24. University of Colorado, Boulder	45
24. Michigan Technological University	45
28. SUNY, Buffalo	44
29. University of Florida	43
29. University of Oklahoma	43
29. Virginia Tech	43
32. Michigan State University	42
33. Auburn University	39
34. Univ. of California Santa Barbara	38
34. University of Kansas	38
34. Rose-Hulman Inst. of Technology	38
37. Brigham Young University	36
38. University of Notre Dame	35
39. University of Dayton	34
39. University of Missouri, Columbia	34
39. University of Pittsburgh	34
39. University of Toledo	34
43. Rensselaer Polytechnic Institute	33
44. Arizona State University	32
44. Clemson University	32
44. Columbia University	32
44. Drexel University	32
48. University of Arizona	31
48. University of Cincinnati	31
48. University of Missouri, Rolla	31
48. Northeastern University	31
48. University of South Carolina	31
48. University of Utah	31

155 schools reported.

CIVIL ENGINEERING DEGREES AWARDED BY SCHOOL

1. Texas A&M University	203
2. Purdue University	180
3. California Poly. State Univ., SLO	176
4. Pennsylvania State University	167
5. North Carolina State University	166
6. Georgia Institute of Technology	156
7. Polytechnic Univ. of Puerto Rico	150
8. Virginia Tech	145
9. University of Florida	136
10. Univ. of Illinois, Urbana-Champaign	113
11. Michigan Technological University	111
12. Auburn University	108
13. California State Poly. U., Pomona	105
13. University of Washington	105
15. University of California Davis	103
16. University of California Berkeley	102
16. Univ. of Wisconsin Madison	102
18. Clemson University	97
18. Univ. of Puerto Rico, Mayaguez	97
20. Brigham Young University	96
21. University of Minnesota, Twin Cities	94
22. University of Central Florida	92
22. Iowa State University	92
24. University of California San Diego	87
25. University of Kentucky	84
26. North Dakota State University	83
27. University of Texas, Austin	82
27. Utah State University	82
29. FAMU-FSU College of Eng.	81
30. University of Missouri, Rolla	78
31. Colorado State University	77
31. Ohio State University	77
33. San Diego State University	75
34. Michigan State University	72
35. Oregon State University	71
35. University of Pittsburgh	71
37. Florida International University	70
38. Louisiana State University	67
39. Texas Tech University	64
40. Montana State University	63
41. University of Texas, San Antonio	62
42. Clarkson University	61
42. SUNY, Buffalo	61
42. Worcester Polytechnic Institute	61
45. Northeastern University	60
45. University of Tennessee, Knoxville	60
45. University of Utah	60
48. University of Nebraska, Lincoln	59
48. Univ. of North Carolina, Charlotte	59
50. Manhattan College	58
50. Univ. of Maryland, College Park	58

211 schools reported.

Industrial/Manufacturing Engineering Degrees Awarded by School

1. Georgia Institute of Technology	266
2. University of Michigan	186
3. Ohio State University	158
4. Purdue University	149
5. Pennsylvania State University	138
6. Cornell University	101
7. Virginia Tech	99
8. University of Florida	84
9. Columbia University	79
10. Iowa State University	65
11. Northwestern University	64
12. California Poly. State U., SLO	63
12. Texas A&M University	63
14. Univ. of Puerto Rico Mayaguez	62
15. Stanford University	58
16. North Carolina State University	57
17. Oregon State University	55
18. University of Wisconsin Madison	53
19. Arizona State University	46
19. University of Pittsburgh	46
21. Clemson University	45
22. University of California, Berkeley	44
23. San Jose State University	41
24. California State Poly. Univ., Pomona	40
25. University of Arkansas	39
25. Florida International University	39
27. FAMU-FSU College of Eng.	38
27. West Virginia University	38
29. Kettering University	36
29. Lehigh University	36
29. South Dakota Sc. of Mines & Tech.	36
32. Polytechnic University of Puerto Rico	35
32. University of Texas, El Paso	35
34. University of Houston	34
34. University of Southern California	34
36. University of Arizona	33
37. University of Washington	32
38. George Mason University	30
38. Lamar University	30
40. Kansas State University	29
40. SUNY, Buffalo	29
40. North Carolina A & T State Univ.	29
43. Auburn University	28
43. University of Iowa	28
43. Rensselaer Polytechnic Institute	28
43. Rochester Institute of Technology	28
43. Rutgers University	28
48. North Dakota State University	27
49. University of Nebraska Lincoln	26
50. University of Miami	25

111 schools reported

Mechanical Engineering Degrees Awarded by School

1. Purdue University	277
1. Virginia Tech	277
3. Georgia Institute of Technology	273
4. Pennsylvania State University	261
5. Kettering University	257
6. University of Michigan	223
7. Michigan Technological University	222
8. California Poly. State U., SLO	209
9. Iowa State University	207
10. Univ. of Illinois, Urbana-Champaign	205
11. University of Texas, Austin	196
12. Michigan State University	185
13. Univ. of Maryland College Park	172
13. Texas A&M University	172
15. University of Minnesota, Twin Cities	167
16. University of California Berkeley	161
17. Brigham Young University	160
18. Ohio State University	155
19. Clemson University	152
20. Worcester Polytechnic Institute	150
21. University of California Davis	149
21. University of California, San Diego	149
23. North Carolina State University	145
24. University of Wisconsin Madison	141
25. SUNY, Buffalo	138
26. University of Colorado, Boulder	131
26. Rochester Institute of Technology	131
28. Rensselaer Polytechnic Institute	127
29. University of Florida	126
29. University of Oklahoma	126
31. Cornell University	122
31. University of Puerto Rico Mayaguez	122
33. University of Missouri, Rolla	120
34. Massachusetts Inst. of Technology	114
35. Rose-Hulman Inst. of Technology	111
36. Carnegie Mellon University	110
36. Oklahoma State University	110
38. Drexel University	109
38. Oregon State University	109
40. Texas Tech University	105
41. Colorado State University	104
42. University of Missouri-Columbia	103
43. University of Central Florida	101
44. Clarkson University	100
45. Milwaukee School of Engineering	99
45. University of Wisconsin, Platteville	99
47. West Virginia University	95
47. Western Michigan University	95
49. University of Kentucky	93
50. Washington State University	90

276 schools reported

Electrical Engineering Degrees Awarded by School

1. Georgia Institute of Technology	262
2. University of California, San Diego	243
3. California State Poly. U., Pomona	225
4. Univ. of Illinois, Urbana-Champaign	219
5. Pennsylvania State University	189
6. California Poly. State U., SLO	176
6. University of Florida	176
8. Texas A&M University	174
9. Univ. of Maryland, College Park	171
10. North Carolina State University	168
11. University of Washington	162
12. San Jose State University	150
13. Virginia Tech	147
14. Univ. of California, Los Angeles	146
15. University of Michigan	143
16. University of Minnesota, Twin Cities	130
17. Univ. of Puerto Rico, Mayaguez	129
18. University of California, Irvine	125
19. Arizona State University	122
20. University of Texas, Dallas	121
21. Iowa State University	110
22. Rensselaer Polytechnic Institute	105
23. Michigan Technological University	102
24. University of Wisconsin, Madison	100
25. University of Central Florida	99
26. Polytechnic Univ. of Puerto Rico	96
26. Utah State University	96
28. New Jersey Inst. of Technology	94
28. Northeastern University	94
30. San Diego State University	90
31. SUNY, Buffalo	89
31. University of California, Davis	89
33. Rochester Inst. of Technology	88
33. University of Illinois at Chicago	88
33. University of Michigan, Dearborn	88
33. University of Texas, El Paso	88
37. University of Houston	86
38. Michigan State University	85
39. University of Southern California	83
40. Drexel University	82
41. University of Arizona	81
42. Florida International University	80
42. Louisiana State University	80
44. Auburn University	79
45. FAMU-FSU College of Eng.	78
46. Kettering University	77
47. University of Utah	72
48. California State U., Long Beach	70
48. Texas Tech University	70
50. Stanford University	69

255 schools reported.

COMPUTER ENGINEERING DEGREES AWARDED BY SCHOOL

1. Purdue University	315
2. Pennsylvania State University	149
3. Iowa State University	135
4. Univ. of Illinois, Urbana-Champaign	127
5. University of Florida	122
6. University of California, Irvine	121
7. North Carolina State University	113
8. Virginia Tech	99
9. Georgia Institute of Technology	96
10. Arizona State University	87
10. California Poly. State U., SLO	87
12. University of Central Florida	72
13. University of Michigan	71
14. Rensselaer Polytechnic Institute	70
14. San Jose State University	70
16. New Jersey Inst. of Technology	67
16. Rochester Inst. of Technology	67
18. University of Washington	66
19. University of Arizona	58
20. California State U., Sacramento	57
20. Milwaukee School of Engineering	57
22. Univ. of Maryland, College Park	56
23. Univ. of Puerto Rico, Mayaguez	55
24. Stevens Institute of Technology	54
25. Univ. of California, Santa Barbara	52
25. Polytechnic University	52
27. University of Wisconsin, Madison	49
28. Drexel University	48
28. University of Michigan, Dearborn	48
28. University of Minnesota, Twin Cities	48
28. West Virginia University	48
32. University of Pittsburgh	46
33. University of Illinois at Chicago	42
33. University of Missouri, Kansas City	42
35. Rose-Hulman Inst. of Technology	41
35. San Diego State University	41
37. Clarkson University	39
37. University of Missouri, Rolla	39
39. Univ. of Maryland, Baltimore County	38
40. University of California, Santa Cruz	37
40. Florida International University	37
42. Clemson University	36
42. Michigan State University	36
44. Case Western Reserve University	35
45. University of Kansas	33
45. Michigan Technological University	33
47. Florida Institute of Technology	32
47. Univ. of Massachusetts, Amherst	32
47. Northeastern University	32
47. Oregon State University	32

165 schools reported

ELECTRICAL/COMPUTER ENGINEERING DEGREES AWARDED BY SCHOOL

1. University of Texas, Austin	328
2. University of California, Berkeley	240
3. Massachusetts Inst. of Technology	198
4. Ohio State University	185
5. Rutgers University	162
6. Brigham Young University	145
7. Cornell University	134
8. Carnegie Mellon University	126
9. Vanderbilt University	99
10. Stony Brook University	89
11. Worcester Polytechnic Institute	82
12. Univ. of California, Los Angeles	73
13. University of Texas, San Antonio	69
14. Colorado State University	57
15. University of Florida	56
16. Southern Illinois Univ., Carbondale	48
17. University of Colorado, Boulder	47
18. Temple University	42
19. University of Toledo	41
20. University of Pennsylvania	39

48 total schools reported.

COMPUTER SCIENCE (OUTSIDE ENG.) DEGREES AWARDED BY SCHOOL*

1. University of California, Irvine	266
2. Georgia Institute of Technology	226
3. Univ. of Maryland, College Park	177
4. Brigham Young University	141
4. Rochester Institute of Technology	141
6. Rensselaer Polytechnic Institute	116
7. Carnegie Mellon University	115
8. University of California, Davis	104
9. University of California, Berkeley	97
10. Worcester Polytechnic Institute	86
11. New Jersey Inst. of Technology	83
12. FAMU-FSU College of Eng.	81
13. Univ. of Massachusetts, Amherst	76
14. University of Arizona	75
15. University of Florida	72
16. University of Pittsburgh	69
17. Wentworth Inst. of Technology	64
18. University of Texas, San Antonio	51
19. University of Nebraska, Lincoln	48
20. Illinois Institute of Technology	46

62 schools reported
*ASEE collects only a fraction of all computer science degrees awarded outside of engineering colleges.

COMPUTER SCIENCE (INSIDE ENG.) DEGREES AWARDED BY SCHOOL

1. University of California, San Diego	211
2. University of Central Florida	210
3. Univ. of Illinois at Urbana-Champaign	183
4. University of Texas, Dallas	181
5. Stony Brook University	169
6. University of North Texas	162
7. Virginia Tech	155
8. Florida International University	150
9. North Carolina State University	133
10. Texas A&M University	124
11. Univ. of Maryland, Baltimore County	119
12. University of Minnesota, Twin Cities	114
13. California State Univ., Northridge	110
14. University of Southern California	107
15. George Mason University	102
16. Arizona State University	99
16. Oregon State University	99
18. California Poly. State Univ., SLO	96
19. California State Univ., Long Beach	95
20. Drexel University	90
21. California State Univ., Fullerton	89
21. University of California, Riverside	89
23. New York Institute of Technology	87
24. University of California, Berkeley	86
24. University of Colorado, Boulder	86
24. University of Texas, Arlington	86
27. California State Univ., Sacramento	83
28. Ohio State University	82
28. Stanford University	82
30. SUNY, Binghamton	81
31. University of Washington	79
32. Cornell University	75
32. Michigan State University	75
34. University of Connecticut	74
34. Polytechnic University	74
36. University of Pennsylvania	72
37. Florida Atlantic University	71
38. University of Utah	69
39. University of Michigan	66
40. University of California, Davis	65
41. SUNY, Buffalo	64
41. Univ. of Wisconsin, Milwaukee	64
43. Univ. of California, Santa Barbara	62
44. Univ. of California, Los Angeles	61
44. University of Nevada, Las Vegas	61
46. Portland State University	60
47. Auburn University	57
48. University of Michigan, Dearborn	56
49. University of California, Santa Cruz	54
50. City College of the CUNY	52
50. University of Texas, El Paso	52
50. University of Virginia	52

148 total schools reported.

ENGINEERING UNDERGRADUATE ENROLLMENT BY SCHOOL*

1. Georgia Institute of Technology	7,203	
2. Texas A&M University	6,544	
3. Purdue University	6,281	
4. Pennsylvania State University	5,831	
5. North Carolina State University	5,823	
6. Univ. of Illinois, Urbana-Champaign	5,597	
7. Virginia Tech	5,483	
8. California Poly. State Univ., SLO	5,150	
9. University of Texas, Austin	5,047	
10. University of Michigan	4,912	
11. Univ. of Puerto Rico, Mayaguez	4,692	
12. Iowa State University	4,611	
13. University of Florida	4,573	
14. Ohio State University	4,362	
15. University of Central Florida	4,250	
16. California State Poly. U., Pomona	3,973	
17. Arizona State University	3,843	
18. University of California, San Diego	3,820	
19. Polytechnic Univ. of Puerto Rico	3,806	
20. Drexel University	3,425	
21. University of Missouri, Rolla	3,404	
22. University of Minnesota, Twin Cities	3,383	

23. Michigan Technological University	3,187
24. University of Wisconsin, Madison	3,179
25. Clemson University	3,159
26. Colorado School of Mines	3,154
27. Oregon State University	3,110
28. University of California, Berkeley	3,045
29. Rensselaer Polytechnic Institute	3,042
30. Cornell University	3,003
31. Auburn University	2,842
32. Michigan State University	2,826
33. University of California, Davis	2,814
34. Kansas State University	2,776
35. University of Colorado, Boulder	2,743
36. Texas Tech University	2,740
37. University of South Florida	2,727
38. Univ. of Maryland, College Park	2,547
39. Mississippi State University	2,536
40. University of Arizona	2,494
41. Louisiana State University	2,413
42. Rochester Inst. of Technology	2,373
43. Rutgers University	2,343
44. Univ. of California, Los Angeles	2,313

45. San Jose State University	2,309
46. City College of the CUNY	2,263
47. California State Univ., Long Beach	2,252
48. University of Nebraska, Lincoln	2,231
49. SUNY, Buffalo	2,230
50. University of California, Irvine	2,210
51. George Mason University	2,115
52. University of Texas, El Paso	2,106
53. University of Utah	2,093
54. West Virginia University	2,092
55. Florida International University	2,090
56. Oklahoma State University	2,058
57. Brigham Young University	2,044
58. University of Virginia	2,036
59. Kettering University	2,025
60. University of Oklahoma	2,024
61. Stanford University	1,970
62. University of Washington	1,946
63. University of Pittsburgh	1,931
64. FAMU-FSU College of Eng.	1,920
65. New Jersey Inst. of Technology	1,865
66. University of Alabama	1,856

331 schools reported.
* Some schools do not permit formal enrollment in their engineering colleges until the second or third year. Enrollment is full-time plus part-time students.

UNDERGRADUATE ENROLLMENT BY ENGINEERING DISCIPLINE:* 373,074

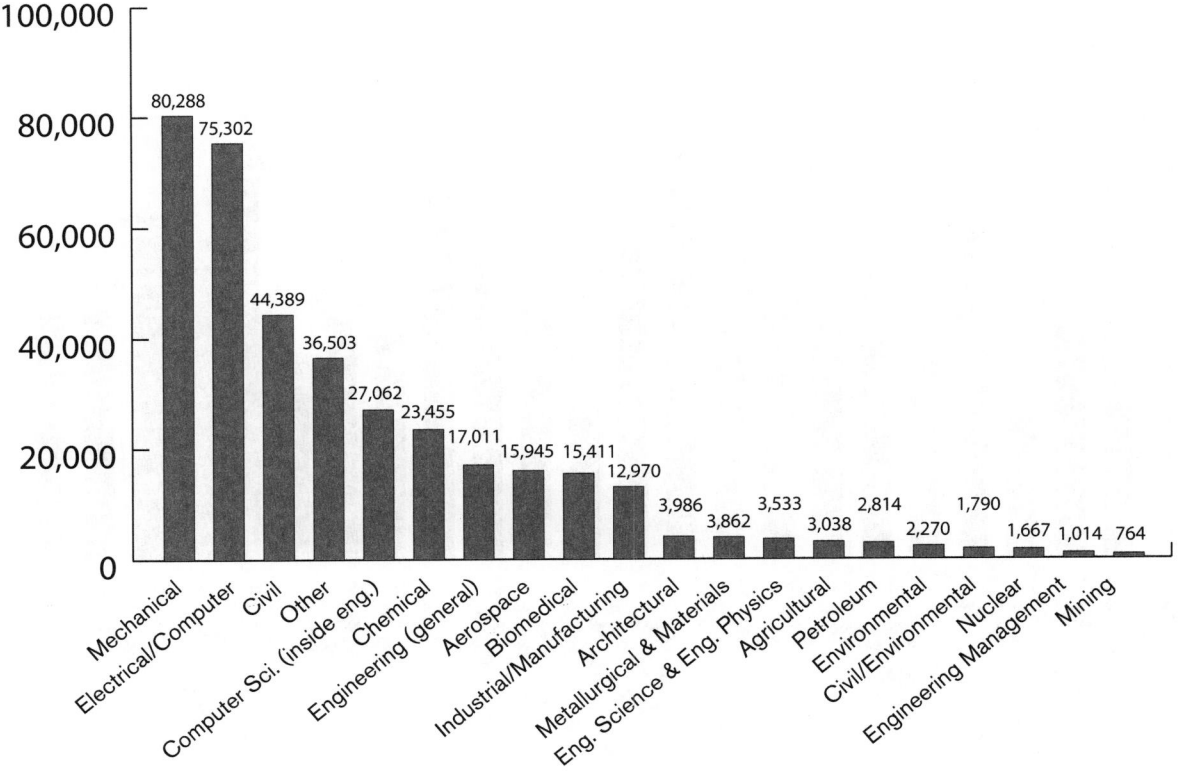

* Enrollment is for full-time bachelor's degree candidates in engineering.

MASTER'S DEGREES BY ENGINEERING DISCIPLINE: 39,015

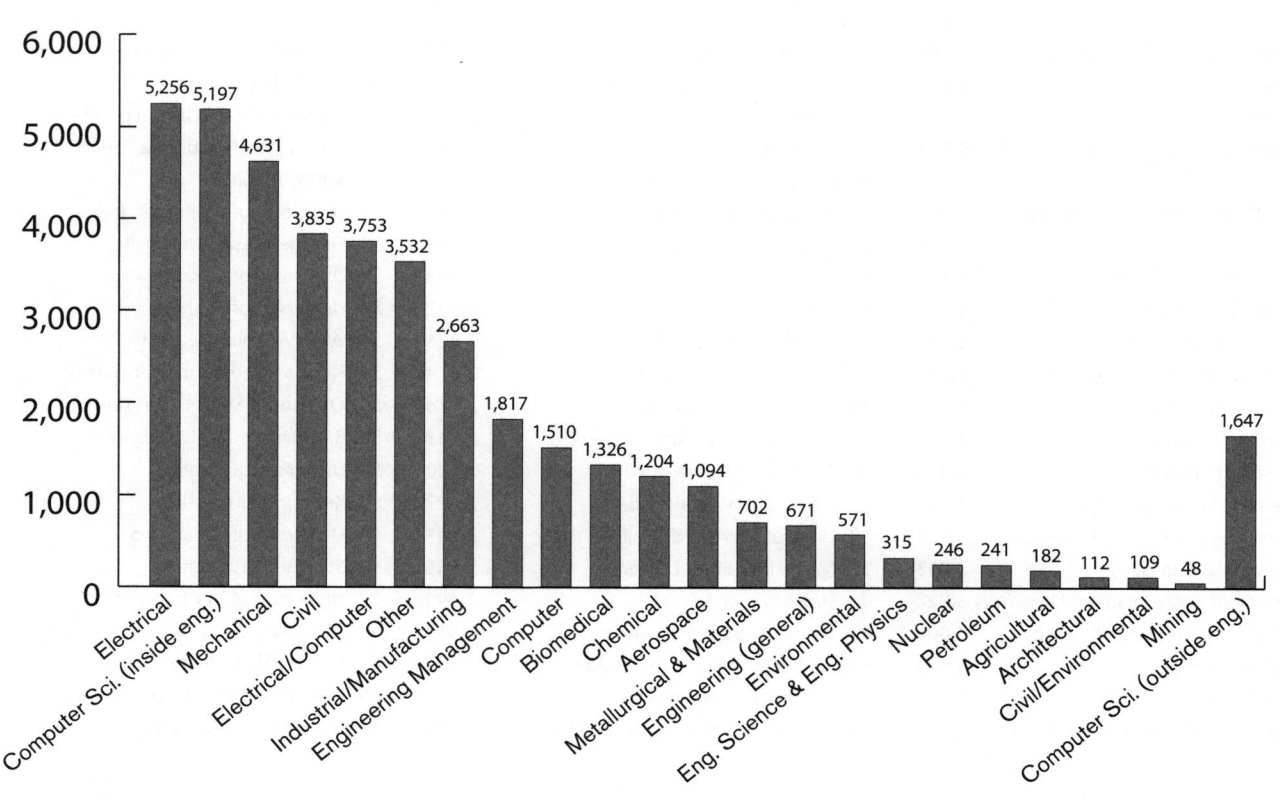

PERCENTAGE OF MASTER'S DEGREES AWARDED TO WOMEN BY DISCIPLINE: 22.5%

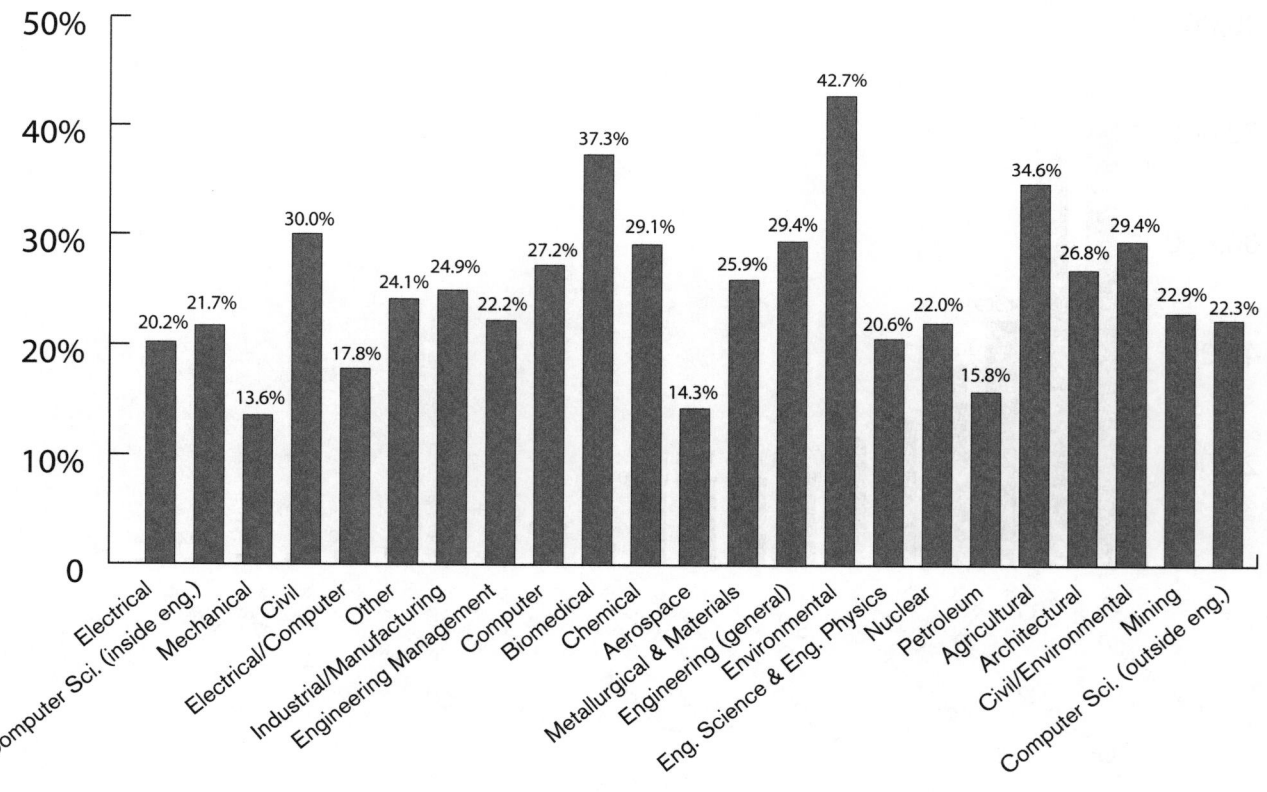

ENGINEERING MASTER'S DEGREES AWARDED BY SCHOOL

1. University of Southern California	1,190
2. Stanford University	1,015
3. Johns Hopkins University	811
4. Georgia Institute of Technology	751
5. Massachusetts Inst. of Technology	745
6. University of Michigan	730
7. San Jose State University	628
8. Air Force Institute of Technology	573
9. University of Texas, Arlington	565
10. Univ. of Illinois, Urbana-Champaign	554
11. Cornell University	508
12. Purdue University	461
13. University of Florida	449
14. University of Texas, Austin	447
15. Texas A&M University	445
16. Virginia Tech	438
17. North Carolina State University	437
18. Columbia University	431
19. George Washington University	419
20. George Mason University	405
21. New Jersey Inst. of Technology	371
22. Wayne State University	364
23. Univ. of Maryland, College Park	361
24. Univ. of Minnesota, Twin Cities	360
25. University of Wisconsin, Madison	353
26. Southern Methodist University	340
27. University of California, Berkeley	335
28. University of Pennsylvania	334
29. University of Colorado, Boulder	330
29. Pennsylvania State University	330
31. University of Washington	308
32. SUNY, Buffalo	304
33. Univ. of California, Los Angeles	301
34. University of Missouri, Rolla	300
35. New York Institute of Technology	299
36. Polytechnic University	297
37. Florida Atlantic University	296
38. Carnegie Mellon University	294
39. University of Texas, Dallas	291
40. Arizona State University	285
41. Illinois Institute of Technology	284
42. Old Dominion University	280
43. University of Central Florida	274
44. Ohio State University	272
45. Stevens Institute of Technology	264
46. Northwestern University	262
47. University of California, San Diego	253
47. University of Cincinnati	253
47. University of Louisville	253
50. University of Michigan, Dearborn	247

249 schools reported.

MASTER'S DEGREES BY ETHNICITY*

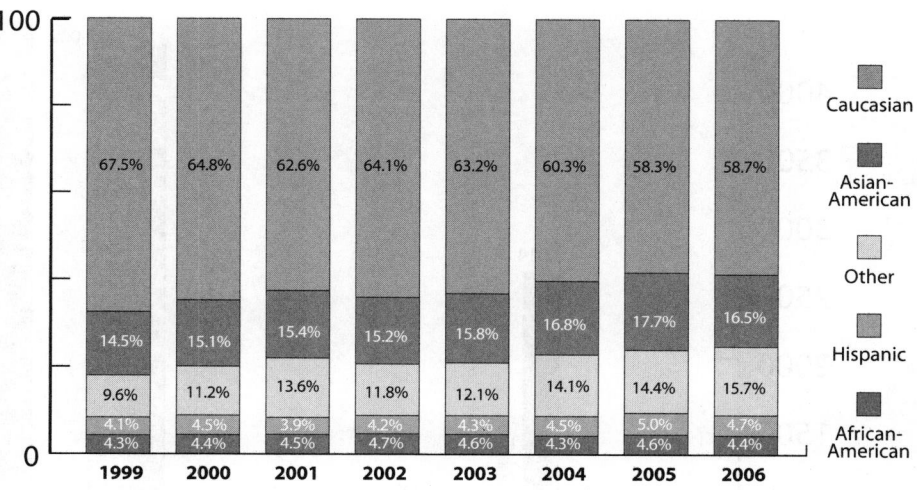

* Data on ethnicity does not include schools from Puerto Rico or foreign nationals.

MASTER'S DEGREES BY RESIDENCY

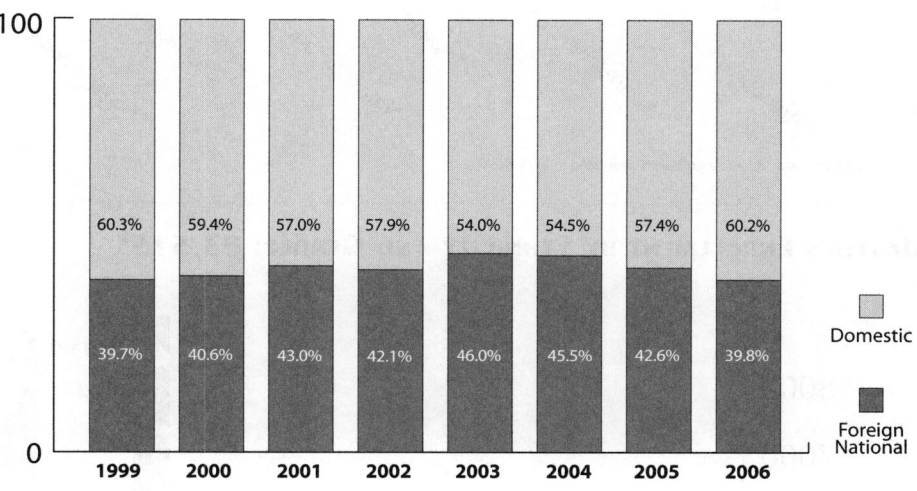

MASTER'S DEGREES BY GENDER

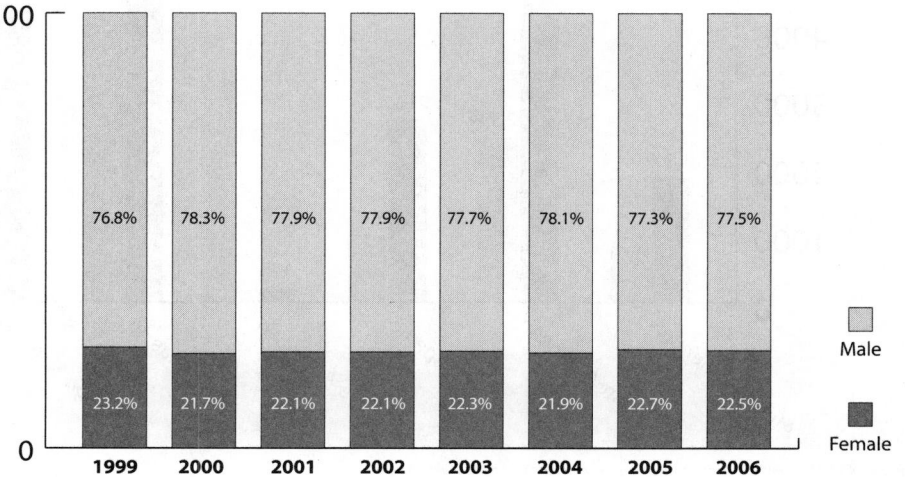

MASTER'S DEGREES BY ETHNICITY AND GENDER: 39,015*

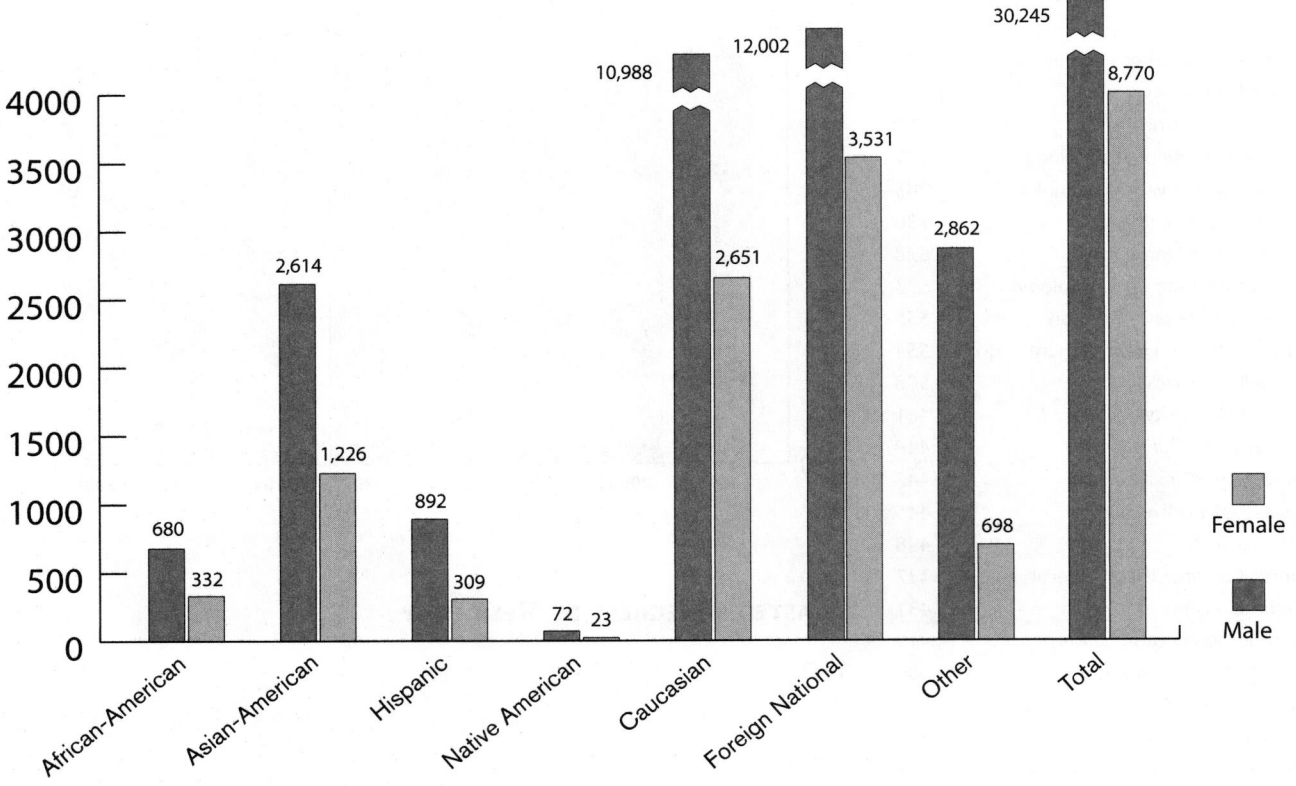

* Includes 73 male and 38 female graduates from schools in Puerto Rico.

MASTER'S ENROLLMENT BY ETHNICITY AND GENDER: 83,515*

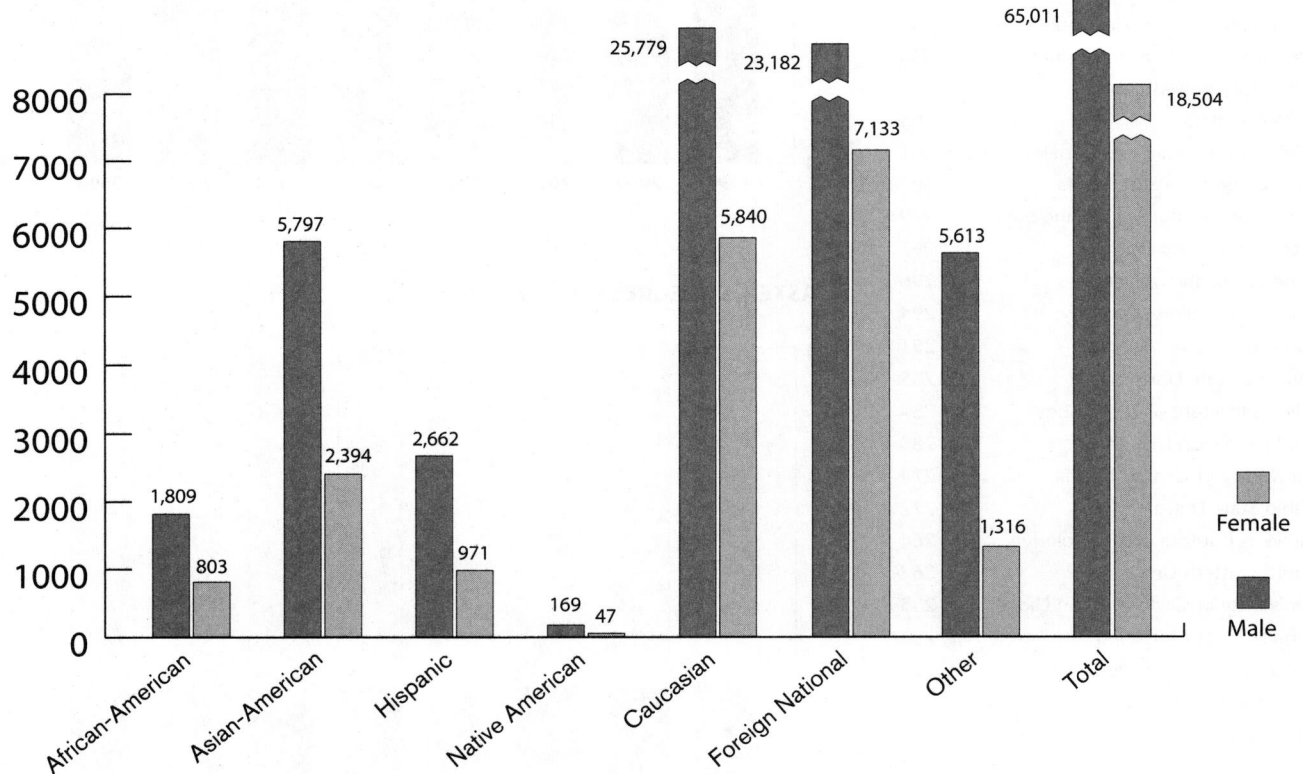

* Includes 423 male and 274 female enrolled students from schools in Puerto Rico

ENGINEERING GRADUATE ENROLLMENT BY SCHOOL

1. University of Southern California	3,819
2. Stanford University	3,377
3. Georgia Institute of Technology	3,360
4. Massachusetts Inst. of Technology	2,662
5. Johns Hopkins University	2,604
6. Univ. of Illinois, Urbana-Champaign	2,472
7. University of Michigan	2,450
8. Texas A&M University	2,265
9. University of Florida	2,205
10. University of Texas, Austin	2,125
11. Purdue University	2,121
12. North Carolina State University	1,903
13. Virginia Tech	1,870
14. Univ. of Minnesota, Twin Cities	1,827
15. University of Maryland, College Park	1,661
16. University of California, Berkeley	1,639
17. Pennsylvania State University	1,611
18. Arizona State University	1,603
19. San Jose State University	1,566
20. George Mason University	1,524
21. University of Colorado, Boulder	1,489
22. University of Texas, Arlington	1,444
23. University of Washington	1,440
24. George Washington University	1,368
25. Columbia University	1,338
26. University of Wisconsin, Madison	1,333
27. Univ. of California, Los Angeles	1,295
28. Cornell University	1,295
29. Ohio State University	1,209
30. University of California, San Diego	1,195
31. New Jersey Institute of Technology	1,171
32. University of California, Davis	1,133
33. University of Pennsylvania	1,070
34. Northwestern University	1,053
35. Illinois Institute of Technology	1,025
36. University of Missouri, Rolla	1,019
37. University of Central Florida	994
38. SUNY, Buffalo	991
39. Polytechnic University	975
40. University of Texas, Dallas	973
41. Drexel University	961
42. University of Cincinnati	959
43. Wayne State University	951
44. Old Dominion University	942
45. Carnegie Mellon University	930
46. Southern Methodist University	927
47. Stony Brook University	895
48. University of Illinois, Chicago	875
49. Iowa State University	862
50. Northeastern University	842

250 total schools reported.

ENGINEERING DOCTORAL DEGREES AWARDED BY SCHOOL

1. Massachusetts Inst. of Technology	288
2. Georgia Institute of Technology	276
3. Stanford University	243
4. Univ. of Illinois, Urbana-Champaign	240
5. University of Michigan	218
6. University of California, Berkeley	206
7. Purdue University	192
8. University of Texas, Austin	191
9. University of Florida	181
10. Pennsylvania State University	176
11. Texas A&M University	153
12. University of Southern California	151
13. Virginia Tech	149
14. Univ. of California, Los Angeles	142
15. Ohio State University	136
16. University of Minnesota, Twin Cities	131
17. Univ. of Maryland, College Park	130
18. Cornell University	122
19. North Carolina State University	119
19. Northwestern University	119
21. Univ. of California, Santa Barbara	107
21. University of Washington	107
23. University of California, San Diego	106
24. Arizona State University	100
25. University of Wisconsin, Madison	97
26. Carnegie Mellon University	86
26. Rensselaer Polytechnic Institute	86
28. Iowa State University	84
29. Princeton University	81
30. University of California, Davis	80
31. California Institute of Technology	78
32. University of Cincinnati	77
32. Columbia University	77
34. University of Colorado, Boulder	76
35. William Marsh Rice University	73
36. Stony Brook University	71
37. University of California, Irvine	70
37. Case Western Reserve University	70
39. Johns Hopkins University	66
40. George Washington University	61
40. Michigan State University	61
42. University of Hawaii, Manoa	60
43. University of Arizona	59
43. University of Delaware	59
45. University of Central Florida	55
48. Auburn University	52
47. University of Missouri, Rolla	52
46. SUNY, Buffalo	52
49. Drexel University	51
49. University of Utah	51
49. University of Virginia	51

184 total schools reported.

PERCENTAGE OF MASTER'S DEGREES AWARDED TO WOMEN BY SCHOOL*

1. San Jose State University	51.8%
2. Marquette University	40.9%
3. Catholic University of America	37.2%
4. University of Delaware	35.2%
5. University of Iowa	34.2%
6. Univ. of Maryland, Baltimore County	33.9%
6. University of Rochester	33.9%
8. University of Toledo	33.8%
9. OGI School of Science & Eng., OHSU	33.7%
10. Stony Brook University	33.0%
11. Colorado School of Mines	32.9%
12. University of Puerto Rico, Mayaguez	32.2%
13. Wright State University	32.1%
14. Vanderbilt University	31.9%
15. University of Akron	31.7%
15. Howard University	31.7%
17. Boston University	31.1%
18. University of California, Berkeley	30.7%
19. University of Arizona	30.4%
19. Southern Illinois Univ. Edwardsville	30.4%

* Minimum of 35 total master's degrees awarded
197 schools met this criterion.

PERCENTAGE OF DOCTORAL DEGREES AWARDED TO WOMEN BY SCHOOL*

1. Northeastern University	37.0%
1. William Marsh Rice University	37.0%
3. Columbia University	32.5%
4. New Jersey Inst. of Technology	32.4%
5. Colorado School of Mines	30.8%
6. University of Connecticut	30.0%
7. Univ. of California, Riverside	29.7%
8. University of Kentucky	29.4%
8. University of Virginia	29.4%
10. Univ. of Tennessee, Knoxville	29.3%
11. Clemson University	29.2%
12. Stony Brook University	28.2%
13. George Washington University	27.9%
14. Vanderbilt University	27.5%
15. Johns Hopkins University	27.3%
16. University of Pennsylvania	27.1%
17. University of Notre Dame	26.5%
18. Cornell University	26.2%
18. Boston University	26.2%
20. Princeton University	25.9%

* Minimum of 25 total doctoral degrees awarded
93 schools fit this criterion.

DOCTORAL DEGREES BY ENGINEERING DISCIPLINE: 8,351

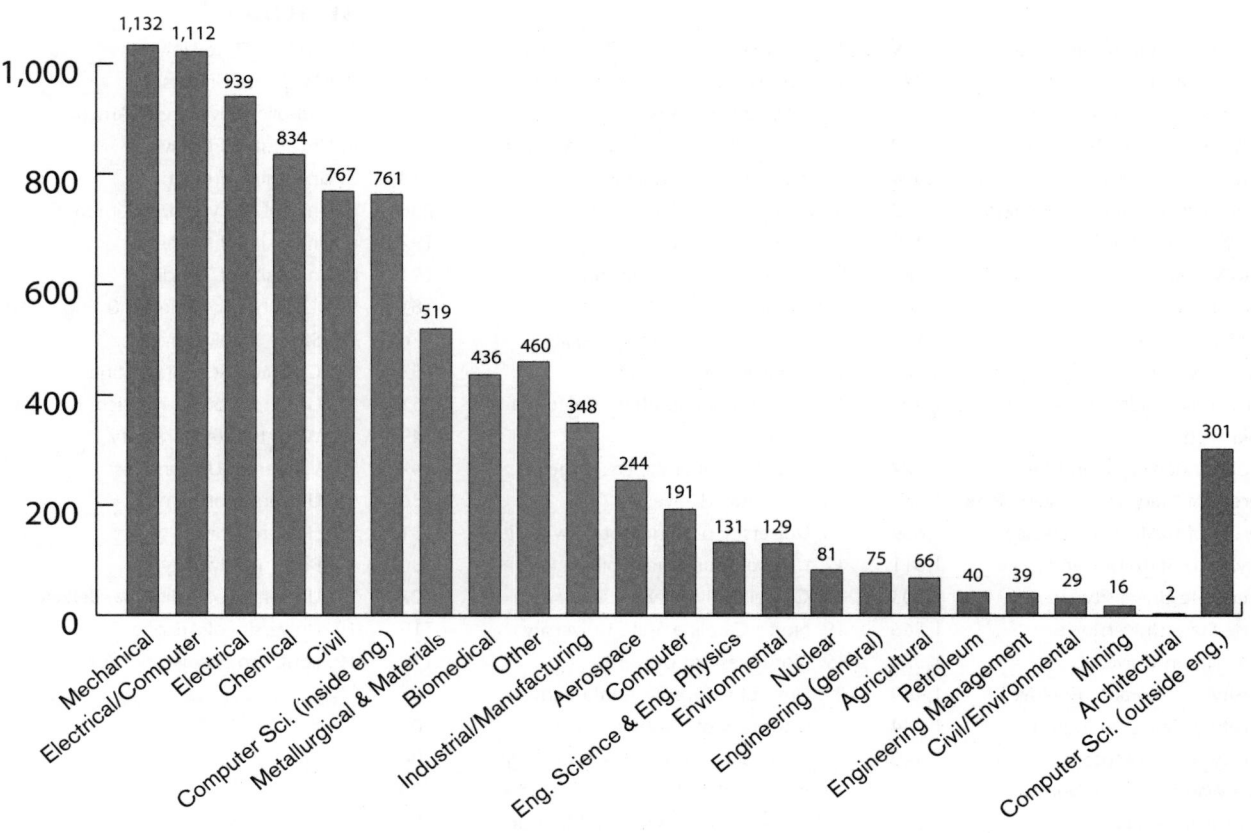

PERCENTAGE OF DOCTORAL DEGREES AWARDED TO WOMEN BY DISCIPLINE: 20.2%

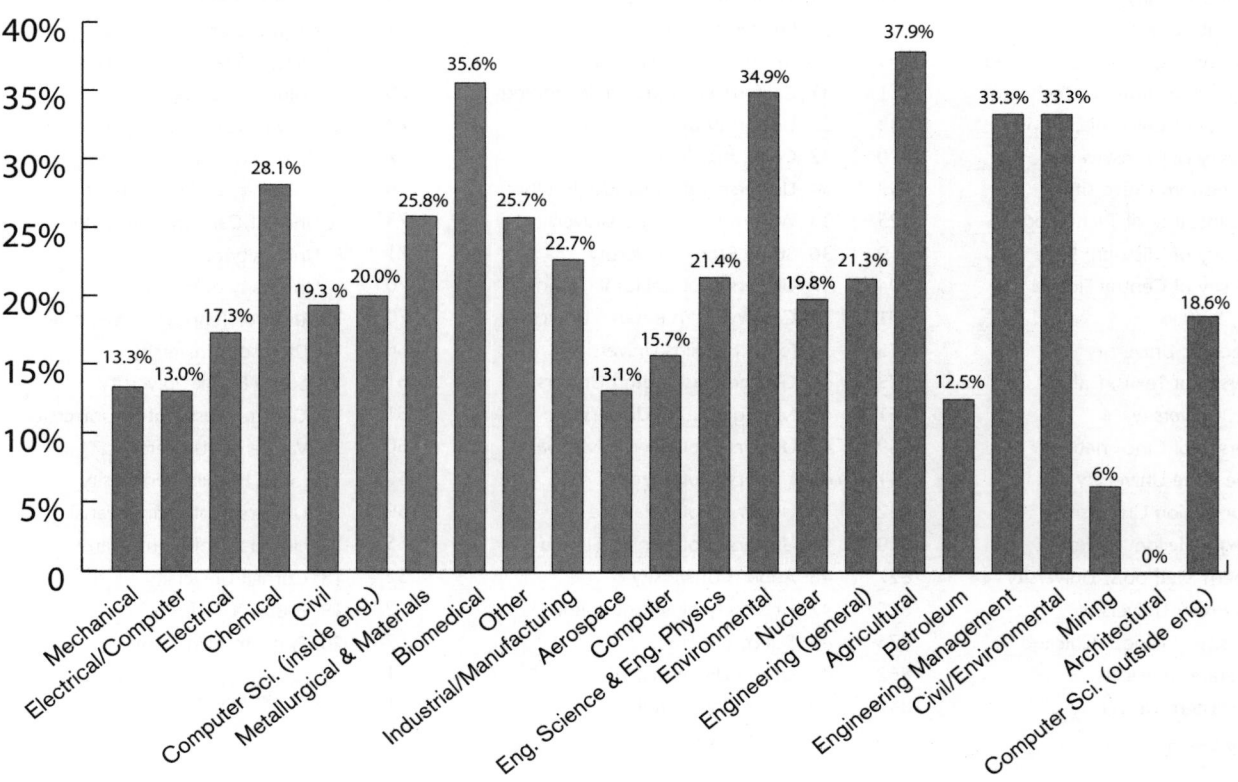

DOCTORAL DEGREES AWARDED TO FOREIGN NATIONALS BY SCHOOL

1. Georgia Institute of Technology	162
2. Univ. of Illinois, Urbana-Champaign	156
3. Purdue University	144
4. Massachusetts Inst. of Technology	135
5. University of Texas, Austin	130
6. University of Michigan	128
6. Texas A&M University	128
8. University of Southern California	123
8. Stanford University	123
10. University of Florida	122
11. Ohio State University	115
11. Pennsylvania State University	115
13. Univ. of California, Los Angeles	99
14. Univ. of Maryland, College Park	95
14. University of Minnesota, Twin Cities	95
16. University of California, Berkeley	92
16. Virginia Tech	92
18. North Carolina State University	85
19. Arizona State University	76
20. Cornell University	73
21. University of Cincinnati	68
22. Univ. of California, Santa Barbara	63
23. Iowa State University	62
24. Northwestern University	58
24. Rensselaer Polytechnic Institute	58
24. University of Washington	58
27. University of California, San Diego	55
27. University of Wisconsin, Madison	55
29. Carnegie Mellon University	54
29. Stony Brook University	54
31. Columbia University	53
32. California Institute of Technology	48
32. Princeton University	48
34. University of Hawaii, Manoa	47
35. Michigan State University	46
36. University of Arizona	41
36. University of Delaware	41
36. SUNY, Buffalo	41
36. William Marsh Rice University	41
40. University of Missouri, Rolla	40
41. Johns Hopkins University	38
41. University of Texas, Dallas	38
43. Auburn University	37
43. University of California, Davis	37
43. Case Western Reserve University	37
46. University of Central Florida	36
47. University of Connecticut	35
48. University of Houston	34
49. New Jersey Institute of Technology	33
50. Louisiana State University	32
50. University of Utah	32

184 total schools reported.

DOCTORAL DEGREES BY ETHNICITY*

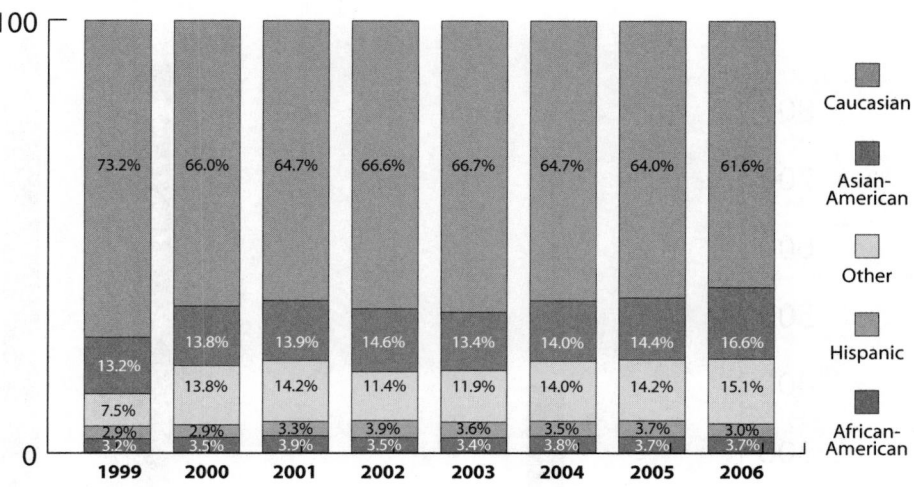

* Data on ethnicity does not include schools from Puerto Rico or foreign nationals.

DOCTORAL DEGREES BY RESIDENCY

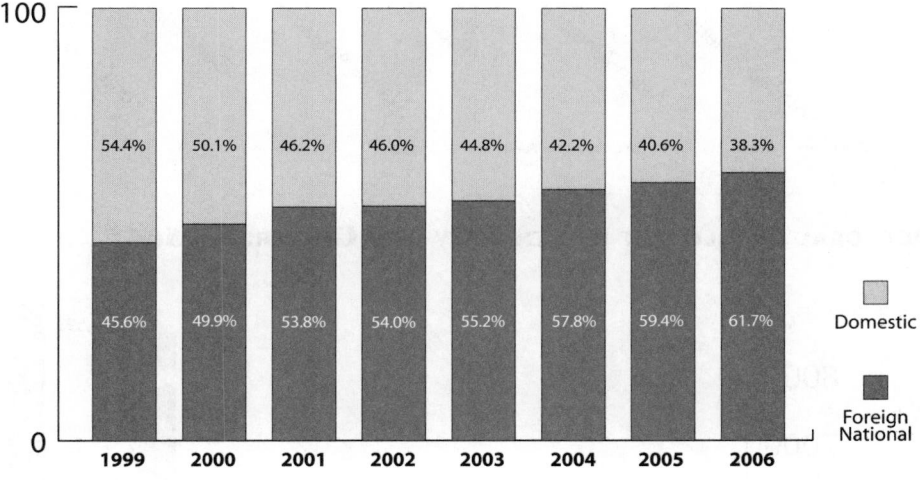

DOCTORAL DEGREES BY GENDER

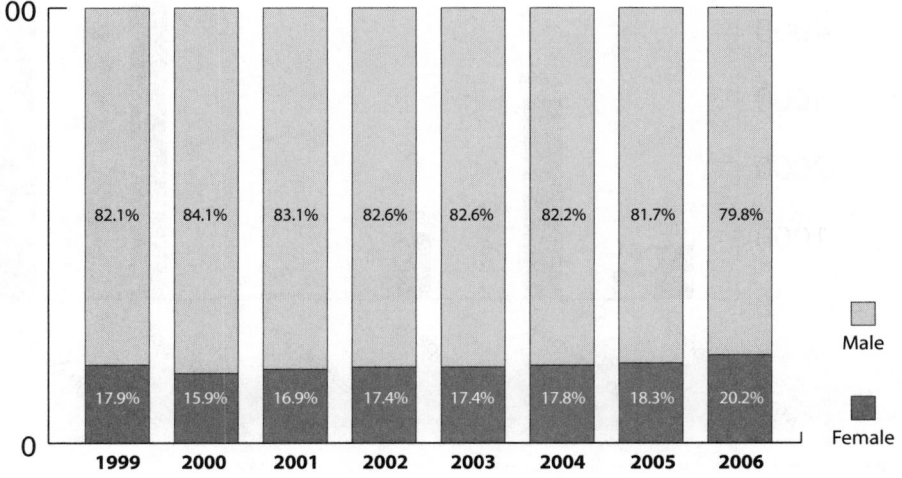

DOCTORAL DEGREES BY ETHNICITY AND GENDER: 8,351*

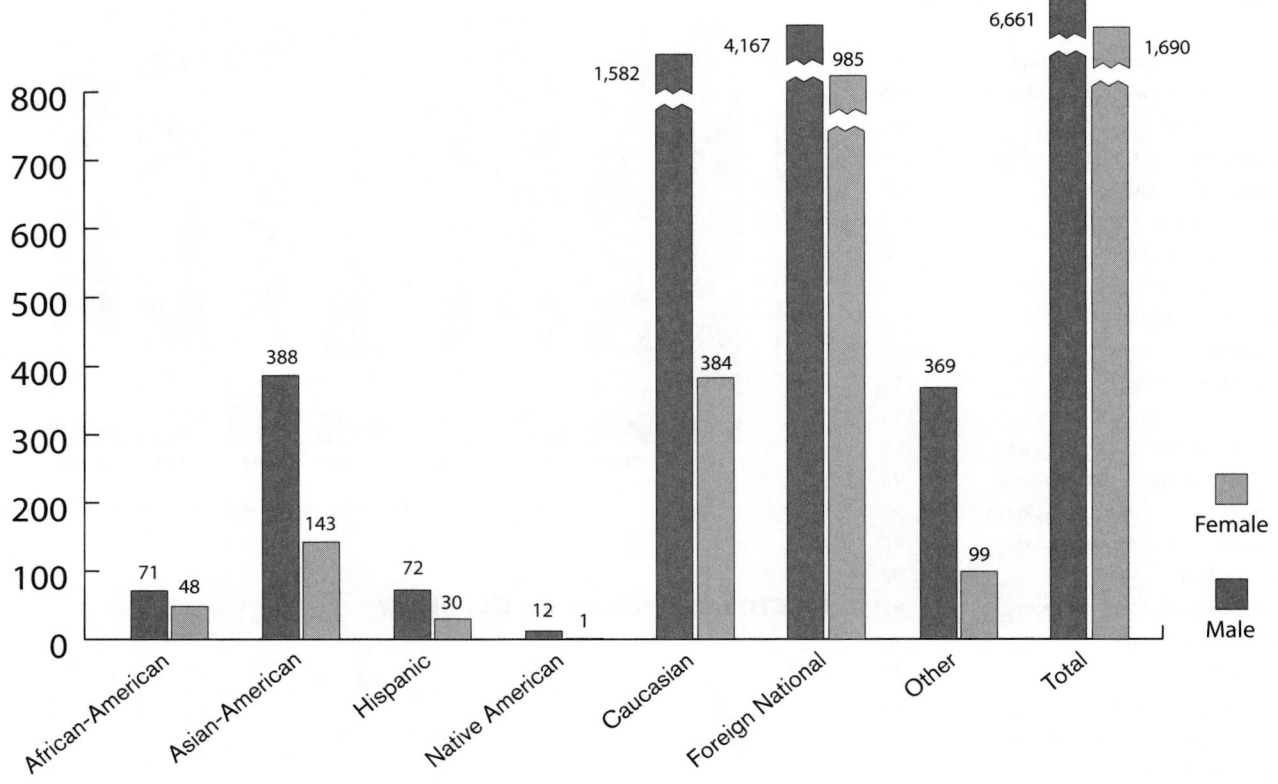

* Includes 7 male and 1 female graduates from University of Puerto Rico, Mayaguez.

DOCTORAL ENROLLMENT BY ETHNICITY AND GENDER: 57,566*

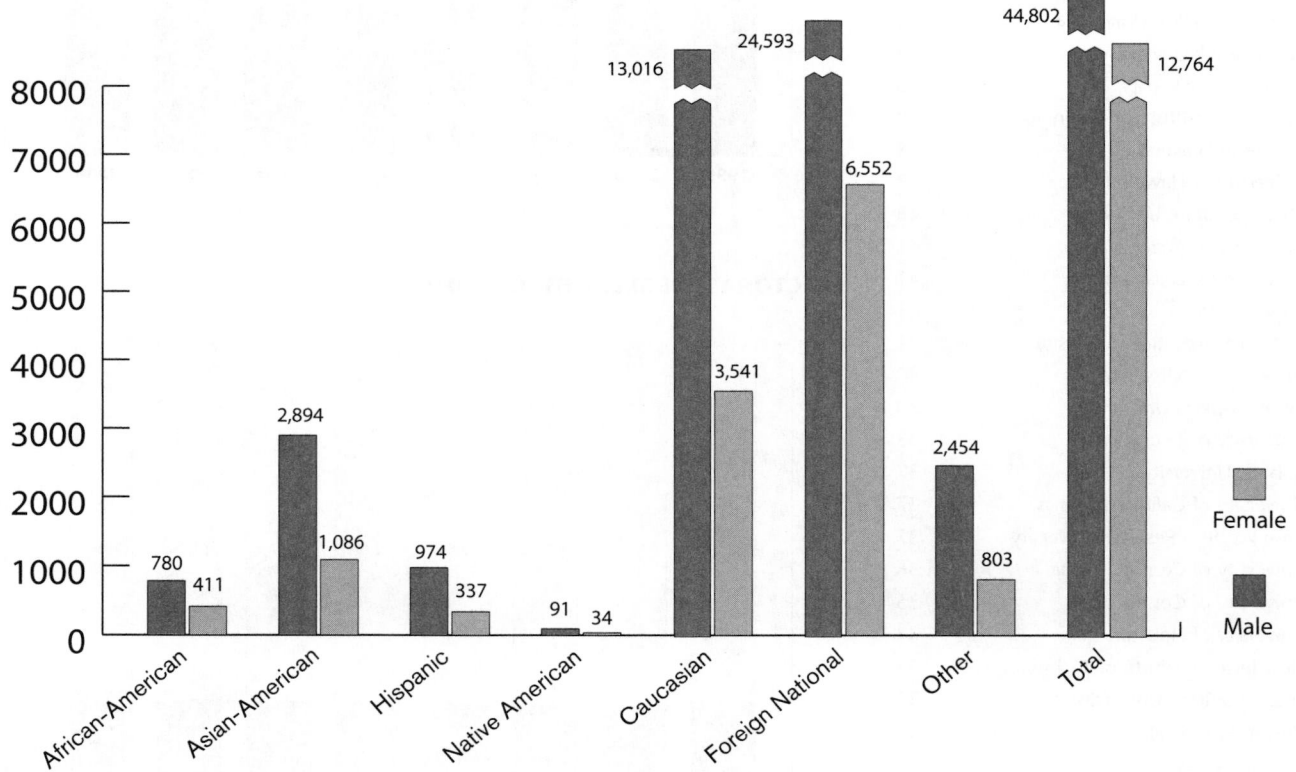

* Includes 58 male and 20 female enrolled students from schools in Puerto Rico. Enrollment is for full-time students.

ENGINEERING BACHELOR'S DEGREES AWARDED BY SCHOOL (EXCLUDING COMPUTER SCIENCE)

1.	Georgia Institute of Technology	1,391
2.	Pennsylvania State University	1,319
3.	Purdue University	1,238
4.	Univ. of Illinois, Urbana-Champaign	1,054
5.	Virginia Tech	1,032
6.	University of Michigan	984
7.	University of Texas, Austin	980
8.	Texas A&M University	942
9.	Iowa State University	932
10.	North Carolina State University	907
11.	California Poly. State Univ., SLO	878
12.	University of Florida	867
13.	University of California Berkeley	796
14.	Ohio State University	766
15.	University of California San Diego	744
16.	Univ. of Maryland College Park	657
17.	University of Washington	652
18.	University of Wisconsin Madison	641
19.	Cornell University	629
20.	University of Minnesota, Twin Cities	624
21.	Michigan Technological University	616
22.	Univ. of Puerto Rico, Mayaguez	606
23.	Massachusetts Inst. of Technology	578
24.	Arizona State University	574
25.	Rensselaer Polytechnic Institute	550
26.	Michigan State University	515
27.	California State Poly. Univ., Pomona	513
28.	University of California, Davis	508
29.	University of Missouri, Rolla	504
30.	Oregon State University	493
31.	Colorado School of Mines	482
32.	Clemson University	478
33.	Univ. of California, Los Angeles	473
34.	University of California Irvine	466
35.	University of Colorado, Boulder	458
36.	University of Arizona	448
37.	Brigham Young University	437
38.	SUNY, Buffalo	436
39.	San Jose State University	432
40.	University of Central Florida	430
41.	Drexel University	419
42.	Rutgers University	415
43.	Auburn University	406
44.	Worcester Polytechnic Institute	400
45.	Louisiana State University	398
46.	Kettering University	392
47.	Polytechnic Univ. of Puerto Rico	387
48.	Kansas State University	384
49.	Rochester Institute of Technology	379
50.	University of Pittsburgh	371

334 schools reported.

ENGINEERING MASTER'S DEGREES AWARDED BY SCHOOL (EXCLUDING COMPUTER SCIENCE)

1.	Stanford University	861
2.	University of Southern California	837
3.	Georgia Institute of Technology	751
4.	Massachusetts Inst. of Technology	745
5.	University of Michigan	730
6.	San Jose State University	628
7.	Air Force Institute of Technology	562
8.	Johns Hopkins University	547
9.	Purdue University	461
10.	University of Florida	449
11.	Univ. of Illinois, Urbana-Champaign	447
11.	University of Texas, Austin	447
13.	University of Texas, Arlington	426
14.	Texas A&M University	402
15.	Virginia Tech	394
16.	Cornell University	383
17.	New Jersey Institute of Technology	371
18.	Wayne State University	365
19.	Univ. of Maryland College Park	361
20.	North Carolina State University	355
21.	University of Wisconsin Madison	353
22.	George Mason University	351
23.	Columbia University	344
24.	Southern Methodist University	316
25.	George Washington University	310
26.	Pennsylvania State University	309
27.	University of Washington	308
28.	University of Colorado, Boulder	305
29.	University of Missouri, Rolla	300
30.	University of California Berkeley	295
31.	Carnegie Mellon University	294
32.	Illinois Institute of Technology	284
32.	University of Minnesota, Twin Cities	284
34.	Old Dominion University	280
35.	Stevens Institute of Technology	264
36.	Northwestern University	262
37.	University of Louisville	253
37.	University of Pennsylvania	253
39.	Ohio State University	252
40.	Arizona State University	236
40.	Univ. of California Los Angeles	236
40.	University of Cincinnati	236
43.	Syracuse University	230
44.	University of Arkansas	228
45.	University of Michigan Dearborn	213
46.	Rensselaer Polytechnic Institute	225
46.	Santa Clara University	225
48.	Northeastern University	224
49.	SUNY, Buffalo	220
50.	Iowa State University	214

249 schools reported.

ENGINEERING DOCTORAL DEGREES AWARDED BY SCHOOL (EXCLUDING COMPUTER SCIENCE)

1.	Massachusetts Inst. of Technology	288
2.	Georgia Institute of Technology	276
3.	University of Michigan	218
4.	Stanford University	215
5.	Purdue University	192
6.	University of Texas, Austin	191
7.	Univ. of Illinois, Urbana-Champaign	183
8.	University of Florida	181
9.	University of California Berkeley	154
10.	Pennsylvania State University	153
11.	Virginia Tech	138
12.	Texas A&M University	131
13.	Univ. of Maryland, College Park	130
14.	University of Southern California	121
15.	Northwestern University	119
15.	Ohio State University	119
17.	Cornell University	109
18.	Univ. of California Los Angeles	107
18.	University of Minnesota, Twin Cities	107
18.	North Carolina State University	107
18.	University of Washington	107
22.	University of Wisconsin Madison	97
23.	Univ. of California Santa Barbara	94
24.	Carnegie Mellon University	86
24.	Rensselaer Polytechnic Institute	86
26.	Iowa State University	84
27.	University of California, San Diego	83
28.	Arizona State University	79
29.	University of Cincinnati	77
30.	California Institute of Technology	75
31.	University of California Irvine	70
32.	University of California Davis	68
32.	William Marsh Rice University	68
34.	Case Western Reserve University	66
35.	Princeton University	65
36.	University of Colorado, Boulder	64
36.	Columbia University	64
38.	University of Hawaii, Manoa	60
39.	University of Arizona	59
39.	University of Delaware	59
39.	Stony Brook University	59
42.	Johns Hopkins University	55
43.	George Washington University	52
43.	University of Missouri, Rolla	52
45.	Michigan State University	50
46.	University of Notre Dame	49
46.	University of Pittsburgh	49
48.	Auburn University	48
48.	Drexel University	48
48.	University of Utah	48

184 schools reported.

Note: All enrollment and degree data in this book includes computer science programs administered by the engineering colleges. This page displays the largest degree programs at each level without the computer science programs.

NUMBER OF TEACHING PERSONNEL BY ENGINEERING DISCIPLINE:* 26,699

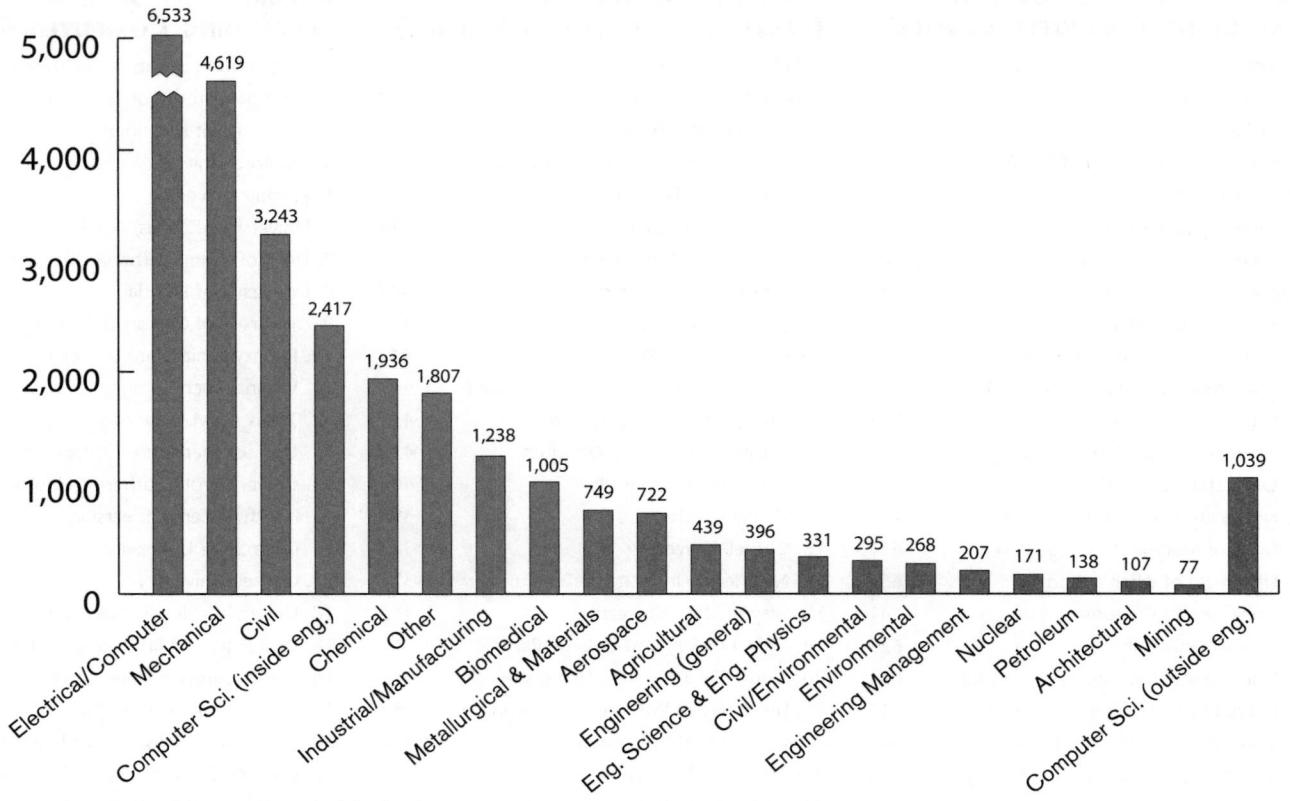

Note: These numbers were determined by adding tenured/tenure-track faculty, full-time nontenure-track teaching personnel and the full-time equivalent of part-time teaching personnel.

PERCENTAGE OF WOMEN TENURED/TENURE-TRACK TEACHING FACULTY BY DISCIPLINE: 11.3%

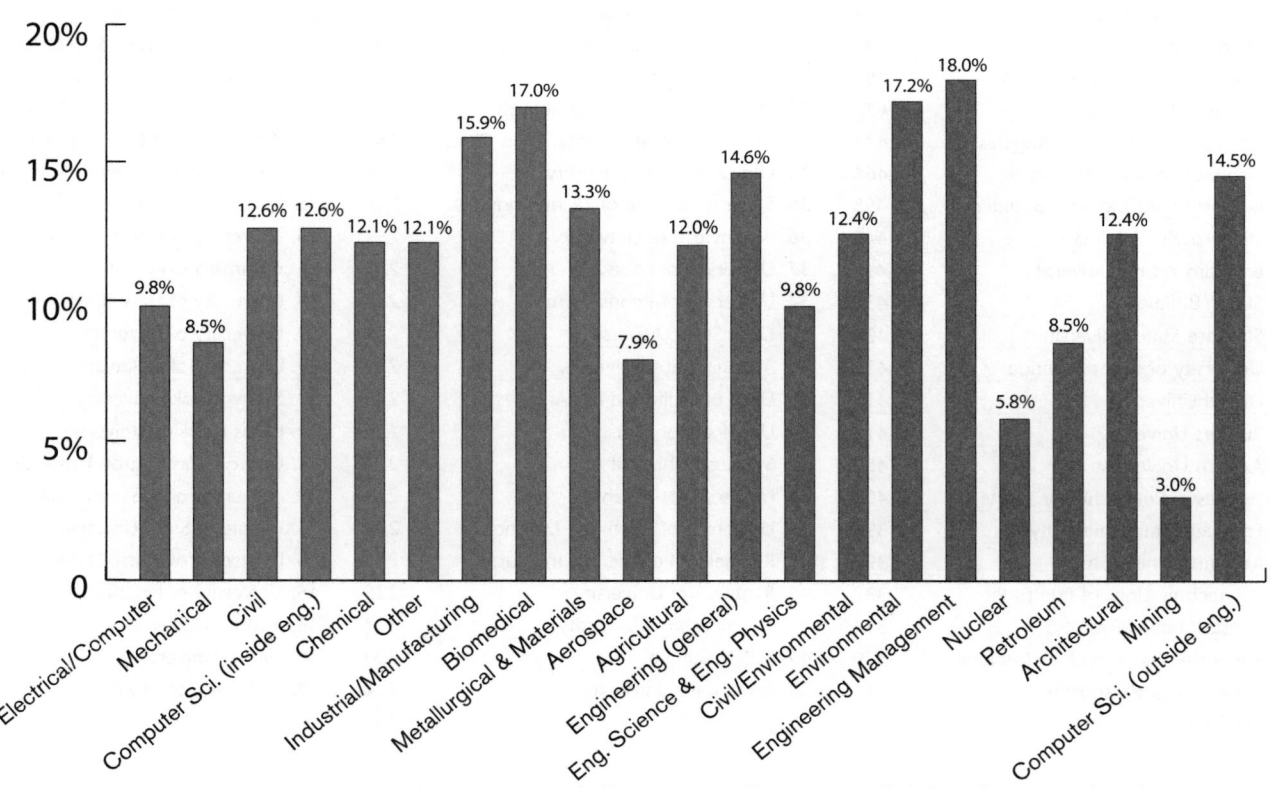

NUMBER OF TEACHING PERSONNEL BY SCHOOL*

1. Univ. of Illinois, Urbana-Champaign	441
2. Georgia Institute of Technology	419
3. Texas A&M University	376
4. Massachusetts Inst. of Technology	372
4. Virginia Tech	372
6. North Carolina State University	354
7. University of Michigan	337
8. Pennsylvania State University	334
9. University of Florida	311
10. Purdue University	309
11. Ohio State University	291
12. University of Texas, Austin	275
13. University of Minnesota, Twin Cities	268
14. Cornell University	260
15. University of Washington	257
16. Iowa State University	248
17. University of California, Berkeley	244
18. Clemson University	229
19. Arizona State University	228
20. University of Nebraska, Lincoln	216
21. Stanford University	213
22. University of California, Davis	212
23. Colorado School of Mines	210
24. Univ. of Maryland, College Park	209
25. California Poly. State U., SLO	193
26. University of Colorado, Boulder	188
26. United States Military Academy	188
28. University of California, San Diego	186
29. University of Wisconsin, Madison	183
30. University of Missouri, Rolla	176
31. University of Southern California	175
32. Michigan State University	172
33. Univ. of Puerto Rico, Mayaguez	167
34. University of Kentucky	166
35. Univ. of California, Los Angeles	165
36. University of Central Florida	162
36. New Jersey Institute of Technology	162
38. Northwestern University	161
39. University of Tennessee, Knoxville	156
40. Auburn University	155
41. Carnegie Mellon University	151
41. University of Virginia	151
43. University of Cincinnati	148
44. University of Utah	147
45. George Mason University	146
46. Rensselaer Polytechnic Institute	145
47. Kansas State University	144
47. Stony Brook University	144
49. Johns Hopkins University	142
50. Drexel University	141

323 schools reported.
* These numbers were determined by adding tenured/tenure-track faculty, full-time nontenure-track teaching personnel and the full-time equivalent of part-time teaching personnel.

NUMBER OF ENGINEERING TEACHING PERSONNEL BY RANK

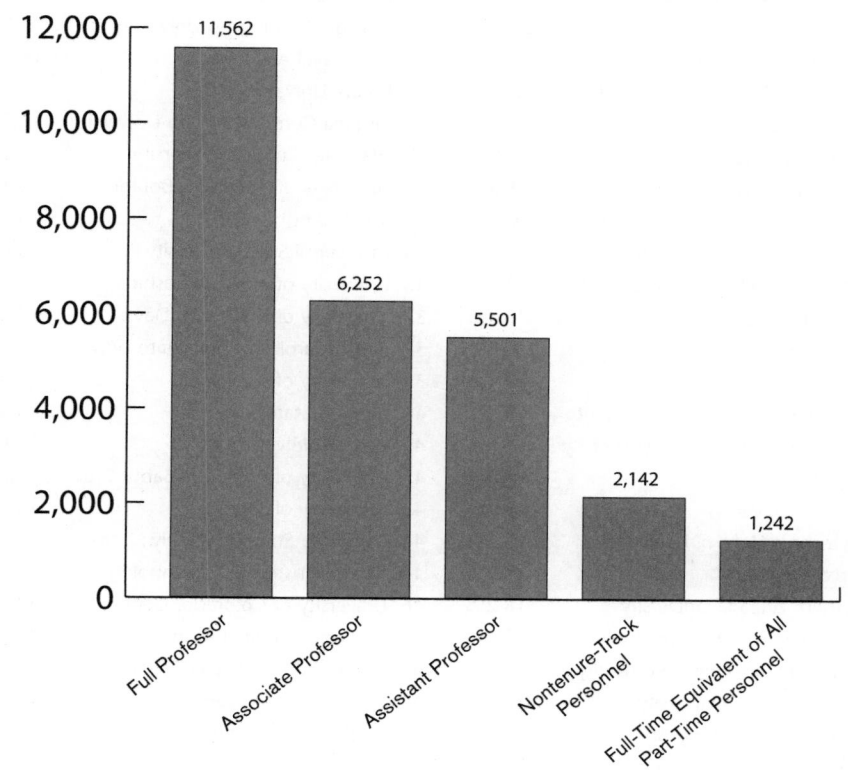

PERCENTAGE OF WOMEN TENURED/TENURE-TRACK FACULTY MEMBERS BY LEVEL

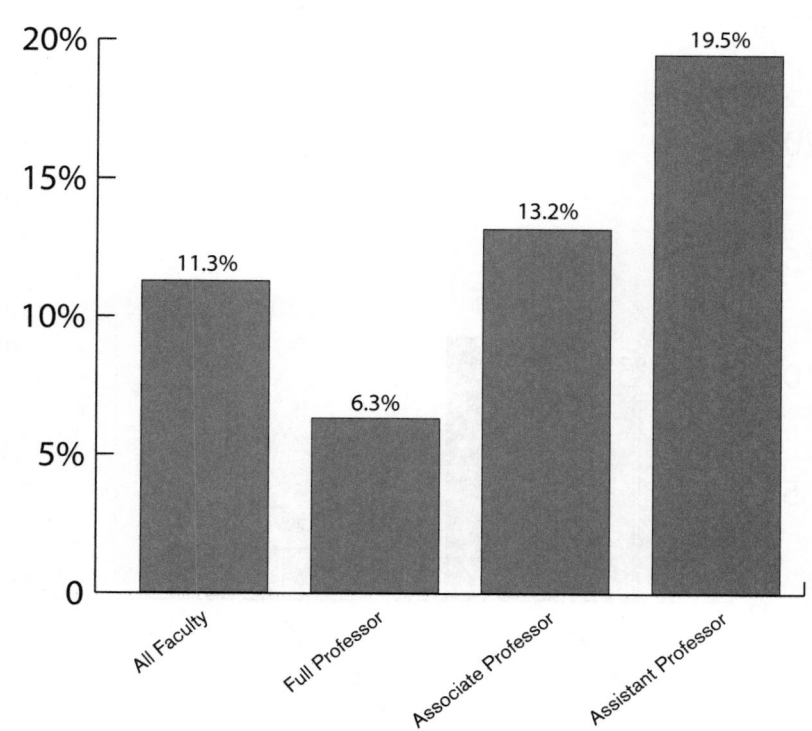

PERCENTAGE OF WOMEN TENURED /TENURE-TRACK TEACHING FACULTY MEMBERS BY SCHOOL*

1. Santa Clara University	29.4%	
2. Boise State University	25.0%	
3. OGI School of Science & Eng., OHSU	22.2%	
3. Tennessee State University	22.2%	
5. Lafayette College	21.9%	
5. Rowan University	21.9%	
7. Univ. of Maryland, Baltimore County	20.7%	
8. Univ. of Tennessee, Chattanooga	20.6%	
9. California State Univ., Los Angeles	20.5%	
10. Bucknell University	20.4%	
11. Clarkson University	20.0%	
11. Syracuse University	20.0%	
13. California State Univ., Sacramento	19.4%	
14. Lawrence Technological University	18.8%	
15. Tufts University	18.5%	
16. Oakland University	18.4%	
17. Polytechnic Univ. of Puerto Rico	18.3%	
18. Mercer University	18.2%	
18. Northern Arizona University	18.2%	
20. Rose-Hulman Inst. of Technology	18.0%	
21. California State Univ., Northridge	17.9%	
22. Cleveland State University	17.6%	
23. University of Washington	17.3%	
24. University of Alabama, Huntsville	17.2%	
25. Duke University	17.0%	
25. George Mason University	17.0%	
27. Drexel University	16.9%	
28. George Washington University	16.7%	
28. U.S. Naval Academy	16.7%	
30. Miami University	16.3%	
30. Virginia Commonwealth University	16.3%	
32. Washington State University	16.2%	
33. University of Colorado, Boulder	16.1%	
33. SUNY, Binghamton	16.1%	
35. Mississippi State University	16.0%	
36. University of New Hampshire	15.8%	
37. University of California, Davis	15.5%	
37. North Carolina A & T State Univ.	15.5%	
39. University of the Pacific	15.4%	
40. Oregon State University	15.3%	
41. Purdue University	15.0%	
42. University of California-Santa Cruz	14.9%	
42. University of Toledo	14.9%	
44. California State Poly. Univ., Pomona	14.8%	
44. Oregon Institute of Technology	14.8%	
46. University of Colorado, Denver	14.7%	
46. University of Pittsburgh	14.7%	
46. William Marsh Rice University	14.7%	
49. Stony Brook University	14.5%	
49. Portland State University	14.5%	

231 schools fit this criterion.
* Minimum of 25 faculty members.

WOMEN TENURED/TENURE-TRACK TEACHING FACULTY MEMBERS BY SCHOOL

1. Massachusetts Inst. of Technology	52
2. Georgia Institute of Technology	48
3. Virginia Tech	46
4. Purdue University	45
5. University of Michigan	43
6. Pennsylvania State University	42
7. Texas A&M University	40
8. Univ. of Illinois, Urbana-Champaign	35
9. University of Washington	33
10. University of California, Davis	32
11. North Carolina State University	29
12. University of California, Berkeley	28
12. Stanford University	28
14. University of Colorado at Boulder	27
14. Ohio State University	27
16. University of Texas, Austin	26
17. University of Florida	25
18. Arizona State University	24
18. Cornell University	24
18. Iowa State University	24

317 total schools reported.

PERCENTAGE OF WOMEN AND MINORITY FACULTY MEMBERS, 2001-2006*

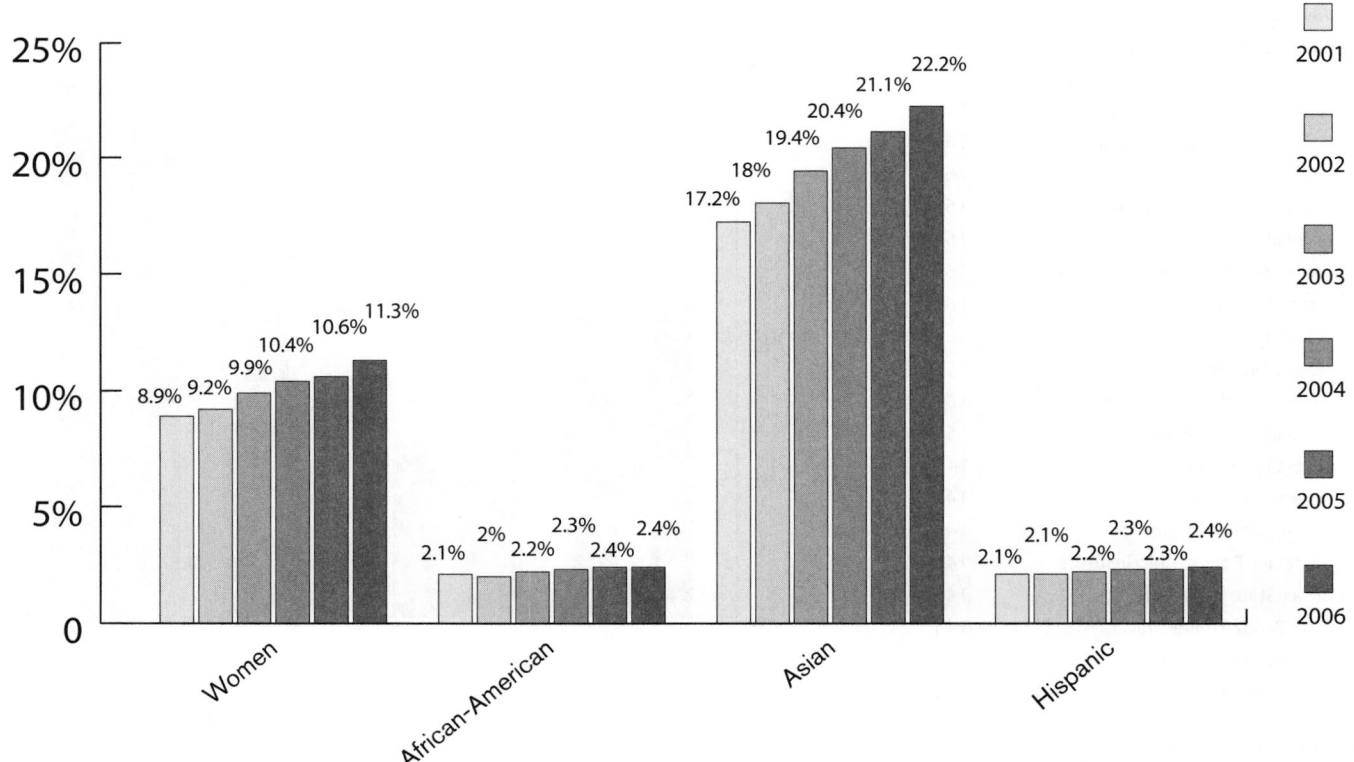

*Note: only data on women includes faculty from University of Puerto Rico, Mayaguez and Polytechnic University of Puerto Rico

NUMBER OF FULL PROFESSORS BY RACE/ETHNICITY (TEACHING): 11,562*

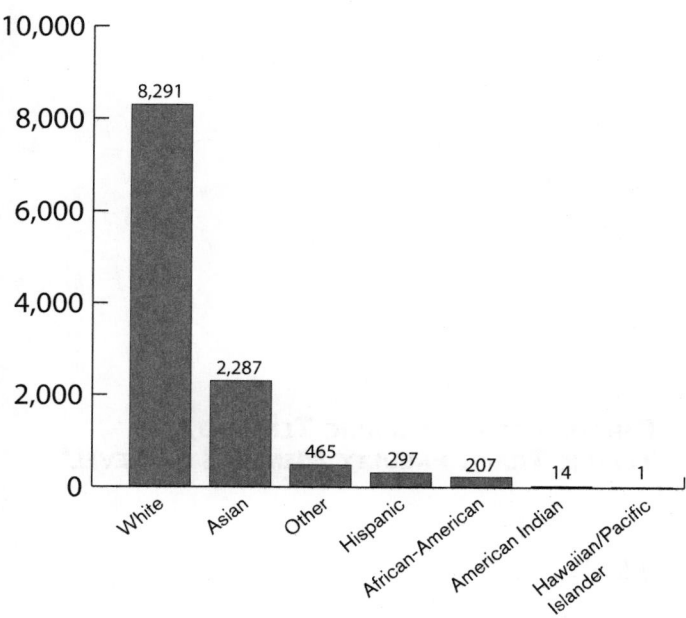

Note: Includes 101 Hispanic faculty from University of Puerto Rico, Mayaguez and Polytechnic University of Puerto Rico

NUMBER OF ASSISTANT PROFESSORS BY RACE/ETHNICITY (TEACHING): 5,501*

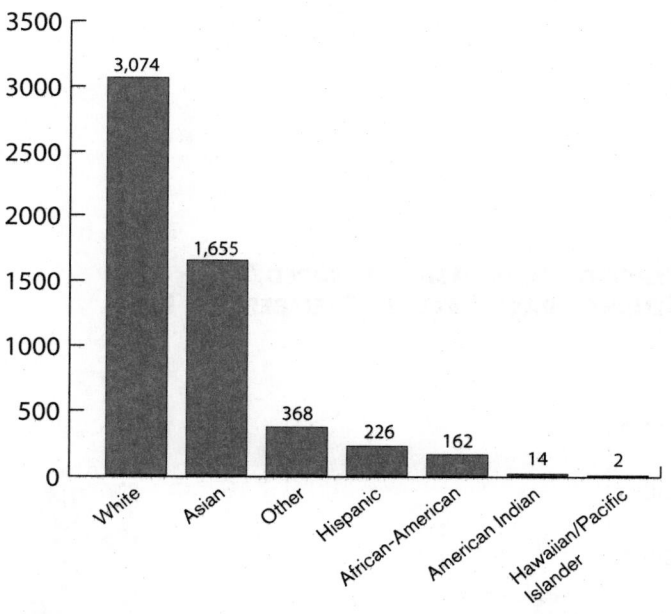

* Note: Includes 67 Hispanic faculty from University of Puerto Rico, Mayaguez and Polytechnic University of Puerto Rico.

NUMBER OF ASSOCIATE PROFESSORS BY RACE/ETHNICITY (TEACHING): 6,252*

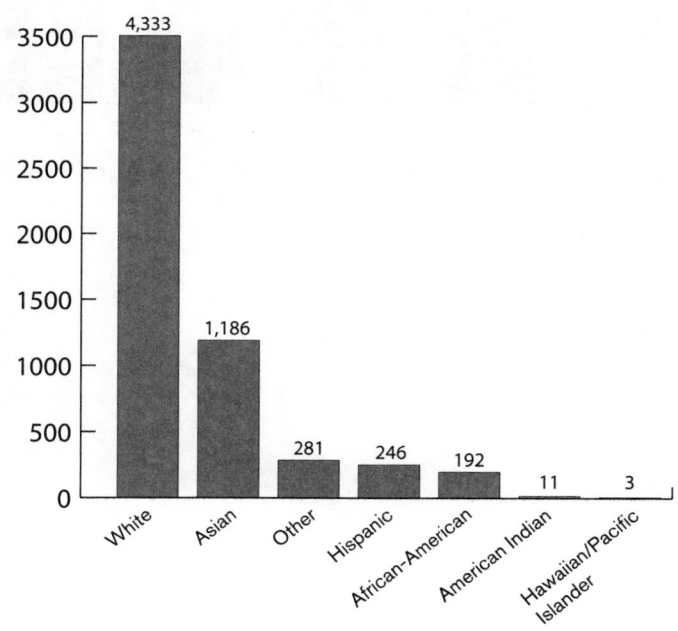

Note: Includes 68 Hispanic faculty from University of Puerto Rico, Mayaguez and Polytechnic University of Puerto Rico.

PERCENTAGE OF AFRICAN-AMERICAN TENURED/TENURE-TRACK FACULTY MEMBERS BY LEVEL*

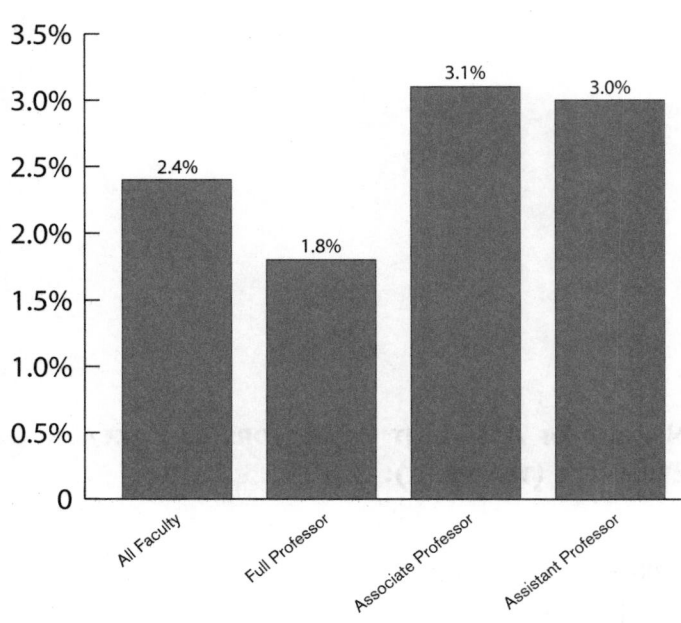

PERCENTAGE OF HISPANIC TENURED/ TENURE-TRACK FACULTY MEMBERS BY LEVEL*

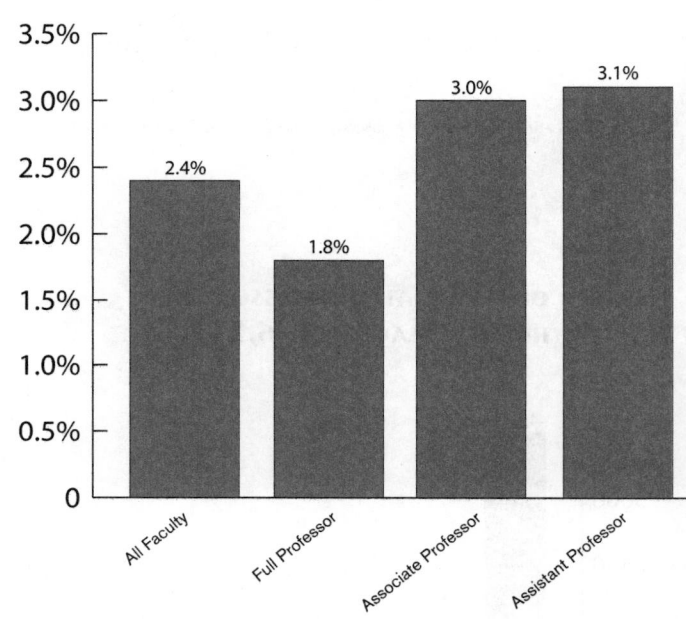

PERCENTAGE OF ASIAN TENURED/ TENURE-TRACK FACULTY MEMBERS BY LEVEL*

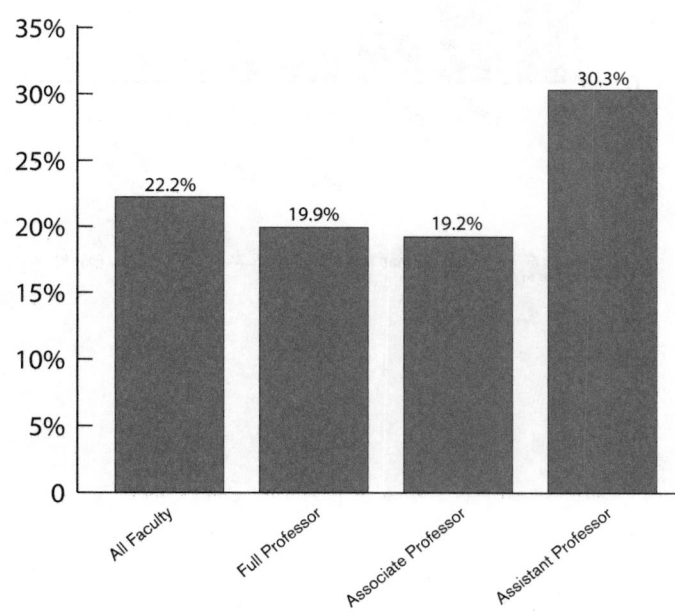

* Does not include ethnicity data from University of Puerto Rico, Mayaguez and Polytechnic University of Puerto Rico.

AFRICAN-AMERICAN TENURED/ TENURE-TRACK TEACHING FACULTY MEMBERS BY SCHOOL

1. Howard University	25
2. North Carolina A & T State Univ.	22
3. Morgan State University	20
4. Prairie View A&M University	19
5. Southern Univ. and A&M College	18
6. FAMU-FSU College of Eng.	17
7. Georgia Institute of Technology	15
8. Massachusetts Inst. of Technology	14
8. Tuskegee University	14
10. University of Michigan	10
10. Virginia Tech	10
12. Florida International University	9
13. North Carolina State University	8
14. Clemson University	7
14. Cornell University	7
14. Univ. of Illinois, Urbana-Champaign	7
14. Pennsylvania State University	7
14. Tennessee State University	7
19. University of Central Florida	6
19. University of Florida	6
19. New Jersey Institute of Technology	6
19. Purdue University	6
19. Stevens Institute of Technology	6
19. Texas A&M University	6

317 total schools reported.

ASIAN TENURED/TENURE-TRACK TEACHING FACULTY MEMBERS BY SCHOOL

1. Univ. of Illinois, Urbana-Champaign	103
2. Texas A&M University	90
3. University of Florida	85
4. Georgia Institute of Technology	84
5. Purdue University	81
6. Virginia Tech	74
7. Ohio State University	68
8. Iowa State University	64
9. University of Michigan	63
10. University of Central Florida	62
11. Arizona State University	61
11. North Carolina State University	61
13. Univ. of California, Los Angeles	57
14. University of Minnesota, Twin Cities	56
15. University of California, Davis	54
16. Michigan State University	50
17. University of Cincinnati	49
17. Massachusetts Inst. of Technology	49
19. University of Missouri, Columbia	47
20. SUNY, Buffalo	45

317 total schools reported.

HISPANIC TENURED/TENURE-TRACK TEACHING FACULTY MEMBERS BY SCHOOL

1. Univ. of Puerto Rico, Mayaguez	130
2. Polytechnic Univ. of Puerto Rico	78
3. Texas A&M University	19
4. University of Texas at El Paso	15
5. Pennsylvania State University	13
5. Virginia Tech	13
7. Florida International University	12
8. University of California, Berkeley	11
8. Univ. of Illinois, Urbana-Champaign	11
8. New Mexico State University	11
8. Purdue University	11
12. University of South Florida	10
12. University of Texas, Austin	10
14. Arizona State University	9
14. Massachusetts Inst. of Technology	9
16. University of Cincinnati	8
16. Georgia Institute of Technology	8
16. Stanford University	8
19. California Poly. State Univ., SLO	7
19. Univ. of Maryland, College Park	7
19. Northwestern University	7

317 total schools reported.

PERCENTAGE OF AFRICAN-AMERICAN TENURED/TENURE-TRACK TEACHING FACULTY MEMBERS BY DISCIPLINE: 2.4%

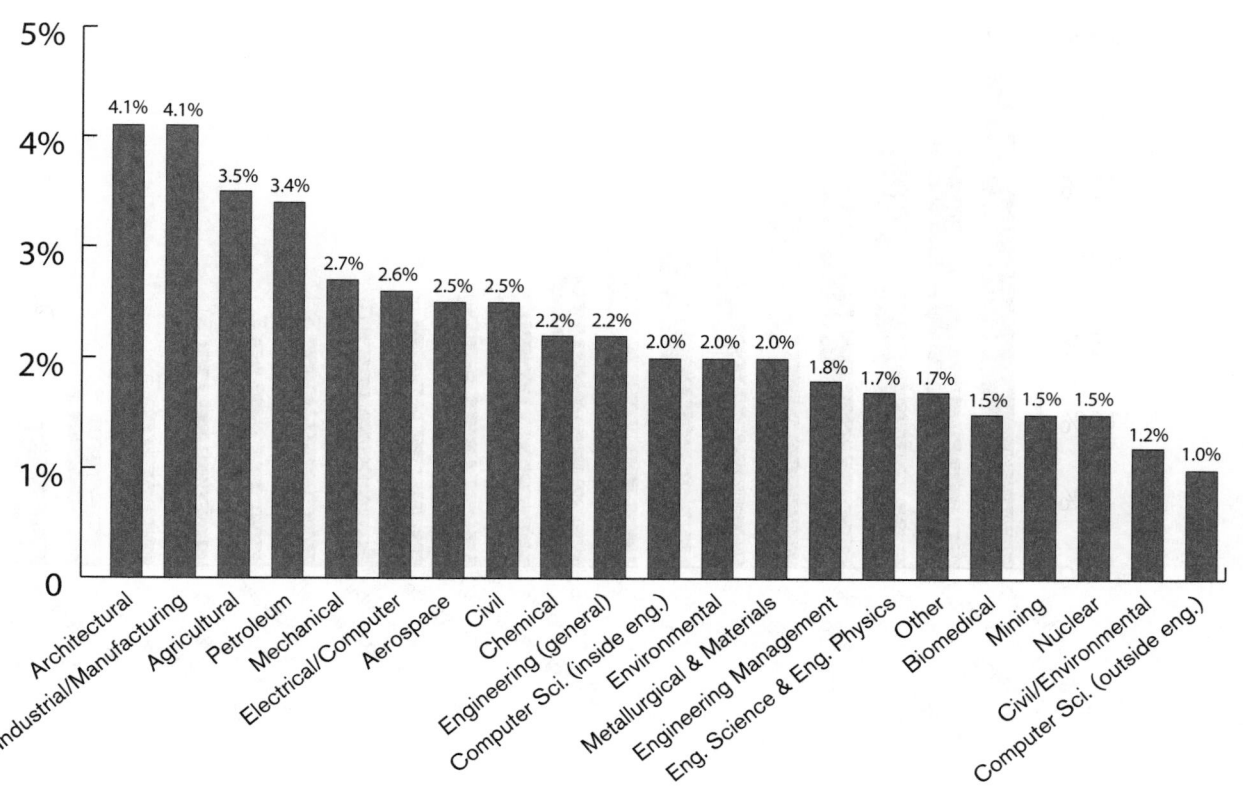

PERCENTAGE OF HISPANIC TENURED/TENURE-TRACK TEACHING FACULTY MEMBERS BY DISCIPLINE: 2.4%

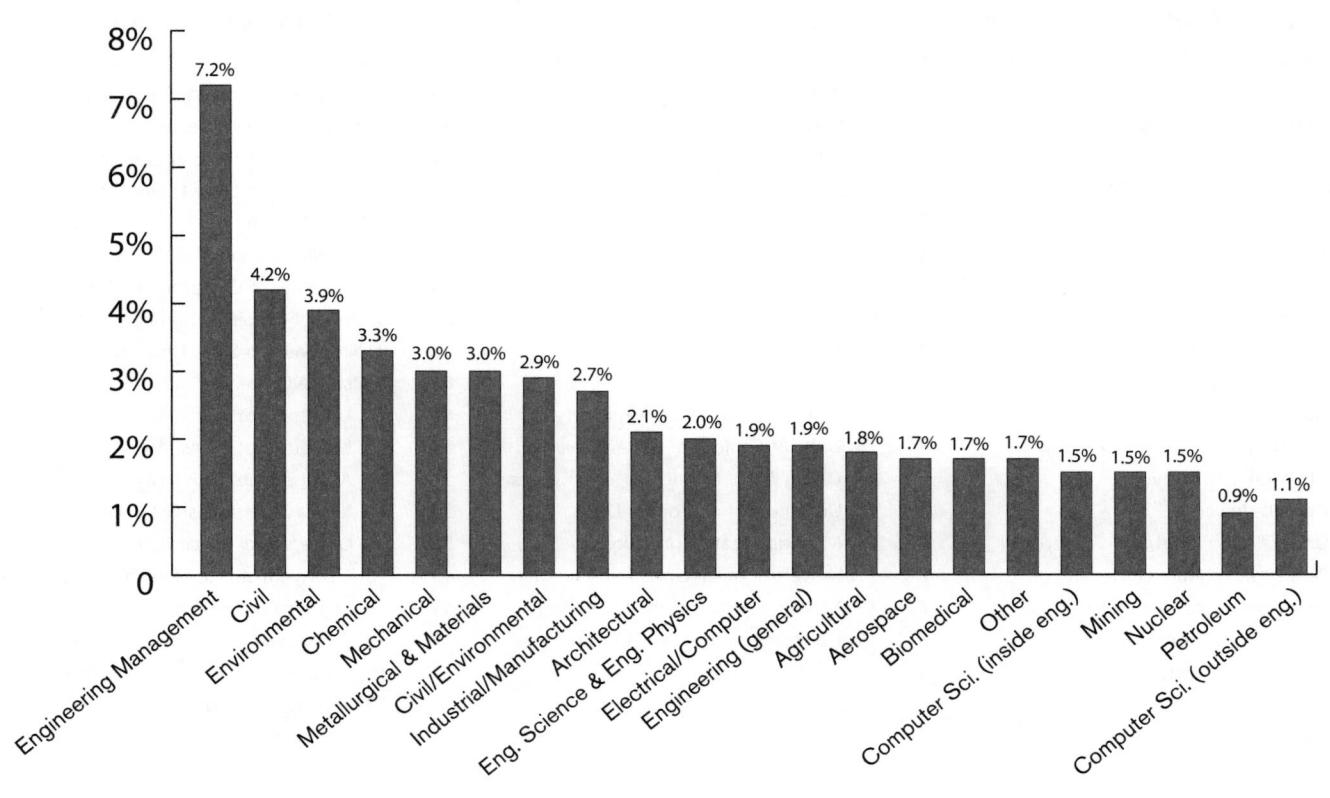

PERCENTAGE OF ASIAN-AMERICAN TENURED/TENURE-TRACK TEACHING FACULTY MEMBERS BY DISCIPLINE: 22.2%

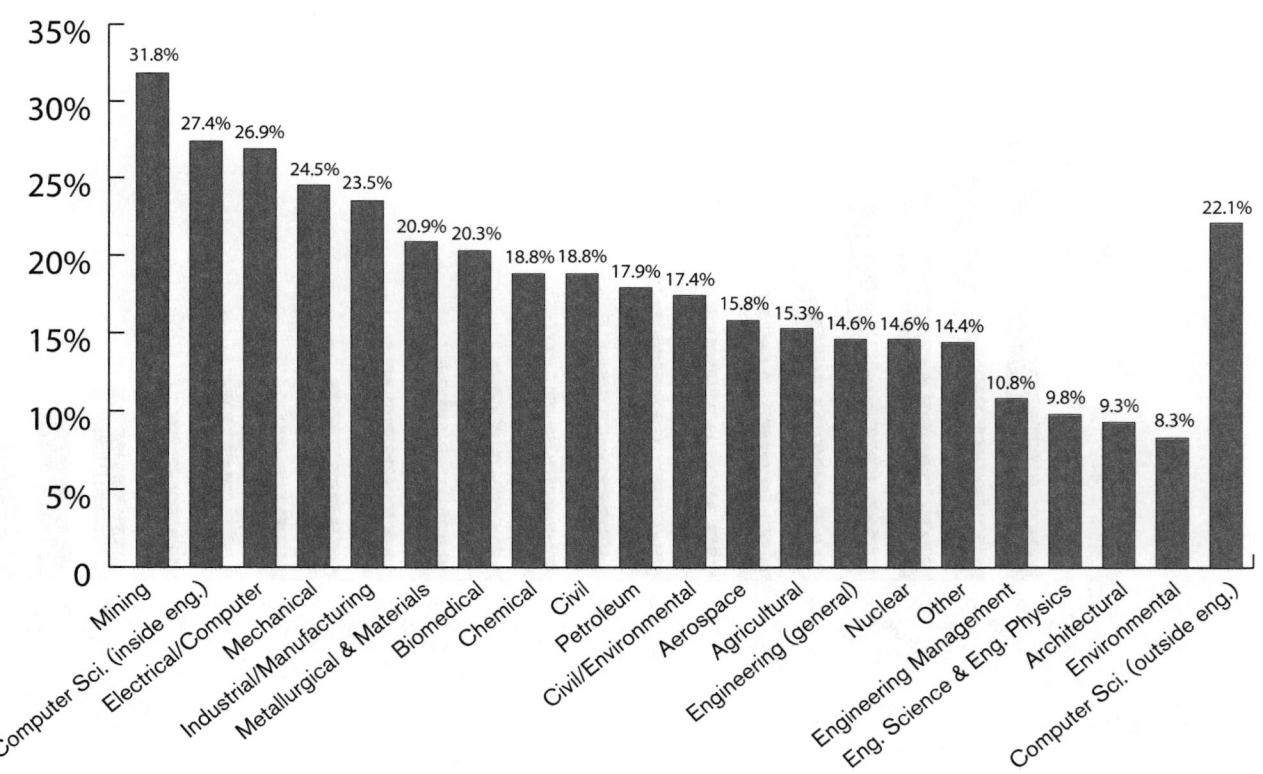

ENGINEERING RESEARCH EXPENDITURES BY SCHOOL

(IN MILLIONS)

1. Massachusetts Inst. of Technology	$234.5
2. Georgia Institute of Technology	$203.7
3. Univ. of Illinois, Urbana-Champaign	$200.1
4. Texas A&M University	$196.1
5. University of Southern California	$169.8
6. Carnegie Mellon University	$159.0
7. Stanford University	$152.4
8. University of Michigan	$145.7
9. Univ. of Maryland, College Park	$145.4
10. University of California, San Diego	$138.6
11. University of Texas, Austin	$124.0
12. University of California, Berkeley	$119.8
13. Cornell University	$118.7
14. Pennsylvania State University	$118.1
15. Purdue University	$112.3
16. Ohio State University	$108.4
17. University of Wisconsin, Madison	$108.0
18. University of Florida	$107.8
19. North Carolina State University	$103.0
20. University of Rochester	$100.4
21. University of Washington	$92.2
22. Virginia Tech	$89.3
23. Univ. of California, Los Angeles	$89.2
24. California Institute of Technology	$80.4
25. Univ. of Minnesota, Twin Cities	$71.7
26. University of Dayton	$66.7
27. University of California, Irvine	$66.1
28. Iowa State University	$65.5
29. University of Pennsylvania	$64.0
30. University of California, Davis	$61.7
31. Boston University	$59.6
32. University of Colorado, Boulder	$56.7
33. Duke University	$55.4
34. Johns Hopkins University	$54.3
35. University of Virginia	$54.2
36. University of Pittsburgh	$53.6
37. Princeton University	$52.1
38. University of Central Florida	$51.5
39. Arizona State University	$50.2
40. Colorado State University	$50.1
41. Rensselaer Polytechnic Institute	$48.9
42. SUNY, Buffalo	$48.7
43. Vanderbilt University	$43.4
44. University of Utah	$43.0
45. Mississippi State University	$40.6
46. University of Delaware	$37.7
47. Case Western Reserve Univ.	$37.1
48. Drexel University	$36.8
49. Auburn University	$36.3
50. Harvard University	$35.2

194 total schools reported.

TOTAL RESEARCH EXPENDITURES BY SOURCE IN MILLIONS OF DOLLARS

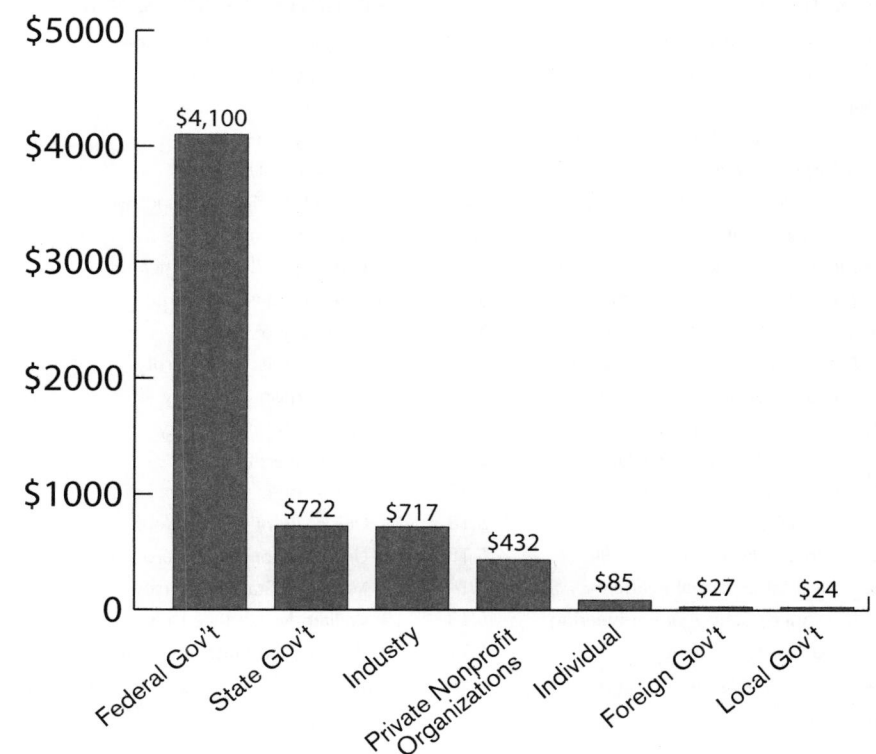

COMPUTER SCIENCE RESEARCH EXPENDITURES LOCATED OUTSIDE OF ENGINEERING BY SCHOOL

(IN MILLIONS)

1. Carnegie Mellon University	$85.0
2. Univ. of Massachusetts, Amherst	$14.9
3. Purdue University	$9.5
4. Univ. of Maryland, College Park	$6.2
5. University of Tennessee, Knoxville	$4.5
6. Univ. of North Carolina, Charlotte	$4.1
7. Dartmouth College	$3.5
8. University of Houston	$3.2
9. University of Pittsburgh	$3.0
9. Rensselaer Polytechnic Institute	$3.0
11. Northeastern University	$2.2
12. University of Nebraska, Lincoln	$1.8
13. University of Delaware	$1.7
13. Illinois Institute of Technology	$1.7
13. University of Rochester	$1.7
16. New Jersey Inst. of Technology	$1.6
17. Worcester Polytechnic Institute	$1.1
18. Louisiana State University	$0.9
18. University of Missouri, Rolla	$0.9
20. Brigham Young University	$0.7

23 total schools reported.
* Schools are not required to report this data to ASEE.

HIGH RATIO OF BACHELOR'S DEGREES TO FACULTY MEMBERS BY SCHOOL*

1. University of North Florida	7.45
2. California Poly. State Univ., SLO	6.81
3. Kettering University	6.43
4. California State Univ., Long Beach	6.40
5. California State Poly. U., Pomona	6.33
6. San Jose State University	6.26
7. Texas A&M Univ., Kingsville	5.93
8. United States Coast Guard Academy	5.77
9. Univ. of California, San Diego	5.52
10. California State University, Chico	5.45
11. Embry Riddle Aero. U., Prescott	5.41
12. California State Univ., Fullerton	5.37
13. Lawrence Technological University	5.31
13. Michigan Technological University	5.31
15. Brigham Young University	5.27
16. Clarkson University	5.18
16. Southern Illinois, Edwardsville	5.18
18. United States Naval Academy	5.14
19. Milwaukee School of Engineering	5.13
20. Ohio Northern University	5.11

*Minimum 50 degrees awarded.
254 schools fit the criteria for this table.
Faculty members refers to tenured/tenure-track faculty.*

HIGHEST RATIO OF DOCTORAL DEGREES TO RESEARCH EXPENDITURES BY SCHOOL*

1. University of Hawaii, Manoa	5.94
2. University of Cincinnati	4.28
3. University of Alabama	3.81
4. University of Houston	3.56
5. Stony Brook University	3.01
6. University of Texas, Arlington	2.68
7. Texas Tech University	2.65
8. University of Illinois, Chicago	2.63
8. University of Notre Dame	2.63
10. University of Arizona	2.57
11. Louisiana State University	2.50
12. Washington University	2.41
13. Wayne State University	2.40
14. Yale University	2.37
15. University of Louisville	2.33
16. University of Connecticut	2.31
17. University of South Carolina	2.28
18. Michigan State University	2.26
19. William Marsh Rice University	2.20
20. Washington State University	2.09

*Minimum of 25 doctoral degrees awarded. Ratios were derived by dividing degrees awarded by millions of research dollars.
87 schools fit this criterion.*

HIGHEST PERCENTAGE OF DOCTORAL DEGREES TO FOREIGN NATIONALS BY SCHOOL*

1. Illinois Institute of Technology	92.3%
2. New Jersey Institute of Technology	89.2%
3. Louisiana State University	88.9%
4. University of Cincinnati	88.3%
5. University of Texas, Dallas	86.4%
6. Louisiana Tech University	85.7%
7. Ohio State University	84.6%
8. Texas A&M University	83.7%
9. University of Southern California	81.5%
10. University of Louisville	80.0%
11. SUNY, Buffalo	78.8%
12. University of Hawaii, Manoa	78.3%
13. University of Missouri, Rolla	76.9%
14. Stony Brook University	76.1%
15. Arizona State University	76.0%
15. University of Rochester	76.0%
17. University of Missouri, Columbia	75.8%
17. West Virginia University	75.8%
19. Lehigh University	75.7%
20. Michigan State University	75.4%

*Minimum of 25 doctoral degrees awarded.
94 schools fit this criterion.*

LOW RATIO OF BACHELOR'S DEGREES TO FACULTY MEMBERS BY SCHOOL*

1. George Washington University	1.14
2. California Institute of Technology	1.20
3. Harvard University	1.23
4. Cleveland State University	1.34
5. University of South Florida	1.37
6. Princeton University	1.38
7. University of Mississippi	1.46
8. Massachusetts Inst. of Technology	1.55
9. University of Rochester	1.59
10. Tuskegee University	1.67
11. Wayne State University	1.70
12. Univ. of Tennessee, Chattanooga	1.76
13. North Carolina A&T State Univ.	1.77
14. Brown University	1.78
15. Univ. of Massachusetts, Dartmouth	1.79
15. William Marsh Rice University	1.79
17. Prairie View A&M University	1.81
18. Stanford University	1.83
19. Southern Univ. and A&M College	1.85
20. Univ. of Massachusetts, Lowell	1.86

*Minimum 50 degrees awarded.
254 schools fit the criteria for this table.
Faculty members refers to tenured/tenure-track faculty.*

LOWEST RATIO OF DOCTORAL DEGREES TO RESEARCH EXPENDITURES BY SCHOOL*

1. University of Rochester	0.25
2. Colorado State University	0.54
2. Carnegie Mellon University	0.54
4. Boston University	0.71
5. University of Pennsylvania	0.75
6. University of California, San Diego	0.76
7. Duke University	0.78
7. Texas A&M University	0.78
9. Harvard University	0.82
10. Univ. of Maryland, College Park	0.89
10. University of Southern California	0.89
12. University of Wisconsin, Madison	0.90
13. University of Pittsburgh	0.91
14. Vanderbilt University	0.92
15. University of Virginia	0.94
16. California Institute of Technology	0.97
17. Cornell University	1.03
18. University of California, Irvine	1.06
19. University of Central Florida	1.07
19. SUNY, Buffalo	1.07

*Minimum of 25 doctoral degrees awarded. Ratios were derived by dividing degrees awarded by millions of research dollars.
87 schools fit this criterion.*

LOWEST PERCENTAGE OF DOCTORAL DEGREES TO FOREIGN NATIONALS BY SCHOOL*

1. University of Colorado, Boulder	32.9%
2. Boston University	40.5%
3. George Washington University	41.0%
4. Colorado School of Mines	43.6%
5. University of California, Berkeley	44.7%
6. University of Alabama	44.8%
7. University of California, Davis	46.3%
8. Massachusetts Inst. of Technology	46.9%
9. Drexel University	47.1%
10. Harvard University	48.3%
11. Northwestern University	48.7%
12. University of Virginia	49.0%
13. Stanford University	50.6%
14. University of California, San Diego	51.9%
15. University of Pennsylvania	52.1%
16. Case Western Reserve University	52.9%
17. University of Notre Dame	53.1%
17. University of Pittsburgh	53.1%
19. University of Texas, Arlington	54.0%
20. University of Washington	54.2%

*Minimum of 25 doctoral degrees awarded.
94 schools fit this criterion.*

BACHELOR'S DEGREES BY DISCIPLINE 1999-2006

Bachelor's Degrees	1999	2000	2001	2002	2003	2004	2005	2006
Aerospace Engineering	1,174	1,296	1,558	1,711	2,011	2,232	2,371	2,722
Agricultural Engineering	536	583	549	556	603	601	635	646
Architectural Engineering	497	559	554	513	627	590	722	631
Biomedical Engineering	1,016	1,156	1,138	1,315	1,628	2,019	2,410	2,917
Chemical Engineering	6,199	6,023	5,740	5,529	5,233	4,801	4,521	4,452
Civil Engineering	9,416	8,653	8,027	8,066	8,192	8,142	8,247	8,935
Civil/Environmental Engineering[1]	—	—	—	—	—	—	212	291
Computer Engineering	3,117	3,972	4,519	4,720	5,746	5,838	5,455	4,901
Computer Science (inside engineering)	4,177	5,510	6,062	6,842	8,649	9,156	8,419	7,330
Electrical Engineering	10,955	11,211	11,096	11,402	11,994	12,500	12,459	11,915
Electrical/Computer Engineering	2,374	2,126	2,444	2,597	2,782	2,700	2,924	2,825
Engineering (General)	814	944	992	1,069	1,105	1,138	1,179	1,176
Engineering Management	171	186	187	227	296	302	303	238
Engr. Science and Engr. Physics	547	535	475	489	451	501	383	431
Environmental Engineering	604	588	510	465	516	576	522	437
Industrial/Manufacturing Engineering	3,524	3,555	3,474	3,575	3,769	3,790	3,647	3,664
Mechanical Engineering	12,859	12,992	12,921	13,247	13,801	14,182	14,947	16,063
Metallurgical and Matrls. Engineering	875	904	791	838	859	817	840	909
Mining Engineering	173	164	150	112	96	85	92	120
Nuclear Engineering	114	134	118	145	135	202	275	342
Other Engineering Disciplines	2,192	2,478	2,627	3,106	2,422	2,488	2,724	2,902
Petroleum Engineering	219	251	268	257	250	233	315	339
TOTAL	**61,553**	**63,820**	**64,200**	**66,781**	**71,165**	**72,893**	**73,602**	**74,186**

[1] *New discipline added in 2005.*

ENROLLMENT BY CLASS 1999-2006

UNDERGRADUATE ENROLLMENT	1999	2000	2001	2002	2003	2004	2005	2006
Freshmen	89,101	89,605	96,426	97,817	97,170	96,978	95,425	101,291
Sophomores	69,961	73,411	76,184	77,720	80,381	79,696	77,930	79,331
Juniors	72,069	76,409	78,320	78,373	80,685	80,265	77,986	78,963
Seniors	100,817	101,495	106,926	113,455	117,252	117,942	114,695	113,489
TOTAL FULL TIME	**331,948**	**340,920**	**357,856**	**367,365**	**375,488**	**374,881**	**366,046**	**373,074**
TOTAL PART TIME	**32,910**	**32,153**	**32,137**	**30,513**	**33,278**	**31,872**	**31,076**	**31,430**

MASTER'S DEGREES BY DISCIPLINE 1999-2006

MASTERS DEGREES	1999	2000	2001	2002	2003	2004	2005	2006
Aerospace Engineering	641	705	633	735	720	915	1,043	1,094
Agricultural Engineering	163	194	143	150	139	191	173	182
Architectural Engineering	88	115	119	98	111	160	164	112
Biomedical Engineering	428	476	526	652	762	862	1,007	1,326
Chemical Engineering	1,270	1,161	1,133	1,054	1,136	1,321	1,404	1,204
Civil Engineering	3,692	3,530	3,399	3,410	3,638	3,745	3,875	3,835
Civil/Environmental Engineering[1]	—	—	—	—	—	—	78	109
Computer Engineering	1,177	1,329	1,717	1,485	1,800	1,735	1,557	1,510
Computer Science (inside engineering)	4,141	3,573	3,845	4,096	5,163	5,797	5,735	5,197
Electrical Engineering	3,960	3,699	3,528	3,597	4,419	5,656	5,615	5,256
Electrical/Computer Engineering	3,188	3,293	3,556	3,348	3,653	4,393	4,243	3,753
Engineering (General)	288	350	426	377	607	642	539	671
Engineering Management	1,105	1,101	1,145	1,352	1,663	1,764	1,818	1,817
Engr. Science and Engr. Physics	437	409	372	417	344	315	282	315
Environmental Engineering	619	572	557	517	488	579	635	571
Industrial/Manufacturing Engineering	2,180	2,455	2,475	2,502	2,766	3,262	3,138	2,663
Mechanical Engineering	3,307	3,399	3,594	3,566	3,680	4,461	4,767	4,631
Metallurgical and Matrls. Engineering	692	735	605	568	642	737	743	702
Mining Engineering	33	23	39	34	27	46	38	48
Nuclear Engineering	161	150	161	141	212	197	181	246
Other Engineering Disciplines	2,119	2,738	2,497	2,809	3,026	2,826	3,259	3,532
Petroleum Engineering	107	153	199	181	200	233	256	241
TOTAL	29,796	30,160	30,669	31,089	35,196	39,837	40,550	39,015

[1] *New discipline added in 2005.*

DOCTORAL DEGREES BY DISCIPLINE 1999-2006

DOCTORAL DEGREES	1999	2000	2001	2002	2003	2004	2005	2006
Aerospace Engineering	208	214	216	211	197	210	259	244
Agricultural Engineering	68	66	72	68	69	90	68	66
Architectural Engineering	5	2	2	4	2	7	6	2
Biomedical Engineering	187	203	219	213	240	339	333	436
Chemical Engineering	592	653	645	632	592	655	805	834
Civil Engineering	578	529	574	628	618	644	725	767
Civil/Environmental Engineering[1]	—	—	—	—	—	—	20	29
Computer Engineering	87	69	80	76	95	125	115	191
Computer Science (inside engineering)	405	399	381	350	410	494	606	761
Electrical Engineering	651	767	691	627	644	720	834	939
Electrical/Computer Engineering	761	792	840	776	761	901	938	1,112
Engineering (General)	30	31	36	32	47	44	46	75
Engineering Management	47	28	32	26	30	40	35	39
Engr. Science and Engr. Physics	137	120	132	100	102	109	111	131
Environmental Engineering	75	77	57	83	89	124	112	129
Industrial/Manufacturing Engineering	243	234	231	274	275	306	302	348
Mechanical Engineering	842	838	858	796	792	855	964	1,132
Metallurgical and Matrls. Engineering	421	392	408	342	388	442	464	519
Mining Engineering	11	11	11	11	12	7	11	16
Nuclear Engineering	78	95	84	64	81	61	76	81
Other Engineering Disciplines	444	443	443	429	398	403	457	460
Petroleum Engineering	34	36	32	30	28	28	46	40
TOTAL	**5,904**	**5,999**	**6,044**	**5,772**	**5,870**	**6,604**	**7,333**	**8,351**

[1] *New discipline added in 2005.*

UNDERGRADUATE ENROLLMENT BY DISCIPLINE 1999-2006

UNDERGRADUATE ENROLLMENT	1999		2000		2001	
	Full Time	Part Time	Full Time	Part Time	Full Time	Part Time
AEROSPACE ENGINEERING	7,584	378	8,422	420	9,410	346
AGRICULTURAL ENGINEERING	2,373	77	2,375	76	2,503	56
ARCHITECTURAL ENGINEERING	2,015	152	2,360	97	2,404	110
BIOMEDICAL ENGINEERING	5,183	60	6,262	78	7,093	72
CHEMICAL ENGINEERING	27,379	1,740	25,118	1,655	23,534	1,392
CIVIL ENGINEERING	38,213	3,829	37,310	3,750	37,449	3,769
CIVIL/ENVIRONMENTAL ENGINEERING[1]	—	—	—	—	—	—
COMPUTER SCIENCE (INSIDE ENGINEERING)	25,496	3,572	30,063	3,349	33,695	3,778
ELECTRICAL/COMPUTER ENGINEERING	91,852	11,701	98,578	12,370	102,943	12,173
ENGINEERING (GENERAL)	4,534	324	4,822	286	6,305	411
ENGINEERING MANAGEMENT	477	42	543	56	595	52
ENGR. SCIENCE AND ENGR. PHYSICS	1,742	95	1,584	73	1,761	57
ENVIRONMENTAL ENGINEERING	605	10	740	49	729	51
INDUSTRIAL/MANUFACTURING ENGINEERING	11,929	1,147	12,377	1,015	13,076	1,053
MECHANICAL ENGINEERING	64,404	7,146	64,005	6,843	66,608	6,880
METALLURGICAL AND MATRLS. ENGINEERING	3,424	174	3,268	125	3,063	117
MINING ENGINEERING	635	20	502	37	482	36
NUCLEAR ENGINEERING	666	36	709	20	845	28
OTHER ENGINEERING DISCIPLINES	42,087	2,375	40,613	1,809	44,061	1,702
PETROLEUM ENGINEERING	1,350	32	1,269	45	1,300	54
TOTAL	331,948	32,910	340,920	32,153	357,856	32,137

[1] New discipline added in 2005.

Note: ASEE collected enrollment data at the department level until 2004. Enrollment data for 2005 was collected at the degree program level. This method is more accurate. However, some longitudinal continuity is lost between 1999-2004 and 2005. For example, some aerospace data was grouped with mechanical data prior to 2005 because mechanical engineering departments often award aerospace degrees. Consequently, the aerospace total is much larger in 2005. This effect is also apparent for some other disciplines.

2002		2003		2004		2005		2006	
Full Time	**Part Time**	**Full Time**	**Part Time**	**Full Time**	**Part Time**	**Full Time**	**Part Time**	**Full Time**	**Part Time**
9,386	386	10,834	476	11,436	709	15,882	588	15,945	654
2,816	58	2,878	68	2,629	47	2,978	72	3,038	68
2,537	102	2,793	126	2,878	116	4,392	134	3,986	187
9,178	146	10,716	230	12,566	647	14,213	464	15,411	481
22,641	1,328	21,926	1,310	22,088	1,497	21,727	1,323	23,455	1,269
39,031	3,451	41,442	3,911	43,590	4,230	42,007	3,448	44,389	3,783
—	—	—	—	—	—	1,264	185	1,790	245
32,668	4,077	35,448	4,400	31,646	4,390	27,577	4,678	27,062	4,355
102,983	11,158	99,658	11,525	91,366	11,221	79,883	8,977	75,302	8,979
6,649	277	6,392	400	5,837	499	14,925	544	17,011	625
663	65	921	62	911	47	1,239	37	1,014	35
2,310	88	2,246	48	2,332	39	3,161	486	3,533	525
734	56	850	77	793	60	2,007	112	2,270	128
13,376	1,116	13,621	1,122	13,573	1,254	13,065	1,170	12,970	1,054
71,902	6,345	76,482	7,255	80,863	7,134	78,202	6,636	80,288	6,786
3,087	126	3,181	110	3,215	191	3,577	175	3,862	184
456	47	450	20	566	48	626	26	764	37
960	39	1,259	42	1,371	60	1,562	61	1,667	75
44,497	1,576	42,760	2,045	45,393	2,664	35,943	1,865	36,503	1,877
1,491	72	1,631	51	1,828	44	2,131	95	2,814	83
367,365	**30,513**	**375,488**	**33,278**	**374,881**	**34,897**	**366,361**	**31,076**	**373,074**	**31,430**

MASTER'S ENROLLMENT BY DISCIPLINE 1999-2006

MASTER'S ENROLLMENT	1999			2000			2001		
	Full Time	Part Time	Total	Full Time	Part Time	Total	Full Time	Part Time	Total
Aerospace Engineering	1,171	324	1,495	1,413	342	1,755	1,406	335	1,741
Agricultural Engineering	310	61	371	286	74	360	315	43	358
Architectural Engineering	161	33	194	168	50	218	160	12	172
Biomedical Engineering	796	259	1,055	958	260	1,218	1,130	231	1,361
Chemical Engineering	2,064	982	3,046	1,920	945	2,865	1,887	842	2,729
Civil Engineering	5,580	3,314	8,894	5,820	2,829	8,649	5,836	2,885	8,721
Civil/Environmental Engineering[1]	—	—	—	—	—	—	—	—	—
Computer Science (inside engineering)	4,215	2,717	6,932	5,415	2,842	8,257	6,425	3,316	9,741
Electrical/Computer Engineering	12,557	8,589	21,146	14,223	8,287	22,510	16,009	8,434	24,443
Engineering (General)	128	74	202	199	104	303	347	366	713
Engineering Management	324	1,443	1,767	470	1,870	2,340	569	1,357	1,926
Engr. Science and Engr. Physics	412	662	1,074	350	484	834	199	214	413
Environmental Engineering	212	143	355	234	154	388	206	172	378
Industrial/Manufacturing Engineering	2,631	2,383	5,014	3,588	2,512	6,100	3,944	2,474	6,418
Mechanical Engineering	6,449	3,614	10,063	6,688	3,381	10,069	7,234	3,492	10,726
Metallurgical and Matrls. Engineering	1,065	421	1,486	1,072	322	1,394	942	328	1,270
Mining Engineering	69	17	86	92	22	114	78	29	107
Nuclear Engineering	264	35	299	273	26	299	255	52	307
Other Engineering Disciplines	2,773	4,114	6,887	3,470	3,837	7,307	3,136	3,907	7,043
Petroleum Engineering	308	78	386	300	88	388	311	69	380
TOTAL	41,489	29,263	70,752	46,939	28,429	75,368	50,389	28,558	78,947

[1] New discipline added in 2005.

Note: ASEE collected enrollment data at the department level until 2004. Enrollment data for 2005 was collected at the degree program level. This method is more accurate. However, some longitudinal continuity is lost between 1999-2004 and 2005. For example, some aerospace data was grouped with mechanical data prior to 2005 because mechanical engineering departments often award aerospace degrees. Consequently, the aeros total is much larger in 2005. This effect is also apparent for some other disciplines.

2002			2003			2004			2005			2006		
Full Time	Part Time	Total	Full Time	Part Time	Total	Full Time	Part Time	Total	Full Time	Part Time	Total	Full Time	Part Time	Total
1,338	293	1,631	1,507	477	1,984	1,621	541	2,162	1,853	575	2,428	1,758	627	2,385
318	52	370	363	58	421	311	58	369	338	61	399	309	55	364
173	31	204	194	27	221	229	21	250	256	32	288	104	40	144
1,376	342	1,718	1,567	462	2,029	1,775	539	2,314	1,701	612	2,313	1,795	595	2,390
2,036	922	2,958	1,874	980	2,854	1,791	955	2,746	1,527	801	2,328	1,285	678	1,963
6,086	3,094	9,180	6,065	3,370	9,435	5,975	3,323	9,298	4,955	2,599	7,554	5,067	2,432	7,499
—	—	—	—	—	—	—	—	—	92	119	211	127	125	252
6,552	4,263	10,815	6,680	5,452	12,132	5,509	5,388	10,897	6,040	4,933	10,973	6,240	4,595	10,835
18,551	9,574	28,125	17,611	10,809	28,420	15,311	10,738	26,049	13,799	8,995	22,794	14,868	8,731	23,599
503	505	1,008	498	634	1,132	475	734	1,209	669	1,067	1,736	698	1,012	1,710
633	1,734	2,367	499	1,800	2,299	633	2,351	2,984	1,384	2,826	4,210	1,390	3,397	4,787
249	244	493	260	239	499	190	174	364	210	167	377	193	134	327
198	254	452	371	368	739	330	254	584	852	445	1,297	767	507	1,274
4,524	2,596	7,120	4,060	2,814	6,874	3,496	2,572	6,068	3,608	2,105	5,713	3,542	1,963	5,505
8,199	3,791	11,990	8,179	4,161	12,340	7,458	4,208	11,666	7,126	3,564	10,690	6,762	3,529	10,291
951	278	1,229	895	214	1,109	784	243	1,027	920	293	1,213	904	303	1,207
73	37	110	78	32	110	77	35	112	82	30	112	72	43	115
231	53	284	250	62	312	253	57	310	379	96	475	422	100	522
3,724	5,199	8,923	3,529	4,737	8,266	3,702	5,310	9,012	3,089	4,400	7,489	3,421	4,369	7,790
375	90	465	393	96	489	385	108	493	387	128	515	362	194	556
56,090	33,352	89,442	54,873	36,792	91,665	50,305	37,609	87,914	49,267	33,848	82,991	50,086	33,429	83,515

DOCTORAL ENROLLMENT BY DISCIPLINE 1999-2006

DOCTORAL ENROLLMENT	1999			2000			2001		
	Full Time	Part Time	Total	Full Time	Part Time	Total	Full Time	Part Time	Total
Aerospace Engineering	944	235	1,179	1,027	148	1,175	1,041	159	1,200
Agricultural Engineering	317	46	363	297	55	352	303	47	350
Architectural Engineering	34	6	40	41	4	45	56	1	57
Biomedical Engineering	1,185	250	1,435	1,440	203	1,643	1,777	172	1,949
Chemical Engineering	3,565	366	3,931	3,530	323	3,853	3,652	340	3,992
Civil Engineering	3,061	813	3,874	3,222	707	3,929	3,400	734	4,134
Civil/Environmental Engineering[1]	—	—	—	—	—	—	—	—	—
Computer Science (inside engineering)	2,135	377	2,512	2,316	463	2,779	2,745	519	3,264
Electrical/Computer Engineering	9,051	2,024	11,075	9,725	1,837	11,562	10,301	1,769	12,070
Engineering (General)	85	32	117	135	24	159	124	44	168
Engineering Management	69	111	180	80	133	213	145	154	299
Engr. Science and Engr. Physics	542	90	632	559	75	634	646	56	702
Environmental Engineering	173	10	183	178	18	196	246	24	270
Industrial/Manufacturing Engineering	1,144	421	1,565	1,395	392	1,787	1,423	427	1,850
Mechanical Engineering	4,411	1,093	5,504	4,603	868	5,471	4,803	781	5,584
Metallurgical and Matrls. Engineering	1,829	316	2,145	1,895	188	2,083	2,063	172	2,235
Mining Engineering	63	8	71	57	12	69	51	11	62
Nuclear Engineering	334	51	385	374	24	398	389	29	418
Other Engineering Disciplines	1,965	725	2,690	2,230	697	2,927	2,015	668	2,683
Petroleum Engineering	161	13	174	158	34	192	133	26	159
TOTAL	31,068	6,987	38,055	33,262	6,205	39,467	35,313	6,133	41,446

[1] *New discipline added in 2005.*

Note: ASEE collected enrollment data at the department level until 2004. Enrollment data for 2005 was collected at the degree program level. This method is more accurate. However, some longitudinal continuity is lost between 1999-2004 and 2005. For example, some aerospace data was grouped with mechanical data prior to 2005 because mechanical engineering departments often award aerospace degrees. Consequently, the aerospace total is much larger in 2005. This effect is also apparent for some other disciplines.

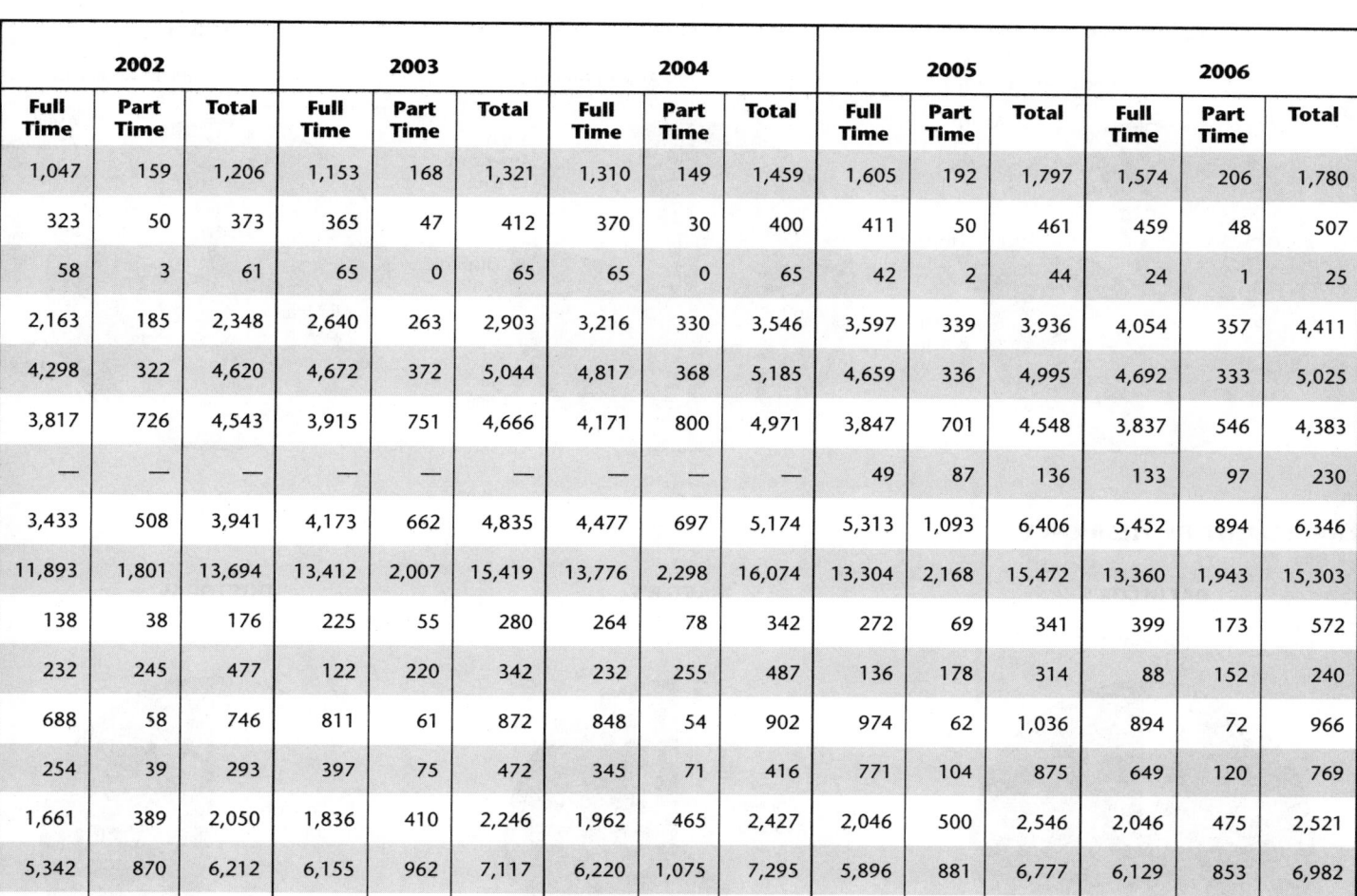

	2002			2003			2004			2005			2006	
Full Time	Part Time	Total	Full Time	Part Time	Total	Full Time	Part Time	Total	Full Time	Part Time	Total	Full Time	Part Time	Total
1,047	159	1,206	1,153	168	1,321	1,310	149	1,459	1,605	192	1,797	1,574	206	1,780
323	50	373	365	47	412	370	30	400	411	50	461	459	48	507
58	3	61	65	0	65	65	0	65	42	2	44	24	1	25
2,163	185	2,348	2,640	263	2,903	3,216	330	3,546	3,597	339	3,936	4,054	357	4,411
4,298	322	4,620	4,672	372	5,044	4,817	368	5,185	4,659	336	4,995	4,692	333	5,025
3,817	726	4,543	3,915	751	4,666	4,171	800	4,971	3,847	701	4,548	3,837	546	4,383
—	—	—	—	—	—	—	—	—	49	87	136	133	97	230
3,433	508	3,941	4,173	662	4,835	4,477	697	5,174	5,313	1,093	6,406	5,452	894	6,346
11,893	1,801	13,694	13,412	2,007	15,419	13,776	2,298	16,074	13,304	2,168	15,472	13,360	1,943	15,303
138	38	176	225	55	280	264	78	342	272	69	341	399	173	572
232	245	477	122	220	342	232	255	487	136	178	314	88	152	240
688	58	746	811	61	872	848	54	902	974	62	1,036	894	72	966
254	39	293	397	75	472	345	71	416	771	104	875	649	120	769
1,661	389	2,050	1,836	410	2,246	1,962	465	2,427	2,046	500	2,546	2,046	475	2,521
5,342	870	6,212	6,155	962	7,117	6,220	1,075	7,295	5,896	881	6,777	6,129	853	6,982
2,172	253	2,425	2,472	218	2,690	2,614	217	2,831	3,060	221	3,281	3,035	267	3,302
50	13	63	59	10	69	71	18	89	80	13	93	51	20	71
376	33	409	427	26	453	446	18	464	529	51	580	538	51	589
2,581	860	3,441	2,496	704	3,200	2,895	769	3,664	2,573	628	3,201	2,540	788	3,328
153	32	185	155	43	198	170	40	210	209	29	238	171	40	211
40,679	6,584	47,263	45,550	7,054	52,604	48,269	7,732	56,001	49,373	7,704	57,077	50,125	7,436	57,561

ENROLLMENT BY ETHNICITY

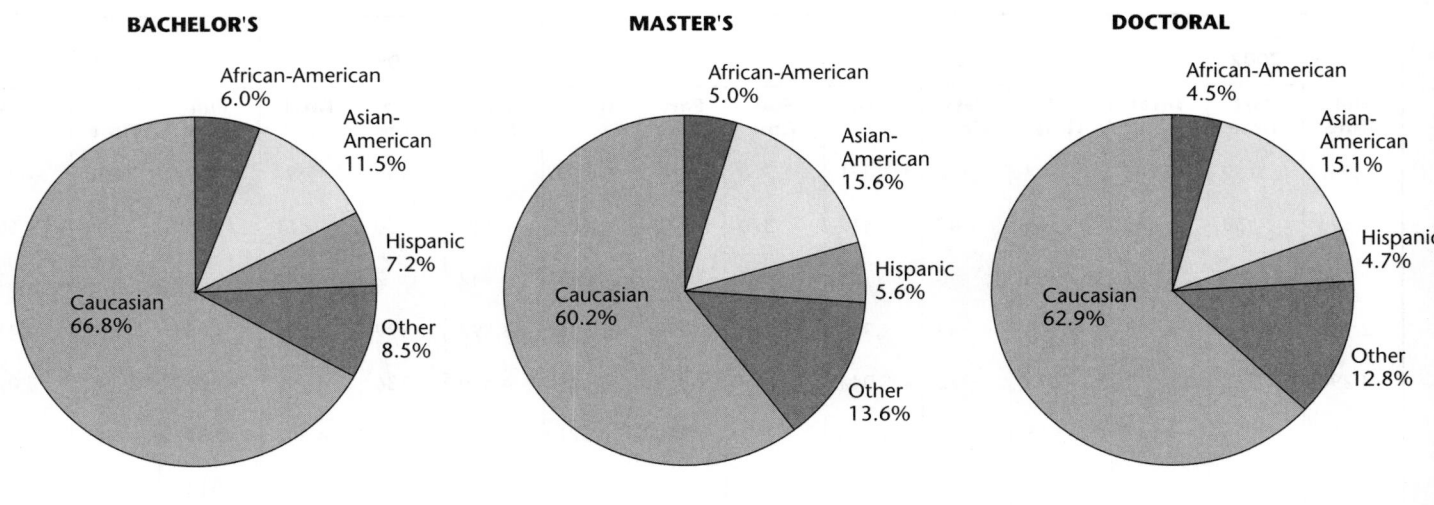

BACHELOR'S
- African-American 6.0%
- Asian-American 11.5%
- Hispanic 7.2%
- Other 8.5%
- Caucasian 66.8%

MASTER'S
- African-American 5.0%
- Asian-American 15.6%
- Hispanic 5.6%
- Other 13.6%
- Caucasian 60.2%

DOCTORAL
- African-American 4.5%
- Asian-American 15.1%
- Hispanic 4.7%
- Other 12.8%
- Caucasian 62.9%

ENROLLMENT BY RESIDENCY

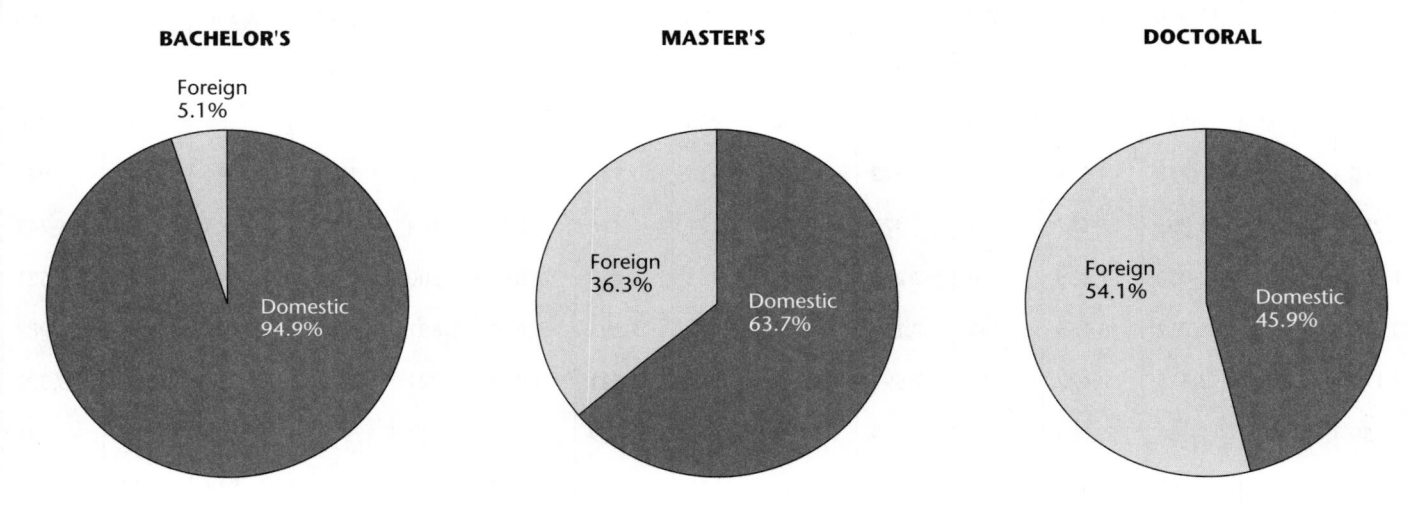

BACHELOR'S
- Foreign 5.1%
- Domestic 94.9%

MASTER'S
- Foreign 36.3%
- Domestic 63.7%

DOCTORAL
- Foreign 54.1%
- Domestic 45.9%

ENROLLMENT BY GENDER

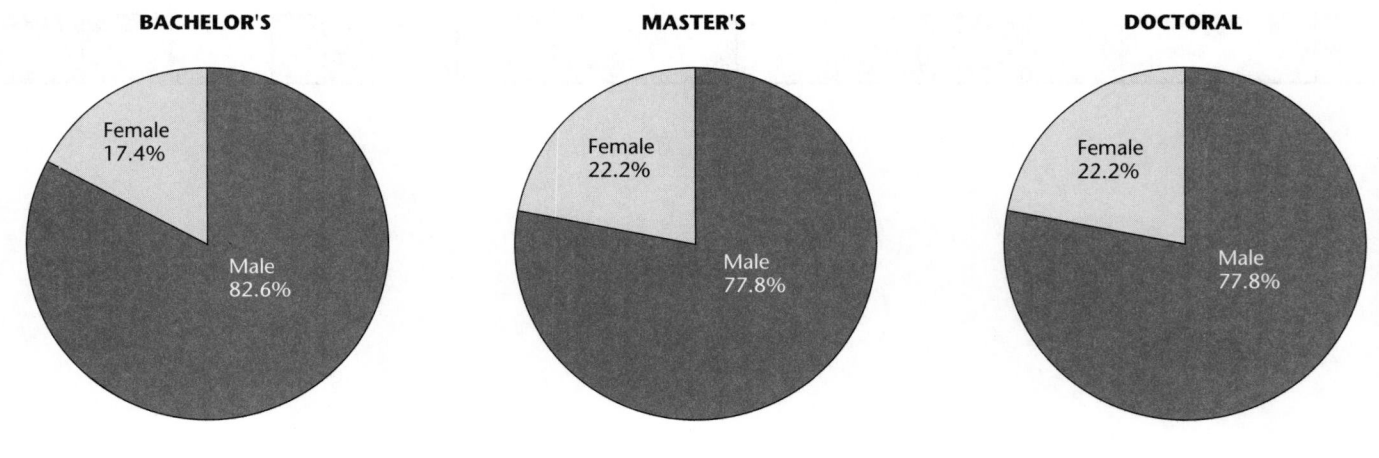

BACHELOR'S
- Female 17.4%
- Male 82.6%

MASTER'S
- Female 22.2%
- Male 77.8%

DOCTORAL
- Female 22.2%
- Male 77.8%

BACHELOR'S TOTAL	MASTER'S TOTAL	DOCTORAL TOTAL
373,074	83,515	57,566

QUANSER
INNOVATE. EDUCATE.

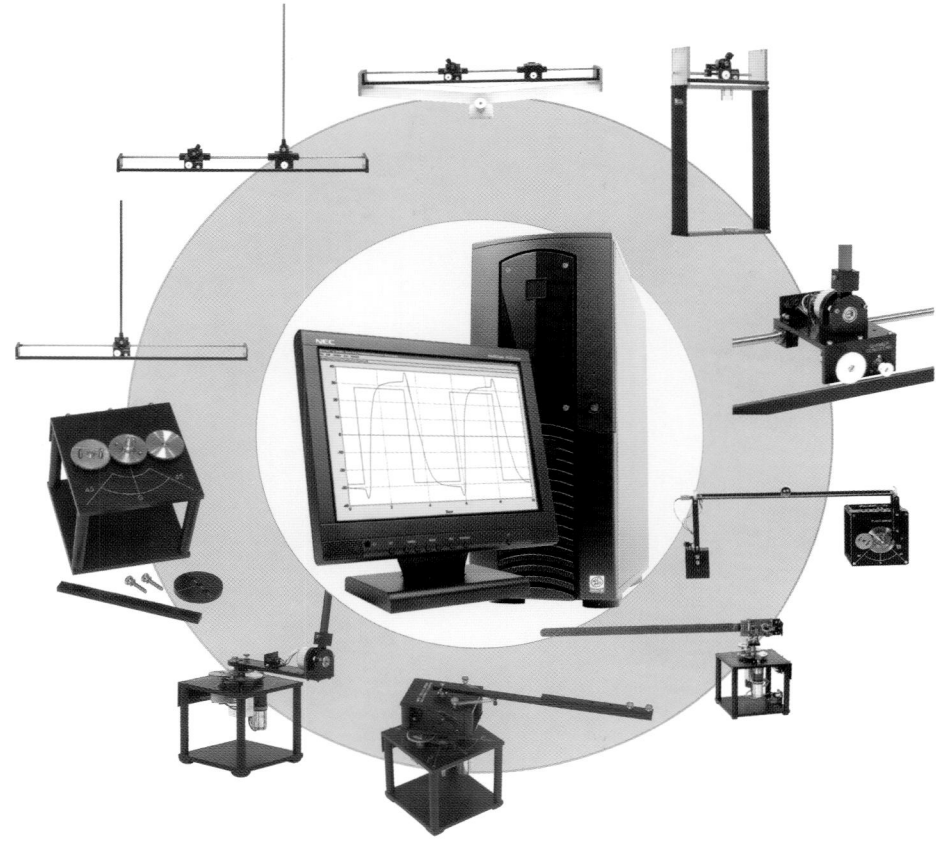

ANSYS Academic Solutions

ANSYS, Inc. is at the forefront of providing engineering simulation software worldwide for academic users, both for teaching and research applications.

At release 11.0, ANSYS® software provides a scalable academic product portfolio based on three usage tiers: Associate, Research and Teaching. Each usage tier includes a range of noncommercial products covering a variety of physics and more advanced coupled field (multiphysics) solver capability. ANSYS also offers several Academic Toolbox products that address high-performance computing (HPC) and specialized pre-processing concerns.

The ANSYS academic community consists of thousands of universities and colleges worldwide using analysis solutions in a variety of disciplines such as:

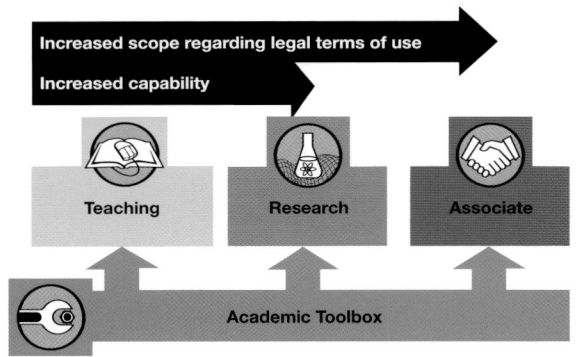

- Mechanical engineering
- Aeronautical engineering
- Civil engineering
- Electromagnetics
- Biomechanics
- Microsystems (MEMS)
- Electronic engineering

Flexible, scalable software solutions exist for undergraduate teaching environments, graduate research, and academic partnerships.

Learn more about the ANSYS Academic Solutions at www.ansys.com/academic, call toll-free 1.866.267.9724 or send email to education@ansys.com.

ANSYS®

www.ansys.com

ANSYS, INC. I SOUTHPOINTE I 275 TECHNOLOGY DRIVE I CANONSBURG, PA 15317 I USA I 724.746.3304 I 1.866.267.9724

ENGINEERING TECHNOLOGY BACHELOR'S DEGREES AWARDED BY SCHOOL

1. Ferris State University	362
2. Indiana U. Purdue U., Indianapolis	284
3. Wentworth Institute of Technology	282
4. Purdue University	230
5. Southern Polytechnic State Univ.	198
5. University of Toledo	198
7. Rochester Institute of Technology	188
8. University of Houston	174
9. Old Dominion University	154
10. Oklahoma State University	149
10. Oregon Institute of Technology	149
12. New Jersey Inst. of Technology	119
13. University of Central Florida	116
14. Texas A&M University	113
15. Arizona State Univ., Polytechnic	101
16. Alfred State College	95
17. Weber State University	92
18. University of Maine	91
19. Northeastern University	90
19. University of North Texas	90
21. California State Poly. U., Pomona	87
22. Univ. of North Carolina, Charlotte	76
22. Northern Illinois University	76
24. Brigham Young University	72
25. Pennsylvania State Univ., Erie	70
26. Montana State University	68
27. Pittsburg State University	66
27. Texas Tech University	66
29. Michigan Technological University	64
30. New Mexico State University	62
31. University of Dayton	60
32. Minnesota State Univ., Mankato	55
33. Capitol College	54
33. Univ. of Massachusetts Lowell	54
35. University of Hartford	51
36. University of Nebraska, Lincoln	50
36. Wayne State University	50
38. South Dakota State University	47
39. Lawrence Technological University	44
40. Youngstown State University	43
41. California Maritime Academy	42
42. Western Carolina University	41
43. Prairie View A&M University	39
43. Temple University	39
45. Buffalo State College	38
46. University of Memphis	36
46. Pennsylvania State Univ. Harrisburg	36
48. Louisiana Tech University	35
48. Milwaukee School of Engineering	35
50. Metropolitan State College of Denver	33

69 total schools reported.

ENGINEERING TECHNOLOGY BACHELOR'S DEGREES BY DISCIPLINE

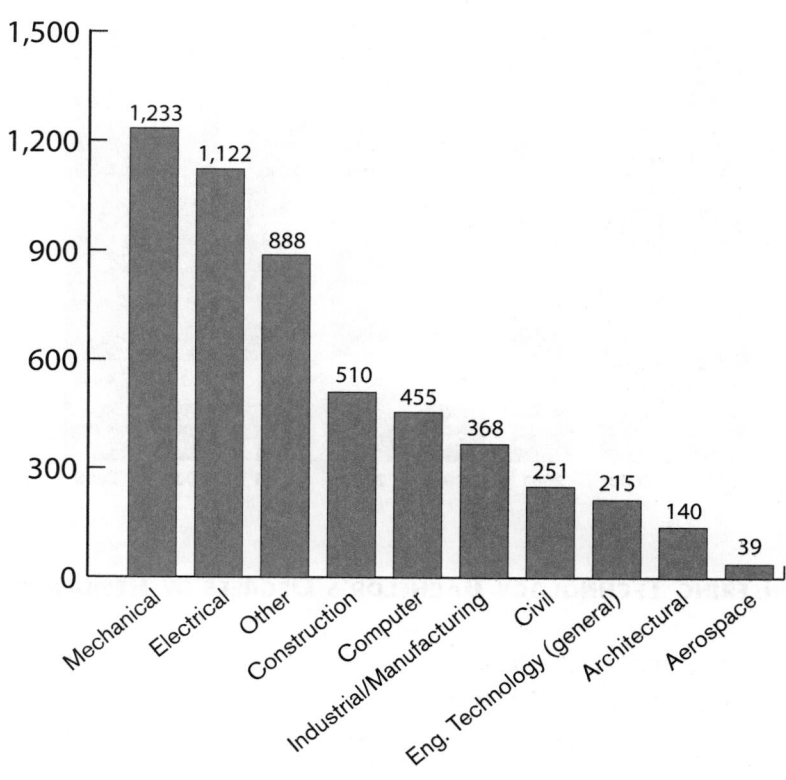

FULL-TIME ENGINEERING TECHNOLOGY ENROLLMENT BY DISCIPLINE*

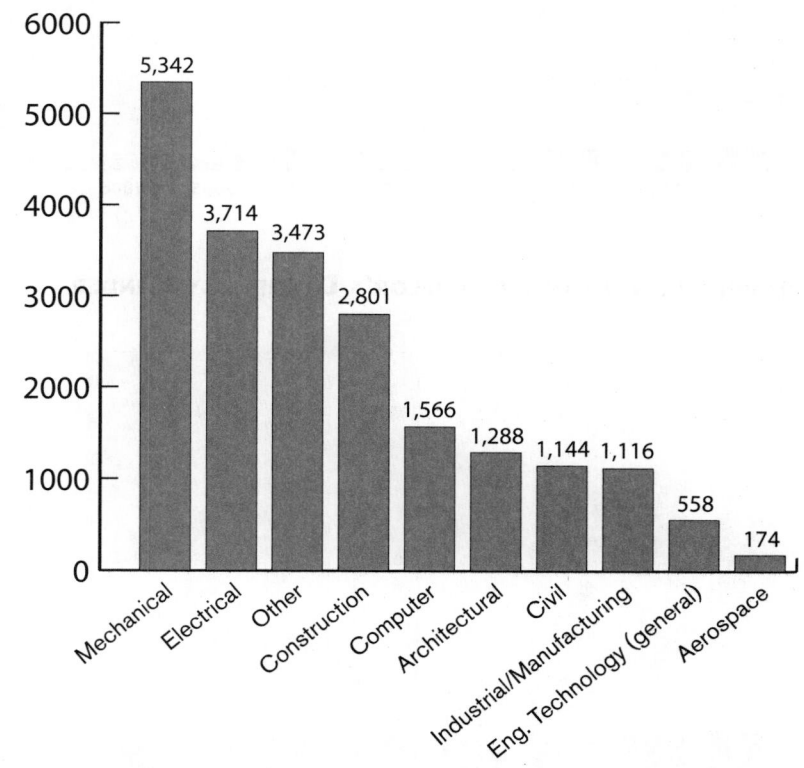

* Enrollment is for full-time bachelor's degree candidates in engineering technology.

ENGINEERING TECHNOLOGY BACHELOR'S DEGREES BY ETHNICITY

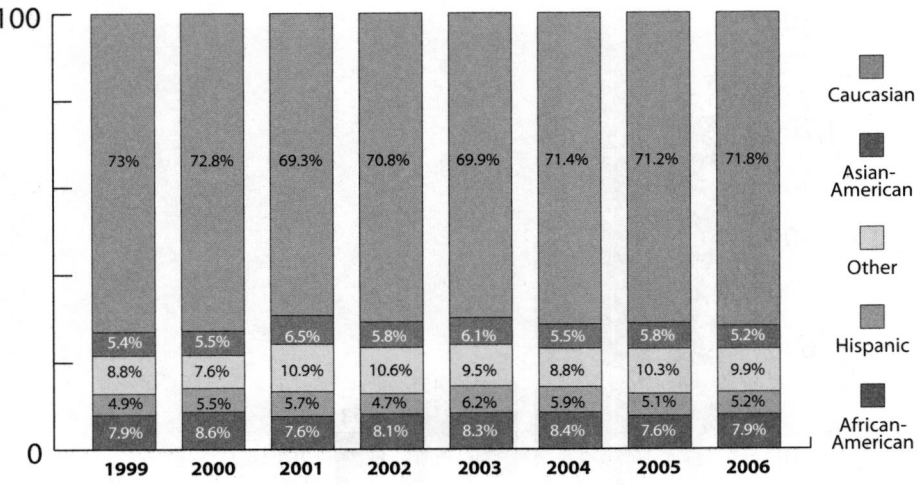

Legend: Caucasian, Asian-American, Other, Hispanic, African-American

ENGINEERING TECHNOLOGY BACHELOR'S DEGREES BY RESIDENCY

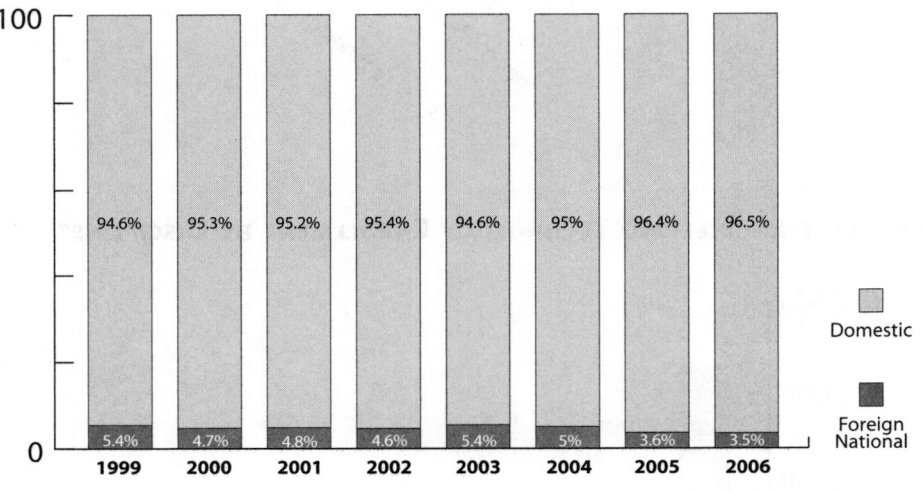

Legend: Domestic, Foreign National

ENGINEERING TECHNOLOGY BACHELOR'S DEGREES BY GENDER

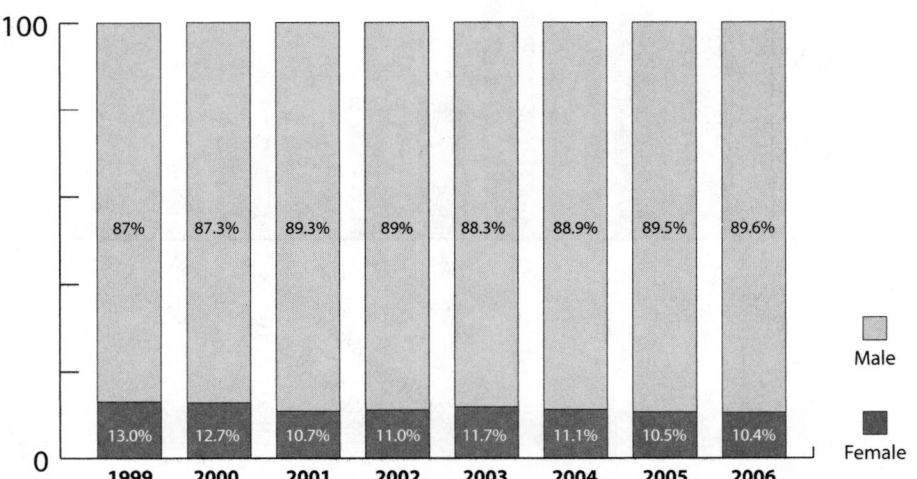

Legend: Male, Female

ENGINEERING TECHNOLOGY DEGREES AWARDED TO WOMEN BY SCHOOL

1.	Indiana U. Purdue U., Indianapolis	62
2.	Wentworth Institute of Technology	38
3.	Ferris State University	33
4.	Southern Polytechnic State Univ.	29
5.	University of Houston	25
6.	Weber State University	19
7.	Old Dominion University	16
8.	Purdue University	14
9.	Arizona State Univ., Polytechnic	13
9.	Metropolitan State College of Denver	13
9.	Rochester Institute of Technology	13
12.	University of Central Florida	12
12.	New Jersey Institute of Technology	12
14.	University of North Texas	11
15.	University of Massachusetts Lowell	10
15.	Prairie View A&M University	10
15.	Texas A&M University	10
15.	University of Toledo	10
19.	Alfred State College	9
19.	Capitol College	9
19.	University of Hartford	9
22.	California Maritime Academy	7
22.	University of Dayton	7
22.	University of Memphis	7
22.	Northeastern University	7
22.	Northern Illinois University	7
22.	Temple University	7
28.	California State Poly. Univ., Pomona	6
28.	New Mexico State University	6
28.	Oregon Institute of Technology	6
28.	Wayne State University	6
32.	University of North Carolina, Charlotte	5
32.	Pennsylvania State Univ., Erie	5
32.	Buffalo State College	5
32.	Colorado State University, Pueblo	5
32.	Colorado Technical University	5
32.	Indiana U. Purdue U., Fort Wayne	5
32.	Lawrence Technological University	5
32.	Southern University and A&M College	5
40.	Montana State University	4
40.	Oklahoma State University	4
40.	Pittsburg State University	4
40.	Youngstown State University	4
44.	Alabama A&M University	3
44.	McNeese State University	3
44.	Michigan Technological University	3
44.	Pennsylvania State Univ. Harrisburg	3
44.	Western Carolina University	3
49.	10 schools tied with 2	

69 total schools reported.

ENGINEERING TECHNOLOGY ENROLLMENT BY SCHOOL*

1. Ferris State University	2,093
2. Wentworth Institute of Technology	1,669
3. Southern Polytechnic State University	1,549
4. Rochester Institute of Technology	1,173
5. Purdue University	1,144
6. University of Toledo	949
7. Indiana U. Purdue U., Indianapolis	915
8. Old Dominion University	813
9. Oklahoma State University	783
10. Alfred State College	725
11. University of Houston	709
12. Univ. of North Carolina, Charlotte	632
13. Oregon Institute of Technology	621
14. Weber State University	598
15. California State Poly. Univ., Pomona	524
16. University of Central Florida	523
17. Indiana U. Purdue U., Fort Wayne	521
18. Arizona State University, Polytechnic	501
19. Metropolitan State College of Denver	462
20. Northeastern University	427
21. University of Hartford	423
22. New Jersey Institute of Technology	419
23. Montana State University	398
24. Minnesota State University, Mankato	388
25. University of Maine	385
26. Pennsylvania State University, Erie	373
27. South Dakota State University	357
28. Texas Tech University	349
29. Texas A&M University	340
30. University of North Texas	330
31. New Mexico State University	308
32. Michigan Technological University	303
33. University of Dayton	259
34. Pennsylvania State Univ., Harrisburg	250
35. Western Michigan University	235
36. Youngstown State University	230
37. Northern Illinois University	225
38. University of Memphis	224
39. University of Nebraska, Lincoln	218
40. Capitol College	217
41. California State Univ., Sacramento	205
42. Louisiana Tech University	196
43. University of Arkansas, Little Rock	191
44. Wayne State University	186
45. University of Massachusetts Lowell	184
46. Buffalo State College	182
47. Southern University and A&M College	178
48. Lawrence Technological University	177
49. California Maritime Academy	161
50. McNeese State University	160

66 total schools reported.
*Enrollment is for full-time and part-time bachelor's degree candidates in engineering technology.

ENGINEERING TECHNOLOGY ENROLLMENT BY ETHNICITY

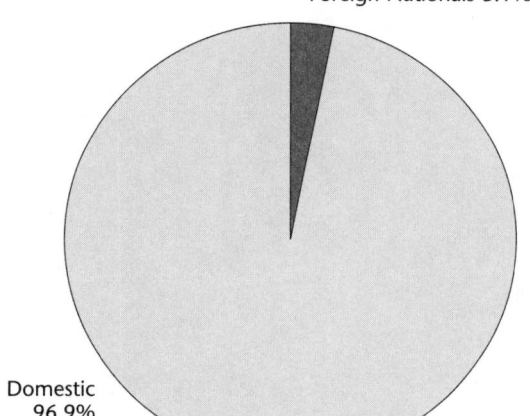

Other 7%
African-American 7.9%
Hispanic 5.8%
Asian-American 4.3%
Caucasian 75%

ENGINEERING TECHNOLOGY ENROLLMENT BY RESIDENCY

Foreign Nationals 3.1%
Domestic 96.9%

ENGINEERING TECHNOLOGY ENROLLMENT BY GENDER

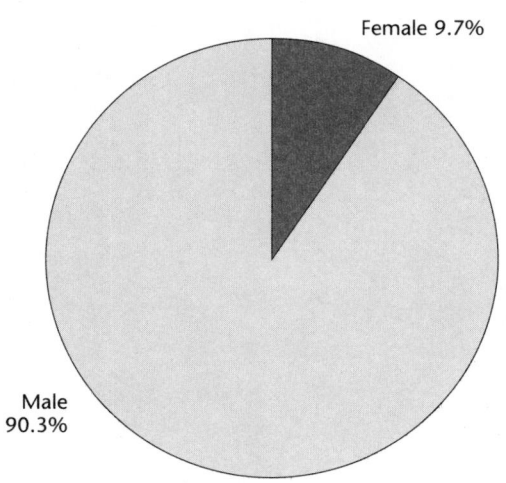

Female 9.7%
Male 90.3%

2006 Statistical Tables of Engineering Colleges

AKR-CAR

INSTITUTION		FRESHMEN (FT)	SOPHOMORES (FT)	JUNIORS (FT)	SENIORS (FT)	ENROLLMENT TOTAL			(PT)
						M	F (FT)	TOTAL	
The University of Akron	OH	642	243	251	293	1,258	171	1,429	180
Alabama A&M University	AL	176	166	107	217	497	169	666	0
University of Alabama at Birmingham	AL	176	105	95	138	395	119	514	168
The University of Alabama in Huntsville	AL	331	183	253	317	888	196	1,084	289
The University of Alabama	AL	653	399	323	370	1,431	314	1,745	111
University of Alaska Fairbanks	AK	88	64	56	94	243	59	302	53
Alfred University, NY State College of Ceramics	NY	87	63	66	75	231	60	291	22
The University of Arizona	AZ	538	565	563	828	2,019	475	2,494	0
Arizona State University	AZ	671	702	701	1,130	2,625	579	3,204	639
University of Arkansas	AR	459	251	254	380	1,140	204	1,344	195
Arkansas State University	AR	79	42	42	60	212	11	223	26
Arkansas Tech University	AR	103	73	57	58	262	29	291	23
University of Arkansas at Little Rock	AR	60	36	35	54	163	22	185	0
Auburn University	AL	925	505	522	731	2,294	389	2,683	159
Baylor University	TX	216	117	86	116	452	83	535	2
Boise State University	ID	308	203	167	193	770	101	871	418
Boston University	MA	328	291	274	277	909	261	1,170	5
Bradley University	IL	129	121	135	176	497	64	561	25
University of Bridgeport	CT	17	7	5	7	30	6	36	5
Brigham Young University	UT	468	326	401	849	1,816	228	2,044	0
Brown University	RI	152	70	64	63	229	120	349	0
Bucknell University	PA	182	156	140	150	476	152	628	0
California Institute of Technology	CA	0	117	107	88	248	64	312	0
California Maritime Academy	CA	36	33	22	14	94	11	105	0
California Polytechnic State University	CA	1,399	796	834	1,876	4,166	739	4,905	245
California State Polytechnic University, Pomona	CA	1,254	461	747	1,511	3,457	516	3,973	0
California State University, Chico	CA	246	116	164	281	716	91	807	47
California State University, Fresno	CA	326	181	267	338	955	157	1,112	187
California State University, Fullerton	CA	212	129	137	263	645	96	741	280
California State University, Long Beach	CA	462	328	287	703	1,487	293	1,780	472
California State University, Los Angeles	CA	175	131	187	443	792	144	936	0
California State University, Northridge	CA	293	175	257	475	1,047	153	1,200	337
California State University, Sacramento	CA	359	140	278	617	1,238	156	1,394	338
University of California, Berkeley	CA	229	362	468	697	1,395	361	1,756	1,289
University of California, Davis	CA	873	518	525	898	2,266	548	2,814	0
University of California, Irvine	CA	583	387	404	836	1,775	435	2,210	0
University of California, Los Angeles	CA	365	422	547	979	1,882	431	2,313	0
University of California, Riverside	CA	380	268	221	333	1,061	141	1,202	57
University of California, San Diego	CA	801	668	729	1,622	2,985	835	3,820	0
University of California, Santa Barbara	CA	289	309	316	405	1,151	168	1,319	0
University of California-Santa Cruz	CA	346	202	135	188	759	112	871	0
Calvin College	MI	108	72	69	79	287	41	328	3
Capitol College	MD	38	18	19	14	76	13	89	20
Carnegie Mellon University	PA	435	386	356	383	1,159	401	1,560	23
Carroll College	MT	24	14	8	19	55	10	65	0

UNDERGRADUATE ENROLLMENTS

INSTITUTION		FRESHMEN (FT)	SOPHOMORES (FT)	JUNIORS (FT)	SENIORS (FT)	ENROLLMENT TOTAL			(PT)
						M	(FT) F	TOTAL	
Case Western Reserve University	OH	13	267	229	375	713	171	884	99
The Catholic University of America	DC	64	41	44	46	158	37	195	8
Cedarville University	OH	115	76	56	53	287	13	300	0
University of Central Florida	FL	1,109	575	615	1,100	2,895	504	3,399	851
Christian Brothers University	TN	58	43	36	36	143	30	173	7
Christopher Newport University	VA	34	17	6	16	67	6	73	13
University of Cincinnati	OH	583	378	578	278	1,558	259	1,817	0
The Citadel	SC	131	66	64	59	311	9	320	39
Clarkson University	NY	321	292	309	303	1,081	144	1,225	1
Clemson University	SC	975	715	596	642	2,426	502	2,928	231
Cleveland State University	OH	92	86	103	312	515	78	593	66
Colorado School of Mines	CO	1,015	717	582	840	2,461	693	3,154	0
Colorado State University	CO	319	217	271	438	1,037	208	1,245	133
Colorado State University, Pueblo	CO	30	12	12	16	58	12	70	13
Colorado Technical University	CO	55	25	25	21	111	15	126	0
University of Colorado at Boulder	CO	659	592	585	907	2,256	487	2,743	0
University of Colorado at Colorado Springs	CO	89	81	81	115	312	54	366	35
University of Colorado at Denver	CO	62	42	66	155	269	56	325	183
Columbia University	NY	315	325	378	387	997	408	1,405	2
University of Connecticut	CT	375	421	393	537	1,480	246	1,726	0
The Cooper Union	NY	109	131	126	119	359	126	485	0
Cornell University	NY	811	733	717	742	2,164	839	3,003	0
Dartmouth College	NH	93	66	52	61	185	87	272	0
University of Dayton	OH	223	215	149	182	624	145	769	86
University of Delaware	DE	322	277	252	322	942	231	1,173	33
University of Denver	CO	48	27	16	35	103	23	126	4
University of Detroit Mercy	MI	53	33	26	46	123	35	158	65
University of the District of Columbia	DC	47	43	43	48	144	37	181	38
Drexel University	PA	763	893	838	641	2,629	506	3,135	290
Duke University Pratt School of Engineering	NC	301	326	231	219	800	277	1,077	2
Embry Riddle Aeronautical Univ., Daytona Beach	FL	610	306	277	428	1,372	249	1,621	80
Embry Riddle Aeronautical University, Prescott	AZ	208	102	115	135	472	88	560	20
University of Evansville	IN	109	50	68	69	252	44	296	40
Fairfield University	CT	38	28	27	30	107	16	123	53
Fairleigh Dickinson University	NJ	22	14	13	8	46	11	57	10
Ferris State University	MI	14	28	24	51	114	3	117	0
University of Florida	FL	705	1,049	1,107	1,712	3,644	929	4,573	0
Florida Atlantic University	FL	195	136	163	275	665	104	769	583
Florida Institute of Technology	FL	402	217	205	286	917	193	1,110	42
Florida International University	FL	19	83	434	520	835	221	1,056	1,034
FAMU-FSU College of Engineering	FL	525	329	446	620	1,522	398	1,920	0
Gannon University	PA	29	21	21	32	91	12	103	19
George Mason University	VA	409	327	356	461	1,327	226	1,553	562
The George Washington University	DC	138	149	81	108	316	160	476	22
University of Georgia	GA	59	37	41	63	156	44	200	9

CAS-GEO

UNDERGRADUATE ENROLLMENTS

UNDERGRADUATE ENROLLMENTS

INSTITUTION		FRESHMEN (FT)	SOPHOMORES (FT)	JUNIORS (FT)	SENIORS (FT)	ENROLLMENT TOTAL M (FT)	F (FT)	TOTAL	(PT)
Georgia Institute of Technology	GA	1,995	1,412	1,517	1,937	5,410	1,451	6,861	342
Gonzaga University	WA	137	115	95	111	388	70	458	0
Grand Valley State University	MI	150	105	96	156	410	97	507	1
Grove City College	PA	96	82	69	50	266	31	297	1
University of Hartford	CT	96	60	67	64	257	30	287	55
Harvard University	MA	0	90	95	119	223	81	304	0
Harvey Mudd College	CA	72	80	69	65	204	82	286	0
University of Hawaii at Manoa	HI	149	152	163	235	560	139	699	103
Henry Cogswell College	WA	13	9	10	10	39	3	42	30
Hofstra University	NY	60	35	34	34	150	13	163	12
University of Houston, Cullen School of Engineering	TX	344	200	236	393	909	264	1,173	443
Howard University	DC	136	84	105	119	300	144	444	15
Humboldt State University	CA	18	17	32	82	108	41	149	26
University of Idaho	ID	298	208	217	380	952	151	1,103	59
Idaho State University	ID	151	119	82	94	400	46	446	0
Illinois Institute of Technology	IL	288	226	210	305	824	205	1,029	75
University of Illinois at Chicago	IL	395	230	286	548	1,234	225	1,459	165
University of Illinois at Urbana-Champaign	IL	1,261	1,190	1,172	1,974	4,721	876	5,597	0
Indiana Institute of Technology	IN	36	28	32	36	113	19	132	0
Indiana University Purdue University at Indianapolis	IN	113	69	59	77	282	36	318	106
Indiana University-Purdue University Fort Wayne	IN	101	49	28	18	179	17	196	70
The University of Iowa	IA	431	295	281	250	1,024	233	1,257	0
Iowa State University	IA	1,247	858	908	1,280	3,679	614	4,293	318
John Brown University	AR	35	14	14	16	66	13	79	0
The Johns Hopkins University	MD	419	360	277	295	918	433	1,351	7
University of Kansas	KS	418	287	285	401	1,118	273	1,391	68
Kansas State University	KS	791	537	534	906	2,435	333	2,768	8
University of Kentucky	KY	464	289	348	576	1,454	223	1,677	129
Kettering University formerly GMI	MI	331	460	394	840	1,728	297	2,025	0
Lafayette College	PA	156	124	101	113	370	124	494	12
Lake Superior State University	MI	26	20	27	52	115	10	125	11
Lamar University	TX	213	110	98	149	483	87	570	187
Lawrence Technological University	MI	135	103	130	155	457	66	523	271
Lehigh University	PA	414	419	304	430	1,242	325	1,567	11
LeTourneau University	TX	139	91	83	71	347	37	384	10
Louisiana State University	LA	611	512	495	657	1,897	378	2,275	138
Louisiana Tech University	LA	448	238	208	299	1,039	154	1,193	40
University of Louisiana at Lafayette	LA	364	170	145	198	782	95	877	94
University of Louisville	KY	451	260	186	245	963	179	1,142	341
Loyola College in Maryland	MD	34	21	12	13	64	16	80	1
Loyola Marymount University	CA	68	65	54	60	194	53	247	0
University of Maine	ME	160	189	144	189	579	103	682	45
Maine Maritime Academy	ME	24	16	26	7	70	3	73	0
Manhattan College	NY	171	149	144	157	487	134	621	1
Marietta College	OH	43	30	20	28	104	17	121	0

GEO-MAR

INSTITUTION		FRESHMEN (FT)	SOPHOMORES (FT)	JUNIORS (FT)	SENIORS (FT)	M	(FT) F	TOTAL	(PT)
Marquette University	WI	246	251	245	268	814	196	1,010	39
University of Maryland, Baltimore County	MD	286	231	298	366	1,032	149	1,181	192
University of Maryland, College Park	MD	603	562	570	695	2,011	419	2,430	117
Massachusetts Institute of Technology	MA	0	566	601	556	1,064	659	1,723	26
University of Massachusetts Amherst	MA	301	236	250	313	961	139	1,100	36
University of Massachusetts Dartmouth	MA	303	196	141	149	715	74	789	58
University of Massachusetts Lowell	MA	425	173	179	176	845	108	953	97
McNeese State University	LA	139	63	63	71	286	50	336	33
The University of Memphis	TN	154	81	48	123	342	64	406	108
Mercer University	GA	131	90	53	102	272	104	376	34
Merrimack College	MA	32	26	16	27	92	9	101	25
Messiah College	PA	33	25	32	38	114	14	128	1
University of Miami	FL	180	172	137	349	591	247	838	30
Miami University	OH	298	190	142	165	660	135	795	50
University of Michigan	MI	992	1,083	1,189	1,494	3,616	1,142	4,758	154
Michigan State University	MI	917	582	541	786	2,341	485	2,826	0
Michigan Technological University	MI	841	691	644	778	2,465	489	2,954	233
University of Michigan, Dearborn	MI	229	170	182	218	659	140	799	392
Milwaukee School of Engineering	WI	558	349	264	304	1,308	167	1,475	58
Minnesota State University, Mankato	MN	112	96	69	151	400	28	428	22
University of Minnesota, Duluth	MN	211	180	160	244	725	70	795	0
University of Minnesota -Twin Cities	MN	538	982	450	1,413	2,911	472	3,383	0
The University of Mississippi	MS	243	126	103	136	502	106	608	39
Mississippi State University	MS	464	336	338	1,134	1,895	377	2,272	264
University of Missouri-Columbia	MO	406	326	391	587	1,505	205	1,710	69
University of Missouri - Rolla	MO	849	668	664	977	2,583	575	3,158	246
Monmouth University	NJ	14	8	7	0	25	4	29	1
Montana State University	MT	413	271	277	417	1,206	172	1,378	121
Montana Tech of the University of Montana	MT	255	149	150	203	757	0	757	0
Morgan State University	MD	177	150	136	138	431	170	601	56
University of Nebraska, Lincoln	NE	599	405	445	627	1,811	265	2,076	155
University of Nevada, Las Vegas	NV	201	150	143	296	667	123	790	394
University of Nevada, Reno	NV	267	195	201	264	765	162	927	187
University of New Hampshire	NH	238	199	191	216	744	100	844	0
University of New Haven	CT	75	43	24	41	164	19	183	89
New Jersey Institute of Technology	NJ	341	365	431	485	1,347	275	1,622	243
The College of New Jersey	NJ	117	93	78	72	298	62	360	7
The University of New Mexico	NM	157	143	188	298	649	137	786	210
New Mexico Institute of Mining & Technology	NM	134	116	95	135	395	85	480	24
New Mexico State University	NM	319	252	212	376	938	221	1,159	0
University of New Orleans	LA	270	132	98	166	572	94	666	174
New York Institute of Technology	NY	161	149	158	158	540	86	626	109
City College of the City University of New York	NY	443	426	374	365	1,291	317	1,608	655
The State University of New York at Binghamton	NY	328	348	288	337	1,127	174	1,301	100
State University of New York at Buffalo	NY	535	404	430	742	1,857	254	2,111	119

MAR-NEW

UNDERGRADUATE ENROLLMENTS

INSTITUTION		FRESHMEN (FT)	SOPHOMORES (FT)	JUNIORS (FT)	SENIORS (FT)	ENROLLMENT TOTAL M	(FT) F	TOTAL	(PT)
City University of New York, College of Staten Island	NY	24	19	17	20	67	13	80	16
SUNY College of Environmental Science and Forestry	NY	55	52	63	46	187	29	216	10
Stony Brook University	NY	294	210	207	560	1,038	233	1,271	62
North Carolina A & T State University	NC	717	324	216	292	1,081	468	1,549	0
North Carolina State University	NC	1,656	1,074	1,070	1,448	4,453	795	5,248	575
University of North Carolina, Charlotte	NC	349	281	247	379	1,145	111	1,256	137
University of North Dakota	ND	151	171	120	161	546	57	603	192
North Dakota State University	ND	436	394	302	501	1,488	145	1,633	128
University of North Florida	FL	277	131	122	80	560	50	610	186
University of North Texas	TX	160	103	84	70	372	45	417	116
Northeastern University	MA	445	385	664	295	1,497	292	1,789	48
Northern Arizona University	AZ	254	191	165	221	709	122	831	81
Northern Illinois University	IL	142	113	135	223	579	34	613	45
Northwestern University	IL	362	360	361	314	1,019	378	1,397	11
Norwich University	VT	65	46	55	53	194	25	219	0
University of Notre Dame	IN	0	261	271	251	592	191	783	0
Oakland University	MI	268	125	153	193	625	114	739	283
Ohio Northern University	OH	173	91	87	86	372	65	437	24
The Ohio State University	OH	1,021	929	841	1,571	3,777	585	4,362	0
Ohio University	OH	245	203	164	278	797	93	890	59
University of Oklahoma	OK	493	330	377	603	1,469	334	1,803	221
Oklahoma Christian University	OK	95	46	27	36	173	31	204	0
Oklahoma State University	OK	584	395	423	656	1,625	433	2,058	0
Old Dominion University	VA	261	180	131	218	663	127	790	142
Oral Roberts University	OK	30	20	15	13	72	6	78	0
Oregon Institute of Technology	OR	42	30	37	51	139	21	160	8
Oregon State University	OR	938	793	502	716	2,566	383	2,949	161
University of the Pacific	CA	116	69	108	177	371	99	470	8
University of Pennsylvania	PA	407	408	466	447	1,107	423	1,530	0
Pennsylvania State University Harrisburg	PA	18	17	59	59	124	29	153	16
Penn State Erie, The Behrend College	PA	94	107	80	138	361	58	419	10
The Pennsylvania State University	PA	1,346	1,083	1,383	1,852	4,411	1,253	5,664	167
Philadelphia University	PA	19	7	1	5	22	10	32	1
University of Pittsburgh	PA	470	501	466	447	1,497	387	1,884	47
Polytechnic University	NY	386	301	207	192	913	173	1,086	63
Polytechnic University of Puerto Rico	PR	704	743	798	1,561	2,927	879	3,806	0
University of Portland	OR	87	63	96	94	286	54	340	8
Portland State University	OR	211	137	169	305	717	105	822	414
Prairie View A&M University	TX	166	140	152	184	481	161	642	31
Princeton University	NJ	259	192	177	171	536	263	799	0
University of Puerto Rico, Mayaguez Campus	PR	933	732	725	2,302	2,939	1,753	4,692	0
Purdue University, Calumet	IN	77	47	40	8	147	25	172	57
Purdue University	IN	1,817	1,631	1,182	1,300	4,907	1,023	5,930	351
Rensselaer Polytechnic Institute	NY	833	707	679	823	2,455	587	3,042	0
University of Rhode Island	RI	300	176	188	198	734	128	862	60

NEW-RHO

UNDERGRADUATE ENROLLMENTS

UNDERGRADUATE ENGINEERING ENROLLMENTS, FALL 2006

INSTITUTION		FRESHMEN (FT)	SOPHOMORES (FT)	JUNIORS (FT)	SENIORS (FT)	ENROLLMENT TOTAL M	(FT) F	TOTAL	(PT)
William Marsh Rice University	TX	207	220	173	174	544	230	774	14
University of Rochester	NY	187	147	144	88	428	138	566	10
Rochester Institute of Technology	NY	638	446	369	861	2,064	250	2,314	59
Roger Williams University	RI	118	92	63	70	319	24	343	0
Rose-Hulman Institute of Technology	IN	510	431	395	365	1,397	304	1,701	5
Rowan University	NJ	111	128	111	124	406	68	474	12
Rutgers, The State University of New Jersey	NJ	562	548	654	507	1,928	343	2,271	72
Saginaw Valley State University	MI	67	26	56	66	198	17	215	77
Saint Ambrose University	IA	10	9	15	15	41	8	49	0
Saint Cloud State University	MN	80	64	51	106	267	34	301	22
Saint Louis University - Parks College	MO	122	77	83	118	326	74	400	9
Saint Martin's College	WA	31	27	29	32	102	17	119	0
Saint Mary's University	TX	30	29	28	31	97	21	118	15
University of Saint Thomas	MN	49	32	32	58	141	30	171	0
University of San Diego	CA	78	38	36	40	148	44	192	0
San Diego State University	CA	349	215	340	522	1,215	211	1,426	343
San Francisco State University	CA	155	141	146	177	544	75	619	0
San Jose State University	CA	527	187	395	759	1,593	275	1,868	441
Santa Clara University	CA	157	118	110	104	392	97	489	11
Seattle University	WA	39	43	65	128	238	37	275	0
Seattle Pacific University	WA	42	33	22	17	103	11	114	41
Smith College	MA	0	0	0	26	0	26	26	0
University of South Alabama	AL	165	113	89	143	432	78	510	150
University of South Carolina	SC	359	159	198	332	884	164	1,048	125
South Dakota School of Mines and Technology	SD	353	273	205	308	963	176	1,139	119
South Dakota State University	SD	387	197	189	289	963	99	1,062	0
University of South Florida	FL	617	300	352	764	1,720	313	2,033	694
Southeast Missouri State University	MO	20	6	6	8	34	6	40	0
University of Southern California	CA	389	397	428	559	1,329	444	1,773	0
Southern Illinois University Carbondale	IL	187	159	132	253	657	74	731	34
Southern Illinois University Edwardsville	IL	151	157	203	278	716	73	789	127
University of Southern Maine	ME	10	32	6	0	43	5	48	12
Southern Methodist University	TX	1	77	103	127	222	86	308	12
Southern University and A&M College	LA	193	108	105	194	517	83	600	14
Stanford University	CA	687	538	378	367	1,368	602	1,970	0
Stevens Institute of Technology	NJ	262	361	282	212	883	234	1,117	0
Swarthmore College	PA	32	34	21	15	68	34	102	0
Syracuse University	NY	381	232	186	254	818	235	1,053	16
Temple University	PA	223	139	129	189	586	94	680	0
Tennessee State University	TN	175	82	82	124	348	115	463	108
Tennessee Technological University	TN	410	251	232	301	1,084	110	1,194	197
University of Tennessee, Chattanooga	TN	148	82	57	132	366	53	419	109
University of Tennessee, Knoxville	TN	538	383	362	458	1,461	280	1,741	85
University of Tennessee, Martin	TN	82	38	31	66	196	21	217	20
Texas A&M University	TX	2,040	1,345	1,270	1,554	5,016	1,193	6,209	335

UNDERGRADUATE ENROLLMENTS   RIC-TEX

INSTITUTION		FRESHMEN (FT)	SOPHOMORES (FT)	JUNIORS (FT)	SENIORS (FT)	ENROLLMENT TOTAL			
						M	(FT) F	TOTAL	(PT)
Texas A&M University, Galveston	TX	89	47	30	54	180	40	220	10
Texas A&M University - Kingsville	TX	130	105	120	165	438	82	520	64
Texas Christian University	TX	49	40	31	41	134	27	161	0
Texas Tech University	TX	707	548	504	760	2,245	274	2,519	221
The University of Texas at Arlington	TX	214	153	195	402	820	144	964	739
The University of Texas at Austin	TX	1,073	942	1,008	1,637	3,639	1,021	4,660	387
The University of Texas at Dallas	TX	357	208	288	360	1,079	134	1,213	410
University of Texas at El Paso	TX	475	285	274	438	1,161	311	1,472	634
The University of Texas-Pan American	TX	289	139	105	203	612	124	736	116
University of Texas at San Antonio	TX	535	240	178	396	1,194	155	1,349	337
The University of Texas at Tyler	TX	101	35	127	46	264	45	309	63
The University of Toledo	OH	366	252	261	403	1,117	165	1,282	107
Tri-State University	IN	121	74	63	92	316	34	350	15
Trinity University	TX	34	36	19	30	93	26	119	0
Trinity College	CT	29	26	25	16	75	21	96	1
Tufts University	MA	182	183	174	170	497	212	709	3
Tulane University	LA	40	51	80	156	236	91	327	6
University of Tulsa	OK	198	108	116	121	467	76	543	16
Tuskegee University	AL	132	70	87	96	259	126	385	20
Union College	NY	63	78	69	55	231	34	265	2
U.S. Air Force Academy	CO	24	298	240	235	727	70	797	0
U.S. Coast Guard Academy	CT	125	106	80	87	331	67	398	0
U.S. Merchant Marine Academy	NY	114	105	99	94	377	35	412	0
United States Military Academy	NY	0	274	258	187	652	67	719	2
U.S. Naval Academy	MD	0	469	396	396	1,113	148	1,261	0
University of Utah	UT	243	228	308	757	1,358	178	1,536	557
Utah State University	UT	251	230	254	502	1,116	121	1,237	0
Valparaiso University	IN	91	52	69	110	277	45	322	0
Vanderbilt University	TN	308	243	331	338	891	329	1,220	7
University of Vermont	VT	128	130	97	116	398	73	471	18
Villanova University	PA	273	237	216	198	744	180	924	0
University of Virginia	VA	545	510	482	499	1,486	550	2,036	0
Virginia Commonwealth University	VA	268	231	220	256	787	188	975	119
Virginia Military Institute	VA	139	94	89	71	380	13	393	0
Virginia Polytechnic Institute and State University	VA	1,296	1,192	1,204	1,684	4,596	780	5,376	107
Walla Walla College	WA	70	59	46	50	205	20	225	2
University of Washington	WA	67	187	617	923	1,429	365	1,794	152
Washington State University	WA	420	291	376	521	1,429	179	1,608	115
Washington University	MO	306	240	321	388	920	335	1,255	0
Wayne State University	MI	272	116	138	226	574	178	752	361
Webb Institute	NY	26	17	14	15	53	19	72	0
Wentworth Institute of Technology	MA	52	42	40	55	165	24	189	2
West Virginia University Institute of Technology	WV	162	82	70	142	367	89	456	21
West Virginia University	WV	640	441	357	602	1,838	202	2,040	52
Western Kentucky University	KY	145	72	60	100	349	28	377	27

TEX-WES

UNDERGRADUATE ENROLLMENTS

UNDERGRADUATE ENGINEERING ENROLLMENTS, FALL 2006

INSTITUTION		FRESHMEN (FT)	SOPHOMORES (FT)	JUNIORS (FT)	SENIORS (FT)	ENROLLMENT TOTAL			
						M	F (FT)	TOTAL	(PT)
Western Michigan University	MI	384	326	253	367	1,190	140	1,330	175
Western New England College	MA	102	63	82	57	265	39	304	11
Wichita State University	KS	174	120	128	221	547	96	643	254
Widener University	PA	114	64	43	47	240	28	268	7
Wilkes University	PA	55	37	23	34	138	11	149	21
Winona State University	MN	61	30	31	24	136	10	146	2
University of Wisconsin, Stout	WI	48	22	23	41	123	11	134	0
University of Wisconsin, Madison	WI	609	609	633	1,088	2,411	528	2,939	240
University of Wisconsin, Milwaukee	WI	335	292	225	351	1,116	87	1,203	290
University of Wisconsin, Platteville	WI	785	253	279	327	1,475	169	1,644	0
Worcester Polytechnic Institute	MA	262	451	373	463	1,196	353	1,549	23
Wright State University	OH	422	205	138	257	886	136	1,022	144
University of Wyoming	WY	325	199	199	360	936	147	1,083	59
Yale University/Faculty of Engineering	CT	0	0	57	69	94	32	126	0
York College of Pennsylvania	PA	60	23	27	22	124	8	132	2
Youngstown State University	OH	23	84	81	127	264	51	315	30
Totals:		101,291	79,331	78,963	113,489	308,079	64,995	373,074	31,430
CANADIAN INSTITUTIONS:									
University of Alberta	AB	851	835	781	965	2,751	681	3,432	0
University of Calgary	AB	751	541	817	548	2,051	606	2,657	42
Concordia University, Faculty of Engr. and Comp. Sci.	PQ	912	813	572	544	2,416	425	2,841	74
Ecole Polytechnique de Montreal	PQ	1,263	519	588	466	2,261	575	2,836	265
Ecole de Technologie Superieure	PQ	818	764	0	0	1,408	174	1,582	130
McGill University, Faculty of Engineering	PQ	218	612	517	835	1,704	478	2,182	184
University of Ottawa, Faculty of Engineering	ON	384	337	357	741	1,526	293	1,819	216
University of Waterloo	ON	1,303	1,136	879	1,681	4,165	834	4,999	0
Totals:		6,500	5,557	4,512	5,780	18,282	4,066	22,348	911

WES-YOU

UNDERGRADUATE ENROLLMENTS

INSTITUTION		AFRICAN AMERICAN M	F	ASIAN AMERICAN M	F	HISPANIC M	F	NATIVE AMERICAN M	F	CAUCASIAN M	F	FOREIGN M	F	OTHER M	F	TOTAL BY GENDER M	F	TOTAL DEGREES
The University of Akron	OH	6	2	1	3	0	0	2	0	125	27	6	0	3	1	143	33	176
Alabama A&M University	AL	44	26	0	0	0	0	0	0	2	0	0	0	0	0	46	26	72
University of Alabama at Birmingham	AL	7	4	3	2	2	1	0	0	41	6	7	3	0	0	60	16	76
The University of Alabama in Huntsville	AL	12	7	5	0	1	0	1	0	127	31	5	3	1	0	152	42	194
The University of Alabama	AL	14	11	3	1	1	0	1	1	132	40	3	1	0	0	154	54	208
University of Alaska, Anchorage	AK	0	1	0	0	1	0	2	2	9	3	0	0	0	0	12	6	18
University of Alaska Fairbanks	AK	1	0	4	3	1	0	2	0	42	13	0	0	0	0	50	16	66
Alfred University, NY State College of Ceramics	NY	1	0	0	1	2	1	0	0	40	11	0	0	5	0	48	13	61
The University of Arizona	AZ	7	6	20	9	42	12	2	1	240	52	48	9	0	0	359	89	448
Arizona State University	AZ	9	4	52	28	47	18	5	1	322	61	57	14	42	13	534	139	673
University of Arkansas	AR	2	2	4	5	2	0	4	1	158	28	11	1	4	1	185	38	223
Arkansas State University	AR	0	1	0	0	0	1	0	0	21	3	2	0	0	0	23	5	28
Arkansas Tech University	AR	1	0	0	0	0	0	0	0	50	2	1	0	0	0	52	2	54
University of Arkansas at Little Rock	AR	0	0	0	0	0	1	0	0	13	1	1	0	0	0	14	2	16
Auburn University	AL	15	21	10	2	3	2	1	0	325	68	9	2	5	0	368	95	463
Baylor University	TX	3	1	4	2	7	0	0	0	49	8	1	0	0	0	64	11	75
Boise State University	ID	0	0	4	1	4	0	1	1	88	13	5	0	7	0	109	15	124
Boston University	MA	5	1	48	15	6	5	0	1	134	31	13	5	0	0	206	58	264
Bradley University	IL	2	0	3	2	2	0	0	0	115	18	3	0	0	0	125	20	145
University of Bridgeport	CT	0	0	0	0	0	0	0	0	2	0	1	0	1	0	4	0	4
Brigham Young University	UT	0	0	2	0	3	0	0	0	0	0	15	1	384	32	404	33	437
Brown University	RI	0	2	5	6	1	1	0	0	33	9	4	5	0	0	43	23	66
Bucknell University	PA	0	2	7	2	1	0	2	0	83	32	8	0	1	0	102	36	138
California Institute of Technology	CA	2	1	28	12	9	0	1	0	39	13	6	3	0	0	85	29	114
California Maritime Academy	CA	0	0	4	0	1	0	0	0	15	4	0	0	0	0	20	4	24
California Polytechnic State University	CA	11	2	153	41	68	16	4	1	461	85	7	2	106	17	810	164	974
California State Polytechnic University, Pomona	CA	15	3	179	45	82	17	4	0	112	15	0	0	36	5	428	85	513
California State University, East Bay	CA	1	1	4	0	0	0	0	0	2	0	0	0	3	4	10	5	15
California State University, Chico	CA	2	1	6	1	4	3	1	0	49	6	10	2	21	3	93	16	109
California State University, Fresno	CA	3	1	16	6	31	10	0	0	78	9	20	1	0	0	148	27	175
California State University, Fullerton	CA	3	1	55	13	25	6	2	0	37	4	19	3	18	2	159	29	188
California State University, Long Beach	CA	8	4	62	14	30	6	0	0	95	10	61	11	0	0	256	45	301
California State University, Los Angeles	CA	4	2	15	3	23	4	1	0	11	1	19	4	12	0	85	14	99
California State University, Northridge	CA	13	3	52	7	58	11	0	0	72	11	11	0	28	2	234	34	268
California State University, Sacramento	CA	7	1	80	22	24	5	2	0	79	13	18	4	25	12	235	57	292
University of California, Berkeley	CA	3	3	341	131	38	10	4	0	161	24	60	28	63	20	666	216	882
University of California, Davis	CA	3	0	232	66	28	3	5	2	143	37	18	7	23	6	452	121	573
University of California, Irvine	CA	0	0	0	0	0	0	0	0	0	0	0	0	366	100	366	100	466
University of California, Los Angeles	CA	7	1	174	50	26	4	2	0	118	22	35	19	61	15	423	111	534
University of California, Riverside	CA	9	3	90	23	37	3	0	0	63	6	0	0	14	3	213	38	251
University of California, San Diego	CA	7	1	358	96	39	8	4	0	217	46	66	27	72	14	763	192	955
University of California, Santa Barbara	CA	5	0	46	18	22	2	2	0	114	26	12	3	31	5	232	54	286
University of California-Santa Cruz	CA	3	0	26	9	13	2	1	0	63	5	6	2	18	1	129	19	148
Calvin College	MI	0	0	1	0	0	0	0	0	44	5	11	4	0	0	57	9	66
Capitol College	MD	0	0	0	0	0	0	0	0	0	0	0	0	19	3	19	3	22

BACHELOR'S DEGREES AWARDED   AKR-CAP

INSTITUTION		AFRICAN AMERICAN		ASIAN AMERICAN		HISPANIC		NATIVE AMERICAN		CAUCASIAN		FOREIGN		OTHER		TOTAL BY GENDER		TOTAL DEGREES
		M	F	M	F	M	F	M	F	M	F	M	F	M	F	M	F	
Carnegie Mellon University	PA	11	6	46	21	15	2	0	1	114	26	33	13	19	6	238	75	313
Carroll College	MT	0	0	0	0	0	0	0	0	5	1	0	0	0	0	5	1	6
Case Western Reserve University	OH	4	1	30	15	3	0	0	0	188	44	10	12	3	1	238	73	311
The Catholic University of America	DC	2	0	1	0	0	0	0	0	21	4	3	1	1	0	28	5	33
Cedarville University	OH	0	0	0	0	0	0	0	0	0	0	0	0	58	5	58	5	63
University of Central Florida	FL	32	8	33	16	68	10	2	2	350	51	28	15	23	2	536	104	640
Christian Brothers University	TN	2	2	5	0	0	1	0	0	16	5	2	1	1	0	26	9	35
Christopher Newport University	VA	0	0	0	1	0	0	0	0	11	2	0	0	0	0	11	3	14
University of Cincinnati	OH	10	1	9	1	3	2	1	1	194	44	0	0	4	4	221	53	274
The Citadel	SC	3	0	2	0	2	0	0	0	54	2	3	0	0	0	64	2	66
Clarkson University	NY	5	0	3	5	7	0	1	0	252	27	10	1	0	0	278	33	311
Clemson University	SC	23	18	8	3	4	0	0	0	341	77	6	4	31	8	413	110	523
Cleveland State University	OH	9	0	0	1	0	0	0	0	70	8	3	0	0	0	82	9	91
Colorado School of Mines	CO	5	0	21	11	21	14	3	1	348	81	19	3	0	0	417	110	527
Colorado State University	CO	0	0	7	2	8	3	1	0	194	42	0	0	19	3	229	50	279
Colorado State University, Pueblo	CO	0	0	0	0	1	0	0	0	0	1	0	0	0	1	1	2	3
Colorado Technical University	CO	1	0	0	0	0	0	0	0	0	0	3	0	28	7	32	7	39
University of Colorado at Boulder	CO	10	4	44	13	17	7	1	0	376	56	10	6	0	0	458	86	544
University of Colorado at Colorado Springs	CO	4	0	9	7	5	2	0	0	55	11	1	1	2	1	76	22	98
University of Colorado at Denver	CO	5	1	12	2	12	3	0	1	66	6	13	2	8	1	116	16	132
Columbia University	NY	7	4	95	21	13	4	0	0	104	35	36	8	38	13	293	85	378
University of Connecticut	CT	7	2	20	13	9	2	0	0	172	37	3	0	6	2	217	56	273
The Cooper Union	NY	3	1	28	11	7	1	1	0	39	7	11	2	0	0	89	22	111
Cornell University	NY	9	7	145	56	16	6	3	0	265	82	72	24	11	8	521	183	704
Dartmouth College	NH	2	1	10	2	5	1	1	0	57	21	11	5	2	0	88	30	118
University of Dayton	OH	2	0	1	2	5	0	0	0	0	0	1	1	113	35	122	38	160
University of Delaware	DE	2	2	7	2	5	1	0	0	140	42	2	2	0	0	156	49	205
University of Denver	CO	0	0	2	1	2	1	0	0	12	2	4	1	0	0	20	5	25
University of Detroit Mercy	MI	10	6	1	0	2	0	0	0	26	5	1	0	2	1	42	12	54
University of the District of Columbia	DC	14	3	8	0	1	0	0	0	10	1	5	3	0	0	38	7	45
Drexel University	PA	31	7	63	17	6	7	1	0	237	52	40	9	34	5	412	97	509
Duke University Pratt School of Engineering	NC	0	0	0	0	0	0	0	0	0	0	0	0	185	59	185	59	244
Embry Riddle Aeronautical Univ, Daytona Beach	FL	7	3	8	1	9	1	0	0	120	31	23	1	19	3	186	40	226
Embry Riddle Aeronautical University, Prescott	AZ	0	0	5	1	2	3	0	1	62	11	3	0	4	0	76	16	92
University of Evansville	IN	0	0	0	0	0	0	0	0	0	0	0	0	47	4	47	4	51
Fairfield University	CT	1	0	3	0	2	0	0	0	21	2	1	2	0	0	28	4	32
Fairleigh Dickinson University	NJ	0	0	0	0	0	0	0	0	8	1	0	0	0	0	8	1	9
Ferris State University	MI	0	0	0	0	0	0	0	0	30	4	0	0	2	1	32	5	37
University of Florida	FL	27	8	66	17	110	28	5	2	477	104	21	2	0	0	706	161	867
Florida Atlantic University	FL	18	7	22	4	26	7	0	0	80	15	23	10	0	0	169	43	212
Florida Institute of Technology	FL	6	1	6	3	5	1	0	1	79	26	56	11	19	6	171	49	220
Florida International University	FL	35	10	17	5	191	57	1	0	48	9	68	22	1	0	361	103	464
FAMU-FSU College of Engineering	FL	86	28	4	1	17	4	1	0	102	31	27	12	0	0	237	76	313
Gannon University	PA	0	0	0	0	0	0	0	0	29	5	7	0	0	0	36	5	41
George Mason University	VA	23	11	86	23	27	6	1	1	150	28	32	14	27	9	346	92	438

BACHELOR'S DEGREES AWARDED

CAR-GEO

BACHELOR'S DEGREES AWARDED IN ENGINEERING, 2005-2006

INSTITUTION		AFRICAN AMERICAN		ASIAN AMERICAN		HISPANIC		NATIVE AMERICAN		CAUCASIAN		FOREIGN		OTHER		TOTAL BY GENDER		TOTAL DEGREES
		M	F	M	F	M	F	M	F	M	F	M	F	M	F	M	F	
The George Washington University	DC	3	1	5	7	0	1	0	0	33	10	11	4	5	2	57	25	82
University of Georgia	GA	2	0	2	0	1	0	0	0	19	5	0	0	1	0	25	5	30
Georgia Institute of Technology	GA	88	32	160	55	35	19	0	2	714	172	75	25	13	1	1,085	306	1,391
Gonzaga University	WA	0	0	4	1	3	0	1	0	72	11	2	0	0	0	82	12	94
Grand Valley State University	MI	0	0	0	0	0	0	0	0	55	7	0	0	0	0	55	7	62
Grove City College	PA	0	0	0	0	0	0	0	0	35	8	0	0	0	0	35	8	43
University of Hartford	CT	1	0	2	0	2	0	0	0	32	9	4	6	0	0	41	15	56
Harvard University	MA	2	1	12	6	3	0	0	0	33	10	8	4	0	0	58	21	79
Harvey Mudd College	CA	0	0	15	8	2	0	0	0	22	5	2	0	7	1	48	14	62
University of Hawaii at Manoa	HI	0	0	51	19	1	0	0	0	11	2	0	0	32	1	95	22	117
Henry Cogswell College	WA	0	0	2	1	0	0	0	0	13	1	0	0	0	0	15	2	17
Hofstra University	NY	2	1	0	0	2	1	0	0	6	6	1	0	2	1	13	9	22
University of Houston, Cullen School of Engineering	TX	10	7	51	17	31	13	0	0	57	16	24	8	7	4	180	65	245
Howard University	DC	82	24	0	0	0	0	0	0	0	0	0	0	0	0	82	24	106
Humboldt State University	CA	0	1	1	0	0	0	1	0	10	4	0	0	2	2	14	7	21
University of Idaho	ID	0	0	9	3	5	0	1	0	171	31	0	0	20	3	206	37	243
Idaho State University	ID	0	0	0	0	1	0	0	0	34	2	3	0	0	0	38	2	40
Illinois Institute of Technology	IL	4	4	19	5	6	2	0	0	82	17	40	8	8	0	159	36	195
University of Illinois at Chicago	IL	17	5	73	40	24	14	1	0	134	18	0	0	15	2	264	79	343
University of Illinois at Urbana-Champaign	IL	17	11	198	48	30	9	2	0	666	115	90	33	16	2	1,019	218	1,237
Indiana Institute of Technology	IN	0	0	0	0	0	2	0	0	11	2	0	0	3	1	14	5	19
Indiana University Purdue University at Indianapolis	IN	6	2	10	2	2	0	0	0	53	7	6	2	3	0	80	13	93
Indiana University-Purdue University Fort Wayne	IN	1	0	0	1	0	0	0	0	12	2	4	1	0	0	17	4	21
The University of Iowa	IA	2	1	2	5	2	0	0	0	150	47	4	1	5	0	165	54	219
Iowa State University	IA	25	8	29	9	9	6	3	1	632	110	54	8	36	2	788	144	932
John Brown University	AR	0	0	0	0	0	0	0	0	9	1	5	1	0	0	14	2	16
The Johns Hopkins University	MD	7	4	59	21	9	2	2	2	122	31	18	8	0	0	217	68	285
University of Kansas	KS	2	2	2	2	1	0	1	2	171	32	31	14	0	0	207	48	255
Kansas State University	KS	9	0	2	2	10	3	3	1	323	45	7	2	15	2	367	54	421
University of Kentucky	KY	3	3	5	5	2	0	1	1	238	40	7	3	4	1	260	52	312
Kettering University formerly GMI	MI	7	9	15	6	6	3	2	0	263	39	10	4	22	6	325	67	392
Lafayette College	PA	3	1	2	0	1	0	0	0	78	30	5	2	0	0	89	33	122
Lake Superior State University	MI	0	0	1	0	0	0	0	0	16	1	3	0	0	0	20	1	21
Lamar University	TX	7	4	7	1	3	1	1	0	72	15	3	0	0	2	93	23	116
Lawrence Technological University	MI	6	3	7	2	3	0	1	0	107	20	6	1	13	1	143	27	170
Lehigh University	PA	4	1	19	4	6	2	1	0	0	0	9	5	252	57	291	69	360
LeTourneau University	TX	0	1	0	0	0	0	0	0	42	2	1	0	1	0	44	3	47
Louisiana State University	LA	13	10	14	4	8	5	0	0	226	62	36	10	9	1	306	92	398
Louisiana Tech University	LA	10	10	3	1	0	0	2	0	127	24	17	4	2	0	161	39	200
University of Louisiana at Lafayette	LA	7	2	0	0	0	0	0	0	72	13	15	2	0	0	94	17	111
University of Louisville	KY	8	4	8	4	2	0	0	0	131	16	6	4	0	0	155	28	183
Loyola College in Maryland	MD	1	1	0	0	0	0	0	0	5	2	0	0	0	1	6	4	10
Loyola Marymount University	CA	2	1	14	3	4	3	0	0	27	3	2	1	5	3	54	14	68
University of Maine	ME	0	1	1	2	1	0	4	0	117	22	3	2	1	0	127	27	154
Maine Maritime Academy	ME	0	0	0	0	0	0	0	0	9	2	1	0	0	0	10	2	12

GEO-MAI

BACHELOR'S DEGREES AWARDED

INSTITUTION		AFRICAN AMERICAN		ASIAN AMERICAN		HISPANIC		NATIVE AMERICAN		CAUCASIAN		FOREIGN		OTHER		TOTAL BY GENDER		TOTAL DEGREES
		M	F	M	F	M	F	M	F	M	F	M	F	M	F	M	F	
Manhattan College	NY	10	5	3	4	13	6	0	0	71	16	0	0	37	5	134	36	170
Marietta College	OH	0	0	0	0	0	0	0	0	14	0	0	0	0	0	14	0	14
Marquette University	WI	2	0	5	2	4	1	0	0	92	41	14	4	0	0	117	48	165
University of Maryland, Baltimore County	MD	17	8	31	6	5	2	0	0	120	19	9	3	7	0	189	38	227
University of Maryland, College Park	MD	48	14	102	33	27	4	0	0	311	64	20	4	27	3	535	122	657
Massachusetts Institute of Technology	MA	25	5	76	76	50	9	8	5	169	57	33	13	38	14	399	179	578
Massachusetts Maritime Academy	MA	1	0	1	0	1	0	0	0	62	9	0	0	0	0	65	9	74
University of Massachusetts Amherst	MA	10	1	22	2	7	1	0	0	136	28	7	1	0	0	182	33	215
University of Massachusetts Dartmouth	MA	6	0	1	0	2	1	0	0	94	5	3	0	5	1	111	7	118
University of Massachusetts Lowell	MA	9	1	7	6	11	2	1	1	61	17	6	0	20	1	115	28	143
McNeese State University	LA	2	2	0	0	0	0	0	0	31	8	2	0	0	0	35	10	45
The University of Memphis	TN	5	1	7	3	0	0	0	0	27	3	0	1	1	0	40	8	48
Mercer University	GA	4	7	5	2	1	0	0	0	46	24	2	1	1	0	59	34	93
Merrimack College	MA	0	0	0	0	0	0	0	0	19	2	0	0	0	0	19	2	21
Messiah College	PA	0	0	0	0	0	0	0	0	22	3	2	0	0	0	24	3	27
University of Miami	FL	13	11	6	4	31	15	0	0	44	20	11	6	1	1	106	57	163
Miami University	OH	0	1	2	2	1	0	1	0	98	23	2	0	4	0	108	26	134
University of Michigan	MI	31	34	119	49	34	10	6	1	435	162	104	30	26	9	755	295	1,050
Michigan State University	MI	13	12	47	13	8	1	1	1	362	90	37	5	0	0	468	122	590
Michigan Technological University	MI	3	2	6	1	7	0	4	0	430	98	34	7	19	5	503	113	616
University of Michigan, Dearborn	MI	4	5	28	20	3	1	0	0	167	34	12	3	0	0	214	63	277
Milwaukee School of Engineering	WI	5	3	10	1	8	1	2	0	206	28	6	0	2	0	239	33	272
Minnesota State University, Mankato	MN	0	0	1	1	0	0	0	0	33	5	14	2	22	1	70	9	79
University of Minnesota, Duluth	MN	0	0	2	0	0	0	0	0	110	6	8	3	0	0	120	9	129
University of Minnesota - Twin Cities	MN	21	2	65	14	7	2	3	2	504	61	43	14	0	0	643	95	738
The University of Mississippi	MS	7	1	1	0	0	0	0	0	51	5	1	0	1	0	61	6	67
Mississippi State University	MS	16	15	5	2	2	0	2	0	246	41	3	2	0	0	274	60	334
University of Missouri-Columbia	MO	4	1	9	2	2	0	2	0	253	39	22	2	6	1	298	45	343
University of Missouri - Kansas City	MO	7	0	3	0	4	1	0	0	57	13	37	12	0	0	108	26	134
University of Missouri - Rolla	MO	18	8	7	3	2	2	1	2	367	66	12	4	10	2	417	87	504
Monmouth University	NJ	0	0	0	0	0	0	0	0	2	0	0	0	0	0	2	0	2
Montana State University	MT	0	0	2	0	2	0	3	0	184	25	4	2	7	5	202	32	234
Montana Tech of the University of Montana	MT	0	0	2	1	0	0	0	1	68	16	13	0	5	1	88	19	107
Morgan State University	MD	33	18	2	0	0	0	0	0	2	0	10	1	1	0	48	19	67
University of Nebraska, Lincoln	NE	5	1	5	3	3	0	1	0	288	39	14	2	0	0	316	45	361
University of Nevada, Las Vegas	NV	5	2	20	5	9	2	2	1	57	12	3	2	10	3	106	27	133
University of Nevada, Reno	NV	2	0	21	8	5	2	1	0	107	18	2	1	7	2	145	31	176
University of New Hampshire	NH	0	0	7	0	0	0	0	0	134	23	1	0	0	0	142	23	165
University of New Haven	CT	5	0	0	0	1	0	0	0	0	0	10	0	27	3	43	3	46
New Jersey Institute of Technology	NJ	25	8	56	13	27	10	1	0	85	8	27	5	68	14	289	58	347
The College of New Jersey	NJ	3	0	0	1	0	1	0	0	23	5	0	0	0	0	26	7	33
The University of New Mexico	NM	2	0	6	2	40	17	5	2	76	21	17	2	0	0	146	44	190
New Mexico Institute of Mining & Technology	NM	0	1	4	1	4	8	3	3	39	10	3	0	0	0	53	23	76
New Mexico State University	NM	3	3	2	0	52	13	2	1	40	6	5	0	19	6	123	29	152
University of New Orleans	LA	8	1	7	0	3	0	1	0	40	14	10	1	2	0	71	16	87

BACHELOR'S DEGREES AWARDED   MAN-NEW

INSTITUTION		AFRICAN AMERICAN M	F	ASIAN AMERICAN M	F	HISPANIC M	F	NATIVE AMERICAN M	F	CAUCASIAN M	F	FOREIGN M	F	OTHER M	F	TOTAL BY GENDER M	F	TOTAL DEGREES
New York Institute of Technology	NY	0	0	0	0	0	0	0	0	0	0	0	0	113	33	113	33	146
State University of New York Maritime College	NY	2	0	2	0	1	2	0	0	31	1	0	0	0	0	36	3	39
City College of the City University of New York	NY	20	4	37	11	24	7	0	0	0	0	23	8	60	12	164	42	206
The State University of New York at Binghamton	NY	5	2	23	7	13	0	1	0	103	10	8	1	55	7	208	27	235
State University of New York at Buffalo	NY	13	3	17	6	5	0	3	0	261	43	101	18	26	4	426	74	500
City University of New York, College of Staten Island	NY	0	0	1	0	0	0	0	0	4	0	2	0	0	0	7	0	7
SUNY College of Environmental Science and Forestry	NY	0	1	2	0	0	0	0	0	32	8	1	0	0	0	35	9	44
SUNY, New Paltz	NY	1	0	5	0	5	1	0	0	20	1	6	1	0	0	37	3	40
Stony Brook University	NY	18	12	147	43	10	4	0	0	157	20	34	9	0	0	366	88	454
North Carolina A & T State University	NC	102	36	4	1	1	0	1	0	23	1	1	0	1	1	133	39	172
North Carolina State University	NC	46	18	63	22	18	6	6	1	729	116	8	4	2	1	872	168	1,040
University of North Carolina, Charlotte	NC	9	2	7	1	7	0	1	0	141	19	8	3	0	0	173	25	198
University of North Dakota	ND	0	0	2	0	0	0	0	0	104	25	0	0	0	0	106	25	131
North Dakota State University	ND	1	1	1	0	2	0	0	0	279	30	0	0	0	0	283	31	314
University of North Florida	FL	4	0	7	1	5	0	0	1	53	6	3	0	2	0	74	8	82
University of North Texas	TX	8	1	3	0	13	4	5	0	96	6	20	4	1	1	146	16	162
Northeastern University	MA	5	1	18	2	9	3	1	0	151	37	6	4	70	11	260	58	318
Northern Arizona University	AZ	1	1	1	0	5	3	5	2	94	10	0	1	0	0	106	17	123
Northern Illinois University	IL	4	1	9	1	6	0	0	0	75	4	3	0	3	0	100	6	106
Northwestern University	IL	3	4	60	35	11	3	0	0	111	34	31	18	9	5	225	99	324
Norwich University	VT	0	0	0	0	1	0	0	0	22	6	3	0	0	0	26	6	32
University of Notre Dame	IN	2	2	9	3	5	2	0	0	160	37	9	5	0	0	185	49	234
Oakland University	MI	1	4	4	4	3	1	0	3	134	35	10	1	0	0	152	48	200
Ohio Northern University	OH	0	0	0	0	0	0	0	0	79	18	0	0	0	0	79	18	97
The Ohio State University	OH	22	8	47	15	16	3	2	0	523	85	101	26	0	0	711	137	848
Ohio University	OH	4	1	1	0	0	0	0	2	130	15	0	0	4	0	139	18	157
University of Oklahoma	OK	9	7	34	6	9	5	20	4	213	36	22	10	0	0	307	68	375
Oklahoma Christian University	OK	0	0	0	0	1	0	0	0	29	2	1	0	0	0	31	2	33
Oklahoma State University	OK	4	1	5	3	5	1	10	2	195	56	35	12	0	0	254	75	329
Old Dominion University	VA	12	3	7	4	4	0	1	0	68	15	9	5	13	1	114	28	142
Oral Roberts University	OK	2	0	1	1	0	0	0	0	9	3	0	0	0	0	12	4	16
Oregon Institute of Technology	OR	0	0	1	1	1	0	0	0	19	3	0	0	2	0	23	4	27
Oregon State University	OR	5	1	17	6	18	2	3	1	397	59	15	4	53	11	508	84	592
University of the Pacific	CA	2	0	14	7	8	1	0	0	25	7	1	1	7	1	57	17	74
University of Pennsylvania	PA	2	2	58	20	8	4	0	0	100	37	31	14	29	10	228	87	315
Penn State Erie, The Behrend College	PA	1	0	0	0	2	0	0	0	72	5	0	0	0	0	75	5	80
The Pennsylvania State University	PA	19	9	78	13	21	8	0	0	936	161	56	17	0	0	1,110	209	1,319
Philadelphia University	PA	0	0	0	0	0	0	0	0	1	0	0	0	0	0	1	0	1
University of Pittsburgh	PA	12	8	18	2	0	2	0	0	248	71	6	4	0	0	284	87	371
Polytechnic University	NY	14	7	80	20	11	3	0	0	80	10	18	1	15	1	218	42	260
Polytechnic University of Puerto Rico	PR	0	0	0	0	294	93	0	0	0	0	0	0	0	0	294	93	387
University of Portland	OR	0	0	6	4	1	0	0	0	62	18	0	1	0	0	69	23	92
Portland State University	OR	2	1	18	8	3	1	2	0	122	16	13	2	13	1	173	29	202
Prairie View A&M University	TX	40	20	0	0	4	0	0	0	4	0	7	1	0	0	55	21	76
Princeton University	NJ	10	5	23	13	7	0	0	0	67	26	12	5	0	0	119	49	168

BACHELOR'S DEGREES AWARDED

NEW-PRI

Institution	State	African American M	F	Asian American M	F	Hispanic M	F	Native American M	F	Caucasian M	F	Foreign M	F	Other M	F	Total by Gender M	F	Total Degrees
University of Puerto Rico, Mayaguez Campus	PR	0	0	0	0	370	236	0	0	0	0	0	0	0	0	370	236	606
Purdue University, Calumet	IN	6	1	2	0	3	1	0	0	23	2	0	0	12	5	46	9	55
Purdue University	IN	8	4	64	17	12	5	1	2	672	153	218	47	29	6	1,004	234	1,238
Rensselaer Polytechnic Institute	NY	13	2	53	21	10	7	2	1	329	85	17	10	0	0	424	126	550
University of Rhode Island	RI	0	0	5	1	7	3	0	0	93	25	0	3	12	3	117	35	152
William Marsh Rice University	TX	5	4	18	10	17	5	0	0	72	23	9	3	9	6	130	53	183
University of Rochester	NY	1	1	12	4	1	0	0	0	50	26	4	0	16	1	84	32	116
Rochester Institute of Technology	NY	8	3	24	3	9	1	3	0	234	41	19	7	27	0	324	55	379
Roger Williams University	RI	0	0	2	0	0	0	0	0	45	3	0	0	0	0	47	3	50
Rose-Hulman Institute of Technology	IN	3	1	11	1	5	3	0	0	262	58	0	0	1	0	282	63	345
Rowan University	NJ	1	0	0	0	0	1	0	0	58	10	0	0	0	0	59	11	70
Rutgers, The State University of New Jersey	NJ	14	10	96	30	16	3	1	0	180	44	18	3	0	0	325	90	415
Saginaw Valley State University	MI	0	0	0	0	0	0	0	0	36	3	10	2	1	0	47	5	52
Saint Ambrose University	IA	0	0	0	0	0	0	0	0	5	2	1	0	0	0	6	2	8
Saint Cloud State University	MN	1	0	0	2	0	0	0	0	21	2	12	2	7	0	41	6	47
Saint Louis University - Parks College	MO	5	1	5	1	1	0	0	0	37	18	0	0	5	4	53	24	77
Saint Martin's College	WA	0	0	0	0	0	0	0	0	22	4	0	1	0	0	22	5	27
Saint Mary's University	TX	0	0	1	0	8	2	0	0	1	0	1	1	0	0	11	3	14
University of Saint Thomas	MN	0	0	1	0	1	0	0	0	28	3	0	1	0	0	30	4	34
University of San Diego	CA	1	0	3	0	2	2	0	0	11	3	2	1	1	0	20	6	26
San Diego State University	CA	9	2	56	19	34	7	1	0	81	21	14	1	28	7	223	57	280
San Francisco State University	CA	2	1	30	13	13	2	0	0	24	6	8	3	0	0	77	25	102
San Jose State University	CA	14	2	176	59	36	9	2	0	65	11	48	10	0	0	341	91	432
Santa Clara University	CA	0	0	24	8	8	1	1	0	41	6	5	3	2	1	81	19	100
Seattle University	WA	1	2	12	10	3	1	0	0	24	6	12	2	7	0	59	21	80
Seattle Pacific University	WA	0	0	1	1	0	0	0	0	20	2	0	0	0	0	21	3	24
Smith College	MA	0	1	0	3	0	3	0	0	0	14	0	9	0	3	0	33	33
University of South Alabama	AL	4	0	4	2	0	0	0	0	57	10	16	2	3	1	84	15	99
University of South Carolina	SC	20	5	16	3	7	0	0	0	143	21	14	1	14	1	214	31	245
South Dakota School of Mines and Technology	SD	1	0	2	2	0	0	2	1	161	28	3	0	6	1	175	32	207
South Dakota State University	SD	0	0	1	0	0	0	1	0	116	12	0	0	0	0	118	12	130
University of South Florida	FL	6	1	10	5	13	2	0	0	68	18	9	4	4	1	110	31	141
Southeast Missouri State University	MO	0	0	0	0	0	0	0	0	2	1	0	0	0	0	2	1	3
University of Southern California	CA	12	7	65	38	25	10	1	1	121	22	48	20	8	2	280	100	380
Southern Illinois University Carbondale	IL	6	2	4	0	3	0	0	0	93	10	13	0	5	0	124	12	136
Southern Illinois University Edwardsville	IL	3	2	10	1	6	0	1	0	172	12	0	0	0	0	192	15	207
University of Southern Maine	ME	0	0	0	0	0	0	0	0	12	0	1	0	0	0	13	0	13
Southern Methodist University	TX	3	4	10	7	7	3	0	0	40	16	4	2	0	0	64	32	96
Southern University and A&M College	LA	40	13	0	0	0	0	0	0	1	0	6	1	0	0	47	14	61
Stanford University	CA	20	18	74	41	26	7	5	1	112	24	33	9	9	4	279	104	383
Stevens Institute of Technology	NJ	3	7	25	10	12	8	0	0	83	23	11	2	17	12	151	62	213
Swarthmore College	PA	1	0	3	1	0	0	0	0	15	4	3	1	0	0	22	6	28
Syracuse University	NY	11	8	9	2	4	1	0	0	118	21	7	1	0	0	149	33	182
Temple University	PA	9	3	12	2	0	0	0	0	29	7	11	2	0	0	61	14	75
Tennessee State University	TN	33	27	0	1	1	0	0	0	1	1	1	1	0	0	36	30	66

BACHELOR'S DEGREES AWARDED

PUE-TEN

INSTITUTION		AFRICAN AMERICAN		ASIAN AMERICAN		HISPANIC		NATIVE AMERICAN		CAUCASIAN		FOREIGN		OTHER		TOTAL BY GENDER		TOTAL DEGREES
		M	F	M	F	M	F	M	F	M	F	M	F	M	F	M	F	
Tennessee Technological University	TN	2	0	4	0	3	0	0	0	147	20	5	2	0	0	161	22	183
University of Tennessee, Chattanooga	TN	1	0	1	0	1	0	0	0	47	6	4	0	0	0	54	6	60
University of Tennessee, Knoxville	TN	11	8	10	1	2	0	0	0	185	46	5	5	0	0	213	60	273
University of Tennessee, Martin	TN	0	0	0	0	0	0	0	0	28	6	1	1	0	0	29	7	36
Texas A&M University	TX	14	6	49	21	85	26	5	1	601	156	75	17	6	4	835	231	1,066
Texas A&M University, Galveston	TX	0	0	0	1	0	3	0	0	18	0	0	1	0	0	18	5	23
Texas A&M University - Kingsville	TX	3	2	1	0	82	14	0	0	45	9	3	1	0	0	134	26	160
Texas Christian University	TX	1	0	0	1	0	0	0	0	12	2	2	1	0	0	15	4	19
Texas Tech University	TX	8	0	8	3	40	5	2	1	238	42	16	1	2	0	314	52	366
The University of Texas at Arlington	TX	15	1	24	4	20	4	1	0	115	16	43	4	0	0	218	29	247
The University of Texas at Austin	TX	8	13	210	50	75	31	4	0	411	103	58	17	0	0	766	214	980
The University of Texas at Dallas	TX	10	5	56	17	14	3	2	0	138	21	25	10	1	0	246	56	302
University of Texas at El Paso	TX	0	0	4	2	136	41	0	0	13	6	59	12	0	0	212	61	273
The University of Texas-Pan American	TX	1	0	0	0	57	14	1	0	7	1	16	6	2	1	84	22	106
University of Texas at San Antonio	TX	4	1	12	2	71	14	1	0	61	13	4	3	0	0	153	33	186
The University of Texas at Tyler	TX	2	0	2	0	5	0	0	0	24	1	2	0	1	1	36	2	38
The University of Toledo	OH	2	1	2	1	2	0	0	0	198	43	9	3	0	0	213	48	261
Tri-State University	IN	0	0	1	1	0	0	0	0	41	15	2	0	4	1	48	17	65
Trinity University	TX	0	0	0	0	0	0	0	0	0	0	0	0	23	10	23	10	33
Trinity College	CT	0	0	0	0	0	1	0	0	13	0	2	0	0	0	15	1	16
Tufts University	MA	6	1	23	14	3	3	0	0	0	0	4	2	92	52	128	72	200
Tulane University	LA	7	4	7	5	4	0	1	0	0	0	2	3	77	26	98	38	136
University of Tulsa	OK	1	0	2	0	1	0	4	1	44	11	23	3	5	0	80	15	95
Tuskegee University	AL	39	22	0	0	0	1	0	0	0	0	0	0	9	5	48	27	75
Union College	NY	1	0	2	1	4	0	0	0	45	12	1	0	1	0	54	13	67
U.S. Air Force Academy	CO	6	0	9	0	7	1	2	0	0	0	2	0	169	24	195	25	220
U.S. Coast Guard Academy	CT	2	0	2	0	3	4	0	0	50	12	2	0	0	0	59	16	75
U.S. Merchant Marine Academy	NY	0	0	5	1	0	1	0	0	66	6	3	1	0	0	74	9	83
United States Military Academy	NY	8	4	12	3	8	0	0	0	164	13	5	0	1	1	198	21	219
U.S. Naval Academy	MD	16	2	17	3	27	2	10	1	262	28	2	0	0	0	334	36	370
University of Utah	UT	0	0	6	7	12	1	3	0	279	34	14	5	1	15	315	62	377
Utah State University	UT	0	0	0	0	0	0	0	0	259	16	0	0	0	0	259	16	275
Valparaiso University	IN	1	0	0	0	0	0	1	0	49	11	3	0	0	0	54	11	65
Vanderbilt University	TN	11	8	23	2	11	5	0	2	149	60	17	14	18	2	229	93	322
University of Vermont	VT	1	0	3	0	0	0	0	0	81	15	1	0	1	1	87	16	103
Villanova University	PA	3	1	10	0	7	1	0	0	131	34	4	1	0	0	148	36	184
University of Virginia	VA	16	5	54	13	6	1	0	0	207	67	7	7	20	7	310	100	410
Virginia Commonwealth University	VA	6	6	19	6	4	0	1	0	99	14	0	0	6	1	135	27	162
Virginia Military Institute	VA	3	0	4	1	1	0	0	0	60	0	0	0	0	0	68	1	69
Virginia Polytechnic Institute and State University	VA	33	14	104	21	15	4	0	0	723	144	70	13	42	4	987	200	1,187
Walla Walla College	WA	0	0	3	0	1	0	0	0	25	1	5	0	0	0	34	1	35
University of Washington	WA	11	3	151	50	14	4	3	0	304	59	35	14	74	9	592	139	731
Washington State University	WA	1	2	5	7	7	1	1	0	179	31	13	5	24	5	230	51	281
Washington University	MO	17	7	21	6	4	1	0	0	122	56	20	7	16	6	200	83	283
Wayne State University	MI	7	6	15	4	2	3	0	0	52	17	16	5	2	0	94	35	129

BACHELOR'S DEGREES AWARDED   TEN-WAY

Bachelor's Degrees Awarded in Engineering, 2005-2006

Institution		African American M	African American F	Asian American M	Asian American F	Hispanic M	Hispanic F	Native American M	Native American F	Caucasian M	Caucasian F	Foreign M	Foreign F	Other M	Other F	Total by Gender M	Total by Gender F	Total Degrees
Webb Institute	NY	0	0	0	0	0	0	0	0	16	6	0	0	0	0	16	6	22
Wentworth Institute of Technology	MA	0	0	0	0	0	0	0	0	21	0	0	0	0	0	21	0	21
West Virginia University Institute of Technology	WV	0	0	2	0	0	0	0	0	62	5	6	1	0	0	70	6	76
West Virginia University	WV	10	2	1	3	2	0	0	0	260	40	8	3	3	1	284	49	333
Western Kentucky University	KY	0	0	0	3	0	0	0	0	22	5	0	0	0	0	22	5	27
Western Michigan University	MI	4	4	4	0	0	0	1	0	200	27	37	5	0	0	246	36	282
Western New England College	MA	0	0	1	0	1	2	0	0	44	8	1	0	3	0	50	10	60
Wichita State University	KS	2	0	16	6	6	1	0	0	0	0	28	2	65	8	117	17	134
Widener University	PA	0	0	2	1	1	0	0	0	48	5	5	0	0	0	56	6	62
Wilkes University	PA	0	0	0	0	0	0	0	0	34	3	1	0	0	0	35	3	38
Winona State University	MN	0	0	0	0	0	0	0	0	11	2	1	0	0	0	12	2	14
University of Wisconsin, Stout	WI	0	0	1	0	0	0	0	0	18	2	0	0	0	0	19	2	21
University of Wisconsin, Madison	WI	7	2	25	4	5	6	1	0	427	96	40	14	11	3	516	125	641
University of Wisconsin, Milwaukee	WI	5	0	7	0	6	1	0	0	159	21	7	3	0	0	184	25	209
University of Wisconsin, Platteville	WI	0	0	3	1	0	0	0	0	204	34	0	0	0	0	207	35	242
Worcester Polytechnic Institute	MA	2	1	16	6	6	4	2	1	265	80	3	2	8	4	302	98	400
Wright State University	OH	6	3	6	1	0	1	0	0	119	18	5	2	7	2	143	27	170
University of Wyoming	WY	0	0	1	1	5	1	1	1	127	28	5	3	7	1	146	35	181
Yale University/Faculty of Engineering	CT	0	0	0	0	0	0	0	0	0	0	0	0	29	14	29	14	43
York College of Pennsylvania	PA	0	0	0	0	0	0	0	0	0	0	0	0	19	2	19	2	21
Youngstown State University	OH	0	0	0	0	1	0	0	0	50	19	7	1	0	0	58	20	78
Totals:		2,357	1,021	7,070	2,328	3,878	1,209	278	82	37,758	7,478	4,162	1,183	4,398	984	59,901	14,285	74,186
CANADIAN INSTITUTIONS:																		
University of Alberta	AB	0	0	0	0	0	0	0	0	0	0	0	0	495	125	495	125	620
University of Calgary	AB	0	0	0	0	0	0	0	0	0	0	7	1	315	84	322	85	407
Concordia University, Faculty of Engr. and Comp. Sci.	PQ	0	0	0	0	0	0	0	0	0	0	27	5	294	74	321	79	400
Ecole Polytechnique de Montreal	PQ	0	0	0	0	0	0	0	0	0	0	0	0	484	141	484	141	625
Ecole de Technologie Superieure	PQ	0	0	0	0	0	0	0	0	0	0	0	0	610	46	610	46	656
McGill University, Faculty of Engineering	PQ	0	0	0	0	0	0	0	0	0	0	0	0	320	104	320	104	424
University of Ottawa, Faculty of Engineering	ON	0	0	0	0	0	0	0	0	0	0	39	10	365	83	404	93	497
University of Waterloo	ON	0	0	0	0	0	0	0	0	0	0	0	0	584	163	584	163	747
Totals:		0	0	0	0	0	0	0	0	0	0	73	16	3,467	820	3,540	836	4,376

BACHELOR'S DEGREES AWARDED   WEB-YOU

BACHELOR'S DEGREES AWARDED IN AEROSPACE ENGINEERING, 2005-2006

INSTITUTION		AFRICAN AMERICAN		ASIAN AMERICAN		HISPANIC		NATIVE AMERICAN		CAUCASIAN		FOREIGN		OTHER		TOTAL BY GENDER		TOTAL DEGREES
		M	F	M	F	M	F	M	F	M	F	M	F	M	F	M	F	
The University of Alabama	AL	0	0	0	0	0	0	0	0	2	3	0	0	0	0	2	3	5
The University of Arizona	AZ	0	0	0	0	4	0	0	0	21	2	3	1	0	0	28	3	31
Arizona State University	AZ	0	0	2	0	4	0	1	0	16	1	3	0	4	1	30	2	32
Auburn University	AL	1	1	1	1	1	0	1	0	26	9	0	0	0	0	30	11	41
Boston University	MA	0	0	3	1	0	0	0	1	22	2	0	0	0	0	25	4	29
California Polytechnic State University	CA	1	0	5	1	3	1	0	0	30	10	0	0	3	2	42	14	56
California State Polytechnic University, Pomona	CA	1	0	7	1	7	1	0	0	7	1	0	0	5	0	27	3	30
California State University, Long Beach	CA	2	0	2	0	1	0	0	0	4	1	1	0	0	0	10	1	11
University of California, Davis	CA	0	0	0	1	0	0	0	0	7	0	0	0	0	0	7	1	8
University of California, Irvine	CA	0	0	0	0	0	0	0	0	0	0	0	0	13	6	13	6	19
University of California, Los Angeles	CA	0	0	11	4	2	0	0	0	14	5	3	0	5	1	35	10	45
University of California, San Diego	CA	1	0	16	3	2	0	0	0	23	6	2	0	3	0	47	9	56
Case Western Reserve University	OH	0	0	0	0	0	0	0	0	9	1	0	0	0	0	9	1	10
University of Central Florida	FL	1	1	0	2	7	2	0	1	13	2	2	1	0	0	23	9	32
University of Cincinnati	OH	1	0	1	0	1	0	0	0	31	4	0	0	1	2	35	6	41
Clarkson University	NY	1	0	0	0	0	0	0	0	27	3	2	1	0	0	30	4	34
University of Colorado at Boulder	CO	2	1	1	2	1	0	0	0	54	6	0	0	0	0	58	9	67
Embry Riddle Aeronautical Univ., Daytona Beach	FL	6	2	8	1	9	1	0	0	106	30	18	1	17	3	164	38	202
Embry Riddle Aeronautical University, Prescott	AZ	0	0	5	1	2	3	0	1	49	6	3	0	3	0	62	11	73
University of Florida	FL	1	0	0	1	6	0	0	0	24	8	0	0	0	0	31	9	40
Florida Institute of Technology	FL	1	0	0	0	2	0	0	0	12	5	2	0	1	3	18	8	26
Georgia Institute of Technology	GA	6	1	9	1	4	2	0	1	88	16	4	1	3	0	114	22	136
Illinois Institute of Technology	IL	0	0	1	0	0	0	0	0	9	2	1	0	3	0	14	2	16
University of Illinois at Urbana-Champaign	IL	1	0	8	1	2	0	0	0	46	12	1	1	0	0	58	14	72
Iowa State University	IA	1	0	2	0	0	1	0	0	55	8	2	0	3	0	63	9	72
University of Kansas	KS	0	0	0	0	0	0	0	0	9	1	2	0	0	0	11	1	12
University of Maryland, College Park	MD	4	1	9	0	3	0	0	0	51	9	0	1	1	1	68	12	80
Massachusetts Institute of Technology	MA	8	1	3	4	7	0	0	1	21	9	6	0	6	1	51	16	67
University of Miami	FL	0	0	0	0	2	0	0	0	1	1	1	0	0	0	4	1	5
University of Michigan	MI	2	2	6	2	4	0	1	0	48	14	6	0	2	1	69	19	88
University of Minnesota -Twin Cities	MN	1	0	4	1	1	0	0	0	44	4	0	0	0	0	50	5	55
Mississippi State University	MS	1	0	0	0	0	0	0	0	18	1	1	0	0	1	20	2	22
University of Missouri - Rolla	MO	2	0	1	0	0	0	0	0	24	5	1	0	1	0	29	5	34
State University of New York at Buffalo	NY	1	1	2	0	0	0	0	0	20	6	9	1	1	0	33	8	41
North Carolina State University	NC	1	0	1	0	2	0	0	0	24	3	1	0	0	0	29	3	32
University of Notre Dame	IN	1	1	1	1	1	0	0	0	21	6	1	1	0	0	25	9	34
The Ohio State University	OH	0	1	1	4	0	0	0	0	23	8	4	0	0	0	28	13	41
University of Oklahoma	OK	1	0	2	0	0	0	2	0	19	4	0	0	0	0	24	4	28
Oklahoma State University	OK	1	0	0	0	0	0	1	0	15	5	3	1	0	0	20	6	26
The Pennsylvania State University	PA	0	1	3	0	2	1	0	0	65	7	4	0	0	0	74	9	83
Polytechnic University	NY	1	1	2	2	1	0	0	0	3	2	1	0	0	1	8	6	14
Purdue University	IN	1	0	4	1	2	3	0	0	80	22	12	3	2	0	101	29	130
Rensselaer Polytechnic Institute	NY	0	0	2	0	1	1	0	0	38	4	1	0	0	0	42	5	47
Saint Louis University - Parks College	MO	2	0	1	0	0	0	0	0	10	4	0	0	3	4	16	8	24
San Diego State University	CA	0	0	2	0	2	0	0	0	3	3	0	0	5	0	12	3	15

ALA-SAN

AEROSPACE ENGINEERING

BACHELOR'S DEGREES AWARDED IN AEROSPACE ENGINEERING, 2005-2006

INSTITUTION		AFRICAN AMERICAN		ASIAN AMERICAN		HISPANIC		NATIVE AMERICAN		CAUCASIAN		FOREIGN		OTHER		TOTAL BY GENDER		TOTAL DEGREES
		M	F	M	F	M	F	M	F	M	F	M	F	M	F	M	F	
San Jose State University	CA	0	0	1	1	2	1	0	0	4	0	2	1	0	0	9	3	12
University of Southern California	CA	0	1	0	0	2	1	0	0	10	1	1	0	0	0	13	3	16
Syracuse University	NY	0	0	0	0	0	0	0	0	13	2	2	0	0	0	15	2	17
University of Tennessee, Knoxville	TN	0	0	0	0	0	0	0	0	15	5	1	0	0	0	16	5	21
Texas A&M University	TX	0	0	3	0	2	4	0	0	27	9	3	0	0	0	35	13	48
The University of Texas at Arlington	TX	1	0	1	0	3	1	0	0	10	4	5	1	0	0	20	6	26
The University of Texas at Austin	TX	0	1	13	1	11	2	1	0	27	15	2	2	0	0	54	21	75
Tuskegee University	AL	4	2	0	0	0	0	0	0	0	0	0	0	1	1	5	3	8
U.S. Air Force Academy	CO	0	0	3	0	1	1	1	0	0	0	1	0	76	12	82	13	95
U.S. Naval Academy	MD	1	0	2	0	6	1	1	0	49	5	0	0	0	0	59	6	65
University of Virginia	VA	1	0	0	0	1	0	0	0	7	2	0	0	0	1	9	3	12
Virginia Polytechnic Institute and State University	VA	5	0	6	2	1	0	0	0	64	19	0	1	2	1	78	23	101
University of Washington	WA	0	0	5	3	1	1	0	0	27	11	1	0	6	0	40	15	55
Washington University	MO	0	0	0	0	0	0	0	0	4	1	0	0	1	0	5	1	6
West Virginia University	WV	1	0	0	0	0	0	0	0	28	3	0	0	1	0	30	3	33
Western Michigan University	MI	0	1	1	0	0	0	0	0	16	1	5	1	0	0	22	3	25
Wichita State University	KS	0	0	1	0	3	1	0	0	0	0	6	1	16	2	26	4	30
Worcester Polytechnic Institute	MA	0	0	1	1	1	0	0	0	10	2	0	0	0	0	12	3	15
Totals:		**67**	**20**	**163**	**44**	**121**	**29**	**9**	**5**	**1,543**	**341**	**128**	**21**	**188**	**43**	**2,219**	**503**	**2,722**

AEROSPACE ENGINEERING

SAN-WOR

BACHELOR'S DEGREES AWARDED IN AGRICULTURAL ENGINEERING, 2005-2006

INSTITUTION		AFRICAN AMERICAN M	AFRICAN AMERICAN F	ASIAN AMERICAN M	ASIAN AMERICAN F	HISPANIC M	HISPANIC F	NATIVE AMERICAN M	NATIVE AMERICAN F	CAUCASIAN M	CAUCASIAN F	FOREIGN M	FOREIGN F	OTHER M	OTHER F	TOTAL BY GENDER M	TOTAL BY GENDER F	TOTAL DEGREES
The University of Arizona	AZ	0	0	0	1	0	1	0	0	2	2	1	0	0	0	3	4	7
Auburn University	AL	0	0	0	0	0	1	0	0	6	3	0	0	0	0	6	4	10
University of California, Davis	CA	1	0	17	9	2	0	0	0	0	2	1	0	1	1	22	12	34
Clemson University	SC	1	2	0	2	0	0	0	0	12	11	0	0	3	0	16	15	31
Cornell University	NY	0	2	16	5	0	1	0	0	26	23	3	5	1	4	46	40	86
University of Florida	FL	1	0	0	1	1	1	0	0	11	7	0	0	0	0	13	9	22
University of Georgia	GA	1	0	1	0	1	0	0	0	16	1	0	0	0	0	20	1	21
University of Idaho	ID	0	0	0	0	0	0	0	0	1	0	0	0	0	0	1	0	1
University of Illinois at Urbana-Champaign	IL	1	0	0	0	0	0	0	0	18	2	0	0	0	0	19	2	21
Iowa State University	IA	0	0	0	0	0	0	0	0	27	4	0	0	4	0	31	4	35
Kansas State University	KS	0	0	0	0	0	0	0	0	9	4	0	0	0	0	9	4	13
University of Kentucky	KY	1	0	0	1	0	0	0	0	7	3	0	0	0	0	8	4	12
Louisiana State University	LA	2	4	0	1	2	2	0	0	13	10	0	0	1	0	18	17	35
University of Maryland, College Park	MD	4	1	6	4	1	1	0	0	6	9	0	0	1	0	18	15	33
Michigan State University	MI	0	0	1	2	1	0	1	0	10	8	0	0	0	0	13	10	23
Mississippi State University	MS	1	1	1	2	0	0	0	0	22	11	0	1	0	0	24	15	39
University of Nebraska, Lincoln	NE	1	0	0	1	0	0	0	0	17	6	1	0	0	0	18	7	25
North Carolina A & T State University	NC	1	1	0	0	0	0	0	0	3	0	0	0	0	0	4	1	5
North Carolina State University	NC	0	2	1	2	0	0	0	1	6	5	0	1	0	0	7	11	18
North Dakota State University	ND	0	0	0	0	0	0	0	0	12	0	0	0	0	0	12	0	12
The Ohio State University	OH	2	0	0	0	0	0	0	0	12	3	2	1	0	0	16	4	20
Oklahoma State University	OK	0	0	0	0	1	0	1	1	10	3	2	1	0	0	14	5	19
The Pennsylvania State University	PA	0	2	0	1	0	0	0	0	7	6	0	0	0	0	7	9	16
Purdue University	IN	0	0	0	0	0	0	0	0	15	4	1	1	0	1	16	6	22
South Dakota State University	SD	0	0	0	0	0	0	0	0	12	2	0	0	0	0	12	2	14
University of Tennessee, Knoxville	TN	0	0	0	0	0	0	0	0	2	1	0	0	0	0	2	1	3
Texas A&M University	TX	0	0	2	1	1	0	0	0	15	8	1	0	0	0	19	9	28
Utah State University	UT	0	0	0	0	0	0	0	0	14	3	0	0	0	0	14	3	17
Virginia Polytechnic Institute and State University	VA	0	0	1	1	0	0	0	0	6	15	1	0	0	0	8	16	24
Totals:		16	15	46	34	10	7	2	2	317	156	13	10	12	6	416	230	646

ARI-VIR

AGRICULTURAL ENGINEERING

INSTITUTION		AFRICAN AMERICAN		ASIAN AMERICAN		HISPANIC		NATIVE AMERICAN		CAUCASIAN		FOREIGN		OTHER		TOTAL BY GENDER		TOTAL DEGREES
		M	F	M	F	M	F	M	F	M	F	M	F	M	F	M	F	
California Polytechnic State University	CA	1	0	2	5	3	3	0	0	24	6	0	0	7	1	37	15	52
University of Colorado at Boulder	CO	0	0	0	1	0	0	1	0	22	5	2	1	0	0	25	7	32
Drexel University	PA	1	0	2	0	0	0	0	0	18	7	1	2	5	1	27	11	38
Illinois Institute of Technology	IL	0	0	2	0	0	1	0	0	10	1	2	0	1	0	15	1	16
University of Kansas	KS	0	1	0	0	0	0	0	0	16	5	0	0	0	0	16	6	22
Kansas State University	KS	1	0	1	1	1	0	0	0	37	4	1	0	0	1	41	6	47
University of Miami	FL	1	2	0	1	2	0	0	0	4	6	2	1	0	0	9	10	19
Milwaukee School of Engineering	WI	0	1	1	0	0	1	0	0	35	16	0	0	0	0	36	18	54
University of Missouri - Rolla	MO	0	0	0	1	0	0	0	0	17	3	0	0	0	0	17	4	21
University of Nebraska, Lincoln	NE	3	0	0	1	0	0	1	0	54	9	0	0	0	0	58	10	68
North Carolina A & T State University	NC	10	7	2	0	0	0	0	0	1	0	1	0	0	0	14	7	21
University of Oklahoma	OK	0	0	0	0	0	0	0	0	2	1	0	0	0	0	2	1	3
Oklahoma State University	OK	0	0	0	0	0	1	0	0	1	1	0	0	0	0	1	2	3
The Pennsylvania State University	PA	1	0	5	0	1	2	0	0	61	18	4	0	0	0	72	20	92
Tennessee State University	TN	2	2	0	0	0	0	0	0	0	0	0	0	0	0	2	2	4
The University of Texas at Austin	TX	0	1	3	4	2	3	0	0	20	11	1	2	0	0	26	21	47
United States Military Academy	NY	2	1	2	3	3	0	0	0	44	3	0	0	0	0	51	7	58
University of Wyoming	WY	0	0	0	0	1	1	0	1	19	10	2	0	0	0	22	12	34
Totals:		22	15	20	17	13	12	2	1	385	106	16	6	13	3	471	160	631

ARCHITECTURAL ENGINEERING   CAL-WYO

BACHELOR'S DEGREES AWARDED IN BIOMEDICAL ENGINEERING, 2005-2006

INSTITUTION		AFRICAN AMERICAN		ASIAN AMERICAN		HISPANIC		NATIVE AMERICAN		CAUCASIAN		FOREIGN		OTHER		TOTAL BY GENDER		TOTAL DEGREES
		M	F	M	F	M	F	M	F	M	F	M	F	M	F	M	F	
The University of Akron	OH	2	0	0	0	0	0	0	0	5	4	0	0	0	0	7	4	11
University of Alabama at Birmingham	AL	0	0	0	1	0	1	0	0	8	1	0	1	0	0	8	4	12
Alfred University, NY State College of Ceramics	NY	0	0	0	0	0	0	0	0	1	0	0	0	0	0	1	0	1
Arizona State University	AZ	0	1	7	6	5	5	1	1	21	16	5	3	3	3	42	35	77
Boston University	MA	2	1	15	5	1	1	0	0	26	14	2	3	0	0	46	24	70
Brown University	RI	0	1	2	4	0	0	0	0	6	4	2	1	0	0	10	10	20
California Polytechnic State University	CA	0	0	2	0	3	0	0	0	9	0	0	0	5	0	19	0	19
University of California, Berkeley	CA	0	1	33	30	1	0	0	0	6	2	1	4	5	2	46	39	85
University of California, Davis	CA	0	0	2	3	0	0	0	0	6	3	0	0	0	0	8	6	14
University of California, Irvine	CA	0	0	0	0	0	0	0	0	0	0	0	0	30	27	30	27	57
University of California, San Diego	CA	1	0	63	31	3	0	0	0	28	9	5	5	15	5	115	50	165
University of California-Santa Cruz	CA	0	0	1	0	0	0	0	0	1	0	1	0	1	1	4	1	5
Case Western Reserve University	OH	1	1	14	14	0	0	0	0	27	26	2	8	1	0	45	49	94
The Catholic University of America	DC	1	0	0	0	0	0	0	0	2	1	1	1	0	0	4	2	6
University of Cincinnati	OH	2	0	0	0	0	0	0	0	5	6	0	0	0	0	7	6	13
Columbia University	NY	1	2	21	7	2	1	0	0	16	8	4	0	3	2	47	20	67
University of Connecticut	CT	0	0	5	2	1	1	0	0	15	11	0	0	0	1	21	15	36
Drexel University	PA	0	3	7	2	1	0	0	0	14	12	4	2	0	1	26	20	46
Duke University Pratt School of Engineering	NC	0	0	0	0	0	0	0	0	0	0	0	0	88	34	88	34	122
Florida International University	FL	0	0	0	0	2	3	0	0	0	2	3	1	0	0	5	6	11
FAMU-FSU College of Engineering	FL	2	2	0	0	0	0	0	0	2	3	0	0	0	0	4	5	9
The George Washington University	DC	0	0	1	2	0	0	0	0	2	1	1	0	0	0	4	3	7
Georgia Institute of Technology	GA	2	2	9	9	1	0	0	0	31	18	3	1	1	0	47	30	77
University of Hartford	CT	0	0	0	0	0	0	0	0	3	4	0	4	0	0	3	8	11
University of Houston, Cullen School of Engineering	TX	0	0	1	0	0	0	0	0	0	0	0	0	0	0	1	0	1
Illinois Institute of Technology	IL	0	0	3	5	0	0	0	0	8	1	0	2	2	0	13	8	21
University of Illinois at Chicago	IL	1	0	13	16	1	1	0	0	6	6	0	0	0	0	21	23	44
University of Illinois at Urbana-Champaign	IL	0	1	1	0	0	0	0	0	1	0	1	0	0	0	3	1	4
The University of Iowa	IA	0	1	0	2	1	0	0	0	20	22	2	0	1	0	24	25	49
The Johns Hopkins University	MD	2	2	34	13	2	2	2	1	32	8	11	5	0	0	83	31	114
Louisiana Tech University	LA	1	5	2	1	0	0	0	0	11	7	4	0	1	0	19	13	32
Marquette University	WI	1	0	1	2	0	0	0	0	23	22	3	4	0	0	28	28	56
Mercer University	GA	1	1	4	0	0	0	0	0	5	9	0	0	0	0	10	10	20
University of Miami	FL	4	4	3	1	4	8	0	0	10	5	1	1	1	1	23	20	43
University of Michigan	MI	1	1	10	2	0	0	0	0	20	6	4	0	1	0	36	9	45
Michigan Technological University	MI	0	0	0	0	0	0	0	0	12	15	2	0	1	1	15	16	31
Milwaukee School of Engineering	WI	1	1	0	1	0	0	0	0	6	4	0	0	0	0	7	6	13
University of Minnesota-Twin Cities	MN	0	0	9	3	0	0	0	0	21	11	2	0	0	0	32	14	46
University of Missouri-Columbia	MO	0	0	1	0	0	0	0	0	12	7	1	0	0	0	15	7	22
New Jersey Institute of Technology	NJ	1	3	9	8	1	4	0	0	4	2	3	1	6	6	24	24	48
City College of the City University of New York	NY	0	0	2	2	1	2	0	0	0	0	0	1	2	0	5	5	10
The State University of New York at Binghamton	NY	0	0	2	1	0	0	0	0	8	2	1	0	6	3	17	6	23
Stony Brook University	NY	1	0	4	3	0	1	0	0	4	3	2	0	0	0	11	7	18
North Carolina State University	NC	1	2	1	1	0	1	0	0	14	15	0	0	0	0	16	19	35
Northwestern University	IL	0	0	26	14	0	1	0	0	18	15	2	3	2	3	48	36	84

BIOMEDICAL ENGINEERING

AKR-NOR

INSTITUTION		AFRICAN AMERICAN		ASIAN AMERICAN		HISPANIC		NATIVE AMERICAN		CAUCASIAN		FOREIGN		OTHER		TOTAL BY GENDER		TOTAL DEGREES
		M	F	M	F	M	F	M	F	M	F	M	F	M	F	M	F	
Oral Roberts University	OK	0	0	0	0	0	0	0	0	0	2	0	0	0	0	0	2	2
Oregon State University	OR	0	0	0	0	0	0	0	0	6	7	0	0	2	2	8	9	17
University of the Pacific	CA	1	0	2	0	2	1	0	0	1	3	0	0	1	0	7	4	11
University of Pennsylvania	PA	0	0	22	9	0	2	0	0	15	14	10	3	9	4	56	32	88
The Pennsylvania State University	PA	0	0	3	0	0	0	0	0	11	12	0	1	0	0	14	13	27
University of Pittsburgh	PA	0	3	2	1	0	0	0	0	16	13	2	0	0	0	20	17	37
Rensselaer Polytechnic Institute	NY	0	0	4	9	2	1	0	0	12	18	2	2	0	0	20	30	50
University of Rhode Island	RI	0	0	0	0	0	0	0	0	4	7	0	1	0	0	4	8	12
William Marsh Rice University	TX	1	1	9	7	1	2	0	0	8	4	3	2	0	1	22	17	39
University of Rochester	NY	0	0	5	2	0	0	0	0	9	14	2	0	2	0	18	16	34
Rose-Hulman Institute of Technology	IN	2	0	0	0	0	0	0	0	8	12	0	0	0	0	10	12	22
Rutgers, The State University of New Jersey	NJ	2	1	11	7	0	0	0	0	18	13	3	0	0	0	34	21	55
Saint Louis University - Parks College	MO	0	0	3	0	1	0	0	0	10	11	0	0	2	0	16	11	27
University of Southern California	CA	0	1	16	12	3	1	0	1	9	3	2	3	2	0	32	21	53
Stevens Institute of Technology	NJ	0	1	2	2	0	0	0	0	6	4	0	0	1	1	9	8	17
Syracuse University	NY	0	0	1	0	1	0	0	0	10	8	0	1	0	0	12	9	21
University of Tennessee, Knoxville	TN	2	4	0	1	0	0	0	0	10	7	0	0	0	0	12	12	24
Texas A&M University	TX	2	1	4	5	1	3	1	0	17	12	3	0	0	1	28	22	50
The University of Texas at Austin	TX	0	3	26	6	3	3	1	0	19	8	2	4	0	0	51	24	75
The University of Toledo	OH	0	0	0	0	0	0	0	0	12	12	0	0	0	0	12	12	24
Tulane University	LA	2	0	2	2	1	0	1	0	0	0	2	1	14	12	22	15	37
University of Utah	UT	0	0	0	2	0	0	0	0	26	11	0	1	0	0	26	14	40
Vanderbilt University	TN	0	3	11	0	3	1	0	0	29	23	0	4	4	1	47	32	79
University of Virginia	VA	0	0	4	4	1	1	0	0	13	18	1	1	5	0	24	24	48
Virginia Commonwealth University	VA	0	1	7	2	0	0	0	0	9	5	0	0	0	1	16	9	25
University of Washington	WA	0	0	7	3	0	0	0	0	9	8	0	1	3	1	19	13	32
Washington University	MO	4	1	10	4	0	1	0	0	21	18	4	2	4	3	43	29	72
Western New England College	MA	0	0	0	0	0	0	0	0	0	3	1	0	0	0	1	4	5
University of Wisconsin, Madison	WI	0	0	2	1	0	0	0	0	23	8	1	0	0	0	26	9	35
Worcester Polytechnic Institute	MA	0	0	1	1	0	0	0	1	14	18	1	0	0	1	16	21	37
Wright State University	OH	0	1	0	0	0	0	0	0	8	4	0	1	2	0	10	7	17
Yale University/Faculty of Engineering	CT	0	0	0	0	0	1	0	0	0	0	0	0	6	5	6	5	11
Totals:		45	56	462	271	49	50	6	4	822	605	112	79	233	123	1,729	1,188	2,917

BIOMEDICAL ENGINEERING   ORA-YAL

INSTITUTION		AFRICAN AMERICAN M	F	ASIAN AMERICAN M	F	HISPANIC M	F	NATIVE AMERICAN M	F	CAUCASIAN M	F	FOREIGN M	F	OTHER M	F	TOTAL BY GENDER M	F	TOTAL DEGREES
The University of Akron	OH	0	2	0	0	0	0	0	0	17	3	3	0	0	1	20	6	26
The University of Alabama in Huntsville	AL	0	0	0	0	0	0	0	0	5	2	2	0	0	0	7	2	9
The University of Alabama	AL	0	2	0	1	0	0	0	0	9	11	1	1	0	0	10	15	25
The University of Arizona	AZ	0	1	2	0	4	1	0	0	12	10	1	0	0	0	19	12	31
Arizona State University	AZ	1	0	3	1	1	2	0	0	8	8	5	0	1	2	19	13	32
University of Arkansas	AR	0	1	1	2	0	0	1	0	14	5	2	0	1	0	19	8	27
Auburn University	AL	0	3	0	1	0	0	0	0	21	13	0	0	1	0	22	17	39
Brigham Young University	UT	0	0	0	0	0	0	0	0	0	0	0	0	34	2	34	2	36
Brown University	RI	0	0	1	0	0	0	0	0	2	1	0	0	0	0	3	1	4
Bucknell University	PA	0	1	1	0	0	0	0	0	14	12	2	0	0	0	17	13	30
California Institute of Technology	CA	0	0	2	3	0	0	0	0	6	4	0	0	0	0	8	7	15
California State Polytechnic University, Pomona	CA	0	0	5	8	4	3	0	0	3	2	0	0	0	0	12	13	25
California State University, Long Beach	CA	1	1	6	2	4	1	0	0	6	0	5	2	0	0	22	6	28
University of California, Berkeley	CA	1	0	10	15	2	0	0	0	5	4	10	9	3	0	31	28	59
University of California, Davis	CA	0	0	13	9	2	0	0	0	7	7	4	3	5	0	31	19	50
University of California, Irvine	CA	0	0	0	0	0	0	0	0	0	0	0	0	14	3	14	3	17
University of California, Los Angeles	CA	0	0	15	6	1	0	0	0	14	3	1	3	7	3	38	15	53
University of California, Riverside	CA	0	0	4	4	3	0	0	0	2	1	0	0	2	0	11	5	16
University of California, San Diego	CA	0	0	3	7	2	0	0	0	4	1	2	1	0	0	11	9	20
University of California, Santa Barbara	CA	0	0	4	3	0	1	0	0	14	12	0	1	3	0	21	17	38
Carnegie Mellon University	PA	1	2	9	4	2	1	0	0	12	9	1	0	4	0	29	16	45
Case Western Reserve University	OH	0	0	2	0	0	0	0	0	15	2	0	0	0	0	17	2	19
Christian Brothers University	TN	1	0	0	0	0	1	0	0	0	3	1	0	0	0	2	4	6
University of Cincinnati	OH	0	0	0	1	2	1	0	0	16	11	0	0	0	0	18	13	31
Clarkson University	NY	0	0	0	2	2	0	0	0	22	4	0	0	0	0	22	6	28
Clemson University	SC	0	4	0	1	0	0	0	0	23	3	0	0	1	1	24	8	32
Cleveland State University	OH	0	0	0	1	0	0	0	0	6	1	0	0	0	0	6	2	8
Colorado School of Mines	CO	0	0	1	1	3	3	0	0	29	7	1	0	0	0	34	11	45
Colorado State University	CO	0	0	0	1	1	2	0	0	5	11	0	0	2	0	8	14	22
University of Colorado at Boulder	CO	1	2	2	1	2	1	0	0	26	10	0	0	0	0	31	14	45
Columbia University	NY	1	0	8	1	1	0	0	0	7	5	1	2	4	2	22	10	32
University of Connecticut	CT	1	0	0	0	0	0	0	0	8	6	0	0	2	0	11	6	17
The Cooper Union	NY	0	0	6	3	2	0	0	0	10	3	1	1	0	0	19	7	26
Cornell University	NY	0	2	10	10	3	2	0	0	15	11	2	0	1	2	31	27	58
University of Dayton	OH	0	0	0	2	0	0	0	0	0	0	0	0	18	14	18	16	34
University of Delaware	DE	0	0	1	1	0	0	0	0	37	13	0	0	0	0	38	14	52
Drexel University	PA	3	1	2	2	0	0	1	0	11	6	3	2	0	1	20	12	32
University of Florida	FL	2	1	5	0	5	2	0	1	19	8	0	0	0	0	31	12	43
Florida Institute of Technology	FL	0	0	0	0	0	0	0	0	2	1	3	2	1	0	6	3	9
FAMU-FSU College of Engineering	FL	5	4	0	0	1	0	0	0	5	2	2	0	0	0	13	6	19
Georgia Institute of Technology	GA	4	4	4	3	1	2	0	0	37	9	8	1	0	0	54	19	73
University of Houston, Cullen School of Engineering	TX	1	4	7	8	5	1	0	0	6	4	3	4	3	1	25	22	47
Howard University	DC	10	10	0	0	0	0	0	0	0	0	0	0	0	0	10	10	20
University of Idaho	ID	0	0	0	0	0	0	0	0	10	4	0	0	0	0	10	4	14
Illinois Institute of Technology	IL	0	0	3	0	0	1	0	0	4	5	3	1	0	0	10	7	17

CHEMICAL ENGINEERING

AKR-ILL

INSTITUTION		AFRICAN AMERICAN M	F	ASIAN AMERICAN M	F	HISPANIC M	F	NATIVE AMERICAN M	F	CAUCASIAN M	F	FOREIGN M	F	OTHER M	F	TOTAL BY GENDER M	F	TOTAL DEGREES
University of Illinois at Chicago	IL	3	0	0	4	0	0	0	0	8	2	0	0	0	0	11	6	17
University of Illinois at Urbana-Champaign	IL	0	1	5	4	2	1	0	0	18	8	6	7	0	1	31	22	53
The University of Iowa	IA	0	0	0	1	0	0	0	0	11	5	1	1	1	0	13	7	20
Iowa State University	IA	0	3	0	1	0	1	0	1	25	17	1	2	1	0	27	25	52
The Johns Hopkins University	MD	0	0	2	2	0	0	0	1	9	2	1	0	0	0	12	5	17
University of Kansas	KS	0	0	0	0	1	0	0	0	25	10	1	1	0	0	27	11	38
Kansas State University	KS	0	0	0	0	0	0	0	0	15	2	0	0	2	0	17	2	19
University of Kentucky	KY	0	0	1	1	0	0	0	0	11	7	2	0	0	0	14	8	22
Lafayette College	PA	0	0	0	0	1	0	0	0	11	3	1	1	0	0	13	4	17
Lamar University	TX	0	1	0	0	1	1	0	0	13	12	0	0	0	2	14	16	30
Lehigh University	PA	0	0	3	0	0	0	0	0	0	0	0	2	17	4	20	6	26
Louisiana State University	LA	2	3	1	1	0	1	0	0	28	12	2	1	3	0	36	18	54
Louisiana Tech University	LA	0	1	0	0	0	0	0	0	7	2	1	0	0	0	8	3	11
University of Louisiana at Lafayette	LA	1	2	0	0	0	0	0	0	5	6	1	0	0	0	7	8	15
University of Louisville	KY	0	1	1	0	0	0	0	0	11	2	2	0	0	0	14	3	17
University of Maine	ME	0	0	0	1	0	0	0	0	17	6	0	0	0	0	17	7	24
Manhattan College	NY	2	3	3	3	1	0	0	0	11	2	0	0	0	0	17	8	25
University of Maryland, Baltimore County	MD	1	3	2	0	0	1	0	0	15	3	0	2	1	0	19	9	28
University of Maryland, College Park	MD	3	1	0	1	0	1	0	0	8	8	2	1	2	0	15	12	27
Massachusetts Institute of Technology	MA	3	0	8	11	2	3	0	2	11	9	0	3	3	2	27	30	57
University of Massachusetts Amherst	MA	0	0	2	0	1	1	0	0	9	7	1	1	0	0	13	9	22
University of Massachusetts Lowell	MA	0	0	1	1	0	0	0	0	0	1	0	0	1	0	2	2	4
McNeese State University	LA	0	0	0	0	0	0	0	0	8	3	0	0	0	0	8	3	11
University of Michigan	MI	0	5	3	4	0	1	0	0	21	23	3	2	2	1	29	36	65
Michigan State University	MI	1	1	3	0	0	0	0	0	20	14	2	1	0	0	26	16	42
Michigan Technological University	MI	0	0	1	0	1	0	0	0	27	13	1	1	0	1	30	15	45
University of Minnesota, Duluth	MN	0	0	0	0	0	0	0	0	26	2	0	2	0	0	26	4	30
University of Minnesota -Twin Cities	MN	0	0	3	3	2	1	0	0	38	7	8	9	0	0	51	20	71
The University of Mississippi	MS	1	0	0	0	0	0	0	0	5	0	1	0	0	0	7	0	7
Mississippi State University	MS	1	5	0	0	0	0	0	0	14	9	0	0	0	0	15	14	29
University of Missouri-Columbia	MO	0	0	2	0	0	0	0	0	20	6	4	0	1	1	27	7	34
University of Missouri - Rolla	MO	3	3	0	0	0	0	0	0	20	2	1	0	2	0	26	5	31
Montana State University	MT	0	0	1	0	0	0	0	0	11	8	0	1	0	1	12	10	22
University of Nebraska, Lincoln	NE	0	0	0	0	0	0	0	0	7	4	0	0	0	0	7	4	11
University of Nevada, Reno	NV	0	0	1	3	1	0	0	0	5	3	1	0	1	1	9	7	16
University of New Hampshire	NH	0	0	1	0	0	0	0	0	12	2	0	0	0	0	13	2	15
University of New Haven	CT	1	0	0	0	0	0	0	0	0	0	2	0	0	1	3	1	4
New Jersey Institute of Technology	NJ	1	0	3	1	1	0	0	0	3	1	0	2	1	1	9	5	14
The University of New Mexico	NM	1	0	0	0	2	3	0	0	2	4	0	1	0	0	5	8	13
New Mexico Institute of Mining & Technology	NM	0	1	2	0	2	2	0	0	3	4	0	0	0	0	7	7	14
New Mexico State University	NM	0	0	0	0	2	2	1	0	0	0	0	0	1	1	4	3	7
City College of the City University of New York	NY	0	1	5	2	1	1	0	0	0	0	2	0	0	0	8	4	12
State University of New York at Buffalo	NY	1	0	3	1	0	0	0	0	14	9	7	7	2	0	27	17	44
North Carolina A &T State University	NC	7	6	0	0	0	0	0	0	2	0	0	0	0	0	9	6	15
North Carolina State University	NC	0	1	2	0	0	0	0	0	41	16	0	1	0	0	43	18	61

ILL-NOR

CHEMICAL ENGINEERING

INSTITUTION		AFRICAN AMERICAN		ASIAN AMERICAN		HISPANIC		NATIVE AMERICAN		CAUCASIAN		FOREIGN		OTHER		TOTAL BY GENDER		TOTAL DEGREES
		M	F	M	F	M	F	M	F	M	F	M	F	M	F	M	F	
University of North Dakota	ND	0	0	2	0	0	0	0	0	17	4	0	0	0	0	19	4	23
Northeastern University	MA	0	0	2	0	1	0	0	0	13	6	0	0	5	4	21	10	31
Northwestern University	IL	1	0	1	3	1	0	0	0	9	3	0	0	1	1	13	7	20
University of Notre Dame	IN	1	1	1	0	1	1	0	0	18	9	2	2	0	0	22	13	35
The Ohio State University	OH	0	0	5	1	2	0	0	0	47	3	16	6	0	0	70	10	80
Ohio University	OH	0	0	0	0	0	0	0	2	6	1	0	0	0	0	6	3	9
University of Oklahoma	OK	2	3	3	1	1	1	3	0	15	9	1	4	0	0	25	18	43
Oklahoma State University	OK	0	0	1	0	0	0	1	0	10	6	4	0	0	0	16	6	22
Oregon State University	OR	1	0	1	0	2	0	0	0	24	13	1	1	4	0	33	14	47
University of Pennsylvania	PA	0	0	2	2	0	0	0	0	10	4	1	0	3	0	16	6	22
The Pennsylvania State University	PA	2	3	2	3	0	2	0	0	65	22	4	2	0	0	73	32	105
University of Pittsburgh	PA	1	0	2	0	1	0	0	0	19	11	1	0	0	0	23	11	34
Polytechnic University of Puerto Rico	PR	0	0	0	0	5	5	0	0	0	0	0	0	0	0	5	5	10
Prairie View A&M University	TX	7	4	0	0	0	0	0	0	0	0	2	0	0	0	9	4	13
Princeton University	NJ	1	1	4	5	0	0	0	0	7	7	2	0	0	0	14	13	27
University of Puerto Rico, Mayaguez Campus	PR	0	0	0	0	39	80	0	0	0	0	0	0	0	0	39	80	119
Purdue University	IN	1	1	3	3	1	1	0	0	49	18	10	3	2	0	66	25	91
Rensselaer Polytechnic Institute	NY	1	1	2	1	1	1	1	0	20	5	1	0	0	0	25	8	33
University of Rhode Island	RI	0	0	0	0	0	0	0	0	9	5	0	1	1	0	10	6	16
William Marsh Rice University	TX	0	0	3	2	2	1	0	2	6	4	0	0	1	2	12	11	23
University of Rochester	NY	0	0	1	0	0	0	0	0	7	5	1	0	1	0	10	5	15
Rose-Hulman Institute of Technology	IN	0	0	0	1	0	1	0	0	23	13	0	0	0	0	23	15	38
Rowan University	NJ	0	0	0	0	0	1	0	0	7	3	0	0	0	0	7	4	11
Rutgers, The State University of New Jersey	NJ	0	3	4	7	1	0	0	0	8	8	0	0	0	0	13	18	31
San Jose State University	CA	0	0	0	0	4	6	0	0	2	0	2	0	0	0	8	6	14
University of South Alabama	AL	2	0	0	1	0	0	0	0	12	4	0	1	0	1	14	7	21
University of South Carolina	SC	2	1	3	2	0	0	0	0	17	3	2	0	0	1	24	7	31
South Dakota School of Mines and Technology	SD	0	0	0	0	0	0	0	0	13	5	0	0	1	0	14	5	19
University of South Florida	FL	1	0	1	1	0	1	0	0	1	1	0	0	0	1	3	4	7
University of Southern California	CA	0	1	1	3	1	4	1	0	4	2	0	1	0	0	7	11	18
Stanford University	CA	0	1	6	1	0	1	0	0	4	2	2	0	2	0	14	5	19
Stevens Institute of Technology	NJ	0	0	2	2	0	1	0	0	3	1	1	2	1	0	7	6	13
Syracuse University	NY	1	0	0	0	0	0	0	0	3	3	0	0	0	0	4	3	7
Tennessee Technological University	TN	0	0	2	0	0	0	0	0	9	2	0	0	0	0	11	2	13
University of Tennessee, Chattanooga	TN	0	0	0	0	0	0	0	0	3	0	0	0	0	0	3	0	3
University of Tennessee, Knoxville	TN	0	0	0	0	0	0	0	0	10	6	0	0	0	0	10	6	16
Texas A&M University	TX	3	2	3	3	2	5	0	0	44	21	3	4	1	0	56	35	91
Texas A&M University - Kingsville	TX	1	0	0	0	11	4	0	0	5	3	2	0	0	0	19	7	26
Texas Tech University	TX	1	0	0	1	2	0	0	0	7	5	1	1	0	0	11	7	18
The University of Texas at Austin	TX	0	2	13	9	6	7	0	0	32	20	3	4	0	0	54	42	96
The University of Toledo	OH	0	1	0	0	1	0	0	0	18	11	3	0	0	0	22	12	34
Tri-State University	IN	0	0	0	0	0	0	0	0	4	3	1	0	2	0	7	3	10
Tufts University	MA	1	1	2	6	0	0	0	0	0	0	0	1	4	10	7	18	25
Tulane University	LA	1	1	0	1	1	0	0	0	0	0	0	0	7	4	9	6	15
University of Tulsa	OK	0	0	1	0	0	0	0	1	6	1	2	1	0	0	9	3	12

CHEMICAL ENGINEERING

NOR-TUL

BACHELOR'S DEGREES AWARDED IN CHEMICAL ENGINEERING, 2005-2006

INSTITUTION		AFRICAN AMERICAN		ASIAN AMERICAN		HISPANIC		NATIVE AMERICAN		CAUCASIAN		FOREIGN		OTHER		TOTAL BY GENDER		TOTAL DEGREES
		M	F	M	F	M	F	M	F	M	F	M	F	M	F	M	F	
Tuskegee University	AL	4	10	0	0	0	0	0	0	0	0	0	0	1	0	5	10	15
University of Utah	UT	0	0	0	1	0	0	0	0	22	6	0	0	0	2	22	9	31
Vanderbilt University	TN	1	1	0	0	1	0	0	0	9	8	3	2	2	1	16	12	28
Villanova University	PA	0	0	2	0	0	0	0	0	14	5	0	1	0	0	16	6	22
University of Virginia	VA	0	0	4	1	0	0	0	0	9	4	1	1	1	1	15	7	22
Virginia Commonwealth University	VA	0	0	2	1	0	0	0	0	3	1	0	0	0	0	5	2	7
Virginia Polytechnic Institute and State University	VA	1	2	2	1	0	0	0	0	22	10	1	1	2	1	28	15	43
University of Washington	WA	0	0	11	7	2	1	1	0	24	10	3	4	6	2	47	24	71
Washington State University	WA	0	0	0	0	1	0	0	0	10	3	1	0	2	1	14	4	18
Washington University	MO	2	1	1	0	0	0	0	0	9	11	0	0	0	1	12	13	25
Wayne State University	MI	0	0	0	0	0	2	0	0	8	6	1	2	0	0	9	10	19
West Virginia University Institute of Technology	WV	0	0	0	0	0	0	0	0	5	1	1	1	0	0	6	2	8
West Virginia University	WV	0	0	0	1	0	0	0	0	11	3	0	0	0	0	11	4	15
Western Michigan University	MI	0	0	0	0	0	0	0	0	6	2	1	0	0	0	7	2	9
Widener University	PA	0	0	1	0	0	0	0	0	8	2	2	0	0	0	11	2	13
University of Wisconsin, Madison	WI	0	0	6	1	0	1	0	0	37	17	9	6	0	1	52	26	78
Worcester Polytechnic Institute	MA	0	0	0	0	0	1	0	0	15	11	2	0	0	0	17	12	29
University of Wyoming	WY	0	0	0	1	0	0	1	0	11	2	0	2	1	0	13	5	18
Yale University/Faculty of Engineering	CT	0	0	0	0	0	0	0	0	0	0	0	0	2	1	2	1	3
Youngstown State University	OH	0	0	0	0	1	0	0	0	2	6	1	0	0	0	4	6	10
Totals:		103	128	291	220	161	171	12	10	1,866	853	212	136	203	86	2,848	1,604	4,452
CANADIAN INSTITUTIONS:																		
University of Alberta	AB	0	0	0	0	0	0	0	0	0	0	0	0	57	29	57	29	86
University of Calgary	AB	0	0	0	0	0	0	0	0	0	0	1	0	29	23	30	23	53
Ecole Polytechnique de Montreal	PQ	0	0	0	0	0	0	0	0	0	0	0	0	19	21	19	21	40
McGill University, Faculty of Engineering	PQ	0	0	0	0	0	0	0	0	0	0	0	0	38	26	38	26	64
University of Ottawa, Faculty of Engineering	ON	0	0	0	0	0	0	0	0	0	0	0	0	18	16	18	16	34
University of Waterloo	ON	0	0	0	0	0	0	0	0	0	0	0	0	32	30	32	30	62
Totals:		0	0	0	0	0	0	0	0	0	0	1	0	193	145	194	145	339

CHEMICAL ENGINEERING   TUS-YOU

INSTITUTION		AFRICAN AMERICAN		ASIAN AMERICAN		HISPANIC		NATIVE AMERICAN		CAUCASIAN		FOREIGN		OTHER		TOTAL BY GENDER		TOTAL DEGREES
		M	F	M	F	M	F	M	F	M	F	M	F	M	F	M	F	
The University of Akron	OH	0	0	0	0	0	0	2	0	13	11	0	0	1	0	16	11	27
Alabama A&M University	AL	1	1	0	0	0	0	0	0	1	0	0	0	0	0	2	1	3
University of Alabama at Birmingham	AL	2	1	0	0	0	0	0	0	11	1	1	0	0	0	14	2	16
The University of Alabama in Huntsville	AL	0	1	0	0	0	0	0	0	7	2	0	1	0	0	7	4	11
The University of Alabama	AL	0	4	0	0	1	0	0	0	30	9	0	0	0	0	31	13	44
The University of Arizona	AZ	0	0	0	0	4	2	0	0	24	5	3	0	0	0	31	7	38
University of Arkansas	AR	0	0	0	0	0	0	1	0	28	2	2	0	0	0	31	2	33
Auburn University	AL	1	1	3	0	1	0	0	0	84	14	0	1	3	0	92	16	108
Boise State University	ID	0	0	0	0	2	0	0	0	9	2	0	0	1	0	12	2	14
Bradley University	IL	0	0	0	1	1	0	0	0	23	4	0	0	0	0	24	5	29
Brigham Young University	UT	0	0	1	0	0	0	0	0	0	0	3	1	76	15	80	16	96
Brown University	RI	0	0	0	1	0	0	0	0	2	0	0	0	0	0	2	0	2
Bucknell University	PA	0	0	0	1	1	0	1	0	12	10	2	0	1	0	18	11	29
California Polytechnic State University	CA	1	0	10	7	15	3	1	1	96	23	0	0	15	4	138	38	176
California State Polytechnic University, Pomona	CA	3	0	25	6	25	5	0	0	27	8	0	0	5	1	85	20	105
California State University, Chico	CA	0	1	2	0	1	1	0	0	16	5	0	0	8	1	27	8	35
California State University, Fresno	CA	0	0	3	1	8	4	0	0	11	2	1	0	0	0	23	7	30
California State University, Fullerton	CA	0	0	9	3	4	3	0	0	3	0	2	0	2	0	20	6	26
California State University, Long Beach	CA	0	1	4	0	7	1	0	0	9	1	4	1	0	0	24	4	28
California State University, Los Angeles	CA	0	1	1	3	2	2	0	0	0	0	1	0	2	0	6	6	12
California State University, Northridge	CA	2	1	1	0	9	3	0	0	6	2	0	0	5	0	23	6	29
California State University, Sacramento	CA	0	1	7	4	1	4	0	0	13	6	0	0	5	4	26	19	45
University of California, Berkeley	CA	0	0	28	23	6	3	0	0	19	5	8	1	5	4	66	36	102
University of California, Davis	CA	1	0	39	15	4	1	1	2	24	10	0	1	2	3	71	32	103
University of California, Irvine	CA	0	0	0	0	0	0	0	0	0	0	0	0	34	16	34	16	50
University of California, Los Angeles	CA	1	0	9	9	3	2	1	0	14	4	2	3	3	1	32	19	51
University of California, San Diego	CA	0	0	19	8	5	4	0	0	32	10	1	1	5	2	62	25	87
Carnegie Mellon University	PA	0	0	1	1	2	0	0	0	9	3	0	1	0	2	12	8	20
Carroll College	MT	0	0	0	0	0	0	0	0	5	1	0	0	0	0	5	1	6
Case Western Reserve University	OH	2	0	1	0	0	0	0	0	13	2	0	0	0	0	16	2	18
The Catholic University of America	DC	0	0	1	0	0	0	0	0	6	2	0	0	0	0	7	2	9
University of Central Florida	FL	4	1	0	0	9	3	0	1	50	12	0	7	5	0	68	24	92
Christian Brothers University	TN	0	0	1	0	0	0	0	0	5	0	0	1	0	0	6	1	7
University of Cincinnati	OH	1	0	0	0	0	0	1	0	29	7	0	0	0	0	31	7	38
The Citadel	SC	0	0	1	0	1	0	0	0	34	1	1	0	0	0	37	1	38
Clarkson University	NY	0	0	1	1	2	0	1	0	44	8	4	0	0	0	52	9	61
Clemson University	SC	4	1	1	0	0	0	0	0	69	17	0	1	3	1	77	20	97
Cleveland State University	OH	0	0	0	0	0	0	0	0	7	1	1	0	0	0	8	1	9
Colorado State University	CO	0	0	2	1	4	1	0	0	57	8	0	0	3	1	66	11	77
University of Colorado at Boulder	CO	0	1	2	0	2	1	0	0	35	7	0	1	0	0	39	10	49
University of Colorado at Denver	CO	0	1	1	0	4	2	0	1	21	2	0	0	1	0	27	6	33
Columbia University	NY	0	1	1	1	0	0	0	0	11	4	4	1	7	7	23	14	37
University of Connecticut	CT	0	0	1	1	2	1	0	0	29	4	0	0	0	0	32	6	38
The Cooper Union	NY	0	0	8	2	2	1	0	0	5	0	1	1	0	0	16	4	20
Cornell University	NY	2	1	2	6	1	0	0	0	15	7	0	2	1	0	21	16	37

CIVIL ENGINEERING

AKR-COR

BACHELOR'S DEGREES AWARDED IN CIVIL ENGINEERING, 2005-2006

INSTITUTION		AFRICAN AMERICAN		ASIAN AMERICAN		HISPANIC		NATIVE AMERICAN		CAUCASIAN		FOREIGN		OTHER		TOTAL BY GENDER		TOTAL DEGREES
		M	F	M	F	M	F	M	F	M	F	M	F	M	F	M	F	
University of Dayton	OH	0	0	0	0	1	0	0	0	0	0	0	0	20	9	21	9	30
University of Delaware	DE	1	0	1	0	1	1	0	0	30	17	0	1	0	0	33	19	52
University of Detroit Mercy	MI	1	0	0	0	0	0	0	0	2	0	0	0	0	0	3	0	3
University of the District of Columbia	DC	2	0	1	0	0	0	0	0	2	0	0	1	0	0	5	1	6
Drexel University	PA	1	0	3	1	1	2	0	0	26	8	1	0	3	0	35	11	46
Duke University Pratt School of Engineering	NC	0	0	0	0	0	0	0	0	0	0	0	0	11	16	11	16	27
Embry Riddle Aeronautical Univ, Daytona Beach	FL	0	0	0	0	0	0	0	0	5	0	1	0	1	0	7	0	7
University of Evansville	IN	0	0	0	0	0	0	0	0	0	0	0	0	11	0	11	0	11
University of Florida	FL	2	1	2	2	21	3	0	0	79	23	3	0	0	0	107	29	136
Florida Atlantic University	FL	2	1	4	0	3	2	0	0	14	4	0	2	0	0	23	9	32
Florida Institute of Technology	FL	1	0	0	0	1	0	0	0	6	5	2	1	0	0	10	6	16
Florida International University	FL	7	2	1	1	29	18	0	0	1	2	7	2	0	0	45	25	70
FAMU-FSU College of Engineering	FL	9	1	1	1	7	2	0	0	39	12	5	3	0	0	62	19	81
George Mason University	VA	1	0	2	2	3	1	0	0	14	2	1	1	0	0	21	6	27
The George Washington University	DC	0	0	1	0	0	1	0	0	4	0	0	0	2	0	7	1	8
Georgia Institute of Technology	GA	4	6	4	5	5	5	0	1	97	23	2	2	2	0	114	42	156
Gonzaga University	WA	0	0	1	1	1	0	0	0	31	6	1	0	0	0	34	7	41
University of Hartford	CT	0	0	0	0	0	0	0	0	2	1	1	1	0	0	3	2	5
University of Hawaii at Manoa	HI	0	0	14	4	0	0	0	0	2	2	0	0	11	0	27	6	33
University of Houston, Cullen School of Engineering	TX	0	0	10	1	5	1	0	0	11	6	1	1	0	0	27	9	36
Howard University	DC	7	1	0	0	0	0	0	0	0	0	0	0	0	0	7	1	8
University of Idaho	ID	0	0	0	0	1	0	0	0	23	5	0	0	1	0	25	5	30
Idaho State University	ID	0	0	0	0	0	0	0	0	6	0	0	0	0	0	6	0	6
Illinois Institute of Technology	IL	0	2	0	0	1	0	0	0	2	0	0	1	0	0	3	3	6
University of Illinois at Chicago	IL	2	0	9	3	3	2	0	0	20	4	0	0	5	0	39	9	48
University of Illinois at Urbana-Champaign	IL	0	0	9	5	8	2	0	0	70	14	3	2	0	0	90	23	113
Iowa State University	IA	2	1	1	0	2	0	0	0	62	19	2	0	3	0	72	20	92
The Johns Hopkins University	MD	2	0	1	0	0	0	0	0	3	5	1	0	0	0	7	5	12
University of Kansas	KS	0	0	0	0	0	0	0	0	21	9	0	1	0	0	21	10	31
Kansas State University	KS	0	0	1	0	0	1	0	0	20	6	1	0	3	0	25	7	32
University of Kentucky	KY	0	0	0	0	1	0	0	0	67	15	0	0	1	0	69	15	84
Lafayette College	PA	0	0	0	0	0	0	0	0	17	9	0	0	0	0	17	9	26
Lamar University	TX	0	1	1	0	1	0	0	0	11	0	0	0	0	0	13	1	14
Lawrence Technological University	MI	0	1	0	0	1	0	0	0	10	5	0	0	3	0	14	6	20
Lehigh University	PA	0	1	0	0	2	0	0	0	0	0	0	0	25	11	27	12	39
Louisiana State University	LA	2	0	0	1	0	0	0	0	46	11	7	0	0	0	55	12	67
Louisiana Tech University	LA	1	0	0	0	0	0	0	0	27	6	0	0	0	0	28	6	34
University of Louisiana at Lafayette	LA	2	0	0	0	0	0	0	0	15	1	0	0	0	0	17	1	18
University of Louisville	KY	0	0	0	0	1	0	0	0	24	1	0	2	0	0	25	3	28
Loyola Marymount University	CA	0	0	4	2	2	3	0	0	6	2	0	0	1	1	13	8	21
University of Maine	ME	0	0	0	0	1	0	1	0	36	11	0	0	1	0	39	11	50
Manhattan College	NY	1	2	0	0	3	3	0	0	37	12	0	0	0	0	41	17	58
University of Maryland, College Park	MD	0	2	8	1	1	0	0	0	29	13	3	0	0	1	41	17	58
Massachusetts Institute of Technology	MA	1	0	2	0	3	0	0	1	2	3	0	0	1	0	9	4	13
University of Massachusetts Amherst	MA	1	0	2	1	3	0	0	0	29	10	0	0	0	0	35	11	46

DAY-MAS

CIVIL ENGINEERING

BACHELOR'S DEGREES AWARDED IN CIVIL ENGINEERING, 2005-2006

INSTITUTION		AFRICAN AMERICAN		ASIAN AMERICAN		HISPANIC		NATIVE AMERICAN		CAUCASIAN		FOREIGN		OTHER		TOTAL BY GENDER		TOTAL DEGREES
		M	F	M	F	M	F	M	F	M	F	M	F	M	F	M	F	
University of Massachusetts Lowell	MA	3	1	0	0	1	1	1	0	1	7	1	0	4	1	11	10	21
McNeese State University	LA	1	1	0	0	0	0	0	0	3	4	0	0	0	0	4	5	9
The University of Memphis	TN	0	0	0	1	0	0	0	0	7	1	0	0	0	0	7	2	9
Merrimack College	MA	0	0	0	0	0	0	0	0	12	1	0	0	0	0	12	1	13
University of Miami	FL	0	1	1	1	5	1	0	0	2	1	0	3	0	0	9	7	16
University of Michigan	MI	3	0	5	0	1	0	0	0	23	9	2	1	2	0	36	10	46
Michigan State University	MI	0	1	4	1	3	0	0	0	48	14	1	0	0	0	56	16	72
Michigan Technological University	MI	0	0	1	0	0	0	1	0	87	15	3	0	2	2	94	17	111
Minnesota State University, Mankato	MN	0	0	0	0	0	0	0	0	8	1	1	0	1	0	10	1	11
University of Minnesota -Twin Cities	MN	4	0	3	0	0	0	0	0	73	11	2	1	0	0	82	12	94
The University of Mississippi	MS	2	0	0	0	0	0	0	0	15	1	0	0	0	0	17	1	18
Mississippi State University	MS	0	0	0	0	0	0	1	0	39	4	1	0	0	0	41	4	45
University of Missouri-Columbia	MO	1	0	0	0	0	0	0	0	44	10	0	0	0	0	45	10	55
University of Missouri - Kansas City	MO	0	0	0	0	2	0	0	0	7	1	1	0	0	0	10	1	11
University of Missouri - Rolla	MO	0	0	0	2	0	0	0	1	61	9	3	0	2	0	66	12	78
Montana State University	MT	0	0	0	0	0	0	1	0	48	9	0	0	2	3	51	12	63
Morgan State University	MD	7	3	0	0	0	0	0	0	2	0	1	0	0	0	10	3	13
University of Nebraska, Lincoln	NE	0	0	0	0	1	0	0	0	47	9	2	0	0	0	50	9	59
University of Nevada, Las Vegas	NV	1	0	3	1	2	0	1	1	9	6	0	0	0	1	16	9	25
University of New Hampshire	NH	0	0	1	0	0	0	0	0	37	10	0	0	0	0	38	10	48
University of New Haven	CT	0	0	0	0	0	0	0	0	0	0	0	0	1	0	1	0	1
New Jersey Institute of Technology	NJ	5	1	7	0	4	0	0	0	11	2	1	0	8	2	36	5	41
The University of New Mexico	NM	0	0	1	0	4	2	3	0	12	6	0	0	0	0	20	8	28
New Mexico State University	NM	0	1	0	0	10	2	0	0	7	2	3	0	4	1	24	6	30
University of New Orleans	LA	0	1	0	0	0	0	1	0	9	5	1	1	0	0	11	7	18
City College of the City University of New York	NY	0	1	1	0	1	0	0	0	0	0	2	1	7	4	11	6	17
State University of New York at Buffalo	NY	2	0	1	0	0	0	0	0	42	6	4	1	3	1	53	8	61
North Carolina A & T State University	NC	2	1	0	0	1	0	0	0	3	0	0	0	0	0	6	1	7
North Carolina State University	NC	3	0	2	4	2	1	0	0	135	19	0	0	0	0	142	24	166
University of North Carolina, Charlotte	NC	2	0	0	1	2	0	1	0	43	10	0	0	0	0	47	12	59
University of North Dakota	ND	0	0	0	0	0	0	0	0	18	5	0	0	0	0	18	5	23
North Dakota State University	ND	0	0	0	1	0	0	0	0	72	10	0	0	0	0	73	10	83
University of North Florida	FL	1	0	0	1	2	0	0	1	16	2	1	0	1	0	21	4	25
Northeastern University	MA	1	0	2	1	1	0	0	0	30	15	1	0	8	1	43	17	60
Northern Arizona University	AZ	0	0	0	0	0	0	1	1	11	3	0	0	0	0	12	4	16
Northwestern University	IL	0	0	2	1	0	2	0	0	5	3	3	0	0	0	10	6	16
Norwich University	VT	0	0	0	0	1	0	0	0	9	1	1	0	0	0	11	1	12
University of Notre Dame	IN	1	0	1	0	1	0	0	0	14	6	2	0	0	0	19	6	25
Ohio Northern University	OH	0	0	0	0	0	0	0	0	18	8	0	0	0	0	18	8	26
The Ohio State University	OH	2	1	2	2	1	0	0	0	56	12	1	0	0	0	62	15	77
Ohio University	OH	0	0	0	0	0	0	0	0	28	5	0	0	0	0	28	5	33
University of Oklahoma	OK	0	0	1	0	1	1	2	0	16	1	2	1	0	0	22	3	25
Oklahoma State University	OK	1	0	0	0	1	0	1	0	20	10	2	1	0	0	25	11	36
Old Dominion University	VA	2	0	0	0	1	0	1	0	15	3	1	1	4	0	23	5	28
Oregon Institute of Technology	OR	0	0	0	1	1	0	0	0	14	2	0	0	2	0	17	3	20

CIVIL ENGINEERING   MAS-ORE

BACHELOR'S DEGREES AWARDED IN CIVIL ENGINEERING, 2005-2006

INSTITUTION		AFRICAN AMERICAN		ASIAN AMERICAN		HISPANIC		NATIVE AMERICAN		CAUCASIAN		FOREIGN		OTHER		TOTAL BY GENDER		TOTAL DEGREES
		M	F	M	F	M	F	M	F	M	F	M	F	M	F	M	F	
Oregon State University	OR	0	0	0	1	0	1	0	0	54	6	2	0	7	0	63	8	71
University of the Pacific	CA	0	0	2	2	2	0	0	0	2	1	0	1	1	1	7	5	12
The Pennsylvania State University	PA	1	0	10	0	4	0	0	0	126	23	3	0	0	0	144	23	167
University of Pittsburgh	PA	1	3	0	0	0	1	0	0	47	17	0	2	0	0	48	23	71
Polytechnic University	NY	2	1	10	3	0	3	0	0	7	0	1	0	1	0	21	7	28
Polytechnic University of Puerto Rico	PR	0	0	0	0	115	35	0	0	0	0	0	0	0	0	115	35	150
University of Portland	OR	0	0	3	1	0	0	0	0	11	8	0	1	0	0	14	10	24
Portland State University	OR	0	0	3	1	0	0	0	0	19	4	1	0	4	1	27	6	33
University of Puerto Rico, Mayaguez Campus	PR	0	0	0	0	67	30	0	0	0	0	0	0	0	0	67	30	97
Purdue University	IN	0	0	4	1	3	0	0	0	124	30	14	2	1	1	146	34	180
Rensselaer Polytechnic Institute	NY	0	0	1	1	0	1	0	0	22	10	2	1	0	0	25	13	38
University of Rhode Island	RI	0	0	0	0	1	2	0	0	14	4	0	0	0	0	15	6	21
William Marsh Rice University	TX	1	0	0	0	2	0	0	0	7	5	1	0	0	0	11	5	16
Rose-Hulman Institute of Technology	IN	0	0	0	0	0	1	0	0	23	6	0	0	0	0	23	7	30
Rowan University	NJ	0	0	0	0	0	0	0	0	19	4	0	0	0	0	19	4	23
Rutgers, The State University of New Jersey	NJ	0	0	0	0	0	0	0	0	30	7	0	0	0	0	30	7	37
Saint Martin's College	WA	0	1	1	3	0	0	0	0	12	4	0	0	0	0	12	4	16
San Diego State University	CA	2	0	7	4	10	2	1	0	28	13	3	0	4	1	55	20	75
San Francisco State University	CA	0	0	6	2	2	0	0	0	4	3	3	0	0	0	13	5	18
San Jose State University	CA	1	1	15	6	6	0	0	0	9	2	8	2	0	0	39	11	50
Santa Clara University	CA	0	0	4	1	5	0	0	0	11	1	1	0	0	1	21	3	24
Seattle University	WA	0	1	1	3	0	0	0	0	3	1	0	0	0	0	4	5	9
University of South Alabama	AL	1	0	0	0	0	0	0	0	17	1	1	0	1	0	20	1	21
South Dakota School of Mines and Technology	SD	0	0	0	0	0	0	2	0	13	3	0	0	0	1	15	5	20
South Dakota State University	SD	0	0	0	0	0	0	0	0	35	6	0	0	0	0	35	6	41
University of South Florida	FL	1	0	0	0	0	0	0	0	7	4	3	0	1	0	12	4	16
University of Southern California	CA	1	0	4	4	2	2	0	0	7	3	3	0	0	0	17	9	26
Southern Illinois University Carbondale	IL	0	2	0	0	1	0	0	0	38	5	1	0	3	0	43	7	50
Southern Illinois University Edwardsville	IL	0	0	0	0	1	0	0	0	31	3	0	0	0	0	32	3	35
Southern Methodist University	TX	0	0	0	0	0	0	0	0	0	0	2	1	0	0	2	1	3
Southern University and A&M College	LA	6	2	0	0	0	0	0	0	0	0	0	0	0	0	6	2	8
Stanford University	CA	2	1	6	5	2	2	0	1	8	3	0	0	1	1	19	14	33
Stevens Institute of Technology	NJ	0	1	3	1	1	2	0	0	11	3	0	0	1	1	16	8	24
Syracuse University	NY	1	3	0	1	0	1	0	0	15	3	0	0	0	0	16	8	24
Temple University	PA	2	1	0	0	0	0	0	0	9	3	3	0	0	0	14	4	18
Tennessee State University	TN	2	2	0	0	0	0	0	0	0	0	0	0	0	0	2	2	4
Tennessee Technological University	TN	1	0	0	0	0	0	0	0	34	10	0	0	0	0	35	10	45
University of Tennessee, Chattanooga	TN	0	0	0	0	0	0	0	0	8	0	1	0	0	0	9	0	9
University of Tennessee, Knoxville	TN	3	0	2	0	0	0	0	0	42	12	0	1	0	0	47	13	60
Texas A&M University	TX	1	1	5	1	23	5	0	0	121	41	2	1	1	1	153	50	203
Texas A&M University - Kingsville	TX	0	0	0	0	25	2	0	0	7	1	1	1	0	0	33	4	37
Texas Tech University	TX	1	0	0	0	9	2	0	0	40	11	1	0	0	0	51	13	64
The University of Texas at Arlington	TX	0	0	0	0	4	0	0	0	17	2	2	0	0	0	23	2	25
The University of Texas at Austin	TX	1	0	7	4	8	2	1	0	39	15	5	0	0	0	61	21	82
University of Texas at El Paso	TX	0	0	0	0	16	8	0	0	0	0	2	1	0	0	18	9	27

ORE-TEX

CIVIL ENGINEERING

INSTITUTION		AFRICAN AMERICAN		ASIAN AMERICAN		HISPANIC		NATIVE AMERICAN		CAUCASIAN		FOREIGN		OTHER		TOTAL BY GENDER		TOTAL DEGREES
		M	F	M	F	M	F	M	F	M	F	M	F	M	F	M	F	
University of Texas at San Antonio	TX	0	1	1	0	26	6	1	0	21	5	0	1	0	0	49	13	62
The University of Toledo	OH	0	0	0	0	0	0	0	0	22	3	2	0	0	0	24	3	27
Tri-State University	IN	0	0	0	0	0	0	0	0	6	5	1	0	1	1	8	6	14
Tufts University	MA	2	0	3	4	0	0	0	0	0	0	0	1	14	12	19	17	36
Tulane University	LA	0	1	0	1	1	0	0	0	0	0	0	1	12	5	13	8	21
U.S. Air Force Academy	CO	2	0	0	0	0	0	0	0	0	0	0	0	26	5	28	5	33
U.S. Coast Guard Academy	CT	0	0	2	0	0	2	0	0	19	7	0	0	0	0	21	9	30
United States Military Academy	NY	2	1	4	0	0	0	0	0	38	2	0	0	0	0	44	3	47
University of Utah	UT	0	0	0	2	4	1	0	0	45	4	0	1	0	3	49	11	60
Utah State University	UT	0	0	0	0	0	0	0	0	75	7	0	0	0	0	75	7	82
Valparaiso University	IN	0	0	0	0	0	0	1	0	10	3	0	0	0	0	11	3	14
University of Vermont	VT	0	0	0	0	0	0	0	0	24	9	1	0	1	0	25	9	34
Villanova University	PA	1	0	0	1	0	0	0	0	30	15	1	0	0	0	32	15	47
University of Virginia	VA	1	1	3	0	1	0	0	0	34	11	0	1	1	1	40	14	54
Virginia Military Institute	VA	0	0	0	0	0	0	0	0	23	0	0	0	0	0	23	0	23
Virginia Polytechnic Institute and State University	VA	2	2	3	3	2	1	0	0	103	20	5	0	4	0	119	26	145
University of Washington	WA	3	1	18	2	2	0	0	0	52	11	1	1	14	0	90	15	105
Washington State University	WA	0	0	0	1	2	1	0	0	33	10	3	0	3	1	41	13	54
Washington University	MO	0	2	2	0	2	0	0	0	12	5	3	0	5	0	24	7	31
Wayne State University	MI	0	0	0	0	1	0	0	0	8	3	0	0	0	0	9	3	12
West Virginia University Institute of Technology	WV	0	0	0	0	0	0	0	0	19	3	0	0	0	0	19	3	22
West Virginia University	WV	3	0	0	0	0	0	0	0	32	5	0	0	1	1	36	6	42
Western Kentucky University	KY	0	0	0	0	0	0	0	0	8	1	0	0	0	0	8	1	9
Western Michigan University	MI	0	0	0	0	0	0	0	0	10	0	0	0	0	0	10	0	10
Widener University	PA	0	0	1	1	0	0	0	0	11	1	0	0	0	0	12	2	14
University of Wisconsin, Madison	WI	3	0	0	0	1	1	0	0	70	22	1	2	2	0	77	25	102
University of Wisconsin, Milwaukee	WI	1	0	1	0	1	0	0	0	30	5	0	0	0	0	33	5	38
University of Wisconsin, Platteville	WI	0	0	0	0	0	0	0	0	37	7	0	0	0	0	37	7	44
Worcester Polytechnic Institute	MA	0	0	1	0	0	0	0	0	42	13	0	1	2	1	46	15	61
University of Wyoming	WY	0	0	0	0	1	0	1	0	31	7	0	0	1	1	33	8	41
Youngstown State University	OH	0	0	0	0	0	0	0	0	7	2	5	0	0	0	12	2	14
Totals:		173	82	440	199	644	218	30	15	5,006	1,217	212	82	462	155	6,967	1,968	8,935

CANADIAN INSTITUTIONS:

INSTITUTION		AFRICAN AMERICAN		ASIAN AMERICAN		HISPANIC		NATIVE AMERICAN		CAUCASIAN		FOREIGN		OTHER		TOTAL BY GENDER		TOTAL DEGREES
		M	F	M	F	M	F	M	F	M	F	M	F	M	F	M	F	
University of Alberta	AB	0	0	0	0	0	0	0	0	0	0	0	0	77	29	77	29	106
University of Calgary	AB	0	0	0	0	0	0	0	0	0	0	1	0	53	17	54	17	71
Concordia University, Faculty of Engr. and Comp. Sci.	PQ	0	0	0	0	0	0	0	0	0	0	2	0	13	7	15	7	22
Ecole Polytechnique de Montreal	PQ	0	0	0	0	0	0	0	0	0	0	0	0	19	9	19	9	28
Ecole de Technologie Superieure	PQ	0	0	0	0	0	0	0	0	0	0	0	0	60	16	60	16	76
McGill University, Faculty of Engineering	PQ	0	0	0	0	0	0	0	0	0	0	0	0	44	29	44	29	73
University of Ottawa, Faculty of Engineering	ON	0	0	0	0	0	0	0	0	0	0	3	0	25	10	28	10	38
University of Waterloo	ON	0	0	0	0	0	0	0	0	0	0	0	0	60	18	60	18	78
Totals:		0	0	0	0	0	0	0	0	0	0	6	0	351	135	357	135	492

TEX-YOU

CIVIL ENGINEERING

Bachelor's Degrees Awarded in Civil/Environmental Engineering, 2005-2006

INSTITUTION		AFRICAN AMERICAN		ASIAN AMERICAN		HISPANIC		NATIVE AMERICAN		CAUCASIAN		FOREIGN		OTHER		TOTAL BY GENDER		TOTAL DEGREES
		M	F	M	F	M	F	M	F	M	F	M	F	M	F	M	F	
University of Alaska Fairbanks	AK	1	0	1	2	0	0	1	0	13	9	0	0	0	0	16	11	27
Arizona State University	AZ	1	1	3	2	5	5	0	0	38	11	1	1	6	1	54	21	75
The University of Iowa	IA	1	0	0	0	0	0	0	0	27	7	0	0	1	0	29	7	36
Marquette University	WI	0	0	1	0	1	1	0	0	25	8	1	0	0	0	28	9	37
University of Massachusetts Dartmouth	MA	0	0	0	0	1	1	0	0	10	0	0	0	0	0	11	1	12
University of Nevada, Las Vegas	NV	0	0	0	0	0	0	0	0	3	2	1	0	1	0	5	2	7
University of Nevada, Reno	NV	1	0	3	2	0	2	0	0	31	8	0	1	1	1	36	14	50
Prairie View A&M University	TX	5	2	0	0	0	0	0	0	1	0	0	0	0	0	6	2	8
University of South Carolina	SC	1	1	1	0	0	0	0	0	27	7	0	0	2	0	31	8	39
Totals:		10	4	9	6	7	9	1	0	175	52	3	2	11	2	216	75	291

CIVIL/ENVIRONMENTAL ENGINEERING   ALA-SOU

Bachelor's Degrees Awarded in Computer Engineering, 2005-2006

INSTITUTION		AFRICAN AMERICAN M	F	ASIAN AMERICAN M	F	HISPANIC M	F	NATIVE AMERICAN M	F	CAUCASIAN M	F	FOREIGN M	F	OTHER M	F	TOTAL BY GENDER M	F	TOTAL DEGREES
The University of Alabama in Huntsville	AL	1	0	1	0	0	0	0	0	22	4	1	0	0	0	25	4	29
The University of Arizona	AZ	2	0	1	1	6	1	0	1	31	3	9	3	0	0	49	9	58
Arizona State University	AZ	2	0	8	3	5	4	0	0	50	5	4	2	4	0	73	14	87
University of Arkansas	AR	0	0	0	2	0	0	0	0	16	2	2	0	0	0	18	4	22
Boston University	MA	0	0	9	1	1	0	0	0	12	1	5	0	0	0	27	2	29
University of Bridgeport	CT	0	0	0	0	0	0	0	0	2	0	0	0	0	0	2	0	2
Brown University	RI	0	0	0	0	0	0	0	0	6	1	2	2	0	0	8	3	11
California Polytechnic State University	CA	0	0	27	5	3	1	0	0	38	3	1	1	7	1	76	11	87
California State Polytechnic University, Pomona	CA	1	0	10	1	2	0	1	0	2	0	0	0	0	0	16	1	17
California State University, Chico	CA	1	0	1	1	2	0	0	0	2	0	5	0	2	2	13	3	16
California State University, Fresno	CA	0	0	1	0	2	0	0	0	2	1	5	0	0	0	10	1	11
California State University, Fullerton	CA	0	0	10	2	7	0	0	0	3	0	2	2	2	0	24	4	28
California State University, Long Beach	CA	0	0	2	0	1	0	0	0	5	1	8	1	0	0	16	2	18
California State University, Northridge	CA	1	0	6	2	7	1	0	0	4	0	1	0	1	0	20	3	23
California State University, Sacramento	CA	3	0	28	3	4	0	0	0	9	1	4	2	2	1	50	7	57
University of California, Davis	CA	1	0	15	2	0	0	0	0	5	0	1	0	0	0	22	2	24
University of California, Irvine	CA	0	0	0	0	0	0	0	0	0	0	0	0	108	13	108	13	121
University of California, Riverside	CA	0	0	6	1	4	0	0	0	4	0	0	0	0	0	14	1	15
University of California, San Diego	CA	0	0	10	1	2	0	0	0	3	0	1	0	3	0	19	1	20
University of California, Santa Barbara	CA	2	0	16	1	4	0	0	0	22	0	4	0	3	0	51	1	52
University of California-Santa Cruz	CA	2	0	6	2	5	1	0	0	12	0	2	0	7	0	34	3	37
Capitol College	MD	0	0	0	0	0	0	0	0	0	0	0	0	5	1	5	1	6
Case Western Reserve University	OH	1	0	0	1	0	0	0	0	31	1	0	1	0	0	32	3	35
Cedarville University	OH	0	0	0	0	0	0	0	0	0	0	0	0	7	0	7	0	7
University of Central Florida	FL	8	2	2	1	10	1	0	0	35	3	5	2	2	1	62	10	72
Christopher Newport University	VA	0	0	0	1	0	0	0	0	11	2	0	0	0	0	11	3	14
University of Cincinnati	OH	0	0	2	0	0	0	0	0	14	1	0	0	1	0	17	1	18
Clarkson University	NY	0	0	0	0	2	0	0	0	33	3	1	0	0	0	36	3	39
Clemson University	SC	2	1	0	0	0	0	0	0	28	1	2	0	2	0	34	2	36
Cleveland State University	OH	1	0	0	0	0	0	0	0	9	1	0	0	0	0	10	1	11
Colorado Technical University	CO	0	0	0	0	0	0	0	0	4	0	1	0	7	3	8	3	11
University of Colorado at Colorado Springs	CO	1	0	0	0	1	0	0	0	4	0	0	1	1	1	7	2	9
Columbia University	NY	3	0	4	0	2	0	0	0	5	1	3	0	2	0	19	1	20
University of Connecticut	CT	0	0	2	0	0	0	0	0	5	0	0	0	0	0	7	0	7
University of Dayton	OH	0	0	1	0	1	0	0	0	0	0	1	1	10	2	13	3	16
University of Delaware	DE	0	1	3	0	1	0	0	0	15	0	1	0	0	0	20	1	21
University of Denver	CO	0	0	1	0	1	0	0	0	3	1	2	1	1	0	7	2	9
Drexel University	PA	8	0	9	1	0	1	0	0	17	2	7	2	1	0	42	6	48
Embry Riddle Aeronautical Univ., Daytona Beach	FL	1	1	0	0	0	0	0	0	4	1	0	0	1	0	6	2	8
Embry Riddle Aeronautical University, Prescott	AZ	0	0	0	0	0	0	0	0	4	4	0	0	0	0	4	4	8
University of Evansville	IN	0	0	0	0	0	0	0	0	0	0	0	0	4	1	4	1	5
Fairfield University	CT	0	0	1	0	2	0	0	0	6	0	1	0	0	0	10	0	10
University of Florida	FL	1	0	14	6	16	4	0	0	69	9	3	0	0	0	103	19	122
Florida Atlantic University	FL	2	2	4	3	1	2	0	0	7	3	5	2	0	0	19	12	31
Florida Institute of Technology	FL	1	0	1	1	2	0	0	0	9	0	15	1	2	0	30	2	32

COMPUTER ENGINEERING

ALA-FLO

BACHELOR'S DEGREES AWARDED IN COMPUTER ENGINEERING, 2005-2006

INSTITUTION		AFRICAN AMERICAN M	F	ASIAN AMERICAN M	F	HISPANIC M	F	NATIVE AMERICAN M	F	CAUCASIAN M	F	FOREIGN M	F	OTHER M	F	TOTAL BY GENDER M	F	TOTAL DEGREES
Florida International University	FL	0	0	2	0	14	7	0	0	1	0	10	3	0	0	27	10	37
FAMU-FSU College of Engineering	FL	12	3	0	0	1	0	0	0	4	0	1	0	0	0	18	3	21
George Mason University	VA	2	0	10	2	2	1	0	0	4	0	5	0	2	0	25	3	28
The George Washington University	DC	0	0	1	0	0	0	0	0	1	0	0	0	0	0	2	0	2
Georgia Institute of Technology	GA	5	2	20	3	2	0	0	0	42	3	16	2	1	0	86	10	96
Gonzaga University	WA	0	0	2	0	0	0	1	0	4	1	1	0	0	0	8	1	9
Grand Valley State University	MI	0	0	0	0	0	0	0	0	7	0	0	0	0	0	7	0	7
University of Hartford	CT	0	0	1	0	1	0	0	0	1	2	1	0	0	0	4	2	6
Hofstra University	NY	0	0	0	0	0	0	0	0	1	0	0	0	0	0	1	0	1
University of Houston, Cullen School of Engineering	TX	1	0	0	0	1	1	0	0	3	0	1	0	0	0	6	1	7
University of Idaho	ID	0	0	1	0	0	0	0	0	6	1	0	0	2	1	9	2	11
Illinois Institute of Technology	IL	1	1	5	0	1	0	0	0	11	0	12	0	0	0	30	1	31
University of Illinois at Chicago	IL	0	0	11	4	0	1	0	0	22	3	0	0	1	0	34	8	42
University of Illinois at Urbana-Champaign	IL	2	0	21	4	3	0	0	0	63	7	19	3	5	0	113	14	127
Indiana Institute of Technology	IN	0	0	0	0	0	0	0	0	2	0	0	0	0	0	2	0	2
Indiana University Purdue University at Indianapolis	IN	1	0	2	1	0	0	0	0	2	0	3	0	0	0	8	2	10
Iowa State University	IA	3	0	6	2	0	0	1	0	92	10	16	0	4	1	122	13	135
The Johns Hopkins University	MD	1	0	5	0	0	0	1	0	4	0	1	0	0	0	11	0	11
University of Kansas	KS	0	0	1	0	0	0	0	0	22	3	6	1	0	0	29	4	33
Kansas State University	KS	0	0	0	0	0	0	0	0	25	2	1	0	3	0	29	2	31
Kettering University formerly GMI	MI	3	0	2	0	0	0	0	0	13	0	1	1	2	0	21	1	22
Lake Superior State University	MI	0	0	0	0	0	0	0	0	5	0	1	0	0	0	6	0	6
Lawrence Technological University	MI	0	0	1	2	0	0	0	0	16	0	0	0	0	0	17	2	19
Lehigh University	PA	1	0	1	0	0	0	0	0	0	0	2	0	15	0	19	0	19
University of Maine	ME	0	0	0	0	0	0	0	0	8	0	1	0	0	0	9	0	9
Manhattan College	NY	4	0	0	0	4	0	0	0	5	0	0	0	0	1	13	1	14
Marquette University	WI	0	0	1	0	0	0	0	0	2	2	3	0	0	0	6	2	8
University of Maryland, Baltimore County	MD	6	1	6	0	0	0	0	0	19	0	5	0	1	0	37	1	38
University of Maryland, College Park	MD	1	0	14	5	2	1	0	0	23	1	4	1	4	0	48	8	56
University of Massachusetts Amherst	MA	4	0	7	0	1	0	0	0	19	0	1	0	0	0	32	0	32
University of Massachusetts Dartmouth	MA	2	0	0	0	1	0	0	0	9	0	2	0	0	0	14	0	14
University of Massachusetts Lowell	MA	0	0	2	0	0	0	0	0	6	0	1	0	2	0	11	0	11
The University of Memphis	TN	0	0	1	0	0	0	0	0	6	0	0	0	0	0	7	0	7
Mercer University	GA	3	0	0	0	1	0	0	0	5	0	0	0	0	0	9	0	9
University of Miami	FL	2	0	0	0	6	0	0	0	4	1	2	0	0	0	14	1	15
Miami University	OH	0	0	0	0	0	0	0	0	2	0	0	0	0	0	2	0	2
University of Michigan	MI	1	2	16	2	2	0	0	0	37	2	6	1	2	0	64	7	71
Michigan State University	MI	1	1	5	0	2	0	0	0	23	0	5	1	0	0	34	2	36
Michigan Technological University	MI	0	0	0	0	0	0	0	0	24	4	5	0	0	0	29	4	33
University of Michigan, Dearborn	MI	1	1	5	3	1	0	0	0	30	4	3	0	0	0	40	8	48
Milwaukee School of Engineering	WI	3	0	2	0	1	0	1	0	47	0	2	0	1	0	57	0	57
Minnesota State University, Mankato	MN	0	0	0	0	0	0	0	0	0	1	4	1	2	1	6	3	9
University of Minnesota -Twin Cities	MN	1	0	9	0	0	0	0	0	32	2	4	0	0	0	46	2	48
Mississippi State University	MS	3	1	1	0	1	0	0	0	17	2	0	0	0	0	22	3	25
University of Missouri-Columbia	MO	0	0	1	0	0	0	1	0	19	0	6	2	0	0	27	2	29

FLO-MIS

COMPUTER ENGINEERING

BACHELOR'S DEGREES AWARDED IN COMPUTER ENGINEERING, 2005-2006

INSTITUTION		AFRICAN AMERICAN M	F	ASIAN AMERICAN M	F	HISPANIC M	F	NATIVE AMERICAN M	F	CAUCASIAN M	F	FOREIGN M	F	OTHER M	F	TOTAL BY GENDER M	F	TOTAL DEGREES
University of Missouri - Kansas City	MO	1	0	1	0	0	0	0	0	17	2	17	4	0	0	36	6	42
University of Missouri - Rolla	MO	2	0	2	0	0	0	0	0	29	2	2	1	1	0	36	3	39
Montana State University	MT	0	0	1	0	0	0	0	0	11	0	0	1	0	0	12	1	13
University of Nevada, Las Vegas	NV	2	0	0	0	0	0	0	0	3	0	1	0	0	0	6	0	6
University of Nevada, Reno	NV	0	0	0	0	0	0	0	0	6	0	0	0	0	0	6	0	6
University of New Hampshire	NH	0	0	1	0	0	0	0	0	5	1	0	0	0	0	6	1	7
University of New Haven	CT	0	0	0	0	0	0	0	0	0	0	0	0	2	0	2	0	2
New Jersey Institute of Technology	NJ	2	2	15	0	6	1	0	0	22	0	7	0	10	2	62	5	67
The College of New Jersey	NJ	2	0	0	0	0	0	0	0	1	0	0	0	0	0	3	0	3
The University of New Mexico	NM	0	0	2	0	5	1	0	0	1	2	1	0	0	0	9	3	12
City College of the City University of New York	NY	0	0	6	1	2	0	0	0	0	0	0	0	9	3	17	4	21
The State University of New York at Binghamton	NY	0	0	3	2	0	0	0	0	13	0	0	0	4	0	20	2	22
State University of New York at Buffalo	NY	1	0	1	0	1	0	0	0	10	0	12	1	2	0	27	1	28
SUNY, New Paltz	NY	0	0	0	0	0	0	0	0	7	1	2	0	0	0	9	1	10
North Carolina State University	NC	4	0	14	3	4	0	1	0	79	7	1	0	0	0	103	10	113
University of North Carolina, Charlotte	NC	1	1	4	0	0	0	0	0	10	2	2	1	0	0	17	4	21
North Dakota State University	ND	0	0	0	0	0	0	0	0	6	1	0	0	0	0	6	1	7
Northeastern University	MA	1	0	1	0	2	1	0	0	11	1	0	0	14	1	29	3	32
Northwestern University	IL	0	0	0	1	1	0	0	0	9	1	0	1	2	0	12	2	14
Norwich University	VT	0	0	0	0	0	0	0	0	0	0	1	0	0	0	1	0	1
University of Notre Dame	IN	0	0	1	0	1	0	0	0	11	0	1	0	0	0	14	0	14
Oakland University	MI	0	1	0	2	0	1	0	2	18	4	1	0	0	0	19	10	29
Ohio Northern University	OH	0	0	0	0	0	0	0	0	13	0	0	0	0	0	13	0	13
University of Oklahoma	OK	0	1	4	0	0	0	0	0	20	0	3	1	0	0	27	2	29
Oklahoma Christian University	OK	0	0	0	0	0	0	0	0	4	0	0	0	0	0	4	0	4
Old Dominion University	VA	3	1	0	1	0	0	1	0	4	0	1	1	0	0	9	3	12
Oregon State University	OR	0	0	3	2	0	0	0	0	21	2	1	0	3	0	28	4	32
Penn State Erie, The Behrend College	PA	1	0	0	0	2	0	0	0	19	1	0	0	0	0	22	1	23
The Pennsylvania State University	PA	0	1	6	3	6	0	0	0	109	12	10	2	0	0	131	18	149
University of Pittsburgh	PA	3	1	4	0	0	0	0	0	38	0	0	0	0	0	45	1	46
Polytechnic University	NY	5	0	18	2	3	0	0	0	15	0	6	0	3	0	50	2	52
Polytechnic University of Puerto Rico	PR	0	0	0	0	8	1	0	0	0	0	0	0	0	0	8	1	9
Portland State University	OR	0	1	0	1	1	0	0	0	4	1	5	0	0	0	10	3	13
University of Puerto Rico, Mayaguez Campus	PR	0	0	0	0	40	15	0	0	0	0	0	0	0	0	40	15	55
Purdue University, Calumet	IN	1	0	0	0	0	0	0	0	1	1	0	1	2	1	4	2	6
Purdue University	IN	5	1	33	7	1	0	0	0	122	15	96	22	11	2	268	47	315
Rensselaer Polytechnic Institute	NY	4	0	11	1	1	0	1	0	44	3	3	2	0	0	64	6	70
University of Rhode Island	RI	0	0	1	0	1	0	0	0	9	0	0	0	1	0	12	0	12
Rochester Institute of Technology	NY	2	0	8	0	2	1	0	0	39	5	3	1	6	0	60	7	67
Rose-Hulman Institute of Technology	IN	0	0	4	0	0	0	0	0	34	3	0	0	0	0	38	3	41
Saint Cloud State University	MN	0	0	0	0	0	0	0	0	0	0	3	1	0	0	3	1	4
Saint Mary's University	TX	0	0	1	0	4	1	0	0	0	0	1	0	0	0	6	1	7
San Diego State University	CA	2	0	14	5	5	0	0	0	6	0	4	0	4	1	35	6	41
San Jose State University	CA	2	0	35	9	1	1	0	0	7	3	12	0	0	0	57	13	70
Santa Clara University	CA	0	0	7	1	0	0	0	0	7	1	3	1	1	0	18	3	21

COMPUTER ENGINEERING   MIS-SAN

Bachelor's Degrees Awarded in Computer Engineering, 2005-2006

INSTITUTION		AFRICAN AMERICAN		ASIAN AMERICAN		HISPANIC		NATIVE AMERICAN		CAUCASIAN		FOREIGN		OTHER		TOTAL BY GENDER		TOTAL DEGREES
		M	F	M	F	M	F	M	F	M	F	M	F	M	F	M	F	
University of South Carolina	SC	6	0	1	0	0	0	0	0	12	2	4	0	0	0	23	2	25
South Dakota School of Mines and Technology	SD	0	0	0	0	0	0	0	0	15	1	0	0	1	0	16	1	17
Southern Illinois University Edwardsville	IL	1	0	4	0	0	0	0	0	7	0	0	0	0	0	12	0	12
Southern Methodist University	TX	0	0	2	1	2	0	0	0	4	1	0	0	0	0	8	2	10
Stevens Institute of Technology	NJ	2	1	10	4	6	2	0	0	10	7	5	0	5	2	38	16	54
Syracuse University	NY	4	1	2	0	0	0	0	0	19	0	2	0	0	0	27	1	28
Tennessee Technological University	TN	0	0	0	0	0	0	0	0	13	0	0	0	0	0	13	0	13
University of Tennessee, Knoxville	TN	3	0	0	0	1	0	0	0	10	3	0	1	0	0	14	4	18
Texas Tech University	TX	1	0	1	0	0	0	0	0	2	0	0	0	0	0	4	0	4
Tri-State University	IN	0	0	0	0	0	0	0	0	6	0	0	0	0	0	6	0	6
Tufts University	MA	0	0	6	0	1	1	0	0	0	0	1	0	8	1	16	2	18
Tulane University	LA	0	0	2	0	0	0	0	0	0	0	0	0	5	1	7	1	8
Union College	NY	0	0	1	0	1	0	0	0	6	0	0	0	0	0	8	0	8
U.S. Air Force Academy	CO	0	0	1	1	1	0	1	0	0	0	1	0	6	0	9	0	9
University of Utah	UT	0	0	0	1	1	0	0	0	9	0	0	0	0	0	10	1	11
Valparaiso University	IN	0	0	0	0	0	0	0	0	5	0	1	0	0	0	6	0	6
Villanova University	PA	0	0	1	0	0	0	0	0	19	0	0	0	0	0	20	0	20
University of Virginia	VA	2	0	5	0	0	0	0	0	17	1	2	0	2	0	28	1	29
Virginia Commonwealth University	VA	1	0	1	0	0	0	1	0	4	0	0	0	1	0	8	0	8
Virginia Polytechnic Institute and State University	VA	2	0	16	1	1	0	0	0	63	2	11	1	2	0	95	4	99
University of Washington	WA	0	0	20	6	1	0	0	0	29	2	4	0	4	0	58	8	66
Washington State University	WA	0	0	0	0	0	0	0	0	8	0	1	0	3	1	12	1	13
Washington University	MO	3	0	1	0	0	0	0	0	8	0	2	0	0	0	14	0	14
West Virginia University Institute of Technology	WV	0	0	0	0	0	0	0	0	4	0	0	0	0	0	4	0	4
West Virginia University	WV	2	0	0	1	0	0	0	0	36	4	3	2	0	0	41	7	48
Western Michigan University	MI	0	0	0	0	0	0	0	0	11	0	6	1	0	0	17	1	18
Wichita State University	KS	0	0	3	2	0	0	0	0	0	0	8	1	7	0	18	3	21
University of Wisconsin, Madison	WI	0	0	3	0	1	0	0	0	37	3	4	0	1	0	46	3	49
Wright State University	OH	0	0	2	0	0	0	0	0	11	1	2	0	1	0	16	1	17
University of Wyoming	WY	0	0	1	0	0	0	0	0	2	0	0	0	1	0	4	1	5
Totals:		180	31	647	127	252	54	9	3	2,399	204	511	86	353	45	4,351	550	4,901
CANADIAN INSTITUTIONS:																		
University of Alberta	AB	0	0	0	0	0	0	0	0	0	0	0	0	54	10	54	10	64
University of Calgary	AB	0	0	0	0	0	0	0	0	0	0	0	0	35	5	35	5	40
Concordia University, Faculty of Engr. and Comp. Sci.	PQ	0	0	0	0	0	0	0	0	0	0	10	1	61	7	71	8	79
Ecole Polytechnique de Montreal	PQ	0	0	0	0	0	0	0	0	0	0	0	0	130	23	130	23	153
Ecole de Technologie Superieure	PQ	0	0	0	0	0	0	0	0	0	0	0	0	54	1	54	1	55
University of Ottawa, Faculty of Engineering	ON	0	0	0	0	0	0	0	0	0	0	11	3	71	6	82	9	91
University of Waterloo	ON	0	0	0	0	0	0	0	0	0	0	0	0	190	20	190	20	210
Totals:		0	0	0	0	0	0	0	0	0	0	21	4	595	72	616	76	692

SOU-WYO

COMPUTER ENGINEERING

INSTITUTION		AFRICAN AMERICAN		ASIAN AMERICAN		HISPANIC		NATIVE AMERICAN		CAUCASIAN		FOREIGN		OTHER		TOTAL BY GENDER		TOTAL DEGREES
		M	F	M	F	M	F	M	F	M	F	M	F	M	F	M	F	
Alabama A&M University	AL	21	19	0	0	0	0	0	0	0	0	0	0	0	0	21	19	40
The University of Alabama	AL	3	1	0	0	0	0	0	1	8	6	1	0	0	0	12	8	20
Arizona State University	AZ	0	0	6	3	4	1	1	0	62	2	15	0	3	2	91	8	99
University of Arkansas	AR	0	0	0	0	0	0	0	0	15	2	1	0	1	0	17	2	19
University of Arkansas at Little Rock	AR	0	0	0	0	0	1	0	0	4	0	1	0	0	0	5	1	6
Auburn University	AL	5	7	2	0	0	0	0	0	39	2	1	0	1	0	48	9	57
Baylor University	TX	2	0	2	0	3	0	0	0	24	4	1	0	0	0	30	4	34
Boise State University	ID	0	0	1	1	0	0	0	0	14	0	0	0	2	0	17	1	18
University of Bridgeport	CT	0	0	0	0	0	0	0	0	0	0	1	0	1	0	2	0	2
Bucknell University	PA	0	0	3	0	0	0	0	0	8	2	0	0	0	0	11	2	13
California Institute of Technology	CA	0	0	2	0	4	0	0	0	10	0	1	1	0	0	17	1	18
California Polytechnic State University	CA	1	0	14	11	4	0	0	0	49	1	3	0	12	1	83	13	96
California State University, Fresno	CA	1	0	3	1	1	1	0	0	11	0	5	0	0	0	21	2	23
California State University, Fullerton	CA	3	1	23	6	5	1	2	0	23	3	9	1	10	2	75	14	89
California State University, Long Beach	CA	3	1	29	8	3	2	0	0	32	3	9	5	0	0	76	19	95
California State University, Los Angeles	CA	1	0	8	0	5	1	0	0	4	0	5	1	3	0	26	2	28
California State University, Northridge	CA	6	0	28	4	12	1	0	0	34	8	5	0	12	0	97	13	110
California State University, Sacramento	CA	3	0	18	8	10	0	1	0	17	4	8	1	10	3	67	16	83
University of California, Berkeley	CA	0	0	42	7	0	0	0	0	17	2	8	0	8	2	75	11	86
University of California, Davis	CA	0	0	32	4	3	0	0	0	18	0	5	0	2	1	60	5	65
University of California, Los Angeles	CA	0	0	18	7	4	0	0	0	12	4	3	7	6	0	43	18	61
University of California, Riverside	CA	6	2	30	6	7	0	0	0	30	2	0	0	6	0	79	10	89
University of California, San Diego	CA	0	0	91	14	4	1	0	0	48	3	27	11	12	0	182	29	211
University of California, Santa Barbara	CA	1	0	7	6	3	0	0	0	25	5	4	1	9	1	49	13	62
University of California-Santa Cruz	CA	1	0	9	2	5	0	0	0	29	1	1	0	6	0	51	3	54
Case Western Reserve University	OH	0	0	1	0	0	0	0	0	27	2	1	0	0	1	29	3	32
The Catholic University of America	DC	1	0	0	0	0	0	0	0	4	0	0	0	0	0	5	0	5
Cedarville University	OH	0	0	0	0	0	0	0	0	0	0	0	0	5	2	5	2	7
University of Central Florida	FL	8	1	8	5	20	0	0	0	132	10	12	2	11	1	191	19	210
University of Cincinnati	OH	1	0	3	0	0	0	0	1	14	1	0	0	0	0	18	2	20
Clemson University	SC	2	0	3	0	0	0	0	0	30	3	0	0	6	1	41	4	45
Colorado School of Mines	CO	0	0	4	1	2	1	0	0	27	10	0	0	0	0	33	12	45
University of Colorado at Boulder	CO	0	0	13	4	1	0	0	0	60	3	4	1	0	0	78	8	86
University of Colorado at Colorado Springs	CO	2	0	5	3	0	0	0	0	18	6	1	0	0	0	26	9	35
University of Colorado at Denver	CO	1	0	5	1	3	0	0	0	14	1	4	0	0	0	27	2	29
Columbia University	NY	0	0	16	2	0	0	0	0	11	1	0	0	2	1	29	4	33
University of Connecticut	CT	1	2	5	8	3	0	0	0	48	5	1	0	1	0	59	15	74
Cornell University	NY	0	0	17	1	1	0	0	0	40	4	7	2	3	0	68	7	75
University of Detroit Mercy	MI	1	2	0	0	0	0	0	0	2	0	0	0	0	0	3	2	5
University of the District of Columbia	DC	7	1	4	0	0	0	0	0	4	1	3	1	0	0	18	3	21
Drexel University	PA	2	1	13	4	1	1	0	0	48	4	7	1	7	1	78	12	90
Embry Riddle Aeronautical Univ., Daytona Beach	FL	0	0	0	0	0	0	0	0	5	0	4	0	0	0	9	0	9
University of Evansville	IN	0	0	0	0	0	0	0	0	0	0	0	0	1	1	1	1	2
Florida Atlantic University	FL	9	2	7	0	8	0	0	0	27	3	9	6	0	0	60	11	71
Florida Institute of Technology	FL	2	0	1	0	0	0	0	0	20	1	13	3	6	0	42	4	46

COMPUTER SCIENCE (INSIDE ENGR.)   ALA-FLO

INSTITUTION		AFRICAN AMERICAN		ASIAN AMERICAN		HISPANIC		NATIVE AMERICAN		CAUCASIAN		FOREIGN		OTHER		TOTAL BY GENDER		TOTAL DEGREES
		M	F	M	F	M	F	M	F	M	F	M	F	M	F	M	F	
Florida International University	FL	8	4	8	2	60	13	0	0	21	4	23	7	0	0	120	30	150
Gannon University	PA	0	0	0	0	0	0	0	0	4	2	0	0	0	0	4	2	6
George Mason University	VA	1	0	24	8	3	1	0	1	38	4	6	8	7	1	79	23	102
The George Washington University	DC	1	1	1	1	0	0	0	0	19	3	2	0	2	1	25	6	31
Harvard University	MA	1	0	5	2	1	0	0	0	14	1	2	1	0	0	23	4	27
Howard University	DC	27	7	0	0	0	0	0	0	0	0	0	0	0	0	27	7	34
University of Idaho	ID	0	0	3	2	1	0	0	0	26	1	0	0	5	0	35	3	38
Idaho State University	ID	0	0	0	0	0	0	0	0	2	0	1	0	0	0	3	0	3
University of Illinois at Chicago	IL	0	0	5	1	2	1	1	0	15	0	0	0	3	1	26	3	29
University of Illinois at Urbana-Champaign	IL	4	0	41	7	3	0	0	0	101	8	12	5	1	1	162	21	183
The Johns Hopkins University	MD	1	0	5	1	0	0	0	0	24	2	1	0	0	0	31	3	34
University of Kansas	KS	0	0	1	0	0	0	0	0	29	0	4	5	0	0	34	5	39
Kansas State University	KS	1	0	0	0	3	0	0	0	28	3	1	0	1	0	34	3	37
University of Kentucky	KY	0	1	3	3	1	0	0	0	35	1	1	0	1	0	41	5	46
Lehigh University	PA	0	0	4	0	0	0	0	0	0	0	0	2	39	3	43	5	48
Louisiana Tech University	LA	1	2	0	0	0	0	0	0	10	2	4	1	0	0	15	5	20
University of Louisville	KY	1	0	5	2	1	0	0	0	22	1	1	1	0	0	30	4	34
University of Maryland, Baltimore County	MD	7	2	19	3	5	1	0	0	63	10	4	1	4	0	102	17	119
University of Massachusetts Dartmouth	MA	1	0	0	0	0	0	0	0	28	1	1	0	3	1	33	2	35
Miami University	OH	0	0	1	0	0	0	0	0	24	3	1	0	3	0	29	3	32
University of Michigan	MI	2	1	10	1	3	0	1	0	36	2	8	2	0	0	60	6	66
Michigan State University	MI	1	0	6	3	1	0	0	0	55	3	6	0	0	0	69	6	75
University of Michigan, Dearborn	MI	0	1	2	5	0	0	0	0	38	7	3	0	0	0	43	13	56
University of Minnesota, Duluth	MN	0	0	0	0	0	0	0	0	20	0	3	1	0	0	23	1	24
University of Minnesota - Twin Cities	MN	2	0	10	1	1	0	0	0	89	9	1	1	0	0	103	11	114
The University of Mississippi	MS	2	1	1	0	0	0	0	0	5	0	0	0	0	0	8	1	9
Mississippi State University	MS	3	3	0	0	0	0	1	0	35	2	0	0	0	0	39	5	44
University of Missouri-Columbia	MO	0	1	2	0	0	0	0	0	31	0	4	0	0	0	37	1	38
University of Missouri - Kansas City	MO	3	0	2	0	1	1	0	0	12	8	9	7	0	0	27	16	43
Montana State University	MT	0	0	0	0	1	0	1	0	32	1	2	0	2	0	38	1	39
University of Nebraska, Lincoln	NE	0	0	0	0	0	0	0	0	20	2	2	0	0	0	22	2	24
University of Nevada, Las Vegas	NV	1	0	12	3	3	0	0	0	27	2	1	2	8	2	52	9	61
University of Nevada, Reno	NV	1	0	5	2	1	0	1	0	18	1	1	0	2	0	29	3	32
University of New Hampshire	NH	0	0	1	0	0	0	0	0	25	2	1	0	0	0	27	2	29
University of New Haven	CT	0	0	0	0	0	0	0	0	0	0	3	0	3	1	6	1	7
The University of New Mexico	NM	0	0	0	1	5	2	0	0	9	1	3	0	0	0	17	4	21
New York Institute of Technology	NY	0	0	0	0	0	0	0	0	0	0	0	0	66	21	66	21	87
City College of the City University of New York	NY	3	2	5	2	7	0	0	0	0	0	3	2	26	2	44	8	52
The State University of New York at Binghamton	NY	0	0	5	1	10	0	0	0	38	2	3	1	20	1	76	5	81
State University of New York at Buffalo	NY	1	1	1	1	1	0	0	0	33	2	21	0	2	1	59	5	64
Stony Brook University	NY	2	0	53	16	3	0	0	0	65	9	16	5	0	0	139	30	169
North Carolina A & T State University	NC	15	7	2	0	0	0	0	0	2	0	0	0	0	0	19	7	26
North Carolina State University	NC	7	2	12	3	0	0	1	0	101	5	1	1	0	0	122	11	133
University of North Texas	TX	8	1	3	0	13	4	5	1	96	6	20	4	1	0	146	16	162
Northern Arizona University	AZ	0	0	1	0	2	0	0	1	14	1	0	0	0	0	17	2	19

COMPUTER SCIENCE (INSIDE ENGR.)   FLO-NOR

BACHELOR'S DEGREES AWARDED IN COMPUTER SCIENCE (INSIDE ENGINEERING), 2005-2006

INSTITUTION		AFRICAN AMERICAN		ASIAN AMERICAN		HISPANIC		NATIVE AMERICAN		CAUCASIAN		FOREIGN		OTHER		TOTAL BY GENDER		TOTAL DEGREES
		M	F	M	F	M	F	M	F	M	F	M	F	M	F	M	F	
Northwestern University	IL	1	0	5	2	0	0	0	0	9	0	2	0	1	0	18	2	20
University of Notre Dame	IN	0	0	1	0	0	0	0	0	22	1	0	1	0	0	23	2	25
Oakland University	MI	0	1	2	1	0	0	0	0	22	4	2	1	0	0	26	7	33
Ohio Northern University	OH	0	0	0	0	0	0	0	0	9	0	0	0	0	0	9	0	9
The Ohio State University	OH	1	0	8	0	1	0	0	0	47	3	16	6	0	0	73	9	82
Ohio University	OH	2	0	0	0	0	0	0	0	12	0	0	0	1	0	15	0	15
University of Oklahoma	OK	0	0	2	1	0	0	3	0	14	1	0	0	0	0	19	2	21
Oklahoma Christian University	OK	0	0	0	0	0	0	0	0	6	0	0	0	0	0	6	0	6
Oregon State University	OR	0	0	6	1	1	0	0	0	67	10	0	3	9	2	83	16	99
University of the Pacific	CA	0	0	2	0	3	0	0	0	4	0	0	0	1	0	10	0	10
University of Pennsylvania	PA	1	0	8	4	4	1	0	0	32	6	6	3	6	1	57	15	72
Polytechnic University	NY	3	1	17	9	4	0	0	0	31	5	1	0	3	0	59	15	74
University of Portland	OR	0	0	0	1	0	0	0	0	8	2	0	0	0	0	8	2	10
Portland State University	OR	0	0	9	2	0	1	0	0	38	2	5	2	1	0	53	7	60
Prairie View A&M University	TX	2	1	0	0	1	0	0	0	1	0	0	0	0	0	4	1	5
Princeton University	NJ	0	0	4	2	2	0	0	0	6	0	0	0	0	0	12	2	14
William Marsh Rice University	TX	0	0	1	0	4	1	0	0	15	1	1	0	0	0	21	2	23
Roger Williams University	RI	0	0	0	0	0	0	0	0	3	0	0	0	0	0	3	0	3
Rose-Hulman Institute of Technology	IN	0	0	2	0	2	0	0	0	40	3	0	0	0	0	44	3	47
Seattle University	WA	0	1	4	5	1	1	0	0	9	2	6	2	2	0	22	11	33
University of South Carolina	SC	4	2	4	0	3	0	0	0	26	3	5	1	2	0	44	6	50
South Dakota School of Mines and Technology	SD	0	0	2	1	0	0	0	0	15	2	0	0	0	0	17	3	20
South Dakota State University	SD	0	0	0	0	0	0	0	0	10	0	0	0	0	0	10	0	10
University of South Florida	FL	0	0	4	3	2	1	0	0	20	1	2	0	2	0	30	5	35
University of Southern California	CA	6	1	22	6	5	1	0	0	45	5	9	5	2	0	89	18	107
Southern Illinois University Edwardsville	IL	0	0	3	1	2	0	0	0	35	3	0	0	0	0	40	4	44
Southern Methodist University	TX	0	0	2	1	1	0	0	0	7	1	0	0	0	0	10	2	12
Stanford University	CA	5	2	13	8	5	0	0	0	31	1	10	3	4	0	68	14	82
Syracuse University	NY	3	2	2	0	2	0	0	0	21	2	3	0	0	0	31	4	35
Tennessee State University	TN	16	11	0	1	0	0	0	0	1	1	0	1	0	0	17	14	31
University of Tennessee, Chattanooga	TN	0	0	0	0	1	0	0	0	18	1	1	0	0	0	20	1	21
Texas A&M University	TX	0	0	8	2	8	0	0	0	88	6	10	2	0	0	114	10	124
Texas A&M University - Kingsville	TX	0	0	0	0	2	0	0	0	0	0	0	0	0	0	2	0	2
Texas Tech University	TX	0	0	2	0	4	1	0	0	28	3	3	0	0	0	37	4	41
The University of Texas at Arlington	TX	5	0	10	2	4	0	1	0	32	4	27	1	0	0	79	7	86
The University of Texas at Dallas	TX	4	2	25	9	7	2	1	0	94	13	19	5	0	0	150	31	181
University of Texas at El Paso	TX	0	0	1	0	22	6	0	0	2	0	18	3	0	0	43	9	52
The University of Texas at Tyler	TX	1	0	2	0	2	0	0	0	19	1	2	0	0	1	26	2	28
Tufts University	MA	0	0	1	0	0	0	0	0	0	0	0	0	7	1	8	1	9
Tulane University	LA	0	0	2	1	0	0	0	0	0	0	0	0	9	0	11	1	12
University of Tulsa	OK	0	0	0	0	0	0	1	0	18	3	0	0	1	0	21	3	24
Union College	NY	0	0	0	1	1	0	0	0	3	0	0	0	0	0	4	1	5
U.S. Air Force Academy	CO	1	0	2	0	2	0	0	0	0	0	0	0	6	0	11	0	11
University of Utah	UT	0	0	2	1	1	0	1	0	49	5	9	1	0	0	62	7	69
Vanderbilt University	TN	1	1	2	0	1	0	0	0	19	2	2	0	2	0	27	3	30

COMPUTER SCIENCE (INSIDE ENGR.)　　　　NOR-VAN

Bachelor's Degrees Awarded in Computer Science (Inside Engineering), 2005-2006

VER-WYO

Institution		African American		Asian American		Hispanic		Native American		Caucasian		Foreign		Other		Total by Gender		Total Degrees
		M	F	M	F	M	F	M	F	M	F	M	F	M	F	M	F	
University of Vermont	VT	0	0	1	0	0	0	0	0	11	1	0	0	0	0	12	1	13
University of Virginia	VA	2	0	15	3	1	0	0	0	23	5	1	0	2	0	44	8	52
Virginia Commonwealth University	VA	0	4	0	3	0	0	0	0	26	5	0	0	0	0	26	12	38
Virginia Polytechnic Institute and State University	VA	8	0	24	2	2	0	0	0	98	3	10	1	7	0	149	6	155
University of Washington	WA	0	0	10	5	0	1	0	0	30	5	10	1	15	2	65	14	79
Washington State University	WA	0	0	1	3	1	0	0	0	23	4	1	3	5	0	31	10	41
Washington University	MO	2	1	3	0	1	0	0	0	23	3	2	1	1	0	32	5	37
West Virginia University Institute of Technology	WV	0	0	1	0	0	0	0	0	9	1	0	0	0	0	10	1	11
Western Michigan University	MI	0	0	0	0	0	0	0	0	30	0	9	3	0	0	39	3	42
University of Wisconsin, Milwaukee	WI	0	0	2	0	2	0	0	0	46	7	5	2	0	0	55	9	64
University of Wisconsin, Platteville	WI	0	0	1	1	0	0	0	0	12	1	0	0	0	0	13	2	15
Wright State University	OH	0	0	1	0	0	0	0	0	31	3	1	0	1	0	34	3	37
University of Wyoming	WY	0	0	0	0	2	0	0	0	18	2	1	0	1	0	22	2	24
Totals:		265	106	970	270	355	50	22	5	3,724	357	555	152	436	63	6,327	1,003	7,330
CANADIAN INSTITUTIONS:																		
University of Calgary	AB	0	0	0	0	0	0	0	0	0	0	0	0	19	2	19	2	21
University of Ottawa, Faculty of Engineering	ON	0	0	0	0	0	0	0	0	0	0	6	5	60	16	66	21	87
Totals:		0	0	0	0	0	0	0	0	0	0	6	5	79	18	85	23	108

COMPUTER SCIENCE (INSIDE ENGR.)

BACHELOR'S DEGREES AWARDED IN COMPUTER SCIENCE (OUTSIDE ENGINEERING), 2005-2006

INSTITUTION		AFRICAN AMERICAN M	F	ASIAN AMERICAN M	F	HISPANIC M	F	NATIVE AMERICAN M	F	CAUCASIAN M	F	FOREIGN M	F	OTHER M	F	TOTAL BY GENDER M	F	TOTAL DEGREES
University of Alaska Fairbanks	AK	0	0	5	0	0	0	0	0	6	0	0	0	0	0	11	0	11
The University of Arizona	AZ	0	0	7	1	9	1	0	0	48	7	10	2	0	0	74	11	85
University of Arkansas	AR	0	0	0	0	0	0	0	0	2	1	0	0	1	0	3	1	4
Arkansas Tech University	AR	0	0	1	0	0	0	0	0	9	2	1	0	0	0	11	2	13
Brigham Young University	UT	0	0	0	0	4	0	1	1	0	0	10	1	108	5	123	7	130
University of California, Berkeley	CA	0	0	38	9	0	0	0	0	32	2	10	2	6	5	86	18	104
University of California, Davis	CA	0	0	27	8	5	0	0	0	21	3	1	0	3	0	57	11	68
University of California, Irvine	CA	0	0	0	0	0	0	0	0	0	0	0	0	242	47	242	47	289
Carnegie Mellon University	PA	2	2	29	7	8	0	0	0	45	9	22	3	9	3	115	24	139
Clarkson University	NY	0	0	0	0	0	0	0	0	18	0	1	0	0	0	19	0	19
Dartmouth College	NH	0	0	1	0	0	0	0	0	8	3	3	0	1	0	13	3	16
Embry Riddle Aeronautical University, Prescott	AZ	0	0	0	0	0	0	0	0	4	4	0	0	0	0	4	4	8
University of Florida	FL	2	1	3	0	6	3	0	0	48	3	3	0	0	0	62	7	69
FAMU-FSU College of Engineering	FL	1	2	4	1	5	1	0	0	45	6	0	0	0	0	55	10	65
Georgia Institute of Technology	GA	7	1	30	2	5	1	0	0	162	15	19	6	3	1	226	26	252
Grove City College	PA	0	0	0	0	0	0	0	0	9	0	0	0	0	0	9	0	9
University of Houston, Cullen School of Engineering	TX	0	0	15	2	4	0	0	0	8	3	7	0	2	0	36	5	41
Illinois Institute of Technology	IL	1	0	5	3	1	0	0	0	19	1	14	5	3	0	43	9	52
Indiana University-Purdue University Fort Wayne	IN	0	0	0	0	0	0	0	0	9	2	0	0	1	1	10	3	13
The University of Iowa	IA	3	0	3	0	1	0	1	1	31	5	1	0	4	1	44	7	51
Lamar University	TX	0	0	0	0	0	0	6	0	0	0	1	0	0	0	7	0	7
LeTourneau University	TX	0	0	0	0	0	0	0	0	4	1	0	0	0	0	4	1	5
Louisiana State University	LA	3	0	1	1	0	0	0	0	30	3	3	3	3	0	40	3	47
University of Louisiana at Lafayette	LA	0	0	1	0	0	0	0	0	19	2	0	0	0	0	20	2	22
Loyola College in Maryland	MD	0	1	1	0	1	0	0	0	6	3	0	0	0	0	8	4	12
Marquette University	WI	0	0	0	0	0	0	0	0	9	1	1	0	0	0	10	1	11
University of Maryland, College Park	MD	13	4	41	8	7	0	1	0	87	5	15	3	11	2	175	22	197
University of Massachusetts Amherst	MA	3	0	9	0	2	0	0	0	51	1	5	1	5	0	75	2	77
University of Massachusetts Lowell	MA	0	0	0	0	0	0	0	0	0	1	0	0	0	0	0	1	1
The University of Memphis	TN	1	1	1	1	1	0	0	0	5	0	3	1	0	0	11	3	14
University of Michigan	MI	1	1	9	0	2	0	1	0	22	2	3	1	2	0	40	4	44
Michigan Technological University	MI	0	0	1	0	0	0	0	0	36	3	5	0	3	0	45	3	48
Montana Tech of the University of Montana	MT	0	0	0	0	0	0	0	0	2	0	1	0	0	0	3	0	3
University of Nebraska, Lincoln	NE	1	0	0	2	0	0	0	0	26	4	5	0	0	0	32	6	38
New Jersey Institute of Technology	NJ	3	0	23	9	6	2	0	0	36	0	5	1	10	4	83	16	99
Norwich University	VT	0	0	0	0	0	0	0	0	1	0	0	0	0	0	1	0	1
University of Pittsburgh	PA	3	0	5	1	2	0	0	0	56	2	0	0	3	0	69	3	72
Purdue University, Calumet	IN	0	0	0	0	0	0	0	0	2	0	0	0	0	0	2	0	2
Rensselaer Polytechnic Institute	NY	2	0	13	3	3	1	0	0	92	5	4	0	1	1	115	10	125
University of Rochester	NY	0	0	5	0	1	0	0	0	18	0	0	0	2	1	26	1	27
Rochester Institute of Technology	NY	3	0	11	1	3	1	1	0	105	3	5	3	13	3	141	11	152
Saint Cloud State University	MN	0	0	0	0	0	0	0	0	11	2	5	1	3	0	19	3	22
Santa Clara University	CA	1	0	3	3	1	0	0	0	11	0	0	0	2	0	18	3	21
University of South Alabama	AL	2	4	1	1	0	0	0	0	23	5	4	2	0	0	30	12	42
Southern Illinois University Carbondale	IL	1	0	1	0	0	0	0	0	13	0	3	0	0	0	18	0	18

COMPUTER SCIENCE (OUTSIDE ENGR.)   ALA-SOU

BACHELOR'S DEGREES AWARDED IN COMPUTER SCIENCE (OUTSIDE ENGINEERING), 2005-2006

INSTITUTION		AFRICAN AMERICAN		ASIAN AMERICAN		HISPANIC		NATIVE AMERICAN		CAUCASIAN		FOREIGN		OTHER		TOTAL BY GENDER		TOTAL DEGREES
		M	F	M	F	M	F	M	F	M	F	M	F	M	F	M	F	
Stevens Institute of Technology	NJ	1	0	9	1	1	0	0	0	19	2	3	0	3	0	36	3	39
Tennessee Technological University	TN	0	0	0	0	0	0	0	0	14	0	0	0	0	0	14	0	14
University of Tennessee, Knoxville	TN	2	0	0	0	1	0	0	0	16	2	0	0	0	0	19	2	21
University of Texas at San Antonio	TX	5	0	4	0	14	4	0	0	24	3	3	1	0	0	50	8	58
Tri-State University	IN	0	0	0	0	0	0	0	0	5	0	0	0	0	1	5	1	6
Valparaiso University	IN	0	0	1	0	0	0	0	0	8	0	0	0	0	0	9	0	9
University of Vermont	VT	0	0	0	0	0	0	0	0	6	1	0	0	1	0	7	1	8
Wentworth Institute of Technology	MA	1	0	4	1	3	1	1	0	44	5	4	0	4	0	61	7	68
West Virginia University	WV	0	0	1	0	0	0	0	0	27	2	2	0	1	1	31	3	34
Worcester Polytechnic Institute	MA	0	0	7	0	0	0	1	0	67	3	4	0	7	0	86	3	89
Totals:		62	17	319	64	95	15	13	2	1,421	127	186	37	457	76	2,553	338	2,891
CANADIAN INSTITUTIONS:																		
Concordia University, Faculty of Engr. and Comp. Sci.	PQ	0	0	0	0	0	0	0	0	0	0	14	3	112	29	126	32	158
Totals:		0	0	0	0	0	0	0	0	0	0	14	3	112	29	126	32	158

STE-WOR

COMPUTER SCIENCE (OUTSIDE ENGR.)

BACHELOR'S DEGREES AWARDED IN ELECTRICAL ENGINEERING, 2005-2006

INSTITUTION		AFRICAN AMERICAN		ASIAN AMERICAN		HISPANIC		NATIVE AMERICAN		CAUCASIAN		FOREIGN		OTHER		TOTAL BY GENDER		TOTAL DEGREES
		M	F	M	F	M	F	M	F	M	F	M	F	M	F	M	F	
Alabama A&M University	AL	15	5	0	0	0	0	0	0	0	0	0	0	0	0	15	5	20
University of Alabama at Birmingham	AL	4	0	3	1	0	0	0	0	9	1	6	2	0	0	22	4	26
The University of Alabama in Huntsville	AL	5	3	3	0	1	0	0	1	40	8	1	2	1	0	51	14	65
The University of Alabama	AL	6	1	2	0	0	0	1	0	28	4	1	0	0	0	38	5	43
Alfred University, NY State College of Ceramics	NY	1	0	0	1	2	0	0	0	6	3	0	0	2	0	11	4	15
The University of Arizona	AZ	1	1	10	5	4	1	0	0	35	2	20	2	0	0	70	11	81
Arizona State University	AZ	3	0	14	10	9	0	2	0	51	3	13	4	12	1	104	18	122
University of Arkansas	AR	1	1	0	0	0	0	1	0	25	1	2	1	1	0	30	3	33
Arkansas Tech University	AR	1	0	0	0	0	0	0	0	11	0	1	0	0	0	13	0	13
Auburn University	AL	3	3	1	0	1	1	0	0	58	7	5	0	0	0	68	11	79
Boise State University	ID	0	0	2	0	0	0	0	0	24	1	5	0	2	0	33	1	34
Boston University	MA	1	0	11	4	2	0	0	0	36	6	2	1	0	0	52	11	63
Bradley University	IL	2	0	1	0	0	0	0	0	20	4	2	0	0	0	25	4	29
Brown University	RI	0	0	2	1	0	1	0	0	8	1	0	2	0	0	10	5	15
Bucknell University	PA	0	0	1	1	0	0	1	0	21	2	3	0	0	0	26	3	29
California Institute of Technology	CA	0	0	13	3	0	0	0	0	6	1	3	2	0	0	23	6	29
California Polytechnic State University	CA	5	1	57	3	10	2	1	0	71	4	1	1	17	3	162	14	176
California State Polytechnic University, Pomona	CA	9	2	102	24	29	6	0	0	29	3	0	0	18	3	187	38	225
California State University, Chico	CA	0	0	2	0	1	0	1	0	4	1	3	2	1	0	12	3	15
California State University, Fresno	CA	0	0	0	1	5	0	0	0	13	0	7	1	0	0	25	2	27
California State University, Fullerton	CA	0	0	11	2	3	1	0	0	3	0	4	0	3	0	24	3	27
California State University, Long Beach	CA	1	0	10	4	5	1	0	0	17	2	28	2	0	0	61	9	70
California State University, Los Angeles	CA	3	1	2	0	11	1	1	0	5	1	9	3	3	0	34	6	40
California State University, Northridge	CA	3	0	9	1	17	3	0	0	11	1	2	0	4	1	46	6	52
California State University, Sacramento	CA	0	0	20	6	5	1	0	0	25	2	5	1	4	3	59	13	72
University of California, Davis	CA	0	0	49	12	4	0	1	0	15	2	3	2	1	0	73	16	89
University of California, Irvine	CA	0	0	0	0	0	0	0	0	0	0	0	0	109	16	109	16	125
University of California, Los Angeles	CA	2	0	63	12	5	0	1	0	19	1	14	4	21	4	125	21	146
University of California, Riverside	CA	2	0	23	3	9	1	0	0	10	0	0	0	4	0	48	4	52
University of California, San Diego	CA	4	1	111	22	8	1	1	0	39	5	21	6	20	4	204	39	243
University of California, Santa Barbara	CA	1	0	11	5	3	0	1	0	23	2	3	1	4	1	46	9	55
University of California-Santa Cruz	CA	0	0	7	2	2	0	0	0	7	1	1	1	1	0	18	4	22
Capitol College	MD	0	0	0	0	0	0	0	0	0	0	0	0	12	2	12	2	14
Case Western Reserve University	OH	0	0	3	0	0	0	0	0	30	0	3	0	1	0	37	0	37
The Catholic University of America	DC	0	0	0	0	0	0	0	0	4	1	2	0	1	0	7	1	8
Cedarville University	OH	0	0	0	0	0	0	0	0	0	0	0	0	10	1	10	1	11
University of Central Florida	FL	8	1	15	6	11	1	1	0	43	2	6	2	3	0	87	12	99
The Citadel	SC	3	0	1	0	2	1	0	0	20	1	2	0	0	0	27	1	28
Clarkson University	NY	1	0	0	1	0	0	0	0	43	4	2	0	0	0	44	5	49
Clemson University	SC	6	3	4	0	1	0	0	0	38	3	3	1	3	2	55	9	64
Cleveland State University	OH	5	0	0	0	0	0	0	0	22	1	1	0	0	0	28	1	29
Colorado Technical University	CO	1	0	0	0	0	0	0	0	0	0	2	0	21	4	24	4	28
University of Colorado at Boulder	CO	3	0	6	2	2	1	0	0	24	3	1	0	0	0	36	6	42
University of Colorado at Colorado Springs	CO	1	0	4	2	3	2	0	0	12	0	0	0	1	0	21	4	25
University of Colorado at Denver	CO	2	0	5	1	0	1	0	0	19	1	7	2	5	1	38	6	44

ELECTRICAL ENGINEERING   ALA-COL

INSTITUTION		AFRICAN AMERICAN		ASIAN AMERICAN		HISPANIC		NATIVE AMERICAN		CAUCASIAN		FOREIGN		OTHER		TOTAL BY GENDER		TOTAL DEGREES
		M	F	M	F	M	F	M	F	M	F	M	F	M	F	M	F	
Columbia University	NY	1	0	8	2	2	0	0	0	4	1	4	1	2	0	21	4	25
University of Connecticut	CT	4	0	2	0	1	0	0	0	16	0	2	0	1	0	26	0	26
The Cooper Union	NY	1	0	7	3	1	0	0	0	9	0	7	0	0	0	25	3	28
University of Dayton	OH	2	0	0	0	2	0	0	0	0	0	0	0	20	4	24	4	28
University of Delaware	DE	1	0	1	1	0	0	0	0	11	2	0	0	0	0	13	3	16
University of Denver	CO	0	0	0	1	1	1	0	0	3	1	2	0	0	0	7	3	10
University of Detroit Mercy	MI	2	1	0	0	0	0	0	0	4	2	1	0	0	0	7	3	10
University of the District of Columbia	DC	3	1	3	0	0	0	0	0	3	0	1	1	0	0	10	2	12
Drexel University	PA	11	0	18	5	1	0	0	0	28	3	10	0	6	0	74	8	82
Duke University Pratt School of Engineering	NC	0	0	0	0	0	0	0	0	0	0	0	0	15	6	15	6	21
Embry Riddle Aeronautical University, Prescott	AZ	0	0	0	0	0	0	0	0	9	1	0	0	1	0	10	1	11
University of Evansville	IN	0	0	0	0	0	0	0	0	0	0	0	0	6	2	6	2	8
Fairfield University	CT	1	0	2	0	0	0	0	0	2	2	0	0	0	0	5	2	7
Fairleigh Dickinson University	NJ	0	0	1	0	0	0	0	0	8	1	0	0	0	0	8	1	9
University of Florida	FL	6	1	20	3	26	3	1	0	108	5	3	0	0	0	164	12	176
Florida Atlantic University	FL	3	2	6	1	8	1	0	0	15	3	5	0	0	0	37	7	44
Florida Institute of Technology	FL	1	0	2	2	0	0	0	0	2	0	10	2	3	1	18	5	23
Florida International University	FL	10	1	5	1	42	3	1	0	9	0	6	1	1	0	74	6	80
FAMU-FSU College of Engineering	FL	33	9	1	0	4	1	0	0	18	3	7	2	0	0	63	15	78
Gannon University	PA	0	0	0	0	0	0	1	0	11	1	2	0	0	0	13	1	14
George Mason University	VA	5	2	13	3	3	0	0	0	13	2	11	1	3	1	48	9	57
The George Washington University	DC	0	0	0	0	0	0	0	0	1	1	1	3	1	0	3	4	7
Georgia Institute of Technology	GA	33	6	50	11	8	1	0	0	109	13	24	5	2	0	226	36	262
Gonzaga University	WA	0	0	0	0	1	0	0	0	9	0	0	0	0	0	10	0	10
Grand Valley State University	MI	0	0	0	0	0	0	0	0	11	2	0	0	0	0	11	2	13
Grove City College	PA	0	0	0	0	0	0	0	0	10	3	0	0	0	0	10	3	13
University of Hartford	CT	0	0	1	0	0	0	0	0	5	0	1	1	0	0	7	1	8
University of Hawaii at Manoa	HI	0	0	27	15	1	0	0	0	5	0	0	0	14	0	47	15	62
Henry Cogswell College	WA	0	0	2	1	0	0	0	0	5	0	0	0	0	0	7	1	8
Hofstra University	NY	1	0	0	0	0	0	0	0	3	1	1	0	1	0	6	1	7
University of Houston, Cullen School of Engineering	TX	4	1	27	4	10	1	0	0	21	1	12	2	2	1	76	10	86
University of Idaho	ID	0	0	4	1	1	0	0	0	38	8	0	0	5	1	48	10	58
Idaho State University	ID	0	0	0	0	0	0	0	0	6	0	2	0	0	0	8	0	8
Illinois Institute of Technology	IL	3	1	4	0	3	1	0	0	16	2	19	2	1	0	46	6	52
University of Illinois at Chicago	IL	7	5	23	8	10	3	0	0	26	1	0	0	4	1	70	18	88
University of Illinois at Urbana-Champaign	IL	4	3	62	16	1	1	2	0	72	9	33	13	3	0	177	42	219
Indiana Institute of Technology	IN	0	0	0	0	0	1	0	0	0	0	0	0	2	0	2	1	3
Indiana University Purdue University at Indianapolis	IN	2	2	6	0	1	0	0	0	23	0	2	1	2	0	36	3	39
Indiana University-Purdue University Fort Wayne	IN	0	0	0	1	0	0	0	0	5	1	1	1	0	0	6	3	9
Iowa State University	IA	8	1	14	2	1	1	1	0	55	4	18	3	2	0	99	11	110
John Brown University	AR	0	0	0	0	0	0	0	0	1	0	4	0	0	0	5	0	5
The Johns Hopkins University	MD	0	2	6	1	2	0	0	0	18	3	1	0	0	0	27	6	33
University of Kansas	KS	1	1	0	0	0	0	0	0	16	0	11	6	0	0	28	7	35
Kansas State University	KS	5	0	0	1	1	0	0	0	34	3	2	2	0	0	42	6	48
University of Kentucky	KY	2	0	0	0	0	0	0	0	29	5	2	1	1	1	34	7	41

ELECTRICAL ENGINEERING

COL-KEN

BACHELOR'S DEGREES AWARDED IN ELECTRICAL ENGINEERING, 2005-2006

Institution		African American M	African American F	Asian American M	Asian American F	Hispanic M	Hispanic F	Native American M	Native American F	Caucasian M	Caucasian F	Foreign M	Foreign F	Other M	Other F	Total by Gender M	Total by Gender F	Total Degrees
Kettering University formerly GMI	MI	1	1	7	1	0	0	0	0	53	3	4	1	4	2	69	8	77
Lake Superior State University	MI	0	0	1	0	0	0	0	0	2	0	0	0	0	0	3	0	3
Lamar University	TX	1	0	3	1	0	0	1	0	11	0	2	0	0	0	18	1	19
Lawrence Technological University	MI	4	2	3	0	1	0	0	0	31	5	5	1	5	1	49	9	58
Lehigh University	PA	1	0	5	0	0	1	0	0	0	0	0	0	28	3	34	4	38
Louisiana State University	LA	5	2	6	0	4	2	0	0	44	5	9	1	1	1	69	11	80
Louisiana Tech University	LA	5	1	1	0	0	0	0	0	26	2	5	2	1	0	38	5	43
University of Louisiana at Lafayette	LA	3	0	0	0	0	0	0	0	30	3	8	1	0	0	41	4	45
University of Louisville	KY	5	1	1	1	0	0	0	0	28	7	2	1	0	0	36	10	46
Loyola Marymount University	CA	2	0	6	0	0	0	0	0	10	1	2	1	1	1	21	3	24
University of Maine	ME	0	0	0	1	0	0	0	0	15	1	2	1	0	0	17	3	20
Manhattan College	NY	3	0	0	0	3	0	0	0	12	0	0	0	2	1	20	1	21
Marquette University	WI	0	0	0	0	0	0	0	0	20	6	3	0	0	0	23	6	29
University of Maryland, College Park	MD	28	3	38	16	6	0	0	0	58	5	6	1	10	0	146	25	171
Massachusetts Institute of Technology	MA	2	0	8	12	4	2	0	0	14	4	6	1	4	3	38	22	60
University of Massachusetts Amherst	MA	1	1	7	0	0	0	0	0	21	4	3	0	0	0	32	5	37
University of Massachusetts Dartmouth	MA	3	0	0	0	0	0	0	0	25	1	0	0	1	0	29	1	30
University of Massachusetts Lowell	MA	4	0	2	5	6	1	0	1	16	2	3	0	7	0	38	9	47
McNeese State University	LA	0	0	0	0	0	0	0	0	10	1	2	0	0	0	12	1	13
The University of Memphis	TN	4	1	4	2	0	0	0	0	7	1	0	0	0	0	15	4	19
Mercer University	GA	0	3	1	0	0	0	0	0	11	2	0	0	0	0	12	5	17
Merrimack College	MA	0	0	0	0	0	0	0	0	7	1	0	0	0	0	7	1	8
University of Miami	FL	2	1	0	0	4	1	0	0	11	0	1	0	1	0	19	2	21
Miami University	OH	0	0	0	0	0	0	0	0	1	0	0	0	0	0	1	0	1
University of Michigan	MI	8	5	21	7	4	3	1	0	51	8	28	5	2	0	115	28	143
Michigan State University	MI	6	2	13	3	0	0	0	0	41	6	12	2	0	0	72	13	85
Michigan Technological University	MI	1	0	2	0	0	0	0	0	75	4	14	4	2	0	94	8	102
University of Michigan, Dearborn	MI	2	0	13	10	1	0	0	0	47	10	3	2	0	0	66	22	88
Milwaukee School of Engineering	WI	0	1	2	0	3	0	0	0	29	3	2	0	1	0	37	4	41
Minnesota State University, Mankato	MN	0	0	1	1	0	0	0	0	7	1	8	0	6	0	22	2	24
University of Minnesota -Twin Cities	MN	11	2	17	5	1	1	0	0	76	4	13	0	0	0	118	12	130
The University of Mississippi	MS	1	0	0	0	0	0	0	0	7	1	0	0	0	0	8	1	9
Mississippi State University	MS	2	2	0	0	0	0	0	0	30	1	0	0	0	0	32	3	35
University of Missouri-Columbia	MO	1	0	1	0	1	0	1	0	35	0	2	0	1	0	42	0	42
University of Missouri - Rolla	MO	3	4	2	0	0	0	0	0	45	5	4	1	2	1	56	11	67
Montana State University	MT	0	0	0	0	0	0	1	0	19	2	0	0	2	0	22	2	24
Morgan State University	MD	21	13	2	0	0	0	0	0	0	0	9	1	1	0	33	14	47
University of Nebraska, Lincoln	NE	0	0	1	1	0	0	0	0	54	4	6	0	0	0	61	5	66
University of Nevada, Las Vegas	NV	1	1	2	1	4	2	1	0	5	0	0	1	0	0	13	5	18
University of Nevada, Reno	NV	0	0	6	0	2	0	0	0	16	1	0	0	1	0	25	1	26
University of New Hampshire	NH	0	0	3	0	0	0	0	0	18	1	0	0	0	0	21	1	22
University of New Haven	CT	2	0	0	0	0	0	0	0	0	0	2	0	10	0	14	0	14
New Jersey Institute of Technology	NJ	12	1	15	3	8	1	0	0	19	1	11	1	19	3	84	10	94
The College of New Jersey	NJ	1	0	0	0	0	0	0	0	3	2	0	0	0	0	4	2	6
The University of New Mexico	NM	0	0	1	1	10	6	1	1	18	2	7	1	0	0	37	11	48

ELECTRICAL ENGINEERING

KET-NEW

Bachelor's Degrees Awarded in Electrical Engineering, 2005–2006

Institution	State	African American M	African American F	Asian American M	Asian American F	Hispanic M	Hispanic F	Native American M	Native American F	Caucasian M	Caucasian F	Foreign M	Foreign F	Other M	Other F	Total M	Total F	Total Degrees
New Mexico Institute of Mining & Technology	NM	0	0	2	1	3	1	1	1	19	1	3	0	0	0	28	4	32
New Mexico State University	NM	2	1	1	0	25	5	0	0	18	1	1	0	6	3	53	10	63
University of New Orleans	LA	5	0	4	0	2	0	0	0	13	6	0	0	0	0	24	6	30
City College of the City University of New York	NY	8	0	11	5	10	3	0	0	0	0	9	3	11	1	49	12	61
The State University of New York at Binghamton	NY	2	1	7	1	3	0	0	0	8	0	2	0	8	1	30	3	33
State University of New York at Buffalo	NY	3	0	5	1	2	0	1	0	39	1	26	4	6	1	82	7	89
SUNY, New Paltz	NY	1	0	5	0	5	0	0	0	13	1	4	1	0	0	28	2	30
North Carolina A & T State University	NC	23	4	0	1	0	0	0	0	3	0	1	0	0	0	27	5	32
North Carolina State University	NC	13	4	21	5	4	1	3	0	104	11	1	1	0	0	146	22	168
University of North Carolina, Charlotte	NC	5	0	0	0	2	0	0	0	21	2	4	1	0	0	32	3	35
University of North Dakota	ND	0	0	0	0	0	0	0	0	21	2	0	0	0	0	21	2	23
North Dakota State University	ND	0	1	0	0	0	0	0	0	52	9	0	0	0	0	52	10	62
University of North Florida	FL	0	0	4	0	0	0	0	0	21	4	2	0	0	0	27	4	31
Northeastern University	MA	1	1	8	1	2	0	1	0	41	3	3	2	28	3	84	10	94
Northern Illinois University	IL	3	1	8	1	5	0	0	0	36	2	3	0	1	0	56	4	60
Northwestern University	IL	0	1	4	5	3	0	0	0	12	2	5	2	2	0	26	10	36
Norwich University	VT	0	0	0	0	0	0	0	0	5	2	1	0	0	0	6	2	8
University of Notre Dame	IN	0	0	2	1	2	1	0	0	26	3	2	1	0	0	32	6	38
Oakland University	MI	1	2	2	0	2	0	0	0	29	12	5	0	0	0	39	14	53
Ohio Northern University	OH	0	0	0	0	0	0	0	0	11	6	0	0	0	0	11	6	17
Ohio University	OH	2	1	1	0	0	0	0	0	40	2	0	0	1	0	44	3	47
University of Oklahoma	OK	2	0	8	2	0	0	2	0	15	2	6	1	0	0	33	5	38
Oklahoma Christian University	OK	0	0	0	0	1	0	0	0	7	1	1	0	0	0	9	1	10
Oklahoma State University	OK	2	0	1	1	0	0	0	0	26	3	7	3	0	0	36	7	43
Old Dominion University	VA	4	1	4	2	1	0	0	0	22	4	6	2	3	0	40	9	49
Oregon State University	OR	1	0	3	1	4	1	0	0	40	1	4	0	7	0	59	3	62
University of Pennsylvania	PA	0	0	10	2	0	0	0	0	9	0	6	3	3	0	28	5	33
Penn State Erie, The Behrend College	PA	0	0	0	0	0	0	0	0	17	2	0	0	0	0	17	2	19
The Pennsylvania State University	PA	6	0	17	2	3	0	0	0	137	7	16	1	0	0	179	10	189
University of Pittsburgh	PA	3	0	6	0	0	0	0	0	39	4	2	2	0	0	50	6	56
Polytechnic University	NY	3	3	27	4	2	0	0	0	9	1	8	0	5	0	54	8	62
Polytechnic University of Puerto Rico	PR	0	0	0	0	82	14	0	0	0	0	0	0	0	0	82	14	96
University of Portland	OR	0	0	2	3	1	0	0	0	20	1	0	0	0	0	23	4	27
Portland State University	OR	2	0	4	4	2	0	1	0	34	4	2	0	4	0	49	8	57
Prairie View A&M University	TX	18	11	0	0	0	0	0	0	2	0	3	1	0	0	23	12	35
Princeton University	NJ	0	0	5	0	1	0	0	0	9	2	3	1	0	0	18	3	21
University of Puerto Rico, Mayaguez Campus	PR	0	0	1	0	86	42	0	0	0	0	0	0	0	0	87	42	129
Purdue University, Calumet	IN	4	0	1	0	2	1	0	0	13	1	0	0	9	4	29	6	35
Rensselaer Polytechnic Institute	NY	2	0	24	6	3	1	0	0	52	7	5	5	0	0	86	19	105
University of Rhode Island	RI	0	0	2	0	2	0	0	0	18	5	0	1	4	0	26	6	32
William Marsh Rice University	TX	2	0	6	1	2	0	0	0	12	0	1	0	3	1	26	2	28
Rochester Institute of Technology	NY	4	0	6	1	3	0	0	0	54	5	8	4	3	0	78	10	88
Rose-Hulman Institute of Technology	IN	1	0	2	0	3	0	0	0	39	5	0	0	1	0	46	5	51
Saginaw Valley State University	MI	0	0	0	0	0	0	0	0	15	0	9	1	1	0	25	1	26
Saint Cloud State University	MN	1	0	0	0	0	0	0	0	10	2	7	1	2	0	20	3	23

ELECTRICAL ENGINEERING

NEW-SAI

BACHELOR'S DEGREES AWARDED IN ELECTRICAL ENGINEERING, 2005-2006

INSTITUTION		AFRICAN AMERICAN M	F	ASIAN AMERICAN M	F	HISPANIC M	F	NATIVE AMERICAN M	F	CAUCASIAN M	F	FOREIGN M	F	OTHER M	F	TOTAL BY GENDER M	F	TOTAL DEGREES
Saint Louis University - Parks College	MO	2	0	1	0	0	0	0	0	7	2	0	0	0	0	10	2	12
Saint Mary's University	TX	0	0	0	0	4	1	0	0	1	0	0	0	0	0	5	1	6
University of Saint Thomas	MN	0	0	1	0	0	0	0	0	7	1	0	0	0	0	8	1	9
University of San Diego	CA	1	0	1	0	0	0	0	0	2	0	1	0	0	0	5	0	5
San Diego State University	CA	4	2	24	6	15	3	0	0	21	2	4	0	7	2	75	15	90
San Francisco State University	CA	1	0	18	9	7	1	0	0	15	3	5	2	0	0	46	15	61
San Jose State University	CA	6	0	67	25	9	1	1	0	23	1	14	3	0	0	120	30	150
Santa Clara University	CA	0	0	9	4	0	0	1	0	4	1	0	2	1	0	16	7	23
Seattle University	WA	1	0	5	2	0	0	0	0	6	3	4	0	3	0	19	5	24
Seattle Pacific University	WA	0	0	1	1	0	0	0	0	20	2	0	0	0	0	21	3	24
University of South Carolina	SC	4	0	4	1	0	0	0	0	21	2	3	0	4	0	36	3	39
South Dakota School of Mines and Technology	SD	0	0	0	0	0	0	0	0	16	2	0	0	1	0	17	2	19
South Dakota State University	SD	0	0	1	0	0	0	0	0	24	2	0	0	0	0	25	2	27
University of South Florida	FL	4	0	3	0	4	0	0	0	21	3	0	1	0	0	32	4	36
University of Southern California	CA	5	0	14	3	9	0	0	0	21	2	19	6	2	2	70	13	83
Southern Illinois University Edwardsville	IL	0	1	2	0	1	0	0	0	31	3	0	0	0	0	34	4	38
University of Southern Maine	ME	0	0	0	0	0	0	0	0	12	0	1	0	0	0	13	0	13
Southern Methodist University	TX	2	3	4	3	3	1	0	0	11	2	1	0	0	0	21	9	30
Southern University and A&M College	LA	25	8	0	0	0	0	0	0	0	0	6	1	0	0	31	9	40
Stanford University	CA	5	0	28	7	6	0	1	0	10	0	9	3	0	0	59	10	69
Stevens Institute of Technology	NJ	1	2	5	0	2	0	0	0	14	1	1	0	5	4	28	7	35
Syracuse University	NY	2	0	1	0	0	0	0	0	10	2	0	0	0	0	13	2	15
Tennessee State University	TN	7	10	0	0	0	0	0	0	0	0	0	0	0	0	7	10	17
Tennessee Technological University	TN	0	0	1	0	1	0	0	0	27	1	3	2	0	0	32	3	35
University of Tennessee, Chattanooga	TN	1	0	1	0	0	0	0	0	5	2	1	0	0	0	8	2	10
University of Tennessee, Knoxville	TN	3	1	2	0	13	3	0	0	21	0	2	1	0	0	28	2	30
Texas A&M University	TX	2	0	13	6	13	3	0	0	89	10	31	6	0	1	148	26	174
Texas A&M University - Kingsville	TX	1	0	0	0	14	1	0	0	6	3	0	0	0	0	21	4	25
Texas Tech University	TX	0	0	2	0	9	1	1	0	48	2	5	0	1	0	67	3	70
The University of Texas at Arlington	TX	5	1	2	1	4	0	0	0	17	2	2	0	0	0	30	4	34
The University of Texas at Dallas	TX	6	3	31	8	7	1	1	0	44	8	6	5	1	0	96	25	121
University of Texas at El Paso	TX	0	0	2	1	46	11	0	0	5	2	19	2	0	0	72	16	88
The University of Texas-Pan American	TX	0	0	0	0	19	3	0	0	2	0	5	1	1	0	27	4	31
The University of Texas at Tyler	TX	1	0	0	0	0	0	0	0	1	0	0	0	1	0	3	0	3
The University of Toledo	OH	1	0	2	1	0	0	0	0	34	1	0	1	0	0	37	3	40
Tri-State University	IN	0	0	0	0	0	0	0	0	5	2	0	0	1	0	6	2	8
Tufts University	MA	0	0	4	2	1	1	0	0	0	0	1	0	14	4	20	7	27
Tulane University	LA	3	1	0	0	0	0	0	0	0	0	0	0	7	0	10	1	11
University of Tulsa	OK	0	0	0	0	1	0	2	0	3	1	3	1	0	0	9	2	11
Tuskegee University	AL	15	7	0	0	0	0	0	0	0	0	0	0	4	2	19	9	28
Union College	NY	1	0	0	0	1	0	0	0	11	2	1	0	0	0	14	2	16
U.S. Air Force Academy	CO	1	0	2	0	0	0	0	0	0	0	0	0	15	1	18	1	19
U.S. Coast Guard Academy	CT	0	0	0	0	2	2	0	0	9	2	2	0	0	0	13	4	17
United States Military Academy	NY	0	0	0	0	1	0	0	0	11	0	3	0	0	0	15	0	15
U.S. Naval Academy	MD	2	1	2	0	1	0	0	0	23	3	0	0	0	0	28	4	32

SAI-USN

ELECTRICAL ENGINEERING

BACHELOR'S DEGREES AWARDED IN ELECTRICAL ENGINEERING, 2005-2006

INSTITUTION		AFRICAN AMERICAN M	F	ASIAN AMERICAN M	F	HISPANIC M	F	NATIVE AMERICAN M	F	CAUCASIAN M	F	FOREIGN M	F	OTHER M	F	TOTAL BY GENDER M	F	TOTAL DEGREES
University of Utah	UT	0	0	4	0	4	0	1	0	54	3	3	1	1	1	67	5	72
Utah State University	UT	0	0	0	0	0	0	0	0	92	4	0	0	0	0	92	4	96
Valparaiso University	IN	1	0	0	0	0	0	0	0	9	4	1	0	0	0	11	4	15
University of Vermont	VT	1	0	2	0	0	0	0	0	17	2	0	0	0	1	20	3	23
Villanova University	PA	0	0	5	0	0	0	0	0	12	0	2	0	0	0	19	0	19
University of Virginia	VA	5	0	6	2	1	0	0	0	19	3	0	2	2	0	33	7	40
Virginia Commonwealth University	VA	3	0	2	0	1	0	0	0	17	0	0	0	1	0	24	0	24
Virginia Military Institute	VA	1	0	1	0	0	0	0	0	8	0	0	0	0	0	10	0	10
Virginia Polytechnic Institute and State University	VA	7	3	25	1	2	0	0	0	64	7	25	4	8	1	131	16	147
University of Washington	WA	7	1	50	13	3	0	0	0	53	3	10	4	17	1	140	22	162
Washington State University	WA	0	0	0	2	0	0	0	0	25	3	5	2	5	2	35	9	44
Washington University	MO	1	0	3	0	0	0	0	0	11	1	7	1	1	0	23	2	25
Wayne State University	MI	5	3	10	3	0	0	0	0	15	3	11	3	1	0	42	12	54
West Virginia University Institute of Technology	WV	0	0	0	0	0	0	0	0	10	0	2	0	0	0	12	0	12
West Virginia University	WV	2	1	0	1	1	0	0	0	32	1	1	1	0	0	36	4	40
Western Kentucky University	KY	0	0	0	0	0	0	0	0	3	1	0	0	0	0	3	1	4
Western Michigan University	MI	2	0	2	0	0	0	0	0	20	1	9	0	0	0	33	1	34
Western New England College	MA	0	0	0	0	1	1	0	0	18	1	0	0	1	0	20	2	22
Wichita State University	KS	0	0	10	4	1	0	0	0	0	0	3	0	20	2	34	6	40
Widener University	PA	0	0	0	0	1	0	0	0	11	0	3	0	0	0	15	0	15
Wilkes University	PA	0	0	0	0	0	0	0	0	9	2	1	0	0	0	10	2	12
University of Wisconsin, Madison	WI	3	0	7	1	1	0	0	0	59	4	19	4	1	1	90	10	100
University of Wisconsin, Milwaukee	WI	2	0	3	0	2	0	0	0	39	3	2	0	0	0	48	3	51
University of Wisconsin, Platteville	WI	0	0	1	0	0	0	0	0	30	2	0	0	0	0	31	2	33
Worcester Polytechnic Institute	MA	0	0	0	0	0	0	0	0	6	0	0	0	0	0	6	0	6
Wright State University	OH	4	0	2	1	0	0	0	0	19	5	0	1	3	1	28	8	36
University of Wyoming	WY	0	0	0	0	0	0	0	0	20	0	1	1	1	0	22	1	23
Yale University/Faculty of Engineering	CT	0	0	0	0	0	0	0	0	0	0	0	0	12	1	12	1	13
Youngstown State University	OH	0	0	0	0	0	0	0	0	16	3	1	0	0	0	17	3	20
Totals:		685	189	1,683	447	815	164	43	4	5,254	538	1,004	224	744	121	10,228	1,687	11,915

CANADIAN INSTITUTIONS:

INSTITUTION		AFRICAN AMERICAN M	F	ASIAN AMERICAN M	F	HISPANIC M	F	NATIVE AMERICAN M	F	CAUCASIAN M	F	FOREIGN M	F	OTHER M	F	TOTAL BY GENDER M	F	TOTAL DEGREES
University of Alberta	AB	0	0	0	0	0	0	0	0	0	0	0	0	107	24	107	24	131
University of Calgary	AB	0	0	0	0	0	0	0	0	0	0	5	1	45	9	50	10	60
Concordia University, Faculty of Engr. and Comp. Sci.	PQ	0	0	0	0	0	0	0	0	0	0	4	3	76	22	80	25	105
Ecole Polytechnique de Montreal	PQ	0	0	0	0	0	0	0	0	0	0	0	0	127	18	127	18	145
Ecole de Technologie Superieure	PQ	0	0	0	0	0	0	0	0	0	0	0	0	166	10	166	10	176
University of Ottawa, Faculty of Engineering	ON	0	0	0	0	0	0	0	0	0	0	10	1	79	14	89	15	104
University of Waterloo	ON	0	0	0	0	0	0	0	0	0	0	0	0	98	18	98	18	116
Totals:		0	0	0	0	0	0	0	0	0	0	19	5	698	115	717	120	837

UTA-YOU

ELECTRICAL ENGINEERING

BACHELOR'S DEGREES AWARDED IN ELECTRICAL/COMPUTER ENGINEERING, 2005-2006

INSTITUTION		AFRICAN AMERICAN M	F	ASIAN AMERICAN M	F	HISPANIC M	F	NATIVE AMERICAN M	F	CAUCASIAN M	F	FOREIGN M	F	OTHER M	F	TOTAL BY GENDER M	F	TOTAL DEGREES
The University of Akron	OH	3	0	1	2	0	0	0	0	34	1	0	0	1	0	39	3	42
University of Alaska Fairbanks	AK	0	0	1	1	1	0	1	0	13	1	0	0	0	0	16	2	18
Auburn University	AL	1	0	1	0	0	0	0	0	21	2	0	0	0	0	23	2	25
Baylor University	TX	3	1	2	2	3	0	0	0	10	3	0	0	0	0	18	6	24
Brigham Young University	UT	0	0	1	0	3	0	0	0	0	0	8	0	126	7	138	7	145
University of California, Berkeley	CA	0	2	117	26	5	0	0	0	40	2	18	5	19	6	199	41	240
University of California, Davis	CA	0	0	8	0	0	0	1	0	0	1	0	0	0	0	9	1	10
University of California, Los Angeles	CA	3	0	24	4	6	1	0	0	15	2	4	0	11	3	63	10	73
University of California, San Diego	CA	0	0	0	0	0	0	0	0	2	2	0	0	0	0	2	2	4
Carnegie Mellon University	PA	7	2	21	7	6	1	0	0	35	5	26	9	6	1	101	25	126
Case Western Reserve University	OH	0	0	2	0	0	0	0	0	4	0	2	3	1	0	9	3	12
Christian Brothers University	TN	1	2	4	0	0	0	0	0	2	1	1	0	1	0	9	3	12
University of Cincinnati	OH	3	1	2	0	0	0	0	0	27	3	0	0	0	1	32	5	37
Colorado State University	CO	0	0	4	0	2	0	0	0	36	4	0	0	10	1	52	5	57
University of Colorado at Boulder	CO	1	0	7	0	3	1	0	0	31	2	1	1	0	0	43	4	47
Cornell University	NY	2	1	40	12	3	0	2	0	33	2	32	5	1	1	113	21	134
Duke University Pratt School of Engineering	NC	0	0	0	0	1	0	0	0	0	0	0	0	32	0	32	0	32
University of Florida	FL	2	0	9	0	4	0	1	0	38	1	1	0	0	0	55	1	56
Howard University	DC	28	3	0	0	0	0	0	0	0	0	0	0	0	0	28	3	31
The University of Iowa	IA	1	0	1	0	0	0	0	0	29	3	1	0	1	0	33	3	36
Lafayette College	PA	0	1	1	0	0	0	0	0	11	5	2	1	0	0	14	7	21
Louisiana State University	LA	1	0	5	0	1	0	0	0	8	2	1	1	1	0	17	3	20
Massachusetts Institute of Technology	MA	5	1	38	16	17	2	3	0	69	7	17	6	15	2	164	34	198
University of Minnesota, Duluth	MN	0	0	2	0	0	0	0	0	17	0	5	0	0	0	24	0	24
University of Missouri - Kansas City	MO	2	0	0	0	1	0	0	0	9	2	7	1	0	0	19	3	22
University of Nebraska, Lincoln	NE	1	1	4	0	0	0	0	0	8	0	0	1	0	0	14	2	16
New York Institute of Technology	NY	0	0	0	0	0	0	0	0	0	0	0	0	26	6	26	6	32
Stony Brook University	NY	5	2	40	2	1	0	0	0	28	0	10	1	0	0	84	5	89
Northern Arizona University	AZ	0	0	0	0	1	1	0	0	13	1	0	0	0	0	14	2	16
The Ohio State University	OH	7	1	14	2	4	0	0	0	109	9	35	4	0	0	169	16	185
Oklahoma State University	OK	0	0	1	1	0	0	2	0	18	3	2	2	0	0	23	6	29
University of the Pacific	CA	1	0	7	4	0	0	0	0	3	2	0	0	2	0	13	6	19
University of Pennsylvania	PA	0	1	7	0	1	0	0	0	12	5	6	4	3	0	29	10	39
Penn State Erie, The Behrend College	PA	0	0	0	0	0	0	0	0	4	0	0	0	0	0	4	0	4
William Marsh Rice University	TX	1	0	0	0	2	0	0	0	2	0	1	0	0	0	6	0	6
University of Rochester	NY	0	1	3	0	0	0	0	0	12	0	0	0	1	1	16	2	18
Rowan University	NJ	0	0	0	0	0	0	0	0	12	1	0	0	0	0	12	1	13
Rutgers, The State University of New Jersey	NJ	8	3	61	8	10	0	0	0	53	8	8	3	0	0	140	22	162
University of South Alabama	AL	1	0	4	0	0	0	0	0	14	3	13	1	2	0	34	4	38
University of Southern California	CA	0	0	1	1	0	0	0	0	2	0	0	0	0	0	3	1	4
Southern Illinois University Carbondale	IL	3	0	2	0	0	0	0	0	34	2	5	0	2	0	46	2	48
Temple University	PA	6	2	10	2	0	0	0	0	13	2	5	2	0	0	34	8	42
The University of Texas at Austin	TX	4	4	108	18	26	5	0	0	118	14	27	4	0	0	283	45	328
University of Texas at San Antonio	TX	3	0	8	2	28	4	0	0	17	5	1	1	0	0	57	12	69
The University of Toledo	OH	0	0	0	0	0	0	0	0	37	2	1	1	0	0	38	3	41

ELECTRICAL/COMPUTER ENGINEERING   AKR-TOL

BACHELOR'S DEGREES AWARDED IN ELECTRICAL/COMPUTER ENGINEERING, 2005-2006

INSTITUTION		AFRICAN AMERICAN		ASIAN AMERICAN		HISPANIC		NATIVE AMERICAN		CAUCASIAN		FOREIGN		OTHER		TOTAL BY GENDER		TOTAL DEGREES
		M	F	M	F	M	F	M	F	M	F	M	F	M	F	M	F	
Vanderbilt University	TN	7	2	8	2	2	1	0	2	41	16	7	6	5	0	70	29	99
Worcester Polytechnic Institute	MA	1	0	9	1	1	1	1	0	60	6	0	0	2	0	74	8	82
Totals:		111	31	578	113	131	17	11	2	1,094	130	248	62	268	29	2,441	384	2,825
CANADIAN INSTITUTIONS:																		
McGill University, Faculty of Engineering	PQ	0	0	0	0	0	0	0	0	0	0	0	0	124	27	124	27	151
Totals:		0	0	0	0	0	0	0	0	0	0	0	0	124	27	124	27	151

ELECTRICAL/COMPUTER ENGINEERING   VAN-WOR

Bachelor's Degrees Awarded in Engineering (General), 2005-2006

Institution		African American		Asian American		Hispanic		Native American		Caucasian		Foreign		Other		Total by Gender		Total Degrees
		M	F	M	F	M	F	M	F	M	F	M	F	M	F	M	F	
The University of Arizona	AZ	1	0	0	0	0	1	0	0	2	0	0	0	0	0	3	1	4
Arkansas State University	AR	0	1	0	0	0	1	0	0	21	3	2	0	0	0	23	5	28
Baylor University	TX	0	0	0	0	1	0	0	0	2	0	0	0	0	0	3	0	3
California State University, East Bay	CA	1	1	4	0	0	0	0	0	2	0	0	0	3	4	10	5	15
California State University, Long Beach	CA	0	1	0	0	0	0	0	0	1	0	0	0	0	0	1	1	2
Calvin College	MI	0	0	1	0	0	0	1	0	44	5	11	4	0	0	57	9	66
Colorado School of Mines	CO	3	0	8	5	12	4	2	0	158	29	5	0	0	0	188	38	226
Colorado State University, Pueblo	CO	0	0	0	0	1	0	0	0	0	1	0	0	0	1	1	2	3
The Cooper Union	NY	1	0	5	2	0	0	0	0	5	0	1	0	0	0	12	2	14
Dartmouth College	NH	2	1	10	2	5	1	1	0	57	21	11	5	2	0	88	30	118
Gonzaga University	WA	0	0	0	0	0	0	0	0	2	0	0	0	0	0	2	0	2
Harvey Mudd College	CA	0	0	15	8	2	0	0	0	22	5	2	0	7	1	48	14	62
University of Illinois at Urbana-Champaign	IL	0	3	9	0	4	2	0	0	77	20	2	0	1	0	93	25	118
Indiana University Purdue University at Indianapolis	IN	1	0	0	0	0	0	0	0	3	2	1	0	0	0	5	2	7
The Johns Hopkins University	MD	0	0	0	0	0	0	0	0	3	0	0	0	0	0	3	0	3
LeTourneau University	TX	0	1	0	0	0	0	0	0	42	2	1	0	1	0	44	3	47
University of Maryland, College Park	MD	0	0	1	0	0	0	0	0	5	0	0	0	1	0	7	0	7
Messiah College	PA	0	0	0	0	0	0	0	0	22	3	2	0	0	0	24	3	27
Miami University	OH	0	0	0	0	0	0	0	0	1	0	0	0	0	0	1	0	1
Michigan Technological University	MI	0	0	0	0	1	0	0	0	8	1	0	1	3	0	12	2	14
The University of Mississippi	MS	0	0	0	0	0	0	0	0	3	0	0	0	0	0	3	0	3
Montana Tech of the University of Montana	MT	0	0	2	1	0	0	0	1	39	3	0	0	4	1	45	6	51
University of New Haven	CT	0	0	0	0	0	0	0	0	0	0	0	0	2	0	2	0	2
North Carolina State University	NC	0	0	0	0	0	0	0	0	14	1	0	0	1	0	15	1	16
Northwestern University	IL	0	0	0	1	0	0	0	0	0	0	0	0	0	0	0	1	1
Oral Roberts University	OK	2	0	1	1	0	0	0	0	8	1	0	0	0	0	11	2	13
University of Pennsylvania	PA	0	0	7	1	0	1	0	0	5	2	3	1	0	2	15	7	22
University of Rochester	NY	0	0	0	1	0	0	0	0	0	0	0	0	1	0	1	1	2
Roger Williams University	RI	0	0	2	0	0	0	0	0	23	1	2	1	0	0	25	1	26
San Jose State University	CA	1	0	4	3	1	0	1	0	0	0	0	0	0	0	7	3	10
Stanford University	CA	1	4	8	9	3	1	1	0	18	7	0	0	0	1	31	22	53
Swarthmore College	PA	1	0	3	1	0	0	0	0	15	4	3	1	0	0	22	6	28
University of Tennessee, Martin	TN	0	0	0	0	0	0	0	0	28	6	1	1	0	0	29	7	36
Texas Christian University	TX	1	0	0	1	0	0	0	0	12	2	2	1	0	0	15	4	19
Trinity University	TX	0	0	0	0	0	0	0	0	0	0	0	0	23	10	23	10	33
Trinity College	CT	0	0	0	0	0	1	0	0	13	0	2	0	0	0	15	1	16
Tufts University	MA	0	0	1	1	0	0	0	0	0	0	0	0	2	3	3	4	7
U.S. Air Force Academy	CO	1	0	0	0	2	0	0	0	0	0	0	0	7	0	10	0	10
U.S. Naval Academy	MD	3	0	2	0	4	0	1	0	12	4	0	0	0	0	22	4	26
Walla Walla College	WA	0	0	3	0	1	0	0	0	25	1	5	0	0	0	34	1	35
Totals:		19	12	86	37	37	12	7	1	692	124	51	14	61	23	953	223	1,176

ARI-WAL

ENGINEERING (GENERAL)

BACHELOR'S DEGREES AWARDED IN ENGINEERING MANAGEMENT, 2005-2006

INSTITUTION		AFRICAN AMERICAN		ASIAN AMERICAN		HISPANIC		NATIVE AMERICAN		CAUCASIAN		FOREIGN		OTHER		TOTAL BY GENDER		TOTAL DEGREES
		M	F	M	F	M	F	M	F	M	F	M	F	M	F	M	F	
The University of Arizona	AZ	1	0	0	0	6	2	1	0	16	2	3	0	0	0	27	4	31
University of California-Santa Cruz	CA	0	0	3	3	1	1	0	0	14	3	1	1	3	0	22	8	30
Colorado School of Mines	CO	0	0	3	1	1	1	0	0	17	5	1	0	0	0	22	7	29
University of Evansville	IN	0	0	0	0	0	0	0	0	0	0	0	0	5	0	5	0	5
University of Illinois at Chicago	IL	0	0	0	0	0	0	0	0	1	0	0	0	0	0	1	0	1
Mercer University	GA	0	2	0	0	0	0	0	0	3	0	0	0	0	0	3	2	5
Miami University	OH	0	0	1	1	0	0	0	0	22	6	0	0	0	0	23	7	30
University of Missouri - Rolla	MO	5	1	0	0	1	1	0	0	25	12	1	0	1	0	33	14	47
The College of New Jersey	NJ	0	0	0	0	0	0	0	0	2	2	0	0	0	0	2	2	4
University of the Pacific	CA	0	0	1	1	1	0	0	0	0	0	0	0	0	0	2	1	3
University of Portland	OR	0	0	0	0	0	0	0	0	1	0	0	0	0	0	1	0	1
Southern Methodist University	TX	1	0	1	0	0	0	0	0	5	7	0	0	0	0	7	7	14
Stevens Institute of Technology	NJ	0	2	1	0	1	1	0	0	8	3	2	0	1	1	13	7	20
Syracuse University	NY	0	0	0	0	0	0	0	0	1	0	0	0	0	0	1	0	1
Tri-State University	IN	0	0	0	0	0	0	0	0	1	0	0	0	0	0	1	0	1
United States Military Academy	NY	3	2	0	0	0	0	0	0	0	6	1	0	0	1	4	9	13
University of Vermont	VT	0	0	0	0	0	0	0	0	3	0	0	0	0	0	3	0	3
Totals:		10	7	10	6	11	6	1	0	119	46	9	1	10	2	170	68	238

ARI-VER

ENGINEERING MANAGEMENT

BACHELOR'S DEGREES AWARDED IN ENGINEERING SCIENCE AND ENGINEERING PHYSICS, 2005-2006

INSTITUTION		AFRICAN AMERICAN		ASIAN AMERICAN		HISPANIC		NATIVE AMERICAN		CAUCASIAN		FOREIGN		OTHER		TOTAL BY GENDER		TOTAL DEGREES
		M	F	M	F	M	F	M	F	M	F	M	F	M	F	M	F	
The University of Arizona	AZ	0	0	0	0	0	0	0	0	4	0	0	0	0	0	4	0	4
California Institute of Technology	CA	0	1	4	3	3	0	0	0	7	4	1	0	0	0	15	8	23
California State University, Fullerton	CA	0	0	0	0	0	0	0	0	0	0	1	0	0	0	1	0	1
University of California, Berkeley	CA	0	0	7	0	2	0	0	0	7	0	0	0	5	0	21	0	21
University of California, Davis	CA	0	0	9	4	1	0	0	0	5	0	3	0	2	0	20	4	24
Case Western Reserve University	OH	0	0	0	0	1	0	0	0	0	0	0	0	0	0	1	0	1
Colorado School of Mines	CO	2	0	2	0	0	0	1	0	46	8	0	0	0	0	51	8	59
Colorado State University	CO	0	0	0	0	0	0	0	0	3	2	0	0	1	0	4	2	6
University of Colorado at Boulder	CO	0	0	0	0	0	0	0	0	10	0	0	1	0	0	10	1	11
Columbia University	NY	0	0	0	0	0	0	0	0	7	1	1	0	4	0	12	1	13
University of Connecticut	CT	0	0	0	0	0	0	0	0	1	0	0	0	0	0	1	0	1
Cornell University	NY	0	0	4	2	1	0	0	0	14	0	3	1	1	0	23	3	26
Hofstra University	NY	0	1	0	0	1	0	0	0	1	2	0	0	1	1	3	4	7
University of Illinois at Urbana-Champaign	IL	0	0	7	3	0	0	0	0	23	3	3	0	1	0	34	6	40
University of Kansas	KS	0	0	0	0	0	0	0	0	1	0	0	0	0	0	1	0	1
Lehigh University	PA	0	0	1	1	0	0	0	0	0	0	0	0	3	0	4	1	5
Loyola College in Maryland	MD	1	1	0	0	0	0	0	0	5	2	0	0	0	1	6	4	10
University of Maine	ME	0	0	0	0	0	0	0	0	3	1	0	0	0	0	3	1	4
University of Michigan	MI	0	0	1	0	2	0	0	0	4	0	0	1	0	0	7	1	8
University of Nevada, Reno	NV	0	0	0	0	0	0	0	0	1	0	0	0	0	0	1	0	1
New Jersey Institute of Technology	NJ	1	0	2	1	0	0	0	0	0	0	0	0	0	0	3	1	4
New Mexico State University	NM	1	0	1	0	0	0	0	0	0	0	0	0	0	0	2	0	2
City University of New York, College of Staten Island	NY	0	0	1	0	0	0	1	0	3	0	2	0	0	0	7	0	7
Stony Brook University	NY	1	3	2	0	2	0	0	0	3	0	2	0	0	0	10	3	13
Oakland University	MI	0	0	1	0	0	0	0	0	1	0	0	0	0	0	2	0	2
University of Oklahoma	OK	0	0	0	0	0	0	0	0	7	0	0	0	0	0	7	0	7
Oral Roberts University	OK	0	0	0	0	0	0	0	0	1	0	0	0	0	0	1	0	1
University of the Pacific	CA	0	0	0	0	0	0	0	0	5	0	1	0	1	0	7	0	7
The Pennsylvania State University	PA	0	0	0	0	0	0	0	0	19	4	0	0	1	0	20	4	24
University of Pittsburgh	PA	0	0	0	0	0	0	0	0	6	1	0	0	0	0	6	1	7
Rensselaer Polytechnic Institute	NY	0	0	0	0	0	0	0	0	1	1	0	0	0	0	1	1	2
Smith College	MA	0	1	0	3	0	3	0	0	0	14	0	9	0	3	0	33	33
University of South Florida	FL	0	0	0	0	0	0	0	0	1	4	0	0	0	0	1	4	5
Southeast Missouri State University	MO	0	0	0	0	0	0	0	0	2	1	0	0	0	0	2	1	3
Texas Tech University	TX	0	0	0	0	0	0	0	0	0	2	0	0	0	0	0	2	2
Tufts University	MA	0	0	0	0	0	0	0	0	1	0	0	0	0	0	1	0	1
University of Tulsa	OK	0	0	0	0	0	0	0	0	0	1	0	0	0	0	0	1	1
University of Virginia	VA	1	0	0	0	0	0	0	0	7	3	0	1	0	0	8	4	12
Virginia Polytechnic Institute and State University	VA	0	3	0	0	0	0	0	0	12	4	0	0	0	1	12	8	20
Wilkes University	PA	0	0	0	0	0	0	0	0	1	0	0	0	0	0	1	0	1
University of Wisconsin, Madison	WI	0	0	0	0	0	0	0	0	1	0	0	0	1	0	2	0	2
University of Wisconsin, Platteville	WI	0	0	0	0	0	0	0	0	6	0	0	0	0	0	6	0	6
Wright State University	OH	0	0	0	0	0	0	0	0	3	0	0	0	0	0	3	0	3
Totals:		**7**	**10**	**42**	**17**	**13**	**3**	**2**	**0**	**222**	**58**	**17**	**13**	**21**	**6**	**324**	**107**	**431**

ENGR. SCIENCE AND ENGR. PHYSICS   ARI-WRI

BACHELOR'S DEGREES AWARDED IN ENGINEERING SCIENCE AND ENGINEERING PHYSICS, 2005-2006

INSTITUTION		AFRICAN AMERICAN		ASIAN AMERICAN		HISPANIC		NATIVE AMERICAN		CAUCASIAN		FOREIGN		OTHER		TOTAL BY GENDER		TOTAL DEGREES
		M	F	M	F	M	F	M	F	M	F	M	F	M	F	M	F	
CANADIAN INSTITUTIONS:																		
University of Alberta	AB	0	0	0	0	0	0	0	0	0	0	0	0	17	2	17	2	19
Ecole Polytechnique de Montreal	PQ	0	0	0	0	0	0	0	0	0	0	0	0	23	2	23	2	25
Totals:		0	0	0	0	0	0	0	0	0	0	0	0	40	4	40	4	44

ALB-ECO

ENGR. SCIENCE AND ENGR. PHYSICS

INSTITUTION		AFRICAN AMERICAN M	F	ASIAN AMERICAN M	F	HISPANIC M	F	NATIVE AMERICAN M	F	CAUCASIAN M	F	FOREIGN M	F	OTHER M	F	TOTAL BY GENDER M	F	TOTAL DEGREES
California Polytechnic State University	CA	0	0	0	2	0	2	0	0	4	5	0	0	2	1	6	10	16
University of California, Irvine	CA	0	0	0	0	0	0	0	0	0	0	0	0	0	1	0	1	1
University of California, Riverside	CA	0	0	2	1	1	0	0	0	2	0	0	0	0	2	5	3	8
University of Central Florida	FL	0	0	0	0	0	1	1	0	6	6	0	0	0	0	7	7	14
Colorado State University	CO	0	0	0	0	0	0	0	0	5	7	0	0	1	0	6	7	13
University of Colorado at Boulder	CO	0	0	0	0	0	0	0	0	5	2	0	0	0	0	5	2	7
University of Connecticut	CT	0	0	0	0	0	0	0	0	1	2	0	0	0	0	1	2	3
Cornell University	NY	0	0	0	1	0	0	0	0	2	2	0	0	0	0	2	3	5
University of Delaware	DE	0	0	0	1	0	0	0	0	2	0	0	1	0	0	2	1	3
Drexel University	PA	0	0	0	0	0	1	0	0	0	1	1	0	0	1	1	3	4
University of Florida	FL	1	0	0	0	1	1	0	1	7	3	0	0	0	0	9	5	14
FAMU-FSU College of Engineering	FL	0	0	1	0	0	0	0	0	1	3	0	0	0	0	1	3	4
Humboldt State University	CA	0	1	1	0	0	0	1	0	10	4	0	0	2	2	14	7	21
The Johns Hopkins University	MD	0	0	0	0	0	0	0	0	1	2	0	1	0	0	1	3	4
Lehigh University	PA	0	0	0	0	0	0	0	0	0	0	0	0	2	2	2	2	4
Louisiana State University	LA	0	0	0	0	0	0	0	0	1	7	0	0	0	0	1	7	8
Manhattan College	NY	0	0	0	0	0	1	0	0	6	2	0	0	0	0	6	3	9
Massachusetts Institute of Technology	MA	0	0	0	1	0	0	0	0	1	3	0	0	0	1	1	5	6
Mercer University	GA	0	0	0	0	0	0	0	0	2	2	0	0	0	0	2	2	4
University of Miami	FL	0	0	0	0	0	0	0	0	1	2	1	1	0	0	2	3	5
Michigan Technological University	MI	0	0	0	0	0	0	0	0	12	12	1	1	1	1	14	14	28
University of Missouri - Rolla	MO	0	0	0	0	0	1	0	0	0	1	0	0	0	0	0	2	2
Montana Tech of the University of Montana	MT	0	0	0	0	0	0	0	0	3	2	1	0	0	0	4	2	6
University of New Hampshire	NH	0	0	0	0	0	0	0	0	1	0	0	0	0	0	1	0	1
New Jersey Institute of Technology	NJ	0	0	0	0	0	0	0	0	1	0	0	0	0	0	1	0	1
New Mexico Institute of Mining & Technology	NM	0	0	0	0	0	0	0	1	1	2	0	0	0	0	1	3	4
State University of New York at Buffalo	NY	0	0	0	0	0	0	1	0	4	0	0	0	0	1	5	1	6
North Carolina State University	NC	0	0	0	1	0	0	0	0	8	4	0	0	0	0	8	5	13
Northern Arizona University	AZ	0	0	0	0	0	0	2	0	4	0	0	1	0	0	6	1	7
Northwestern University	IL	0	0	0	0	0	0	0	0	2	2	0	2	0	0	2	4	6
University of Notre Dame	IN	0	0	1	1	0	0	0	0	0	1	0	0	0	0	1	2	3
University of Oklahoma	OK	0	0	1	0	0	0	0	0	2	2	0	0	0	0	3	2	5
Old Dominion University	VA	1	1	0	0	0	0	0	0	0	3	0	0	0	0	1	4	5
Oregon State University	OR	0	0	0	1	0	0	1	0	8	2	0	0	1	2	10	4	14
Polytechnic University of Puerto Rico	PR	0	0	0	0	12	9	0	0	0	0	0	0	0	0	12	9	21
Princeton University	NJ	3	1	0	0	0	0	0	0	7	8	0	2	0	0	10	11	21
Rensselaer Polytechnic Institute	NY	0	0	0	0	0	0	0	0	8	4	1	0	0	0	9	4	13
William Marsh Rice University	TX	0	0	0	0	1	0	0	0	1	1	0	0	1	0	3	1	4
San Diego State University	CA	1	0	0	1	0	1	0	0	1	1	1	0	1	1	4	4	8
South Dakota School of Mines and Technology	SD	0	0	0	0	0	0	0	0	0	2	0	0	0	0	0	2	2
University of Southern California	CA	0	0	1	1	0	0	0	0	0	0	0	1	0	0	1	2	3
Southern Methodist University	TX	0	1	0	0	0	0	0	0	2	1	0	0	0	0	2	2	4
Stevens Institute of Technology	NJ	0	0	0	0	0	0	0	0	1	1	0	0	0	0	1	1	2
Texas Tech University	TX	0	0	0	0	0	0	0	0	3	2	0	0	0	0	3	2	5
Tufts University	MA	0	0	0	1	0	0	0	0	0	0	0	0	5	5	5	6	11

ENVIRONMENTAL ENGINEERING   CAL-TUF

BACHELOR'S DEGREES AWARDED IN ENVIRONMENTAL ENGINEERING, 2005-2006

INSTITUTION		AFRICAN AMERICAN		ASIAN AMERICAN		HISPANIC		NATIVE AMERICAN		CAUCASIAN		FOREIGN		OTHER		TOTAL BY GENDER		TOTAL DEGREES
		M	F	M	F	M	F	M	F	M	F	M	F	M	F	M	F	
Tulane University	LA	0	0	0	0	0	0	0	0	0	0	0	0	1	2	1	2	3
U.S. Air Force Academy	CO	0	0	0	0	0	0	0	0	0	0	0	0	4	2	4	2	6
United States Military Academy	NY	0	0	0	0	0	0	0	0	22	0	0	0	0	0	22	0	22
Vanderbilt University	TN	0	0	0	0	2	0	0	0	11	9	0	1	1	0	14	10	24
Wentworth Institute of Technology	MA	0	0	0	0	0	0	0	0	3	0	0	0	0	0	3	0	3
Wilkes University	PA	0	0	0	0	0	0	0	0	6	1	0	0	0	0	6	1	7
University of Wisconsin, Platteville	WI	0	0	0	0	0	0	0	0	9	6	0	0	0	0	9	6	15
University of Wyoming	WY	0	0	0	0	0	0	0	0	2	2	0	0	0	0	2	2	4
Yale University/Faculty of Engineering	CT	0	0	0	0	0	0	0	0	0	0	0	0	2	3	2	3	5
Totals:		7	4	6	11	17	16	6	2	179	122	4	11	25	27	244	193	437

CANADIAN INSTITUTIONS:

		AFRICAN AMERICAN		ASIAN AMERICAN		HISPANIC		NATIVE AMERICAN		CAUCASIAN		FOREIGN		OTHER		TOTAL BY GENDER		TOTAL DEGREES
		M	F	M	F	M	F	M	F	M	F	M	F	M	F	M	F	
University of Waterloo	ON	0	0	0	0	0	0	0	0	0	0	0	0	32	21	32	21	53
Totals:		0	0	0	0	0	0	0	0	0	0	0	0	32	21	32	21	53

TUL-YAL

ENVIRONMENTAL ENGINEERING

BACHELOR'S DEGREES AWARDED IN INDUSTRIAL/MANUFACTURING ENGINEERING, 2005-2006

INSTITUTION		AFRICAN AMERICAN		ASIAN AMERICAN		HISPANIC		NATIVE AMERICAN		CAUCASIAN		FOREIGN		OTHER		TOTAL BY GENDER		TOTAL DEGREES
		M	F	M	F	M	F	M	F	M	F	M	F	M	F	M	F	
The University of Alabama in Huntsville	AL	0	0	0	0	0	0	0	0	4	2	0	0	0	0	4	2	6
The University of Alabama	AL	1	2	0	0	0	0	0	0	8	3	0	0	0	0	9	5	14
The University of Arizona	AZ	1	1	1	2	5	1	0	0	9	6	4	3	0	0	20	13	33
Arizona State University	AZ	3	1	3	2	3	0	0	0	19	8	5	3	1	1	31	15	46
University of Arkansas	AR	1	0	1	0	0	0	0	0	24	10	2	0	0	1	28	11	39
Auburn University	AL	1	2	1	0	0	0	0	0	12	11	0	1	0	0	14	14	28
Boston University	MA	0	0	3	0	0	4	0	0	7	2	2	1	0	0	12	7	19
Bradley University	IL	0	0	0	1	0	0	0	0	15	5	1	0	0	0	16	6	22
California Polytechnic State University	CA	1	1	8	3	4	3	1	0	19	10	0	0	11	2	44	19	63
California State Polytechnic University, Pomona	CA	0	1	11	4	5	2	1	0	12	1	0	0	3	0	32	8	40
California State University, Fresno	CA	0	0	3	1	2	0	0	0	1	1	1	0	0	0	7	2	9
California State University, Northridge	CA	0	1	0	0	3	1	0	0	2	0	1	0	1	0	7	2	9
University of California, Berkeley	CA	0	0	11	13	4	0	0	0	7	2	1	4	2	0	25	19	44
University of Central Florida	FL	1	1	2	0	3	1	0	0	6	3	2	1	0	0	14	6	20
Clemson University	SC	5	6	0	1	0	0	0	0	18	11	0	1	3	0	26	19	45
Cleveland State University	OH	0	0	0	0	0	0	0	0	4	3	0	0	0	0	4	3	7
Columbia University	NY	0	1	27	6	1	3	0	0	16	2	15	2	6	0	65	14	79
University of Connecticut	CT	0	0	1	1	0	0	0	0	7	2	0	0	1	0	9	3	12
Cornell University	NY	1	1	27	13	1	0	0	0	29	10	13	5	0	1	71	30	101
University of Detroit Mercy	MI	3	1	0	0	0	0	0	0	0	0	0	0	0	0	3	1	4
Drexel University	PA	0	0	0	0	0	0	0	0	1	0	0	0	0	0	1	0	1
University of Florida	FL	4	2	5	2	14	11	1	0	23	16	5	1	0	0	52	32	84
Florida International University	FL	1	0	0	1	13	8	0	0	0	0	10	6	0	0	24	15	39
FAMU-FSU College of Engineering	FL	13	6	0	0	2	2	0	0	5	3	6	3	0	0	26	12	38
George Mason University	VA	2	0	2	1	5	1	0	0	11	1	4	0	2	0	26	4	30
Georgia Institute of Technology	GA	12	10	36	17	7	8	0	0	97	55	11	11	2	0	165	101	266
Grand Valley State University	MI	0	0	0	0	0	0	0	0	2	0	0	0	0	0	2	0	2
Hofstra University	NY	0	0	0	0	1	1	0	0	0	1	0	0	0	0	1	2	3
University of Houston, Cullen School of Engineering	TX	4	2	3	4	3	2	0	0	6	0	6	1	2	1	24	10	34
University of Illinois at Chicago	IL	1	0	6	2	2	1	0	0	3	1	0	0	0	0	12	4	16
University of Illinois at Urbana-Champaign	IL	0	0	1	3	1	0	0	0	9	6	1	1	0	0	12	10	22
Indiana Institute of Technology	IN	0	0	0	0	0	1	0	0	5	1	0	0	0	1	5	3	8
The University of Iowa	IA	0	0	0	0	1	0	0	0	19	6	0	0	1	0	21	7	28
Iowa State University	IA	0	0	3	3	2	0	0	0	31	16	4	2	4	0	44	21	65
Kansas State University	KS	1	0	0	0	0	0	0	0	15	11	1	0	0	1	17	12	29
Kettering University formerly GMI	MI	0	3	1	0	0	1	0	0	14	12	1	1	2	1	18	18	36
Lamar University	TX	6	2	2	0	0	0	0	0	16	3	1	0	0	0	25	5	30
Lehigh University	PA	0	0	0	0	1	0	0	0	0	0	6	1	19	9	26	10	36
Louisiana State University	LA	0	1	0	0	0	0	0	0	7	4	3	6	0	0	10	12	22
Louisiana Tech University	LA	1	0	0	0	0	0	1	0	3	2	1	0	0	0	6	2	8
University of Louisville	KY	1	2	0	0	0	0	0	0	10	4	0	0	0	0	11	6	17
University of Massachusetts Amherst	MA	2	0	0	1	1	0	0	0	5	2	0	0	0	0	8	3	11
Mercer University	GA	0	0	0	0	0	0	0	0	7	4	1	1	1	0	9	7	16
University of Miami	FL	2	3	1	1	6	4	0	0	1	4	3	0	0	0	13	12	25
Miami University	OH	0	0	0	0	0	0	1	0	14	3	1	0	0	0	16	3	19

INDUSTRIAL/MANUFACTURING ENGR.   ALA-MIA

INSTITUTION		AFRICAN AMERICAN		ASIAN AMERICAN		HISPANIC		NATIVE AMERICAN		CAUCASIAN		FOREIGN		OTHER		TOTAL BY GENDER		TOTAL DEGREES
		M	F	M	F	M	F	M	F	M	F	M	F	M	F	M	F	
University of Michigan	MI	5	14	20	19	3	2	2	0	37	48	20	11	4	1	91	95	186
University of Michigan, Dearborn	MI	0	0	4	0	0	1	0	0	5	2	1	1	0	0	10	4	14
Milwaukee School of Engineering	WI	0	0	0	0	0	0	0	0	6	1	1	0	0	0	7	1	8
University of Minnesota, Duluth	MN	0	0	0	0	0	0	0	0	14	2	0	0	0	0	14	2	16
Mississippi State University	MS	2	3	0	0	0	0	0	0	11	8	0	0	0	0	13	11	24
University of Missouri-Columbia	MO	0	0	0	0	0	0	0	0	11	8	1	0	0	0	12	8	20
Montana State University	MT	0	0	0	0	0	0	0	0	12	2	0	0	0	1	12	3	15
Morgan State University	MD	5	2	0	0	0	0	0	0	0	0	0	0	0	0	5	2	7
University of Nebraska, Lincoln	NE	0	0	0	0	1	0	0	0	17	5	2	1	0	0	20	6	26
University of New Haven	CT	1	0	0	0	0	0	0	0	0	0	2	0	1	0	4	0	4
New Jersey Institute of Technology	NJ	2	1	1	0	4	3	0	0	1	0	0	0	2	0	10	4	14
New Mexico State University	NM	0	1	0	0	2	3	0	0	1	0	0	0	0	1	3	5	8
The State University of New York at Binghamton	NY	1	0	3	0	0	0	0	0	11	2	0	0	4	1	19	3	22
State University of New York at Buffalo	NY	2	0	0	2	0	0	0	0	10	5	5	1	4	0	21	8	29
North Carolina A & T State University	NC	20	8	0	0	0	0	0	0	0	1	0	0	0	0	20	9	29
North Carolina State University	NC	8	5	3	1	2	1	0	0	30	4	2	0	1	0	46	11	57
North Dakota State University	ND	0	0	0	0	1	0	0	0	24	2	0	0	0	0	25	2	27
Northeastern University	MA	0	0	1	0	2	0	0	0	6	2	1	0	3	1	13	3	16
Northwestern University	IL	0	1	13	4	4	0	0	0	18	2	13	8	0	1	48	16	64
The Ohio State University	OH	4	5	9	3	4	3	1	0	85	22	13	9	0	0	116	42	158
Ohio University	OH	0	0	0	0	0	0	0	0	4	3	0	0	0	0	4	3	7
University of Oklahoma	OK	2	0	0	1	2	1	1	1	6	6	0	1	0	0	11	10	21
Oklahoma State University	OK	0	0	0	1	1	0	0	0	9	8	1	2	0	0	11	11	22
Oregon State University	OR	2	0	3	0	3	0	0	0	33	6	5	0	2	1	48	7	55
The Pennsylvania State University	PA	3	0	12	4	2	2	0	0	68	25	12	10	0	0	97	41	138
University of Pittsburgh	PA	1	1	2	0	0	0	0	0	25	17	0	0	0	0	28	18	46
Polytechnic University of Puerto Rico	PR	0	0	0	0	19	16	0	0	0	0	0	0	0	0	19	16	35
University of Puerto Rico, Mayaguez Campus	PR	0	0	0	0	25	37	0	0	0	0	0	0	0	0	25	37	62
Purdue University	IN	0	1	5	3	7	3	0	1	64	14	40	10	2	0	118	31	149
Rensselaer Polytechnic Institute	NY	1	0	1	1	0	1	0	0	12	10	3	0	0	0	17	11	28
University of Rhode Island	RI	0	0	1	1	0	0	0	0	1	0	0	0	2	1	4	2	6
Rochester Institute of Technology	NY	0	1	1	1	0	0	0	0	13	6	3	2	1	0	18	10	28
Rutgers, The State University of New Jersey	NJ	2	0	5	3	1	3	0	0	11	1	2	0	0	0	21	7	28
Saint Ambrose University	IA	0	0	0	0	0	0	0	0	5	2	1	0	0	0	6	2	8
Saint Cloud State University	MN	0	0	0	2	0	0	0	0	1	0	1	0	0	0	2	2	4
Saint Mary's University	TX	0	0	0	0	0	0	0	0	0	0	0	1	0	0	0	1	1
University of San Diego	CA	0	0	2	0	2	2	0	0	5	1	1	1	0	0	10	4	14
San Jose State University	CA	1	1	17	9	3	0	0	0	5	1	2	2	0	0	28	13	41
South Dakota School of Mines and Technology	SD	0	0	0	0	0	0	0	0	28	7	0	0	1	0	29	7	36
University of South Florida	FL	0	1	1	0	0	0	0	0	3	3	1	2	0	0	5	6	11
University of Southern California	CA	0	1	1	4	1	1	0	0	9	3	10	4	0	0	21	13	34
Southern Illinois University Edwardsville	IL	0	0	1	0	0	0	0	0	10	2	0	0	0	0	12	2	14
Stanford University	CA	3	10	7	6	3	2	0	0	12	5	6	1	2	0	34	24	58
Tennessee Technological University	TN	0	0	0	0	0	0	0	0	7	3	0	0	0	0	7	3	10
University of Tennessee, Chattanooga	TN	0	0	0	0	0	0	0	0	1	0	0	0	0	0	1	0	1

INDUSTRIAL/MANUFACTURING ENGR.   MIC-TEN

BACHELOR'S DEGREES AWARDED IN INDUSTRIAL/MANUFACTURING ENGINEERING, 2005-2006

INSTITUTION		AFRICAN AMERICAN		ASIAN AMERICAN		HISPANIC		NATIVE AMERICAN		CAUCASIAN		FOREIGN		OTHER		TOTAL BY GENDER		TOTAL DEGREES
		M	F	M	F	M	F	M	F	M	F	M	F	M	F	M	F	
University of Tennessee, Knoxville	TN	0	2	4	0	0	0	0	0	8	4	1	2	0	0	13	8	21
Texas A&M University	TX	1	1	2	2	7	2	0	0	23	11	10	3	1	0	44	19	63
Texas Tech University	TX	0	0	0	2	1	0	0	0	7	9	1	0	0	0	9	11	20
The University of Texas at Arlington	TX	2	0	1	1	0	3	0	0	1	1	2	1	0	0	6	6	12
University of Texas at El Paso	TX	0	0	0	0	11	5	0	0	0	1	14	4	0	0	25	10	35
The University of Texas-Pan American	TX	0	0	0	0	7	2	0	0	0	1	4	5	0	0	11	8	19
The University of Toledo	OH	1	0	0	0	0	0	0	0	7	2	0	0	0	0	8	2	10
Virginia Polytechnic Institute and State University	VA	2	3	11	3	0	1	0	0	42	21	12	1	2	1	69	30	99
University of Washington	WA	0	0	9	5	1	0	2	0	7	1	2	2	2	1	23	9	32
Wayne State University	MI	0	1	2	0	0	0	0	0	5	3	0	0	1	0	8	4	12
West Virginia University	WV	1	1	0	0	0	0	0	0	25	11	0	0	0	0	26	12	38
Western Michigan University	MI	1	3	0	0	0	0	0	0	9	8	2	0	0	0	12	11	23
Western New England College	MA	0	0	0	0	0	0	0	0	5	1	0	0	0	0	5	1	6
Wichita State University	KS	1	0	0	0	0	0	0	0	0	0	3	0	6	2	10	2	12
University of Wisconsin, Stout	WI	0	0	1	0	0	0	0	0	18	2	0	0	0	0	19	2	21
University of Wisconsin, Madison	WI	0	2	2	0	1	3	0	0	22	18	3	1	1	0	29	24	53
University of Wisconsin, Milwaukee	WI	1	0	0	0	0	1	0	0	3	4	0	0	0	0	4	5	9
University of Wisconsin, Platteville	WI	0	0	0	0	0	0	0	0	11	6	0	0	0	0	11	6	17
Worcester Polytechnic Institute	MA	0	0	0	1	2	1	0	0	12	3	0	0	0	1	14	6	20
Wright State University	OH	1	1	0	0	0	0	0	0	3	1	0	0	0	0	4	2	6
Youngstown State University	OH	0	0	0	0	0	0	0	0	6	3	0	1	0	0	6	4	10
Totals:		141	120	308	164	209	151	12	2	1,368	597	315	143	103	31	2,456	1,208	3,664
CANADIAN INSTITUTIONS:																		
University of Calgary	AB	0	0	0	0	0	0	0	0	0	0	0	0	22	3	22	3	25
Concordia University, Faculty of Engr. and Comp. Sci.	PQ	0	0	0	0	0	0	0	0	0	0	0	0	16	8	16	8	24
Ecole Polytechnique de Montreal	PQ	0	0	0	0	0	0	0	0	0	0	0	0	36	28	36	28	64
Ecole de Technologie Superieure	PQ	0	0	0	0	0	0	0	0	0	0	0	0	118	4	118	4	122
Totals:		0	0	0	0	0	0	0	0	0	0	0	0	192	43	192	43	235

INDUSTRIAL/MANUFACTURING ENGR.　　TEN-YOU

BACHELOR'S DEGREES AWARDED IN MECHANICAL ENGINEERING, 2005-2006

INSTITUTION		AFRICAN AMERICAN		ASIAN AMERICAN		HISPANIC		NATIVE AMERICAN		CAUCASIAN		FOREIGN		OTHER		TOTAL BY GENDER		TOTAL DEGREES
		M	F	M	F	M	F	M	F	M	F	M	F	M	F	M	F	
The University of Akron	OH	1	0	0	1	0	0	0	0	56	8	3	0	1	0	61	9	70
Alabama A&M University	AL	7	1	0	0	0	0	0	0	1	0	0	0	0	0	8	1	9
University of Alabama at Birmingham	AL	0	0	0	0	2	0	0	0	13	2	0	0	0	0	15	2	17
The University of Alabama in Huntsville	AL	6	3	1	0	0	0	1	0	45	11	1	0	0	0	54	14	68
The University of Alabama	AL	2	1	1	0	0	0	0	0	38	4	0	0	0	0	41	5	46
University of Alaska, Anchorage	AK	0	1	0	0	1	0	2	2	9	3	0	0	0	0	12	6	18
University of Alaska Fairbanks	AK	0	0	2	0	0	0	0	0	15	1	0	0	0	0	17	1	18
Alfred University, NY State College of Ceramics	NY	0	0	0	0	0	0	0	0	13	1	0	0	1	0	14	1	15
The University of Arizona	AZ	1	1	3	0	3	1	1	0	56	4	3	0	0	0	67	6	73
Arizona State University	AZ	1	1	5	1	10	1	0	0	49	7	6	1	6	1	77	12	89
University of Arkansas	AR	0	0	1	1	2	0	1	0	24	2	0	0	1	0	29	3	32
Arkansas Tech University	AR	0	0	0	0	0	0	0	0	39	2	0	0	0	0	39	2	41
Auburn University	AL	3	2	1	0	0	0	0	0	55	4	3	0	0	0	62	6	68
Baylor University	TX	0	0	0	0	0	0	0	0	13	1	0	0	0	0	13	1	14
Boise State University	ID	0	0	1	0	1	0	0	0	23	4	0	0	0	0	25	4	29
Boston University	MA	2	0	7	4	2	0	0	0	30	6	2	0	0	0	43	10	53
Bradley University	IL	0	0	2	0	1	0	0	0	57	5	0	0	0	0	60	5	65
Brigham Young University	UT	0	0	0	0	0	0	0	0	0	0	4	0	148	8	152	8	160
Brown University	RI	0	1	0	0	0	0	0	0	6	1	1	0	0	0	7	2	9
Bucknell University	PA	0	1	1	0	0	0	0	0	28	6	1	0	0	0	30	7	37
California Institute of Technology	CA	1	0	5	1	2	0	0	0	7	4	1	0	0	0	16	5	21
California Maritime Academy	CA	0	0	4	0	1	0	0	0	15	4	0	0	0	0	20	4	24
California Polytechnic State University	CA	1	0	26	4	23	1	0	0	110	14	2	0	27	1	189	20	209
California State Polytechnic University, Pomona	CA	1	0	19	1	10	0	2	0	32	0	0	0	5	1	69	2	71
California State University, Chico	CA	0	0	0	0	0	2	2	0	17	0	2	0	8	0	27	2	29
California State University, Fresno	CA	0	0	2	0	4	0	0	0	12	1	1	0	0	0	19	1	20
California State University, Fullerton	CA	0	0	2	0	6	1	0	0	5	1	1	0	1	0	15	2	17
California State University, Long Beach	CA	1	0	9	0	9	1	0	0	21	2	6	0	0	0	46	3	49
California State University, Los Angeles	CA	0	0	4	0	5	0	0	0	2	0	4	0	4	0	19	0	19
California State University, Northridge	CA	1	1	8	0	10	2	0	0	15	0	2	0	5	1	41	4	45
California State University, Sacramento	CA	1	0	7	1	4	0	1	0	15	0	1	0	4	1	33	2	35
University of California, Berkeley	CA	1	0	55	9	13	6	0	0	44	4	10	2	13	4	136	25	161
University of California, Davis	CA	0	0	47	7	12	2	2	0	55	12	1	0	10	1	127	22	149
University of California, Irvine	CA	0	0	0	0	0	0	0	0	0	0	0	0	54	17	54	17	71
University of California, Los Angeles	CA	1	1	21	6	4	1	1	0	28	3	8	1	7	2	70	14	84
University of California, Riverside	CA	1	1	15	2	12	2	0	0	10	2	0	0	2	1	40	8	48
University of California, San Diego	CA	1	0	45	10	13	2	3	0	38	10	7	3	14	3	121	28	149
University of California, Santa Barbara	CA	1	0	8	3	12	1	1	0	30	7	1	0	12	3	65	14	79
Carnegie Mellon University	PA	3	1	14	7	5	0	0	0	55	7	5	2	9	2	91	19	110
Case Western Reserve University	OH	0	0	7	0	2	0	0	0	29	6	2	0	0	0	40	6	46
The Catholic University of America	DC	0	0	0	0	0	0	0	0	5	0	0	0	0	0	5	0	5
Cedarville University	OH	0	0	0	0	0	0	0	0	0	0	0	0	36	2	36	2	38
University of Central Florida	FL	2	1	6	2	8	1	0	0	65	13	1	0	2	0	84	17	101
Christian Brothers University	TN	0	0	0	0	0	0	0	0	9	1	0	0	0	0	9	1	10
University of Cincinnati	OH	2	0	1	0	0	2	0	0	58	11	0	0	2	0	63	13	76

AKR–CIN

MECHANICAL ENGINEERING

INSTITUTION		AFRICAN AMERICAN		ASIAN AMERICAN		HISPANIC		NATIVE AMERICAN		CAUCASIAN		FOREIGN		OTHER		TOTAL BY GENDER		TOTAL DEGREES
		M	F	M	F	M	F	M	F	M	F	M	F	M	F	M	F	
Clarkson University	NY	3	0	2	1	3	0	0	0	83	5	3	0	0	0	94	6	100
Clemson University	SC	3	0	0	0	3	0	0	0	112	20	1	1	10	2	129	23	152
Cleveland State University	OH	3	0	0	0	0	0	0	0	22	1	1	0	0	0	26	1	27
Colorado State University	CO	0	0	1	0	1	0	1	0	88	10	2	0	2	1	93	11	104
University of Colorado at Boulder	CO	3	0	10	2	6	3	0	0	92	12	2	1	0	0	113	18	131
University of Colorado at Colorado Springs	CO	0	0	0	2	1	0	0	0	21	5	0	0	0	0	22	7	29
University of Colorado at Denver	CO	2	0	1	0	5	0	0	0	12	2	2	0	2	0	24	2	26
Columbia University	NY	0	0	8	0	3	0	0	0	16	7	1	0	4	0	32	7	39
University of Connecticut	CT	1	0	4	0	2	0	0	0	35	6	0	0	1	0	43	6	49
The Cooper Union	NY	1	1	2	1	2	0	1	0	10	4	1	0	0	0	17	6	23
Cornell University	NY	3	0	17	2	5	3	0	0	63	14	10	2	3	0	101	21	122
University of Dayton	OH	0	0	0	0	1	0	0	0	0	0	0	0	45	6	46	6	52
University of Delaware	DE	0	1	1	0	3	0	0	0	45	10	1	0	0	0	50	11	61
University of Denver	CO	0	0	0	0	0	0	0	0	6	0	0	0	0	0	6	0	6
University of Detroit Mercy	MI	3	2	1	0	2	0	0	0	18	3	0	0	2	1	26	6	32
University of the District of Columbia	DC	2	1	0	0	1	0	0	0	1	0	1	0	0	0	5	1	6
Drexel University	PA	4	2	8	1	2	2	0	0	65	9	6	0	10	0	95	14	109
Duke University Pratt School of Engineering	NC	0	0	0	0	0	0	0	0	0	0	0	0	38	3	38	3	41
University of Evansville	IN	0	0	0	0	0	0	0	0	0	0	0	0	20	0	20	0	20
Fairfield University	CT	0	0	0	0	0	0	0	0	13	0	0	2	0	0	13	2	15
University of Florida	FL	5	0	6	1	14	2	1	0	75	16	5	1	0	0	106	20	126
Florida Atlantic University	FL	2	0	1	0	6	1	0	0	8	0	4	0	0	0	21	1	22
Florida Institute of Technology	FL	0	0	2	0	0	1	0	0	15	3	10	0	3	1	30	5	35
Florida International University	FL	6	2	1	0	19	2	0	0	6	0	6	1	0	0	38	5	43
FAMU-FSU College of Engineering	FL	12	3	2	0	2	1	0	0	27	4	6	3	0	0	49	11	60
Gannon University	PA	0	0	0	0	0	0	0	0	14	2	5	0	0	0	19	2	21
The George Washington University	DC	2	0	1	4	0	0	0	0	5	3	2	1	0	1	10	9	19
Georgia Institute of Technology	GA	20	1	23	6	6	0	0	0	188	21	5	1	1	1	243	30	273
Gonzaga University	WA	0	0	1	0	1	0	0	0	26	4	0	0	0	0	28	4	32
Grand Valley State University	MI	0	0	0	0	0	0	0	0	35	5	0	0	0	0	35	5	40
Grove City College	PA	0	0	0	0	0	0	0	0	25	5	0	0	0	0	25	5	30
University of Hartford	CT	1	0	0	0	1	0	0	0	21	2	1	0	0	0	24	2	26
University of Hawaii at Manoa	HI	0	0	10	0	0	0	1	0	4	0	0	0	7	1	21	1	22
Henry Cogswell College	WA	0	0	0	0	0	0	0	0	8	1	0	0	0	0	8	1	9
Hofstra University	NY	1	0	0	0	1	0	0	0	1	2	0	0	1	0	2	2	4
University of Houston, Cullen School of Engineering	TX	0	0	3	0	7	7	0	0	10	5	1	0	0	1	21	13	34
Howard University	DC	10	3	0	0	0	0	0	0	0	0	0	0	0	0	10	3	13
University of Idaho	ID	0	0	0	0	2	0	1	0	52	8	0	0	3	1	58	9	67
Idaho State University	ID	0	0	0	0	1	0	0	0	20	2	0	0	0	0	21	2	23
Illinois Institute of Technology	IL	0	0	1	0	1	0	0	0	16	5	3	1	1	0	22	6	28
University of Illinois at Chicago	IL	3	0	6	2	6	5	0	0	33	1	0	0	2	0	50	8	58
University of Illinois at Urbana-Champaign	IL	4	1	27	4	3	3	0	0	135	16	8	0	4	0	181	24	205
Indiana Institute of Technology	IN	0	0	0	0	0	0	0	0	4	1	0	0	1	0	5	1	6
Indiana University-Purdue University at Indianapolis	IN	2	0	2	1	1	0	0	0	25	4	0	1	1	0	31	6	37
Indiana University-Purdue University Fort Wayne	IN	1	0	0	0	0	0	0	0	7	1	3	0	0	0	11	1	12

MECHANICAL ENGINEERING

CLA-IND

BACHELOR'S DEGREES AWARDED IN MECHANICAL ENGINEERING, 2005-2006

INSTITUTION		AFRICAN AMERICAN M	F	ASIAN AMERICAN M	F	HISPANIC M	F	NATIVE AMERICAN M	F	CAUCASIAN M	F	FOREIGN M	F	OTHER M	F	TOTAL BY GENDER M	F	TOTAL DEGREES
The University of Iowa	IA	0	0	1	1	0	0	0	0	44	4	0	0	0	0	45	5	50
Iowa State University	IA	6	3	3	0	1	1	0	0	154	17	10	1	10	1	184	23	207
John Brown University	AR	0	0	0	0	0	0	0	0	8	1	1	1	0	0	9	2	11
The Johns Hopkins University	MD	1	0	2	3	4	0	0	0	21	5	0	0	0	0	28	8	36
University of Kansas	KS	1	0	0	0	0	0	0	0	32	4	5	0	0	0	38	4	42
Kansas State University	KS	0	0	0	0	2	0	0	0	71	7	0	0	3	0	76	7	83
University of Kentucky	KY	0	2	1	0	0	0	1	0	80	7	1	1	0	0	83	10	93
Kettering University formerly GMI	MI	3	5	5	5	6	2	2	0	183	24	4	1	14	3	217	40	257
Lafayette College	PA	1	0	1	0	0	0	0	0	30	9	2	0	0	0	34	9	43
Lake Superior State University	MI	0	0	0	0	0	0	0	0	9	1	2	0	0	0	11	1	12
Lamar University	TX	0	0	1	0	1	0	0	0	21	0	0	0	0	0	23	0	23
Lawrence Technological University	MI	2	0	3	0	1	0	1	0	50	10	1	0	5	0	63	10	73
Lehigh University	PA	1	0	3	1	2	0	1	0	0	0	0	0	70	6	77	7	84
Louisiana State University	LA	1	0	2	0	1	0	0	0	61	6	0	1	2	0	67	7	74
Louisiana Tech University	LA	1	1	0	0	0	0	1	0	43	3	2	1	0	0	47	5	52
University of Louisiana at Lafayette	LA	1	0	0	0	0	0	0	0	22	3	6	1	0	0	29	4	33
University of Louisville	KY	1	0	1	0	0	0	0	0	36	1	1	1	0	0	39	2	41
Loyola Marymount University	CA	0	1	4	1	2	0	0	0	11	0	0	0	3	1	20	3	23
University of Maine	ME	0	0	1	0	0	0	2	0	35	3	0	0	0	0	38	3	41
Manhattan College	NY	0	0	0	1	2	2	0	0	0	0	0	0	35	3	37	6	43
Marquette University	WI	1	0	2	0	1	0	0	0	24	3	4	0	0	0	32	3	35
University of Maryland, Baltimore County	MD	3	2	4	3	0	0	0	0	23	6	0	0	1	0	31	11	42
University of Maryland, College Park	MD	8	3	24	5	13	1	0	0	93	14	5	0	5	1	148	24	172
Massachusetts Institute of Technology	MA	3	3	9	21	16	1	4	1	32	11	2	2	7	2	73	41	114
University of Massachusetts Amherst	MA	2	0	4	0	1	0	0	0	53	5	2	0	0	0	62	5	67
University of Massachusetts Dartmouth	MA	0	0	1	0	0	0	0	0	20	2	0	0	1	0	22	2	24
University of Massachusetts Lowell	MA	2	0	1	0	4	0	0	0	33	1	1	0	5	0	46	1	47
McNeese State University	LA	1	1	0	0	0	0	0	0	10	0	0	0	0	0	11	1	12
The University of Memphis	TN	1	0	2	0	0	0	0	0	7	2	0	0	1	0	11	2	13
Mercer University	GA	0	0	0	0	0	0	0	0	12	5	1	0	0	0	13	5	18
University of Miami	FL	1	0	0	0	2	1	0	0	10	0	0	0	0	0	13	1	14
Miami University	OH	0	0	0	0	1	0	0	0	16	5	0	0	0	0	17	5	22
University of Michigan	MI	8	3	19	6	10	2	0	0	108	26	21	6	9	5	175	48	223
Michigan State University	MI	3	2	8	1	2	1	0	0	126	31	11	0	0	0	150	35	185
Michigan Technological University	MI	2	2	2	1	4	0	2	0	168	27	8	0	6	0	192	30	222
University of Michigan, Dearborn	MI	1	2	4	2	1	0	0	0	44	9	2	0	0	0	52	13	65
Milwaukee School of Engineering	WI	1	0	5	0	4	0	1	0	83	4	1	0	0	0	95	4	99
Minnesota State University, Mankato	MN	0	0	0	0	0	0	0	0	18	2	1	1	13	0	32	3	35
University of Minnesota, Duluth	MN	0	0	0	0	0	0	0	0	33	2	0	0	0	0	33	2	35
University of Minnesota - Twin Cities	MN	2	0	9	1	2	0	2	2	121	12	13	3	0	0	149	18	167
The University of Mississippi	MS	1	0	0	0	0	0	0	0	6	1	0	0	1	0	8	1	9
Mississippi State University	MS	3	0	3	0	0	0	0	0	60	3	2	0	0	0	68	3	71
University of Missouri-Columbia	MO	2	1	2	1	0	0	0	0	81	8	4	0	3	0	93	10	103
University of Missouri - Kansas City	MO	1	0	0	0	0	0	0	0	12	0	3	0	0	0	16	0	16
University of Missouri - Rolla	MO	3	0	0	0	1	0	1	1	100	13	0	0	1	0	106	14	120

IOW-MIS

MECHANICAL ENGINEERING

INSTITUTION		AFRICAN AMERICAN		ASIAN AMERICAN		HISPANIC		NATIVE AMERICAN		CAUCASIAN		FOREIGN		OTHER		TOTAL BY GENDER		TOTAL DEGREES
		M	F	M	F	M	F	M	F	M	F	M	F	M	F	M	F	
Montana State University	MT	0	0	0	0	1	0	0	0	51	3	2	0	1	0	55	3	58
University of Nebraska, Lincoln	NE	0	0	1	0	0	0	0	0	63	0	0	0	0	0	64	0	64
University of Nevada, Las Vegas	NV	0	1	3	0	0	0	0	0	10	1	0	0	1	0	14	2	16
University of Nevada, Reno	NV	0	0	4	0	1	0	0	0	28	4	0	0	2	0	35	4	39
University of New Hampshire	NH	0	0	0	0	0	0	0	0	36	7	0	0	0	0	36	7	43
University of New Haven	CT	1	0	0	0	1	0	0	0	0	0	1	0	8	1	11	1	12
New Jersey Institute of Technology	NJ	1	0	4	0	3	1	1	0	24	2	5	1	22	0	60	4	64
The College of New Jersey	NJ	0	0	0	1	0	1	0	0	17	1	0	0	0	0	17	3	20
The University of New Mexico	NM	1	0	0	0	13	2	1	1	28	5	5	0	0	0	48	8	56
New Mexico Institute of Mining & Technology	NM	0	0	0	0	0	2	0	0	5	0	0	0	0	0	5	2	7
New Mexico State University	NM	0	0	1	0	12	1	0	1	13	3	1	0	8	0	35	5	40
University of New Orleans	LA	3	0	2	0	1	0	0	0	14	2	4	0	2	0	26	2	28
New York Institute of Technology	NY	0	0	7	0	0	0	0	0	0	0	0	0	21	6	21	6	27
City College of the City University of New York	NY	9	0	7	0	2	1	0	0	0	0	9	0	3	1	30	3	33
The State University of New York at Binghamton	NY	2	1	3	2	0	0	1	0	25	4	2	0	13	1	46	8	54
State University of New York at Buffalo	NY	2	1	4	1	0	0	1	0	89	14	17	3	6	0	119	19	138
Stony Brook University	NY	3	1	18	3	3	1	0	0	28	1	2	2	0	0	54	8	62
North Carolina A & T State University	NC	24	2	0	0	0	0	0	0	9	0	0	0	1	1	34	3	37
North Carolina State University	NC	9	0	4	0	2	1	0	0	116	10	2	0	0	1	133	12	145
University of North Carolina, Charlotte	NC	1	1	3	0	3	0	1	0	67	5	2	0	0	0	77	6	83
University of North Dakota	ND	0	0	0	0	0	0	0	0	46	13	0	0	0	0	46	13	59
North Dakota State University	ND	1	0	0	0	1	0	0	0	69	5	2	0	1	0	71	5	76
University of North Florida	FL	3	0	3	0	3	0	0	0	16	0	0	0	1	0	26	0	26
Northeastern University	MA	2	0	4	0	1	2	0	0	50	10	1	2	12	1	70	15	85
Northern Arizona University	AZ	0	1	0	0	2	2	1	0	16	3	0	0	0	0	19	6	25
Northern Illinois University	IL	1	0	1	0	1	0	0	0	39	2	0	0	2	0	44	2	46
Northwestern University	IL	1	2	5	1	1	0	0	0	19	5	2	0	1	0	29	8	37
Norwich University	VT	0	0	0	0	0	0	0	0	8	3	0	0	0	0	8	3	11
University of Notre Dame	IN	0	0	1	0	1	0	0	0	46	11	1	0	0	0	49	11	60
Oakland University	MI	0	0	0	0	1	0	0	1	60	12	1	0	0	0	62	13	75
Ohio Northern University	OH	0	0	0	0	0	0	0	0	28	4	0	0	0	0	28	4	32
The Ohio State University	OH	5	0	5	1	3	0	1	0	109	17	14	0	0	0	137	18	155
Ohio University	OH	0	0	0	0	0	0	0	0	40	4	0	0	2	0	42	4	46
University of Oklahoma	OK	2	2	12	0	4	1	4	2	86	6	7	0	0	0	115	11	126
Oklahoma Christian University	OK	0	0	0	0	0	0	0	0	12	1	0	0	0	0	12	1	13
Oklahoma State University	OK	0	1	2	0	1	0	4	1	75	13	12	1	0	0	94	16	110
Old Dominion University	VA	2	0	3	0	2	0	0	0	27	5	1	1	6	1	41	7	48
Oregon State University	OR	0	0	1	0	1	0	0	0	82	8	2	0	12	3	98	11	109
University of the Pacific	CA	0	0	0	0	0	0	0	0	10	1	0	0	1	0	11	1	12
University of Pennsylvania	PA	1	1	2	1	3	0	0	0	13	3	2	0	2	3	23	8	31
Penn State Erie, The Behrend College	PA	0	0	0	0	0	0	0	0	32	2	0	0	0	0	32	2	34
The Pennsylvania State University	PA	3	1	14	0	3	0	0	0	218	19	2	1	0	0	240	21	261
University of Pittsburgh	PA	3	0	2	0	0	1	0	0	53	9	1	0	0	0	59	10	69
Polytechnic University	NY	0	1	6	0	1	0	0	0	15	2	1	1	3	0	26	4	30
Polytechnic University of Puerto Rico	PR	0	0	0	0	53	13	0	0	0	0	0	0	0	0	53	13	66

MECHANICAL ENGINEERING

MON-POL

Bachelor's Degrees Awarded in Mechanical Engineering, 2005-2006

INSTITUTION		AFRICAN AMERICAN M	F	ASIAN AMERICAN M	F	HISPANIC M	F	NATIVE AMERICAN M	F	CAUCASIAN M	F	FOREIGN M	F	OTHER M	F	TOTAL BY GENDER M	F	TOTAL DEGREES
University of Portland	OR	0	0	1	0	0	0	0	0	22	7	0	0	0	0	23	7	30
Portland State University	OR	0	0	2	0	0	0	1	0	27	5	0	0	4	0	34	5	39
Prairie View A&M University	TX	8	2	0	0	3	0	0	0	0	0	2	0	0	0	13	2	15
Princeton University	NJ	3	1	3	3	3	0	0	0	17	1	2	0	0	0	28	5	33
University of Puerto Rico, Mayaguez Campus	PR	0	0	0	0	96	26	0	0	0	0	0	0	0	0	96	26	122
Purdue University, Calumet	IN	1	1	1	0	1	0	0	0	9	0	0	0	1	0	13	1	14
Purdue University	IN	1	1	7	1	2	0	0	1	171	34	42	6	10	0	234	43	277
Rensselaer Polytechnic Institute	NY	2	1	8	2	2	1	0	0	93	18	0	0	0	0	105	22	127
University of Rhode Island	RI	0	0	1	0	3	1	0	0	32	2	0	0	4	2	40	5	45
William Marsh Rice University	TX	0	3	2	0	2	0	0	0	14	3	1	1	4	1	23	8	31
University of Rochester	NY	1	0	1	0	1	0	0	0	13	5	1	0	7	0	24	5	29
Rochester Institute of Technology	NY	2	1	4	0	3	0	3	0	90	17	1	0	10	0	113	18	131
Rose-Hulman Institute of Technology	IN	0	1	3	0	0	1	0	0	92	14	0	0	0	0	95	16	111
Rowan University	NJ	1	0	0	0	0	0	0	0	20	2	0	0	0	0	21	2	23
Rutgers, The State University of New Jersey	NJ	2	1	10	4	3	0	0	0	48	3	4	0	0	0	67	8	75
Saginaw Valley State University	MI	0	0	0	0	0	0	0	0	21	3	1	1	0	0	22	4	26
Saint Cloud State University	MN	0	0	0	0	0	0	0	0	10	0	1	0	5	0	16	0	16
Saint Louis University - Parks College	MO	1	1	0	1	0	0	0	0	10	1	0	0	0	0	11	3	14
Saint Martin's College	WA	0	0	0	0	0	0	0	0	10	0	0	1	0	0	10	1	11
University of Saint Thomas	MN	0	0	0	0	1	0	0	0	21	2	0	1	0	0	22	3	25
University of San Diego	CA	0	0	0	0	0	0	0	0	4	2	0	0	1	0	5	2	7
San Diego State University	CA	0	0	9	3	2	1	0	0	22	2	2	1	7	2	42	9	51
San Francisco State University	CA	1	1	6	2	4	1	0	0	5	0	2	1	0	0	18	5	23
San Jose State University	CA	3	0	37	5	8	0	0	0	14	4	7	2	0	0	69	11	80
Santa Clara University	CA	0	0	4	2	2	1	0	0	19	3	1	0	0	0	26	6	32
Seattle University	WA	0	0	2	0	2	0	0	0	6	0	2	0	2	0	14	0	14
University of South Alabama	AL	0	0	0	1	0	0	0	0	14	2	2	0	0	0	16	3	19
University of South Carolina	SC	3	1	3	0	4	0	0	0	40	4	0	0	6	0	56	5	61
South Dakota School of Mines and Technology	SD	3	0	0	0	0	0	0	0	51	3	3	0	1	0	56	3	59
South Dakota State University	SD	0	0	0	0	0	0	0	0	30	1	1	0	0	0	30	1	31
University of South Florida	FL	0	0	1	0	7	0	0	0	16	3	2	1	1	0	27	4	31
University of Southern California	CA	0	2	2	4	1	0	0	0	10	0	2	0	1	0	16	6	22
Southern Illinois University Carbondale	IL	3	0	2	0	2	0	0	0	17	3	7	0	0	0	31	3	34
Southern Illinois University Edwardsville	IL	2	0	0	0	1	0	1	0	37	1	0	0	0	0	41	1	42
Southern Methodist University	TX	0	0	1	2	1	2	0	0	11	4	1	1	0	0	14	9	23
Southern University and A&M College	LA	9	3	0	0	0	0	0	0	1	0	0	0	0	0	10	3	13
Stanford University	CA	4	0	6	5	7	1	2	0	27	6	6	1	0	2	52	15	67
Stevens Institute of Technology	NJ	0	0	2	1	2	2	0	0	30	3	2	0	3	3	39	9	48
Syracuse University	NY	0	2	3	1	0	0	0	0	26	1	1	0	0	0	30	4	34
Temple University	PA	1	0	2	0	0	0	0	0	7	2	3	0	0	0	13	2	15
Tennessee State University	TN	6	2	0	0	1	0	0	0	0	0	1	0	0	0	8	2	10
Tennessee Technological University	TN	1	0	1	0	2	0	0	0	57	4	2	0	0	0	63	4	67
University of Tennessee, Chattanooga	TN	0	0	0	0	0	0	0	0	12	3	1	0	0	0	13	3	16
University of Tennessee, Knoxville	TN	0	0	1	0	1	0	0	0	42	4	1	0	0	0	45	4	49
Texas A&M University	TX	5	0	5	0	18	2	1	0	115	18	6	0	1	1	151	21	172

POR-TEX

MECHANICAL ENGINEERING

INSTITUTION		AFRICAN AMERICAN M	F	ASIAN AMERICAN M	F	HISPANIC M	F	NATIVE AMERICAN M	F	CAUCASIAN M	F	FOREIGN M	F	OTHER M	F	TOTAL BY GENDER M	F	TOTAL DEGREES
Texas A&M University - Kingsville	TX	0	1	1	0	6	3	0	0	15	0	0	0	0	0	22	4	26
Texas Tech University	TX	4	0	2	0	11	1	0	1	79	6	1	0	0	0	97	8	105
The University of Texas at Arlington	TX	2	0	10	5	5	0	0	0	38	3	5	1	0	0	60	4	64
The University of Texas at Austin	TX	3	2	27	5	14	5	1	0	113	15	10	1	0	0	168	28	196
University of Texas at El Paso	TX	0	0	0	0	29	7	0	0	4	3	5	2	0	0	38	12	50
The University of Texas-Pan American	TX	1	0	0	0	31	9	1	0	5	0	7	0	1	1	46	10	56
University of Texas at San Antonio	TX	1	0	3	0	17	4	0	0	23	3	3	1	0	0	47	8	55
The University of Texas at Tyler	TX	0	0	0	0	3	0	0	0	4	0	0	0	0	0	7	0	7
The University of Toledo	OH	0	0	0	0	1	0	0	0	68	12	3	1	0	0	72	13	85
Tri-State University	IN	0	0	1	1	0	0	0	0	19	5	0	0	0	0	20	6	26
Tufts University	MA	2	0	4	0	1	0	0	0	0	0	2	0	27	12	36	12	48
Tulane University	LA	1	1	1	0	1	0	0	0	0	0	0	1	22	2	25	4	29
University of Tulsa	OK	1	0	1	0	0	0	1	0	14	4	6	0	4	0	27	4	31
Tuskegee University	AL	16	3	0	0	0	0	0	0	0	0	0	0	3	2	19	5	24
Union College	NY	0	0	1	0	1	0	0	0	25	10	0	0	1	0	28	10	38
U.S. Air Force Academy	CO	1	0	1	0	1	0	1	0	0	0	0	0	29	4	33	4	37
U.S. Coast Guard Academy	CT	2	0	0	0	1	0	0	0	15	1	0	0	0	0	18	1	19
United States Military Academy	NY	1	0	6	0	4	0	0	0	49	2	1	0	1	0	62	2	64
U.S. Naval Academy	MD	4	0	2	0	4	0	2	0	53	3	0	0	0	0	65	3	68
University of Utah	UT	0	0	0	0	2	0	1	0	71	4	1	0	0	9	75	13	88
Utah State University	UT	0	0	0	0	0	0	0	0	78	2	0	0	0	0	78	2	80
Valparaiso University	IN	0	0	0	0	0	0	0	0	25	4	1	0	0	0	26	4	30
Vanderbilt University	TN	2	1	2	0	2	3	0	0	40	2	5	1	4	0	55	7	62
University of Vermont	VT	0	0	0	0	0	0	0	0	26	3	1	0	0	0	27	3	30
Villanova University	PA	2	1	2	0	0	0	0	0	56	14	1	0	0	0	61	15	76
University of Virginia	VA	4	4	4	2	1	0	0	0	30	6	0	0	2	0	41	12	53
Virginia Commonwealth University	VA	2	1	7	0	3	0	0	0	40	3	0	0	4	0	56	4	60
Virginia Military Institute	VA	2	0	3	1	1	0	0	0	29	0	0	0	0	0	35	1	36
Virginia Polytechnic Institute and State University	VA	5	1	13	3	6	2	0	0	201	27	4	0	15	0	244	33	277
University of Washington	WA	0	0	12	2	3	1	0	0	50	0	3	0	5	0	73	3	76
Washington State University	WA	1	0	3	0	3	0	1	0	69	7	2	0	4	0	83	7	90
Washington University	MO	4	0	1	0	0	0	0	0	17	10	0	1	4	0	26	11	37
Wayne State University	MI	2	2	3	1	1	1	0	0	16	2	4	0	0	0	26	6	32
West Virginia University Institute of Technology	WV	0	0	1	0	0	0	0	0	15	0	3	0	0	0	19	0	19
West Virginia University	WV	1	0	1	0	1	0	0	0	81	7	3	0	1	0	88	7	95
Western Kentucky University	KY	0	0	0	0	0	0	0	0	11	3	0	0	0	0	11	3	14
Western Michigan University	MI	1	0	3	1	1	1	1	0	74	13	5	0	0	0	82	13	95
Western New England College	MA	0	0	1	0	0	0	0	0	21	3	0	0	2	0	24	3	27
Wichita State University	KS	1	0	2	0	2	0	0	0	0	0	8	0	16	2	29	2	31
Widener University	PA	0	0	0	0	0	0	0	0	18	2	0	0	0	0	18	2	20
Wilkes University	PA	0	0	0	0	0	0	0	0	18	0	0	0	0	0	18	0	18
University of Wisconsin, Madison	WI	1	0	3	1	1	1	0	0	113	15	3	0	2	0	124	17	141
University of Wisconsin, Milwaukee	WI	1	0	1	0	1	0	0	0	38	2	0	1	0	0	41	3	44
University of Wisconsin, Platteville	WI	0	0	1	0	0	0	0	0	87	11	0	0	0	0	88	11	99
Worcester Polytechnic Institute	MA	1	1	4	2	2	1	0	0	106	27	0	1	4	1	117	33	150

MECHANICAL ENGINEERING   TEX-WOR

BACHELOR'S DEGREES AWARDED IN MECHANICAL ENGINEERING, 2005-2006

INSTITUTION		AFRICAN AMERICAN		ASIAN AMERICAN		HISPANIC		NATIVE AMERICAN		CAUCASIAN		FOREIGN		OTHER		TOTAL BY GENDER		TOTAL DEGREES
		M	F	M	F	M	F	M	F	M	F	M	F	M	F	M	F	
Wright State University	OH	1	0	1	0	0	0	0	0	42	3	1	0	0	1	45	4	49
University of Wyoming	WY	0	0	0	0	1	0	0	0	24	4	1	0	1	0	27	4	31
Yale University/Faculty of Engineering	CT	0	0	0	0	0	0	0	0	0	0	0	0	7	4	7	4	11
York College of Pennsylvania	PA	0	0	0	0	0	0	0	0	0	0	0	0	19	2	19	2	21
Youngstown State University	OH	0	0	0	0	0	0	0	0	19	5	0	0	0	0	19	5	24
Totals:		417	123	969	206	843	173	71	14	9,977	1,346	578	83	1,103	160	13,958	2,105	16,063

CANADIAN INSTITUTIONS:

INSTITUTION		AFRICAN AMERICAN		ASIAN AMERICAN		HISPANIC		NATIVE AMERICAN		CAUCASIAN		FOREIGN		OTHER		TOTAL BY GENDER		TOTAL DEGREES
		M	F	M	F	M	F	M	F	M	F	M	F	M	F	M	F	
University of Alberta	AB	0	0	0	0	0	0	0	0	0	0	0	0	130	21	130	21	151
University of Calgary	AB	0	0	0	0	0	0	0	0	0	0	0	0	74	10	74	10	84
Concordia University, Faculty of Engr. and Comp. Sci.	PQ	0	0	0	0	0	0	0	0	0	0	8	1	89	15	97	16	113
Ecole Polytechnique de Montreal	PQ	0	0	0	0	0	0	0	0	0	0	0	0	122	35	122	35	157
Ecole de Technologie Superieure	PQ	0	0	0	0	0	0	0	0	0	0	0	0	212	15	212	15	227
McGill University, Faculty of Engineering	PQ	0	0	0	0	0	0	0	0	0	0	0	0	94	18	94	18	112
University of Ottawa, Faculty of Engineering	ON	0	0	0	0	0	0	0	0	0	0	4	0	63	14	67	14	81
University of Waterloo	ON	0	0	0	0	0	0	0	0	0	0	0	0	123	25	123	25	148
Totals:		0	0	0	0	0	0	0	0	0	0	12	1	907	153	919	154	1,073

WRI-YOU

MECHANICAL ENGINEERING

INSTITUTION		AFRICAN AMERICAN M	F	ASIAN AMERICAN M	F	HISPANIC M	F	NATIVE AMERICAN M	F	CAUCASIAN M	F	FOREIGN M	F	OTHER M	F	TOTAL BY GENDER M	F	TOTAL DEGREES
University of Alabama at Birmingham	AL	1	3	0	0	0	0	0	0	0	1	0	0	0	0	1	4	5
The University of Alabama	AL	2	0	0	0	0	0	0	0	9	0	0	0	0	0	11	0	11
Alfred University, NY State College of Ceramics	NY	0	0	0	0	0	1	0	0	5	3	0	0	2	0	7	4	11
The University of Arizona	AZ	0	1	1	0	0	0	0	0	10	3	0	0	0	0	11	4	15
Arizona State University	AZ	1	0	1	0	1	0	0	0	8	0	0	0	2	1	13	1	14
Auburn University	AL	0	0	0	0	0	0	0	0	1	0	0	0	0	0	1	0	1
Brown University	RI	0	0	0	1	0	0	0	0	3	1	0	0	0	0	3	2	5
California Polytechnic State University	CA	0	0	1	0	0	0	0	0	5	3	0	0	0	0	6	3	9
University of California, Berkeley	CA	0	0	9	2	3	0	0	0	1	1	0	1	0	0	13	4	17
University of California, Davis	CA	0	0	1	0	0	0	0	0	1	0	0	1	0	0	2	1	3
University of California, Irvine	CA	0	0	0	0	0	0	0	0	0	0	0	0	4	1	4	1	5
University of California, Los Angeles	CA	0	0	13	2	1	0	0	0	2	0	0	1	1	1	17	4	21
Carnegie Mellon University	PA	0	1	1	2	0	0	0	0	3	2	1	1	0	1	5	7	12
Case Western Reserve University	OH	0	0	0	0	0	0	0	0	1	1	0	0	0	0	1	1	2
Clemson University	SC	0	1	0	0	0	0	0	0	11	8	0	0	0	1	11	10	21
Colorado School of Mines	CO	0	0	1	2	1	3	0	1	17	6	0	1	0	0	19	13	32
Columbia University	NY	0	0	0	1	0	0	0	0	3	0	0	0	0	0	3	1	4
University of Connecticut	CT	0	0	0	1	0	0	0	0	5	1	0	0	0	1	5	3	8
Cornell University	NY	1	0	12	3	1	0	0	0	18	2	1	2	0	0	33	7	40
Drexel University	PA	0	0	0	0	0	0	0	0	8	0	0	0	0	0	8	0	8
University of Florida	FL	1	3	4	1	1	0	0	0	18	8	1	0	0	0	25	12	37
FAMU-FSU College of Engineering	FL	0	0	0	0	0	0	0	0	1	1	0	1	0	0	1	2	3
Georgia Institute of Technology	GA	0	0	1	0	1	0	0	0	7	4	2	1	1	0	12	5	17
University of Idaho	ID	0	0	0	0	0	0	0	0	11	0	0	0	3	0	14	0	14
Illinois Institute of Technology	IL	0	0	0	0	0	0	0	0	6	1	0	1	0	0	6	2	8
University of Illinois at Urbana-Champaign	IL	1	2	5	4	2	0	0	0	25	5	1	1	0	0	34	12	46
Iowa State University	IA	0	0	0	1	0	0	0	0	19	7	0	0	3	0	22	8	30
The Johns Hopkins University	MD	0	0	1	0	0	0	0	0	0	1	0	0	0	0	1	1	2
University of Kentucky	KY	0	0	0	0	0	0	0	0	3	2	1	1	0	0	4	3	7
Lehigh University	PA	0	0	0	0	0	0	0	0	0	0	0	0	17	5	17	5	22
University of Maryland, College Park	MD	0	0	0	0	0	0	0	0	6	1	0	0	2	0	8	1	9
Massachusetts Institute of Technology	MA	1	0	6	10	0	1	0	0	11	7	1	1	2	1	21	20	41
University of Michigan	MI	0	1	3	3	1	0	0	0	14	10	2	1	1	1	21	16	37
Michigan State University	MI	0	1	3	2	0	0	0	0	17	4	0	0	0	0	20	7	27
Michigan Technological University	MI	0	0	0	0	0	0	1	0	11	3	0	0	0	0	12	3	15
University of Minnesota - Twin Cities	MN	0	0	1	0	0	0	1	0	6	1	0	0	0	0	8	1	9
University of Missouri - Rolla	MO	0	0	1	0	0	0	0	0	10	5	0	0	0	0	11	5	16
Montana Tech of the University of Montana	MT	0	0	0	0	0	0	0	0	4	3	3	0	0	0	7	3	10
University of Nevada, Reno	NV	0	0	2	1	0	0	0	0	2	1	0	0	0	0	4	2	6
New Mexico Institute of Mining & Technology	NM	0	0	0	0	0	1	0	1	5	0	0	0	0	0	5	2	7
North Carolina State University	NC	0	0	1	0	1	0	1	0	21	7	0	0	0	0	24	7	31
Northwestern University	IL	0	0	3	3	1	0	0	0	10	2	3	2	0	0	17	7	24
The Ohio State University	OH	1	0	3	2	1	0	0	0	20	8	0	0	0	0	25	10	35
University of Pennsylvania	PA	0	0	0	1	0	0	0	0	4	3	0	0	0	0	4	4	8
The Pennsylvania State University	PA	1	0	2	0	0	1	0	1	14	1	0	0	0	0	17	3	20

METALLURGICAL AND MATERIALS ENGR.   ALA-PEN

METALLURGICAL AND MATERIALS ENGINEERING

BACHELOR'S DEGREES AWARDED IN METALLURGICAL AND MATERIALS ENGINEERING, 2005-2006

INSTITUTION		AFRICAN AMERICAN		ASIAN AMERICAN		HISPANIC		NATIVE AMERICAN		CAUCASIAN		FOREIGN		OTHER		TOTAL BY GENDER		TOTAL DEGREES
		M	F	M	F	M	F	M	F	M	F	M	F	M	F	M	F	
University of Pittsburgh	PA	0	0	0	0	0	0	0	0	5	0	0	0	0	0	5	0	5
Purdue University	IN	0	0	1	1	0	0	0	0	22	8	1	0	0	0	24	9	33
Rensselaer Polytechnic Institute	NY	0	0	0	1	0	0	0	1	5	3	0	0	0	0	5	5	10
William Marsh Rice University	TX	0	0	0	0	0	0	0	0	0	1	0	0	0	0	0	1	1
San Jose State University	CA	0	0	0	1	2	0	0	0	1	0	1	0	0	0	4	1	5
South Dakota School of Mines and Technology	SD	0	0	0	1	0	0	0	0	5	0	0	0	0	0	5	1	6
Stanford University	CA	0	0	0	0	0	0	0	0	2	0	0	0	0	0	2	0	2
University of Tennessee, Knoxville	TN	0	0	0	0	0	0	0	0	6	1	0	0	0	0	6	1	7
University of Texas at El Paso	TX	0	0	1	1	12	4	0	0	2	0	1	0	0	0	16	5	21
University of Utah	UT	0	0	0	0	0	0	0	0	3	1	1	1	0	0	4	2	6
Virginia Polytechnic Institute and State University	VA	1	0	0	2	0	0	0	0	12	4	0	0	0	0	13	6	19
University of Washington	WA	0	0	7	1	1	0	0	0	16	3	1	1	1	2	26	7	33
Washington State University	WA	0	0	0	0	0	0	0	0	6	1	0	0	0	0	6	1	7
University of Wisconsin, Madison	WI	0	0	1	0	0	0	0	0	15	3	0	1	0	1	16	5	21
University of Wisconsin, Milwaukee	WI	0	0	0	0	0	0	0	0	3	0	0	0	0	0	3	0	3
Wright State University	OH	0	1	0	0	0	0	0	0	2	1	1	0	0	0	3	2	5
Totals:		**11**	**14**	**86**	**50**	**30**	**11**	**4**	**4**	**460**	**143**	**22**	**19**	**39**	**16**	**652**	**257**	**909**
CANADIAN INSTITUTIONS:																		
University of Alberta	AB	0	0	0	0	0	0	0	0	0	0	0	0	21	6	21	6	27
Ecole Polytechnique de Montreal	PQ	0	0	0	0	0	0	0	0	0	0	0	0	5	0	5	0	5
Totals:		**0**	**0**	**0**	**0**	**0**	**0**	**0**	**0**	**0**	**0**	**0**	**0**	**26**	**6**	**26**	**6**	**32**

METALLURGICAL AND MATERIALS ENGR.   PIT-WRI

BACHELOR'S DEGREES AWARDED IN MINING ENGINEERING, 2005-2006

INSTITUTION		AFRICAN AMERICAN		ASIAN AMERICAN		HISPANIC		NATIVE AMERICAN		CAUCASIAN		FOREIGN		OTHER		TOTAL BY GENDER		TOTAL DEGREES
		M	F	M	F	M	F	M	F	M	F	M	F	M	F	M	F	
University of Alaska Fairbanks	AK	0	0	0	0	0	0	0	0	1	2	0	0	0	0	1	2	3
The University of Arizona	AZ	0	0	0	0	1	0	0	0	0	6	1	0	0	0	2	6	8
Colorado School of Mines	CO	0	0	0	1	1	0	0	0	12	0	2	0	0	0	15	1	16
Columbia University	NY	0	0	0	0	0	0	0	0	0	3	0	0	0	0	0	3	3
University of Kentucky	KY	0	0	0	0	0	0	0	0	6	0	0	0	1	0	7	0	7
Michigan Technological University	MI	0	0	0	0	0	0	0	0	0	0	0	0	4	0	4	0	4
University of Missouri - Rolla	MO	0	0	0	0	0	0	0	0	11	1	0	1	0	1	11	3	14
Montana Tech of the University of Montana	MT	0	0	0	0	0	0	0	0	5	1	4	0	0	0	9	1	10
New Mexico Institute of Mining & Technology	NM	0	0	0	0	0	2	1	0	1	2	0	0	0	0	2	4	6
South Dakota School of Mines and Technology	SD	0	0	0	0	0	0	0	0	2	1	0	0	0	0	2	1	3
Southern Illinois University Carbondale	IL	0	0	0	0	0	0	0	0	4	0	0	0	0	0	4	0	4
Virginia Polytechnic Institute and State University	VA	0	0	2	0	1	0	0	0	23	11	0	0	0	0	26	11	37
West Virginia University	WV	0	0	0	0	0	0	0	0	4	1	0	0	0	0	4	1	5
Totals:		0	0	2	1	3	2	1	0	69	28	7	1	5	1	87	33	120
CANADIAN INSTITUTIONS:																		
University of Alberta	AB	0	0	0	0	0	0	0	0	0	0	0	0	10	4	10	4	14
Ecole Polytechnique de Montreal	PQ	0	0	0	0	0	0	0	0	0	0	0	0	1	0	1	0	1
McGill University, Faculty of Engineering	PQ	0	0	0	0	0	0	0	0	0	0	0	0	20	4	20	4	24
Totals:		0	0	0	0	0	0	0	0	0	0	0	0	31	8	31	8	39

ALA-WES

MINING ENGINEERING

BACHELOR'S DEGREES AWARDED IN NUCLEAR ENGINEERING, 2005-2006

INSTITUTION		AFRICAN AMERICAN		ASIAN AMERICAN		HISPANIC		NATIVE AMERICAN		CAUCASIAN		FOREIGN		OTHER		TOTAL BY GENDER		TOTAL DEGREES
		M	F	M	F	M	F	M	F	M	F	M	F	M	F	M	F	
University of California, Berkeley	CA	0	0	2	1	0	0	0	0	0	2	1	1	0	0	3	4	7
University of Florida	FL	1	0	1	0	1	1	0	0	7	0	0	0	0	0	10	1	11
Georgia Institute of Technology	GA	1	0	4	0	0	0	0	0	16	1	0	0	0	0	21	1	22
University of Illinois at Urbana-Champaign	IL	0	0	2	0	1	0	0	0	8	2	0	0	1	0	12	2	14
Massachusetts Institute of Technology	MA	2	0	2	1	1	0	1	0	5	2	0	0	0	2	11	5	16
University of Michigan	MI	1	0	2	3	3	1	1	1	19	4	0	1	1	0	27	10	37
University of Missouri - Rolla	MO	0	0	0	0	0	0	0	0	11	5	0	0	0	0	11	5	16
The University of New Mexico	NM	0	0	2	0	1	1	0	0	6	1	1	0	0	0	10	2	12
North Carolina State University	NC	0	0	1	0	1	1	0	0	16	1	0	0	0	0	18	1	19
Oregon State University	OR	0	1	0	1	3	0	0	0	18	3	0	0	2	1	23	6	29
The Pennsylvania State University	PA	1	0	2	0	0	0	0	0	26	3	0	0	0	0	29	3	32
Purdue University	IN	0	0	3	0	0	0	0	0	12	4	1	0	1	0	17	4	21
Rensselaer Polytechnic Institute	NY	2	0	0	0	0	0	0	0	22	2	1	0	0	0	25	2	27
University of Tennessee, Knoxville	TN	0	1	1	0	0	0	0	0	17	3	0	0	0	0	18	4	22
Texas A&M University	TX	0	0	1	1	5	1	1	0	23	4	0	1	1	1	31	8	39
University of Wisconsin, Madison	WI	0	0	0	0	0	0	0	0	16	0	0	0	2	0	18	0	18
Totals:		8	2	23	7	16	4	3	1	222	37	4	3	8	4	284	58	342

NUCLEAR ENGINEERING

CAL-WIS

BACHELOR'S DEGREES AWARDED IN OTHER ENGINEERING DISCIPLINES, 2005-2006

INSTITUTION		AFRICAN AMERICAN		ASIAN AMERICAN		HISPANIC		NATIVE AMERICAN		CAUCASIAN		FOREIGN		OTHER		TOTAL BY GENDER		TOTAL DEGREES
		M	F	M	F	M	F	M	F	M	F	M	F	M	F	M	F	
The University of Alabama in Huntsville	AL	0	0	0	0	0	0	0	0	4	2	0	0	0	0	4	2	6
Alfred University, NY State College of Ceramics	NY	0	0	0	0	0	0	0	0	15	4	0	0	0	0	15	4	19
The University of Arizona	AZ	0	1	2	0	5	1	0	0	18	7	0	0	0	0	25	9	34
University of Arkansas	AR	0	0	1	0	0	0	0	1	12	4	0	0	0	0	13	5	18
University of Arkansas at Little Rock	AR	0	0	0	0	0	0	0	0	9	1	0	0	0	0	9	1	10
Auburn University	AL	0	0	0	0	0	0	0	0	2	3	0	0	0	0	2	5	7
Boise State University	ID	0	2	0	0	1	0	1	1	18	6	0	0	2	0	22	7	29
Boston University	MA	0	0	0	0	0	0	0	0	1	0	0	0	0	0	1	0	1
California Institute of Technology	CA	1	0	2	2	0	0	0	0	3	0	0	0	0	0	6	2	8
California Polytechnic State University	CA	0	0	1	0	0	0	1	0	6	6	0	0	0	1	8	7	15
California State University, Chico	CA	2	0	0	0	0	0	0	0	10	0	0	0	2	0	14	0	14
California State University, Fresno	CA	2	1	4	2	9	5	0	0	28	4	0	0	0	0	43	12	55
University of California, Berkeley	CA	1	0	27	5	2	1	0	0	15	0	3	1	3	2	51	9	60
University of California, Riverside	CA	0	0	10	6	1	0	0	0	5	1	0	0	0	0	16	7	23
Capitol College	MD	0	0	0	0	0	0	0	0	0	0	0	0	2	0	2	0	2
Case Western Reserve University	OH	0	0	0	0	0	0	0	0	2	3	0	0	0	0	2	3	5
Colorado School of Mines	CO	0	0	1	0	0	1	0	0	24	12	1	1	0	0	26	14	40
University of Colorado at Boulder	CO	0	0	3	1	0	0	0	0	17	6	0	0	0	0	20	7	27
Columbia University	NY	1	0	2	1	2	0	0	0	8	2	3	2	4	1	20	6	26
University of Connecticut	CT	0	0	0	0	0	0	0	0	2	0	0	0	0	0	2	0	2
Cornell University	NY	0	0	0	1	0	0	1	0	10	7	1	0	0	0	12	8	20
Drexel University	PA	1	0	1	0	0	0	0	0	1	0	0	0	2	0	5	0	5
Duke University Pratt School of Engineering	NC	0	0	0	0	0	0	0	0	0	0	0	0	1	0	1	0	1
Ferris State University	MI	0	0	0	0	0	0	0	0	30	4	0	0	2	1	32	5	37
Florida Atlantic University	FL	0	0	0	0	0	1	0	0	9	2	0	0	0	0	9	3	12
Florida Institute of Technology	FL	0	1	0	0	0	0	0	1	13	11	1	2	3	1	17	16	33
Florida International University	FL	3	1	0	0	12	3	0	0	10	1	3	1	0	0	28	6	34
George Mason University	VA	12	9	35	7	11	2	0	0	70	19	5	3	13	7	147	47	194
The George Washington University	DC	0	0	0	0	0	0	0	0	1	2	5	0	0	0	6	2	8
University of Georgia	GA	1	0	1	0	0	0	0	0	3	4	0	0	0	0	5	4	9
Georgia Institute of Technology	GA	1	0	0	0	0	1	0	0	2	9	0	0	0	0	3	10	13
Harvard University	MA	1	1	7	4	2	0	0	0	19	9	6	3	0	0	35	17	52
University of Idaho	ID	0	0	1	0	0	0	0	0	4	4	0	0	1	0	6	4	10
Iowa State University	IA	5	0	0	0	3	2	0	0	112	8	1	0	2	0	124	10	134
The Johns Hopkins University	MD	0	0	3	1	1	0	0	0	7	3	2	2	0	0	13	6	19
Kansas State University	KS	1	0	0	0	3	2	0	0	69	3	0	0	3	0	77	5	82
Lafayette College	PA	2	0	0	0	0	0	0	0	9	4	0	0	0	0	11	4	15
Lehigh University	PA	1	0	2	2	1	1	0	0	0	0	1	0	17	14	22	17	39
University of Maine	ME	0	1	0	0	0	0	0	0	4	1	0	0	0	0	4	2	6
Maine Maritime Academy	ME	0	0	0	0	0	0	0	0	9	2	1	0	0	0	10	2	12
University of Maryland, College Park	MD	0	3	2	1	1	0	0	0	32	4	0	0	1	0	36	8	44
Massachusetts Institute of Technology	MA	0	0	0	0	0	0	0	0	3	2	1	0	0	0	4	2	6
Massachusetts Maritime Academy	MA	1	0	1	0	0	1	0	0	62	9	0	0	0	0	65	9	74
University of Massachusetts Dartmouth	MA	0	0	0	0	0	0	0	0	2	1	0	0	0	0	2	1	3
University of Massachusetts Lowell	MA	0	0	1	0	0	0	0	0	5	6	0	0	1	0	7	6	13

OTHER ENGINEERING DISCIPLINES   ALA-MAS

INSTITUTION		AFRICAN AMERICAN		ASIAN AMERICAN		HISPANIC		NATIVE AMERICAN		CAUCASIAN		FOREIGN		OTHER		TOTAL BY GENDER		TOTAL DEGREES
		M	F	M	F	M	F	M	F	M	F	M	F	M	F	M	F	
Mercer University	GA	0	1	0	0	0	0	0	0	1	2	0	0	0	0	1	3	4
Miami University	OH	0	1	0	1	0	0	0	0	18	6	0	0	1	0	19	8	27
University of Michigan	MI	0	0	3	0	1	1	0	0	17	9	4	0	0	0	25	10	35
Michigan State University	MI	1	4	4	1	1	0	0	1	22	10	0	1	0	0	28	17	45
Michigan Technological University	MI	0	0	0	0	1	0	0	0	6	4	0	0	0	0	7	4	11
University of Michigan, Dearborn	MI	0	1	0	0	0	0	0	0	3	2	0	0	0	0	3	3	6
University of Minnesota - Twin Cities	MN	0	0	0	0	0	0	0	0	4	0	0	0	0	0	4	0	4
The University of Mississippi	MS	0	0	0	0	0	0	0	0	10	2	0	0	0	0	10	2	12
University of Missouri - Rolla	MO	0	0	0	0	0	0	0	0	9	3	0	0	0	0	9	3	12
Monmouth University	NJ	0	0	0	0	0	0	0	0	2	0	0	0	0	0	2	0	2
Montana Tech of the University of Montana	MT	0	0	0	0	0	0	0	0	2	3	0	0	0	0	2	3	5
University of Nebraska, Lincoln	NE	0	0	0	0	1	0	0	0	1	0	0	0	0	0	2	0	2
New Mexico Institute of Mining & Technology	NM	0	0	0	0	0	0	0	0	3	0	0	0	0	0	3	0	3
New Mexico State University	NM	0	0	0	0	1	0	1	0	0	0	0	0	0	0	2	0	2
University of New Orleans	LA	0	0	1	0	0	0	0	0	4	1	5	0	0	0	10	1	11
State University of New York Maritime College	NY	2	0	2	0	1	2	0	0	31	1	0	0	0	0	36	3	39
SUNY College of Environmental Science and Forestry	NY	0	1	2	0	0	0	0	0	32	8	1	0	0	0	35	9	44
Stony Brook University	NY	6	6	30	19	1	2	0	0	27	7	4	1	0	0	68	35	103
North Carolina State University	NC	0	2	0	2	0	1	0	0	20	8	0	0	0	0	20	13	33
University of North Dakota	ND	0	0	0	0	0	0	0	0	2	1	0	0	0	0	2	1	3
North Dakota State University	ND	0	0	0	0	0	0	0	0	44	3	0	0	0	0	44	3	47
Northern Arizona University	AZ	1	0	0	0	0	0	1	0	36	2	0	0	0	0	38	2	40
Northwestern University	IL	0	0	1	0	0	0	0	0	0	0	1	0	0	0	2	0	2
Oakland University	MI	0	0	0	1	0	0	0	0	4	3	0	0	0	0	4	4	8
The Ohio State University	OH	0	0	0	0	0	0	0	0	15	0	0	0	0	0	15	0	15
University of Oklahoma	OK	0	0	0	0	0	0	0	0	1	0	0	0	0	0	1	0	1
Oklahoma State University	OK	0	0	0	0	1	0	0	0	11	4	2	1	0	0	14	5	19
Oregon Institute of Technology	OR	0	0	1	0	0	0	0	0	5	1	0	0	0	0	6	1	7
Oregon State University	OR	1	0	0	0	4	0	2	1	44	1	0	0	4	0	55	2	57
The Pennsylvania State University	PA	1	1	0	0	0	0	0	0	11	2	1	0	0	0	13	3	16
Philadelphia University	PA	0	0	0	0	0	0	0	0	1	0	0	0	0	0	1	0	1
Princeton University	NJ	3	2	7	3	1	0	0	0	21	8	5	2	0	0	37	15	52
University of Puerto Rico, Mayaguez Campus	PR	0	0	0	0	16	6	0	0	0	0	0	0	0	0	16	6	22
Purdue University	IN	0	0	0	0	0	0	0	0	13	4	1	0	0	2	14	6	20
University of Rhode Island	RI	0	0	0	0	0	0	0	0	6	2	0	0	0	0	6	2	8
William Marsh Rice University	TX	0	0	1	1	1	1	0	0	3	3	1	0	0	1	6	6	12
University of Rochester	NY	0	0	2	1	0	0	0	0	9	2	0	0	4	0	15	3	18
Rochester Institute of Technology	NY	0	1	5	1	1	0	0	0	38	8	4	0	7	0	55	10	65
Roger Williams University	RI	0	0	0	0	0	0	0	0	19	2	0	0	0	0	19	2	21
Rose-Hulman Institute of Technology	IN	0	0	0	0	0	0	0	0	3	2	0	0	0	0	3	2	5
Rutgers, The State University of New Jersey	NJ	0	2	5	1	1	0	1	0	12	4	1	0	0	0	20	7	27
South Dakota School of Mines and Technology	SD	0	0	0	0	0	0	0	0	3	2	0	0	1	0	4	2	6
South Dakota State University	SD	0	0	0	0	0	0	1	0	5	1	0	0	0	0	6	1	7
University of Southern California	CA	0	0	3	0	0	0	0	0	3	2	0	0	1	0	7	2	9
Southern Illinois University Edwardsville	IL	0	1	0	0	0	0	0	0	21	0	0	0	0	0	21	1	22

MER-SOU

OTHER ENGINEERING DISCIPLINES

BACHELOR'S DEGREES AWARDED IN OTHER ENGINEERING DISCIPLINES, 2005-2006

INSTITUTION		AFRICAN AMERICAN M	F	ASIAN AMERICAN M	F	HISPANIC M	F	NATIVE AMERICAN M	F	CAUCASIAN M	F	FOREIGN M	F	OTHER M	F	TOTAL BY GENDER M	F	TOTAL DEGREES
University of Tennessee, Knoxville	TN	0	0	0	0	0	0	0	0	2	0	0	0	0	0	2	0	2
Texas A&M University	TX	0	0	2	0	2	1	0	0	20	6	1	0	0	0	25	7	32
Texas A&M University, Galveston	TX	0	0	0	1	0	3	0	0	18	0	0	1	0	0	18	5	23
Texas A&M University - Kingsville	TX	1	1	0	0	24	4	0	0	12	2	0	0	0	0	37	7	44
Tufts University	MA	1	0	2	0	0	1	0	0	0	0	0	0	10	4	13	5	18
U.S. Coast Guard Academy	CT	0	0	0	0	0	0	0	0	7	2	0	0	0	0	7	2	9
U.S. Merchant Marine Academy	NY	0	0	5	1	0	1	0	0	66	6	3	1	0	0	74	9	83
U.S. Naval Academy	MD	6	1	9	3	12	1	6	1	125	13	2	0	0	0	160	19	179
University of Virginia	VA	0	0	13	1	0	0	0	0	48	14	2	2	5	3	68	20	88
Virginia Polytechnic Institute and State University	VA	0	0	1	1	0	0	0	0	13	2	1	3	0	0	15	6	21
University of Washington	WA	1	1	2	3	0	0	0	0	7	5	0	0	1	0	11	9	20
Washington State University	WA	1	2	1	1	0	0	0	0	5	3	0	0	2	0	8	6	14
Washington University	MO	1	2	0	2	1	0	0	0	17	7	2	3	0	1	21	15	36
Webb Institute	NY	0	0	0	0	0	0	0	0	16	6	0	0	0	0	16	6	22
Wentworth Institute of Technology	MA	0	0	0	0	0	0	0	0	18	0	0	0	0	0	18	0	18
West Virginia University	WV	0	0	0	0	0	0	0	0	8	4	0	0	0	0	8	4	12
Western Michigan University	MI	0	0	0	0	0	0	0	0	24	2	0	0	0	0	24	2	26
Winona State University	MN	0	0	0	0	0	0	0	0	11	2	1	0	0	0	12	2	14
University of Wisconsin, Madison	WI	0	0	1	0	0	0	0	0	34	6	0	0	1	0	36	6	42
University of Wisconsin, Platteville	WI	0	0	0	0	0	0	0	0	12	1	0	0	0	0	12	1	13
Totals:		60	50	211	77	126	44	18	6	1,690	380	76	30	96	38	2,277	625	2,902

CANADIAN INSTITUTIONS:

INSTITUTION		AFRICAN AMERICAN M	F	ASIAN AMERICAN M	F	HISPANIC M	F	NATIVE AMERICAN M	F	CAUCASIAN M	F	FOREIGN M	F	OTHER M	F	TOTAL BY GENDER M	F	TOTAL DEGREES
University of Calgary	AB	0	0	0	0	0	0	0	0	0	0	0	0	28	13	28	13	41
Concordia University, Faculty of Engr. and Comp. Sci.	PQ	0	0	0	0	0	0	0	0	0	0	3	0	39	15	42	15	57
Ecole Polytechnique de Montreal	PQ	0	0	0	0	0	0	0	0	0	0	0	0	2	5	2	5	7
University of Ottawa, Faculty of Engineering	ON	0	0	0	0	0	0	0	0	0	0	5	1	49	7	54	8	62
University of Waterloo	ON	0	0	0	0	0	0	0	0	0	0	0	0	49	31	49	31	80
Totals:		0	0	0	0	0	0	0	0	0	0	8	1	167	71	175	72	247

OTHER ENGINEERING DISCIPLINES   TEN-WIS

Bachelor's Degrees Awarded in Petroleum Engineering, 2005-2006

INSTITUTION		AFRICAN AMERICAN		ASIAN AMERICAN		HISPANIC		NATIVE AMERICAN		CAUCASIAN		FOREIGN		OTHER		TOTAL BY GENDER		TOTAL DEGREES
		M	F	M	F	M	F	M	F	M	F	M	F	M	F	M	F	
Colorado School of Mines	CO	0	0	1	0	1	1	0	0	18	4	9	1	0	0	29	6	35
University of Kansas	KS	0	0	0	0	0	0	0	0	0	0	2	0	0	0	2	0	2
Louisiana State University	LA	0	0	0	0	0	0	0	0	18	5	14	0	1	0	33	5	38
Marietta College	OH	0	0	0	0	0	0	0	0	14	0	0	0	0	0	14	0	14
University of Missouri - Rolla	MO	0	0	1	0	0	0	0	0	5	0	0	1	0	0	6	1	7
Montana Tech of the University of Montana	MT	0	0	0	0	0	0	0	0	15	4	6	0	0	0	21	4	25
New Mexico Institute of Mining & Technology	NM	0	0	0	0	0	0	0	0	2	1	0	0	0	0	2	1	3
University of Oklahoma	OK	0	1	1	1	1	1	3	1	10	4	3	2	0	0	18	10	28
University of Southern California	CA	0	0	0	0	1	0	0	0	1	1	2	0	0	0	4	1	5
Texas A&M University	TX	0	1	1	0	3	0	2	0	19	10	5	0	1	0	31	11	42
Texas Tech University	TX	0	0	1	0	4	0	1	0	24	2	4	0	1	0	35	2	37
The University of Texas at Austin	TX	0	0	13	3	5	4	0	0	43	5	8	0	0	0	69	12	81
University of Tulsa	OK	0	0	0	0	0	0	0	0	3	1	11	1	0	0	14	2	16
West Virginia University	WV	0	0	0	0	0	0	0	0	3	1	1	0	0	0	4	1	5
University of Wyoming	WY	0	0	0	0	0	0	0	0	0	0	0	0	1	0	1	0	1
Totals:		0	2	18	4	15	6	6	1	175	38	65	5	4	0	283	56	339
CANADIAN INSTITUTIONS:																		
University of Alberta	AB	0	0	0	0	0	0	0	0	0	0	0	0	22	0	22	0	22
University of Calgary	AB	0	0	0	0	0	0	0	0	0	0	0	0	10	2	10	2	12
Totals:		0	0	0	0	0	0	0	0	0	0	0	0	32	2	32	2	34

COL-WYO

PETROLEUM ENGINEERING

GRADUATE ENGINEERING ENROLLMENTS, FALL 2006

INSTITUTION		MASTER'S (FT)	MASTER'S (PT)	MASTER'S M	MASTER'S F	TOTAL MASTER'S	PH.D. (FT)	PH.D. (PT)	PH.D. M	PH.D. F	TOTAL PH.D.	TOTAL GRAD ENROLLMENT
Air Force Institute of Technology	OH	711	13	656	68	724	110	4	102	12	114	838
The University of Akron	OH	116	38	115	39	154	93	19	88	24	112	266
University of Alabama at Birmingham	AL	93	51	97	47	144	51	28	61	18	79	223
The University of Alabama in Huntsville	AL	117	257	293	81	374	50	114	128	36	164	538
The University of Alabama	AL	82	59	101	40	141	79	40	95	24	119	260
University of Alaska Fairbanks	AK	63	25	65	23	88	22	7	23	6	29	117
Alfred University,NY State College of Ceramics	NY	29	7	26	10	36	9	4	8	5	13	49
The University of Arizona	AZ	333	0	247	86	333	338	0	251	87	338	671
Arizona State University	AZ	529	362	683	208	891	578	134	567	145	712	1,603
University of Arkansas	AR	281	222	369	134	503	118	34	120	32	152	655
Auburn University	AL	207	166	299	74	373	171	132	219	84	303	676
Baylor University	TX	35	3	29	9	38	0	0	0	0	0	38
Boise State University	ID	54	72	98	28	126	2	3	5	0	5	131
Boston University	MA	153	47	152	48	200	353	12	270	95	365	565
Bradley University	IL	68	100	135	33	168	0	0	0	0	0	168
University of Bridgeport	CT	374	210	499	85	584	2	2	4	0	4	588
Brigham Young University	UT	187	0	174	13	187	107	0	95	12	107	294
Brown University	RI	18	7	19	6	25	106	1	84	23	107	132
Bucknell University	PA	38	4	31	11	42	0	0	0	0	0	42
California Institute of Technology	CA	66	3	58	11	69	568	0	439	129	568	637
California Polytechnic State University	CA	172	99	212	59	271	0	0	0	0	0	271
California State University, East Bay	CA	4	9	7	6	13	0	0	0	0	0	13
California State University, Fresno	CA	94	0	78	16	94	0	0	0	0	0	94
California State University, Fullerton	CA	43	463	394	112	506	0	0	0	0	0	506
California State University, Long Beach	CA	149	325	375	99	474	0	0	0	0	0	474
California State University, Los Angeles	CA	277	0	225	52	277	0	0	0	0	0	277
California State University, Northridge	CA	143	310	360	93	453	0	0	0	0	0	453
California State University, Sacramento	CA	178	227	318	87	405	0	0	0	0	0	405
University of California, Berkeley	CA	195	12	137	70	207	1,315	117	1,082	350	1,432	1,639
University of California, Davis	CA	297	32	246	83	329	763	41	585	219	804	1,133
University of California, Irvine	CA	180	0	135	45	180	348	0	261	87	348	528
University of California, Los Angeles	CA	495	0	390	105	495	800	0	642	158	800	1,295
University of California, Riverside	CA	36	21	45	12	57	233	20	179	74	253	310
University of California, San Diego	CA	366	0	308	58	366	829	0	657	172	829	1,195
University of California, Santa Barbara	CA	97	0	76	21	97	577	0	454	123	577	674
University of California-Santa Cruz	CA	72	11	57	26	83	178	35	165	48	213	296
Carnegie Mellon University	PA	286	32	252	66	318	576	36	450	162	612	930
Case Western Reserve University	OH	127	122	213	36	249	280	98	288	90	378	627
The Catholic University of America	DC	14	96	75	35	110	8	35	35	8	43	153
University of Central Florida	FL	215	265	396	84	480	451	63	406	108	514	994
University of Cincinnati	OH	458	54	407	105	512	437	10	354	93	447	959
Clarkson University	NY	119	1	97	23	120	84	0	71	13	84	204
Clemson University	SC	339	70	321	88	409	292	35	243	84	327	736
Cleveland State University	OH	13	340	263	90	353	4	57	46	15	61	414
Colorado School of Mines	CO	292	154	337	109	446	152	139	218	72	291	737

GRADUATE ENROLLMENTS

AIR-COL

GRADUATE ENGINEERING ENROLLMENTS, FALL 2006

INSTITUTION		MASTER'S (FT)	(PT)	M	F	TOTAL MASTER'S	(FT)	(PT)	PH.D. M	F	TOTAL PH.D.	TOTAL GRAD ENROLLMENT
Colorado State University	CO	223	73	217	79	296	151	97	194	54	248	544
Colorado State University, Pueblo	CO	6	20	19	7	26	0	0	0	0	0	26
University of Colorado at Boulder	CO	697	301	775	223	998	491	0	375	116	491	1,489
University of Colorado at Colorado Springs	CO	80	109	146	43	189	25	17	36	6	42	231
University of Colorado at Denver	CO	167	119	202	84	286	11	6	15	2	17	303
Columbia University	NY	375	392	600	167	767	535	36	454	117	571	1,338
University of Connecticut	CT	111	72	143	40	183	228	57	218	67	285	468
Cornell University	NY	484	0	373	111	484	811	0	613	198	811	1,295
Dartmouth College	NH	79	1	62	18	80	46	1	31	16	47	127
University of Dayton	OH	160	171	263	68	331	54	32	69	17	86	417
University of Delaware	DE	96	52	111	37	148	387	22	291	118	409	557
University of Denver	CO	23	6	21	8	29	7	2	6	3	9	38
University of Detroit Mercy	MI	88	53	114	27	141	0	10	9	1	10	151
Drexel University	PA	163	439	465	137	602	204	155	261	98	359	961
Duke University Pratt School of Engineering	NC	149	0	102	47	149	334	0	234	100	334	483
Embry Riddle Aeronautical Univ, Daytona Beach	FL	87	10	80	17	97	0	0	0	0	0	97
Fairleigh Dickinson University	NJ	102	33	97	38	135	0	0	0	0	0	135
University of Florida	FL	943	0	749	194	943	1,262	0	1,004	258	1,262	2,205
Florida Atlantic University	FL	131	168	215	84	299	55	35	65	25	90	389
Florida Institute of Technology	FL	161	312	369	104	473	50	35	71	14	85	558
Florida International University	FL	257	277	381	153	534	194	57	179	72	251	785
FAMU-FSU College of Engineering	FL	126	0	95	31	126	145	0	118	27	145	271
Gannon University	PA	134	35	135	34	169	0	0	0	0	0	169
George Mason University	VA	251	915	899	267	1,166	43	315	294	64	358	1,524
The George Washington University	DC	392	596	713	275	988	89	291	281	99	380	1,368
University of Georgia	GA	18	3	16	5	21	14	2	12	4	16	37
Georgia Institute of Technology	GA	844	578	1,173	249	1,422	1,780	158	1,520	418	1,938	3,360
Grand Valley State University	MI	14	57	62	9	71	0	0	0	0	0	71
University of Hartford	CT	52	69	91	30	121	0	0	0	0	0	121
Harvard University	MA	31	8	33	6	39	306	0	231	75	306	345
University of Hawaii at Manoa	HI	89	39	92	36	128	57	16	59	14	73	201
University of Houston, Cullen School of Engineering	TX	180	174	273	81	354	171	58	176	53	229	583
Howard University	DC	28	21	40	9	49	9	9	14	4	18	67
University of Idaho	ID	89	149	211	27	238	29	45	66	8	74	312
Idaho State University	ID	21	19	35	5	40	9	14	19	4	23	63
Illinois Institute of Technology	IL	537	272	642	167	809	89	127	175	41	216	1,025
University of Illinois at Chicago	IL	296	150	330	116	446	343	86	325	104	429	875
University of Illinois at Urbana-Champaign	IL	727	67	651	143	794	1,678	0	1,379	299	1,678	2,472
Indiana University Purdue University at Indianapolis	IN	38	46	69	15	84	0	0	0	0	0	84
The University of Iowa	IA	123	0	91	32	123	227	0	162	65	227	350
Iowa State University	IA	370	0	305	65	370	492	0	391	101	492	862
The Johns Hopkins University	MD	169	1,866	1,578	457	2,035	553	16	416	153	569	2,604
University of Kansas	KS	107	378	391	94	485	79	76	124	31	155	640
Kansas State University	KS	220	129	275	74	349	90	15	75	30	105	454
University of Kentucky	KY	312	100	315	97	412	239	22	213	48	261	673

GRADUATE ENROLLMENTS

COL-KEN

GRADUATE ENGINEERING ENROLLMENTS, FALL 2006

INSTITUTION		MASTER'S					PH.D.					TOTAL GRAD ENROLLMENT
		(FT)	(PT)	M	F	TOTAL MASTER'S	(FT)	(PT)	M	F	TOTAL PH.D.	
Kettering University formerly GMI	MI	3	50	45	8	53	0	0	0	0	0	53
Lamar University	TX	213	62	232	43	275	17	12	23	6	29	304
Lawrence Technological University	MI	18	320	289	49	338	1	34	31	4	35	373
Lehigh University	PA	134	100	179	55	234	328	0	254	74	328	562
Louisiana State University	LA	170	50	168	52	220	216	30	196	50	246	466
Louisiana Tech University	LA	174	55	170	59	229	108	18	102	24	126	355
University of Louisiana at Lafayette	LA	125	0	101	24	125	38	0	34	4	38	163
University of Louisville	KY	164	164	271	57	328	139	27	129	37	166	494
Loyola College in Maryland	MD	22	14	32	4	36	0	0	0	0	0	36
Loyola Marymount University	CA	69	48	88	29	117	0	0	0	0	0	117
University of Maine	ME	61	24	69	16	85	47	16	52	11	63	148
Manhattan College	NY	98	56	127	27	154	0	0	0	0	0	154
Marquette University	WI	79	95	125	49	174	45	25	56	14	70	244
University of Maryland, Baltimore County	MD	84	101	148	37	185	91	100	150	41	191	376
University of Maryland, College Park	MD	352	437	589	200	789	762	110	688	184	872	1,661
Massachusetts Institute of Technology	MA	1,094	4	826	272	1,098	1,556	8	1,192	372	1,564	2,662
University of Massachusetts Amherst	MA	204	12	161	55	216	192	0	155	37	192	408
University of Massachusetts Dartmouth	MA	139	108	189	58	247	5	18	19	4	23	270
University of Massachusetts Lowell	MA	139	150	219	70	289	43	22	54	11	65	354
McNeese State University	LA	67	13	65	15	80	0	0	0	0	0	80
The University of Memphis	TN	99	34	103	30	133	34	11	33	12	45	178
Mercer University	GA	23	75	68	30	98	0	0	0	0	0	98
University of Miami	FL	95	24	84	35	119	108	8	95	21	116	235
Miami University	OH	22	8	21	9	30	0	0	0	0	0	30
University of Michigan	MI	920	207	888	239	1,127	1,278	45	1,031	292	1,323	2,450
Michigan State University	MI	204	0	160	44	204	374	0	307	67	374	578
Michigan Technological University	MI	193	78	206	65	271	179	31	156	54	210	481
University of Michigan, Dearborn	MI	58	577	514	121	635	0	0	0	0	0	635
Milwaukee School of Engineering	WI	6	44	41	9	50	0	0	0	0	0	50
Minnesota State University, Mankato	MN	18	24	37	5	42	0	0	0	0	0	42
University of Minnesota -Twin Cities	MN	880	0	724	156	880	947	0	772	175	947	1,827
The University of Mississippi	MS	95	28	98	25	123	58	14	51	21	72	195
Mississippi State University	MS	168	77	195	50	245	172	56	181	47	228	473
University of Missouri-Columbia	MO	200	0	160	40	200	204	0	161	43	204	404
University of Missouri - Rolla	MO	378	409	625	162	787	203	29	182	50	232	1,019
Monmouth University	NJ	5	76	61	20	81	0	0	0	0	0	81
Montana State University	MT	53	47	89	11	100	10	35	36	9	45	145
Montana Tech of the University of Montana	MT	27	6	27	6	33	0	0	0	0	0	33
Morgan State University	MD	19	19	28	10	38	18	22	28	12	40	78
Naval Postgraduate School	CA	393	0	368	25	393	0	0	0	0	0	393
University of Nebraska, Lincoln	NE	149	78	182	45	227	124	42	133	33	166	393
University of Nevada, Las Vegas	NV	64	153	162	55	217	15	39	46	8	54	271
University of Nevada, Reno	NV	63	106	140	29	169	34	53	70	17	87	256
University of New Hampshire	NH	73	85	120	38	158	37	36	55	18	73	231
University of New Haven	CT	119	106	195	30	225	0	0	0	0	0	225

GRADUATE ENROLLMENTS   KET-NEW

INSTITUTION		MASTER'S (FT)	(PT)	M	F	TOTAL MASTER'S	PH.D. (FT)	(PT)	M	F	TOTAL PH.D.	TOTAL GRAD ENROLLMENT
New Jersey Institute of Technology	NJ	558	439	738	259	997	166	8	124	50	174	1,171
The University of New Mexico	NM	345	0	274	71	345	245	0	199	46	245	590
New Mexico Institute of Mining & Technology	NM	82	11	71	22	93	0	0	0	0	0	93
New Mexico State University	NM	319	0	249	70	319	86	0	69	17	86	405
University of New Orleans	LA	23	73	66	30	96	47	21	57	11	68	164
New York Institute of Technology	NY	475	0	377	98	475	0	0	0	0	0	475
City College of the City University of New York	NY	41	388	332	97	429	190	12	153	49	202	631
The State University of New York at Binghamton	NY	260	190	347	103	450	85	75	136	24	160	610
State University of New York at Buffalo	NY	482	159	525	116	641	334	16	278	72	350	991
SUNY College of Environmental Science and Forestry	NY	25	25	34	16	50	12	17	22	7	29	79
Stony Brook University	NY	308	113	307	114	421	446	28	347	127	474	895
North Carolina A & T State University	NC	197	0	141	56	197	71	0	55	16	71	268
North Carolina State University	NC	630	321	756	195	951	849	103	751	201	952	1,903
University of North Carolina at Chapel Hill	NC	24	0	10	14	24	26	0	16	10	26	50
University of North Carolina, Charlotte	NC	133	83	167	49	216	43	52	78	17	95	311
University of North Dakota	ND	35	45	65	15	80	0	0	0	0	0	80
North Dakota State University	ND	27	75	90	12	102	22	30	43	9	52	154
University of North Texas	TX	93	22	89	26	115	35	13	33	15	48	163
Northeastern University	MA	338	268	488	118	606	216	20	173	63	236	842
Northern Arizona University	AZ	12	12	23	1	24	0	0	0	0	0	24
Northern Illinois University	IL	76	44	95	25	120	0	0	0	0	0	120
Northwestern University	IL	120	250	289	81	370	674	9	484	199	683	1,053
University of Notre Dame	IN	43	1	29	15	44	346	3	270	79	349	393
Oakland University	MI	187	236	341	82	423	45	65	89	21	110	533
The Ohio State University	OH	376	0	297	79	376	833	0	652	181	833	1,209
Ohio University	OH	169	28	172	25	197	71	16	74	13	87	284
University of Oklahoma	OK	164	114	224	54	278	160	63	174	49	223	501
Oklahoma State University	OK	470	0	372	98	470	140	0	119	21	140	610
Old Dominion University	VA	79	679	624	134	758	71	113	150	34	184	942
OGI School of Science & Engineering at OHSU	OR	17	181	137	61	198	59	36	56	39	95	293
Oregon State University	OR	259	65	259	65	324	205	25	191	39	230	554
University of Pennsylvania	PA	303	350	494	159	653	400	17	298	119	417	1,070
The Pennsylvania State University	PA	435	75	406	104	510	1,019	82	861	240	1,101	1,611
University of Pittsburgh	PA	141	114	205	50	255	247	27	182	92	274	529
Polytechnic University	NY	474	368	684	158	842	77	56	103	30	133	975
Polytechnic University of Puerto Rico	PR	397	0	212	185	397	0	0	0	0	0	397
Portland State University	OR	218	207	317	108	425	57	32	68	22	89	514
Prairie View A&M University	TX	63	27	65	25	90	11	3	14	0	14	104
Princeton University	NJ	24	0	17	7	24	476	0	358	118	476	500
University of Puerto Rico, Mayaguez Campus	PR	300	0	211	89	300	78	0	58	20	78	378
Purdue University, Calumet	IN	57	22	67	12	79	0	0	0	0	0	79
Purdue University	IN	411	327	582	156	738	1,161	222	1,126	257	1,383	2,121
Rensselaer Polytechnic Institute	NY	84	58	110	32	142	446	28	360	114	474	616
University of Rhode Island	RI	57	65	94	28	122	39	20	44	15	59	181
William Marsh Rice University	TX	27	9	30	6	36	470	6	351	125	476	512

NEW-RIC

GRADUATE ENROLLMENTS

INSTITUTION		MASTER'S					PH.D.					TOTAL GRAD ENROLLMENT
		(FT)	(PT)	M	F	TOTAL MASTER'S	(FT)	(PT)	M	F	TOTAL PH.D.	
University of Rochester	NY	92	17	80	29	109	260	21	205	76	281	390
Rochester Institute of Technology	NY	183	201	294	90	384	19	3	19	3	22	406
Rose-Hulman Institute of Technology	IN	34	14	39	9	48	0	0	0	0	0	48
Rowan University	NJ	16	10	25	1	26	0	0	0	0	0	26
Rutgers, The State University of New Jersey	NJ	151	139	212	78	290	281	108	281	108	389	679
Saint Cloud State University	MN	44	27	55	16	71	0	0	0	0	0	71
Saint Louis University - Parks College	MO	0	0	0	0	0	5	0	3	2	5	5
Saint Martin's College	WA	40	0	31	9	40	0	0	0	0	0	40
Saint Mary's University	TX	28	31	46	13	59	0	0	0	0	0	59
University of Saint Thomas	MN	48	161	168	41	209	0	0	0	0	0	209
San Diego State University	CA	149	167	234	82	316	0	9	9	0	9	325
San Francisco State University	CA	16	29	31	14	45	0	0	0	0	0	45
San Jose State University	CA	616	950	886	680	1,566	0	0	0	0	0	1,566
Santa Clara University	CA	110	344	354	100	454	17	28	37	8	45	499
University of South Alabama	AL	213	28	193	48	241	0	0	0	0	0	241
University of South Carolina	SC	89	48	115	22	137	164	57	172	49	221	358
South Dakota School of Mines and Technology	SD	91	40	102	29	131	20	12	27	5	32	163
South Dakota State University	SD	150	0	126	24	150	20	0	16	4	20	170
University of South Florida	FL	175	195	278	92	370	204	101	223	82	305	675
University of Southern California	CA	1,294	1,513	2,217	590	2,807	933	79	809	203	1,012	3,819
Southern Illinois University Carbondale	IL	181	88	212	57	269	45	33	64	14	78	347
Southern Illinois University Edwardsville	IL	124	97	162	59	221	0	0	0	0	0	221
Southern Methodist University	TX	108	701	643	166	809	76	42	97	21	118	927
Stanford University	CA	1,509	362	1,456	415	1,871	1,480	26	1,174	332	1,506	3,377
Stevens Institute of Technology	NJ	200	470	543	127	670	103	40	109	34	143	813
Syracuse University	NY	498	151	481	168	649	114	44	133	25	158	807
Temple University	PA	36	37	50	23	73	3	13	12	4	16	89
Tennessee State University	TN	29	23	32	20	52	3	9	12	0	12	64
Tennessee Technological University	TN	80	24	79	25	104	19	25	37	7	44	148
University of Tennessee, Chattanooga	TN	27	75	83	19	102	7	7	12	2	14	116
University of Tennessee, Knoxville	TN	214	256	376	94	470	165	123	225	63	288	758
Texas A&M University	TX	1,103	182	1,016	269	1,285	856	124	835	145	980	2,265
Texas A&M University - Kingsville	TX	274	122	317	79	396	15	16	21	10	31	427
Texas Tech University	TX	245	107	284	68	352	154	47	169	32	201	553
The University of Texas at Arlington	TX	520	560	843	237	1,080	93	271	288	76	364	1,444
The University of Texas at Austin	TX	782	243	815	210	1,025	850	250	904	196	1,100	2,125
The University of Texas at Dallas	TX	454	269	539	184	723	183	67	208	42	250	973
University of Texas at El Paso	TX	196	146	258	84	342	73	41	83	31	114	456
University of Texas at San Antonio	TX	69	81	116	34	150	34	25	41	18	59	209
The University of Texas at Tyler	TX	16	27	37	6	43	0	0	0	0	0	43
The University of Toledo	OH	127	76	161	42	203	82	16	81	17	98	301
Tri-State University	IN	2	5	6	1	7	0	0	0	0	0	7
Tufts University	MA	201	138	234	105	339	118	36	97	57	154	493
Tulane University	LA	22	5	19	8	27	69	2	44	27	71	98
University of Tulsa	OK	114	42	126	30	156	27	22	36	13	49	205

ROC-TUL

GRADUATE ENROLLMENTS

GRADUATE ENGINEERING ENROLLMENTS, FALL 2006

TUS-YOU

INSTITUTION		MASTER'S					PH.D.					TOTAL GRAD ENROLLMENT
		(FT)	(PT)	M	F	TOTAL MASTER'S	(FT)	(PT)	M	F	TOTAL PH.D.	
Tuskegee University	AL	40	1	32	9	41	15	0	7	8	15	56
U.S. Merchant Marine Academy	NY	0	12	12	0	12	0	0	0	0	0	12
University of Utah	UT	247	160	344	63	407	278	87	292	73	365	772
Utah State University	UT	217	3	192	28	220	106	1	91	16	107	327
Vanderbilt University	TN	47	23	50	20	70	320	7	237	90	327	397
University of Vermont	VT	13	38	40	11	51	24	35	43	16	59	110
Villanova University	PA	59	256	246	69	315	10	0	7	3	10	325
University of Virginia	VA	189	84	199	74	273	447	0	344	103	447	720
Virginia Commonwealth University	VA	53	70	84	39	123	43	15	41	17	58	181
Virginia Polytechnic Institute and State University	VA	611	264	688	187	875	888	107	798	197	995	1,870
University of Washington	WA	379	237	459	157	616	778	46	626	198	824	1,440
Washington State University	WA	105	133	188	50	238	157	31	143	45	188	426
Washington University	MO	139	374	399	114	513	295	12	237	70	307	820
Wayne State University	MI	433	301	560	174	734	170	47	172	45	217	951
West Virginia University	WV	332	133	357	108	465	144	37	160	21	181	646
Western Michigan University	MI	211	83	233	61	294	37	13	39	11	50	344
Wichita State University	KS	207	282	422	67	489	29	42	62	9	71	560
Widener University	PA	14	31	37	8	45	0	0	0	0	0	45
Wilkes University	PA	24	4	16	12	28	0	0	0	0	0	28
University of Wisconsin, Madison	WI	392	200	502	90	592	667	74	597	144	741	1,333
University of Wisconsin, Milwaukee	WI	37	104	106	35	141	38	50	70	18	88	229
Worcester Polytechnic Institute	MA	217	135	282	70	352	95	8	78	25	103	455
Wright State University	OH	301	110	311	100	411	91	23	92	22	114	525
University of Wyoming	WY	69	32	79	22	101	78	13	69	22	91	192
Yale University/Faculty of Engineering	CT	12	4	13	3	16	216	0	156	60	216	232
Youngstown State University	OH	12	18	26	4	30	0	0	0	0	0	30
Totals:		50,086	33,429	65,011	18,504	83,515	50,130	7,436	44,802	12,764	57,566	141,081
CANADIAN INSTITUTIONS:												
University of Alberta	AB	586	0	456	130	586	482	0	402	80	482	1,068
University of Calgary	AB	592	247	655	184	839	260	21	230	51	281	1,120
Concordia University, Faculty of Engr. and Comp. Sci.	PQ	1,323	91	1,142	272	1,414	370	7	319	58	377	1,791
Ecole Polytechnique de Montreal	PQ	601	88	525	164	689	445	0	354	91	445	1,134
Ecole de Technologie Superieure	PQ	295	172	386	81	467	196	5	167	34	201	668
McGill University, Faculty of Engineering	PQ	281	35	236	80	316	310	4	257	57	314	630
University of Ottawa, Faculty of Engineering	ON	282	110	292	100	392	217	18	189	46	235	627
University of Waterloo	ON	417	202	449	170	619	463	47	422	88	510	1,129
Totals:		4,377	945	4,141	1,181	5,322	2,743	102	2,340	505	2,845	8,167

GRADUATE ENROLLMENTS

MASTER'S DEGREES AWARDED IN ENGINEERING, 2005-2006

INSTITUTION		AFRICAN AMERICAN		ASIAN AMERICAN		HISPANIC		NATIVE AMERICAN		CAUCASIAN		FOREIGN		OTHER		TOTAL BY GENDER		TOTAL DEGREES
		M	F	M	F	M	F	M	F	M	F	M	F	M	F	M	F	
Air Force Institute of Technology	OH	1	0	0	0	0	0	0	0	18	1	0	0	513	40	532	41	573
The University of Akron	OH	2	0	2	1	0	0	0	0	13	3	23	15	1	0	41	19	60
University of Alabama at Birmingham	AL	2	1	2	0	0	0	0	0	17	1	39	7	6	3	66	12	78
The University of Alabama in Huntsville	AL	2	2	0	0	1	0	0	0	66	18	33	3	0	1	102	24	126
The University of Alabama	AL	1	2	15	5	0	0	0	0	39	2	14	4	0	0	69	13	82
University of Alaska Fairbanks	AK	0	0	0	1	0	0	0	0	6	2	13	2	0	0	24	5	29
Alfred University, NY State College of Ceramics	NY	1	1	0	0	0	0	0	0	11	5	3	4	0	0	15	10	25
The University of Arizona	AZ	0	0	4	3	6	4	0	1	38	19	71	25	0	0	119	52	171
Arizona State University	AZ	1	1	9	1	4	4	0	0	54	15	136	36	18	6	222	63	285
University of Arkansas	AR	16	9	4	0	5	0	0	0	103	26	43	15	11	4	182	54	236
Auburn University	AL	5	0	3	3	1	1	1	0	45	10	36	15	1	1	92	30	122
Baylor University	TX	0	0	3	1	0	0	1	0	11	0	0	0	0	0	15	1	16
Boise State University	ID	0	0	2	1	0	0	0	0	17	3	3	5	0	0	22	9	31
Boston University	MA	2	1	20	14	2	0	0	0	21	7	28	11	0	0	73	33	106
Bradley University	IL	2	0	0	0	2	0	0	0	17	4	59	9	0	0	80	13	93
University of Bridgeport	CT	1	0	1	1	0	0	0	0	1	0	110	22	0	0	113	23	136
Brigham Young University	UT	0	0	2	0	0	0	0	0	0	0	14	3	95	3	111	6	117
Brown University	RI	0	0	1	2	1	0	0	0	3	3	9	1	0	0	14	6	20
Bucknell University	PA	1	0	1	1	0	2	2	0	75	27	1	0	0	0	80	30	110
California Institute of Technology	CA	0	0	7	0	3	4	0	0	27	6	30	9	0	0	67	19	86
California Polytechnic State University	CA	1	1	11	1	5	3	0	0	46	9	2	1	8	4	73	19	92
California State University, Fresno	CA	0	0	7	3	1	0	0	0	3	1	28	3	0	0	39	7	46
California State University, Fullerton	CA	2	1	48	9	8	1	0	0	23	6	49	10	19	3	149	29	178
California State University, Long Beach	CA	2	1	16	3	5	0	0	0	20	5	26	5	0	0	69	14	83
California State University, Los Angeles	CA	2	0	12	1	11	5	0	0	7	2	22	6	9	2	63	16	79
California State University, Northridge	CA	2	2	35	15	19	4	0	0	41	8	8	0	24	7	129	36	165
California State University, Sacramento	CA	0	0	17	12	3	1	0	0	18	3	83	31	17	1	138	48	186
University of California, Berkeley	CA	2	3	43	11	9	7	0	0	80	47	79	28	17	7	232	103	335
University of California, Davis	CA	2	1	24	14	3	0	1	0	56	15	28	13	17	6	131	49	180
University of California, Irvine	CA	0	0	0	0	0	0	0	0	0	0	0	0	132	46	132	46	178
University of California, Los Angeles	CA	2	0	88	24	12	2	1	0	63	6	48	21	22	12	236	65	301
University of California, Riverside	CA	0	1	5	3	1	0	0	0	3	1	0	0	27	7	36	12	48
University of California, San Diego	CA	1	1	48	6	10	5	0	0	78	25	50	17	9	3	196	57	253
University of California, Santa Barbara	CA	1	0	13	11	0	0	0	1	20	7	43	11	29	2	107	31	138
University of California-Santa Cruz	CA	0	0	8	8	1	0	0	0	17	1	7	3	5	2	38	14	52
Carnegie Mellon University	PA	7	1	22	4	4	2	0	1	66	12	133	33	6	3	238	56	294
Case Western Reserve University	OH	1	0	7	4	2	1	0	0	72	16	26	11	4	1	112	33	145
The Catholic University of America	DC	1	2	0	1	0	3	0	0	4	2	17	4	5	4	27	16	43
University of Central Florida	FL	9	5	11	3	8	5	0	1	82	21	95	30	3	1	208	66	274
University of Cincinnati	OH	4	2	2	2	3	0	0	0	33	8	162	35	1	0	205	48	253
Clarkson University	NY	0	2	0	0	0	0	0	0	18	6	15	4	0	0	33	12	45
Clemson University	SC	4	2	4	0	1	0	0	0	92	17	88	29	7	1	196	49	245
Cleveland State University	OH	0	0	3	3	1	0	0	0	31	6	80	20	0	0	115	29	144
Colorado School of Mines	CO	3	1	8	1	7	1	0	0	86	58	41	10	0	0	145	71	216
Colorado State University	CO	0	1	0	1	2	0	0	0	56	23	0	0	29	5	87	30	117

MASTER'S DEGREES AWARDED

AIR-COL

Master's Degrees Awarded in Engineering, 2005-2006

Institution		African American		Asian American		Hispanic		Native American		Caucasian		Foreign		Other		Total by Gender		Total Degrees
		M	F	M	F	M	F	M	F	M	F	M	F	M	F	M	F	
Colorado State University, Pueblo	CO	0	0	0	0	0	0	0	0	1	1	1	1	0	0	2	2	4
University of Colorado at Boulder	CO	5	2	8	4	6	3	1	0	176	52	61	12	0	0	257	73	330
University of Colorado at Colorado Springs	CO	1	0	2	0	1	0	1	0	29	2	3	3	5	0	42	5	47
University of Colorado at Denver	CO	1	0	9	4	8	2	1	0	47	15	20	10	4	5	90	36	126
Columbia University	NY	4	0	36	15	9	0	0	0	69	11	154	43	64	26	336	95	431
University of Connecticut	CT	0	0	5	1	2	0	0	0	28	9	34	18	5	4	74	32	106
Cornell University	NY	3	1	68	25	9	5	1	1	133	31	154	57	16	4	384	124	508
Dartmouth College	NH	2	0	1	0	2	1	0	0	21	5	5	3	7	2	38	11	49
University of Dayton	OH	1	0	0	0	0	0	0	0	56	14	37	9	3	0	97	23	120
University of Delaware	DE	0	2	0	0	0	0	1	0	20	8	25	15	0	0	46	25	71
University of Denver	CO	0	0	0	0	0	0	0	0	4	1	7	1	0	0	11	2	13
University of Detroit Mercy	MI	1	0	5	0	5	1	0	0	13	2	21	1	5	3	50	7	57
Drexel University	PA	5	4	14	6	1	0	0	0	62	12	68	30	18	5	168	57	225
Duke University Pratt School of Engineering	NC	0	0	0	0	0	0	0	0	0	0	0	0	84	27	84	27	111
Embry Riddle Aeronautical Univ, Daytona Beach	FL	1	0	1	0	2	0	1	0	6	0	12	2	2	1	24	3	27
Fairleigh Dickinson University	NJ	1	1	3	0	2	0	0	0	9	2	31	3	0	0	46	6	52
University of Florida	FL	13	5	30	4	17	7	1	0	167	56	119	30	0	0	347	102	449
Florida Atlantic University	FL	4	2	7	4	6	4	0	0	16	8	235	10	0	0	268	28	296
Florida Institute of Technology	FL	5	2	3	1	9	0	0	0	65	19	32	14	16	4	130	40	170
Florida International University	FL	12	2	5	5	45	12	0	1	17	5	82	21	1	0	162	46	208
FAMU-FSU College of Engineering	FL	5	3	2	0	2	0	0	0	14	1	15	4	0	0	38	8	46
Gannon University	PA	0	0	0	0	0	0	0	0	9	0	15	9	0	0	24	9	33
George Mason University	VA	17	5	58	32	10	2	0	0	131	28	54	37	24	7	294	111	405
The George Washington University	DC	19	12	52	19	9	7	2	0	110	39	80	22	39	9	311	108	419
University of Georgia	GA	0	0	0	0	0	0	0	0	2	1	1	0	0	0	3	1	4
Georgia Institute of Technology	GA	18	11	28	18	17	3	1	1	274	47	255	69	8	1	601	150	751
Grand Valley State University	MI	0	0	0	0	0	0	0	0	6	2	0	0	0	0	6	2	8
University of Hartford	CT	0	0	1	0	0	0	0	0	17	0	7	0	1	0	26	0	26
Harvard University	MA	0	0	6	2	0	0	1	0	22	3	20	3	0	0	49	8	57
University of Hawaii at Manoa	HI	0	0	34	15	3	1	0	0	5	0	18	11	32	5	93	32	125
University of Houston, Cullen School of Engineering	TX	3	2	10	4	7	1	0	0	33	7	66	14	5	4	124	32	156
Howard University	DC	9	6	0	0	1	0	0	0	2	0	16	7	0	0	28	13	41
University of Idaho	ID	0	0	3	1	3	0	0	0	49	1	0	0	35	11	90	13	103
Idaho State University	ID	0	0	0	0	0	0	0	0	6	3	5	0	0	0	11	3	14
Illinois Institute of Technology	IL	1	1	7	1	4	1	1	0	48	10	172	36	2	0	235	49	284
University of Illinois at Chicago	IL	4	10	70	33	8	1	0	0	70	15	0	0	22	5	174	64	238
University of Illinois at Urbana-Champaign	IL	7	2	44	12	11	7	0	0	246	27	151	42	4	1	463	91	554
Indiana University Purdue University at Indianapolis	IN	6	1	10	5	0	0	0	0	5	4	9	1	1	0	31	11	42
The University of Iowa	IA	0	0	2	2	0	0	0	0	28	14	17	9	1	0	48	25	73
Iowa State University	IA	3	0	3	0	4	1	0	0	108	20	54	15	5	1	177	37	214
The Johns Hopkins University	MD	22	21	61	26	20	2	0	1	448	116	68	26	0	0	619	192	811
University of Kansas	KS	1	0	1	0	0	0	0	0	55	11	75	17	0	1	132	29	161
Kansas State University	KS	2	0	3	1	1	0	0	0	41	11	53	14	1	0	101	26	127
University of Kentucky	KY	1	0	2	1	1	0	1	0	45	8	84	14	3	3	137	26	163
Kettering University formerly GMI	MI	1	1	2	0	1	0	0	0	10	1	2	0	7	2	23	4	27

MASTER'S DEGREES AWARDED

COL-KET

MASTER'S DEGREES AWARDED IN ENGINEERING, 2005-2006

INSTITUTION		AFRICAN AMERICAN M	F	ASIAN AMERICAN M	F	HISPANIC M	F	NATIVE AMERICAN M	F	CAUCASIAN M	F	FOREIGN M	F	OTHER M	F	TOTAL BY GENDER M	F	TOTAL DEGREES
Lamar University	TX	2	0	1	1	1	0	0	0	1	2	122	21	0	0	127	24	151
Lawrence Technological University	MI	3	2	8	2	1	0	0	0	38	9	7	0	5	1	62	14	76
Lehigh University	PA	0	1	2	1	2	2	0	0	0	0	38	7	69	13	111	24	135
Louisiana State University	LA	2	2	1	0	2	0	0	0	10	5	79	30	0	0	92	37	129
Louisiana Tech University	LA	1	0	0	0	0	0	0	0	4	0	140	40	0	0	145	40	185
University of Louisiana at Lafayette	LA	1	1	0	0	0	0	0	0	8	2	35	12	0	0	44	15	59
University of Louisville	KY	9	8	8	3	2	3	0	1	127	19	52	21	0	0	199	54	253
Loyola College in Maryland	MD	0	0	0	0	0	0	0	0	11	1	0	0	0	0	11	1	12
Loyola Marymount University	CA	3	1	2	3	0	2	1	0	11	3	6	1	0	0	23	10	33
University of Maine	ME	0	0	1	0	0	0	0	0	16	7	4	1	0	0	21	8	29
Manhattan College	NY	1	0	9	2	2	1	0	0	20	5	6	0	14	1	52	9	61
Marquette University	WI	0	1	1	2	0	0	0	0	27	19	11	6	0	0	39	27	66
University of Maryland, Baltimore County	MD	1	1	1	1	0	2	0	0	16	2	21	14	0	0	39	20	59
University of Maryland, College Park	MD	8	4	21	6	5	3	1	0	106	25	125	35	13	9	279	82	361
Massachusetts Institute of Technology	MA	9	3	67	43	22	7	6	1	194	58	196	55	64	20	558	187	745
University of Massachusetts Amherst	MA	0	0	2	0	3	1	0	0	30	7	24	6	7	0	66	14	80
University of Massachusetts Dartmouth	MA	0	0	0	0	0	0	0	0	9	2	35	11	1	0	45	13	58
University of Massachusetts Lowell	MA	5	0	5	8	1	0	0	0	31	8	33	12	4	1	79	29	108
McNeese State University	LA	0	0	0	0	0	0	0	0	0	0	15	9	0	0	15	9	24
The University of Memphis	TN	2	1	2	0	0	0	0	0	8	2	19	7	0	0	31	10	41
Mercer University	GA	1	1	0	1	1	0	0	0	0	1	15	0	3	2	20	5	25
University of Miami	FL	1	1	2	1	11	7	0	0	13	7	14	1	1	0	42	17	59
Miami University	OH	0	0	1	1	0	0	0	0	2	0	6	3	0	0	9	4	13
University of Michigan	MI	12	6	52	21	13	3	6	1	255	69	205	63	22	2	565	165	730
Michigan State University	MI	3	3	4	2	0	1	0	0	0	0	28	11	26	6	61	23	84
Michigan Technological University	MI	0	0	1	0	1	1	0	0	39	11	37	11	6	1	84	24	108
University of Michigan, Dearborn	MI	9	9	23	8	5	5	1	0	107	24	24	9	18	5	187	60	247
Milwaukee School of Engineering	WI	0	0	0	0	0	0	0	0	4	3	0	0	1	0	5	3	8
Minnesota State University, Mankato	MN	0	0	0	0	0	0	0	0	2	2	6	0	2	0	10	2	12
University of Minnesota-Twin Cities	MN	8	2	14	7	2	1	1	1	175	32	93	25	0	0	293	67	360
The University of Mississippi	MS	2	2	3	1	1	0	0	0	19	4	13	4	5	1	43	12	55
Mississippi State University	MS	6	5	0	0	0	0	0	0	35	8	43	13	0	0	84	26	110
University of Missouri-Columbia	MO	0	0	3	0	2	0	0	0	33	7	45	18	1	0	84	25	109
University of Missouri-Kansas City	MO	0	0	2	0	0	0	0	0	9	3	61	15	0	0	72	18	90
University of Missouri-Rolla	MO	12	3	8	2	5	0	1	1	139	28	72	21	8	1	244	56	300
Monmouth University	NJ	0	0	2	1	2	1	0	0	13	4	3	2	3	1	23	9	32
Montana State University	MT	0	0	0	0	0	0	0	0	23	3	17	2	1	0	41	5	46
Montana Tech of the University of Montana	MT	0	0	0	0	0	0	0	0	6	1	2	1	0	0	8	2	10
Morgan State University	MD	8	5	0	0	0	0	0	0	1	0	4	3	1	0	14	8	22
Naval Postgraduate School	CA	8	0	6	0	5	1	0	0	166	11	27	1	0	0	212	13	225
University of Nebraska, Lincoln	NE	1	0	8	1	0	1	0	0	47	13	33	10	0	0	89	25	114
University of Nevada, Las Vegas	NV	0	0	4	0	0	0	0	0	18	3	51	20	3	1	76	24	100
University of Nevada, Reno	NV	2	0	3	1	0	0	0	0	15	3	23	7	3	0	46	11	57
University of New Hampshire	NH	0	0	0	0	0	0	0	0	30	2	6	7	0	0	37	9	46
University of New Haven	CT	4	0	4	0	2	2	0	0	24	1	17	4	0	0	51	8	59

LAM-NEW

MASTER'S DEGREES AWARDED

Master's Degrees Awarded in Engineering, 2005-2006

Institution		African American		Asian American		Hispanic		Native American		Caucasian		Foreign		Other		Total by Gender		Total Degrees
		M	F	M	F	M	F	M	F	M	F	M	F	M	F	M	F	
New Jersey Institute of Technology	NJ	13	7	30	17	13	6	0	0	53	19	136	61	15	1	260	111	371
The University of New Mexico	NM	1	0	0	2	9	5	0	1	50	9	64	20	0	0	124	37	161
New Mexico Institute of Mining & Technology	NM	1	0	1	1	2	1	0	0	23	4	16	4	0	0	43	10	53
New Mexico State University	NM	0	0	1	1	10	5	2	0	13	2	34	14	13	3	73	25	98
University of New Orleans	LA	2	1	1	1	1	0	0	0	9	0	19	7	0	0	32	9	41
New York Institute of Technology	NY	0	0	0	0	0	0	0	0	0	0	0	0	229	70	229	70	299
City College of the City University of New York	NY	4	2	14	6	20	2	0	0	0	0	64	21	8	0	110	31	141
The State University of New York at Binghamton	NY	0	0	7	3	0	0	0	0	22	1	73	14	11	3	113	21	134
State University of New York at Buffalo	NY	3	3	3	0	1	0	0	0	42	5	189	53	3	1	242	62	304
SUNY College of Environmental Science and Forestry	NY	0	0	0	0	0	0	0	0	10	4	4	0	0	0	14	4	18
Stony Brook University	NY	4	3	12	7	5	0	0	0	27	16	104	49	0	0	152	75	227
North Carolina A & T State University	NC	28	9	4	1	0	0	0	0	6	1	8	2	0	0	46	13	59
North Carolina State University	NC	9	6	18	13	8	1	0	0	193	24	121	44	0	0	349	88	437
University of North Carolina at Chapel Hill	NC	0	1	0	1	0	0	0	0	0	0	1	4	0	0	1	6	7
University of North Carolina, Charlotte	NC	3	3	5	2	0	0	0	0	26	11	37	10	0	0	71	26	97
University of North Dakota	ND	0	0	0	0	0	1	0	0	22	3	0	0	0	0	22	4	26
North Dakota State University	ND	0	0	11	7	0	0	0	0	13	1	0	0	0	0	24	8	32
University of North Texas	TX	0	0	2	0	0	0	0	0	11	0	8	2	34	10	55	12	67
Northeastern University	MA	5	1	13	2	3	0	0	0	49	5	87	27	27	5	184	40	224
Northern Arizona University	AZ	0	0	1	0	0	0	1	0	1	0	1	0	0	0	4	0	4
Northern Illinois University	IL	0	0	1	0	0	0	0	0	3	0	23	5	0	1	27	6	33
Northwestern University	IL	7	2	20	6	9	0	1	0	97	44	54	9	12	1	200	62	262
University of Notre Dame	IN	0	0	2	1	3	0	0	0	35	3	28	7	0	0	68	11	79
Oakland University	MI	1	1	10	8	2	0	0	0	65	17	40	21	0	0	118	47	165
The Ohio State University	OH	2	0	6	1	2	1	0	0	119	23	91	26	0	0	221	51	272
Ohio University	OH	0	0	0	0	0	0	0	0	8	4	35	2	0	0	43	6	49
University of Oklahoma	OK	4	0	8	1	3	1	3	0	33	6	72	25	0	0	123	33	156
Oklahoma State University	OK	2	0	0	1	0	0	2	0	44	14	104	36	0	0	152	51	203
Old Dominion University	VA	7	5	3	5	5	0	2	0	145	26	63	5	12	2	237	43	280
OGI School of Science & Engineering at OHSU	OR	2	1	15	7	4	0	0	0	25	16	7	5	4	0	57	29	86
Oregon State University	OR	0	0	2	0	2	0	0	0	48	13	51	9	6	0	109	22	131
University of Pennsylvania	PA	4	5	30	16	1	1	0	0	87	30	119	33	7	1	248	86	334
The Pennsylvania State University	PA	7	1	6	4	4	0	0	0	135	41	99	21	9	3	260	70	330
University of Pittsburgh	PA	3	2	5	1	0	1	0	0	62	16	19	7	0	0	89	27	116
Polytechnic University	NY	10	3	41	9	5	0	1	0	54	6	79	19	57	13	247	50	297
Polytechnic University of Puerto Rico	PR	0	0	0	0	14	10	0	0	0	0	0	0	0	0	14	10	24
Portland State University	OR	2	0	5	3	4	1	1	0	35	12	56	30	14	1	117	47	164
Prairie View A&M University	TX	4	1	1	1	0	0	0	0	0	0	1	1	0	0	6	3	9
Princeton University	NJ	1	0	2	0	0	0	0	0	9	3	2	3	3	0	17	6	23
University of Puerto Rico, Mayaguez Campus	PR	0	0	0	0	59	28	0	0	0	0	0	0	0	0	59	28	87
Purdue University, Calumet	IN	0	1	0	1	0	0	0	0	0	0	6	2	11	2	18	6	24
Purdue University	IN	7	2	20	10	6	1	0	0	182	36	132	41	18	6	365	96	461
Rensselaer Polytechnic Institute	NY	6	1	17	3	12	4	0	0	97	14	40	9	19	3	191	34	225
University of Rhode Island	RI	0	0	1	0	0	0	0	0	15	1	15	4	1	1	32	6	38
William Marsh Rice University	TX	0	1	6	4	6	0	0	0	18	3	16	3	4	1	50	12	62

NEW-RIC

MASTER'S DEGREES AWARDED

INSTITUTION		AFRICAN AMERICAN		ASIAN AMERICAN		HISPANIC		NATIVE AMERICAN		CAUCASIAN		FOREIGN		OTHER		TOTAL BY GENDER		TOTAL DEGREES
		M	F	M	F	M	F	M	F	M	F	M	F	M	F	M	F	
University of Rochester	NY	1	0	1	4	0	1	0	0	9	6	23	6	3	2	37	19	56
Rochester Institute of Technology	NY	3	3	8	3	4	2	0	0	62	22	30	15	14	1	121	46	167
Rose-Hulman Institute of Technology	IN	0	0	8	2	0	0	0	0	18	4	0	0	2	0	28	6	34
Rowan University	NJ	1	0	2	0	2	0	0	0	10	3	0	0	0	0	15	3	18
Rutgers, The State University of New Jersey	NJ	1	3	5	4	4	2	0	0	27	7	93	22	0	0	130	38	168
Saint Cloud State University	MN	0	0	1	0	0	0	0	0	0	0	16	4	0	0	17	4	21
Saint Martin's College	WA	0	0	1	0	0	0	0	0	6	0	0	1	0	0	7	1	8
Saint Mary's University	TX	0	0	0	0	0	1	0	0	7	0	0	2	0	0	7	3	10
University of Saint Thomas	MN	1	0	0	0	0	0	0	0	30	4	1	0	0	0	32	4	36
San Diego State University	CA	1	0	6	2	0	1	0	0	13	4	26	7	8	2	54	16	70
San Francisco State University	CA	0	0	0	0	0	0	0	0	0	0	0	0	15	6	15	6	21
San Jose State University	CA	4	0	224	279	11	5	0	2	25	19	0	0	39	20	303	325	628
Santa Clara University	CA	0	1	47	20	7	2	0	0	35	6	45	24	30	8	164	61	225
University of South Alabama	AL	2	0	1	2	0	0	0	0	6	2	53	11	0	0	62	15	77
University of South Carolina	SC	3	0	4	1	1	1	0	1	25	6	22	12	3	0	58	21	79
South Dakota School of Mines and Technology	SD	2	0	0	2	0	0	1	0	18	5	20	10	1	0	42	17	59
South Dakota State University	SD	0	0	0	0	0	0	0	0	9	3	26	8	0	0	35	11	46
University of South Florida	FL	0	0	5	3	3	3	0	0	18	9	28	13	0	0	54	28	82
University of Southern California	CA	7	4	134	37	18	3	1	1	154	44	607	131	44	5	965	225	1190
Southern Illinois University Carbondale	IL	0	1	1	0	1	0	0	0	18	3	82	22	0	0	102	26	128
Southern Illinois University Edwardsville	IL	0	2	0	0	0	1	0	0	22	4	49	24	0	0	71	31	102
Southern Methodist University	TX	24	8	41	6	13	5	2	0	150	41	43	7	0	0	273	67	340
Stanford University	CA	7	7	126	57	18	7	0	1	225	60	318	80	81	28	775	240	1015
Stevens Institute of Technology	NJ	6	0	25	9	5	0	1	0	69	18	55	19	47	10	208	56	264
Syracuse University	NY	3	0	4	4	5	2	0	1	42	6	128	35	5	0	182	48	230
Temple University	PA	0	0	17	3	0	0	0	0	27	3	0	0	0	0	44	6	50
Tennessee State University	TN	4	3	1	0	1	0	0	0	5	1	2	0	0	0	12	4	16
Tennessee Technological University	TN	3	0	0	0	0	0	0	0	19	2	18	9	0	0	40	11	51
University of Tennessee, Chattanooga	TN	0	0	0	0	1	0	0	0	4	0	2	1	0	0	7	1	8
University of Tennessee, Knoxville	TN	3	1	4	2	0	0	0	1	98	21	40	11	3	0	149	35	184
Texas A&M University	TX	3	7	13	5	15	3	0	0	130	22	194	49	3	1	358	87	445
Texas A&M University - Kingsville	TX	1	0	1	0	3	2	0	0	4	1	168	45	0	0	177	48	225
Texas Tech University	TX	1	0	5	2	8	3	0	0	74	12	54	7	0	1	146	27	173
The University of Texas at Arlington	TX	7	6	28	18	6	3	4	2	53	12	324	108	0	0	418	147	565
The University of Texas at Austin	TX	3	1	33	6	17	8	1	0	174	46	125	33	0	0	353	94	447
The University of Texas at Dallas	TX	3	0	24	11	3	1	0	0	37	7	142	63	0	0	209	82	291
University of Texas at El Paso	TX	1	0	0	0	26	11	0	0	10	1	48	21	0	0	85	33	118
University of Texas at San Antonio	TX	2	0	0	1	7	0	0	0	13	1	21	9	0	0	43	11	54
The University of Texas at Tyler	TX	0	0	4	3	0	0	0	0	2	0	4	0	0	0	10	3	13
The University of Toledo	OH	0	0	0	0	0	0	0	0	17	7	32	18	0	0	49	25	74
Tri-State University	IN	0	0	0	0	0	0	0	0	1	0	0	0	1	0	2	0	2
Tufts University	MA	0	0	11	3	3	1	0	0	0	0	17	9	78	30	110	43	153
Tulane University	LA	1	1	1	0	0	0	0	0	0	0	7	2	11	6	20	9	29
University of Tulsa	OK	0	0	0	1	1	0	0	0	15	2	37	8	6	0	59	11	70
Tuskegee University	AL	3	1	0	1	0	0	0	0	0	0	1	0	5	1	9	3	12

MASTER'S DEGREES AWARDED   ROC-TUS

INSTITUTION		AFRICAN AMERICAN		ASIAN AMERICAN		HISPANIC		NATIVE AMERICAN		CAUCASIAN		FOREIGN		OTHER		TOTAL BY GENDER		TOTAL DEGREES
		M	F	M	F	M	F	M	F	M	F	M	F	M	F	M	F	
University of Utah	UT	0	1	6	2	3	0	0	0	98	4	35	11	1	2	143	20	163
Utah State University	UT	0	0	0	0	0	0	0	0	51	0	50	0	0	0	101	0	101
Vanderbilt University	TN	0	1	0	1	1	1	1	0	23	12	16	5	6	2	47	22	69
University of Vermont	VT	0	0	0	0	1	0	0	0	23	4	2	1	0	0	26	5	31
Villanova University	PA	0	0	3	0	0	0	0	0	56	9	27	9	0	0	86	18	104
University of Virginia	VA	4	4	15	3	1	0	0	0	90	24	34	15	3	1	147	47	194
Virginia Commonwealth University	VA	10	3	4	2	6	0	0	3	9	6	29	11	0	0	58	25	83
Virginia Polytechnic Institute and State University	VA	9	2	16	10	4	4	1	0	190	46	119	33	3	1	342	96	438
University of Washington	WA	2	1	16	13	10	2	1	0	126	43	36	11	33	14	224	84	308
Washington State University	WA	2	0	2	1	0	1	1	0	38	8	14	3	20	12	77	25	102
Washington University	MO	4	5	12	8	5	1	0	0	106	34	24	12	16	2	167	62	229
Wayne State University	MI	5	1	14	7	0	1	0	0	61	20	203	39	9	4	292	72	364
West Virginia University	WV	3	0	3	1	0	0	0	0	69	18	88	33	1	1	164	53	217
Western Michigan University	MI	2	0	4	2	1	0	0	0	19	4	106	35	0	0	132	41	173
Wichita State University	KS	0	0	3	1	0	0	0	0	0	0	108	15	18	4	129	20	149
Widener University	PA	2	0	3	0	0	0	0	0	7	2	10	2	0	0	22	4	26
Wilkes University	PA	0	0	0	0	0	0	0	0	0	0	3	0	0	0	3	0	3
University of Wisconsin, Madison	WI	3	0	9	1	3	3	0	0	129	30	119	32	18	6	281	72	353
University of Wisconsin, Milwaukee	WI	1	0	5	0	2	0	0	0	27	5	21	16	0	0	56	21	77
Worcester Polytechnic Institute	MA	1	0	4	1	3	0	0	0	77	24	23	11	2	0	110	36	146
Wright State University	OH	4	2	6	2	2	0	0	0	44	15	90	50	0	0	146	69	215
University of Wyoming	WY	0	0	0	0	2	0	0	0	16	1	8	3	1	1	27	5	32
Yale University/Faculty of Engineering	CT	0	0	0	0	0	0	0	0	0	0	0	0	76	26	76	26	102
Youngstown State University	OH	0	0	0	0	0	0	0	0	0	0	7	0	4	1	11	1	12
Totals:		**680**	**332**	**2,614**	**1,226**	**892**	**309**	**72**	**23**	**10,988**	**2,651**	**12,002**	**3,531**	**2,862**	**698**	**30,245**	**8,770**	**39,015**
CANADIAN INSTITUTIONS:																		
University of Alberta	AB	0	0	0	0	0	0	0	0	0	0	0	0	129	45	129	45	174
University of Calgary	AB	0	0	0	0	0	0	0	0	0	0	36	6	73	22	109	28	137
Concordia University, Faculty of Engr. and Comp. Sci.	PQ	0	0	0	0	0	0	0	0	0	0	42	9	304	57	346	66	412
Ecole Polytechnique de Montreal	PQ	0	0	0	0	0	0	0	0	0	0	0	0	179	34	179	34	213
Ecole de Technologie Superieure	PQ	0	0	0	0	0	0	0	0	0	0	0	0	110	13	110	13	123
University of Guelph	ON	0	0	0	0	0	0	0	0	0	0	5	1	23	6	28	7	35
McGill University, Faculty of Engineering	PQ	0	0	0	0	0	0	0	0	0	0	0	0	107	38	107	38	145
University of Ottawa, Faculty of Engineering	ON	0	0	0	0	0	0	0	0	0	0	19	11	86	41	105	52	157
University of Waterloo	ON	0	0	0	0	0	0	0	0	0	0	0	0	207	73	207	73	280
Totals:		**0**	**0**	**0**	**0**	**0**	**0**	**0**	**0**	**0**	**0**	**102**	**27**	**1,218**	**329**	**1,320**	**356**	**1,676**

MASTER'S DEGREES AWARDED   UTA-YOU

MASTER'S DEGREES AWARDED IN AEROSPACE ENGINEERING, 2005-2006

INSTITUTION		AFRICAN AMERICAN M	F	ASIAN AMERICAN M	F	HISPANIC M	F	NATIVE AMERICAN M	F	CAUCASIAN M	F	FOREIGN M	F	OTHER M	F	TOTAL BY GENDER M	F	TOTAL DEGREES
Air Force Institute of Technology	OH	0	0	0	0	0	0	0	0	6	1	0	0	172	13	178	14	192
The University of Alabama in Huntsville	AL	0	0	0	0	1	0	0	0	18	7	5	1	0	0	24	8	32
The University of Alabama	AL	0	0	2	0	0	0	0	0	6	0	3	0	0	0	11	0	11
The University of Arizona	AZ	0	0	0	0	0	0	0	0	2	0	5	1	0	0	7	1	8
Arizona State University	AZ	0	0	1	0	0	0	0	0	2	0	1	0	0	0	4	0	4
Auburn University	AL	0	0	0	0	0	0	0	0	1	0	5	1	0	0	6	1	7
Boston University	MA	0	0	0	0	0	0	0	0	2	0	0	0	0	0	2	0	2
California Institute of Technology	CA	0	0	0	0	1	1	0	0	3	1	2	1	0	0	6	3	9
California Polytechnic State University	CA	0	0	1	0	2	0	0	0	8	3	0	0	1	1	12	4	16
California State University, Long Beach	CA	1	0	0	0	0	0	0	0	0	0	2	0	0	0	3	0	3
University of California, Los Angeles	CA	0	0	2	0	1	0	0	0	3	1	0	0	1	0	7	1	8
University of California, San Diego	CA	0	0	1	0	0	0	0	0	3	0	0	0	0	0	4	0	4
Case Western Reserve University	OH	0	0	0	0	0	0	0	0	2	0	0	0	0	0	2	0	2
University of Central Florida	FL	0	0	0	0	0	0	0	0	4	2	1	0	0	0	5	2	7
University of Cincinnati	OH	0	0	0	0	1	0	0	0	5	2	3	3	1	0	10	5	15
Clemson University	SC	0	0	0	0	0	0	0	0	2	0	0	1	0	0	2	1	3
University of Colorado at Boulder	CO	0	0	0	2	1	1	0	0	25	9	2	0	0	0	28	12	40
Cornell University	NY	0	0	1	1	0	0	1	0	2	0	1	0	0	0	5	1	6
University of Dayton	OH	1	0	0	0	0	0	0	0	2	0	2	0	0	0	5	0	5
Embry Riddle Aeronautical Univ., Daytona Beach	FL	1	0	1	0	0	0	0	0	4	0	6	0	1	0	13	0	13
University of Florida	FL	0	0	0	0	0	0	1	0	5	2	3	0	0	0	9	2	11
Florida Institute of Technology	FL	1	0	0	0	0	0	0	0	3	0	1	0	1	0	6	0	6
Georgia Institute of Technology	GA	3	0	5	1	1	0	0	0	49	4	30	6	1	0	89	11	100
University of Houston, Cullen School of Engineering	TX	0	0	0	0	0	0	0	0	1	0	0	0	0	0	1	0	1
University of Illinois at Urbana-Champaign	IL	1	0	1	0	0	0	0	0	15	1	4	0	0	0	21	1	22
Iowa State University	IA	0	0	0	0	1	0	0	0	9	0	3	0	0	0	13	0	13
University of Kansas	KS	0	0	0	0	0	0	0	0	2	0	3	1	0	0	5	1	6
University of Maryland, College Park	MD	0	1	0	0	1	0	1	0	22	3	7	4	1	1	32	9	41
Massachusetts Institute of Technology	MA	0	0	4	3	1	1	2	0	20	5	22	2	8	1	57	12	69
University of Michigan	MI	3	0	1	1	0	0	0	0	20	0	12	3	2	0	38	4	42
University of Minnesota - Twin Cities	MN	0	0	0	0	0	0	0	0	7	1	8	1	0	0	15	2	17
Mississippi State University	MS	1	0	0	0	0	0	0	0	2	1	2	0	0	0	5	1	6
University of Missouri - Rolla	MO	0	0	1	0	0	0	0	0	3	1	0	0	0	0	4	1	5
State University of New York at Buffalo	NY	0	0	0	0	0	0	0	0	1	0	5	0	0	0	6	0	6
North Carolina State University	NC	0	0	0	0	1	1	0	0	10	1	0	0	0	0	11	2	13
University of Notre Dame	IN	0	0	1	0	0	0	0	0	6	0	4	1	0	0	11	1	12
The Ohio State University	OH	0	0	0	0	0	0	0	0	8	0	0	2	0	0	8	2	10
University of Oklahoma	OK	0	0	0	0	0	0	0	0	0	0	0	1	0	0	0	1	1
Old Dominion University	VA	1	0	0	0	0	0	0	0	1	1	5	1	0	0	7	2	9
The Pennsylvania State University	PA	0	0	1	0	0	0	0	0	8	0	3	0	0	0	12	0	12
Purdue University	IN	0	0	2	1	3	0	0	0	28	2	26	6	6	1	65	10	75
Rensselaer Polytechnic Institute	NY	1	0	0	0	0	0	0	0	1	0	0	0	0	0	2	0	2
San Diego State University	CA	0	0	0	0	0	0	0	0	1	0	2	0	0	0	3	0	3
San Jose State University	CA	0	0	5	0	0	0	0	0	1	1	0	0	3	0	9	1	10
University of Southern California	CA	0	0	2	0	0	0	0	0	4	2	2	0	1	0	9	2	11

AEROSPACE ENGINEERING

AIR-SOU

INSTITUTION		AFRICAN AMERICAN		ASIAN AMERICAN		HISPANIC		NATIVE AMERICAN		CAUCASIAN		FOREIGN		OTHER		TOTAL BY GENDER		TOTAL DEGREES
		M	F	M	F	M	F	M	F	M	F	M	F	M	F	M	F	
Stanford University	CA	0	0	6	3	3	0	0	0	22	6	6	5	7	2	44	16	60
Syracuse University	NY	1	0	0	0	0	0	0	0	1	0	3	0	0	0	5	0	5
University of Tennessee, Knoxville	TN	0	0	0	0	0	0	0	0	3	0	2	0	0	0	5	0	5
Texas A&M University	TX	0	0	0	1	2	0	0	0	7	2	9	0	1	0	19	3	22
The University of Texas at Arlington	TX	0	0	0	0	0	0	0	0	1	0	6	0	0	0	7	0	7
The University of Texas at Austin	TX	0	0	5	1	1	0	0	0	14	4	3	0	0	0	23	5	28
Virginia Polytechnic Institute and State University	VA	0	0	1	1	0	0	0	0	13	3	5	0	0	0	19	4	23
University of Washington	WA	0	0	4	1	0	0	0	0	14	3	2	1	3	2	23	7	30
Washington University	MO	0	0	0	0	0	0	0	0	6	0	0	0	1	0	7	0	7
West Virginia University	WV	0	0	0	0	0	0	0	0	3	0	1	1	0	0	4	1	5
Wichita State University	KS	0	0	0	0	0	0	0	0	0	0	8	0	2	2	10	2	12
Totals:		15	1	48	16	21	4	5	0	411	69	225	43	213	23	938	156	1,094
CANADIAN INSTITUTIONS:																		
Concordia University, Faculty of Engr. and Comp. Sci.	PQ	0	0	0	0	0	0	0	0	0	0	1	0	12	3	13	3	16
Ecole Polytechnique de Montreal	PQ	0	0	0	0	0	0	0	0	0	0	0	0	8	1	8	1	9
Ecole de Technologie Superieure	PQ	0	0	0	0	0	0	0	0	0	0	0	0	4	0	4	0	4
Totals:		0	0	0	0	0	0	0	0	0	0	1	0	24	4	25	4	29

STA-WIC

AEROSPACE ENGINEERING

Master's Degrees Awarded in Agricultural Engineering, 2005-2006

INSTITUTION		AFRICAN AMERICAN M	F	ASIAN AMERICAN M	F	HISPANIC M	F	NATIVE AMERICAN M	F	CAUCASIAN M	F	FOREIGN M	F	OTHER M	F	TOTAL BY GENDER M	F	TOTAL DEGREES
The University of Arizona	AZ	0	0	0	0	0	0	0	0	1	1	5	2	0	0	6	3	9
University of Arkansas	AR	0	0	0	0	0	0	0	0	0	0	1	0	0	0	1	0	1
University of California, Davis	CA	0	0	1	0	0	0	0	0	3	1	0	0	1	1	5	2	7
Clemson University	SC	0	0	0	0	0	0	0	0	5	0	0	1	0	0	5	1	6
Cornell University	NY	0	0	2	0	0	1	0	0	6	2	1	3	1	0	10	6	16
University of Florida	FL	0	0	1	0	0	0	0	0	4	1	7	1	0	0	12	2	14
University of Georgia	GA	0	0	0	0	0	0	0	0	0	0	1	0	0	0	1	0	1
University of Idaho	ID	0	0	0	0	0	0	0	0	0	1	0	0	1	0	1	1	2
University of Illinois at Urbana-Champaign	IL	0	0	0	0	0	0	0	0	3	3	2	0	0	0	5	3	8
Iowa State University	IA	1	0	0	0	0	0	0	0	8	5	1	3	0	1	10	9	19
Kansas State University	KS	0	0	0	0	0	0	0	0	2	0	0	1	0	0	2	1	3
University of Kentucky	KY	0	0	0	0	0	0	0	0	2	0	0	0	0	0	2	0	2
Louisiana State University	LA	0	1	0	0	0	0	0	0	0	1	2	1	0	0	2	3	5
University of Maryland, College Park	MD	0	0	0	0	0	1	0	0	0	4	0	0	0	0	0	5	5
Michigan State University	MI	0	0	0	1	0	0	0	0	0	0	0	0	0	0	1	1	2
Mississippi State University	MS	0	0	0	0	0	0	0	0	0	2	5	0	0	0	5	2	7
University of Nebraska, Lincoln	NE	0	0	0	0	0	0	0	0	2	2	1	0	0	0	3	2	5
North Carolina State University	NC	0	0	0	0	0	0	0	0	6	1	0	1	0	0	6	2	8
North Dakota State University	ND	0	0	1	0	0	0	0	0	0	0	0	0	0	0	1	0	1
The Ohio State University	OH	0	0	0	0	0	0	0	0	1	1	3	1	0	0	4	2	6
Oklahoma State University	OK	0	0	0	0	0	0	0	0	0	2	3	0	0	0	3	2	5
The Pennsylvania State University	PA	0	0	0	0	1	0	0	0	2	0	2	1	0	0	5	1	6
Purdue University	IN	0	0	0	0	0	0	0	0	9	1	2	4	0	0	11	5	16
South Dakota State University	SD	0	0	0	0	0	0	0	0	1	1	0	0	0	0	1	1	2
University of Tennessee, Knoxville	TN	0	1	0	0	0	0	0	0	1	1	0	0	1	0	2	2	4
Texas A&M University	TX	0	0	0	0	0	0	0	0	7	2	1	3	0	0	8	5	13
Utah State University	UT	0	0	0	0	0	0	0	0	2	0	4	0	0	0	6	0	6
Virginia Polytechnic Institute and State University	VA	0	0	1	0	0	0	0	0	0	1	0	1	0	0	1	2	3
Totals:		1	2	6	1	1	2	0	0	65	33	41	23	5	2	119	63	182

ARI-VIR

AGRICULTURAL ENGINEERING

MASTER'S DEGREES AWARDED IN ARCHITECTURAL ENGINEERING, 2005-2006

INSTITUTION		AFRICAN AMERICAN		ASIAN AMERICAN		HISPANIC		NATIVE AMERICAN		CAUCASIAN		FOREIGN		OTHER		TOTAL BY GENDER		TOTAL DEGREES
		M	F	M	F	M	F	M	F	M	F	M	F	M	F	M	F	
University of Hartford	CT	0	0	0	0	0	0	0	0	9	0	0	0	0	0	9	0	9
Illinois Institute of Technology	IL	0	0	0	0	0	0	0	0	2	0	0	0	0	0	2	0	2
University of Kansas	KS	0	0	0	0	0	0	0	0	0	0	3	1	0	1	3	2	5
Kansas State University	KS	0	0	1	1	0	0	0	0	9	5	1	0	0	0	11	6	17
University of Nebraska, Lincoln	NE	1	0	0	0	0	0	0	0	22	5	0	0	0	0	23	5	28
The Pennsylvania State University	PA	0	1	2	0	1	0	0	0	26	12	3	2	0	0	32	15	47
The University of Texas at Austin	TX	0	0	0	0	0	0	0	0	1	1	1	1	0	0	2	2	4
Totals:		1	1	3	1	1	0	0	0	69	23	8	4	0	1	82	30	112

HAR-TEX

ARCHITECTURAL ENGINEERING

Master's Degrees Awarded in Biomedical Engineering, 2005-2006

INSTITUTION		AFRICAN AMERICAN		ASIAN AMERICAN		HISPANIC		NATIVE AMERICAN		CAUCASIAN		FOREIGN		OTHER		TOTAL BY GENDER		TOTAL DEGREES
		M	F	M	F	M	F	M	F	M	F	M	F	M	F	M	F	
The University of Akron	OH	0	0	0	1	0	0	0	0	1	0	3	3	0	0	4	4	8
University of Alabama at Birmingham	AL	0	0	0	0	0	0	0	0	0	0	2	2	1	1	3	3	6
Alfred University,NY State College of Ceramics	NY	0	1	0	0	0	0	0	0	1	0	1	0	0	0	2	1	3
The University of Arizona	AZ	0	0	0	0	0	1	0	0	1	3	1	0	0	0	2	4	6
Arizona State University	AZ	0	1	1	0	1	0	0	0	8	1	2	5	0	1	12	8	20
Baylor University	TX	0	0	0	0	0	0	0	0	2	0	0	0	0	0	2	0	2
Boston University	MA	1	0	0	3	0	0	0	0	5	4	1	1	0	0	7	8	15
Brown University	RI	0	0	0	1	0	0	0	0	0	1	0	0	0	0	0	2	2
California Institute of Technology	CA	0	0	0	0	0	0	0	0	0	0	1	0	0	0	1	0	1
University of California, Davis	CA	0	0	3	0	0	0	0	0	1	5	1	0	0	1	5	6	11
University of California, Irvine	CA	0	0	0	0	0	0	0	0	0	0	0	0	32	14	32	14	46
University of California, Los Angeles	CA	0	0	11	3	2	0	0	0	4	1	6	4	6	2	29	10	39
University of California, San Diego	CA	0	1	12	3	2	2	0	0	10	6	0	1	0	0	24	13	37
University of California-Santa Cruz	CA	0	0	0	0	1	0	0	0	2	0	0	0	0	0	3	0	3
Carnegie Mellon University	PA	0	0	0	0	0	0	0	0	0	0	1	0	0	0	1	0	1
Case Western Reserve University	OH	0	0	3	1	1	0	0	0	3	4	2	3	0	0	9	8	17
The Catholic University of America	DC	0	0	0	1	0	1	0	0	3	1	7	3	1	2	11	8	19
Clemson University	SC	1	1	0	0	0	0	0	0	6	5	0	3	0	0	7	9	16
Columbia University	NY	1	0	3	3	0	0	0	0	2	2	6	1	6	2	18	8	26
University of Connecticut	CT	0	0	1	0	0	0	0	0	1	4	6	2	2	0	10	6	16
Cornell University	NY	0	0	4	4	1	0	0	0	0	3	3	7	0	0	8	14	22
Drexel University	PA	0	3	4	1	0	0	0	0	12	3	14	13	1	0	31	20	51
Duke University Pratt School of Engineering	NC	0	0	0	0	0	0	0	0	0	0	0	0	11	3	11	3	14
University of Florida	FL	0	0	0	1	1	0	0	0	2	2	0	0	0	0	3	3	6
Florida International University	FL	0	1	0	0	4	0	0	0	0	2	4	0	0	0	8	3	11
FAMU-FSU College of Engineering	FL	0	0	0	0	1	0	0	0	1	0	0	0	0	0	2	0	2
Georgia Institute of Technology	GA	0	0	0	1	1	0	0	0	1	5	5	0	0	0	6	6	12
University of Houston, Cullen School of Engineering	TX	0	0	0	0	0	0	0	0	0	0	0	1	0	0	0	1	1
University of Illinois at Chicago	IL	1	9	8	1	1	0	0	0	6	3	0	0	0	0	16	13	29
University of Illinois at Urbana-Champaign	IL	0	0	0	0	1	0	0	0	1	1	1	0	0	0	2	1	3
Indiana University Purdue University at Indianapolis	IN	0	0	0	0	0	0	0	0	2	0	0	0	0	0	2	0	2
The University of Iowa	IA	0	0	1	2	0	0	0	0	4	7	5	2	1	0	11	11	22
The Johns Hopkins University	MD	0	2	3	2	1	0	0	0	12	1	4	5	0	0	20	10	30
University of Kentucky	KY	0	0	0	0	0	0	0	0	0	0	0	2	0	0	0	2	2
Louisiana Tech University	LA	1	0	0	0	0	0	0	0	1	0	99	27	0	0	101	27	128
Marquette University	WI	0	0	0	2	0	0	0	0	3	13	3	1	0	0	6	16	22
University of Maryland, College Park	MD	0	0	0	1	0	1	0	0	0	0	0	0	0	0	0	2	2
Massachusetts Institute of Technology	MA	0	0	2	0	0	1	0	0	1	0	1	1	0	1	4	3	7
The University of Memphis	TN	0	0	0	0	0	0	0	0	1	0	1	1	0	0	2	1	3
University of Miami	FL	0	0	0	0	2	3	0	0	2	2	3	0	0	0	7	5	12
University of Michigan	MI	0	1	9	3	1	1	0	1	23	12	10	4	3	0	46	22	68
University of Minnesota -Twin Cities	MN	0	0	0	0	0	0	0	0	3	3	1	0	0	0	4	3	7
University of Missouri-Columbia	MO	0	0	0	0	0	0	0	0	3	2	3	0	0	0	6	2	8
New Jersey Institute of Technology	NJ	4	0	4	2	0	0	0	0	1	1	6	7	1	1	16	11	27
City College of the City University of New York	NY	0	0	1	0	0	0	0	0	0	0	2	0	0	0	3	0	3

BIOMEDICAL ENGINEERING

AKR-NEW

MASTER'S DEGREES AWARDED IN BIOMEDICAL ENGINEERING, 2005-2006

INSTITUTION		AFRICAN AMERICAN M	F	ASIAN AMERICAN M	F	HISPANIC M	F	NATIVE AMERICAN M	F	CAUCASIAN M	F	FOREIGN M	F	OTHER M	F	TOTAL BY GENDER M	F	TOTAL DEGREES
Stony Brook University	NY	0	0	2	2	0	0	0	0	2	2	4	2	0	0	8	6	14
North Carolina State University	NC	0	0	0	0	0	0	0	0	0	0	1	0	0	0	1	0	1
Northwestern University	IL	0	1	2	2	0	0	0	0	4	5	1	3	1	0	8	11	19
The Ohio State University	OH	0	0	0	0	0	0	0	0	5	1	1	1	0	0	6	2	8
OGI School of Science & Engineering at OHSU	OR	0	0	0	1	1	0	0	0	1	0	1	1	0	0	3	2	5
Oregon State University	OR	0	0	0	0	0	0	0	0	1	1	0	0	1	0	2	1	3
University of Pennsylvania	PA	0	0	0	0	0	0	0	0	0	0	2	1	0	0	2	1	3
The Pennsylvania State University	PA	0	0	0	0	0	0	0	0	2	2	3	0	0	0	5	2	7
University of Pittsburgh	PA	0	1	1	0	0	1	0	0	6	5	2	2	0	0	9	9	18
Polytechnic University	NY	0	0	0	0	0	0	0	0	5	1	1	0	3	1	9	2	11
Purdue University	IN	0	0	0	1	0	0	0	0	2	0	0	0	1	0	3	1	4
Rensselaer Polytechnic Institute	NY	0	0	0	1	0	0	0	0	1	1	0	1	0	0	1	3	4
William Marsh Rice University	TX	0	0	1	0	0	0	0	0	0	1	0	0	0	0	1	1	2
University of Rochester	NY	0	0	0	1	0	0	0	0	1	0	3	2	1	0	5	3	8
Rose-Hulman Institute of Technology	IN	0	0	1	0	0	0	0	0	1	2	0	0	0	0	2	2	4
Rutgers, The State University of New Jersey	NJ	0	1	0	2	1	0	0	0	1	0	1	0	0	0	2	3	5
University of Southern California	CA	1	0	9	0	3	0	0	0	10	6	28	8	5	0	53	14	67
Stanford University	CA	0	0	1	4	1	0	0	0	1	3	3	0	2	0	8	7	15
Syracuse University	NY	0	0	0	2	0	0	0	0	1	1	2	1	1	0	4	4	8
Temple University	PA	0	0	1	0	0	0	0	0	0	0	0	0	0	0	1	0	1
Tennessee State University	TN	0	0	0	0	1	0	0	0	1	0	0	0	0	0	2	0	2
Texas A&M University	TX	0	0	0	0	3	0	0	0	2	1	1	3	0	0	6	4	10
The University of Texas at Arlington	TX	0	2	0	4	0	1	0	0	3	1	31	19	0	0	34	27	61
The University of Texas at Austin	TX	0	0	2	1	1	1	0	0	3	3	1	0	0	0	7	5	12
The University of Toledo	OH	0	0	0	0	0	0	0	0	3	2	7	5	0	0	10	7	17
Tufts University	MA	0	0	1	0	0	0	0	0	0	0	0	2	2	1	3	3	6
Tulane University	LA	0	1	1	0	0	0	0	0	0	0	0	0	1	2	2	3	5
University of Utah	UT	0	1	1	1	1	0	0	0	15	1	1	3	0	0	18	6	24
Vanderbilt University	TN	0	0	0	0	1	0	0	0	5	3	1	1	2	0	9	4	13
University of Vermont	VT	0	0	0	0	0	0	0	0	2	0	0	1	0	0	2	1	3
University of Virginia	VA	0	0	0	0	0	0	0	0	0	1	0	0	0	0	0	1	1
Virginia Commonwealth University	VA	3	0	0	0	0	0	0	0	4	5	7	5	0	0	14	10	24
Virginia Polytechnic Institute and State University	VA	0	0	0	0	0	0	0	0	2	0	0	1	0	0	2	1	3
University of Washington	WA	0	0	1	2	0	0	0	0	6	3	2	0	1	2	12	7	19
Washington University	MO	0	0	0	3	2	1	0	0	5	4	2	1	0	0	8	8	16
Wayne State University	MI	0	1	0	3	0	0	0	0	6	4	10	7	1	2	17	17	34
University of Wisconsin, Madison	WI	0	0	1	0	0	1	0	0	12	1	15	0	0	0	28	2	30
Worcester Polytechnic Institute	MA	0	0	0	0	0	0	0	0	5	2	0	3	0	0	5	5	10
Wright State University	OH	1	0	0	0	0	0	0	0	5	5	17	14	0	0	22	19	41
Totals:		14	28	95	66	30	14	1	1	251	164	353	186	87	36	831	495	1,326

CANADIAN INSTITUTIONS:

INSTITUTION		AFRICAN AMERICAN M	F	ASIAN AMERICAN M	F	HISPANIC M	F	NATIVE AMERICAN M	F	CAUCASIAN M	F	FOREIGN M	F	OTHER M	F	TOTAL BY GENDER M	F	TOTAL DEGREES
Ecole Polytechnique de Montreal	PQ	0	0	0	0	0	0	0	0	0	0	0	0	8	5	8	5	13
Totals:		0	0	0	0	0	0	0	0	0	0	0	0	8	5	8	5	13

BIOMEDICAL ENGINEERING

STO-WRI

MASTER'S DEGREES AWARDED IN CHEMICAL ENGINEERING, 2005-2006

INSTITUTION		AFRICAN AMERICAN		ASIAN AMERICAN		HISPANIC		NATIVE AMERICAN		CAUCASIAN		FOREIGN		OTHER		TOTAL BY GENDER		TOTAL DEGREES
		M	F	M	F	M	F	M	F	M	F	M	F	M	F	M	F	
The University of Akron	OH	0	0	0	0	0	0	0	0	2	0	2	5	0	0	4	5	9
The University of Alabama in Huntsville	AL	0	0	0	0	0	0	0	0	1	0	4	0	0	0	5	0	5
The University of Alabama	AL	0	1	0	1	0	0	0	0	3	0	1	0	0	0	4	2	6
The University of Arizona	AZ	0	0	0	1	0	0	0	0	1	1	0	1	0	0	1	3	4
Arizona State University	AZ	0	0	0	0	0	1	0	0	2	1	0	0	1	1	3	3	6
University of Arkansas	AR	1	0	0	0	0	0	0	0	0	1	0	0	0	0	1	1	2
Auburn University	AL	1	0	0	0	0	0	0	0	1	0	1	0	0	1	3	1	4
Brigham Young University	UT	0	0	0	0	0	0	0	0	0	0	1	0	4	0	5	0	5
Bucknell University	PA	0	0	0	0	0	1	0	0	11	14	1	0	0	0	12	15	27
California Institute of Technology	CA	0	0	2	0	1	0	0	0	5	1	2	0	0	0	10	1	11
University of California, Berkeley	CA	0	0	0	0	0	0	0	0	2	0	0	0	0	0	2	0	2
University of California, Davis	CA	0	0	1	0	0	0	0	0	1	0	1	0	0	0	3	0	3
University of California, Irvine	CA	0	0	0	0	0	0	0	0	0	0	0	0	9	2	9	2	11
University of California, Los Angeles	CA	0	0	2	3	0	0	0	0	3	0	0	0	0	0	5	3	8
University of California, Riverside	CA	0	1	0	0	0	0	0	0	1	1	0	0	2	1	3	3	6
University of California, San Diego	CA	0	0	1	0	0	0	0	0	0	1	2	1	0	0	3	2	5
University of California, Santa Barbara	CA	0	0	0	0	0	0	0	0	0	4	2	0	2	0	4	4	8
Carnegie Mellon University	PA	1	0	0	0	1	1	0	0	3	1	7	1	0	1	12	4	16
Case Western Reserve University	OH	0	0	0	1	0	0	0	0	7	2	0	2	0	0	7	5	12
University of Cincinnati	OH	0	0	0	0	1	0	0	0	3	0	6	2	0	0	9	2	11
Clarkson University	NY	0	1	0	0	0	0	0	0	1	0	3	1	0	0	4	2	6
Clemson University	SC	0	0	0	0	0	0	0	0	2	0	0	0	0	0	2	0	2
Cleveland State University	OH	0	0	1	0	0	0	0	0	4	0	16	5	0	0	21	5	26
Colorado School of Mines	CO	1	0	1	0	0	0	0	0	6	0	4	0	0	0	12	0	12
Colorado State University	CO	0	0	0	0	1	0	0	0	1	1	0	0	0	0	2	1	3
University of Colorado at Boulder	CO	0	0	0	0	0	0	1	0	2	0	1	1	0	0	4	1	5
Columbia University	NY	0	0	0	1	2	0	0	0	5	0	2	0	0	0	9	1	10
University of Connecticut	CT	0	0	0	0	0	0	0	0	3	3	4	3	0	0	7	6	13
Cornell University	NY	0	0	1	2	1	1	0	0	6	2	4	1	1	0	13	6	19
University of Dayton	OH	0	0	0	0	0	0	0	0	1	1	2	1	0	0	3	2	5
University of Delaware	DE	0	0	0	0	0	0	0	0	1	0	3	2	0	0	4	2	6
Drexel University	PA	0	0	1	1	0	0	0	0	0	1	3	1	0	0	4	3	7
University of Florida	FL	0	0	0	0	1	0	0	0	1	1	5	0	0	0	7	1	8
Florida Institute of Technology	FL	0	0	0	0	0	0	0	0	2	0	0	1	0	0	2	1	3
FAMU-FSU College of Engineering	FL	0	0	0	0	0	0	0	0	2	1	0	0	0	0	2	1	3
Georgia Institute of Technology	GA	0	2	0	1	0	1	0	0	9	2	2	6	0	0	11	12	23
University of Houston, Cullen School of Engineering	TX	1	0	0	2	0	0	1	0	8	1	1	0	0	0	11	3	14
Howard University	DC	0	2	0	0	0	0	0	0	0	0	3	2	0	0	3	4	7
University of Idaho	ID	0	0	0	0	0	0	0	0	2	0	0	0	0	0	2	0	2
Illinois Institute of Technology	IL	0	0	1	0	2	0	0	0	5	2	22	3	0	0	30	5	35
University of Illinois at Chicago	IL	1	0	1	1	1	0	0	0	1	1	0	0	0	0	4	2	6
University of Illinois at Urbana-Champaign	IL	0	0	2	2	0	0	0	0	10	2	3	0	0	0	15	4	19
The University of Iowa	IA	0	0	0	0	0	0	0	0	2	1	0	1	0	0	2	2	4
Iowa State University	IA	0	0	0	0	0	0	0	0	0	1	0	0	0	0	0	1	1
The Johns Hopkins University	MD	0	0	1	1	0	0	0	0	5	0	2	0	0	0	8	1	9

CHEMICAL ENGINEERING   AKR-JOH

MASTER'S DEGREES AWARDED IN CHEMICAL ENGINEERING, 2005-2006

INSTITUTION		AFRICAN AMERICAN		ASIAN AMERICAN		HISPANIC		NATIVE AMERICAN		CAUCASIAN		FOREIGN		OTHER		TOTAL BY GENDER		TOTAL DEGREES
		M	F	M	F	M	F	M	F	M	F	M	F	M	F	M	F	
University of Kansas	KS	0	0	0	0	0	0	0	0	5	0	2	0	0	0	7	0	7
Kansas State University	KS	0	0	0	0	0	0	0	0	1	0	5	0	0	0	6	0	6
University of Kentucky	KY	0	0	0	0	0	0	0	0	1	0	0	0	1	0	2	0	2
Lamar University	TX	0	0	0	0	1	0	0	0	0	1	33	5	0	0	34	6	40
Lehigh University	PA	0	0	0	0	0	0	0	0	0	0	2	1	9	2	11	3	14
Louisiana State University	LA	0	1	0	0	0	0	0	0	2	0	1	1	0	0	3	2	5
University of Louisiana at Lafayette	LA	0	0	0	0	0	0	0	0	0	0	8	1	0	0	8	1	9
University of Louisville	KY	0	0	0	0	0	0	0	0	10	2	1	1	0	0	11	3	14
University of Maine	ME	0	0	1	0	0	0	0	0	0	0	1	1	0	0	2	1	3
Manhattan College	NY	0	0	6	1	0	1	0	0	1	1	0	0	0	0	7	3	10
University of Maryland, Baltimore County	MD	0	0	0	0	0	1	0	0	2	0	1	2	0	0	3	3	6
University of Maryland, College Park	MD	0	0	0	0	0	0	0	0	1	1	1	0	0	0	2	1	3
Massachusetts Institute of Technology	MA	0	0	2	4	0	0	0	0	13	0	13	4	1	3	29	11	40
University of Massachusetts Amherst	MA	0	0	0	0	0	0	0	0	0	0	3	0	0	0	3	0	3
University of Massachusetts Lowell	MA	0	0	0	1	0	0	0	0	1	1	3	1	0	0	4	3	7
McNeese State University	LA	0	0	0	0	0	0	0	0	0	0	0	1	0	0	0	1	1
University of Michigan	MI	0	0	1	0	1	0	0	0	13	4	3	1	0	0	18	5	23
Michigan State University	MI	0	0	0	0	0	0	0	0	0	0	4	2	1	0	5	2	7
Michigan Technological University	MI	0	0	0	0	0	0	0	0	2	0	1	2	1	0	4	2	6
University of Minnesota - Twin Cities	MN	0	0	0	0	0	0	0	0	1	0	2	0	0	0	3	0	3
The University of Mississippi	MS	1	0	1	0	0	0	0	0	0	0	1	1	0	0	3	1	4
Mississippi State University	MS	0	0	0	0	0	0	0	0	1	2	0	2	0	0	1	4	5
University of Missouri-Columbia	MO	0	0	0	0	0	0	0	0	1	1	2	0	0	0	3	1	4
University of Missouri - Rolla	MO	0	0	0	0	0	0	0	0	1	1	8	0	0	0	9	1	10
Montana State University	MT	0	0	0	0	0	0	0	0	2	0	0	0	0	0	2	0	2
University of Nebraska, Lincoln	NE	0	0	0	0	0	0	0	0	1	1	0	1	0	0	1	2	3
University of Nevada, Reno	NV	1	0	0	0	0	0	0	0	1	0	0	2	0	0	2	2	4
University of New Hampshire	NH	0	0	0	0	0	0	0	0	1	1	1	1	0	0	2	2	4
New Jersey Institute of Technology	NJ	2	3	3	1	0	1	0	0	4	4	9	6	1	0	19	15	34
The University of New Mexico	NM	0	0	0	0	1	1	0	0	2	2	1	0	0	0	4	3	7
New Mexico State University	NM	0	0	0	0	0	1	0	0	2	1	3	1	0	0	5	3	8
City College of the City University of New York	NY	0	0	2	0	1	0	0	0	0	0	3	3	1	0	7	3	10
State University of New York at Buffalo	NY	0	1	0	0	0	0	0	0	3	0	4	2	0	0	7	3	10
North Carolina A & T State University	NC	4	0	0	0	0	0	0	0	1	0	1	0	0	0	6	0	6
North Carolina State University	NC	1	0	0	1	1	0	0	0	6	4	6	1	0	0	14	6	20
University of North Dakota	ND	0	0	0	0	0	0	0	0	6	1	0	0	0	0	6	1	7
Northeastern University	MA	0	0	0	0	0	0	0	0	1	0	0	0	0	0	1	0	1
University of Notre Dame	IN	0	0	0	1	1	0	0	0	6	0	4	0	0	0	11	1	12
The Ohio State University	OH	0	0	0	0	0	0	0	0	1	0	1	0	0	0	2	0	2
Ohio University	OH	0	0	0	0	0	0	0	0	0	1	4	0	0	0	4	1	5
University of Oklahoma	OK	0	0	0	0	0	0	0	0	3	0	3	0	0	0	6	0	6
Oklahoma State University	OK	0	0	0	0	0	0	0	0	3	0	4	7	0	0	7	7	14
Oregon State University	OR	0	0	0	1	0	0	0	0	2	0	1	1	0	0	3	1	4
University of Pennsylvania	PA	0	0	3	1	0	0	0	0	7	1	4	1	1	0	15	3	18
The Pennsylvania State University	PA	0	0	0	0	0	0	0	0	1	1	2	1	0	0	3	2	5

CHEMICAL ENGINEERING

KAN-PEN

MASTER'S DEGREES AWARDED IN CHEMICAL ENGINEERING, 2005-2006

INSTITUTION		AFRICAN AMERICAN		ASIAN AMERICAN		HISPANIC		NATIVE AMERICAN		CAUCASIAN		FOREIGN		OTHER		TOTAL BY GENDER		TOTAL DEGREES
		M	F	M	F	M	F	M	F	M	F	M	F	M	F	M	F	
University of Pittsburgh	PA	1	0	0	0	0	0	0	0	3	2	3	0	0	0	7	2	9
Polytechnic University	NY	0	0	1	0	0	0	0	0	2	0	1	0	2	0	6	0	6
Prairie View A&M University	TX	1	1	0	0	0	0	0	0	0	0	0	1	0	0	1	2	3
University of Puerto Rico, Mayaguez Campus	PR	0	0	0	0	2	6	0	0	0	0	0	0	0	0	2	6	8
Purdue University	IN	0	0	0	0	0	0	0	0	3	0	3	1	0	0	6	1	7
Rensselaer Polytechnic Institute	NY	0	0	1	0	0	0	0	0	1	0	3	1	0	0	5	1	6
University of Rhode Island	RI	0	0	0	0	0	0	0	0	0	0	2	0	0	0	2	0	2
William Marsh Rice University	TX	0	0	0	1	0	0	0	0	0	1	0	0	0	0	0	2	2
University of Rochester	NY	0	0	0	1	0	0	0	0	1	2	1	1	1	1	3	5	8
Rose-Hulman Institute of Technology	IN	0	0	0	2	0	0	0	0	0	0	0	0	0	0	0	2	2
Rowan University	NJ	0	0	0	0	0	0	0	0	2	1	0	0	0	0	2	1	3
Rutgers, The State University of New Jersey	NJ	0	1	0	0	0	0	0	0	4	2	3	0	0	0	7	3	10
San Jose State University	CA	0	0	3	5	0	0	0	0	0	2	0	0	2	0	5	7	12
University of South Alabama	AL	0	0	0	2	0	0	0	0	0	2	5	0	0	0	5	4	9
University of South Carolina	SC	0	0	1	0	0	0	0	0	0	1	1	1	0	0	2	2	4
South Dakota School of Mines and Technology	SD	1	0	0	0	0	0	0	0	1	0	5	2	0	0	7	2	9
University of South Florida	FL	0	0	1	0	0	0	0	0	0	0	0	0	0	0	1	0	1
University of Southern California	CA	0	0	3	1	0	0	0	0	2	5	14	3	0	0	19	9	28
Stanford University	CA	0	0	3	4	1	1	0	0	11	2	7	5	2	2	24	14	38
Stevens Institute of Technology	NJ	0	0	0	1	0	0	0	0	2	0	15	1	0	0	17	2	19
Syracuse University	NY	0	0	0	0	0	0	0	0	2	0	9	3	0	0	11	3	14
Tennessee Technological University	TN	0	0	0	0	0	0	0	0	3	0	2	0	0	0	5	0	5
University of Tennessee, Knoxville	TN	0	0	0	0	0	0	0	0	4	0	2	0	0	0	6	0	6
Texas A&M University	TX	0	1	2	0	0	0	0	0	4	0	4	5	0	0	10	6	16
Texas A&M University - Kingsville	TX	0	0	0	0	0	0	0	0	2	1	17	4	0	0	19	5	24
Texas Tech University	TX	0	0	0	0	1	1	0	0	0	0	1	0	0	0	2	1	3
The University of Texas at Austin	TX	1	1	0	0	0	0	0	0	6	3	1	2	0	0	8	6	14
The University of Toledo	OH	0	0	0	0	0	0	0	0	1	1	1	1	0	0	2	2	4
Tufts University	MA	0	0	0	0	0	1	0	0	0	0	1	0	5	3	7	3	10
Tulane University	LA	0	0	0	0	0	0	0	0	0	0	0	0	2	1	2	1	3
University of Tulsa	OK	0	0	0	0	0	0	0	0	0	0	5	1	1	0	6	1	7
University of Utah	UT	0	0	0	0	0	0	0	0	4	0	2	2	0	0	6	2	8
Vanderbilt University	TN	0	0	0	0	0	0	0	0	0	0	0	1	0	0	0	1	1
Villanova University	PA	0	0	0	0	0	0	0	0	3	1	2	1	0	0	5	2	7
University of Virginia	VA	0	0	0	0	0	0	0	0	5	1	3	1	0	0	8	2	10
Virginia Polytechnic Institute and State University	VA	0	0	0	0	0	0	0	0	4	0	1	0	0	0	5	0	5
University of Washington	WA	0	0	0	1	0	0	0	0	2	0	1	3	1	0	4	4	8
Washington State University	WA	0	0	1	0	0	0	0	0	3	1	0	0	4	1	8	2	10
Washington University	MO	0	0	0	0	0	0	0	0	5	0	1	2	1	1	7	3	10
Wayne State University	MI	0	0	0	0	0	0	0	0	0	1	4	2	0	0	4	3	7
West Virginia University	WV	0	0	0	0	0	0	0	0	2	1	2	3	0	1	4	5	9
Widener University	PA	0	0	0	0	0	0	0	0	2	1	1	0	0	0	3	1	4
University of Wisconsin, Madison	WI	0	0	0	0	1	0	0	0	3	0	1	0	0	0	5	0	5
Worcester Polytechnic Institute	MA	0	0	0	0	0	0	0	0	1	0	1	1	0	0	2	1	3
Youngstown State University	OH	0	0	0	0	0	0	0	0	0	0	2	0	0	0	2	0	2

CHEMICAL ENGINEERING

PIT-YOU

INSTITUTION	AFRICAN AMERICAN		ASIAN AMERICAN		HISPANIC		NATIVE AMERICAN		CAUCASIAN		FOREIGN		OTHER		TOTAL BY GENDER		TOTAL DEGREES
	M	F	M	F	M	F	M	F	M	F	M	F	M	F	M	F	
Totals:	19	16	50	45	22	18	1	0	319	109	385	142	58	20	854	350	1,204
CANADIAN INSTITUTIONS:																	
University of Alberta AB	0	0	0	0	0	0	0	0	0	0	0	0	17	12	17	12	29
University of Calgary AB	0	0	0	0	0	0	0	0	0	0	22	1	17	6	39	7	46
Ecole Polytechnique de Montreal PQ	0	0	0	0	0	0	0	0	0	0	0	0	10	4	10	4	14
McGill University, Faculty of Engineering PQ	0	0	0	0	0	0	0	0	0	0	0	0	8	9	8	9	17
University of Ottawa, Faculty of Engineering ON	0	0	0	0	0	0	0	0	0	0	2	2	8	1	10	3	13
University of Waterloo ON	0	0	0	0	0	0	0	0	0	0	0	0	9	10	9	10	19
Totals:	0	0	0	0	0	0	0	0	0	0	24	3	69	42	93	45	138

CHEMICAL ENGINEERING

ALB-WAT

MASTER'S DEGREES AWARDED IN CIVIL ENGINEERING, 2005-2006

INSTITUTION		AFRICAN AMERICAN M	F	ASIAN AMERICAN M	F	HISPANIC M	F	NATIVE AMERICAN M	F	CAUCASIAN M	F	FOREIGN M	F	OTHER M	F	TOTAL BY GENDER M	F	TOTAL DEGREES
The University of Akron	OH	0	0	0	0	0	0	0	0	2	1	5	3	0	0	7	4	11
University of Alabama at Birmingham	AL	0	0	0	0	0	0	0	0	0	0	13	0	4	2	17	3	20
The University of Alabama in Huntsville	AL	0	0	0	0	0	0	0	0	1	1	6	0	0	0	7	1	8
The University of Alabama	AL	1	0	1	0	0	0	0	0	6	1	1	1	0	0	9	2	11
The University of Arizona	AZ	0	0	0	0	0	0	0	0	1	0	2	3	0	0	3	3	6
Arizona State University	AZ	0	0	1	0	0	0	0	0	1	0	9	1	0	1	11	2	13
University of Arkansas	AR	0	0	0	0	0	0	0	0	2	2	3	1	0	0	5	3	8
Auburn University	AL	1	0	0	0	1	0	0	0	18	4	0	1	0	0	20	5	25
Boise State University	ID	0	0	0	1	0	0	0	0	3	1	1	0	0	0	4	2	6
Bradley University	IL	0	0	0	0	0	0	0	0	1	0	4	1	0	0	5	1	6
Brigham Young University	UT	0	0	0	0	0	0	0	0	0	0	3	1	34	3	37	4	41
Bucknell University	PA	0	0	0	0	0	1	2	0	18	5	0	0	0	0	20	6	26
California Institute of Technology	CA	0	0	0	0	1	0	0	0	1	0	0	0	0	0	2	0	2
California Polytechnic State University	CA	0	0	0	0	2	2	0	0	6	0	0	0	0	0	8	2	10
California State University, Fresno	CA	0	0	2	0	0	0	0	0	0	0	0	0	0	0	2	0	2
California State University, Fullerton	CA	0	0	3	1	3	0	0	0	4	2	3	0	2	0	15	3	18
California State University, Long Beach	CA	0	0	2	1	2	0	0	0	5	1	1	2	0	0	10	4	14
California State University, Los Angeles	CA	0	0	3	1	2	1	0	0	1	1	2	1	5	1	13	5	18
California State University, Sacramento	CA	0	0	2	1	1	0	0	0	9	0	2	1	1	0	15	2	17
University of California, Berkeley	CA	1	1	14	10	2	2	2	0	40	34	30	12	7	6	96	65	161
University of California, Davis	CA	0	0	2	1	0	0	0	0	10	7	7	4	3	2	22	14	36
University of California, Irvine	CA	0	0	0	0	0	0	0	0	0	0	0	0	9	3	9	3	12
University of California, Los Angeles	CA	1	0	7	2	3	0	0	0	9	0	6	5	4	3	30	10	40
University of California, San Diego	CA	0	0	0	0	3	1	0	0	14	6	3	0	1	0	21	8	29
Carnegie Mellon University	PA	2	1	1	0	0	0	0	0	12	6	11	3	0	0	26	10	36
Case Western Reserve University	OH	0	0	0	0	0	0	0	0	2	0	1	0	0	1	3	1	4
The Catholic University of America	DC	0	0	0	0	0	0	0	0	0	0	4	1	1	2	5	3	8
University of Central Florida	FL	0	0	0	0	1	0	0	1	5	1	14	1	1	0	21	3	24
University of Cincinnati	OH	1	0	0	0	0	0	0	0	4	2	19	3	0	0	24	5	29
Clarkson University	NY	0	1	0	0	0	0	0	0	2	2	1	2	0	0	3	5	8
Clemson University	SC	0	0	1	0	1	0	0	0	32	8	13	3	2	0	49	11	60
Cleveland State University	OH	0	0	0	0	0	0	0	0	3	4	8	2	0	0	11	6	17
University of Colorado at Boulder	CO	0	0	1	1	3	1	0	0	47	27	1	1	0	0	52	30	82
University of Colorado at Denver	CO	0	0	0	1	2	1	0	0	12	8	4	0	0	1	18	11	29
Columbia University	NY	0	0	1	0	2	0	0	0	9	2	6	2	3	5	21	9	30
University of Connecticut	CT	0	0	1	0	0	0	0	0	7	0	4	1	0	1	12	2	14
Cornell University	NY	0	0	3	1	3	2	0	0	18	17	13	4	4	1	41	25	66
University of Dayton	OH	0	0	0	0	0	0	0	0	1	0	2	0	0	0	3	0	3
University of Delaware	DE	0	1	0	0	0	0	0	0	9	3	7	3	0	0	16	7	23
University of Detroit Mercy	MI	0	0	0	0	0	0	0	0	2	0	1	0	1	0	4	0	4
Drexel University	PA	0	0	0	0	0	0	0	0	5	1	1	1	2	0	8	2	10
Duke University Pratt School of Engineering	NC	0	0	0	0	0	0	0	0	0	0	0	0	3	0	3	0	3
University of Florida	FL	4	0	3	0	2	0	0	0	23	11	17	6	0	0	49	17	66
Florida Atlantic University	FL	0	0	0	0	0	0	0	0	5	0	0	0	0	0	5	0	5
Florida Institute of Technology	FL	0	0	0	0	0	0	0	0	0	1	5	2	0	0	5	3	8

CIVIL ENGINEERING

AKR-FLO

INSTITUTION		AFRICAN AMERICAN		ASIAN AMERICAN		HISPANIC		NATIVE AMERICAN		CAUCASIAN		FOREIGN		OTHER		TOTAL BY GENDER		TOTAL DEGREES
		M	F	M	F	M	F	M	F	M	F	M	F	M	F	M	F	
Florida International University	FL	3	0	2	1	6	1	0	0	1	0	6	2	0	0	18	4	22
FAMU-FSU College of Engineering	FL	0	1	0	0	0	0	0	0	1	0	2	0	0	0	3	1	4
George Mason University	VA	0	0	0	1	0	0	0	0	0	5	1	0	1	1	2	7	9
Georgia Institute of Technology	GA	3	2	0	1	3	1	0	1	29	8	13	6	1	0	49	19	68
University of Hartford	CT	0	0	0	0	0	0	0	0	1	0	1	0	0	0	2	0	2
University of Hawaii at Manoa	HI	0	0	12	14	2	0	0	0	0	0	8	7	11	3	33	24	57
University of Houston, Cullen School of Engineering	TX	0	0	1	1	2	0	0	0	5	2	10	1	1	0	19	4	23
Howard University	DC	2	1	0	0	0	0	0	0	0	0	1	0	0	0	3	1	4
University of Idaho	ID	0	0	0	1	0	0	0	0	11	0	0	0	10	2	21	3	24
Idaho State University	ID	0	0	0	0	0	0	0	0	2	1	0	0	0	0	2	1	3
Illinois Institute of Technology	IL	0	0	0	0	1	1	0	0	7	4	12	5	1	0	21	10	31
University of Illinois at Chicago	IL	0	1	4	3	0	0	0	0	13	2	0	0	0	0	17	6	23
University of Illinois at Urbana-Champaign	IL	2	0	2	2	4	4	0	0	55	3	21	8	0	0	84	17	101
The University of Iowa	IA	0	0	0	0	0	0	0	0	9	2	4	3	0	0	13	5	18
Iowa State University	IA	0	0	1	0	0	0	0	0	13	4	10	3	0	0	24	7	31
The Johns Hopkins University	MD	0	1	0	0	0	0	0	0	1	3	2	1	0	0	3	5	8
University of Kansas	KS	0	0	0	0	0	0	0	0	11	7	0	0	0	0	11	7	18
Kansas State University	KS	0	0	0	0	0	0	0	0	2	0	6	1	1	0	9	1	10
University of Kentucky	KY	1	0	1	0	0	0	1	0	23	6	12	2	1	0	39	8	47
Lamar University	TX	1	0	1	1	0	0	0	0	0	1	40	9	0	0	42	11	53
Lawrence Technological University	MI	0	0	1	0	0	0	0	0	3	0	1	0	0	0	5	1	6
Lehigh University	PA	0	0	0	0	0	0	0	0	0	0	5	0	3	1	8	1	9
Louisiana State University	LA	0	0	1	0	0	0	0	0	2	4	6	4	0	0	9	8	17
University of Louisiana at Lafayette	LA	0	0	0	0	0	0	0	0	0	1	6	1	0	0	6	2	8
University of Louisville	KY	1	0	2	0	1	1	0	0	51	7	1	2	0	0	56	10	66
Loyola Marymount University	CA	1	1	0	1	0	1	0	0	2	2	0	0	0	0	4	5	9
University of Maine	ME	0	0	0	0	0	0	0	0	7	5	0	0	0	0	7	5	12
Manhattan College	NY	0	0	0	0	0	0	0	0	10	3	0	0	0	0	10	3	13
Marquette University	WI	0	0	0	0	0	0	0	0	10	3	2	1	0	0	12	4	16
University of Maryland, Baltimore County	MD	0	0	0	0	0	1	0	0	0	0	1	0	0	0	1	1	2
University of Maryland, College Park	MD	2	0	0	1	1	0	0	0	11	1	16	6	1	2	31	10	41
Massachusetts Institute of Technology	MA	0	1	2	7	1	2	0	0	13	12	27	14	5	3	48	39	87
University of Massachusetts Amherst	MA	0	0	0	0	1	0	0	0	9	2	1	2	0	0	11	4	15
University of Massachusetts Lowell	MA	3	0	0	1	0	0	0	0	4	0	1	2	1	0	9	3	12
The University of Memphis	TN	0	0	1	0	0	0	0	0	4	1	2	1	0	0	7	2	9
University of Miami	FL	0	0	0	0	0	0	0	0	1	0	0	0	0	0	1	0	1
University of Michigan	MI	0	0	1	2	3	0	0	0	9	6	9	6	2	0	24	14	38
Michigan State University	MI	0	0	1	1	0	0	0	0	0	0	2	2	1	2	4	5	9
Michigan Technological University	MI	0	0	0	0	0	0	0	0	8	1	4	1	1	0	13	2	15
Milwaukee School of Engineering	WI	0	0	0	0	0	0	0	0	1	0	0	0	0	0	1	0	1
University of Minnesota - Twin Cities	MN	2	0	0	0	0	0	0	0	22	3	6	4	0	0	30	7	37
The University of Mississippi	MS	0	0	0	0	0	0	0	0	4	2	2	0	2	0	8	2	10
Mississippi State University	MS	0	0	0	0	0	0	0	0	6	0	1	0	0	0	7	1	8
University of Missouri-Columbia	MO	0	0	0	0	1	0	0	0	6	1	5	2	1	0	13	3	16
University of Missouri - Kansas City	MO	0	0	0	0	0	0	0	0	2	1	0	1	0	0	2	2	4

FLO-MIS

CIVIL ENGINEERING

MASTER'S DEGREES AWARDED IN CIVIL ENGINEERING, 2005-2006

INSTITUTION		AFRICAN AMERICAN		ASIAN AMERICAN		HISPANIC		NATIVE AMERICAN		CAUCASIAN		FOREIGN		OTHER		TOTAL BY GENDER		TOTAL DEGREES
		M	F	M	F	M	F	M	F	M	F	M	F	M	F	M	F	
University of Missouri - Rolla	MO	0	0	0	0	1	0	0	0	23	3	2	4	1	0	27	7	34
Montana State University	MT	0	0	0	0	0	0	0	0	6	2	0	0	0	0	6	2	8
University of Nebraska, Lincoln	NE	0	0	0	1	0	0	0	0	9	1	2	1	0	0	11	3	14
University of New Hampshire	NH	0	0	0	0	0	0	0	0	8	0	0	2	0	0	8	2	10
New Jersey Institute of Technology	NJ	0	1	1	2	2	1	0	0	13	3	7	3	3	0	26	10	36
The University of New Mexico	NM	0	0	0	0	0	2	0	0	9	2	6	1	0	0	15	5	20
New Mexico State University	NM	0	0	0	0	0	0	1	0	3	1	5	1	0	0	9	2	11
University of New Orleans	LA	1	0	1	1	1	0	0	0	7	0	16	5	0	0	26	6	32
City College of the City University of New York	NY	0	0	2	1	6	0	0	0	0	0	6	0	2	0	16	1	17
State University of New York at Buffalo	NY	0	0	0	0	0	0	0	0	7	0	17	9	1	1	25	10	35
North Carolina A & T State University	NC	4	2	0	1	0	0	0	0	0	0	2	0	0	0	6	3	9
North Carolina State University	NC	0	0	1	0	1	0	0	0	34	5	10	5	0	0	46	10	56
University of North Carolina, Charlotte	NC	0	0	0	1	0	0	0	0	8	6	3	1	0	0	11	8	19
University of North Dakota	ND	0	0	0	0	0	0	0	0	4	0	0	0	0	0	4	0	4
North Dakota State University	ND	0	0	2	0	0	0	0	0	3	0	0	0	0	0	5	0	5
Northeastern University	MA	0	0	0	1	0	0	0	0	6	1	7	1	2	0	15	3	18
Northwestern University	IL	0	0	2	0	0	0	0	0	6	6	11	1	2	0	21	7	28
University of Notre Dame	IN	0	0	0	0	0	0	0	0	2	0	0	0	0	0	2	0	2
The Ohio State University	OH	1	0	0	0	0	0	0	0	8	1	11	4	0	0	20	5	25
Ohio University	OH	0	0	0	0	0	0	0	0	1	1	3	1	0	0	4	2	6
University of Oklahoma	OK	2	0	1	0	0	0	0	0	3	0	5	1	0	0	11	1	12
Oklahoma State University	OK	0	0	0	0	0	0	2	0	4	0	3	4	0	0	9	4	13
Old Dominion University	VA	0	0	0	0	1	0	0	0	5	2	2	0	0	0	8	2	10
Oregon State University	OR	0	0	0	0	0	0	0	0	6	4	4	1	0	0	10	5	15
The Pennsylvania State University	PA	0	0	0	0	0	0	0	0	7	4	5	4	0	0	12	8	20
University of Pittsburgh	PA	0	0	0	0	0	0	0	0	26	1	0	2	0	0	26	3	29
Polytechnic University	NY	2	1	4	0	0	0	0	0	6	1	2	2	5	1	19	5	24
Polytechnic University of Puerto Rico	PR	0	0	0	0	4	1	0	0	0	0	0	0	0	0	4	1	5
Portland State University	OR	1	0	0	0	0	0	0	0	3	5	1	0	1	0	6	5	11
Princeton University	NJ	0	0	0	0	0	0	0	0	4	3	0	0	0	0	4	3	7
University of Puerto Rico, Mayaguez Campus	PR	0	0	0	0	15	6	0	0	0	0	0	0	0	0	15	6	21
Purdue University	IN	0	1	2	3	2	0	0	0	19	4	16	7	0	2	39	17	56
Rensselaer Polytechnic Institute	NY	0	0	1	0	0	0	0	0	7	1	1	1	0	0	9	2	11
University of Rhode Island	RI	0	0	0	0	0	0	0	0	2	0	4	1	0	1	6	2	8
Rowan University	NJ	0	0	0	0	1	0	0	0	2	1	0	0	0	0	3	1	4
Rutgers, The State University of New Jersey	NJ	0	0	0	0	1	0	0	0	3	5	10	6	0	0	14	11	25
Saint Martin's College	WA	0	0	0	0	0	0	0	0	2	0	0	0	0	0	2	0	2
San Diego State University	CA	0	0	0	0	0	1	0	0	1	1	1	0	1	1	3	3	6
San Jose State University	CA	0	0	10	18	1	0	0	0	2	3	0	0	4	0	17	21	38
South Dakota School of Mines and Technology	SD	1	0	0	0	0	0	0	0	6	4	4	4	0	0	11	8	19
South Dakota State University	SD	0	0	0	0	0	0	0	0	3	0	3	0	0	0	6	0	6
University of Southern California	CA	0	0	7	2	2	1	0	0	19	4	31	4	2	1	61	10	71
Southern Illinois University Carbondale	IL	0	0	1	0	1	0	0	0	8	2	5	1	0	0	15	3	18
Southern Illinois University Edwardsville	IL	0	1	0	0	0	0	0	0	6	3	6	2	0	0	12	7	19
Southern Methodist University	TX	0	0	0	0	0	1	0	0	1	0	2	0	0	0	3	1	4

CIVIL ENGINEERING

MIS-SOU

MASTER'S DEGREES AWARDED IN CIVIL ENGINEERING, 2005-2006

INSTITUTION		AFRICAN AMERICAN M	F	ASIAN AMERICAN M	F	HISPANIC M	F	NATIVE AMERICAN M	F	CAUCASIAN M	F	FOREIGN M	F	OTHER M	F	TOTAL BY GENDER M	F	TOTAL DEGREES
Stanford University	CA	1	1	9	5	3	1	0	1	25	18	29	12	7	5	74	43	117
Stevens Institute of Technology	NJ	0	0	1	2	1	0	0	0	6	3	4	0	0	0	12	5	17
Syracuse University	NY	1	0	0	0	0	0	0	0	2	1	6	1	0	0	9	2	11
Temple University	PA	0	0	0	0	0	0	0	0	7	1	0	0	0	0	7	1	8
Tennessee Technological University	TN	0	0	0	0	0	0	0	0	3	2	1	1	0	0	4	3	7
University of Tennessee, Knoxville	TN	0	0	0	0	0	0	0	0	16	9	0	2	0	0	16	11	27
Texas A&M University	TX	0	0	2	0	1	2	0	0	23	7	27	9	0	1	53	19	72
Texas A&M University - Kingsville	TX	0	0	0	0	0	1	0	0	0	0	9	3	0	0	9	4	13
Texas Tech University	TX	1	0	1	0	1	0	0	0	15	5	7	2	0	0	25	7	32
The University of Texas at Arlington	TX	2	0	3	0	1	0	0	0	6	2	17	7	0	0	29	9	38
The University of Texas at Austin	TX	0	0	1	0	3	1	0	0	36	16	21	7	0	0	61	24	85
University of Texas at El Paso	TX	0	0	0	0	1	1	0	0	0	0	5	1	0	0	6	2	8
University of Texas at San Antonio	TX	2	0	0	0	0	0	0	0	5	0	0	2	0	0	7	2	9
The University of Toledo	OH	0	0	0	0	0	0	0	0	2	2	3	5	0	0	5	7	12
Tufts University	MA	0	0	0	2	0	1	1	0	0	0	0	1	7	12	8	16	24
Tulane University	LA	0	0	0	0	0	0	0	0	0	0	2	0	2	0	4	0	4
University of Utah	UT	0	0	1	0	1	0	0	0	23	1	5	0	1	1	30	2	32
Utah State University	UT	0	0	0	0	0	0	0	0	25	0	19	0	0	0	44	0	44
Vanderbilt University	TN	0	0	0	0	1	0	0	0	7	4	2	0	1	0	11	4	15
University of Vermont	VT	0	0	0	0	0	1	0	0	4	0	0	0	1	0	5	1	6
Villanova University	PA	0	0	0	0	0	0	0	0	9	0	0	0	0	0	9	0	9
University of Virginia	VA	0	0	0	0	1	0	0	0	8	4	6	1	0	0	15	5	20
Virginia Polytechnic Institute and State University	VA	1	0	2	2	1	0	0	0	36	7	28	3	0	1	68	13	81
University of Washington	WA	0	1	2	1	4	0	0	0	26	12	3	1	1	3	37	18	55
Washington State University	WA	0	0	0	0	0	0	0	0	1	2	4	1	6	2	11	5	16
Washington University	MO	1	3	0	0	2	0	0	0	13	4	3	2	3	0	22	9	31
Wayne State University	MI	2	0	2	1	0	0	0	0	5	7	16	4	2	0	27	12	39
West Virginia University	WV	1	0	0	0	0	0	0	0	5	2	5	1	0	0	11	3	14
Widener University	PA	0	0	0	0	0	0	0	0	1	0	0	0	0	0	1	0	1
University of Wisconsin, Madison	WI	0	0	0	0	1	1	0	0	21	5	6	2	0	1	28	9	37
Worcester Polytechnic Institute	MA	0	0	0	0	1	0	0	0	5	6	0	0	0	0	6	6	12
University of Wyoming	WY	0	0	0	0	0	0	0	0	6	0	3	0	0	0	9	0	9
Youngstown State University	OH	0	0	0	0	0	0	0	0	0	0	1	0	0	0	1	0	1
Totals:		**56**	**24**	**140**	**103**	**122**	**45**	**11**	**3**	**1,362**	**464**	**925**	**317**	**185**	**78**	**2,801**	**1,034**	**3,835**

CANADIAN INSTITUTIONS:

INSTITUTION		AFRICAN AMERICAN M	F	ASIAN AMERICAN M	F	HISPANIC M	F	NATIVE AMERICAN M	F	CAUCASIAN M	F	FOREIGN M	F	OTHER M	F	TOTAL BY GENDER M	F	TOTAL DEGREES
University of Alberta	AB	0	0	0	0	0	0	0	0	0	0	0	0	61	20	61	20	81
University of Calgary	AB	0	0	0	0	0	0	0	0	0	0	2	1	8	4	10	5	15
Concordia University, Faculty of Engr. and Comp. Sci.	PQ	0	0	0	0	0	0	0	0	0	0	3	1	42	6	45	7	52
Ecole Polytechnique de Montreal	PQ	0	0	0	0	0	0	0	0	0	0	0	0	6	2	6	2	8
Ecole de Technologie Superieure	PQ	0	0	0	0	0	0	0	0	0	0	0	0	16	2	16	2	18
McGill University, Faculty of Engineering	PQ	0	0	0	0	0	0	0	0	0	0	0	0	18	9	18	9	27
University of Ottawa, Faculty of Engineering	ON	0	0	0	0	0	0	0	0	0	0	2	1	9	6	11	7	18
University of Waterloo	ON	0	0	0	0	0	0	0	0	0	0	0	0	31	9	31	9	40
Totals:		**0**	**0**	**0**	**0**	**0**	**0**	**0**	**0**	**0**	**0**	**7**	**3**	**191**	**58**	**198**	**61**	**259**

STA-YOU

CIVIL ENGINEERING

INSTITUTION		AFRICAN AMERICAN		ASIAN AMERICAN		HISPANIC		NATIVE AMERICAN		CAUCASIAN		FOREIGN		OTHER		TOTAL BY GENDER		TOTAL DEGREES
		M	F	M	F	M	F	M	F	M	F	M	F	M	F	M	F	
University of Alaska Fairbanks	AK	0	0	0	1	0	0	0	0	2	0	1	0	0	0	3	1	4
Colorado State University	CO	0	0	0	1	0	0	0	0	23	13	0	1	4	1	27	15	42
The George Washington University	DC	0	0	1	0	0	0	0	0	1	0	6	1	1	0	9	1	10
University of Massachusetts Dartmouth	MA	0	0	0	0	0	0	0	0	2	0	0	0	0	0	2	0	2
University of Nevada, Las Vegas	NV	0	0	2	0	0	0	0	0	9	2	5	5	2	0	18	7	25
University of Nevada, Reno	NV	1	0	2	1	0	0	0	0	2	3	6	0	0	0	11	4	15
University of North Dakota	ND	0	0	0	0	0	1	0	0	2	0	0	0	0	0	2	1	3
Northern Arizona University	AZ	0	0	0	0	0	0	1	0	0	0	0	0	0	0	1	0	1
University of South Carolina	SC	0	0	0	0	0	0	0	0	3	3	0	0	1	0	4	3	7
Totals:		1	0	5	3	0	1	1	0	44	21	18	6	8	1	77	32	109

CIVIL/ENVIRONMENTAL ENGINEERING   ALA-SOU

MASTER'S DEGREES AWARDED IN COMPUTER ENGINEERING, 2005-2006

INSTITUTION		AFRICAN AMERICAN		ASIAN AMERICAN		HISPANIC		NATIVE AMERICAN		CAUCASIAN		FOREIGN		OTHER		TOTAL BY GENDER		TOTAL DEGREES
		M	F	M	F	M	F	M	F	M	F	M	F	M	F	M	F	
Air Force Institute of Technology	OH	0	0	0	0	0	0	0	0	0	0	0	0	8	0	8	0	8
The University of Alabama in Huntsville	AL	0	1	0	0	0	0	0	0	7	2	1	0	0	1	8	4	12
University of Arkansas	AR	1	0	0	0	0	0	0	0	6	0	5	1	0	0	12	1	13
Boise State University	ID	0	0	0	0	0	0	0	0	6	0	0	0	0	0	6	0	6
Boston University	MA	0	0	6	6	0	0	0	0	3	1	4	3	0	0	13	10	23
University of Bridgeport	CT	0	0	0	0	0	0	0	0	0	0	15	5	0	0	15	5	20
California State University, Sacramento	CA	0	0	2	1	0	0	0	0	0	0	0	0	0	0	2	1	3
University of California-Santa Cruz	CA	0	0	4	4	0	0	0	0	4	1	2	2	1	1	11	8	19
Case Western Reserve University	OH	0	0	0	0	0	0	0	0	6	0	2	1	0	0	8	1	9
University of Central Florida	FL	1	0	3	1	0	1	0	0	14	2	5	3	0	0	23	7	30
University of Cincinnati	OH	0	0	1	0	0	0	0	0	2	0	30	5	0	0	33	5	38
Clemson University	SC	1	0	0	0	0	0	0	0	2	0	6	0	3	0	12	0	12
Columbia University	NY	0	0	3	0	0	0	0	0	2	0	2	1	1	0	8	1	9
University of Denver	CO	0	0	0	0	0	0	0	0	1	0	2	0	0	0	3	0	3
Drexel University	PA	2	0	1	1	1	0	0	0	3	1	7	1	1	1	15	4	19
Embry Riddle Aeronautical Univ., Daytona Beach	FL	0	0	0	0	2	0	0	0	2	0	6	2	1	1	11	3	14
University of Florida	FL	0	0	4	0	3	2	0	0	22	2	19	7	0	0	48	11	59
Florida Atlantic University	FL	1	0	1	0	0	0	0	0	3	0	5	6	0	0	10	6	16
Florida Institute of Technology	FL	0	1	0	0	0	0	0	0	8	2	2	1	3	0	13	4	17
Florida International University	FL	0	0	0	0	0	0	0	0	0	0	5	2	0	0	5	2	7
Gannon University	PA	0	0	0	0	0	0	0	0	1	0	3	3	0	0	4	3	7
George Mason University	VA	0	1	8	9	1	0	0	0	24	4	7	8	5	1	45	23	68
The George Washington University	DC	0	1	1	1	0	0	0	0	5	0	5	0	1	0	12	2	14
University of Idaho	ID	0	0	0	0	0	0	0	0	3	0	0	0	1	0	4	0	4
Illinois Institute of Technology	IL	0	0	1	0	0	0	0	0	5	0	17	5	0	0	23	5	28
Iowa State University	IA	1	0	0	0	1	0	0	0	11	1	11	3	0	0	24	4	28
University of Kansas	KS	0	0	0	0	0	0	0	0	4	1	4	1	0	0	8	2	10
Lehigh University	PA	0	0	0	0	1	0	0	0	0	0	1	1	5	0	7	1	8
University of Louisiana at Lafayette	LA	0	0	0	0	0	0	0	0	1	1	7	2	0	0	8	3	11
University of Louisville	KY	2	2	2	0	0	0	0	0	10	1	0	0	0	0	14	3	17
University of Maine	ME	0	0	0	0	0	0	0	0	1	0	0	0	0	0	1	0	1
Manhattan College	NY	1	0	2	1	1	0	0	0	3	0	1	0	2	0	10	1	11
University of Maryland, Baltimore County	MD	0	0	1	0	0	0	0	0	0	0	1	0	0	0	2	0	2
University of Massachusetts Dartmouth	MA	0	0	0	0	0	0	0	0	0	0	4	0	1	0	5	0	5
University of Massachusetts Lowell	MA	0	0	1	3	0	0	0	0	4	1	5	1	1	1	12	5	17
Mercer University	GA	1	1	0	0	0	0	0	0	0	0	8	0	1	2	10	3	13
University of Michigan, Dearborn	MI	0	0	0	0	0	0	0	0	4	0	2	2	0	0	6	2	8
University of Minnesota -Twin Cities	MN	1	1	1	0	0	0	0	0	4	2	5	2	0	0	11	5	16
Mississippi State University	MS	0	0	0	0	0	0	0	0	2	0	5	1	0	0	7	1	8
University of Missouri-Columbia	MO	0	0	0	0	0	0	0	0	0	0	1	3	0	0	1	3	4
University of Missouri - Rolla	MO	0	0	0	1	0	0	0	0	2	0	7	2	0	0	9	3	12
University of Nevada, Reno	NV	0	0	0	0	0	0	0	0	0	0	1	1	1	0	2	1	3
New Jersey Institute of Technology	NJ	0	0	3	1	2	0	0	0	1	0	10	2	2	0	18	3	21
The University of New Mexico	NM	0	0	0	1	0	0	0	0	2	0	4	1	0	0	6	2	8
The State University of New York at Binghamton	NY	0	0	0	0	0	0	0	0	0	0	0	0	1	0	1	0	1

AIR-NEW

COMPUTER ENGINEERING

INSTITUTION		AFRICAN AMERICAN		ASIAN AMERICAN		HISPANIC		NATIVE AMERICAN		CAUCASIAN		FOREIGN		OTHER		TOTAL BY GENDER		TOTAL DEGREES
		M	F	M	F	M	F	M	F	M	F	M	F	M	F	M	F	
North Carolina State University	NC	0	1	9	4	1	0	0	0	24	2	15	8	0	0	49	15	64
University of North Texas	TX	0	0	0	0	0	0	0	0	0	0	3	0	0	0	3	0	3
University of Notre Dame	IN	0	0	1	0	1	0	0	0	10	0	3	0	0	0	15	0	15
Old Dominion University	VA	0	0	1	0	0	0	0	0	2	1	5	0	0	0	8	1	9
Polytechnic University	NY	0	0	4	1	0	0	0	0	2	0	5	1	3	0	14	2	16
University of Puerto Rico, Mayaguez Campus	PR	0	0	0	0	9	3	0	0	0	0	0	0	0	0	9	3	12
Rensselaer Polytechnic Institute	NY	2	0	5	1	1	0	0	0	14	1	3	0	5	0	30	2	32
Rochester Institute of Technology	NY	0	0	1	0	0	0	0	0	9	0	3	1	0	0	13	1	14
Saint Mary's University	TX	0	0	0	0	0	0	0	0	2	0	0	1	0	0	2	1	3
San Jose State University	CA	2	0	94	120	0	0	0	2	4	6	0	0	10	10	110	138	248
Santa Clara University	CA	0	1	15	10	1	0	0	0	7	1	27	10	8	3	58	25	83
University of Southern California	CA	0	0	6	0	0	0	0	0	7	1	7	1	0	0	20	2	22
Southern Methodist University	TX	0	0	0	0	0	0	0	0	3	0	1	0	0	0	4	0	4
Stevens Institute of Technology	NJ	0	0	0	1	0	0	0	0	1	0	6	0	4	2	11	3	14
Syracuse University	NY	0	0	3	0	0	0	0	1	2	1	40	8	0	0	45	10	55
University of Tennessee, Knoxville	TN	0	0	0	0	0	0	0	0	1	0	0	0	0	0	1	0	1
The University of Texas at Dallas	TX	0	0	2	0	0	0	0	0	1	0	9	3	0	0	12	3	15
University of Texas at El Paso	TX	0	0	0	0	1	0	0	0	0	0	1	3	0	0	2	3	5
Villanova University	PA	0	0	1	0	0	0	0	0	14	1	2	0	0	0	17	1	18
University of Virginia	VA	0	0	0	0	0	0	0	0	1	0	1	1	0	0	2	1	3
Virginia Polytechnic Institute and State University	VA	0	0	2	1	0	0	0	0	10	0	7	1	0	0	19	2	21
University of Washington	WA	1	0	4	3	1	1	0	0	30	8	16	3	14	0	66	15	81
Washington State University	WA	0	0	0	0	0	0	0	0	2	0	1	1	0	1	3	2	5
Washington University	MO	0	0	0	0	0	0	0	0	3	0	3	0	0	0	6	0	6
Wayne State University	MI	0	0	1	1	0	0	0	0	0	0	10	4	1	1	12	6	18
West Virginia University	WV	0	0	1	0	0	0	0	0	10	5	3	1	0	0	14	6	20
Western Michigan University	MI	0	0	0	1	0	0	0	0	3	2	19	12	0	0	22	15	37
Widener University	PA	0	0	2	0	0	0	0	0	0	0	0	1	0	0	2	1	3
Wright State University	OH	1	0	0	0	0	0	0	0	7	1	8	4	0	0	16	5	21
Totals:		18	10	197	173	28	7	0	3	347	52	425	142	84	24	1,099	411	1,510
CANADIAN INSTITUTIONS:																		
Ecole Polytechnique de Montreal	PQ	0	0	0	0	0	0	0	0	0	0	0	0	37	5	37	5	42
Ecole de Technologie Superieure	PQ	0	0	0	0	0	0	0	0	0	0	0	0	8	4	8	4	12
Totals:		0	0	0	0	0	0	0	0	0	0	0	0	45	9	45	9	54

COMPUTER ENGINEERING   NOR-WRI

INSTITUTION		AFRICAN AMERICAN		ASIAN AMERICAN		HISPANIC		NATIVE AMERICAN		CAUCASIAN		FOREIGN		OTHER		TOTAL BY GENDER		TOTAL DEGREES
		M	F	M	F	M	F	M	F	M	F	M	F	M	F	M	F	
Air Force Institute of Technology	OH	0	0	0	0	0	0	0	0	1	0	0	0	9	1	10	1	11
The University of Alabama	AL	0	0	3	3	0	0	0	0	8	0	2	0	0	0	13	3	16
Arizona State University	AZ	1	0	1	1	1	0	0	0	9	3	23	8	2	0	37	12	49
University of Arkansas	AR	0	0	0	0	0	0	0	0	1	0	3	4	0	0	4	4	8
Auburn University	AL	1	0	2	2	0	0	1	0	8	0	3	6	0	0	15	8	23
Baylor University	TX	0	0	3	1	0	0	1	0	0	0	0	0	0	0	4	1	5
Boise State University	ID	0	0	1	0	0	0	0	0	3	0	0	2	0	0	4	2	6
University of Bridgeport	CT	0	0	1	1	0	0	0	0	0	0	20	8	0	0	21	9	30
California Institute of Technology	CA	0	0	2	0	0	0	0	0	1	0	4	0	0	0	7	2	9
California Polytechnic State University	CA	1	0	2	0	0	0	0	0	8	0	1	1	4	1	16	2	18
California State University, Fresno	CA	0	0	4	3	1	0	0	0	0	1	24	3	0	0	29	7	36
California State University, Fullerton	CA	1	0	34	8	3	1	0	0	15	4	38	8	14	3	105	24	129
California State University, Long Beach	CA	0	0	6	1	1	0	0	0	5	2	4	3	0	0	16	6	22
California State University, Los Angeles	CA	1	0	0	0	0	0	0	0	1	0	0	1	1	0	3	1	4
California State University, Northridge	CA	0	0	3	3	0	0	0	0	5	0	1	0	2	1	11	4	15
California State University, Sacramento	CA	0	0	3	6	1	1	0	0	3	2	20	7	5	1	32	17	49
University of California, Berkeley	CA	0	1	12	0	0	0	0	0	5	0	14	2	4	1	36	4	40
University of California, Davis	CA	2	0	6	4	0	0	0	0	9	0	4	1	4	0	25	5	30
University of California, Los Angeles	CA	0	0	23	4	3	1	1	0	18	2	8	1	4	0	57	8	65
University of California, Riverside	CA	0	0	2	2	1	0	0	0	0	0	0	0	14	4	17	6	23
University of California, San Diego	CA	1	0	12	1	1	0	0	0	21	1	12	8	3	1	50	11	61
University of California, Santa Barbara	CA	1	0	2	4	0	0	1	0	1	2	12	6	13	0	30	12	42
University of California-Santa Cruz	CA	0	0	1	1	0	0	0	0	8	0	3	0	2	1	14	2	16
Case Western Reserve University	OH	0	0	2	1	2	0	0	0	4	2	1	0	2	0	9	2	11
The Catholic University of America	DC	0	0	0	0	0	0	0	0	0	0	4	0	3	0	7	0	7
University of Central Florida	FL	1	0	2	0	1	0	0	0	26	3	28	11	1	0	59	14	73
University of Cincinnati	OH	1	0	0	1	0	0	0	0	3	1	7	4	0	0	11	6	17
Clemson University	SC	0	0	0	0	0	0	0	0	13	1	17	5	1	0	31	6	37
Colorado School of Mines	CO	0	0	2	1	0	0	0	0	10	5	0	1	0	0	12	7	19
University of Colorado at Boulder	CO	0	0	1	1	1	0	0	0	14	6	1	1	0	0	17	8	25
University of Colorado at Colorado Springs	CO	0	0	2	0	0	0	0	0	6	1	2	0	5	0	15	1	16
University of Colorado at Denver	CO	0	0	6	2	4	0	0	0	21	1	9	9	1	3	41	15	56
Columbia University	NY	0	0	6	1	1	0	0	0	15	3	24	6	24	7	70	17	87
University of Connecticut	CT	0	0	0	1	2	0	0	0	3	0	7	7	1	1	13	9	22
Cornell University	NY	0	0	18	2	2	0	0	0	32	1	49	15	5	1	106	19	125
University of Detroit Mercy	MI	0	0	0	0	0	0	0	0	0	0	5	1	1	1	6	2	8
Drexel University	PA	0	0	4	2	0	0	0	0	14	0	13	4	5	1	36	7	43
Florida Atlantic University	FL	1	1	5	2	2	3	0	0	7	7	85	4	0	0	235	17	252
Florida Institute of Technology	FL	0	0	1	0	1	1	0	0	7	2	6	3	3	2	18	7	25
Florida International University	FL	1	0	0	1	4	3	0	0	2	0	12	2	0	0	19	6	25
Gannon University	PA	0	0	0	0	0	0	0	0	5	3	5	0	0	0	10	3	13
George Mason University	VA	1	0	6	1	0	0	0	0	19	1	13	12	1	0	40	14	54
The George Washington University	DC	6	1	9	4	0	1	0	0	30	6	33	10	7	1	86	23	109
Harvard University	MA	0	0	4	1	0	0	0	0	9	0	2	0	0	0	15	1	16
Howard University	DC	4	3	0	0	0	0	0	0	0	0	3	3	0	0	7	6	13

COMPUTER SCIENCE (INSIDE ENGR.)   AIR–HOW

MASTER'S DEGREES AWARDED IN COMPUTER SCIENCE (INSIDE ENGINEERING), 2005-2006

INSTITUTION		AFRICAN AMERICAN M	F	ASIAN AMERICAN M	F	HISPANIC M	F	NATIVE AMERICAN M	F	CAUCASIAN M	F	FOREIGN M	F	OTHER M	F	TOTAL BY GENDER M	F	TOTAL DEGREES
University of Idaho	ID	0	0	1	0	0	0	0	0	6	0	0	0	2	3	9	3	12
University of Illinois at Chicago	IL	0	0	12	18	1	0	0	0	19	2	0	0	1	1	33	21	54
University of Illinois at Urbana-Champaign	IL	2	0	9	0	1	0	0	0	36	2	48	7	2	0	98	9	107
The Johns Hopkins University	MD	5	4	28	10	6	0	0	0	149	27	24	11	0	0	212	52	264
University of Kansas	KS	0	0	1	0	0	0	0	0	9	0	16	4	0	0	26	4	30
Kansas State University	KS	0	0	0	0	0	0	0	0	5	1	25	7	0	0	30	8	38
University of Kentucky	KY	0	0	1	0	1	0	0	0	6	0	30	5	0	3	38	8	46
Lehigh University	PA	0	0	0	0	0	0	0	0	0	0	5	1	13	0	18	1	19
Louisiana Tech University	LA	0	0	0	0	0	0	0	0	2	0	14	6	0	0	16	6	22
University of Maryland, Baltimore County	MD	0	1	0	1	0	0	0	0	9	1	9	5	0	0	18	8	26
University of Massachusetts Dartmouth	MA	0	0	0	0	0	0	0	0	4	0	16	5	0	0	20	5	25
Miami University	OH	0	0	0	1	0	0	0	0	1	0	2	3	0	0	4	4	8
Michigan State University	MI	1	1	1	0	0	0	0	0	0	0	7	3	9	0	18	4	22
University of Michigan, Dearborn	MI	1	0	5	2	0	0	0	0	12	2	6	5	0	0	25	9	34
University of Minnesota - Twin Cities	MN	0	0	3	3	1	0	0	0	40	4	16	9	0	0	60	16	76
The University of Mississippi	MS	1	2	2	1	1	0	0	0	4	0	4	3	3	1	15	7	22
Mississippi State University	MS	4	4	0	0	0	0	0	0	6	1	9	0	0	0	19	5	24
University of Missouri-Columbia	MO	0	0	1	0	0	0	0	0	6	0	8	3	0	0	15	3	18
University of Missouri - Kansas City	MO	0	0	2	0	0	0	0	0	5	2	48	13	0	0	55	15	70
Montana State University	MT	0	0	0	0	0	0	0	0	2	0	2	1	0	0	4	1	5
University of Nevada, Las Vegas	NV	0	0	1	0	0	0	0	0	3	0	4	8	0	0	8	8	16
University of Nevada, Reno	NV	0	0	1	0	2	0	0	0	5	0	4	0	1	0	11	0	11
University of New Hampshire	NH	0	0	0	0	0	0	1	0	3	0	4	2	0	0	8	2	10
University of New Haven	CT	1	0	1	0	1	1	0	0	16	1	2	3	0	0	21	5	26
The University of New Mexico	NM	0	0	0	1	0	0	0	0	8	0	27	10	0	0	35	11	46
New York Institute of Technology	NY	0	0	0	0	0	0	0	0	0	0	0	0	96	44	96	44	140
City College of the City University of New York	NY	0	1	2	3	3	0	0	0	0	0	22	6	2	0	29	10	39
The State University of New York at Binghamton	NY	0	0	3	2	0	0	0	0	9	1	34	4	1	0	47	7	54
State University of New York at Buffalo	NY	1	0	1	0	0	0	0	0	9	2	57	13	1	0	69	15	84
Stony Brook University	NY	1	0	1	2	0	0	0	0	6	0	65	20	0	0	73	22	95
North Carolina A & T State University	NC	6	5	1	0	0	0	0	0	2	0	1	0	0	0	10	5	15
North Carolina State University	NC	0	1	3	7	2	0	0	0	27	1	28	13	0	0	60	22	82
University of North Texas	TX	0	0	2	0	0	0	0	0	9	0	0	0	34	10	45	10	55
Oakland University	MI	0	0	5	3	0	0	0	0	15	3	15	10	0	0	35	16	51
The Ohio State University	OH	0	0	1	0	1	0	0	0	6	1	10	2	0	0	17	3	20
University of Oklahoma	OK	0	0	1	1	0	0	0	0	4	3	10	4	0	0	15	8	23
OGI School of Science & Engineering at OHSU	OR	0	0	10	3	1	0	0	0	9	3	2	1	2	0	24	7	31
Oregon State University	OR	0	0	0	0	1	0	0	0	2	0	13	2	1	0	17	2	19
University of Pennsylvania	PA	0	0	1	2	0	0	0	0	15	5	46	10	2	0	64	17	81
The Pennsylvania State University	PA	1	0	0	0	1	0	0	0	8	2	8	1	0	0	18	3	21
Polytechnic University	NY	2	1	20	4	2	0	1	0	23	4	14	4	22	9	84	22	106
Portland State University	OR	0	0	1	0	0	0	0	0	9	2	10	12	5	1	26	15	41
Prairie View A&M University	TX	1	0	1	1	0	0	0	0	0	0	0	0	0	0	2	1	3
Princeton University	NJ	0	0	0	0	0	0	0	0	1	0	0	0	0	0	1	0	1
William Marsh Rice University	TX	0	0	1	1	0	0	0	0	6	0	4	0	0	0	11	1	12

COMPUTER SCIENCE (INSIDE ENGR.)   IDA-RIC

MASTER'S DEGREES AWARDED IN COMPUTER SCIENCE (INSIDE ENGINEERING), 2005-2006

INSTITUTION		AFRICAN AMERICAN		ASIAN AMERICAN		HISPANIC		NATIVE AMERICAN		CAUCASIAN		FOREIGN		OTHER		TOTAL BY GENDER		TOTAL DEGREES
		M	F	M	F	M	F	M	F	M	F	M	F	M	F	M	F	
University of South Carolina	SC	0	0	0	1	0	0	0	0	7	0	7	4	0	0	14	5	19
South Dakota School of Mines and Technology	SD	0	0	0	2	0	0	0	0	1	0	1	0	0	0	2	2	4
South Dakota State University	SD	0	0	0	0	0	0	0	0	0	0	11	3	0	0	11	3	14
University of South Florida	FL	0	0	0	1	0	1	0	0	2	1	3	2	0	0	5	5	10
University of Southern California	CA	2	0	30	12	6	0	0	0	27	6	201	56	9	4	275	78	353
Southern Illinois University Edwardsville	IL	0	0	0	0	0	0	0	0	3	0	15	13	0	0	18	13	31
Southern Methodist University	TX	0	0	1	0	1	0	0	0	10	1	9	2	0	0	21	3	24
Stanford University	CA	0	1	25	8	2	1	0	0	48	1	46	9	11	2	132	22	154
University of Tennessee, Chattanooga	TN	0	0	0	0	1	1	0	0	3	0	0	0	0	0	4	0	4
Texas A&M University	TX	1	0	1	1	1	0	0	0	15	1	20	3	0	0	38	5	43
Texas A&M University - Kingsville	TX	0	0	1	0	0	0	0	0	0	0	51	11	0	0	52	11	63
Texas Tech University	TX	0	0	1	1	1	0	0	1	15	1	7	1	0	0	24	4	28
The University of Texas at Arlington	TX	1	0	14	7	2	1	0	0	9	4	72	29	0	0	98	41	139
The University of Texas at Dallas	TX	2	0	13	9	2	1	0	0	20	6	79	43	0	0	116	59	175
University of Texas at El Paso	TX	1	0	0	0	6	4	0	0	6	0	5	2	0	0	18	6	24
The University of Texas at Tyler	TX	0	0	3	3	0	0	0	0	0	0	2	0	0	0	5	3	8
Tufts University	MA	0	0	4	0	1	0	0	0	0	0	3	3	16	4	24	7	31
University of Tulsa	OK	0	0	0	1	1	0	0	0	12	2	8	2	3	0	24	5	29
University of Utah	UT	0	0	1	0	0	0	0	0	8	0	3	2	0	0	12	2	14
University of Vermont	VT	0	0	0	0	0	0	0	0	4	1	2	0	0	0	6	1	7
University of Virginia	VA	0	0	3	0	0	0	0	0	11	1	12	8	0	0	26	9	35
Virginia Commonwealth University	VA	6	3	0	0	3	0	0	3	3	1	12	4	0	0	24	11	35
Virginia Polytechnic Institute and State University	VA	0	0	1	0	1	1	0	0	12	1	17	11	0	0	31	13	44
Washington State University	WA	0	0	1	1	0	0	0	0	8	1	1	0	3	1	13	3	16
Washington University	MO	1	1	3	1	1	0	0	0	19	3	8	4	4	0	36	9	45
West Virginia University	WV	1	0	1	0	0	0	0	0	11	2	13	4	0	0	26	6	32
Western Michigan University	MI	0	0	0	0	0	0	0	0	0	0	5	0	0	0	5	0	5
University of Wisconsin, Milwaukee	WI	0	0	0	0	0	0	0	0	6	0	5	5	0	0	12	5	17
Wright State University	OH	0	0	0	0	0	0	0	0	9	1	5	9	0	0	14	10	24
University of Wyoming	WY	0	0	0	0	0	0	0	0	2	1	1	0	1	1	4	2	6
Totals:		66	31	418	179	85	20	7	4	1,157	162	1,815	618	385	115	4,068	1,129	5,197

SOU-WYO

COMPUTER SCIENCE (INSIDE ENGR.)

INSTITUTION		AFRICAN AMERICAN		ASIAN AMERICAN		HISPANIC		NATIVE AMERICAN		CAUCASIAN		FOREIGN		OTHER		TOTAL BY GENDER		TOTAL DEGREES
		M	F	M	F	M	F	M	F	M	F	M	F	M	F	M	F	
University of Alaska Fairbanks	AK	0	0	1	0	0	0	0	0	1	1	2	0	1	0	5	1	6
The University of Arizona	AZ	0	0	0	0	1	0	0	0	11	1	8	4	0	0	20	5	25
Brigham Young University	UT	0	0	0	0	0	0	0	0	0	0	3	1	19	3	22	4	26
University of California, Irvine	CA	0	0	0	6	0	0	0	0	0	0	0	0	51	14	51	14	65
Carnegie Mellon University	PA	0	0	4	6	3	0	1	0	34	12	101	25	20	5	163	48	211
Clarkson University	NY	0	0	0	2	0	0	0	0	2	0	2	1	0	0	4	3	7
Dartmouth College	NH	0	0	0	0	0	0	0	0	2	1	3	0	0	0	5	1	6
University of Delaware	DE	0	0	0	0	0	0	0	0	12	2	6	4	0	0	18	6	24
University of Florida	FL	0	0	0	0	1	1	0	0	0	0	8	1	0	0	9	2	11
FAMU-FSU College of Engineering	FL	0	0	0	0	1	0	0	0	31	8	9	7	0	0	41	15	56
Georgia Institute of Technology	GA	2	2	6	1	2	0	0	0	39	4	46	11	3	0	98	18	116
University of Houston, Cullen School of Engineering	TX	0	0	2	3	0	0	0	0	4	0	31	15	1	3	38	21	59
Illinois Institute of Technology	IL	1	0	7	2	1	0	0	0	13	1	79	29	2	0	103	32	135
The University of Iowa	IA	0	0	0	1	1	0	0	0	10	0	10	4	3	0	24	5	29
Lamar University	TX	0	0	0	0	0	0	0	0	1	0	29	9	0	0	30	9	39
Louisiana State University	LA	0	0	1	1	1	0	0	0	1	0	19	4	0	0	22	5	27
University of Louisiana at Lafayette	LA	0	0	0	0	0	0	0	0	4	1	35	9	0	0	39	10	49
Loyola College in Maryland	MD	0	1	0	0	0	0	0	0	9	0	2	0	0	0	11	1	12
University of Maryland, College Park	MD	0	1	0	0	0	0	0	0	11	2	13	5	0	1	24	9	33
University of Massachusetts Amherst	MA	0	0	3	0	1	0	18	3	9	4	0	0	2	0	33	7	40
The University of Memphis	TN	0	1	0	0	0	0	0	0	0	0	3	2	0	0	3	3	6
Michigan Technological University	MI	0	0	0	1	0	0	0	0	5	0	10	2	0	0	15	3	18
University of Nebraska, Lincoln	NE	0	0	1	1	0	0	0	0	3	0	7	5	0	0	11	6	17
New Jersey Institute of Technology	NJ	4	1	32	10	4	0	0	0	21	3	103	43	10	1	174	58	232
University of Pittsburgh	PA	0	0	0	2	0	0	0	0	7	2	5	2	0	0	12	6	18
Purdue University	IN	0	0	0	0	1	0	0	0	11	1	11	4	1	0	24	5	29
Rensselaer Polytechnic Institute	NY	1	0	5	1	0	0	1	0	37	8	10	3	7	0	61	12	73
University of Rochester	NY	0	0	0	0	0	0	0	0	3	1	8	1	1	0	12	2	14
Rochester Institute of Technology	NY	1	0	2	1	1	0	0	0	23	3	21	3	1	1	49	8	57
Saint Cloud State University	MN	0	0	0	0	0	0	0	0	0	0	9	2	0	0	9	2	11
University of South Alabama	AL	0	0	2	0	0	0	0	0	8	0	27	12	2	0	39	12	51
Southern Illinois University Carbondale	IL	0	0	0	0	0	0	0	0	2	1	21	8	0	0	23	9	32
Stevens Institute of Technology	NJ	0	0	5	1	0	0	0	0	13	2	10	1	5	1	33	5	38
University of Tennessee, Knoxville	TN	0	0	0	0	1	0	0	0	12	0	1	3	0	0	14	3	17
University of Texas at San Antonio	TX	0	0	0	1	2	2	0	0	6	1	2	3	0	0	10	7	17
Worcester Polytechnic Institute	MA	2	0	0	0	0	0	0	0	23	5	6	5	0	0	31	10	41
Totals:		11	6	71	34	21	3	20	3	368	64	660	228	129	29	1,280	367	1,647

CANADIAN INSTITUTIONS:

INSTITUTION		AFRICAN AMERICAN		ASIAN AMERICAN		HISPANIC		NATIVE AMERICAN		CAUCASIAN		FOREIGN		OTHER		TOTAL BY GENDER		TOTAL DEGREES
		M	F	M	F	M	F	M	F	M	F	M	F	M	F	M	F	
Concordia University, Faculty of Engr. and Comp. Sci.	PQ	0	0	0	0	0	0	0	0	0	0	8	4	65	23	73	27	100
Totals:		0	0	0	0	0	0	0	0	0	0	8	4	65	23	73	27	100

ALA-WOR

COMPUTER SCIENCE (OUTSIDE ENGR.)

MASTER'S DEGREES AWARDED IN ELECTRICAL ENGINEERING, 2005-2006

INSTITUTION		AFRICAN AMERICAN M	F	ASIAN AMERICAN M	F	HISPANIC M	F	NATIVE AMERICAN M	F	CAUCASIAN M	F	FOREIGN M	F	OTHER M	F	TOTAL BY GENDER M	F	TOTAL DEGREES
Air Force Institute of Technology	OH	0	0	0	0	0	0	0	0	6	0	0	0	54	2	60	2	62
University of Alabama at Birmingham	AL	1	0	1	0	0	0	0	0	15	1	15	5	0	0	32	6	38
The University of Alabama in Huntsville	AL	1	0	0	0	0	0	0	0	22	3	12	1	0	0	35	4	39
The University of Alabama	AL	0	0	3	0	0	0	0	0	4	0	2	2	0	0	9	2	11
University of Alaska Fairbanks	AK	0	0	0	0	0	0	0	0	1	0	2	2	0	0	3	2	5
Alfred University, NY State College of Ceramics	NY	0	0	0	0	0	0	0	0	2	0	0	2	0	0	2	2	4
Arizona State University	AZ	0	0	3	0	0	1	0	0	17	3	49	10	6	0	75	14	89
University of Arkansas	AR	0	0	0	0	0	0	0	0	2	0	14	5	2	0	18	5	23
Boise State University	ID	0	0	0	0	0	0	0	0	1	1	2	2	0	0	3	3	6
Boston University	MA	1	1	10	3	2	0	0	0	7	2	11	4	0	0	31	10	41
Bradley University	IL	1	0	0	0	1	0	0	0	6	0	27	4	0	0	35	4	39
University of Bridgeport	CT	0	0	0	0	0	0	0	0	1	0	35	5	0	0	36	5	41
Bucknell University	PA	0	0	0	1	0	0	0	0	25	6	0	0	0	0	25	7	32
California Institute of Technology	CA	0	0	2	0	0	1	0	0	6	0	15	3	0	0	23	4	27
California Polytechnic State University	CA	0	0	2	0	0	1	0	0	13	0	1	0	1	0	17	1	18
California State University, Fresno	CA	0	0	0	0	0	0	0	0	1	0	3	0	0	0	4	0	4
California State University, Fullerton	CA	1	0	7	0	1	0	0	0	2	0	8	2	2	0	21	2	23
California State University, Los Angeles	CA	1	0	8	0	6	3	0	0	4	0	12	4	0	1	31	8	39
California State University, Northridge	CA	0	0	14	5	1	1	0	0	14	2	4	0	13	2	46	10	56
California State University, Sacramento	CA	0	0	9	3	0	0	0	0	3	1	52	21	8	0	72	25	97
University of California, Los Angeles	CA	1	0	31	5	2	0	0	0	11	1	18	8	2	4	65	18	83
University of California, Riverside	CA	0	0	2	1	0	0	0	0	0	0	0	0	9	1	11	2	13
University of California, San Diego	CA	0	0	1	0	1	0	0	0	2	2	2	0	1	0	7	2	9
University of California-Santa Cruz	CA	0	0	3	3	0	0	0	0	3	0	2	1	2	0	10	4	14
Case Western Reserve University	OH	0	0	1	0	1	0	0	0	9	1	7	0	0	0	18	1	19
The Catholic University of America	DC	1	0	0	0	0	1	0	0	0	0	2	0	0	0	3	1	4
University of Central Florida	FL	2	2	3	0	1	0	0	0	7	1	20	6	0	0	33	9	42
Clarkson University	NY	0	0	0	0	0	0	0	0	5	2	8	1	0	0	13	3	16
Clemson University	SC	1	0	2	0	0	0	0	0	9	1	31	7	0	0	43	8	51
University of Colorado at Colorado Springs	CO	0	0	0	0	1	0	0	0	10	1	1	0	0	0	12	1	13
University of Colorado at Denver	CO	1	0	2	0	0	0	0	0	5	0	1	0	2	0	11	0	11
Columbia University	NY	2	0	12	1	1	0	0	0	11	0	33	3	15	7	74	11	85
University of Connecticut	CT	0	0	2	0	0	0	0	0	2	0	7	1	0	0	11	1	12
University of Dayton	OH	0	0	0	0	0	0	0	0	4	3	15	4	2	0	21	7	28
University of Denver	CO	0	0	0	0	0	0	0	0	1	0	2	1	0	0	3	1	4
Drexel University	PA	1	0	2	1	0	0	0	0	7	0	12	6	0	0	22	7	29
Fairleigh Dickinson University	NJ	1	1	3	0	2	0	0	0	9	2	31	3	0	0	46	6	52
University of Florida	FL	2	2	11	2	5	0	0	0	34	6	26	7	0	0	78	17	95
Florida Atlantic University	FL	1	1	1	2	2	0	0	0	0	0	4	0	0	0	8	3	11
Florida Institute of Technology	FL	3	0	0	0	2	0	0	0	10	1	11	2	3	0	29	3	32
Florida International University	FL	0	0	1	0	4	0	0	0	0	0	8	1	0	0	13	1	14
FAMU-FSU College of Engineering	FL	0	0	0	0	1	0	0	0	0	0	2	0	0	0	3	0	3
Gannon University	PA	0	0	0	0	0	0	0	0	2	0	4	3	0	0	6	3	9
George Mason University	VA	1	0	2	2	1	0	0	0	6	1	6	4	1	0	17	7	24
The George Washington University	DC	1	0	5	4	3	2	0	0	9	3	4	4	2	0	24	13	37

ELECTRICAL ENGINEERING

AIR-GEO

MASTER'S DEGREES AWARDED IN ELECTRICAL ENGINEERING, 2005-2006

INSTITUTION		AFRICAN AMERICAN		ASIAN AMERICAN		HISPANIC		NATIVE AMERICAN		CAUCASIAN		FOREIGN		OTHER		TOTAL BY GENDER		TOTAL DEGREES
		M	F	M	F	M	F	M	F	M	F	M	F	M	F	M	F	
University of Hartford	CT	0	0	1	0	0	0	0	0	1	0	6	0	1	0	9	0	9
University of Hawaii at Manoa	HI	0	0	14	1	1	1	0	0	0	0	8	4	11	1	34	7	41
University of Houston, Cullen School of Engineering	TX	0	1	5	1	2	0	0	0	7	0	16	4	1	0	31	6	37
University of Idaho	ID	0	0	2	0	2	0	0	0	12	0	0	0	15	6	31	6	37
Illinois Institute of Technology	IL	0	0	2	0	1	0	0	0	11	1	63	14	0	0	77	15	92
Indiana University Purdue University at Indianapolis	IN	2	0	10	5	0	0	0	0	3	4	2	1	0	0	17	10	27
Iowa State University	IA	0	0	1	0	0	0	0	0	6	1	3	2	0	0	10	3	13
University of Kansas	KS	0	0	0	0	0	0	0	0	5	0	10	3	0	0	15	3	18
Lamar University	TX	1	0	0	0	0	0	0	0	0	0	14	3	0	0	15	3	18
Lehigh University	PA	0	0	0	0	0	1	0	0	0	0	6	2	5	0	11	3	14
University of Louisville	KY	0	0	3	2	1	0	0	0	18	3	29	12	0	0	51	17	68
Loyola Marymount University	CA	0	0	0	2	0	1	0	0	5	0	5	1	0	0	10	4	14
University of Maine	ME	0	0	0	0	0	0	0	0	4	1	0	0	0	0	4	1	5
Manhattan College	NY	0	0	0	0	1	0	0	0	0	0	2	0	6	0	9	0	9
University of Maryland, Baltimore County	MD	0	0	0	0	0	0	0	0	2	0	4	5	0	0	6	5	11
Massachusetts Institute of Technology	MA	0	0	0	0	1	0	0	0	0	0	0	0	0	0	1	0	1
University of Massachusetts Dartmouth	MA	0	0	0	0	0	0	0	0	1	0	10	6	0	0	11	6	17
University of Massachusetts Lowell	MA	2	0	2	1	0	0	0	0	8	1	4	3	1	0	17	5	22
McNeese State University	LA	0	0	0	0	0	0	0	0	0	0	8	4	0	0	8	4	12
The University of Memphis	TN	0	0	0	0	0	0	0	0	1	0	8	4	0	0	9	4	13
Mercer University	GA	0	0	0	1	1	0	0	0	0	0	5	0	1	0	7	1	8
University of Michigan	MI	2	0	10	2	2	0	0	0	17	1	22	1	1	0	54	4	58
Michigan Technological University	MI	2	0	1	0	0	0	0	0	4	0	7	4	0	0	12	4	16
University of Michigan, Dearborn	MI	2	1	5	2	1	0	0	0	0	0	3	0	18	5	29	8	37
Minnesota State University, Mankato	MN	0	0	0	0	0	0	0	0	2	2	4	0	2	0	8	2	10
The University of Mississippi	MS	0	0	0	0	0	0	0	0	6	1	0	0	0	0	6	1	7
Mississippi State University	MS	0	0	0	0	0	0	0	0	5	0	11	7	0	0	16	7	23
University of Missouri-Columbia	MO	0	0	1	0	0	0	0	0	3	3	17	5	0	0	21	8	29
University of Missouri - Kansas City	MO	0	0	0	0	0	0	0	0	2	0	10	1	0	0	12	1	13
University of Missouri - Rolla	MO	0	0	1	0	0	0	0	0	9	1	14	3	0	0	24	4	28
Montana State University	MT	0	0	0	0	0	0	0	0	6	1	5	0	0	0	11	1	12
University of Nebraska, Lincoln	NE	0	0	0	0	0	0	0	0	3	0	9	1	0	0	12	1	13
University of Nevada, Reno	NV	0	0	0	0	0	0	0	0	5	1	5	0	0	0	10	1	11
New Jersey Institute of Technology	NJ	2	1	9	2	1	1	0	0	5	1	53	23	6	0	70	28	98
New Mexico State University	NM	0	0	0	0	4	1	1	0	3	0	21	8	6	1	35	10	45
City College of the City University of New York	NY	3	1	3	1	8	0	0	0	0	0	26	9	2	0	42	11	53
The State University of New York at Binghamton	NY	0	0	3	1	0	0	0	0	11	0	17	6	4	1	35	8	43
State University of New York at Buffalo	NY	2	1	1	0	0	0	0	0	6	0	45	19	0	0	55	20	75
Stony Brook University	NY	0	0	2	1	0	0	0	0	0	1	19	8	0	0	21	10	31
North Carolina A & T State University	NC	8	2	2	0	0	0	0	0	1	1	2	1	0	0	13	4	17
North Carolina State University	NC	2	1	2	1	1	0	0	0	18	1	30	3	0	0	53	6	59
University of North Dakota	ND	0	0	0	0	0	0	0	0	6	0	0	0	0	0	6	0	6
North Dakota State University	ND	0	0	1	7	0	0	0	0	2	0	0	0	0	0	3	7	10
Northern Illinois University	IL	0	0	1	0	0	0	0	0	2	0	12	3	0	0	15	3	18
University of Notre Dame	IN	0	0	0	0	0	0	0	0	5	1	13	2	0	0	18	3	21

ELECTRICAL ENGINEERING

HAR-NOT

INSTITUTION		AFRICAN AMERICAN		ASIAN AMERICAN		HISPANIC		NATIVE AMERICAN		CAUCASIAN		FOREIGN		OTHER		TOTAL BY GENDER		TOTAL DEGREES
		M	F	M	F	M	F	M	F	M	F	M	F	M	F	M	F	
Ohio University	OH	0	0	0	0	0	0	0	0	7	3	13	0	0	0	20	3	23
Old Dominion University	VA	0	1	1	1	0	0	0	0	4	1	11	0	0	1	16	4	20
University of Pennsylvania	PA	1	0	5	1	0	0	0	0	4	0	17	2	0	0	27	3	30
The Pennsylvania State University	PA	4	0	2	1	0	0	0	0	15	4	18	1	0	0	39	6	45
University of Pittsburgh	PA	0	0	1	0	0	0	0	0	11	1	4	1	0	0	16	2	18
Polytechnic University	NY	0	1	7	2	1	0	0	0	12	0	39	9	11	0	70	12	82
Polytechnic University of Puerto Rico	PR	0	0	0	0	3	0	0	0	0	0	0	0	0	0	3	0	3
Prairie View A&M University	TX	0	0	0	0	0	0	0	0	0	0	1	0	0	0	1	0	1
Princeton University	NJ	1	0	1	0	0	0	0	0	1	0	1	2	3	0	7	2	9
University of Puerto Rico, Mayaguez Campus	PR	0	0	0	0	21	5	0	0	0	0	0	0	0	0	21	5	26
Purdue University, Calumet	IN	0	1	0	1	1	0	0	0	0	0	6	2	11	2	18	6	24
Rensselaer Polytechnic Institute	NY	2	0	4	1	3	1	0	0	17	1	17	1	4	1	47	4	51
William Marsh Rice University	TX	0	0	3	1	2	0	0	0	1	0	2	1	2	0	10	2	12
Rochester Institute of Technology	NY	1	1	0	0	1	0	0	0	12	1	12	7	2	0	28	9	37
Rose-Hulman Institute of Technology	IN	0	0	1	0	0	0	0	0	2	1	0	0	0	0	3	1	4
Saint Mary's University	TX	0	0	0	0	0	0	0	0	3	0	0	1	0	0	3	1	4
San Diego State University	CA	1	0	6	2	0	0	0	0	8	1	18	6	5	1	38	10	48
San Jose State University	CA	2	0	45	72	3	1	0	0	3	1	0	0	3	2	56	76	132
Santa Clara University	CA	0	0	14	4	3	0	0	0	15	1	9	8	11	0	52	13	65
University of South Alabama	AL	2	0	1	0	0	0	0	0	5	0	32	10	0	0	40	10	50
University of South Carolina	SC	1	0	2	0	0	0	0	0	4	0	10	7	0	0	17	7	24
South Dakota State University	SD	0	0	0	0	0	0	0	0	0	0	6	3	0	0	6	3	9
University of South Florida	FL	0	0	2	1	0	0	0	0	6	0	14	5	0	0	22	6	28
University of Southern California	CA	4	2	60	17	9	2	0	0	45	7	217	36	17	0	352	65	417
Southern Methodist University	TX	0	1	0	0	1	0	0	0	4	1	12	2	0	0	17	4	21
Stanford University	CA	1	1	35	8	2	0	0	0	40	3	100	17	20	6	198	35	233
Stevens Institute of Technology	NJ	2	0	12	1	2	0	0	0	10	2	10	3	10	1	46	7	53
Syracuse University	NY	0	0	0	1	0	0	0	0	12	0	43	15	0	0	55	16	71
Tennessee State University	TN	1	0	0	0	0	0	0	0	0	0	0	0	0	0	1	0	1
University of Tennessee, Chattanooga	TN	0	0	0	0	0	0	0	0	0	0	1	1	0	0	1	1	2
Texas A&M University	TX	0	1	2	2	3	0	0	0	18	1	35	13	0	0	58	17	75
Texas A&M University - Kingsville	TX	0	0	0	0	0	0	0	0	1	0	50	17	0	0	51	17	68
The University of Texas at Arlington	TX	2	0	8	6	1	1	0	0	11	3	115	38	0	0	137	47	184
The University of Texas at Dallas	TX	1	0	9	2	1	0	0	0	16	1	54	17	0	0	81	20	101
University of Texas at El Paso	TX	0	0	0	0	5	2	0	0	2	0	16	6	0	0	23	8	31
University of Texas at San Antonio	TX	0	0	0	1	6	0	0	0	5	1	17	6	0	0	28	8	36
The University of Texas at Tyler	TX	0	0	1	0	0	0	0	0	2	0	2	0	0	0	5	0	5
University of Toledo	OH	0	0	0	0	0	0	0	0	3	0	7	2	0	0	10	2	12
Tufts University	MA	0	0	2	0	1	0	0	0	0	0	2	0	13	3	18	3	21
Tulane University	LA	1	0	0	0	0	0	0	0	0	0	1	1	3	2	5	3	8
Vanderbilt University	TN	0	1	0	0	0	1	0	0	7	4	6	1	2	1	15	8	23
University of Vermont	VT	0	0	0	0	0	0	0	0	8	1	0	0	0	0	8	1	9
Villanova University	PA	0	0	1	0	0	0	0	0	11	1	14	4	0	0	26	5	31
University of Virginia	VA	1	1	1	1	0	0	0	0	10	0	2	1	0	0	14	3	17
Virginia Polytechnic Institute and State University	VA	4	1	4	2	0	0	1	0	31	4	12	3	0	0	52	10	62

ELECTRICAL ENGINEERING   OHI-VIR

INSTITUTION		AFRICAN AMERICAN		ASIAN AMERICAN		HISPANIC		NATIVE AMERICAN		CAUCASIAN		FOREIGN		OTHER		TOTAL BY GENDER		TOTAL DEGREES
		M	F	M	F	M	F	M	F	M	F	M	F	M	F	M	F	
University of Washington	WA	1	0	2	2	1	0	0	0	17	3	5	2	4	3	30	10	40
Washington State University	WA	0	0	0	0	0	0	0	0	1	0	0	1	1	0	2	1	3
Washington University	MO	0	0	3	2	0	0	0	0	6	0	3	1	1	0	13	3	16
Wayne State University	MI	2	0	3	1	0	0	0	0	11	1	38	7	1	0	55	9	64
West Virginia University	WV	1	0	0	1	0	0	0	0	3	0	32	17	1	0	37	18	55
Western Michigan University	MI	0	0	1	1	0	0	0	0	1	0	36	18	0	0	38	19	57
Wichita State University	KS	0	0	3	1	0	0	0	0	0	0	47	11	9	2	59	14	73
Widener University	PA	0	0	0	0	0	0	0	0	0	0	5	1	0	0	5	1	6
Wilkes University	PA	0	0	0	0	0	0	0	0	0	0	3	0	0	0	3	0	3
Wright State University	OH	2	0	5	1	0	0	0	0	8	0	46	18	0	0	61	19	80
University of Wyoming	WY	0	0	0	0	2	0	0	0	4	0	2	2	0	0	8	2	10
Totals:		88	27	472	200	137	27	3	1	930	116	2,232	634	333	56	4,195	1,061	5,256
CANADIAN INSTITUTIONS:																		
University of Calgary	AB	0	0	0	0	0	0	0	0	0	0	3	0	21	5	24	5	29
Ecole Polytechnique de Montreal	PQ	0	0	0	0	0	0	0	0	0	0	0	0	31	10	31	10	41
Ecole de Technologie Superieure	PQ	0	0	0	0	0	0	0	0	0	0	0	0	20	1	20	1	21
University of Ottawa, Faculty of Engineering	ON	0	0	0	0	0	0	0	0	0	0	6	4	34	9	40	13	53
Totals:		0	0	0	0	0	0	0	0	0	0	9	4	106	25	115	29	144

WAS-WYO

ELECTRICAL ENGINEERING

INSTITUTION		AFRICAN AMERICAN M	F	ASIAN AMERICAN M	F	HISPANIC M	F	NATIVE AMERICAN M	F	CAUCASIAN M	F	FOREIGN M	F	OTHER M	F	TOTAL BY GENDER M	F	TOTAL DEGREES
Air Force Institute of Technology	OH	0	0	0	0	0	0	0	0	0	0	0	0	26	0	26	0	26
The University of Akron	OH	0	0	0	0	0	0	0	0	0	0	4	3	0	0	4	3	7
The University of Arizona	AZ	0	0	0	0	0	0	0	0	7	2	29	7	0	0	36	9	45
Auburn University	AL	1	0	0	1	0	0	0	0	7	1	14	4	1	0	23	6	29
Baylor University	TX	0	0	0	0	0	0	0	0	7	0	0	0	0	0	7	0	7
Brigham Young University	UT	0	0	1	0	0	0	0	0	0	0	4	1	19	0	24	1	25
Brown University	RI	0	0	0	1	0	0	0	0	2	1	5	0	0	0	7	2	9
California State University, Long Beach	CA	0	1	4	0	1	0	0	0	3	1	12	0	0	0	20	2	22
University of California, Berkeley	CA	0	1	4	0	0	1	0	0	10	2	11	1	2	0	27	5	32
University of California, Davis	CA	0	0	5	5	1	0	0	0	7	0	2	3	4	2	19	10	29
University of California, Irvine	CA	0	0	0	0	0	0	0	1	0	0	0	0	51	17	51	17	68
University of California, San Diego	CA	0	0	15	1	1	0	0	0	13	6	16	4	1	2	46	13	59
University of California, Santa Barbara	CA	0	0	9	5	0	0	0	0	12	1	22	4	8	2	51	12	63
Carnegie Mellon University	PA	2	0	21	4	2	0	0	0	37	3	96	25	5	2	163	34	197
Case Western Reserve University	OH	0	0	0	0	0	0	0	0	1	0	0	0	1	0	2	0	2
University of Cincinnati	OH	1	0	0	0	0	0	0	1	3	0	22	5	0	0	26	6	32
Cleveland State University	OH	0	0	0	2	0	0	0	0	10	1	29	11	0	0	39	14	53
Colorado State University	CO	0	0	0	0	0	0	0	0	9	1	0	0	16	4	25	5	30
University of Colorado at Boulder	CO	1	0	4	0	0	0	0	0	23	2	20	7	0	0	48	9	57
Cornell University	NY	0	0	13	3	2	0	0	0	12	1	32	6	0	1	59	11	70
University of Delaware	DE	0	1	0	0	0	0	0	0	7	0	10	6	0	0	17	7	24
University of Detroit Mercy	MI	0	0	1	0	0	1	0	0	1	0	7	0	1	1	10	2	12
Drexel University	PA	0	0	0	0	0	0	0	0	3	0	7	1	1	0	11	1	12
Duke University Pratt School of Engineering	NC	0	0	0	0	0	0	0	0	0	0	0	0	12	6	12	6	18
Florida International University	FL	0	0	0	1	4	1	0	1	2	0	9	2	0	0	15	5	20
The George Washington University	DC	0	0	1	0	1	0	0	0	2	0	3	0	0	0	7	0	7
Georgia Institute of Technology	GA	3	3	15	3	4	0	1	0	65	5	89	15	4	0	181	26	207
University of Houston, Cullen School of Engineering	TX	0	0	0	0	0	0	0	0	0	0	3	0	0	1	3	1	4
Howard University	DC	3	0	0	0	1	0	0	0	0	0	9	2	0	0	13	2	15
Illinois Institute of Technology	IL	0	0	1	0	0	0	0	0	5	1	12	3	1	0	19	4	23
University of Illinois at Chicago	IL	1	0	14	4	2	1	0	0	9	3	0	0	7	2	33	10	43
University of Illinois at Urbana-Champaign	IL	1	0	20	4	1	1	0	0	53	2	33	9	0	1	108	17	125
The University of Iowa	IA	0	0	0	0	0	0	0	0	6	0	2	0	0	0	8	0	8
The Johns Hopkins University	MD	3	2	15	5	5	2	0	0	84	18	15	3	0	0	122	30	152
Kansas State University	KS	0	0	1	0	1	0	0	0	10	1	4	2	0	0	16	3	19
University of Kentucky	KY	0	0	0	0	0	0	0	0	5	0	15	3	0	0	20	3	23
Lawrence Technological University	MI	1	0	2	0	0	0	0	0	4	0	0	0	1	0	8	0	8
Lehigh University	PA	0	0	1	0	0	0	0	0	0	0	1	0	0	0	2	0	2
Louisiana State University	LA	0	0	0	0	0	0	0	0	3	0	22	12	0	0	25	12	37
Marquette University	WI	0	0	1	0	0	0	0	0	4	1	5	3	0	0	10	4	14
University of Maryland, College Park	MD	3	1	6	1	0	0	0	0	11	4	59	16	1	1	80	23	103
Massachusetts Institute of Technology	MA	6	1	34	18	13	2	2	0	59	11	44	16	24	4	182	52	234
University of Massachusetts Amherst	MA	0	0	2	0	1	1	0	0	18	3	14	4	3	0	38	8	46
University of Miami	FL	0	0	0	0	3	0	0	0	2	0	4	0	0	0	9	0	9
University of Michigan	MI	1	0	11	4	0	0	0	0	45	3	38	13	2	0	97	20	117

ELECTRICAL/COMPUTER ENGINEERING   AIR-MIC

INSTITUTION		AFRICAN AMERICAN M	F	ASIAN AMERICAN M	F	HISPANIC M	F	NATIVE AMERICAN M	F	CAUCASIAN M	F	FOREIGN M	F	OTHER M	F	TOTAL BY GENDER M	F	TOTAL DEGREES
Michigan State University	MI	2	2	2	0	0	1	0	0	0	0	13	2	5	0	22	5	27
University of Minnesota - Twin Cities	MN	4	0	6	3	0	0	0	0	48	6	33	7	0	0	91	16	107
University of Nebraska, Lincoln	NE	0	0	4	0	0	0	0	0	0	0	0	0	0	0	4	0	4
University of Nevada, Las Vegas	NV	0	0	0	0	0	0	0	0	2	1	18	4	1	0	21	5	26
University of New Hampshire	NH	0	0	0	0	0	0	0	0	10	1	0	2	0	0	10	3	13
University of New Haven	CT	1	0	2	0	0	0	0	0	2	0	10	0	0	0	15	0	15
New Jersey Institute of Technology	NJ	0	0	2	0	1	0	0	0	0	0	21	3	0	0	24	3	27
The University of New Mexico	NM	1	0	0	0	2	0	0	1	14	3	14	8	0	0	31	12	43
New York Institute of Technology	NY	0	0	0	0	0	0	0	0	0	0	0	0	70	12	70	12	82
University of North Carolina, Charlotte	NC	2	0	3	0	0	0	0	0	7	3	18	4	0	0	30	7	37
Northeastern University	MA	1	0	5	0	1	0	0	0	22	0	28	8	8	1	65	9	74
Northwestern University	IL	1	0	5	0	0	0	0	0	25	5	14	1	0	0	45	6	51
Oakland University	MI	0	1	2	3	1	0	0	0	7	4	8	6	0	0	18	14	32
The Ohio State University	OH	0	0	2	0	0	0	0	0	26	2	22	6	0	0	50	8	58
University of Oklahoma	OK	0	0	2	0	1	0	2	0	9	0	12	7	0	0	26	7	33
Oklahoma State University	OK	0	0	0	0	0	0	0	0	10	0	31	10	0	0	41	10	51
Oregon State University	OR	0	0	2	0	0	0	0	0	16	1	18	4	3	0	39	5	44
Polytechnic University	NY	1	0	2	0	1	0	0	0	2	0	9	1	4	2	19	3	22
Portland State University	OR	0	0	4	3	2	0	0	0	17	2	21	13	6	0	50	18	68
Purdue University	IN	1	0	2	2	0	1	0	0	16	0	25	8	1	0	45	11	56
University of Rhode Island	RI	0	0	0	0	0	0	0	0	7	1	6	3	0	0	13	4	17
William Marsh Rice University	TX	0	0	1	0	0	0	0	0	3	0	2	1	0	0	6	1	7
University of Rochester	NY	0	0	1	0	0	0	0	0	3	1	11	0	1	0	16	1	17
Rose-Hulman Institute of Technology	IN	0	0	2	0	0	0	0	0	1	0	0	0	0	0	3	0	3
Rowan University	NJ	1	0	2	0	0	0	0	0	2	0	0	0	0	0	5	0	5
Rutgers, The State University of New Jersey	NJ	1	0	5	0	0	1	0	0	8	0	39	11	0	0	53	12	65
Saint Cloud State University	MN	0	0	0	0	0	0	0	0	0	0	2	1	0	0	2	1	3
South Dakota School of Mines and Technology	SD	0	0	0	0	0	0	0	0	4	0	3	3	0	0	7	3	10
Southern Illinois University Carbondale	IL	0	0	0	0	0	0	0	0	7	0	65	18	0	0	72	18	90
Southern Illinois University Edwardsville	IL	0	1	0	0	0	0	0	0	12	0	15	4	0	0	27	5	32
Temple University	PA	0	0	16	3	0	0	0	0	10	1	0	0	0	0	26	4	30
Tennessee Technological University	TN	3	0	0	0	0	0	0	0	4	0	10	6	0	0	17	6	23
University of Tennessee, Knoxville	TN	1	0	1	2	0	0	0	0	20	1	15	4	0	0	37	7	44
Texas Tech University	TX	0	0	2	0	1	0	0	0	13	6	14	1	0	0	30	8	38
The University of Texas at Austin	TX	0	0	18	1	7	3	1	0	56	4	50	13	0	0	132	21	153
The University of Toledo	OH	0	0	0	0	0	0	0	0	0	0	0	1	0	0	0	1	1
University of Utah	UT	0	0	2	1	1	0	0	0	22	1	7	2	0	0	32	4	36
Utah State University	UT	0	0	0	0	0	0	0	0	22	0	21	0	0	0	43	0	43
University of Wisconsin, Madison	WI	0	0	1	1	0	0	0	0	16	0	45	17	4	1	66	19	85
Worcester Polytechnic Institute	MA	1	0	2	0	1	0	0	0	18	2	6	3	2	0	30	5	35
Youngstown State University	OH	0	0	0	0	0	0	0	0	0	0	1	0	1	0	2	0	2
Totals:		48	14	299	81	62	16	6	4	1,022	119	1,350	373	297	62	3,084	669	3,753

ELECTRICAL/COMPUTER ENGINEERING   MIC-YOU

INSTITUTION		AFRICAN AMERICAN		ASIAN AMERICAN		HISPANIC		NATIVE AMERICAN		CAUCASIAN		FOREIGN		OTHER		TOTAL BY GENDER		TOTAL DEGREES
		M	F	M	F	M	F	M	F	M	F	M	F	M	F	M	F	
CANADIAN INSTITUTIONS:																		
University of Alberta	AB	0	0	0	0	0	0	0	0	0	0	0	0	22	8	22	8	30
University of Calgary	AB	0	0	0	0	0	0	0	0	0	0	0	0	7	3	7	3	10
Concordia University, Faculty of Engr. and Comp. Sci.	PQ	0	0	0	0	0	0	0	0	0	0	20	3	121	28	141	31	172
Ecole de Technologie Superieure	PQ	0	0	0	0	0	0	0	0	0	0	0	0	22	3	22	3	25
McGill University, Faculty of Engineering	PQ	0	0	0	0	0	0	0	0	0	0	0	0	44	12	44	12	56
University of Waterloo	ON	0	0	0	0	0	0	0	0	0	0	0	0	42	8	42	8	50
Totals:		**0**	**0**	**0**	**0**	**0**	**0**	**0**	**0**	**0**	**0**	**20**	**3**	**258**	**62**	**278**	**65**	**343**

ELECTRICAL/COMPUTER ENGINEERING

ALB-WAT

Master's Degrees Awarded in Engineering (General), 2005-2006

AKR-WIS

INSTITUTION		AFRICAN AMERICAN		ASIAN AMERICAN		HISPANIC		NATIVE AMERICAN		CAUCASIAN		FOREIGN		OTHER		TOTAL BY GENDER		TOTAL DEGREES
		M	F	M	F	M	F	M	F	M	F	M	F	M	F	M	F	
The University of Akron	OH	1	0	1	0	0	0	0	0	2	2	1	0	1	0	6	2	8
The University of Arizona	AZ	0	0	1	0	3	0	0	1	5	4	9	2	0	0	18	7	25
Arizona State University	AZ	0	0	0	0	0	1	0	0	0	0	2	1	0	0	2	2	4
University of Arkansas	AR	0	0	1	0	0	0	0	0	2	0	3	2	0	0	6	2	8
California Polytechnic State University	CA	0	0	1	0	0	0	0	0	0	0	0	0	0	0	1	0	1
California State University, Long Beach	CA	0	0	2	0	0	0	0	0	0	0	2	0	0	0	4	0	4
University of California, Irvine	CA	0	0	0	0	0	0	0	0	0	0	0	0	0	1	0	1	1
Case Western Reserve University	OH	0	0	0	0	0	0	0	0	8	3	1	0	0	0	9	3	12
Colorado School of Mines	CO	0	0	3	0	1	1	0	0	10	5	1	0	0	0	15	6	21
University of Colorado at Denver	CO	0	0	0	0	1	1	1	0	6	6	4	1	0	1	12	9	21
Dartmouth College	NH	0	0	0	0	0	0	0	0	4	2	1	1	3	1	8	4	12
University of Illinois at Chicago	IL	1	0	8	1	0	0	0	0	3	1	0	0	3	1	15	3	18
University of Illinois at Urbana-Champaign	IL	0	0	0	0	0	0	0	0	3	1	2	2	0	0	5	3	8
Iowa State University	IA	1	0	0	0	1	0	0	0	28	6	2	2	4	1	36	9	45
Kettering University formerly GMI	MI	1	0	2	0	0	0	0	0	7	1	2	2	5	2	17	3	20
University of Maryland, College Park	MD	3	2	12	3	3	1	0	0	37	6	21	7	4	1	80	20	100
Michigan Technological University	MI	0	0	0	0	0	0	0	0	2	0	2	3	1	0	5	3	8
Milwaukee School of Engineering	WI	0	0	0	0	0	0	0	0	2	1	0	0	0	0	2	1	3
Morgan State University	MD	5	3	0	0	0	0	0	0	1	0	2	3	1	0	9	6	15
University of Nebraska, Lincoln	NE	0	0	2	0	0	1	0	0	3	2	2	1	0	0	7	4	11
North Carolina State University	NC	1	1	2	0	0	0	0	0	7	0	1	0	0	0	11	1	12
Northern Arizona University	AZ	0	0	1	0	0	0	0	0	1	0	1	0	0	0	3	0	3
Oklahoma State University	OK	1	0	0	1	0	0	0	0	17	5	2	0	0	0	20	6	26
San Francisco State University	CA	0	0	0	0	0	0	0	0	0	0	0	0	15	6	15	6	21
San Jose State University	CA	0	0	50	52	3	1	0	0	10	6	0	0	12	5	75	64	139
Stanford University	CA	1	0	2	5	0	1	0	0	7	3	1	0	3	0	14	9	23
Texas Tech University	TX	0	0	0	0	1	1	3	0	0	0	7	0	0	0	11	1	12
The University of Toledo	OH	0	0	0	0	0	0	0	0	4	2	0	0	0	0	4	2	6
Virginia Commonwealth University	VA	1	0	4	2	3	0	0	0	2	0	10	2	0	0	20	4	24
University of Wisconsin, Milwaukee	WI	1	0	5	0	1	0	0	0	21	5	16	11	0	0	44	16	60
Totals:		17	6	97	64	17	8	4	1	192	61	95	38	52	19	474	197	671

CANADIAN INSTITUTIONS:

INSTITUTION		AFRICAN AMERICAN		ASIAN AMERICAN		HISPANIC		NATIVE AMERICAN		CAUCASIAN		FOREIGN		OTHER		TOTAL BY GENDER		TOTAL DEGREES
		M	F	M	F	M	F	M	F	M	F	M	F	M	F	M	F	
Ecole de Technologie Superieure	PQ	0	0	0	0	0	0	0	0	0	0	0	0	9	1	9	1	10
Totals:		0	0	0	0	0	0	0	0	0	0	0	0	9	1	9	1	10

ENGINEERING (GENERAL)

MASTER'S DEGREES AWARDED IN ENGINEERING MANAGEMENT, 2005-2006

INSTITUTION		AFRICAN AMERICAN		ASIAN AMERICAN		HISPANIC		NATIVE AMERICAN		CAUCASIAN		FOREIGN		OTHER		TOTAL BY GENDER		TOTAL DEGREES
		M	F	M	F	M	F	M	F	M	F	M	F	M	F	M	F	
Air Force Institute of Technology	OH	0	0	0	0	0	0	0	0	0	0	0	0	16	2	16	2	18
University of Alaska Fairbanks	AK	0	0	0	0	0	0	0	0	1	1	0	0	0	0	1	1	2
University of Bridgeport	CT	0	0	0	0	0	0	0	0	0	0	6	1	0	0	6	1	7
California Polytechnic State University	CA	0	0	3	0	0	0	0	0	9	5	0	0	1	2	13	7	20
California State University, Northridge	CA	2	2	8	4	12	1	0	0	13	5	3	0	4	2	42	14	56
Case Western Reserve University	OH	1	0	1	2	0	1	0	0	16	2	3	4	1	0	22	9	31
The Catholic University of America	DC	0	2	0	0	0	1	0	0	1	0	0	0	0	0	1	3	4
Colorado School of Mines	CO	0	0	1	0	2	0	0	0	18	5	8	4	0	0	29	9	38
University of Colorado at Boulder	CO	0	0	0	0	0	0	0	0	23	2	8	3	0	0	31	5	36
Dartmouth College	NH	2	0	1	0	2	1	0	0	17	3	4	2	4	1	30	7	37
University of Dayton	OH	0	0	0	0	0	0	0	0	27	5	2	0	0	0	29	5	34
University of Detroit Mercy	MI	1	0	3	0	3	0	0	0	2	0	5	0	0	0	14	0	14
Drexel University	PA	1	1	0	0	0	0	0	0	6	4	0	0	7	2	14	7	21
Duke University Pratt School of Engineering	NC	0	0	0	0	0	0	0	0	0	0	0	0	51	14	51	14	65
Florida Institute of Technology	FL	1	1	2	1	5	0	0	0	28	5	3	2	6	1	45	10	55
Florida International University	FL	5	0	2	0	6	1	0	0	2	0	6	2	0	0	21	3	24
FAMU-FSU College of Engineering	FL	1	0	0	0	0	0	0	0	3	0	0	0	0	0	4	0	4
The George Washington University	DC	8	5	31	7	2	3	1	0	30	23	17	3	15	7	104	48	152
University of Illinois at Urbana-Champaign	IL	0	0	0	0	0	1	0	0	2	1	3	1	0	0	5	3	8
University of Kansas	KS	1	0	0	0	0	0	0	0	12	0	22	5	0	0	35	5	40
Kansas State University	KS	2	0	0	0	0	0	0	0	1	1	0	0	0	0	3	1	4
Lawrence Technological University	MI	1	1	0	0	0	0	0	0	4	2	0	0	1	0	6	3	9
University of Louisiana at Lafayette	LA	0	1	0	0	0	0	0	0	1	0	4	2	0	0	5	3	8
University of Louisville	KY	3	2	0	0	0	0	1	0	7	3	12	5	0	0	23	10	33
Marquette University	WI	0	0	0	0	0	0	0	0	1	1	0	1	0	0	1	2	3
University of Maryland, Baltimore County	MD	0	0	0	0	0	0	0	0	2	0	0	1	0	0	2	1	3
Massachusetts Institute of Technology	MA	0	0	7	1	0	0	0	0	7	0	11	0	16	1	41	2	43
University of Massachusetts Amherst	MA	0	0	0	0	0	0	0	0	0	0	0	0	1	0	1	0	1
McNeese State University	LA	0	0	0	0	0	0	0	0	0	0	4	2	0	0	4	2	6
Mercer University	GA	0	0	0	0	0	0	0	0	0	0	0	0	1	0	1	0	1
University of Miami	FL	0	0	1	0	1	2	0	0	6	3	1	0	1	0	10	5	15
University of Michigan, Dearborn	MI	3	5	6	0	2	1	0	0	32	13	1	1	0	0	44	20	64
University of Missouri - Rolla	MO	8	1	4	0	3	0	0	0	54	13	6	4	2	0	77	18	95
New Jersey Institute of Technology	NJ	2	2	4	6	4	3	0	0	15	7	6	2	8	0	39	20	59
New Mexico Institute of Mining & Technology	NM	0	0	0	0	0	0	0	0	0	0	2	0	0	0	2	0	2
University of New Orleans	LA	1	1	0	0	0	0	0	0	1	0	3	2	0	0	5	3	8
University of North Carolina, Charlotte	NC	0	3	1	1	0	0	0	0	4	1	3	2	0	0	8	7	15
Northeastern University	MA	2	0	0	1	1	0	0	0	6	1	9	3	3	1	21	6	27
Northwestern University	IL	2	0	3	0	4	0	0	0	12	2	2	0	0	0	23	2	25
Oakland University	MI	0	0	0	0	0	0	0	0	14	4	7	2	0	0	21	6	27
Old Dominion University	VA	3	2	1	1	4	0	1	0	121	16	8	1	11	0	149	20	169
OGI School of Science & Engineering at OHSU	OR	1	0	5	0	2	0	0	0	13	10	2	1	2	0	25	11	36
University of Pennsylvania	PA	3	4	7	2	1	0	0	0	22	5	16	2	1	0	50	13	63
Portland State University	OR	0	0	0	0	2	1	0	0	2	2	20	3	2	0	26	6	32
Rose-Hulman Institute of Technology	IN	0	0	2	0	0	0	0	0	12	1	0	0	1	0	15	1	16

AIR-ROS

ENGINEERING MANAGEMENT

INSTITUTION		AFRICAN AMERICAN		ASIAN AMERICAN		HISPANIC		NATIVE AMERICAN		CAUCASIAN		FOREIGN		OTHER		TOTAL BY GENDER		TOTAL DEGREES
		M	F	M	F	M	F	M	F	M	F	M	F	M	F	M	F	
Saint Cloud State University	MN	0	0	0	0	0	0	0	0	0	0	8	3	0	0	8	3	11
Saint Martin's College	WA	0	0	1	0	0	0	0	0	4	0	0	1	0	0	5	1	6
Saint Mary's University	TX	0	0	0	0	0	0	0	0	2	0	0	0	0	0	2	0	2
Santa Clara University	CA	0	0	17	5	1	1	0	0	9	4	9	5	8	2	44	17	61
University of Southern California	CA	0	1	7	2	0	0	0	0	6	3	36	7	6	0	55	13	68
Southern Methodist University	TX	2	1	5	2	0	1	1	0	28	12	2	0	0	0	38	16	54
Stevens Institute of Technology	NJ	0	0	2	1	0	0	0	0	2	6	2	1	0	0	6	8	14
Syracuse University	NY	1	0	0	0	0	0	0	0	8	1	9	6	1	0	19	7	26
University of Tennessee, Chattanooga	TN	0	0	0	0	0	0	0	0	1	0	1	0	0	0	2	0	2
The University of Texas at Austin	TX	2	0	2	2	3	1	0	0	12	2	3	0	0	0	22	5	27
Tufts University	MA	0	0	2	0	0	0	0	0	0	0	5	1	22	3	29	4	33
Washington State University	WA	2	0	0	0	0	0	0	0	10	2	0	0	0	0	12	2	14
Washington University	MO	1	0	0	1	1	0	0	0	6	0	0	0	0	0	8	1	9
Wayne State University	MI	0	0	1	1	0	1	0	0	27	5	0	1	1	0	29	8	37
Western Michigan University	MI	0	0	0	0	0	0	0	0	7	1	4	1	0	0	11	2	13
Wichita State University	KS	0	0	0	0	0	0	0	0	0	0	2	1	1	0	3	1	4
Widener University	PA	0	0	0	0	0	0	0	0	2	0	0	0	0	0	2	0	2
Worcester Polytechnic Institute	MA	0	0	0	0	0	0	0	0	1	1	2	0	0	0	3	1	4
Totals:		62	35	130	40	61	20	4	0	672	183	290	88	194	38	1,413	404	1,817
CANADIAN INSTITUTIONS:																		
University of Ottawa, Faculty of Engineering	ON	0	0	0	0	0	0	0	0	0	0	7	2	32	11	39	13	52
University of Waterloo	ON	0	0	0	0	0	0	0	0	0	0	0	0	47	17	47	17	64
Totals:		0	0	0	0	0	0	0	0	0	0	7	2	79	28	86	30	116

ENGINEERING MANAGEMENT

SAI-WOR

INSTITUTION		AFRICAN AMERICAN		ASIAN AMERICAN		HISPANIC		NATIVE AMERICAN		CAUCASIAN		FOREIGN		OTHER		TOTAL BY GENDER		TOTAL DEGREES
		M	F	M	F	M	F	M	F	M	F	M	F	M	F	M	F	
Air Force Institute of Technology	OH	0	0	0	0	0	0	0	0	2	0	0	0	17	4	19	4	23
California Institute of Technology	CA	0	0	0	0	0	1	0	0	4	2	1	0	0	0	5	3	8
California State University, Fullerton	CA	0	0	2	0	0	0	0	0	0	0	0	0	0	0	2	0	2
University of California, Davis	CA	0	0	1	2	0	0	1	0	4	0	4	4	1	0	11	6	17
Colorado School of Mines	CO	0	0	0	0	0	0	0	0	2	2	0	1	0	0	2	3	5
Cornell University	NY	0	0	4	1	0	0	0	1	8	2	5	3	1	0	18	7	25
University of Illinois at Urbana-Champaign	IL	0	0	1	1	2	0	0	0	21	4	15	4	2	0	41	9	50
The Johns Hopkins University	MD	1	0	0	0	0	0	0	0	11	2	0	0	0	0	12	2	14
Louisiana State University	LA	0	0	0	0	0	0	0	0	1	0	17	2	0	0	18	2	20
Louisiana Tech University	LA	0	0	0	0	0	0	0	0	1	0	27	7	0	0	28	7	35
Loyola College in Maryland	MD	0	0	0	0	0	0	0	0	11	1	0	0	0	0	11	1	12
Northwestern University	IL	0	0	1	0	1	0	1	0	3	5	0	0	1	0	7	5	12
University of Oklahoma	OK	0	0	0	0	0	0	0	0	0	0	2	0	0	0	2	0	2
The Pennsylvania State University	PA	1	0	0	0	0	0	0	0	8	0	5	1	0	0	14	1	15
Rensselaer Polytechnic Institute	NY	0	0	0	0	0	0	0	0	15	4	7	1	7	1	29	6	35
South Dakota State University	SD	0	0	0	0	0	0	0	0	2	0	0	0	0	0	2	0	2
University of South Florida	FL	0	0	0	1	0	0	0	0	0	3	1	0	0	0	1	4	5
University of Tennessee, Knoxville	TN	1	0	0	0	0	0	0	0	3	2	4	1	0	0	8	3	11
University of Virginia	VA	1	0	0	0	0	0	0	0	3	0	2	0	1	0	7	0	7
Virginia Polytechnic Institute and State University	VA	0	0	1	0	0	0	0	0	10	1	1	1	1	0	13	2	15
Totals:		4	0	10	5	3	1	2	1	109	28	91	25	31	5	250	65	315
CANADIAN INSTITUTIONS:																		
Ecole Polytechnique de Montreal	PQ	0	0	0	0	0	0	0	0	0	0	0	0	10	0	10	0	10
Totals:		0	0	0	0	0	0	0	0	0	0	0	0	10	0	10	0	10

AIR-VIR

ENGR. SCIENCE AND ENGR. PHYSICS

INSTITUTION		AFRICAN AMERICAN		ASIAN AMERICAN		HISPANIC		NATIVE AMERICAN		CAUCASIAN		FOREIGN		OTHER		TOTAL BY GENDER		TOTAL DEGREES
		M	F	M	F	M	F	M	F	M	F	M	F	M	F	M	F	
Air Force Institute of Technology	OH	0	0	0	0	0	0	0	0	0	0	0	0	9	1	9	1	10
The University of Alabama	AL	0	0	0	0	0	0	0	0	1	0	2	0	0	0	3	0	3
University of Alaska Fairbanks	AK	0	0	0	0	0	0	0	0	1	1	4	0	0	0	5	1	6
The University of Arizona	AZ	0	0	0	1	0	0	0	0	3	2	2	0	0	0	5	3	8
Arizona State University	AZ	0	0	1	0	0	0	0	0	2	3	4	3	2	3	9	9	18
University of Arkansas	AR	0	0	0	0	0	0	0	0	0	0	0	0	1	0	1	0	1
University of California, Irvine	CA	0	0	0	0	0	0	0	0	0	1	0	0	4	1	4	1	5
University of Central Florida	FL	0	0	1	0	0	0	0	0	1	0	1	0	0	0	3	0	3
Clarkson University	NY	0	0	0	0	0	0	0	0	1	1	0	0	0	0	1	1	2
Clemson University	SC	0	1	1	0	0	0	0	0	2	1	2	1	0	0	5	3	8
Cleveland State University	OH	0	0	2	1	0	0	0	0	6	1	0	0	0	0	8	2	10
Colorado School of Mines	CO	0	0	0	0	0	0	0	0	8	21	2	0	0	0	10	21	31
University of Connecticut	CT	0	0	0	0	0	0	0	0	1	1	0	0	1	1	2	2	4
Drexel University	PA	0	0	0	0	0	0	0	0	2	1	1	2	0	1	3	4	7
University of Florida	FL	0	1	0	0	1	1	0	0	8	4	5	1	0	0	14	7	21
Florida International University	FL	0	0	0	0	1	1	0	0	1	0	6	4	1	0	9	5	14
Georgia Institute of Technology	GA	1	0	0	3	0	0	0	0	7	3	1	3	0	0	9	9	18
University of Hartford	CT	0	0	0	0	0	0	0	0	6	0	0	0	0	0	6	0	6
University of Houston, Cullen School of Engineering	TX	0	0	1	0	0	0	0	0	1	1	3	3	0	2	5	6	11
Idaho State University	ID	0	0	0	0	0	0	0	0	1	1	1	0	0	0	2	1	3
Illinois Institute of Technology	IL	0	0	1	1	0	0	0	0	2	1	2	1	0	0	5	3	8
University of Illinois at Urbana-Champaign	IL	0	0	1	1	1	0	0	0	3	3	3	10	0	0	8	14	22
The Johns Hopkins University	MD	0	0	1	1	0	0	0	0	10	12	3	4	0	0	14	17	31
University of Kansas	KS	0	0	0	0	0	0	0	0	0	1	0	0	0	0	0	1	1
Lehigh University	PA	0	0	0	0	0	0	0	0	0	0	0	0	2	0	2	0	2
Manhattan College	NY	0	0	1	0	0	0	0	0	6	1	0	0	0	0	7	1	8
University of Massachusetts Amherst	MA	0	0	0	0	0	0	0	0	3	1	0	0	2	0	5	1	6
University of Massachusetts Lowell	MA	0	0	0	0	0	0	0	0	4	1	0	0	0	1	4	2	6
University of Michigan	MI	0	0	0	0	0	0	0	0	3	1	0	1	0	0	3	2	5
Michigan State University	MI	0	0	0	0	2	0	0	0	0	0	0	1	2	0	2	1	3
Michigan Technological University	MI	0	0	0	0	0	0	0	0	5	4	3	0	0	1	8	5	13
Milwaukee School of Engineering	WI	0	0	0	0	0	0	0	0	1	2	0	0	1	0	2	2	4
University of Missouri - Rolla	MO	0	0	1	0	0	0	0	0	2	2	6	0	0	0	9	2	11
Montana State University	MT	0	0	0	0	0	0	0	0	0	0	1	0	0	0	1	0	1
Montana Tech of the University of Montana	MT	0	0	0	0	0	0	0	0	2	1	0	0	0	0	2	1	3
University of Nebraska, Lincoln	NE	0	0	0	0	0	0	0	0	2	0	2	1	0	0	4	1	5
University of New Haven	CT	1	0	0	0	0	0	0	0	0	0	2	1	0	0	3	1	4
New Jersey Institute of Technology	NJ	0	0	0	1	0	0	0	0	0	0	1	6	0	0	1	7	8
New Mexico Institute of Mining & Technology	NM	0	0	0	0	0	0	0	0	2	0	2	1	0	0	4	1	5
New Mexico State University	NM	0	0	0	0	2	0	0	0	0	0	1	0	0	0	3	0	3
University of North Carolina at Chapel Hill	NC	0	1	0	1	0	0	0	0	0	0	1	4	0	0	1	6	7
University of Notre Dame	IN	0	0	0	0	1	0	0	0	2	1	0	0	0	0	3	1	4
University of Oklahoma	OK	0	0	0	0	0	0	0	0	0	0	3	0	0	0	3	0	3
Oklahoma State University	OK	0	0	0	0	0	0	0	0	2	4	3	4	0	0	5	8	13
Old Dominion University	VA	1	2	0	0	0	0	0	0	0	1	3	1	1	0	5	4	9

ENVIRONMENTAL ENGINEERING

AIR-OLD

MASTER'S DEGREES AWARDED IN ENVIRONMENTAL ENGINEERING, 2005-2006

INSTITUTION		AFRICAN AMERICAN		ASIAN AMERICAN		HISPANIC		NATIVE AMERICAN		CAUCASIAN		FOREIGN		OTHER		TOTAL BY GENDER		TOTAL DEGREES
		M	F	M	F	M	F	M	F	M	F	M	F	M	F	M	F	
OGI School of Science & Engineering at OHSU	OR	1	1	0	3	0	0	0	0	2	3	2	2	0	0	5	9	14
Polytechnic University	NY	1	0	0	1	0	0	0	0	1	0	0	1	0	0	2	2	4
Rensselaer Polytechnic Institute	NY	0	0	0	0	0	0	0	0	0	2	1	0	0	0	1	2	3
William Marsh Rice University	TX	0	0	0	0	0	0	0	0	1	1	0	0	0	0	1	1	2
Rose-Hulman Institute of Technology	IN	0	0	0	0	0	0	0	0	0	0	0	0	1	0	1	0	1
San Diego State University	CA	0	0	0	0	0	0	0	0	2	1	1	1	2	0	5	2	7
University of South Florida	FL	0	0	0	0	0	0	0	0	3	2	6	1	0	0	9	3	12
University of Southern California	CA	0	0	1	1	0	0	0	0	1	0	9	5	1	0	12	6	18
Southern Methodist University	TX	0	0	0	0	0	0	0	0	4	0	0	2	0	0	4	2	6
Stevens Institute of Technology	NJ	0	0	0	0	1	0	0	0	1	0	1	7	0	0	3	7	10
Syracuse University	NY	0	0	0	0	0	1	0	0	4	0	3	1	0	0	7	2	9
Tennessee State University	TN	2	2	0	0	0	0	0	0	3	1	0	0	0	0	5	3	8
University of Tennessee, Knoxville	TN	0	0	0	0	0	0	0	0	5	1	0	0	0	0	5	1	6
Texas A&M University - Kingsville	TX	0	0	0	0	3	1	0	0	0	0	8	5	0	0	11	6	17
Texas Tech University	TX	0	0	0	0	0	0	0	0	0	0	2	1	0	0	2	1	3
The University of Texas at Austin	TX	0	0	0	0	0	0	0	0	4	8	1	1	0	0	5	9	14
University of Texas at El Paso	TX	0	0	0	0	1	1	0	0	0	0	2	0	0	0	3	1	4
Tulane University	LA	0	0	0	0	0	0	0	0	0	0	1	1	0	1	1	2	3
Vanderbilt University	TN	0	0	0	1	0	0	0	0	1	0	2	1	0	1	3	3	6
Virginia Polytechnic Institute and State University	VA	0	0	0	2	0	0	0	0	8	6	3	4	1	0	12	12	24
Washington State University	WA	0	0	0	0	0	1	1	0	2	1	2	0	1	3	6	5	11
Washington University	MO	0	0	0	0	0	0	0	0	1	3	0	0	1	1	2	4	6
Worcester Polytechnic Institute	MA	0	0	0	0	0	0	0	0	4	2	0	2	0	0	4	4	8
University of Wyoming	WY	0	0	0	0	0	0	0	0	0	0	1	0	0	0	1	0	1
Totals:		7	8	12	18	11	7	1	0	148	108	115	87	33	16	327	244	571

OGI-WYO

ENVIRONMENTAL ENGINEERING

MASTER'S DEGREES AWARDED IN INDUSTRIAL/MANUFACTURING ENGINEERING, 2005-2006

INSTITUTION		AFRICAN AMERICAN M	AFRICAN AMERICAN F	ASIAN AMERICAN M	ASIAN AMERICAN F	HISPANIC M	HISPANIC F	NATIVE AMERICAN M	NATIVE AMERICAN F	CAUCASIAN M	CAUCASIAN F	FOREIGN M	FOREIGN F	OTHER M	OTHER F	TOTAL BY GENDER M	TOTAL BY GENDER F	TOTAL DEGREES
Air Force Institute of Technology	OH	0	0	0	0	0	0	0	0	1	0	0	0	16	5	17	5	22
The University of Alabama in Huntsville	AL	0	1	0	0	0	0	0	0	16	3	3	1	0	0	19	5	24
The University of Alabama	AL	0	0	0	0	0	0	0	0	2	0	1	1	0	0	3	1	4
The University of Arizona	AZ	0	0	2	0	2	0	0	0	6	0	8	5	0	0	18	5	23
Arizona State University	AZ	0	0	0	0	2	1	0	0	2	3	22	6	1	0	27	10	37
University of Arkansas	AR	0	0	0	0	0	0	0	0	6	1	9	2	0	0	15	3	18
Auburn University	AL	1	0	1	0	0	0	0	0	1	3	6	1	0	0	9	4	13
Boston University	MA	0	0	1	1	0	0	0	0	2	0	10	3	0	0	13	4	17
Bradley University	IL	0	0	0	1	1	0	0	0	4	2	7	2	0	0	12	4	16
California Polytechnic State University	CA	0	1	1	1	0	0	0	0	0	1	0	0	1	0	2	3	5
California State University, Northridge	CA	0	0	4	1	0	0	0	0	1	0	0	0	1	1	6	2	8
University of California, Berkeley	CA	0	0	3	1	0	4	0	0	1	1	7	7	1	0	12	13	25
University of Central Florida	FL	4	3	2	1	3	4	0	0	23	6	10	6	1	1	43	21	64
Clemson University	SC	0	0	0	0	0	0	0	0	1	0	7	3	0	1	8	4	12
Cleveland State University	OH	0	0	0	0	1	0	0	0	6	0	11	0	0	0	18	0	18
Colorado State University, Pueblo	CO	0	0	0	0	0	0	0	0	1	1	1	1	0	0	2	2	4
Columbia University	NY	0	0	9	8	1	0	0	0	12	2	53	22	6	2	81	34	115
Cornell University	NY	1	1	16	6	0	0	0	0	21	0	35	16	4	0	77	23	100
University of Florida	FL	5	1	3	1	3	2	0	0	30	13	15	3	0	0	56	20	76
Florida International University	FL	0	0	0	0	1	0	0	0	0	0	5	2	0	0	6	2	8
FAMU-FSU College of Engineering	FL	3	2	1	0	0	0	0	0	1	0	4	1	0	0	9	3	12
George Mason University	VA	3	0	4	4	4	0	0	0	29	6	2	1	3	1	45	12	57
Georgia Institute of Technology	GA	2	0	1	5	4	0	0	0	19	7	64	25	0	0	90	37	127
Grand Valley State University	MI	0	0	0	0	0	0	0	0	2	0	0	0	0	0	2	0	2
University of Houston, Cullen School of Engineering	TX	0	0	0	0	1	1	0	0	1	3	13	2	0	0	15	6	21
Illinois Institute of Technology	IL	0	0	0	0	0	0	0	0	0	0	1	0	0	0	1	0	1
University of Illinois at Chicago	IL	0	0	9	3	1	0	0	0	3	0	0	0	0	0	13	3	16
University of Illinois at Urbana-Champaign	IL	0	0	0	0	0	0	0	0	2	0	1	0	0	0	3	0	3
The University of Iowa	IA	0	0	0	0	0	0	0	0	4	2	1	2	0	0	5	4	9
Iowa State University	IA	0	0	0	0	0	0	0	0	4	0	16	1	1	0	21	1	22
Kansas State University	KS	0	0	1	0	0	0	0	0	2	0	4	2	0	0	7	2	9
University of Kentucky	KY	0	0	0	0	0	0	0	0	4	0	4	0	0	0	8	0	8
Kettering University formerly GMI	MI	0	1	0	0	1	0	0	0	3	0	0	0	2	0	6	1	7
Lamar University	TX	0	0	0	0	0	0	0	0	0	0	14	3	0	0	14	3	17
Lawrence Technological University	MI	0	1	1	1	0	0	0	0	9	1	0	0	0	1	10	3	13
Lehigh University	PA	0	0	1	1	0	1	0	0	0	0	12	2	9	3	22	7	29
Louisiana State University	LA	1	0	0	0	0	0	0	0	0	0	14	0	0	0	15	0	15
University of Louisville	KY	2	4	1	0	0	1	0	0	15	2	4	0	0	0	22	7	29
University of Massachusetts Amherst	MA	0	0	0	0	1	0	0	0	0	0	1	0	0	0	2	0	2
University of Miami	FL	1	1	1	1	5	2	0	0	0	2	4	1	0	0	11	7	18
University of Michigan	MI	2	2	4	5	2	1	2	0	30	9	29	17	3	0	72	34	106
University of Michigan, Dearborn	MI	0	1	2	1	0	2	1	0	12	3	2	1	0	0	17	8	25
University of Minnesota - Twin Cities	MN	0	0	0	0	0	0	0	0	1	1	6	1	0	0	7	2	9
Mississippi State University	MS	0	0	0	0	0	0	0	0	2	0	10	3	0	0	12	3	15
University of Missouri-Columbia	MO	0	0	1	0	0	0	0	0	2	0	5	2	0	0	8	2	10

INDUSTRIAL/MANUFACTURING ENGR. AIR-MIS

MASTER'S DEGREES AWARDED IN INDUSTRIAL/MANUFACTURING ENGINEERING, 2005-2006

INSTITUTION		AFRICAN AMERICAN		ASIAN AMERICAN		HISPANIC		NATIVE AMERICAN		CAUCASIAN		FOREIGN		OTHER		TOTAL BY GENDER		TOTAL DEGREES
		M	F	M	F	M	F	M	F	M	F	M	F	M	F	M	F	
University of Missouri - Rolla	MO	3	2	1	1	1	0	0	1	25	5	6	2	4	1	40	12	52
Montana State University	MT	0	0	0	0	0	0	0	0	2	0	6	1	1	0	9	1	10
University of Nebraska, Lincoln	NE	0	0	0	0	0	0	0	0	2	2	11	1	0	0	13	3	16
University of New Haven	CT	1	1	1	0	1	1	0	0	1	0	3	0	0	0	7	2	9
New Jersey Institute of Technology	NJ	2	0	1	0	1	0	0	0	3	1	12	1	0	0	19	2	21
The University of New Mexico	NM	0	0	0	0	1	0	0	0	1	0	3	0	0	0	5	0	5
New Mexico State University	NM	0	0	0	1	2	3	0	0	3	0	2	1	5	2	12	7	19
The State University of New York at Binghamton	NY	0	0	1	0	0	0	0	0	2	0	15	2	1	1	18	3	21
State University of New York at Buffalo	NY	0	1	0	0	1	0	0	0	6	2	30	7	1	0	38	10	48
North Carolina State University	NC	2	2	1	0	1	0	0	0	8	4	21	8	0	0	33	14	47
North Dakota State University	ND	0	0	4	0	0	0	0	0	0	1	0	0	0	0	4	1	5
Northeastern University	MA	0	0	0	0	0	0	0	0	0	0	4	1	0	0	4	1	5
Northwestern University	IL	1	0	4	1	0	0	0	0	21	9	21	3	2	1	49	14	63
The Ohio State University	OH	0	0	1	1	0	0	0	0	18	3	17	5	0	0	36	9	45
Ohio University	OH	0	0	0	0	0	0	0	0	0	0	4	0	0	0	4	0	4
University of Oklahoma	OK	0	0	1	1	0	0	0	0	4	0	8	3	0	0	13	3	16
Oklahoma State University	OK	1	0	0	0	0	0	0	0	3	1	36	7	0	0	40	8	48
Oregon State University	OR	0	0	0	0	0	0	0	0	2	3	8	1	0	0	10	4	14
The Pennsylvania State University	PA	0	0	1	0	0	0	0	0	0	0	16	3	9	3	26	6	32
University of Pittsburgh	PA	2	1	0	1	0	0	0	0	4	5	9	2	0	0	15	9	24
Polytechnic University	NY	1	0	1	1	1	0	0	0	0	0	5	1	1	0	9	2	11
Polytechnic University of Puerto Rico	PR	0	0	0	0	7	9	0	0	0	0	0	0	0	0	7	9	16
University of Puerto Rico, Mayaguez Campus	PR	0	0	0	0	3	6	0	0	0	0	0	0	0	0	3	6	9
Purdue University	IN	0	1	4	1	0	0	0	0	6	3	29	9	1	0	40	14	54
Rensselaer Polytechnic Institute	NY	1	1	1	0	1	2	0	0	1	1	1	1	0	0	5	5	10
University of Rhode Island	RI	0	0	0	0	0	0	0	0	0	0	0	0	1	0	1	0	1
Rochester Institute of Technology	NY	0	1	0	1	0	1	0	0	9	5	8	3	1	0	18	11	29
Rutgers, The State University of New Jersey	NJ	0	1	0	2	0	0	0	0	2	0	21	2	0	0	23	5	28
Saint Mary's University	TX	0	0	0	0	0	1	0	0	0	0	0	0	0	0	0	1	1
University of Saint Thomas	MN	1	0	0	0	0	0	0	0	23	3	0	0	0	0	24	3	27
San Jose State University	CA	0	0	7	7	1	2	0	0	0	0	0	0	1	1	9	10	19
South Dakota State University	SD	0	0	0	0	0	0	0	0	2	2	3	2	0	0	5	4	9
University of South Florida	FL	0	0	1	0	2	2	0	0	6	3	4	4	0	0	13	9	22
University of Southern California	CA	0	1	6	1	0	0	0	0	4	0	30	3	0	0	40	5	45
Stanford University	CA	1	4	20	10	2	1	0	0	21	8	59	21	9	2	112	46	158
Syracuse University	NY	0	0	0	0	0	0	0	0	1	0	3	0	0	0	4	0	4
Tennessee State University	TN	1	1	0	0	0	0	0	0	1	0	2	0	0	0	4	1	5
University of Tennessee, Knoxville	TN	1	0	0	0	0	0	0	0	6	1	2	0	0	0	9	1	10
Texas A&M University	TX	0	1	3	0	2	0	0	0	8	1	23	3	0	0	36	5	41
Texas A&M University - Kingsville	TX	0	0	0	0	0	0	0	0	0	0	15	0	0	0	15	0	15
Texas Tech University	TX	0	0	0	1	0	1	0	0	8	0	1	0	0	1	9	3	12
The University of Texas at Arlington	TX	2	4	1	1	0	1	0	0	12	2	54	8	0	0	69	16	85
The University of Texas at Austin	TX	0	0	0	0	0	0	0	0	2	1	7	2	0	0	9	3	12
University of Texas at El Paso	TX	0	0	0	0	5	2	0	0	0	0	8	7	0	0	13	9	22
The University of Toledo	OH	0	0	0	0	0	0	0	0	0	0	1	0	0	0	1	0	1

INDUSTRIAL/MANUFACTURING ENGR.   MIS-TOL

MASTER'S DEGREES AWARDED IN INDUSTRIAL/MANUFACTURING ENGINEERING, 2005-2006

INSTITUTION		AFRICAN AMERICAN		ASIAN AMERICAN		HISPANIC		NATIVE AMERICAN		CAUCASIAN		FOREIGN		OTHER		TOTAL BY GENDER		TOTAL DEGREES
		M	F	M	F	M	F	M	F	M	F	M	F	M	F	M	F	
Virginia Polytechnic Institute and State University	VA	0	1	1	0	0	2	0	0	10	8	37	8	0	0	48	19	67
University of Washington	WA	0	0	0	1	0	0	0	0	1	1	4	0	0	1	5	3	8
Wayne State University	MI	1	0	2	0	0	0	0	0	1	2	50	5	1	0	55	7	62
West Virginia University	WV	0	0	0	0	0	0	0	0	26	6	13	4	0	0	39	10	49
Western Michigan University	MI	0	0	2	0	0	0	0	0	2	0	20	2	0	0	24	2	26
Wichita State University	KS	0	0	0	0	0	0	0	0	0	0	19	2	3	0	22	2	24
University of Wisconsin, Madison	WI	1	0	1	0	0	0	0	0	7	9	24	10	0	2	33	21	54
Worcester Polytechnic Institute	MA	0	0	0	0	0	0	0	0	4	3	1	0	0	0	5	3	8
Wright State University	OH	0	2	0	0	0	0	0	0	5	4	5	4	0	0	10	10	20
Youngstown State University	OH	0	0	0	0	0	0	0	0	0	0	2	0	2	0	4	0	4
Totals:		47	44	135	71	65	53	3	1	554	171	1,104	294	91	30	1,999	664	2,663
CANADIAN INSTITUTIONS:																		
University of Calgary	AB	0	0	0	0	0	0	0	0	0	0	1	0	5	1	6	1	7
Ecole Polytechnique de Montreal	PQ	0	0	0	0	0	0	0	0	0	0	0	0	25	3	25	3	28
Ecole de Technologie Superieure	PQ	0	0	0	0	0	0	0	0	0	0	0	0	13	1	13	1	14
Totals:		0	0	0	0	0	0	0	0	0	0	1	0	43	5	44	5	49

INDUSTRIAL/MANUFACTURING ENGR.   VIR-YOU

MASTER'S DEGREES AWARDED IN MECHANICAL ENGINEERING, 2005-2006

INSTITUTION		AFRICAN AMERICAN		ASIAN AMERICAN		HISPANIC		NATIVE AMERICAN		CAUCASIAN		FOREIGN		OTHER		TOTAL BY GENDER		TOTAL DEGREES
		M	F	M	F	M	F	M	F	M	F	M	F	M	F	M	F	
The University of Akron	OH	1	0	1	0	0	0	0	0	6	0	8	1	0	0	16	1	17
University of Alabama at Birmingham	AL	1	0	1	0	0	0	0	0	2	0	6	0	0	0	10	0	10
The University of Alabama in Huntsville	AL	1	0	0	0	0	0	0	0	0	2	2	0	0	0	3	2	5
The University of Alabama	AL	0	0	2	0	0	0	0	0	6	0	2	0	0	0	10	0	10
University of Alaska Fairbanks	AK	0	0	2	0	0	0	0	0	0	0	1	0	0	0	3	0	3
Alfred University, NY State College of Ceramics	NY	0	0	0	0	0	0	0	0	2	0	0	0	0	0	2	0	2
The University of Arizona	AZ	0	0	1	0	1	1	0	0	5	1	10	0	0	0	17	2	19
Arizona State University	AZ	0	0	0	0	0	0	0	0	1	1	21	1	3	0	25	2	27
University of Arkansas	AR	0	0	0	0	0	0	0	0	3	0	2	0	0	0	5	0	5
Auburn University	AL	0	0	0	0	0	0	0	0	8	1	5	1	0	0	13	2	15
Baylor University	TX	0	0	0	0	0	0	0	0	2	0	0	0	0	0	2	0	2
Boise State University	ID	0	0	1	0	0	0	0	0	3	0	0	1	0	0	4	1	5
Boston University	MA	0	0	3	1	0	0	0	0	2	0	2	0	0	0	7	1	8
Bradley University	IL	1	0	0	0	0	0	0	0	6	2	21	2	0	0	28	4	32
University of Bridgeport	CT	1	0	0	0	0	0	0	0	0	0	34	3	0	0	35	3	38
Brigham Young University	UT	0	0	1	0	0	0	0	0	0	0	6	1	38	0	45	1	46
Bucknell University	PA	1	0	1	0	0	0	0	0	21	2	0	0	0	0	23	2	25
California Institute of Technology	CA	0	0	0	0	0	0	0	0	4	0	3	2	0	0	7	2	9
California Polytechnic State University	CA	0	0	1	0	1	0	0	0	2	0	0	0	0	0	4	0	4
California State University, Fresno	CA	0	0	1	0	0	0	0	0	2	0	1	0	0	0	4	0	4
California State University, Fullerton	CA	0	0	2	0	1	0	0	0	2	0	0	0	1	0	6	0	6
California State University, Long Beach	CA	1	0	2	1	1	0	0	0	7	1	5	0	0	0	16	2	18
California State University, Los Angeles	CA	0	0	1	0	3	1	0	0	1	1	8	0	3	0	16	2	18
California State University, Northridge	CA	0	0	4	1	1	1	0	0	3	0	0	0	2	1	10	3	13
California State University, Sacramento	CA	0	0	1	1	1	0	0	0	3	0	9	2	3	0	17	3	20
University of California, Berkeley	CA	0	0	8	0	6	0	0	0	13	3	16	2	0	0	43	5	48
University of California, Davis	CA	0	1	4	2	2	0	0	0	21	2	8	1	2	0	37	6	43
University of California, Irvine	CA	0	0	0	0	0	0	0	0	0	0	0	0	23	6	23	6	29
University of California, Los Angeles	CA	0	0	9	5	1	0	0	0	14	0	8	2	5	3	37	10	47
University of California, Riverside	CA	0	0	1	0	0	0	0	0	2	0	0	0	2	1	5	1	6
University of California, San Diego	CA	0	0	4	0	2	2	0	0	13	3	13	1	2	0	34	6	40
University of California, Santa Barbara	CA	0	0	1	2	0	0	0	0	4	0	5	1	3	0	13	3	16
Carnegie Mellon University	PA	2	0	0	0	1	0	0	0	10	0	7	2	1	1	21	3	24
Case Western Reserve University	OH	0	0	0	0	0	1	0	0	10	0	4	1	0	0	14	2	16
The Catholic University of America	DC	0	0	0	0	0	0	0	0	0	1	0	0	0	0	0	1	1
University of Central Florida	FL	1	0	0	0	1	0	0	0	2	5	8	2	0	0	12	7	19
University of Cincinnati	OH	1	0	1	1	0	0	0	0	8	2	60	8	0	0	70	11	81
Clarkson University	NY	0	0	0	0	0	0	0	0	9	1	3	0	0	0	12	1	13
Clemson University	SC	1	0	1	0	0	0	0	0	15	1	8	2	0	0	25	3	28
Cleveland State University	OH	0	0	0	0	0	0	0	0	2	0	16	2	0	0	18	2	20
Colorado State University	CO	0	0	0	0	0	0	0	0	17	2	0	0	7	0	24	2	26
University of Colorado at Boulder	CO	1	0	2	0	1	1	0	0	26	3	15	0	0	0	45	4	49
University of Colorado at Colorado Springs	CO	0	0	0	0	0	0	0	0	2	0	0	0	0	0	2	0	2
University of Colorado at Denver	CO	0	0	1	1	1	0	0	0	3	0	2	0	1	0	8	1	9
Columbia University	NY	1	0	0	0	0	0	0	0	4	0	14	1	4	3	23	4	27

MECHANICAL ENGINEERING

AKR–COL

Master's Degrees Awarded in Mechanical Engineering, 2005-2006

INSTITUTION		AFRICAN AMERICAN		ASIAN AMERICAN		HISPANIC		NATIVE AMERICAN		CAUCASIAN		FOREIGN		OTHER		TOTAL BY GENDER		TOTAL DEGREES
		M	F	M	F	M	F	M	F	M	F	M	F	M	F	M	F	
University of Connecticut	CT	0	0	0	0	0	0	0	0	7	0	2	3	1	0	10	3	13
Cornell University	NY	1	0	5	2	0	0	0	0	20	1	6	1	0	0	32	4	36
University of Dayton	OH	0	0	0	0	0	0	0	0	14	1	9	2	0	0	23	3	26
University of Delaware	DE	0	0	0	0	0	0	1	0	3	3	4	4	0	0	8	7	15
University of Denver	CO	0	0	0	0	0	0	0	0	2	1	3	0	0	0	5	1	6
University of Detroit Mercy	MI	0	0	0	0	0	0	0	0	0	1	3	0	0	0	3	1	4
Drexel University	PA	1	0	2	0	0	0	0	0	8	1	7	0	1	0	19	1	20
Duke University Pratt School of Engineering	NC	0	0	0	0	0	0	0	0	0	0	0	0	7	4	7	4	11
University of Florida	FL	1	0	3	0	0	0	0	0	21	3	16	3	0	0	41	6	47
Florida Atlantic University	FL	0	0	0	0	1	1	0	0	1	0	3	0	0	0	5	1	6
Florida Institute of Technology	FL	0	0	0	0	1	0	0	0	2	0	1	1	0	0	4	1	5
Florida International University	FL	0	0	0	0	2	0	0	0	1	0	10	1	0	0	13	1	14
FAMU-FSU College of Engineering	FL	1	0	1	0	0	0	0	0	6	1	7	2	0	0	15	3	18
Gannon University	PA	0	0	0	0	0	0	0	0	1	0	3	0	0	0	4	0	4
The George Washington University	DC	0	0	0	2	2	0	0	0	13	1	5	2	7	0	27	5	32
Georgia Institute of Technology	GA	6	4	6	1	5	1	0	0	81	8	47	6	1	1	146	21	167
Grand Valley State University	MI	0	0	0	0	0	0	0	0	4	2	0	0	0	0	4	2	6
University of Hawaii at Manoa	HI	0	0	8	0	0	0	1	0	0	0	1	0	10	1	20	1	21
University of Houston, Cullen School of Engineering	TX	0	0	0	0	2	0	0	0	3	0	10	2	1	0	16	2	18
Howard University	DC	0	0	0	0	0	0	0	0	2	0	0	0	0	0	2	0	2
University of Idaho	ID	0	0	0	0	1	0	0	0	13	0	0	0	4	0	18	0	18
Idaho State University	ID	0	0	0	0	0	0	0	0	0	1	0	0	0	0	0	1	1
Illinois Institute of Technology	IL	1	0	1	0	0	0	1	0	8	0	41	2	0	0	52	2	54
University of Illinois at Chicago	IL	0	0	13	1	1	0	0	0	14	3	1	0	11	1	39	5	44
University of Illinois at Urbana-Champaign	IL	1	0	7	0	1	1	0	0	35	3	9	0	0	0	53	4	57
Indiana University Purdue University at Indianapolis	IN	4	1	0	0	0	0	1	0	0	0	7	0	0	0	12	1	13
The University of Iowa	IA	0	0	1	0	0	0	0	0	3	2	5	1	0	0	9	3	12
Iowa State University	IA	0	0	0	1	1	0	0	0	26	0	6	0	0	0	34	1	35
The Johns Hopkins University	MD	0	0	1	0	0	0	0	0	26	4	8	1	0	0	35	6	41
University of Kansas	KS	0	0	0	0	0	0	0	1	6	0	8	1	0	0	14	2	16
Kansas State University	KS	0	0	0	0	0	0	0	0	5	1	7	1	0	0	12	2	14
University of Kentucky	KY	0	0	0	1	0	0	0	0	4	2	22	2	1	0	27	5	32
Lamar University	TX	0	0	0	0	0	0	0	0	1	0	21	1	0	0	22	1	23
Lawrence Technological University	MI	1	0	0	1	1	0	0	0	15	4	1	0	1	0	19	5	24
Lehigh University	PA	0	1	0	0	1	0	0	0	0	0	5	0	13	4	19	5	24
Louisiana State University	LA	0	0	0	0	0	0	0	0	1	0	12	7	0	0	13	7	20
University of Louisiana at Lafayette	LA	0	0	0	0	0	0	0	0	0	0	3	3	0	0	3	3	6
University of Louisville	KY	1	0	0	1	0	0	0	0	16	1	5	2	0	0	22	4	26
Loyola Marymount University	CA	2	0	2	0	0	0	0	0	4	1	1	0	0	0	9	1	10
University of Maine	ME	0	0	0	0	0	0	0	0	3	0	1	0	0	0	4	0	4
Manhattan College	NY	0	0	0	0	0	0	0	0	0	0	3	0	6	1	9	1	10
Marquette University	WI	0	0	0	0	0	0	0	0	9	1	1	0	0	0	10	1	11
University of Maryland, Baltimore County	MD	1	0	0	0	0	0	0	0	1	1	5	1	0	0	7	2	9
University of Maryland, College Park	MD	0	0	2	0	0	0	0	0	9	0	11	1	2	0	24	1	25
Massachusetts Institute of Technology	MA	1	0	10	5	6	1	1	1	45	11	36	8	6	4	105	30	135

MECHANICAL ENGINEERING CON-MAS

Master's Degrees Awarded in Mechanical Engineering, 2005-2006

Institution		African American M	African American F	Asian American M	Asian American F	Hispanic M	Hispanic F	Native American M	Native American F	Caucasian M	Caucasian F	Foreign M	Foreign F	Other M	Other F	Total by Gender M	Total by Gender F	Total Degrees
University of Massachusetts Amherst	MA	0	0	0	0	0	0	0	0	0	1	5	0	1	0	6	1	7
University of Massachusetts Dartmouth	MA	0	0	0	0	0	0	0	0	1	1	3	0	0	0	4	1	5
University of Massachusetts Lowell	MA	0	0	2	0	0	0	0	0	2	2	6	0	0	0	10	2	12
McNeese State University	LA	0	0	0	0	0	0	0	0	0	0	2	1	0	0	2	1	3
The University of Memphis	TN	2	1	1	0	0	0	0	0	2	1	8	1	0	0	13	3	16
Mercer University	GA	0	0	0	0	0	0	0	0	0	0	1	0	0	0	1	0	1
University of Miami	FL	0	0	0	0	0	0	0	0	2	0	2	0	0	0	4	0	4
University of Michigan	MI	3	3	5	0	2	1	0	0	44	10	41	3	2	0	98	17	115
Michigan State University	MI	0	0	0	0	0	0	1	0	0	0	0	1	6	4	7	5	12
Michigan Technological University	MI	0	0	0	0	1	0	0	0	14	4	18	1	3	0	36	5	41
University of Michigan, Dearborn	MI	3	1	3	1	1	1	0	0	34	5	0	0	0	0	41	8	49
Minnesota State University, Mankato	MN	0	0	0	0	0	0	0	0	0	0	2	0	0	0	2	0	2
University of Minnesota - Twin Cities	MN	1	0	1	1	0	1	0	0	22	6	11	0	0	0	35	8	43
The University of Mississippi	MS	0	0	0	0	0	0	0	0	4	0	4	0	0	0	8	0	8
Mississippi State University	MS	1	1	0	0	0	0	0	0	11	1	0	0	0	0	12	2	14
University of Missouri-Columbia	MO	0	0	0	0	1	0	0	0	11	0	3	2	0	0	15	2	17
University of Missouri - Kansas City	MO	0	0	0	0	0	0	0	0	0	0	3	0	0	0	3	0	3
University of Missouri - Rolla	MO	1	0	0	0	0	0	0	0	8	2	16	3	1	0	26	5	31
Montana State University	MT	0	0	0	0	0	0	0	0	5	0	3	0	0	0	8	0	8
University of Nebraska, Lincoln	NE	0	0	1	0	0	0	0	0	3	0	4	3	0	0	8	3	11
University of Nevada, Las Vegas	NV	0	0	1	0	3	1	0	0	1	0	24	3	0	0	29	4	33
University of Nevada, Reno	NV	0	0	0	0	2	0	0	0	2	0	2	3	0	0	6	3	9
University of New Hampshire	NH	0	0	0	0	0	0	0	0	4	0	1	0	0	0	5	0	5
University of New Haven	CT	0	0	0	0	0	0	0	0	5	0	0	0	0	0	5	0	5
New Jersey Institute of Technology	NJ	1	0	0	1	0	0	0	0	7	1	10	3	0	0	18	5	23
The University of New Mexico	NM	0	0	0	0	3	1	0	0	6	0	7	0	0	0	16	1	17
New Mexico State University	NM	0	0	1	0	2	0	0	0	2	0	2	3	2	0	9	3	12
City College of the City University of New York	NY	0	0	4	1	2	2	0	0	1	0	5	3	1	0	13	6	19
The State University of New York at Binghamton	NY	0	0	0	0	0	0	0	0	0	0	6	0	5	0	11	0	11
State University of New York at Buffalo	NY	0	0	1	0	0	0	0	0	10	1	31	3	0	0	42	4	46
Stony Brook University	NY	0	0	1	1	1	0	0	0	6	0	2	2	0	0	10	3	13
North Carolina A & T State University	NC	6	0	2	0	1	0	0	0	0	0	2	1	0	0	11	1	12
North Carolina State University	NC	0	0	0	0	0	0	0	0	31	3	4	1	0	0	35	4	39
University of North Carolina, Charlotte	NC	1	0	1	0	0	0	0	0	7	1	13	3	0	0	22	4	26
University of North Dakota	ND	0	0	0	0	0	0	0	0	4	2	0	0	0	0	4	2	6
North Dakota State University	ND	0	0	3	0	0	0	0	0	0	0	8	0	0	0	11	0	11
Northeastern University	MA	1	0	2	0	1	0	0	0	6	0	8	1	5	0	23	1	24
Northern Illinois University	IL	1	0	0	0	0	0	0	0	11	2	0	1	0	0	12	3	15
Northwestern University	IL	0	0	0	0	0	0	0	0	0	0	5	0	4	0	9	0	9
University of Notre Dame	IN	0	0	0	0	0	0	0	0	4	1	4	4	0	0	8	5	13
Oakland University	MI	1	0	3	1	1	0	0	0	23	5	9	2	0	0	37	8	45
The Ohio State University	OH	1	0	1	0	1	1	0	0	35	9	19	3	0	0	57	13	70
Ohio University	OH	0	0	0	0	0	0	0	0	0	0	11	0	0	0	11	0	11
University of Oklahoma	OK	0	0	2	0	1	0	1	0	7	0	5	2	0	0	16	2	18
Oklahoma State University	OK	0	0	0	0	0	0	0	0	5	1	22	4	0	0	27	5	32

MECHANICAL ENGINEERING

MAS-OKL

INSTITUTION		AFRICAN AMERICAN M	F	ASIAN AMERICAN M	F	HISPANIC M	F	NATIVE AMERICAN M	F	CAUCASIAN M	F	FOREIGN M	F	OTHER M	F	TOTAL BY GENDER M	F	TOTAL DEGREES
Old Dominion University	VA	0	0	0	0	0	0	0	0	3	0	29	2	0	0	32	2	34
Oregon State University	OR	0	0	0	0	0	0	0	0	11	1	3	0	1	0	15	1	16
University of Pennsylvania	PA	0	0	0	0	0	0	0	0	8	1	6	2	1	0	15	3	18
The Pennsylvania State University	PA	1	0	0	0	0	0	0	0	25	3	14	1	0	0	40	4	44
University of Pittsburgh	PA	0	0	2	0	0	0	0	0	11	0	0	0	0	0	13	0	13
Polytechnic University	NY	3	0	2	0	0	0	0	0	1	0	3	0	6	0	15	0	15
Portland State University	OR	1	0	0	0	0	0	0	0	2	1	2	2	0	0	5	3	8
Prairie View A&M University	TX	2	0	0	0	0	0	0	0	0	0	0	0	0	0	2	0	2
Princeton University	NJ	0	0	0	0	0	0	0	0	3	0	1	1	0	0	4	1	5
University of Puerto Rico, Mayaguez Campus	PR	0	0	0	0	9	2	0	0	0	0	0	0	0	0	9	2	11
Purdue University	IN	2	0	2	0	0	0	0	0	30	6	11	2	4	0	49	8	57
Rensselaer Polytechnic Institute	NY	0	0	5	0	7	0	0	0	34	3	5	1	3	0	54	4	58
University of Rhode Island	RI	0	0	1	0	0	0	0	0	3	0	3	0	0	0	7	0	7
William Marsh Rice University	TX	0	0	0	0	0	0	0	0	2	0	1	0	0	1	3	1	4
University of Rochester	NY	0	0	0	0	0	1	0	0	2	0	3	0	0	0	5	1	6
Rochester Institute of Technology	NY	1	0	3	1	0	0	0	0	17	12	1	2	4	0	26	15	41
Rose-Hulman Institute of Technology	IN	0	0	1	0	0	0	0	0	2	0	0	0	0	0	3	0	3
Rowan University	NJ	0	0	0	0	1	0	0	0	4	1	0	0	0	0	5	1	6
Rutgers, The State University of New Jersey	NJ	0	0	0	0	3	1	0	0	3	0	16	2	0	0	22	3	25
Saint Cloud State University	MN	0	0	1	0	0	0	0	0	0	0	6	0	0	0	7	0	7
San Diego State University	CA	0	0	0	0	0	0	0	0	1	0	4	0	0	1	5	1	6
San Jose State University	CA	0	0	8	3	3	1	0	0	4	0	0	0	3	1	18	5	23
Santa Clara University	CA	0	0	1	0	2	1	0	0	4	0	0	0	2	1	9	2	11
University of South Alabama	AL	0	0	0	0	0	0	0	0	1	0	16	1	0	0	17	1	18
University of South Carolina	SC	2	0	1	0	1	1	0	1	8	1	4	0	0	0	16	3	19
South Dakota School of Mines and Technology	SD	0	0	0	0	0	0	0	0	5	0	0	0	1	0	6	0	6
South Dakota State University	SD	0	0	0	0	0	0	0	0	1	0	3	0	0	0	4	0	4
University of South Florida	FL	0	0	1	0	1	0	1	0	0	1	0	0	0	0	3	1	4
University of Southern California	CA	0	0	3	1	2	0	0	0	10	2	14	3	0	0	29	6	35
Southern Illinois University Carbondale	IL	0	1	0	0	0	0	0	0	3	1	8	3	0	0	11	5	16
Southern Illinois University Edwardsville	IL	0	0	0	0	0	0	0	0	1	1	13	5	0	0	14	6	20
Southern Methodist University	TX	0	0	0	0	1	0	0	0	2	0	0	0	0	0	3	0	3
Stanford University	CA	0	0	18	7	3	2	0	0	37	12	53	5	15	9	128	35	163
Stevens Institute of Technology	NJ	0	0	3	0	0	0	0	0	19	0	7	1	16	3	45	4	49
Syracuse University	NY	0	0	1	1	0	1	0	0	5	1	10	0	3	0	19	3	22
Temple University	PA	0	0	0	0	0	0	0	0	10	1	0	0	0	0	10	1	11
Tennessee Technological University	TN	0	0	0	0	0	0	0	0	9	0	5	2	0	0	14	2	16
University of Tennessee, Knoxville	TN	0	0	0	0	0	0	1	0	6	1	6	0	1	0	14	1	15
Texas A&M University	TX	0	0	2	1	2	1	0	0	29	1	42	1	2	0	77	4	81
Texas A&M University - Kingsville	TX	0	0	0	0	0	0	0	0	1	0	7	4	0	0	8	4	12
Texas Tech University	TX	0	0	0	0	0	0	1	0	16	0	6	0	0	0	23	0	23
The University of Texas at Arlington	TX	0	0	1	0	1	0	0	0	11	0	24	4	0	0	37	4	41
The University of Texas at Austin	TX	0	0	4	0	2	1	0	0	32	4	12	1	0	0	50	6	56
University of Texas at El Paso	TX	0	0	0	0	6	0	0	0	1	0	9	2	0	0	16	2	18
University of Texas at San Antonio	TX	0	0	0	0	1	0	0	0	3	0	4	1	0	0	8	1	9

OLD-TEX

MECHANICAL ENGINEERING

Master's Degrees Awarded in Mechanical Engineering, 2005-2006

MECHANICAL ENGINEERING — TOL-YOU

INSTITUTION		African American M	African American F	Asian American M	Asian American F	Hispanic M	Hispanic F	Native American M	Native American F	Caucasian M	Caucasian F	Foreign M	Foreign F	Other M	Other F	Total by Gender M	Total by Gender F	Total Degrees
The University of Toledo	OH	0	0	0	0	0	0	0	0	4	0	13	4	0	0	17	4	21
Tufts University	MA	0	0	1	0	0	0	0	0	0	0	3	2	12	2	16	4	20
Tulane University	LA	0	0	0	0	0	0	0	0	0	0	3	0	3	0	6	0	6
University of Tulsa	OK	0	0	0	0	0	0	0	0	3	0	5	0	1	0	9	0	9
Tuskegee University	AL	3	1	0	1	0	0	0	0	0	0	1	0	5	1	9	3	12
University of Utah	UT	0	0	0	0	1	0	0	0	24	1	15	2	0	1	40	4	44
Vanderbilt University	TN	0	0	0	0	0	0	0	0	3	0	2	0	1	0	6	0	6
University of Vermont	VT	0	0	0	0	0	0	0	0	4	1	0	0	0	0	4	1	5
Villanova University	PA	0	0	0	0	0	0	0	0	10	2	7	3	0	0	17	5	22
University of Virginia	VA	0	0	0	0	0	0	0	0	16	2	3	0	1	0	20	2	22
Virginia Polytechnic Institute and State University	VA	2	0	1	0	2	1	0	0	35	4	7	0	0	0	47	5	52
University of Washington	WA	0	0	3	2	2	0	0	0	17	3	3	0	5	1	30	6	36
Washington State University	WA	0	0	0	0	0	0	0	0	6	1	1	0	5	1	12	2	14
Washington University	MO	0	0	3	0	0	0	0	0	15	8	2	0	2	1	22	9	31
Wayne State University	MI	0	0	5	0	0	0	0	0	10	0	72	6	2	0	89	6	95
West Virginia University	WV	0	0	1	0	0	0	0	0	9	2	14	0	0	0	24	2	26
Western Michigan University	MI	1	0	0	0	1	0	0	0	5	0	17	0	0	0	24	0	24
Wichita State University	KS	0	0	0	0	0	0	0	0	0	0	32	1	3	0	35	1	36
Widener University	PA	2	0	1	0	0	0	0	0	2	1	4	0	0	0	9	1	10
University of Wisconsin, Madison	WI	1	0	1	0	0	0	0	0	30	7	12	0	5	0	49	7	56
Worcester Polytechnic Institute	MA	0	0	1	0	0	0	0	0	23	5	2	0	0	0	26	5	31
Wright State University	OH	0	0	1	1	2	0	0	0	8	2	5	1	0	0	16	4	20
University of Wyoming	WY	0	0	0	0	0	0	0	0	2	0	1	0	0	0	3	0	3
Youngstown State University	OH	0	0	0	0	0	0	0	0	0	0	1	0	1	1	2	1	3
Totals:		83	16	232	52	118	32	10	3	1,648	244	1,598	223	313	59	4,002	629	4,631
CANADIAN INSTITUTIONS:																		
University of Alberta	AB	0	0	0	0	0	0	0	0	0	0	0	0	29	5	29	5	34
University of Calgary	AB	0	0	0	0	0	0	0	0	0	0	1	0	8	1	9	1	10
Concordia University, Faculty of Engr. and Comp. Sci.	PQ	0	0	0	0	0	0	0	0	0	0	12	4	85	10	97	14	111
Ecole Polytechnique de Montreal	PQ	0	0	0	0	0	0	0	0	0	0	0	0	18	2	18	2	20
Ecole de Technologie Superieure	PQ	0	0	0	0	0	0	0	0	0	0	0	0	18	1	18	1	19
McGill University, Faculty of Engineering	PQ	0	0	0	0	0	0	0	0	0	0	0	0	29	4	29	4	33
University of Ottawa, Faculty of Engineering	ON	0	0	0	0	0	0	0	0	0	0	2	2	3	14	5	16	21
University of Waterloo	ON	0	0	0	0	0	0	0	0	0	0	0	0	54	9	54	9	63
Totals:		0	0	0	0	0	0	0	0	0	0	15	6	244	46	259	52	311

INSTITUTION		AFRICAN AMERICAN		ASIAN AMERICAN		HISPANIC		NATIVE AMERICAN		CAUCASIAN		FOREIGN		OTHER		TOTAL BY GENDER		TOTAL DEGREES
		M	F	M	F	M	F	M	F	M	F	M	F	M	F	M	F	
University of Alabama at Birmingham	AL	0	0	0	0	0	0	0	0	0	0	3	0	1	0	4	0	4
The University of Alabama	AL	0	1	4	1	0	0	0	0	3	1	0	0	0	0	7	3	10
Alfred University, NY State College of Ceramics	NY	0	0	0	0	0	0	0	0	3	1	1	1	0	0	4	2	6
The University of Arizona	AZ	0	0	0	1	0	1	0	0	0	1	0	1	0	0	0	4	4
Arizona State University	AZ	0	0	0	0	0	0	0	0	4	0	3	1	3	0	10	1	11
Auburn University	AL	0	0	0	0	0	1	0	0	1	1	1	0	0	0	2	2	4
California Institute of Technology	CA	0	0	1	0	0	0	0	0	3	2	2	0	0	0	6	2	8
California State University, Northridge	CA	0	0	1	1	2	0	0	0	2	1	0	0	1	0	6	2	8
University of California, Berkeley	CA	0	0	2	0	0	0	0	0	5	5	0	1	1	0	8	6	14
University of California, Davis	CA	0	0	1	0	0	0	0	0	0	0	1	0	1	0	3	0	3
University of California, Irvine	CA	0	0	0	0	0	0	0	0	0	0	0	0	4	2	4	2	6
University of California, Los Angeles	CA	0	0	3	2	0	1	0	0	1	1	2	1	0	0	6	5	11
University of California, San Diego	CA	0	0	2	1	0	0	0	0	2	0	2	1	1	0	7	2	9
University of California, Santa Barbara	CA	0	0	1	0	0	0	0	0	3	0	2	0	3	0	9	0	9
Carnegie Mellon University	PA	0	0	0	0	0	0	0	0	1	1	6	1	0	0	7	2	9
Case Western Reserve University	OH	0	0	0	0	0	0	0	0	3	0	5	0	0	0	8	0	8
University of Central Florida	FL	0	0	0	1	1	0	0	0	0	1	8	1	0	0	9	3	12
University of Cincinnati	OH	0	1	0	0	0	0	0	0	3	0	13	4	0	0	16	5	21
Clemson University	SC	0	0	0	0	0	0	0	0	3	0	4	3	0	0	7	3	10
Colorado School of Mines	CO	0	0	0	0	0	0	0	0	6	6	4	0	0	0	10	6	16
Columbia University	NY	0	0	1	0	0	0	0	0	1	0	7	1	0	0	9	1	10
University of Connecticut	CT	0	0	1	0	0	0	0	0	4	1	4	1	0	1	9	3	12
Cornell University	NY	0	0	0	2	0	0	0	0	4	1	4	1	0	0	8	4	12
University of Dayton	OH	0	0	0	0	0	0	0	0	3	4	4	1	0	0	7	5	12
University of Delaware	DE	0	0	0	0	0	0	0	0	0	2	1	0	0	0	1	2	3
Drexel University	PA	0	0	0	0	0	0	0	0	2	0	3	0	0	0	5	0	5
University of Florida	FL	1	1	1	0	0	1	0	0	9	7	6	2	0	0	17	11	28
Florida International University	FL	0	0	0	0	2	0	0	0	0	0	2	0	0	0	4	0	4
Georgia Institute of Technology	GA	0	0	1	0	0	0	0	0	6	1	3	0	1	0	11	1	12
University of Houston, Cullen School of Engineering	TX	0	0	1	0	0	0	0	0	2	0	2	0	0	0	5	0	5
University of Idaho	ID	0	0	0	0	0	0	0	0	2	0	0	0	2	0	4	0	4
Illinois Institute of Technology	IL	0	0	0	0	0	0	0	0	2	1	1	1	0	0	3	2	5
University of Illinois at Chicago	IL	0	0	1	1	1	0	0	0	2	0	0	0	0	0	4	1	5
University of Illinois at Urbana-Champaign	IL	0	0	0	2	1	0	0	0	2	1	3	1	0	0	6	4	10
Iowa State University	IA	0	0	0	0	0	0	0	0	3	2	2	0	0	0	5	2	7
The Johns Hopkins University	MD	0	0	0	0	0	0	0	0	5	2	2	0	0	0	7	2	9
University of Kentucky	KY	0	0	0	0	0	0	0	0	0	0	1	0	0	0	1	0	1
Lehigh University	PA	0	0	0	0	0	0	0	0	0	0	0	0	7	0	7	0	7
University of Maryland, College Park	MD	0	0	0	0	0	0	0	0	1	0	0	0	0	1	1	1	2
Massachusetts Institute of Technology	MA	0	0	1	1	0	0	0	0	10	6	8	0	1	1	20	8	28
University of Michigan	MI	0	0	2	0	1	0	0	0	4	2	3	0	0	0	10	2	12
Michigan Technological University	MI	0	0	0	0	0	0	0	0	4	0	0	0	0	0	4	0	4
University of Missouri - Rolla	MO	0	0	0	0	0	0	0	0	3	0	4	3	0	0	7	3	10
Montana Tech of the University of Montana	MT	0	0	0	0	0	0	0	0	1	0	1	0	0	0	2	0	2
University of Nevada, Reno	NV	0	0	0	0	0	0	0	0	0	0	3	0	1	0	4	0	4

METALLURGICAL AND MATERIALS ENGR.   ALA-NEV

MASTER'S DEGREES AWARDED IN METALLURGICAL AND MATERIALS ENGINEERING, 2005-2006

INSTITUTION		AFRICAN AMERICAN		ASIAN AMERICAN		HISPANIC		NATIVE AMERICAN		CAUCASIAN		FOREIGN		OTHER		TOTAL BY GENDER		TOTAL DEGREES
		M	F	M	F	M	F	M	F	M	F	M	F	M	F	M	F	
University of New Hampshire	NH	0	0	0	0	0	0	0	0	2	0	0	0	0	0	2	0	2
New Mexico Institute of Mining & Technology	NM	0	0	0	0	1	0	0	0	5	0	4	1	0	0	10	1	11
The State University of New York at Binghamton	NY	0	0	0	0	0	0	0	0	0	0	0	1	0	0	0	1	1
Stony Brook University	NY	0	0	0	1	0	0	0	0	2	1	5	4	0	0	7	6	13
North Carolina State University	NC	2	0	0	0	0	0	0	0	10	1	0	1	0	0	12	2	14
University of North Texas	TX	0	0	0	0	0	0	0	0	2	0	5	2	0	0	7	2	9
Northwestern University	IL	0	0	0	0	2	0	0	0	5	0	2	1	0	0	9	1	10
The Ohio State University	OH	0	0	1	0	1	0	0	0	9	5	7	1	0	0	18	6	24
Oregon State University	OR	0	0	0	0	0	0	0	0	1	0	0	0	0	0	1	0	1
University of Pennsylvania	PA	0	0	0	0	0	0	0	0	1	0	6	1	0	0	7	1	8
The Pennsylvania State University	PA	0	0	0	1	0	0	0	0	5	3	2	1	0	0	7	5	12
University of Pittsburgh	PA	0	0	1	0	0	0	0	0	1	2	1	0	0	0	3	2	5
Purdue University	IN	0	0	0	0	0	0	0	0	3	1	1	1	0	0	4	2	6
Rensselaer Polytechnic Institute	NY	0	0	0	0	0	0	0	0	3	0	0	0	0	1	3	1	4
University of Rochester	NY	0	0	0	1	0	0	0	0	0	0	0	1	0	0	0	2	2
San Jose State University	CA	0	0	2	2	0	0	0	0	1	0	0	0	1	1	4	3	7
South Dakota School of Mines and Technology	SD	0	0	0	0	0	0	1	0	0	1	7	1	0	0	8	2	10
University of Southern California	CA	0	0	0	0	1	0	0	0	1	0	16	4	1	0	19	4	23
Stanford University	CA	1	0	4	1	1	0	0	0	7	3	9	4	5	0	27	8	35
University of Tennessee, Knoxville	TN	0	0	1	0	0	0	0	0	4	1	6	3	0	0	11	4	15
The University of Texas at Arlington	TX	0	0	1	0	1	0	0	0	0	0	5	3	0	0	7	3	10
The University of Texas at Austin	TX	0	0	0	0	0	0	0	0	0	0	0	1	0	0	0	1	1
University of Texas at El Paso	TX	0	0	0	0	1	1	0	0	1	0	2	0	0	0	4	2	6
University of Utah	UT	0	0	1	0	0	0	0	0	1	0	2	0	0	0	4	0	4
Vanderbilt University	TN	0	0	0	0	0	0	0	0	1	1	3	1	0	0	3	2	5
University of Vermont	VT	0	0	0	0	0	0	0	0	1	0	0	0	0	0	1	0	1
University of Virginia	VA	0	0	0	0	0	0	0	0	5	1	1	1	0	0	6	2	8
Virginia Polytechnic Institute and State University	VA	2	0	0	0	0	0	0	0	0	3	1	0	0	0	3	3	6
University of Washington	WA	0	0	0	0	0	0	0	0	1	1	0	1	2	0	3	2	5
Washington State University	WA	0	0	0	0	0	0	0	0	4	0	4	0	0	1	8	1	9
Wayne State University	MI	0	0	0	0	0	0	0	0	0	0	3	3	0	0	3	3	6
University of Wisconsin, Madison	WI	0	0	0	0	0	0	0	0	5	1	8	3	0	0	13	5	18
Worcester Polytechnic Institute	MA	0	0	1	1	0	0	0	0	2	0	2	0	0	0	5	1	6
Wright State University	OH	0	0	0	0	0	0	0	0	3	2	4	0	0	0	7	2	9
Totals:		**6**	**3**	**36**	**20**	**16**	**6**	**1**	**0**	**198**	**79**	**227**	**66**	**36**	**8**	**520**	**182**	**702**

CANADIAN INSTITUTIONS:

INSTITUTION		AFRICAN AMERICAN		ASIAN AMERICAN		HISPANIC		NATIVE AMERICAN		CAUCASIAN		FOREIGN		OTHER		TOTAL BY GENDER		TOTAL DEGREES
		M	F	M	F	M	F	M	F	M	F	M	F	M	F	M	F	
Ecole Polytechnique de Montreal	PQ	0	0	0	0	0	0	0	0	0	0	0	0	6	0	6	0	6
Totals:		**0**	**0**	**0**	**0**	**0**	**0**	**0**	**0**	**0**	**0**	**0**	**0**	**6**	**0**	**6**	**0**	**6**

METALLURGICAL AND MATERIALS ENGR.   NEW-WRI

METALLURGICAL AND MATERIALS ENGR.

MASTER'S DEGREES AWARDED IN MINING ENGINEERING, 2005-2006

INSTITUTION		AFRICAN AMERICAN		ASIAN AMERICAN		HISPANIC		NATIVE AMERICAN		CAUCASIAN		FOREIGN		OTHER		TOTAL BY GENDER		TOTAL DEGREES
		M	F	M	F	M	F	M	F	M	F	M	F	M	F	M	F	
University of Alaska Fairbanks	AK	0	0	1	0	0	0	0	0	0	0	2	0	0	0	3	0	3
Colorado School of Mines	CO	0	0	0	0	1	0	0	0	5	1	5	0	0	0	11	1	12
Columbia University	NY	0	0	0	0	0	0	0	0	3	2	3	2	2	0	8	4	12
Michigan Technological University	MI	0	0	0	0	0	0	0	0	0	0	1	0	0	0	1	0	1
University of Missouri - Rolla	MO	0	0	0	0	0	0	0	0	2	0	0	0	0	0	2	0	2
Montana Tech of the University of Montana	MT	0	0	0	0	0	0	0	0	0	0	1	0	0	0	1	0	1
New Mexico Institute of Mining & Technology	NM	0	0	0	0	0	0	0	0	3	2	0	0	0	0	3	2	5
Southern Illinois University Carbondale	IL	0	0	0	0	0	0	0	0	0	0	4	0	0	0	4	0	4
Virginia Polytechnic Institute and State University	VA	0	0	0	0	0	0	0	0	2	2	0	0	1	0	3	2	5
West Virginia University	WV	0	0	0	0	0	0	0	0	0	0	1	2	0	0	1	2	3
Totals:		**0**	**0**	**1**	**0**	**1**	**0**	**0**	**0**	**15**	**7**	**17**	**4**	**3**	**0**	**37**	**11**	**48**
CANADIAN INSTITUTIONS:																		
Ecole Polytechnique de Montreal	PQ	0	0	0	0	0	0	0	0	0	0	0	0	8	0	8	0	8
McGill University, Faculty of Engineering	PQ	0	0	0	0	0	0	0	0	0	0	0	0	8	4	8	4	12
Totals:		**0**	**0**	**0**	**0**	**0**	**0**	**0**	**0**	**0**	**0**	**0**	**0**	**16**	**4**	**16**	**4**	**20**

ALA-WES

MINING ENGINEERING

MASTER'S DEGREES AWARDED IN NUCLEAR ENGINEERING, 2005-2006

INSTITUTION		AFRICAN AMERICAN		ASIAN AMERICAN		HISPANIC		NATIVE AMERICAN		CAUCASIAN		FOREIGN		OTHER		TOTAL BY GENDER		TOTAL DEGREES
		M	F	M	F	M	F	M	F	M	F	M	F	M	F	M	F	
Air Force Institute of Technology	OH	0	0	0	0	0	0	0	0	0	0	0	0	7	0	7	0	7
University of California, Berkeley	CA	0	0	0	0	0	0	0	0	3	2	1	3	1	0	5	5	10
University of Cincinnati	OH	0	1	0	0	2	0	0	0	2	1	2	1	0	0	6	3	9
University of Florida	FL	0	0	4	0	1	1	0	0	8	4	0	0	0	0	13	5	18
Georgia Institute of Technology	GA	0	0	0	2	0	0	0	0	8	3	0	0	0	0	8	5	13
Idaho State University	ID	0	0	0	0	0	0	0	0	2	0	0	0	0	0	2	0	2
University of Illinois at Urbana-Champaign	IL	0	2	1	0	0	0	0	0	5	0	3	0	0	0	9	2	11
Kansas State University	KS	0	0	0	0	0	0	0	0	3	0	1	0	0	0	4	0	4
University of Maryland, College Park	MD	0	0	0	0	0	0	0	0	2	0	0	0	0	0	2	0	2
Massachusetts Institute of Technology	MA	1	0	0	0	0	0	1	0	8	2	7	1	0	0	17	3	20
University of Michigan	MI	0	0	0	1	0	0	1	0	12	3	3	3	1	0	17	7	24
University of Missouri-Columbia	MO	0	0	0	0	0	0	0	0	1	0	1	1	0	0	2	1	3
University of Missouri - Rolla	MO	0	0	0	0	0	0	0	0	2	0	1	0	0	0	3	0	3
The University of New Mexico	NM	0	0	0	0	2	0	0	0	6	2	0	0	0	0	8	2	10
North Carolina State University	NC	0	0	0	0	0	0	0	0	7	0	1	0	0	0	8	0	8
The Ohio State University	OH	0	0	0	0	0	0	1	0	2	0	0	1	0	0	3	1	4
Oregon State University	OR	0	0	0	0	1	0	0	0	6	3	2	0	0	0	9	3	12
The Pennsylvania State University	PA	0	0	0	0	0	0	0	0	6	2	2	0	0	0	8	2	10
Purdue University	IN	0	0	0	0	0	0	0	0	7	2	4	1	1	0	12	3	15
Rensselaer Polytechnic Institute	NY	0	0	0	0	0	0	0	0	3	1	0	0	0	0	3	1	4
University of South Carolina	SC	0	0	0	0	0	0	0	0	3	1	0	0	2	0	5	1	6
University of Tennessee, Knoxville	TN	0	0	1	0	0	0	0	0	12	3	2	1	1	0	16	4	20
Texas A&M University	TX	0	1	0	0	0	0	0	0	9	3	1	0	0	0	10	4	14
University of Utah	UT	0	0	0	0	0	0	0	0	1	0	0	0	0	0	1	0	1
University of Wisconsin, Madison	WI	0	0	1	0	0	0	0	0	7	2	1	0	5	0	14	2	16
Totals:		1	4	7	3	6	1	3	0	125	34	32	12	18	0	192	54	246

CANADIAN INSTITUTIONS:

INSTITUTION		AFRICAN AMERICAN		ASIAN AMERICAN		HISPANIC		NATIVE AMERICAN		CAUCASIAN		FOREIGN		OTHER		TOTAL BY GENDER		TOTAL DEGREES
		M	F	M	F	M	F	M	F	M	F	M	F	M	F	M	F	
Ecole Polytechnique de Montreal	PQ	0	0	0	0	0	0	0	0	0	0	0	0	4	1	4	1	5
Totals:		0	0	0	0	0	0	0	0	0	0	0	0	4	1	4	1	5

NUCLEAR ENGINEERING

AIR-WIS

INSTITUTION		AFRICAN AMERICAN		ASIAN AMERICAN		HISPANIC		NATIVE AMERICAN		CAUCASIAN		FOREIGN		OTHER		TOTAL BY GENDER		TOTAL DEGREES
		M	F	M	F	M	F	M	F	M	F	M	F	M	F	M	F	
Air Force Institute of Technology	OH	1	0	0	0	0	0	0	0	2	0	0	0	179	12	182	12	194
The University of Alabama in Huntsville	AL	0	0	0	0	0	0	0	0	1	0	0	0	0	0	1	0	1
Alfred University, NY State College of Ceramics	NY	1	0	0	0	0	0	0	0	3	4	1	1	0	0	5	5	10
The University of Arizona	AZ	0	0	0	0	0	1	0	0	6	4	0	3	0	0	6	8	14
Arizona State University	AZ	0	0	1	0	0	0	0	0	6	0	0	0	0	0	7	0	7
University of Arkansas	AR	14	9	3	0	5	0	0	0	81	22	3	0	8	4	114	35	149
Auburn University	AL	0	0	0	0	0	0	0	0	0	0	1	1	0	0	1	1	2
Boise State University	ID	0	0	0	0	0	0	0	0	1	1	0	0	0	0	1	1	2
Brown University	RI	0	0	1	0	1	0	0	0	1	1	4	1	0	0	7	2	9
California Institute of Technology	CA	0	0	0	0	0	1	0	0	0	0	0	1	0	0	0	2	2
California State University, Northridge	CA	0	0	1	0	3	1	0	0	3	0	0	0	1	0	8	1	9
University of California, Berkeley	CA	1	0	0	0	0	0	0	0	1	0	0	0	1	0	3	0	3
University of California, Davis	CA	0	0	0	0	0	0	0	0	0	0	0	0	1	0	1	0	1
Carnegie Mellon University	PA	0	0	0	0	0	0	0	0	3	1	5	1	0	0	8	3	11
Case Western Reserve University	OH	0	0	0	0	0	0	0	0	1	0	0	0	0	1	1	1	2
Colorado School of Mines	CO	2	0	1	0	0	0	0	0	12	12	7	3	0	0	22	15	37
Colorado State University	CO	0	1	0	0	1	0	0	0	6	6	0	0	2	0	9	7	16
University of Colorado at Boulder	CO	3	2	0	0	0	0	0	0	16	2	13	0	0	0	32	4	36
University of Colorado at Colorado Springs	CO	1	0	0	0	0	0	0	0	12	0	0	3	0	0	13	3	16
Columbia University	NY	0	0	1	1	2	0	0	0	5	1	4	3	3	0	15	5	20
Cornell University	NY	1	0	1	1	0	1	0	0	4	1	1	0	0	1	7	4	11
University of Dayton	OH	0	0	0	0	0	0	0	0	4	0	1	1	1	0	6	1	7
University of Detroit Mercy	MI	0	0	1	0	2	0	0	0	8	1	0	0	2	1	13	2	15
Drexel University	PA	0	0	0	0	0	0	0	0	0	0	0	0	0	1	0	1	1
Florida Atlantic University	FL	1	0	0	0	1	0	0	0	0	0	3	1	0	0	5	1	6
Florida Institute of Technology	FL	0	0	0	0	0	0	0	0	7	8	1	2	0	1	8	11	19
Florida International University	FL	3	1	0	2	11	5	0	0	8	3	9	3	0	0	31	14	45
George Mason University	VA	12	4	38	15	4	2	0	0	53	11	25	12	13	4	145	48	193
The George Washington University	DC	4	5	4	1	0	1	1	0	20	6	7	2	6	1	42	16	58
University of Georgia	GA	0	0	0	0	0	0	0	0	2	1	0	0	0	0	2	1	3
Georgia Institute of Technology	GA	0	0	0	0	0	0	0	0	0	1	1	2	0	0	1	3	4
Harvard University	MA	0	0	2	1	0	0	1	0	13	3	18	3	0	0	34	7	41
University of Hawaii at Manoa	HI	0	0	0	0	0	0	0	0	5	0	1	0	0	0	6	0	6
Idaho State University	ID	0	0	0	0	0	0	0	0	1	0	4	0	0	0	5	0	5
Illinois Institute of Technology	IL	0	1	0	0	0	0	0	0	1	0	1	2	0	0	2	3	5
The Johns Hopkins University	MD	13	12	12	7	8	0	0	0	145	47	8	1	0	0	186	67	253
University of Kansas	KS	0	0	0	0	0	0	0	0	1	2	0	0	0	0	1	2	3
Kansas State University	KS	0	0	0	0	0	0	0	0	1	2	0	0	0	0	1	2	3
Lawrence Technological University	MI	0	0	4	1	0	0	0	0	3	1	5	0	2	0	14	2	16
Lehigh University	PA	0	0	0	0	0	0	0	0	0	0	1	0	3	3	4	3	7
University of Louisiana at Lafayette	LA	1	0	0	0	0	0	0	0	6	0	7	3	0	0	14	3	17
University of Maine	ME	0	0	0	0	0	0	0	0	1	1	2	0	0	0	3	1	4
University of Maryland, College Park	MD	0	0	1	0	0	0	0	0	12	6	10	1	4	3	27	10	37
Massachusetts Institute of Technology	MA	1	1	5	4	0	0	0	0	18	11	27	9	3	2	54	27	81
University of Massachusetts Dartmouth	MA	0	0	0	0	0	0	0	0	1	1	2	0	0	0	3	1	4

OTHER ENGINEERING DISCIPLINES

AIR-MAS

MASTER'S DEGREES AWARDED IN OTHER ENGINEERING DISCIPLINES, 2005-2006

INSTITUTION		AFRICAN AMERICAN		ASIAN AMERICAN		HISPANIC		NATIVE AMERICAN		CAUCASIAN		FOREIGN		OTHER		TOTAL BY GENDER		TOTAL DEGREES
		M	F	M	F	M	F	M	F	M	F	M	F	M	F	M	F	
University of Massachusetts Lowell	MA	0	0	0	2	0	0	0	0	8	2	14	5	1	0	23	9	32
McNeese State University	LA	0	0	0	0	0	0	0	0	0	0	1	1	0	0	1	1	2
Mercer University	GA	0	0	0	0	0	0	0	0	0	1	1	0	0	0	1	1	2
Miami University	OH	0	0	0	0	0	0	0	0	1	0	4	0	0	0	5	0	5
University of Michigan	MI	1	0	8	3	1	0	2	0	35	18	35	11	6	2	88	34	122
Michigan State University	MI	0	0	0	0	0	0	0	0	0	0	1	0	1	0	2	0	2
Michigan Technological University	MI	0	0	0	0	0	0	0	0	0	2	1	0	0	1	1	3	4
University of Michigan, Dearborn	MI	0	1	2	2	0	1	0	0	13	1	10	0	0	0	25	5	30
University of Minnesota -Twin Cities	MN	0	1	3	0	1	0	1	0	27	6	5	1	0	0	37	8	45
The University of Mississippi	MS	0	0	0	0	0	0	0	0	1	1	2	0	0	0	3	1	4
University of Missouri - Rolla	MO	0	0	0	0	0	0	0	0	4	0	0	0	0	0	4	0	4
Monmouth University	NJ	0	0	2	1	2	1	0	0	13	4	3	2	3	1	23	9	32
Montana Tech of the University of Montana	MT	0	0	0	0	0	0	0	0	3	0	0	1	0	0	3	1	4
Morgan State University	MD	3	2	0	0	0	0	0	0	0	0	2	0	0	0	5	2	7
Naval Postgraduate School	CA	8	0	6	0	5	1	0	0	166	11	27	1	0	0	212	13	225
University of Nebraska, Lincoln	NE	0	0	1	0	0	0	0	0	0	0	2	1	0	0	3	1	4
University of New Hampshire	NH	0	0	0	0	0	0	0	0	2	0	0	0	0	0	2	0	2
New Jersey Institute of Technology	NJ	0	0	3	1	2	0	0	0	4	1	1	5	0	0	10	7	17
The University of New Mexico	NM	0	0	0	0	0	1	0	0	2	0	2	0	0	0	4	1	5
New Mexico Institute of Mining & Technology	NM	1	0	1	1	1	1	0	0	12	2	1	0	0	0	16	4	20
University of New Orleans	LA	0	0	0	0	0	0	0	0	1	0	0	0	0	0	1	0	1
New York Institute of Technology	NY	0	0	0	0	0	0	0	0	0	0	0	0	63	14	63	14	77
The State University of New York at Binghamton	NY	0	0	0	0	0	0	0	0	0	0	1	1	0	1	1	2	3
SUNY College of Environmental Science and Forestry	NY	0	0	0	0	0	0	0	0	10	4	4	0	0	0	14	4	18
Stony Brook University	NY	3	3	6	1	4	0	0	0	11	12	9	12	0	0	33	28	61
North Carolina State University	NC	1	0	0	0	0	0	0	0	5	1	4	3	0	0	10	4	14
Northeastern University	MA	1	1	6	0	0	0	0	0	9	2	31	14	8	3	55	20	75
Northwestern University	IL	2	1	3	3	0	0	0	0	21	12	2	0	1	0	29	16	45
Oakland University	MI	0	0	0	1	0	0	0	0	6	1	1	1	0	0	7	3	10
University of Oklahoma	OK	0	0	1	0	1	0	0	0	3	3	5	4	0	0	10	7	17
Oklahoma State University	OK	0	0	0	0	0	0	0	0	0	1	0	0	0	0	0	1	1
Old Dominion University	VA	2	0	0	3	0	0	0	0	9	4	0	0	0	1	12	8	20
Oregon State University	OR	0	0	0	0	0	0	0	0	1	0	2	0	0	0	3	0	3
University of Pennsylvania	PA	0	1	14	10	0	1	0	0	30	18	22	14	2	1	68	45	113
The Pennsylvania State University	PA	0	0	0	2	1	0	0	0	22	8	16	5	0	0	39	15	54
Portland State University	OR	0	0	0	0	0	0	0	0	2	0	2	0	0	0	4	0	4
Princeton University	NJ	0	0	1	0	0	0	0	0	0	0	0	0	0	1	1	0	1
Purdue University	IN	4	0	8	2	2	1	0	0	59	17	15	2	4	3	91	24	115
Rensselaer Polytechnic Institute	NY	0	0	0	0	0	1	0	0	0	0	2	2	0	0	2	3	5
University of Rhode Island	RI	0	0	0	0	0	0	0	0	3	0	0	0	0	0	3	0	3
William Marsh Rice University	TX	0	1	0	1	4	0	0	0	5	0	7	1	2	0	18	3	21
University of Rochester	NY	1	0	0	1	0	0	0	0	2	3	5	2	0	1	8	7	15
Rochester Institute of Technology	NY	1	1	4	1	3	1	0	0	15	4	6	2	7	1	36	10	46
Rose-Hulman Institute of Technology	IN	0	0	1	0	0	0	0	0	0	0	0	0	0	0	1	0	1
Rutgers, The State University of New Jersey	NJ	0	0	0	0	0	0	0	0	6	0	3	1	0	0	9	1	10

OTHER ENGINEERING DISCIPLINES   MAS-RUT

INSTITUTION		AFRICAN AMERICAN		ASIAN AMERICAN		HISPANIC		NATIVE AMERICAN		CAUCASIAN		FOREIGN		OTHER		TOTAL BY GENDER		TOTAL DEGREES
		M	F	M	F	M	F	M	F	M	F	M	F	M	F	M	F	
University of Saint Thomas	MN	0	0	0	0	0	0	0	0	7	1	1	0	0	0	8	1	9
Santa Clara University	CA	0	0	0	1	0	0	0	0	0	0	0	0	1	2	1	4	5
South Dakota School of Mines and Technology	SD	0	0	0	0	0	0	0	0	1	0	0	0	0	0	1	0	1
University of Southern California	CA	0	0	0	0	0	0	0	0	17	10	1	0	1	0	19	10	29
Southern Methodist University	TX	22	6	34	4	11	3	1	0	98	27	17	1	0	0	183	41	224
Stanford University	CA	0	0	3	2	0	0	0	0	6	1	5	2	0	0	14	5	19
Stevens Institute of Technology	NJ	4	0	7	3	1	0	1	0	28	7	10	6	17	4	68	20	88
Syracuse University	NY	0	0	0	0	0	0	0	0	4	1	0	0	0	0	4	1	5
University of Tennessee, Knoxville	TN	0	0	1	0	0	0	0	0	17	1	1	0	0	0	19	1	20
Texas A&M University	TX	1	1	0	0	0	0	0	0	3	2	7	3	0	0	11	6	17
Texas Tech University	TX	0	0	0	0	3	0	0	0	1	0	9	2	0	0	13	2	15
Tri-State University	IN	0	0	0	0	0	0	0	0	1	0	0	0	1	0	2	0	2
Tufts University	MA	0	0	1	1	0	0	0	0	0	0	3	0	1	2	5	3	8
Utah State University	UT	0	0	0	0	0	0	0	0	2	0	6	0	0	0	8	0	8
Villanova University	PA	0	0	1	0	0	0	0	0	9	4	2	1	0	0	12	5	17
University of Virginia	VA	2	3	11	2	0	0	0	0	31	14	4	2	1	1	49	22	71
Virginia Polytechnic Institute and State University	VA	0	0	2	2	0	0	0	0	17	6	0	0	0	0	19	8	27
University of Washington	WA	0	0	0	0	0	1	0	0	12	9	0	0	2	2	14	12	26
Washington State University	WA	0	0	0	0	0	0	0	0	1	0	1	0	0	2	2	2	4
Washington University	MO	1	1	3	1	0	1	0	0	27	11	2	2	3	0	36	16	52
Wayne State University	MI	0	0	0	0	0	0	0	0	1	1	0	0	0	1	1	1	2
Western Michigan University	MI	1	0	1	0	0	0	0	0	1	1	5	2	0	0	8	3	11
University of Wisconsin, Madison	WI	1	0	4	0	1	0	0	0	28	5	7	0	4	2	45	7	52
Worcester Polytechnic Institute	MA	0	0	0	0	1	0	0	0	14	3	9	0	0	0	24	5	29
University of Wyoming	WY	0	0	0	0	0	0	0	0	2	0	0	1	0	0	2	1	3
Yale University/Faculty of Engineering	CT	0	0	0	0	0	0	0	0	0	0	0	0	76	26	76	26	102
Totals:		119	59	214	84	81	25	9	1	1,312	402	511	177	434	104	2,680	852	3,532

CANADIAN INSTITUTIONS:

INSTITUTION		AFRICAN AMERICAN		ASIAN AMERICAN		HISPANIC		NATIVE AMERICAN		CAUCASIAN		FOREIGN		OTHER		TOTAL BY GENDER		TOTAL DEGREES
		M	F	M	F	M	F	M	F	M	F	M	F	M	F	M	F	
University of Calgary	AB	0	0	0	0	0	0	0	0	0	0	7	4	7	2	14	6	20
Concordia University, Faculty of Engr. and Comp. Sci.	PQ	0	0	0	0	0	0	0	0	0	0	6	1	44	10	50	11	61
Ecole Polytechnique de Montreal	PQ	0	0	0	0	0	0	0	0	0	0	0	0	8	1	8	1	9
University of Waterloo	ON	0	0	0	0	0	0	0	0	0	0	0	0	24	20	24	20	44
Totals:		0	0	0	0	0	0	0	0	0	0	13	5	83	33	96	38	134

OTHER ENGINEERING DISCIPLINES

SAI-YAL

MASTER'S DEGREES AWARDED IN PETROLEUM ENGINEERING, 2005-2006

INSTITUTION		AFRICAN AMERICAN		ASIAN AMERICAN		HISPANIC		NATIVE AMERICAN		CAUCASIAN		FOREIGN		OTHER		TOTAL BY GENDER		TOTAL DEGREES
		M	F	M	F	M	F	M	F	M	F	M	F	M	F	M	F	
University of Alaska Fairbanks	AK	0	0	2	0	0	0	0	0	1	0	3	0	0	0	6	0	6
Colorado School of Mines	CO	0	1	0	0	3	0	0	0	9	1	10	1	0	0	22	3	25
University of Houston, Cullen School of Engineering	TX	2	1	2	0	0	0	0	0	5	0	8	1	1	1	18	3	21
University of Kansas	KS	0	0	0	0	0	0	0	0	0	0	7	0	0	0	7	0	7
Louisiana State University	LA	1	0	0	0	0	0	0	0	1	0	5	3	0	0	7	3	10
University of Missouri - Rolla	MO	0	0	0	0	0	0	0	0	1	0	2	0	0	0	3	0	3
New Mexico Institute of Mining & Technology	NM	0	0	0	0	0	0	0	0	1	0	7	2	0	0	8	2	10
University of Oklahoma	OK	2	0	0	0	0	1	0	0	1	0	19	3	0	0	21	4	25
University of Southern California	CA	0	0	0	0	0	0	0	0	1	0	1	1	0	0	2	1	3
Texas A&M University	TX	1	1	1	0	1	0	0	0	5	1	24	7	0	0	32	9	41
Texas A&M University - Kingsville	TX	1	0	0	0	0	0	0	0	0	0	11	1	0	0	12	1	13
Texas Tech University	TX	0	0	1	0	0	0	0	0	6	0	0	0	0	0	7	0	7
The University of Texas at Austin	TX	0	0	1	1	0	1	0	0	8	0	25	5	0	0	34	7	41
University of Tulsa	OK	0	0	0	0	0	0	0	0	0	0	19	5	1	0	20	5	25
West Virginia University	WV	0	0	0	0	0	0	0	0	0	0	4	0	0	0	4	0	4
Totals:		7	3	7	1	4	2	0	0	38	2	145	29	2	1	203	38	241

ALA-WES

PETROLEUM ENGINEERING

INSTITUTION		AFRICAN AMERICAN		ASIAN AMERICAN		HISPANIC		NATIVE AMERICAN		CAUCASIAN		FOREIGN		OTHER		TOTAL BY GENDER		TOTAL DEGREES
		M	F	M	F	M	F	M	F	M	F	M	F	M	F	M	F	
Air Force Institute of Technology	OH	0	0	0	0	0	0	0	0	7	0	0	0	7	7	14	7	21
The University of Akron	OH	0	0	0	0	0	0	0	0	0	0	19	4	0	0	19	4	23
University of Alabama at Birmingham	AL	0	1	1	0	0	0	0	0	6	2	8	1	0	0	15	4	19
The University of Alabama in Huntsville	AL	1	1	0	0	0	0	0	0	6	2	7	0	0	0	14	3	17
The University of Alabama	AL	1	1	9	1	0	0	0	0	3	1	10	3	0	0	23	6	29
Alfred University, NY State College of Ceramics	NY	0	0	0	0	0	0	0	0	3	0	0	0	0	0	3	0	3
The University of Arizona	AZ	0	0	1	0	1	0	0	0	14	2	35	6	0	0	51	8	59
Arizona State University	AZ	0	0	6	1	0	1	0	0	12	2	65	11	2	0	85	15	100
University of Arkansas	AR	1	0	2	0	0	0	0	0	6	0	8	2	0	1	17	3	20
Auburn University	AL	0	1	1	1	0	0	0	0	11	1	31	6	0	0	43	9	52
Boston University	MA	1	1	7	2	1	0	0	0	8	5	14	3	0	0	31	11	42
Brigham Young University	UT	0	0	0	0	0	0	0	0	0	0	8	1	6	0	14	1	15
Brown University	RI	0	1	0	0	0	0	0	0	2	1	4	2	0	0	6	4	10
California Institute of Technology	CA	1	0	2	1	0	0	0	0	18	8	38	10	0	0	59	19	78
University of California, Berkeley	CA	2	0	25	14	4	1	0	0	48	8	77	15	10	2	166	40	206
University of California, Davis	CA	0	0	5	0	1	0	0	0	22	6	31	6	6	3	65	15	80
University of California, Irvine	CA	0	0	0	0	0	0	0	0	0	0	0	0	55	15	55	15	70
University of California, Los Angeles	CA	0	0	14	5	0	1	0	0	14	3	87	12	4	2	119	23	142
University of California, Riverside	CA	0	1	0	0	0	0	0	0	1	0	0	0	25	10	26	11	37
University of California, San Diego	CA	0	0	6	1	0	1	1	0	26	8	42	13	6	2	81	25	106
University of California, Santa Barbara	CA	0	0	4	1	0	0	1	0	22	6	49	14	8	2	84	23	107
University of California-Santa Cruz	CA	0	0	4	0	0	0	0	0	5	0	12	4	0	1	21	5	26
Carnegie Mellon University	PA	0	0	2	2	2	1	0	0	17	2	39	15	4	2	64	22	86
Case Western Reserve University	OH	0	0	7	3	0	0	0	0	18	4	31	6	1	0	57	13	70
The Catholic University of America	DC	0	0	0	0	0	0	0	0	0	1	3	0	0	0	3	1	4
University of Central Florida	FL	0	0	0	0	2	1	1	0	10	5	31	5	0	0	44	11	55
University of Cincinnati	OH	0	0	2	0	0	0	0	0	6	1	55	13	0	0	63	14	77
Clarkson University	NY	0	0	0	0	0	0	0	0	5	2	11	5	0	0	16	7	23
Clemson University	SC	1	0	0	0	0	0	0	0	15	5	18	9	0	0	34	14	48
Cleveland State University	OH	0	0	0	0	2	0	0	0	0	0	2	0	5	1	9	1	10
Colorado School of Mines	CO	0	0	0	0	1	0	0	0	14	7	12	5	0	0	27	12	39
Colorado State University	CO	0	0	0	0	1	0	0	0	8	0	0	0	16	2	25	2	27
University of Colorado at Boulder	CO	1	0	0	1	2	0	1	0	36	10	22	3	0	0	62	14	76
University of Colorado at Colorado Springs	CO	0	0	0	0	0	0	0	0	4	1	1	1	0	0	5	2	7
Columbia University	NY	0	1	1	3	0	0	0	0	6	2	38	15	7	4	52	25	77
University of Connecticut	CT	0	0	1	1	3	1	0	0	5	1	24	11	2	1	35	15	50
Cornell University	NY	0	1	4	3	3	1	0	0	26	8	56	17	1	2	90	32	122
Dartmouth College	NH	0	0	0	0	0	0	0	0	0	0	3	2	2	1	5	3	8
University of Dayton	OH	0	0	0	0	0	0	0	0	4	1	13	0	0	0	17	1	18
University of Delaware	DE	0	0	1	1	1	1	0	0	12	2	32	9	0	0	46	13	59
University of Denver	CO	0	0	0	0	0	0	0	0	1	0	1	0	0	0	2	0	2
Drexel University	PA	0	1	5	1	0	0	0	0	15	2	20	4	2	1	42	9	51
Duke University Pratt School of Engineering	NC	0	0	0	0	0	0	0	0	0	0	0	0	35	8	35	8	43
University of Florida	FL	2	3	3	4	3	2	0	0	31	11	101	21	0	0	140	41	181
Florida Atlantic University	FL	0	0	2	0	0	0	0	0	1	0	5	1	0	0	8	1	9

DOCTORAL DEGREES AWARDED   AIR-FLO

INSTITUTION		AFRICAN AMERICAN M	F	ASIAN AMERICAN M	F	HISPANIC M	F	NATIVE AMERICAN M	F	CAUCASIAN M	F	FOREIGN M	F	OTHER M	F	TOTAL BY GENDER M	F	TOTAL DEGREES
Florida Institute of Technology	FL	0	0	0	0	0	0	0	0	3	1	3	0	1	0	7	1	8
Florida International University	FL	0	0	0	0	0	1	0	0	1	0	14	2	0	0	15	3	18
FAMU-FSU College of Engineering	FL	0	4	0	0	0	0	0	0	3	0	12	3	0	0	15	7	22
George Mason University	VA	0	0	0	4	0	0	0	0	5	0	10	1	0	0	15	5	20
The George Washington University	DC	1	2	4	0	1	0	0	1	19	8	19	6	0	0	44	17	61
University of Georgia	GA	0	0	0	0	0	0	0	0	0	0	2	0	0	0	2	0	2
Georgia Institute of Technology	GA	10	1	11	8	2	0	0	0	59	19	137	25	4	0	223	53	276
Harvard University	MA	0	0	0	1	0	0	0	0	9	5	13	1	0	0	22	7	29
University of Hawaii at Manoa	HI	0	0	6	1	0	0	0	0	0	0	37	10	4	2	47	13	60
University of Houston, Cullen School of Engineering	TX	0	0	2	0	1	0	0	0	7	0	29	5	2	0	41	5	46
Howard University	DC	0	0	0	0	0	0	0	0	0	0	1	0	0	0	1	0	1
University of Idaho	ID	1	0	1	0	0	0	0	0	5	0	0	0	4	0	11	0	11
Idaho State University	ID	0	0	0	0	0	0	0	0	0	1	1	0	0	0	1	1	2
Illinois Institute of Technology	IL	0	0	1	0	0	0	0	0	1	1	19	5	0	0	21	5	26
University of Illinois at Chicago	IL	0	0	27	7	0	0	1	0	11	1	0	0	0	0	39	8	47
University of Illinois at Urbana-Champaign	IL	2	1	13	1	0	1	1	0	55	8	133	23	2	0	206	34	240
The University of Iowa	IA	0	1	0	0	0	0	0	0	5	4	23	3	0	0	28	8	36
Iowa State University	IA	1	0	0	0	0	0	0	0	12	6	49	13	2	1	64	20	84
The Johns Hopkins University	MD	0	1	1	2	1	0	0	0	18	5	28	10	0	0	48	18	66
University of Kansas	KS	0	0	7	1	0	0	0	0	2	0	2	0	0	0	11	1	12
Kansas State University	KS	0	0	0	0	0	0	0	0	2	0	11	3	0	0	13	3	16
University of Kentucky	KY	1	1	1	2	0	0	0	0	3	0	16	5	3	2	24	10	34
Lamar University	TX	0	0	1	0	0	0	0	0	1	0	1	0	0	0	3	0	3
Lawrence Technological University	MI	0	0	0	0	0	0	0	0	2	1	0	0	0	0	2	1	3
Lehigh University	PA	0	0	0	0	0	1	0	0	0	0	22	6	7	1	29	8	37
Louisiana State University	LA	0	0	0	0	0	0	0	0	3	0	26	6	1	0	30	6	36
Louisiana Tech University	LA	0	0	0	0	0	0	0	0	3	0	11	7	0	0	14	7	21
University of Louisiana at Lafayette	LA	0	0	0	0	0	0	0	0	0	0	4	0	0	0	4	0	4
University of Louisville	KY	0	0	1	0	0	0	0	0	5	0	18	6	0	0	24	6	30
University of Maine	ME	0	0	0	0	0	0	0	0	2	1	3	0	0	0	5	1	6
Marquette University	WI	0	0	0	0	0	0	0	0	4	1	2	1	0	0	6	2	8
University of Maryland, Baltimore County	MD	1	0	0	0	0	0	0	0	2	0	11	8	0	0	14	8	22
University of Maryland, College Park	MD	2	2	6	2	0	0	0	0	14	5	78	17	3	1	103	27	130
Massachusetts Institute of Technology	MA	6	0	18	9	0	0	0	0	80	17	101	34	21	1	227	61	288
University of Massachusetts Amherst	MA	0	0	0	1	0	0	1	0	3	1	11	4	1	0	15	6	21
University of Massachusetts Dartmouth	MA	0	0	0	0	0	0	0	0	1	0	3	0	0	0	4	0	4
University of Massachusetts Lowell	MA	0	0	1	0	0	0	0	0	0	0	15	2	0	0	16	2	18
The University of Memphis	TN	0	0	0	0	0	0	0	0	0	0	3	1	0	0	3	1	4
University of Miami	FL	0	0	0	0	0	0	0	0	0	0	11	1	0	0	11	1	12
University of Michigan	MI	2	1	18	4	3	0	0	0	50	10	109	19	2	0	184	34	218
Michigan State University	MI	0	1	5	1	1	1	0	0	6	0	42	4	0	0	54	7	61
Michigan Technological University	MI	1	0	1	0	0	0	1	0	5	3	15	3	0	0	23	3	26
University of Minnesota -Twin Cities	MN	1	0	6	3	0	0	0	0	24	2	69	26	0	0	100	31	131
The University of Mississippi	MS	0	0	1	0	0	0	0	0	2	1	2	3	0	0	5	4	9
Mississippi State University	MS	0	0	1	1	0	0	0	0	1	0	16	1	0	0	18	2	20

FLO-MIS

DOCTORAL DEGREES AWARDED

DOCTORAL DEGREES AWARDED IN ENGINEERING, 2005-2006

INSTITUTION		AFRICAN AMERICAN M	F	ASIAN AMERICAN M	F	HISPANIC M	F	NATIVE AMERICAN M	F	CAUCASIAN M	F	FOREIGN M	F	OTHER M	F	TOTAL BY GENDER M	F	TOTAL DEGREES
University of Missouri-Columbia	MO	0	0	0	0	2	1	0	0	3	1	22	3	0	1	27	6	33
University of Missouri - Kansas City	MO	0	0	0	0	0	0	0	0	0	0	8	0	0	0	8	0	8
University of Missouri - Rolla	MO	1	0	0	0	1	0	0	0	7	3	31	9	0	0	40	12	52
Montana State University	MT	0	0	0	0	0	0	0	0	2	2	2	1	0	0	4	3	7
Morgan State University	MD	4	2	1	0	0	0	0	0	0	0	0	1	0	0	5	3	8
University of Nebraska, Lincoln	NE	0	1	1	0	0	0	0	0	2	1	11	2	0	0	14	4	18
University of Nevada, Las Vegas	NV	0	0	0	0	0	0	0	0	2	1	5	0	1	0	8	1	9
University of Nevada, Reno	NV	0	0	0	0	1	0	0	0	3	2	14	0	0	0	18	2	20
University of New Hampshire	NH	0	0	0	0	0	0	0	0	2	0	2	1	0	0	4	1	5
New Jersey Institute of Technology	NJ	0	0	1	0	0	0	0	0	3	0	21	12	0	0	25	12	37
The University of New Mexico	NM	0	0	1	0	2	0	0	0	5	3	25	4	0	0	33	7	40
New Mexico State University	NM	0	0	0	0	0	0	0	0	1	0	3	0	3	0	7	0	7
University of New Orleans	LA	0	0	1	0	0	0	0	0	1	1	2	3	0	0	4	4	8
City College of the City University of New York	NY	2	0	4	1	0	0	0	0	0	0	11	4	3	1	20	6	26
The State University of New York at Binghamton	NY	0	0	0	0	0	0	0	0	0	0	13	1	3	0	16	1	17
State University of New York at Buffalo	NY	0	0	0	0	0	0	0	0	8	1	33	8	2	0	43	9	52
SUNY College of Environmental Science and Forestry	NY	0	0	0	0	0	0	0	0	1	0	5	1	0	0	6	1	7
Stony Brook University	NY	3	0	2	1	1	0	0	0	7	3	38	16	0	0	51	20	71
North Carolina A & T State University	NC	2	3	1	0	0	0	0	0	0	0	4	2	0	0	7	5	12
North Carolina State University	NC	0	0	3	3	1	0	0	0	22	5	69	16	0	0	95	24	119
University of North Carolina at Chapel Hill	NC	0	0	0	0	0	0	0	0	2	0	2	1	0	0	4	1	5
University of North Carolina, Charlotte	NC	1	0	0	0	0	0	0	0	2	2	4	2	0	0	7	4	11
North Dakota State University	ND	0	0	4	0	0	0	0	0	1	0	0	0	0	0	5	0	5
University of North Texas	TX	0	0	0	0	0	0	0	0	3	0	4	0	3	1	10	1	11
Northeastern University	MA	0	0	1	0	0	0	0	0	4	0	11	8	1	2	17	10	27
Northwestern University	IL	0	1	7	6	1	1	0	0	32	10	48	10	3	0	91	28	119
University of Notre Dame	IN	1	2	1	0	0	0	0	0	15	4	19	7	0	0	36	13	49
Oakland University	MI	1	0	1	0	0	0	0	0	4	0	3	1	0	0	9	1	10
The Ohio State University	OH	0	0	1	0	0	0	0	0	18	2	88	27	0	0	107	29	136
Ohio University	OH	0	0	0	0	0	0	0	0	1	0	9	0	0	0	10	0	10
University of Oklahoma	OK	0	0	0	1	0	0	0	0	6	1	16	3	1	0	23	5	28
Oklahoma State University	OK	0	0	0	0	0	0	0	0	6	0	16	2	0	0	22	2	24
Old Dominion University	VA	0	0	0	0	0	0	0	0	5	1	8	2	1	0	14	3	17
OGI School of Science & Engineering at OHSU	OR	0	0	1	0	2	0	0	0	6	2	3	0	0	0	12	2	14
Oregon State University	OR	0	0	0	0	0	0	0	0	8	1	18	5	0	0	26	6	32
University of Pennsylvania	PA	0	1	4	0	0	0	0	0	12	4	17	8	2	0	35	13	48
The Pennsylvania State University	PA	1	0	3	2	0	0	0	0	45	10	92	23	0	0	141	35	176
University of Pittsburgh	PA	0	1	2	1	0	0	0	0	17	2	20	6	0	0	39	10	49
Polytechnic University	NY	0	0	1	1	0	0	0	0	2	0	13	1	3	0	19	2	21
Portland State University	OR	0	0	0	1	0	0	0	0	0	0	5	0	0	0	5	1	6
Princeton University	NJ	0	0	7	5	0	0	0	0	18	3	35	13	0	0	60	21	81
University of Puerto Rico, Mayaguez Campus	PR	0	0	0	0	7	1	0	0	0	0	0	0	0	0	7	1	8
Purdue University	IN	2	1	3	1	4	0	0	0	21	8	128	16	3	5	161	31	192
Rensselaer Polytechnic Institute	NY	0	1	6	0	2	0	0	0	16	2	45	13	0	1	69	17	86
University of Rhode Island	RI	0	0	0	0	0	0	0	0	3	0	5	2	0	0	8	2	10

DOCTORAL DEGREES AWARDED   MIS-RHO

INSTITUTION		AFRICAN AMERICAN		ASIAN AMERICAN		HISPANIC		NATIVE AMERICAN		CAUCASIAN		FOREIGN		OTHER		TOTAL BY GENDER		TOTAL DEGREES
		M	F	M	F	M	F	M	F	M	F	M	F	M	F	M	F	
William Marsh Rice University	TX	0	1	4	1	0	2	0	0	16	8	26	15	0	0	46	27	73
University of Rochester	NY	0	0	0	0	0	0	0	0	6	0	14	5	0	0	20	5	25
Rochester Institute of Technology	NY	0	0	1	0	0	0	0	0	1	0	2	0	0	0	4	0	4
Rutgers, The State University of New Jersey	NJ	0	0	1	1	0	3	0	0	8	3	21	2	0	0	30	9	39
Santa Clara University	CA	0	0	2	0	0	0	0	0	0	0	3	0	0	0	5	0	5
University of South Carolina	SC	1	0	0	0	0	0	0	0	7	2	23	6	0	0	31	8	39
South Dakota School of Mines and Technology	SD	0	0	0	0	0	0	0	0	1	1	1	0	0	0	2	1	3
University of South Florida	FL	0	0	0	0	0	0	0	0	2	0	1	0	0	0	3	0	3
University of Southern California	CA	0	0	5	1	1	0	0	0	11	2	100	23	7	1	124	27	151
Southern Illinois University Carbondale	IL	0	0	0	0	0	0	0	0	0	1	6	0	0	0	6	1	7
Southern Methodist University	TX	0	0	0	0	0	0	0	0	0	2	14	0	0	0	14	2	16
Stanford University	CA	2	1	18	5	3	1	0	0	61	15	98	25	14	0	196	47	243
Stevens Institute of Technology	NJ	0	0	0	0	0	0	0	0	2	0	10	6	0	0	12	6	18
Syracuse University	NY	0	0	0	1	0	0	0	0	1	0	14	1	0	0	15	2	17
Tennessee Technological University	TN	0	0	0	0	0	0	0	0	2	0	4	1	0	0	6	1	7
University of Tennessee, Chattanooga	TN	0	0	0	0	0	0	0	0	1	0	0	0	0	0	1	0	1
University of Tennessee, Knoxville	TN	0	0	0	0	0	0	0	0	12	1	17	11	0	0	29	12	41
Texas A&M University	TX	1	1	3	2	0	2	0	0	13	2	110	18	1	0	128	25	153
Texas A&M University - Kingsville	TX	1	0	0	0	0	0	0	0	1	1	1	0	0	0	3	1	4
Texas Tech University	TX	0	0	0	0	1	1	0	0	7	0	23	2	0	0	31	3	34
The University of Texas at Arlington	TX	0	0	13	3	0	0	0	0	7	0	22	5	0	0	42	8	50
The University of Texas at Austin	TX	1	0	7	4	1	0	0	0	33	15	114	16	0	0	156	35	191
The University of Texas at Dallas	TX	0	0	1	0	0	0	0	0	5	0	35	3	0	0	41	3	44
University of Texas at El Paso	TX	0	0	0	0	1	0	0	0	0	0	3	0	0	0	4	0	4
The University of Toledo	OH	0	0	0	0	0	0	0	0	2	0	11	7	0	0	13	7	20
Tufts University	MA	0	0	0	0	0	0	0	0	0	0	3	4	1	1	4	5	9
Tulane University	LA	0	0	0	0	0	0	0	0	0	0	5	0	4	1	9	1	10
University of Tulsa	OK	0	0	0	0	0	0	0	0	0	0	7	2	0	0	7	2	9
Tuskegee University	AL	2	0	0	0	0	0	0	0	0	0	0	0	0	0	2	0	2
University of Utah	UT	0	0	1	0	0	0	0	0	16	0	28	4	1	1	46	5	51
Utah State University	UT	0	0	0	0	0	0	0	0	10	0	8	0	0	0	18	0	18
Vanderbilt University	TN	0	0	0	0	0	0	0	0	12	3	16	6	1	2	29	11	40
University of Vermont	VT	0	0	0	0	0	0	0	0	0	1	1	1	0	0	1	2	3
University of Virginia	VA	1	0	1	2	0	0	0	0	17	5	17	8	0	0	36	15	51
Virginia Commonwealth University	VA	0	0	4	2	0	0	0	0	4	1	0	0	0	1	8	4	12
Virginia Polytechnic Institute and State University	VA	1	2	3	2	2	0	0	0	38	9	75	17	0	0	119	30	149
University of Washington	WA	0	0	7	2	0	1	0	0	25	7	44	14	5	1	82	25	107
Washington State University	WA	0	0	0	0	0	0	0	0	4	0	16	5	7	0	27	5	32
Washington University	MO	0	0	0	0	0	0	0	0	8	1	25	6	4	0	37	7	44
Wayne State University	MI	1	0	6	0	0	0	4	0	1	1	17	3	0	0	29	4	33
West Virginia University	WV	0	0	0	0	0	0	0	0	7	1	23	2	0	0	30	3	33
Western Michigan University	MI	0	0	1	0	0	0	0	0	1	0	4	1	0	0	6	1	7
Wichita State University	KS	0	0	2	0	0	0	0	0	0	0	3	1	0	0	5	1	6
University of Wisconsin, Madison	WI	2	2	1	0	2	2	0	0	18	7	48	7	7	1	78	19	97
University of Wisconsin, Milwaukee	WI	0	0	1	0	0	0	0	0	2	0	9	1	0	0	12	1	13

RIC-WIS

DOCTORAL DEGREES AWARDED

DOCTORAL DEGREES AWARDED IN ENGINEERING, 2005-2006

INSTITUTION		AFRICAN AMERICAN		ASIAN AMERICAN		HISPANIC		NATIVE AMERICAN		CAUCASIAN		FOREIGN		OTHER		TOTAL BY GENDER		TOTAL DEGREES
		M	F	M	F	M	F	M	F	M	F	M	F	M	F	M	F	
Worcester Polytechnic Institute	MA	0	0	0	0	0	0	0	0	3	2	9	2	0	0	12	4	16
Wright State University	OH	0	0	1	0	0	0	0	0	4	1	6	1	0	0	11	2	13
University of Wyoming	WY	0	0	0	0	0	0	0	0	1	0	7	1	0	0	8	1	9
Yale University/Faculty of Engineering	CT	0	0	0	0	0	0	0	0	0	0	0	0	27	4	27	4	31
Totals:		71	48	388	143	72	30	12	1	1,582	384	4,167	985	369	99	6,661	1,690	8,351
CANADIAN INSTITUTIONS:																		
University of Alberta	AB	0	0	0	0	0	0	0	0	0	0	0	0	45	5	45	5	50
University of Calgary	AB	0	0	0	0	0	0	0	0	0	0	14	0	14	3	28	3	31
Concordia University, Faculty of Engr. and Comp. Sci.	PQ	0	0	0	0	0	0	0	0	0	0	8	1	18	2	26	3	29
Ecole Polytechnique de Montreal	PQ	0	0	0	0	0	0	0	0	0	0	0	0	34	8	34	8	42
Ecole de Technologie Superieure	PQ	0	0	0	0	0	0	0	0	0	0	0	0	10	3	10	3	13
McGill University, Faculty of Engineering	PQ	0	0	0	0	0	0	0	0	0	0	0	0	42	10	42	10	52
University of Ottawa, Faculty of Engineering	ON	0	0	0	0	0	0	0	0	0	0	1	1	19	4	20	5	25
University of Waterloo	ON	0	0	0	0	0	0	0	0	0	0	0	0	57	5	57	5	62
Totals:		0	0	0	0	0	0	0	0	0	0	23	2	239	41	262	42	304

DOCTORAL DEGREES AWARDED

WOR-YAL

INSTITUTION		AFRICAN AMERICAN		ASIAN AMERICAN		HISPANIC		NATIVE AMERICAN		CAUCASIAN		FOREIGN		OTHER		TOTAL BY GENDER		TOTAL DEGREES
		M	F	M	F	M	F	M	F	M	F	M	F	M	F	M	F	
Air Force Institute of Technology	OH	0	0	0	0	0	0	0	0	2	0	0	0	4	0	6	0	6
The University of Alabama	AL	0	0	1	0	0	0	0	0	1	0	1	0	0	0	3	0	3
The University of Arizona	AZ	0	0	0	0	0	0	0	0	2	0	0	0	0	0	2	0	2
California Institute of Technology	CA	0	0	0	0	0	0	0	0	0	0	4	1	0	0	4	1	5
University of California, Los Angeles	CA	0	0	1	0	0	0	0	0	0	0	1	0	0	0	2	0	2
University of California, San Diego	CA	0	0	0	0	0	0	0	0	0	1	2	1	0	0	2	2	4
University of Cincinnati	OH	0	0	0	0	0	0	0	0	0	0	6	1	0	0	6	1	7
University of Colorado at Boulder	CO	1	0	0	0	0	0	0	0	8	0	2	0	0	0	11	0	11
University of Colorado at Colorado Springs	CO	0	0	0	0	0	0	0	0	4	1	1	1	0	0	5	2	7
Cornell University	NY	0	0	0	0	0	0	0	0	1	0	2	1	0	0	3	1	4
University of Florida	FL	0	0	0	0	0	0	0	0	2	0	10	2	0	0	12	2	14
Georgia Institute of Technology	GA	1	0	0	0	0	0	0	0	6	0	16	2	0	0	23	2	25
University of Illinois at Chicago	IL	0	0	0	0	0	0	0	0	1	0	0	0	0	0	1	0	1
University of Illinois at Urbana-Champaign	IL	0	0	0	0	0	0	0	0	0	0	2	0	0	0	2	0	2
Iowa State University	IA	1	0	0	0	0	0	0	0	0	0	2	3	0	0	3	3	6
University of Kansas	KS	0	0	1	0	0	0	0	0	0	0	1	0	0	0	2	0	2
University of Maryland, College Park	MD	0	0	2	0	0	0	0	0	3	1	6	0	0	0	11	1	12
Massachusetts Institute of Technology	MA	1	0	1	0	0	0	0	0	1	3	8	3	1	0	12	6	18
University of Michigan	MI	0	0	2	0	0	0	0	0	6	0	9	0	0	0	17	0	17
University of Minnesota - Twin Cities	MN	0	0	0	0	0	0	0	0	1	0	0	0	0	0	1	0	1
State University of New York at Buffalo	NY	0	0	0	0	0	0	0	0	0	0	1	0	1	0	2	0	2
North Carolina State University	NC	0	0	0	0	0	0	0	0	1	1	1	0	0	0	2	1	3
University of Oklahoma	OK	0	0	0	1	0	0	0	0	0	0	1	0	0	0	1	1	2
Old Dominion University	VA	0	0	0	0	0	0	0	0	0	0	1	1	1	0	2	1	3
The Pennsylvania State University	PA	0	0	0	0	0	0	0	0	2	0	7	0	0	0	9	0	9
Purdue University	IN	1	0	0	0	0	0	0	0	3	1	9	0	1	0	14	1	15
University of Southern California	CA	0	0	1	1	0	0	0	0	2	0	5	1	0	0	8	2	10
Stanford University	CA	0	0	3	0	0	0	0	0	5	2	7	2	0	0	15	4	19
Texas A&M University	TX	0	0	0	0	0	0	0	0	0	0	8	0	0	0	8	0	8
The University of Texas at Arlington	TX	0	0	0	0	0	0	0	0	1	0	1	0	0	0	2	0	2
The University of Texas at Austin	TX	0	0	0	0	0	0	0	0	2	0	3	0	0	0	5	0	5
Virginia Polytechnic Institute and State University	VA	0	0	0	0	0	0	0	0	3	0	6	1	0	0	9	1	10
University of Washington	WA	0	0	0	0	0	0	0	0	4	0	0	0	0	0	4	0	4
Washington University	MO	0	0	0	0	0	0	0	0	0	0	1	0	0	0	1	0	1
West Virginia University	WV	0	0	0	0	0	0	0	0	0	0	2	0	0	0	2	0	2
Totals:		5	0	12	2	0	0	0	0	61	10	126	20	8	0	212	32	244

AEROSPACE ENGINEERING   AIR-WES

DOCTORAL DEGREES AWARDED IN AGRICULTURAL ENGINEERING, 2005-2006

INSTITUTION		AFRICAN AMERICAN		ASIAN AMERICAN		HISPANIC		NATIVE AMERICAN		CAUCASIAN		FOREIGN		OTHER		TOTAL BY GENDER		TOTAL DEGREES
		M	F	M	F	M	F	M	F	M	F	M	F	M	F	M	F	
The University of Arizona	AZ	0	0	0	0	0	0	0	0	1	0	2	1	0	0	3	1	4
University of California, Davis	CA	0	0	0	0	0	0	0	0	2	1	5	0	0	0	7	1	8
Clemson University	SC	0	0	0	0	0	0	0	0	1	1	1	0	0	0	2	1	3
Cornell University	NY	0	1	0	0	0	0	0	0	2	0	2	0	0	0	4	1	5
University of Florida	FL	0	0	0	0	0	0	0	0	1	1	1	3	0	0	2	4	6
University of Idaho	ID	0	0	0	0	0	0	0	0	0	0	0	0	1	0	1	0	1
University of Illinois at Urbana-Champaign	IL	0	1	1	0	0	1	0	0	0	0	1	1	0	0	2	3	5
Iowa State University	IA	0	0	0	0	0	0	0	0	2	2	1	2	1	1	4	5	9
Kansas State University	KS	0	0	0	0	0	0	0	0	0	0	1	0	0	0	1	0	1
University of Kentucky	KY	0	0	0	0	0	0	0	0	0	0	0	0	1	1	1	1	2
Michigan State University	MI	0	0	0	0	0	0	0	0	0	0	1	0	0	0	1	0	1
The Ohio State University	OH	0	0	0	0	0	0	0	0	2	0	1	1	0	0	3	1	4
Oklahoma State University	OK	0	0	0	0	0	0	0	0	0	0	1	1	0	0	1	1	2
Purdue University	IN	0	1	0	0	1	0	0	0	0	0	4	1	0	0	5	2	7
University of Tennessee, Knoxville	TN	0	0	0	0	0	0	0	0	0	0	0	3	0	0	0	3	3
Texas A&M University	TX	0	0	0	0	0	0	0	0	1	0	0	1	1	0	2	1	3
Utah State University	UT	0	0	0	0	0	0	0	0	0	0	1	0	0	0	1	0	1
Virginia Polytechnic Institute and State University	VA	0	0	0	0	0	0	0	0	0	0	1	0	0	0	1	0	1
Totals:		0	3	1	0	1	1	0	0	12	5	23	14	4	2	41	25	66

AGRICULTURAL ENGINEERING   ARI-VIR

DOCTORAL DEGREES AWARDED IN ARCHITECTURAL ENGINEERING, 2005-2006

INSTITUTION		AFRICAN AMERICAN		ASIAN AMERICAN		HISPANIC		NATIVE AMERICAN		CAUCASIAN		FOREIGN		OTHER		TOTAL BY GENDER		TOTAL DEGREES
		M	F	M	F	M	F	M	F	M	F	M	F	M	F	M	F	
The Pennsylvania State University	PA	0	0	0	0	0	0	0	0	1	0	1	0	0	0	2	0	2
Totals:		0	0	0	0	0	0	0	0	1	0	1	0	0	0	2	0	2

PEN-PEN

ARCHITECTURAL ENGINEERING

DOCTORAL DEGREES AWARDED IN BIOMEDICAL ENGINEERING, 2005-2006

INSTITUTION		AFRICAN AMERICAN		ASIAN AMERICAN		HISPANIC		NATIVE AMERICAN		CAUCASIAN		FOREIGN		OTHER		TOTAL BY GENDER		TOTAL DEGREES
		M	F	M	F	M	F	M	F	M	F	M	F	M	F	M	F	
The University of Akron	OH	0	0	0	0	0	0	0	0	0	0	1	0	0	0	1	0	1
University of Alabama at Birmingham	AL	0	1	0	0	0	0	0	0	2	1	3	1	0	0	5	3	8
The University of Arizona	AZ	0	0	0	0	0	0	0	0	2	1	0	1	0	0	2	2	4
Arizona State University	AZ	0	0	0	0	0	1	0	0	0	1	0	1	0	0	0	3	3
Boston University	MA	1	0	1	1	1	0	0	0	4	4	2	2	0	0	9	7	16
California Institute of Technology	CA	0	0	0	0	0	0	0	0	1	0	0	0	0	0	1	0	1
University of California, Berkeley	CA	0	0	3	1	0	0	0	0	1	0	0	1	2	0	6	2	8
University of California, Davis	CA	0	0	0	0	0	0	0	0	1	2	0	0	0	2	1	4	5
University of California, Irvine	CA	0	0	0	0	0	0	0	0	0	0	0	0	5	2	5	2	7
University of California, Los Angeles	CA	0	0	3	2	0	0	0	0	2	1	4	2	2	0	11	5	16
University of California, San Diego	CA	0	0	1	0	0	0	0	0	6	2	0	1	1	1	8	4	12
Carnegie Mellon University	PA	0	0	0	0	0	0	0	0	1	0	0	1	0	0	1	1	2
Case Western Reserve University	OH	0	0	2	1	0	0	0	0	6	0	4	2	0	0	12	3	15
Clemson University	SC	0	0	0	0	0	0	0	0	2	1	0	1	0	0	2	2	4
Cleveland State University	OH	0	0	0	0	0	0	0	0	0	0	0	0	3	1	3	1	4
Columbia University	NY	0	1	0	0	0	0	0	0	0	1	0	1	0	0	0	3	3
University of Connecticut	CT	0	0	0	0	1	1	0	0	1	1	0	1	0	0	2	3	5
Cornell University	NY	0	0	1	0	0	0	0	0	2	0	0	1	0	0	3	1	4
Drexel University	PA	0	1	0	1	0	0	0	0	2	0	0	0	0	0	2	2	4
Duke University Pratt School of Engineering	NC	0	0	0	0	0	0	0	0	0	0	0	0	11	5	11	5	16
University of Florida	FL	0	0	0	0	0	0	0	0	1	2	0	0	0	0	1	2	3
Florida International University	FL	0	0	0	0	0	0	0	0	0	0	0	1	0	0	0	1	1
FAMU-FSU College of Engineering	FL	0	0	0	0	0	0	0	0	0	0	1	0	0	0	1	0	1
Georgia Institute of Technology	GA	0	0	1	2	0	0	0	0	2	6	4	1	0	0	7	9	16
Illinois Institute of Technology	IL	0	0	0	0	0	0	0	0	0	0	2	0	0	0	2	0	2
University of Illinois at Chicago	IL	0	0	4	2	0	0	0	0	1	0	0	0	0	0	5	2	7
The University of Iowa	IA	0	0	0	0	0	0	0	0	1	0	4	1	0	0	5	1	6
The Johns Hopkins University	MD	0	1	0	1	1	0	0	0	1	1	2	3	0	0	4	6	10
University of Kentucky	KY	0	1	0	0	0	0	0	0	0	1	1	1	0	0	1	2	3
Louisiana Tech University	LA	0	0	0	0	0	0	0	0	1	0	2	1	0	0	3	1	4
Marquette University	WI	0	0	0	0	0	0	0	0	3	1	0	0	0	0	3	1	4
University of Maryland, College Park	MD	0	0	0	0	0	0	0	0	0	0	0	1	0	0	0	1	1
Massachusetts Institute of Technology	MA	0	0	2	1	0	0	0	0	2	1	5	3	2	0	11	5	16
University of Miami	FL	0	0	0	0	0	0	0	0	0	0	3	0	0	0	3	0	3
University of Michigan	MI	0	0	2	1	1	0	0	0	7	2	2	3	0	0	12	6	18
University of Minnesota-Twin Cities	MN	0	0	1	0	0	0	0	0	1	0	3	1	0	0	5	1	6
University of Missouri-Columbia	MO	0	0	0	0	0	0	0	0	1	0	1	0	0	0	2	0	2
University of Nevada, Reno	NV	0	0	0	0	0	0	0	0	1	1	0	0	0	0	1	1	2
New Jersey Institute of Technology	NJ	0	0	1	0	0	0	0	0	0	0	0	0	0	0	1	0	1
City College of the City University of New York	NY	0	0	1	0	0	0	0	0	0	0	0	0	0	1	1	1	2
Stony Brook University	NY	0	0	1	0	0	0	0	0	2	3	3	0	0	0	6	3	9
Northwestern University	IL	0	0	0	1	0	0	0	0	4	0	1	2	0	0	5	3	8
The Ohio State University	OH	0	0	1	0	0	0	0	0	0	0	1	2	0	0	2	2	4
OGI School of Science & Engineering at OHSU	OR	0	0	0	0	1	0	0	0	0	0	1	0	0	0	2	0	2
Oregon State University	OR	0	0	0	0	0	0	0	0	0	0	1	0	0	0	1	0	1

BIOMEDICAL ENGINEERING   AKR-ORE

DOCTORAL DEGREES AWARDED IN BIOMEDICAL ENGINEERING, 2005-2006

INSTITUTION		AFRICAN AMERICAN		ASIAN AMERICAN		HISPANIC		NATIVE AMERICAN		CAUCASIAN		FOREIGN		OTHER		TOTAL BY GENDER		TOTAL DEGREES
		M	F	M	F	M	F	M	F	M	F	M	F	M	F	M	F	
University of Pennsylvania	PA	0	1	2	0	0	0	0	0	4	2	2	1	1	0	9	4	13
The Pennsylvania State University	PA	0	0	0	0	0	0	0	0	1	1	1	2	0	0	2	3	5
University of Pittsburgh	PA	0	0	0	1	0	0	0	0	7	1	1	0	0	0	8	2	10
Purdue University	IN	1	0	0	1	0	0	0	0	1	1	0	2	0	1	2	5	7
Rensselaer Polytechnic Institute	NY	0	1	1	0	0	0	0	0	1	0	0	0	0	0	2	2	4
William Marsh Rice University	TX	0	1	2	0	0	0	0	0	7	3	3	2	0	0	12	6	18
University of Rochester	NY	0	0	0	0	0	0	0	0	1	0	0	1	0	0	1	1	2
Rutgers, The State University of New Jersey	NJ	0	0	0	0	0	0	0	0	3	0	2	0	0	0	5	0	5
University of Southern California	CA	0	0	1	0	1	0	0	0	2	0	5	3	0	0	9	3	12
Stanford University	CA	0	0	0	0	0	0	0	0	1	1	0	0	0	0	1	1	2
Syracuse University	NY	0	0	0	0	0	0	0	0	1	0	0	0	0	0	1	0	1
Texas A&M University	TX	0	0	0	0	0	0	0	0	1	0	6	1	0	0	7	1	8
The University of Texas at Arlington	TX	0	0	0	0	0	0	0	0	0	0	1	0	0	0	1	0	1
The University of Texas at Austin	TX	0	0	1	0	0	0	0	0	2	4	3	2	0	0	6	6	12
The University of Toledo	OH	0	0	0	0	0	0	0	0	0	0	4	1	0	0	4	1	5
Tufts University	MA	0	0	0	0	0	0	0	0	0	0	0	1	0	0	0	1	1
Tulane University	LA	0	0	0	0	0	0	0	0	0	0	0	0	2	1	2	1	3
University of Utah	UT	0	0	1	0	0	0	0	0	6	0	1	0	0	0	8	0	8
Vanderbilt University	TN	0	0	0	0	0	0	0	0	5	1	0	0	0	0	5	1	6
University of Virginia	VA	0	0	0	1	0	0	0	0	2	2	2	0	0	0	4	3	7
Virginia Commonwealth University	VA	0	0	3	1	0	0	0	0	1	1	0	0	0	0	4	2	6
Virginia Polytechnic Institute and State University	VA	0	0	0	0	0	0	0	0	0	1	1	0	0	0	1	1	2
University of Washington	WA	0	0	1	1	1	1	0	0	6	1	3	2	0	1	11	6	17
Washington University	MO	0	0	0	0	0	0	0	0	0	0	3	1	0	0	3	1	4
Wayne State University	MI	0	0	1	0	0	0	0	0	0	0	1	0	0	0	2	1	3
University of Wisconsin, Madison	WI	0	1	0	0	0	0	0	0	1	1	1	0	0	0	2	2	4
Totals:		2	9	38	19	7	3	0	0	114	51	91	57	29	16	281	155	436

CANADIAN INSTITUTIONS:

INSTITUTION		AFRICAN AMERICAN		ASIAN AMERICAN		HISPANIC		NATIVE AMERICAN		CAUCASIAN		FOREIGN		OTHER		TOTAL BY GENDER		TOTAL DEGREES
		M	F	M	F	M	F	M	F	M	F	M	F	M	F	M	F	
Ecole Polytechnique de Montreal	PQ	0	0	0	0	0	0	0	0	0	0	0	0	1	4	1	4	5
Totals:		0	0	0	0	0	0	0	0	0	0	0	0	1	4	1	4	5

PEN-WIS

BIOMEDICAL ENGINEERING

INSTITUTION		AFRICAN AMERICAN		ASIAN AMERICAN		HISPANIC		NATIVE AMERICAN		CAUCASIAN		FOREIGN		OTHER		TOTAL BY GENDER		TOTAL DEGREES
		M	F	M	F	M	F	M	F	M	F	M	F	M	F	M	F	
The University of Akron	OH	0	0	0	0	0	0	0	0	0	0	5	1	0	0	5	1	6
The University of Alabama	AL	0	0	2	1	0	0	0	0	1	0	1	0	0	0	4	1	5
The University of Arizona	AZ	0	0	0	0	0	0	0	0	2	0	5	1	0	0	7	1	8
Arizona State University	AZ	0	0	0	0	0	0	0	0	0	0	0	2	0	0	0	2	2
University of Arkansas	AR	0	0	0	0	0	0	0	0	0	0	3	1	0	0	3	1	4
Auburn University	AL	0	1	0	0	0	0	0	0	2	0	4	1	0	0	6	1	7
Brigham Young University	UT	0	0	0	0	0	0	0	0	0	0	4	1	2	0	6	1	7
California Institute of Technology	CA	0	0	1	1	0	0	0	0	5	1	2	1	0	0	8	3	11
University of California, Berkeley	CA	0	0	2	2	0	0	0	0	12	1	0	0	2	0	16	3	19
University of California, Davis	CA	0	0	0	0	0	0	0	0	2	1	2	0	1	0	5	1	6
University of California, Irvine	CA	0	0	0	0	0	0	0	0	0	0	0	0	3	1	3	1	4
University of California, Los Angeles	CA	0	0	0	2	0	1	0	0	0	0	1	0	0	1	1	4	5
University of California, Riverside	CA	0	0	0	0	0	0	0	0	0	0	0	0	7	1	7	1	8
University of California, San Diego	CA	0	0	0	0	0	0	0	0	0	1	0	0	1	0	1	1	2
University of California, Santa Barbara	CA	0	0	1	0	0	0	0	0	3	3	8	1	0	0	12	4	16
Carnegie Mellon University	PA	0	0	1	0	1	1	0	0	10	0	4	2	1	0	17	3	20
Case Western Reserve University	OH	0	0	1	0	0	0	0	0	3	1	3	0	0	0	7	1	8
University of Cincinnati	OH	0	0	0	0	0	0	0	0	1	0	1	1	0	0	2	1	3
Clarkson University	NY	0	0	0	0	0	0	0	0	2	0	3	2	0	0	5	2	7
Clemson University	SC	0	0	0	0	0	0	0	0	0	0	2	1	0	0	2	1	3
Colorado School of Mines	CO	0	0	0	0	0	0	0	0	0	0	1	0	0	0	1	0	1
Colorado State University	CO	0	0	0	0	0	0	0	0	3	0	0	0	1	1	4	1	5
University of Colorado at Boulder	CO	0	0	0	0	0	0	0	0	8	4	1	0	0	0	9	4	13
Columbia University	NY	0	0	0	0	0	0	0	0	0	0	1	1	0	0	1	1	2
University of Connecticut	CT	0	0	0	0	0	0	0	0	0	0	8	4	0	0	8	4	12
Cornell University	NY	0	0	0	0	0	0	0	0	0	1	6	1	0	0	6	2	8
University of Delaware	DE	0	0	1	0	0	1	0	0	8	0	1	2	0	0	11	3	14
Drexel University	PA	0	0	0	0	0	0	0	0	2	0	3	1	0	1	5	2	7
University of Florida	FL	0	1	0	0	0	1	0	0	3	1	5	0	0	0	8	3	11
FAMU-FSU College of Engineering	FL	0	0	0	0	0	0	0	0	0	0	4	2	0	0	4	2	6
Georgia Institute of Technology	GA	3	0	0	2	1	0	0	0	5	7	2	2	1	0	12	11	23
University of Houston, Cullen School of Engineering	TX	0	0	0	0	1	0	0	0	4	0	8	2	0	0	13	2	15
University of Idaho	ID	0	0	0	0	0	0	0	0	2	0	0	0	0	0	2	0	2
Illinois Institute of Technology	IL	0	0	0	0	0	0	0	0	1	0	2	4	0	0	3	4	7
University of Illinois at Chicago	IL	0	0	3	0	0	0	0	0	0	0	0	0	0	0	3	0	3
University of Illinois at Urbana-Champaign	IL	0	0	1	0	0	0	0	0	3	0	3	1	0	0	7	1	8
The University of Iowa	IA	0	0	0	0	0	0	0	0	1	3	1	1	0	0	2	4	6
Iowa State University	IA	0	0	0	0	0	0	0	0	1	2	2	0	0	0	3	2	5
The Johns Hopkins University	MD	0	0	1	0	0	0	0	0	5	1	3	1	0	0	9	2	11
University of Kansas	KS	0	0	1	0	0	0	0	0	0	0	0	0	0	0	1	0	1
Kansas State University	KS	0	0	0	0	0	0	0	0	0	0	0	1	0	0	0	1	1
University of Kentucky	KY	0	0	0	0	0	0	0	0	0	0	2	1	0	0	2	1	3
Lamar University	TX	0	0	1	0	0	0	0	0	0	0	0	0	0	0	1	0	1
Lehigh University	PA	0	0	0	0	0	0	0	0	0	0	1	0	0	0	1	0	1
Louisiana State University	LA	0	0	0	0	0	0	0	0	1	0	2	0	0	0	3	0	3

CHEMICAL ENGINEERING

AKR-LOU

DOCTORAL DEGREES AWARDED IN CHEMICAL ENGINEERING, 2005-2006

INSTITUTION		AFRICAN AMERICAN		ASIAN AMERICAN		HISPANIC		NATIVE AMERICAN		CAUCASIAN		FOREIGN		OTHER		TOTAL BY GENDER		TOTAL DEGREES
		M	F	M	F	M	F	M	F	M	F	M	F	M	F	M	F	
University of Louisville	KY	0	0	0	0	0	0	0	0	0	0	4	1	0	0	4	1	5
University of Maine	ME	0	0	0	0	0	0	0	0	1	0	1	0	0	0	2	0	2
University of Maryland, Baltimore County	MD	1	0	0	0	0	0	0	0	0	0	0	1	0	0	1	1	2
University of Maryland, College Park	MD	0	1	1	1	0	0	0	0	1	0	3	3	0	0	5	5	10
Massachusetts Institute of Technology	MA	0	0	2	0	0	0	1	0	13	2	6	3	5	0	27	5	32
University of Massachusetts Amherst	MA	0	0	0	1	0	0	0	0	2	0	3	3	0	0	5	4	9
University of Michigan	MI	1	0	1	1	0	0	0	0	4	2	6	2	0	0	12	5	17
Michigan State University	MI	0	1	0	0	0	0	0	0	1	1	5	1	0	0	6	3	9
Michigan Technological University	MI	0	0	0	0	0	0	0	0	0	0	1	0	0	0	1	0	1
University of Minnesota - Twin Cities	MN	1	0	1	0	0	0	0	0	5	1	8	5	0	0	15	6	21
Mississippi State University	MS	0	0	0	0	0	0	0	0	1	0	0	1	0	0	1	1	2
University of Missouri-Columbia	MO	0	0	0	0	0	0	0	0	0	1	2	0	0	0	2	1	3
University of Missouri - Rolla	MO	0	0	0	0	0	0	0	0	0	0	4	0	0	0	4	0	4
University of Nevada, Reno	NV	0	0	0	0	0	0	0	0	0	0	2	0	0	0	2	0	2
New Jersey Institute of Technology	NJ	0	0	0	0	0	0	0	0	0	0	2	0	0	0	2	0	2
The University of New Mexico	NM	0	0	0	0	0	0	0	0	0	1	6	0	0	0	6	1	7
New Mexico State University	NM	0	0	0	0	0	0	0	0	0	0	0	0	1	0	1	0	1
City College of the City University of New York	NY	0	0	1	0	0	0	0	0	0	0	2	1	0	0	3	1	4
State University of New York at Buffalo	NY	0	0	0	0	0	0	0	0	0	0	5	5	0	0	5	5	10
North Carolina State University	NC	0	0	1	0	0	0	0	0	7	1	8	2	0	0	16	3	19
Northeastern University	MA	0	0	0	0	0	0	0	0	0	0	0	1	0	1	0	2	2
Northwestern University	IL	0	1	1	2	0	1	0	0	8	2	5	1	0	0	14	7	21
University of Notre Dame	IN	0	2	0	0	0	0	0	0	8	2	0	3	0	0	8	7	15
The Ohio State University	OH	0	0	0	0	2	0	0	0	0	0	12	7	0	0	14	7	21
Ohio University	OH	0	0	0	0	0	0	0	0	0	0	1	0	0	0	1	0	1
University of Oklahoma	OK	0	0	0	0	0	0	0	0	0	0	1	1	0	0	1	1	2
Oklahoma State University	OK	0	0	0	0	0	0	0	0	1	0	2	0	0	0	3	0	3
Oregon State University	OR	0	0	0	0	0	0	0	0	1	0	2	0	0	0	3	0	3
University of Pennsylvania	PA	0	0	2	0	0	0	0	0	0	0	1	2	0	0	3	2	5
The Pennsylvania State University	PA	0	0	0	0	0	0	0	0	5	5	4	1	0	0	9	6	15
University of Pittsburgh	PA	0	0	0	0	0	0	0	0	2	0	5	1	0	0	7	1	8
Polytechnic University	NY	0	0	0	0	0	0	0	0	0	0	0	0	1	0	1	0	1
Princeton University	NJ	0	0	1	1	0	0	0	0	4	0	3	2	0	0	8	3	11
University of Puerto Rico, Mayaguez Campus	PR	0	0	0	0	2	1	0	0	0	0	0	0	0	0	2	1	3
Purdue University	IN	0	0	0	0	0	0	0	0	4	0	8	1	0	1	12	2	14
Rensselaer Polytechnic Institute	NY	0	0	2	0	0	0	0	0	0	0	4	2	0	1	6	3	9
University of Rhode Island	RI	0	0	0	0	0	0	0	0	0	0	0	1	0	0	0	1	1
William Marsh Rice University	TX	0	0	1	0	0	0	0	0	1	2	6	2	0	0	8	4	12
University of Rochester	NY	0	0	0	1	0	0	0	0	1	0	3	0	0	0	4	1	5
Rutgers, The State University of New Jersey	NJ	0	0	0	1	0	1	0	0	0	2	3	1	0	0	3	5	8
University of South Carolina	SC	0	0	0	0	0	0	0	0	2	0	5	2	0	0	7	2	9
University of Southern California	CA	0	0	1	0	0	0	0	0	0	0	8	3	0	0	9	3	12
Stanford University	CA	0	0	1	2	0	0	0	0	6	2	2	1	0	0	9	5	14
Stevens Institute of Technology	NJ	0	0	0	0	0	0	0	0	1	0	0	0	0	0	1	0	1
Syracuse University	NY	0	0	0	1	0	0	0	0	0	0	0	0	0	0	0	1	1

LOU-SYR

CHEMICAL ENGINEERING

DOCTORAL DEGREES AWARDED IN CHEMICAL ENGINEERING, 2005-2006

INSTITUTION		AFRICAN AMERICAN		ASIAN AMERICAN		HISPANIC		NATIVE AMERICAN		CAUCASIAN		FOREIGN		OTHER		TOTAL BY GENDER		TOTAL DEGREES
		M	F	M	F	M	F	M	F	M	F	M	F	M	F	M	F	
University of Tennessee, Knoxville	TN	0	0	0	0	0	0	0	0	1	0	2	2	0	0	3	2	5
Texas A&M University	TX	0	0	1	0	0	1	0	0	2	0	14	1	0	0	17	2	19
The University of Texas at Austin	TX	0	0	1	2	0	0	0	0	11	6	11	5	0	0	23	13	36
The University of Toledo	OH	0	0	0	0	0	0	0	0	0	0	2	2	0	0	2	2	4
Tufts University	MA	0	0	0	0	0	0	0	0	0	0	1	3	0	1	1	4	5
Tulane University	LA	0	0	0	0	0	0	0	0	0	0	2	0	0	0	2	0	2
University of Tulsa	OK	0	0	0	0	0	0	0	0	0	0	0	1	0	0	0	1	1
University of Utah	UT	0	0	0	0	0	0	0	0	3	0	9	1	0	0	12	1	13
Vanderbilt University	TN	0	0	0	0	0	0	0	0	3	2	3	2	0	0	6	4	10
University of Virginia	VA	0	0	1	0	0	0	0	0	2	0	0	2	0	0	3	2	5
Virginia Polytechnic Institute and State University	VA	0	0	1	0	0	0	0	0	4	2	0	1	0	0	5	3	8
University of Washington	WA	0	0	2	0	0	0	0	0	2	2	4	1	0	0	8	3	11
Washington University	MO	0	0	0	0	0	0	0	0	0	1	7	1	0	0	7	2	9
Wayne State University	MI	0	0	0	0	0	0	0	0	0	0	1	1	0	0	1	1	2
West Virginia University	WV	0	0	0	0	0	0	0	0	0	0	2	0	0	0	2	0	2
University of Wisconsin, Madison	WI	0	0	0	0	0	1	0	0	8	1	7	0	1	0	16	2	18
Worcester Polytechnic Institute	MA	0	0	0	0	0	0	0	0	1	1	2	0	0	0	3	1	4
University of Wyoming	WY	0	0	0	0	0	0	0	0	0	0	0	1	0	0	0	1	1
Totals:		6	7	38	20	7	11	1	0	208	64	313	123	27	9	600	234	834
CANADIAN INSTITUTIONS:																		
University of Alberta	AB	0	0	0	0	0	0	0	0	0	0	0	0	8	2	8	2	10
University of Calgary	AB	0	0	0	0	0	0	0	0	0	0	0	0	1	1	1	1	2
Ecole Polytechnique de Montreal	PQ	0	0	0	0	0	0	0	0	0	0	0	0	4	0	4	0	4
McGill University, Faculty of Engineering	PQ	0	0	0	0	0	0	0	0	0	0	0	0	5	3	5	3	8
University of Ottawa, Faculty of Engineering	ON	0	0	0	0	0	0	0	0	0	0	0	0	2	0	2	0	2
University of Waterloo	ON	0	0	0	0	0	0	0	0	0	0	0	0	7	1	7	1	8
Totals:		0	0	0	0	0	0	0	0	0	0	0	0	27	7	27	7	34

TEN-WYO

CHEMICAL ENGINEERING

INSTITUTION		AFRICAN AMERICAN		ASIAN AMERICAN		HISPANIC		NATIVE AMERICAN		CAUCASIAN		FOREIGN		OTHER		TOTAL BY GENDER		TOTAL DEGREES
		M	F	M	F	M	F	M	F	M	F	M	F	M	F	M	F	
The University of Akron	OH	0	0	0	0	0	0	0	0	0	0	6	1	0	0	6	1	7
University of Alabama at Birmingham	AL	0	0	0	0	0	0	0	0	1	0	1	0	0	0	2	0	2
The University of Alabama in Huntsville	AL	0	1	0	0	0	0	0	0	0	0	1	0	0	0	1	1	2
The University of Alabama	AL	0	0	0	0	0	0	0	0	1	1	1	0	0	0	2	1	3
The University of Arizona	AZ	0	0	0	0	0	0	0	0	0	0	4	0	0	0	4	0	4
Arizona State University	AZ	0	0	1	0	0	0	0	0	0	0	2	0	0	0	3	0	3
University of Arkansas	AR	0	0	0	0	0	0	0	0	1	0	2	0	0	0	3	0	3
Auburn University	AL	0	0	1	0	0	0	0	0	1	0	1	0	0	0	3	0	3
University of California, Berkeley	CA	0	0	1	2	0	0	0	0	3	1	8	3	0	0	12	6	18
University of California, Davis	CA	0	0	2	0	0	0	0	0	4	1	3	1	0	0	9	2	11
University of California, Irvine	CA	0	0	0	0	0	0	0	0	0	0	0	0	8	2	8	2	10
University of California, Los Angeles	CA	0	0	2	0	0	0	0	0	1	0	10	2	0	0	13	2	15
University of California, San Diego	CA	0	0	1	0	0	0	0	0	4	1	5	1	1	0	11	2	13
Carnegie Mellon University	PA	0	0	0	0	0	0	0	0	1	0	5	3	0	0	6	3	9
Case Western Reserve University	OH	0	0	0	0	0	0	0	0	0	0	3	0	0	0	3	0	3
University of Central Florida	FL	0	0	0	0	0	0	0	0	2	0	2	0	0	0	4	0	4
University of Cincinnati	OH	0	0	0	0	0	0	0	0	0	1	8	3	0	0	9	4	13
Clarkson University	NY	0	0	0	0	0	0	0	0	0	2	3	0	0	0	3	2	5
Clemson University	SC	0	0	0	0	0	0	0	0	1	0	3	2	0	0	4	2	6
University of Colorado at Boulder	CO	0	0	0	0	2	0	0	0	4	3	6	1	0	0	12	4	16
Columbia University	NY	0	0	0	0	0	0	0	0	1	0	5	0	0	0	6	0	6
University of Connecticut	CT	0	0	0	0	0	0	0	0	0	0	1	1	0	0	1	1	2
University of Delaware	DE	0	0	0	0	0	0	0	0	1	0	9	1	0	0	10	1	11
Drexel University	PA	0	0	0	0	0	0	0	0	1	0	3	1	0	0	4	1	5
Duke University Pratt School of Engineering	NC	0	0	0	0	0	0	0	0	0	0	0	0	5	1	5	1	6
University of Florida	FL	0	0	0	0	0	0	0	0	2	1	8	1	0	0	10	2	12
Florida International University	FL	0	0	0	0	0	0	0	0	0	0	2	0	0	0	2	0	2
FAMU-FSU College of Engineering	FL	0	1	0	0	0	0	0	0	2	0	3	1	0	0	5	2	7
Georgia Institute of Technology	GA	0	0	1	0	0	0	0	0	7	0	15	4	0	0	23	4	27
University of Hawaii at Manoa	HI	0	0	3	0	0	0	0	0	0	0	12	0	1	1	16	1	17
University of Houston, Cullen School of Engineering	TX	0	0	0	0	0	0	0	0	0	0	2	1	0	0	2	1	3
University of Idaho	ID	0	0	0	0	0	0	0	0	1	0	0	0	1	0	2	0	2
Illinois Institute of Technology	IL	0	0	0	0	0	0	0	0	0	0	1	0	0	0	1	0	1
University of Illinois at Chicago	IL	0	0	3	0	0	0	0	0	1	1	0	0	0	0	4	1	5
University of Illinois at Urbana-Champaign	IL	1	0	0	1	0	0	0	0	2	1	18	2	0	0	21	4	25
The University of Iowa	IA	0	1	0	0	0	0	0	0	1	1	5	0	0	0	6	2	8
Iowa State University	IA	0	0	0	0	0	0	0	0	2	0	7	1	0	0	9	1	10
The Johns Hopkins University	MD	0	0	0	0	0	0	0	0	1	0	2	0	0	0	3	0	3
University of Kansas	KS	0	0	1	1	0	0	0	0	0	0	0	1	0	0	1	1	2
Kansas State University	KS	0	0	0	0	0	0	0	0	1	0	1	0	0	0	2	0	2
University of Kentucky	KY	0	0	0	1	0	0	0	0	0	0	3	1	1	0	4	2	6
Lamar University	TX	0	0	0	0	0	0	0	0	1	0	0	0	0	0	1	0	1
Lehigh University	PA	0	0	0	0	0	0	0	0	0	0	5	1	1	0	6	1	7
Louisiana State University	LA	0	0	0	0	0	0	0	0	1	0	6	3	1	0	8	3	11
University of Louisville	KY	0	0	0	0	0	0	0	0	0	0	2	0	0	0	2	0	2

CIVIL ENGINEERING

AKR-LOU

DOCTORAL DEGREES AWARDED IN CIVIL ENGINEERING, 2005-2006

INSTITUTION		AFRICAN AMERICAN M	F	ASIAN AMERICAN M	F	HISPANIC M	F	NATIVE AMERICAN M	F	CAUCASIAN M	F	FOREIGN M	F	OTHER M	F	TOTAL BY GENDER M	F	TOTAL DEGREES
University of Maryland, College Park	MD	0	0	0	1	0	0	0	0	1	1	6	2	1	0	8	4	12
Massachusetts Institute of Technology	MA	0	0	0	0	0	0	0	0	0	1	14	4	2	0	16	5	21
University of Massachusetts Amherst	MA	0	0	0	0	0	0	0	0	0	1	0	1	1	0	1	2	3
University of Miami	FL	0	0	0	0	0	0	0	0	0	0	1	0	0	0	1	0	1
University of Michigan	MI	0	0	0	0	0	0	0	0	1	0	9	1	0	0	10	1	11
Michigan State University	MI	0	0	0	1	0	0	0	0	0	0	6	0	0	0	6	1	7
Michigan Technological University	MI	1	0	0	0	0	0	0	0	0	0	0	0	0	0	1	0	1
University of Minnesota - Twin Cities	MN	0	0	0	0	0	0	0	0	4	0	5	2	0	0	9	2	11
The University of Mississippi	MS	0	0	1	0	0	0	0	0	0	0	0	0	0	0	1	0	1
University of Missouri-Columbia	MO	0	0	0	0	1	1	0	0	0	0	3	0	0	0	4	1	5
University of Missouri - Kansas City	MO	0	0	0	0	0	0	0	0	0	0	1	0	0	0	1	0	1
University of Missouri - Rolla	MO	0	0	0	0	0	0	0	0	1	0	7	1	0	0	8	1	9
New Jersey Institute of Technology	NJ	0	0	0	0	0	0	0	0	0	0	2	0	0	0	2	0	2
The University of New Mexico	NM	0	0	0	0	0	0	0	0	0	0	1	0	0	0	1	0	1
New Mexico State University	NM	0	0	0	0	0	0	0	0	0	0	1	0	0	0	1	0	1
City College of the City University of New York	NY	0	0	0	0	0	0	0	0	0	0	1	2	1	0	2	2	4
State University of New York at Buffalo	NY	0	0	0	0	0	0	0	0	2	0	9	0	0	0	11	0	11
North Carolina State University	NC	0	0	0	0	0	0	0	0	1	2	9	1	0	0	10	3	13
University of North Carolina, Charlotte	NC	1	0	0	0	0	0	0	0	0	0	0	0	0	0	1	0	1
North Dakota State University	ND	0	0	1	0	0	0	0	0	0	0	0	0	0	0	1	0	1
Northeastern University	MA	0	0	0	0	0	0	0	0	1	0	1	0	0	0	2	0	2
Northwestern University	IL	0	0	0	1	0	0	0	0	1	2	3	3	1	0	5	6	11
University of Notre Dame	IN	1	0	0	0	0	0	0	0	2	2	2	1	0	0	5	3	8
The Ohio State University	OH	0	0	0	0	0	0	0	0	0	0	8	1	0	0	8	1	9
University of Oklahoma	OK	0	0	0	0	0	0	0	0	1	1	1	0	0	0	2	1	3
Oklahoma State University	OK	0	0	0	0	0	0	0	0	1	0	0	0	0	0	1	0	1
Old Dominion University	VA	0	0	0	0	0	0	0	0	0	0	5	1	0	0	5	1	6
Oregon State University	OR	0	0	0	0	0	0	0	0	1	0	1	0	0	0	2	0	2
The Pennsylvania State University	PA	0	0	0	1	0	0	0	0	3	0	7	0	0	0	10	1	11
University of Pittsburgh	PA	0	0	0	0	0	0	0	0	0	0	3	2	0	0	3	2	5
Polytechnic University	NY	0	0	0	1	0	0	0	0	1	0	1	0	0	0	2	1	3
Princeton University	NJ	0	0	0	1	0	0	0	0	0	1	0	2	0	0	0	4	4
University of Puerto Rico, Mayaguez Campus	PR	0	0	0	0	5	0	0	0	0	0	0	0	0	0	5	0	5
Purdue University	IN	0	0	0	0	2	0	0	0	3	2	19	5	0	0	24	7	31
Rensselaer Polytechnic Institute	NY	0	0	0	0	0	0	0	0	2	0	2	0	0	0	4	0	4
William Marsh Rice University	TX	0	0	0	0	0	0	0	0	0	0	2	0	0	0	2	0	2
Rutgers, The State University of New Jersey	NJ	0	0	0	0	0	0	0	0	2	0	2	0	0	0	4	0	4
University of Southern California	CA	0	0	0	0	0	0	0	0	0	0	4	0	0	0	4	0	4
Southern Illinois University Carbondale	IL	0	0	0	0	0	0	0	0	0	1	6	0	0	0	6	1	7
Stanford University	CA	0	1	1	1	1	0	0	0	5	1	14	4	1	0	22	7	29
Syracuse University	NY	0	0	0	0	0	0	0	0	0	0	2	0	0	0	2	0	2
Tennessee Technological University	TN	0	0	0	0	0	0	0	0	2	0	4	1	0	0	6	1	7
University of Tennessee, Knoxville	TN	0	0	0	0	0	0	0	0	2	0	5	1	0	0	7	1	8
Texas A&M University	TX	0	0	0	0	0	1	0	0	0	1	9	3	0	0	9	5	14
Texas Tech University	TX	0	0	0	0	0	0	0	0	1	0	4	2	0	0	5	2	7

CIVIL ENGINEERING

MAR-TEX

Doctoral Degrees Awarded in Civil Engineering, 2005-2006

INSTITUTION		AFRICAN AMERICAN		ASIAN AMERICAN		HISPANIC		NATIVE AMERICAN		CAUCASIAN		FOREIGN		OTHER		TOTAL BY GENDER		TOTAL DEGREES
		M	F	M	F	M	F	M	F	M	F	M	F	M	F	M	F	
The University of Texas at Arlington	TX	0	0	2	0	0	0	0	0	2	0	3	0	0	0	7	0	7
The University of Texas at Austin	TX	0	0	1	0	1	0	0	0	6	2	22	3	0	0	30	5	35
The University of Toledo	OH	0	0	0	0	0	0	0	0	0	0	2	0	0	0	2	0	2
Tulane University	LA	0	0	0	0	0	0	0	0	0	0	0	0	1	0	1	0	1
University of Utah	UT	0	0	0	0	0	0	0	0	2	0	2	1	1	0	5	1	6
Utah State University	UT	0	0	0	0	0	0	0	0	5	0	4	0	0	0	9	0	9
Vanderbilt University	TN	0	0	0	0	0	0	0	0	1	0	3	0	0	0	4	0	4
University of Vermont	VT	0	0	0	0	0	0	0	0	0	1	0	1	0	0	0	2	2
University of Virginia	VA	0	0	0	0	0	0	0	0	1	0	3	0	0	0	4	0	4
Virginia Polytechnic Institute and State University	VA	0	1	0	0	0	0	0	0	5	1	10	2	0	0	15	4	19
University of Washington	WA	0	0	1	0	0	0	0	0	0	2	3	0	2	0	6	2	8
Washington State University	WA	0	0	0	0	0	0	0	0	2	0	2	0	1	0	5	0	5
Washington University	MO	0	0	0	0	0	0	0	0	0	0	1	2	0	0	1	2	3
Wayne State University	MI	1	0	1	0	0	0	0	0	0	1	6	0	0	0	8	1	9
West Virginia University	WV	0	0	0	0	0	0	0	0	0	1	3	0	0	0	3	1	4
University of Wisconsin, Madison	WI	0	1	0	0	0	0	0	0	0	1	7	1	0	0	7	3	10
Totals:		5	6	24	12	12	2	0	0	112	39	435	86	31	3	619	148	767
CANADIAN INSTITUTIONS:																		
University of Alberta	AB	0	0	0	0	0	0	0	0	0	0	0	0	17	0	17	0	17
University of Calgary	AB	0	0	0	0	0	0	0	0	0	0	3	0	3	0	6	0	6
Concordia University, Faculty of Engr. and Comp. Sci.	PQ	0	0	0	0	0	0	0	0	0	0	1	1	3	0	4	1	5
Ecole Polytechnique de Montreal	PQ	0	0	0	0	0	0	0	0	0	0	0	0	1	0	1	0	1
McGill University, Faculty of Engineering	PQ	0	0	0	0	0	0	0	0	0	0	0	0	4	1	4	1	5
University of Ottawa, Faculty of Engineering	ON	0	0	0	0	0	0	0	0	0	0	0	0	6	1	6	1	7
University of Waterloo	ON	0	0	0	0	0	0	0	0	0	0	0	0	6	0	6	0	6
Totals:		0	0	0	0	0	0	0	0	0	0	4	1	40	2	44	3	47

TEX-WIS

CIVIL ENGINEERING

DOCTORAL DEGREES AWARDED IN CIVIL/ENVIRONMENTAL ENGINEERING, 2005-2006

INSTITUTION		AFRICAN AMERICAN		ASIAN AMERICAN		HISPANIC		NATIVE AMERICAN		CAUCASIAN		FOREIGN		OTHER		TOTAL BY GENDER		TOTAL DEGREES
		M	F	M	F	M	F	M	F	M	F	M	F	M	F	M	F	
Colorado State University	CO	0	0	0	0	0	0	0	0	3	0	0	0	3	0	6	0	6
The George Washington University	DC	0	0	0	0	0	0	0	0	1	0	1	0	0	0	2	0	2
University of Illinois at Urbana-Champaign	IL	0	0	0	0	0	0	0	0	2	0	2	0	0	0	4	0	4
University of Nevada, Las Vegas	NV	0	0	0	0	0	0	0	0	2	0	2	0	0	0	4	0	4
University of Nevada, Reno	NV	0	0	0	0	1	0	0	0	1	0	5	0	0	0	7	0	7
University of South Carolina	SC	0	0	0	0	0	0	0	0	1	0	3	2	0	0	4	2	6
Totals:		0	0	0	0	1	0	0	0	10	0	13	2	3	0	27	2	29

CIVIL/ENVIRONMENTAL ENGINEERING   COL-SOU

INSTITUTION		AFRICAN AMERICAN		ASIAN AMERICAN		HISPANIC		NATIVE AMERICAN		CAUCASIAN		FOREIGN		OTHER		TOTAL BY GENDER		TOTAL DEGREES
		M	F	M	F	M	F	M	F	M	F	M	F	M	F	M	F	
University of Alabama at Birmingham	AL	0	0	0	0	0	0	0	0	1	0	3	0	0	0	4	0	4
The University of Alabama in Huntsville	AL	0	0	0	0	0	0	0	0	0	0	2	0	0	0	2	0	2
Boston University	MA	0	0	2	0	0	0	0	0	1	0	2	0	0	0	5	0	5
University of California, San Diego	CA	0	0	0	1	0	0	0	0	0	0	1	0	0	0	1	1	2
University of California-Santa Cruz	CA	0	0	0	0	0	0	0	0	0	0	6	2	0	0	6	2	8
Case Western Reserve University	OH	0	0	1	0	0	0	0	0	1	0	0	1	0	0	2	1	3
University of Central Florida	FL	0	0	0	0	0	0	0	0	1	0	3	0	0	0	4	0	4
University of Cincinnati	OH	0	0	0	0	0	0	0	0	0	0	11	4	0	0	11	4	15
Clemson University	SC	0	0	0	0	0	0	0	0	1	0	0	0	0	0	1	0	1
University of Florida	FL	0	0	0	0	0	0	0	0	4	0	14	0	0	0	18	0	18
Florida Atlantic University	FL	0	0	1	0	0	0	0	0	1	0	4	0	0	0	6	0	6
Florida Institute of Technology	FL	0	0	0	0	0	0	0	0	1	0	2	0	0	0	3	0	3
The George Washington University	DC	0	0	0	0	0	0	0	0	0	1	2	0	0	0	2	1	3
Iowa State University	IA	0	0	0	0	0	0	0	0	2	1	9	2	0	0	11	3	14
Lehigh University	PA	0	0	0	0	0	0	0	0	0	0	2	0	0	0	2	0	2
University of Louisiana at Lafayette	LA	0	0	0	0	0	0	0	0	0	0	4	0	0	0	4	0	4
University of Louisville	KY	0	0	1	0	0	0	0	0	2	0	4	1	0	0	7	1	8
University of Maryland, Baltimore County	MD	0	0	0	0	0	0	0	0	0	0	1	0	0	0	1	0	1
Mississippi State University	MS	0	0	1	1	0	0	0	0	0	0	3	0	0	0	4	1	5
University of Missouri - Rolla	MO	0	0	0	0	0	0	0	0	0	0	1	0	0	0	1	0	1
University of Nevada, Reno	NV	0	0	0	0	0	0	0	0	0	1	1	0	0	0	1	1	2
New Jersey Institute of Technology	NJ	0	0	0	0	0	0	0	0	0	0	4	3	0	0	4	3	7
The University of New Mexico	NM	0	0	0	0	0	0	0	0	1	0	1	1	0	0	2	1	3
North Carolina State University	NC	0	0	0	0	0	0	0	0	1	0	6	3	0	0	7	3	10
Northeastern University	MA	0	0	0	0	0	0	0	0	0	0	2	2	0	0	2	2	4
University of Notre Dame	IN	0	0	0	0	0	0	0	0	1	0	2	0	0	0	3	0	3
Rensselaer Polytechnic Institute	NY	0	0	0	0	0	0	0	0	0	0	3	0	0	0	3	0	3
Santa Clara University	CA	0	0	0	0	0	0	0	0	0	0	2	0	0	0	2	0	2
University of Southern California	CA	0	0	0	0	0	0	0	0	0	1	5	1	0	0	5	2	7
Southern Methodist University	TX	0	0	0	0	0	0	0	0	0	0	1	0	0	0	1	0	1
Stevens Institute of Technology	NJ	0	0	0	0	0	0	0	0	0	0	1	1	0	0	1	1	2
Syracuse University	NY	0	0	0	0	0	0	0	0	0	0	2	0	0	0	2	0	2
University of Tennessee, Chattanooga	TN	0	0	0	0	0	0	0	0	1	0	0	0	0	0	1	0	1
University of Texas at El Paso	TX	0	0	0	0	1	0	0	0	0	0	3	0	0	0	4	0	4
Virginia Polytechnic Institute and State University	VA	0	0	0	0	1	0	0	0	0	0	4	0	0	0	5	0	5
University of Washington	WA	0	0	2	1	0	0	0	0	9	0	11	1	0	0	22	2	24
Wayne State University	MI	0	0	0	0	0	0	0	0	0	0	0	1	0	0	0	1	1
West Virginia University	WV	0	0	0	0	0	0	0	0	0	0	1	0	0	0	1	0	1
Totals:		**0**	**0**	**8**	**3**	**2**	**0**	**0**	**0**	**28**	**4**	**123**	**23**	**0**	**0**	**161**	**30**	**191**
CANADIAN INSTITUTIONS:																		
Ecole Polytechnique de Montreal	PQ	0	0	0	0	0	0	0	0	0	0	0	0	5	0	5	0	5
Totals:		**0**	**0**	**0**	**0**	**0**	**0**	**0**	**0**	**0**	**0**	**0**	**0**	**5**	**0**	**5**	**0**	**5**

ALA-WES

COMPUTER ENGINEERING

Doctoral Degrees Awarded in Computer Science (Inside Engineering), 2005-2006

Institution		African American M	African American F	Asian American M	Asian American F	Hispanic M	Hispanic F	Native American M	Native American F	Caucasian M	Caucasian F	Foreign M	Foreign F	Other M	Other F	Total by Gender M	Total by Gender F	Total Degrees
The University of Alabama	AL	0	0	0	0	0	0	0	0	0	0	1	1	0	0	1	1	2
Arizona State University	AZ	0	0	0	0	0	0	0	0	3	1	13	3	1	0	17	4	21
University of Arkansas	AR	0	0	1	0	0	0	0	0	1	0	1	0	0	0	3	0	3
Auburn University	AL	0	0	0	0	0	0	0	0	3	0	1	0	0	0	4	0	4
California Institute of Technology	CA	0	0	0	0	0	0	0	0	1	0	2	0	0	0	3	0	3
University of California, Berkeley	CA	1	0	7	3	0	0	0	0	10	2	22	3	3	1	43	9	52
University of California, Davis	CA	0	0	1	0	0	0	0	0	4	0	5	0	1	1	11	1	12
University of California, Los Angeles	CA	0	0	4	1	0	0	0	0	5	0	19	5	1	0	29	6	35
University of California, Riverside	CA	0	1	0	0	0	0	0	0	1	0	0	0	7	7	8	8	16
University of California, San Diego	CA	0	0	3	0	0	1	0	0	1	1	12	4	1	0	17	6	23
University of California, Santa Barbara	CA	0	0	0	0	0	0	0	0	0	0	7	5	1	0	8	5	13
University of California-Santa Cruz	CA	0	0	2	0	0	0	0	0	5	0	3	1	0	1	10	2	12
Case Western Reserve University	OH	0	0	0	1	0	0	0	0	0	0	2	0	1	0	3	1	4
University of Central Florida	FL	0	0	0	0	0	0	0	0	3	1	11	2	0	0	14	3	17
Clemson University	SC	0	0	0	0	0	0	0	0	2	0	1	0	0	0	3	0	3
Colorado School of Mines	CO	0	0	0	0	0	0	0	0	0	0	0	3	0	0	0	3	3
University of Colorado at Boulder	CO	0	0	0	0	0	0	0	0	5	1	5	1	0	0	10	2	12
Columbia University	NY	0	0	0	1	0	0	0	0	1	1	3	3	3	1	7	6	13
University of Connecticut	CT	0	0	0	1	0	0	0	0	3	0	0	2	0	1	3	4	7
Cornell University	NY	0	0	0	0	0	0	0	0	3	1	8	1	0	0	11	2	13
Drexel University	PA	0	0	0	0	0	0	0	0	0	0	2	0	1	0	3	0	3
Florida Institute of Technology	FL	0	0	0	0	0	0	0	0	0	1	0	0	0	0	0	1	1
Florida International University	FL	0	0	0	0	0	0	0	0	0	0	5	1	0	0	5	1	6
George Mason University	VA	0	0	0	1	0	0	0	0	0	0	3	0	0	0	3	1	4
The George Washington University	DC	0	1	1	0	0	0	0	0	2	1	4	0	0	0	7	2	9
Harvard University	MA	0	0	0	1	0	0	0	0	0	2	3	0	0	0	3	3	6
University of Idaho	ID	1	0	0	0	0	0	0	0	0	0	0	0	1	0	2	0	2
University of Illinois at Chicago	IL	0	0	4	4	0	0	0	0	0	0	0	0	0	0	4	4	8
University of Illinois at Urbana-Champaign	IL	0	0	6	0	0	0	0	0	5	2	38	6	0	0	49	8	57
The Johns Hopkins University	MD	0	0	0	0	0	0	0	0	4	0	6	1	0	0	10	1	11
University of Kansas	KS	0	0	2	0	0	0	0	0	1	0	0	0	0	0	3	0	3
University of Kentucky	KY	1	0	0	0	0	0	0	0	0	0	1	1	0	0	2	1	3
Lehigh University	PA	0	0	0	0	0	0	0	0	0	0	2	0	1	0	3	0	3
University of Maryland, Baltimore County	MD	0	0	0	0	0	0	0	0	1	0	3	2	0	0	4	2	6
Michigan State University	MI	0	0	1	0	0	0	0	0	1	0	8	1	0	0	10	1	11
Michigan Technological University	MI	0	0	0	0	0	0	0	0	1	0	0	0	0	0	1	0	1
University of Minnesota-Twin Cities	MN	0	0	2	1	0	0	0	0	6	0	11	4	0	0	19	5	24
The University of Mississippi	MS	0	0	0	0	0	0	0	0	0	0	3	0	0	0	3	0	3
Mississippi State University	MS	0	0	0	0	0	0	0	0	0	0	5	0	0	0	5	0	5
University of Missouri-Columbia	MO	0	0	0	0	0	0	0	0	0	0	5	0	0	0	5	0	5
University of Missouri - Kansas City	MO	0	0	0	0	0	0	0	0	0	0	6	0	0	0	6	0	6
Montana State University	MT	0	0	0	0	0	0	0	0	0	0	1	0	0	0	1	0	1
University of Nevada, Las Vegas	NV	0	0	0	0	0	0	0	0	0	1	0	0	0	0	0	1	1
University of New Hampshire	NH	0	0	0	0	0	0	0	0	1	0	0	0	0	0	1	0	1
The University of New Mexico	NM	0	0	1	0	0	0	0	0	1	1	1	0	0	0	3	1	4

COMPUTER SCIENCE (INSIDE ENGR.)   ALA-NEW

DOCTORAL DEGREES AWARDED IN COMPUTER SCIENCE (INSIDE ENGINEERING), 2005-2006

INSTITUTION		AFRICAN AMERICAN		ASIAN AMERICAN		HISPANIC		NATIVE AMERICAN		CAUCASIAN		FOREIGN		OTHER		TOTAL BY GENDER		TOTAL DEGREES
		M	F	M	F	M	F	M	F	M	F	M	F	M	F	M	F	
The State University of New York at Binghamton	NY	0	0	0	0	0	0	0	0	0	0	3	0	1	0	4	0	4
State University of New York at Buffalo	NY	0	0	0	0	0	0	0	0	1	1	8	2	0	0	9	3	12
Stony Brook University	NY	1	0	0	0	0	0	0	0	3	0	7	1	0	0	11	1	12
North Carolina State University	NC	0	0	1	2	0	0	0	0	2	0	6	1	0	0	9	3	12
University of North Texas	TX	0	0	0	0	0	0	0	0	2	0	4	0	0	0	6	0	6
The Ohio State University	OH	0	0	0	0	0	0	0	0	1	0	12	4	0	0	13	4	17
University of Oklahoma	OK	0	0	0	0	0	0	0	0	2	0	2	0	0	0	4	0	4
OGI School of Science & Engineering at OHSU	OR	0	0	0	0	0	0	0	0	4	1	1	0	0	0	5	1	6
Oregon State University	OR	0	0	0	0	0	0	0	0	1	0	0	0	0	0	1	0	1
University of Pennsylvania	PA	0	0	0	0	0	0	0	0	5	1	3	2	1	0	9	3	12
The Pennsylvania State University	PA	0	0	0	0	0	0	0	0	1	0	15	7	0	0	16	7	23
Polytechnic University	NY	0	0	1	0	0	0	0	0	0	0	5	0	0	0	6	0	6
Portland State University	OR	0	0	0	0	0	0	0	0	0	0	1	0	0	0	1	0	1
Princeton University	NJ	0	0	0	1	0	0	0	0	3	1	9	2	0	0	12	4	16
William Marsh Rice University	TX	0	0	0	0	0	0	0	0	2	0	3	0	0	0	5	0	5
University of South Carolina	SC	1	0	0	0	0	0	0	0	1	0	3	0	0	0	5	0	5
University of Southern California	CA	0	0	1	0	0	0	0	0	2	0	19	4	3	1	25	5	30
Southern Methodist University	TX	0	0	0	0	0	0	0	0	0	0	3	0	0	0	3	0	3
Stanford University	CA	0	0	2	0	0	0	0	0	3	3	12	3	5	0	22	6	28
Texas A&M University	TX	0	0	1	2	0	0	0	0	1	0	15	3	0	0	17	5	22
Texas Tech University	TX	0	0	0	0	0	0	0	0	1	0	4	0	0	0	5	0	5
The University of Texas at Arlington	TX	0	0	3	1	0	0	0	0	3	0	3	1	0	0	9	2	11
The University of Texas at Dallas	TX	0	0	1	0	0	0	0	0	2	0	15	3	0	0	18	3	21
Tulane University	LA	0	0	0	0	0	0	0	0	0	0	3	0	1	0	4	0	4
University of Utah	UT	0	0	0	0	0	0	0	0	1	0	2	0	0	0	3	0	3
Vanderbilt University	TN	0	0	0	0	0	0	0	0	0	0	2	2	0	1	2	3	5
University of Vermont	VT	0	0	0	0	0	0	0	0	0	0	1	0	0	0	1	0	1
University of Virginia	VA	0	0	0	0	0	0	0	0	0	1	2	1	0	0	2	2	4
Virginia Polytechnic Institute and State University	VA	0	1	0	0	0	0	0	0	4	1	4	1	0	0	8	3	11
Washington State University	WA	0	0	0	0	0	0	0	0	0	0	0	1	2	0	2	1	3
Washington University	MO	0	0	0	0	0	0	0	0	1	0	3	0	3	0	7	0	7
West Virginia University	WV	0	0	0	0	0	0	0	0	0	0	4	0	0	0	4	0	4
Western Michigan University	MI	0	0	0	0	0	0	0	0	1	0	2	0	0	0	3	0	3
Wright State University	OH	0	0	0	0	0	0	0	0	0	0	3	0	0	0	4	0	4
Totals:		5	3	45	20	0	1	0	0	121	25	400	89	38	14	609	152	761

COMPUTER SCIENCE (INSIDE ENGR.)   NEW-WRI

INSTITUTION		AFRICAN AMERICAN		ASIAN AMERICAN		HISPANIC		NATIVE AMERICAN		CAUCASIAN		FOREIGN		OTHER		TOTAL BY GENDER		TOTAL DEGREES
		M	F	M	F	M	F	M	F	M	F	M	F	M	F	M	F	
The University of Arizona	AZ	0	0	0	0	0	0	0	0	1	1	1	0	0	0	2	1	3
Brigham Young University	UT	0	0	0	0	0	0	0	0	0	0	1	0	3	1	4	1	5
University of California, Irvine	CA	0	0	0	0	0	0	0	0	0	0	0	0	17	2	17	2	19
Carnegie Mellon University	PA	0	0	1	0	0	0	1	0	4	2	30	9	9	0	45	11	56
Dartmouth College	NH	0	0	0	0	0	0	0	0	1	0	7	3	0	0	8	3	11
University of Delaware	DE	0	0	0	0	1	0	0	0	1	1	6	1	0	0	8	2	10
FAMU-FSU College of Engineering	FL	2	0	0	0	0	0	0	0	0	0	3	0	0	0	5	0	5
Georgia Institute of Technology	GA	2	1	3	2	0	0	0	0	13	0	15	3	0	0	33	6	39
University of Houston, Cullen School of Engineering	TX	0	0	0	0	0	0	0	0	0	1	3	1	1	0	4	2	6
Illinois Institute of Technology	IL	0	0	1	0	0	0	0	0	6	2	5	0	1	0	13	2	15
The University of Iowa	IA	0	0	0	0	0	0	0	0	1	0	1	0	0	0	2	0	2
Louisiana State University	LA	0	0	0	0	0	0	0	0	1	0	3	4	0	0	4	4	8
University of Louisiana at Lafayette	LA	0	0	0	0	0	0	0	0	0	0	2	0	0	0	2	0	2
University of Maryland, College Park	MD	0	0	0	0	1	0	0	0	7	2	19	5	1	0	28	7	35
University of Massachusetts Amherst	MA	0	0	0	0	0	0	0	0	5	0	8	1	1	0	14	1	15
Michigan Technological University	MI	0	0	0	0	0	0	0	0	0	0	1	0	0	0	1	0	1
University of Nebraska, Lincoln	NE	0	0	0	0	0	0	0	0	0	0	5	2	0	0	5	2	7
New Jersey Institute of Technology	NJ	0	0	1	1	0	0	0	0	0	0	9	1	0	0	10	2	12
Purdue University	IN	0	0	1	0	0	0	0	0	4	0	10	2	0	0	15	2	17
Rensselaer Polytechnic Institute	NY	0	0	0	1	0	0	0	0	4	1	7	2	0	0	11	4	15
University of Rochester	NY	0	0	0	0	0	0	0	0	1	0	1	0	0	0	2	0	2
University of Tennessee, Knoxville	TN	0	0	0	0	0	0	0	0	1	1	1	0	0	0	2	1	3
Wayne State University	MI	0	0	0	0	0	0	0	0	0	0	4	2	0	0	4	2	6
Worcester Polytechnic Institute	MA	0	0	0	1	0	0	0	0	0	0	6	1	0	0	6	1	7
Totals:		4	1	7	4	2	0	1	0	50	11	148	37	33	3	245	56	301

CANADIAN INSTITUTIONS:

		M	F	M	F	M	F	M	F	M	F	M	F	M	F	M	F	
Concordia University, Faculty of Engr. and Comp. Sci.	PQ	0	0	0	0	0	0	0	0	0	0	0	0	8	1	8	1	9
Totals:		0	0	0	0	0	0	0	0	0	0	0	0	8	1	8	1	9

COMPUTER SCIENCE (OUTSIDE ENGR.)   ARI-WOR

Doctoral Degrees Awarded in Electrical Engineering, 2005-2006

Institution	State	African American		Asian American		Hispanic		Native American		Caucasian		Foreign		Other		Total by Gender		Total Degrees
		M	F	M	F	M	F	M	F	M	F	M	F	M	F	M	F	
Air Force Institute of Technology	OH	0	0	0	0	0	0	0	0	1	0	0	0	0	7	1	7	8
The University of Alabama in Huntsville	AL	0	0	0	0	0	0	0	0	2	0	2	0	0	0	4	0	4
The University of Alabama	AL	0	0	0	0	0	0	0	0	0	0	4	1	0	0	4	1	5
Arizona State University	AZ	0	0	3	0	0	0	0	0	4	0	30	4	0	0	37	4	41
University of Arkansas	AR	0	0	0	0	0	0	0	0	2	0	1	1	0	0	3	1	4
Boston University	MA	0	1	2	1	0	0	0	0	2	0	3	1	0	0	7	3	10
California Institute of Technology	CA	0	0	1	0	0	0	0	0	1	1	12	1	0	0	14	2	16
University of California, Los Angeles	CA	0	0	1	0	0	0	0	0	6	0	27	0	1	1	35	1	36
University of California, Riverside	CA	0	0	0	0	0	0	0	0	0	0	0	0	7	1	7	1	8
University of California, San Diego	CA	0	0	0	0	0	0	0	0	3	1	6	1	0	0	9	2	11
University of California-Santa Cruz	CA	0	0	2	0	0	0	0	0	0	0	3	1	0	0	5	1	6
Case Western Reserve University	OH	0	0	2	0	0	0	0	0	0	0	0	1	0	0	2	1	3
The Catholic University of America	DC	0	0	0	0	0	0	0	0	0	1	1	0	0	0	1	1	2
University of Central Florida	FL	0	0	0	0	0	0	1	0	0	0	6	3	0	0	7	3	10
University of Cincinnati	OH	0	0	1	0	0	0	0	0	2	0	14	2	0	0	17	2	19
Clemson University	SC	1	0	0	0	0	0	0	0	5	0	2	0	0	0	8	0	8
Columbia University	NY	0	0	1	0	0	0	0	0	0	0	12	3	1	0	14	3	17
University of Connecticut	CT	0	0	0	0	2	0	0	0	0	0	6	1	1	0	9	1	10
University of Dayton	OH	0	0	0	0	0	0	0	0	0	0	5	0	0	0	5	0	5
Drexel University	PA	0	0	1	0	0	0	0	0	1	0	5	0	0	0	7	0	7
University of Florida	FL	0	0	1	1	0	0	0	0	2	0	25	7	0	0	28	8	36
Florida Atlantic University	FL	0	0	0	0	0	0	0	0	0	0	1	0	0	0	1	0	1
Florida Institute of Technology	FL	0	0	0	0	0	0	0	0	1	0	0	0	1	0	2	0	2
Florida International University	FL	0	0	0	0	0	0	0	0	1	0	4	1	0	0	5	1	6
FAMU-FSU College of Engineering	FL	0	0	0	0	0	0	0	0	1	0	0	0	0	0	1	0	1
The George Washington University	DC	0	0	0	0	0	0	0	0	0	0	1	3	0	0	1	3	4
University of Hawaii at Manoa	HI	0	0	2	1	0	0	0	0	0	0	15	7	2	1	19	9	28
University of Houston, Cullen School of Engineering	TX	0	0	1	0	0	0	0	0	2	0	10	1	2	0	15	1	16
University of Idaho	ID	0	0	0	0	0	0	0	0	1	0	1	0	0	0	2	0	2
Iowa State University	IA	0	0	0	0	0	0	0	0	0	0	15	4	0	0	15	4	19
Lehigh University	PA	0	0	0	0	0	0	0	0	0	0	5	2	0	0	5	2	7
University of Louisville	KY	0	0	0	0	0	0	0	0	0	0	4	1	0	0	4	1	5
University of Maine	ME	0	0	0	0	0	0	0	0	1	0	0	0	0	0	1	0	1
University of Maryland, Baltimore County	MD	0	0	0	0	0	0	0	0	1	0	4	5	0	0	5	5	10
University of Michigan	MI	1	0	2	0	1	0	0	0	7	0	15	3	0	0	26	3	29
Michigan Technological University	MI	0	0	0	0	0	0	0	0	2	0	2	1	0	0	4	1	5
Mississippi State University	MS	0	0	0	0	0	0	0	0	0	0	4	0	0	0	4	0	4
University of Missouri-Columbia	MO	0	0	0	0	0	0	0	0	1	1	5	0	0	0	6	1	7
University of Missouri - Kansas City	MO	0	0	0	0	0	0	0	0	0	0	1	0	0	0	1	0	1
University of Missouri - Rolla	MO	0	0	0	0	0	0	0	0	2	0	0	6	0	0	2	6	8
University of Nevada, Reno	NV	0	0	0	0	0	0	0	0	1	0	3	0	0	0	4	0	4
New Jersey Institute of Technology	NJ	0	0	0	0	0	0	0	0	1	0	9	6	0	0	10	6	16
New Mexico State University	NM	0	0	0	0	0	0	0	0	0	0	1	0	2	0	3	0	3
The State University of New York at Binghamton	NY	0	0	0	0	0	0	0	0	0	0	2	0	1	0	3	0	3
State University of New York at Buffalo	NY	0	0	0	0	0	0	0	0	1	0	3	1	0	0	4	1	5

AIR-NEW

ELECTRICAL ENGINEERING

INSTITUTION		AFRICAN AMERICAN		ASIAN AMERICAN		HISPANIC		NATIVE AMERICAN		CAUCASIAN		FOREIGN		OTHER		TOTAL BY GENDER		TOTAL DEGREES
		M	F	M	F	M	F	M	F	M	F	M	F	M	F	M	F	
Stony Brook University	NY	0	0	1	0	0	0	0	0	0	0	10	2	0	0	11	2	13
North Carolina A & T State University	NC	1	1	0	0	0	0	0	0	0	0	2	2	0	0	3	3	6
North Carolina State University	NC	0	0	0	1	0	0	0	0	4	0	16	5	0	0	20	6	26
Northeastern University	MA	0	0	1	0	0	0	0	0	1	0	3	3	1	1	6	4	10
University of Notre Dame	IN	0	0	1	0	0	0	0	0	1	0	12	2	0	0	13	2	15
Ohio University	OH	0	0	0	0	0	0	0	0	1	0	8	0	0	0	9	0	9
The Pennsylvania State University	PA	0	0	0	1	0	0	0	0	8	0	19	3	0	0	27	4	31
University of Pittsburgh	PA	0	0	2	0	0	0	0	0	2	0	2	1	0	0	6	1	7
Rensselaer Polytechnic Institute	NY	0	0	2	0	1	0	0	0	4	0	18	5	0	0	25	5	30
Santa Clara University	CA	0	0	0	0	0	0	0	0	0	0	1	0	0	0	1	0	1
University of South Carolina	SC	0	0	0	0	0	0	0	0	0	1	7	1	0	0	7	2	9
University of South Florida	FL	0	0	0	0	0	0	0	0	1	0	1	0	0	0	2	0	2
University of Southern California	CA	0	0	1	0	0	0	0	0	4	0	46	8	4	0	55	8	63
Southern Methodist University	TX	0	0	0	0	0	0	0	0	0	1	4	0	0	0	4	1	5
Stanford University	CA	0	0	4	0	1	0	0	0	19	3	30	6	3	0	57	9	66
Stevens Institute of Technology	NJ	0	0	0	0	0	0	0	0	0	0	4	1	0	0	4	1	5
Syracuse University	NY	0	0	0	0	0	0	0	0	0	0	9	1	0	0	9	1	10
Texas A&M University	TX	1	0	0	0	0	0	0	0	2	0	22	6	0	0	25	6	31
The University of Texas at Arlington	TX	0	0	5	1	0	0	0	0	1	0	8	3	0	0	14	4	18
The University of Texas at Dallas	TX	0	0	0	0	0	0	0	0	3	0	17	0	0	0	20	0	20
The University of Toledo	OH	0	0	0	0	0	0	0	0	1	0	2	0	0	0	3	0	3
Vanderbilt University	TN	0	0	0	0	0	0	0	0	2	0	5	1	0	0	7	1	8
University of Virginia	VA	1	0	0	1	0	0	0	0	2	1	8	3	0	0	11	5	16
Virginia Polytechnic Institute and State University	VA	0	0	2	1	0	0	0	0	5	0	30	4	0	0	37	5	42
University of Washington	WA	0	0	1	0	0	0	0	0	2	0	13	4	2	0	18	4	22
Washington State University	WA	0	0	0	0	0	0	0	0	1	0	2	2	0	0	3	2	5
Washington University	MO	0	0	0	0	0	0	0	0	0	0	0	0	1	0	1	0	1
Wayne State University	MI	0	0	1	0	0	0	0	0	0	0	3	0	0	0	4	0	4
West Virginia University	WV	0	0	0	0	0	0	0	0	1	0	1	0	0	0	2	0	2
Wichita State University	KS	0	0	1	0	0	0	0	0	0	0	1	0	0	0	2	0	2
University of Wyoming	WY	0	0	0	0	0	0	0	0	0	0	4	0	0	0	4	0	4
Totals:		6	2	41	8	5	1	1	0	119	10	574	130	31	11	777	162	939
CANADIAN INSTITUTIONS:																		
Ecole Polytechnique de Montreal	PQ	0	0	0	0	0	0	0	0	0	0	0	0	8	1	8	1	9
University of Ottawa, Faculty of Engineering	ON	0	0	0	0	0	0	0	0	0	0	1	1	8	3	9	4	13
Totals:		0	0	0	0	0	0	0	0	0	0	1	1	16	4	17	5	22

STO-WYO

ELECTRICAL ENGINEERING

DOCTORAL DEGREES AWARDED IN ELECTRICAL/COMPUTER ENGINEERING, 2005-2006

INSTITUTION		AFRICAN AMERICAN		ASIAN AMERICAN		HISPANIC		NATIVE AMERICAN		CAUCASIAN		FOREIGN		OTHER		TOTAL BY GENDER		TOTAL DEGREES
		M	F	M	F	M	F	M	F	M	F	M	F	M	F	M	F	
Air Force Institute of Technology	OH	0	0	0	0	0	0	0	0	1	0	0	0	0	0	1	0	1
The University of Akron	OH	0	0	0	0	0	0	0	0	0	0	4	1	0	0	4	1	5
The University of Arizona	AZ	0	0	0	0	0	0	0	0	2	0	6	2	0	0	8	2	10
Auburn University	AL	0	0	0	1	0	0	0	0	4	0	10	4	0	0	14	5	19
Brigham Young University	UT	0	0	0	0	0	0	0	0	0	0	1	0	2	0	3	0	3
Brown University	RI	0	1	0	0	0	0	0	0	1	0	0	2	0	0	1	3	4
University of California, Berkeley	CA	0	0	4	2	0	0	0	0	13	0	7	1	1	0	25	3	28
University of California, Davis	CA	0	0	2	0	0	0	0	0	1	0	5	4	1	0	9	4	13
University of California, Irvine	CA	0	0	0	0	0	0	0	0	0	0	0	0	19	7	19	7	26
University of California, San Diego	CA	0	0	1	0	0	0	1	0	3	0	7	4	0	1	12	5	17
University of California, Santa Barbara	CA	0	0	2	0	0	0	1	0	8	0	26	2	5	1	42	3	45
Carnegie Mellon University	PA	0	0	1	0	0	0	0	0	2	0	12	3	2	1	17	4	21
Case Western Reserve University	OH	0	0	0	0	0	0	0	0	0	0	4	0	0	0	4	0	4
Clarkson University	NY	0	0	0	1	0	0	0	0	2	0	2	1	0	0	4	1	5
Cleveland State University	OH	0	0	0	0	0	0	0	0	0	0	0	0	2	0	2	0	2
Colorado State University	CO	0	0	0	0	0	0	0	0	1	0	0	0	9	0	10	0	10
University of Colorado at Boulder	CO	0	0	0	0	0	0	0	0	10	1	5	1	0	0	15	2	17
Cornell University	NY	0	0	0	1	0	0	0	0	8	1	17	4	1	0	26	6	32
University of Delaware	DE	0	0	0	0	0	0	0	0	0	0	10	2	0	0	10	2	12
Duke University Pratt School of Engineering	NC	0	0	0	0	0	0	0	0	0	0	0	0	14	1	14	1	15
George Mason University	VA	0	0	0	0	0	0	0	0	0	0	0	1	0	0	0	1	1
Georgia Institute of Technology	GA	2	0	2	2	0	0	0	0	17	1	54	4	0	0	75	7	82
Illinois Institute of Technology	IL	0	0	1	0	0	0	0	0	0	0	12	1	0	0	13	1	14
University of Illinois at Chicago	IL	0	0	8	0	0	0	0	0	0	0	0	0	0	0	8	0	8
University of Illinois at Urbana-Champaign	IL	0	0	3	0	0	0	0	0	12	2	31	5	0	0	46	7	53
The University of Iowa	IA	0	0	0	0	0	0	0	0	0	0	5	0	0	0	5	0	5
The Johns Hopkins University	MD	0	0	0	0	0	0	0	0	2	0	10	1	0	0	12	1	13
University of Kansas	KS	0	0	1	0	0	0	0	0	1	0	1	0	0	0	3	0	3
Kansas State University	KS	0	0	0	0	0	0	0	0	0	0	4	0	0	0	4	0	4
University of Kentucky	KY	0	0	1	0	0	0	0	0	2	0	6	0	0	0	9	0	9
Lehigh University	PA	0	0	0	0	0	0	0	0	0	0	0	1	0	0	0	1	1
Louisiana State University	LA	0	0	0	0	0	0	0	0	0	0	4	1	0	0	4	1	5
Marquette University	WI	0	0	0	0	0	0	0	0	0	0	2	0	0	0	2	0	2
University of Maryland, College Park	MD	0	0	2	0	0	0	0	0	4	1	23	5	1	0	30	6	36
Massachusetts Institute of Technology	MA	3	0	11	5	0	0	0	0	36	4	27	7	7	0	84	16	100
University of Massachusetts Amherst	MA	0	0	0	0	0	0	0	0	0	0	5	0	0	0	5	0	5
University of Massachusetts Dartmouth	MA	0	0	0	0	0	0	0	0	1	0	3	0	0	0	4	0	4
University of Massachusetts Lowell	MA	0	0	1	0	0	0	0	0	0	0	7	0	0	0	8	0	8
University of Miami	FL	0	0	0	0	0	0	0	0	0	0	3	1	0	0	3	1	4
University of Michigan	MI	0	0	6	0	1	0	0	0	11	0	16	2	0	0	33	2	35
Michigan State University	MI	0	0	0	0	0	0	0	0	2	0	9	1	0	0	12	1	13
University of Minnesota - Twin Cities	MN	0	0	0	1	0	0	0	0	6	0	28	6	0	0	34	7	41
Montana State University	MT	0	0	0	0	0	0	0	0	0	0	1	1	0	0	1	1	2
University of Nevada, Las Vegas	NV	0	0	0	0	0	0	0	0	0	0	1	0	1	0	2	0	2
University of New Hampshire	NH	0	0	0	0	0	0	0	0	1	0	2	1	0	0	3	1	4

ELECTRICAL/COMPUTER ENGINEERING   AIR-NEW

INSTITUTION		AFRICAN AMERICAN		ASIAN AMERICAN		HISPANIC		NATIVE AMERICAN		CAUCASIAN		FOREIGN		OTHER		TOTAL BY GENDER		TOTAL DEGREES
		M	F	M	F	M	F	M	F	M	F	M	F	M	F	M	F	
The University of New Mexico	NM	0	0	0	0	1	0	0	0	0	1	11	2	0	0	12	3	15
City College of the City University of New York	NY	1	0	1	1	0	0	0	0	0	0	5	0	2	0	9	1	10
University of North Carolina, Charlotte	NC	0	0	0	0	0	0	0	0	0	0	2	2	0	0	2	2	4
North Dakota State University	ND	0	0	1	0	0	0	0	0	1	0	0	0	0	0	2	0	2
Northwestern University	IL	0	0	2	0	0	0	0	0	5	0	18	2	1	0	26	2	28
The Ohio State University	OH	0	0	0	0	0	0	0	0	8	0	23	5	0	0	31	5	36
University of Oklahoma	OK	0	0	0	0	0	0	0	0	0	0	4	1	1	0	5	1	6
Oklahoma State University	OK	0	0	0	0	0	0	0	0	1	0	9	0	0	0	10	0	10
Old Dominion University	VA	0	0	0	0	0	0	0	0	2	1	0	0	0	0	2	1	3
Oregon State University	OR	0	0	0	0	0	0	0	0	2	0	8	2	0	0	10	2	12
University of Pennsylvania	PA	0	0	0	0	0	0	0	0	0	0	4	1	0	0	4	1	5
Polytechnic University	NY	0	0	0	0	0	0	0	0	0	0	6	1	2	0	8	1	9
Portland State University	OR	0	0	0	1	0	0	0	0	0	0	2	0	0	0	2	1	3
Princeton University	NJ	0	0	4	1	0	0	0	0	3	0	15	4	0	0	22	5	27
Purdue University	IN	0	0	1	0	1	0	0	0	2	0	47	4	2	1	53	5	58
University of Rhode Island	RI	0	0	0	0	0	0	0	0	3	0	0	1	0	0	3	1	4
William Marsh Rice University	TX	0	0	0	0	0	0	0	0	2	0	5	1	0	0	7	1	8
University of Rochester	NY	0	0	0	0	0	0	0	0	1	0	5	1	0	0	6	1	7
Rutgers, The State University of New Jersey	NJ	0	0	0	0	0	2	0	0	1	0	7	0	0	0	8	2	10
University of Tennessee, Knoxville	TN	0	0	0	0	0	0	0	0	1	0	1	2	0	0	2	2	4
Texas Tech University	TX	0	0	0	0	1	0	0	0	5	0	4	0	0	0	10	0	10
The University of Texas at Austin	TX	1	0	4	0	0	0	0	0	8	2	46	0	0	0	59	2	61
University of Utah	UT	0	0	0	0	0	0	0	0	2	0	5	1	0	0	7	1	8
Utah State University	UT	0	0	0	0	0	0	0	0	2	0	2	0	0	0	4	0	4
University of Wisconsin, Madison	WI	1	0	0	0	0	0	0	0	2	0	13	2	3	0	19	2	21
Worcester Polytechnic Institute	MA	0	0	0	0	0	0	0	0	1	0	3	0	0	0	4	0	4
Totals:		8	1	59	15	4	2	2	0	203	14	615	101	76	12	967	145	1,112
CANADIAN INSTITUTIONS:																		
University of Alberta	AB	0	0	0	0	0	0	0	0	0	0	0	0	13	2	13	2	15
University of Calgary	AB	0	0	0	0	0	0	0	0	0	0	6	0	6	0	12	0	12
Concordia University, Faculty of Engr. and Comp. Sci.	PQ	0	0	0	0	0	0	0	0	0	0	1	0	9	0	10	0	10
McGill University, Faculty of Engineering	PQ	0	0	0	0	0	0	0	0	0	0	0	0	9	2	9	2	11
University of Waterloo	ON	0	0	0	0	0	0	0	0	0	0	0	0	28	3	28	3	31
Totals:		0	0	0	0	0	0	0	0	0	0	7	0	65	7	72	7	79

ELECTRICAL/COMPUTER ENGINEERING — NEW-WOR

INSTITUTION		AFRICAN AMERICAN		ASIAN AMERICAN		HISPANIC		NATIVE AMERICAN		CAUCASIAN		FOREIGN		OTHER		TOTAL BY GENDER		TOTAL DEGREES
		M	F	M	F	M	F	M	F	M	F	M	F	M	F	M	F	
Colorado School of Mines	CO	0	0	0	0	0	0	0	0	1	0	0	0	0	0	1	0	1
Dartmouth College	NH	0	0	0	0	0	0	0	0	0	0	3	2	2	1	5	3	8
University of Denver	CO	0	0	0	0	0	0	0	0	0	0	1	0	0	0	1	0	1
Louisiana Tech University	LA	0	0	0	0	0	0	0	0	1	0	8	2	0	0	9	2	11
The University of Memphis	TN	0	0	0	0	0	0	0	0	0	0	3	1	0	0	3	1	4
Morgan State University	MD	4	2	1	0	0	0	0	0	0	0	0	1	0	0	5	3	8
University of Nebraska, Lincoln	NE	0	1	1	0	0	0	0	0	2	1	11	2	0	0	14	4	18
North Dakota State University	ND	0	0	2	0	0	0	0	0	0	0	0	0	0	0	2	0	2
University of Oklahoma	OK	0	0	0	0	0	0	0	0	1	0	0	0	0	0	1	0	1
Tuskegee University	AL	2	0	0	0	0	0	0	0	0	0	0	0	0	0	2	0	2
Virginia Commonwealth University	VA	0	0	1	1	0	0	0	0	3	0	0	0	0	1	4	2	6
University of Wisconsin, Milwaukee	WI	0	0	1	0	0	0	0	0	2	0	9	1	0	0	12	1	13
Totals:		6	3	6	1	0	0	0	0	10	1	35	9	2	2	59	16	75

COL-WIS

ENGINEERING (GENERAL)

DOCTORAL DEGREES AWARDED IN ENGINEERING MANAGEMENT, 2005-2006

INSTITUTION		AFRICAN AMERICAN		ASIAN AMERICAN		HISPANIC		NATIVE AMERICAN		CAUCASIAN		FOREIGN		OTHER		TOTAL BY GENDER		TOTAL DEGREES
		M	F	M	F	M	F	M	F	M	F	M	F	M	F	M	F	
Colorado School of Mines	CO	0	0	0	0	1	0	0	0	0	1	0	1	0	0	1	2	3
The George Washington University	DC	1	1	2	0	1	0	0	1	7	5	8	2	0	0	19	9	28
University of Illinois at Urbana-Champaign	IL	0	0	0	0	0	0	0	0	2	0	0	0	0	0	2	0	2
University of Missouri - Rolla	MO	1	0	0	0	0	0	0	0	0	2	1	0	0	0	2	2	4
Portland State University	OR	0	0	0	0	0	0	0	0	0	0	2	0	0	0	2	0	2
Totals:		2	1	2	0	2	0	0	1	9	8	11	3	0	0	26	13	39
CANADIAN INSTITUTIONS:																		
University of Waterloo	ON	0	0	0	0	0	0	0	0	0	0	0	0	1	0	1	0	1
Totals:		0	0	0	0	0	0	0	0	0	0	0	0	1	0	1	0	1

COL-POR

ENGINEERING MANAGEMENT

INSTITUTION		AFRICAN AMERICAN		ASIAN AMERICAN		HISPANIC		NATIVE AMERICAN		CAUCASIAN		FOREIGN		OTHER		TOTAL BY GENDER		TOTAL DEGREES
		M	F	M	F	M	F	M	F	M	F	M	F	M	F	M	F	
Air Force Institute of Technology	OH	0	0	0	0	0	0	0	0	2	0	0	0	0	0	2	0	2
California Institute of Technology	CA	0	0	1	0	0	0	0	0	0	3	6	4	0	0	7	7	14
University of California, Davis	CA	0	0	0	0	0	0	0	0	4	0	1	0	1	0	6	0	6
Colorado School of Mines	CO	0	0	0	0	0	0	0	0	0	1	1	0	0	0	1	1	2
Columbia University	NY	0	0	0	1	0	0	0	0	3	1	3	2	0	0	6	4	10
Cornell University	NY	0	0	0	0	1	0	0	0	2	1	0	2	0	0	3	3	6
Idaho State University	ID	0	0	0	0	0	0	0	0	0	1	1	0	0	0	1	1	2
University of Illinois at Urbana-Champaign	IL	0	0	2	0	0	0	1	0	17	1	20	2	2	0	42	3	45
Louisiana State University	LA	0	0	0	0	0	0	0	0	1	0	4	1	0	0	5	1	6
Mississippi State University	MS	0	0	0	0	0	0	0	0	0	0	2	0	0	0	2	0	2
Northwestern University	IL	0	0	1	0	0	0	0	0	0	2	0	0	0	0	1	2	3
The Pennsylvania State University	PA	0	0	1	0	0	0	0	0	4	0	7	3	0	0	12	3	15
Rensselaer Polytechnic Institute	NY	0	0	0	0	0	0	0	0	1	0	2	1	0	0	3	1	4
University of Tennessee, Knoxville	TN	0	0	0	0	0	0	0	0	1	0	0	1	0	0	1	1	2
University of Virginia	VA	0	0	0	0	0	0	0	0	5	0	0	0	0	0	5	0	5
Virginia Polytechnic Institute and State University	VA	0	0	0	0	0	0	0	0	2	0	4	1	0	0	6	1	7
Totals:		0	0	5	1	1	0	1	0	42	10	51	17	3	0	103	28	131
CANADIAN INSTITUTIONS:																		
Ecole Polytechnique de Montreal	PQ	0	0	0	0	0	0	0	0	0	0	0	0	4	1	4	1	5
Totals:		0	0	0	0	0	0	0	0	0	0	0	0	4	1	4	1	5

ENGR. SCIENCE AND ENGR. PHYSICS   AIR-VIR

INSTITUTION		AFRICAN AMERICAN		ASIAN AMERICAN		HISPANIC		NATIVE AMERICAN		CAUCASIAN		FOREIGN		OTHER		TOTAL BY GENDER		TOTAL DEGREES
		M	F	M	F	M	F	M	F	M	F	M	F	M	F	M	F	
The University of Arizona	AZ	0	0	0	0	0	0	0	0	0	0	2	1	0	0	2	1	3
Arizona State University	AZ	0	0	1	0	0	0	0	0	0	0	4	0	0	0	5	0	5
University of Central Florida	FL	0	0	0	0	0	0	0	0	0	1	1	0	0	0	1	1	2
University of Cincinnati	OH	0	0	0	0	0	0	0	0	2	0	9	2	0	0	11	2	13
Clarkson University	NY	0	0	0	0	0	0	0	0	0	0	1	0	0	0	1	0	1
Clemson University	SC	0	0	0	0	0	0	0	0	1	1	1	3	0	0	2	4	6
Colorado School of Mines	CO	0	0	0	0	0	0	0	0	1	0	0	0	0	0	1	0	1
Columbia University	NY	0	0	0	1	0	0	0	0	0	0	3	1	0	0	3	2	5
Cornell University	NY	0	0	0	0	0	0	0	0	0	0	5	3	0	1	5	4	9
Drexel University	PA	0	0	0	0	0	0	0	0	1	0	0	0	0	0	1	0	1
University of Florida	FL	0	0	1	0	1	0	0	0	2	2	5	1	0	0	9	3	12
Georgia Institute of Technology	GA	0	0	1	0	0	0	0	0	1	0	2	4	1	0	5	4	9
University of Houston, Cullen School of Engineering	TX	0	0	0	0	0	0	0	0	1	0	3	0	0	0	4	0	4
Illinois Institute of Technology	IL	0	0	0	0	0	0	0	0	0	0	1	0	0	0	1	0	1
The Johns Hopkins University	MD	0	0	0	1	0	0	0	0	2	2	0	2	0	0	2	5	7
Lehigh University	PA	0	0	0	0	0	0	0	0	0	0	1	0	0	0	1	0	1
University of Michigan	MI	0	0	0	0	0	0	0	0	1	0	4	1	0	0	5	1	6
Michigan State University	MI	0	0	0	0	0	0	0	0	0	0	2	1	0	0	2	1	3
Michigan Technological University	MI	0	0	0	0	0	0	0	0	0	0	1	0	0	0	1	0	1
Montana State University	MT	0	0	0	0	0	0	0	0	0	1	0	0	0	0	0	1	1
New Jersey Institute of Technology	NJ	0	0	0	0	0	0	0	0	0	0	0	1	0	0	0	1	1
University of North Carolina at Chapel Hill	NC	0	0	0	0	0	0	0	0	2	0	2	1	0	0	4	1	5
Old Dominion University	VA	0	0	0	0	0	0	0	0	1	0	0	0	0	0	1	0	1
OGI School of Science & Engineering at OHSU	OR	0	0	1	0	1	0	0	0	2	1	1	0	0	0	5	1	6
William Marsh Rice University	TX	0	0	0	0	0	0	0	0	0	0	1	3	0	0	1	3	4
University of Southern California	CA	0	0	0	0	0	0	0	0	0	0	5	2	0	0	5	2	7
Stevens Institute of Technology	NJ	0	0	0	0	0	0	0	0	0	0	1	3	0	0	1	3	4
Texas A&M University - Kingsville	TX	1	0	0	0	0	0	0	0	1	1	1	0	0	0	3	1	4
Vanderbilt University	TN	0	0	0	0	0	0	0	0	0	0	0	1	1	1	1	2	3
Virginia Polytechnic Institute and State University	VA	0	0	0	0	0	0	0	0	0	0	0	1	0	0	0	1	1
Washington University	MO	0	0	0	0	0	0	0	0	0	0	1	1	0	0	1	1	2
Totals:		1	0	4	2	2	0	0	0	18	9	57	32	2	2	84	45	129

ENVIRONMENTAL ENGINEERING

ARI-WAS

DOCTORAL DEGREES AWARDED IN INDUSTRIAL/MANUFACTURING ENGINEERING, 2005-2006

INSTITUTION		AFRICAN AMERICAN		ASIAN AMERICAN		HISPANIC		NATIVE AMERICAN		CAUCASIAN		FOREIGN		OTHER		TOTAL BY GENDER		TOTAL DEGREES
		M	F	M	F	M	F	M	F	M	F	M	F	M	F	M	F	
Air Force Institute of Technology	OH	0	0	0	0	0	0	0	0	0	0	0	0	3	0	3	0	3
The University of Alabama in Huntsville	AL	1	0	0	0	0	0	0	0	3	2	0	0	0	0	4	2	6
The University of Arizona	AZ	0	0	0	0	1	0	0	0	1	0	7	0	0	0	9	0	9
Arizona State University	AZ	0	0	0	1	0	0	0	0	3	0	0	0	1	0	4	1	5
University of Arkansas	AR	0	0	0	0	0	0	0	0	1	0	1	0	0	0	2	0	2
Auburn University	AL	0	0	0	0	0	0	0	0	0	1	0	0	0	0	0	1	1
Boston University	MA	0	0	0	0	0	0	0	0	0	0	3	1	0	0	3	1	4
University of California, Berkeley	CA	0	0	0	0	0	0	0	0	1	0	5	0	0	0	6	0	6
University of Central Florida	FL	0	0	0	0	2	1	0	0	3	2	0	0	0	0	5	3	8
Clemson University	SC	0	0	0	0	0	0	0	0	1	2	0	0	0	0	1	2	3
Cleveland State University	OH	0	0	0	0	2	0	0	0	0	0	1	0	0	0	3	0	3
Columbia University	NY	0	0	0	0	0	0	0	0	0	0	5	1	0	0	5	1	6
Cornell University	NY	0	0	1	1	0	0	0	0	1	0	3	1	0	0	5	2	7
University of Florida	FL	1	0	0	0	0	0	0	0	0	0	5	0	0	0	6	0	6
Florida International University	FL	0	0	0	0	0	0	0	0	0	0	1	0	0	0	1	0	1
FAMU-FSU College of Engineering	FL	0	1	0	0	0	0	0	0	0	0	1	0	0	0	1	1	2
Georgia Institute of Technology	GA	0	1	3	1	0	0	0	0	8	3	20	4	2	0	33	9	42
University of Houston, Cullen School of Engineering	TX	0	0	0	0	0	0	0	0	0	0	2	0	0	0	2	0	2
University of Illinois at Chicago	IL	0	0	0	1	0	0	0	0	0	0	0	1	0	0	0	1	1
University of Illinois at Urbana-Champaign	IL	0	0	0	0	0	0	0	0	0	1	0	0	0	0	0	1	1
The University of Iowa	IA	0	0	0	0	0	0	0	0	1	0	1	1	0	0	2	1	3
Iowa State University	IA	0	0	0	0	0	0	0	0	0	0	4	0	0	0	4	0	4
Kansas State University	KS	0	0	0	0	0	0	0	0	0	0	2	1	0	0	2	1	3
Lamar University	TX	0	0	0	0	0	0	0	0	0	0	1	0	0	0	1	0	1
Lawrence Technological University	MI	0	0	0	0	0	0	0	0	2	1	0	0	0	0	2	1	3
Lehigh University	PA	0	0	0	0	0	1	0	0	0	0	1	0	1	0	2	1	3
University of Louisville	KY	0	0	0	0	0	0	0	0	2	0	2	1	0	0	4	1	5
University of Massachusetts Amherst	MA	0	0	0	0	0	0	0	0	0	0	1	0	0	0	1	0	1
University of Michigan	MI	0	0	0	1	0	0	0	0	2	1	7	0	1	0	10	2	12
University of Minnesota - Twin Cities	MN	0	0	0	0	0	0	0	0	0	0	1	0	0	0	1	0	1
Mississippi State University	MS	0	0	0	0	0	0	0	0	0	0	2	0	0	0	2	0	2
Montana State University	MT	0	0	0	0	0	0	0	0	0	1	0	0	0	0	0	1	1
New Jersey Institute of Technology	NJ	0	0	0	0	0	0	0	0	0	0	1	0	0	0	1	0	1
State University of New York at Buffalo	NY	0	0	0	0	0	0	0	0	1	0	3	0	1	0	5	0	5
North Carolina A & T State University	NC	0	2	0	0	0	0	0	0	0	0	0	0	0	0	0	2	2
North Carolina State University	NC	0	0	0	0	0	0	0	0	0	0	3	3	0	0	3	3	6
University of North Texas	TX	0	0	0	0	0	0	0	0	1	0	0	0	3	1	4	1	5
Northeastern University	MA	0	0	0	0	0	0	0	0	1	0	1	0	0	0	1	0	1
Northwestern University	IL	0	0	0	0	0	0	0	0	0	1	5	1	0	0	5	1	6
The Ohio State University	OH	0	0	0	0	0	0	0	0	3	0	7	1	0	0	10	1	11
University of Oklahoma	OK	0	0	0	0	0	0	0	0	1	0	4	0	0	0	5	0	5
Oklahoma State University	OK	0	0	0	0	0	0	0	0	0	0	1	0	0	0	2	0	2
Oregon State University	OR	0	0	0	0	0	0	0	0	0	0	3	3	0	0	3	3	6
The Pennsylvania State University	PA	0	0	0	0	0	0	0	0	0	1	5	0	0	0	5	1	6
University of Pittsburgh	PA	0	1	0	0	0	0	0	0	1	1	3	1	0	0	4	3	7

INDUSTRIAL/MANUFACTURING ENGR.

AIR-PIT

DOCTORAL DEGREES AWARDED IN INDUSTRIAL/MANUFACTURING ENGINEERING, 2005-2006

INSTITUTION		AFRICAN AMERICAN		ASIAN AMERICAN		HISPANIC		NATIVE AMERICAN		CAUCASIAN		FOREIGN		OTHER		TOTAL BY GENDER		TOTAL DEGREES
		M	F	M	F	M	F	M	F	M	F	M	F	M	F	M	F	
Purdue University	IN	0	0	0	0	0	0	0	0	1	0	10	2	0	1	11	3	14
Rensselaer Polytechnic Institute	NY	0	0	0	0	0	0	0	0	0	0	5	2	0	0	5	2	7
University of Rhode Island	RI	0	0	0	0	0	0	0	0	0	0	2	0	0	0	2	0	2
Rutgers, The State University of New Jersey	NJ	0	0	0	0	0	0	0	0	0	0	4	0	0	0	4	0	4
University of South Florida	FL	0	0	0	0	0	0	0	0	1	0	0	0	0	0	1	0	1
University of Southern California	CA	0	0	0	0	0	0	0	0	1	1	3	1	0	0	4	2	6
Stanford University	CA	0	0	1	0	1	0	0	0	2	0	10	4	0	0	14	4	18
University of Tennessee, Knoxville	TN	0	0	0	0	0	0	0	0	2	1	3	0	0	0	5	1	6
Texas A&M University	TX	0	0	0	0	0	0	0	0	1	0	7	1	0	0	8	1	9
Texas Tech University	TX	0	0	0	0	0	1	0	0	0	0	5	0	0	0	5	1	6
The University of Texas at Arlington	TX	0	0	2	1	0	0	0	0	0	0	2	1	0	0	4	2	6
The University of Texas at Austin	TX	0	0	0	0	0	0	0	0	0	1	0	1	0	0	0	2	2
The University of Toledo	OH	0	0	0	0	0	0	0	0	0	0	1	0	0	0	1	0	1
Virginia Polytechnic Institute and State University	VA	1	0	0	1	1	0	0	0	3	3	7	4	0	0	12	8	20
University of Washington	WA	0	0	0	0	0	0	0	0	0	0	2	1	0	0	2	1	3
Wayne State University	MI	0	0	0	0	0	0	0	0	0	0	5	0	0	0	5	0	5
West Virginia University	WV	0	0	0	0	0	0	0	0	2	0	2	1	0	0	4	1	5
Western Michigan University	MI	0	0	0	0	0	0	0	0	0	0	2	0	0	0	2	0	2
University of Wisconsin, Madison	WI	0	0	0	0	1	1	0	0	1	0	5	2	0	0	7	3	10
Worcester Polytechnic Institute	MA	0	0	0	0	0	0	0	0	0	0	1	0	0	0	1	0	1
Totals:		3	5	7	7	8	4	0	0	52	22	187	39	12	2	269	79	348
CANADIAN INSTITUTIONS:																		
University of Calgary	AB	0	0	0	0	0	0	0	0	0	0	0	0	3	2	3	2	5
Ecole de Technologie Superieure	PQ	0	0	0	0	0	0	0	0	0	0	0	0	10	3	10	3	13
Totals:		0	0	0	0	0	0	0	0	0	0	0	0	13	5	13	5	18

INDUSTRIAL/MANUFACTURING ENGR.   PUR-WOR

DOCTORAL DEGREES AWARDED IN MECHANICAL ENGINEERING, 2005-2006

INSTITUTION		AFRICAN AMERICAN		ASIAN AMERICAN		HISPANIC		NATIVE AMERICAN		CAUCASIAN		FOREIGN		OTHER		TOTAL BY GENDER		TOTAL DEGREES
		M	F	M	F	M	F	M	F	M	F	M	F	M	F	M	F	
The University of Akron	OH	0	0	0	0	0	0	0	0	0	0	3	1	0	0	3	1	4
The University of Alabama in Huntsville	AL	0	0	0	0	0	0	0	0	0	0	1	0	0	0	1	0	1
The University of Alabama	AL	0	0	4	0	0	0	0	0	0	0	2	1	0	0	6	1	7
The University of Arizona	AZ	0	0	0	0	0	0	0	0	0	0	3	0	0	0	3	0	3
Arizona State University	AZ	0	0	0	0	0	0	0	0	1	0	10	0	0	0	11	0	11
Auburn University	AL	0	0	0	0	0	0	0	0	0	0	8	0	0	0	8	0	8
Boston University	MA	0	0	1	0	0	0	0	0	1	0	1	0	0	0	3	0	3
Brigham Young University	UT	0	0	0	0	0	0	0	0	0	0	3	0	2	0	5	0	5
California Institute of Technology	CA	0	0	0	0	0	0	0	0	4	0	2	2	0	0	6	2	8
University of California, Berkeley	CA	0	0	4	3	3	0	0	0	7	2	26	2	1	1	41	8	49
University of California, Davis	CA	0	0	0	0	0	0	0	0	2	0	3	0	2	0	7	0	7
University of California, Irvine	CA	0	0	0	0	0	0	0	0	0	0	0	0	14	2	14	2	16
University of California, Los Angeles	CA	0	0	2	0	0	0	0	0	0	1	17	1	0	0	19	2	21
University of California, Riverside	CA	0	0	0	0	0	0	0	0	0	0	0	0	4	1	4	1	5
University of California, San Diego	CA	0	0	0	0	0	0	0	0	3	0	8	0	2	0	13	0	13
University of California, Santa Barbara	CA	0	0	1	0	0	0	0	0	2	2	3	4	1	1	7	7	14
Carnegie Mellon University	PA	0	0	0	0	1	0	0	0	1	1	9	1	0	0	11	2	13
Case Western Reserve University	OH	0	0	1	1	0	0	0	0	6	2	9	0	0	0	16	3	19
The Catholic University of America	DC	0	0	0	0	0	0	0	0	0	0	2	0	0	0	2	0	4
University of Central Florida	FL	0	0	0	0	0	0	0	0	1	1	2	0	0	0	3	1	4
University of Cincinnati	OH	0	0	0	0	0	0	0	0	0	0	5	0	0	0	5	0	5
Clarkson University	NY	0	0	0	0	0	0	0	0	1	0	1	2	0	0	2	2	4
Clemson University	SC	0	0	0	0	0	0	0	0	1	0	2	1	0	0	3	1	4
Cleveland State University	OH	0	0	0	0	0	0	0	0	0	0	1	0	0	0	1	0	1
Colorado State University	CO	0	0	0	0	0	0	0	0	0	0	0	0	1	0	1	0	1
University of Colorado at Boulder	CO	0	0	0	1	0	0	1	0	1	1	3	0	0	0	5	2	7
Columbia University	NY	0	0	0	0	0	0	0	0	0	0	5	2	1	0	6	2	8
University of Connecticut	CT	0	0	1	0	0	0	0	0	0	0	3	0	1	0	6	0	6
Cornell University	NY	0	0	0	0	0	0	0	0	1	0	7	0	0	0	8	0	8
University of Dayton	OH	0	0	0	0	0	0	0	0	3	0	4	0	0	0	7	0	7
University of Delaware	DE	0	0	0	0	0	0	0	0	2	0	10	3	0	0	12	3	15
Drexel University	PA	0	0	1	0	0	0	0	0	2	1	5	1	1	0	9	2	11
Duke University Pratt School of Engineering	NC	0	0	0	0	0	0	0	0	0	0	0	0	5	1	5	1	6
University of Florida	FL	0	0	0	0	1	0	0	0	4	2	12	1	0	0	17	3	20
Florida Atlantic University	FL	0	0	1	0	0	0	0	0	0	0	0	1	0	0	1	1	2
Florida Institute of Technology	FL	0	0	0	0	0	0	0	0	1	0	0	0	0	0	1	0	1
Florida International University	FL	0	0	0	0	0	0	0	0	0	0	2	0	0	0	2	0	2
FAMU-FSU College of Engineering	FL	0	0	0	2	0	0	0	0	0	0	3	0	0	0	3	2	5
The George Washington University	DC	0	0	0	0	0	0	0	0	1	0	1	0	0	0	2	0	2
Georgia Institute of Technology	GA	3	0	3	1	1	0	0	0	12	1	23	3	0	0	42	5	47
University of Hawaii at Manoa	HI	0	0	1	0	0	0	0	0	0	0	8	2	1	1	10	3	13
University of Houston, Cullen School of Engineering	TX	0	0	0	0	0	0	0	0	0	0	4	0	0	0	9	0	5
Howard University	DC	0	0	0	0	0	0	0	0	0	0	1	0	0	0	1	0	1
University of Idaho	ID	0	0	1	0	0	0	0	0	1	0	0	0	0	0	2	0	2
University of Illinois at Chicago	IL	0	0	4	0	0	0	0	0	8	0	0	0	0	0	12	0	12

MECHANICAL ENGINEERING

AKR-ILL

Doctoral Degrees Awarded in Mechanical Engineering, 2005-2006

Institution	State	African American M	F	Asian American M	F	Hispanic M	F	Native American M	F	Caucasian M	F	Foreign M	F	Other M	F	Total by Gender M	F	Total Degrees
University of Illinois at Urbana-Champaign	IL	0	0	0	0	0	0	0	0	7	1	9	1	0	0	16	2	18
The University of Iowa	IA	0	0	0	0	0	0	0	0	1	0	7	0	0	0	8	0	8
Iowa State University	IA	0	0	0	0	0	0	0	0	3	0	6	1	1	0	10	1	11
The Johns Hopkins University	MD	0	0	0	0	0	0	0	0	2	1	3	1	0	0	5	2	7
University of Kansas	KS	0	0	1	0	0	0	0	0	0	0	0	0	0	0	1	0	1
Kansas State University	KS	0	0	0	0	0	0	0	0	1	0	3	1	0	0	4	1	5
University of Kentucky	KY	0	0	0	1	0	0	0	0	1	0	3	0	0	0	4	1	5
Louisiana State University	LA	0	0	0	0	0	0	0	0	0	0	6	1	0	0	6	1	7
University of Louisville	KY	0	0	0	0	0	0	0	0	1	0	2	2	0	0	3	2	5
University of Maine	ME	0	0	0	0	0	0	0	0	0	1	1	0	0	0	1	1	2
Marquette University	WI	0	0	0	0	0	0	0	0	1	0	0	1	0	0	1	1	2
University of Maryland, Baltimore County	MD	0	0	0	0	0	0	0	0	0	0	3	0	0	0	3	0	3
University of Maryland, College Park	MD	1	0	1	0	0	0	0	0	5	1	30	2	1	0	38	3	41
Massachusetts Institute of Technology	MA	2	0	0	1	0	0	0	0	18	1	18	5	0	0	38	7	45
University of Massachusetts Amherst	MA	0	0	0	0	0	0	0	0	1	0	2	0	0	0	3	0	3
University of Massachusetts Lowell	MA	0	0	0	0	0	0	0	0	0	0	3	1	0	0	3	1	4
University of Miami	FL	0	0	0	0	0	0	0	0	0	0	4	0	0	0	4	0	4
University of Michigan	MI	0	1	2	0	0	0	0	0	3	3	29	2	0	0	34	6	40
Michigan State University	MI	0	0	2	0	0	0	0	0	1	0	11	0	0	0	14	0	14
Michigan Technological University	MI	0	0	1	0	0	0	1	0	0	0	9	2	0	0	11	2	13
University of Minnesota -Twin Cities	MN	0	0	2	0	0	0	0	0	0	0	8	3	0	0	10	3	13
The University of Mississippi	MS	0	0	0	0	0	0	0	0	0	0	1	0	0	0	1	0	1
University of Missouri-Columbia	MO	0	0	0	0	0	0	0	0	1	0	5	2	0	0	6	2	8
University of Missouri - Rolla	MO	0	0	0	0	0	0	0	0	0	1	9	0	0	0	9	1	10
University of Nevada, Las Vegas	NV	0	0	0	0	0	0	0	0	0	0	2	0	0	0	2	0	2
University of Nevada, Reno	NV	0	0	0	0	0	0	0	0	0	0	2	0	0	0	2	0	2
New Jersey Institute of Technology	NJ	0	0	0	0	0	0	0	0	2	0	3	2	0	0	5	2	7
The University of New Mexico	NM	0	0	0	0	0	0	0	0	2	0	3	1	0	0	5	1	6
New Mexico State University	NM	0	0	0	0	0	0	0	0	1	0	1	0	0	0	2	0	2
City College of the City University of New York	NY	1	0	1	0	0	0	0	0	0	0	3	1	0	0	5	1	6
The State University of New York at Binghamton	NY	0	0	0	0	0	0	0	0	0	0	1	1	0	0	1	1	2
State University of New York at Buffalo	NY	0	0	0	0	0	0	0	0	3	0	4	0	0	0	7	0	7
Stony Brook University	NY	0	0	0	0	0	0	0	0	0	0	7	0	0	0	7	0	7
North Carolina A & T State University	NC	1	0	1	0	0	0	0	0	0	0	2	0	0	0	4	0	4
North Carolina State University	NC	0	0	1	0	0	0	0	0	1	0	7	0	0	0	9	0	9
University of North Carolina, Charlotte	NC	0	0	0	0	0	0	0	0	2	2	2	0	0	0	4	2	6
Northeastern University	MA	0	0	0	0	0	0	0	0	0	0	5	2	0	0	5	2	7
Northwestern University	IL	0	0	1	1	0	0	0	0	5	0	10	0	0	0	16	1	17
University of Notre Dame	IN	0	0	0	0	0	0	0	0	4	0	3	1	0	0	7	1	8
Oakland University	MI	0	0	0	0	0	0	0	0	0	0	2	1	0	0	2	1	3
The Ohio State University	OH	0	0	0	0	0	0	0	0	1	2	11	1	0	0	12	3	15
University of Oklahoma	OK	0	0	0	0	0	0	0	0	1	0	0	1	0	0	1	1	2
Oklahoma State University	OK	0	0	1	0	0	0	0	0	2	0	3	1	0	0	5	1	6
Old Dominion University	VA	0	0	0	0	0	0	0	0	1	0	2	0	0	0	3	0	3
Oregon State University	OR	0	0	0	0	0	0	0	0	1	1	2	0	0	0	3	1	4

MECHANICAL ENGINEERING

ILL-ORE

Doctoral Degrees Awarded in Mechanical Engineering, 2005-2006

INSTITUTION		AFRICAN AMERICAN		ASIAN AMERICAN		HISPANIC		NATIVE AMERICAN		CAUCASIAN		FOREIGN		OTHER		TOTAL BY GENDER		TOTAL DEGREES
		M	F	M	F	M	F	M	F	M	F	M	F	M	F	M	F	
University of Pennsylvania	PA	0	0	0	0	0	0	0	0	0	1	1	1	0	0	1	2	3
The Pennsylvania State University	PA	1	0	0	0	0	0	0	0	5	1	10	1	0	0	16	2	18
University of Pittsburgh	PA	0	0	0	0	0	0	0	0	4	0	3	1	0	0	7	1	8
Polytechnic University	NY	0	0	0	0	0	0	0	0	1	0	1	0	0	0	2	0	2
Princeton University	NJ	0	0	2	1	0	0	0	0	6	1	5	0	0	0	13	2	15
Purdue University	IN	0	0	2	0	0	0	0	0	5	3	27	1	0	0	34	4	38
Rensselaer Polytechnic Institute	NY	0	0	0	0	1	0	0	0	4	0	9	1	0	0	14	1	15
University of Rhode Island	RI	0	0	0	0	0	0	0	0	0	0	3	0	0	0	3	0	3
William Marsh Rice University	TX	0	0	0	0	0	0	0	0	1	0	2	0	0	0	3	0	3
University of Rochester	NY	0	0	0	0	0	0	0	0	0	0	0	1	0	0	0	1	1
Rutgers, The State University of New Jersey	NJ	0	0	1	0	0	0	0	0	2	0	1	1	0	0	4	1	5
Santa Clara University	CA	0	0	2	0	0	0	0	0	0	0	0	0	0	0	2	0	2
University of South Carolina	SC	0	0	0	0	0	0	0	0	3	1	5	1	0	0	8	2	10
Southern Methodist University	TX	0	0	0	0	0	0	0	0	0	0	5	0	0	0	5	0	5
Stanford University	CA	2	0	3	2	0	1	0	0	18	1	15	2	3	0	41	6	47
Stevens Institute of Technology	NJ	0	0	0	0	0	0	0	0	0	0	2	0	0	0	2	0	2
Syracuse University	NY	0	0	0	0	0	0	0	0	0	0	1	0	0	0	1	0	1
University of Tennessee, Knoxville	TN	0	0	0	0	0	0	0	0	1	0	1	0	0	0	2	0	2
Texas A&M University	TX	0	0	1	0	0	0	0	0	1	1	23	1	0	0	25	2	27
Texas Tech University	TX	0	0	0	0	0	0	0	0	0	0	3	0	0	0	3	0	3
The University of Texas at Arlington	TX	0	0	1	0	0	0	0	0	0	0	3	0	0	0	4	0	4
The University of Texas at Austin	TX	0	0	0	0	0	0	0	0	3	0	8	1	0	0	11	1	12
The University of Toledo	OH	0	0	0	0	0	0	0	0	1	0	0	4	0	0	1	4	5
Tufts University	MA	0	0	0	0	0	0	0	0	0	0	1	0	1	0	2	0	2
University of Tulsa	OK	0	0	0	0	0	0	0	0	0	0	2	0	0	0	2	0	2
University of Utah	UT	0	0	0	0	0	0	0	0	2	0	6	1	0	0	8	1	9
Utah State University	UT	0	0	0	0	0	0	0	0	3	0	1	0	0	0	4	0	4
Vanderbilt University	TN	0	0	0	0	0	0	0	0	1	0	2	0	0	0	3	0	3
University of Virginia	VA	0	0	0	0	0	0	0	0	1	0	0	1	0	0	1	1	2
Virginia Polytechnic Institute and State University	VA	0	0	0	0	0	0	0	0	9	0	5	1	0	0	14	1	15
University of Washington	WA	0	0	0	0	0	0	0	0	2	1	6	2	0	0	8	3	11
Washington State University	WA	0	0	0	0	0	0	0	0	1	0	5	0	1	0	7	0	7
Washington University	MO	0	0	0	0	0	0	0	0	2	0	5	0	0	0	7	0	7
Wayne State University	MI	0	0	2	0	0	0	4	0	1	0	0	0	0	0	7	0	7
West Virginia University	WV	0	0	0	0	0	0	0	0	2	0	6	1	0	0	8	1	9
Wichita State University	KS	0	0	1	0	0	0	0	0	0	0	2	1	0	0	3	1	4
University of Wisconsin, Madison	WI	0	0	0	0	0	0	0	0	1	0	9	0	1	0	11	0	11
Worcester Polytechnic Institute	MA	0	0	0	0	0	0	0	0	1	0	3	1	0	0	4	1	5
Totals:		11	3	54	12	7	1	6	0	220	38	640	89	44	7	982	150	1,132
CANADIAN INSTITUTIONS:																		
University of Alberta	AB	0	0	0	0	0	0	0	0	0	0	0	0	7	1	7	1	8
Concordia University, Faculty of Engr. and Comp. Sci.	PQ	0	0	0	0	0	0	0	0	0	0	4	0	4	0	8	0	8
Ecole Polytechnique de Montreal	PQ	0	0	0	0	0	0	0	0	0	0	0	0	2	0	2	0	2

MECHANICAL ENGINEERING

PEN-WOR

It makes Airplanes Fly and Kids Play: It's CATIA

Doug (age 13) programs CATIA NC

CATIA is not just a CAD software. It also offers complete NC programming functions, integrated finite element simulation, and all the applications that an engineer will ever need in a single package. That is why Boeing, Toyota, DaimlerChrysler, and Nokia have adopted Dassault Systemes technology, together with 90,000 other customers in 80 countries in all types of industries.

CATIA prepare students for the most exciting careers in engineering.

Dassault Systèmes has built a powerful range of products, all of which are leaders in their field: **Cosmic Blobs**, **SolidWorks**, **CATIA**, **DELMIA**, **ENOVIA** (VPLM, SmarTeam, MatrixOne), **SIMULIA** (ABAQUS) and **Virtools**.

www.3ds.com

DASSAULT SYSTEMES

NEW FOCUS,
Same Title

NOW AVAILABLE

The research journal for engineering education

Doctoral Degrees Awarded in Mechanical Engineering, 2005-2006

INSTITUTION		AFRICAN AMERICAN M	F	ASIAN AMERICAN M	F	HISPANIC M	F	NATIVE AMERICAN M	F	CAUCASIAN M	F	FOREIGN M	F	OTHER M	F	TOTAL BY GENDER M	F	TOTAL DEGREES
McGill University, Faculty of Engineering	PQ	0	0	0	0	0	0	0	0	0	0	0	0	12	2	12	2	14
University of Ottawa, Faculty of Engineering	ON	0	0	0	0	0	0	0	0	0	0	0	0	3	0	3	0	3
University of Waterloo	ON	0	0	0	0	0	0	0	0	0	0	0	0	5	0	5	0	5
Totals:		0	0	0	0	0	0	0	0	0	0	4	0	33	3	37	3	40

MCG-WAT

MECHANICAL ENGINEERING

DOCTORAL DEGREES AWARDED IN METALLURGICAL AND MATERIALS ENGINEERING, 2005-2006

INSTITUTION		AFRICAN AMERICAN		ASIAN AMERICAN		HISPANIC		NATIVE AMERICAN		CAUCASIAN		FOREIGN		OTHER		TOTAL BY GENDER		TOTAL DEGREES
		M	F	M	F	M	F	M	F	M	F	M	F	M	F	M	F	
University of Alabama at Birmingham	AL	0	0	1	0	0	0	0	0	2	1	1	0	0	0	4	1	5
The University of Alabama	AL	1	1	2	0	0	0	0	0	0	0	0	0	0	0	3	1	4
The University of Arizona	AZ	0	0	1	0	0	0	0	0	1	0	1	0	0	0	3	0	3
Arizona State University	AZ	0	0	1	0	0	0	0	0	1	0	6	1	0	0	8	1	9
Auburn University	AL	0	0	0	0	0	0	0	0	1	0	3	0	0	0	4	0	4
Brown University	RI	0	0	0	0	0	0	0	0	0	1	0	0	0	0	0	1	1
California Institute of Technology	CA	0	0	0	0	0	0	0	0	1	1	1	0	0	0	2	1	3
University of California, Berkeley	CA	0	0	2	1	0	0	0	0	1	1	3	4	0	0	6	6	12
University of California, Davis	CA	0	0	0	0	0	0	0	0	1	1	7	1	0	0	8	2	10
University of California, Irvine	CA	0	0	0	0	0	0	0	0	0	0	0	0	6	1	6	1	7
University of California, Los Angeles	CA	0	0	1	0	0	0	0	0	0	1	8	2	0	0	9	3	12
University of California, San Diego	CA	0	0	0	0	0	0	0	0	4	1	0	1	0	0	4	2	6
University of California, Santa Barbara	CA	0	0	0	1	0	0	0	0	9	1	5	2	1	0	15	4	19
Carnegie Mellon University	PA	0	0	0	1	0	0	0	0	2	0	5	0	0	1	7	2	9
Case Western Reserve University	OH	0	0	0	0	0	0	0	0	1	0	3	2	0	0	4	2	6
University of Central Florida	FL	0	0	0	0	0	0	0	0	0	0	6	0	0	0	6	0	6
Clemson University	SC	0	0	0	0	0	0	0	0	0	0	6	1	0	0	6	1	7
Colorado School of Mines	CO	0	0	0	0	0	0	0	0	5	2	5	0	0	0	10	2	12
Columbia University	NY	0	0	0	0	0	0	0	0	0	0	2	1	1	2	3	3	6
University of Connecticut	CT	0	0	0	0	0	0	0	0	0	0	6	2	0	0	6	2	8
Cornell University	NY	0	0	1	1	0	0	0	0	1	0	1	2	0	0	3	3	6
University of Dayton	OH	0	0	0	0	0	0	0	0	1	0	1	0	0	0	2	0	2
University of Delaware	DE	0	0	0	1	0	0	0	0	1	2	2	1	0	0	3	4	7
University of Denver	CO	0	0	0	0	0	0	0	0	1	0	0	0	0	0	1	0	1
Drexel University	PA	0	0	3	0	0	0	0	0	6	1	2	1	0	0	11	2	13
University of Florida	FL	0	2	1	3	1	1	0	0	7	2	13	5	0	0	22	13	35
University of Houston, Cullen School of Engineering	TX	0	0	0	0	0	0	0	0	0	0	0	1	0	0	0	1	1
Illinois Institute of Technology	IL	0	0	0	0	0	0	0	0	0	0	1	0	0	0	1	0	1
University of Illinois at Chicago	IL	0	0	1	0	0	0	1	0	0	0	0	0	0	0	2	0	2
University of Illinois at Urbana-Champaign	IL	1	0	0	0	0	0	0	0	4	0	7	4	0	0	12	4	16
Iowa State University	IA	0	0	0	0	0	0	0	0	2	1	3	0	0	0	5	1	6
The Johns Hopkins University	MD	0	0	0	0	0	0	0	0	1	0	1	1	0	0	2	1	3
University of Kentucky	KY	0	0	0	0	0	0	0	0	0	0	0	1	1	0	1	1	2
Lehigh University	PA	0	0	0	0	0	0	0	0	0	0	0	0	4	1	4	1	5
University of Maryland, College Park	MD	1	0	0	0	0	0	0	0	0	0	5	4	0	1	6	5	11
Massachusetts Institute of Technology	MA	0	0	1	1	0	0	0	0	3	2	14	4	2	0	20	7	27
University of Michigan	MI	0	0	2	0	0	0	0	0	2	1	4	1	0	0	8	2	10
Michigan Technological University	MI	0	0	0	0	0	0	0	0	0	0	1	0	0	0	1	0	1
University of Minnesota - Twin Cities	MN	0	0	0	1	0	0	0	0	0	1	5	5	0	0	5	7	12
University of Missouri - Rolla	MO	0	0	0	0	0	1	0	0	2	0	5	2	0	0	8	2	10
University of Nevada, Reno	NV	0	0	0	0	0	0	0	0	0	0	1	0	0	0	1	0	1
The State University of New York at Binghamton	NY	0	0	0	0	0	0	0	0	0	0	1	0	0	0	1	0	1
Stony Brook University	NY	1	0	0	0	0	0	0	0	1	0	3	2	0	0	6	2	8
North Carolina State University	NC	0	0	0	0	1	0	0	0	5	1	6	1	0	0	12	2	14
Northwestern University	IL	0	0	2	1	0	0	0	0	9	4	7	1	1	0	19	6	25

METALLURGICAL AND MATERIALS ENGR.   ALA-NOR

DOCTORAL DEGREES AWARDED IN METALLURGICAL AND MATERIALS ENGINEERING, 2005-2006

INSTITUTION		AFRICAN AMERICAN		ASIAN AMERICAN		HISPANIC		NATIVE AMERICAN		CAUCASIAN		FOREIGN		OTHER		TOTAL BY GENDER		TOTAL DEGREES
		M	F	M	F	M	F	M	F	M	F	M	F	M	F	M	F	
The Ohio State University	OH	0	0	0	0	0	0	0	0	1	0	12	5	0	0	13	5	18
Oregon State University	OR	0	0	0	0	0	0	0	0	1	0	0	0	0	0	1	0	1
University of Pennsylvania	PA	0	0	0	0	0	0	0	0	3	0	6	1	0	0	9	1	10
The Pennsylvania State University	PA	0	0	1	0	0	0	0	0	7	2	11	2	0	0	19	4	23
University of Pittsburgh	PA	0	0	0	0	0	0	0	0	1	0	3	0	0	0	4	0	4
Purdue University	IN	0	0	0	0	0	0	0	0	1	1	0	0	0	1	1	2	3
Rensselaer Polytechnic Institute	NY	0	0	1	0	0	0	0	0	4	2	2	1	0	0	7	3	10
South Dakota School of Mines and Technology	SD	0	0	0	0	0	0	0	0	0	0	1	0	0	0	1	0	1
Stanford University	CA	0	0	2	0	0	0	0	0	2	2	5	3	2	0	11	5	16
University of Tennessee, Knoxville	TN	0	0	0	0	0	0	0	0	4	0	5	2	0	0	9	2	11
The University of Texas at Arlington	TX	0	0	0	0	0	0	0	0	0	0	1	0	0	0	1	0	1
The University of Texas at Austin	TX	0	0	0	1	0	0	0	0	1	0	10	3	0	0	11	4	15
The University of Texas at Dallas	TX	0	0	0	0	0	0	0	0	0	0	3	0	0	0	3	0	3
University of Utah	UT	0	0	0	0	0	0	0	0	0	0	3	1	0	1	3	1	4
Vanderbilt University	TN	0	0	0	0	0	0	0	0	0	0	1	0	0	0	1	0	1
University of Virginia	VA	0	0	0	0	0	0	0	0	0	0	1	0	0	0	1	0	1
Virginia Polytechnic Institute and State University	VA	0	0	0	0	0	0	0	0	3	1	1	1	0	0	4	2	6
University of Washington	WA	0	0	0	0	0	0	0	0	0	1	2	3	1	0	3	4	7
Washington State University	WA	0	0	0	0	0	0	0	0	0	0	4	0	1	0	5	0	5
Washington University	MO	0	0	0	0	0	0	0	0	0	0	1	0	0	0	1	0	1
Wayne State University	MI	0	0	1	0	0	0	0	0	0	0	1	0	0	0	2	0	2
University of Wisconsin, Madison	WI	0	0	0	0	0	0	0	0	3	0	1	1	1	0	5	1	6
Worcester Polytechnic Institute	MA	0	0	0	0	0	0	0	0	0	0	0	1	0	0	0	1	1
Totals:		**4**	**3**	**24**	**12**	**4**	**1**	**1**	**0**	**106**	**34**	**225**	**76**	**21**	**8**	**385**	**134**	**519**

CANADIAN INSTITUTIONS:

INSTITUTION		AFRICAN AMERICAN		ASIAN AMERICAN		HISPANIC		NATIVE AMERICAN		CAUCASIAN		FOREIGN		OTHER		TOTAL BY GENDER		TOTAL DEGREES
		M	F	M	F	M	F	M	F	M	F	M	F	M	F	M	F	
Ecole Polytechnique de Montreal	PQ	0	0	0	0	0	0	0	0	0	0	0	0	2	1	2	1	3
Totals:		**0**	**0**	**0**	**0**	**0**	**0**	**0**	**0**	**0**	**0**	**0**	**0**	**2**	**1**	**2**	**1**	**3**

METALLURGICAL AND MATERIALS ENGR.   OHI-WOR

METALLURGICAL AND MATERIALS ENGINEERING

INSTITUTION		AFRICAN AMERICAN		ASIAN AMERICAN		HISPANIC		NATIVE AMERICAN		CAUCASIAN		FOREIGN		OTHER		TOTAL BY GENDER		TOTAL DEGREES
		M	F	M	F	M	F	M	F	M	F	M	F	M	F	M	F	
The University of Arizona	AZ	0	0	0	0	0	0	0	0	1	0	1	0	0	0	2	0	2
Colorado School of Mines	CO	0	0	0	0	0	0	0	0	0	0	1	0	0	0	1	0	1
University of Kentucky	KY	0	0	0	0	0	0	0	0	0	0	0	0	0	1	0	1	1
Michigan Technological University	MI	0	0	0	0	0	0	0	0	1	0	0	0	0	0	1	0	1
University of Missouri - Rolla	MO	0	0	0	0	0	0	0	0	2	0	3	0	0	0	5	0	5
Virginia Polytechnic Institute and State University	VA	0	0	0	0	0	0	0	0	0	0	2	0	0	0	2	0	2
West Virginia University	WV	0	0	0	0	0	0	0	0	2	0	2	0	0	0	4	0	4
Totals:		0	0	0	0	0	0	0	0	6	0	9	0	0	1	15	1	16
CANADIAN INSTITUTIONS:																		
Ecole Polytechnique de Montreal	PQ	0	0	0	0	0	0	0	0	0	0	0	0	3	1	3	1	4
McGill University, Faculty of Engineering	PQ	0	0	0	0	0	0	0	0	0	0	0	0	12	2	12	2	14
Totals:		0	0	0	0	0	0	0	0	0	0	0	0	15	3	15	3	18

ARI-WES

MINING ENGINEERING

INSTITUTION		AFRICAN AMERICAN		ASIAN AMERICAN		HISPANIC		NATIVE AMERICAN		CAUCASIAN		FOREIGN		OTHER		TOTAL BY GENDER		TOTAL DEGREES
		M	F	M	F	M	F	M	F	M	F	M	F	M	F	M	F	
University of California, Berkeley	CA	0	0	1	0	0	0	0	0	0	0	5	1	0	0	6	1	7
University of Cincinnati	OH	0	0	1	0	0	0	0	0	0	0	1	0	0	0	2	0	2
University of Florida	FL	1	0	0	0	0	0	0	0	3	0	3	1	0	0	7	1	8
Georgia Institute of Technology	GA	1	0	0	0	0	0	0	0	0	0	0	0	0	0	1	0	1
University of Illinois at Urbana-Champaign	IL	0	0	0	0	0	0	0	0	1	0	2	1	0	0	3	1	4
Massachusetts Institute of Technology	MA	0	0	0	0	0	0	0	0	6	1	6	4	2	1	14	6	20
University of Michigan	MI	0	0	0	0	1	0	0	0	5	1	3	1	0	0	9	2	11
University of Missouri-Columbia	MO	0	0	0	0	1	0	0	0	0	0	1	0	0	1	2	1	3
The University of New Mexico	NM	0	0	0	0	1	0	0	0	1	0	0	0	0	0	2	0	2
North Carolina State University	NC	0	0	0	0	0	0	0	0	0	0	5	0	0	0	5	0	5
The Ohio State University	OH	0	0	0	0	0	0	0	0	0	0	1	0	0	0	1	0	1
Oregon State University	OR	0	0	0	0	0	0	0	0	1	0	1	0	0	0	2	0	2
The Pennsylvania State University	PA	0	0	0	0	0	0	0	0	1	0	1	2	0	0	2	2	4
Purdue University	IN	0	0	0	0	0	0	0	0	1	0	4	0	0	0	5	0	5
Texas A&M University	TX	0	0	0	0	0	0	0	0	1	0	0	0	0	0	1	0	1
University of Wisconsin, Madison	WI	0	0	1	0	0	0	0	0	0	0	2	1	0	1	3	2	5
Totals:		2	0	3	0	3	0	0	0	20	2	35	11	2	3	65	16	81

CAL-WIS

NUCLEAR ENGINEERING

DOCTORAL DEGREES AWARDED IN OTHER ENGINEERING DISCIPLINES, 2005-2006

INSTITUTION		AFRICAN AMERICAN		ASIAN AMERICAN		HISPANIC		NATIVE AMERICAN		CAUCASIAN		FOREIGN		OTHER		TOTAL BY GENDER		TOTAL DEGREES
		M	F	M	F	M	F	M	F	M	F	M	F	M	F	M	F	
Air Force Institute of Technology	OH	0	0	0	0	0	0	0	0	1	0	0	0	0	0	1	0	1
The University of Alabama in Huntsville	AL	0	0	0	0	0	0	0	0	1	0	1	0	0	0	2	0	2
Alfred University, NY State College of Ceramics	NY	0	0	0	0	0	0	0	0	3	0	0	0	0	0	3	0	3
The University of Arizona	AZ	0	0	0	0	0	0	0	0	2	1	4	0	0	0	6	1	7
University of Arkansas	AR	1	0	1	0	0	0	0	0	1	0	0	0	0	1	3	1	4
Auburn University	AL	0	0	0	0	0	0	0	0	0	0	4	2	0	0	4	2	6
Boston University	MA	0	0	1	0	0	0	0	0	0	0	3	0	0	0	4	0	4
Brown University	RI	0	0	0	0	0	0	0	0	1	0	4	0	0	0	5	0	5
California Institute of Technology	CA	0	0	0	0	0	0	0	0	5	2	9	1	0	0	14	3	17
University of California, Berkeley	CA	1	0	1	0	1	1	0	0	0	1	1	0	1	0	5	2	7
University of California, Davis	CA	0	0	0	0	1	0	0	0	1	0	0	0	0	0	2	0	2
University of California, San Diego	CA	0	0	0	0	0	0	0	0	2	0	1	0	0	0	3	0	3
Carnegie Mellon University	PA	0	0	0	1	0	0	0	0	0	1	4	5	1	0	5	7	12
Case Western Reserve University	OH	0	0	0	0	0	0	0	0	1	1	3	0	0	0	4	1	5
Clarkson University	NY	0	0	0	0	0	0	0	0	0	0	1	0	0	0	1	0	1
Colorado School of Mines	CO	0	0	0	0	0	0	0	0	6	2	2	0	0	1	8	3	11
Colorado State University	CO	0	0	0	0	1	0	0	0	1	0	0	0	2	1	4	1	5
Columbia University	NY	0	0	0	0	0	0	0	0	0	0	1	0	0	0	1	0	1
Cornell University	NY	0	0	1	0	2	1	0	0	5	4	5	1	0	1	13	7	20
University of Dayton	OH	0	0	0	0	0	0	0	0	0	1	3	0	0	0	3	1	4
Florida Institute of Technology	FL	0	0	0	0	0	0	0	0	0	0	1	0	0	0	1	0	1
George Mason University	VA	0	0	0	3	0	0	0	0	5	0	7	0	0	0	12	3	15
The George Washington University	DC	0	0	1	0	0	0	0	0	8	1	2	1	0	0	11	2	13
University of Georgia	GA	0	0	0	0	0	0	0	0	0	0	2	0	0	0	2	0	2
Georgia Institute of Technology	GA	0	0	0	0	0	0	0	0	1	1	1	1	0	0	2	2	4
Harvard University	MA	0	0	0	0	0	0	0	0	9	3	10	1	0	0	19	4	23
University of Hawaii at Manoa	HI	0	0	0	0	0	0	0	0	0	0	2	0	0	0	2	0	2
The Johns Hopkins University	MD	0	0	0	0	0	0	0	0	0	0	1	0	0	0	1	0	1
Lehigh University	PA	0	0	0	0	0	0	0	0	0	0	5	2	0	0	5	2	7
Louisiana Tech University	LA	0	0	0	0	0	0	0	0	1	0	1	4	0	0	2	4	6
University of Maine	ME	0	0	0	0	0	0	0	0	0	0	1	0	0	0	1	0	1
University of Maryland, College Park	MD	0	1	0	0	0	0	0	0	0	1	5	0	0	0	5	2	7
Massachusetts Institute of Technology	MA	0	0	1	1	0	0	0	0	1	2	3	1	0	0	5	4	9
University of Massachusetts Lowell	MA	0	0	0	0	0	0	0	0	0	0	5	1	0	0	5	1	6
University of Michigan	MI	0	0	1	1	0	0	0	0	1	0	5	3	1	0	8	4	12
Michigan State University	MI	0	0	2	0	0	0	0	0	1	0	0	0	0	0	3	0	3
Michigan Technological University	MI	0	0	0	0	0	0	0	0	2	0	0	0	0	0	2	0	2
University of Minnesota - Twin Cities	MN	0	0	1	0	0	0	0	0	0	0	0	0	0	0	1	0	1
The University of Mississippi	MS	0	0	0	1	0	0	0	0	2	0	1	2	0	0	3	3	6
Montana State University	MT	0	0	0	0	0	0	0	0	2	0	0	0	0	0	2	0	2
The University of New Mexico	NM	0	0	0	0	0	0	0	0	0	0	2	0	0	0	2	0	2
University of New Orleans	LA	0	0	0	0	0	0	0	0	1	1	2	3	1	0	4	4	8
The State University of New York at Binghamton	NY	0	0	0	0	0	0	0	0	0	0	6	0	1	0	7	0	7
SUNY College of Environmental Science and Forestry	NY	0	0	0	0	0	0	0	0	1	0	5	1	0	0	6	1	7
Stony Brook University	NY	1	0	0	1	0	0	0	0	1	0	8	11	0	0	10	12	22

OTHER ENGINEERING DISCIPLINES

AIR-NEW

DOCTORAL DEGREES AWARDED IN OTHER ENGINEERING DISCIPLINES, 2005-2006

INSTITUTION		AFRICAN AMERICAN		ASIAN AMERICAN		HISPANIC		NATIVE AMERICAN		CAUCASIAN		FOREIGN		OTHER		TOTAL BY GENDER		TOTAL DEGREES
		M	F	M	F	M	F	M	F	M	F	M	F	M	F	M	F	
North Carolina State University	NC	0	0	0	0	0	0	0	0	0	0	2	0	0	0	2	0	2
Northeastern University	MA	0	0	0	0	0	0	0	0	1	0	0	0	0	0	1	0	1
Oakland University	MI	1	0	1	0	0	0	0	0	4	0	1	0	0	0	7	0	7
Old Dominion University	VA	0	0	0	0	0	0	0	0	1	0	0	0	0	0	1	0	1
The Pennsylvania State University	PA	0	0	1	0	0	0	0	0	7	0	4	2	0	0	12	2	14
Princeton University	NJ	0	0	1	0	0	0	0	0	2	0	3	3	0	0	5	3	8
William Marsh Rice University	TX	0	0	1	1	0	1	0	0	3	4	4	7	0	0	8	13	21
University of Rochester	NY	0	0	0	0	0	0	0	0	3	0	6	1	0	0	9	1	10
Rochester Institute of Technology	NY	0	0	1	0	0	0	0	0	1	0	2	0	0	0	4	0	4
Rutgers, The State University of New Jersey	NJ	0	0	0	0	0	0	0	0	0	1	2	0	0	0	2	1	3
South Dakota School of Mines and Technology	SD	0	0	0	0	0	0	0	0	1	1	0	0	0	0	1	1	2
Southern Methodist University	TX	0	0	0	0	0	0	0	0	0	1	1	0	0	0	1	1	2
Stanford University	CA	0	0	1	0	0	0	0	0	0	0	3	0	0	0	4	0	4
Stevens Institute of Technology	NJ	0	0	0	0	0	0	0	0	1	0	2	1	0	0	3	1	4
Texas A&M University	TX	0	1	0	0	0	0	0	0	2	0	4	0	0	0	6	1	7
Tufts University	MA	0	0	0	0	0	0	0	0	0	0	1	0	0	0	1	0	1
University of Virginia	VA	0	0	0	0	0	0	0	0	4	1	1	1	0	0	5	2	7
Washington State University	WA	0	0	0	0	0	0	0	0	0	0	3	2	2	0	5	2	7
Washington University	MO	0	0	0	0	0	0	0	0	5	0	3	1	0	0	8	1	9
Western Michigan University	MI	0	0	1	0	0	0	0	0	0	0	0	1	0	0	1	1	2
University of Wisconsin, Madison	WI	1	0	0	0	1	0	0	0	2	4	3	0	1	0	8	4	12
Worcester Polytechnic Institute	MA	0	0	0	0	0	0	0	0	0	1	0	0	0	0	0	1	1
Wright State University	OH	0	0	1	0	0	0	0	0	3	1	3	1	0	0	7	2	9
University of Wyoming	WY	0	0	0	0	0	0	0	0	1	0	1	0	0	0	2	0	2
Yale University/Faculty of Engineering	CT	0	0	0	0	0	0	0	0	0	0	0	0	27	4	27	4	31
Totals:		5	2	17	8	6	3	0	0	108	37	170	61	36	7	342	118	460
CANADIAN INSTITUTIONS:																		
University of Calgary	AB	0	0	0	0	0	0	0	0	0	0	5	0	1	0	6	0	6
Concordia University, Faculty of Engr. and Comp. Sci.	PQ	0	0	0	0	0	0	0	0	0	0	2	0	2	2	4	2	6
Ecole Polytechnique de Montreal	PQ	0	0	0	0	0	0	0	0	0	0	0	0	4	0	4	0	4
University of Guelph	ON	0	0	0	0	0	0	0	0	0	0	0	1	3	1	3	2	5
University of Waterloo	ON	0	0	0	0	0	0	0	0	0	0	0	0	10	1	10	1	11
Totals:		0	0	0	0	0	0	0	0	0	0	7	1	20	4	27	5	32

NOR-YAL

OTHER ENGINEERING DISCIPLINES

DOCTORAL DEGREES AWARDED IN PETROLEUM ENGINEERING, 2005-2006

INSTITUTION		AFRICAN AMERICAN		ASIAN AMERICAN		HISPANIC		NATIVE AMERICAN		CAUCASIAN		FOREIGN		OTHER		TOTAL BY GENDER		TOTAL DEGREES
		M	F	M	F	M	F	M	F	M	F	M	F	M	F	M	F	
Colorado School of Mines	CO	0	0	0	0	0	0	0	0	1	1	2	0	0	0	3	1	4
Louisiana State University	LA	0	0	0	0	0	0	0	0	0	0	4	0	0	0	4	0	4
University of Missouri - Rolla	MO	0	0	0	0	0	0	0	0	0	0	1	0	0	0	1	0	1
University of Oklahoma	OK	0	0	0	0	0	0	0	0	0	0	3	0	0	0	3	0	3
Texas A&M University	TX	0	0	0	0	0	0	0	0	1	0	2	1	0	0	3	1	4
Texas Tech University	TX	0	0	0	0	0	0	0	0	0	0	3	0	0	0	3	0	3
The University of Texas at Austin	TX	0	0	0	0	0	0	0	0	0	0	11	1	0	0	11	2	13
University of Tulsa	OK	0	0	0	0	0	0	0	0	0	0	5	1	0	0	5	1	6
University of Wyoming	WY	0	0	0	0	0	0	0	0	0	0	2	0	0	0	2	0	2
Totals:		0	0	0	1	0	0	0	0	2	1	33	3	0	0	35	5	40

COL-WYO

PETROLEUM ENGINEERING

2006 Statistical Tables of Engineering Faculty and Research Expenditures

FACULTY, FALL 2006

INSTITUTION		TEACHING FACULTY							RESEARCH FACULTY			TOTAL FTE
		FULL-TIME				NON T/T-T	PART-TIME		FULL-TIME	PART-TIME		
		TENURE/TENURE-TRACK				NON-TENURE	TOTAL FACULTY	FTE (PT)	RESEARCH (FT)	RESEARCH (PT)	FTE (PT) RESEARCH	
		PROFESSOR	ASSOCIATE	ASSISTANT	TOTAL T/T-T							
Air Force Institute of Technology	OH	26	24	83	133	5	0	0	0	0	0	138
The University of Akron	OH	23	28	9	60	2	9	2.33	2	0	0	66.33
Alabama A&M University	AL	8	10	16	34	1	0	0	0	0	0	35
University of Alabama at Birmingham	AL	14	18	7	39	9	4	2.71	4	0	0	54.71
The University of Alabama in Huntsville	AL	27	21	10	58	6	32	9.66	4	0	0	77.66
The University of Alabama	AL	38	41	22	101	11	2	0.5	0	0	0	112.5
University of Alaska, Anchorage	AK	7	9	0	16	16	14	7	7	2	1	47
University of Alaska Fairbanks	AK	15	9	9	33	10	0	0	11	0	0	54
Alfred University, NY State College of Ceramics	NY	17	8	2	27	0	0	0	0	0	0	27
The University of Arizona	AZ	80	31	27	138	2	16	0	29	12	0	169
Arizona State University	AZ	102	51	48	201	20	25	7.08	36	17	6.76	270.84
University of Arkansas	AR	47	32	19	98	15	8	2.9	29	3	2	146.9
Arkansas State University	AR	3	2	5	10	2	1	0.25	0	0	0	12.25
Arkansas Tech University	AR	4	3	4	11	1	3	0.83	0	0	0	12.83
University of Arkansas at Little Rock	AR	10	8	12	30	1	2	0	2	0	0	33
Auburn University	AL	76	44	31	151	1	6	3.28	30	0	0	185.28
Baker College	MI	0	0	4	4	2	10	3	0	0	0	9
Baylor University	TX	12	8	6	26	7	0	0	0	0	0	33
Boise State University	ID	11	21	12	44	2	12	0	3	2	0	49
Boston University	MA	58	44	28	130	7	0	0	0	0	0	137
Bradley University	IL	20	17	9	46	2	19	5	0	0	0	53
University of Bridgeport	CT	4	2	5	11	6	33	16	0	1	0.5	33.5
Brigham Young University	UT	42	25	16	83	0	23	0	1	0	0	84
Brown University	RI	22	10	5	37	1	19	5.75	2	2	0	45.75
Bucknell University	PA	17	16	16	49	4	2	1	5	0	2.25	61.25
California Institute of Technology	CA	70	7	18	95	3	28	23.33	127	45	11.25	259.58
California Maritime Academy	CA	2	4	1	7	0	0	0	0	0	0	7
California Polytechnic State University	CA	66	35	42	143	15	56	34.93	0	0	0	192.93
California State Polytechnic University, Pomona	CA	55	24	2	81	5	61	0	0	2	0	86
California State University, East Bay	CA	2	0	2	4	0	0	0	0	0	0	4
California State University, Chico	CA	16	1	3	20	3	13	5.56	0	0	0	28.56
California State University, Fullerton	CA	26	5	4	35	4	39	0	0	0	0	39
California State University, Long Beach	CA	37	8	2	47	0	0	0	0	0	0	47
California State University, Los Angeles	CA	27	6	6	39	4	5	0	0	0	0	43
California State University, Northridge	CA	32	10	14	56	0	0	0	0	0	0	56
California State University, Sacramento	CA	41	6	20	67	4	44	16.99	0	0	0	87.99
University of California, Berkeley	CA	170	40	26	236	8	0	0	0	0	0	244
University of California, Davis	CA	139	26	42	207	1	9	3.63	89	14	6.7	307.33
University of California, Irvine	CA	62	17	20	99	7	16	2.26	47	18	8.8	164.06
University of California, Los Angeles	CA	107	12	33	152	5	70	8.45	7	15	0	172.45
University of California, Riverside	CA	37	15	18	70	3	11	0	28	2	0	101
University of California, San Diego	CA	114	28	31	173	7	21	5.81	25	18	8.76	219.57
University of California, Santa Barbara	CA	104	17	13	134	0	0	4.8	0	0	0	138.8
University of California-Santa Cruz	CA	34	18	22	74	1	26	10.3	25	8	3.8	114.1
Calvin College	MI	8	3	3	14	0	6	0	0	0	0	14

FACULTY

AIR-CAL

INSTITUTION		TEACHING FACULTY							RESEARCH FACULTY			TOTAL FTE
		FULL-TIME					PART-TIME		FULL-TIME	PART-TIME		
		TENURE/TENURE-TRACK				NON T/T-T						
		PROFESSOR	ASSOCIATE	ASSISTANT	TOTAL T/T-T	NON-TENURE	TOTAL FACULTY	FTE (PT)	RESEARCH (FT)	RESEARCH (PT)	FTE (PT) RESEARCH	
Capitol College	MD	15	39	0	54	5	10	2	1	0	0	62
Carnegie Mellon University	PA	90	18	27	135	9	18	6.9	24	3	1.2	176.1
Carroll College	MT	2	7	1	10	10	4	2	0	0	0	22
Case Western Reserve University	OH	61	30	25	116	0	0	0	9	1	0.5	125.5
The Catholic University of America	DC	7	5	14	26	0	23	7.67	0	0	0	33.67
Cedarville University	OH	7	6	3	16	1	0	0	0	0	0	17
University of Central Florida	FL	60	43	34	137	17	23	7.94	17	2	1	179.94
Christian Brothers University	TN	15	4	2	21	1	2	0	0	0	0	22
University of Cincinnati	OH	77	41	22	140	8	22	0	38	1	0	186
The Citadel	SC	3	6	7	16	0	0	0	0	0	0	16
Clarkson University	NY	26	21	13	60	1	4	2.25	0	0	0	63.25
Clemson University	SC	79	60	59	198	27	9	3.87	24	3	1.13	254
Cleveland State University	OH	35	24	9	68	0	0	0	0	0	0	68
Colorado School of Mines	CO	76	50	32	158	30	78	22.25	37	15	7.2	254.45
Colorado State University	CO	58	20	17	95	1	14	3.52	104	14	7.04	210.56
Colorado State University, Pueblo	CO	2	2	1	5	0	5	0	1	0	0	6
University of Colorado at Boulder	CO	83	43	42	168	20	49	0	12	0	0	200
University of Colorado at Colorado Springs	CO	14	9	4	27	5	15	0	0	0	0	32
University of Colorado at Denver	CO	17	10	7	34	4	2	1.25	1	0	1	41.25
University of Connecticut	CT	44	21	36	101	2	28	9	30	22	11.44	153.44
The Cooper Union	NY	20	5	7	32	0	47	29.5	4	5	2.5	68
Cornell University	NY	147	47	47	241	16	6	2.8	35	8	3.2	298
Dartmouth College	NH	16	10	2	28	22	12	0	37	10	0	87
University of Dayton	OH	29	13	8	50	0	0	0	5	0	0	55
University of Delaware	DE	57	17	26	100	0	0	0	0	0	0	100
University of Detroit Mercy	MI	10	7	3	20	0	0	0	0	0	0	20
Drexel University	PA	55	33	42	130	11	5	0	5	0	0	146
Duke University Pratt School of Engineering	NC	45	24	25	94	9	13	0	83	3	0	186
Embry Riddle Aeronautical Univ., Daytona Beach	FL	20	21	13	54	20	13	0	0	0	0	74
Embry Riddle Aeronautical University, Prescott	AZ	1	9	7	17	4	0	0	0	0	0	21
University of Evansville	IN	7	10	3	20	1	4	0	0	0	0	21
Fairfield University	CT	2	11	1	14	0	90	29.98	0	0	0	43.98
Ferris State University	MI	3	1	3	7	0	1	0	0	0	0	7
University of Florida	FL	121	94	72	287	24	1	0.15	41	5	2.43	354.58
Florida Atlantic University	FL	44	11	13	68	8	12	3.98	5	1	0.1	85.08
Florida Institute of Technology	FL	20	26	20	66	0	23	7.25	0	1	0	73.25
Florida International University	FL	31	39	31	101	25	0	0	0	0	0	126
FAMU-FSU College of Engineering	FL	31	30	21	82	1	11	3.24	10	1	0.7	96.94
Gannon University	PA	6	7	6	19	1	8	0	0	0	0	20
George Mason University	VA	38	31	19	88	22	113	35.5	16	6	3	164.5
The George Washington University	DC	46	10	16	72	6	128	30.16	11	5	2.5	121.66
University of Georgia	GA	11	8	4	23	0	3	0	21	0	0	44
Georgia Institute of Technology	GA	231	111	70	412	7	25	0	195	0	0	614
Gonzaga University	WA	13	8	2	23	1	0	0	0	0	0	24
Grand Valley State University	MI	7	4	10	21	2	0	0	0	0	0	23

CAP-GRA

FACULTY

INSTITUTION		TEACHING FACULTY							RESEARCH FACULTY			TOTAL FTE
		FULL-TIME					PART-TIME		FULL-TIME	PART-TIME		
		TENURE/TENURE-TRACK			TOTAL T/T-T	NON T/T-T	TOTAL FACULTY	FTE (PT)	RESEARCH (FT)	RESEARCH (PT)	FTE (PT) RESEARCH	
		PROFESSOR	ASSOCIATE	ASSISTANT		NON-TENURE						
Grove City College	PA	0	0	0	0	10	3	1	0	0	0	11
University of Hartford	CT	6	6	6	18	3	19	0	2	0	0	23
Harvard University	MA	39	11	14	64	0	7	2.75	95	6	3	164.75
Harvey Mudd College	CA	9	3	5	17	0	1	0.5	0	0	0	17.5
University of Hawaii at Manoa	HI	21	22	14	57	0	3	1	18	0	0	76
Hofstra University	NY	5	8	1	14	0	2	0.66	0	0	0	14.66
University of Houston, Cullen School of Engineering	TX	47	26	18	91	5	37	18.8	22	0	0	136.8
Howard University	DC	18	13	7	38	1	5	0	0	0	0	39
Humboldt State University	CA	7	1	2	10	0	7	2.04	0	0	0	12.04
University of Idaho	ID	45	16	12	73	0	29	0	27	19	0	100
Idaho State University	ID	7	8	5	20	5	0	0	0	0	0	25
Illinois Institute of Technology	IL	31	28	21	80	9	27	14	13	0	0	116
University of Illinois at Chicago	IL	48	37	24	109	6	19	6.73	0	0	0	121.73
University of Illinois at Urbana-Champaign	IL	233	84	98	415	18	16	8.18	173	53	24.95	639.13
Indiana Institute of Technology	IN	1	5	4	10	0	6	0	0	0	0	10
Indiana University Purdue University at Indianapolis	IN	12	8	13	33	3	5	4	13	0	0	53
Indiana University-Purdue University Fort Wayne	IN	4	5	8	17	0	2	0.5	0	0	0	17.5
The University of Iowa	IA	44	22	17	83	0	2	0.75	0	0	0	83.75
Iowa State University	IA	99	68	50	217	27	9	3.52	28	4	2.13	277.65
John Brown University	AR	3	2	1	6	0	0	0	0	0	0	6
The Johns Hopkins University	MD	84	13	38	135	7	264	0	17	35	0	159
University of Kansas	KS	48	34	24	106	0	14	0	0	0	0	106
Kansas State University	KS	62	45	23	130	13	7	1.3	3	1	0	147.3
University of Kentucky	KY	68	41	35	144	14	15	7.5	10	13	6.5	182
Kettering University formerly GMI	MI	35	20	6	61	5	0	0	0	0	0	66
Lafayette College	PA	8	13	11	32	3	2	1	0	2	1	37
Lake Superior State University	MI	1	3	5	9	0	2	0.6	2	0	0	11.6
Lamar University	TX	16	9	9	34	0	6	2.6	1	1	0.5	38.1
Lawrence Technological University	MI	12	11	9	32	4	40	16.2	0	0	0	52.2
Lehigh University	PA	70	21	28	119	5	0	0	48	0	0	172
LeTourneau University	TX	6	0	5	11	0	0	0	0	0	0	11
Louisiana State University	LA	51	39	28	118	15	13	5	4	0	0	142
Louisiana Tech University	LA	24	20	34	78	21	18	6	24	30	7.85	136.85
University of Louisiana at Lafayette	LA	20	7	6	33	2	5	0.6	7	0	0	42.6
University of Louisville	KY	46	13	18	77	5	17	8.4	3	0	3	96.4
Loyola College in Maryland	MD	2	1	1	4	1	3	1.08	0	0	0	6.08
Loyola Marymount University	CA	15	2	5	22	0	9	3	0	0	0	25
University of Maine	ME	31	23	13	67	5	3	1	1	0	0	74
Manhattan College	NY	17	16	4	37	0	0	0	0	0	0	37
Marietta College	OH	1	3	2	6	0	0	0	0	0	0	6
Marquette University	WI	22	24	9	55	5	13	6.5	4	5	3	73.5
University of Maryland, Baltimore County	MD	28	17	13	58	8	18	0	19	15	0	85
University of Maryland, College Park	MD	110	59	27	196	5	45	7.99	206	28	14.41	429.4
Massachusetts Institute of Technology	MA	255	67	50	372	0	0	0	0	0	0	372
University of Massachusetts Amherst	MA	41	28	18	87	1	7	3.44	24	6	2.9	118.34

GRO-MAS

FACULTY

INSTITUTION		TEACHING FACULTY							RESEARCH FACULTY			TOTAL FTE
		FULL-TIME					PART-TIME		FULL-TIME	PART-TIME		
		TENURE/TENURE-TRACK				NON T/T-T						
		PROFESSOR	ASSOCIATE	ASSISTANT	TOTAL T/T-T	NON-TENURE	TOTAL FACULTY	FTE (PT)	RESEARCH (FT)	RESEARCH (PT)	FTE (PT) RESEARCH	
University of Massachusetts Dartmouth	MA	31	16	19	66	3	7	1.83	0	0	0	70.83
University of Massachusetts Lowell	MA	51	11	15	77	15	12	0	4	0	0	96
McNeese State University	LA	8	4	2	14	2	4	0	0	0	0	16
The University of Memphis	TN	19	10	11	40	2	8	1.6	7	1	0.5	51.1
Mercer University	GA	10	14	9	33	0	0	0	0	0	0	33
Messiah College	PA	2	2	4	8	10	0	0	2	0	0	20
University of Miami	FL	28	12	7	47	16	0	0	0	0	0	63
Miami University	OH	13	12	18	43	7	16	7	0	0	0	57
University of Michigan	MI	186	75	51	312	16	18	8.8	52	27	14.44	403.24
Michigan State University	MI	73	47	41	161	7	10	4.36	38	31	14.5	224.86
Michigan Technological University	MI	40	49	27	116	17	7	4.08	1	11	3.39	141.47
University of Michigan, Dearborn	MI	21	23	17	61	0	14	5.07	13	4	2.26	81.33
Milwaukee School of Engineering	WI	21	21	11	53	4	28	12.61	0	0	0	69.61
Minnesota State University, Mankato	MN	13	3	6	22	0	3	1.25	0	0	0	23.25
University of Minnesota, Duluth	MN	13	12	11	36	6	5	0	2	0	0	44
University of Minnesota - Twin Cities	MN	145	52	48	245	0	39	23.4	0	5	3.45	271.85
The University of Mississippi	MS	16	17	13	46	3	7	0	5	2	0	54
Mississippi State University	MS	50	30	39	119	12	10	4.5	22	4	1.8	159.3
University of Missouri-Columbia	MO	34	42	32	108	25	13	5.38	4	3	2	144.38
University of Missouri - Kansas City	MO	9	9	12	30	0	0	0	0	0	0	30
University of Missouri - Rolla	MO	67	47	33	147	21	28	8.3	30	15	7.96	214.26
Monmouth University	NJ	1	6	0	7	1	0	0	0	0	0	8
Montana State University	MT	25	21	16	62	5	15	6.45	39	19	8.05	120.5
Montana Tech of the University of Montana	MT	20	4	10	34	38	1.98	39.98	0	0	0	111.98
Morgan State University	MD	9	13	11	33	0	0	0	0	0	0	33
Naval Postgraduate School	CA	23	12	4	39	16	0	0	7	0	0	62
University of Nebraska, Lincoln	NE	71	67	36	174	42	18	0	0	0	0	216
University of Nevada, Las Vegas	NV	28	18	15	61	2	3	0	0	0	0	63
University of Nevada, Reno	NV	25	17	14	56	1	2	0	6	0	0	63
University of New Hampshire	NH	34	17	6	57	6	7	3.33	12	1	0.5	78.83
University of New Haven	CT	21	7	1	29	0	0	0	0	0	0	29
New Jersey Institute of Technology	NJ	70	34	13	117	14	92	30.68	7	0	0	168.68
The College of New Jersey	NJ	5	4	10	19	18	9	0	0	0	0	37
The University of New Mexico	NM	44	23	23	90	17	34	8.02	22	25	10.3	147.32
New Mexico State University	NM	30	32	19	81	0	16	7.94	3	1	0.05	91.99
University of New Orleans	LA	16	9	4	29	0	22	6.25	0	0	0	35.25
City College of the City University of New York	NY	57	26	22	105	0	31	15.5	3	0	0	123.5
The State University of New York at Binghamton	NY	19	19	24	62	6	27	7.75	4	0	0	79.75
State University of New York at Buffalo	NY	66	28	26	120	13	24	6.89	5	7	4.95	149.84
SUNY College of Environmental Science and Forestry	NY	9	7	4	20	1	0	0	6	0	0	27
SUNY, New Paltz	NY	2	3	3	8	0	0	0	0	0	0	8
Stony Brook University	NY	47	39	31	117	19	26	8.26	0	0	0	144.26
North Carolina A & T State University	NC	38	31	28	97	14	0	0	20	3	0	131
North Carolina State University	NC	164	85	57	306	40	22	7.88	195	28	14.65	563.53
University of North Carolina at Chapel Hill	NC	20	3	34	57	0	0	0	0	0	0	57

MAS-NOR

FACULTY

FACULTY, FALL 2006

INSTITUTION		TEACHING FACULTY							RESEARCH FACULTY			TOTAL FTE
		FULL-TIME				NON T/T-T	PART-TIME		FULL-TIME	PART-TIME		
		TENURE/TENURE-TRACK										
		PROFESSOR	ASSOCIATE	ASSISTANT	TOTAL T/T-T	NON-TENURE	TOTAL FACULTY	FTE (PT)	RESEARCH (FT)	RESEARCH (PT)	FTE (PT) RESEARCH	
University of North Carolina, Charlotte	NC	21	22	24	67	6	6	1.42	28	6	3.25	105.67
University of North Dakota	ND	7	11	12	30	1	2	1.5	3	0	200	235.5
North Dakota State University	ND	18	24	20	62	4	26	0	0	0	0	66
University of North Florida	FL	2	4	5	11	5	6	1.75	1	0	0	18.75
University of North Texas	TX	7	1	4	12	0	0	0	0	0	0	12
Northeastern University	MA	42	26	22	90	7	27	8.97	24	0	0	129.97
Northern Arizona University	AZ	9	13	11	33	6	6	2.9	1	2	1.2	44.1
Northern Illinois University	IL	11	6	5	22	4	0	0	0	0	0	26
Northwestern University	IL	102	34	25	161	0	0	0	0	0	0	161
Norwich University	VT	6	3	3	12	1	2	1.5	0	0	0	14.5
University of Notre Dame	IN	51	22	20	93	4	10	5	12	0	0	114
Oakland University	MI	20	17	12	49	0	21	0	0	21	0	49
Ohio Northern University	OH	7	8	4	19	1	1	0	0	0	0	20
The Ohio State University	OH	144	72	43	259	14	39	18	54	31	14.29	359.29
Ohio University	OH	31	33	13	77	2	4	0	34	0	0	113
University of Oklahoma	OK	67	28	28	123	2	18	5.94	25	4	2.1	158.04
Oklahoma Christian University	OK	9	6	1	16	0	0	0	0	0	0	16
Oklahoma State University	OK	49	41	34	124	2	9	4.69	4	3	1.39	136.08
Old Dominion University	VA	35	18	13	66	1	21	0	9	0	0	76
Oral Roberts University	OK	2	1	1	4	1	0	0	0	0	0	5
OGI School of Science & Engineering at OHSU	OR	18	8	19	45	2	61	0	4	1	0.75	51.75
Oregon Institute of Technology	OR	10	7	10	27	4	2	0.88	0	0	0	31.88
Oregon State University	OR	35	46	43	124	7	9	4.5	15	0	0	150.5
University of the Pacific	CA	9	9	8	26	2	4	0	2	0	0	30
University of Pennsylvania	PA	57	17	23	97	9	43	22.5	56	0	56	240.5
Pennsylvania State University Harrisburg	PA	2	10	9	21	6	20	6	2	0	0	35
Penn State Erie, The Behrend College	PA	2	2	14	18	12	12	6	0	0	0	36
The Pennsylvania State University	PA	188	93	53	334	0	0	0	0	0	0	334
Philadelphia University	PA	3	3	2	8	8	0	0	1	0	0	17
University of Pittsburgh	PA	41	30	31	102	6	17	10.9	25	40	23.12	167.02
Polytechnic University	NY	25	22	13	60	14	52	0	11	0	0	85
Polytechnic University of Puerto Rico	PR	15	33	34	82	0	78	22.5	0	0	0	104.5
University of Portland	OR	7	10	5	22	0	0	0	0	0	0	22
Portland State University	OR	25	23	14	62	16	11	1.31	14	9	1.8	95.11
Prairie View A&M University	TX	16	14	12	42	4	0	0	0	0	0	46
Princeton University	NJ	85	11	26	122	5	12	2.11	81	0	0	210.11
University of Puerto Rico, Mayaguez Campus	PR	86	35	33	154	13	7	0	4	2	0	171
Purdue University, Calumet	IN	11	3	2	16	0	6	1.45	0	0	0	17.45
Purdue University	IN	151	79	70	300	9	11	0	40	8	0	349
Rensselaer Polytechnic Institute	NY	71	30	37	138	7	1	0	11	6	0	156
University of Rhode Island	RI	50	10	12	72	8	0	0	2	1	0	82
William Marsh Rice University	TX	62	13	27	102	12	30	12.21	12	1	0.6	138.81
University of Rochester	NY	42	8	23	73	0	20	10	25	2	1.3	109.3
Rochester Institute of Technology	NY	31	28	23	82	7	5	2.5	1	0	0	92.5
Roger Williams University	RI	6	3	4	13	0	7	2.75	0	0	0	15.75

NOR–ROG

FACULTY

INSTITUTION		TEACHING FACULTY							RESEARCH FACULTY			TOTAL FTE
		FULL-TIME					PART-TIME		FULL-TIME	PART-TIME		
		TENURE/TENURE-TRACK				NON T/T-T						
		PROFESSOR	ASSOCIATE	ASSISTANT	TOTAL T/T-T	NON-TENURE	TOTAL FACULTY	FTE (PT)	RESEARCH (FT)	RESEARCH (PT)	FTE (PT) RESEARCH	
Rose-Hulman Institute of Technology	IN	35	36	29	100	0	0	0	0	0	0	100
Rowan University	NJ	9	18	5	32	0	6	2	0	0	0	34
Rutgers, The State University of New Jersey	NJ	76	25	30	131	9	8	0	0	0	0	140
Saginaw Valley State University	MI	7	3	1	11	0	5	2.11	0	0	0	13.11
Saint Cloud State University	MN	8	3	7	18	0	2	0.21	0	0	0	18.21
Saint Louis University - Parks College	MO	5	8	4	17	1	7	0	1	0	0	19
University of Saint Thomas	MN	2	1	4	7	0	0	0	0	0	0	7
University of San Diego	CA	3	8	4	15	0	4	1.5	0	0	0	16.5
San Diego State University	CA	32	6	17	55	2	8	0	9	0	0	66
San Francisco State University	CA	15	1	4	20	2	17	9.5	0	0	0	31.5
San Jose State University	CA	37	17	15	69	7	110	31.93	0	0	0	107.93
Santa Clara University	CA	13	14	7	34	4	47	23.05	0	0	0	61.05
Seattle University	WA	4	7	12	23	0	0	0	0	0	0	23
Seattle Pacific University	WA	1	1	1	3	1	1	0	0	0	0	4
Smith College	MA	1	2	6	9	1	0	0	2	0	0	12
University of South Alabama	AL	12	6	14	32	0	0	0	0	0	0	32
University of South Carolina	SC	28	30	29	87	2	0	0	51	25	0	140
South Dakota School of Mines and Technology	SD	32	12	21	65	5	6	0	5	0	0	75
South Dakota State University	SD	33	14	22	69	23	10	4.45	4	2	1	101.45
University of South Florida	FL	50	23	30	103	12	17	6	66	0	0	187
Southeast Missouri State University	MO	3	2	2	7	0	1	0.5	0	0	0	7.5
University of Southern California	CA	112	30	24	166	9	48	0	66	3	0	241
Southern Illinois University Carbondale	IL	28	12	13	53	3	2	1	3	6	1	61
Southern Illinois University Edwardsville	IL	20	8	12	40	5	14	2.81	5	0	0	52.81
University of Southern Maine	ME	2	5	0	7	0	0	0	0	0	0	7
Southern Methodist University	TX	23	13	13	49	0	0	0	0	0	0	49
Southern University and A&M College	LA	17	9	7	33	0	3	0	0	0	0	33
Stanford University	CA	120	36	53	209	4	0	0	11	3	1.5	225.5
Stevens Institute of Technology	NJ	28	11	15	54	19	35	13.08	2	0	0	88.08
Swarthmore College	PA	7	1	1	9	0	0	0	0	0	0	9
Syracuse University	NY	45	14	6	65	3	28	6.87	14	0	0	88.87
Temple University	PA	12	8	6	26	4	14	9	6	6	6	51
Tennessee State University	TN	15	8	4	27	5	6	1.4	0	0	0	33.4
Tennessee Technological University	TN	28	24	17	69	0	4	1	4	0	0	74
University of Tennessee, Chattanooga	TN	23	8	3	34	6	6	2.76	9	0	0	51.76
University of Tennessee, Knoxville	TN	65	41	26	132	8	51	15.95	30	16	8.57	194.52
University of Tennessee, Martin	TN	1	3	6	10	0	2	1	0	0	0	11
Texas A&M University	TX	165	73	108	346	20	23	9.82	43	15	6.42	425.24
Texas A&M University - Kingsville	TX	0	16	11	27	6	4	2	0	0	0	35
Texas Christian University	TX	2	3	0	5	3	1	0.5	0	0	0	8.5
Texas Tech University	TX	50	35	34	119	11	16	5.03	0	0	0	135.03
The University of Texas at Arlington	TX	54	24	43	121	0	0	0	15	5	1.3	137.3
The University of Texas at Austin	TX	142	45	58	245	12	43	17.52	94	50	26.87	395.39
The University of Texas at Dallas	TX	42	31	19	92	13	13	4.75	3	0	0	112.75
University of Texas at El Paso	TX	29	19	25	73	0	0	0	0	0	0	73

ROS-TEX

FACULTY

FACULTY, FALL 2006

INSTITUTION		TEACHING FACULTY							RESEARCH FACULTY			TOTAL FTE
		FULL-TIME					PART-TIME		FULL-TIME	PART-TIME		
		TENURE/TENURE-TRACK				NON T/T-T						
		PROFESSOR	ASSOCIATE	ASSISTANT	TOTAL T/T-T	NON-TENURE	TOTAL FACULTY	FTE (PT)	RESEARCH (FT)	RESEARCH (PT)	FTE (PT) RESEARCH	
The University of Texas-Pan American	TX	5	10	11	26	2	4	0	0	21	0	28
University of Texas at San Antonio	TX	18	15	13	46	5	13	5.35	5	9	7.5	68.85
The University of Texas at Tyler	TX	7	10	6	23	1	7	2.8	0	0	0	26.8
The University of Toledo	OH	37	18	12	67	3	10	3.5	21	1	0.5	95
Tri-State University	IN	6	12	5	23	22	6	1.75	0	0	0	46.75
Trinity University	TX	2	4	3	9	0	0	0	0	0	0	9
Trinity College	CT	3	2	1	6	1	1	0.4	0	0	0	7.4
Tufts University	MA	31	22	12	65	11	24	0.63	3	2	0	79.63
Tulane University	LA	18	8	13	39	0	0	0	0	0	0	39
University of Tulsa	OK	16	12	9	37	7	7	3.5	10	2	0.5	58
Tuskegee University	AL	15	14	16	45	2	2	0	0	0	0	47
Union College	NY	12	4	8	24	5	3	1.75	0	0	0	30.75
U.S. Air Force Academy	CO	16	16	38	70	43	0	0	19	2	0	132
U.S. Coast Guard Academy	CT	6	4	3	13	14	0	0	0	0	0	27
U.S. Merchant Marine Academy	NY	8	8	6	22	4	6	4	2	2	1	33
United States Military Academy	NY	0	0	0	0	183	3	1.5	0	0	0	184.5
U.S. Naval Academy	MD	26	23	23	72	55	10	3.16	4	0	0	134.16
University of Utah	UT	57	32	37	126	14	13	6.92	57	5	1.6	205.52
Utah State University	UT	36	13	20	69	14	0	0	0	0	0	83
Valparaiso University	IN	5	5	9	19	0	2	1	0	0	0	20
Vanderbilt University	TN	42	19	21	82	21	17	0	21	0	0	124
University of Vermont	VT	14	9	13	36	5	10	1.49	4	3	2.2	48.69
Villanova University	PA	19	19	15	53	10	32	10	0	0	0	73
University of Virginia	VA	75	38	27	140	9	16	2.24	8	0	0	159.24
Virginia Commonwealth University	VA	11	18	14	43	3	4	1.25	0	0	0	47.25
Virginia Military Institute	VA	16	4	3	23	0	4	0	8	0	0	31
Virginia Polytechnic Institute and State University	VA	146	113	74	333	28	31	10.95	79	41	18.97	469.92
Walla Walla College	WA	7	3	2	12	0	0	0	1	0	0	13
University of Washington	WA	104	53	34	191	49	49	17.49	39	9	4.6	301.09
Washington State University	WA	52	27	26	105	12	2	0.95	26	5	3.15	147.1
Washington University	MO	45	17	27	89	0	137	0	26	3	1.75	116.75
Wayne State University	MI	42	21	13	76	5	59	19.64	16	0	0	116.64
Webb Institute	NY	8	1	1	10	0	0	0	0	0	0	10
Wentworth Institute of Technology	MA	6	12	10	28	0	0	0	0	0	0	28
West Virginia University Institute of Technology	WV	13	4	8	25	2	0	0	0	0	0	27
West Virginia University	WV	59	24	27	110	1	23	4.39	16	0	0.76	132.15
Western Kentucky University	KY	3	5	5	13	0	0	0	0	0	0	13
Western Michigan University	MI	43	34	16	93	0	21	0	0	0	0	93
Western New England College	MA	7	8	4	19	0	0	0	0	0	0	19
Wichita State University	KS	20	14	10	44	1	11	2.75	0	0	0	47.75
Widener University	PA	4	10	5	19	2	19	9	0	0	0	30
Wilkes University	PA	6	8	1	15	16	5	2.5	0	0	0	33.5
Winona State University	MN	4	0	1	5	0	1	0.25	0	0	0	5.25
University of Wisconsin, Stout	WI	9	3	5	17	2	6	3.5	4	0	0	26.5
University of Wisconsin, Madison	WI	109	32	42	183	0	0	0	0	0	0	183

TEX-WIS

FACULTY

INSTITUTION		TEACHING FACULTY							RESEARCH FACULTY			TOTAL FTE
		FULL-TIME				NON T/T-T	PART-TIME		FULL-TIME	PART-TIME		
		TENURE/TENURE-TRACK										
		PROFESSOR	ASSOCIATE	ASSISTANT	TOTAL T/T-T	NON-TENURE	TOTAL FACULTY	FTE (PT)	RESEARCH (FT)	RESEARCH (PT)	FTE (PT) RESEARCH	
University of Wisconsin, Milwaukee	WI	18	24	18	60	6	0	0	8	1	0	74
University of Wisconsin, Platteville	WI	25	14	15	54	2	1	0.5	0	0	0	56.5
Worcester Polytechnic Institute	MA	37	34	14	85	3	17	2.74	6	0	0	96.74
Wright State University	OH	27	20	16	63	8	30	14	9	2	1.25	95.25
University of Wyoming	WY	34	21	21	76	9	1	0.5	30	0	0	115.5
Yale University/Faculty of Engineering	CT	32	10	15	57	1	47	0	53	0	0	111
York College of Pennsylvania	PA	0	3	4	7	0	6	0	0	0	0	7
Youngstown State University	OH	17	2	3	22	0	3	0.65	0	0	0	22.65
Totals:		11,562	6,252	5,501	23,315	2,142	4,575	1,242	3,971	1,047	657	31,327
CANADIAN INSTITUTIONS:												
University of Alberta	AB	82	31	37	150	8	58	11.95	0	0	0	169.95
University of Calgary	AB	61	42	30	133	24	24	20.32	6	12	7.75	191.07
Concordia University, Faculty of Engr. and Comp. Sci.	PQ	50	51	45	146	5	65	14.64	32	14	8.7	206.34
Ecole Polytechnique de Montreal	PQ	128	55	47	230	0	0	0	0	0	0	230
Ecole de Technologie Superieure	PQ	55	72	24	151	19	197	50	0	0	0	220
McGill University, Faculty of Engineering	PQ	45	42	38	125	2	60	0	76	0	0	203
University of Ottawa, Faculty of Engineering	ON	42	28	35	105	6	72	22.04	0	0	0	133.04
University of Waterloo	ON	87	67	50	204	11	0	0	6	0	0	221
Totals:		550	388	306	1,244	75	476	119	120	26	16	1,574

WIS-YOU

FACULTY

Am Ind - American Indian or Alaska Native: A person having origins in any of the original peoples of North and South American (including Central America), and who maintains tribal affiliation or community attachment.

Asian: A person having origins in any of the original peoples of the Far East, Southeast Asia, or the Indian subcontinent including, for example, Cambodia, China, India, Japan, Korea, Malaysia, Pakistan, the Philippine Islands, Thailand, and Vietnam.

B/AfrA- Black or Afrian American: A person having origins in any of the black racial groups of Africa. Terms such as "Haitian" or "Negro" can be used in addition to "Black or African American."

Hisp - Hispanic or Latino: A person of Cuban, Mexican, Puerto Rican, South or Central American, or other Spanish culture or origin, regardless of race. The term, "Spanish origin," can be used in addition to "Hispanic or Latino."

Haw - Native Hawaiian or Other Pacific Islander: A person having origins in any of the original peoples of Hawaii, Guam, Samoa, or other Pacific Islands.

Caucasian: A person having origins in any of the original peoples of Europe, the Middle East, or North Africa.

Tenured/Tenure-Track Faculty

AIR-CAL

TENURED/TENURE-TRACK FACULTY

INSTITUTION		AM IND M	AM IND F	ASIAN M	ASIAN F	B/AFRA M	B/AFRA F	HISP M	HISP F	HAW M	HAW F	CAUCASIAN M	CAUCASIAN F	OTHER M	OTHER F	TOTAL BY GENDER M	TOTAL BY GENDER F	TOTAL
Air Force Institute of Technology	OH	2	0	3	1	0	0	1	0	0	0	120	3	2	1	128	5	133
The University of Akron	OH	1	0	20	1	3	0	1	0	0	0	28	5	0	1	53	7	60
Alabama A&M University	AL	0	0	22	0	4	0	1	0	0	0	7	0	0	0	34	0	34
University of Alabama at Birmingham	AL	0	0	11	1	1	0	0	0	0	0	24	2	0	0	36	3	39
The University of Alabama in Huntsville	AL	0	0	11	0	1	0	1	0	0	0	35	10	0	0	48	10	58
The University of Alabama	AL	0	0	16	3	3	1	1	0	0	0	70	6	1	0	91	10	101
University of Alaska, Anchorage	AK	0	0	1	1	0	1	0	0	0	0	13	0	0	0	14	2	16
University of Alaska Fairbanks	AK	1	0	17	0	0	0	1	0	0	0	12	2	0	0	31	2	33
Alfred University, NY State College of Ceramics	NY	0	0	7	0	0	0	0	0	0	0	17	3	0	0	24	3	27
The University of Arizona	AZ	0	0	20	3	1	0	5	1	0	0	83	9	14	2	123	15	138
Arizona State University	AZ	0	0	53	8	1	0	6	3	0	0	117	13	0	0	177	24	201
University of Arkansas	AR	1	0	20	3	0	0	1	0	0	0	62	6	4	1	88	10	98
Arkansas State University	AR	0	0	0	0	0	0	0	0	0	0	8	0	2	0	10	0	10
Arkansas Tech University	AR	0	0	1	1	0	0	0	0	0	0	8	1	0	0	9	2	11
University of Arkansas at Little Rock	AR	0	0	15	0	1	0	0	0	0	0	6	0	8	1	29	1	30
Auburn University	AL	0	0	39	3	4	1	2	2	0	0	93	7	0	0	138	13	151
Baker College	MI	0	0	0	0	0	0	0	0	0	0	2	2	0	0	2	2	4
Baylor University	TX	0	0	0	1	0	0	0	0	0	0	24	1	0	0	24	2	26
Boise State University	ID	0	0	5	0	0	0	0	0	0	0	28	11	0	0	33	11	44
Boston University	MA	0	0	6	5	1	0	1	0	0	0	107	10	0	0	115	15	130
Bradley University	IL	0	0	4	0	1	0	1	0	0	0	37	3	0	0	43	3	46
University of Bridgeport	CT	0	0	6	0	0	0	0	0	0	0	3	1	0	1	9	2	11
Brigham Young University	UT	0	0	1	0	0	0	1	0	0	0	81	0	0	0	83	0	83
Brown University	RI	0	0	8	0	0	0	0	0	0	0	25	4	0	0	33	4	37
Bucknell University	PA	0	0	4	1	0	0	0	1	0	0	35	7	0	1	39	10	49
California Institute of Technology	CA	0	0	12	1	1	1	0	0	0	0	70	10	0	0	83	12	95
California Maritime Academy	CA	0	0	3	0	0	0	1	0	0	0	2	1	0	0	6	1	7
California Polytechnic State University	CA	0	0	15	8	3	0	7	0	0	0	92	11	6	1	123	20	143
California State Polytechnic University, Pomona	CA	0	0	16	5	3	0	2	0	0	0	42	7	6	0	69	12	81
California State University, East Bay	CA	0	0	0	1	0	0	0	0	0	0	2	1	0	0	2	2	4
California State University, Chico	CA	0	0	7	1	1	0	0	0	0	0	11	0	0	0	19	1	20
California State University, Fullerton	CA	0	0	18	2	0	0	0	0	0	0	11	3	1	0	30	5	35
California State University, Long Beach	CA	0	0	12	2	1	0	2	0	0	1	26	3	0	0	41	6	47
California State University, Los Angeles	CA	0	0	13	3	2	0	0	0	0	0	16	5	0	0	31	8	39
California State University, Northridge	CA	0	0	0	0	0	0	0	0	0	0	0	0	46	10	46	10	56

INSTITUTION		AM IND M	AM IND F	ASIAN M	ASIAN F	B/AFRA M	B/AFRA F	HISP M	HISP F	HAW M	HAW F	CAUCASIAN M	CAUCASIAN F	OTHER M	OTHER F	TOTAL BY GENDER M	TOTAL BY GENDER F	TOTAL
California State University, Sacramento	CA	0	0	20	6	2	1	1	0	0	0	31	6	0	0	54	13	67
University of California, Berkeley	CA	0	0	38	6	1	0	10	1	0	0	159	21	0	0	208	28	236
University of California, Davis	CA	1	0	46	8	3	0	4	1	0	0	121	23	0	0	175	32	207
University of California, Irvine	CA	0	0	0	0	0	0	0	0	0	0	0	0	88	11	88	11	99
University of California, Los Angeles	CA	0	0	53	4	0	0	2	1	0	0	83	9	0	0	138	14	152
University of California, Riverside	CA	0	0	23	2	1	0	2	0	0	0	38	4	0	0	64	6	70
University of California, San Diego	CA	0	0	0	0	0	0	0	0	0	0	0	0	157	16	157	16	173
University of California, Santa Barbara	CA	0	0	27	2	0	0	3	0	0	0	93	9	0	0	123	11	134
University of California-Santa Cruz	CA	0	0	9	3	0	0	4	1	0	0	38	5	12	2	63	11	74
Calvin College	MI	0	0	0	0	0	0	1	0	0	0	11	2	0	0	12	2	14
Capitol College	MD	0	0	0	0	0	0	0	0	0	0	0	0	41	13	41	13	54
Carnegie Mellon University	PA	0	0	24	3	5	0	4	0	0	1	81	12	4	1	118	17	135
Carroll College	MT	0	0	0	0	0	0	0	0	0	0	8	2	0	0	8	2	10
Case Western Reserve University	OH	1	0	24	3	1	0	2	0	0	0	76	9	0	0	104	12	116
The Catholic University of America	DC	0	0	7	0	1	0	0	0	0	0	12	2	4	0	24	2	26
Cedarville University	OH	0	0	0	0	0	0	0	0	0	0	0	0	15	1	15	1	16
University of Central Florida	FL	0	0	59	3	2	4	3	0	0	0	56	10	0	0	120	17	137
Christian Brothers University	TN	0	0	7	0	0	0	1	0	0	0	13	0	0	0	21	0	21
University of Cincinnati	OH	0	0	49	0	4	0	7	1	0	0	79	0	0	0	139	1	140
The Citadel	SC	0	0	2	0	0	0	0	0	0	0	14	0	0	0	16	0	16
Clarkson University	NY	0	0	13	1	0	0	0	0	0	0	33	11	2	0	48	12	60
Clemson University	SC	0	0	33	1	7	0	3	1	0	0	139	14	0	0	182	16	198
Cleveland State University	OH	0	0	20	2	2	1	4	0	0	0	30	9	0	0	56	12	68
Colorado School of Mines	CO	0	0	12	3	0	0	3	2	0	0	107	13	15	3	137	21	158
Colorado State University	CO	0	0	14	1	0	0	5	1	0	0	70	4	0	0	89	6	95
Colorado State University, Pueblo	CO	0	0	0	0	0	0	0	0	0	0	2	1	2	0	4	1	5
University of Colorado at Boulder	CO	0	0	22	3	4	0	4	0	0	0	111	24	0	0	141	27	168
University of Colorado at Colorado Springs	CO	0	1	7	0	0	0	2	0	0	0	17	0	0	0	26	1	27
University of Colorado at Denver	CO	0	0	6	0	0	2	2	0	0	0	21	3	0	0	29	5	34
University of Connecticut	CT	0	0	27	9	4	0	1	0	0	0	57	3	0	0	89	12	101
The Cooper Union	NY	0	0	3	0	1	0	0	0	0	0	26	2	0	0	30	2	32
Cornell University	NY	1	0	21	3	6	1	5	0	0	0	184	20	0	0	217	24	241
Dartmouth College	NH	0	0	1	0	0	0	0	0	0	0	22	4	1	0	24	4	28
University of Dayton	OH	0	0	15	0	0	0	1	0	0	0	29	3	2	0	47	3	50
University of Delaware	DE	0	0	21	3	4	0	3	0	0	0	60	9	0	0	88	12	100
University of Detroit Mercy	MI	0	0	4	1	0	0	0	0	0	0	13	2	0	0	17	3	20
Drexel University	PA	0	0	32	5	1	1	0	1	0	0	71	15	4	0	108	22	130
Duke University Pratt School of Engineering	NC	0	0	15	2	1	0	2	0	0	0	60	13	0	0	78	16	94
Embry Riddle Aeronautical Univ., Daytona Beach	FL	0	0	11	0	1	1	0	0	0	0	41	1	0	0	53	1	54
Embry Riddle Aeronautical University, Prescott	AZ	0	0	1	2	0	0	0	0	0	0	14	0	0	0	15	2	17
University of Evansville	IN	0	0	0	0	0	0	0	0	0	0	0	0	18	2	18	2	20
Fairfield University	CT	0	0	4	0	0	0	0	0	0	0	8	2	0	0	12	2	14
Ferris State University	MI	0	0	1	0	0	0	0	0	0	0	5	0	1	0	7	0	7
University of Florida	FL	0	0	77	8	5	1	6	0	0	0	174	16	0	0	262	25	287
Florida Atlantic University	FL	0	0	11	2	2	0	4	1	0	0	45	3	0	0	62	6	68

TENURED/TENURE-TRACK FACULTY   CAL-FLO

TENURED/TENURE-TRACK FACULTY   FLO-LOY

INSTITUTION		AM IND M	AM IND F	ASIAN M	ASIAN F	B/AFRA M	B/AFRA F	HISP M	HISP F	HAW M	HAW F	CAUCASIAN M	CAUCASIAN F	OTHER M	OTHER F	TOTAL BY GENDER M	TOTAL BY GENDER F	TOTAL
Florida Institute of Technology	FL	0	0	10	0	0	0	1	1	0	0	42	1	11	0	64	2	66
Florida International University	FL	0	0	33	5	9	0	10	2	0	0	38	4	0	0	90	11	101
FAMU-FSU College of Engineering	FL	0	0	25	3	15	2	2	1	0	0	30	4	0	0	72	10	82
Gannon University	PA	0	0	6	2	0	0	0	1	0	0	9	1	0	0	15	4	19
George Mason University	VA	0	0	17	3	0	0	2	0	0	0	54	12	0	0	73	15	88
The George Washington University	DC	0	0	10	5	1	0	2	0	0	0	47	7	0	0	60	12	72
University of Georgia	GA	0	0	5	0	1	0	0	0	0	0	16	1	0	0	22	1	23
Georgia Institute of Technology	GA	0	1	73	11	13	2	7	1	0	0	271	33	0	0	364	48	412
Gonzaga University	WA	0	0	4	0	0	0	1	0	0	0	15	3	0	0	20	3	23
Grand Valley State University	MI	0	0	3	1	1	0	0	0	0	0	15	1	0	0	19	2	21
University of Hartford	CT	0	0	3	2	1	1	0	0	0	0	10	1	0	0	14	4	18
Harvard University	MA	0	0	13	1	1	1	0	0	0	0	46	2	0	0	60	4	64
Harvey Mudd College	CA	0	0	2	1	0	0	0	1	0	0	9	4	0	0	11	6	17
University of Hawaii at Manoa	HI	0	0	21	2	0	0	3	0	0	0	27	4	0	0	51	6	57
Hofstra University	NY	0	0	1	0	0	0	1	0	0	0	10	1	0	1	12	2	14
University of Houston, Cullen School of Engineering	TX	0	0	27	3	0	0	1	0	0	0	52	5	2	1	82	9	91
Howard University	DC	0	0	5	0	21	4	0	0	0	0	4	0	4	0	34	4	38
Humboldt State University	CA	0	0	0	0	0	0	0	0	0	0	7	3	0	0	7	3	10
University of Idaho	ID	2	0	8	0	1	0	0	0	0	0	58	2	2	0	71	2	73
Idaho State University	ID	0	0	4	0	0	0	1	0	0	0	11	2	3	0	18	2	20
Illinois Institute of Technology	IL	1	0	18	3	1	0	3	0	0	0	52	2	0	0	75	5	80
University of Illinois at Chicago	IL	0	0	36	4	0	1	2	1	0	0	57	9	0	0	95	14	109
University of Illinois at Urbana-Champaign	IL	0	0	95	8	6	1	11	0	0	0	265	26	3	0	380	35	415
Indiana Institute of Technology	IN	0	0	1	0	0	0	0	0	0	0	5	2	2	0	8	2	10
Indiana University Purdue University at Indianapolis	IN	0	0	11	1	1	0	1	0	0	0	17	2	0	0	30	3	33
Indiana University–Purdue University Fort Wayne	IN	1	0	3	3	0	0	0	0	0	0	8	1	0	0	13	4	17
The University of Iowa	IA	0	0	25	1	0	1	0	0	0	0	51	5	0	0	76	7	83
Iowa State University	IA	0	0	60	4	2	0	1	0	0	0	130	20	0	0	193	24	217
John Brown University	AR	0	0	1	0	0	0	0	0	0	0	5	0	0	0	6	0	6
The Johns Hopkins University	MD	0	0	14	0	2	0	2	0	0	0	78	12	24	3	120	15	135
University of Kansas	KS	0	0	16	1	1	0	5	0	0	0	67	13	3	0	92	14	106
Kansas State University	KS	0	0	35	3	0	0	0	0	0	0	80	12	0	0	115	15	130
University of Kentucky	KY	0	0	31	2	1	2	0	0	0	0	96	12	0	0	128	16	144
Kettering University formerly GMI	MI	0	0	8	2	1	0	1	0	0	0	43	6	0	0	53	8	61
Lafayette College	PA	0	0	1	0	0	0	0	0	0	0	24	6	0	1	25	7	32
Lake Superior State University	MI	0	0	0	0	0	0	0	0	0	0	9	0	0	0	9	0	9
Lamar University	TX	0	0	15	2	0	0	0	0	0	0	16	0	1	0	32	2	34
Lawrence Technological University	MI	0	0	3	0	0	0	0	0	0	0	23	6	0	0	26	6	32
Lehigh University	PA	0	0	19	4	0	0	4	0	1	0	83	4	2	2	109	10	119
LeTourneau University	TX	0	0	2	0	0	0	2	0	0	0	7	0	0	0	11	0	11
Louisiana State University	LA	0	0	30	0	3	1	3	0	0	0	66	4	10	1	112	6	118
Louisiana Tech University	LA	0	0	17	1	0	1	1	1	0	0	49	7	1	0	68	10	78
University of Louisiana at Lafayette	LA	0	0	3	1	1	0	0	0	0	0	26	2	0	0	30	3	33
University of Louisville	KY	0	0	11	2	0	1	3	0	0	0	52	8	0	0	66	11	77
Loyola College in Maryland	MD	0	0	0	0	0	0	0	0	0	0	4	0	0	0	4	0	4

FACULTY, FALL 2006

INSTITUTION		AM IND M	AM IND F	ASIAN M	ASIAN F	B/AFRA M	B/AFRA F	HISP M	HISP F	HAW M	HAW F	CAUCASIAN M	CAUCASIAN F	OTHER M	OTHER F	TOTAL BY GENDER M	TOTAL BY GENDER F	TOTAL
Loyola Marymount University	CA	0	0	4	1	0	0	1	0	0	0	13	3	0	0	18	4	22
University of Maine	ME	1	0	5	1	0	0	0	0	1	0	52	7	0	0	59	8	67
Manhattan College	NY	0	0	2	0	0	0	0	0	0	0	31	4	0	0	33	4	37
Marietta College	OH	0	0	0	0	0	0	0	0	0	0	6	0	0	0	6	0	6
Marquette University	WI	0	0	8	0	1	0	0	0	0	0	42	4	0	0	51	4	55
University of Maryland, Baltimore County	MD	0	0	14	1	1	1	1	0	0	0	27	8	3	2	46	12	58
University of Maryland, College Park	MD	0	0	38	2	4	1	4	3	0	0	123	12	8	1	177	19	196
Massachusetts Institute of Technology	MA	0	0	45	4	12	2	7	2	0	0	256	44	0	0	320	52	372
University of Massachusetts Amherst	MA	0	0	17	1	0	0	1	2	0	0	62	4	0	0	80	7	87
University of Massachusetts Dartmouth	MA	0	0	12	2	2	0	0	0	0	0	34	6	9	1	57	9	66
University of Massachusetts Lowell	MA	0	0	10	4	2	0	0	0	0	0	43	4	12	2	67	10	77
McNeese State University	LA	0	0	3	0	0	0	0	0	0	0	9	0	2	0	14	0	14
The University of Memphis	TN	0	0	7	0	2	0	0	0	0	0	28	3	0	0	37	3	40
Mercer University	GA	0	0	6	0	2	0	1	0	0	0	18	6	0	0	27	6	33
Messiah College	PA	0	0	0	0	0	0	0	0	0	0	7	1	0	0	7	1	8
University of Miami	FL	0	0	18	1	1	0	1	1	0	0	24	4	0	0	44	3	47
Miami University	OH	1	0	10	2	1	0	0	0	0	0	23	5	1	0	36	7	43
University of Michigan	MI	1	0	55	8	8	2	4	0	0	0	200	33	1	0	269	43	312
Michigan State University	MI	0	0	42	8	4	0	3	0	0	0	95	9	0	0	144	17	161
Michigan Technological University	MI	0	0	20	1	0	0	0	0	0	0	62	11	20	2	102	14	116
University of Michigan, Dearborn	MI	0	0	36	2	1	0	2	0	0	0	20	0	0	0	59	2	61
Milwaukee School of Engineering	WI	0	0	4	1	1	0	0	0	0	0	40	6	1	0	46	7	53
Minnesota State University, Mankato	MN	0	0	2	1	0	0	1	0	0	0	10	1	7	0	20	2	22
University of Minnesota, Duluth	MN	0	0	6	0	1	0	1	0	0	0	27	1	0	0	35	1	36
University of Minnesota -Twin Cities	MN	0	0	54	2	2	1	2	0	0	0	164	20	0	0	222	23	245
The University of Mississippi	MS	0	0	8	1	1	0	0	0	0	0	24	4	8	0	41	5	46
Mississippi State University	MS	0	0	13	2	2	1	5	0	0	0	81	17	1	0	100	19	119
University of Missouri-Columbia	MO	0	0	44	3	1	0	2	0	0	0	52	5	1	0	100	8	108
University of Missouri - Kansas City	MO	0	0	5	1	0	0	0	0	0	0	14	1	9	0	28	2	30
University of Missouri - Rolla	MO	0	0	37	2	3	0	4	0	0	0	94	7	0	0	138	9	147
Monmouth University	NJ	0	0	1	0	0	0	0	0	0	0	5	1	0	0	6	1	7
Montana State University	MT	1	0	7	0	0	0	0	0	0	0	51	3	0	0	59	3	62
Montana Tech of the University of Montana	MT	0	0	3	0	0	0	0	0	0	0	28	3	0	0	31	3	34
Morgan State University	MD	0	0	8	1	16	4	1	0	0	0	2	1	0	0	27	6	33
Naval Postgraduate School	CA	0	0	8	2	0	0	4	0	0	0	20	4	7	0	35	4	39
University of Nebraska, Lincoln	NE	0	0	38	5	1	1	3	0	0	0	118	8	0	0	160	14	174
University of Nevada, Las Vegas	NV	0	0	5	1	0	0	0	1	0	0	50	4	0	0	55	6	61
University of Nevada, Reno	NV	0	0	12	1	1	0	2	0	0	0	37	3	0	0	52	4	56
University of New Hampshire	NH	0	0	7	2	0	0	1	0	0	0	39	7	1	0	48	9	57
University of New Haven	CT	0	0	0	0	0	0	0	0	0	0	26	3	0	0	26	3	29
New Jersey Institute of Technology	NJ	3	0	19	3	4	2	1	0	0	0	67	5	13	0	107	10	117
The College of New Jersey	NJ	0	0	3	2	0	0	1	0	0	0	9	2	2	0	15	4	19
The University of New Mexico	NM	1	0	15	1	0	1	4	0	0	0	59	8	1	0	80	10	90
New Mexico State University	NM	0	0	18	0	1	0	9	2	0	1	40	2	8	0	76	5	81
University of New Orleans	LA	0	0	5	0	1	0	1	0	0	0	18	4	0	0	25	4	29

LOY-NEW

TENURED/TENURE-TRACK FACULTY

INSTITUTION		AM IND M	AM IND F	ASIAN M	ASIAN F	B/AFRA M	B/AFRA F	HISP M	HISP F	HAW M	HAW F	CAUCASIAN M	CAUCASIAN F	OTHER M	OTHER F	TOTAL BY GENDER M	TOTAL BY GENDER F	TOTAL
City College of the City University of New York	NY	0	0	14	5	4	0	2	1	0	0	63	8	8	0	91	14	105
The State University of New York at Binghamton	NY	0	0	20	6	0	0	1	0	0	0	31	4	0	0	52	10	62
State University of New York at Buffalo	NY	0	0	39	6	0	0	3	0	0	0	68	4	0	0	110	10	120
SUNY College of Environmental Science and Forestry	NY	0	0	5	0	1	0	0	0	0	0	12	2	0	0	18	2	20
SUNY, New Paltz	NY	0	0	1	0	0	0	1	0	0	0	6	0	0	0	8	0	8
Stony Brook University	NY	0	0	36	6	4	0	1	0	0	0	59	11	0	0	100	17	117
North Carolina A & T State University	NC	0	0	28	6	17	5	2	0	0	0	26	3	9	1	82	15	97
North Carolina State University	NC	0	0	56	5	6	2	2	1	0	0	212	21	1	0	277	29	306
University of North Carolina at Chapel Hill	NC	0	0	0	0	0	0	1	0	0	0	51	5	0	0	52	5	57
University of North Carolina, Charlotte	NC	0	0	20	1	1	2	1	0	0	0	37	5	0	0	59	8	67
University of North Dakota	ND	0	0	11	1	0	0	0	0	0	0	18	0	0	0	29	1	30
North Dakota State University	ND	0	0	23	4	2	0	0	0	0	0	32	1	0	0	57	5	62
University of North Florida	FL	0	0	3	1	1	0	0	0	0	0	5	1	0	0	9	2	11
University of North Texas	TX	0	0	6	0	0	0	0	0	0	0	6	0	0	0	12	0	12
Northeastern University	MA	0	0	9	6	0	1	1	0	0	0	67	6	0	0	77	13	90
Northern Arizona University	AZ	0	1	2	1	1	0	1	0	0	0	24	4	0	0	27	6	33
Northern Illinois University	IL	0	0	10	0	0	0	0	0	0	0	12	0	0	0	22	0	22
Northwestern University	IL	0	0	26	5	2	0	5	2	0	0	111	10	0	0	144	17	161
Norwich University	VT	0	0	0	0	0	0	0	0	0	0	10	1	1	0	11	1	12
University of Notre Dame	IN	0	0	6	4	1	0	4	0	0	0	71	7	0	0	82	11	93
Oakland University	MI	1	0	20	4	1	0	0	0	0	0	18	5	0	0	40	9	49
Ohio Northern University	OH	0	0	4	1	0	0	0	0	0	0	13	1	0	0	17	2	19
The Ohio State University	OH	0	0	64	4	4	0	5	0	0	0	153	22	6	1	232	27	259
Ohio University	OH	0	0	16	0	0	0	1	1	0	0	54	5	0	0	71	6	77
University of Oklahoma	OK	0	0	35	4	1	0	4	0	0	0	71	8	0	0	111	12	123
Oklahoma Christian University	OK	0	0	0	0	0	0	0	0	0	0	16	0	0	0	16	0	16
Oklahoma State University	OK	2	2	23	2	0	0	2	0	0	0	88	5	0	0	115	9	124
Old Dominion University	VA	0	0	22	2	5	0	2	0	0	0	33	2	0	0	62	4	66
Oral Roberts University	OK	0	0	1	0	0	0	0	0	0	0	3	0	0	0	4	0	4
OGI School of Science & Engineering at OHSU	OR	0	0	1	4	1	0	2	0	0	0	29	6	2	0	35	10	45
Oregon Institute of Technology	OR	0	0	2	0	0	0	0	0	0	0	21	4	0	0	23	4	27
Oregon State University	OR	0	0	28	4	1	0	3	0	0	0	73	15	0	0	105	19	124
University of the Pacific	CA	0	0	2	0	1	0	1	0	0	0	16	4	2	0	22	4	26
University of Pennsylvania	PA	0	0	20	2	1	1	3	0	0	0	64	6	0	0	88	9	97
Pennsylvania State University Harrisburg	PA	0	0	3	2	1	0	1	0	1	0	9	4	0	0	15	6	21
Penn State Erie, The Behrend College	PA	0	0	5	1	0	0	0	0	0	0	11	1	0	0	16	2	18
The Pennsylvania State University	PA	0	0	9	0	6	1	10	3	0	0	267	38	0	0	292	42	334
Philadelphia University	PA	0	0	1	0	0	0	1	0	0	0	4	2	0	0	6	2	8
University of Pittsburgh	PA	0	0	25	4	2	0	2	0	0	0	58	11	0	0	87	15	102
Polytechnic University	NY	0	0	18	1	0	0	0	0	0	0	34	6	1	0	53	7	60
Polytechnic University of Puerto Rico	PR	0	0	0	0	0	0	64	14	0	0	3	1	0	0	67	15	82
University of Portland	OR	0	0	7	0	0	0	0	0	0	0	13	2	0	0	20	2	22
Portland State University	OR	1	0	8	2	1	0	0	0	0	0	35	7	8	0	53	9	62
Prairie View A&M University	TX	0	0	19	0	14	5	1	0	0	0	2	0	1	0	37	5	42
Princeton University	NJ	0	0	21	4	2	0	3	1	0	0	79	12	0	0	105	17	122

TENURED/TENURE-TRACK FACULTY   NEW-PRI

FACULTY, FALL 2006

INSTITUTION		AM IND M	AM IND F	ASIAN M	ASIAN F	B/AFRA M	B/AFRA F	HISP M	HISP F	HAW M	HAW F	CAUCASIAN M	CAUCASIAN F	OTHER M	OTHER F	TOTAL BY GENDER M	TOTAL BY GENDER F	TOTAL
University of Puerto Rico, Mayaguez Campus	PR	0	0	14	1	1	1	114	16	0	0	5	0	2	0	136	18	154
Purdue University, Calumet	IN	0	0	0	2	1	0	0	0	0	0	13	0	0	0	14	2	16
Purdue University	IN	0	0	71	10	5	1	9	2	0	0	168	32	2	0	255	45	300
Rensselaer Polytechnic Institute	NY	0	0	34	3	2	0	3	2	0	0	82	10	2	0	123	15	138
University of Rhode Island	RI	1	0	15	1	2	1	0	1	0	0	45	6	0	0	63	9	72
William Marsh Rice University	TX	0	0	0	0	0	0	0	0	0	0	0	0	87	15	87	15	102
University of Rochester	NY	0	0	12	0	1	0	1	0	0	0	54	5	0	0	68	5	73
Rochester Institute of Technology	NY	0	0	17	3	1	0	5	1	0	0	51	4	0	0	74	8	82
Roger Williams University	RI	0	0	2	1	0	0	0	0	0	0	8	2	0	0	10	3	13
Rose-Hulman Institute of Technology	IN	0	0	6	1	0	1	2	0	0	0	71	13	3	3	82	18	100
Rowan University	NJ	0	0	7	4	1	0	1	1	0	0	16	2	0	0	25	7	32
Rutgers, The State University of New Jersey	NJ	0	0	39	2	3	0	2	0	0	0	73	12	0	0	117	14	131
Saginaw Valley State University	MI	0	0	0	1	0	0	0	0	0	0	11	0	0	0	11	0	11
Saint Cloud State University	MN	0	0	7	3	0	0	0	0	0	0	8	0	0	0	15	3	18
Saint Louis University - Parks College	MO	0	0	7	0	0	0	0	0	0	0	7	3	0	0	14	3	17
University of Saint Thomas	MN	0	0	0	0	0	0	0	0	0	0	6	1	0	0	6	1	7
University of San Diego	CA	0	0	2	0	1	0	0	1	0	0	9	2	0	0	12	3	15
San Diego State University	CA	0	0	28	1	1	0	2	0	0	0	20	3	0	0	51	4	55
San Francisco State University	CA	0	0	6	1	0	0	0	0	0	0	12	1	0	0	18	2	20
San Jose State University	CA	0	0	24	4	3	0	0	0	0	0	25	5	8	0	60	9	69
Santa Clara University	CA	0	0	5	2	2	0	1	0	0	0	16	6	0	2	24	10	34
Seattle University	WA	0	0	2	1	0	0	0	0	0	0	11	5	1	3	14	9	23
Seattle Pacific University	WA	0	0	0	0	0	0	0	0	0	0	1	2	0	0	1	2	3
Smith College	MA	0	0	0	0	0	0	0	0	0	0	3	6	0	0	3	6	9
University of South Alabama	AL	0	0	11	0	1	0	0	0	0	0	19	1	0	0	31	1	32
University of South Carolina	SC	0	0	0	0	0	0	0	0	0	0	0	0	80	7	80	7	87
South Dakota School of Mines and Technology	SD	0	0	10	3	0	0	2	0	0	0	45	5	0	0	57	8	65
South Dakota State University	SD	0	0	10	1	0	0	0	0	0	0	52	6	0	0	62	7	69
University of South Florida	FL	1	0	30	3	3	2	7	3	0	0	47	4	3	0	91	12	103
Southeast Missouri State University	MO	0	0	2	0	0	0	0	0	0	0	4	1	0	0	6	1	7
University of Southern California	CA	0	0	40	4	1	0	6	0	0	0	109	6	0	0	156	10	166
Southern Illinois University Carbondale	IL	0	0	19	0	1	0	1	0	0	0	29	3	0	0	50	3	53
Southern Illinois University Edwardsville	IL	0	0	17	1	2	0	0	0	0	0	18	2	0	0	37	3	40
University of Southern Maine	ME	0	0	0	0	0	0	0	0	0	0	6	1	0	0	6	1	7
Southern Methodist University	TX	0	0	9	1	0	0	2	0	0	0	35	2	0	0	46	3	49
Southern University and A&M College	LA	0	0	11	0	15	3	0	0	0	0	4	0	0	0	30	3	33
Stanford University	CA	0	0	24	5	5	0	8	0	0	0	144	23	0	0	181	28	209
Stevens Institute of Technology	NJ	0	0	15	3	6	0	1	0	0	0	27	2	0	0	49	5	54
Swarthmore College	PA	0	0	1	0	0	0	0	0	0	0	1	1	5	1	7	2	9
Syracuse University	NY	0	0	18	2	0	0	1	0	0	0	29	9	4	2	52	13	65
Temple University	PA	0	0	7	0	2	1	1	0	0	0	13	2	0	0	23	3	26
Tennessee State University	TN	0	0	8	3	4	3	0	0	0	0	9	0	0	0	21	6	27
Tennessee Technological University	TN	0	0	17	4	2	0	3	0	0	0	38	5	0	0	60	9	69
University of Tennessee, Chattanooga	TN	0	0	1	1	3	0	0	0	0	0	23	6	0	0	27	7	34
University of Tennessee, Knoxville	TN	0	0	35	4	3	1	1	0	0	0	87	1	0	0	126	6	132

TENURED/TENURE-TRACK FACULTY   PUE-TEN

FACULTY, FALL 2006

TENURED/TENURE-TRACK FACULTY TEN-WES

INSTITUTION		AM IND M	AM IND F	ASIAN M	ASIAN F	B/AFRA M	B/AFRA F	HISP M	HISP F	HAW M	HAW F	CAUCASIAN M	CAUCASIAN F	OTHER M	OTHER F	TOTAL BY GENDER M	TOTAL BY GENDER F	TOTAL
University of Tennessee, Martin	TN	0	0	1	0	0	0	0	0	0	0	9	0	0	0	10	0	10
Texas A&M University	TX	1	0	80	10	4	2	14	5	0	0	207	23	0	0	306	40	346
Texas A&M University - Kingsville	TX	0	0	4	2	0	0	4	0	0	0	9	1	7	0	24	3	27
Texas Christian University	TX	0	0	2	0	0	0	0	0	0	0	3	0	0	0	5	0	5
Texas Tech University	TX	1	0	24	7	1	0	3	1	0	0	74	8	0	0	103	16	119
The University of Texas at Arlington	TX	0	0	38	5	1	0	2	0	0	0	49	5	21	0	111	10	121
The University of Texas at Austin	TX	1	1	42	2	4	1	9	1	0	0	163	21	0	0	219	26	245
The University of Texas at Dallas	TX	0	0	39	5	1	0	2	0	0	0	42	3	0	0	84	8	92
University of Texas at El Paso	TX	1	0	11	0	1	0	13	2	0	0	30	3	9	3	65	8	73
The University of Texas-Pan American	TX	0	0	4	0	0	0	3	1	0	0	10	0	7	1	24	2	26
University of Texas at San Antonio	TX	0	0	16	1	1	0	4	0	0	0	22	1	1	0	44	2	46
The University of Texas at Tyler	TX	0	0	6	0	1	1	0	0	0	0	15	1	0	0	22	1	23
The University of Toledo	OH	0	0	19	1	0	1	0	2	0	0	38	6	0	0	57	10	67
Tri-State University	IN	0	0	3	0	0	0	1	0	0	0	18	1	0	0	22	1	23
Trinity University	TX	0	0	1	0	1	0	0	0	0	0	5	1	1	0	8	1	9
Trinity College	CT	0	0	1	0	1	0	0	0	0	0	4	0	0	0	6	0	6
Tufts University	MA	2	0	6	0	2	1	0	0	0	0	43	11	0	0	53	12	65
Tulane University	LA	0	0	11	0	1	0	0	0	0	0	26	1	0	0	38	1	39
University of Tulsa	OK	1	0	8	0	0	0	1	0	0	0	12	2	13	0	35	2	37
Tuskegee University	AL	0	0	24	2	11	3	0	0	0	0	4	1	0	0	39	6	45
Union College	NY	0	0	3	0	0	0	1	0	0	0	19	2	0	0	22	2	24
U.S. Air Force Academy	CO	0	0	4	1	0	0	5	0	0	0	58	6	1	0	63	7	70
U.S. Coast Guard Academy	CT	0	0	0	0	0	0	0	0	0	0	11	2	0	0	11	2	13
U.S. Merchant Marine Academy	NY	0	0	1	0	0	0	1	0	0	0	19	1	0	0	21	1	22
U.S. Naval Academy	MD	0	0	0	0	5	0	0	1	0	0	55	11	0	0	60	12	72
University of Utah	UT	0	0	13	1	0	0	3	0	0	0	83	10	14	2	113	13	126
Utah State University	UT	0	0	9	1	1	0	4	0	0	0	47	4	3	0	64	5	69
Valparaiso University	IN	0	0	0	0	1	0	0	0	0	0	17	1	0	0	18	1	19
Vanderbilt University	TN	0	0	16	2	1	0	0	0	0	0	57	6	0	0	74	8	82
University of Vermont	VT	0	0	7	0	0	0	1	0	0	0	23	5	0	0	31	5	36
Villanova University	PA	0	0	15	1	0	0	1	0	0	0	31	5	0	0	47	6	53
University of Virginia	VA	0	0	11	2	5	0	5	0	0	0	103	14	0	0	124	16	140
Virginia Commonwealth University	VA	0	0	11	0	1	2	0	1	0	0	24	4	0	0	36	7	43
Virginia Military Institute	VA	0	0	0	0	0	0	0	0	0	0	23	0	0	0	23	0	23
Virginia Polytechnic Institute and State University	VA	0	0	65	9	8	2	11	2	0	0	203	33	0	0	287	46	333
Walla Walla College	WA	0	0	2	0	0	0	0	0	0	0	8	2	0	0	10	2	12
University of Washington	WA	0	0	38	5	2	1	3	0	0	0	114	26	1	1	158	33	191
Washington State University	WA	0	0	20	5	1	0	3	0	0	0	49	11	15	1	88	17	105
Washington University	MO	0	0	24	1	0	0	0	0	0	0	58	6	0	0	82	7	89
Wayne State University	MI	0	0	35	2	4	0	0	0	0	0	30	5	0	0	69	7	76
Webb Institute	NY	0	0	0	0	0	0	0	0	0	0	10	0	0	0	10	0	10
Wentworth Institute of Technology	MA	0	0	1	0	0	0	2	0	0	0	24	1	0	0	27	1	28
West Virginia University Institute of Technology	WV	0	0	10	0	1	0	0	0	0	0	9	0	5	0	25	0	25
West Virginia University	WV	0	0	19	2	2	0	1	0	0	0	82	4	0	0	104	6	110
Western Kentucky University	KY	0	0	0	0	0	0	0	0	0	0	12	1	0	0	12	1	13

INSTITUTION		AM IND M	AM IND F	ASIAN M	ASIAN F	B/AFRA M	B/AFRA F	HISP M	HISP F	HAW M	HAW F	CAUCASIAN M	CAUCASIAN F	OTHER M	OTHER F	TOTAL BY GENDER M	TOTAL BY GENDER F	TOTAL
Western Michigan University	MI	0	0	18	0	2	0	1	0	0	0	58	9	5	0	84	9	93
Western New England College	MA	0	0	0	0	0	0	0	0	0	0	16	3	0	0	16	3	19
Wichita State University	KS	0	0	3	0	0	0	0	1	0	0	39	1	0	0	42	2	44
Widener University	PA	0	0	6	1	0	0	0	0	0	0	9	3	0	0	15	4	19
Wilkes University	PA	0	0	3	0	0	0	0	0	0	0	10	1	1	0	14	1	15
Winona State University	MN	0	0	0	0	1	0	0	0	0	0	3	1	0	0	4	1	5
University of Wisconsin, Stout	WI	0	0	2	0	0	0	0	0	0	0	12	3	0	0	14	3	17
University of Wisconsin, Madison	WI	0	0	19	3	1	0	5	0	0	0	133	20	2	0	160	23	183
University of Wisconsin, Milwaukee	WI	0	0	22	5	0	0	3	0	0	0	27	2	1	0	53	7	60
University of Wisconsin, Platteville	WI	0	0	13	0	1	0	0	1	0	0	35	4	0	0	49	5	54
Worcester Polytechnic Institute	MA	0	0	10	4	0	0	2	0	0	0	56	8	5	0	73	12	85
Wright State University	OH	0	0	27	3	0	1	0	0	0	0	30	2	0	0	57	6	63
University of Wyoming	WY	0	0	8	0	0	0	0	1	0	0	61	6	0	0	69	7	76
Yale University/Faculty of Engineering	CT	0	0	8	1	0	0	0	1	0	0	45	2	0	0	53	4	57
York College of Pennsylvania	PA	0	0	0	1	0	0	0	0	0	0	6	0	0	0	6	1	7
Youngstown State University	OH	0	0	2	0	0	0	0	0	0	0	18	2	0	0	20	2	22
Totals:		33	6	4,581	547	467	94	661	108	3	3	13,955	1,743	986	128	20,686	2,629	23,315
CANADIAN INSTITUTIONS:																		
University of Alberta	AB	0	0	0	0	0	0	0	0	0	0	0	0	139	11	139	11	150
University of Calgary	AB	0	0	0	0	0	0	0	0	0	0	0	0	116	17	116	17	133
Concordia University, Faculty of Engr. and Comp. Sci.	PQ	0	0	0	0	0	0	0	0	0	0	0	0	127	19	127	19	146
Ecole Polytechnique de Montreal	PQ	0	0	0	0	0	0	0	0	0	0	0	0	207	23	207	23	230
Ecole de Technologie Superieure	PQ	0	0	0	0	0	0	0	0	0	0	0	0	134	17	134	17	151
McGill University, Faculty of Engineering	PQ	0	0	0	0	0	0	0	0	0	0	0	0	114	11	114	11	125
University of Ottawa, Faculty of Engineering	ON	0	0	14	1	4	0	0	0	0	0	73	13	0	0	91	14	105
University of Waterloo	ON	0	0	0	0	0	0	0	0	0	0	0	0	177	27	177	27	204
Totals:		0	0	14	1	4	0	0	0	0	0	73	13	1,014	125	1,105	139	1,145

TENURED/TENURE-TRACK FACULTY WES-YOU

ENGINEERING-RELATED RESEARCH EXPENDITURES, FISCAL 2006

INSTITUTION		GRANTS	FEDERAL	STATE	FOREIGN	INDUSTRY	NON-PROFIT	INDIVIDUAL	LOCAL	TOTAL FUNDING
Air Force Institute of Technology	OH	218	$5,728,000	$2,000		$296,000				$6,026,000
The University of Akron	OH	119	$1,921,000	$2,540,855		$632,000	$483,000		$29,000	$5,605,855
University of Alabama at Birmingham	AL	149	$8,080,705	$3,128		$325,009	$435,293		$73,045	$8,917,180
The University of Alabama	AL	172	$6,799,000	$468,000			$349,000			$7,616,000
Alfred University, NY State College of Ceramics	NY	187	$1,368,000	$1,037,000	$64,000	$1,398,000	$12,000			$3,879,000
The University of Arizona	AZ	0	$19,254,815	$458,817	$187,374	$2,840,250	$140,189	$14,281	$34,611	$22,930,337
Arizona State University	AZ	0	$29,786,472	$4,754,888	$290,433	$8,939,440	$6,151,839		$230,968	$50,154,040
University of Arkansas	AR	304	$5,308,514	$2,577,670		$3,539,168	$3,610,818		$67,680	$15,103,850
Auburn University	AL	549	$22,400,000	$9,485,000	$322,000	$2,953,000	$1,171,000			$36,331,000
Baylor University	TX	17	$206,671			$484,323	$7,632			$698,626
Boise State University	ID	44	$3,569,186	$30,155		$121,900				$3,721,241
Boston University	MA	0	$53,616,355			$5,957,372				$59,573,727
Bradley University	IL	69	$348,094			$954,880	$68,127			$1,371,100
Brigham Young University	UT	238	$319,200	$7,542,700	$959,300	$2,927,700	$525,700	$78,200	$1,300	$12,354,100
California Institute of Technology	CA	680	$69,217,000	$50,000		$1,412,000	$9,713,000			$80,392,000
California Polytechnic State University	CA	62	$944,977	$748,923		$593,643	$432,362	$65,005		$2,784,910
California State University, Fullerton	CA	0	$176,000	$50,000						$226,000
University of California, Berkeley	CA	0	$65,479,000	$13,871,000		$16,814,000	$21,948,000	$1,127,000	$564,000	$119,803,000
University of California, Davis	CA	480	$31,764,000	$15,698,000			$14,191,000			$61,653,000
University of California, Irvine	CA	747	$46,595,215	$11,355,053		$5,809,637	$2,254,264	$62,092		$66,076,262
University of California, Los Angeles	CA	1,570	$50,514,603	$17,579,972		$21,116,199				$89,210,774
University of California, Riverside	CA	431	$20,072,350	$8,416,479			$4,539,682	$672,910	$365,817	$34,067,238
University of California, San Diego	CA	1,120	$86,480,999	$17,195,716		$34,424,240	$485,125			$138,586,080
University of California-Santa Cruz	CA	229	$13,235,000	$318,000		$678,000	$1,479,000	$18,000		$15,728,000
Carnegie Mellon University	PA	731	$134,385,640	$3,756,300	$2,518,300	$17,360,560	$927,600		$18,600	$158,967,000
Case Western Reserve University	OH	778	$23,767,000	$3,626,000		$5,850,000	$2,360,000	$1,460,000		$37,063,000
University of Central Florida	FL	1,037	$30,739,057	$6,133,604	$690,416	$10,518,417	$2,553,829	$169,244	$718,265	$51,522,832
University of Cincinnati	OH	0	$13,669,669	$2,120,743	$66,381	$1,416,578	$638,974		$78,724	$17,991,069
Clarkson University	NY	201	$4,103,875	$1,118,686			$1,423,396			$6,645,957
Clemson University	SC	488	$22,183,000	$3,012,000	$187,000	$1,303,000	$2,951,000		$9,000	$29,645,000
Colorado School of Mines	CO	405	$19,888,636	$1,869,298		$7,538,917				$29,296,851
Colorado State University	CO	640	$41,012,000	$1,127,000	$159,000	$6,075,000	$1,741,000			$50,114,000
Colorado State University, Pueblo	CO	0		$97,852		$8,600				$106,452
University of Colorado at Boulder	CO	753	$40,462,656	$544,240	$86,110	$6,610,990	$3,506,393	$5,469,815		$56,680,204
University of Connecticut	CT	388	$17,833,000	$1,348,000	$208,000	$1,276,000	$663,000	$9,000	$263,000	$21,600,000
Cornell University	NY	0	$87,546,740	$6,436,305	$176,602	$12,266,540	$7,860,692	$4,409,200		$118,696,079
Dartmouth College	NH	125	$15,300,000			$1,500,000	$300,000			$17,100,000
University of Dayton	OH	0	$55,878,000	$4,845,000	$273,000	$4,294,000	$1,128,000		$143,000	$66,561,000
University of Delaware	DE	0	$26,900,000	$1,532,000		$3,224,000	$4,307,000	$1,717,000		$37,680,000
Drexel University	PA	166	$31,440,058	$756,010		$2,276,172	$1,521,804	$538,814	$224,341	$36,757,199
Duke University Pratt School of Engineering	NC	0					$55,431,815			$55,431,815
Embry Riddle Aeronautical Univ, Daytona Beach	FL	9	$82,886				$77,256			$160,142
University of Florida	FL	1,448	$66,377,000	$26,977,000	$495,000	$5,405,000	$4,674,000	$3,703,000	$135,000	$107,766,000
Florida Atlantic University	FL	0	$4,105,887	$256,702		$141,959	$1,362,426		$54,316	$5,921,290
Florida Institute of Technology	FL	129	$2,750,940	$536,600		$392,219	$91,812			$3,771,571

AIR-FLO

RESEARCH EXPENDITURES

INSTITUTION		GRANTS	FEDERAL	STATE	FOREIGN	INDUSTRY	NON-PROFIT	INDIVIDUAL	LOCAL	TOTAL FUNDING
Florida International University	FL	200	$8,431,267	$904,462		$385,657	$1,480,860		$190,470	$11,392,716
FAMU-FSU College of Engineering	FL	257	$20,758,000	$2,237,000		$1,501,999	$270,000	$617,000		$25,383,999
George Mason University	VA	0	$10,218,710	$153,213	$33,064	$10,951	$184,062			$10,600,000
University of Georgia	GA	0	$1,238,707	$946,738		$1,260,354			$125,919	$3,571,718
Georgia Institute of Technology	GA	0	$103,329,000	$56,300,000	$988,000	$6,407,000	$30,176,000	$6,415,000	$62,000	$203,677,000
Grand Valley State University	MI	0	$75,000							$75,000
University of Hartford	CT	0	$1,072,000	$365,602		$180,000				$1,617,602
Harvard University	MA	0	$35,175,000			$25,000				$35,200,000
University of Hawaii at Manoa	HI	113	$9,044,290	$449,851		$457,343	$141,823			$10,093,307
University of Houston, Cullen School of Engineering	TX	0	$5,817,229	$4,099,472		$968,536	$1,455,905		$588,191	$12,929,333
University of Idaho	ID	0	$16,894,888	$2,044,959		$1,216,214	$295,375			$20,451,436
Idaho State University	ID	28	$1,165,315	$137,700		$393,989	$8,000			$1,705,004
Illinois Institute of Technology	IL	201	$16,759,599	$1,144,915					$1,914,872	$19,819,386
University of Illinois at Chicago	IL	0	$13,970,096	$804,977		$2,487,151	$435,288		$182,688	$17,880,200
University of Illinois at Urbana-Champaign	IL	0	$162,137,000	$5,723,000		$32,258,000				$200,118,000
The University of Iowa	IA	0	$13,371,000	$1,280,200		$7,183,500	$760,500	$4,699,200		$27,294,400
Iowa State University	IA	357	$41,039,000	$10,315,000	$107,000	$9,972,000	$3,588,000	$299,000	$171,000	$65,491,000
The Johns Hopkins University	MD	622	$47,586,000	$44,000	$398,000	$1,017,000	$3,766,000	$1,531,000		$54,342,000
University of Kansas	KS	0	$11,273,362	$1,391,767	$114,998	$635,499	$317,539		$61,917	$13,795,082
Kansas State University	KS	367	$12,544,000	$2,034,000		$3,894,000	$222,000			$18,694,000
Kettering University formerly GMI	MI	16	$102,257	$64,478		$879,577	$11,773			$1,058,085
Lamar University	TX	59	$1,722,779	$513,260		$13,166	$5,402			$2,254,607
Lawrence Technological University	MI	0	$3,288,000			$198,000				$3,486,000
Lehigh University	PA	1,019	$13,848,188	$10,505,401		$6,705,571	$452,855		$5,248	$31,517,263
Louisiana State University	LA	640	$3,769,150	$6,929,842	$48,823	$1,590,833	$2,068,114			$14,406,762
Louisiana Tech University	LA		$4,803,216	$4,649,317		$671,145				$10,123,678
University of Louisville	KY	171	$9,445,000	$1,511,000		$1,422,000	$497,000			$12,875,000
University of Maine	ME	348	$10,924,924	$29,372		$2,021,270	$637,665			$13,613,231
Marquette University	WI	45	$848,554	$184,796		$332,052	$293,468		$36,273	$1,695,143
University of Maryland, Baltimore County	MD	0	$5,514,237	$213,603		$423,491	$1,832,271		$119,344	$8,102,946
University of Maryland, College Park	MD	1,111	$80,252,930	$31,322,655	$241,288	$28,033,549	$1,477,060	$2,304,755	$1,807,099	$145,439,336
Massachusetts Institute of Technology	MA	0	$169,025,000	$1,292,000	$7,206,000	$44,540,000	$12,445,000			$234,508,000
University of Massachusetts Amherst	MA	472	$13,010,108	$6,041,435		$3,428,107	$705,707		$588,672	$23,774,029
University of Massachusetts Dartmouth	MA	220	$6,864,000	$5,784,000			$662,000	$10,000		$13,320,000
The University of Memphis	TN	63	$2,102,000	$163,000		$325,000	$1,058,000		$254,000	$3,902,000
University of Miami	FL	78	$2,028,041	$202,530		$643,307	$85,151		$239,380	$3,198,409
Miami University	OH	0	$837,479			$222,475				$1,059,954
University of Michigan	MI	1,874	$115,747,000	$11,817,000	$6,000	$14,703,000	$1,327,000	$2,140,000	- $10,000	$145,730,000
Michigan State University	MI	255	$14,665,000	$4,822,000	$94,000	$5,433,000	$1,828,000		$167,000	$27,009,000
Michigan Technological University	MI	0	$10,577,000	$323,000	$87,000	$3,355,000	$136,000			$14,478,000
University of Michigan, Dearborn	MI	124	$1,689,000	$209,000	$3,000	$1,034,000				$2,935,000
Milwaukee School of Engineering	WI	214	$786,067	$776		$1,444,611	$701,727			$2,933,181
University of Minnesota - Twin Cities	MN	1,578	$51,849,185	$8,951,526		$10,860,633				$71,661,344
The University of Mississippi	MS	62	$9,658,658	$215,897		$76,090	$590,393	$24,767		$10,565,805
Mississippi State University	MS	378	$30,372,394	$3,752,298		$2,181,379	$3,823,556		$519,479	$40,649,106

FLO-MIS

RESEARCH EXPENDITURES

INSTITUTION		GRANTS	FEDERAL	STATE	FOREIGN	INDUSTRY	NON-PROFIT	INDIVIDUAL	LOCAL	TOTAL FUNDING
University of Missouri-Columbia	MO	330	$14,297,684	$1,533,141	$26,572	$1,841,503	$654,937		$33,660	$18,387,497
University of Missouri - Rolla	MO	1,104	$17,575,110	$1,026,091		$4,652,727	$2,235,131		$376,337	$25,865,396
Monmouth University	NJ	0	$2,703,382							$2,703,382
Montana State University	MT	263	$9,459,597	$2,901,524		$624,309	$640,364	$40,000	$53,224	$13,719,018
University of Nebraska, Lincoln	NE	0	$10,479,000	$2,887,000		$3,068,000	$1,299,000		$555,000	$18,288,000
University of Nevada, Reno	NV	0	$9,036,121	$1,568,098			$536,365		$103,681	$11,244,265
University of New Hampshire	NH	172	$16,009,669							$16,009,669
University of New Haven	CT	0	$40,000							$40,000
New Jersey Institute of Technology	NJ	0	$20,011,500	$8,179,630		$3,444,401				$31,635,531
The University of New Mexico	NM	0	$25,099,000	$3,234,000		$585,000			$36,000	$28,954,000
New Mexico State University	NM	328	$13,607,663	$3,241,270		$567,736	$133,311		$60,188	$17,610,168
University of New Orleans	LA	0	$1,413,761	$810,620		$21,447	$1,826,291	$646		$4,072,765
City College of the City University of New York	NY	105	$9,907,200	$3,962,880		$660,480	$1,816,320		$165,120	$16,512,000
The State University of New York at Binghamton	NY	123	$6,446,965	$3,384,110		$4,011,520	$72,254			$13,914,849
State University of New York at Buffalo	NY	765	$31,549,000	$3,734,000		$7,029,000	$6,165,000	$136,000	$117,000	$48,730,000
SUNY College of Environmental Science and Forestry	NY	93	$1,603,201	$86,430	$49,036	$516,295	$372,824		$5,531	$2,633,317
Stony Brook University	NY	434	$17,799,794	$3,407,874	$109,966	$1,202,005	$683,027		$381,579	$23,584,245
North Carolina A&T State University	NC	0	$9,664,343	$12,438		$4,253	$390,783			$10,071,817
North Carolina State University	NC	0	$59,327,000	$36,297,000		$2,896,000	$4,509,000			$103,029,000
University of North Carolina, Charlotte	NC	129	$3,158,000	$712,000		$1,067,000	$21,000		$153,000	$5,111,000
University of North Texas	TX	0	$2,456,768	$141,949		$749,351				$3,348,068
Northeastern University	MA	97	$16,864,343	$204,889		$1,497,340	$481,194	$1,095,213		$20,142,979
Northern Arizona University	AZ	44	$6,187,109	$318,806		$298,331	$782,844			$7,587,090
Northern Illinois University	IL	14	$2,796,528			$5,250,000		$234,955	$339,375	$8,620,858
University of Notre Dame	IN	298	$13,916,773	$1,839,538			$2,892,531			$18,648,842
Oakland University	MI	101	$2,455,435	$140,843		$732,832	$279,032			$3,608,142
The Ohio State University	OH	1,892	$43,928,000	$13,359,000	$71,000	$47,235,000	$3,337,000	$339,000	$109,000	$108,378,000
Ohio University	OH	112	$14,166,450							$14,166,450
University of Oklahoma	OK	262	$9,003,909	$4,971,240		$3,724,920	$857,193			$18,557,262
Oklahoma State University	OK	317	$14,913,354	$2,016,658		$2,320,546	$72,783			$19,323,341
Old Dominion University	VA	0	$24,746,451							$24,746,451
OGI School of Science & Engineering at OHSU	OR	129	$6,814,260	$1,955,059		$287,949	$490,909		$10,272	$9,558,449
Oregon State University	OR	280	$19,608,068	$904,697	$31,803	$2,488,908	$2,257,640			$25,291,116
University of Pennsylvania	PA	351	$47,758,471			$2,307,000	$13,898,000			$63,963,471
The Pennsylvania State University	PA	0	$77,613,911	$14,503,425		$19,137,430	$6,814,427		$12,611	$118,081,804
University of Pittsburgh	PA	409	$41,599,000	$2,077,000		$6,685,000	$1,081,000	$75,000	$2,106,000	$53,623,000
Polytechnic University	NY	176	$7,187,108	$1,570,365		$2,235,647				$10,993,120
Prairie View A&M University	TX	0	$3,104,036	$1,365,139		$287,720	$258,000			$5,014,895
Princeton University	NJ	659	$39,880,837	$848,175		$3,448,356	$998,800	$6,956,558		$52,132,726
University of Puerto Rico, Mayaguez Campus	PR	0	$9,168,636							$9,168,636
Purdue University	IN	0	$57,385,093	$19,981,377	$283,884	$25,878,781	$1,170,021	$7,607,726		$112,306,882
Rensselaer Polytechnic Institute	NY	0	$31,565,825	$9,421,484	$41,244	$4,978,642	$2,701,490	$215,340	$1,995	$48,926,020
University of Rhode Island	RI	128	$2,983,487	$546,606		$529,564	$586,937			$4,646,594
William Marsh Rice University	TX	180	$25,136,883	$1,295,605		$1,074,330	$2,705,678	$2,987,504		$33,200,000
University of Rochester	NY	236	$91,143,000	$2,919,000	$5,000	$4,103,000	$2,226,000	$9,000		$100,405,000

RESEARCH EXPENDITURES

MIS-ROC

INSTITUTION		GRANTS	FEDERAL	STATE	FOREIGN	INDUSTRY	NON-PROFIT	INDIVIDUAL	LOCAL	TOTAL FUNDING
Rochester Institute of Technology	NY	193	$9,857,000	$189,000		$1,796,000	$478,000			$12,320,000
Rose-Hulman Institute of Technology	IN	32	$1,689,702	$75,077		$26,124	$497,298			$2,288,201
Rowan University	NJ	98	$1,106,494	$197,284		$69,640	$196,463		$13,388	$1,583,269
Saint Louis University - Parks College	MO	0	$350,000	$104,000		$66	$75,000			$529,066
Santa Clara University	CA	18	$311,065	$10,885		$29,944	$19,230			$371,124
University of South Alabama	AL	16	$377,000	$39,218		$47,120	$8,790			$472,128
University of South Carolina	SC	0	$14,695,378	$428,247		$1,451,326	$492,115		$2,968	$17,070,034
South Dakota School of Mines and Technology	SD	447	$9,525,133	$1,389,601		$128,904	$169,834		$33,721	$11,247,193
South Dakota State University	SD	70	$2,352,227	$454,065		$8,352	$299			$2,814,943
University of Southern California	CA	0	$125,663,987	$859,426		$8,117,147	$23,460,061	$11,724,847		$169,825,468
Southern Illinois University Carbondale	IL	84	$415,000	$2,092,000	$29,000	$938,000			$68,000	$3,542,000
Southern Illinois University Edwardsville	IL	21	$450,396	$2,000		$137,684				$590,080
Southern Methodist University	TX	0	$1,807,441	$590,632		$218,115	$76,389			$2,692,577
Stanford University	CA	1,581	$105,640,010	$1,483,946	$4,800,878	$13,223,048	$22,505,010	$4,764,448		$152,417,340
Stevens Institute of Technology	NJ	0	$15,187,565	$2,025,503			$3,582,597			$20,795,665
Syracuse University	NY	168	$10,594,000	$3,310,000		$952,000	$1,262,000			$16,118,000
Temple University	PA	0	$1,200,000	$268,000						$1,468,000
Tennessee State University	TN	0	$2,567,748							$2,567,748
Tennessee Technological University	TN	89	$3,654,651	$489,777	$10,000	$875,022			$43,382	$5,072,832
University of Tennessee, Chattanooga	TN	0	$1,943,652	$1,683,716		$792,195				$4,419,563
University of Tennessee, Knoxville	TN	888	$18,077,000	$7,993,000	$291,000	$5,621,000	$1,946,000	$744,000	$1,000	$34,673,000
Texas A&M University	TX	0	$78,055,000	$77,511,000	$470,000	$20,832,000	$18,974,000		$210,000	$196,052,000
Texas A&M University - Kingsville	TX	25	$255,582	$302,441		$5,769	$62,839		$59,067	$685,699
Texas Tech University	TX	0	$8,583,439	$1,447,534	$1,002,322	$1,337,421	$384,434	$52,079	$5,500	$12,812,729
The University of Texas at Arlington	TX	220	$11,257,000	$3,599,000		$488,000	$3,167,000	$7,000	$130,000	$18,648,000
The University of Texas at Austin	TX	1,848	$75,256,920	$14,571,008	$504,177	$20,025,177	$13,693,644		- $210	$124,050,716
The University of Texas at Dallas	TX	154	$6,308,823	$13,149,738			$2,939,176		$892,483	$23,290,220
University of Texas at San Antonio	TX	0	$73,000	$199,700			$20,000		$10,000	$302,700
The University of Texas at Tyler	TX	0	$346,823	$14,288			$5,514			$366,625
The University of Toledo	OH	178	$8,149,436	$2,991,395		$1,679,731	$54,502		$110,366	$12,985,430
Tufts University	MA	146	$8,959,713	$139,965	$33,022	$422,949	$514,366		$39,505	$10,109,520
Tulane University	LA	122	$4,953,246	$248,648		$78,529	$94,567			$5,374,990
University of Utah	UT	460	$33,876,000	$852,000		$6,393,000	$1,872,000		$7,000	$43,000,000
Vanderbilt University	TN	425	$39,959,000	$729,000		$1,909,000	$711,000		$96,000	$43,404,000
University of Vermont	VT	0	$1,504,798	- $2,400		$466,545	$103,092			$2,072,035
Villanova University	PA	101	$4,243,771	$527,754	$11,654	$2,735,194	$1,871,025		$25,734	$9,415,132
University of Virginia	VA	695	$36,061,745	$2,135,770		$6,538,229	$2,842,849		$6,597,367	$54,175,960
Virginia Commonwealth University	VA	82	$4,533,823	$95,831		$657,911	$48,674			$5,336,239
Virginia Polytechnic Institute and State University	VA	2,373	$50,723,449	$26,101,283	$82,098	$8,286,129	$3,778,618	$8,107,000	$305,766	$89,277,343
University of Washington	WA	0	$68,405,000	$2,854,000	$2,840,000	$3,001,000	$6,517,000		$459,000	$92,183,000
Washington State University	WA	454	$12,868,000	$729,000	$54,000	$682,000	$714,000	$54,000	$226,000	$15,327,000
Washington University	MO	0	$13,518,937			$2,464,988	$2,244,187			$18,228,112
Wayne State University	MI	0	$7,173,215	$1,097,457		$4,854,881		$602,779	$4,550	$13,732,882
West Virginia University	WV	325	$13,569,454	$2,582,523	$57,106	$3,831,036	$2,449,264	$1,227,432	$4,840	$23,721,655
Western Michigan University	MI	44	$1,174,751	$361,485		$1,967,470				$3,503,706

RESEARCH EXPENDITURES

ROC–WES

INSTITUTION		GRANTS	FEDERAL	STATE	FOREIGN	INDUSTRY	NON-PROFIT	INDIVIDUAL	LOCAL	TOTAL FUNDING
Wichita State University	KS	0	$8,095,460	$3,083,941		$2,047,615	$34,221			$13,261,237
Widener University	PA	0	$93,000			$29,000				$122,000
University of Wisconsin, Madison	WI	0	$71,543,000	$9,610,000		$22,381,000	$4,489,000			$108,023,000
University of Wisconsin, Milwaukee	WI	103	$1,694,085	$405,000		$259,000	$159,117		$146,380	$2,663,582
Worcester Polytechnic Institute	MA	0	$11,303,362	$30,766		$1,185,635	$4,875,627			$17,395,390
Wright State University	OH	126	$4,986,000	$3,417,000		$401,000			$41,000	$8,845,000
University of Wyoming	WY	217	$5,446,808	$2,176,279	$102,690	$821,022	$243,530			$8,790,329
Yale University/Faculty of Engineering	CT	0	$10,327,093	$68,847	$137,695	$413,084	$2,134,266			$13,080,985
Totals:		46,889	$4,099,577,737	$722,226,329	$27,054,236	$717,274,134	$431,530,560	$84,534,809	$24,186,599	$6,106,384,404
CANADIAN INSTITUTIONS:										
University of Alberta	AB	830	$20,096,000	$10,267,000	$227,000	$5,627,000	$1,344,000		$264,000	$37,825,000
University of Calgary	AB	563	$17,034,000	$8,590,000	$2,595,000	$4,381,000	$2,359,000		$532,000	$35,491,000
Concordia University, Faculty of Engr. and Comp. Sci.	PQ	596	$6,568,313	$1,262,122	$262,000	$3,839,000	$11,000			$11,942,435
Ecole Polytechnique de Montreal	PQ	0	$33,838,931			$10,150,377				$43,989,308
University of Ottawa, Faculty of Engineering	ON	277	$7,243,213			$1,445,553			$512,779	$9,201,545
University of Waterloo	ON	349	$16,728,000	$3,726,000		$2,599,000		$1,652,000		$24,705,000
Totals:		2,615	$101,508,457	$23,845,122	$3,084,000	$28,041,930	$3,714,000	$1,652,000	$1,308,779	$163,154,288

RESEARCH EXPENDITURES

WIC-YAL

2006 Statistical Tables of Engineering Technology Colleges

ENGINEERING TECHNOLOGY ENROLLMENTS, FALL 2006

INSTITUTION		FRESHMEN (FT)	SOPHOMORES (FT)	JUNIORS (FT)	SENIORS (FT)	ENROLLMENT TOTAL (FT) M	(FT) F	TOTAL	(PT)
Alfred State College	NY	219	219	142	139	646	73	719	6
Arizona State University, Polytechnic	AZ	64	83	111	135	326	67	393	108
University of Arkansas at Little Rock	AR	41	45	34	48	146	22	168	23
Bradley University	IL	12	24	36	55	119	8	127	11
Brigham Young University	UT	10	15	30	74	118	11	129	0
Buffalo State College	NY	47	20	27	24	108	10	118	64
California Maritime Academy	CA	49	39	47	26	144	17	161	0
California State Polytechnic University, Pomona	CA	132	44	107	241	471	53	524	0
California State University, Sacramento	CA	24	15	48	74	145	16	161	44
Capitol College	MD	86	46	44	41	171	46	217	0
University of Central Florida	FL	23	34	59	153	230	39	269	254
Colorado State University, Pueblo	CO	14	15	18	16	56	7	63	15
University of Dayton	OH	42	53	67	49	178	33	211	48
University of the District of Columbia	DC	10	9	9	9	33	4	37	8
Eastern Washington University	WA	12	19	44	31	105	1	106	0
Ferris State University	MI	458	463	436	736	1942	151	2,093	0
University of Hartford	CT	148	79	78	77	316	66	382	41
University of Houston, College of Technology	TX	42	62	114	234	415	37	452	257
Indiana University Purdue University at Indianapolis	IN	92	117	174	179	408	154	562	353
Indiana University-Purdue University Fort Wayne	IN	152	71	20	18	247	14	261	260
Kansas State University	KS	7	5	12	23	45	2	47	1
Lake Superior State University	MI	8	6	9	18	41	0	41	12
Lawrence Technological University	MI	11	6	17	15	43	6	49	128
LeTourneau University	TX	25	12	12	13	60	2	62	3
Louisiana Tech University	LA	28	47	33	67	165	10	175	21
University of Maine	ME	78	93	80	98	333	16	349	36
University of Massachusetts Lowell	MA	0	1	0	3	4	0	4	180
McNeese State University	LA	37	33	29	30	117	12	129	31
The University of Memphis	TN	41	23	23	49	109	27	136	88
Metropolitan State College of Denver	CO	98	41	51	63	227	26	253	209
Miami University	OH	8	10	13	12	41	2	43	73
Michigan Technological University	MI	58	57	60	100	265	10	275	28
Milwaukee School of Engineering	WI	0	0	31	14	43	2	45	97
Minnesota State University, Mankato	MN	66	82	67	149	354	10	364	24
Montana State University	MT	80	72	96	114	349	13	362	36
University of Nebraska, Lincoln	NE	29	37	42	52	140	20	160	58
New Jersey Institute of Technology	NJ	16	35	92	91	207	27	234	185
New Mexico State University	NM	33	50	76	149	257	51	308	0
University of North Carolina, Charlotte	NC	118	99	125	103	411	34	445	187
University of North Texas	TX	72	61	46	64	224	19	243	87
Northeastern University	MA	0	48	89	102	214	25	239	188
Northern Illinois University	IL	14	20	54	73	150	11	161	64
Oklahoma State University	OK	98	181	219	285	734	49	783	0
Old Dominion University	VA	89	89	103	148	367	62	429	187
Oregon Institute of Technology	OR	114	67	98	141	402	18	420	201

ENGINEERING TECHNOLOGY ENROLLMENTS   ALF-ORE

ENGINEERING TECHNOLOGY ENROLLMENTS, FALL 2006

INSTITUTION		FRESHMEN (FT)	SOPHOMORES (FT)	JUNIORS (FT)	SENIORS (FT)	ENROLLMENT TOTAL			
						M (FT)	F (FT)	TOTAL	(PT)
Pennsylvania State University Harrisburg	PA	24	11	88	105	202	26	228	22
Penn State Erie, The Behrend College	PA	80	56	97	119	330	22	352	21
Pittsburg State University	KS	58	0	0	0	54	4	58	0
Prairie View A&M University	TX	31	26	32	55	107	37	144	7
Purdue University College of Technology	IN	219	262	249	414	1092	52	1,144	0
Rochester Institute of Technology	NY	234	187	193	387	929	72	1,001	172
Saint Louis University - Parks College	MO	3	6	5	4	18	0	18	0
South Dakota State University	SD	73	96	101	87	347	10	357	0
Southern Illinois University Carbondale	IL	3	9	8	23	39	4	43	7
Southern Polytechnic State University	GA	297	226	200	288	922	89	1,011	538
Southern University and A&M College	LA	61	36	29	47	148	25	173	5
Temple University	PA	16	21	24	64	114	11	125	0
Texas A&M University	TX	38	41	76	149	282	22	304	36
Texas Tech University	TX	46	53	76	125	288	12	300	49
The University of Toledo	OH	183	152	146	242	675	48	723	226
Tri-State University	IN	9	11	14	13	44	3	47	1
Wayne State University	MI	0	6	16	23	40	5	45	141
Weber State University	UT	94	54	55	78	246	35	281	317
Wentworth Institute of Technology	MA	581	436	312	232	1300	261	1,561	108
Western Michigan University	MI	40	43	45	67	181	14	195	40
Youngstown State University	OH	53	31	29	44	143	14	157	73
Totals:		**4,948**	**4,410**	**4,917**	**6,901**	**19,127**	**2,049**	**21,176**	**5,576**

ENGINEERING TECHNOLOGY ENROLLMENTS   PEN-YOU

ENGINEERING TECHNOLOGY DEGREES, 2005-2006

INSTITUTION		AFRICAN AMERICAN		ASIAN AMERICAN		HISPANIC		NATIVE AMERICAN		CAUCASIAN		FOREIGN		OTHER		TOTAL BY GENDER		TOTAL DEGREES
		M	F	M	F	M	F	M	F	M	F	M	F	M	F	M	F	
Alabama A&M University	AL	8	3	0	0	0	0	0	0	7	0	0	0	0	0	15	3	18
Alfred State College	NY	2	0	2	0	1	0	0	0	81	9	0	0	0	0	86	9	95
Arizona State University, Polytechnic	AZ	0	0	12	2	10	0	0	0	63	11	0	0	3	0	88	13	101
University of Arkansas at Little Rock	AR	5	1	0	0	0	0	0	0	10	1	2	0	0	0	17	2	19
Bradley University	IL	0	0	1	0	0	0	0	0	23	2	0	0	0	0	24	2	26
Brigham Young University	UT	0	0	1	0	1	0	0	0	0	0	10	0	58	2	70	2	72
Buffalo State College	NY	1	1	0	0	1	0	0	0	30	4	0	0	1	0	33	5	38
California Maritime Academy	CA	1	2	3	1	1	0	0	0	30	4	0	0	0	0	35	7	42
California State Polytechnic University, Pomona	CA	0	0	31	1	24	5	0	0	18	0	0	0	7	0	81	6	87
California State University, Sacramento	CA	2	0	4	1	3	0	1	0	9	1	0	0	9	0	27	2	29
Capitol College	MD	0	0	0	0	0	0	0	0	0	0	0	0	45	9	45	9	54
University of Central Florida	FL	6	1	4	1	13	1	3	0	76	9	2	0	0	0	104	12	116
Colorado State University, Pueblo	CO	0	0	0	0	3	3	0	0	6	0	0	0	7	2	16	5	21
Colorado Technical University	CO	0	0	0	0	0	0	0	0	0	0	0	0	16	5	16	5	21
University of Dayton	OH	0	2	2	0	0	1	1	0	0	0	0	0	50	4	53	7	60
University of the District of Columbia	DC	3	1	0	0	1	0	0	0	1	1	1	0	0	0	6	2	8
Eastern Washington University	WA	0	0	1	0	3	0	0	0	11	1	1	0	1	0	16	1	17
Ferris State University	MI	7	3	6	1	5	1	1	0	290	26	0	0	20	2	329	33	362
University of Hartford	CT	3	1	1	0	2	2	0	0	36	6	0	0	0	0	42	9	51
University of Houston, College of Technology	TX	26	8	29	3	26	5	0	0	58	6	10	3	0	0	149	25	174
Indiana University Purdue University at Indianapolis	IN	19	12	7	6	3	0	2	0	185	41	3	3	3	0	222	62	284
Indiana University-Purdue University Fort Wayne	IN	0	0	0	0	0	0	0	1	21	3	0	0	2	1	23	5	28
Kansas State University	KS	0	0	0	0	0	0	0	0	9	2	0	0	1	0	10	2	12
Lake Superior State University	MI	0	0	0	0	0	0	2	0	4	1	3	0	0	0	9	1	10
Lawrence Technological University	MI	2	0	1	0	0	0	0	0	29	3	3	1	4	1	39	5	44
LeTourneau University	TX	0	0	1	0	0	0	0	0	10	0	0	0	1	0	12	0	12
Louisiana Tech University	LA	4	0	0	0	1	0	0	0	29	1	0	0	0	0	34	1	35
University of Maine	ME	0	0	1	0	0	0	0	0	89	1	0	0	0	0	90	1	91
University of Massachusetts Lowell	MA	4	1	2	0	2	1	0	0	25	7	1	0	10	1	44	10	54
McNeese State University	LA	2	1	0	0	0	0	0	0	8	2	1	0	0	0	11	3	14
The University of Memphis	TN	9	6	1	1	0	0	0	0	17	0	2	0	0	0	29	7	36
Metropolitan State College of Denver	CO	3	2	2	4	2	1	0	0	10	5	1	0	2	1	20	13	33
Miami University	OH	0	0	0	0	0	0	1	0	23	0	0	0	0	0	24	0	24
Michigan Technological University	MI	1	0	3	0	0	0	0	0	56	3	0	0	1	0	61	3	64
Milwaukee School of Engineering	WI	1	0	0	0	0	0	0	0	28	2	0	0	4	0	33	2	35
Minnesota State University, Mankato	MN	0	0	1	0	0	0	0	0	30	2	6	0	16	0	53	2	55
Montana State University	MT	0	0	0	0	0	0	1	0	63	4	0	0	1	0	64	4	68
University of Nebraska, Lincoln	NE	2	0	3	0	0	0	0	0	44	0	1	0	0	0	50	0	50
New Jersey Institute of Technology	NJ	15	1	8	4	17	1	0	0	39	2	5	1	23	3	107	12	119
New Mexico State University	NM	2	0	1	0	27	5	0	0	17	1	0	0	9	0	56	6	62
University of North Carolina, Charlotte	NC	8	0	2	1	0	0	0	0	61	4	0	0	0	0	71	5	76
University of North Texas	TX	5	0	0	5	5	4	0	0	40	1	28	1	1	0	79	11	90
Northeastern University	MA	8	2	9	2	6	1	0	0	54	2	6	0	0	0	83	7	90
Northern Illinois University	IL	11	5	4	1	3	1	0	0	49	0	1	0	1	0	69	7	76
Oklahoma State University	OK	3	0	2	0	1	0	13	1	125	3	1	0	0	0	145	4	149

ENGINEERING TECHNOLOGY DEGREES — ALA-OKL

ENGINEERING TECHNOLOGY DEGREES, 2005-2006

INSTITUTION		AFRICAN AMERICAN		ASIAN AMERICAN		HISPANIC		NATIVE AMERICAN		CAUCASIAN		FOREIGN		OTHER		TOTAL BY GENDER		TOTAL DEGREES
		M	F	M	F	M	F	M	F	M	F	M	F	M	F	M	F	
Old Dominion University	VA	8	6	2	1	2	1	2	0	116	8	1	0	7	0	138	16	154
Oregon Institute of Technology	OR	2	0	9	1	4	0	0	0	115	5	1	0	12	0	143	6	149
Pennsylvania State University Harrisburg	PA	2	0	1	0	1	0	0	0	28	2	1	0	0	0	33	3	36
Penn State Erie, The Behrend College	PA	0	0	0	0	1	0	0	0	64	5	0	0	0	0	65	5	70
Pittsburg State University	KS	0	0	0	0	0	0	0	0	62	4	0	0	0	0	62	4	66
Prairie View A&M University	TX	27	7	0	0	1	3	0	0	0	0	1	0	0	0	29	10	39
Purdue University College of Technology	IN	4	0	6	0	1	1	0	0	203	12	2	1	0	0	216	14	230
Rochester Institute of Technology	NY	14	2	11	1	4	1	1	0	119	8	5	1	21	0	175	13	188
Saint Louis University - Parks College	MO	0	0	0	0	0	0	0	0	3	0	0	0	0	0	3	0	3
South Dakota State University	SD	0	0	0	0	0	0	0	0	45	2	0	0	0	0	45	2	47
Southern Illinois University Carbondale	IL	2	1	0	0	1	0	0	0	22	0	1	0	1	0	27	1	28
Southern Polytechnic State University	GA	30	11	16	1	5	0	0	0	88	10	28	6	2	1	169	29	198
Southern University and A&M College	LA	18	5	0	0	0	0	0	0	0	0	1	0	0	0	19	5	24
Temple University	PA	3	1	0	0	0	0	0	0	27	6	2	0	0	0	32	7	39
Texas A&M University	TX	2	2	5	0	8	3	1	0	86	5	0	0	1	0	103	10	113
Texas Tech University	TX	0	0	2	0	11	0	0	0	52	1	0	0	0	0	65	1	66
The University of Toledo	OH	4	2	4	0	1	1	0	0	166	7	13	0	0	0	188	10	198
Tri-State University	IN	0	0	0	0	0	0	0	0	10	1	0	0	0	0	10	1	11
Wayne State University	MI	4	0	1	0	1	0	0	0	26	2	9	2	3	2	44	6	50
Weber State University	UT	2	0	3	0	0	0	0	0	51	11	0	0	17	8	73	19	92
Wentworth Institute of Technology	MA	17	2	19	0	15	2	0	0	162	28	10	2	21	4	244	38	282
Western Carolina University	NC	0	0	0	0	0	0	0	0	0	0	0	0	38	3	38	3	41
Western Michigan University	MI	1	0	0	0	2	0	0	0	27	2	0	0	0	0	30	2	32
Youngstown State University	OH	2	2	0	0	0	0	0	0	37	2	0	0	0	0	39	4	43
Totals:		305	94	224	39	219	44	29	2	3,323	292	162	21	418	49	4,680	541	5,221

ENGINEERING TECHNOLOGY DEGREES   OLD-YOU

ENGINEERING TECHNOLOGY DEGREES

GRADUATE ENGINEERING TECHNOLOGY ENROLLMENTS AND DEGREES AWARDED, FALL 2005

GRADUATE ENGINEERING TECHNOLOGY ENROLLMENTS

ARI-TRI

INSTITUTION		MASTER'S				
		(FT)	(PT)	M	F	TOTAL MASTER'S
Arizona State University, Polytechnic	AZ	76	108	114	70	184
Brigham Young University	UT	10	0	9	1	10
University of Houston, College of Technology	TX	15	12	11	16	27
Montana State University	MT	2	0	1	1	2
University of North Texas	TX	11	13	19	5	24
Pittsburg State University	KS	34	0	31	3	34
Purdue University College of Technology	IN	216	0	148	68	216
Rochester Institute of Technology	NY	32	29	47	14	61
Southern Polytechnic State University	GA	27	104	96	35	131
Tri-State University	IN	2	3	4	1	5
Totals:		425	269	480	214	694

GRADUATE ENGINEERING TECHNOLOGY DEGREES AWARDED

ARI-TRI

INSTITUTION		AFRICAN AMERICAN		ASIAN AMERICAN		HISPANIC		NATIVE AMERICAN		CAUCASIAN		FOREIGN		OTHER		TOTAL BY GENDER		TOTAL DEGREES
		M	F	M	F	M	F	M	F	M	F	M	F	M	F	M	F	
Arizona State University, Polytechnic	AZ	0	0	9	7	1	0	0	0	8	5	14	2	0	2	32	16	48
Brigham Young University	UT	0	0	0	0	0	0	0	0	1	0	0	0	11	2	12	2	14
University of Houston, College of Technology	TX	1	0	1	0	1	0	0	0	2	3	0	0	0	0	5	3	8
Montana State University	MT	0	0	0	0	0	0	0	0	0	0	4	0	0	0	4	0	4
University of North Texas	TX	0	0	8	0	0	0	0	0	0	0	2	1	0	0	10	1	11
Pittsburg State University	KS	0	0	0	0	0	0	0	0	0	0	19	0	0	0	19	0	19
Purdue University College of Technology	IN	1	1	0	0	0	0	0	1	0	0	25	11	4	15	31	27	58
Rochester Institute of Technology	NY	0	0	0	0	1	0	0	0	8	1	3	0	0	0	12	1	13
Southern Polytechnic State University	GA	3	5	2	0	0	0	0	0	6	1	11	2	0	0	22	8	30
Tri-State University	IN	0	0	0	0	0	0	0	0	0	0	1	0	1	0	2	0	2
Totals:		5	6	20	7	3	0	1	0	25	10	79	16	16	19	149	58	207

2006 Profiles of Engineering Colleges

Air Force Institute of Technology

INSTITUTION INFORMATION

Graduate School of Engineering and Management
AFIT/EN, 2950 Hobson Way
Wright-Patterson AFB, OH 45433
Phone: (937) 255-3636
Fax: (937) 255-6569
Web: http://www.afit.edu

GENERAL INFORMATION

[All Students - Fall 2006]

Undergraduate Enrollment	0
Graduate Enrollment	838
Professional Enrollment	0
Total Enrollment	**838**

ENGINEERING COLLEGE INFORMATION

HEAD OF ENGINEERING

Marlin U Thomas
Dean
Graduate School of Engineering and Management
Air Force Institute of Technology
AFIT/EN
2950 Hobson Way, Bld 640
Wright-Patterson AFB, OH 45433
Phone: (937) 255-3636
Fax: (937) 255-6569
Email: marlin.thomas@afit.edu

ENGINEERING COLLEGE INQUIRIES

Dr. William F Adams
Air Force Institute of Technology
AFIT/EN, 2950 Hobson Way
Wright-Patterson AFB, OH 45433-7765
Phone: (937) 255-3636
Fax: (937) 255-6569
Email: william.adams@afit.edu

TYPES OF ENGINEERING DEGREES

Bachelor's:
Master's: M.S. with thesis, M.S. without thesis, but with project or report
Doctoral: Ph.D.

GRADUATE INFORMATION

ESTIMATED STUDENT EXPENSES (FALL 2006)

[Expenses are for the 2006-2007 nine-month academic year and are based on an average credit load of: Graduate: N/A]

	Other Group 1	Other Group 2
Tuition and Fees:	$13,440	$18,144
Campus and Room and Board:		
Books and Supplies:		$1,200
Other Expenses:		
Total Estimated Expenses:	**$13,440**	**$19,344**

Note: Air Force and all external funding sources: 25 projects at $1,411,000

NEW APPLICANTS/NEWLY ENROLLED STUDENTS

[Numbers are for the graduate engineering college for the Fall 2006 term]

Number of Applicants (a):	0
Of those, Number Offered Admission (b):	0
Of those, Number Enrolled Fall 2006 (c):	838

The University of Akron

INSTITUTION INFORMATION

Akron, OH 44325
Phone: (330) 972-7111
Web: http://www.uakron.edu

GENERAL INFORMATION

[All Students - Fall 2006]

Undergraduate Enrollment	19,673
Graduate Enrollment	3,327
Professional Enrollment	539
Total Enrollment	**23,539**

ENGINEERING COLLEGE INFORMATION

HEAD OF ENGINEERING

Dr. George K Haritos
Dean, College of Engineering
College of Engineering
The University of Akron
Akron, OH 44325-3901
Phone: (330) 972-6978
Fax: (330) 972-5162
Email: haritos@uakron.edu

HEAD OF ENGINEERING

Paul C. Lam
Associate Dean, Undergraduate Studies & Diversity Programs, Engineering
Engineering Undergraduate Studies & Diversity Programs
The University of Akron
Akron, OH 44325-3901
Phone: (330) 972-7817
Fax: (330) 972-5162
Email: plam@uakron.edu

HEAD OF ENGINEERING

S. I. Hariharan
Associate Dean, Graduate Studies & Research, Engineering
Engineering Graduate Studies & Research
The University of Akron
Akron, OH 44325-3901
Phone: (330) 972-6580
Fax: (330) 972-5162
Email: hari@uakron.edu

TYPES OF ENGINEERING DEGREES

Bachelor's: B.S.
Master's: M.S. with thesis, M.S. without thesis, but with project or report
Doctoral: Ph.D.

UNDERGRADUATE INFORMATION

ESTIMATED STUDENT EXPENSES (FALL 2006)

[Expenses are for the 2006-2007 nine-month academic year and are based on an average credit load of: Undergraduate: 15]

	In-State	Out-of-State
Tuition and Fees:	$8,382	$17,631
Campus and Room and Board:	$7,640	$7,640
Books and Supplies:	$900	$900
Other Expenses:	$3,150	$3,150
Total Estimated Expenses:	**$20,072**	**$29,321**

NEW APPLICANTS/NEWLY ENROLLED STUDENTS

[Numbers are for the undergraduate engineering college for the Fall 2006 term]

Number of Applicants (a):	1,098
Of those, Number Offered Admission (b):	938
Of those, Number Enrolled Fall 2006 (c):	456

GRADUATE INFORMATION

ESTIMATED STUDENT EXPENSES (FALL 2006)

[Expenses are for the 2006-2007 nine-month academic year and are based on an average credit load of: Graduate: 9]

	In-State	Out-of-State
Tuition and Fees:	$6,971	$11,381
Campus and Room and Board:	$7,640	$7,640
Books and Supplies:	$900	$900
Other Expenses:	$3,676	$3,676
Total Estimated Expenses:	**$19,187**	**$23,597**

NEW APPLICANTS/NEWLY ENROLLED STUDENTS

[Numbers are for the graduate engineering college for the Fall 2006 term]

Number of Applicants (a):	427
Of those, Number Offered Admission (b):	156
Of those, Number Enrolled Fall 2006 (c):	70

Alabama A&M University

INSTITUTION INFORMATION

P.O. Box 1357
PS New School of Business
Normal, AL 35762
Phone: (256) 372-5000
Fax: (256) 372-5244
Web: http://www.aamu.edu

GENERAL INFORMATION

[All Students - Fall 2006]

Undergraduate Enrollment	5,047
Graduate Enrollment	1,135
Professional Enrollment	0
Total Enrollment	**6,182**

ENGINEERING COLLEGE INFORMATION

HEAD OF ENGINEERING

Vernell T Montgomery
Dean
Engineering & Technology
Alabama A&M University
P.O. Box 1148
227 ETB
Normal, AL 35762-1146
Phone: (256) 372-5560
Fax: (256) 372-5580
Email: trent.montgomery@aamu.edu

TYPES OF ENGINEERING DEGREES

Bachelor's: B.S.
Master's: M.S. with thesis, M.S. without thesis, but with project or report
Doctoral:

UNDERGRADUATE INFORMATION

ADMISSION INQUIRIES

Ruben Rojas-Oviedo
Chair/Associate Professopr
Alabama A&M University
P.O. Box 1163, 117 Carver Complex North
Normal, AL 35762-1163
Phone: (256) 851-5000
Fax: (256) 851-5580
Email: rojaso@aamu.edu

ADMISSION INQUIRIES

Juan Alexander
Director, Admissions
Alabama A&M University
P.O. Box 908, 111 Patton Hall
Normal, AL 35762
Phone: (256) 372-5245
Fax: (256) 372-5249

ESTIMATED STUDENT EXPENSES (FALL 2006)

[Expenses are for the 2006-2007 nine-month academic year and are based on an average credit load of: Undergraduate: 16]

	In-State	Out-of-State
Tuition and Fees:	$4,420	$8,320
Campus and Room and Board:	$4,470	$4,770
Books and Supplies:	$900	$900
Other Expenses:	$2,500	$2,900
Total Estimated Expenses:	**$12,290**	**$16,890**

GRADUATE INFORMATION

ADMISSION INQUIRIES

Chandra Reddy
Dean, Graduate Studies
Alabama A&M University
P.O. Box 998, 300 Patton Hall
Normal, AL 35762-0998
Phone: (256) 851-5000
Fax: (256) 851-5269
Email: reddyc@aamu.edu

ADMISSION INQUIRIES

Caula Beyl
Interim Dean, Graduate Studies
Alabama A&M University
P.O. Box 998, 300 Patton Hall
Normal, AL 35762
Phone: (256) 372-5266
Fax: (256) 372-5244

ESTIMATED STUDENT EXPENSES (FALL 2006)

[Expenses are for the 2006-2007 nine-month academic year and are based on an average credit load of: Graduate: 9]

	In-State	Out-of-State
Tuition and Fees:	$2,736	$5,112
Campus and Room and Board:	$4,770	$4,770
Books and Supplies:	$900	$900
Other Expenses:	$2,500	$2,900
Total Estimated Expenses:	**$10,906**	**$13,682**

University of Alabama at Birmingham

INSTITUTION INFORMATION

HOEN 101
1530 3rd Avenue South
Birmingham, AL 35294-4440
Phone: (205) 934-8400
Fax: (205) 934-8437
Web: http://www.uab.edu

GENERAL INFORMATION

[All Students - Fall 2006]

Undergraduate Enrollment	11,284
Graduate Enrollment	4,302
Professional Enrollment	2,005
Total Enrollment	**17,591**

ENGINEERING COLLEGE INFORMATION

HEAD OF ENGINEERING

Linda C Lucas
Dean; Professor
School of Engineering; Biomedical Engineering
University of Alabama at Birmingham
HOEN 100
1530 3rd Avenue South
Birmingham, AL 35294-4440
Phone: (205) ,20-5934
Fax: (205) ,20-8437
Email: lucas@uab.edu

ENGINEERING COLLEGE INQUIRIES

Melinda M Lalor
Associate Dean and Associate Professor
University of Alabama at Birmingham
HOEN 101, 1530 3rd Avenue South
Birmingham, AL 35294-4440
Phone: (205) 934-8400
Fax: (205) 934-8437

ENGINEERING COLLEGE INQUIRIES

Zoe Dwyer
Assistant Professor; Director of Outreach and Retention
University of Alabama at Birmingham
HOEN 100, 1530 3rd Avenue South
Birmingham, AL 35294-4440
Phone: (205) 934-8400
Fax: (205) 934-8437
Email: zdwyer@uab.edu

TYPES OF ENGINEERING DEGREES

Bachelor's: B.S.
Master's: M.S. with thesis, M.S. without thesis, but with project or report
Doctoral: Ph.D.

UNDERGRADUATE INFORMATION

ADMISSION INQUIRIES

Melinda M Lalor
Associate Dean and Associate Professor
University of Alabama at Birmingham
HOEN 101, 1530 3rd Avenue South
Birmingham, AL 35294-4440
Phone: (205) 934-8400
Fax: (205) 934-8437

ESTIMATED STUDENT EXPENSES (FALL 2006)

[Expenses are for the 2006-2007 nine-month academic year and are based on an average credit load of: Undergraduate: 15]

	In-State	Out-of-State
Tuition and Fees:	$5,362	$4,900
Campus and Room and Board:	$6,300	$6,300
Books and Supplies:	$1,200	$1,200
Other Expenses:	$2,400	$2,400
Total Estimated Expenses:	**$15,262**	**$14,800**

Note: Room and board based on 12 months on-campus housing.

NEW APPLICANTS/NEWLY ENROLLED STUDENTS

[Numbers are for the undergraduate engineering college for the Fall 2006 term]

Number of Applicants (a):	573
Of those, Number Offered Admission (b):	417
Of those, Number Enrolled Fall 2006 (c):	191

Note: Information available on only 74 of the 191 entering freshmen. Of that number 36 ranked in the top 25% of their HS class.

GRADUATE INFORMATION

ADMISSION INQUIRIES

Melinda M Lalor
Associate Dean and Associate Professor
University of Alabama at Birmingham
HOEN 101, 1530 3rd Avenue South
Birmingham , AL 35294-4440
Phone: (205) 934-8400
Fax: (205) 934-8437

ADMISSION INQUIRIES

Bryan D Noe
Dean
University of Alabama at Birmingham
HUC 504, 1530 3rd Avenue South
Birmingham , AL 35294-4440
Phone: (205) 934-8257
Fax: (205) 975-7677
Email: bnoe@uab.edu

ESTIMATED STUDENT EXPENSES (FALL 2006)

[Expenses are for the 2006-2007 nine-month academic year and are based on an average credit load of: Graduate: 12]

	In-State	Out-of-State
Tuition and Fees:	$11,302	$11,020
Campus and Room and Board:	$6,300	$6,300
Books and Supplies:	$1,200	$1,200
Other Expenses:	$2,400	$2,400
Total Estimated Expenses:	**$21,202**	**$20,920**

Note: Room and board based on 12 months on-campus housing.

NEW APPLICANTS/NEWLY ENROLLED STUDENTS

[Numbers are for the graduate engineering college for the Fall 2006 term]

Number of Applicants (a):	273
Of those, Number Offered Admission (b):	114
Of those, Number Enrolled Fall 2006 (c):	48

The University of Alabama in Huntsville

INSTITUTION INFORMATION

301 Sparkman Drive
Huntsville, AL 35899
Phone: (256) 824-1000
Web: http://www.uah.edu

GENERAL INFORMATION

[All Students - Fall 2006]

Undergraduate Enrollment	5,719
Graduate Enrollment	1,372
Professional Enrollment	0
Total Enrollment	**7,091**

ENGINEERING COLLEGE INFORMATION

HEAD OF ENGINEERING

Jorge I. Aunon
Dean
College of Engineering
The University of Alabama in Huntsville
301 Sparkman Drive
Huntsville, AL 35899
Phone: (256) 824-6474
Fax: (256) 824-6843
Email: dean@eb.uah.edu

ENGINEERING COLLEGE INQUIRIES

Mark V. Bower
Chair
The University of Alabama in Huntsville
301 Sparkman Drive
Huntsville, AL 35899
Phone: (256) 824-6154
Fax: (256) 824-6758
Email: mbower@mae.uah.edu

TYPES OF ENGINEERING DEGREES

Bachelor's: B.S.
Master's: M.S. with thesis, M.S. without thesis, but with project or report
Doctoral: Ph.D.

UNDERGRADUATE INFORMATION

ADMISSION INQUIRIES

Mark V. Bower
Chair
The University of Alabama in Huntsville
301 Sparkman Drive
Huntsville, AL 35899
Phone: (256) 824-6154
Fax: (256) 824-6758
Email: mbower@mae.uah.edu

ESTIMATED STUDENT EXPENSES (FALL 2006)

[Expenses are for the 2006-2007 nine-month academic year and are based on an average credit load of: Undergraduate: N/A]

	Other Group 1	Other Group 2
Tuition and Fees:	$4,848	$10,224
Campus and Room and Board:	$6,820	$6,820
Books and Supplies:	$720	$720
Other Expenses:	$1,350	$1,350
Total Estimated Expenses:	**$13,738**	**$19,114**

NEW APPLICANTS/NEWLY ENROLLED STUDENTS

[Numbers are for the undergraduate engineering college for the Fall 2006 term]

Number of Applicants (a):	678
Of those, Number Offered Admission (b):	639
Of those, Number Enrolled Fall 2006 (c):	398

Note: High School rank is not a factor for admission; therefore, not all students report this data.

GRADUATE INFORMATION

ADMISSION INQUIRIES

Debra M Moriarity
Dean
The University of Alabama in Huntsville
301 Sparkman Drive
Huntsville , AL 35899
Phone: (256) 824-6605
Fax: (256) 824-6349
Email: moriard@uah.edu

ESTIMATED STUDENT EXPENSES (FALL 2006)

[Expenses are for the 2006-2007 nine-month academic year and are based on an average credit load of: Graduate: N/A]

	Other Group 1	Other Group 2
Tuition and Fees:	$6,072	$12,476
Campus and Room and Board:	$6,820	$6,820
Books and Supplies:	$720	$720
Other Expenses:	$1,350	$1,350
Total Estimated Expenses:	**$14,962**	**$21,366**

NEW APPLICANTS/NEWLY ENROLLED STUDENTS

[Numbers are for the graduate engineering college for the Fall 2006 term]

Number of Applicants (a):	408
Of those, Number Offered Admission (b):	251
Of those, Number Enrolled Fall 2006 (c):	117

The University of Alabama

INSTITUTION INFORMATION

College of Engineering
Box 870200
Tuscaloosa, AL 35487-0200
Phone: (205) 348-6400
Fax: (205) 348-8573
Web: http://www.eng.ua.edu

GENERAL INFORMATION

[All Students - Fall 2006]

Undergraduate Enrollment	19,474
Graduate Enrollment	3,781
Professional Enrollment	623
Total Enrollment	**23,878**

ENGINEERING COLLEGE INFORMATION

HEAD OF ENGINEERING

Charles L Karr
Dean
Engineering Dean
The University of Alabama
College of Engineering
Box 870200

Tuscaloosa, AL 35487-0200
Phone: (205) 348-6405
Fax: (205) 348-8573
Email: ckarr@eng.ua.edu

ENGINEERING COLLEGE INQUIRIES
Gregory L Singleton
Director/Mulitcultural Engineering Progam Coordinator
The University of Alabama
College of Engineering, Box 870200
Tuscaloosa, AL 35487-0200
Phone: (481) 447-1447
Fax: (480) 591-0591
Email: gsingleton@eng.ua.edu

TYPES OF ENGINEERING DEGREES
Bachelor's: B.S.
Master's: M.S. with thesis, M.S. without thesis, but with project or report
Doctoral: Ph.D.

UNDERGRADUATE INFORMATION

ESTIMATED STUDENT EXPENSES (FALL 2006)
[Expenses are for the 2006-2007 nine-month academic year and are based on an average credit load of: Undergraduate: 14]

	In-State	Out-of-State
Tutition and Fees:	$5,278	$15,294
Campus and Room and Board:	$5,380	$5,380
Books and Supplies:	$950	$950
Other Expenses:	$2,103	$2,103
Total Estimated Expenses:	**$13,711**	**$23,727**

NEW APPLICANTS/NEWLY ENROLLED STUDENTS
[Numbers are for the undergraduate engineering college for the Fall 2006 term]

Number of Applicants (a):	1,186
Of those, Number Offered Admission (b):	1,125
Of those, Number Enrolled Fall 2006 (c):	506

GRADUATE INFORMATION

ESTIMATED STUDENT EXPENSES (FALL 2006)
[Expenses are for the 2006-2007 nine-month academic year and are based on an average credit load of: Graduate: 9]

	In-State	Out-of-State
Tutition and Fees:	$5,278	$15,294
Campus and Room and Board:	$5,380	$5,380
Books and Supplies:	$950	$950
Other Expenses:	$2,103	$2,103
Total Estimated Expenses:	**$13,711**	**$23,727**

NEW APPLICANTS/NEWLY ENROLLED STUDENTS
[Numbers are for the graduate engineering college for the Fall 2006 term]

Number of Applicants (a):	283
Of those, Number Offered Admission (b):	144
Of those, Number Enrolled Fall 2006 (c):	61

University of Alaska Fairbanks

INSTITUTION INFORMATION
P.O. Box 755960
357 Duckering
Fairbanks, AK 99775-5640
Phone: (907) 474-7366
Fax: (907) 474-6994
Web: http://www.uaf.edu/cem/

GENERAL INFORMATION
[All Students - Fall 2006]

Undergraduate Enrollment	7,247
Graduate Enrollment	1,067
Professional Enrollment	0
Total Enrollment	**8,314**

ENGINEERING COLLEGE INFORMATION

HEAD OF ENGINEERING
Douglas J Goering
Acting Dean
College of Engineering and Mines
University of Alaska Fairbanks
PO Box 755960
357 Duckering
Fairbanks, AK 99775-5960

Phone: (907) 474-7730
Fax: (907) 474-6994
Email: ffdjg@uaf.edu

TYPES OF ENGINEERING DEGREES
Bachelor's: B.S.
Master's: M.S. with thesis, M.S. without thesis, but with project or report
Doctoral: Ph.D.

UNDERGRADUATE INFORMATION

ESTIMATED STUDENT EXPENSES (FALL 2006)
[Expenses are for the 2006-2007 nine-month academic year and are based on an average credit load of: Undergraduate: 15]

	In-State	Out-of-State
Tutition and Fees:	$4,553	$13,090
Campus and Room and Board:	$6,030	$6,030
Books and Supplies:	$1,400	$1,400
Other Expenses:	$2,250	$2,250
Total Estimated Expenses:	**$14,233**	**$22,770**

Note: Tuition and fee calculations based on academic year. Single semester costs would be half of the reported figures.

NEW APPLICANTS/NEWLY ENROLLED STUDENTS
[Numbers are for the undergraduate engineering college for the Fall 2006 term]

Number of Applicants (a):	174
Of those, Number Offered Admission (b):	104
Of those, Number Enrolled Fall 2006 (c):	72

Note: Number reflects only those students who were offered admission and were then actually admitted to the University.

GRADUATE INFORMATION

ESTIMATED STUDENT EXPENSES (FALL 2006)
[Expenses are for the 2006-2007 nine-month academic year and are based on an average credit load of: Graduate: 9]

	In-State	Out-of-State
Tutition and Fees:	$5,526	$10,649
Campus and Room and Board:	$6,030	$6,030
Books and Supplies:	$1,400	$1,400
Other Expenses:	$2,250	$2,250
Total Estimated Expenses:	**$15,206**	**$20,329**

Note: Tuition and fee calculations based on academic year. Single semester costs would be half of the reported figures.

NEW APPLICANTS/NEWLY ENROLLED STUDENTS
[Numbers are for the graduate engineering college for the Fall 2006 term]

Number of Applicants (a):	122
Of those, Number Offered Admission (b):	47
Of those, Number Enrolled Fall 2006 (c):	29

University of Alberta

INSTITUTION INFORMATION
114 Street - 89 Avenue
Edmonton, AB T6G 2M7
Phone: (780) 492-3111
Fax: (780) 492-0500
Web: http://www.ualberta.ca

GENERAL INFORMATION
[All Students - Fall 2006]

Undergraduate Enrollment	29,317
Graduate Enrollment	6,073
Professional Enrollment	0
Total Enrollment	**35,390**

ENGINEERING COLLEGE INFORMATION

HEAD OF ENGINEERING
David T Lynch
Dean
Faculty of Engineering
University of Alberta
E6-050 Engineering Teaching & Learning Complex
Edmonton, AB T6G2V4
Phone: (780) 492-3596
Fax: (780) 492-3973
Email: engginfo@engineering.ualberta.ca

TYPES OF ENGINEERING DEGREES
Bachelor's: B.S.
Master's: M.S. with thesis, M.S. without thesis, but with

project or report, M.Eng.
Doctoral: Ph.D.

UNDERGRADUATE INFORMATION

ESTIMATED STUDENT EXPENSES (FALL 2006)
[Expenses are for the 2006-2007 nine-month academic year and are based on an average credit load of: Undergraduate: N/A]

	Canadian Citizen	Non-Canadian
Tutition and Fees:	$5,402	$17,381
Campus and Room and Board:		
Books and Supplies:		
Other Expenses:		
Total Estimated Expenses:	**$5,402**	**$17,381**

NEW APPLICANTS/NEWLY ENROLLED STUDENTS
[Numbers are for the undergraduate engineering college for the Fall 2006 term]

Number of Applicants (a):	1,924
Of those, Number Offered Admission (b):	995
Of those, Number Enrolled Fall 2006 (c):	851

GRADUATE INFORMATION

ESTIMATED STUDENT EXPENSES (FALL 2006)
[Expenses are for the 2006-2007 nine-month academic year and are based on an average credit load of: Graduate: N/A]

	Canadian Citizen	Non-Canadian
Tutition and Fees:	$3,971	$7,563
Campus and Room and Board:		
Books and Supplies:		
Other Expenses:		
Total Estimated Expenses:	**$3,971**	**$7,563**

Alfred University, NY State College of Ceramics

INSTITUTION INFORMATION
Kazuo Inamori School of Engineering
2 Pine Street
Alfred, NY 14802
Phone: (607) 871-2422
Fax: (607) 871-2354
Web: http://www.alfred.edu/

GENERAL INFORMATION
[All Students - Fall 2006]

Undergraduate Enrollment	1,924
Graduate Enrollment	227
Professional Enrollment	2,151
Total Enrollment	**4,302**

ENGINEERING COLLEGE INFORMATION

HEAD OF ENGINEERING
Alastair N Cormack
VanDerck Frechette Professor of Ceramic Science
Kazuo Inamori School of Engineering
Alfred University, NY State College of Ceramics
Binns-Merrill Hall 160
2 Pine Street
Alfred, NY 14802
Phone: (607) 871-2422
Fax: (607) 871-2354
Email: cormack@alfred.edu

ENGINEERING COLLEGE INQUIRIES
Alastair N Cormack
VanDerck Frechette Professor of Ceramic Science
Alfred University, NY State College of Ceramics
Binns-Merrill Hall 160, 2 Pine Street
Alfred, NY 14802
Phone: (607) 871-2422
Fax: (607) 871-2354
Email: cormack@alfred.edu

TYPES OF ENGINEERING DEGREES
Bachelor's: B.S.
Master's: M.S. with thesis
Doctoral: Ph.D.

UNDERGRADUATE INFORMATION

ADMISSION INQUIRIES
Jeremy Spencer
Director of Admissions
Alfred University, NY State College of Ceramics

Alumni Hall, Saxon Drive
Alfred, NY 14802
Phone: (607) 871-2115
Fax: (607) 871-2198
Email: spencer@alfred.edu

ESTIMATED STUDENT EXPENSES (FALL 2006)

[Expenses are for the 2006-2007 nine-month academic year and are based on an average credit load of: Undergraduate: 17]

	In-State	Out-of-State
Tuition and Fees:	$12,500	$17,200
Campus and Room and Board:	$9,900	$9,900
Books and Supplies:	$850	$850
Other Expenses:	$850	$850
Total Estimated Expenses:	**$24,100**	**$28,800**

NEW APPLICANTS/NEWLY ENROLLED STUDENTS

[Numbers are for the undergraduate engineering college for the Fall 2006 term]

Number of Applicants (a):	337
Of those, Number Offered Admission (b):	272
Of those, Number Enrolled Fall 2006 (c):	69

GRADUATE INFORMATION

ADMISSION INQUIRIES

Valerie Stephens
Assistant Director of Admissions
Alfred University, NY State College of Ceramics
Alumni Hall, Saxon Drive
Alfred , NY 14802
Phone: (607) 871-2115
Fax: (601) 871-2198
Email: stephens@alfred.edu

ESTIMATED STUDENT EXPENSES (FALL 2006)

[Expenses are for the 2006-2007 nine-month academic year and are based on an average credit load of: Graduate: 15]

	In-State	Out-of-State
Tuition and Fees:	$17,530	$17,530
Campus and Room and Board:	$9,900	$9,900
Books and Supplies:	$950	$950
Other Expenses:	$850	$850
Total Estimated Expenses:	**$29,230**	**$29,230**

NEW APPLICANTS/NEWLY ENROLLED STUDENTS

[Numbers are for the graduate engineering college for the Fall 2006 term]

Number of Applicants (a):	67
Of those, Number Offered Admission (b):	31
Of those, Number Enrolled Fall 2006 (c):	17

The University of Arizona

INSTITUTION INFORMATION

Robert L. Nugent Bldg.
PO Box 210040
Tucson, AZ 85721-0040
Phone: (520) 621-3237
Fax: (520) 621-9799
Web: http://www.arizona.edu

GENERAL INFORMATION

[All Students - Fall 2006]

Undergraduate Enrollment	28,442
Graduate Enrollment	7,084
Professional Enrollment	1,279
Total Enrollment	**36,805**

ENGINEERING COLLEGE INFORMATION

HEAD OF ENGINEERING

Thomas W. Peterson
Dean
College of Engineering
The University of Arizona
Civil Engr. Bldg., Rm. 100
P.O. Box 210072
Tucson, AZ 85721-0072
Phone: (520) 621-6594
Fax: (520) 621-2232
Email: peterson@erc.arizona.edu

TYPES OF ENGINEERING DEGREES

Bachelor's: B.A., B.S.
Master's: M.S. with thesis, M.S. without thesis, but with project or report
Doctoral: Ph.D.

UNDERGRADUATE INFORMATION

ESTIMATED STUDENT EXPENSES (FALL 2006)

[Expenses are for the 2006-2007 nine-month academic year and are based on an average credit load of: Undergraduate: 12]

	In-State	Out-of-State
Tuition and Fees:	$4,766	$14,972
Campus and Room and Board:	$7,850	$7,850
Books and Supplies:	$816	$816
Other Expenses:	$2,520	$2,520
Total Estimated Expenses:	**$15,952**	**$26,158**

NEW APPLICANTS/NEWLY ENROLLED STUDENTS

[Numbers are for the undergraduate engineering college for the Fall 2006 term]

Number of Applicants (a):	1,310
Of those, Number Offered Admission (b):	1,012
Of those, Number Enrolled Fall 2006 (c):	578

GRADUATE INFORMATION

ESTIMATED STUDENT EXPENSES (FALL 2006)

[Expenses are for the 2006-2007 nine-month academic year and are based on an average credit load of: Graduate: 12]

	In-State	Out-of-State
Tuition and Fees:	$5,452	$15,242
Campus and Room and Board:	$7,850	$7,850
Books and Supplies:	$816	$816
Other Expenses:	$2,520	$2,520
Total Estimated Expenses:	**$16,638**	**$26,428**

NEW APPLICANTS/NEWLY ENROLLED STUDENTS

[Numbers are for the graduate engineering college for the Fall 2006 term]

Number of Applicants (a):	887
Of those, Number Offered Admission (b):	305
Of those, Number Enrolled Fall 2006 (c):	121

Arizona State University

INSTITUTION INFORMATION

Arizona State University
Tempe, AZ 85287
Phone: (480) 965-9011
Fax: (480) 965-8095
Web: http://www.asu.edu

GENERAL INFORMATION

[All Students - Fall 2006]

Undergraduate Enrollment	41,815
Graduate Enrollment	9,419
Professional Enrollment	0
Total Enrollment	**51,234**

ENGINEERING COLLEGE INFORMATION

HEAD OF ENGINEERING

Paul C Johnson
Executive Dean
Ira A Fulton School of Engineering
Arizona State University
Ira A Fulton School of Engineering
Box 879309
Tempe, AZ 85287-9309
Phone: (480) 965-1722
Fax: (480) 965-8855
Email: PAUL.C.JOHNSON@asu.edu

TYPES OF ENGINEERING DEGREES

Bachelor's: B.S.
Master's: M.S. with thesis, M.Eng.,MCS, MSE
Doctoral: Ph.D.

UNDERGRADUATE INFORMATION

ADMISSION INQUIRIES

Martha Byrd
Dean
Arizona State University
Box 870112
Tempe, AZ 85287-0112
Phone: (480) 965-5078
Fax: (480) 965-3610

ADMISSION INQUIRIES

James Collofello
Associate Dean

Arizona State University
Ira A Fulton School of Engineering, Box 875506
Tempe, AZ 85287-5506
Phone: (480) 965-1726
Fax: (480) 965-8095

ESTIMATED STUDENT EXPENSES (FALL 2006)

[Expenses are for the 2006-2007 nine-month academic year and are based on an average credit load of: Undergraduate: N/A]

	In-State	Out-of-State
Tuition and Fees:	$4,689	$15,848
Campus and Room and Board:	$6,900	$6,900
Books and Supplies:	$950	$950
Other Expenses:		
Total Estimated Expenses:	**$12,539**	**$23,698**

NEW APPLICANTS/NEWLY ENROLLED STUDENTS

[Numbers are for the undergraduate engineering college for the Fall 2006 term]

Number of Applicants (a):	1,922
Of those, Number Offered Admission (b):	1,456
Of those, Number Enrolled Fall 2006 (c):	687

GRADUATE INFORMATION

ADMISSION INQUIRIES

Michael Dickson
Assistant Dean
Arizona State University
Box 871003
Tempe , AZ 85287-1003
Phone: (480) 965-6113
Fax: (480) 965-5158
Email: asugrad@asu.edu

ESTIMATED STUDENT EXPENSES (FALL 2006)

[Expenses are for the 2006-2007 nine-month academic year and are based on an average credit load of: Graduate: N/A]

	In-State	Out-of-State
Tuition and Fees:	$6,026	$16,612
Campus and Room and Board:	$7,400	$7,400
Books and Supplies:	$950	$950
Other Expenses:		
Total Estimated Expenses:	**$14,376**	**$24,962**

NEW APPLICANTS/NEWLY ENROLLED STUDENTS

[Numbers are for the graduate engineering college for the Fall 2006 term]

Number of Applicants (a):	3,123
Of those, Number Offered Admission (b):	1,378
Of those, Number Enrolled Fall 2006 (c):	493

University of Arkansas

INSTITUTION INFORMATION

3189 Bell Engineering Center
800 West Dickson
Fayetteville, AR 72701
Phone: (479) 575-6012
Fax: (479) 575-7744
Web: http://www.engr.uark.edu

GENERAL INFORMATION

[All Students - Fall 2006]

Undergraduate Enrollment	13,876
Graduate Enrollment	3,021
Professional Enrollment	1,029
Total Enrollment	**17,926**

ENGINEERING COLLEGE INFORMATION

HEAD OF ENGINEERING

Ashok Saxena
Dean of Engineering, Distinguished Professor
Engineering Dean
University of Arkansas
4187 Bell Engineering Center
Fayetteville, AR 72701
Phone: (479) 575-3054
Fax: (479) 575-4346
Email: asaxena@uark.edu

ENGINEERING COLLEGE INQUIRIES

Terry W Martin
Associate Dean for Academic Affairs
University of Arkansas
4188 Bell Engineering Center, 800 West Dickson
Fayetteville, AR 72701

Phone: (479) 575-6012
Fax: (479) 575-7744
Email: tmartin@uark.edu

TYPES OF ENGINEERING DEGREES
Bachelor's: B.S.
Master's: M.S. with thesis, M.S. without thesis, but with project or report
Doctoral: Ph.D.

UNDERGRADUATE INFORMATION

ADMISSION INQUIRIES
Terry W Martin
Associate Dean for Academic Affairs
University of Arkansas
4188 Bell Engineering Center, 800 West Dickson
Fayetteville, AR 72701
Phone: (479) 575-6012
Fax: (479) 575-7744
Email: tmartin@uark.edu

ESTIMATED STUDENT EXPENSES (FALL 2006)
[Expenses are for the 2006-2007 nine-month academic year and are based on an average credit load of: Undergraduate: 15]

	In-State	Out-of-State
Tutition and Fees:	$6,252	$14,386
Campus and Room and Board:	$6,522	$6,522
Books and Supplies:	$1,383	$1,383
Other Expenses:		
Total Estimated Expenses:	**$14,157**	**$22,291**

NEW APPLICANTS/NEWLY ENROLLED STUDENTS
[Numbers are for the undergraduate engineering college for the Fall 2006 term]
Number of Applicants (a): 988
Of those, Number Offered Admission (b): 741
Of those, Number Enrolled Fall 2006 (c): 384
Note: High school ranking not surveyed.

GRADUATE INFORMATION

ESTIMATED STUDENT EXPENSES (FALL 2006)
[Expenses are for the 2006-2007 nine-month academic year and are based on an average credit load of: Graduate: 9]

	In-State	Out-of-State
Tutition and Fees:	$5,914	$12,551
Campus and Room and Board:	$6,522	$6,522
Books and Supplies:	$1,383	$1,383
Other Expenses:		
Total Estimated Expenses:	**$13,819**	**$20,456**

NEW APPLICANTS/NEWLY ENROLLED STUDENTS
[Numbers are for the graduate engineering college for the Fall 2006 term]
Number of Applicants (a): 761
Of those, Number Offered Admission (b): 350
Of those, Number Enrolled Fall 2006 (c): 207

Arkansas State University

INSTITUTION INFORMATION
P.O. Box 1740
State University, AR 72467
Phone: (870) 972-2088
Fax: (870) 972-3948
Web: http://www.astate.edu

GENERAL INFORMATION
[All Students - Fall 2006]
Undergraduate Enrollment 9,340
Graduate Enrollment 1,387
Professional Enrollment 0
Total Enrollment **10,727**

ENGINEERING COLLEGE INFORMATION

HEAD OF ENGINEERING
Gregory C Phillips
Dean
Engineering
Arkansas State University
P.O. Box 1080
State University, AR 72467
Phone: (870) 972-2085
Fax: (870) 972-3948
Email: gphillips@astate.edu

ENGINEERING COLLEGE INQUIRIES
Rick Clifft
Associate Dean
Arkansas State University
P.O. Box 1740
State University, AR 72467
Phone: (870) 972-2088
Fax: (870) 972-3948
Email: rclifft@astate.edu

TYPES OF ENGINEERING DEGREES
Bachelor's: B.S.
Master's:
Doctoral:

UNDERGRADUATE INFORMATION

ESTIMATED STUDENT EXPENSES (FALL 2006)
[Expenses are for the 2006-2007 nine-month academic year and are based on an average credit load of: Undergraduate: 15]

	In-State	Out-of-State
Tutition and Fees:	$5,710	$12,760
Campus and Room and Board:	$4,190	$4,190
Books and Supplies:	$1,000	$1,000
Other Expenses:	$3,055	$3,055
Total Estimated Expenses:	**$13,955**	**$21,005**

NEW APPLICANTS/NEWLY ENROLLED STUDENTS
[Numbers are for the undergraduate engineering college for the Fall 2006 term]
Number of Applicants (a): 182
Of those, Number Offered Admission (b): 143
Of those, Number Enrolled Fall 2006 (c): 87

Arkansas Tech University

INSTITUTION INFORMATION
1815 Coliseum Drive
CES 112
Russellville, AR 72801
Phone: (479) 964-0877
Fax: (479) 964-0882
Web: http://www.atu.edu

GENERAL INFORMATION
[All Students - Fall 2006]
Undergraduate Enrollment 5,865
Graduate Enrollment 603
Professional Enrollment 0
Total Enrollment **6,468**

ENGINEERING COLLEGE INFORMATION

HEAD OF ENGINEERING
John Watson
Dean, School of System Science
School of System Science
Arkansas Tech University
Corley 112
1814 N. Boulder
Russellville, AR 72801
Phone: (479) 968-0353
Fax: (479) 968-0667
Email: john.watson@atu.edu

ENGINEERING COLLEGE INQUIRIES
Carla Terry
Administrative Assistant
Arkansas Tech University
CES 112, 1815 Coliseum Dr.
Russellville, AR 72801
Phone: (479) 964-0877
Fax: (479) 964-0882
Email: carla.terry@atu.edu

TYPES OF ENGINEERING DEGREES
Bachelor's: B.S.
Master's:
Doctoral:

UNDERGRADUATE INFORMATION

ADMISSION INQUIRIES
Shauna Donnell
Director of Admissions
Arkansas Tech University
Bryan Student Services Building
Russellville, AR 72801

Phone: (479) 964-0844
Email: tech.enroll@atu.edu

ESTIMATED STUDENT EXPENSES (FALL 2006)
[Expenses are for the 2006-2007 nine-month academic year and are based on an average credit load of: Undergraduate: N/A]

	In-State	Out-of-State
Tutition and Fees:	$4,880	$9,350
Campus and Room and Board:	$3,948	$3,948
Books and Supplies:	$800	$800
Other Expenses:		
Total Estimated Expenses:	**$9,628**	**$14,098**

NEW APPLICANTS/NEWLY ENROLLED STUDENTS
[Numbers are for the undergraduate engineering college for the Fall 2006 term]
Number of Applicants (a): 208
Of those, Number Offered Admission (b): 126
Of those, Number Enrolled Fall 2006 (c): 93

University of Arkansas at Little Rock

INSTITUTION INFORMATION
ETAS Building Room 202
2801 South University Avenue
Little Rock, AR 72204
Phone: (501) 683-7117
Fax: (501) 569-8002
Web: http://technologize.ualr.edu/

GENERAL INFORMATION
[All Students - Fall 2006]
Undergraduate Enrollment 9,400
Graduate Enrollment 2,155
Professional Enrollment 500
Total Enrollment **12,055**

ENGINEERING COLLEGE INFORMATION

HEAD OF ENGINEERING
Mary L. Good
Dean
Donaghey College of Info. Science & Systems Engr.
University of Arkansas at Little Rock
UALR - ETAS 202
2801 South University
Little Rock, AR 72204
Phone: (501) 569-8188
Fax: (501) 569-8002
Email: mlgood@ualr.edu

HEAD OF ENGINEERING
Seshadri Mohan
Chair, Systems Engineering
Donaghey College of Info.Science & Systems Eng./
Systems Engineering
University of Arkansas at Little Rock
ETAS Building Room 300
2801 South University Avenue
Little Rock, AR 72204
Phone: (501) 683-7475
Fax: (501) 569-8698
Email: sxmohan@ualr.edu

TYPES OF ENGINEERING DEGREES
Bachelor's: B.S.
Master's: M.S. with thesis, M.S. without thesis, but with project or report
Doctoral:

UNDERGRADUATE INFORMATION

ESTIMATED STUDENT EXPENSES (FALL 2006)
[Expenses are for the 2006-2007 nine-month academic year and are based on an average credit load of: Undergraduate: 16]

	In-State	Out-of-State
Tutition and Fees:	$4,736	$12,432
Campus and Room and Board:	$4,500	$4,500
Books and Supplies:	$1,000	$1,000
Other Expenses:	$3,000	$3,000
Total Estimated Expenses:	**$13,236**	**$20,932**

GRADUATE INFORMATION

ESTIMATED STUDENT EXPENSES (FALL 2006)
[Expenses are for the 2006-2007 nine-month academic year and are based on an average credit load of: Graduate: 12]

	In-State	Out-of-State
Tuition and Fees:	$5,000	$11,000
Campus and Room and Board:	$4,500	$4,500
Books and Supplies:	$1,000	$1,000
Other Expenses:	$3,000	$3,000
Total Estimated Expenses:	**$13,500**	**$19,500**

Auburn University

INSTITUTION INFORMATION
Undergraduate Admissions: 202 Mary Martin Hall
Graduate Admissions: 106 Hargis Hall
Auburn University, AL 36849-3501
Phone: (133) 484-4400
Fax: (133) 484-6436
Web: http://www.auburn.edu

GENERAL INFORMATION
[All Students - Fall 2006]

Undergraduate Enrollment	19,367
Graduate Enrollment	3,245
Professional Enrollment	935
Total Enrollment	**23,547**

ENGINEERING COLLEGE INFORMATION

HEAD OF ENGINEERING
Larry D Benefield
Dean, Col. of Engr. & Prof., Civil Eng.
Samuel Ginn College of Engineering
Auburn University
108 Ramsay Hall
Auburn University, AL 36849
Phone: (334) 844-2303
Fax: (334) 844-4487
Email: benefld@eng.auburn.edu

ENGINEERING COLLEGE INQUIRIES
C R Karcher
Director
Auburn University
Samuel Ginn College of Engineering, 104 Ramsay Hall
Auburn University, AL 36849
Phone: (334) 844-4310
Fax: (334) 844-2349
Email: karchcr@auburn.edu

TYPES OF ENGINEERING DEGREES
Bachelor's: B.S.
Master's: M.S. with thesis, M.Eng.
Doctoral: Ph.D.

UNDERGRADUATE INFORMATION

ESTIMATED STUDENT EXPENSES (FALL 2006)
[Expenses are for the 2006-2007 nine-month academic year and are based on an average credit load of: Undergraduate: 15]

	In-State	Out-of-State
Tuition and Fees:	$5,496	$15,496
Campus and Room and Board:	$7,564	$7,564
Books and Supplies:	$1,000	$1,000
Other Expenses:	$4,188	$4,188
Total Estimated Expenses:	**$18,248**	**$28,248**

Note: Auburn University has no formal board plan.

NEW APPLICANTS/NEWLY ENROLLED STUDENTS
[Numbers are for the undergraduate engineering college for the Fall 2006 term]

Number of Applicants (a):	2,469
Of those, Number Offered Admission (b):	2,023
Of those, Number Enrolled Fall 2006 (c):	891

Note: In an effort to ensure a high level of retention, tutorial assistance is offered through Engineering Student Services and the Minority Engineering Program.

GRADUATE INFORMATION

ADMISSION INQUIRIES
Stephen L McFarland
Acting Associate Provost for Academic Affairs and Dean, Grad. School
Auburn University

106D Hargis Hall
Auburn University , AL 36849
Phone: (334) 844-2125
Email: mcfarsl@auburn.edu

ESTIMATED STUDENT EXPENSES (FALL 2006)
[Expenses are for the 2006-2007 nine-month academic year and are based on an average credit load of: Graduate: 10]

	In-State	Out-of-State
Tuition and Fees:	$5,496	$15,496
Campus and Room and Board:	$7,564	$7,564
Books and Supplies:	$1,000	$1,000
Other Expenses:	$4,188	$4,188
Total Estimated Expenses:	**$18,248**	**$28,248**

Note: Auburn University has no formal board plan.

NEW APPLICANTS/NEWLY ENROLLED STUDENTS
[Numbers are for the graduate engineering college for the Fall 2006 term]

Number of Applicants (a):	993
Of those, Number Offered Admission (b):	585
Of those, Number Enrolled Fall 2006 (c):	173

Baker College

INSTITUTION INFORMATION
Technology Center
1050 W Bristol RD
Flint, MI 48507
Phone: (810) 766-4190
Fax: (810) 766-4042
Web: https://www.baker.edu/campusresources/Flint/techcenter/main.cfm

GENERAL INFORMATION
[All Students - Fall 2006]

Undergraduate Enrollment	6,000
Graduate Enrollment	0
Professional Enrollment	0
Total Enrollment	**6,000**

ENGINEERING COLLEGE INFORMATION

HEAD OF ENGINEERING
James Riddell
Dean, Engineering & Technology
Engineering Dept.
Baker College
Technology Center
1050 W Bristol RD
Flint, MI 48507
Phone: (810) 766-4190
Fax: (810) 766-4042
Email: jridde01@baker.edu

ENGINEERING COLLEGE INQUIRIES
James Riddell
Dean, Engineering & Technology
Baker College
Technology Center, 1050 W Bristol RD
Flint, MI 48507
Phone: (810) 766-4190
Fax: (810) 766-4042
Email: jridde01@baker.edu

TYPES OF ENGINEERING DEGREES
Bachelor's: B.S.
Master's:
Doctoral:

Baylor University

INSTITUTION INFORMATION
One Bear Place #97356
Waco, TX 76798
Phone: (254) 710-3871
Fax: (254) 710-3839
Web: http://www.baylor.edu

GENERAL INFORMATION
[All Students - Fall 2006]

Undergraduate Enrollment	11,831
Graduate Enrollment	1,278
Professional Enrollment	931
Total Enrollment	**14,040**

ENGINEERING COLLEGE INFORMATION

HEAD OF ENGINEERING
Benjamin S Kelley
Dean
School of Engineering and Computer Science
Baylor University
One Bear Place # 97356
Waco, TX 76798
Phone: (254) 710-3871
Fax: (254) 710-3839
Email: Ben_Kelley@baylor.edu

ENGINEERING COLLEGE INQUIRIES
Benjamin S Kelley
Dean
Baylor University
One Bear Place # 97356
Waco, TX 76798
Phone: (254) 710-3871
Fax: (254) 710-3839
Email: Ben_Kelley@baylor.edu

TYPES OF ENGINEERING DEGREES
Bachelor's: B.A., B.S.
Master's: M.S. with thesis, M.S. without thesis, but with project or report
Doctoral:

UNDERGRADUATE INFORMATION

ADMISSION INQUIRIES
Jennifer Carron
Director of Admissions Services
Baylor University
One Bear Place #97056
Waco, TX 76798
Phone: (254) 710-3435
Fax: (254) 710-3436
Email: Jennifer_Carron@baylor.edu

ESTIMATED STUDENT EXPENSES (FALL 2006)
[Expenses are for the 2006-2007 nine-month academic year and are based on an average credit load of: Undergraduate: 15]

	All Students
Tuition and fees:	$22,814
Campus and Room and Board:	$7,222
Books and Supplies:	$1,502
Other Expenses:	
Total Estimated Expenses:	**$31,538**

GRADUATE INFORMATION

ADMISSION INQUIRIES
Michael W Thompson
Associate Professor of Electrical & Computer Engineering & Graduate Program Director
Baylor University
One Bear Place # 97356
Waco , TX 76798
Phone: (254) 710-4188
Fax: (254) 710-3839
Email: Michael_W_Thompson@baylor.edu

ADMISSION INQUIRIES
David B Sturgill
Assistant Professor of Computer Science& Graduate Program Director
Baylor University
One Bear Place #97356
Waco , TX 76798
Phone: (254) 710-3876
Fax: (254) 710-3839
Email: David_Sturgill@baylor.edu

ESTIMATED STUDENT EXPENSES (FALL 2006)
[Expenses are for the 2006-2007 nine-month academic year and are based on an average credit load of: Graduate: 9]

	All Students
Tuition and fees:	$17,217
Campus and Room and Board:	$6,934
Books and Supplies:	$1,502
Other Expenses:	
Total Estimated Expenses:	**$25,653**

NEW APPLICANTS/NEWLY ENROLLED STUDENTS
[Numbers are for the graduate engineering college for the Fall 2006 term]

Number of Applicants (a):	61

Of those, Number Offered Admission (b): 19
Of those, Number Enrolled Fall 2006 (c): 11

Boise State University

INSTITUTION INFORMATION
College of Engineering
1910 University Dr., MS2100
Boise, ID 83725
Phone: (208) 426-1153
Fax: (208) 426-4466
Web: http://coen.boisestate.edu

GENERAL INFORMATION
[All Students - Fall 2006]
Undergraduate Enrollment	16,017
Graduate Enrollment	1,786
Professional Enrollment	1,073
Total Enrollment	**18,876**

ENGINEERING COLLEGE INFORMATION

HEAD OF ENGINEERING
Cheryl B Schrader
Dean
College of Engineering
Boise State University
1910 University Drive
MS 2100
Boise, ID 83725
Phone: (208) 426-1153
Fax: (208) 426-4466
Email: schrader@boisestate.edu

TYPES OF ENGINEERING DEGREES
Bachelor's: B.S.
Master's: M.S. with thesis, M.Eng.
Doctoral: Ph.D.

UNDERGRADUATE INFORMATION

ESTIMATED STUDENT EXPENSES (FALL 2006)
[Expenses are for the 2006-2007 nine-month academic year and are based on an average credit load of: Undergraduate: 12]

	In-State	Out-of-State
Tuition and Fees:	$4,154	$11,932
Campus and Room and Board:	$5,778	$5,778
Books and Supplies:	$1,050	$1,050
Other Expenses:	$3,532	$3,532
Total Estimated Expenses:	**$14,514**	**$22,292**

NEW APPLICANTS/NEWLY ENROLLED STUDENTS
[Numbers are for the undergraduate engineering college for the Fall 2006 term]
Number of Applicants (a):	416
Of those, Number Offered Admission (b):	314
Of those, Number Enrolled Fall 2006 (c):	178

GRADUATE INFORMATION

ESTIMATED STUDENT EXPENSES (FALL 2006)
[Expenses are for the 2006-2007 nine-month academic year and are based on an average credit load of: Graduate: 6]

	In-State	Out-of-State
Tuition and Fees:	$4,944	$12,722
Campus and Room and Board:	$5,778	$5,778
Books and Supplies:	$1,050	$1,050
Other Expenses:	$3,532	$3,532
Total Estimated Expenses:	**$15,304**	**$23,082**

NEW APPLICANTS/NEWLY ENROLLED STUDENTS
[Numbers are for the graduate engineering college for the Fall 2006 term]
Number of Applicants (a):	101
Of those, Number Offered Admission (b):	53
Of those, Number Enrolled Fall 2006 (c):	33

Boston University

INSTITUTION INFORMATION
College of Engineering
44 Cummington Street
Boston, MA 02215
Phone: (617) 353-2800
Fax: (617) 353-7285
Web: http://www.bu.edu/eng

GENERAL INFORMATION
[All Students - Fall 2006]
Undergraduate Enrollment	16,231
Graduate Enrollment	7,456
Professional Enrollment	1,033
Total Enrollment	**24,720**

ENGINEERING COLLEGE INFORMATION

HEAD OF ENGINEERING
Kenneth R Lutchen
Dean
College of Engineering
Boston University
College of Engineering
44 Cummington Street
Boston, MA 02215
Phone: (617) 353-2800
Fax: (617) 353-5929
Email: klutch@bu.edu

TYPES OF ENGINEERING DEGREES
Bachelor's: B.S.
Master's: M.S. with thesis, M.S. without thesis, but with project or report
Doctoral: Ph.D.

UNDERGRADUATE INFORMATION

ADMISSION INQUIRIES
Solomon R Eisenberg
Chair, College of Engineering
Boston University
College of Engineering, 44 Cummington Street
Boston, MA 02215
Phone: (617) 353-2800
Fax: (617) 353-5929
Email: sre@bu.edu

ADMISSION INQUIRIES
Joanne Cornell
Director, Undergraduate Programs Office
Boston University
College of Engineering, 44 Cummington Street
Boston, MA 02215
Phone: (617) 353-6447
Fax: (617) 353-7285
Email: jcornell@bu.edu

ESTIMATED STUDENT EXPENSES (FALL 2006)
[Expenses are for the 2006-2007 nine-month academic year and are based on an average credit load of: Undergraduate: 16]

	All Students
Tuition and fees:	$33,792
Campus and Room and Board:	$10,480
Books and Supplies:	$792
Other Expenses:	$1,636
Total Estimated Expenses:	**$46,700**

Note: Breakdown of total room and board expenses is 6760 for room and 3720 for board.

NEW APPLICANTS/NEWLY ENROLLED STUDENTS
[Numbers are for the undergraduate engineering college for the Fall 2006 term]
Number of Applicants (a):	2,246
Of those, Number Offered Admission (b):	1,480
Of those, Number Enrolled Fall 2006 (c):	327

GRADUATE INFORMATION

ADMISSION INQUIRIES
Mark N. Horenstein
Associate Dean for Graduate Programs and Research
Boston University
College of Engineering, 44 Cummington Street
Boston , MA 02215
Phone: (617) 353-2800
Fax: (617) 353-5929
Email: mnh@bu.edu

ADMISSION INQUIRIES
Cheryl Kelley
Director, Graduate Programs Office
Boston University
College of Engineering, 48 Cummington Street
Boston , MA 02215
Phone: (617) 353-9760
Fax: (617) 353-0259
Email: cdk@bu.edu

ESTIMATED STUDENT EXPENSES (FALL 2006)
[Expenses are for the 2006-2007 nine-month academic year and are based on an average credit load of: Graduate: 16]

	All Students
Tuition and fees:	$33,792
Campus and Room and Board:	$10,480
Books and Supplies:	$1,286
Other Expenses:	$1,575
Total Estimated Expenses:	**$47,133**

Note: Breakdown of total room and board expenses is 6760 for room and 3720 for board.

NEW APPLICANTS/NEWLY ENROLLED STUDENTS
[Numbers are for the graduate engineering college for the Fall 2006 term]
Number of Applicants (a):	1,738
Of those, Number Offered Admission (b):	462
Of those, Number Enrolled Fall 2006 (c):	193

Bradley University

INSTITUTION INFORMATION
Jobst Hall 124
Peoria, IL 61625
Phone: (309) 677-2720
Fax: (309) 677-3670
Web: http://www.bradley.edu

GENERAL INFORMATION
[All Students - Fall 2006]
Undergraduate Enrollment	5,314
Graduate Enrollment	800
Professional Enrollment	0
Total Enrollment	**6,114**

ENGINEERING COLLEGE INFORMATION

HEAD OF ENGINEERING
Richard T Johnson
Dean, College of Engineering & Technology
124 Jobst
Bradley University
Peoria, IL 61625
Phone: (309) 677-2721
Fax: (309) 677-3670
Email: rtj@bradley.edu

ENGINEERING COLLEGE INQUIRIES
Sharon L McBride
Undergraduate Student Advisor
Bradley University
125 Jobst Hall
Peoria, IL 61625
Phone: (309) 677-2975
Fax: (309) 677-3670
Email: mcbride@bradley.edu

TYPES OF ENGINEERING DEGREES
Bachelor's: B.S.
Master's: M.S. with thesis, M.S. without thesis, but with project or report
Doctoral:

UNDERGRADUATE INFORMATION

ADMISSION INQUIRIES
Tom Richmond
Admissions Marketing & Communications Director
Bradley University
Visitors Center
Peoria, IL 61625
Phone: (309) 677-3144
Fax: (309) 677-2797
Email: richmond@adm.bradley.edu

ESTIMATED STUDENT EXPENSES (FALL 2006)
[Expenses are for the 2006-2007 nine-month academic year and are based on an average credit load of: Undergraduate: 16]

	All Students
Tuition and fees:	$19,900
Campus and Room and Board:	$6,750
Books and Supplies:	$1,200
Other Expenses:	$150
Total Estimated Expenses:	**$28,000**

Note: Undergraduate tuition and fees is for 12-16 semester hours.

Room & board is for a double room.

NEW APPLICANTS/NEWLY ENROLLED STUDENTS
[Numbers are for the undergraduate engineering college for the Fall 2006 term]

Number of Applicants (a):	593
Of those, Number Offered Admission (b):	447
Of those, Number Enrolled Fall 2006 (c):	149

GRADUATE INFORMATION

ADMISSION INQUIRIES
Lynne Franks
Director Graduate International Admissions and Student Services
Bradley University
200 Bradley Hall
Peoria , IL 61625
Phone: (309) 677-2375
Fax: (309) 677-3343
Email: lrf@bradley.edu

ESTIMATED STUDENT EXPENSES (FALL 2006)
[Expenses are for the 2006-2007 nine-month academic year and are based on an average credit load of: Graduate: 9]

	All Students
Tuition and fees:	$11,880
Campus and Room and Board:	$6,750
Books and Supplies:	$1,200
Other Expenses:	$150
Total Estimated Expenses:	**$19,980**

Note: Graduate tuition is based on 9 semester hours at $565/credit hour

Room & board is for a double room.

NEW APPLICANTS/NEWLY ENROLLED STUDENTS
[Numbers are for the graduate engineering college for the Fall 2006 term]

Number of Applicants (a):	292
Of those, Number Offered Admission (b):	167
Of those, Number Enrolled Fall 2006 (c):	76

University of Bridgeport

INSTITUTION INFORMATION
126 Park Avenue
Bridgeport, CT 06604
Phone: (203) 576-4000
Fax: (203) 576-4941
Web: http://www.bridgeport.edu

GENERAL INFORMATION
[All Students - Fall 2006]

Undergraduate Enrollment	1,694
Graduate Enrollment	2,128
Professional Enrollment	196
Total Enrollment	**4,018**

ENGINEERING COLLEGE INFORMATION

HEAD OF ENGINEERING
Tarek M Sobh
Dean
School of Engineering
University of Bridgeport
Engineering Technology Building
221 University Avenue
Bridgeport, CT 06604
Phone: (203) 576-4111
Fax: (203) 576-4766
Email: sobh@bridgeport.edu

TYPES OF ENGINEERING DEGREES
Bachelor's: B.S.
Master's: M.S. with thesis, M.S. without thesis, but with project or report
Doctoral: Ph.D.

UNDERGRADUATE INFORMATION

ESTIMATED STUDENT EXPENSES (FALL 2006)
[Expenses are for the 2006-2007 nine-month academic year and are based on an average credit load of: Undergraduate: 15]

	All Students
Tuition and fees:	$21,710
Campus and Room and Board:	$9,600
Books and Supplies:	$1,500
Other Expenses:	$4,257
Total Estimated Expenses:	**$37,067**

NEW APPLICANTS/NEWLY ENROLLED STUDENTS
[Numbers are for the undergraduate engineering college for the Fall 2006 term]

Number of Applicants (a):	173
Of those, Number Offered Admission (b):	78
Of those, Number Enrolled Fall 2006 (c):	7

GRADUATE INFORMATION

ESTIMATED STUDENT EXPENSES (FALL 2006)
[Expenses are for the 2006-2007 nine-month academic year and are based on an average credit load of: Graduate: 9]

	All Students
Tuition and fees:	$10,650
Campus and Room and Board:	$8,200
Books and Supplies:	$1,500
Other Expenses:	$1,800
Total Estimated Expenses:	**$22,150**

NEW APPLICANTS/NEWLY ENROLLED STUDENTS
[Numbers are for the graduate engineering college for the Fall 2006 term]

Number of Applicants (a):	1,725
Of those, Number Offered Admission (b):	1,288
Of those, Number Enrolled Fall 2006 (c):	272

Brigham Young University

INSTITUTION INFORMATION
270 CB
Provo, UT 84602
Phone: (801) 422-4326
Web: http://www.byu.edu

GENERAL INFORMATION
[All Students - Fall 2006]

Undergraduate Enrollment	30,964
Graduate Enrollment	3,678
Professional Enrollment	0
Total Enrollment	**34,642**

ENGINEERING COLLEGE INFORMATION

HEAD OF ENGINEERING
Alan R Parkinson
Dean
Ira A. Fulton College of Engineering & Technology
Brigham Young University
270 Clyde Building
Provo, UT 84602
Phone: (801) ,80-1422
Fax: (801) ,80-0218
Email: parkinson@byu.edu

TYPES OF ENGINEERING DEGREES
Bachelor's: B.S.
Master's: M.S. with thesis, M.S. without thesis, but with project or report
Doctoral: Ph.D.

UNDERGRADUATE INFORMATION

ADMISSION INQUIRIES
Pamela O Williamson
Supervisor
Brigham Young University
264 CB
Provo, UT 84602
Phone: (801) 422-4325
Fax: (801) 422-0218
Email: olson@byu.edu

ESTIMATED STUDENT EXPENSES (FALL 2006)
[Expenses are for the 2006-2007 nine-month academic year and are based on an average credit load of: Undergraduate: 14516]

	Other Group 1	Other Group 2
Tuition and Fees:	$3,620	$7,240
Campus and Room and Board:	$5,816	$5,816
Books and Supplies:	$1,380	$1,380
Other Expenses:	$3,700	$3,700
Total Estimated Expenses:	**$14,516**	**$18,136**

Note: Other 1: LDS Students; Other 2: Non-LDS Students

NEW APPLICANTS/NEWLY ENROLLED STUDENTS
[Numbers are for the undergraduate engineering college for the Fall 2006 term]

Number of Applicants (a):	782
Of those, Number Offered Admission (b):	600
Of those, Number Enrolled Fall 2006 (c):	454

Note: These numbers are based on our Fall 2002 admittance to the Professional Program which students typically enter after their sophomore year.

GRADUATE INFORMATION

ESTIMATED STUDENT EXPENSES (FALL 2006)
[Expenses are for the 2006-2007 nine-month academic year and are based on an average credit load of: Graduate: 15476]

	Other Group 1	Other Group 2
Tuition and Fees:	$4,580	$9,160
Campus and Room and Board:	$5,816	$5,816
Books and Supplies:	$1,380	$1,380
Other Expenses:	$3,700	$3,700
Total Estimated Expenses:	**$15,476**	**$20,056**

Note: Other 1: LDS Students; Other 2: Non-LDS Students

NEW APPLICANTS/NEWLY ENROLLED STUDENTS
[Numbers are for the graduate engineering college for the Fall 2006 term]

Number of Applicants (a):	285
Of those, Number Offered Admission (b):	171
Of those, Number Enrolled Fall 2006 (c):	118

Brown University

INSTITUTION INFORMATION
Box D
Providence, RI 02912
Phone: (401) 863-1425
Fax: (401) 863-1238
Web: http://www.engin.brown.edu

GENERAL INFORMATION
[All Students - Fall 2006]

Undergraduate Enrollment	5,701
Graduate Enrollment	1,568
Professional Enrollment	326
Total Enrollment	**7,595**

ENGINEERING COLLEGE INFORMATION

HEAD OF ENGINEERING
Gregory P Crawford
Dean of Engineering
Division of Engineering
Brown University
182 Hope Street
Providence, RI 02912
Phone: (401) 863-1422
Fax: (401) 863-1238
Email: gregory_crawford@brown.edu

TYPES OF ENGINEERING DEGREES
Bachelor's: B.A., B.S., S.B.
Master's: M.S. with thesis, M.S. without thesis, but with project or report
Doctoral: Ph.D.

UNDERGRADUATE INFORMATION

ADMISSION INQUIRIES
Virginia Novak
Manager, Office of Student Affairs
Brown University
182 Hope Street
Providence, RI 02912
Phone: (401) 863-2679
Fax: (401) 863-1238
Email: Virginia_Novak@brown.edu

GRADUATE INFORMATION

ADMISSION INQUIRIES
Virginia Novak
Manager, Office of Student Affairs
Brown University
182 Hope Street
Providence , RI 02912
Phone: (401) 863-2679
Fax: (401) 863-1238
Email: Virginia_Novak@brown.edu

Bucknell University

INSTITUTION INFORMATION

235 Dana
College of Engineering
Lewisburg, PA 17837
Phone: (570) 577-3711
Fax: (570) 577-3579
Web: http://www.eg.bucknell.edu

GENERAL INFORMATION

[All Students - Fall 2006]

Undergraduate Enrollment	3,607
Graduate Enrollment	164
Professional Enrollment	32
Total Enrollment	**3,803**

ENGINEERING COLLEGE INFORMATION

HEAD OF ENGINEERING

James G. Orbison
Dean
Office of the Dean
Bucknell University
235 Dana
College of Engineering
Lewisburg, PA 17837
Phone: (570) 577-3711
Fax: (570) 577-3579
Email: jorbison@bucknell.edu

ENGINEERING COLLEGE INQUIRIES

Karen Marosi
Associate Dean
Bucknell University
235 Dana, College of Engineering
Lewisburg, PA 17837
Phone: (570) 577-3705
Fax: (570) 577-3579
Email: ktmarosi@bucknell.edu

TYPES OF ENGINEERING DEGREES

Bachelor's: B.S.
Master's: M.S. with thesis
Doctoral:

UNDERGRADUATE INFORMATION

ADMISSION INQUIRIES

Kurt Thiede
Dean of Admissions
Bucknell University
8 Freas Hall
Lewisburg, PA 17837
Phone: (570) 577-1618
Fax: (570) 577-3538
Email: kthiede@bucknell.edu

ESTIMATED STUDENT EXPENSES (FALL 2006)

[Expenses are for the 2006-2007 nine-month academic year and are based on an average credit load of: Undergraduate: 4]

	All Students
Tuition and fees:	$36,000
Campus and Room and Board:	$7,366
Books and Supplies:	$700
Other Expenses:	$196
Total Estimated Expenses:	**$44,262**

Note: Graduate student expenses are based on $3,725 per course credit for a typical course.

NEW APPLICANTS/NEWLY ENROLLED STUDENTS

[Numbers are for the undergraduate engineering college for the Fall 2006 term]

Number of Applicants (a):	1,800
Of those, Number Offered Admission (b):	646
Of those, Number Enrolled Fall 2006 (c):	184

GRADUATE INFORMATION

ADMISSION INQUIRIES

M. Lois Huffines
Associate Vice President for Academic Affairs
Bucknell University
217 Marts Hall
Lewisburg , PA 17837
Phone: (570) 577-1561
Fax: (570) 577-3369
Email: huffines@bucknell.edu

University of Calgary

INSTITUTION INFORMATION

2500 University Drive NW
Calgary, AB T2N 1N4
Phone: (403) 220-5110
Fax: (403) 282-7298
Web: http://www.ucalgary.ca

GENERAL INFORMATION

[All Students - Fall 2006]

Undergraduate Enrollment	20,371
Graduate Enrollment	5,647
Professional Enrollment	2,304
Total Enrollment	**28,322**

ENGINEERING COLLEGE INFORMATION

HEAD OF ENGINEERING

Elizabeth Cannon
Dean, Schulich School of Engineering
Schulich School of Engineering
University of Calgary
2500 University Drive, NW
Calgary, AB T2N1N4
Phone: (403) 220-5738
Fax: (403) 284-3697
Email: cannon@ucalgary.ca

TYPES OF ENGINEERING DEGREES

Bachelor's: B.S.
Master's: M.S. with thesis, M.S. without thesis, but with project or report, M.Eng.
Doctoral: Ph.D.

UNDERGRADUATE INFORMATION

ADMISSION INQUIRIES

Eleanor Sit
Advisor/Administrator, Undergraduate Studies Office
University of Calgary
Undergraduate Studies Office, 2500 University Drive, NW
Calgary, AB T2N1N4
Phone: (403) 220-7841
Fax: (403) 284-3697
Email: esit@ucalgary.ca

ESTIMATED STUDENT EXPENSES (FALL 2006)

[Expenses are for the 2006-2007 nine-month academic year and are based on an average credit load of: Undergraduate: 10]

	Canadian Citizen	Non-Canadian
Tuition and Fees:	$5,600	$14,500
Campus and Room and Board:	$3,900	$3,900
Books and Supplies:	$1,400	$1,400
Other Expenses:	$3,000	$3,000
Total Estimated Expenses:	**$13,900**	**$22,800**

Note: Our academic year is from September to April (8 months).
Group 1 is Canadian Citizen/Landed Immigrants.
Group 2 is International Students.
1 single semester course = 2.0 credit

NEW APPLICANTS/NEWLY ENROLLED STUDENTS

[Numbers are for the undergraduate engineering college for the Fall 2006 term]

Number of Applicants (a):	1,422
Of those, Number Offered Admission (b):	802
Of those, Number Enrolled Fall 2006 (c):	583

GRADUATE INFORMATION

ESTIMATED STUDENT EXPENSES (FALL 2006)

[Expenses are for the 2006-2007 nine-month academic year and are based on an average credit load of: Graduate: 4]

	Canadian Citizen	Non-Canadian
Tuition and Fees:	$2,200	$4,300
Campus and Room and Board:	$3,900	$3,900
Books and Supplies:	$600	$600
Other Expenses:	$3,000	$3,000
Total Estimated Expenses:	**$9,700**	**$11,800**

Note: Our academic year is from September to April (8 months).
Group 1 is Canadian Citizen/Landed Immigrants.
Group 2 is International Students.
1 single semester course = 2.0 credit

NEW APPLICANTS/NEWLY ENROLLED STUDENTS

[Numbers are for the graduate engineering college for the Fall 2006 term]

Number of Applicants (a):	947
Of those, Number Offered Admission (b):	335
Of those, Number Enrolled Fall 2006 (c):	229

California Institute of Technology

INSTITUTION INFORMATION

1200 East California Blvd.
Pasadena, CA 91125
Phone: (626) 395-6811
Fax: (626) 795-1547
Web: http://www.caltech.edu

GENERAL INFORMATION

[All Students - Fall 2006]

Undergraduate Enrollment	864
Graduate Enrollment	1,222
Professional Enrollment	47
Total Enrollment	**2,133**

ENGINEERING COLLEGE INFORMATION

HEAD OF ENGINEERING

David B Rutledge
Kiyo and Eiko Tomiyasu Professor of Electrical Engineering
Chair, Division of Engineering and Applied Science
California Institute of Technology
1200 East California Blvd.
Mail Code 104-44
Pasadena, CA 91125-3100
Phone: (626) 395-4100
Fax: (626) 585-1729
Email: dave.rutledge@caltech.edu

TYPES OF ENGINEERING DEGREES

Bachelor's: B.S.
Master's: M.S. with thesis, M.S. without thesis, but with project or report
Doctoral: Ph.D.

UNDERGRADUATE INFORMATION

ADMISSION INQUIRIES

Richard Bischoff
Director of Admissions
California Institute of Technology
1200 East California Blvd., Mail Code 1-94
Pasadena, CA 91125
Phone: (626) 395-8375
Fax: (626) 683-3026
Email: rbisch@admissions.caltech.edu

ESTIMATED STUDENT EXPENSES (FALL 2006)

[Expenses are for the 2006-2007 nine-month academic year and are based on an average credit load of: Undergraduate: 36]

	All Students
Tuition and fees:	$31,516
Campus and Room and Board:	$10,308
Books and Supplies:	$1,077
Other Expenses:	$1,701
Total Estimated Expenses:	**$44,602**

GRADUATE INFORMATION

ESTIMATED STUDENT EXPENSES (FALL 2006)

[Expenses are for the 2006-2007 nine-month academic year and are based on an average credit load of: Graduate: 36]

	All Students
Tuition and fees:	$29,595
Campus and Room and Board:	$9,750
Books and Supplies:	$926
Other Expenses:	$4,955
Total Estimated Expenses:	**$45,226**

NEW APPLICANTS/NEWLY ENROLLED STUDENTS

[Numbers are for the graduate engineering college for the Fall 2006 term]

Number of Applicants (a):	2,310
Of those, Number Offered Admission (b):	226
Of those, Number Enrolled Fall 2006 (c):	104

California Polytechnic State University

INSTITUTION INFORMATION
1 Grand Avenue
San Luis Obispo, CA 93407
Phone: (805) 756-1111
Web: http://www.calpoly.edu

GENERAL INFORMATION
[All Students - Fall 2006]

Undergraduate Enrollment	17,777
Graduate Enrollment	945
Professional Enrollment	0
Total Enrollment	**18,722**

ENGINEERING COLLEGE INFORMATION

HEAD OF ENGINEERING
Mohammad N Noori
Dean - College of Engineering
College of Engineering
California Polytechnic State University
1 Grand Avenue
San Luis Obispo, CA 93407
Phone: (805) 756-2131
Fax: (805) 756-6503
Email: mnoori@calpoly.edu

ENGINEERING COLLEGE INQUIRIES
Daniel Walsh
Associate Dean-Academic Programs/Administration
California Polytechnic State University
1 Grand Avenue
San Luis Obispo, CA 93407
Phone: (805) 756-2131
Fax: (805) 756-6503
Email: dwalsh@calpoly.edu

TYPES OF ENGINEERING DEGREES
Bachelor's: B.S.
Master's: M.S. with thesis, M.S. without thesis, but with project or report
Doctoral:

UNDERGRADUATE INFORMATION

ADMISSION INQUIRIES
James Maraviglia
Asst. VP of Admissions, Recruitment & Financial Aid
California Polytechnic State University
1 Grand Avenue
San Luis Obispo, CA 93407
Phone: (805) 756-2311
Fax: (805) 756-5400
Email: jmaravig@calpoly.edu

ADMISSION INQUIRIES
Daniel Walsh
Associate Dean-Academic Programs/Administration
California Polytechnic State University
1 Grand Avenue
San Luis Obispo, CA 93407
Phone: (805) 756-2131
Fax: (805) 756-6503
Email: dwalsh@calpoly.edu

ESTIMATED STUDENT EXPENSES (FALL 2006)
[Expenses are for the 2006-2007 nine-month academic year and are based on an average credit load of: Undergraduate: 15]

	In-State	Out-of-State
Tuition and Fees:	$4,350	$14,520
Campus and Room and Board:	$8,453	$8,453
Books and Supplies:	$1,350	$1,350
Other Expenses:	$2,025	$2,025
Total Estimated Expenses:	**$16,178**	**$26,348**

NEW APPLICANTS/NEWLY ENROLLED STUDENTS
[Numbers are for the undergraduate engineering college for the Fall 2006 term]

Number of Applicants (a):	6,490
Of those, Number Offered Admission (b):	3,979
Of those, Number Enrolled Fall 2006 (c):	1,327

GRADUATE INFORMATION

ADMISSION INQUIRIES
Edward Sullivan

Assistant Dean, Graduate Programs/Research
California Polytechnic State University
1 Grand Avenue
San Luis Obispo , CA 93407
Phone: (805) 756-2131
Fax: (805) 756-6503
Email: esulliva@calpoly.edu

NEW APPLICANTS/NEWLY ENROLLED STUDENTS
[Numbers are for the graduate engineering college for the Fall 2006 term]

Number of Applicants (a):	170
Of those, Number Offered Admission (b):	117
Of those, Number Enrolled Fall 2006 (c):	81

California State Polytechnic University, Pomona

INSTITUTION INFORMATION
3801 West Temple Ave
Pomona, CA 91768
Phone: (909) 869-7659
Web: http://www.csupomona.edu

GENERAL INFORMATION
[All Students - Fall 2006]

Undergraduate Enrollment	18,625
Graduate Enrollment	1,313
Professional Enrollment	572
Total Enrollment	**20,510**

ENGINEERING COLLEGE INFORMATION

HEAD OF ENGINEERING
Edward C Hohmann
Dean
College of Engineering
California State Polytechnic University, Pomona
3801 West Temple Avenue
Building 9, Room 225
Pomona, CA 91768
Phone: (909) 869-2472
Fax: (909) 869-4370
Email: echohmann@csupomona.edu

TYPES OF ENGINEERING DEGREES
Bachelor's: B.S.
Master's: M.S. with thesis, M.S. without thesis, but with project or report
Doctoral:

UNDERGRADUATE INFORMATION

ESTIMATED STUDENT EXPENSES (FALL 2006)
[Expenses are for the 2006-2007 nine-month academic year and are based on an average credit load of: Undergraduate: 16]

	In-State	Out-of-State
Tuition and Fees:	$3,036	
Campus and Room and Board:	$7,973	
Books and Supplies:	$1,600	
Other Expenses:	$2,550	
Total Estimated Expenses:	**$15,159**	
Note: Figures are for full-time students, academic year

NEW APPLICANTS/NEWLY ENROLLED STUDENTS
[Numbers are for the undergraduate engineering college for the Fall 2006 term]

Number of Applicants (a):	3,356
Of those, Number Offered Admission (b):	2,189
Of those, Number Enrolled Fall 2006 (c):	884
Note: Figures are for Fall, 2000

GRADUATE INFORMATION

ESTIMATED STUDENT EXPENSES (FALL 2006)
[Expenses are for the 2006-2007 nine-month academic year and are based on an average credit load of: Graduate: 8]

	In-State	Out-of-State
Tuition and Fees:	$3,618	
Campus and Room and Board:	$7,973	
Books and Supplies:	$1,600	
Other Expenses:	$2,550	
Total Estimated Expenses:	**$15,741**	
Note: Figures are for full-time students, academic year

California State University, East Bay

INSTITUTION INFORMATION
25800 Carlos Bee Blvd
Hayward, CA 94542
Phone: (510) 885-2654
Fax: (510) 885-2678
Web: www.csueastbay.edu

GENERAL INFORMATION
[All Students - Fall 2006]

Undergraduate Enrollment	9,215
Graduate Enrollment	3,491
Professional Enrollment	0
Total Enrollment	**12,706**

ENGINEERING COLLEGE INFORMATION

TYPES OF ENGINEERING DEGREES
Bachelor's: B.S.
Master's: M.S. without thesis, but with project or report
Doctoral:

UNDERGRADUATE INFORMATION

ESTIMATED STUDENT EXPENSES (FALL 2006)
[Expenses are for the 2006-2007 nine-month academic year and are based on an average credit load of: Undergraduate: N/A]

	All Students
Tuition and fees:	$990
Campus and Room and Board:	$8,432
Books and Supplies:	
Other Expenses:	
Total Estimated Expenses:	$9,422
Note: International and other non-resident students pay an additional $226 per unit in addition to resident fees.

NEW APPLICANTS/NEWLY ENROLLED STUDENTS
[Numbers are for the undergraduate engineering college for the Fall 2006 term]

Number of Applicants (a):	85
Of those, Number Offered Admission (b):	85
Of those, Number Enrolled Fall 2006 (c):	40

GRADUATE INFORMATION

ESTIMATED STUDENT EXPENSES (FALL 2006)
[Expenses are for the 2006-2007 nine-month academic year and are based on an average credit load of: Graduate: N/A]

	All Students
Tuition and fees:	$1,184
Campus and Room and Board:	
Books and Supplies:	
Other Expenses:	
Total Estimated Expenses:	**$1,184**
Note: International and other non-resident students pay an additional $226 per unit in addition to resident fees.

NEW APPLICANTS/NEWLY ENROLLED STUDENTS
[Numbers are for the graduate engineering college for the Fall 2006 term]

Number of Applicants (a):	20
Of those, Number Offered Admission (b):	20
Of those, Number Enrolled Fall 2006 (c):	13

California State University, Chico

INSTITUTION INFORMATION
400 West First Street
Chico, CA 95929-0003
Phone: (530) 898-5963
Fax: (530) 898-4070
Web: http://www.csuchico.edu

GENERAL INFORMATION
[All Students - Fall 2006]

Undergraduate Enrollment	14,526
Graduate Enrollment	1,393
Professional Enrollment	0
Total Enrollment	**15,919**

ENGINEERING COLLEGE INFORMATION

HEAD OF ENGINEERING
Kenneth N. Derucher
Dean
College of Engr., CSCI, and Construction Mgmt.
California State University, Chico
400 West First Street
OConnell Technology Center, Room 410
Chico, CA 95929-0003
Phone: (530) 898-5963
Fax: (530) 898-4070
Email: kderucher@csuchico.edu

TYPES OF ENGINEERING DEGREES
Bachelor's: B.S.
Master's: M.S. with thesis, M.S. without thesis, but with project or report
Doctoral:

UNDERGRADUATE INFORMATION

ADMISSION INQUIRIES
John Swiney
Director
California State University, Chico
400 West First Street, Colusa Hall, Room 101
Chico, CA 95929-0722
Phone: (530) 898-6322
Fax: (530) 898-6456
Email: jswiney@csuchico.edu

ESTIMATED STUDENT EXPENSES (FALL 2006)
[Expenses are for the 2006-2007 nine-month academic year and are based on an average credit load of: Undergraduate: N/A]

	In-State	Out-of-State
Tutition and Fees:	$3,412	$13,582
Campus and Room and Board:	$8,314	$8,314
Books and Supplies:	$1,219	$1,219
Other Expenses:	$2,132	$2,132
Total Estimated Expenses:	**$15,077**	**$25,247**

Note: Student expenses are for the 2005-2006 academic year. Non-residents of California pay an additional tuition of $339 per unit (included in tuition and fees above).

NEW APPLICANTS/NEWLY ENROLLED STUDENTS
[Numbers are for the undergraduate engineering college for the Fall 2006 term]

Number of Applicants (a):	899
Of those, Number Offered Admission (b):	756
Of those, Number Enrolled Fall 2006 (c):	151

Note: High school rank not available.

GRADUATE INFORMATION

ESTIMATED STUDENT EXPENSES (FALL 2006)
[Expenses are for the 2006-2007 nine-month academic year and are based on an average credit load of: Graduate: N/A]

	In-State	Out-of-State
Tutition and Fees:	$3,412	$13,582
Campus and Room and Board:	$8,314	$8,314
Books and Supplies:	$1,219	$1,219
Other Expenses:	$2,132	$2,132
Total Estimated Expenses:	**$15,077**	**$25,247**

Note: Student expenses are for the 2005-2006 academic year. Non-residents of California pay an additional tuition of $339 per unit (included in tuition and fees above).

California State University, Fullerton

INSTITUTION INFORMATION
College of Engineering & Computer Science
P.O. Box 6870
Fullerton, CA 92834
Phone: (714) 278-3362
Fax: (714) 278-7108
Web: http://www.fullerton.edu/ecs

GENERAL INFORMATION
[All Students - Fall 2006]

Undergraduate Enrollment	29,026
Graduate Enrollment	5,361
Professional Enrollment	0
Total Enrollment	**34,387**

ENGINEERING COLLEGE INFORMATION

TYPES OF ENGINEERING DEGREES
Bachelor's: B.S.
Master's: M.S. with thesis, M.S. without thesis, but with project or report
Doctoral:

UNDERGRADUATE INFORMATION

ESTIMATED STUDENT EXPENSES (FALL 2006)
[Expenses are for the 2006-2007 nine-month academic year and are based on an average credit load of: Undergraduate: 12]

	In-State	Out-of-State
Tuition and Fees:	$3,030	$12,000
Campus and Room and Board:	$8,000	$8,000
Books and Supplies:	$700	$700
Other Expenses:	$4,000	$5,236
Total Estimated Expenses:	**$15,730**	**$25,936**

*Note: *Estimated Student Expenses are based on one academic year.*
**Group 1-Undergraduate Room & Board estimated amount is based on living in Campus Housing, all Room & Board amounts are variable.*
***Group 1-Undergraduate and Graduate Estimated Avg. credit load per term is 7 units or more.*

NEW APPLICANTS/NEWLY ENROLLED STUDENTS
[Numbers are for the undergraduate engineering college for the Fall 2006 term]

Number of Applicants (a):	2,589
Of those, Number Offered Admission (b):	1,591
Of those, Number Enrolled Fall 2006 (c):	323

GRADUATE INFORMATION

ESTIMATED STUDENT EXPENSES (FALL 2006)
[Expenses are for the 2006-2007 nine-month academic year and are based on an average credit load of: Graduate: 6]

	In-State	Out-of-State
Tuition and Fees:	$3,612	$12,500
Campus and Room and Board:	$8,000	$8,000
Books and Supplies:	$700	$700
Other Expenses:	$4,000	$5,000
Total Estimated Expenses:	**$16,312**	**$26,200**

*Note: *Estimated Student Expenses are based on one academic year.*
**Group 1-Undergraduate Room & Board estimated amount is based on living in Campus Housing, all Room & Board amounts are variable.*
***Group 1-Undergraduate and Graduate Estimated Avg. credit load per term is 7 units or more.*

NEW APPLICANTS/NEWLY ENROLLED STUDENTS
[Numbers are for the graduate engineering college for the Fall 2006 term]

Number of Applicants (a):	420
Of those, Number Offered Admission (b):	287
Of those, Number Enrolled Fall 2006 (c):	153

California State University, Long Beach

INSTITUTION INFORMATION
1250 Bellflower Boulevard
Long Beach, CA 90840
Phone: (562) 985-4111
Web: http://www.csulb.edu

GENERAL INFORMATION
[All Students - Fall 2006]

Undergraduate Enrollment	29,578
Graduate Enrollment	5,998
Professional Enrollment	0
Total Enrollment	**35,576**

ENGINEERING COLLEGE INFORMATION

HEAD OF ENGINEERING
Sandy Cynar
Interim Dean
California State University, Long Beach
1250 Bellflower Boulevard
Long Beach, CA 90840
Phone: (562) 985-4111

ENGINEERING COLLEGE INQUIRIES
Hamid Hefazi
Chair of Mechanical and Aerospace Engineering
California State University, Long Beach
1250 Bellflower Boulevard
Long Beach, CA 90840
Phone: (562) 985-1502

ENGINEERING COLLEGE INQUIRIES
Rajendra Kumar
Chair of Electrical Engineering
California State University, Long Beach
1250 Bellflower Boulevard
Long Beach, CA 90840
Phone: (562) 985-1556
Email: kumar@csulb.edu

ENGINEERING COLLEGE INQUIRIES
Larry Jang
Chair of Chemical Engineering
California State University, Long Beach
1250 Bellflower Boulevard
Long Beach, CA 90840
Phone: (562) 985-7533

ENGINEERING COLLEGE INQUIRIES
Steve Tsai
Chair, Civil Engineering and Construction Engineering Management
California State University, Long Beach
1250 Bellflower Boulevard
Long Beach, CA 90840
Phone: (562) 985-4111

ENGINEERING COLLEGE INQUIRIES
Tesfai Goitom
Construction Engineering Management Coordinator
California State University, Long Beach
1250 Bellflower Boulevard
Long Beach, CA 90840
Phone: (562) 985-4111
Email: tgg@csulb.edu

TYPES OF ENGINEERING DEGREES
Bachelor's: B.S.
Master's: M.S. with thesis, M.S. without thesis, but with project or report
Doctoral: Ph.D.

UNDERGRADUATE INFORMATION

ADMISSION INQUIRIES
Wayne Dick
Chair of Computer Engineering and Computer Science
California State University, Long Beach
1250 Bellflower Boulevard
Long Beach, CA 90840
Phone: (562) 985-1551

ESTIMATED STUDENT EXPENSES (FALL 2006)
[Expenses are for the 2006-2007 nine-month academic year and are based on an average credit load of: Undergraduate: N/A]

	In-State	Out-of-State
Tutition and Fees:	$2,864	$11,000
Campus and Room and Board:		
Books and Supplies:		
Other Expenses:		
Total Estimated Expenses:	**$2,864**	**$11,000**

GRADUATE INFORMATION

ESTIMATED STUDENT EXPENSES (FALL 2006)
[Expenses are for the 2006-2007 nine-month academic year and are based on an average credit load of: Graduate: N/A]

	In-State	Out-of-State
Tutition and Fees:	$3,446	$11,000
Campus and Room and Board:		
Books and Supplies:		
Other Expenses:		
Total Estimated Expenses:	**$3,446**	**$11,000**

California State University, Los Angeles

INSTITUTION INFORMATION
Engineering, Computer Science, and Technology
5151 State University Drive

Los Angeles, CA 90032
Phone: (323) 343-4500
Fax: (323) 343-4555
Web: http://ecst.calstatela.edu

GENERAL INFORMATION
[All Students - Fall 2006]
Undergraduate Enrollment   14,955
Graduate Enrollment   5,079
Professional Enrollment   0
Total Enrollment   20,034

ENGINEERING COLLEGE INFORMATION

HEAD OF ENGINEERING
Keith Moo-Young
Dean
College of Engineering, Computer Science, and Technology
California State University, Los Angeles
5151 State University Drive
Los Angeles, CA 90032
Phone: (323) 343-4500
Fax: (323) 343-4555
Email: kmooyou@calstatela.edu

ENGINEERING COLLEGE INQUIRIES
David Linnevers
Outreach, Advising and Retention Director
California State University, Los Angeles
5151 State University Drive
Los Angeles, CA 90032
Phone: (323) 343-5604
Fax: (323) 343-4555
Email: dlinnev@calstatela.edu

TYPES OF ENGINEERING DEGREES
Bachelor's: B.S.
Master's: M.S. with thesis, M.S. without thesis, but with project or report
Doctoral:

UNDERGRADUATE INFORMATION

ADMISSION INQUIRIES
David Linnevers
Outreach, Advising and Retention Director
California State University, Los Angeles
5151 State University Drive
Los Angeles, CA 90032
Phone: (323) 343-5604
Fax: (323) 343-4555
Email: dlinnev@calstatela.edu

ESTIMATED STUDENT EXPENSES (FALL 2006)
[Expenses are for the 2006-2007 nine-month academic year and are based on an average credit load of: Undergraduate: 12]

	In-State	Out-of-State
Tuition and Fees:	$3,077	$11,213
Campus and Room and Board:	$3,717	$3,717
Books and Supplies:	$3,000	$3,000
Other Expenses:	$3,500	$3,500
Total Estimated Expenses:	**$13,294**	**$21,430**

Note: Not Reflected in these totals, non-residents pay an $226/unit for out of state tuition plus the normal student per quarter fees.

NEW APPLICANTS/NEWLY ENROLLED STUDENTS
[Numbers are for the undergraduate engineering college for the Fall 2006 term]
Number of Applicants (a):   2,018
Of those, Number Offered Admission (b):   1,111
Of those, Number Enrolled Fall 2006 (c):   250
Note: Total includes transfer students. Transfer students make up a significant portion of our enrollment.

GRADUATE INFORMATION

ADMISSION INQUIRIES
David Linnevers
Outreach, Advising and Retention Director
California State University, Los Angeles
5151 State University Drive
Los Angeles , CA 90032
Phone: (323) 343-5604
Fax: (323) 343-4555
Email: dlinnev@calstatela.edu

ESTIMATED STUDENT EXPENSES (FALL 2006)
[Expenses are for the 2006-2007 nine-month academic year and are based on an average credit load of: Graduate: 12]

	In-State	Out-of-State
Tuition and Fees:	$3,659	$11,795
Campus and Room and Board:	$3,717	$3,717
Books and Supplies:	$3,000	$3,000
Other Expenses:	$3,500	$3,500
Total Estimated Expenses:	**$13,876**	**$22,012**

Note: Not Reflected in these totals, non-residents pay an $226/unit for out of state tuition plus the normal student per quarter fees.

California State University, Northridge

INSTITUTION INFORMATION
18111 Nordhoff Street
Northridge, CA 91330
Phone: (818) 677-1200
Web: http://www.csun.edu

GENERAL INFORMATION
[All Students - Fall 2006]
Undergraduate Enrollment   28,281
Graduate Enrollment   6,279
Professional Enrollment   0
Total Enrollment   34,560

ENGINEERING COLLEGE INFORMATION

HEAD OF ENGINEERING
S.K. Ramesh
Dean
Dean's Office
California State University, Northridge
College of Engineering and Computer Science
18111 Nordhoff Street
Northridge, CA 91330-8295
Phone: (818) 677-4501
Fax: (818) 677-2140
Email: mau@csun.edu

ENGINEERING COLLEGE INQUIRIES
Yervant Aghishian
Academic Advisor
California State University, Northridge
18111 Nordhoff Street
Northridge, CA 91330-8295
Phone: (818) 677-2569
Fax: (818) 677-2140
Email: yervant.aghishian@csun.edu

TYPES OF ENGINEERING DEGREES
Bachelor's: B.S.
Master's: M.S. with thesis, M.S. without thesis, but with project or report
Doctoral:

UNDERGRADUATE INFORMATION

ADMISSION INQUIRIES
Yervant Aghishian
Academic Advisor
California State University, Northridge
18111 Nordhoff Street
Northridge, CA 91330-8295
Phone: (818) 677-2569
Fax: (818) 677-2140
Email: yervant.aghishian@csun.edu

ESTIMATED STUDENT EXPENSES (FALL 2006)
[Expenses are for the 2006-2007 nine-month academic year and are based on an average credit load of: Undergraduate: N/A]

	In-State	Out-of-State
Tuition and Fees:	$3,042	
Campus and Room and Board:	$9,328	
Books and Supplies:	$1,314	
Other Expenses:	$2,520	
Total Estimated Expenses:	**$16,204**	

Note: Tuition and fees are based on an academic year for full-time students. Fees do not include an additional $542 in miscellaneous fees per semester.

NEW APPLICANTS/NEWLY ENROLLED STUDENTS
[Numbers are for the undergraduate engineering college for the Fall 2006 term]

Number of Applicants (a):   1,419
Of those, Number Offered Admission (b):   965
Of those, Number Enrolled Fall 2006 (c):   454
Note: Top 25% cannot be listed because the CSU system has to accept the top third of high school students who apply.

GRADUATE INFORMATION

ADMISSION INQUIRIES
Ali Amini
Professor
California State University, Northridge
18111 Nordhoff Street
Northridge , CA 91330-8346
Phone: (818) 677-3609
Fax: (818) 677-7062
Email: amini@ecs.csun.edu

ADMISSION INQUIRIES
Sidney H Schwartz
Professor and Chair, Mechanical Engineering Department
California State University, Northridge
College of Engineering and Comp. Science, 18111 Nordhoff Street
Northridge , CA 91330-8295
Phone: (818) 677-3884
Fax: (818) 677-7062
Email: sid.schwartz@csun.edu

ADMISSION INQUIRIES
Bonita Campbell
Professor and Department Chair
California State University, Northridge
College of Engineering and Computer Science, 18111 Nordhoff Street
Northridge , CA 91330-8332
Phone: (818) 677-2484
Fax: (818) 677-6427
Email: bjc20362@csun.edu

ADMISSION INQUIRIES
Roger Di Julio
Professor
California State University, Northridge
College of Engineering and Computer Sci., 18111 Nordhoff Street
Northridge , CA 91330-8347
Phone: (818) 677-3904
Fax: (818) 677-5810
Email: rdijulio@csun.edu

ADMISSION INQUIRIES
Richard J Lorentz
Professor
California State University, Northridge
College of Engineering and Computer Sci., 18111 Nordhoff Street
Northridge , CA 91330-8281
Phone: (818) 677-3388
Fax: (818) 677-7208
Email: lorentz@csun.edu

ESTIMATED STUDENT EXPENSES (FALL 2006)
[Expenses are for the 2006-2007 nine-month academic year and are based on an average credit load of: Graduate: N/A]

	In-State	Out-of-State
Tuition and Fees:	$3,642	
Campus and Room and Board:	$8,800	
Books and Supplies:	$1,242	
Other Expenses:	$2,500	
Total Estimated Expenses:	**$16,184**	

Note: Tuition and fees are based on an academic year for full-time students. Fees do not include an additional $542 in miscellaneous fees per semester.

NEW APPLICANTS/NEWLY ENROLLED STUDENTS
[Numbers are for the graduate engineering college for the Fall 2006 term]
Number of Applicants (a):   461
Of those, Number Offered Admission (b):   271
Of those, Number Enrolled Fall 2006 (c):   190

University of California, Berkeley

INSTITUTION INFORMATION
University of California, Berkeley
Berkeley, CA 94720

Phone: (510) 642-6000
Web: http://www.berkeley.edu

GENERAL INFORMATION

[All Students - Fall 2006]
Undergraduate Enrollment 23,863
Graduate Enrollment 7,342
Professional Enrollment 2,728
Total Enrollment **33,933**

ENGINEERING COLLEGE INFORMATION

HEAD OF ENGINEERING

A Richard Newton
Dean
College of Engineering
University of California, Berkeley
320 McLaughlin Hall # 1700
University of California
Berkeley, CA 94720-1700
Phone: (510) 642-5771
Fax: (510) 642-9178
Email: newton@coe.berkeley.edu

ENGINEERING COLLEGE INQUIRIES

Fiona M Doyle
Executive Associate Dean
University of California, Berkeley
308 McLaughlin Hall # 1702
Berkeley, CA 94720-1702
Phone: (510) 642-7594
Fax: (510) 643-8653
Email: fmdoyle@berkeley.edu

TYPES OF ENGINEERING DEGREES

Bachelor's: B.A., B.S.
Master's: M.S. with thesis, M.S. without thesis, but with project or report, M.Eng.
Doctoral: Ph.D., D.Eng

UNDERGRADUATE INFORMATION

ADMISSION INQUIRIES

Fiona M Doyle
Executive Associate Dean
University of California, Berkeley
308 McLaughlin Hall # 1702
Berkeley, CA 94720-1702
Phone: (510) 642-7594
Fax: (510) 643-8653
Email: fmdoyle@berkeley.edu

ESTIMATED STUDENT EXPENSES (FALL 2006)

[Expenses are for the 2006-2007 nine-month academic year and are based on an average credit load of: Undergraduate: 15]

	In-State	Out-of-State
Tuition and Fees:	$7,704	
Campus and Room and Board:	$13,074	
Books and Supplies:	$1,326	
Other Expenses:	$1,388	
Total Estimated Expenses:	**$23,492**	

NEW APPLICANTS/NEWLY ENROLLED STUDENTS

[Numbers are for the undergraduate engineering college for the Fall 2006 term]
Number of Applicants (a): 6,894
Of those, Number Offered Admission (b): 1,553
Of those, Number Enrolled Fall 2006 (c): 657

GRADUATE INFORMATION

ADMISSION INQUIRIES

Gregory L Fenves
Chair
University of California, Berkeley
760 Davis Hall # 1710
Berkeley, CA 94720-1710
Phone: (510) 642-3261
Fax: (510) 643-5264
Email: fenves@berkeley.edu

ADMISSION INQUIRIES

Albert P Pisano
Chair
University of California, Berkeley
6195 Etcheverry Hall # 1740
Berkeley, CA 94720-1740
Phone: (510) 642-1338
Fax: (510) 642-6163
Email: appisano@me.berkeley.edu

ADMISSION INQUIRIES

Robert O Ritchie
Chair
University of California, Berkeley
210 Hearst Memorial Mining Bldg # 1760
Berkeley, CA 94720-1760
Phone: (510) 642-3801
Fax: (510) 643-5792
Email: ritchie@berkeley.edu

ADMISSION INQUIRIES

Dorian Liepmann
Chair
University of California, Berkeley
459 Evans Hall # 1762
Berkeley, CA 94720-1762
Phone: (510) 642-5833
Fax: (510) 642-5835
Email: liepmann@me.berkeley.edu

ADMISSION INQUIRIES

Jeffrey A Reimer
Chair
University of California, Berkeley
201 Gilman Hall # 1462
Berkeley, CA 94720-1462
Phone: (510) 642-2291
Fax: (510) 642-4778
Email: reimer@berkeley.edu

ADMISSION INQUIRIES

Jasmina L Vujic
Chair
University of California, Berkeley
4155 Etcheverry Hall # 1730
Berkeley, CA 94720-1730
Phone: (510) 642-0574
Fax: (510) 643-9685
Email: vujic@nuc.berkeley.edu

ADMISSION INQUIRIES

Edward A Lee
Chair
University of California, Berkeley
231 Cory Hall # 1770
Berkeley, CA 94720-1770
Phone: (510) 642-0253
Fax: (510) 642-2845
Email: eal@eecs.berkeley.edu

ADMISSION INQUIRIES

Ilan Adler
Chair
University of California, Berkeley
4175 Etcheverry Hall # 1777
Berkeley, CA 94720-1777
Phone: (510) 642-5484
Fax: (510) 643-8992
Email: adler@ieor.berkeley.edu

ESTIMATED STUDENT EXPENSES (FALL 2006)

[Expenses are for the 2006-2007 nine-month academic year and are based on an average credit load of: Graduate: 12]

	In-State	Out-of-State
Tuition and Fees:	$8,867	
Campus and Room and Board:	$14,608	
Books and Supplies:	$1,006	
Other Expenses:	$2,262	
Total Estimated Expenses:	**$26,743**	

NEW APPLICANTS/NEWLY ENROLLED STUDENTS

[Numbers are for the graduate engineering college for the Fall 2006 term]
Number of Applicants (a): 4,988
Of those, Number Offered Admission (b): 918
Of those, Number Enrolled Fall 2006 (c): 394

University of California, Davis

INSTITUTION INFORMATION

Engineering Dean's Office
One Shields Avenue
Davis, CA 95616
Phone: (530) 752-1979
Fax: (530) 752-8058
Web: http://engineering.ucdavis.edu

GENERAL INFORMATION

[All Students - Fall 2006]
Undergraduate Enrollment 23,546
Graduate Enrollment 4,150
Professional Enrollment 1,932
Total Enrollment **29,628**

ENGINEERING COLLEGE INFORMATION

HEAD OF ENGINEERING

Enrique J Lavernia
Dean
College of Engineering
University of California, Davis
One Shields Avenue
Davis, CA 95616
Phone: (530) 752-0554
Fax: (530) 752-8058
Email: lavernia@ucdavis.edu

TYPES OF ENGINEERING DEGREES

Bachelor's: B.S.
Master's: M.S. with thesis, M.S. without thesis, but with project or report, M.Eng.
Doctoral: Ph.D., D.Eng

UNDERGRADUATE INFORMATION

ADMISSION INQUIRIES

Gary Ford
Associate Dean, Undergraduate Studies
University of California, Davis
One Shields Avenue
Davis, CA 95616
Phone: (530) 752-0556
Fax: (530) 752-2123
Email: geford@ucdavis.edu

ADMISSION INQUIRIES

Wesley Young
Director, Services to International Students and Scholars
University of California, Davis
One Shields Avenue
Davis, CA 95616
Phone: (530) 752-7879
Fax: (530) 752-5822
Email: wryoung@ucdavis.edu

ESTIMATED STUDENT EXPENSES (FALL 2006)

[Expenses are for the 2006-2007 nine-month academic year and are based on an average credit load of: Undergraduate: 15]

	In-State	Out-of-State
Tuition and Fees:	$8,323	$27,007
Campus and Room and Board:	$11,239	$11,239
Books and Supplies:	$1,514	$1,514
Other Expenses:	$2,167	$2,167
Total Estimated Expenses:	**$23,243**	**$41,927**

NEW APPLICANTS/NEWLY ENROLLED STUDENTS

[Numbers are for the undergraduate engineering college for the Fall 2006 term]
Number of Applicants (a): 5,369
Of those, Number Offered Admission (b): 3,364
Of those, Number Enrolled Fall 2006 (c): 701

GRADUATE INFORMATION

ADMISSION INQUIRIES

Donna Davies
Student Affairs Office, Graduate Engineering
University of California, Davis
Engineering Dean's Office, One Shields Avenue
Davis, CA 95616
Phone: (530) 752-0592
Fax: (530) 752-8058
Email: dedavies@ucdavis.edu

ADMISSION INQUIRIES

Karen McDonald
Associate Dean, Research and Graduate Studies
University of California, Davis
One Shields Avenue
Davis, CA 95616
Phone: (530) 752-0559
Fax: (530) 752-8058
Email: kamcdonald@ucdavis.edu

ADMISSION INQUIRIES
Wesley Young
Director, Services to International Students and Scholars
University of California, Davis
One Shields Avenue
Davis , CA 95616
Phone: (530) 752-7879
Fax: (530) 752-5822
Email: wryoung@ucdavis.edu

ESTIMATED STUDENT EXPENSES (FALL 2006)
[Expenses are for the 2006-2007 nine-month academic year and are based on an average credit load of: Graduate: 15]

	In-State	Out-of-State
Tuition and Fees:	$9,142	$24,103
Campus and Room and Board:	$11,004	$11,004
Books and Supplies:	$1,102	$1,102
Other Expenses:	$3,549	$3,549
Total Estimated Expenses:	**$24,797**	**$39,758**

NEW APPLICANTS/NEWLY ENROLLED STUDENTS
[Numbers are for the graduate engineering college for the Fall 2006 term]
Number of Applicants (a): 2,216
Of those, Number Offered Admission (b): 761
Of those, Number Enrolled Fall 2006 (c): 246

University of California, Irvine

INSTITUTION INFORMATION
305 Rockwell Engineering Center
The Henry Samueli School of Engineering
Irvine, CA 92697-2700
Phone: (949) 824-4333
Fax: (949) 824-7966
Web: http://www.uci.edu

GENERAL INFORMATION
[All Students - Fall 2006]
Undergraduate Enrollment 20,698
Graduate Enrollment 3,799
Professional Enrollment 2,145
Total Enrollment **26,642**

ENGINEERING COLLEGE INFORMATION

HEAD OF ENGINEERING
Nicolaos G Alexopoulos
Henry Samueli School of Engineering Dean, Professor
Engineering Dean's Office, Electrical Engineering &
Computer Science
University of California, Irvine
305 Rockwell Engineering Center
Henry Samueli School of Engineering
Irvine, CA 92697-2700
Phone: (949) 824-6002
Fax: (949) 824-7966
Email: alfios@uci.edu

TYPES OF ENGINEERING DEGREES
Bachelor's: B.S.
Master's: M.S. with thesis, M.S. without thesis, but with project or report
Doctoral: Ph.D.

UNDERGRADUATE INFORMATION

ADMISSION INQUIRIES
Kimberly S Perry
Engineering Admissions Counselor
University of California, Irvine
204 Administration, Admissions & Relations with Schools
Irvine, CA 92697-1075
Phone: (949) 824-2552
Fax: (949) 824-2951
Email: ksperry@uci.edu

ESTIMATED STUDENT EXPENSES (FALL 2006)
[Expenses are for the 2006-2007 nine-month academic year and are based on an average credit load of: Undergraduate: 16]

	In-State	Out-of-State
Tuition and Fees:	$7,607	$26,291
Campus and Room and Board:	$9,815	$9,815
Books and Supplies:	$1,631	$1,631
Other Expenses:	$2,898	$2,898
Total Estimated Expenses:	**$21,951**	**$40,635**

Note: Tuition and fees are subject to change without notice.

NEW APPLICANTS/NEWLY ENROLLED STUDENTS
[Numbers are for the undergraduate engineering college for the Fall 2006 term]
Number of Applicants (a): 5,812
Of those, Number Offered Admission (b): 3,336
Of those, Number Enrolled Fall 2006 (c): 567

GRADUATE INFORMATION

ADMISSION INQUIRIES
Sonja Krause-Burkins
Interim Director, Graduate Student Affairs
University of California, Irvine
101 Engineering & Computing Trailer, Henry Samueli
School of Engineering
Irvine , CA 92697-2710
Phone: (949) 824-3562
Fax: (949) 824-3440
Email: skrauseb@uci.edu

ESTIMATED STUDENT EXPENSES (FALL 2006)
[Expenses are for the 2006-2007 nine-month academic year and are based on an average credit load of: Graduate: 12]

	In-State	Out-of-State
Tuition and Fees:	$9,670	$24,631
Campus and Room and Board:	$14,425	$14,425
Books and Supplies:	$2,729	$2,729
Other Expenses:	$3,958	$3,958
Total Estimated Expenses:	**$30,782**	**$45,743**

Note: Tuition and fees are subject to change without notice.

NEW APPLICANTS/NEWLY ENROLLED STUDENTS
[Numbers are for the graduate engineering college for the Fall 2006 term]
Number of Applicants (a): 2,005
Of those, Number Offered Admission (b): 539
Of those, Number Enrolled Fall 2006 (c): 175

University of California, Los Angeles

INSTITUTION INFORMATION
Henry Samueli School of Engineering & Applied Science
6412 Boelter Hall, UCLA Box 90095-1601
Los Angeles, CA 90095-1601
Phone: (310) 825-2942
Fax: (310) 825-2473
Web: http://www.engineer.ucla.edu/

GENERAL INFORMATION
[All Students - Fall 2006]
Undergraduate Enrollment 25,432
Graduate Enrollment 9,247
Professional Enrollment 3,539
Total Enrollment **38,218**

ENGINEERING COLLEGE INFORMATION

HEAD OF ENGINEERING
Vijay K. Dhir
Dean
Henry Samueli School of Engineering and Applied
Science
University of California, Los Angeles
7400 Boelter Hall
405 Hilgard Ave.
Los Angeles, CA 90095
Phone: (310) 825-8507
Email: vdhir@seas.ucla.edu

TYPES OF ENGINEERING DEGREES
Bachelor's: B.S.
Master's: M.S. with thesis, M.S. without thesis, but with project or report
Doctoral: Ph.D.

UNDERGRADUATE INFORMATION

ESTIMATED STUDENT EXPENSES (FALL 2006)
[Expenses are for the 2006-2007 nine-month academic year and are based on an average credit load of: Undergraduate: 16]

	In-State	Out-of-State
Tuition and Fees:	$7,143	$25,827
Campus and Room and Board:	$12,312	$12,312
Books and Supplies:	$1,554	$1,554

| Other Expenses: | $2,283 | $2,283 |
| **Total Estimated Expenses:** | **$23,292** | **$41,976** |

NEW APPLICANTS/NEWLY ENROLLED STUDENTS
[Numbers are for the undergraduate engineering college for the Fall 2006 term]
Number of Applicants (a): 7,430
Of those, Number Offered Admission (b): 2,143
Of those, Number Enrolled Fall 2006 (c): 664
Note: We do not have separate Math ACT scores.

GRADUATE INFORMATION

ESTIMATED STUDENT EXPENSES (FALL 2006)
[Expenses are for the 2006-2007 nine-month academic year and are based on an average credit load of: Graduate: 12]

	In-State	Out-of-State
Tuition and Fees:	$8,285	$23,246
Campus and Room and Board:	$12,927	$12,927
Books and Supplies:	$1,881	$1,881
Other Expenses:	$5,100	$5,100
Total Estimated Expenses:	**$28,193**	**$43,154**

NEW APPLICANTS/NEWLY ENROLLED STUDENTS
[Numbers are for the graduate engineering college for the Fall 2006 term]
Number of Applicants (a): 2,913
Of those, Number Offered Admission (b): 1,043
Of those, Number Enrolled Fall 2006 (c): 404

University of California, Riverside

INSTITUTION INFORMATION
Bourns College of Engineering
College of Engineering
Riverside, CA 92521
Phone: (951) 827-5190
Fax: (951) 827-3188
Web: http://www.engr.ucr.edu/

GENERAL INFORMATION
[All Students - Fall 2006]
Undergraduate Enrollment 14,792
Graduate Enrollment 2,034
Professional Enrollment 49
Total Enrollment **16,875**

ENGINEERING COLLEGE INFORMATION

HEAD OF ENGINEERING
Reza Abbaschian
Dean
The Marlan & Rosemary Bourns College of Engrg.
University of California, Riverside
Office of the Dean
College of Engineering
Riverside, CA 92521
Phone: (951) 827-6374
Fax: (951) 827-3188
Email: rabba@engr.ucr.edu

TYPES OF ENGINEERING DEGREES
Bachelor's: B.S.
Master's: M.S. with thesis, M.S. without thesis, but with project or report
Doctoral: Ph.D.

UNDERGRADUATE INFORMATION

ESTIMATED STUDENT EXPENSES (FALL 2006)
[Expenses are for the 2006-2007 nine-month academic year and are based on an average credit load of: Undergraduate: 16]

	In-State	Out-of-State
Tuition and Fees:	$7,316	$26,000
Campus and Room and Board:	$10,200	$10,200
Books and Supplies:	$1,700	$1,700
Other Expenses:	$4,000	$4,000
Total Estimated Expenses:	**$23,216**	**$41,900**

Note: Room & Board expenses are for on-campus undergrads & off-campus grads.

NEW APPLICANTS/NEWLY ENROLLED STUDENTS
[Numbers are for the undergraduate engineering college for the Fall 2006 term]
Number of Applicants (a): 3,522

Of those, Number Offered Admission (b): 3,037
Of those, Number Enrolled Fall 2006 (c): 413

GRADUATE INFORMATION

ESTIMATED STUDENT EXPENSES (FALL 2006)
[Expenses are for the 2006-2007 nine-month academic year and are based on an average credit load of: Graduate: 12]

	In-State	Out-of-State
Tuition and Fees:	$8,934	$23,895
Campus and Room and Board:	$10,200	$10,200
Books and Supplies:	$1,700	$1,700
Other Expenses:	$4,000	$4,000
Total Estimated Expenses:	**$24,834**	**$39,795**

Note: Room & Board expenses are for on-campus under-grads & off-campus grads.

NEW APPLICANTS/NEWLY ENROLLED STUDENTS
[Numbers are for the graduate engineering college for the Fall 2006 term]

Number of Applicants (a): 645
Of those, Number Offered Admission (b): 195
Of those, Number Enrolled Fall 2006 (c): 81

University of California, San Diego

INSTITUTION INFORMATION
Jacobs School of Engineering
9500 Gilman Drive
La Jolla, CA 92093
Phone: (858) 534-2230
Web: http://www.ucsd.edu

GENERAL INFORMATION
[All Students - Fall 2006]

Undergraduate Enrollment	21,369
Graduate Enrollment	4,050
Professional Enrollment	1,287
Total Enrollment	**26,706**

ENGINEERING COLLEGE INFORMATION

HEAD OF ENGINEERING
Frieder Seible
Dean, Jacobs School of Engineering
Jacobs School of Engineering
University of California, San Diego
9500 Gilman Drive #0403
La Jolla, CA 92093
Phone: (858) 534-6237
Fax: (858) 822-3904
Email: fseible@ucsd.edu

TYPES OF ENGINEERING DEGREES
Bachelor's: B.A., B.S.
Master's: M.S. with thesis, M.S. without thesis, but with project or report, M.Eng.
Doctoral: Ph.D.

UNDERGRADUATE INFORMATION

ADMISSION INQUIRIES
Undergraduate Admission Inquiries
University of California, San Diego
Jacobs School of Engineering, 9500 Gilman Drive #0429
a Jolla, CA 92093
Phone: (858) 534-6105
Fax: (858) 534-2095
Email: ess@soe.ucsd.edu

ESTIMATED STUDENT EXPENSES (FALL 2006)
[Expenses are for the 2006-2007 nine-month academic year and are based on an average credit load of: Undergraduate: 16]

	In-State	Out-of-State
Tuition and Fees:	$7,423	$18,684
Campus and Room and Board:	$9,657	$9,657
Books and Supplies:	$1,505	$1,505
Other Expenses:	$3,505	$3,505
Total Estimated Expenses:	**$22,090**	**$33,351**

NEW APPLICANTS/NEWLY ENROLLED STUDENTS
[Numbers are for the undergraduate engineering college for the Fall 2006 term]

Number of Applicants (a): 6,856
Of those, Number Offered Admission (b): 3,477
Of those, Number Enrolled Fall 2006 (c): 863

GRADUATE INFORMATION

ADMISSION INQUIRIES
Graduate Admission Inquiries
University of California, San Diego
Jacobs School of Engineering, 9500 Gilman Drive #0429
La Jolla , CA 92093
Phone: (858) 534-6105
Fax: (858) 534-2095
Email: ess@soe.ucsd.edu

ESTIMATED STUDENT EXPENSES (FALL 2006)
[Expenses are for the 2006-2007 nine-month academic year and are based on an average credit load of: Graduate: 12]

	In-State	Out-of-State
Tuition and Fees:	$8,612	$23,573
Campus and Room and Board:	$9,657	$9,657
Books and Supplies:	$1,505	$1,505
Other Expenses:	$3,505	$3,505
Total Estimated Expenses:	**$23,279**	**$38,240**

NEW APPLICANTS/NEWLY ENROLLED STUDENTS
[Numbers are for the graduate engineering college for the Fall 2006 term]

Number of Applicants (a): 4,197
Of those, Number Offered Admission (b): 922
Of those, Number Enrolled Fall 2006 (c): 347

University of California, Santa Barbara

INSTITUTION INFORMATION
University of California, Santa Barbara
Santa Barbara, CA 93106
Phone: (805) 893-8000
Web: http://www.ucsb.edu

ENGINEERING COLLEGE INFORMATION

HEAD OF ENGINEERING
Gary S Hansen
Associate Dean, Technology Management Programs
College of Engineering
University of California, Santa Barbara
Santa Barbara, CA 93106-5130
Phone: (805) 893-5328

HEAD OF ENGINEERING
Matthew Tirrell
Dean
College of Engineering
University of California, Santa Barbara
College of Engineering
Engr. I, room 1030
Santa Barbara, CA 93106-5130
Phone: (805) 893-4802
Fax: (805) 893-8124
Email: tirrell@engineering.ucsb.edu

TYPES OF ENGINEERING DEGREES
Bachelor's: B.S.
Master's: M.S. with thesis, M.S. without thesis, but with project or report
Doctoral: Ph.D.

UNDERGRADUATE INFORMATION

ADMISSION INQUIRIES
Glenn E Beltz
Associate Dean for Undergraduate Studies
University of California, Santa Barbara
Harold Frank Hall, Room 1004
Santa Barbara, CA 93106-5130
Phone: (805) 893-3354
Fax: (805) 893-8124
Email: beltz@engineering.ucsb.edu

ESTIMATED STUDENT EXPENSES (FALL 2006)
[Expenses are for the 2006-2007 nine-month academic year and are based on an average credit load of: Undergraduate: 15]

	In-State	Out-of-State
Tuition and Fees:	$7,010	$25,694
Campus and Room and Board:	$11,178	$11,178
Books and Supplies:	$1,505	$1,505
Other Expenses:	$432	$432
Total Estimated Expenses:	**$20,125**	**$38,809**

Note: R&B is for On-Campus dorms.

NEW APPLICANTS/NEWLY ENROLLED STUDENTS
[Numbers are for the undergraduate engineering college for the Fall 2006 term]

Number of Applicants (a): 3,732
Of those, Number Offered Admission (b): 1,952
Of those, Number Enrolled Fall 2006 (c): 297

GRADUATE INFORMATION

ADMISSION INQUIRIES
Gale Morrison
Acting Dean
University of California, Santa Barbara
Santa Barbara , CA 93106-2070
Phone: (805) 893-2277

ESTIMATED STUDENT EXPENSES (FALL 2006)
[Expenses are for the 2006-2007 nine-month academic year and are based on an average credit load of: Graduate: 12]

	In-State	Out-of-State
Tuition and Fees:	$7,501	$22,462
Campus and Room and Board:	$8,986	$8,986
Books and Supplies:	$1,505	$1,505
Other Expenses:	$432	$432
Total Estimated Expenses:	**$18,424**	**$33,385**

Note: R&B is for On-Campus dorms.

University of California-Santa Cruz

INSTITUTION INFORMATION
Baskin School of Engineering
1156 High Street
Santa Cruz, CA 95064
Phone: (831) 459-2158
Fax: (831) 459-4046
Web: http://www.soe.ucsc.edu

GENERAL INFORMATION
[All Students - Fall 2006]

Undergraduate Enrollment	13,941
Graduate Enrollment	1,419
Professional Enrollment	0
Total Enrollment	**15,360**

ENGINEERING COLLEGE INFORMATION

HEAD OF ENGINEERING
Sung-Mo (Steve) Kang
Dean
School of Engineering
University of California-Santa Cruz
University of California
1156 High Street
Santa Cruz, CA 95064
Phone: (831) 459-2158
Fax: (831) 459-4046
Email: dean@soe.ucsc.edu

ENGINEERING COLLEGE INQUIRIES
Glen T Winans
Assistant Dean
University of California-Santa Cruz
Baskin School of Engineering, 1156 High Street
Santa Cruz, CA 95064
Phone: (831) 459-2158
Fax: (831) 459-4046
Email: dean@soe.ucsc.edu

TYPES OF ENGINEERING DEGREES
Bachelor's: B.A., B.S.
Master's: M.S. with thesis, M.S. without thesis, but with project or report
Doctoral: Ph.D.

UNDERGRADUATE INFORMATION

ADMISSION INQUIRIES
Charles McDowell
Professor and Associate Dean for Undergraduate Affairs
University of California-Santa Cruz
1156 High Street
Santa Cruz, CA 95064
Phone: (831) 459-4772
Fax: (831) 459-4482
Email: advising@soe.ucsc.edu

ESTIMATED STUDENT EXPENSES (FALL 2006)

[Expenses are for the 2006-2007 nine-month academic year and are based on an average credit load of: Undergraduate: 15]

	In-State	Out-of-State
Tuition and Fees:	$7,962	$26,646
Campus and Room and Board:	$11,805	$11,805
Books and Supplies:	$1,395	$1,395
Other Expenses:	$2,328	$2,328
Total Estimated Expenses:	**$23,490**	**$42,174**

NEW APPLICANTS/NEWLY ENROLLED STUDENTS

[Numbers are for the undergraduate engineering college for the Fall 2006 term]

Number of Applicants (a):	1,457
Of those, Number Offered Admission (b):	1,193
Of those, Number Enrolled Fall 2006 (c):	176

Note: See complete admission requirements.

GRADUATE INFORMATION

ADMISSION INQUIRIES

Darrell Long
Professor and Associate Dean for Graduate Studies and Research
University of California-Santa Cruz
1156 High Street
Santa Cruz , CA 95064
Phone: (831) 459-2158
Fax: (831) 459-4046
Email: soegradadm@soe.ucsc.edu

ESTIMATED STUDENT EXPENSES (FALL 2006)

[Expenses are for the 2006-2007 nine-month academic year and are based on an average credit load of: Graduate: 12]

	In-State	Out-of-State
Tuition and Fees:	$9,775	$24,736
Campus and Room and Board:	$12,816	$12,816
Books and Supplies:	$1,395	$1,395
Other Expenses:	$4,026	$4,026
Total Estimated Expenses:	**$28,012**	**$42,973**

NEW APPLICANTS/NEWLY ENROLLED STUDENTS

[Numbers are for the graduate engineering college for the Fall 2006 term]

Number of Applicants (a):	684
Of those, Number Offered Admission (b):	241
Of those, Number Enrolled Fall 2006 (c):	87

Capitol College

INSTITUTION INFORMATION

11301 Springfield Road
Laurel, MD 20708
Phone: (800) 950-1992
Fax: (301) 953-1442
Web: http://www.capitol-college.edu

ENGINEERING COLLEGE INFORMATION

HEAD OF ENGINEERING

Robert L Weiler
Vice President for Academic Affairs
Computers Engineering and Technology
Capitol College
11301 Springfield Road
Laurel, MD 20708
Phone: (301) 369-2800
Email: rweiler@capitol-college.edu

TYPES OF ENGINEERING DEGREES

Bachelor's: B.S.
Master's: M.S. without thesis, but with project or report
Doctoral:

UNDERGRADUATE INFORMATION

ADMISSION INQUIRIES

Robert L Weiler
Dean
Capitol College
11301 Springfield Road
Laurel, MD 20708
Phone: (301) 369-2800
Email: rweiler@capitol-college.edu

Carnegie Mellon University

INSTITUTION INFORMATION

College of Engineering, Dean's Office
Scaife Hall, Room 110
Pittsburgh, PA 15213
Phone: (412) 268-2479
Fax: (412) 268-6421
Web: http://www.cit.cmu.edu/

GENERAL INFORMATION

[All Students - Fall 2006]

Undergraduate Enrollment	5,580
Graduate Enrollment	4,451
Professional Enrollment	89
Total Enrollment	**10,120**

ENGINEERING COLLEGE INFORMATION

HEAD OF ENGINEERING

Pradeep K Khosla
Dean
Dean's Office, College of Engineering
Carnegie Mellon University
5000 Forbes Ave.
Pittsburgh, PA 15213
Phone: (412) 268-5090
Fax: (412) 268-6421
Email: pkk@ece.cmu.edu

TYPES OF ENGINEERING DEGREES

Bachelor's: B.S.
Master's: M.S. with thesis, M.S. without thesis, but with project or report
Doctoral: Ph.D.

UNDERGRADUATE INFORMATION

ADMISSION INQUIRIES

Michael Steidel
Director of Admissions
Carnegie Mellon University
5000 Forbes Ave.
Pittsburgh, PA 15213
Phone: (412) 268-2082
Fax: (412) 268-7838
Email: ms44@andrew.cmu.edu

ESTIMATED STUDENT EXPENSES (FALL 2006)

[Expenses are for the 2006-2007 nine-month academic year and are based on an average credit load of: Undergraduate: 12]

	All Students
Tuition and fees:	$34,768
Campus and Room and Board:	$9,280
Books and Supplies:	$945
Other Expenses:	$1,315
Total Estimated Expenses:	**$46,308**

Note: Other expenses include transportation, insurance & miscellaneous expenses.

NEW APPLICANTS/NEWLY ENROLLED STUDENTS

[Numbers are for the undergraduate engineering college for the Fall 2006 term]

Number of Applicants (a):	4,508
Of those, Number Offered Admission (b):	1,935
Of those, Number Enrolled Fall 2006 (c):	435

GRADUATE INFORMATION

ESTIMATED STUDENT EXPENSES (FALL 2006)

[Expenses are for the 2006-2007 nine-month academic year and are based on an average credit load of: Graduate: 12]

	All Students
Tuition and fees:	$32,788
Campus and Room and Board:	$10,150
Books and Supplies:	$945
Other Expenses:	$1,915
Total Estimated Expenses:	**$45,798**

Note: Other expenses include transportation, insurance & miscellaneous expenses.

Case Western Reserve University

INSTITUTION INFORMATION

10900 Euclid Avenue
Cleveland, OH 44106-7220
Phone: (216) 368-4436
Fax: (216) 368-6939
Web: http://www.engineering.case.edu

GENERAL INFORMATION

[All Students - Fall 2006]

Undergraduate Enrollment	4,305
Graduate Enrollment	3,941
Professional Enrollment	1,681
Total Enrollment	**9,927**

ENGINEERING COLLEGE INFORMATION

HEAD OF ENGINEERING

Robert F Savinell
Professor and Dean
Engineering Dean
Case Western Reserve University
10900 Euclid Avenue
500 Nord Hall
Cleveland, OH 44106-7220
Phone: (216) 368-4436
Fax: (216) 368-6939
Email: rfs2@case.edu

ENGINEERING COLLEGE INQUIRIES

James D McGuffin-Cawley
Professor and Associate Dean for Undergraduate Programs
Case Western Reserve University
10900 Euclid Avenue
Cleveland, OH 44106
Phone: (216) 368-6482
Fax: (216) 368-0327
Email: jxc41@po.cwru.edu

TYPES OF ENGINEERING DEGREES

Bachelor's: B.A., B.S.
Master's: M.S. with thesis, M.S. without thesis, but with project or report, M.Eng.
Doctoral: Ph.D.

UNDERGRADUATE INFORMATION

ADMISSION INQUIRIES

James D McGuffin-Cawley
Professor and Associate Dean for Undergraduate Programs
Case Western Reserve University
10900 Euclid Avenue
Cleveland, OH 44106
Phone: (216) 368-6482
Fax: (216) 368-0327
Email: jxc41@po.cwru.edu

ESTIMATED STUDENT EXPENSES (FALL 2006)

[Expenses are for the 2006-2007 nine-month academic year and are based on an average credit load of: Undergraduate: 12]

	All Students
Tuition and fees:	$30,240
Campus and Room and Board:	$7,802
Books and Supplies:	$1,400
Other Expenses:	$212
Total Estimated Expenses:	**$39,654 Note:**

All residential students are assessed a $400 technology fee to provide for technology access in the residence halls.

NEW APPLICANTS/NEWLY ENROLLED STUDENTS

[Numbers are for the undergraduate engineering college for the Fall 2006 term]

Number of Applicants (a):	7,508
Of those, Number Offered Admission (b):	5,002
Of those, Number Enrolled Fall 2006 (c):	1,015

Note: Represents applications for class entering 2006. Students apply to the university as a whole, not to the Case School of Engineering.

GRADUATE INFORMATION

ADMISSION INQUIRIES

John Blackwell
Professor and Associate Dean for Research & Graduate

Programs
Case Western Reserve University
10900 Euclid Avenue
Cleveland , OH 44106
Phone: (216) 368-4436
Fax: (216) 368-6939
Email: jxb6@cwru.edu

ESTIMATED STUDENT EXPENSES (FALL 2006)
[Expenses are for the 2006-2007 nine-month academic year and are based on an average credit load of: Graduate: 9]

	All Students
Tuition and fees:	$21,078
Campus and Room and Board:	$6,000
Books and Supplies:	$900
Other Expenses:	$10
Total Estimated Expenses:	**$27,988**

Note: All residential students are assessed a $400 technology fee to provide for technology access in the residence halls.

NEW APPLICANTS/NEWLY ENROLLED STUDENTS
[Numbers are for the graduate engineering college for the Fall 2006 term]

Number of Applicants (a):	1,174
Of those, Number Offered Admission (b):	329
Of those, Number Enrolled Fall 2006 (c):	85

The Catholic University of America

INSTITUTION INFORMATION
Pangborn Hall, Room 102
620 Michigan Avenue, N.E.
Washington, DC 20064
Phone: (202) 319-5160
Fax: (202) 319-4499
Web: http://engineering.cua.edu

GENERAL INFORMATION
[All Students - Fall 2006]

Undergraduate Enrollment	3,053
Graduate Enrollment	2,070
Professional Enrollment	1,007
Total Enrollment	**6,130**

ENGINEERING COLLEGE INFORMATION

HEAD OF ENGINEERING
Charles C. Nguyen
Dean, School of Engineering
Office of the Dean
The Catholic University of America
Pangborn Hall, Room 102
620 Michigan Avenue, N.E.
Washington, DC 20064
Phone: (202) 319-5160
Fax: (202) 319-4499
Email: nguyen@cua.edu

TYPES OF ENGINEERING DEGREES
Bachelor's: B.S.
Master's: M.S. with thesis, M.S. without thesis, but with project or report
Doctoral: Ph.D., D.Eng

Cedarville University

INSTITUTION INFORMATION
251 N. Main St.
Cedarville, OH 45314
Phone: (937) 766-7680
Fax: (937) 766-7689
Web: http://www.cedarville.edu/index.html

GENERAL INFORMATION
[All Students - Fall 2006]

Undergraduate Enrollment	3,064
Graduate Enrollment	0
Professional Enrollment	0
Total Enrollment	**3,064**

ENGINEERING COLLEGE INFORMATION

HEAD OF ENGINEERING
Stanley K. Baczek

Dean
School of Engineering, Nursing, and Science
Cedarville University
251 N. Main St.
Cedarville, OH 45314
Phone: (937) 766-7680
Email: sbaczek@cedarville.edu

TYPES OF ENGINEERING DEGREES
Bachelor's: B.S.
Master's:
Doctoral:

UNDERGRADUATE INFORMATION

ESTIMATED STUDENT EXPENSES (FALL 2006)
[Expenses are for the 2006-2007 nine-month academic year and are based on an average credit load of: Undergraduate: N/A]

	All Students
Tuition and fees:	$18,400
Campus and Room and Board:	$4,784
Books and Supplies:	$800
Other Expenses:	$1,300
Total Estimated Expenses:	**$25,284**

Note: Engineering Students average 17.5 credit hours per semester to graduate in four years; board expenses reflect 14-meal plan.

University of Central Florida

INSTITUTION INFORMATION
4000 Central Florida Blvd.
Orlando, FL 32816
Phone: (407) 823-2000
Web: http://www.ucf.edu

GENERAL INFORMATION
[All Students - Fall 2006]

Undergraduate Enrollment	39,964
Graduate Enrollment	5,950
Professional Enrollment	1,312
Total Enrollment	**47,226**

ENGINEERING COLLEGE INFORMATION

HEAD OF ENGINEERING
Neal Gallagher
Dean, Professor of Electrical Engineering
College of Engineering and Computer Science (CECS)
University of Central Florida
4000 Central Florida Blvd.
P.O. Box 162993
Orlando, FL 32816-2993
Phone: (407) 823-2156
Fax: (407) 823-5483
Email: nealg@mail.ucf.edu

ENGINEERING COLLEGE INQUIRIES
Melissa Falls
Director of Academic Support Services
University of Central Florida
P.O. Box 162993
Orlando, FL 32816-2993
Phone: (407) 823-0040
Fax: (407) 823-6334
Email: mfalls@mail.ucf.edu

TYPES OF ENGINEERING DEGREES
Bachelor's: B.S.
Master's: M.S. with thesis, M.S. without thesis, but with project or report
Doctoral: Ph.D.

UNDERGRADUATE INFORMATION

ESTIMATED STUDENT EXPENSES (FALL 2006)
[Expenses are for the 2006-2007 nine-month academic year and are based on an average credit load of: Undergraduate: 15]

	In-State	Out-of-State
Tuition and Fees:	$3,492	$17,017
Campus and Room and Board:	$8,528	$8,528
Books and Supplies:	$888	$888
Other Expenses:	$4,000	$4,000
Total Estimated Expenses:	**$16,908**	**$30,433**

Note: Full time Fall/Spring

NEW APPLICANTS/NEWLY ENROLLED STUDENTS
[Numbers are for the undergraduate engineering college for the Fall 2006 term]

Number of Applicants (a):	2,961
Of those, Number Offered Admission (b):	1,764
Of those, Number Enrolled Fall 2006 (c):	1,080

GRADUATE INFORMATION

ADMISSION INQUIRIES
Kerry Ann Hall
Coordinator, Academic Support Services, Graduate Programs
University of Central Florida
P.O. Box 162993
Orlando, FL 32816-2993
Phone: (407) 823-3874
Fax: (407) 823-6334
Email: knhall@mail.ucf.edu

ADMISSION INQUIRIES
Patricia J. Bishop
Vice Provost/Dean of Graduate Studies
University of Central Florida
PO Box 160112
Orlando , FL 32816-0112
Phone: (407) 823-6432
Fax: (407) 823-6442
Email: pbishop@mail.ucf.edu

ESTIMATED STUDENT EXPENSES (FALL 2006)
[Expenses are for the 2006-2007 nine-month academic year and are based on an average credit load of: Graduate: 12]

	In-State	Out-of-State
Tuition and Fees:	$6,167	$22,790
Campus and Room and Board:	$8,528	$8,528
Books and Supplies:	$888	$888
Other Expenses:	$4,000	$4,000
Total Estimated Expenses:	**$19,583**	**$36,206**

Note: Full time Fall/Spring

NEW APPLICANTS/NEWLY ENROLLED STUDENTS
[Numbers are for the graduate engineering college for the Fall 2006 term]

Number of Applicants (a):	1,111
Of those, Number Offered Admission (b):	471
Of those, Number Enrolled Fall 2006 (c):	221

Christian Brothers University

INSTITUTION INFORMATION
650 East Parkway South
Memphis, TN 38104
Phone: (901) 321-3000
Fax: (901) 321-3494
Web: http://www.cbu.edu

GENERAL INFORMATION
[All Students - Fall 2006]

Undergraduate Enrollment	1,420
Graduate Enrollment	304
Professional Enrollment	0
Total Enrollment	**1,724**

ENGINEERING COLLEGE INFORMATION

HEAD OF ENGINEERING
Eric B Welch
Dean, School of Engineering
School of Engineering
Christian Brothers University
650 East Parkway South
Memphis, TN 38104
Phone: (901) 321-3425
Fax: (901) 321-3402
Email: ewelch@cbu.edu

TYPES OF ENGINEERING DEGREES
Bachelor's: B.S.
Master's: Engineering Management
Doctoral:

UNDERGRADUATE INFORMATION

ADMISSION INQUIRIES
Tracy Dysart-Ford
Dean of Admissions

Christian Brothers University
650 East Parkway South
Memphis, TN 38104
Phone: (901) 321-4213
Fax: (901) 321-3202
Email: tdysart@cbu.edu

ESTIMATED STUDENT EXPENSES (FALL 2006)
[Expenses are for the 2006-2007 nine-month academic year and are based on an average credit load of: Undergraduate: 15]

	All Students
Tuition and fees:	$19,560
Campus and Room and Board:	$5,350
Books and Supplies:	$900
Other Expenses:	
Total Estimated Expenses:	**$25,810**

NEW APPLICANTS/NEWLY ENROLLED STUDENTS
[Numbers are for the undergraduate engineering college for the Fall 2006 term]

Number of Applicants (a):	171
Of those, Number Offered Admission (b):	125
Of those, Number Enrolled Fall 2006 (c):	53

GRADUATE INFORMATION

ADMISSION INQUIRIES
Neal Jackson
Director of Engineering Management Masters Program
Christian Brothers University
650 East Parkway South
Memphis , TN 38104
Phone: (901) 321-3283
Fax: (901) 321-3402
Email: njackson@cbu.edu

ESTIMATED STUDENT EXPENSES (FALL 2006)
[Expenses are for the 2006-2007 nine-month academic year and are based on an average credit load of: Graduate: 5]

	All Students
Tuition and fees:	$3,060
Campus and Room and Board:	
Books and Supplies:	$450
Other Expenses:	
Total Estimated Expenses:	**$3,510**

University of Cincinnati

INSTITUTION INFORMATION
Nancy L. Zimpher
625 University Pavilion
Cincinnati, OH 45221-0063
Phone: (513) 556-2201
Fax: (513) 556-3010
Web: http://www.uc.edu/

GENERAL INFORMATION
[All Students - Fall 2006]

Undergraduate Enrollment	1,828
Graduate Enrollment	7,402
Professional Enrollment	1,751
Total Enrollment	**10,981**

ENGINEERING COLLEGE INFORMATION

HEAD OF ENGINEERING
Carlo Montemagno
Dean
College of Engineering
University of Cincinnati
Engineering Research Center
801 ERC ML 0018
Cincinnati, OH 45221
Phone: (513) 556-2933
Fax: (513) 556-3626

TYPES OF ENGINEERING DEGREES
Bachelor's: B.S.
Master's: M.S. with thesis, M.S. without thesis, but with project or report
Doctoral: Ph.D.

UNDERGRADUATE INFORMATION

ESTIMATED STUDENT EXPENSES (FALL 2006)
[Expenses are for the 2006-2007 nine-month academic year

and are based on an average credit load of: Undergraduate: N/A]

	In-State	Out-of-State
Tuition and Fees:	$9,380	$23,900
Campus and Room and Board:	$8,286	$8,286
Books and Supplies:	$1,185	$1,185
Other Expenses:	$4,150	$4,150
Total Estimated Expenses:	**$23,001**	**$37,521**

NEW APPLICANTS/NEWLY ENROLLED STUDENTS
[Numbers are for the undergraduate engineering college for the Fall 2006 term]

Number of Applicants (a):	1,469
Of those, Number Offered Admission (b):	1,225
Of those, Number Enrolled Fall 2006 (c):	570

GRADUATE INFORMATION

NEW APPLICANTS/NEWLY ENROLLED STUDENTS
[Numbers are for the graduate engineering college for the Fall 2006 term]

Number of Applicants (a):	2,073
Of those, Number Offered Admission (b):	629
Of those, Number Enrolled Fall 2006 (c):	283

The Citadel

INSTITUTION INFORMATION
171 Moultrie Street
Charleston, SC 29409
Phone: (843) 225-3294
Fax: (843) 953-6937
Web: http://www.citadel.edu

GENERAL INFORMATION
[All Students - Fall 2006]

Undergraduate Enrollment	2,238
Graduate Enrollment	952
Professional Enrollment	116
Total Enrollment	**3,306**

ENGINEERING COLLEGE INFORMATION

HEAD OF ENGINEERING
Dennis J Fallon
Dean
School of Engineering
The Citadel
The Citadel
171 Moultrie St.
Charleston, SC 29409
Phone: (843) 953-6588
Fax: (843) 953-6328
Email: fallond@citadel.edu

TYPES OF ENGINEERING DEGREES
Bachelor's: B.S.
Master's:
Doctoral:

UNDERGRADUATE INFORMATION

ESTIMATED STUDENT EXPENSES (FALL 2006)
[Expenses are for the 2006-2007 nine-month academic year and are based on an average credit load of: Undergraduate: N/A]

	In-State	Out-of-State
Tuition and Fees:	$7,168	$17,487
Campus and Room and Board:	$5,090	$5,090
Books and Supplies:		
Other Expenses:	$500	$500
Total Estimated Expenses:	**$12,758**	**$23,077**

NEW APPLICANTS/NEWLY ENROLLED STUDENTS
[Numbers are for the undergraduate engineering college for the Fall 2006 term]

Number of Applicants (a):	1,999
Of those, Number Offered Admission (b):	1,494
Of those, Number Enrolled Fall 2006 (c):	538

Note: We do not have admissions information broken down by major. The figures for all categories are for the Corps of Cadets.

GRADUATE INFORMATION

ESTIMATED STUDENT EXPENSES (FALL 2006)
[Expenses are for the 2006-2007 nine-month academic year and are based on an average credit load of: Graduate: N/A]

	In-State	Out-of-State
Tuition and Fees:	$4,662	$8,676
Campus and Room and Board:		
Books and Supplies:		
Other Expenses:		
Total Estimated Expenses:	**$4,662**	**$8,676**

Clarkson University

INSTITUTION INFORMATION
Box 5557
Potsdam, NY 13699
Phone: (315) 268-6590
Fax: (315) 268-3905
Web: http://www.clarkson.edu

GENERAL INFORMATION
[All Students - Fall 2006]

Undergraduate Enrollment	2,545
Graduate Enrollment	399
Professional Enrollment	20
Total Enrollment	**2,964**

ENGINEERING COLLEGE INFORMATION

HEAD OF ENGINEERING
Goodarz Ahmadi
Dean of Engineering
School of Engineering
Clarkson University
Camp Bldg
Potsdam, NY 13699-5700
Phone: (315) 268-6446
Fax: (315) 268-4494
Email: ahmadi@clarkson.edu

TYPES OF ENGINEERING DEGREES
Bachelor's: B.S.,BPS
Master's: M.S. with thesis
Doctoral: Ph.D.,Dr. of Physical Theraphy

UNDERGRADUATE INFORMATION

ADMISSION INQUIRIES
Brian T Grant
Director of Admission
Clarkson University
Box 5605
Potsdam, NY 13699
Phone: (315) 268-6419
Fax: (315) 268-7647
Email: bgrant@clarkson.edu

ESTIMATED STUDENT EXPENSES (FALL 2006)
[Expenses are for the 2006-2007 nine-month academic year and are based on an average credit load of: Undergraduate: 15]

	All Students
Tuition and fees:	$27,090
Campus and Room and Board:	$9,648
Books and Supplies:	$1,100
Other Expenses:	$1,962
Total Estimated Expenses:	**$39,800**

NEW APPLICANTS/NEWLY ENROLLED STUDENTS
[Numbers are for the undergraduate engineering college for the Fall 2006 term]

Number of Applicants (a):	1,254
Of those, Number Offered Admission (b):	1,127
Of those, Number Enrolled Fall 2006 (c):	373

GRADUATE INFORMATION

NEW APPLICANTS/NEWLY ENROLLED STUDENTS
[Numbers are for the graduate engineering college for the Fall 2006 term]

Number of Applicants (a):	335
Of those, Number Offered Admission (b):	125
Of those, Number Enrolled Fall 2006 (c):	66

Clemson University

INSTITUTION INFORMATION
109 Riggs Hall
Box 340901
Clemson, SC 29634-0901

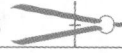
Phone: (864) 656-3201
Web: http://www.clemson.edu

GENERAL INFORMATION
[All Students - Fall 2006]

Undergraduate Enrollment	14,069
Graduate Enrollment	3,112
Professional Enrollment	0
Total Enrollment	**17,181**

ENGINEERING COLLEGE INFORMATION

HEAD OF ENGINEERING
Esin Gulari
Dean
College of Engineering and Science
Clemson University
109 Riggs Hall
Box 340901
Clemson, SC 29634-0901
Phone: (864) 656-3202
Fax: (864) 656-0859
Email: keinath@clemson.edu

TYPES OF ENGINEERING DEGREES
Bachelor's: B.A., B.S.
Master's: M.S. with thesis, M.S. without thesis, but with project or report, M.Eng.
Doctoral: Ph.D.

UNDERGRADUATE INFORMATION

ADMISSION INQUIRIES
Stephen S Melsheimer
Associate Dean for Undergraduate Studies
Clemson University
107 Riggs Hall, Box 340901
Clemson, SC 29634-0901
Phone: (864) 646-4440
Fax: (864) 656-0859
Email: steve.melsheimer@ces.clemson.edu

ADMISSION INQUIRIES
Robert S Barkley
Director of Admissions
Clemson University
106 Sikes Hall
Clemson, SC 29634
Phone: (864) 656-2287
Fax: (864) 656-2464
Email: rbrtbkl@clemson.edu

ESTIMATED STUDENT EXPENSES (FALL 2006)
[Expenses are for the 2006-2007 nine-month academic year and are based on an average credit load of: Undergraduate: 15]

	In-State	Out-of-State
Tuition and Fees:	$9,868	$20,292
Campus and Room and Board:	$5,874	$5,874
Books and Supplies:	$848	$848
Other Expenses:	$4,212	$4,212
Total Estimated Expenses:	**$20,802**	**$31,226**

NEW APPLICANTS/NEWLY ENROLLED STUDENTS
[Numbers are for the undergraduate engineering college for the Fall 2006 term]

Number of Applicants (a):	2,273
Of those, Number Offered Admission (b):	1,732
Of those, Number Enrolled Fall 2006 (c):	803

GRADUATE INFORMATION

ADMISSION INQUIRIES
Robert S Barkley
Director of Admissions
Clemson University
106 Sikes Hall
Clemson , SC 29634
Phone: (864) 656-2287
Fax: (864) 656-2464
Email: rbrtbkl@clemson.edu

ESTIMATED STUDENT EXPENSES (FALL 2006)
[Expenses are for the 2006-2007 nine-month academic year and are based on an average credit load of: Graduate: 12]

	In-State	Out-of-State
Tuition and Fees:	$9,754	$18,978
Campus and Room and Board:	$5,874	$5,874
Books and Supplies:	$848	$848
Other Expenses:	$4,212	$4,212
Total Estimated Expenses:	**$20,688**	**$29,912**

NEW APPLICANTS/NEWLY ENROLLED STUDENTS
[Numbers are for the graduate engineering college for the Fall 2006 term]

Number of Applicants (a):	1,647
Of those, Number Offered Admission (b):	790
Of those, Number Enrolled Fall 2006 (c):	211

Cleveland State University

INSTITUTION INFORMATION
2121 Euclid Avenue
Cleveland, OH 44115
Phone: (216) 687-2555
Fax: (216) 687-9280
Web: http://www.csuohio.edu

ENGINEERING COLLEGE INFORMATION

HEAD OF ENGINEERING
Charles K Alexander
Dean of Engineering
Fenn College of Engineering
Cleveland State University
2121 Euclid Ave.
Stillwell Hall, Room 104
Cleveland, OH 44115-2214
Phone: (216) 216-6876
Fax: (216) 216-9280
Email: c.alexander@ieee.org

ENGINEERING COLLEGE INQUIRIES
Carolyn Kasprzak
Secretary
Cleveland State University
2121 Euclid Avenue, Stilwell Hall Room 104
Cleveland, OH 44115
Phone: (216) 687-2558
Fax: (216) 687-9280
Email: c.kasprzak@csuohio.edu

TYPES OF ENGINEERING DEGREES
Bachelor's: B.S.
Master's: M.S. with thesis, M.S. without thesis, but with project or report
Doctoral: D.Eng.

UNDERGRADUATE INFORMATION

ADMISSION INQUIRIES
Pamela Charity
Director of Undergraduate Affairs & Student Relations
Cleveland State University
2121 Euclid Avenue, Stilwell Hall Room 104
Cleveland, OH 44115
Phone: (216) 687-6912
Fax: (216) 687-9280
Email: p.charity@csuohio.edu

ESTIMATED STUDENT EXPENSES (FALL 2006)
[Expenses are for the 2006-2007 nine-month academic year and are based on an average credit load of: Undergraduate: 12]

	In-State	Out-of-State
Tuition and Fees:	$3,960	$5,332
Campus and Room and Board:	$3,900	$3,900
Books and Supplies:	$400	$400
Other Expenses:	$141	$141
Total Estimated Expenses:	**$8,401**	**$9,773**

NEW APPLICANTS/NEWLY ENROLLED STUDENTS
[Numbers are for the undergraduate engineering college for the Fall 2006 term]

Number of Applicants (a):	0
Of those, Number Offered Admission (b):	0
Of those, Number Enrolled Fall 2006 (c):	93

GRADUATE INFORMATION

ESTIMATED STUDENT EXPENSES (FALL 2006)
[Expenses are for the 2006-2007 nine-month academic year and are based on an average credit load of: Graduate: 13]

	In-State	Out-of-State
Tuition and Fees:	$5,385	$7,314
Campus and Room and Board:	$3,900	$3,900
Books and Supplies:	$400	$400
Other Expenses:	$141	$141
Total Estimated Expenses:	**$9,826**	**$11,755**

Colorado School of Mines

INSTITUTION INFORMATION
1500 Illinois Street
Golden, CO 80401
Phone: (303) 273-3000
Fax: (303) 273-3040
Web: http://www.mines.edu

GENERAL INFORMATION
[All Students - Fall 2006]

Undergraduate Enrollment	3,209
Graduate Enrollment	770
Professional Enrollment	77
Total Enrollment	**4,056**

ENGINEERING COLLEGE INFORMATION

HEAD OF ENGINEERING
Nigel T Middleton
Executive Vice President for Academic Affairs and Dean of Faculty
Academic Affairs
Colorado School of Mines
1500 Illinois St.
Golden, CO 80401
Phone: (303) 273-3610
Fax: (303) 273-3040
Email: nmiddlet@mines.edu

ENGINEERING COLLEGE INQUIRIES
William A Young
Associate Vice President for Student Affairs, Director of Enrollment Management
Colorado School of Mines
1500 Illinois St.
Golden, CO 80401
Phone: (303) 273-3610
Fax: (303) 273-3509
Email: wyoung@mines.edu

TYPES OF ENGINEERING DEGREES
Bachelor's: B.S.
Master's: M.S. with thesis, M.S. without thesis, but with project or report
Doctoral: Ph.D.

UNDERGRADUATE INFORMATION

ADMISSION INQUIRIES
William A Young
Associate Vice President for Student Affairs, Director of Enrollment Management
Colorado School of Mines
1500 Illinois St.
Golden, CO 80401
Phone: (303) 273-3610
Fax: (303) 273-3509
Email: wyoung@mines.edu

ESTIMATED STUDENT EXPENSES (FALL 2006)
[Expenses are for the 2006-2007 nine-month academic year and are based on an average credit load of: Undergraduate: 16]

	In-State	Out-of-State
Tuition and Fees:	$9,060	$21,353
Campus and Room and Board:	$7,000	$7,000
Books and Supplies:	$1,300	$1,300
Other Expenses:	$1,800	$1,800
Total Estimated Expenses:	**$19,160**	**$31,453**

NEW APPLICANTS/NEWLY ENROLLED STUDENTS
[Numbers are for the undergraduate engineering college for the Fall 2006 term]

Number of Applicants (a):	3,932
Of those, Number Offered Admission (b):	2,794
Of those, Number Enrolled Fall 2006 (c):	873

GRADUATE INFORMATION

ADMISSION INQUIRIES
Linda Powell
Graduate Admissions Officer
Colorado School of Mines
1500 Illinois St.
Golden , CO 80401
Phone: (303) 273-3610
Fax: (303) 273-3244
Email: lpowell@mines.edu

ESTIMATED STUDENT EXPENSES (FALL 2006)
[Expenses are for the 2006-2007 nine-month academic year and are based on an average credit load of: Graduate: 9]

	In-State	Out-of-State
Tuition and Fees:	$9,077	$21,353
Campus and Room and Board:	$18,000	$18,000
Books and Supplies:	$1,300	$1,300
Other Expenses:	$1,800	$1,800
Total Estimated Expenses:	**$30,177**	**$42,453**

NEW APPLICANTS/NEWLY ENROLLED STUDENTS
[Numbers are for the graduate engineering college for the Fall 2006 term]

Number of Applicants (a):	792
Of those, Number Offered Admission (b):	577
Of those, Number Enrolled Fall 2006 (c):	264

Colorado State University

INSTITUTION INFORMATION
College of Engineering
1301 Campus Delivery
Fort Collins, CO 80523-1301
Phone: (970) 491-3366
Fax: (970) 491-5569
Web: http://www.colostate.edu

GENERAL INFORMATION
[All Students - Fall 2006]

Undergraduate Enrollment	20,500
Graduate Enrollment	3,636
Professional Enrollment	534
Total Enrollment	**24,670**

ENGINEERING COLLEGE INFORMATION

HEAD OF ENGINEERING
Sandra Woods
Dean
College of Enginering
Colorado State University
Dean of Engineering
1301 Campus Delivery
Fort Collins, CO 80523-1301
Phone: (970) 491-3366
Fax: (970) 491-5569
Email: sandra.woods@colostate.edu

TYPES OF ENGINEERING DEGREES
Bachelor's: B.S.
Master's: M.S. with thesis, M.S. without thesis, but with project or report, M.Eng.
Doctoral: Ph.D.

UNDERGRADUATE INFORMATION

ESTIMATED STUDENT EXPENSES (FALL 2006)
[Expenses are for the 2006-2007 nine-month academic year and are based on an average credit load of: Undergraduate: 12]

	In-State	Out-of-State
Tuition and Fees:	$4,657	$16,185
Campus and Room and Board:	$6,800	$6,800
Books and Supplies:	$900	$900
Other Expenses:	$2,142	$2,842
Total Estimated Expenses:	**$14,499**	**$26,727**

NEW APPLICANTS/NEWLY ENROLLED STUDENTS
[Numbers are for the undergraduate engineering college for the Fall 2006 term]

Number of Applicants (a):	840
Of those, Number Offered Admission (b):	753
Of those, Number Enrolled Fall 2006 (c):	291

GRADUATE INFORMATION

ESTIMATED STUDENT EXPENSES (FALL 2006)
[Expenses are for the 2006-2007 nine-month academic year and are based on an average credit load of: Graduate: 9]

	In-State	Out-of-State
Tuition and Fees:	$5,379	$16,773
Campus and Room and Board:	$6,800	$6,800
Books and Supplies:	$900	$900
Other Expenses:	$2,142	$2,842
Total Estimated Expenses:	**$15,221**	**$27,315**

NEW APPLICANTS/NEWLY ENROLLED STUDENTS
[Numbers are for the graduate engineering college for the

Fall 2006 term]

Number of Applicants (a):	889
Of those, Number Offered Admission (b):	324
Of those, Number Enrolled Fall 2006 (c):	115

Colorado State University, Pueblo

INSTITUTION INFORMATION
2200 Bonforte Boulevard
Pueblo, CO 81001
Phone: (719) 549-2696
Fax: (719) 549-2519
Web: http://www.uscolo.edu/

GENERAL INFORMATION
[All Students - Fall 2006]

Undergraduate Enrollment	3,645
Graduate Enrollment	138
Professional Enrollment	0
Total Enrollment	**3,783**

ENGINEERING COLLEGE INFORMATION

HEAD OF ENGINEERING
Hector R. Carrasco
Dean
College of Education, Engr., & Professional Studies
Colorado State University, Pueblo
2200 Bonforte Boulevard
Pueblo, CO 81001-4901
Phone: (719) 549-2696
Fax: (719) 549-2519
Email: hector.carrasco@colostate-pueblo.edu

TYPES OF ENGINEERING DEGREES
Bachelor's: B.S.
Master's: M.S. with thesis, M.S. without thesis, but with project or report
Doctoral:

UNDERGRADUATE INFORMATION

ADMISSION INQUIRIES
Jane M. Fraser
Chair Engineering
Colorado State University, Pueblo
2200 Bonforte Boulevard
Pueblo, CO 81001
Phone: (719) 549-2036
Fax: (719) 549-2519
Email: jane.fraser@colostate-pueblo.edu

ESTIMATED STUDENT EXPENSES (FALL 2006)
[Expenses are for the 2006-2007 nine-month academic year and are based on an average credit load of: Undergraduate: 9]

	In-State	Out-of-State
Tuition and Fees:	$2,974	$13,543
Campus and Room and Board:	$5,810	$5,810
Books and Supplies:	$1,000	$1,000
Other Expenses:	$200	$200
Total Estimated Expenses:	**$9,984**	**$20,553**

NEW APPLICANTS/NEWLY ENROLLED STUDENTS
[Numbers are for the undergraduate engineering college for the Fall 2006 term]

Number of Applicants (a):	26
Of those, Number Offered Admission (b):	21
Of those, Number Enrolled Fall 2006 (c):	18

GRADUATE INFORMATION

ADMISSION INQUIRIES
Nebojsa Jaksic
Associate Professor Engineering
Colorado State University, Pueblo
2200 Bonforte Boulevard
Pueblo , CO 81001
Phone: (719) 549-2112
Fax: (719) 549-2519
Email: n.jaksic@colostate-pueblo.edu

ESTIMATED STUDENT EXPENSES (FALL 2006)
[Expenses are for the 2006-2007 nine-month academic year and are based on an average credit load of: Graduate: 12]

	In-State	Out-of-State
Tuition and Fees:	$2,974	$13,543

Campus and Room and Board:	$5,810	$5,810
Books and Supplies:	$1,000	$1,000
Other Expenses:	$200	$200
Total Estimated Expenses:	**$9,984**	**$20,553**

NEW APPLICANTS/NEWLY ENROLLED STUDENTS
[Numbers are for the graduate engineering college for the Fall 2006 term]

Number of Applicants (a):	21
Of those, Number Offered Admission (b):	17
Of those, Number Enrolled Fall 2006 (c):	12

University of Colorado at Boulder

INSTITUTION INFORMATION
422 UCB
College of Engineering & Applied Science
Boulder, CO 80309
Phone: (303) 492-5071
Fax: (303) 492-2199
Web: http://engineering.colorado.edu/

GENERAL INFORMATION
[All Students - Fall 2006]

Undergraduate Enrollment	24,815
Graduate Enrollment	4,580
Professional Enrollment	0
Total Enrollment	**29,395**

ENGINEERING COLLEGE INFORMATION

HEAD OF ENGINEERING
Robert H Davis
Dean
College of Engineering and Applied Science
University of Colorado at Boulder
422 UCB
Boulder, CO 80309-0422
Phone: (303) 492-7006
Fax: (303) 492-2199
Email: robert.davis@colorado.edu

TYPES OF ENGINEERING DEGREES
Bachelor's: B.S.
Master's: M.S. with thesis, M.S. without thesis, but with project or report, M.Eng.
Doctoral: Ph.D.

UNDERGRADUATE INFORMATION

ESTIMATED STUDENT EXPENSES (FALL 2006)
[Expenses are for the 2006-2007 nine-month academic year and are based on an average credit load of: Undergraduate: 14]

	In-State	Out-of-State
Tuition and Fees:	$7,083	$24,146
Campus and Room and Board:	$10,448	$10,448
Books and Supplies:	$1,736	$1,736
Other Expenses:	$5,260	$5,260
Total Estimated Expenses:	**$24,527**	**$41,590**

NEW APPLICANTS/NEWLY ENROLLED STUDENTS
[Numbers are for the undergraduate engineering college for the Fall 2006 term]

Number of Applicants (a):	2,092
Of those, Number Offered Admission (b):	1,799
Of those, Number Enrolled Fall 2006 (c):	654
Note: Mean 27.1	

GRADUATE INFORMATION

ESTIMATED STUDENT EXPENSES (FALL 2006)
[Expenses are for the 2006-2007 nine-month academic year and are based on an average credit load of: Graduate: 5]

	In-State	Out-of-State
Tuition and Fees:	$9,108	$24,889
Campus and Room and Board:	$10,448	$10,448
Books and Supplies:	$1,736	$1,736
Other Expenses:	$5,260	$5,260
Total Estimated Expenses:	**$26,552**	**$42,333**

NEW APPLICANTS/NEWLY ENROLLED STUDENTS
[Numbers are for the graduate engineering college for the Fall 2006 term]

Number of Applicants (a):	1,477
Of those, Number Offered Admission (b):	902
Of those, Number Enrolled Fall 2006 (c):	299

University of Colorado at Colorado Springs

INSTITUTION INFORMATION

Post Office Box 7150
1420 Austin Bluffs Parkway
Colorado Springs, CO 80933
Phone: (719) 262-3543
Fax: (719) 262-3542
Web: http://www.eas.uccs.edu

GENERAL INFORMATION

[All Students - Fall 2006]

Undergraduate Enrollment	7,629
Graduate Enrollment	1,678
Professional Enrollment	0
Total Enrollment	**9,307**

ENGINEERING COLLEGE INFORMATION

HEAD OF ENGINEERING

Jeremy Haefner
Dean
College of Engineering and Applied Science
University of Colorado at Colorado Springs
P.O. Box 7150
1420 Austin Bluffs Parkway
Colorado Springs, CO 80933-7150
Phone: (719) 262-3543
Fax: (719) 262-3542
Email: hafner@eas.uccs.edu

TYPES OF ENGINEERING DEGREES

Bachelor's: B.S.
Master's: M.S. with thesis, M.S. without thesis, but with project or report, M.Eng.
Doctoral: Ph.D.

UNDERGRADUATE INFORMATION

ADMISSION INQUIRIES

Chris Duval
Undergraduate Engineering Advisor
University of Colorado at Colorado Springs
Post Office Box 7150, 1420 Austin Bluffs Parkway
Colorado Springs, CO 80933-7150
Phone: (719) 262-3427
Fax: (719) 262-3645
Email: cduval@uccs.edu

NEW APPLICANTS/NEWLY ENROLLED STUDENTS

[Numbers are for the undergraduate engineering college for the Fall 2006 term]

Number of Applicants (a):	1,276
Of those, Number Offered Admission (b):	646
Of those, Number Enrolled Fall 2006 (c):	207

University of Colorado at Denver and Health Sciences Center

INSTITUTION INFORMATION

Campus Box 104
PO Box 173364
Denver, CO 80217
Phone: (303) 556-2870
Fax: (303) 556-2511
Web: http://www.cudenver.edu/academics/colleges/college+of+engineering+and+applied+science/

GENERAL INFORMATION

[All Students - Fall 2006]

Undergraduate Enrollment	7,872
Graduate Enrollment	4,453
Professional Enrollment	12,325
Total Enrollment	**24,650**

ENGINEERING COLLEGE INFORMATION

HEAD OF ENGINEERING

Renjeng Su
Dean
College of Engineering and Applied Science
University of Colorado at Denver

Campus Box 104
PO Box 173364
Denver, CO 80217
Phone: (303) 556-2870
Fax: (303) 556-2511
Email: Renjeng.Su@cudenver.edu

TYPES OF ENGINEERING DEGREES

Bachelor's: B.S.
Master's: M.S. with thesis, M.S. without thesis, but with project or report, M.Eng.
Doctoral: Ph.D.

UNDERGRADUATE INFORMATION

ESTIMATED STUDENT EXPENSES (FALL 2006)

[Expenses are for the 2006-2007 nine-month academic year and are based on an average credit load of: Undergraduate: 12]

	All Students
Tuition and fees:	$4,132
Campus and Room and Board:	$7,641
Books and Supplies:	$1,698
Other Expenses:	$675
Total Estimated Expenses:	**$14,146**

NEW APPLICANTS/NEWLY ENROLLED STUDENTS

[Numbers are for the undergraduate engineering college for the Fall 2006 term]

Number of Applicants (a):	242
Of those, Number Offered Admission (b):	141
Of those, Number Enrolled Fall 2006 (c):	50

Note: Avg 598

GRADUATE INFORMATION

ESTIMATED STUDENT EXPENSES (FALL 2006)

[Expenses are for the 2006-2007 nine-month academic year and are based on an average credit load of: Graduate: 12]

	All Students
Tuition and fees:	$7,766
Campus and Room and Board:	$7,641
Books and Supplies:	$1,698
Other Expenses:	$675
Total Estimated Expenses:	**$17,780**

NEW APPLICANTS/NEWLY ENROLLED STUDENTS

[Numbers are for the graduate engineering college for the Fall 2006 term]

Number of Applicants (a):	247
Of those, Number Offered Admission (b):	189
Of those, Number Enrolled Fall 2006 (c):	78

Columbia University

INSTITUTION INFORMATION

510 Seeley W. Mudd Building
500 West 120th Street
New York, NY 10027
Phone: (212) 854-2931
Fax: (212) 864-0104
Web: http://www.engineering.columbia.edu

GENERAL INFORMATION

[All Students - Fall 2006]

Undergraduate Enrollment	7,407
Graduate Enrollment	6,085
Professional Enrollment	10,911
Total Enrollment	**24,403**

ENGINEERING COLLEGE INFORMATION

HEAD OF ENGINEERING

Zvi Galil
Dean
Fu Foundation School of Engineering and Applied Science
Columbia University
510 Seeley W. Mudd Building
500 West 120th Street
New York, NY 10027
Phone: (212) 854-2993
Fax: (212) 864-0104

TYPES OF ENGINEERING DEGREES

Bachelor's: B.S.
Master's: M.S. with thesis, M.S. without thesis, but with project or report
Doctoral: Ph.D., D.Eng

UNDERGRADUATE INFORMATION

ADMISSION INQUIRIES

Jessica Marinaccio
Director
Columbia University
212 Hamilton Hall, 1130 Amsterdam Avenue
New York, NY 10027
Phone: (212) 854-2522

ESTIMATED STUDENT EXPENSES (FALL 2006)

[Expenses are for the 2006-2007 nine-month academic year and are based on an average credit load of: Undergraduate: 15]

	All Students
Tuition and fees:	$33,664
Campus and Room and Board:	$13,560
Books and Supplies:	$2,500
Other Expenses:	$2,500
Total Estimated Expenses:	**$52,224**

NEW APPLICANTS/NEWLY ENROLLED STUDENTS

[Numbers are for the undergraduate engineering college for the Fall 2006 term]

Number of Applicants (a):	2,700
Of those, Number Offered Admission (b):	635
Of those, Number Enrolled Fall 2006 (c):	315

GRADUATE INFORMATION

ADMISSION INQUIRIES

Tiffany M Simon
Assistant Dean
Columbia University
524 Mudd Building, MC 4708, 500 West 120th Street
New York , NY 10027
Phone: (212) 854-6438
Fax: (212) 854-5900
Email: tms26@columbia.edu

ESTIMATED STUDENT EXPENSES (FALL 2006)

[Expenses are for the 2006-2007 nine-month academic year and are based on an average credit load of: Graduate: 15]

	All Students
Tuition and fees:	$33,660
Campus and Room and Board:	$16,089
Books and Supplies:	$2,500
Other Expenses:	$2,500
Total Estimated Expenses:	**$54,749**

NEW APPLICANTS/NEWLY ENROLLED STUDENTS

[Numbers are for the graduate engineering college for the Fall 2006 term]

Number of Applicants (a):	3,461
Of those, Number Offered Admission (b):	1,016
Of those, Number Enrolled Fall 2006 (c):	501

Concordia University, Faculty of Engr. and Comp. Sci.

INSTITUTION INFORMATION

1455 de Maisonneuve West, EV-139
P.O.Box 2900, Montreal [H3G 2S2]
Montreal, PQ H3G 1M8
Phone: (514) 848-2424
Fax: (514) 848-8646
Web: http://www.encs.concordia.ca

GENERAL INFORMATION

[All Students - Fall 2006]

Undergraduate Enrollment	27,829
Graduate Enrollment	6,077
Professional Enrollment	5,273
Total Enrollment	**39,179**

ENGINEERING COLLEGE INFORMATION

HEAD OF ENGINEERING

Nabil Esmail
Dean, Faculty of Engineering and Computer Science
Faculty of Engineering and Computer Science
Concordia University, Faculty of Engr. and Comp. Sci.
1455 de Maisonneuve Blvd West, EV 2-169
P.O.Box 2900, Montreal [H3G 2S2]
Montreal, PQ H3G 1M8
Phone: (514) 848-2424

Fax: (514) 848-4509
Email: esmail@encs.concordia.ca

TYPES OF ENGINEERING DEGREES
Bachelor's: B.S.
Master's: M.S. with thesis, M.S. without thesis, but with project or report
Doctoral: Ph.D.

UNDERGRADUATE INFORMATION

ADMISSION INQUIRIES
Sabrina Poirer
Undergraduate Program Assistant, Michanical and Industrial Engineering (MIE)
Concordia University, Faculty of Engr. and Comp. Sci.
1455 de Maisonneuve West, EV-139, P.O.Box 2900,
Montreal [H3G 2S2]
Montreal, PQ H3G 1M8
Phone: (514) 848-2424
Fax: (514) 848-8646
Email: sabrina@encs.concordia.ca

ESTIMATED STUDENT EXPENSES (FALL 2006)
[Expenses are for the 2006-2007 nine-month academic year and are based on an average credit load of: Undergraduate: 15]

	Canadian Citizen	Non-Canadian
Tutition and Fees:	$2,900	$13,180
Campus and Room and Board:	$7,072	$7,072
Books and Supplies:	$3,992	$3,992
Other Expenses:	$1,825	$1,825
Total Estimated Expenses:	**$15,789**	**$26,069**

Note: The figures stated are in Canadian funds. The Exchange rate at time of survey is 1 Cdn dollar = 0.85US.

NEW APPLICANTS/NEWLY ENROLLED STUDENTS
[Numbers are for the undergraduate engineering college for the Fall 2006 term]

Number of Applicants (a):	1,907
Of those, Number Offered Admission (b):	1,214
Of those, Number Enrolled Fall 2006 (c):	633

GRADUATE INFORMATION

ADMISSION INQUIRIES
Charlene Wald
Graduate Program Assistant, Mechanical and Industrial Engineering (MIE)
Concordia University, Faculty of Engr. and Comp. Sci.
1455 de Maisonneuve West, EV 4-150, P.O.Box 2900,
Montreal [H3G 2S2]
Montreal, PQ H3G 1M8
Phone: (514) 848-2424
Fax: (514) 848-3175
Email: charlene@alcor.concordia.ca

ADMISSION INQUIRIES
Leslie Hosein
 Graduate Program Assistant, Aerospace,
Concordia University, Faculty of Engr. and Comp. Sci.
1455 de Maisonneuve West, EV 4-152, P.O.Box 2900,
Montreal [H3G 2S2]
Montreal, PQ H3G 1M8
Phone: (514) 848-2424
Fax: (514) 848-3175
Email: hosel@vax2.concordia.ca

ADMISSION INQUIRIES
Halina Monkiewicz
Graduate Advisor, Computer Science (CS)
Concordia University, Faculty of Engr. and Comp. Sci.
1455 de Maisonneuve West, EV 3-152, P.O. BOX 2900,
Montreal [H3G 2S2]
Montreal, PQ H3G 1M8
Phone: (514) 848-2424
Fax: (514) 848-2830
Email: halina@cse.concordia.ca

ADMISSION INQUIRIES
Diane Moffat
Graduate Program Assistant, Electrical and Computer Engineering (ECE)
Concordia University, Faculty of Engr. and Comp. Sci.
1455 de Maisonneuve West, EV 5-168, P.O.Box 2900,
Montreal [H3G 2S2]
Montreal, PQ H3G 1M8
Phone: (514) 848-2424
Fax: (514) 848-2802
Email: diane@ece.concordia.ca

ADMISSION INQUIRIES
Betty Bondo
Graduate Advisor, Building, Civil and Environmental Engineering (BCEE)
Concordia University, Faculty of Engr. and Comp. Sci.
1455 de Maisonneuve West, EV 6-152, P.O. Box 2900,
Montreal, [H3G 2S2]
Montreal, PQ H3G 1M8
Phone: (514) 848-2424
Fax: (514) 848-7965
Email: grad-program-advisor@bcee.concordia.ca

ESTIMATED STUDENT EXPENSES (FALL 2006)
[Expenses are for the 2006-2007 nine-month academic year and are based on an average credit load of: Graduate: 12]

	Canadian Citizen	Non-Canadian
Tutition and Fees:	$1,825	$6,447
Campus and Room and Board:	$7,072	$7,072
Books and Supplies:	$3,992	$3,992
Other Expenses:	$1,825	$1,825
Total Estimated Expenses:	**$14,714**	**$19,336**

Note: The figures stated are in Canadian funds. The Exchange rate at time of survey is 1 Cdn dollar = 0.85US.

NEW APPLICANTS/NEWLY ENROLLED STUDENTS
[Numbers are for the graduate engineering college for the Fall 2006 term]

Number of Applicants (a):	2,415
Of those, Number Offered Admission (b):	1,408
Of those, Number Enrolled Fall 2006 (c):	622

University of Connecticut

INSTITUTION INFORMATION
1262 Storrs Road
Storrs, CT 06269
Phone: (860) 486-2000
Web: http://www.uconn.edu

GENERAL INFORMATION
[All Students - Fall 2006]

Undergraduate Enrollment	20,525
Graduate Enrollment	6,180
Professional Enrollment	1,378
Total Enrollment	**28,083**

ENGINEERING COLLEGE INFORMATION

HEAD OF ENGINEERING
Erling Smith
Interim Dean
School of Engineering
University of Connecticut
261 Glenbrook Road Unit 2237
Storrs, CT 06269-2237
Phone: (860) 486-2221
Fax: (860) 486-0318
Email: faghri@engr.uconn.edu

ENGINEERING COLLEGE INQUIRIES
Erling Smith
Interim Dean
University of Connecticut
261 Glenbrook Road Unit 2237
Storrs, CT 06269-2237
Phone: (860) 486-2221
Fax: (860) 486-0318
Email: faghri@engr.uconn.edu

TYPES OF ENGINEERING DEGREES
Bachelor's: B.S.
Master's: M.S. with thesis, M.S. without thesis, but with project or report, M.Eng.
Doctoral: Ph.D.

UNDERGRADUATE INFORMATION

ADMISSION INQUIRIES
M. E. Wood
Assistant Dean for Undergraduate Education
University of Connecticut
191 Auditorium Road Unit 3187
Storrs, CT 06269-3187
Phone: (860) 486-5466
Fax: (860) 486-3045
Email: marty@engr.uconn.edu

ESTIMATED STUDENT EXPENSES (FALL 2006)
[Expenses are for the 2006-2007 nine-month academic year and are based on an average credit load of: Undergraduate: 15]

	In-State	Out-of-State
Tutition and Fees:	$8,437	$21,637
Campus and Room and Board:	$6,308	$6,308
Books and Supplies:	$725	$725
Other Expenses:	$2,400	$2,800
Total Estimated Expenses:	**$17,870**	**$31,470**

NEW APPLICANTS/NEWLY ENROLLED STUDENTS
[Numbers are for the undergraduate engineering college for the Fall 2006 term]

Number of Applicants (a):	2,006
Of those, Number Offered Admission (b):	1,172
Of those, Number Enrolled Fall 2006 (c):	375

 Note: Percentage based on 227/260 students who had an assigned high school class rank.

GRADUATE INFORMATION

ADMISSION INQUIRIES
Anne Lanzit
Associate Director
University of Connecticut
438 Whitney Road Extension Unit 1006
Storrs , CT 06269-1006
Phone: (860) 486-0974
Fax: (860) 486-6739
Email: anne.lanzit@uconn.edu

ESTIMATED STUDENT EXPENSES (FALL 2006)
[Expenses are for the 2006-2007 nine-month academic year and are based on an average credit load of: Graduate: 12]

	In-State	Out-of-State
Tutition and Fees:	$9,510	$22,290
Campus and Room and Board:	$11,316	$11,316
Books and Supplies:	$600	$600
Other Expenses:	$1,500	$1,500
Total Estimated Expenses:	**$22,926**	**$35,706**

NEW APPLICANTS/NEWLY ENROLLED STUDENTS
[Numbers are for the graduate engineering college for the Fall 2006 term]

Number of Applicants (a):	883
Of those, Number Offered Admission (b):	253
Of those, Number Enrolled Fall 2006 (c):	130

The Cooper Union

INSTITUTION INFORMATION
51 Astor Place
New York, NY 10003
Phone: (212) 353-4285
Fax: (212) 353-4341
Web: http://www.cooper.edu

GENERAL INFORMATION
[All Students - Fall 2006]

Undergraduate Enrollment	968
Graduate Enrollment	48
Professional Enrollment	0
Total Enrollment	**1,016**

ENGINEERING COLLEGE INFORMATION

HEAD OF ENGINEERING
Eleanor Baum
Dean, Engineering; Executive Director, Cooper Union Research Foundation
Dean
The Cooper Union
51 Astor Place
New York, NY 10003
Phone: (212) 353-4285
Fax: (212) 353-4341
Email: baum@cooper.edu

ENGINEERING COLLEGE INQUIRIES
Simon Ben-Avi
Associate Dean, Engineering
The Cooper Union
51 Astor Place
New York, NY 10003
Phone: (212) 353-4289
Fax: (212) 353-4341
Email: benavi@cooper.edu

TYPES OF ENGINEERING DEGREES
Bachelor's: B.S.

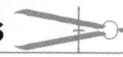

Master's: M.S. with thesis
Doctoral:

UNDERGRADUATE INFORMATION

ADMISSION INQUIRIES
Mitchell Lipton
Dean of Admissions
The Cooper Union
30 Cooper Square, 3rd Floor
New York, NY 10003
Phone: (212) 353-4126
Fax: (212) 353-4342
Email: lipton@cooper.edu

ESTIMATED STUDENT EXPENSES (FALL 2006)
[Expenses are for the 2006-2007 nine-month academic year and are based on an average credit load of: Undergraduate: 17]

	All Students
Tutition and fees:	$25,600
Campus and Room and Board:	$7,900
Books and Supplies:	$1,000
Other Expenses:	$2,275
Total Estimated Expenses:	**$36,775**

Note: Many students live at home or in off campus housing. EVERY STUDENT RECEIVES A FULL TUITION SCHOLARSHIP.

Financial Aid is available in addition.

NEW APPLICANTS/NEWLY ENROLLED STUDENTS
[Numbers are for the undergraduate engineering college for the Fall 2006 term]

Number of Applicants (a):	918
Of those, Number Offered Admission (b):	172
Of those, Number Enrolled Fall 2006 (c):	117

Note: Applicants are requested to self-select based on high entrance requirements.

GRADUATE INFORMATION

ADMISSION INQUIRIES
Mitchell Lipton
Dean of Admissions
The Cooper Union
30 Cooper Square, 3rd Floor
New York , NY 10003
Phone: (212) 353-4126
Fax: (212) 353-4342
Email: lipton@cooper.edu

ESTIMATED STUDENT EXPENSES (FALL 2006)
[Expenses are for the 2006-2007 nine-month academic year and are based on an average credit load of: Graduate: 9]

	All Students
Tutition and fees:	$25,600
Campus and Room and Board:	$7,900
Books and Supplies:	$1,000
Other Expenses:	$2,275
Total Estimated Expenses:	**$36,775**

Note: Many students live at home or in off campus housing. EVERY STUDENT RECEIVES A FULL TUITION SCHOLARSHIP.

Financial Aid is available in addition.

Cornell University

INSTITUTION INFORMATION
College of Engineering
245 Carpenter Hall
Ithaca, NY 14853
Phone: (607) 255-4326
Fax: (607) 255-9606
Web: http://www.engineering.cornell.edu

GENERAL INFORMATION
[All Students - Fall 2006]

Undergraduate Enrollment	13,562
Graduate Enrollment	4,354
Professional Enrollment	2,568
Total Enrollment	**20,484**

ENGINEERING COLLEGE INFORMATION

HEAD OF ENGINEERING
W. Kent Fuchs
Dean, College of Engineering
College of Engineering
Cornell University

242 Carpenter Hall
Cornell University
Ithaca, NY 14853
Phone: (607) 255-9679
Fax: (607) 255-9606
Email: engineering_dean@cornell.edu

TYPES OF ENGINEERING DEGREES
Bachelor's: B.S.
Master's: M.S. with thesis, M.Eng.
Doctoral: Ph.D.

UNDERGRADUATE INFORMATION

ADMISSION INQUIRIES
Mark Spencer
Director
Cornell University
College of Engineering, 102 Hollister Hall
Ithaca, NY 14853
Phone: (607) 255-5008
Fax: (607) 255-0971

ESTIMATED STUDENT EXPENSES (FALL 2006)
[Expenses are for the 2006-2007 nine-month academic year and are based on an average credit load of: Undergraduate: 17]

	All Students
Tutition and fees:	$32,981
Campus and Room and Board:	$10,776
Books and Supplies:	$700
Other Expenses:	$1,420
Total Estimated Expenses:	**$45,877**

NEW APPLICANTS/NEWLY ENROLLED STUDENTS
[Numbers are for the undergraduate engineering college for the Fall 2006 term]

Number of Applicants (a):	5,594
Of those, Number Offered Admission (b):	2,028
Of those, Number Enrolled Fall 2006 (c):	781

GRADUATE INFORMATION

ESTIMATED STUDENT EXPENSES (FALL 2006)
[Expenses are for the 2006-2007 nine-month academic year and are based on an average credit load of: Graduate: 15]

	All Students
Tutition and fees:	$32,870
Campus and Room and Board:	$15,446
Books and Supplies:	$700
Other Expenses:	$1,516
Total Estimated Expenses:	**$50,532**

NEW APPLICANTS/NEWLY ENROLLED STUDENTS
[Numbers are for the graduate engineering college for the Fall 2006 term]

Number of Applicants (a):	4,621
Of those, Number Offered Admission (b):	1,123
Of those, Number Enrolled Fall 2006 (c):	554

Dartmouth College

INSTITUTION INFORMATION
8000 Cummings Hall
Hanover, NH 03755
Phone: (603) 646-2230
Fax: (603) 646-1620
Web: http://www.engineering.dartmouth.edu

GENERAL INFORMATION
[All Students - Fall 2006]

Undergraduate Enrollment	4,110
Graduate Enrollment	1,374
Professional Enrollment	296
Total Enrollment	**5,780**

ENGINEERING COLLEGE INFORMATION

HEAD OF ENGINEERING
Joseph J. Helble
Dean
Thayer School of Engineering
Dartmouth College
8000 Cummings Hall
Hanover, NH 03755
Phone: (603) 646-2238
Fax: (603) 646-2580
Email: joseph.helble@dartmouth.edu

TYPES OF ENGINEERING DEGREES
Bachelor's: B.A.
Master's: M.S. with thesis, M.E.M.
Doctoral: Ph.D.

UNDERGRADUATE INFORMATION

ESTIMATED STUDENT EXPENSES (FALL 2006)
[Expenses are for the 2006-2007 nine-month academic year and are based on an average credit load of: Undergraduate: 9]

	All Students
Tuition and fees:	$33,501
Campus and Room and Board:	$9,840
Books and Supplies:	$2,622
Other Expenses:	
Total Estimated Expenses:	**$45,963**

Note: Credit load based on three courses per term.

NEW APPLICANTS/NEWLY ENROLLED STUDENTS
[Numbers are for the undergraduate engineering college for the Fall 2006 term]

Number of Applicants (a):	1,206
Of those, Number Offered Admission (b):	206
Of those, Number Enrolled Fall 2006 (c):	93

Note: Mean ACT scores for Class of 2006 matriculants was 29.5%

GRADUATE INFORMATION

ESTIMATED STUDENT EXPENSES (FALL 2006)
[Expenses are for the 2006-2007 nine-month academic year and are based on an average credit load of: Graduate: 9]

	All Students
Tutition and fees:	$33,297
Campus and Room and Board:	$13,386
Books and Supplies:	$1,060
Other Expenses:	$5,685
Total Estimated Expenses:	**$53,428**

Note: Credit load based on three courses per term.

NEW APPLICANTS/NEWLY ENROLLED STUDENTS
[Numbers are for the graduate engineering college for the Fall 2006 term]

Number of Applicants (a):	159
Of those, Number Offered Admission (b):	28
Of those, Number Enrolled Fall 2006 (c):	15

University of Dayton

INSTITUTION INFORMATION
300 College Park, KL-266
Dayton, OH 45469-0228
Phone: (937) 229-2736
Fax: (937) 229-2756
Web: http://engineering.udayton.edu

GENERAL INFORMATION
[All Students - Fall 2006]

Undergraduate Enrollment	7,473
Graduate Enrollment	3,030
Professional Enrollment	0
Total Enrollment	**10,503**

ENGINEERING COLLEGE INFORMATION

HEAD OF ENGINEERING
Joseph E Saliba
Dean
School of Engineering
University of Dayton
300 College Park
Dayton, OH 45469-0228
Phone: (937) 229-2736
Fax: (937) 229-2756
Email: Joseph.Saliba@notes.udayton.edu

ENGINEERING COLLEGE INQUIRIES
John Weber
Assistant Dean for Recruitment & Continuous Improvement
University of Dayton
300 College Park
Dayton, OH 45469-0228
Phone: (937) 229-2736
Fax: (937) 229-2756
Email: john.weber@notes.udayton.edu

ENGINEERING COLLEGE INQUIRIES
Riad Alakkad
Assistant Dean for Undergraduate Advising and Retention
University of Dayton
300 College Park
Dayton, OH 45469-0228
Phone: (937) 229-2736
Fax: (937) 229-2756
Email: riad.alakkad@notes.udayton.edu

TYPES OF ENGINEERING DEGREES
Bachelor's: B.S.
Master's: M.S. with thesis, M.S. without thesis, but with project or report
Doctoral: Ph.D., D.Eng

UNDERGRADUATE INFORMATION

ESTIMATED STUDENT EXPENSES (FALL 2006)
[Expenses are for the 2006-2007 nine-month academic year and are based on an average credit load of: Undergraduate: 16]

	All Students
Tuition and fees:	$24,985
Campus and Room and Board:	$7,410
Books and Supplies:	$850
Other Expenses:	$1,300
Total Estimated Expenses:	**$34,545**

NEW APPLICANTS/NEWLY ENROLLED STUDENTS
[Numbers are for the undergraduate engineering college for the Fall 2006 term]

Number of Applicants (a):	1,221
Of those, Number Offered Admission (b):	1,046
Of those, Number Enrolled Fall 2006 (c):	313

GRADUATE INFORMATION

ADMISSION INQUIRIES
Donald L Moon
Associate Dean for Engineering
University of Dayton
300 College Park
Dayton , OH 45469-0228
Phone: (937) 229-2242
Fax: (937) 229-2756
Email: don.moon@notes.udayton.edu

ADMISSION INQUIRIES
Marilyn K Knisley
University of Dayton
300 College Park
Dayton , OH 45469-0228
Phone: (937) 229-2241
Fax: (937) 229-2756
Email: marilyn.knisley@notes.udayton.edu

ESTIMATED STUDENT EXPENSES (FALL 2006)
[Expenses are for the 2006-2007 nine-month academic year and are based on an average credit load of: Graduate: 6]

	All Students
Tuition and fees:	$6,499
Campus and Room and Board:	
Books and Supplies:	$1,200
Other Expenses:	$1,250
Total Estimated Expenses:	**$8,949**

NEW APPLICANTS/NEWLY ENROLLED STUDENTS
[Numbers are for the graduate engineering college for the Fall 2006 term]

Number of Applicants (a):	798
Of those, Number Offered Admission (b):	284
Of those, Number Enrolled Fall 2006 (c):	90

University of Delaware

INSTITUTION INFORMATION
University of Delaware
Newark, DE 19716
Phone: (302) 831-2000
Fax: (302) 831-8000
Web: http://www.udel.edu

GENERAL INFORMATION
[All Students - Fall 2006]

Undergraduate Enrollment	15,849
Graduate Enrollment	3,446

Professional Enrollment	1,085
Total Enrollment	**20,380**

ENGINEERING COLLEGE INFORMATION

HEAD OF ENGINEERING
Eric W Kaler
Dean
College of Engineering
University of Delaware
College of Engineering
102 DuPont Hall
Newark, DE 19716-3101
Phone: (302) 831-3553
Fax: (302) 831-6751
Email: kaler@udel.edu

TYPES OF ENGINEERING DEGREES
Bachelor's: B.S.
Master's: M.S. with thesis
Doctoral: Ph.D.

UNDERGRADUATE INFORMATION

ADMISSION INQUIRIES
Dan L Boulet
Assistant Dean for Undergraduate Affairs
University of Delaware
102 DuPont Hall
Newark, DE 19716
Phone: (302) 831-8659
Fax: (302) 831-8179
Email: boulet@udel.edu

ESTIMATED STUDENT EXPENSES (FALL 2006)
[Expenses are for the 2006-2007 nine-month academic year and are based on an average credit load of: Undergraduate: 15]

	In-State	Out-of-State
Tuition and Fees:	$7,744	$18,454
Campus and Room and Board:	$7,366	$7,366
Books and Supplies:	$800	$800
Other Expenses:	$1,500	$1,500
Total Estimated Expenses:	**$17,410**	**$28,120**

Note: Fees include student health service fee, student center fee, comprehensive student fee.

NEW APPLICANTS/NEWLY ENROLLED STUDENTS
[Numbers are for the undergraduate engineering college for the Fall 2006 term]

Number of Applicants (a):	1,883
Of those, Number Offered Admission (b):	1,074
Of those, Number Enrolled Fall 2006 (c):	292

GRADUATE INFORMATION

ADMISSION INQUIRIES
Mary J Martin
Assistant Provost
University of Delaware
Hullihen Hall
Newark , DE 19716
Phone: (302) 831-2129
Fax: (302) 831-8745
Email: marym@udel.edu

ESTIMATED STUDENT EXPENSES (FALL 2006)
[Expenses are for the 2006-2007 nine-month academic year and are based on an average credit load of: Graduate: 9]

	In-State	Out-of-State
Tuition and Fees:	$7,600	$18,310
Campus and Room and Board:	$9,000	$9,000
Books and Supplies:	$800	$800
Other Expenses:	$1,500	$1,500
Total Estimated Expenses:	**$18,900**	**$29,610**

Note: Fees include student health service fee, student center fee, comprehensive student fee.

NEW APPLICANTS/NEWLY ENROLLED STUDENTS
[Numbers are for the graduate engineering college for the Fall 2006 term]

Number of Applicants (a):	1,653
Of those, Number Offered Admission (b):	423
Of those, Number Enrolled Fall 2006 (c):	185

University of Detroit Mercy

INSTITUTION INFORMATION
4001 W McNichols Rd
Detroit, MI 48221-3038
Phone: (313) 993-1216
Fax: (313) 993-1187
Web: http://www.udmercy.edu

GENERAL INFORMATION
[All Students - Fall 2006]

Undergraduate Enrollment	3,141
Graduate Enrollment	1,307
Professional Enrollment	1,081
Total Enrollment	**5,529**

ENGINEERING COLLEGE INFORMATION

HEAD OF ENGINEERING
Leo E Hanifin
Dean
College of Engineering and Science
University of Detroit Mercy
4001 W. McNichols Rd.
Detroit, MI 48221-3038
Phone: (313) 993-1216
Fax: (313) 993-1187
Email: hanifinl@udmercy.edu

ENGINEERING COLLEGE INQUIRIES
Valeria Clay
Records Manager
University of Detroit Mercy
4001 W McNichols Rd
Detroit, MI 48221-3038
Phone: (313) 993-1216
Fax: (313) 993-1187
Email: clayvc@udmercy.edu

TYPES OF ENGINEERING DEGREES
Bachelor's: B.S.
Master's: M.S. with thesis, M.S. without thesis, but with project or report
Doctoral: D.Eng

UNDERGRADUATE INFORMATION

ESTIMATED STUDENT EXPENSES (FALL 2006)
[Expenses are for the 2006-2007 nine-month academic year and are based on an average credit load of: Undergraduate: 16]

	Other Group 1	Other Group 2
Tuition and Fees:	$25,020	$23,970
Campus and Room and Board:	$7,456	$7,456
Books and Supplies:	$1,796	$1,386
Other Expenses:	$3,931	$3,931
Total Estimated Expenses:	**$38,203**	**$36,743**

NEW APPLICANTS/NEWLY ENROLLED STUDENTS
[Numbers are for the undergraduate engineering college for the Fall 2006 term]

Number of Applicants (a):	215
Of those, Number Offered Admission (b):	128
Of those, Number Enrolled Fall 2006 (c):	36

GRADUATE INFORMATION

ADMISSION INQUIRIES
Valeria Clay
Records Manager
University of Detroit Mercy
4001 W McNichols Rd
Detroit , MI 48221-3038
Phone: (313) 993-1216
Fax: (313) 993-1187
Email: clayvc@udmercy.edu

ESTIMATED STUDENT EXPENSES (FALL 2006)
[Expenses are for the 2006-2007 nine-month academic year and are based on an average credit load of: Graduate: 9]

	Other Group 1	Other Group 2
Tuition and Fees:	$16,590	$16,320
Campus and Room and Board:	$7,456	$7,456
Books and Supplies:	$1,796	$1,386
Other Expenses:	$3,931	$3,931
Total Estimated Expenses:	**$29,773**	**$29,093**

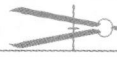

NEW APPLICANTS/NEWLY ENROLLED STUDENTS
[Numbers are for the graduate engineering college for the Fall 2006 term]

Number of Applicants (a):	0
Of those, Number Offered Admission (b):	0
Of those, Number Enrolled Fall 2006 (c):	56

Drexel University

INSTITUTION INFORMATION

3141 Chestnut Street
Philadelphia, PA 19104-2875
Phone: (215) 895-2000
Fax: (215) 895-4929
Web: http://www.drexel.edu

ENGINEERING COLLEGE INFORMATION

HEAD OF ENGINEERING

Selcuk I Guceri
Dean
College of Engineering
Drexel University
LeBow Engineering Center, Suite 239
3141 Chestnut Street
Philadelphia, PA 19104-2875
Phone: (215) 895-2210
Fax: (215) 895-4929
Email: guceri@drexel.edu

TYPES OF ENGINEERING DEGREES

Bachelor's: B.S.
Master's: M.S. with thesis, M.S. without thesis, but with project or report
Doctoral: Ph.D.

UNDERGRADUATE INFORMATION

ADMISSION INQUIRIES

Joan T McDonald
Vice President, Enrollment Management
Drexel University
Main Bldg, Room 212, 3141 Chestnut Street
Philadelphia, PA 19104-2875
Phone: (215) 895-2902
Fax: (215) 895-5939
Email: Mcdonajt@drexel.edu

NEW APPLICANTS/NEWLY ENROLLED STUDENTS

[Numbers are for the undergraduate engineering college for the Fall 2006 term]

Number of Applicants (a):	4,508
Of those, Number Offered Admission (b):	3,031
Of those, Number Enrolled Fall 2006 (c):	679

GRADUATE INFORMATION

ADMISSION INQUIRIES

Joan T McDonald
Vice President, Enrollment Management
Drexel University
Main Bldg, Room 212, 3141 Chestnut Street
Philadelphia , PA 19104-2875
Phone: (215) 895-2902
Fax: (215) 895-5939
Email: Mcdonajt@drexel.edu

NEW APPLICANTS/NEWLY ENROLLED STUDENTS

[Numbers are for the graduate engineering college for the Fall 2006 term]

Number of Applicants (a):	2,394
Of those, Number Offered Admission (b):	922
Of those, Number Enrolled Fall 2006 (c):	380

Duke University Pratt School of Engineering

INSTITUTION INFORMATION

305 Teer Building
Box 90271
Durham, NC 27708-0271
Phone: (919) 660-5386
Fax: (919) 684-4860
Web: http://pratt.duke.edu

GENERAL INFORMATION

[All Students - Fall 2006]

Undergraduate Enrollment	6,179
Graduate Enrollment	2,599
Professional Enrollment	3,770
Total Enrollment	**12,548**

ENGINEERING COLLEGE INFORMATION

HEAD OF ENGINEERING

Kristina M. Johnson
Dean and Professor
Pratt School of Engineering
Duke University Pratt School of Engineering
305 Teer Building
Box 90271
Durham, NC 27708-0271
Phone: (919) 660-5389
Fax: (919) 684-4860
Email: kristina.johnson@duke.edu

TYPES OF ENGINEERING DEGREES

Bachelor's: B.S.
Master's: M.S. with thesis, M.S. without thesis, but with project or report
Doctoral: Ph.D.

UNDERGRADUATE INFORMATION

ESTIMATED STUDENT EXPENSES (FALL 2006)

[Expenses are for the 2006-2007 nine-month academic year and are based on an average credit load of: Undergraduate: N/A]

	All Students
Tuition and fees:	$34,202
Campus and Room and Board:	$9,340
Books and Supplies:	$900
Other Expenses:	$1,608
Total Estimated Expenses:	**$46,050**

GRADUATE INFORMATION

ESTIMATED STUDENT EXPENSES (FALL 2006)

[Expenses are for the 2006-2007 nine-month academic year and are based on an average credit load of: Graduate: N/A]

	All Students
Tuition and fees:	$35,829
Campus and Room and Board:	$8,910
Books and Supplies:	$1,080
Other Expenses:	$6,140
Total Estimated Expenses:	**$51,959**

Ecole Polytechnique de Montreal

INSTITUTION INFORMATION

C.P. 6079
Succursale Centre-ville
Montreal, PQ H3C 3A7
Phone: (514) 340-4711
Fax: (514) 340-4600
Web: http://www.polymtl.ca

GENERAL INFORMATION

[All Students - Fall 2006]

Undergraduate Enrollment	3,101
Graduate Enrollment	1,615
Professional Enrollment	828
Total Enrollment	**5,544**

ENGINEERING COLLEGE INFORMATION

HEAD OF ENGINEERING

Robert L Papineau
Chief Executive Officer
Direction générale
Ecole Polytechnique de Montreal
P.O.Box 6079 Station Centre-ville
Montreal, PQ H3C3A7
Phone: (514) 340-4943
Fax: (514) 340-4600
Email: robert.papineau@polymtl.ca

TYPES OF ENGINEERING DEGREES

Bachelor's: B.A., B.S.
Master's: M.A. with thesis, M.A. without thesis, but with

project or report, M.S. with thesis
Doctoral: Ph.D.

UNDERGRADUATE INFORMATION

ESTIMATED STUDENT EXPENSES (FALL 2006)

[Expenses are for the 2006-2007 nine-month academic year and are based on an average credit load of: Undergraduate: 15]

	In-State	Out-of-State
Tuition and Fees:	$2,400	$10,800
Campus and Room and Board:	$12,000	$12,000
Books and Supplies:	$2,000	$2,000
Other Expenses:	$650	$650
Total Estimated Expenses:	**$17,050**	**$25,450**

NEW APPLICANTS/NEWLY ENROLLED STUDENTS

[Numbers are for the undergraduate engineering college for the Fall 2006 term]

Number of Applicants (a):	1,672
Of those, Number Offered Admission (b):	1,300
Of those, Number Enrolled Fall 2006 (c):	677

GRADUATE INFORMATION

ESTIMATED STUDENT EXPENSES (FALL 2006)

[Expenses are for the 2006-2007 nine-month academic year and are based on an average credit load of: Graduate: 11]

	In-State	Out-of-State
Tuition and Fees:	$2,700	$11,000
Campus and Room and Board:	$12,000	$12,000
Books and Supplies:	$2,000	$2,000
Other Expenses:	$650	$650
Total Estimated Expenses:	**$17,350**	**$25,650**

NEW APPLICANTS/NEWLY ENROLLED STUDENTS

[Numbers are for the graduate engineering college for the Fall 2006 term]

Number of Applicants (a):	1,020
Of those, Number Offered Admission (b):	634
Of those, Number Enrolled Fall 2006 (c):	204

Ecole de Technologie Superieure

INSTITUTION INFORMATION

1100 rue Notre-Dame Ouest
Montreal, PQ H3C 1K3
Phone: (514) 396-8802
Fax: (514) 396-8539
Web: http://www.etsmtl.ca

GENERAL INFORMATION

[All Students - Fall 2006]

Undergraduate Enrollment	4,111
Graduate Enrollment	694
Professional Enrollment	0
Total Enrollment	**4,805**

ENGINEERING COLLEGE INFORMATION

HEAD OF ENGINEERING

Yves Beauchamp
Chief Executive Officer
Direction générale
Ecole de Technologie Superieure
1100 rue Notre Dame Ouest
Montréal, PQ H3C1K3
Phone: (514) 396-8802
Fax: (514) 396-8539
Email: ybeauchamp@etsmtl.ca

TYPES OF ENGINEERING DEGREES

Bachelor's: B. Ing.
Master's: M.S. with thesis, M.S. without thesis, but with project or report
Doctoral: Ph.D.

UNDERGRADUATE INFORMATION

ADMISSION INQUIRIES

Francine Gamache
Registrar
Ecole de Technologie Superieure
1100 rue Notre-Dame Ouest
Montreal, PQ H3C 1K3
Phone: (514) 396-8885

Fax: (514) 396-8931
Email: francine.gamache@etsmtl.ca

ESTIMATED STUDENT EXPENSES (FALL 2006)
[Expenses are for the 2006-2007 nine-month academic year and are based on an average credit load of: Undergraduate: N/A]

	Canadian Citizen	Non-Canadian
Tuition and Fees:	$2,128	$13,231
Campus and Room and Board:	$10,404	$10,404
Books and Supplies:	$2,889	$2,889
Other Expenses:	$1,144	$1,144
Total Estimated Expenses:	**$16,565**	**$27,668**

Note: Expenses are for twelve months (three trimesters) in canadian dollars. Tuition & Fees for non canadian students include health insurance.

NEW APPLICANTS/NEWLY ENROLLED STUDENTS
[Numbers are for the undergraduate engineering college for the Fall 2006 term]

Number of Applicants (a):	1,088
Of those, Number Offered Admission (b):	953
Of those, Number Enrolled Fall 2006 (c):	742

GRADUATE INFORMATION

ADMISSION INQUIRIES
Francine Gamache
Registrar
Ecole de Technologie Superieure
1100 rue Notre-Dame Ouest
Montreal , PQ H3C 1K3
Phone: (514) 396-8885
Fax: (514) 396-8931
Email: francine.gamache@etsmtl.ca

ESTIMATED STUDENT EXPENSES (FALL 2006)
[Expenses are for the 2006-2007 nine-month academic year and are based on an average credit load of: Graduate: N/A]

	Canadian Citizen	Non-Canadian
Tuition and Fees:	$1,800	$9,936
Campus and Room and Board:	$10,404	$10,404
Books and Supplies:	$2,889	$2,889
Other Expenses:	$1,144	$1,144
Total Estimated Expenses:	**$16,237**	**$23,229**

Note: Expenses are for twelve months (three trimesters) in canadian dollars. Tuition & Fees for non canadian students include health insurance.

NEW APPLICANTS/NEWLY ENROLLED STUDENTS
[Numbers are for the graduate engineering college for the Fall 2006 term]

Number of Applicants (a):	248
Of those, Number Offered Admission (b):	185
Of those, Number Enrolled Fall 2006 (c):	123

Embry Riddle Aeronautical Univ., Daytona Beach

INSTITUTION INFORMATION
600 South Clyde Morris Boulevard
Daytona Beach, FL 32114-3900
Phone: (386) 226-6100
Fax: (386) 226-6459
Web: http://www.embryriddle.edu

GENERAL INFORMATION
[All Students - Fall 2006]

Undergraduate Enrollment	4,473
Graduate Enrollment	390
Professional Enrollment	0
Total Enrollment	**4,863**

ENGINEERING COLLEGE INFORMATION

HEAD OF ENGINEERING
Thomas Hilburn
Dean
College of Engineering
Embry Riddle Aeronautical Univ., Daytona Beach
600 S. Clyde Morris Blvd.
Daytona Beach, FL 32114-3900
Phone: (386) 226-6748
Fax: (386) 226-6747
Email: thomas.hilburn@erau.edu

TYPES OF ENGINEERING DEGREES
Bachelor's: B.S.

Master's: M.S. with thesis, M.S. without thesis, but with project or report
Doctoral:

UNDERGRADUATE INFORMATION

ESTIMATED STUDENT EXPENSES (FALL 2006)
[Expenses are for the 2006-2007 nine-month academic year and are based on an average credit load of: Undergraduate: 14]

	All Students
Tuition and fees:	$25,490
Campus and Room and Board:	$7,070
Books and Supplies:	$950
Other Expenses:	$3,600
Total Estimated Expenses:	**$37,110**

NEW APPLICANTS/NEWLY ENROLLED STUDENTS
[Numbers are for the undergraduate engineering college for the Fall 2006 term]

Number of Applicants (a):	1,890
Of those, Number Offered Admission (b):	1,550
Of those, Number Enrolled Fall 2006 (c):	538

Note: Fact Book 2006/Admissions/Overall Applicants (UG)

GRADUATE INFORMATION

ESTIMATED STUDENT EXPENSES (FALL 2006)
[Expenses are for the 2006-2007 nine-month academic year and are based on an average credit load of: Graduate: 7]

	All Students
Tuition and fees:	$13,010
Campus and Room and Board:	$6,360
Books and Supplies:	$950
Other Expenses:	$3,910
Total Estimated Expenses:	**$24,230**

NEW APPLICANTS/NEWLY ENROLLED STUDENTS
[Numbers are for the graduate engineering college for the Fall 2006 term]

Number of Applicants (a):	98
Of those, Number Offered Admission (b):	63
Of those, Number Enrolled Fall 2006 (c):	29

Embry Riddle Aeronautical University, Prescott

INSTITUTION INFORMATION
3700 Willow Creek Road
Prescott, AZ 86301-3720
Phone: (928) 777-3728
Fax: (928) 777-3740
Web: http://www.embryriddle.edu

GENERAL INFORMATION
[All Students - Fall 2006]

Undergraduate Enrollment	1,630
Graduate Enrollment	44
Professional Enrollment	0
Total Enrollment	**1,674**

ENGINEERING COLLEGE INFORMATION

HEAD OF ENGINEERING
Donald A Rabern
Dean
College of Engineering
Embry Riddle Aeronautical University, Prescott
3700 Willow Creek Road
Prescott, AZ 86301-3720
Phone: (928) 777-4052
Fax: (928) 777-6952
Email: don.rabern@erau.edu

ENGINEERING COLLEGE INQUIRIES
Richard F Felton
Professor and Assoc. Dean
Embry Riddle Aeronautical University, Prescott
3700 Willow Creek Road
Prescott, AZ 86301-3720
Phone: (928) 777-3843
Fax: (928) 777-6952
Email: feltonr@erau.edu

TYPES OF ENGINEERING DEGREES
Bachelor's: B.S.
Master's:
Doctoral:

UNDERGRADUATE INFORMATION

ESTIMATED STUDENT EXPENSES (FALL 2006)
[Expenses are for the 2006-2007 nine-month academic year and are based on an average credit load of: Undergraduate: 14]

	All Students
Tuition and fees:	$25,120
Campus and Room and Board:	$7,070
Books and Supplies:	$950
Other Expenses:	$3,600
Total Estimated Expenses:	**$36,740**

NEW APPLICANTS/NEWLY ENROLLED STUDENTS
[Numbers are for the undergraduate engineering college for the Fall 2006 term]

Number of Applicants (a):	546
Of those, Number Offered Admission (b):	484
Of those, Number Enrolled Fall 2006 (c):	190

GRADUATE INFORMATION

ADMISSION INQUIRIES
Richard F Felton
Professor and Assoc. Dean
Embry Riddle Aeronautical University, Prescott
3700 Willow Creek Road
Prescott , AZ 86301-3720
Phone: (928) 777-3843
Fax: (928) 777-6952
Email: feltonr@erau.edu

ESTIMATED STUDENT EXPENSES (FALL 2006)
[Expenses are for the 2006-2007 nine-month academic year and are based on an average credit load of: Graduate: 6]

	All Students
Tuition and fees:	$13,310
Campus and Room and Board:	$6,360
Books and Supplies:	$950
Other Expenses:	$3,910
Total Estimated Expenses:	**$24,530**

University of Evansville

INSTITUTION INFORMATION
1800 Lincoln Avenue
Evansville, IN 47722
Phone: (812) 488-2651
Fax: (812) 488-2780
Web: http://www.evansville.edu

GENERAL INFORMATION
[All Students - Fall 2006]

Undergraduate Enrollment	2,610
Graduate Enrollment	66
Professional Enrollment	203
Total Enrollment	**2,879**

ENGINEERING COLLEGE INFORMATION

HEAD OF ENGINEERING
Philip M Gerhart
Dean
College of Engineering and Computer Science
University of Evansville
1800 Lincoln Ave.
Evansville, IN 47722
Phone: (812) 488-2651
Fax: (812) 488-2780
Email: pg3@evansville.edu

ENGINEERING COLLEGE INQUIRIES
Tina G Newman
Administrative Associate
University of Evansville
1800 Lincoln Ave
Evansville, IN 47722
Phone: (812) 488-2651
Fax: (812) 488-2780
Email: tn2@evansville.edu

TYPES OF ENGINEERING DEGREES
Bachelor's: B.S.
Master's: M.S. with thesis
Doctoral:

UNDERGRADUATE INFORMATION

ESTIMATED STUDENT EXPENSES (FALL 2006)
[Expenses are for the 2006-2007 nine-month academic year and are based on an average credit load of: Undergraduate: 15]

	In-State	Out-of-State
Tuition and Fees:	$22,980	
Campus and Room and Board:	$7,120	
Books and Supplies:	$900	
Other Expenses:		
Total Estimated Expenses:	**$31,000**	

NEW APPLICANTS/NEWLY ENROLLED STUDENTS
[Numbers are for the undergraduate engineering college for the Fall 2006 term]

Number of Applicants (a):	294
Of those, Number Offered Admission (b):	269
Of those, Number Enrolled Fall 2006 (c):	98

Ferris State University

INSTITUTION INFORMATION
College of Technology
1009 E. Campus Dr., Johnson 200
Big Rapids, MI 49307
Phone: (231) 591-2890
Fax: (231) 591-2946
Web: http://www.ferris.edu/

GENERAL INFORMATION
[All Students - Fall 2006]

Undergraduate Enrollment	11,409
Graduate Enrollment	518
Professional Enrollment	648
Total Enrollment	**12,575**

ENGINEERING COLLEGE INFORMATION

HEAD OF ENGINEERING
Thomas E. Oldfield
Dean
College of Technology
Ferris State University
1009 E. Campus Dr., Johnson 200
Big Rapids, MI 49307
Phone: (231) 591-2898
Fax: (231) 591-2946
Email: hoisingr@ferris.edu

TYPES OF ENGINEERING DEGREES
Bachelor's: B.S.
Master's:
Doctoral:

UNDERGRADUATE INFORMATION

ESTIMATED STUDENT EXPENSES (FALL 2006)
[Expenses are for the 2006-2007 nine-month academic year and are based on an average credit load of: Undergraduate: 15]

	In-State	Out-of-State
Tuition and Fees:	$7,342	$14,782
Campus and Room and Board:	$7,220	$7,220
Books and Supplies:	$1,000	$1,000
Other Expenses:	$2,078	$2,078
Total Estimated Expenses:	**$17,640**	**$25,080**

Note: Graduate tuition amount is per credit hour.

GRADUATE INFORMATION

ESTIMATED STUDENT EXPENSES (FALL 2006)
[Expenses are for the 2006-2007 nine-month academic year and are based on an average credit load of: Graduate: 12]

	In-State	Out-of-State
Tuition and Fees:	$8,520	$16,488
Campus and Room and Board:		
Books and Supplies:		
Other Expenses:		
Total Estimated Expenses:	**$8,520**	**$16,488**

Note: Graduate tuition amount is per credit hour.

University of Florida

INSTITUTION INFORMATION
P.O. Box 113150

Gainesville, FL 32611-3150
Phone: (352) 392-1311
Fax: (352) 392-9506
Web: http://www.ufl.edu

GENERAL INFORMATION
[All Students - Fall 2006]

Undergraduate Enrollment	35,110
Graduate Enrollment	11,439
Professional Enrollment	4,363
Total Enrollment	**50,912**

ENGINEERING COLLEGE INFORMATION

HEAD OF ENGINEERING
Pramod P Khargonekar
Dean & Professor
College of Engineering
University of Florida
300 Weil Hall
P.O. Box 116550
Gainesville, FL 32611-6550
Phone: (352) 392-6000
Fax: (352) 392-9673
Email: ppk@eng.ufl.edu

ENGINEERING COLLEGE INQUIRIES
Timothy J Anderson
Associate Dean for Research and Graduate Programs & Professor
University of Florida
300 Weil Hall, P.O. Box 116550
Gainesville, FL 32611-6550
Phone: (352) 392-0946
Fax: (359) 392-9673
Email: tim@ufl.edu

TYPES OF ENGINEERING DEGREES
Bachelor's: B.S.
Master's: M.S. with thesis, M.S. without thesis, but with project or report, M.Eng.
Doctoral: Ph.D., Engineer

UNDERGRADUATE INFORMATION

ADMISSION INQUIRIES
Jonathan F. K. Earle
Associate Dean for Student Affairs & Associate Professor
University of Florida
312 Weil Hall, P.O. Box 116550
Gainesville, FL 32611-6550
Phone: (352) 392-2177
Fax: (352) 392-9673
Email: jearl@eng.ufl.edu

ESTIMATED STUDENT EXPENSES (FALL 2006)
[Expenses are for the 2006-2007 nine-month academic year and are based on an average credit load of: Undergraduate: 15]

	In-State	Out-of-State
Tuition and Fees:	$3,206	$17,791
Campus and Room and Board:	$7,640	$7,640
Books and Supplies:	$920	$920
Other Expenses:	$3,530	$3,530
Total Estimated Expenses:	**$15,296**	**$29,881**

Note: Other Expenses: Local Transportation, clothing, personal/health insurance, and annual computer costs (access is required, ownership is strongly recommended).

NEW APPLICANTS/NEWLY ENROLLED STUDENTS
[Numbers are for the undergraduate engineering college for the Fall 2006 term]

Number of Applicants (a):	0
Of those, Number Offered Admission (b):	0
Of those, Number Enrolled Fall 2006 (c):	1,003

GRADUATE INFORMATION

ADMISSION INQUIRIES
Timothy J Anderson
Associate Dean for Research and Graduate Programs & Professor
University of Florida
300 Weil Hall, P.O. Box 116550
Gainesville , FL 32611-6550
Phone: (352) 392-0946
Fax: (359) 392-9673
Email: tim@ufl.edu

ESTIMATED STUDENT EXPENSES (FALL 2006)
[Expenses are for the 2006-2007 nine-month academic year

---

and are based on an average credit load of: Graduate: 12]

	In-State	Out-of-State
Tuition and Fees:	$6,827	$21,951
Campus and Room and Board:	$7,640	$7,640
Books and Supplies:	$920	$920
Other Expenses:	$3,530	$3,530
Total Estimated Expenses:	**$18,917**	**$34,041**

Note: Other Expenses: Local Transportation, clothing, personal/health insurance, and annual computer costs (access is required, ownership is strongly recommended).

NEW APPLICANTS/NEWLY ENROLLED STUDENTS
[Numbers are for the graduate engineering college for the Fall 2006 term]

Number of Applicants (a):	3,569
Of those, Number Offered Admission (b):	1,547
Of those, Number Enrolled Fall 2006 (c):	608

Florida Atlantic University

INSTITUTION INFORMATION
777 Glades Road
Boca Raton, FL 33431-0991
Phone: (561) 297-2492
Fax: (561) 297-1111
Web: http://www.eng.fau.edu

GENERAL INFORMATION
[All Students - Fall 2006]

Undergraduate Enrollment	19,838
Graduate Enrollment	3,451
Professional Enrollment	2,096
Total Enrollment	**25,385**

ENGINEERING COLLEGE INFORMATION

HEAD OF ENGINEERING
Karl K Stevens
Dean
College of Engineering
Florida Atlantic University
777 Glades Road
Boca Raton, FL 33431-0991
Phone: (561) 297-3487
Fax: (561) 297-1111
Email: stevens@fau.edu

TYPES OF ENGINEERING DEGREES
Bachelor's: B.S.
Master's: M.S. with thesis, M.S. without thesis, but with project or report
Doctoral: Ph.D.

UNDERGRADUATE INFORMATION

ADMISSION INQUIRIES
Sharon M Schlossberg
Assistant Dean, Engineering Student Services
Florida Atlantic University
777 Glades Road
Boca Raton, FL 33431-0991
Phone: (561) 297-2680
Fax: (561) 297-2781
Email: sschloss@fau.edu

ESTIMATED STUDENT EXPENSES (FALL 2006)
[Expenses are for the 2006-2007 nine-month academic year and are based on an average credit load of: Undergraduate: 15]

	In-State	Out-of-State
Tuition and Fees:	$3,327	$16,391
Campus and Room and Board:	$8,280	$8,280
Books and Supplies:	$724	$724
Other Expenses:	$1,458	$1,458
Total Estimated Expenses:	**$13,789**	**$26,853**

Note: Tuition per credit hour

NEW APPLICANTS/NEWLY ENROLLED STUDENTS
[Numbers are for the undergraduate engineering college for the Fall 2006 term]

Number of Applicants (a):	696
Of those, Number Offered Admission (b):	400
Of those, Number Enrolled Fall 2006 (c):	188

GRADUATE INFORMATION

ESTIMATED STUDENT EXPENSES (FALL 2006)
[Expenses are for the 2006-2007 nine-month academic year and are based on an average credit load of: Graduate: 9]

	In-State	Out-of-State
Tuition and Fees:	$4,394	$16,441
Campus and Room and Board:	$8,280	$8,280
Books and Supplies:	$724	$724
Other Expenses:	$1,458	$1,458
Total Estimated Expenses:	**$14,856**	**$26,903**

Note: Tuition per credit hour

NEW APPLICANTS/NEWLY ENROLLED STUDENTS
[Numbers are for the graduate engineering college for the Fall 2006 term]

Number of Applicants (a):	165
Of those, Number Offered Admission (b):	86
Of those, Number Enrolled Fall 2006 (c):	24

Florida Institute of Technology

INSTITUTION INFORMATION

150 W. University Blvd.
Melbourne, FL 32901-6975
Phone: (321) 674-8000
Fax: (321) 984-8461
Web: http://www.fit.edu

GENERAL INFORMATION
[All Students - Fall 2006]

Undergraduate Enrollment	2,365
Graduate Enrollment	2,376
Professional Enrollment	0
Total Enrollment	**4,741**

ENGINEERING COLLEGE INFORMATION

HEAD OF ENGINEERING
Thomas D. Waite
Dean
College of Engineering
Florida Institute of Technology
150 W. University Blvd.
Melbourne, FL 32901-6975
Phone: (321) 674-8020
Fax: (321) 674-7270
Email: twaite@fit.edu

TYPES OF ENGINEERING DEGREES
Bachelor's: B.S.
Master's: M.S. with thesis, M.S. without thesis, but with project or report
Doctoral: Ph.D.

UNDERGRADUATE INFORMATION

ADMISSION INQUIRIES
Judith A Marino
Director, Undergraduate Admission
Florida Institute of Technology
150 West University Blvd.
Melbourne, FL 32901-6975
Phone: (321) 674-7227
Fax: (321) 723-9468
Email: jmarino@fit.edu

ESTIMATED STUDENT EXPENSES (FALL 2006)
[Expenses are for the 2006-2007 nine-month academic year and are based on an average credit load of: Undergraduate: 15]

	All Students
Tuition and fees:	$27,540
Campus and Room and Board:	$7,400
Books and Supplies:	$2,200
Other Expenses:	$1,500
Total Estimated Expenses:	**$38,640**

Note: Eng. & Sci. Programs Tuition $27,540; All Other Programs Tuition $25,100

NEW APPLICANTS/NEWLY ENROLLED STUDENTS
[Numbers are for the undergraduate engineering college for the Fall 2006 term]

Number of Applicants (a):	2,746
Of those, Number Offered Admission (b):	1,748
Of those, Number Enrolled Fall 2006 (c):	335

GRADUATE INFORMATION

ADMISSION INQUIRIES
Carolyn P Farrior
Director, Graduate Admissions
Florida Institute of Technology
150 West University Blvd.
Melbourne , FL 32901-6975
Phone: (321) 674-7118
Fax: (321) 723-9468
Email: cfarrior@fit.edu

ESTIMATED STUDENT EXPENSES (FALL 2006)
[Expenses are for the 2006-2007 nine-month academic year and are based on an average credit load of: Graduate: 9]

	All Students
Tuition and fees:	$900
Campus and Room and Board:	$7,400
Books and Supplies:	$2,200
Other Expenses:	$1,500
Total Estimated Expenses:	**$12,000**

Note: Eng. & Sci. Programs Tuition $27,540; All Other Programs Tuition $25,100

NEW APPLICANTS/NEWLY ENROLLED STUDENTS
[Numbers are for the graduate engineering college for the Fall 2006 term]

Number of Applicants (a):	737
Of those, Number Offered Admission (b):	420
Of those, Number Enrolled Fall 2006 (c):	117

Florida International University

INSTITUTION INFORMATION

University Park
11200 SW 8th Street
Miami, FL 33199
Phone: (305) 348-2522
Web: http://www.fiu.edu

GENERAL INFORMATION
[All Students - Fall 2006]

Undergraduate Enrollment	28,914
Graduate Enrollment	5,416
Professional Enrollment	3,094
Total Enrollment	**37,424**

ENGINEERING COLLEGE INFORMATION

HEAD OF ENGINEERING
Vish Prasad
Executive Dean
College of Engineering and Computing
Florida International University
10555 W. Flagler St
Engineering Center
Miami, FL 33174
Phone: (305) ,30-5348
Fax: (305) 348-1401
Email: prasadv@fiu.edu

TYPES OF ENGINEERING DEGREES
Bachelor's: B.A., B.S.
Master's: M.S. with thesis, M.S. without thesis, but with project or report
Doctoral: Ph.D.

UNDERGRADUATE INFORMATION

ADMISSION INQUIRIES
Carmen A Brown
Director, Admissions
Florida International University
University Park Campus, 11200 SW 8th St.
Miami, FL 33199
Phone: (305) 348-3722
Fax: (305) 348-3648
Email: brownc@fiu.edu

ESTIMATED STUDENT EXPENSES (FALL 2006)
[Expenses are for the 2006-2007 nine-month academic year and are based on an average credit load of: Undergraduate: 15]

	In-State	Out-of-State
Tuition and Fees:	$3,382	$15,813
Campus and Room and Board:	$6,520	$6,520
Books and Supplies:	$872	$872
Other Expenses:	$6,600	$6,600
Total Estimated Expenses:	**$17,374**	**$29,805**

NEW APPLICANTS/NEWLY ENROLLED STUDENTS
[Numbers are for the undergraduate engineering college for the Fall 2006 term]

Number of Applicants (a):	1,517
Of those, Number Offered Admission (b):	860
Of those, Number Enrolled Fall 2006 (c):	434

GRADUATE INFORMATION

ADMISSION INQUIRIES
Agarwal Arvind
Assistant Professor and Graduate Program Director
Florida International University
University Park, 11200 SW 8th Street
Miami, FL 33199
Phone: (305) 348-1701
Fax: (305) 348-1932
Email: arvind.agarwal@fiu.edu

ADMISSION INQUIRIES
Syed Ahmed
Assistant Professor and Graduate Program Director
Florida International University
University Park, 11200 SW 8th Street
Miami, FL 33199
Phone: (305) 348-2730
Fax: (305) 348-6255
Email: syed.ahmed@fiu.edu

ADMISSION INQUIRIES
Albert Gan
Professor and Graduate Program Director
Florida International University
University Park, 11200 SW 8th Street
Miami, FL 33199
Phone: (305) 348-3116
Fax: (305) 348-2802
Email: albert.gan@fiu.edu

ADMISSION INQUIRIES
Berrin Tansel
Associate Professor and Graduate Program Director
Florida International University
University Park, 11200 SW 8th Street
Miami, FL 33199
Phone: (305) 348-2928
Fax: (305) 348-2802
Email: berrin.tansel@fiu.edu

ADMISSION INQUIRIES
Jean Andrian
Professor and Graduate Program Director
Florida International University
University Park, 11200 SW 8th Street
Miami, FL 33199
Phone: (305) 348-2115
Fax: (305) 348-3707
Email: jean.andrian@fiu.edu

ADMISSION INQUIRIES
Amy Diaz
Graduate Coordinator
Florida International University
University Park, 11200 SW 8th Street
Miami, FL 33199
Phone: (305) 348-3526
Fax: (305) 348-6142
Email: amira.diaz@fiu.edu

ADMISSION INQUIRIES
Richard Schoephoerster
Chair and Graduate Program Director, Biomedical Engineering
Florida International University
Engineering Center, 10555 W Flagler St.
Miami, FL 33174
Phone: (305) 348-3722
Fax: (305) 348-6954

ESTIMATED STUDENT EXPENSES (FALL 2006)
[Expenses are for the 2006-2007 nine-month academic year and are based on an average credit load of: Graduate: 9]

	In-State	Out-of-State
Tuition and Fees:	$4,693	$13,842
Campus and Room and Board:	$6,520	$6,520
Books and Supplies:	$872	$872
Other Expenses:	$6,600	$6,600
Total Estimated Expenses:	**$18,685**	**$27,834**

Of those, Number Offered Admission (b): 506
Of those, Number Enrolled Fall 2006 (c): 170

NEW APPLICANTS/NEWLY ENROLLED STUDENTS

[Numbers are for the graduate engineering college for the Fall 2006 term]

Number of Applicants (a):	682
Of those, Number Offered Admission (b):	447
Of those, Number Enrolled Fall 2006 (c):	180

FAMU-FSU College of Engineering

INSTITUTION INFORMATION

2525 Pottsdamer Street
Tallahassee, FL 32310-6046
Phone: (850) 410-6161
Fax: (850) 410-6486
Web: http://www.eng.fsu.edu

GENERAL INFORMATION

[All Students - Fall 2006]

Undergraduate Enrollment	41,049
Graduate Enrollment	9,471
Professional Enrollment	1,864
Total Enrollment	**52,384**

ENGINEERING COLLEGE INFORMATION

HEAD OF ENGINEERING

Ching-Jen Chen
Dean of Engineering
Office of the Dean
FAMU-FSU College of Engineering
2525 Pottsdamer Street
Room B206F
Tallahassee, FL 32310-6046
Phone: (850) 410-6439
Fax: (850) 410-6546
Email: cjchen@eng.fsu.edu

ENGINEERING COLLEGE INQUIRIES

David Edelson
Special Assistant to the Dean
FAMU-FSU College of Engineering
2525 Pottsdamer Street, Room B206H
Tallahassee, FL 32310-6046
Phone: (850) 410-6429
Fax: (850) 410-6546
Email: edelson@eng.fsu.edu

TYPES OF ENGINEERING DEGREES

Bachelor's: B.S.
Master's: M.S. with thesis, M.S. without thesis, but with project or report
Doctoral: Ph.D.

UNDERGRADUATE INFORMATION

ADMISSION INQUIRIES

Sheldon White
Director
FAMU-FSU College of Engineering
2525 Pottsdamer Street, Room B111D
Tallahassee, FL 32310-6046
Phone: (850) 410-6349
Fax: (850) 410-6344
Email: swhite@eng.fsu.edu

ESTIMATED STUDENT EXPENSES (FALL 2006)

[Expenses are for the 2006-2007 nine-month academic year and are based on an average credit load of: Undergraduate: 15]

	In-State	Out-of-State
Tuition and Fees:	$3,360	$17,322
Campus and Room and Board:	$7,800	$7,800
Books and Supplies:	$1,000	$1,000
Other Expenses:	$4,000	$4,000
Total Estimated Expenses:	**$16,160**	**$30,122**

Note: Tuition for FSU students; FAMU tuition is slightly lower. Room & Board based on on-campus housing and meal plan.

GRADUATE INFORMATION

ADMISSION INQUIRIES

Stephanie Gillis
Recruiter
FAMU-FSU College of Engineering
2525 Pottsdamer Street
Tallahassee , FL 32310-6046

Phone: (850) 410-6485
Fax: (850) 410-6224
Email: sgillis@eng.fsu.edu

ESTIMATED STUDENT EXPENSES (FALL 2006)

[Expenses are for the 2006-2007 nine-month academic year and are based on an average credit load of: Graduate: 15]

	In-State	Out-of-State
Tuition and Fees:	$7,228	$27,750
Campus and Room and Board:	$7,800	$7,800
Books and Supplies:	$1,000	$1,000
Other Expenses:	$4,000	$4,000
Total Estimated Expenses:	**$20,028**	**$40,550**

Note: Tuition for FSU students; FAMU tuition is slightly lower. Room & Board based on on-campus housing and meal plan.

Gannon University

INSTITUTION INFORMATION

109 University Square
Erie, PA 16541
Phone: (814) 871-7000
Web: http://www.gannon.edu

GENERAL INFORMATION

[All Students - Fall 2006]

Undergraduate Enrollment	2,675
Graduate Enrollment	1,140
Professional Enrollment	0
Total Enrollment	**3,815**

ENGINEERING COLLEGE INFORMATION

HEAD OF ENGINEERING

Carolynn Masters
Interim Dean
College of Sciences, Engineering and Health Sciences
Gannon University
University Square
Erie, PA 16541
Phone: (814) 871-7605
Email: masters004@gannon.edu

ENGINEERING COLLEGE INQUIRIES

Patricia A Maughn
Coordinator
Gannon University
University Square
Erie, PA 16541
Phone: (814) 871-7408

TYPES OF ENGINEERING DEGREES

Bachelor's: B.S.
Master's: M.S. with thesis, M.S. without thesis, but with project or report
Doctoral:

UNDERGRADUATE INFORMATION

ESTIMATED STUDENT EXPENSES (FALL 2006)

[Expenses are for the 2006-2007 nine-month academic year and are based on an average credit load of: Undergraduate: 16]

	All Students
Tuition and fees:	$21,176
Campus and Room and Board:	$7,880
Books and Supplies:	$1,000
Other Expenses:	$1,790
Total Estimated Expenses:	**$31,846**

GRADUATE INFORMATION

ESTIMATED STUDENT EXPENSES (FALL 2006)

[Expenses are for the 2006-2007 nine-month academic year and are based on an average credit load of: Graduate: 9]

	All Students
Tuition and fees:	$16,232
Campus and Room and Board:	
Books and Supplies:	$1,000
Other Expenses:	
Total Estimated Expenses:	**$17,232**

NEW APPLICANTS/NEWLY ENROLLED STUDENTS

[Numbers are for the graduate engineering college for the Fall 2006 term]

Number of Applicants (a):	715

George Mason University

INSTITUTION INFORMATION

4400 University Drive
Fairfax, VA 22030
Phone: (703) 993-1000
Fax: (703) 993-1633
Web: http://www.gmu.edu

GENERAL INFORMATION

[All Students - Fall 2006]

Undergraduate Enrollment	18,221
Graduate Enrollment	10,906
Professional Enrollment	762
Total Enrollment	**29,889**

ENGINEERING COLLEGE INFORMATION

HEAD OF ENGINEERING

Lloyd J. Griffiths
Dean
School of InformationTechnology and Engineering
George Mason University
4400 University Drive
MS 4A3 - Dean/IT&E
Fairfax, VA 22030-4444
Phone: (703) 993-1500
Fax: (703) 993-1734
Email: IT-Dean@gmu.edu

TYPES OF ENGINEERING DEGREES

Bachelor's: B.S.
Master's: M.S. with thesis, M.S. without thesis, but with project or report
Doctoral: Ph.D., D.Eng

UNDERGRADUATE INFORMATION

ADMISSION INQUIRIES

Andrew Flagel
Dean of Admissions
George Mason University
4400 University Drive
Fairfax, VA 22030
Phone: (703) 993-1515

ESTIMATED STUDENT EXPENSES (FALL 2006)

[Expenses are for the 2006-2007 nine-month academic year and are based on an average credit load of: Undergraduate: 15]

	In-State	Out-of-State
Tuition and Fees:	$6,553	$18,697
Campus and Room and Board:	$6,600	$6,600
Books and Supplies:	$1,400	$1,400
Other Expenses:	$500	$500
Total Estimated Expenses:	**$15,053**	**$27,197**

NEW APPLICANTS/NEWLY ENROLLED STUDENTS

[Numbers are for the undergraduate engineering college for the Fall 2006 term]

Number of Applicants (a):	1,109
Of those, Number Offered Admission (b):	648
Of those, Number Enrolled Fall 2006 (c):	272

GRADUATE INFORMATION

ESTIMATED STUDENT EXPENSES (FALL 2006)

[Expenses are for the 2006-2007 nine-month academic year and are based on an average credit load of: Graduate: 12]

	In-State	Out-of-State
Tuition and Fees:	$9,925	$18,697
Campus and Room and Board:	$6,600	$6,600
Books and Supplies:	$1,400	$1,400
Other Expenses:	$500	$500
Total Estimated Expenses:	**$18,425**	**$27,197**

NEW APPLICANTS/NEWLY ENROLLED STUDENTS

[Numbers are for the graduate engineering college for the Fall 2006 term]

Number of Applicants (a):	1,221
Of those, Number Offered Admission (b):	767
Of those, Number Enrolled Fall 2006 (c):	344

The George Washington University

INSTITUTION INFORMATION
2121 Eye Street, N.W.
Washington, DC 20052
Phone: (202) 994-1000
Fax: (202) 994-0654
Web: http://www.gwu.edu

GENERAL INFORMATION
[All Students - Fall 2006]
Undergraduate Enrollment	10,813
Graduate Enrollment	11,334
Professional Enrollment	2,384
Total Enrollment	**24,531**

ENGINEERING COLLEGE INFORMATION

HEAD OF ENGINEERING
Timothy W Tong
Dean, School of Engineering & Applied Science
School of Engineering and Applied Science
The George Washington University
Tompkins Hall, Suite 106
Washington, DC 20052
Phone: (202) 994-6080
Fax: (202) 994-3394
Email: tong@gwu.edu

ENGINEERING COLLEGE INQUIRIES
Howard N Davis
Director, Undergraduate Student Services, Advising & Records
The George Washington University
Tompkins Hall, Suite 104
Washington, DC 20052
Phone: (202) 994-7133
Fax: (202) 994-1651
Email: hdavis@gwu.edu

TYPES OF ENGINEERING DEGREES
Bachelor's: B.A., B.S.
Master's: M.S. with thesis, M.S. without thesis, but with project or report,Engr.; App.Sc.
Doctoral: D.Sc.

UNDERGRADUATE INFORMATION

ADMISSION INQUIRIES
Howard N Davis
Director, Undergraduate Student Services, Advising & Records
The George Washington University
Tompkins Hall, Suite 104
Washington, DC 20052
Phone: (202) 994-7133
Fax: (202) 994-1651
Email: hdavis@gwu.edu

ESTIMATED STUDENT EXPENSES (FALL 2006)
[Expenses are for the 2006-2007 nine-month academic year and are based on an average credit load of: Undergraduate: 15]
	All Students
Tuition and fees:	$37,790
Campus and Room and Board:	$11,100
Books and Supplies:	$1,000
Other Expenses:	$1,350
Total Estimated Expenses:	**$51,240**

NEW APPLICANTS/NEWLY ENROLLED STUDENTS
[Numbers are for the undergraduate engineering college for the Fall 2006 term]
Number of Applicants (a):	1,023
Of those, Number Offered Admission (b):	558
Of those, Number Enrolled Fall 2006 (c):	132

GRADUATE INFORMATION

ADMISSION INQUIRIES
Leah S Rochelle
Director, Graduate Marketing & Admissions
The George Washington University
Tompkins Hall, Suite 103
Washington , DC 20052
Phone: (202) 994-8675
Fax: (202) 994-1651
Email: lrochell@gwu.edu

ESTIMATED STUDENT EXPENSES (FALL 2006)
[Expenses are for the 2006-2007 nine-month academic year and are based on an average credit load of: Graduate: 9]
	All Students
Tuition and fees:	$17,460
Campus and Room and Board:	$16,380
Books and Supplies:	$1,350
Other Expenses:	$1,230
Total Estimated Expenses:	**$36,420**

NEW APPLICANTS/NEWLY ENROLLED STUDENTS
[Numbers are for the graduate engineering college for the Fall 2006 term]
Number of Applicants (a):	1,102
Of those, Number Offered Admission (b):	808
Of those, Number Enrolled Fall 2006 (c):	443

University of Georgia

INSTITUTION INFORMATION
120 Driftmier Engineering Center
Biological & Ag Engineering Dept.
Athens, GA 30602-4435
Phone: (706) 542-1653
Fax: (706) 542-8806
Web: http://www.engr.uga.edu

GENERAL INFORMATION
[All Students - Fall 2006]
Undergraduate Enrollment	24,885
Graduate Enrollment	6,323
Professional Enrollment	1,604
Total Enrollment	**32,812**

ENGINEERING COLLEGE INFORMATION

HEAD OF ENGINEERING
E. Dale Threadgill
Director
Faculty of Engineering
University of Georgia
Driftmier Engineering Center
Athens, GA 30602-4435
Phone: (706) 542-1653
Fax: (706) 542-8806
Email: tgill@engr.uga.edu

ENGINEERING COLLEGE INQUIRIES
E. Dale Threadgill
Director
University of Georgia
Driftmier Engineering Center
Athens, GA 30602-4435
Phone: (706) 542-1653
Fax: (706) 542-8806
Email: tgill@engr.uga.edu

TYPES OF ENGINEERING DEGREES
Bachelor's: B.S.A.E., B.S.B.E.
Master's: M.S. with thesis
Doctoral: Ph.D.

UNDERGRADUATE INFORMATION

ADMISSION INQUIRIES
Nancy G McDuff
Associate Vice President
University of Georgia
337 Terrell Hall
Athens, GA 30602
Phone: (706) 542-2112
Fax: (706) 542-1466
Email: nancymcduff@admissions.uga.edu

ADMISSION INQUIRIES
Tim Foutz
Professor/Undergraduate Coordinator
University of Georgia
Driftmier Engineering Center
Athens, GA 30602-4435
Phone: (706) 542-0868
Fax: (706) 542-8806
Email: tfoutz@engr.uga.edu

ESTIMATED STUDENT EXPENSES (FALL 2006)
[Expenses are for the 2006-2007 nine-month academic year and are based on an average credit load of: Undergraduate: 12]

	Other Group 1	Other Group 2
Tuition and Fees:	$4,964	$18,040
Campus and Room and Board:	$6,848	$6,848
Books and Supplies:	$800	$800
Other Expenses:	$2,200	$2,200
Total Estimated Expenses:	**$14,812**	**$27,888**

NEW APPLICANTS/NEWLY ENROLLED STUDENTS
[Numbers are for the undergraduate engineering college for the Fall 2006 term]
Number of Applicants (a):	0
Of those, Number Offered Admission (b):	0
Of those, Number Enrolled Fall 2006 (c):	69
Note: This information is not available at this time	

GRADUATE INFORMATION

ADMISSION INQUIRIES
Jan Sandor
Director of Admissions
University of Georgia
Graduate Studies Building
Athens , GA 30602
Phone: (706) 542-1787
Fax: (706) 542-9480
Email: jsandor@uga.edu

ADMISSION INQUIRIES
William S Kisaalita
Professor & Graduate Coordinator
University of Georgia
120 Driftmier Engineering Center, Biological & Ag Engineering Dept.
Athens , GA 30602-4435
Phone: (706) 542-0835
Fax: (706) 542-6063

ESTIMATED STUDENT EXPENSES (FALL 2006)
[Expenses are for the 2006-2007 nine-month academic year and are based on an average credit load of: Graduate: N/A]

	Other Group 1	Other Group 2
Tuition and Fees:	$5,658	$20,778
Campus and Room and Board:	$6,848	$6,848
Books and Supplies:	$800	$800
Other Expenses:	$2,200	$2,200
Total Estimated Expenses:	**$15,506**	**$30,626**

NEW APPLICANTS/NEWLY ENROLLED STUDENTS
[Numbers are for the graduate engineering college for the Fall 2006 term]
Number of Applicants (a):	34
Of those, Number Offered Admission (b):	19
Of those, Number Enrolled Fall 2006 (c):	10

Georgia Institute of Technology

INSTITUTION INFORMATION
225 North Avenue
College of Engineering
Atlanta, GA 30332-0360
Phone: (404) 894-2000
Web: http://www.gatech.edu

GENERAL INFORMATION
[All Students - Fall 2006]
Undergraduate Enrollment	12,360
Graduate Enrollment	5,575
Professional Enrollment	0
Total Enrollment	**17,935**

ENGINEERING COLLEGE INFORMATION

HEAD OF ENGINEERING
Don P. Giddens
Dean - Academic
College of Engineering
Georgia Institute of Technology
225 North Avenue
Atlanta, GA 30332-0360
Phone: (404) 894-6825
Fax: (404) 894-0168
Email: don.giddens@coe.gatech.edu

TYPES OF ENGINEERING DEGREES
Bachelor's: B.S.
Master's: M.S. with thesis, M.S. without thesis, but with

project or report
Doctoral: Ph.D.

UNDERGRADUATE INFORMATION

ESTIMATED STUDENT EXPENSES (FALL 2006)
[Expenses are for the 2006-2007 nine-month academic year and are based on an average credit load of: Undergraduate: 14]

	In-State	Out-of-State
Tuition and Fees:	$4,926	$20,272
Campus and Room and Board:	$7,094	$7,094
Books and Supplies:	$1,000	$1,000
Other Expenses:	$1,500	$1,500
Total Estimated Expenses:	**$14,520**	**$29,866**

NEW APPLICANTS/NEWLY ENROLLED STUDENTS
[Numbers are for the undergraduate engineering college for the Fall 2006 term]

Number of Applicants (a):	6,109
Of those, Number Offered Admission (b):	4,446
Of those, Number Enrolled Fall 2006 (c):	1,997

GRADUATE INFORMATION

ESTIMATED STUDENT EXPENSES (FALL 2006)
[Expenses are for the 2006-2007 nine-month academic year and are based on an average credit load of: Graduate: 16]

	In-State	Out-of-State
Tuition and Fees:	$5,620	$20,244
Campus and Room and Board:	$7,094	$7,094
Books and Supplies:	$1,000	$1,000
Other Expenses:	$1,500	$1,500
Total Estimated Expenses:	**$15,214**	**$29,838**

NEW APPLICANTS/NEWLY ENROLLED STUDENTS
[Numbers are for the graduate engineering college for the Fall 2006 term]

Number of Applicants (a):	5,775
Of those, Number Offered Admission (b):	2,017
Of those, Number Enrolled Fall 2006 (c):	1,062

Georgia Southern University

INSTITUTION INFORMATION
P.O. Box 8046
Statesboro, GA 30458
Phone: (912) 681-5751
Web: www.georgiasouthern.edu

GENERAL INFORMATION
[All Students - Fall 2006]

Undergraduate Enrollment	16,425
Graduate Enrollment	1,996
Professional Enrollment	0
Total Enrollment	**18,421**

ENGINEERING COLLEGE INFORMATION

TYPES OF ENGINEERING DEGREES
Bachelor's:
Master's:
Doctoral:

UNDERGRADUATE INFORMATION

ESTIMATED STUDENT EXPENSES (FALL 2006)
[Expenses are for the 2006-2007 nine-month academic year and are based on an average credit load of: Undergraduate: 12]

	All Students
Tuition and fees:	$1,560
Campus and Room and Board:	$3,950
Books and Supplies:	$500
Other Expenses:	
Total Estimated Expenses:	**$6,010**

GRADUATE INFORMATION

ESTIMATED STUDENT EXPENSES (FALL 2006)
[Expenses are for the 2006-2007 nine-month academic year and are based on an average credit load of: Graduate: 9]

	All Students
Tuition and fees:	$2,000
Campus and Room and Board:	$3,950
Books and Supplies:	$500

Other Expenses:
Total Estimated Expenses: $6,450

Gonzaga University

INSTITUTION INFORMATION
School of Engineering and Applied Science
502 East Boone Avenue
Spokane, WA 99258-0026
Phone: (509) 323-3522
Fax: (509) 323-5871
Web: http://gonzaga.edu

GENERAL INFORMATION
[All Students - Fall 2006]

Undergraduate Enrollment	4,186
Graduate Enrollment	1,614
Professional Enrollment	931
Total Enrollment	**6,731**

ENGINEERING COLLEGE INFORMATION

HEAD OF ENGINEERING
Dennis R Horn
Dean
School of Engineering
Gonzaga University
School of Engineering
502 East Boone Avenue
Spokane, WA 99258-0026
Phone: (509) 323-3522
Fax: (509) 323-5871
Email: horn@gonzaga.edu

TYPES OF ENGINEERING DEGREES
Bachelor's: B.S.
Master's:
Doctoral:

UNDERGRADUATE INFORMATION

ESTIMATED STUDENT EXPENSES (FALL 2006)
[Expenses are for the 2006-2007 nine-month academic year and are based on an average credit load of: Undergraduate: 15]

	All Students
Tuition and fees:	$25,175
Campus and Room and Board:	$6,980
Books and Supplies:	$875
Other Expenses:	$2,900
Total Estimated Expenses:	**$35,930**

NEW APPLICANTS/NEWLY ENROLLED STUDENTS
[Numbers are for the undergraduate engineering college for the Fall 2006 term]

Number of Applicants (a):	552
Of those, Number Offered Admission (b):	363
Of those, Number Enrolled Fall 2006 (c):	118

GRADUATE INFORMATION

ESTIMATED STUDENT EXPENSES (FALL 2006)
[Expenses are for the 2006-2007 nine-month academic year and are based on an average credit load of: Graduate: 6]

	All Students
Tuition and fees:	$8,280
Campus and Room and Board:	$8,775
Books and Supplies:	$450
Other Expenses:	$3,700
Total Estimated Expenses:	**$21,205**

Grand Valley State University

INSTITUTION INFORMATION
School of Engineering
301 West Fulton Street, Suite 718
Grand Rapids, MI 49504
Phone: (616) 331-6750
Fax: (616) 331-7215
Web: http://www.gvsu.edu

GENERAL INFORMATION
[All Students - Fall 2006]

Undergraduate Enrollment	19,578
Graduate Enrollment	3,717

Professional Enrollment	0
Total Enrollment	**23,295**

ENGINEERING COLLEGE INFORMATION

HEAD OF ENGINEERING
Jeffrey L Ray
Director
School of Engineering
Grand Valley State University
301 West Fulton, Suite 718
Grand Rapids, MI 49504
Phone: (616) 331-6750
Fax: (616) 331-7215
Email: rayj@gvsu.edu

TYPES OF ENGINEERING DEGREES
Bachelor's: B.S.E.
Master's: M.S. with thesis, M.S. without thesis, but with project or report
Doctoral:

UNDERGRADUATE INFORMATION

ESTIMATED STUDENT EXPENSES (FALL 2006)
[Expenses are for the 2006-2007 nine-month academic year and are based on an average credit load of: Undergraduate: 16]

	In-State	Out-of-State
Tuition and Fees:	$6,752	$12,721
Campus and Room and Board:	$6,614	$6,614
Books and Supplies:	$900	$900
Other Expenses:	$1,800	$1,800
Total Estimated Expenses:	**$16,066**	**$22,035**

NEW APPLICANTS/NEWLY ENROLLED STUDENTS
[Numbers are for the undergraduate engineering college for the Fall 2006 term]

Number of Applicants (a):	94
Of those, Number Offered Admission (b):	72
Of those, Number Enrolled Fall 2006 (c):	72

Note: All students entering college for the first time.

GRADUATE INFORMATION

ESTIMATED STUDENT EXPENSES (FALL 2006)
[Expenses are for the 2006-2007 nine-month academic year and are based on an average credit load of: Graduate: 9]

	In-State	Out-of-State
Tuition and Fees:	$5,850	$10,800
Campus and Room and Board:	$6,614	$6,614
Books and Supplies:	$750	$750
Other Expenses:	$1,800	$1,800
Total Estimated Expenses:	**$15,014**	**$19,964**

NEW APPLICANTS/NEWLY ENROLLED STUDENTS
[Numbers are for the graduate engineering college for the Fall 2006 term]

Number of Applicants (a):	69
Of those, Number Offered Admission (b):	65
Of those, Number Enrolled Fall 2006 (c):	52

Grove City College

INSTITUTION INFORMATION
100 Campus Drive
Grove City, PA 16127
Phone: (724) 458-2000
Fax: (724) 450-1550
Web: http://www.gcc.edu

GENERAL INFORMATION
[All Students - Fall 2006]

Undergraduate Enrollment	2,473
Graduate Enrollment	0
Professional Enrollment	0
Total Enrollment	**2,473**

ENGINEERING COLLEGE INFORMATION

HEAD OF ENGINEERING
Stacy G Birmingham
Dean, School of Science and Engineering
Hopeman School of Science and Engineering
Grove City College
100 Campus Drive
Box 3115
Grove City, PA 16127

Phone: (724) 458-2033
Fax: (724) 450-1550
Email: sgbirmingham@gcc.edu

TYPES OF ENGINEERING DEGREES
Bachelor's: B.S.
Master's:
Doctoral:

UNDERGRADUATE INFORMATION

ADMISSION INQUIRIES
Jeffrey C Mincey
Director of Admissions
Grove City College
100 Campus Drive
Grove City, PA 16127
Phone: (724) 458-2040
Fax: (724) 458-3395
Email: jcmincey@gcc.edu

ESTIMATED STUDENT EXPENSES (FALL 2006)
[Expenses are for the 2006-2007 nine-month academic year and are based on an average credit load of: Undergraduate: 16]

	All Students
Tuition and fees:	$10,962
Campus and Room and Board:	$5,766
Books and Supplies:	$900
Other Expenses:	$750
Total Estimated Expenses:	**$18,378**

Note: Tuition includes a tablet notebook computer and printer for all full-time freshmen

NEW APPLICANTS/NEWLY ENROLLED STUDENTS
[Numbers are for the undergraduate engineering college for the Fall 2006 term]

Number of Applicants (a):	208
Of those, Number Offered Admission (b):	142
Of those, Number Enrolled Fall 2006 (c):	96

University of Hartford

INSTITUTION INFORMATION
College of Engineering, Technology, and Architecture
200 Bloomfield Avenue
West Hartford, CT 06117
Phone: (860) 768-4112
Fax: (860) 768-5073
Web: http://www.hartford.edu

GENERAL INFORMATION
[All Students - Fall 2006]

Undergraduate Enrollment	5,572
Graduate Enrollment	1,708
Professional Enrollment	23
Total Enrollment	**7,303**

ENGINEERING COLLEGE INFORMATION

HEAD OF ENGINEERING
Lou Manzione
Dean
College of Engineering, Technology, and Architecture
University of Hartford
200 Bloomfield Avenue
West Hartford, CT 06117
Phone: (860) 768-4844
Fax: (860) 768-5073
Email: manzione@hartford.edu

ENGINEERING COLLEGE INQUIRIES
Rachel Bagby
Recruitment Manager
University of Hartford
200 Bloomfield Avenue
West Hartford, CT 06117
Phone: (860) 768-4446
Fax: (860) 768-5073
Email: bagby@hartford.edu

TYPES OF ENGINEERING DEGREES
Bachelor's: B.S.
Master's: M.Eng.
Doctoral:

UNDERGRADUATE INFORMATION

ADMISSION INQUIRIES
Rachel Bagby
Recruitment Manager
University of Hartford
200 Bloomfield Avenue
West Hartford, CT 06117
Phone: (860) 768-4446
Fax: (860) 768-5073
Email: bagby@hartford.edu

ESTIMATED STUDENT EXPENSES (FALL 2006)
[Expenses are for the 2006-2007 nine-month academic year and are based on an average credit load of: Undergraduate: 16]

	All Students
Tuition and fees:	$25,766
Campus and Room and Board:	$10,382
Books and Supplies:	$600
Other Expenses:	
Total Estimated Expenses:	**$36,748**

NEW APPLICANTS/NEWLY ENROLLED STUDENTS
[Numbers are for the undergraduate engineering college for the Fall 2006 term]

Number of Applicants (a):	701
Of those, Number Offered Admission (b):	536
Of those, Number Enrolled Fall 2006 (c):	91

GRADUATE INFORMATION

ADMISSION INQUIRIES
Laurie Granstrand
Manager of Graduate Programs
University of Hartford
200 Bloomfield Avenue
West Hartford , CT 06117
Phone: (860) 768-4858
Fax: (860) 768-5073
Email: granstran@hartford.edu

ESTIMATED STUDENT EXPENSES (FALL 2006)
[Expenses are for the 2006-2007 nine-month academic year and are based on an average credit load of: Graduate: 9]

	All Students
Tuition and fees:	$8,600
Campus and Room and Board:	
Books and Supplies:	$400
Other Expenses:	
Total Estimated Expenses:	**$9,000**

NEW APPLICANTS/NEWLY ENROLLED STUDENTS
[Numbers are for the graduate engineering college for the Fall 2006 term]

Number of Applicants (a):	118
Of those, Number Offered Admission (b):	79
Of those, Number Enrolled Fall 2006 (c):	39

Harvard University

INSTITUTION INFORMATION
110 Pierce Hall
29 Oxford Street
Cambridge, MA 02138
Phone: (617) 495-2833
Fax: (617) 496-4177
Web: http://www.harvard.edu

ENGINEERING COLLEGE INFORMATION

HEAD OF ENGINEERING
Venkatesh Narayanamurti
Dean, Division of Engineering and Applied Sciences
Division of Engineering and Applied Sciences
Harvard University
Pierce Hall 217
29 Oxford Street
Cambridge, MA 02138
Phone: (617) 495-5829
Fax: (617) 496-5264
Email: venky@deas.harvard.edu

ENGINEERING COLLEGE INQUIRIES
Sandra L. Godfrey
Academic Programs Administrator
Harvard University
Pierce Hall 110, 29 Oxford St.
Cambridge, MA 02138

Phone: (617) 495-2833
Fax: (617) 496-4177
Email: godfrey@deas.harvard.edu

TYPES OF ENGINEERING DEGREES
Bachelor's: S.B.,A.B.
Master's: S.M., M.Eng.
Doctoral: Ph.D.

UNDERGRADUATE INFORMATION

ADMISSION INQUIRIES
Sandra L. Godfrey
Academic Programs Administrator
Harvard University
Pierce Hall 110, 29 Oxford St.
Cambridge, MA 02138
Phone: (617) 495-2833
Fax: (617) 496-4177
Email: godfrey@deas.harvard.edu

ADMISSION INQUIRIES
Patricia Ryan
Staff Assistant
Harvard University
Pierce Hall 110, 29 Oxford St.
Cambridge, MA 02138
Phone: (677) 495-2833
Fax: (617) 496-4177
Email: admissions@deas.harvard.edu

ADMISSION INQUIRIES
Marie D Dahleh
Assistant Dean for Academic Programs/Assistant Director of Undergraduate Studies
Harvard University
111 Pierce Hall, 29 Oxford Street
Cambridge, MA 02138
Phone: (617) 495-1485
Fax: (617) 496-4177
Email: mdahleh@deas.harvard.edu

ESTIMATED STUDENT EXPENSES (FALL 2006)
[Expenses are for the 2006-2007 nine-month academic year and are based on an average credit load of: Undergraduate: N/A]

	All Students
Tuition and fees:	$33,709
Campus and Room and Board:	$9,946
Books and Supplies:	$2,795
Other Expenses:	
Total Estimated Expenses:	**$46,450**

NEW APPLICANTS/NEWLY ENROLLED STUDENTS
[Numbers are for the undergraduate engineering college for the Fall 2006 term]

Number of Applicants (a):	22,754
Of those, Number Offered Admission (b):	2,125
Of those, Number Enrolled Fall 2006 (c):	1,684

GRADUATE INFORMATION

ADMISSION INQUIRIES
Julie Holbrook
Director, Graduate Admissions
Harvard University
130 Pierce Hall, 29 Oxford Street
Cambridge , MA 02138
Phone: (617) 495-2747
Fax: (617) 496-4177
Email: holbrook@deas.harvard.edu

ADMISSION INQUIRIES
Lisa Frazier-Zezze
Staff Assistant
Harvard University
110 Pierce Hall, 29 Oxford Street
Cambridge , MA 02138
Phone: (617) 495-2833
Fax: (617) 496-4177
Email: lfrazier@deas.harvard.edu

ESTIMATED STUDENT EXPENSES (FALL 2006)
[Expenses are for the 2006-2007 nine-month academic year and are based on an average credit load of: Graduate: N/A]

	All Students
Tuition and fees:	$32,882
Campus and Room and Board:	$14,670
Books and Supplies:	$900
Other Expenses:	$4,730
Total Estimated Expenses:	**$53,182**

NEW APPLICANTS/NEWLY ENROLLED STUDENTS
[Numbers are for the graduate engineering college for the Fall 2006 term]

Number of Applicants (a):	1,189
Of those, Number Offered Admission (b):	174
Of those, Number Enrolled Fall 2006 (c):	106

University of Hawaii at Manoa

INSTITUTION INFORMATION
2540 Dole Street
Holmes Hall 240
Honolulu, HI 96822
Phone: (808) 956-7727
Fax: (808) 956-2291
Web: http://www.eng.hawaii.edu

GENERAL INFORMATION
[All Students - Fall 2006]

Undergraduate Enrollment	43,439
Graduate Enrollment	6,551
Professional Enrollment	0
Total Enrollment	**49,990**

ENGINEERING COLLEGE INFORMATION

HEAD OF ENGINEERING
Peter E. Crouch
Dean
College of Engineering
University of Hawaii at Manoa
2540 Dole Street, Holmes Hall 240
Honolulu, HI 96822
Phone: (808) 956-7727
Fax: (808) 956-2291
Email: peter.crouch@hawaii.edu

TYPES OF ENGINEERING DEGREES
Bachelor's: B.S.
Master's: M.S. with thesis, M.S. without thesis, but with project or report
Doctoral: Ph.D.

UNDERGRADUATE INFORMATION

ADMISSION INQUIRIES
Tep Dobry
Director of Academic Affairs
University of Hawaii at Manoa
2540 Dole Street, Holmes Hall 240
Honolulu, HI 96822
Phone: (808) 956-8404
Fax: (808) 956-2291

ESTIMATED STUDENT EXPENSES (FALL 2006)
[Expenses are for the 2006-2007 nine-month academic year and are based on an average credit load of: Undergraduate: 15]

	In-State	Out-of-State
Tuition and Fees:	$4,320	$12,192
Campus and Room and Board:	$2,800	$7,200
Books and Supplies:	$1,145	$1,145
Other Expenses:	$1,200	$1,200
Total Estimated Expenses:	**$9,465**	**$21,737**

Note: Undergraduate tuition based on 12 credits as full time. Graduate tuition based on 8 credits as full time. Room and board estimates for in-state are based on living at home; for out-of-state, undergraduate room and board is based on living in the dormitory and graduate room and board is based on living off campus.

NEW APPLICANTS/NEWLY ENROLLED STUDENTS
[Numbers are for the undergraduate engineering college for the Fall 2006 term]

Number of Applicants (a):	307
Of those, Number Offered Admission (b):	280
Of those, Number Enrolled Fall 2006 (c):	129

GRADUATE INFORMATION

ESTIMATED STUDENT EXPENSES (FALL 2006)
[Expenses are for the 2006-2007 nine-month academic year and are based on an average credit load of: Graduate: 8]

	In-State	Out-of-State
Tuition and Fees:	$3,888	$9,136
Campus and Room and Board:	$2,800	$11,200
Books and Supplies:	$1,145	$1,145

Other Expenses: $1,200 $1,200
Total Estimated Expenses: **$9,033** **$22,681**
Note: Undergraduate tuition based on 12 credits as full time. Graduate tuition based on 8 credits as full time. Room and board estimates for in-state are based on living at home; for out-of-state, undergraduate room and board is based on living in the dormitory and graduate room and board is based on living off campus.

NEW APPLICANTS/NEWLY ENROLLED STUDENTS
[Numbers are for the graduate engineering college for the Fall 2006 term]

Number of Applicants (a):	121
Of those, Number Offered Admission (b):	90
Of those, Number Enrolled Fall 2006 (c):	52

Hofstra University

INSTITUTION INFORMATION
Department of Engineering
133 Hofstra University
Hempstead, NY 11549
Phone: (516) 463-5544
Fax: (516) 463-4939
Web: http://www.hofstra.edu/engineering

GENERAL INFORMATION
[All Students - Fall 2006]

Undergraduate Enrollment	8,498
Graduate Enrollment	2,900
Professional Enrollment	1,152
Total Enrollment	**12,550**

ENGINEERING COLLEGE INFORMATION

TYPES OF ENGINEERING DEGREES
Bachelor's: B.A., B.S.
Master's: M.S. without thesis, but with project or report
Doctoral:

UNDERGRADUATE INFORMATION

ADMISSION INQUIRIES
Sunil Samuel
Senior Associate Dean of Admissions
Hofstra University
102 Bernon Hall, Admissions Center
Hempstead, NY 11549
Phone: (516) 463-6697
Fax: (516) 463-5100
Email: Sunil.A. Samuel@hofstra.edu

ESTIMATED STUDENT EXPENSES (FALL 2006)
[Expenses are for the 2006-2007 nine-month academic year and are based on an average credit load of: Undergraduate: 15]

	All Students
Tuition and fees:	$24,830
Campus and Room and Board:	$9,800
Books and Supplies:	$1,000
Other Expenses:	$2,666
Total Estimated Expenses:	**$38,296**

NEW APPLICANTS/NEWLY ENROLLED STUDENTS
[Numbers are for the undergraduate engineering college for the Fall 2006 term]

Number of Applicants (a):	479
Of those, Number Offered Admission (b):	321
Of those, Number Enrolled Fall 2006 (c):	50

GRADUATE INFORMATION

ESTIMATED STUDENT EXPENSES (FALL 2006)
[Expenses are for the 2006-2007 nine-month academic year and are based on an average credit load of: Graduate: 9]

	All Students
Tuition and fees:	$13,320
Campus and Room and Board:	$9,800
Books and Supplies:	$1,000
Other Expenses:	$2,666
Total Estimated Expenses:	**$26,786**

University of Houston, Cullen School of Engineering

INSTITUTION INFORMATION
Cullen College of Engineering
E421 Engineering Bldg2
Houston, TX 77204-4007
Phone: (713) 743-1010
Web: http://www.uh.edu

GENERAL INFORMATION
[All Students - Fall 2006]

Undergraduate Enrollment	27,400
Graduate Enrollment	5,053
Professional Enrollment	1,881
Total Enrollment	**34,334**

ENGINEERING COLLEGE INFORMATION

HEAD OF ENGINEERING
Raymond W. Flumerfelt
Dean; Professor
Engineering, Chemical Engineering
University of Houston
Cullen College of Engineering
E421 Engineering Bldg 2
Houston, TX 77204-4007
Phone: (713) 743-4200
Fax: (713) 743-4214
Email: rwf@uh.edu

ENGINEERING COLLEGE INQUIRIES
Kitty J Karson
Assistant to the Dean
University of Houston
Cullen College of Engineering, E421 Engineering Bldg. 2
Houston, TX 77204-4007
Phone: (713) 743-4242
Fax: (713) 743-4214
Email: rbanks@uh.edu

TYPES OF ENGINEERING DEGREES
Bachelor's: B.S.
Master's: M.S. with thesis, M.S. without thesis, but with project or report
Doctoral: Ph.D.

UNDERGRADUATE INFORMATION

ADMISSION INQUIRIES
Frank (Fritz) Claydon
Professor, Associate Dean Undergraduate Programs & Computer Facilities
University of Houston
Cullen College of Engineering, E421, Engineering Bldg. 2
Houston, TX 77204-4007
Phone: (713) 743-4200
Fax: (713) 743-4214
Email: fclaydon@uh.edu

ESTIMATED STUDENT EXPENSES (FALL 2006)
[Expenses are for the 2006-2007 nine-month academic year and are based on an average credit load of: Undergraduate: 15]

	In-State	Out-of-State
Tuition and Fees:	$6,909	$15,159
Campus and Room and Board:	$6,418	$6,418
Books and Supplies:	$1,050	$1,050
Other Expenses:	$4,182	$4,182
Total Estimated Expenses:	**$18,559**	**$26,809**

*Note: *** Tuition & Fees are based on 15hrs/sem for Undergraduate and 9hrs/sem for Graduate.*

*****Other expenses are:*
Other expenses =$2,958 and
Transportation =$1,224

NEW APPLICANTS/NEWLY ENROLLED STUDENTS
[Numbers are for the undergraduate engineering college for the Fall 2006 term]

Number of Applicants (a):	935
Of those, Number Offered Admission (b):	737
Of those, Number Enrolled Fall 2006 (c):	369

GRADUATE INFORMATION

ADMISSION INQUIRIES
Larry C. Witte
Professor; Associate Dean of Graduate Programs
University of Houston
Cullen College of Engineering, E421 Engineering Bldg 2.
Houston , TX 77204-4007
Phone: (713) 743-4205
Fax: (713) 743-4214
Email: witte@uh.edu

ESTIMATED STUDENT EXPENSES (FALL 2006)
[Expenses are for the 2006-2007 nine-month academic year and are based on an average credit load of: Graduate: 9]

	In-State	Out-of-State
Tuition and Fees:	$6,063	$11,013
Campus and Room and Board:	$6,818	$6,818
Books and Supplies:	$1,050	$1,050
Other Expenses:	$4,182	$4,182
Total Estimated Expenses:	**$18,113**	**$23,063**

*Note: *** Tuition & Fees are based on 15hrs/sem for Undergraduate and 9hrs/sem for Graduate.*

*****Other expenses are:*
Other expenses =$2,958 and
Transportation =$1,224

NEW APPLICANTS/NEWLY ENROLLED STUDENTS
[Numbers are for the graduate engineering college for the Fall 2006 term]

Number of Applicants (a):	637
Of those, Number Offered Admission (b):	374
Of those, Number Enrolled Fall 2006 (c):	151

Humboldt State University

INSTITUTION INFORMATION
1 Harpst Street
Arcata, CA 95521-8299
Web: http://www.humboldt.edu

GENERAL INFORMATION
[All Students - Fall 2006]

Undergraduate Enrollment	6,466
Graduate Enrollment	969
Professional Enrollment	0
Total Enrollment	**7,435**

ENGINEERING COLLEGE INFORMATION

HEAD OF ENGINEERING
James H Howard
Dean
College of Natural Resources and Sciences
Humboldt State University
1 Harpst Street
Arcata, CA 95521
Phone: (707) 826-3256
Fax: (707) 826-3562
Email: howard@humboldt.edu

TYPES OF ENGINEERING DEGREES
Bachelor's: B.S.
Master's: M.S. with thesis
Doctoral:

UNDERGRADUATE INFORMATION

ESTIMATED STUDENT EXPENSES (FALL 2006)
[Expenses are for the 2006-2007 nine-month academic year and are based on an average credit load of: Undergraduate: 12]

	In-State	Out-of-State
Tuition and Fees:	$3,175	$11,311
Campus and Room and Board:	$8,269	$8,269
Books and Supplies:	$1,142	$1,142
Other Expenses:	$1,944	$1,944
Total Estimated Expenses:	**$14,530**	**$22,666**

NEW APPLICANTS/NEWLY ENROLLED STUDENTS
[Numbers are for the undergraduate engineering college for the Fall 2006 term]

Number of Applicants (a):	115
Of those, Number Offered Admission (b):	0
Of those, Number Enrolled Fall 2006 (c):	43

GRADUATE INFORMATION

ESTIMATED STUDENT EXPENSES (FALL 2006)
[Expenses are for the 2006-2007 nine-month academic year and are based on an average credit load of: Graduate: 9]

	In-State	Out-of-State
Tuition and Fees:	$3,757	$9,859
Campus and Room and Board:	$8,269	$8,269
Books and Supplies:	$1,142	$1,142
Other Expenses:	$1,944	$1,944
Total Estimated Expenses:	**$15,112**	**$21,214**

University of Idaho

INSTITUTION INFORMATION
College of Engineering
P.O. Box 441011
Moscow, ID 83844-1011
Phone: (208) 885-6479
Fax: (208) 885-6645
Web: http://www.engr.uidaho.edu

GENERAL INFORMATION
[All Students - Fall 2006]

Undergraduate Enrollment	8,636
Graduate Enrollment	2,013
Professional Enrollment	1,090
Total Enrollment	**11,739**

ENGINEERING COLLEGE INFORMATION

HEAD OF ENGINEERING
Aicha Elshabini
Dean
College of Engineering
University of Idaho
College of Engineering
P.O. Box 441011
Moscow, ID 83844-1011
Phone: (208) 885-6470
Fax: (208) 885-6645
Email: elshabini@uidaho.edu

ENGINEERING COLLEGE INQUIRIES
Howard S Peavy
Professor and Associate Dean
University of Idaho
College of Engineering, P.O. Box 441011
Moscow, ID 83844-1011
Phone: (208) 885-6479
Fax: (208) 885-6645
Email: howardp@uidaho.edu

TYPES OF ENGINEERING DEGREES
Bachelor's: B.S.
Master's: M.S. with thesis, M.Eng.
Doctoral: Ph.D.

UNDERGRADUATE INFORMATION

ADMISSION INQUIRIES
Howard S Peavy
Professor and Associate Dean
University of Idaho
College of Engineering, P.O. Box 441011
Moscow, ID 83844-1011
Phone: (208) 885-6479
Fax: (208) 885-6645
Email: howardp@uidaho.edu

ESTIMATED STUDENT EXPENSES (FALL 2006)
[Expenses are for the 2006-2007 nine-month academic year and are based on an average credit load of: Undergraduate: 16]

	In-State	Out-of-State
Tuition and Fees:	$4,200	$13,800
Campus and Room and Board:	$5,696	$5,696
Books and Supplies:	$1,388	$1,388
Other Expenses:	$4,236	$4,236
Total Estimated Expenses:	**$15,520**	**$25,120**

NEW APPLICANTS/NEWLY ENROLLED STUDENTS
[Numbers are for the undergraduate engineering college for the Fall 2006 term]

Number of Applicants (a):	923
Of those, Number Offered Admission (b):	739
Of those, Number Enrolled Fall 2006 (c):	432

Note: Average ACT Composite Score: 24.770

GRADUATE INFORMATION

ADMISSION INQUIRIES
Charles Hatch
Vice Provost Research / Dean of Graduate Studies
University of Idaho
College of Graduate Studies, P.O. Box 443010
Moscow , ID 83844-3010
Phone: (208) 885-4989
Fax: (208) 885-6198
Email: crhatch@uidaho.edu

ESTIMATED STUDENT EXPENSES (FALL 2006)
[Expenses are for the 2006-2007 nine-month academic year and are based on an average credit load of: Graduate: 9]

	In-State	Out-of-State
Tuition and Fees:	$4,740	$14,340
Campus and Room and Board:	$5,696	$5,696
Books and Supplies:	$1,388	$1,388
Other Expenses:	$4,236	$4,236
Total Estimated Expenses:	**$16,060**	**$25,660**

NEW APPLICANTS/NEWLY ENROLLED STUDENTS
[Numbers are for the graduate engineering college for the Fall 2006 term]

Number of Applicants (a):	323
Of those, Number Offered Admission (b):	137
Of those, Number Enrolled Fall 2006 (c):	58

Idaho State University

INSTITUTION INFORMATION
921 S. 8th Ave.
Pocatello, ID 83209
Phone: (208) 282-0211
Fax: (208) 282-4000
Web: http://www.isu.edu

GENERAL INFORMATION
[All Students - Fall 2006]

Undergraduate Enrollment	12,402
Graduate Enrollment	2,839
Professional Enrollment	1,712
Total Enrollment	**16,953**

ENGINEERING COLLEGE INFORMATION

HEAD OF ENGINEERING
Richard T Jacobsen
Dean and Professor
College of Engineering
Idaho State University
921 S 8th Ave.
MS 8060
Pocatello, ID 83209
Phone: (208) 282-2902
Fax: (208) 282-4538
Email: jacorich@isu.edu

TYPES OF ENGINEERING DEGREES
Bachelor's: B.S.
Master's: M.S. with thesis, M.S. without thesis, but with project or report
Doctoral: Ph.D.

UNDERGRADUATE INFORMATION

ADMISSION INQUIRIES
Alan Frantz
Interim Dir, Admissions
Idaho State University
921 S. 8th Ave., MS 8270
Pocatello, ID 83209
Phone: (208) 282-2661
Fax: (208) 282-4231
Email: franalan@isu.edu

ESTIMATED STUDENT EXPENSES (FALL 2006)
[Expenses are for the 2006-2007 nine-month academic year and are based on an average credit load of: Undergraduate: 15]

	In-State	Out-of-State
Tuition and Fees:	$4,190	$12,460
Campus and Room and Board:	$4,700	$4,700
Books and Supplies:	$550	$1,400
Other Expenses:	$1,200	$1,200
Total Estimated Expenses:	**$10,640**	**$19,760**

Note: Mandatory Health Insurance

GRADUATE INFORMATION

ESTIMATED STUDENT EXPENSES (FALL 2006)
[Expenses are for the 2006-2007 nine-month academic year and are based on an average credit load of: Graduate: 9]

	In-State	Out-of-State
Tuition and Fees:	$4,930	$13,200
Campus and Room and Board:	$4,920	$4,920
Books and Supplies:	$550	$1,400
Other Expenses:	$1,200	$1,200
Total Estimated Expenses:	**$11,600**	**$20,720**

Note: Mandatory Health Insurance

NEW APPLICANTS/NEWLY ENROLLED STUDENTS
[Numbers are for the graduate engineering college for the Fall 2006 term]

Number of Applicants (a):	91
Of those, Number Offered Admission (b):	86
Of those, Number Enrolled Fall 2006 (c):	5

Illinois Institute of Technology

INSTITUTION INFORMATION
3300 South Federal Street
Chicago, IL 60616-3793
Phone: (312) 567-3000
Web: http://www.iit.edu

GENERAL INFORMATION
[All Students - Fall 2006]

Undergraduate Enrollment	2,353
Graduate Enrollment	3,303
Professional Enrollment	1,139
Total Enrollment	**6,795**

ENGINEERING COLLEGE INFORMATION

HEAD OF ENGINEERING
Hamid Arastoopour
Dean
Armour College of Engineering
Illinois Institute of Technology
Rm. 220 E1-bldg
10 W. 32nd St.
Chicago, IL 60616
Phone: (312) 567-3038
Fax: (312) 567-7961
Email: arastoopour@iit.edu

TYPES OF ENGINEERING DEGREES
Bachelor's: B.S.
Master's: M.S. with thesis, M.S. without thesis, but with project or report
Doctoral: Ph.D.

UNDERGRADUATE INFORMATION

ADMISSION INQUIRIES
Mary Ann Rowan
Vice President, Enrollment Management
Illinois Institute of Technology
3300 South Federal Street
Chicago, IL 60616-3793
Phone: (312) 567-3759
Fax: (312) 567-3883
Email: rowan@iit.edu

ESTIMATED STUDENT EXPENSES (FALL 2006)
[Expenses are for the 2006-2007 nine-month academic year and are based on an average credit load of: Undergraduate: 15]

	All Students
Tuition and fees:	$23,329
Campus and Room and Board:	$7,563
Books and Supplies:	$1,147
Other Expenses:	
Total Estimated Expenses:	**$32,039**

Note: Graduate tuition is amount per credit hour.

NEW APPLICANTS/NEWLY ENROLLED STUDENTS
[Numbers are for the undergraduate engineering college for the Fall 2006 term]

Number of Applicants (a):	2,934
Of those, Number Offered Admission (b):	1,637
Of those, Number Enrolled Fall 2006 (c):	323

GRADUATE INFORMATION

ADMISSION INQUIRIES
Suzanne Depeder
Assoc VP, Graduate Enrollment
Illinois Institute of Technology
3300 S. Federal St., Rm. 203 Main Building
Chicago , IL 60616-3793
Phone: (312) 567-3761
Fax: (312) 567-7018
Email: depeder@iit.edu

ADMISSION INQUIRIES
Mary Ann Rowan
Vice President, Enrollment Management
Illinois Institute of Technology
3300 South Federal Street
Chicago , IL 60616-3793
Phone: (312) 567-3759
Fax: (312) 567-3883
Email: rowan@iit.edu

ESTIMATED STUDENT EXPENSES (FALL 2006)
[Expenses are for the 2006-2007 nine-month academic year and are based on an average credit load of: Graduate: 9]

	All Students
Tuition and fees:	$13,840
Campus and Room and Board:	$7,563
Books and Supplies:	$1,147
Other Expenses:	$1,680
Total Estimated Expenses:	**$24,230**

Note: Graduate tuition is amount per credit hour.

NEW APPLICANTS/NEWLY ENROLLED STUDENTS
[Numbers are for the graduate engineering college for the Fall 2006 term]

Number of Applicants (a):	3,894
Of those, Number Offered Admission (b):	2,208
Of those, Number Enrolled Fall 2006 (c):	480

University of Illinois at Chicago

INSTITUTION INFORMATION
2800 University Hall (MC 102)
601 S. Morgan St.
Chicago, IL 60607-7128
Phone: (312) 413-3350
Fax: (312) 413-3393
Web: http://www.uic.edu

GENERAL INFORMATION
[All Students - Fall 2006]

Undergraduate Enrollment	14,998
Graduate Enrollment	7,030
Professional Enrollment	2,497
Total Enrollment	**24,525**

ENGINEERING COLLEGE INFORMATION

HEAD OF ENGINEERING
Prith Banerjee
Dean
College of Engineering
University of Illinois at Chicago
832 Science and Engineering Offices (MC 159)
851 South Morgan Street
Chicago, IL 60607-7043
Phone: (312) 996-2400
Fax: (312) 996-8664
Email: prith@uic.edu

ENGINEERING COLLEGE INQUIRIES
Prith Banerjee
Dean
University of Illinois at Chicago
832 Science and Engineering Offices (MC 159), 851 South Morgan Street
Chicago, IL 60607-7043
Phone: (312) 996-2400
Fax: (312) 996-8664
Email: prith@uic.edu

ENGINEERING COLLEGE INQUIRIES
James T Muench
Director of Engineering Admiss
University of Illinois at Chicago
851 S Morgan (M/C 159), Room 123 SEO

Chicago, IL 60607-7023
Phone: (312) 413-7623
Fax: (312) 413-3365
Email: jmuench@uic.edu

ENGINEERING COLLEGE INQUIRIES
Michael McNallan
Associate Dean for Undergraduate Affairs
University of Illinois at Chicago
851 S. Morgan St, MC 159
Chicago, IL 60607-7128
Phone: (312) 996-3463
Fax: (312) 413-3365

TYPES OF ENGINEERING DEGREES
Bachelor's: B.S.
Master's: M.S. with thesis
Doctoral: Ph.D.

UNDERGRADUATE INFORMATION

ADMISSION INQUIRIES
James T Muench
Director of Engineering Admiss
University of Illinois at Chicago
851 S Morgan (M/C 159), Room 123 SEO
Chicago, IL 60607-7023
Phone: (312) 413-7623
Fax: (312) 413-3365
Email: jmuench@uic.edu

ESTIMATED STUDENT EXPENSES (FALL 2006)
[Expenses are for the 2006-2007 nine-month academic year and are based on an average credit load of: Undergraduate: N/A]

	In-State	Out-of-State
Tuition and Fees:	$11,250	$23,650
Campus and Room and Board:	$10,800	$10,800
Books and Supplies:	$800	$800
Other Expenses:	$2,400	$2,400
Total Estimated Expenses:	**$25,250**	**$37,650**

NEW APPLICANTS/NEWLY ENROLLED STUDENTS
[Numbers are for the undergraduate engineering college for the Fall 2006 term]

Number of Applicants (a):	1,380
Of those, Number Offered Admission (b):	786
Of those, Number Enrolled Fall 2006 (c):	332

Note: Average Composite ACT Score of beginning Freshmen for Fall 2006 was 25.6

GRADUATE INFORMATION

ESTIMATED STUDENT EXPENSES (FALL 2006)
[Expenses are for the 2006-2007 nine-month academic year and are based on an average credit load of: Graduate: N/A]

	In-State	Out-of-State
Tuition and Fees:	$11,810	$23,808
Campus and Room and Board:	$10,800	$10,800
Books and Supplies:	$1,200	$1,200
Other Expenses:	$2,400	$2,400
Total Estimated Expenses:	**$26,210**	**$38,208**

NEW APPLICANTS/NEWLY ENROLLED STUDENTS
[Numbers are for the graduate engineering college for the Fall 2006 term]

Number of Applicants (a):	2,101
Of those, Number Offered Admission (b):	741
Of those, Number Enrolled Fall 2006 (c):	256

University of Illinois at Urbana-Champaign

INSTITUTION INFORMATION
306 Engineering Hall
1308 West Green Street
Urbana, IL 61801
Phone: (217) 333-2150
Fax: (217) 244-7705
Web: http://www.engr.uiuc.edu

GENERAL INFORMATION
[All Students - Fall 2006]

Undergraduate Enrollment	30,453
Graduate Enrollment	9,188
Professional Enrollment	1,029
Total Enrollment	**40,670**

ENGINEERING COLLEGE INFORMATION

HEAD OF ENGINEERING

Ilesanmi Adesida
Dean
College of Engineering
University of Illinois at Urbana-Champaign
306 Engineering Hall, MC-266
1308 West Green Street
Urbana, IL 61801
Phone: (217) 333-2150
Fax: (217) 244-7705
Email: iadesida@uiuc.edu

TYPES OF ENGINEERING DEGREES

Bachelor's: B.S.
Master's: M.S. with thesis, M.S. without thesis, but with project or report
Doctoral: Ph.D.

UNDERGRADUATE INFORMATION

ESTIMATED STUDENT EXPENSES (FALL 2006)

[Expenses are for the 2006-2007 nine-month academic year and are based on an average credit load of: Undergraduate: 15]

	In-State	Out-of-State
Tuition and Fees:	$11,786	$25,872
Campus and Room and Board:	$7,176	$7,176
Books and Supplies:	$950	$950
Other Expenses:	$2,490	$2,820
Total Estimated Expenses:	**$22,402**	**$36,818**

NEW APPLICANTS/NEWLY ENROLLED STUDENTS

[Numbers are for the undergraduate engineering college for the Fall 2006 term]

Number of Applicants (a):	4,308
Of those, Number Offered Admission (b):	2,929
Of those, Number Enrolled Fall 2006 (c):	1,293

GRADUATE INFORMATION

ESTIMATED STUDENT EXPENSES (FALL 2006)

[Expenses are for the 2006-2007 nine-month academic year and are based on an average credit load of: Graduate: 15]

	In-State	Out-of-State
Tuition and Fees:	$12,068	$24,762
Campus and Room and Board:	$9,120	$9,120
Books and Supplies:	$1,250	$1,250
Other Expenses:	$2,561	$2,891
Total Estimated Expenses:	**$24,999**	**$38,023**

NEW APPLICANTS/NEWLY ENROLLED STUDENTS

[Numbers are for the graduate engineering college for the Fall 2006 term]

Number of Applicants (a):	4,502
Of those, Number Offered Admission (b):	1,228
Of those, Number Enrolled Fall 2006 (c):	533

Indiana Institute of Technology

INSTITUTION INFORMATION

1600 East Washington Blvd.
Fort Wayne, IN 46803
Phone: (260) 422-5561
Fax: (260) 426-1732
Web: http://www.indianatech.edu

GENERAL INFORMATION

[All Students - Fall 2006]

Undergraduate Enrollment	3,035
Graduate Enrollment	370
Professional Enrollment	0
Total Enrollment	**3,405**

ENGINEERING COLLEGE INFORMATION

TYPES OF ENGINEERING DEGREES

Bachelor's: B.S.
Master's: M.S. without thesis, but with project or report
Doctoral:

UNDERGRADUATE INFORMATION

ESTIMATED STUDENT EXPENSES (FALL 2006)

[Expenses are for the 2006-2007 nine-month academic year

and are based on an average credit load of: Undergraduate: 15]

	All Students
Tuition and fees:	$18,300
Campus and Room and Board:	$7,088
Books and Supplies:	
Other Expenses:	$3,000
Total Estimated Expenses:	**$28,388**

GRADUATE INFORMATION

ESTIMATED STUDENT EXPENSES (FALL 2006)

[Expenses are for the 2006-2007 nine-month academic year and are based on an average credit load of: Graduate: 9]

	All Students
Tuition and fees:	$7,974
Campus and Room and Board:	
Books and Supplies:	
Other Expenses:	
Total Estimated Expenses:	**$7,974**

Indiana University Purdue University at Indianapolis

INSTITUTION INFORMATION

799 W. Michigan Street
Room 215
Indianapolis, IN 46202
Phone: (317) 274-2533
Fax: (317) 274-4567
Web: http://www.engr.iupui.edu

GENERAL INFORMATION

[All Students - Fall 2006]

Undergraduate Enrollment	19,642
Graduate Enrollment	4,193
Professional Enrollment	4,858
Total Enrollment	**28,693**

ENGINEERING COLLEGE INFORMATION

HEAD OF ENGINEERING

H. Oner Yurtseven
Dean
Engineering and Technology
Indiana University Purdue University at Indianapolis
799 West Michigan St., ET 219
Indianapolis, IN 46202
Phone: (317) 274-0802
Fax: (317) 274-4567
Email: hoyurt7@iupui.edu

TYPES OF ENGINEERING DEGREES

Bachelor's: B.S.
Master's: M.S. with thesis, M.S. without thesis, but with project or report
Doctoral: Ph.D.

GRADUATE INFORMATION

ADMISSION INQUIRIES

Valerie Lim Diemer
Graduate Program Coordinator
Indiana University Purdue University at Indianapolis
723 West Michigan Street, Room 164
Indianapolis, IN 46202
Phone: (317) 278-4960
Fax: (317) 278-2032
Email: wvlim@iupui.edu

Indiana University-Purdue University Fort Wayne

INSTITUTION INFORMATION

2101 East Coliseum Blvd.
Fort Wayne, IN 46805
Phone: (260) 481-6100
Web: http://www.ipfw.edu/

GENERAL INFORMATION

[All Students - Fall 2006]

Undergraduate Enrollment	10,890

Graduate Enrollment	782
Professional Enrollment	0
Total Enrollment	**11,672**

ENGINEERING COLLEGE INFORMATION

HEAD OF ENGINEERING

Gerard Voland
Dean
College of Engineering, Technology, and Computer Sc
Indiana University-Purdue University Fort Wayne
2101 E. Coliseum Blvd.
Fort Wayne, IN 46805-1499
Phone: (260) 481-6839
Fax: (260) 481-5734
Email: volandg@ipfw.edu

ENGINEERING COLLEGE INQUIRIES

Harold Broberg
Associate Dean & Chair
Indiana University-Purdue University Fort Wayne
2101 East Coliseum Blvd.
Fort Wayne, IN 46805
Phone: (260) 481-6341
Fax: (260) 481-5734
Email: broberg@ipfw.edu

TYPES OF ENGINEERING DEGREES

Bachelor's: B.S.
Master's: M.S. with thesis, M.S. without thesis, but with project or report
Doctoral:

UNDERGRADUATE INFORMATION

ESTIMATED STUDENT EXPENSES (FALL 2006)

[Expenses are for the 2006-2007 nine-month academic year and are based on an average credit load of: Undergraduate: 15]

	In-State	Out-of-State
Tuition and Fees:	$201	$461
Campus and Room and Board:	$4,940	
Books and Supplies:	$1,096	$1,096
Other Expenses:		
Total Estimated Expenses:	**$6,237**	**$1,557**

Note: Student Housing: $394-$630 per month.

GRADUATE INFORMATION

ESTIMATED STUDENT EXPENSES (FALL 2006)

[Expenses are for the 2006-2007 nine-month academic year and are based on an average credit load of: Graduate: 12]

	In-State	Out-of-State
Tuition and Fees:	$248	$536
Campus and Room and Board:		
Books and Supplies:		
Other Expenses:		
Total Estimated Expenses:	**$248**	**$536**

Note: Student Housing: $394-$630 per month.

The University of Iowa

INSTITUTION INFORMATION

College of Engineering
3100 Seamans Center
Iowa City, IA 52242
Phone: (319) 335-5764
Fax: (319) 335-6086
Web: http://www.engineering.uiowa.edu/

GENERAL INFORMATION

[All Students - Fall 2006]

Undergraduate Enrollment	20,738
Graduate Enrollment	5,388
Professional Enrollment	3,853
Total Enrollment	**29,979**

ENGINEERING COLLEGE INFORMATION

HEAD OF ENGINEERING

P. Barry Butler
Professor and Dean, College of Engineering
Mechanical Engineering
The University of Iowa
College of Engineering
3100 Seamans Center
Iowa City, IA 52242
Phone: (319) 335-5766

Fax: (319) 335-6086
Email: patrick-butler@uiowa.edu

TYPES OF ENGINEERING DEGREES
Bachelor's: B.S.
Master's: M.S. with thesis, M.S. without thesis, but with project or report
Doctoral: Ph.D.

UNDERGRADUATE INFORMATION

ADMISSION INQUIRIES
Jane M Dorman
Director of Admissions
The University of Iowa
College of Engineering, 3124 Seamans Center
Iowa City, IA 52242
Phone: (319) 335-5763
Fax: (319) 334-0529
Email: jane-dorman@uiowa.edu

ESTIMATED STUDENT EXPENSES (FALL 2006)
[Expenses are for the 2006-2007 nine-month academic year and are based on an average credit load of: Undergraduate: 16]

	In-State	Out-of-State
Tuition and Fees:	$6,373	$18,597
Campus and Room and Board:	$6,912	$6,912
Books and Supplies:	$840	$840
Other Expenses:	$3,260	$3,260
Total Estimated Expenses:	**$17,385**	**$29,609**

NEW APPLICANTS/NEWLY ENROLLED STUDENTS
[Numbers are for the undergraduate engineering college for the Fall 2006 term]

Number of Applicants (a):	1,148
Of those, Number Offered Admission (b):	594
Of those, Number Enrolled Fall 2006 (c):	315

GRADUATE INFORMATION

ESTIMATED STUDENT EXPENSES (FALL 2006)
[Expenses are for the 2006-2007 nine-month academic year and are based on an average credit load of: Graduate: 9]

	In-State	Out-of-State
Tuition and Fees:	$7,217	$18,611
Campus and Room and Board:	$9,180	$9,180
Books and Supplies:	$840	$840
Other Expenses:	$3,130	$3,130
Total Estimated Expenses:	**$20,367**	**$31,761**

NEW APPLICANTS/NEWLY ENROLLED STUDENTS
[Numbers are for the graduate engineering college for the Fall 2006 term]

Number of Applicants (a):	701
Of those, Number Offered Admission (b):	234
Of those, Number Enrolled Fall 2006 (c):	83

Iowa State University

INSTITUTION INFORMATION
Engineering Administration
104 Marston
Ames, IA 50011
Phone: (515) 294-2337
Fax: (515) 294-9273
Web: http://www.iastate.edu

GENERAL INFORMATION
[All Students - Fall 2006]

Undergraduate Enrollment	20,440
Graduate Enrollment	4,583
Professional Enrollment	439
Total Enrollment	**25,462**

ENGINEERING COLLEGE INFORMATION

HEAD OF ENGINEERING
Mark J Kushner
Dean
College of Engineering
Iowa State University
Engineering Administration
104 Marston
Ames, IA 50011
Phone: (515) 294-9988
Fax: (515) 294-9273
Email: mjk@iastate.edu

ENGINEERING COLLEGE INQUIRIES
Diane Rover
Associate Dean/Professor
Iowa State University
Engineering Administration, 104 Marston
Ames, IA 50011
Phone: (515) 294-1309
Fax: (515) 294-9273
Email: drover@iastate.edu

TYPES OF ENGINEERING DEGREES
Bachelor's: B.S.
Master's: M.S. with thesis, M.S. without thesis, but with project or report, M.Eng.
Doctoral: Ph.D.

UNDERGRADUATE INFORMATION

ADMISSION INQUIRIES
Jan Putnam
Classification Officer
Iowa State University
110 Marston
Ames, IA 50011
Phone: (515) 294-3901
Fax: (515) 294-8993
Email: jwputnam@iastate.edu

ESTIMATED STUDENT EXPENSES (FALL 2006)
[Expenses are for the 2006-2007 nine-month academic year and are based on an average credit load of: Undergraduate: 15]

	In-State	Out-of-State
Tuition and Fees:	$6,285	$16,779
Campus and Room and Board:	$6,445	$6,445
Books and Supplies:	$892	$892
Other Expenses:		
Total Estimated Expenses:	**$13,622**	**$24,116**

NEW APPLICANTS/NEWLY ENROLLED STUDENTS
[Numbers are for the undergraduate engineering college for the Fall 2006 term]

Number of Applicants (a):	2,116
Of those, Number Offered Admission (b):	1,997
Of those, Number Enrolled Fall 2006 (c):	1,070

Note: Beginning with Fall Semester 2006, freshmen with estimated rank are excluded from the mean and distribution calculations to be consistent with State of Iowa Board of Regents' policy. Based on this, the percentage of entering Engineering students ranked in the top quarter of their high school would be 71%.

GRADUATE INFORMATION

ADMISSION INQUIRIES
Nancy Knight
Director
Iowa State University
College of Engineering, 104 Marston
Ames, IA 50011
Phone: (515) 294-3241
Fax: (515) 294-9273
Email: nknight@iastate.edu

ESTIMATED STUDENT EXPENSES (FALL 2006)
[Expenses are for the 2006-2007 nine-month academic year and are based on an average credit load of: Graduate: 9]

	In-State	Out-of-State
Tuition and Fees:	$7,135	$17,549
Campus and Room and Board:	$8,143	$8,143
Books and Supplies:	$892	$892
Other Expenses:		
Total Estimated Expenses:	**$16,170**	**$26,584**

NEW APPLICANTS/NEWLY ENROLLED STUDENTS
[Numbers are for the graduate engineering college for the Fall 2006 term]

Number of Applicants (a):	1,284
Of those, Number Offered Admission (b):	287
Of those, Number Enrolled Fall 2006 (c):	161

John Brown University

INSTITUTION INFORMATION
2000 W University St
Siloam Springs, AR 72761
Phone: (479) 524-7244
Fax: (479) 524-7499
Web: http://www.jbu.edu

GENERAL INFORMATION
[All Students - Fall 2006]

Undergraduate Enrollment	1,191
Graduate Enrollment	383
Professional Enrollment	507
Total Enrollment	**2,081**

ENGINEERING COLLEGE INFORMATION

TYPES OF ENGINEERING DEGREES
Bachelor's: B.S.
Master's:
Doctoral:

UNDERGRADUATE INFORMATION

ESTIMATED STUDENT EXPENSES (FALL 2006)
[Expenses are for the 2006-2007 nine-month academic year and are based on an average credit load of: Undergraduate: 15]

	All Students
Tuition and fees:	$14,544
Campus and Room and Board:	$5,630
Books and Supplies:	$250
Other Expenses:	$736
Total Estimated Expenses:	**$21,160**

The Johns Hopkins University

INSTITUTION INFORMATION
120 New Engineering Building
3400 N. Charles Street
Baltimore, MD 21218-2681
Phone: (410) 516-4050
Fax: (410) 516-4090
Web: http://engineering.jhu.edu

GENERAL INFORMATION
[All Students - Fall 2006]

Undergraduate Enrollment	5,827
Graduate Enrollment	10,868
Professional Enrollment	0
Total Enrollment	**16,695**

ENGINEERING COLLEGE INFORMATION

HEAD OF ENGINEERING
Nicholas P. Jones
Dean of Engineering
Whiting School of Engineering
The Johns Hopkins University
120 New Engineering Building
3400 N. Charles Street
Baltimore, MD 21218-2681
Phone: (410) 516-4050
Fax: (410) 516-8627
Email: npjones@jhu.edu

TYPES OF ENGINEERING DEGREES
Bachelor's: B.A., B.S.
Master's: M.A. with thesis, M.A. without thesis, but with project or report, M.S. with thesis, M.S. without thesis, but with project or report
Doctoral: Ph.D.

UNDERGRADUATE INFORMATION

ESTIMATED STUDENT EXPENSES (FALL 2006)
[Expenses are for the 2006-2007 nine-month academic year and are based on an average credit load of: Undergraduate: 17]

	All Students
Tuition and fees:	$33,900
Campus and Room and Board:	$11,206
Books and Supplies:	$1,000
Other Expenses:	$500
Total Estimated Expenses:	**$46,606**

NEW APPLICANTS/NEWLY ENROLLED STUDENTS
[Numbers are for the undergraduate engineering college for the Fall 2006 term]

Number of Applicants (a):	3,616
Of those, Number Offered Admission (b):	1,525
Of those, Number Enrolled Fall 2006 (c):	461

GRADUATE INFORMATION

ESTIMATED STUDENT EXPENSES (FALL 2006)
[Expenses are for the 2006-2007 nine-month academic year and are based on an average credit load of: Graduate: N/A]

	All Students
Tutition and fees:	$33,900
Campus and Room and Board:	$11,300
Books and Supplies:	$1,000
Other Expenses:	$500
Total Estimated Expenses:	**$46,700**

NEW APPLICANTS/NEWLY ENROLLED STUDENTS
[Numbers are for the graduate engineering college for the Fall 2006 term]

Number of Applicants (a):	3,005
Of those, Number Offered Admission (b):	614
Of those, Number Enrolled Fall 2006 (c):	262

University of Kansas

INSTITUTION INFORMATION
1 Eaton Hall, Engineering Dean's Office
1520 W. 15th St.
Lawrence, KS 66045-7621
Phone: (785) 864-3881
Fax: (785) 864-5445
Web: http://www/engr/ku/edu

GENERAL INFORMATION
[All Students - Fall 2006]

Undergraduate Enrollment	21,353
Graduate Enrollment	6,083
Professional Enrollment	2,177
Total Enrollment	**29,613**

ENGINEERING COLLEGE INFORMATION

HEAD OF ENGINEERING
Stuart R Bell
Dean, Professor
Engineering Administration
University of Kansas
1 Eaton Hall
1520 W. 15th St.
Lawrence, KS 66045-7621
Phone: (785) 864-2977
Fax: (785) 864-5445
Email: sbell@ku.edu

TYPES OF ENGINEERING DEGREES
Bachelor's: B.S.
Master's: M.S. with thesis, M.S. without thesis, but with project or report
Doctoral: Ph.D., D.Eng

UNDERGRADUATE INFORMATION

ADMISSION INQUIRIES
Robert Sorem
Associate Dean of Undergraduate Studies, Associate Professor
University of Kansas
1-C Eaton Hall, 1520 W. 15th St.
Lawrence, KS 66045-7621
Phone: (785) 864-2983
Fax: (785) 864-5445
Email: sorem@ku.edu

ESTIMATED STUDENT EXPENSES (FALL 2006)
[Expenses are for the 2006-2007 nine-month academic year and are based on an average credit load of: Undergraduate: 16]

	In-State	Out-of-State
Tuition and Fees:	$7,105	$16,673
Campus and Room and Board:	$6,038	$6,038
Books and Supplies:	$750	$750
Other Expenses:	$2,094	$2,094
Total Estimated Expenses:	**$15,987**	**$25,555**

NEW APPLICANTS/NEWLY ENROLLED STUDENTS
[Numbers are for the undergraduate engineering college for the Fall 2006 term]

Number of Applicants (a):	1,185
Of those, Number Offered Admission (b):	845
Of those, Number Enrolled Fall 2006 (c):	419

GRADUATE INFORMATION

ADMISSION INQUIRIES
Glen Marotz
Professor & Associate Dean for Research and Graduate Studies
University of Kansas
1-B2 Eaton Hall, 1520 W. 15th St.
Lawrence , KS 66045-7621
Phone: (785) 864-2980
Fax: (785) 864-5445
Email: gama@ku.edu

ESTIMATED STUDENT EXPENSES (FALL 2006)
[Expenses are for the 2006-2007 nine-month academic year and are based on an average credit load of: Graduate: 9]

	In-State	Out-of-State
Tutition and Fees:	$5,312	$10,990
Campus and Room and Board:	$7,526	$7,526
Books and Supplies:	$550	$550
Other Expenses:	$2,936	$2,936
Total Estimated Expenses:	**$16,324**	**$22,002**

NEW APPLICANTS/NEWLY ENROLLED STUDENTS
[Numbers are for the graduate engineering college for the Fall 2006 term]

Number of Applicants (a):	575
Of those, Number Offered Admission (b):	319
Of those, Number Enrolled Fall 2006 (c):	138

Kansas State University

INSTITUTION INFORMATION
College of Engineering
1046 Rathbone Hall
Manhattan, KS 66506-5201
Phone: (785) 532-5590
Fax: (785) 532-7810
Web: http://www.engg.ksu.edu/

GENERAL INFORMATION
[All Students - Fall 2006]

Undergraduate Enrollment	18,762
Graduate Enrollment	3,946
Professional Enrollment	433
Total Enrollment	**23,141**

ENGINEERING COLLEGE INFORMATION

HEAD OF ENGINEERING
Richard R Gallagher
Interim Dean
Dean of Engineering Office
Kansas State University
College of Engineering
1046 Rathbone Hall
Manhattan, KS 66506-5201
Phone: (785) 532-5590
Fax: (785) 532-7810
Email: rrgllghr@ksu.edu

TYPES OF ENGINEERING DEGREES
Bachelor's: B.S.
Master's: M.S. with thesis, M.S. without thesis, but with project or report
Doctoral: Ph.D.

UNDERGRADUATE INFORMATION

ADMISSION INQUIRIES
Thomas C Roberts
Assistant Dean for Recruitment & Leadership Development
Kansas State University
College of Engineering, 1056 Rathbone Hall
Manhattan, KS 66506-5201
Phone: (785) 532-5455
Fax: (785) 532-7810
Email: tcr@ksu.edu

ESTIMATED STUDENT EXPENSES (FALL 2006)
[Expenses are for the 2006-2007 nine-month academic year and are based on an average credit load of: Undergraduate: N/A]

	In-State	Out-of-State
Tutition and Fees:	$5,608	$14,694
Campus and Room and Board:	$5,912	$5,912
Books and Supplies:	$900	$900
Other Expenses:		
Total Estimated Expenses:	**$12,420**	**$21,506**

NEW APPLICANTS/NEWLY ENROLLED STUDENTS
[Numbers are for the undergraduate engineering college for the Fall 2006 term]

Number of Applicants (a):	1,456
Of those, Number Offered Admission (b):	1,022
Of those, Number Enrolled Fall 2006 (c):	710

GRADUATE INFORMATION

ESTIMATED STUDENT EXPENSES (FALL 2006)
[Expenses are for the 2006-2007 nine-month academic year and are based on an average credit load of: Graduate: N/A]

	In-State	Out-of-State
Tuition and Fees:	$7,048	$14,952
Campus and Room and Board:	$5,912	$5,912
Books and Supplies:	$900	$900
Other Expenses:		
Total Estimated Expenses:	**$13,860**	**$21,764**

NEW APPLICANTS/NEWLY ENROLLED STUDENTS
[Numbers are for the graduate engineering college for the Fall 2006 term]

Number of Applicants (a):	615
Of those, Number Offered Admission (b):	289
Of those, Number Enrolled Fall 2006 (c):	107

University of Kentucky

INSTITUTION INFORMATION
College of Engineering Dean's Office
351 Ralph G. Anderson Building
Lexington, KY 40506-0503
Phone: (859) 257-1687
Fax: (859) 323-4922
Web: http://www.engr.uky.edu

GENERAL INFORMATION
[All Students - Fall 2006]

Undergraduate Enrollment	19,328
Graduate Enrollment	5,584
Professional Enrollment	2,297
Total Enrollment	**27,209**

ENGINEERING COLLEGE INFORMATION

HEAD OF ENGINEERING
Thomas W Lester
Dean
College of Engineering
University of Kentucky
351 Ralph G. Anderson Building
Lexington, KY 40506-0503
Phone: (859) 257-1687
Fax: (859) 323-4922
Email: lester@engr.uky.edu

ENGINEERING COLLEGE INQUIRIES
Jane Riggs
Director of Student Services
University of Kentucky
351 Ralph G. Anderson Building
Lexington, KY 40506-0503
Phone: (859) 257-1021
Fax: (859) 323-4922
Email: jriggs@engr.uky.edu

TYPES OF ENGINEERING DEGREES
Bachelor's: B.S.
Master's: M.S. with thesis, M.S. without thesis, but with project or report
Doctoral: Ph.D.

UNDERGRADUATE INFORMATION

ADMISSION INQUIRIES
Jane Riggs
Director of Student Services
University of Kentucky
351 Ralph G. Anderson Building
Lexington, KY 40506-0503
Phone: (859) 257-1021
Fax: (859) 323-4922
Email: jriggs@engr.uky.edu

ADMISSION INQUIRIES
Donald E Witt

Director of Undergraduate Admissions & University Registrar
University of Kentucky
11B Funkhouser Building
Lexington, KY 40506-0054
Phone: (859) 257-3458
Fax: (859) 257-9572
Email: dwitt@email.uky.edu

ESTIMATED STUDENT EXPENSES (FALL 2006)
[Expenses are for the 2006-2007 nine-month academic year and are based on an average credit load of: Undergraduate: 15]

	In-State	Out-of-State
Tuition and Fees:	$6,510	$13,970
Campus and Room and Board:	$6,586	$6,586
Books and Supplies:	$800	$800
Other Expenses:		
Total Estimated Expenses:	**$13,896**	**$21,356**

Note: Undergraduate Housing is double occupancy premium residence hall with $1898 Diner-Account. Graduate Housing is one bdrm, single occupancy apt., furnished, utilities, no phone. $3,000 added for meals.

NEW APPLICANTS/NEWLY ENROLLED STUDENTS
[Numbers are for the undergraduate engineering college for the Fall 2006 term]

Number of Applicants (a):	1,094
Of those, Number Offered Admission (b):	945
Of those, Number Enrolled Fall 2006 (c):	571

GRADUATE INFORMATION

ADMISSION INQUIRIES
Jeannine Blackwell
Dean, Graduate School
University of Kentucky
359 Patterson Office Tower
Lexington, KY 40506-0027
Phone: (859) 257-1759
Fax: (859) 323-1928
Email: blackwell@uky.edu

ADMISSION INQUIRIES
Patricia Bond
Academic Coordinator, Graduate Admissions
University of Kentucky
331 Patterson Office Tower
Lexington, KY 40506-0027
Phone: (859) 257-4905
Fax: (859) 323-1928
Email: pbond@pop.uky.edu

ESTIMATED STUDENT EXPENSES (FALL 2006)
[Expenses are for the 2006-2007 nine-month academic year and are based on an average credit load of: Graduate: 9]

	In-State	Out-of-State
Tuition and Fees:	$7,036	$15,154
Campus and Room and Board:	$8,562	$8,562
Books and Supplies:	$1,000	$1,000
Other Expenses:	$800	$800
Total Estimated Expenses:	**$17,398**	**$25,516**

Note: Undergraduate Housing is double occupancy premium residence hall with $1898 Diner-Account. Graduate Housing is one bdrm, single occupancy apt., furnished, utilities, no phone. $3,000 added for meals.

NEW APPLICANTS/NEWLY ENROLLED STUDENTS
[Numbers are for the graduate engineering college for the Fall 2006 term]

Number of Applicants (a):	1,050
Of those, Number Offered Admission (b):	552
Of those, Number Enrolled Fall 2006 (c):	191

Kettering University formerly GMI

INSTITUTION INFORMATION
1700 West Third Avenue
Flint, MI 48504
Phone: (810) 955-4464
Fax: (810) 762-9837
Web: http://www.kettering.edu

GENERAL INFORMATION
[All Students - Fall 2006]

Undergraduate Enrollment	2,290
Graduate Enrollment	519

Professional Enrollment	0
Total Enrollment	**2,809**

ENGINEERING COLLEGE INFORMATION

HEAD OF ENGINEERING
Robert L. Simpson
Interim Vice President for Academic Affairs and Provost
Office of the Provost
Kettering University formerly GMI
1700 West Third Avenue
Flint, MI 48504
Phone: (810) 762-7949
Fax: (810) 762-7885
Email: rsimpson@kettering.edu

ENGINEERING COLLEGE INQUIRIES
Robert L. Simpson
Interim Vice President for Academic Affairs and Provost
Kettering University formerly GMI
1700 West Third Avenue
Flint, MI 48504
Phone: (810) 762-7949
Fax: (810) 762-7885
Email: rsimpson@kettering.edu

TYPES OF ENGINEERING DEGREES
Bachelor's: B.S.
Master's: M.S. with thesis, M.S. without thesis, but with project or report
Doctoral:

UNDERGRADUATE INFORMATION

ESTIMATED STUDENT EXPENSES (FALL 2006)
[Expenses are for the 2006-2007 nine-month academic year and are based on an average credit load of: Undergraduate: 16]

	All Students
Tuition and fees:	$25,050
Campus and Room and Board:	$5,690
Books and Supplies:	$1,000
Other Expenses:	$2,920
Total Estimated Expenses:	**$34,660**

NEW APPLICANTS/NEWLY ENROLLED STUDENTS
[Numbers are for the undergraduate engineering college for the Fall 2006 term]

Number of Applicants (a):	1,668
Of those, Number Offered Admission (b):	1,240
Of those, Number Enrolled Fall 2006 (c):	358

GRADUATE INFORMATION

ADMISSION INQUIRIES
Tony Hain
VP - Graduate Studies, Corporate Connections & Business
Kettering University formerly GMI
1700 West Third Avenue
Flint, MI 48504
Phone: (810) 762-9616
Fax: (810) 762-9935
Email: thain@kettering.edu

ESTIMATED STUDENT EXPENSES (FALL 2006)
[Expenses are for the 2006-2007 nine-month academic year and are based on an average credit load of: Graduate: 5]

	All Students
Tuition and fees:	$9,435
Campus and Room and Board:	
Books and Supplies:	
Other Expenses:	$1,908
Total Estimated Expenses:	**$11,343**

NEW APPLICANTS/NEWLY ENROLLED STUDENTS
[Numbers are for the graduate engineering college for the Fall 2006 term]

Number of Applicants (a):	40
Of those, Number Offered Admission (b):	19
Of those, Number Enrolled Fall 2006 (c):	11

Lafayette College

INSTITUTION INFORMATION
Engineering Division
308 Acopian Engineering Center
Easton, PA 18042-1775
Phone: (610) 330-5403

Fax: (610) 330-5059
Web: http://www.lafayette.edu

GENERAL INFORMATION
[All Students - Fall 2006]

Undergraduate Enrollment	2,381
Graduate Enrollment	0
Professional Enrollment	0
Total Enrollment	**2,381**

ENGINEERING COLLEGE INFORMATION

HEAD OF ENGINEERING
James P. Schaffer
Professor & Director of Engineering
Director of Engineering
Lafayette College
308 Acopian Engineering Center
Easton, PA 18042-1775
Phone: (610) 330-5403
Fax: (610) 330-5059
Email: Engnrdiv@lafayette.edu

TYPES OF ENGINEERING DEGREES
Bachelor's: B.A., B.S.
Master's:
Doctoral:

UNDERGRADUATE INFORMATION

ADMISSION INQUIRIES
Carol A Rowlands
Director of Admissions
Lafayette College
118 Markle Hall
Easton, PA 18042
Phone: (610) 330-5100
Fax: (610) 330-5355
Email: rowlandc@lafayette.edu

ESTIMATED STUDENT EXPENSES (FALL 2006)
[Expenses are for the 2006-2007 nine-month academic year and are based on an average credit load of: Undergraduate: 5]

	All Students
Tuition and fees:	$31,501
Campus and Room and Board:	$9,864
Books and Supplies:	$850
Other Expenses:	$1,168
Total Estimated Expenses:	*$43,383*

Note: Lafayette College is an undergraduate institution, and counts courses per term rather than credits.

NEW APPLICANTS/NEWLY ENROLLED STUDENTS
[Numbers are for the undergraduate engineering college for the Fall 2006 term]

Number of Applicants (a):	5,875
Of those, Number Offered Admission (b):	2,169
Of those, Number Enrolled Fall 2006 (c):	630

Lake Superior State University

INSTITUTION INFORMATION
650 W. Easterday Ave
School of Engineering & Technology
Sault Ste. Marie, MI 49783
Phone: (906) 635-2207
Fax: (906) 635-6663
Web: http://engineering.lssu.edu

ENGINEERING COLLEGE INFORMATION

HEAD OF ENGINEERING
Morrie Walworth
Dean
School of Engineering & Technology
Lake Superior State University
650 W. Easterday Ave
Sault Ste. Marie, MI 49783
Phone: (906) 635-2206
Fax: (906) 635-6663
Email: mwalworth@lssu.edu

ENGINEERING COLLEGE INQUIRIES
Jeanne M Shibley
Special Assistant to the Provost
Lake Superior State University

650 West Easterday Ave
Sault Ste. Marie, MI 49783
Phone: (906) 635-2597
Fax: (906) 635-6663
Email: jmshibly@lssu.edu

ENGINEERING COLLEGE INQUIRIES

Morrie Walworth
Dean
Lake Superior State University
650 W. Easterday Ave
Sault Ste. Marie, MI 49783
Phone: (906) 635-2206
Fax: (906) 635-6663
Email: mwalworth@lssu.edu

TYPES OF ENGINEERING DEGREES

Bachelor's: B.S.
Master's:
Doctoral:

UNDERGRADUATE INFORMATION

ADMISSION INQUIRIES

Morrie Walworth
Dean
Lake Superior State University
650 W. Easterday Ave
Sault Ste. Marie, MI 49783
Phone: (906) 635-2206
Fax: (906) 635-6663
Email: mwalworth@lssu.edu

ESTIMATED STUDENT EXPENSES (FALL 2006)

[Expenses are for the 2006-2007 nine-month academic year and are based on an average credit load of: Undergraduate: 17]

	In-State	Out-of-State
Tuition and Fees:	$6,558	$13,116
Campus and Room and Board:	$6,859	$6,859
Books and Supplies:	$1,500	$1,500
Other Expenses:	$1,500	$1,500
Total Estimated Expenses:	**$16,417**	**$22,975**

Note: In-state tuition rates apply in US dollars to Ontario, Canada residents. Midwest Consortium Agreement State residents: tuition $9840 per year. Room & Board for Grads assumes living in private room or townhouse.

NEW APPLICANTS/NEWLY ENROLLED STUDENTS

[Numbers are for the undergraduate engineering college for the Fall 2006 term]

Number of Applicants (a):	91
Of those, Number Offered Admission (b):	91
Of those, Number Enrolled Fall 2006 (c):	31

GRADUATE INFORMATION

ESTIMATED STUDENT EXPENSES (FALL 2006)

[Expenses are for the 2006-2007 nine-month academic year and are based on an average credit load of: Graduate: 9]

	In-State	Out-of-State
Tuition and Fees:	$2,835	$2,835
Campus and Room and Board:	$8,410	$8,409
Books and Supplies:	$700	$700
Other Expenses:	$700	$700
Total Estimated Expenses:	**$12,645**	**$12,644**

Note: In-state tuition rates apply in US dollars to Ontario, Canada residents. Midwest Consortium Agreement State residents: tuition $9840 per year. Room & Board for Grads assumes living in private room or townhouse.

Lamar University

INSTITUTION INFORMATION

College of Engineering
P.O. Box 10057
Beaumont, TX 77710
Phone: (409) 880-8741
Fax: (409) 880-8121
Web: http://www.lamar.edu

GENERAL INFORMATION

[All Students - Fall 2006]

Undergraduate Enrollment	8,920
Graduate Enrollment	986
Professional Enrollment	0
Total Enrollment	**9,906**

ENGINEERING COLLEGE INFORMATION

HEAD OF ENGINEERING

Jack R Hopper
Dean - College of Engineering, Director- THWRC
Engineering
Lamar University
P.O. Box 10024
Beaumont, TX 77710
Phone: (409) 880-8741
Fax: (409) 880-8121
Email: hopperjr@hal.lamar.edu , jack.hopper@lamar.edu

TYPES OF ENGINEERING DEGREES

Bachelor's: B.S.
Master's: M.S. with thesis, M.S. without thesis, but with project or report
Doctoral: Ph.D., D.Eng

UNDERGRADUATE INFORMATION

ADMISSION INQUIRIES

James Rush
Director
Lamar University
PO Box 10007
Beaumont, TX 77710
Phone: (409) 880-8354
Fax: (409) 880-8463
Email: RUSHJC@HAL.LAMAR.EDU

ESTIMATED STUDENT EXPENSES (FALL 2006)

[Expenses are for the 2006-2007 nine-month academic year and are based on an average credit load of: Undergraduate: 12]

	In-State	Out-of-State
Tuition and Fees:	$4,674	$12,954
Campus and Room and Board:	$5,410	$5,410
Books and Supplies:	$692	$692
Other Expenses:	$1,746	$1,746
Total Estimated Expenses:	**$12,522**	**$20,802**

NEW APPLICANTS/NEWLY ENROLLED STUDENTS

[Numbers are for the undergraduate engineering college for the Fall 2006 term]

Number of Applicants (a):	420
Of those, Number Offered Admission (b):	319
Of those, Number Enrolled Fall 2006 (c):	179

GRADUATE INFORMATION

ESTIMATED STUDENT EXPENSES (FALL 2006)

[Expenses are for the 2006-2007 nine-month academic year and are based on an average credit load of: Graduate: 6]

	In-State	Out-of-State
Tuition and Fees:	$5,810	$12,986
Campus and Room and Board:	$5,410	$5,410
Books and Supplies:	$692	$692
Other Expenses:	$3,908	$3,908
Total Estimated Expenses:	**$15,820**	**$22,996**

NEW APPLICANTS/NEWLY ENROLLED STUDENTS

[Numbers are for the graduate engineering college for the Fall 2006 term]

Number of Applicants (a):	663
Of those, Number Offered Admission (b):	363
Of those, Number Enrolled Fall 2006 (c):	92

Lawrence Technological University

INSTITUTION INFORMATION

21000 West Ten Mile Road
Southfield, MI 48075
Phone: (800) 225-5588
Fax: (248) 204-3727
Web: http://www.ltu.edu

GENERAL INFORMATION

[All Students - Fall 2006]

Undergraduate Enrollment	2,681
Graduate Enrollment	1,368
Professional Enrollment	0
Total Enrollment	**4,049**

ENGINEERING COLLEGE INFORMATION

HEAD OF ENGINEERING

Laird E Johnston
Dean, College of Engineering
Engineering
Lawrence Technological University
21000 West Ten Mile Road
Southfield, MI 48075
Phone: (248) 204-2500
Fax: (248) 204-2509
Email: lejohnston@ltu.edu

ENGINEERING COLLEGE INQUIRIES

Lewis G Frasch
Interim Associate Dean, College of Engineering
Lawrence Technological University
21000 West Ten Mile
Southfield, MI 48075
Phone: (248) 204-2500
Fax: (248) 204-2509
Email: frasch@ltu.edu

TYPES OF ENGINEERING DEGREES

Bachelor's: B.S.
Master's: M.S. with thesis, M.S. without thesis, but with project or report, M.Eng.
Doctoral: D.Eng

UNDERGRADUATE INFORMATION

ADMISSION INQUIRIES

Lewis G Frasch
Interim Associate Dean, College of Engineering
Lawrence Technological University
21000 West Ten Mile
Southfield, MI 48075
Phone: (248) 204-2500
Fax: (248) 204-2509
Email: frasch@ltu.edu

ESTIMATED STUDENT EXPENSES (FALL 2006)

[Expenses are for the 2006-2007 nine-month academic year and are based on an average credit load of: Undergraduate: 15]

	All Students
Tuition and fees:	$19,373
Campus and Room and Board:	$7,266
Books and Supplies:	$1,196
Other Expenses:	$3,498
Total Estimated Expenses:	**$31,333**

*Note: 1.)Room and Board cost shown is for a 2 bedroom 4 person apartment and includes a meal plan.
2.)Apartments are furnished with kitchens, bathrooms and laundry rooms.
3.)Graduate students do not reside on campus.*

NEW APPLICANTS/NEWLY ENROLLED STUDENTS

[Numbers are for the undergraduate engineering college for the Fall 2006 term]

Number of Applicants (a):	615
Of those, Number Offered Admission (b):	481
Of those, Number Enrolled Fall 2006 (c):	175

GRADUATE INFORMATION

ADMISSION INQUIRIES

Lewis G Frasch
Interim Associate Dean, College of Engineering
Lawrence Technological University
21000 West Ten Mile
Southfield , MI 48075
Phone: (248) 204-2500
Fax: (248) 204-2509
Email: frasch@ltu.edu

ESTIMATED STUDENT EXPENSES (FALL 2006)

[Expenses are for the 2006-2007 nine-month academic year and are based on an average credit load of: Graduate: 7]

	All Students
Tuition and fees:	$9,836
Campus and Room and Board:	
Books and Supplies:	$1,196
Other Expenses:	$3,498
Total Estimated Expenses:	**$14,530**

*Note: 1.)Room and Board cost shown is for a 2 bedroom 4 person apartment and includes a meal plan.
2.)Apartments are furnished with kitchens, bathrooms and laundry rooms.
3.)Graduate students do not reside on campus.*

NEW APPLICANTS/NEWLY ENROLLED STUDENTS
[Numbers are for the graduate engineering college for the Fall 2006 term]

Number of Applicants (a):	218
Of those, Number Offered Admission (b):	170
Of those, Number Enrolled Fall 2006 (c):	106

Lehigh University

INSTITUTION INFORMATION

Office of the President
27 Memorial Drive West
Bethlehem, PA 18015
Phone: (610) 758-3155
Fax: (610) 758-3154
Web: http://www.lehigh.edu

GENERAL INFORMATION

[All Students - Fall 2006]

Undergraduate Enrollment	4,743
Graduate Enrollment	2,116
Professional Enrollment	0
Total Enrollment	**6,859**

ENGINEERING COLLEGE INFORMATION

TYPES OF ENGINEERING DEGREES

Bachelor's: B.S.
Master's: M.S. with thesis, M.S. without thesis, but with project or report, M.Eng.,MBA&E
Doctoral: Ph.D.

UNDERGRADUATE INFORMATION

ADMISSION INQUIRIES

J. Bruce Gardiner
Dean of Admissions and Financial Aid
Lehigh University
27 Memorial Drive West
Bethlehem, PA 18015
Phone: (610) 758-3100
Fax: (610) 758-4361
Email: jbg0@lehigh.edu

ESTIMATED STUDENT EXPENSES (FALL 2006)

[Expenses are for the 2006-2007 nine-month academic year and are based on an average credit load of: Undergraduate: 16]

	All Students
Tuition and fees:	$33,770
Campus and Room and Board:	$8,920
Books and Supplies:	$1,000
Other Expenses:	$1,010
Total Estimated Expenses:	**$44,700**

Note: Graduate Tuition for 2006-2007 is $990 per credit hour; full-time graduate students are also assessed a technology fee of $350.
The Books and Supplies and Other Expenses figures are derived from Financial Aid.

NEW APPLICANTS/NEWLY ENROLLED STUDENTS

[Numbers are for the undergraduate engineering college for the Fall 2006 term]

Number of Applicants (a):	2,972
Of those, Number Offered Admission (b):	1,639
Of those, Number Enrolled Fall 2006 (c):	469

GRADUATE INFORMATION

ESTIMATED STUDENT EXPENSES (FALL 2006)

[Expenses are for the 2006-2007 nine-month academic year and are based on an average credit load of: Graduate: 6]

	All Students
Tuition and fees:	$18,120
Campus and Room and Board:	
Books and Supplies:	$1,000
Other Expenses:	$1,010
Total Estimated Expenses:	**$20,130**

Note: Graduate Tuition for 2006-2007 is $990 per credit hour; full-time graduate students are also assessed a technology fee of $350.
The Books and Supplies and Other Expenses figures are derived from Financial Aid.

NEW APPLICANTS/NEWLY ENROLLED STUDENTS

[Numbers are for the graduate engineering college for the Fall 2006 term]

Number of Applicants (a):	1,402
Of those, Number Offered Admission (b):	324
Of those, Number Enrolled Fall 2006 (c):	117

LeTourneau University

INSTITUTION INFORMATION

P.O. Box 7001
2100 S Mobberly
Longview, TX 75607-7001
Phone: (903) 233-3000
Fax: (903) 233-3105
Web: http://www.letu.edu

GENERAL INFORMATION

[All Students - Fall 2006]

Undergraduate Enrollment	3,643
Graduate Enrollment	340
Professional Enrollment	0
Total Enrollment	**3,983**

ENGINEERING COLLEGE INFORMATION

HEAD OF ENGINEERING

Thomas Hellmuth, Ph.D.,P.E.
Dean
School of Engineering and Engineering Technology
LeTourneau University
P.O. Box 7001
Longview, TX 75607-7001
Phone: (903) 233-3900
Fax: (903) 233-3901
Email: TomHellmuth@letu.edu

TYPES OF ENGINEERING DEGREES

Bachelor's: B.S.
Master's:
Doctoral:

UNDERGRADUATE INFORMATION

ESTIMATED STUDENT EXPENSES (FALL 2006)

[Expenses are for the 2006-2007 nine-month academic year and are based on an average credit load of: Undergraduate: 16]

	All Students
Tuition and fees:	$16,920
Campus and Room and Board:	$6,590
Books and Supplies:	$1,240
Other Expenses:	$1,000
Total Estimated Expenses:	**$25,750**

NEW APPLICANTS/NEWLY ENROLLED STUDENTS

[Numbers are for the undergraduate engineering college for the Fall 2006 term]

Number of Applicants (a):	303
Of those, Number Offered Admission (b):	256
Of those, Number Enrolled Fall 2006 (c):	139

Note: These figures include all new engineering and engineering technology students.

Louisiana State University

INSTITUTION INFORMATION

College of Engineering
Louisiana State University
Baton Rouge, LA 70803
Phone: (225) 578-5701
Fax: (225) 578-9162
Web: http://www.lsu.edu

GENERAL INFORMATION

[All Students - Fall 2006]

Undergraduate Enrollment	24,589
Graduate Enrollment	4,360
Professional Enrollment	368
Total Enrollment	**29,317**

ENGINEERING COLLEGE INFORMATION

HEAD OF ENGINEERING

Zaki Bassiouni
Dean
College of Engineering
Louisiana State University
3304 CEBA Building
Louisiana State University
Baton Rouge, LA 70803
Phone: (225) 578-5701
Fax: (225) 578-9162
Email: pezab@lsu.edu

TYPES OF ENGINEERING DEGREES

Bachelor's: B.S.
Master's: M.S. with thesis, M.S. without thesis, but with project or report
Doctoral: Ph.D.

UNDERGRADUATE INFORMATION

ESTIMATED STUDENT EXPENSES (FALL 2006)

[Expenses are for the 2006-2007 nine-month academic year and are based on an average credit load of: Undergraduate: 14]

	In-State	Out-of-State
Tuition and Fees:	$4,617	$12,947
Campus and Room and Board:	$6,498	$6,330
Books and Supplies:	$1,500	$1,500
Other Expenses:	$2,572	$2,572
Total Estimated Expenses:	**$15,187**	**$23,349**

NEW APPLICANTS/NEWLY ENROLLED STUDENTS

[Numbers are for the undergraduate engineering college for the Fall 2006 term]

Number of Applicants (a):	1,309
Of those, Number Offered Admission (b):	955
Of those, Number Enrolled Fall 2006 (c):	536

GRADUATE INFORMATION

ESTIMATED STUDENT EXPENSES (FALL 2006)

[Expenses are for the 2006-2007 nine-month academic year and are based on an average credit load of: Graduate: 9]

	In-State	Out-of-State
Tuition and Fees:	$4,613	$12,913
Campus and Room and Board:	$6,330	$6,330
Books and Supplies:	$1,500	$1,500
Other Expenses:	$2,572	$2,572
Total Estimated Expenses:	**$15,015**	**$23,315**

NEW APPLICANTS/NEWLY ENROLLED STUDENTS

[Numbers are for the graduate engineering college for the Fall 2006 term]

Number of Applicants (a):	590
Of those, Number Offered Admission (b):	284
Of those, Number Enrolled Fall 2006 (c):	103

Louisiana Tech University

INSTITUTION INFORMATION

P.O. Box 10348
600 West Arizona
Ruston, LA 71272
Phone: (318) 257-4647
Fax: (318) 257-2562
Web: http://www.latech.edu

GENERAL INFORMATION

[All Students - Fall 2006]

Undergraduate Enrollment	9,016
Graduate Enrollment	2,216
Professional Enrollment	0
Total Enrollment	**11,232**

ENGINEERING COLLEGE INFORMATION

HEAD OF ENGINEERING

Stan Napper
Dean, College of Engineering and Science; Professor, Biomedical Engineering
College of Engineering and Science
Louisiana Tech University
P.O. Box 10348
600 West Arizona
Ruston, LA 71272
Phone: (318) 257-4647
Fax: (318) 257-2562
Email: san@coes.latech.edu

ENGINEERING COLLEGE INQUIRIES

James D Nelson
Associate Dean for Undergraduate Studies; Professor, Civil Engineering
Louisiana Tech University
P.O. Box 10348, 600 West Arizona
Ruston, LA 71272
Phone: (318) 257-2842

Fax: (318) 257-2562
Email: jdn@coes.latech.edu

TYPES OF ENGINEERING DEGREES
Bachelor's: B.S.
Master's: M.S. with thesis, M.S. without thesis, but with project or report
Doctoral: Ph.D.

UNDERGRADUATE INFORMATION

ADMISSION INQUIRIES
Alicia Boudreaux
Student Success Specialist
Louisiana Tech University
P.O. Box 10348, 600 West Arizona
Ruston, LA 71272
Phone: (318) 257-2260
Fax: (318) 257-2562
Email: aliciab@latech.edu

ADMISSION INQUIRIES
James D Nelson
Associate Dean for Undergraduate Studies; Professor, Civil Engineering
Louisiana Tech University
P.O. Box 10348, 600 West Arizona
Ruston, LA 71272
Phone: (318) 257-2842

Fax: (318) 257-2562
Email: jdn@coes.latech.edu

ESTIMATED STUDENT EXPENSES (FALL 2006)
[Expenses are for the 2006-2007 nine-month academic year and are based on an average credit load of: Undergraduate: N/A]

	In-State	Out-of-State
Tuition and Fees:	$4,634	$9,539
Campus and Room and Board:	$4,390	$4,390
Books and Supplies:	$2,400	$2,400
Other Expenses:		
Total Estimated Expenses:	**$11,424**	**$16,329**

NEW APPLICANTS/NEWLY ENROLLED STUDENTS
[Numbers are for the undergraduate engineering college for the Fall 2006 term]
Number of Applicants (a): 705
Of those, Number Offered Admission (b): 574
Of those, Number Enrolled Fall 2006 (c): 320
Note: Average Math ACT Score: 25.02

GRADUATE INFORMATION

ADMISSION INQUIRIES
Bala Ramachandran
Associate Dean for Research and Graduate Studies; Professor, Chemistry
Louisiana Tech University
P.O. Box 10348, 600 West Arizona
Ruston , LA 71272
Phone: (318) 257-4314
Fax: (318) 257-4339
Email: ramu@latech.edu

ESTIMATED STUDENT EXPENSES (FALL 2006)
[Expenses are for the 2006-2007 nine-month academic year and are based on an average credit load of: Graduate: N/A]

	In-State	Out-of-State
Tuition and Fees:	$4,634	$9,539
Campus and Room and Board:	$4,390	$4,390
Books and Supplies:	$2,100	$2,100
Other Expenses:		
Total Estimated Expenses:	**$11,124**	**$16,029**

NEW APPLICANTS/NEWLY ENROLLED STUDENTS
[Numbers are for the graduate engineering college for the Fall 2006 term]
Number of Applicants (a): 403
Of those, Number Offered Admission (b): 179
Of those, Number Enrolled Fall 2006 (c): 75

University of Louisville

INSTITUTION INFORMATION
J. B. Speed Building, 221
J. B. Speed School of Engineering
Louisville, KY 40292
Phone: (502) 852-6281

Fax: (502) 852-7033
Web: http://speed.louisville.edu

GENERAL INFORMATION
[All Students - Fall 2006]
Undergraduate Enrollment	15,103
Graduate Enrollment	4,655
Professional Enrollment	2,083
Total Enrollment	**21,841**

ENGINEERING COLLEGE INFORMATION

HEAD OF ENGINEERING
Mickey R Wilhelm
Dean
J. B. Speed School of Engineering
University of Louisville
Office of the Dean
Louisville, KY 40292
Phone: (502) 852-5637
Fax: (502) 852-7033
Email: mrwilh01@louisville.edu

ENGINEERING COLLEGE INQUIRIES
Michael L Day
Associate Dean
University of Louisville
J. B. Speed Building, 212, J. B. Speed School of Engineering
Louisville, KY 40292
Phone: (502) 852-6194
Fax: (502) 852-7033
Email: mlday001@louisville.edu

TYPES OF ENGINEERING DEGREES
Bachelor's: B.S.
Master's: M.S. with thesis, M.S. without thesis, but with project or report, M.Eng.
Doctoral: Ph.D.

UNDERGRADUATE INFORMATION

ADMISSION INQUIRIES
Jenny L Sawyer
Exective Director of Admissions
University of Louisville
Houchens, 150, University of Louisville
Louisville, KY 40292
Phone: (502) 852-6194
Fax: (502) 852-4776
Email: jlsawy01@louisville.edu

ESTIMATED STUDENT EXPENSES (FALL 2006)
[Expenses are for the 2006-2007 nine-month academic year and are based on an average credit load of: Undergraduate: 15]

	In-State	Out-of-State
Tuition and Fees:	$6,252	$1,672
Campus and Room and Board:	$6,432	$6,432
Books and Supplies:	$800	$800
Other Expenses:	$5,238	$5,238
Total Estimated Expenses:	**$18,722**	**$14,142**
Note: Excludes travel expenses.

NEW APPLICANTS/NEWLY ENROLLED STUDENTS
[Numbers are for the undergraduate engineering college for the Fall 2006 term]
Number of Applicants (a): 929
Of those, Number Offered Admission (b): 793
Of those, Number Enrolled Fall 2006 (c): 450
Note: Not Available

GRADUATE INFORMATION

ADMISSION INQUIRIES
Ronald M Atlas
Dean of the Graduate School
University of Louisville
105 Houchens Building
Louisville , KY 40292
Phone: (502) 852-6194
Fax: (502) 852-2365
Email: rmatla01@louisville.edu

ADMISSION INQUIRIES
Michael L Day
Associate Dean
University of Louisville
J. B. Speed Building, 212, J. B. Speed School of Engineering
Louisville , KY 40292
Phone: (502) 852-6194

Fax: (502) 852-7033
Email: mlday001@louisville.edu

ESTIMATED STUDENT EXPENSES (FALL 2006)
[Expenses are for the 2006-2007 nine-month academic year and are based on an average credit load of: Graduate: 12]

	In-State	Out-of-State
Tuition and Fees:	$6,786	$17,348
Campus and Room and Board:	$6,432	$6,432
Books and Supplies:	$800	$800
Other Expenses:	$5,238	$5,238
Total Estimated Expenses:	**$19,256**	**$29,818**
Note: Excludes travel expenses.

NEW APPLICANTS/NEWLY ENROLLED STUDENTS
[Numbers are for the graduate engineering college for the Fall 2006 term]
Number of Applicants (a): 318
Of those, Number Offered Admission (b): 206
Of those, Number Enrolled Fall 2006 (c): 95

University of Maine

INSTITUTION INFORMATION
College of Engineering
210 AMC Building
Orono, ME 04469-5769
Phone: (207) 581-2216
Fax: (207) 581-2220
Web: http://www.engineering.umaine.edu

GENERAL INFORMATION
[All Students - Fall 2006]
Undergraduate Enrollment	9,527
Graduate Enrollment	2,270
Professional Enrollment	0
Total Enrollment	**11,797**

ENGINEERING COLLEGE INFORMATION

HEAD OF ENGINEERING
Dana N Humphrey
Interim Dean
Engineering
University of Maine
College of Engineering
200 AMc Building
Orono, ME 04469-5796
Phone: (207) 581-2216
Fax: (207) 581-2220
Email: dana.humphrey@umit.maine.edu

ENGINEERING COLLEGE INQUIRIES
John J McDonough
Associate Dean for Academics
University of Maine
201 AMC Building
Orono, ME 00469-5796
Phone: (207) 581-2217
Fax: (207) 581-2220
Email: johnm@maine.edu

TYPES OF ENGINEERING DEGREES
Bachelor's: B.S.
Master's: M.S. with thesis, M.S. without thesis, but with project or report
Doctoral: Ph.D.

UNDERGRADUATE INFORMATION

ADMISSION INQUIRIES
William J Munsey
Associate Director
University of Maine
115 Chadbourne Hall
Orono, ME 04469-5713
Phone: (207) 581-1561
Fax: (207) 581-1213
Email: um-admit@maine.maine.edu

NEW APPLICANTS/NEWLY ENROLLED STUDENTS
[Numbers are for the undergraduate engineering college for the Fall 2006 term]
Number of Applicants (a): 743
Of those, Number Offered Admission (b): 514
Of those, Number Enrolled Fall 2006 (c): 214

GRADUATE INFORMATION

ADMISSION INQUIRIES
Chet A Rock
Associate Dean for Research and Finance
University of Maine
205 AMC Building
Orono , ME 04469-5796
Phone: (207) 581-2218
Fax: (207) 581-2220
Email: chetrock@maine.edu

NEW APPLICANTS/NEWLY ENROLLED STUDENTS
[Numbers are for the graduate engineering college for the Fall 2006 term]

Number of Applicants (a):	121
Of those, Number Offered Admission (b):	61
Of those, Number Enrolled Fall 2006 (c):	38

Manhattan College

INSTITUTION INFORMATION
School of Engineering
Manhattan College Parkway
Riverdale, NY 10471
Phone: (718) 862-7281
Fax: (718) 862-8015
Web: http://www.engineering.manhattan.edu

GENERAL INFORMATION
[All Students - Fall 2006]

Undergraduate Enrollment	2,994
Graduate Enrollment	360
Professional Enrollment	0
Total Enrollment	**3,354**

ENGINEERING COLLEGE INFORMATION

HEAD OF ENGINEERING
Richard H. Heist
Dean of Engineering
School of Engineering
Manhattan College
Manhattan College Parkway
Riverdale, NY 10471
Phone: (718) 862-7307
Fax: (718) 862-8015
Email: richard.heist@manhattan.edu

TYPES OF ENGINEERING DEGREES
Bachelor's: B.S.
Master's: M.S. with thesis, M.S. without thesis, but with project or report
Doctoral:

UNDERGRADUATE INFORMATION

ADMISSION INQUIRIES
William Bisset
Vice President for Enrollment Management
Manhattan College
Manhattan College Parkway
Riverdale, NY 10471
Phone: (718) 862-7213
Fax: (718) 862-8019
Email: admit@manhattan.edu

ADMISSION INQUIRIES
Richard Schneider
Engineering Academic Advisor
Manhattan College
School of Engineering, Manhattan College Parkway
Riverdale, NY 10471
Phone: (718) 862-7213
Fax: (718) 862-8015
Email: richard.schneider@manhattan.edu

ESTIMATED STUDENT EXPENSES (FALL 2006)
[Expenses are for the 2006-2007 nine-month academic year and are based on an average credit load of: Undergraduate: 17]

	All Students
Tuition and fees:	$20,350
Campus and Room and Board:	$9,000
Books and Supplies:	$1,600
Other Expenses:	$4,000
Total Estimated Expenses:	**$34,950**

Note: Expenses include an $950.00 Program Fee each semester for Engineers= $1,900.00

NEW APPLICANTS/NEWLY ENROLLED STUDENTS
[Numbers are for the undergraduate engineering college for the Fall 2006 term]

Number of Applicants (a):	710
Of those, Number Offered Admission (b):	462
Of those, Number Enrolled Fall 2006 (c):	171

GRADUATE INFORMATION

ADMISSION INQUIRIES
Gordon Silverman
Chairperson, Electrical & Computer Engineering Department
Manhattan College
School of Engineering, Manhattan College Parkway
Riverdale , NY 10471
Phone: (718) 862-7213
Fax: (718) 862-8015
Email: ece@manhattan.edu

ADMISSION INQUIRIES
Bahman Litkouhi
Chairperson, Mechanical Engineering Department
Manhattan College
School of Engineering, Manhattan College Parkway
Riverdale , NY 10471
Phone: (718) 862-7213
Fax: (718) 862-7163
Email: mechdept@manhattan.edu

ADMISSION INQUIRIES
Nada Assaf-Anid
Chairperson, Chemical Engineering
Manhattan College
School of Engineering, Manhattan College Parkway
Riverdale , NY 10471
Phone: (718) 862-7213
Fax: (718) 862-7819
Email: chmldept@manhattan.edu

ADMISSION INQUIRIES
Moujalli Hourani
Chairperson, Civil and Environmental Engineering Department
Manhattan College
School of Engineering, Manhattan College Parkway
Riverdale , NY 10471
Phone: (718) 862-7213
Fax: (718) 862-8015
Email: moujalli.hourani@manhattan.edu

ADMISSION INQUIRIES
Kevin Farley
Director of Environmental Engineering Graduate Program
Manhattan College
School of Engineering, Manhattan College Parkway
Riverdale , NY 10471
Phone: (718) 862-7383
Fax: (718) 862-8015
Email: kevin.farley@manhattan.edu

ESTIMATED STUDENT EXPENSES (FALL 2006)
[Expenses are for the 2006-2007 nine-month academic year and are based on an average credit load of: Graduate: 9]

	All Students
Tuition and fees:	$650
Campus and Room and Board:	
Books and Supplies:	
Other Expenses:	
Total Estimated Expenses:	**$650**

Note: Expenses include an $950.00 Program Fee each semester for Engineers= $1,900.00

NEW APPLICANTS/NEWLY ENROLLED STUDENTS
[Numbers are for the graduate engineering college for the Fall 2006 term]

Number of Applicants (a):	115
Of those, Number Offered Admission (b):	95
Of those, Number Enrolled Fall 2006 (c):	80

Marietta College

INSTITUTION INFORMATION
215 5th Street
Marietta, OH 45750
Phone: (740) 376-4775
Fax: (740) 376-4777
Web: http://www.marietta.edu

GENERAL INFORMATION
[All Students - Fall 2006]

Undergraduate Enrollment	1,350
Graduate Enrollment	200
Professional Enrollment	0
Total Enrollment	**1,550**

ENGINEERING COLLEGE INFORMATION

ENGINEERING COLLEGE INQUIRIES
Robert W Chase
Chair, Professor, PhD
Marietta College
Marietta College, 215 Fifth Street
Marietta, OH 45750
Phone: (740) 376-4776
Fax: (740) 376-4777
Email: chaser@marietta.edu

TYPES OF ENGINEERING DEGREES
Bachelor's: B.S.
Master's:
Doctoral:

UNDERGRADUATE INFORMATION

ESTIMATED STUDENT EXPENSES (FALL 2006)
[Expenses are for the 2006-2007 nine-month academic year and are based on an average credit load of: Undergraduate: N/A]

	All Students
Tuition and fees:	$23,000
Campus and Room and Board:	$7,000
Books and Supplies:	$600
Other Expenses:	$600
Total Estimated Expenses:	**$31,200**

NEW APPLICANTS/NEWLY ENROLLED STUDENTS
[Numbers are for the undergraduate engineering college for the Fall 2006 term]

Number of Applicants (a):	58
Of those, Number Offered Admission (b):	41
Of those, Number Enrolled Fall 2006 (c):	41

Marquette University

INSTITUTION INFORMATION
College of Engineering
P.O. Box 1881
Milwaukee, WI 53201-1881
Phone: (414) 288-7080
Fax: (414) 288-7082
Web: http://www.marquette.edu/engineering/

GENERAL INFORMATION
[All Students - Fall 2006]

Undergraduate Enrollment	8,048
Graduate Enrollment	2,488
Professional Enrollment	1,012
Total Enrollment	**11,548**

ENGINEERING COLLEGE INFORMATION

HEAD OF ENGINEERING
Stanley V Jaskolski
Professor and Dean
College of Engineering
Marquette University
Haggerty Hall
P.O. Box 1881
Milwaukee, WI 53201-1881
Phone: (414) 288-6591
Fax: (414) 288-7082
Email: stan.jaskolski@marquette.edu

ENGINEERING COLLEGE INQUIRIES
Barbara Silver-Thorn
Associate Professor and Associate Dean for Academic Affairs
Marquette University
Olin Engineering Center
Milwaukee, WI 53201-1881
Phone: (414) 288-7080
Fax: (414) 288-7082
Email: barbara.silver-thorn@marquette.edu

TYPES OF ENGINEERING DEGREES
Bachelor's: B.S.

Master's: M.S. with thesis, M.S. without thesis, but with project or report
Doctoral: Ph.D.

UNDERGRADUATE INFORMATION

ADMISSION INQUIRIES
Jon K Jensen
Associate Dean for Enrollment Management
Marquette University
College of Engineering, P.O. Box 1881
Milwaukee, WI 53201-1881
Phone: (414) 288-6720
Fax: (414) 288-7082
Email: jon.jensen@marquette.edu

ADMISSION INQUIRIES
Robert Blust
Dean of Admissions
Marquette University
P.O. Box 1881
Milwaukee, WI 53201-1881
Phone: (414) 288-7004
Fax: (414) 288-3764
Email: roby.blust@marquette.edu

ADMISSION INQUIRIES
David L Bruey
Director of International Programs
Marquette University
PO Box 1881
Milwaukee, WI 53201-1881
Phone: (414) 288-7289
Fax: (414) 288-3701
Email: david.bruey@marquette.edu

ESTIMATED STUDENT EXPENSES (FALL 2006)
[Expenses are for the 2006-2007 nine-month academic year and are based on an average credit load of: Undergraduate: 17]

	All Students
Tuition and fees:	$24,670
Campus and Room and Board:	$8,120
Books and Supplies:	$900
Other Expenses:	$1,350
Total Estimated Expenses:	**$35,040**

NEW APPLICANTS/NEWLY ENROLLED STUDENTS
[Numbers are for the undergraduate engineering college for the Fall 2006 term]

Number of Applicants (a):	1,319
Of those, Number Offered Admission (b):	1,057
Of those, Number Enrolled Fall 2006 (c):	240

GRADUATE INFORMATION

ADMISSION INQUIRIES
Jay R Goldberg
Associate Professor and Director
Marquette University
College of Engineering, P.O. Box 1881
Milwaukee, WI 53201-1881
Phone: (414) 288-6059
Fax: (414) 288-7938
Email: jay.goldberg@marquette.edu

ADMISSION INQUIRIES
Dean C Jeutter
Professor and Director of Graduate Studies
Marquette University
College of Engineering, P.O. Box 1881
Milwaukee, WI 53201-1881
Phone: (414) 288-3375
Fax: (414) 288-7932
Email: dean.jeutter@marquette.edu

ADMISSION INQUIRIES
Stephen M Heinrich
Professor and Director of Graduate Studies
Marquette University
College of Engineering, P.O. Box 1881
Milwaukee, WI 53201-1881
Phone: (414) 288-5466
Fax: (414) 288-7521
Email: stephen.heinrich@marquette.edu

ADMISSION INQUIRIES
Fabien J Josse
Professor and Director; Director of Graduate Studies
Marquette University
College of Engineering, P.O. Box 1881

Milwaukee, WI 53201-1881
Phone: (414) 288-6789
Fax: (414) 288-5579
Email: fabien.josse@marquette.edu

ADMISSION INQUIRIES
James Rice
Associate Professor, Director of Graduate Studies
Marquette University
College of Engineering, P.O. Box 1881
Milwaukee, WI 53201-1881
Phone: (414) 288-5405
Fax: (414) 288-7790
Email: james.rice@marquette.edu

ESTIMATED STUDENT EXPENSES (FALL 2006)
[Expenses are for the 2006-2007 nine-month academic year and are based on an average credit load of: Graduate: 9]

	All Students
Tuition and fees:	$13,500
Campus and Room and Board:	$10,630
Books and Supplies:	$1,120
Other Expenses:	$2,100
Total Estimated Expenses:	**$27,350**

NEW APPLICANTS/NEWLY ENROLLED STUDENTS
[Numbers are for the graduate engineering college for the Fall 2006 term]

Number of Applicants (a):	252
Of those, Number Offered Admission (b):	150
Of those, Number Enrolled Fall 2006 (c):	46

University of Maryland, Baltimore County

INSTITUTION INFORMATION
ITE, Room 217
1000 Hilltop Circle
Baltimore, MD 21250
Phone: (410) 455-3270
Fax: (410) 455-3559
Web: http://www.umbc.edu

GENERAL INFORMATION
[All Students - Fall 2006]

Undergraduate Enrollment	11,798
Graduate Enrollment	2,382
Professional Enrollment	0
Total Enrollment	**14,180**

ENGINEERING COLLEGE INFORMATION

HEAD OF ENGINEERING
Warren R DeVries
Professor and Dean
College of Engineering & Information Technology
University of Maryland, Baltimore County
1000 Hilltop Circle
ITE 217
Baltimore, MD 21250
Phone: (410) 455-3270
Fax: (410) 455-3559
Email: wdevries@umbc.edu

TYPES OF ENGINEERING DEGREES
Bachelor's: B.A., B.S.
Master's: M.S. with thesis, M.S. without thesis, but with project or report
Doctoral: Ph.D.

UNDERGRADUATE INFORMATION

ADMISSION INQUIRIES
Catherine Bielawski
Director, Undergraduate Student Services
University of Maryland, Baltimore County
ITE, 206, 1000 Hilltop Circle
Baltimore, MD 21250
Phone: (410) 455-1614
Fax: (410) 455-3559
Email: bielawsk@umbc.edu

ADMISSION INQUIRIES
Konstantinos Kalpakis
Associate Professor, Undergraduate Coordinator (CSEE)
University of Maryland, Baltimore County
ITE, 348, 1000 Hilltop Circle
Baltimore, MD 21250

Phone: (410) 455-3143
Fax: (410) 455-3969
Email: kalpakis@cs.umbc.edu

ESTIMATED STUDENT EXPENSES (FALL 2006)
[Expenses are for the 2006-2007 nine-month academic year and are based on an average credit load of: Undergraduate: 12]

	In-State	Out-of-State
Tuition and Fees:	$8,520	$16,596
Campus and Room and Board:	$8,342	$8,342
Books and Supplies:	$770	$770
Other Expenses:	$880	$880
Total Estimated Expenses:	**$18,512**	**$26,588**

NEW APPLICANTS/NEWLY ENROLLED STUDENTS
[Numbers are for the undergraduate engineering college for the Fall 2006 term]

Number of Applicants (a):	1,117
Of those, Number Offered Admission (b):	867
Of those, Number Enrolled Fall 2006 (c):	337

GRADUATE INFORMATION

ESTIMATED STUDENT EXPENSES (FALL 2006)
[Expenses are for the 2006-2007 nine-month academic year and are based on an average credit load of: Graduate: 9]

	In-State	Out-of-State
Tuition and Fees:	$8,592	$13,212
Campus and Room and Board:	$8,342	$8,342
Books and Supplies:	$770	$770
Other Expenses:	$880	$880
Total Estimated Expenses:	**$18,584**	**$23,204**

NEW APPLICANTS/NEWLY ENROLLED STUDENTS
[Numbers are for the graduate engineering college for the Fall 2006 term]

Number of Applicants (a):	467
Of those, Number Offered Admission (b):	164
Of those, Number Enrolled Fall 2006 (c):	88

University of Maryland, College Park

INSTITUTION INFORMATION
A. James Clark School of Engineering
Room 3110 Jeong H. Kim Engineering Building
College Park, MD 20742
Phone: (301) 405-8335
Fax: (301) 314-5908
Web: http://www.eng.umd.edu

GENERAL INFORMATION
[All Students - Fall 2006]

Undergraduate Enrollment	25,154
Graduate Enrollment	9,948
Professional Enrollment	0
Total Enrollment	**35,102**

ENGINEERING COLLEGE INFORMATION

HEAD OF ENGINEERING
Nariman Farvardin
Dean
A. James Clark School of Engineering
University of Maryland, College Park
Rm. 3110 Jeong H. Kim Engineering Building
College Park, MD 20742
Phone: (301) 405-3868
Fax: (301) 314-5908
Email: farvardin@umd.edu

TYPES OF ENGINEERING DEGREES
Bachelor's: B.S.
Master's: M.S. with thesis, M.S. without thesis, but with project or report, M.Eng.
Doctoral: Ph.D.

UNDERGRADUATE INFORMATION

ADMISSION INQUIRIES
Meredith DeMoss
Coordinator, Undergraduate Recruitment and Special Programs
University of Maryland, College Park
Rm. 1124 Glenn L. Martin Hall
College Park, MD 20742-3011
Phone: (301) 405-0287

Fax: (301) 314-9867
Email: mdemoss@umd.edu

ESTIMATED STUDENT EXPENSES (FALL 2006)
[Expenses are for the 2006-2007 nine-month academic year and are based on an average credit load of: Undergraduate: 15]

	In-State	Out-of-State
Tuition and Fees:	$7,906	$20,230
Campus and Room and Board:	$13,699	$13,699
Books and Supplies:	$1,002	$1,002
Other Expenses:	$2,880	$2,880
Total Estimated Expenses:	**$25,487**	**$37,811**

Note: Tuition/Fees and Room/Board are per academic year. The amount for Tuition/Fees was calculated based on the estimated average credit load per term. On-campus housing for graduate students is optional.

NEW APPLICANTS/NEWLY ENROLLED STUDENTS
[Numbers are for the undergraduate engineering college for the Fall 2006 term]

Number of Applicants (a):	2,068
Of those, Number Offered Admission (b):	1,363
Of those, Number Enrolled Fall 2006 (c):	566

GRADUATE INFORMATION

ADMISSION INQUIRIES
Johnetta Davis
Director
University of Maryland, College Park
Rm. 2125 Lee Building
College Park, MD 20742
Phone: (301) 405-4183
Fax: (301) 314-9305

ESTIMATED STUDENT EXPENSES (FALL 2006)
[Expenses are for the 2006-2007 nine-month academic year and are based on an average credit load of: Graduate: 9]

	In-State	Out-of-State
Tuition and Fees:	$8,777	$17,317
Campus and Room and Board:	$9,711	$9,711
Books and Supplies:	$1,276	$1,276
Other Expenses:	$4,559	$4,559
Total Estimated Expenses:	**$24,323**	**$32,863**

Note: Tuition/Fees and Room/Board are per academic year. The amount for Tuition/Fees was calculated based on the estimated average credit load per term. On-campus housing for graduate students is optional.

NEW APPLICANTS/NEWLY ENROLLED STUDENTS
[Numbers are for the graduate engineering college for the Fall 2006 term]

Number of Applicants (a):	4,240
Of those, Number Offered Admission (b):	1,037
Of those, Number Enrolled Fall 2006 (c):	594

Massachusetts Institute of Technology

INSTITUTION INFORMATION
Room 1-206
77 Massachusetts Avenue
Cambridge, MA 02139
Phone: (161) 725-3329
Fax: (161) 725-8549
Web: http://web.mit.edu/engineering/

GENERAL INFORMATION
[All Students - Fall 2006]

Undergraduate Enrollment	4,127
Graduate Enrollment	6,126
Professional Enrollment	0
Total Enrollment	**10,253**

ENGINEERING COLLEGE INFORMATION

HEAD OF ENGINEERING
Thomas Magnanti
Institute Professor and Dean
School of Engineering
Massachusetts Institute of Technology
Room 1-206
77 Massachusette Avenue
Cambridge, MA 02139
Phone: (161) 725-3660
Fax: (161) 725-8549
Email: magnanti@mit.edu

TYPES OF ENGINEERING DEGREES
Bachelor's: S.B.
Master's: S.M., M.Eng., Engineer
Doctoral: Ph.D., Sc.D.

UNDERGRADUATE INFORMATION

ESTIMATED STUDENT EXPENSES (FALL 2006)
[Expenses are for the 2006-2007 nine-month academic year and are based on an average credit load of: Undergraduate: N/A]

	All Students
Tuition and fees:	$33,600
Campus and Room and Board:	$9,950
Books and Supplies:	$1,100
Other Expenses:	$1,700
Total Estimated Expenses:	**$46,350**

Note: Does not include transportation and medical expenses.

NEW APPLICANTS/NEWLY ENROLLED STUDENTS
[Numbers are for the undergraduate engineering college for the Fall 2006 term]

Number of Applicants (a):	11,374
Of those, Number Offered Admission (b):	1,514
Of those, Number Enrolled Fall 2006 (c):	1,002

Note: Freshmen do not admit to a major. Data is for all freshmen.

GRADUATE INFORMATION

ESTIMATED STUDENT EXPENSES (FALL 2006)
[Expenses are for the 2006-2007 nine-month academic year and are based on an average credit load of: Graduate: N/A]

	All Students
Tuition and fees:	$33,600
Campus and Room and Board:	$14,250
Books and Supplies:	$1,800
Other Expenses:	$2,700
Total Estimated Expenses:	**$52,350**

Note: Does not include transportation and medical expenses.

NEW APPLICANTS/NEWLY ENROLLED STUDENTS
[Numbers are for the graduate engineering college for the Fall 2006 term]

Number of Applicants (a):	6,460
Of those, Number Offered Admission (b):	1,436
Of those, Number Enrolled Fall 2006 (c):	893

University of Massachusetts Amherst

INSTITUTION INFORMATION
125 Marston Hall
Amherst, MA 01003
Phone: (413) 545-0300
Fax: (413) 545-0724
Web: http://www.ecs.umass.edu

GENERAL INFORMATION
[All Students - Fall 2006]

Undergraduate Enrollment	19,823
Graduate Enrollment	5,770
Professional Enrollment	0
Total Enrollment	**25,593**

ENGINEERING COLLEGE INFORMATION

HEAD OF ENGINEERING
Michael F Malone
Dean
College of Engineering
University of Massachusetts Amherst
125 Marston Hall
Amherst, MA 01003-5210
Phone: (413) 545-6388
Fax: (413) 545-0724
Email: mmalone@ecs.umass.edu

ENGINEERING COLLEGE INQUIRIES
Kathleen G Rubin
Assistant Dean for College Outreach
University of Massachusetts Amherst
129 Marston Hall
Amherst, MA 01003-5210
Phone: (413) 545-4757

Fax: (413) 545-0724
Email: rubin@ecs.umass.edu

TYPES OF ENGINEERING DEGREES
Bachelor's: B.S.
Master's: M.S. with thesis, M.S. without thesis, but with project or report
Doctoral: Ph.D.

UNDERGRADUATE INFORMATION

ADMISSION INQUIRIES
Michael Gargano
Vice Chancellor for Student Affairs and Campus Life
University of Massachusetts Amherst
Whitmore Administration Building
Amherst, MA 01003
Phone: (413) 545-2333
Fax: (413) 545-1838
Email: dunk@stuaf.umass.edu

ESTIMATED STUDENT EXPENSES (FALL 2006)
[Expenses are for the 2006-2007 nine-month academic year and are based on an average credit load of: Undergraduate: N/A]

	In-State	Out-of-State
Tuition and Fees:	$9,598	$18,717
Campus and Room and Board:	$6,989	$6,989
Books and Supplies:	$1,500	$1,500
Other Expenses:	$1,500	$1,500
Total Estimated Expenses:	**$19,587**	**$28,706**

NEW APPLICANTS/NEWLY ENROLLED STUDENTS
[Numbers are for the undergraduate engineering college for the Fall 2006 term]

Number of Applicants (a):	1,742
Of those, Number Offered Admission (b):	1,089
Of those, Number Enrolled Fall 2006 (c):	280

GRADUATE INFORMATION

ADMISSION INQUIRIES
Patricia M Stowell
Registrar
University of Massachusetts Amherst
530 Goodell
Amherst, MA 01003
Phone: (413) 545-0722
Fax: (413) 545-3754
Email: pstowell@resgs.umass.edu

ESTIMATED STUDENT EXPENSES (FALL 2006)
[Expenses are for the 2006-2007 nine-month academic year and are based on an average credit load of: Graduate: N/A]

	In-State	Out-of-State
Tuition and Fees:	$9,877	$18,326
Campus and Room and Board:	$6,989	$6,989
Books and Supplies:	$1,500	$1,500
Other Expenses:	$1,500	$1,500
Total Estimated Expenses:	**$19,866**	**$28,315**

NEW APPLICANTS/NEWLY ENROLLED STUDENTS
[Numbers are for the graduate engineering college for the Fall 2006 term]

Number of Applicants (a):	1,149
Of those, Number Offered Admission (b):	338
Of those, Number Enrolled Fall 2006 (c):	116

University of Massachusetts Dartmouth

INSTITUTION INFORMATION
College of Engineering
285 Old Westport Road
North Dartmouth, MA 02747-2300
Phone: (508) 999-8539
Fax: (508) 999-9137
Web: http://www.umassd.edu

GENERAL INFORMATION
[All Students - Fall 2006]

Undergraduate Enrollment	7,626
Graduate Enrollment	1,130
Professional Enrollment	8,756
Total Enrollment	**17,512**

ENGINEERING COLLEGE INFORMATION

HEAD OF ENGINEERING
Antonio H. Costa
Dean of Engineering
College of Engineering
University of Massachusetts Dartmouth
285 Old Westport Road
North Dartmouth, MA 02747-2300
Phone: (508) 999-8539
Fax: (508) 999-9137
Email: acosta@umassd.edu

ENGINEERING COLLEGE INQUIRIES
Antonio H. Costa
Dean of Engineering
University of Massachusetts Dartmouth
285 Old Westport Road
North Dartmouth, MA 02747-2300
Phone: (508) 999-8539
Fax: (508) 999-9137
Email: acosta@umassd.edu

TYPES OF ENGINEERING DEGREES
Bachelor's: B.S.
Master's: M.S. with thesis, M.S. without thesis, but with project or report,Post Bacclaureate Certificate
Doctoral: Ph.D.

UNDERGRADUATE INFORMATION

ESTIMATED STUDENT EXPENSES (FALL 2006)
[Expenses are for the 2006-2007 nine-month academic year and are based on an average credit load of: Undergraduate: 12]

	In-State	Out-of-State
Tuition and Fees:	$8,309	$17,809
Campus and Room and Board:	$8,483	$8,483
Books and Supplies:	$800	$800
Other Expenses:	$2,690	$2,690
Total Estimated Expenses:	**$20,282**	**$29,782**

Note: Other Expenses are personal & transportation Graduate tuition based on 12 credits per term. Room and board includes a meal plan.

NEW APPLICANTS/NEWLY ENROLLED STUDENTS
[Numbers are for the undergraduate engineering college for the Fall 2006 term]

Number of Applicants (a):	907
Of those, Number Offered Admission (b):	702
Of those, Number Enrolled Fall 2006 (c):	261

GRADUATE INFORMATION

ADMISSION INQUIRIES
Carol A Novo
Administrative Assistant
University of Massachusetts Dartmouth
285 Old Westport Road
North Dartmouth , MA 02747-2300
Phone: (508) 999-8026
Fax: (508) 999-8183
Email: cnovo@umassd.edu

ESTIMATED STUDENT EXPENSES (FALL 2006)
[Expenses are for the 2006-2007 nine-month academic year and are based on an average credit load of: Graduate: 12]

	In-State	Out-of-State
Tuition and Fees:	$9,446	$17,809
Campus and Room and Board:	$8,483	$8,483
Books and Supplies:	$800	$800
Other Expenses:	$2,737	$2,737
Total Estimated Expenses:	**$21,466**	**$29,829**

Note: Other Expenses are personal & transportation Graduate tuition based on 12 credits per term. Room and board includes a meal plan.

NEW APPLICANTS/NEWLY ENROLLED STUDENTS
[Numbers are for the graduate engineering college for the Fall 2006 term]

Number of Applicants (a):	460
Of those, Number Offered Admission (b):	368
Of those, Number Enrolled Fall 2006 (c):	103

University of Massachusetts Lowell

INSTITUTION INFORMATION
1 University Avenue
311 Kitson Hall
Lowell, MA 01854
Phone: (978) 934-2570
Fax: (978) 934-3007
Web: http://www.uml.edu/

GENERAL INFORMATION
[All Students - Fall 2006]

Undergraduate Enrollment	8,649
Graduate Enrollment	2,559
Professional Enrollment	0
Total Enrollment	**11,208**

ENGINEERING COLLEGE INFORMATION

HEAD OF ENGINEERING
John M. Ting
Dean, Professor
Francis College of Engineering
University of Massachusetts Lowell
One University Avenue
Kitson 311
Lowell, MA 01854
Phone: (978) 934-2576
Fax: (978) 934-3007
Email: John_Ting@uml.edu

TYPES OF ENGINEERING DEGREES
Bachelor's: B.S.
Master's: M.S. with thesis, M.S. without thesis, but with project or report,MS without thesis or report/course work only
Doctoral: D.Eng

UNDERGRADUATE INFORMATION

ESTIMATED STUDENT EXPENSES (FALL 2006)
[Expenses are for the 2006-2007 nine-month academic year and are based on an average credit load of: Undergraduate: 12]

	In-State	Out-of-State
Tuition and Fees:	$8,444	$19,714
Campus and Room and Board:	$6,520	$6,520
Books and Supplies:	$725	$725
Other Expenses:	$900	$900
Total Estimated Expenses:	**$16,589**	**$27,859**

NEW APPLICANTS/NEWLY ENROLLED STUDENTS
[Numbers are for the undergraduate engineering college for the Fall 2006 term]

Number of Applicants (a):	968
Of those, Number Offered Admission (b):	695
Of those, Number Enrolled Fall 2006 (c):	304

GRADUATE INFORMATION

ESTIMATED STUDENT EXPENSES (FALL 2006)
[Expenses are for the 2006-2007 nine-month academic year and are based on an average credit load of: Graduate: 12]

	In-State	Out-of-State
Tuition and Fees:	$10,614	$10,497
Campus and Room and Board:	$6,728	$6,728
Books and Supplies:	$725	$725
Other Expenses:	$2,350	$2,350
Total Estimated Expenses:	**$20,417**	**$20,300**

NEW APPLICANTS/NEWLY ENROLLED STUDENTS
[Numbers are for the graduate engineering college for the Fall 2006 term]

Number of Applicants (a):	310
Of those, Number Offered Admission (b):	216
Of those, Number Enrolled Fall 2006 (c):	94

McGill University, Faculty of Engineering

INSTITUTION INFORMATION
3450 University Street
Frank Dawson Adams Building, Room 22
Montreal, PQ H3A 2K6
Phone: (514) 398-7257
Fax: (514) 398-5681
Web: http://www.mcgill.ca/engineering

GENERAL INFORMATION
[All Students - Fall 2006]

Undergraduate Enrollment	22,787
Graduate Enrollment	7,546
Professional Enrollment	2,454
Total Enrollment	**32,787**

ENGINEERING COLLEGE INFORMATION

HEAD OF ENGINEERING
Christophe Pierre
Dean
Faculty of Engineering
McGill University
817 Sherbrooke Street West
Macdonald Engineering Building, Room 382
Montreal, PQ H3A 2K6
Phone: (514) 398-7250
Fax: (514) 398-7379
Email: dean.engineering@mcgill.ca

TYPES OF ENGINEERING DEGREES
Bachelor's: B.Eng
Master's: M.S. with thesis, M.S. without thesis, but with project or report, M.Eng.,M.M.
Doctoral: Ph.D.

UNDERGRADUATE INFORMATION

ESTIMATED STUDENT EXPENSES (FALL 2006)
[Expenses are for the 2006-2007 nine-month academic year and are based on an average credit load of: Undergraduate: 15]

	Canadian Citizen	Non-Canadian
Tuition and Fees:	$6,600	$16,500
Campus and Room and Board:	$6,800	$6,800
Books and Supplies:	$1,000	$1,000
Other Expenses:	$2,000	$2,900
Total Estimated Expenses:	**$16,400**	**$27,200**

NEW APPLICANTS/NEWLY ENROLLED STUDENTS
[Numbers are for the undergraduate engineering college for the Fall 2006 term]

Number of Applicants (a):	3,290
Of those, Number Offered Admission (b):	1,580
Of those, Number Enrolled Fall 2006 (c):	550

GRADUATE INFORMATION

ESTIMATED STUDENT EXPENSES (FALL 2006)
[Expenses are for the 2006-2007 nine-month academic year and are based on an average credit load of: Graduate: N/A]

	Canadian Citizen	Non-Canadian
Tuition and Fees:	$1,670	$10,100
Campus and Room and Board:		$13,000
Books and Supplies:	$800	$800
Other Expenses:	$2,000	$2,700
Total Estimated Expenses:	**$4,470**	**$26,600**

NEW APPLICANTS/NEWLY ENROLLED STUDENTS
[Numbers are for the graduate engineering college for the Fall 2006 term]

Number of Applicants (a):	1,570
Of those, Number Offered Admission (b):	1,690
Of those, Number Enrolled Fall 2006 (c):	225

McNeese State University

INSTITUTION INFORMATION
4300 Ryan Street
P.O.Box 91860
Lake Charles, LA 70609
Phone: (337) 475-5857
Fax: (337) 475-5237
Web: http://www.mcneese.edu

GENERAL INFORMATION
[All Students - Fall 2006]

Undergraduate Enrollment	7,336
Graduate Enrollment	1,007
Professional Enrollment	0
Total Enrollment	**8,343**

ENGINEERING COLLEGE INFORMATION

HEAD OF ENGINEERING
Nikos Kiritsis
Associate Professor, Dean
College of Engineering and Engineering Technology
McNeese State University
P.O. Box 91860
Lake Charles, LA 70609
Phone: (337) 475-5857
Fax: (337) 475-5237
Email: nikosk@mcneese.edu

ENGINEERING COLLEGE INQUIRIES
Nikos Kiritsis
Associate Professor, Dean
McNeese State University
P.O. Box 91860
Lake Charles, LA 70609
Phone: (337) 475-5857
Fax: (337) 475-5237
Email: nikosk@mcneese.edu

TYPES OF ENGINEERING DEGREES
Bachelor's: B.S.
Master's: M.S. with thesis, M.S. without thesis, but with project or report
Doctoral:

UNDERGRADUATE INFORMATION

ADMISSION INQUIRIES
Fred I Denny
Associate Professor, Department Head
McNeese State University
P.O. Box 91735
Lake Charles, LA 70609
Phone: (337) 475-5867
Fax: (337) 475-5286
Email: fdenny@mcneese.edu

ESTIMATED STUDENT EXPENSES (FALL 2006)
[Expenses are for the 2006-2007 nine-month academic year and are based on an average credit load of: Undergraduate: 12]

	In-State	Out-of-State
Tutition and Fees:	$3,200	
Campus and Room and Board:	$5,506	
Books and Supplies:	$700	
Other Expenses:	$200	
Total Estimated Expenses:	**$9,606**	

GRADUATE INFORMATION

ADMISSION INQUIRIES
Janardanan O Uppot
Director of Graduate Studies, Professor of Civil Engineering
McNeese State University
PO Box 91735
Lake Charles , LA 70609
Phone: (318) 475-5868
Fax: (318) 475-5286
Email: juppot@mcneese.edu

ESTIMATED STUDENT EXPENSES (FALL 2006)
[Expenses are for the 2006-2007 nine-month academic year and are based on an average credit load of: Graduate: 9]

	In-State	Out-of-State
Tutition and Fees:	$3,082	
Campus and Room and Board:	$5,506	
Books and Supplies:	$700	
Other Expenses:	$200	
Total Estimated Expenses:	**$9,488**	

The University of Memphis

INSTITUTION INFORMATION
201 Engineering Administration Bldg
Memphis, TN 38152
Phone: (901) 678-2171
Fax: (901) 678-4180
Web: http://www.memphis.edu

GENERAL INFORMATION
[All Students - Fall 2006]

Undergraduate Enrollment	15,984
Graduate Enrollment	4,169
Professional Enrollment	409
Total Enrollment	**20,562**

ENGINEERING COLLEGE INFORMATION

HEAD OF ENGINEERING
Richard C Warder
Dean
Office of the Dean
The University of Memphis
201 Engineering Administration Bldg
Herff College of Engineering
Memphis, TN 38152
Phone: (901) 678-2171
Fax: (901) 678-4180
Email: rcwarder@memphis.edu

TYPES OF ENGINEERING DEGREES
Bachelor's: B.S.
Master's: M.S. with thesis, M.S. without thesis, but with project or report
Doctoral: Ph.D.

UNDERGRADUATE INFORMATION

ADMISSION INQUIRIES
Charles W Bray
Associate Dean for Undergradua
The University of Memphis
Herff College of Engineering
Memphis, TN 38152
Phone: (901) 678-3258
Fax: (901) 678-5030
Email: c-bray@memphis.edu

ESTIMATED STUDENT EXPENSES (FALL 2006)
[Expenses are for the 2006-2007 nine-month academic year and are based on an average credit load of: Undergraduate: 14]

	In-State	Out-of-State
Tuition and Fees:	$5,256	$15,722
Campus and Room and Board:	$6,500	$6,500
Books and Supplies:	$1,200	$1,200
Other Expenses:	$1,000	$1,000
Total Estimated Expenses:	**$13,956**	**$24,422**

NEW APPLICANTS/NEWLY ENROLLED STUDENTS
[Numbers are for the undergraduate engineering college for the Fall 2006 term]

Number of Applicants (a):	180
Of those, Number Offered Admission (b):	150
Of those, Number Enrolled Fall 2006 (c):	84

Note: Data not available.

GRADUATE INFORMATION

ADMISSION INQUIRIES
Steven M Slack
Associate Professor, Associate Dean for Graduate Studies
The University of Memphis
Herff College of Engineering
Memphis , TN 38152
Phone: (901) 678-4791
Fax: (901) 678-5281
Email: s-slack@memphis.edu

ESTIMATED STUDENT EXPENSES (FALL 2006)
[Expenses are for the 2006-2007 nine-month academic year and are based on an average credit load of: Graduate: 12]

	In-State	Out-of-State
Tuition and Fees:	$6,328	$16,488
Campus and Room and Board:	$6,500	$6,500
Books and Supplies:	$1,200	$1,200
Other Expenses:	$1,000	$1,000
Total Estimated Expenses:	**$15,028**	**$25,188**

NEW APPLICANTS/NEWLY ENROLLED STUDENTS
[Numbers are for the graduate engineering college for the Fall 2006 term]

Number of Applicants (a):	175
Of those, Number Offered Admission (b):	142
Of those, Number Enrolled Fall 2006 (c):	70

Mercer University

INSTITUTION INFORMATION
1400 Coleman Avenue
Macon, GA 31207
Phone: (478) 301-2012
Fax: (478) 301-5593
Web: http://www.mercer.edu/engineering

GENERAL INFORMATION
[All Students - Fall 2006]

Undergraduate Enrollment	4,169
Graduate Enrollment	1,355
Professional Enrollment	1,478
Total Enrollment	**7,002**

ENGINEERING COLLEGE INFORMATION

HEAD OF ENGINEERING
M. Dayne Aldridge
Dean
School of Engineering
Mercer University
1400 Coleman Avenue
Macon, GA 31207-0001
Phone: (478) 301-2459
Fax: (478) 301-5593
Email: aldridge_md@mercer.edu

TYPES OF ENGINEERING DEGREES
Bachelor's: B.S.
Master's: M.S. with thesis, M.S. without thesis
Doctoral:

UNDERGRADUATE INFORMATION

ADMISSION INQUIRIES
John P Cole
Vice President for University Admissions
Mercer University
1400 Coleman Avenue
Macon, GA 31207-0001
Phone: (478) 301-2650
Fax: (478) 301-2828
Email: cole_jp@mercer.edu

ESTIMATED STUDENT EXPENSES (FALL 2006)
[Expenses are for the 2006-2007 nine-month academic year and are based on an average credit load of: Undergraduate: 15]

	All Students
Tuition and fees:	$25,056
Campus and Room and Board:	$4,200
Books and Supplies:	$1,100
Other Expenses:	$4,040
Total Estimated Expenses:	**$34,396**

NEW APPLICANTS/NEWLY ENROLLED STUDENTS
[Numbers are for the undergraduate engineering college for the Fall 2006 term]

Number of Applicants (a):	438
Of those, Number Offered Admission (b):	386
Of those, Number Enrolled Fall 2006 (c):	116

GRADUATE INFORMATION

ADMISSION INQUIRIES
Kathy K. Olivier
Assistant to the Dean
Mercer University
1400 Coleman Avenue
Macon , GA 31207-0001
Phone: (478) 301-2459
Fax: (478) 301-5593
Email: olivier_kk@mercer.edu

Messiah College

INSTITUTION INFORMATION
One College Avenue
Box 3034
Grantham, PA 17027
Phone: (717) 766-2511
Fax: (717) 796-5222
Web: http://www.messiah.edu

GENERAL INFORMATION
[All Students - Fall 2006]

Undergraduate Enrollment	2,875
Graduate Enrollment	0
Professional Enrollment	0
Total Enrollment	**2,875**

ENGINEERING COLLEGE INFORMATION

HEAD OF ENGINEERING
W Ray Norman
Dean
Mathematics, Engineering & Business
Messiah College
Box 3056
One College Avenue
Grantham, PA 17027
Phone: (717) 766-2511
Fax: (717) 796-5222
Email: rnorman@messiah.edu

TYPES OF ENGINEERING DEGREES
Bachelor's: B.S.
Master's:
Doctoral:

UNDERGRADUATE INFORMATION

ADMISSION INQUIRIES
William G Strausbaugh
Dean for Enrollment Management
Messiah College
Grantham, PA 17027
Phone: (717) 691-6000
Fax: (717) 796-5374
Email: strausba@messiah.edu

ESTIMATED STUDENT EXPENSES (FALL 2006)
[Expenses are for the 2006-2007 nine-month academic year and are based on an average credit load of: Undergraduate: 17]

	All Students
Tuition and fees:	$23,290
Campus and Room and Board:	$7,300
Books and Supplies:	$1,200
Other Expenses:	$700
Total Estimated Expenses:	**$32,490**

NEW APPLICANTS/NEWLY ENROLLED STUDENTS
[Numbers are for the undergraduate engineering college for the Fall 2006 term]

Number of Applicants (a):	2,730
Of those, Number Offered Admission (b):	2,036
Of those, Number Enrolled Fall 2006 (c):	707
Note: All majors	

University of Miami

INSTITUTION INFORMATION
P.O. Box 248294
1251 Memorial Drive, McArthur Building
Coral Gables, FL 33124-0620
Phone: (305) 284-2404
Fax: (305) 284-3815
Web: http://www.miami.edu/

GENERAL INFORMATION
[All Students - Fall 2006]

Undergraduate Enrollment	10,509
Graduate Enrollment	3,061
Professional Enrollment	2,100
Total Enrollment	**15,670**

ENGINEERING COLLEGE INFORMATION

HEAD OF ENGINEERING
M. Lewis Temares
Dean
College of Engineering, Dean's Office
University of Miami
1251 Memorial Drive
McArthur Building, Room 253
Coral Gables, FL 33146-0620
Phone: (305) 284-6035
Fax: (305) 284-3815
Email: mtemares@miami.edu

TYPES OF ENGINEERING DEGREES
Bachelor's: B.S.
Master's: M.S. with thesis, M.S. without thesis, but with project or report
Doctoral: Ph.D.

UNDERGRADUATE INFORMATION

ADMISSION INQUIRIES
David T Poole
Director of Admission & Recruitment
University of Miami
1251 Memorial Drive, McArthur Building Room 251
Coral Gables, FL 33124-0620
Phone: (305) 284-4773
Fax: (305) 284-3815
Email: dtpoole@miami.edu

ESTIMATED STUDENT EXPENSES (FALL 2006)
[Expenses are for the 2006-2007 nine-month academic year and are based on an average credit load of: Undergraduate: 15]

	All Students
Tuition and fees:	$30,732
Campus and Room and Board:	$9,334
Books and Supplies:	$2,120
Other Expenses:	$1,380
Total Estimated Expenses:	**$43,566**

NEW APPLICANTS/NEWLY ENROLLED STUDENTS
[Numbers are for the undergraduate engineering college for the Fall 2006 term]

Number of Applicants (a):	1,391
Of those, Number Offered Admission (b):	714
Of those, Number Enrolled Fall 2006 (c):	163

GRADUATE INFORMATION

ADMISSION INQUIRIES
David T Poole
Director of Admission & Recruitment
University of Miami
1251 Memorial Drive, McArthur Building Room 251
Coral Gables , FL 33124-0620
Phone: (305) 284-4773
Fax: (305) 284-3815
Email: dtpoole@miami.edu

ESTIMATED STUDENT EXPENSES (FALL 2006)
[Expenses are for the 2006-2007 nine-month academic year and are based on an average credit load of: Graduate: 9]

	All Students
Tuition and fees:	$23,234
Campus and Room and Board:	$9,330
Books and Supplies:	$2,660
Other Expenses:	$1,530
Total Estimated Expenses:	**$36,754**

NEW APPLICANTS/NEWLY ENROLLED STUDENTS
[Numbers are for the graduate engineering college for the Fall 2006 term]

Number of Applicants (a):	221
Of those, Number Offered Admission (b):	131
Of those, Number Enrolled Fall 2006 (c):	50

Miami University

INSTITUTION INFORMATION
School of Engineering & Applied Science
Bonham House, 2nd floor
Oxford, OH 45056
Phone: (513) 529-4036
Fax: (513) 529-4040
Web: http://www.eas.muohio.edu

GENERAL INFORMATION
[All Students - Fall 2006]

Undergraduate Enrollment	18,746
Graduate Enrollment	1,380
Professional Enrollment	0
Total Enrollment	**20,126**

ENGINEERING COLLEGE INFORMATION

HEAD OF ENGINEERING
Marek Dollar
Dean
School of Engineering & Applied Science
Miami University
Bonham House, 2nd floor
Oxford, OH 45056
Phone: (513) 529-4036
Fax: (513) 529-4040
Email: DollarM@muohio.edu

TYPES OF ENGINEERING DEGREES
Bachelor's: B.S.
Master's: M.S. with thesis
Doctoral:

UNDERGRADUATE INFORMATION

ESTIMATED STUDENT EXPENSES (FALL 2006)
[Expenses are for the 2006-2007 nine-month academic year and are based on an average credit load of: Undergraduate: 16]

	In-State	Out-of-State
Tuition and Fees:	$11,863	$31,103
Campus and Room and Board:	$8,140	$8,140
Books and Supplies:	$1,140	$1,140
Other Expenses:	$4,836	$4,836
Total Estimated Expenses:	**$25,979**	**$45,219**

NEW APPLICANTS/NEWLY ENROLLED STUDENTS
[Numbers are for the undergraduate engineering college for the Fall 2006 term]

Number of Applicants (a):	1,182
Of those, Number Offered Admission (b):	955
Of those, Number Enrolled Fall 2006 (c):	247

GRADUATE INFORMATION

ADMISSION INQUIRIES
Douglas A Troy
Chair
Miami University
123 Kreger Hall
Oxford , OH 45056
Phone: (513) 529-5928
Fax: (513) 529-1524

ESTIMATED STUDENT EXPENSES (FALL 2006)
[Expenses are for the 2006-2007 nine-month academic year and are based on an average credit load of: Graduate: 12]

	In-State	Out-of-State
Tuition and Fees:	$11,157	$23,289
Campus and Room and Board:	$6,300	$6,300
Books and Supplies:	$1,060	$1,060
Other Expenses:	$3,000	$3,000
Total Estimated Expenses:	**$21,517**	**$33,649**

NEW APPLICANTS/NEWLY ENROLLED STUDENTS
[Numbers are for the graduate engineering college for the Fall 2006 term]

Number of Applicants (a):	29
Of those, Number Offered Admission (b):	17
Of those, Number Enrolled Fall 2006 (c):	13

University of Michigan

INSTITUTION INFORMATION
Office of the President
2074 Fleming, 503 Thompson St
Ann Arbor, MI 48109-1340
Phone: (734) 764-6270
Fax: (734) 936-3529
Web: http://www.umich.edu/

GENERAL INFORMATION
[All Students - Fall 2006]

Undergraduate Enrollment	25,555
Graduate Enrollment	10,923
Professional Enrollment	3,547
Total Enrollment	**40,025**

ENGINEERING COLLEGE INFORMATION

HEAD OF ENGINEERING
David C Munson
Robert J. Vlasic Dean of Engineering
College of Engineering
University of Michigan
2249 Robert H Lurie Engineering Center
1221 Beal Ave
Ann Arbor, MI 48109-2102
Phone: (734) 647-7010
Fax: (734) 647-7009
Email: munson@umich.edu

TYPES OF ENGINEERING DEGREES
Bachelor's: B.A., B.S.
Master's: M.S. with thesis, M.S. without thesis, but with project or report, M.Eng.
Doctoral: Ph.D., D.Eng

UNDERGRADUATE INFORMATION

ADMISSION INQUIRIES
Sharon R Burch
Director Recruitment and Admissions
University of Michigan
Engineering Undergraduate Education, 1221 Beal Ave, #1112
Ann Arbor, MI 48109-2102
Phone: (734) 647-7101
Fax: (734) 647-7119
Email: sharbu@umich.edu

ESTIMATED STUDENT EXPENSES (FALL 2006)
[Expenses are for the 2006-2007 nine-month academic year and are based on an average credit load of: Undergraduate: 16]

	In-State	Out-of-State
Tuition and Fees:	$10,214	$29,114
Campus and Room and Board:	$7,838	$7,838
Books and Supplies:	$1,002	$1,002
Other Expenses:	$2,124	$2,124
Total Estimated Expenses:	**$21,178**	**$40,078**

NEW APPLICANTS/NEWLY ENROLLED STUDENTS
[Numbers are for the undergraduate engineering college for the Fall 2006 term]

Number of Applicants (a):	4,026
Of those, Number Offered Admission (b):	2,619
Of those, Number Enrolled Fall 2006 (c):	1,087

GRADUATE INFORMATION

ESTIMATED STUDENT EXPENSES (FALL 2006)
[Expenses are for the 2006-2007 nine-month academic year and are based on an average credit load of: Graduate: 9]

	In-State	Out-of-State
Tuition and Fees:	$16,864	$31,760
Campus and Room and Board:	$10,366	$10,366
Books and Supplies:	$1,138	$1,138
Other Expenses:	$4,080	$4,080
Total Estimated Expenses:	**$32,448**	**$47,344**

NEW APPLICANTS/NEWLY ENROLLED STUDENTS
[Numbers are for the graduate engineering college for the Fall 2006 term]

Number of Applicants (a):	4,785
Of those, Number Offered Admission (b):	1,912
Of those, Number Enrolled Fall 2006 (c):	747

Michigan State University

INSTITUTION INFORMATION
Dean of Engineering
3410 Engineering Building
East Lansing, MI 48824
Phone: (517) 355-5114
Fax: (517) 355-2288
Web: http://www.egr.msu.edu

GENERAL INFORMATION
[All Students - Fall 2006]

Undergraduate Enrollment	35,162
Graduate Enrollment	6,773
Professional Enrollment	3,585
Total Enrollment	**45,520**

ENGINEERING COLLEGE INFORMATION

HEAD OF ENGINEERING
Satish Udpa
Dean of Engineering
Office of the Dean
Michigan State University
3410 Engineering Building
East Lansing, MI 48824-1226
Phone: (517) 355-5114
Fax: (517) 355-2288
Email: udpa@egr.msu.edu

ENGINEERING COLLEGE INQUIRIES
Les Leone
Assistant to the Dean
Michigan State University
1410 Engineering Building
East Lansing, MI 48824
Phone: (517) 355-5128

Fax: (517) 432-1356
Email: sarverc@egr.msu.edu

ENGINEERING COLLEGE INQUIRIES
Thomas F Wolff
Associate Dean
Michigan State University
1415 Engineering Bldg
East Lansing, MI 48824-1226
Phone: (517) 355-5128
Fax: (517) 432-1356
Email: wolff@egr.msu.edu

TYPES OF ENGINEERING DEGREES
Bachelor's: B.S.
Master's: M.S. with thesis, M.S. without thesis, but with project or report
Doctoral: Ph.D.

UNDERGRADUATE INFORMATION

ADMISSION INQUIRIES
Drew Kim
Assistant to the Dean for Recruiting and K-12 Outreach
Michigan State University
Engineering Undergraduate Studies, 1410 Engineering Building
East Lansing, MI 48824
Phone: (517) 353-7282
Fax: (517) 432-1356
Email: kima@egr.msu.edu

ESTIMATED STUDENT EXPENSES (FALL 2006)
[Expenses are for the 2006-2007 nine-month academic year and are based on an average credit load of: Undergraduate: 12]

	In-State	Out-of-State
Tuition and Fees:	$8,280	$18,308
Campus and Room and Board:	$6,344	$6,344
Books and Supplies:	$1,500	$1,500
Other Expenses:	$1,700	$1,700
Total Estimated Expenses:	**$17,824**	**$27,852**

NEW APPLICANTS/NEWLY ENROLLED STUDENTS
[Numbers are for the undergraduate engineering college for the Fall 2006 term]

Number of Applicants (a):	2,769
Of those, Number Offered Admission (b):	1,979
Of those, Number Enrolled Fall 2006 (c):	710

Note: At MSU, freshmen are admitted to the University, and can freely declare any major, but admission to Engineering is a competitive process after at least 12 credits and completion of core courses.

GRADUATE INFORMATION

ADMISSION INQUIRIES
Kathleen C Kreh
Executive Secretary
Michigan State University
3410 Engineering
East Lansing , MI 48824-1226
Phone: (517) 432-2464
Fax: (517) 355-2288
Email: kreh@egr.msu.edu

ADMISSION INQUIRIES
Ronald C Rosenberg
Associate Dean for Research and Graduate Studies
Michigan State University
3410 Engineering Building
East Lansing , MI 48824-1226
Phone: (517) 432-2464
Fax: (517) 355-2288
Email: rosenber@egr.msu.edu

ESTIMATED STUDENT EXPENSES (FALL 2006)
[Expenses are for the 2006-2007 nine-month academic year and are based on an average credit load of: Graduate: 9]

	In-State	Out-of-State
Tuition and Fees:	$6,243	$15,142
Campus and Room and Board:	$5,575	$5,575
Books and Supplies:	$1,500	$1,500
Other Expenses:	$3,600	$3,600
Total Estimated Expenses:	**$16,918**	**$25,817**

NEW APPLICANTS/NEWLY ENROLLED STUDENTS
[Numbers are for the graduate engineering college for the Fall 2006 term]

Number of Applicants (a):	1,378

Of those, Number Offered Admission (b):   191
Of those, Number Enrolled Fall 2006 (c):   116

Michigan Technological University

INSTITUTION INFORMATION
1400 Townsend Drive
Houghton, MI 49931-1295
Phone: (906) 487-2005
Fax: (906) 487-2782
Web: http://www.mtu.edu

GENERAL INFORMATION
[All Students - Fall 2006]

Undergraduate Enrollment	5,634
Graduate Enrollment	916
Professional Enrollment	0
Total Enrollment	**6,550**

ENGINEERING COLLEGE INFORMATION

HEAD OF ENGINEERING
Robert O Warrington
Dean of Engineering
College of Engineering
Michigan Technological University
1400 Townsend Drive
701 M&M Bldg.
Houghton, MI 49931-1295
Phone: (906) 487-2005
Fax: (906) 487-2782
Email: row@mtu.edu

TYPES OF ENGINEERING DEGREES
Bachelor's: B.S.
Master's: M.S. with thesis, M.S. without thesis, but with project or report
Doctoral: Ph.D.

UNDERGRADUATE INFORMATION

ESTIMATED STUDENT EXPENSES (FALL 2006)
[Expenses are for the 2006-2007 nine-month academic year and are based on an average credit load of: Undergraduate: 15]

	In-State	Out-of-State
Tuition and Fees:	$8,910	$20,679
Campus and Room and Board:	$6,840	$6,840
Books and Supplies:	$1,000	$1,000
Other Expenses:	$1,763	$2,213
Total Estimated Expenses:	**$18,513**	**$30,732**

Note: Graduate Tuition & Fees are based on 12 credit hours.

NEW APPLICANTS/NEWLY ENROLLED STUDENTS
[Numbers are for the undergraduate engineering college for the Fall 2006 term]

Number of Applicants (a):	2,241
Of those, Number Offered Admission (b):	1,885
Of those, Number Enrolled Fall 2006 (c):	692

GRADUATE INFORMATION

ESTIMATED STUDENT EXPENSES (FALL 2006)
[Expenses are for the 2006-2007 nine-month academic year and are based on an average credit load of: Graduate: 9]

	In-State	Out-of-State
Tuition and Fees:	$12,745	$12,745
Campus and Room and Board:	$7,990	$7,990
Books and Supplies:	$850	$850
Other Expenses:	$2,550	$2,550
Total Estimated Expenses:	**$24,135**	**$24,135**

Note: Graduate Tuition & Fees are based on 12 credit hours.

NEW APPLICANTS/NEWLY ENROLLED STUDENTS
[Numbers are for the graduate engineering college for the Fall 2006 term]

Number of Applicants (a):	798
Of those, Number Offered Admission (b):	351
Of those, Number Enrolled Fall 2006 (c):	146

University of Michigan, Dearborn

INSTITUTION INFORMATION
4901 Evergreen Rd.
Dearborn, MI 48128-1491
Phone: (313) 593-5290
Fax: (313) 593-9967
Web: http://www.umd.umich.edu

GENERAL INFORMATION
[All Students - Fall 2006]
Undergraduate Enrollment	6,612
Graduate Enrollment	1,954
Professional Enrollment	0
Total Enrollment	**8,566**

ENGINEERING COLLEGE INFORMATION

HEAD OF ENGINEERING
Subrata Sengupta
Dean
College of Engineering and Computer Science
University of Michigan, Dearborn
4901 Evergreen Rd.
Dearborn, MI 48128-1491
Phone: (313) 593-5290
Fax: (313) 593-9967
Email: razal@umich.edu

TYPES OF ENGINEERING DEGREES
Bachelor's: B.S.
Master's: M.S. with thesis, M.S. without thesis, but with project or report
Doctoral: D.Eng

UNDERGRADUATE INFORMATION

ESTIMATED STUDENT EXPENSES (FALL 2006)
[Expenses are for the 2006-2007 nine-month academic year and are based on an average credit load of: Undergraduate: 12]
	In-State	Out-of-State
Tutition and Fees:	$7,998	$15,500
Campus and Room and Board:	$6,400	$6,400
Books and Supplies:	$1,500	$1,500
Other Expenses:	$1,800	$1,800
Total Estimated Expenses:	**$17,698**	**$25,200**

NEW APPLICANTS/NEWLY ENROLLED STUDENTS
[Numbers are for the undergraduate engineering college for the Fall 2006 term]
Number of Applicants (a):	534
Of those, Number Offered Admission (b):	398
Of those, Number Enrolled Fall 2006 (c):	182

GRADUATE INFORMATION

ESTIMATED STUDENT EXPENSES (FALL 2006)
[Expenses are for the 2006-2007 nine-month academic year and are based on an average credit load of: Graduate: 9]
	In-State	Out-of-State
Tutition and Fees:	$10,237	$17,753
Campus and Room and Board:	$6,400	$6,400
Books and Supplies:	$1,500	$1,500
Other Expenses:	$1,800	$1,800
Total Estimated Expenses:	**$19,937**	**$27,453**

NEW APPLICANTS/NEWLY ENROLLED STUDENTS
[Numbers are for the graduate engineering college for the Fall 2006 term]
Number of Applicants (a):	250
Of those, Number Offered Admission (b):	165
Of those, Number Enrolled Fall 2006 (c):	132

Milwaukee School of Engineering

INSTITUTION INFORMATION
1025 North Broadway
Milwaukee, WI 53202-3109
Phone: (800) 332-6763
Fax: (414) 277-7475
Web: http://www.msoe.edu

GENERAL INFORMATION
[All Students - Fall 2006]
Undergraduate Enrollment	2,203
Graduate Enrollment	224
Professional Enrollment	0
Total Enrollment	**2,427**

ENGINEERING COLLEGE INFORMATION

HEAD OF ENGINEERING
Roger Frankowski
Vice President of Academics
Academics
Milwaukee School of Engineering
1025 N. Broadway
Milwaukee, WI 53202-3109
Phone: (414) 277-7324
Fax: (414) 277-7477
Email: frankows@msoe.edu

TYPES OF ENGINEERING DEGREES
Bachelor's: B.S.
Master's: M.S. without thesis, but with project or report
Doctoral:

UNDERGRADUATE INFORMATION

ADMISSION INQUIRIES
Paul Borens
Director of Admissions
Milwaukee School of Engineering
1025 North Broadway
Milwaukee, WI 53202-3109
Phone: (414) 277-6765
Fax: (414) 277-7475
Email: borens@msoe.edu

ESTIMATED STUDENT EXPENSES (FALL 2006)
[Expenses are for the 2006-2007 nine-month academic year and are based on an average credit load of: Undergraduate: 15]
	All Students
Tutition and fees:	$24,960
Campus and Room and Board:	$6,189
Books and Supplies:	$1,500
Other Expenses:	$5,140
Total Estimated Expenses:	**$37,789**

NEW APPLICANTS/NEWLY ENROLLED STUDENTS
[Numbers are for the undergraduate engineering college for the Fall 2006 term]
Number of Applicants (a):	1,448
Of those, Number Offered Admission (b):	1,106
Of those, Number Enrolled Fall 2006 (c):	485

GRADUATE INFORMATION

ADMISSION INQUIRIES
Paul Borens
Director of Admissions
Milwaukee School of Engineering
1025 North Broadway
Milwaukee , WI 53202-3109
Phone: (414) 277-6765
Fax: (414) 277-7475
Email: borens@msoe.edu

ESTIMATED STUDENT EXPENSES (FALL 2006)
[Expenses are for the 2006-2007 nine-month academic year and are based on an average credit load of: Graduate: 6]
	All Students
Tutition and fees:	$526
Campus and Room and Board:	$6,189
Books and Supplies:	$1,500
Other Expenses:	$4,000
Total Estimated Expenses:	**$12,215**

NEW APPLICANTS/NEWLY ENROLLED STUDENTS
[Numbers are for the graduate engineering college for the Fall 2006 term]
Number of Applicants (a):	63
Of those, Number Offered Admission (b):	26
Of those, Number Enrolled Fall 2006 (c):	13

Minnesota State University, Mankato

INSTITUTION INFORMATION
131 Trafton Science Center North
Mankato, MN 56001
Phone: (507) 389-5998
Fax: (507) 389-1095
Web: http://www.mnsu.edu

GENERAL INFORMATION
[All Students - Fall 2006]
Undergraduate Enrollment	12,684
Graduate Enrollment	1,651
Professional Enrollment	0
Total Enrollment	**14,335**

ENGINEERING COLLEGE INFORMATION

HEAD OF ENGINEERING
John E Frey
Dean of the College
Science, Engineering and Technology
Minnesota State University, Mankato
131 Trafton Science Center North
Minnesota State University, Mankato
Mankato, MN 56001
Phone: (507) 389-5998
Fax: (507) 389-1095
Email: john.frey@mnsu.edu

ENGINEERING COLLEGE INQUIRIES
Angie Bomier
Student Relations Coordinator
Minnesota State University, Mankato
125 Trafton Science Center
Mankato, MN 56001
Phone: (507) 389-1521
Fax: (507) 389-1095
Email: angie.bomier@mnsu.edu

TYPES OF ENGINEERING DEGREES
Bachelor's: B.S.
Master's: M.S. with thesis, M.S. without thesis, but with project or report
Doctoral:

UNDERGRADUATE INFORMATION

ADMISSION INQUIRIES
Angie Bomier
Student Relations Coordinator
Minnesota State University, Mankato
125 Trafton Science Center
Mankato, MN 56001
Phone: (507) 389-1521
Fax: (507) 389-1095
Email: angie.bomier@mnsu.edu

ADMISSION INQUIRIES
Walter Wolff
Director of Admissions
Minnesota State University, Mankato
122 Taylor Center
Mankato, MN 56001
Phone: (507) 389-6670
Fax: (507) 389-5114
Email: walter.wolff@mnsu.edu

ESTIMATED STUDENT EXPENSES (FALL 2006)
[Expenses are for the 2006-2007 nine-month academic year and are based on an average credit load of: Undergraduate: 15]
	In-State	Out-of-State
Tutition and Fees:	$5,840	$11,668
Campus and Room and Board:	$5,083	$5,083
Books and Supplies:	$920	$920
Other Expenses:	$2,600	$3,000
Total Estimated Expenses:	**$14,443**	**$20,671**

GRADUATE INFORMATION

ESTIMATED STUDENT EXPENSES (FALL 2006)
[Expenses are for the 2006-2007 nine-month academic year and are based on an average credit load of: Graduate: 9]
	In-State	Out-of-State
Tutition and Fees:	$5,320	$8,400
Campus and Room and Board:	$5,083	$5,083
Books and Supplies:	$600	$600

Other Expenses:	$2,600	$3,000
Total Estimated Expenses:	**$13,603**	**$17,083**

University of Minnesota, Duluth

INSTITUTION INFORMATION

1049 University Drive
Duluth, MN 55812
Phone: (218) 726-8000
Web: http://www.d.umn.edu

GENERAL INFORMATION

[All Students - Fall 2006]

Undergraduate Enrollment	9,172
Graduate Enrollment	736
Professional Enrollment	314
Total Enrollment	**10,222**

ENGINEERING COLLEGE INFORMATION

HEAD OF ENGINEERING

James P Riehl
Dean
College of Science and Engineering
University of Minnesota, Duluth
140 Engineering Building
1303 Ordean Court
Duluth, MN 55812
Phone: (218) 726-6397
Fax: (218) 726-6360
Email: cse@d.umn.edu

ENGINEERING COLLEGE INQUIRIES

Janny B Walker
Assistant to the Deans
University of Minnesota, Duluth
140 Engineering Building, 1303 Ordean Court
Duluth, MN 55812
Phone: (218) 726-7806

TYPES OF ENGINEERING DEGREES

Bachelor's: B.S.
Master's: M.S. with thesis, M.S. without thesis, but with project or report
Doctoral:

UNDERGRADUATE INFORMATION

ESTIMATED STUDENT EXPENSES (FALL 2006)

[Expenses are for the 2006-2007 nine-month academic year and are based on an average credit load of: Undergraduate: N/A]

	In-State	Out-of-State
Tuition and Fees:	$8,932	$19,299
Campus and Room and Board:	$5,722	$5,722
Books and Supplies:	$1,100	$1,100
Other Expenses:	$2,528	$2,528
Total Estimated Expenses:	**$18,282**	**$28,649**

NEW APPLICANTS/NEWLY ENROLLED STUDENTS

[Numbers are for the undergraduate engineering college for the Fall 2006 term]

Number of Applicants (a):	2,117
Of those, Number Offered Admission (b):	1,547
Of those, Number Enrolled Fall 2006 (c):	620

GRADUATE INFORMATION

ESTIMATED STUDENT EXPENSES (FALL 2006)

[Expenses are for the 2006-2007 nine-month academic year and are based on an average credit load of: Graduate: N/A]

	In-State	Out-of-State
Tuition and Fees:	$11,038	$18,136
Campus and Room and Board:	$5,722	$5,722
Books and Supplies:	$1,100	$1,100
Other Expenses:	$2,528	$2,528
Total Estimated Expenses:	**$20,388**	**$27,486**

University of Minnesota -Twin Cities

INSTITUTION INFORMATION

117 Pleasant Street S.E.
Institute of Technology
Minneapolis, MN 55455
Phone: (612) 624-2006
Fax: (612) 624-2841
Web: http://www.it.umn.edu

GENERAL INFORMATION

[All Students - Fall 2006]

Undergraduate Enrollment	28,645
Graduate Enrollment	13,929
Professional Enrollment	8,142
Total Enrollment	**50,716**

ENGINEERING COLLEGE INFORMATION

HEAD OF ENGINEERING

Steven L. Crouch
Dean
Institute of Technology
University of Minnesota -Twin Cities
105 Walter Library
117 Pleasant Street S.E.
Minneapolis, MN 55455
Phone: (612) 624-2006
Fax: (612) 624-2841
Email: crouch@umn.edu

ENGINEERING COLLEGE INQUIRIES

Mostafa Kaveh
Associate Dean
University of Minnesota -Twin Cities
105 Walter Library, 117 Pleasant Street S.E.
Minneapolis, MN 55455
Phone: (612) 626-3833
Fax: (612) 624-2841
Email: mos@umn.edu

TYPES OF ENGINEERING DEGREES

Bachelor's: B.S.
Master's: M.S. with thesis, M.S. without thesis, but with project or report, M.Eng.
Doctoral: Ph.D.

UNDERGRADUATE INFORMATION

ADMISSION INQUIRIES

Peter Hudleston
Professor & Associate Dean for Student Affairs
University of Minnesota -Twin Cities
106 Lind Hall, 207 Church St SE
Minneapolis, MN 55455
Phone: (612) 624-5091
Fax: (612) 626-1020
Email: hudlesto@mailbox.mail.umn.edu

ESTIMATED STUDENT EXPENSES (FALL 2006)

[Expenses are for the 2006-2007 nine-month academic year and are based on an average credit load of: Undergraduate: 15]

	In-State	Out-of-State
Tuition and Fees:	$9,410	$21,040
Campus and Room and Board:	$6,824	$6,824
Books and Supplies:	$900	$900
Other Expenses:	$2,124	$2,124
Total Estimated Expenses:	**$19,258**	**$30,888**

NEW APPLICANTS/NEWLY ENROLLED STUDENTS

[Numbers are for the undergraduate engineering college for the Fall 2006 term]

Number of Applicants (a):	3,646
Of those, Number Offered Admission (b):	2,092
Of those, Number Enrolled Fall 2006 (c):	825

GRADUATE INFORMATION

ADMISSION INQUIRIES

Mostafa Kaveh
Associate Dean
University of Minnesota -Twin Cities
105 Walter Library, 117 Pleasant Street S.E.
Minneapolis , MN 55455
Phone: (612) 626-3833
Fax: (612) 624-2841
Email: mos@umn.edu

ESTIMATED STUDENT EXPENSES (FALL 2006)

[Expenses are for the 2006-2007 nine-month academic year and are based on an average credit load of: Graduate: 8]

	In-State	Out-of-State
Tuition and Fees:	$12,248	$19,526
Campus and Room and Board:	$8,932	$8,932

Books and Supplies:	$900	$900
Other Expenses:	$2,750	$2,750
Total Estimated Expenses:	**$24,830**	**$32,108**

NEW APPLICANTS/NEWLY ENROLLED STUDENTS

[Numbers are for the graduate engineering college for the Fall 2006 term]

Number of Applicants (a):	2,877
Of those, Number Offered Admission (b):	1,044
Of those, Number Enrolled Fall 2006 (c):	357

The University of Mississippi

INSTITUTION INFORMATION

Lyceum 123
University, MS 38677-1848
Phone: (662) 915-7111
Fax: (662) 915-5935
Web: http://www.olemiss.edu

GENERAL INFORMATION

[All Students - Fall 2006]

Undergraduate Enrollment	11,763
Graduate Enrollment	1,745
Professional Enrollment	508
Total Enrollment	**14,016**

ENGINEERING COLLEGE INFORMATION

HEAD OF ENGINEERING

Kai-Fong Lee
Dean and Professor of Electrical Engineering
School of Engineering
The University of Mississippi
101 Carrier Hall
PO Box 1848
University, MS 38677-1848
Phone: (662) 915-7407
Fax: (662) 915-1287
Email: engrdean@olemiss.edu

TYPES OF ENGINEERING DEGREES

Bachelor's: B.S.
Master's: M.S. with thesis, M.S. without thesis, but with project or report
Doctoral: Ph.D.

UNDERGRADUATE INFORMATION

ADMISSION INQUIRIES

Marni Kendricks
Assistant to the Dean
The University of Mississippi
120 Carrier Hall, P O Box 1848
University, MS 38677-1848
Phone: (662) 915-5373
Fax: (662) 915-1287
Email: mckendri@olemiss.edu

ESTIMATED STUDENT EXPENSES (FALL 2006)

[Expenses are for the 2006-2007 nine-month academic year and are based on an average credit load of: Undergraduate: 19]

	In-State	Out-of-State
Tuition and Fees:	$4,110	$9,264
Campus and Room and Board:	$4,460	$4,460
Books and Supplies:	$915	$915
Other Expenses:	$3,186	$3,186
Total Estimated Expenses:	**$12,671**	**$17,825**

Note: * R&B $6,048 for 12 month

NEW APPLICANTS/NEWLY ENROLLED STUDENTS

[Numbers are for the undergraduate engineering college for the Fall 2006 term]

Number of Applicants (a):	628
Of those, Number Offered Admission (b):	499
Of those, Number Enrolled Fall 2006 (c):	157

GRADUATE INFORMATION

ADMISSION INQUIRIES

Maurice Eftink
Dean of Graduate School
The University of Mississippi
Lyceum 123
University , MS 38677-1848
Phone: (662) 915-5974

Fax: (662) 915-7577
Email: eftink@olemiss.edu

ESTIMATED STUDENT EXPENSES (FALL 2006)
[Expenses are for the 2006-2007 nine-month academic year and are based on an average credit load of: Graduate: 15]

	In-State	Out-of-State
Tuition and Fees:	$5,626	$11,589
Campus and Room and Board:	$4,346	$4,346
Books and Supplies:	$1,015	$1,015
Other Expenses:	$3,186	$3,186
Total Estimated Expenses:	**$14,173**	**$20,136**

*Note: * R&B $6,048 for 12 month*

NEW APPLICANTS/NEWLY ENROLLED STUDENTS
[Numbers are for the graduate engineering college for the Fall 2006 term]

Number of Applicants (a):	465
Of those, Number Offered Admission (b):	75
Of those, Number Enrolled Fall 2006 (c):	28

Mississippi State University

INSTITUTION INFORMATION
P.O. Box 9544
250 McCain Hall
Mississippi State, MS 39762
Phone: (662) 325-2270
Fax: (662) 325-8573
Web: http://www.msstate.edu

GENERAL INFORMATION
[All Students - Fall 2006]

Undergraduate Enrollment	12,630
Graduate Enrollment	3,312
Professional Enrollment	264
Total Enrollment	**16,206**

ENGINEERING COLLEGE INFORMATION

HEAD OF ENGINEERING
Kirk H Schulz
Dean of Engineering
James Worth Bagley College of Engineering
Mississippi State University
P.O. Box 9544
250 McCain Hall
Mississippi State, MS 39762
Phone: (662) 325-2270
Fax: (662) 325-8573
Email: kschulz@engr.msstate.edu

ENGINEERING COLLEGE INQUIRIES
Donna S Reese
Associate Dean for Academic Affairs and Administration and Professor
Mississippi State University
P.O. Box 9544, 250 McCain Hall
Mississippi State, MS 39762
Phone: (662) 325-7514
Fax: (662) 325-8997
Email: dreese@engr.msstate.edu

TYPES OF ENGINEERING DEGREES
Bachelor's: B.S.
Master's: M.S. with thesis, M.S. without thesis, but with project or report
Doctoral: Ph.D.

UNDERGRADUATE INFORMATION

ADMISSION INQUIRIES
Robert A Green
Undergraduate Coordinator
Mississippi State University
P.O. Box 9544, 160 McCain Engr. Building
Mississippi State, MS 39762
Phone: (662) 325-2267
Fax: (662) 325-9094
Email: Green@engr.msstate.edu

ESTIMATED STUDENT EXPENSES (FALL 2006)
[Expenses are for the 2006-2007 nine-month academic year and are based on an average credit load of: Undergraduate: 15]

	In-State	Out-of-State
Tuition and Fees:	$4,550	$10,506

	$6,968	$6,968
Campus and Room and Board:	$6,968	$6,968
Books and Supplies:	$1,000	$1,000
Other Expenses:	$2,400	$2,400
Total Estimated Expenses:	**$14,918**	**$20,874**

Note: Other expenses include a laptop computer which is required for all engineering students. It does not include additional fees related to international students only, such as required medical insurnace and international fees, totaling approx. $4,900

NEW APPLICANTS/NEWLY ENROLLED STUDENTS
[Numbers are for the undergraduate engineering college for the Fall 2006 term]

Number of Applicants (a):	812
Of those, Number Offered Admission (b):	617
Of those, Number Enrolled Fall 2006 (c):	366

GRADUATE INFORMATION

ADMISSION INQUIRIES
Roger L King
Associate Dean for Research and Graduate Studies and Professsor
Mississippi State University
P.O. Box 9544, 250 McCain
Mississippi State , MS 39762
Phone: (662) 325-3897
Fax: (662) 325-8573
Email: rking@engr.msstate.edu

ESTIMATED STUDENT EXPENSES (FALL 2006)
[Expenses are for the 2006-2007 nine-month academic year and are based on an average credit load of: Graduate: 9]

	In-State	Out-of-State
Tuition and Fees:	$4,550	$10,506
Campus and Room and Board:	$7,319	$7,319
Books and Supplies:	$1,000	$1,000
Other Expenses:	$2,400	$2,400
Total Estimated Expenses:	**$15,269**	**$21,225**

Note: Other expenses include a laptop computer which is required for all engineering students. It does not include ad ditional fees related to international students only, such as required medical insurnace and international fees, totaling approx. $4,900

NEW APPLICANTS/NEWLY ENROLLED STUDENTS
[Numbers are for the graduate engineering college for the Fall 2006 term]

Number of Applicants (a):	531
Of those, Number Offered Admission (b):	185
Of those, Number Enrolled Fall 2006 (c):	96

University of Missouri-Columbia

INSTITUTION INFORMATION
230 Jesse Hall
Columbia, MO 65211
Phone: (573) 882-7786
Fax: (573) 882-7887
Web: http://www.missouri.edu/

GENERAL INFORMATION
[All Students - Fall 2006]

Undergraduate Enrollment	21,551
Graduate Enrollment	5,600
Professional Enrollment	1,102
Total Enrollment	**28,253**

ENGINEERING COLLEGE INFORMATION

HEAD OF ENGINEERING
James E Thompson
Dean
College of Engineering
University of Missouri-Columbia
W1025 Lafferre Hall
Columbia, MO 65211
Phone: (573) 882-4378
Fax: (573) 882-2490
Email: ThompsonJE@missouri.edu

TYPES OF ENGINEERING DEGREES
Bachelor's: B.S.
Master's: M.S. with thesis, M.S. without thesis, but with project or report, M.Eng.
Doctoral: Ph.D.

UNDERGRADUATE INFORMATION

ADMISSION INQUIRIES
Lex A Akers
Associate Dean for Academic Programs
University of Missouri-Columbia
W1025 Thomas and Nell Lafferre Hall
Columbia, MO 65211
Phone: (573) 882-4765
Fax: (573) 882-2490
Email: AkersL@missouri.edu

ESTIMATED STUDENT EXPENSES (FALL 2006)
[Expenses are for the 2006-2007 nine-month academic year and are based on an average credit load of: Undergraduate: 14]

	In-State	Out-of-State
Tuition and Fees:	$7,308	$16,890
Campus and Room and Board:	$7,000	$7,000
Books and Supplies:	$950	$950
Other Expenses:		
Total Estimated Expenses:	**$15,258**	**$24,840**

NEW APPLICANTS/NEWLY ENROLLED STUDENTS
[Numbers are for the undergraduate engineering college for the Fall 2006 term]

Number of Applicants (a):	987
Of those, Number Offered Admission (b):	851
Of those, Number Enrolled Fall 2006 (c):	388

GRADUATE INFORMATION

ADMISSION INQUIRIES
Lex A Akers
Associate Dean for Academic Programs
University of Missouri-Columbia
W1025 Thomas and Nell Lafferre Hall
Columbia , MO 65211
Phone: (573) 882-4765
Fax: (573) 882-2490
Email: AkersL@missouri.edu

ESTIMATED STUDENT EXPENSES (FALL 2006)
[Expenses are for the 2006-2007 nine-month academic year and are based on an average credit load of: Graduate: 9]

	In-State	Out-of-State
Tuition and Fees:	$7,242	$15,108
Campus and Room and Board:	$8,078	$8,078
Books and Supplies:	$890	$890
Other Expenses:		
Total Estimated Expenses:	**$16,210**	**$24,076**

NEW APPLICANTS/NEWLY ENROLLED STUDENTS
[Numbers are for the graduate engineering college for the Fall 2006 term]

Number of Applicants (a):	471
Of those, Number Offered Admission (b):	195
Of those, Number Enrolled Fall 2006 (c):	96

University of Missouri - Rolla

INSTITUTION INFORMATION
1870 Miner Circle
Rolla, MO 65409
Phone: (573) 341-4111
Fax: (573) 341-6963
Web: http://www.umr.edu

GENERAL INFORMATION
[All Students - Fall 2006]

Undergraduate Enrollment	4,515
Graduate Enrollment	1,343
Professional Enrollment	0
Total Enrollment	**5,858**

ENGINEERING COLLEGE INFORMATION

ENGINEERING COLLEGE INQUIRIES
William Perkins
Director
University of Missouri - Rolla
1870 Miner Circle, 211 Engineering Research Lab
Rolla, MO 65409
Phone: (573) 341-4213
Fax: (573) 341-4174
Email: floydh@umr.edu

ENGINEERING COLLEGE INQUIRIES
William Schonberg
Dean
University of Missouri - Rolla
1870 Miner Circle, 101 Engineering Research Lab
Rolla, MO 65409
Phone: (573) 341-4787
Fax: (573) 341-4979
Email: wschon@umr.edu

ENGINEERING COLLEGE INQUIRIES
Jeffrey D Cawlfield
Director
University of Missouri - Rolla
1870 Miner Circle, 125 McNutt Hall
Rolla, MO 65409
Phone: (573) 341-4977
Fax: (573) 341-6935
Email: nhubing@umr.edu

ENGINEERING COLLEGE INQUIRIES
Ralph E Flori, Jr.
Associate Dean
University of Missouri - Rolla
1870 Miner Circle, 101 Engineering Research Lab
Rolla, MO 65409
Phone: (573) 341-7583
Fax: (573) 341-4979
Email: reflori@umr.edu

ENGINEERING COLLEGE INQUIRIES
K Krishnamurthy
Associate Dean
University of Missouri - Rolla
1870 Miner Circle, 101 Engineering Research Lab
Rolla, MO 65409
Phone: (573) 341-4154
Fax: (573) 341-4979
Email: kkrishna@umr.edu

ENGINEERING COLLEGE INQUIRIES
F. Scott Miller
Asst Director
University of Missouri - Rolla
1870 Miner Circle
Rolla, MO 65409
Phone: (573) 341-4977
Fax: (573) 341-6935
Email: smiller@umr.edu

ENGINEERING COLLEGE INQUIRIES
Cecilia Elmore
Director
University of Missouri - Rolla
1870 Miner Circle, 212 Engineering Research Lab
Rolla, MO 65409
Phone: (573) 341-7286
Fax: (573) 341-4890
Email: elmorec@umr.edu

ENGINEERING COLLEGE INQUIRIES
Cindi Vogt
Coordinator
University of Missouri - Rolla
1870 Miner Circle, 212 Engineering Research Lab
Rolla, MO 65409
Phone: (573) 341-4215
Fax: (573) 341-4890
Email: cvogt@umr.edu

ENGINEERING COLLEGE INQUIRIES
Cecilia Elmore
Interim Director
University of Missouri - Rolla
1870 Miner Circle, 212 Engineering Research Lab
Rolla, MO 65409
Phone: (573) 341-4212
Fax: (573) 341-1490
Email: huggansm@umr.edu

TYPES OF ENGINEERING DEGREES
Bachelor's: B.S.
Master's: M.S. with thesis, M.S. without thesis, but with project or report
Doctoral: Ph.D., D.Eng

UNDERGRADUATE INFORMATION

ADMISSION INQUIRIES
Lynn Stichnote
Director of Admissions

University of Missouri - Rolla
1870 Miner Circle
Rolla, MO 65409
Phone: (573) 341-4075
Fax: (573) 341-4082
Email: lynns@umr.edu

ESTIMATED STUDENT EXPENSES (FALL 2006)
[Expenses are for the 2006-2007 nine-month academic year and are based on an average credit load of: Undergraduate: 15]

	In-State	Out-of-State
Tuition and Fees:	$9,404	$19,670
Campus and Room and Board:	$6,185	$6,185
Books and Supplies:	$875	$875
Other Expenses:	$2,129	$2,129
Total Estimated Expenses:	**$18,593**	**$28,859**

Note: The University does not have tuition. The amount listed is student fees for 2 semesters.

NEW APPLICANTS/NEWLY ENROLLED STUDENTS
[Numbers are for the undergraduate engineering college for the Fall 2006 term]
Number of Applicants (a): 0
Of those, Number Offered Admission (b): 0
Of those, Number Enrolled Fall 2006 (c): 786

GRADUATE INFORMATION

ADMISSION INQUIRIES
Lynn Stichnote
Director of Admissions
University of Missouri - Rolla
1870 Miner Circle
Rolla , MO 65409
Phone: (573) 341-4075
Fax: (573) 341-4082
Email: lynns@umr.edu

ESTIMATED STUDENT EXPENSES (FALL 2006)
[Expenses are for the 2006-2007 nine-month academic year and are based on an average credit load of: Graduate: 9]

	In-State	Out-of-State
Tuition and Fees:	$6,756	$14,622
Campus and Room and Board:	$6,185	$6,185
Books and Supplies:	$875	$875
Other Expenses:	$2,129	$2,129
Total Estimated Expenses:	**$15,945**	**$23,811**

Note: The University does not have tuition. The amount listed is student fees for 2 semesters.

Monmouth University

INSTITUTION INFORMATION
400 Cedar Ave.
West Long Branch, NJ 07764
Phone: (732) 571-3400
Fax: (732) 571-4422
Web: http://www.monmouth.edu

GENERAL INFORMATION
[All Students - Fall 2006]

Undergraduate Enrollment	4,621
Graduate Enrollment	1,776
Professional Enrollment	0
Total Enrollment	**6,397**

ENGINEERING COLLEGE INFORMATION

HEAD OF ENGINEERING
Francis C Lutz
Dean, Professor
School of Science, Technology and Engineering
Monmouth University
400 Cedar Ave.
Howard Hall Room 540
West Long Branch, NJ 07764
Phone: (732) 571-7595
Fax: (732) 571-4422
Email: flutz@monmouth.edu

TYPES OF ENGINEERING DEGREES
Bachelor's: B.S.
Master's: M.S. with thesis, M.S. without thesis, but with project or report
Doctoral:

UNDERGRADUATE INFORMATION

ADMISSION INQUIRIES
James McDonald
Associate Professor, Chair of the Department of Software Engineering
Monmouth University
400 Cedar Ave., HH, B-6
West Long Branch, NJ 07764
Phone: (732) 571-4468
Fax: (732) 263-5253
Email: jamesmc@monmouth.edu

ESTIMATED STUDENT EXPENSES (FALL 2006)
[Expenses are for the 2006-2007 nine-month academic year and are based on an average credit load of: Undergraduate: 16]

	All Students
Tuition and fees:	$21,868
Campus and Room and Board:	$8,588
Books and Supplies:	$832
Other Expenses:	$1,957
Total Estimated Expenses:	**$33,245**

Note: Please note that the Graduate "Other Expenses" category reflects costs for a full-time graduate student's off-campus housing, other personal expenses and estimated travel expenses.

NEW APPLICANTS/NEWLY ENROLLED STUDENTS
[Numbers are for the undergraduate engineering college for the Fall 2006 term]
Number of Applicants (a): 31
Of those, Number Offered Admission (b): 19
Of those, Number Enrolled Fall 2006 (c): 14

GRADUATE INFORMATION

ADMISSION INQUIRIES
William Tepfenhart
Associate Professor & Graduate Program Director for Software Engineering
Monmouth University
400 Cedar Ave., HH, B-2
West Long Branch , NJ 07764
Phone: (732) 571-3480
Fax: (732) 263-5253
Email: btepfenh@monmouth.edu

ESTIMATED STUDENT EXPENSES (FALL 2006)
[Expenses are for the 2006-2007 nine-month academic year and are based on an average credit load of: Graduate: 9]

	All Students
Tuition and fees:	$12,734
Campus and Room and Board:	
Books and Supplies:	$624
Other Expenses:	$14,000
Total Estimated Expenses:	**$27,358**

Note: Please note that the Graduate "Other Expenses" category reflects costs for a full-time graduate student's off-campus housing, other personal expenses and estimated travel expenses.

NEW APPLICANTS/NEWLY ENROLLED STUDENTS
[Numbers are for the graduate engineering college for the Fall 2006 term]
Number of Applicants (a): 56
Of those, Number Offered Admission (b): 49
Of those, Number Enrolled Fall 2006 (c): 32

Montana State University

INSTITUTION INFORMATION
College of Engeering
212 Roberts Hall, PO Box 173820
Bozeman, MT 59717-3820
Phone: (406) 994-2272
Fax: (406) 994-6665
Web: http://www.montana.edu/

GENERAL INFORMATION
[All Students - Fall 2006]

Undergraduate Enrollment	10,508
Graduate Enrollment	1,506
Professional Enrollment	324
Total Enrollment	**12,338**

ENGINEERING COLLEGE INFORMATION

HEAD OF ENGINEERING
Robert J Marley
Dean of Engineering
College of Engineering
Montana State University
212 Roberts Hall
P.O. Box 173820
Bozeman, MT 59717-3820
Phone: (406) 994-2272
Fax: (406) 994-6665
Email: marley@coe.montana.edu

ENGINEERING COLLEGE INQUIRIES
Kathleen E Osen
Assistant to the Dean for Administration
Montana State University
College of Engeering, 212 Roberts Hall, PO Box 173820
Bozeman, MT 59717-3820
Phone: (406) 994-2272
Fax: (406) 994-6665
Email: kosen@coe.montana.edu

TYPES OF ENGINEERING DEGREES
Bachelor's: B.S.
Master's: M.S. with thesis, M.S. without thesis, but with project or report
Doctoral: Ph.D.

UNDERGRADUATE INFORMATION

ESTIMATED STUDENT EXPENSES (FALL 2006)
[Expenses are for the 2006-2007 nine-month academic year and are based on an average credit load of: Undergraduate: 12]

	In-State	Out-of-State
Tuition and Fees:	$5,730	$15,580
Campus and Room and Board:	$6,450	$6,450
Books and Supplies:	$1,000	$1,000
Other Expenses:	$2,670	$2,670
Total Estimated Expenses:	**$15,850**	**$25,700**

Note: Tuition & Fees: Does not include a $702 per semester supplemental health insurance fee required of students who do not have proof of insurance coverage.
Room & Board: Food and housing costs will vary depending on a student's living arrangements and lifestyle. Room and board figures are an average of costs incurred by students living on campus in a residence hall and off campus in a shared apartment.

NEW APPLICANTS/NEWLY ENROLLED STUDENTS
[Numbers are for the undergraduate engineering college for the Fall 2006 term]
Number of Applicants (a):	850
Of those, Number Offered Admission (b):	571
Of those, Number Enrolled Fall 2006 (c):	347

GRADUATE INFORMATION

ESTIMATED STUDENT EXPENSES (FALL 2006)
[Expenses are for the 2006-2007 nine-month academic year and are based on an average credit load of: Graduate: 9]

	In-State	Out-of-State
Tuition and Fees:	$5,113	$12,501
Campus and Room and Board:	$6,450	$6,450
Books and Supplies:	$1,000	$1,000
Other Expenses:	$2,670	$2,670
Total Estimated Expenses:	**$15,233**	**$22,621**

Note: Tuition & Fees: Does not include a $702 per semester supplemental health insurance fee required of students who do not have proof of insurance coverage.
Room & Board: Food and housing costs will vary depending on a student's living arrangements and lifestyle. Room and board figures are an average of costs incurred by students living on campus in a residence hall and off campus in a shared apartment.

NEW APPLICANTS/NEWLY ENROLLED STUDENTS
[Numbers are for the graduate engineering college for the Fall 2006 term]
Number of Applicants (a):	137
Of those, Number Offered Admission (b):	69
Of those, Number Enrolled Fall 2006 (c):	45

Montana Tech of the University of Montana

INSTITUTION INFORMATION
1300 West Park Street
Butte, MT 59701
Phone: (406) 496-4133
Fax: (406) 496-4260
Web: http://www.mtech.edu

GENERAL INFORMATION
[All Students - Fall 2006]
Undergraduate Enrollment	2,272
Graduate Enrollment	85
Professional Enrollment	0
Total Enrollment	**2,357**

ENGINEERING COLLEGE INFORMATION

HEAD OF ENGINEERING
Peter H Knudsen
Dean
School of Mines and Engineering
Montana Tech of the University of Montana
Montana Tech
1300 West Park Street
Butte, MT 59701
Phone: (406) 496-4133
Fax: (406) 496-4260
Email: pknudsen@mtech.edu

TYPES OF ENGINEERING DEGREES
Bachelor's: B.S.
Master's: M.S. with thesis, M.S. without thesis, but with project or report
Doctoral:

Morgan State University

INSTITUTION INFORMATION
1700 E. Coldspring Lane
Baltimore, MD 21251
Phone: (443) 885-3231
Fax: (443) 885-8218
Web: http://www.morgan.edu

ENGINEERING COLLEGE INFORMATION

HEAD OF ENGINEERING
Dr. Eugene M. DeLoatch
Dean
School of Engineering
Morgan State University
1700 E. Cold Spring Lane
Baltimore, MD 21251
Phone: (443) 885-3231
Fax: (443) 885-8218
Email: deloatch@eng.morgan.edu

TYPES OF ENGINEERING DEGREES
Bachelor's: B.S.
Master's: M.Eng.
Doctoral: D.Eng

University of Nebraska, Lincoln

INSTITUTION INFORMATION
114 Othmer Hall
P.O. Box 880642
Lincoln, NE 68588
Phone: (402) 472-3181
Fax: (402) 472-7792
Web: http://www.nuengr.unl.edu

GENERAL INFORMATION
[All Students - Fall 2006]
Undergraduate Enrollment	17,371
Graduate Enrollment	4,257
Professional Enrollment	478
Total Enrollment	**22,106**

ENGINEERING COLLEGE INFORMATION

HEAD OF ENGINEERING
David H Allen
Dean College of Engineering
College of Engineering
University of Nebraska, Lincoln
114 Othmer Hall
Lincoln, NE 68588-0642
Phone: (402) 472-3181
Fax: (402) 472-7792
Email: dhallen@unl.edu

TYPES OF ENGINEERING DEGREES
Bachelor's: B.S.
Master's: M.S. with thesis, M.S. without thesis, but with project or report, M.Eng.
Doctoral: Ph.D.

UNDERGRADUATE INFORMATION

ESTIMATED STUDENT EXPENSES (FALL 2006)
[Expenses are for the 2006-2007 nine-month academic year and are based on an average credit load of: Undergraduate: 15]

	In-State	Out-of-State
Tuition and Fees:	$4,800	$14,250
Campus and Room and Board:	$6,183	$6,183
Books and Supplies:	$924	$924
Other Expenses:	$1,167	$1,167
Total Estimated Expenses:	**$13,074**	**$22,524**

Note: Additional fees of $10 and $40 per credit hour for any course offered by the College of Engineering.

NEW APPLICANTS/NEWLY ENROLLED STUDENTS
[Numbers are for the undergraduate engineering college for the Fall 2006 term]
Number of Applicants (a):	745
Of those, Number Offered Admission (b):	660
Of those, Number Enrolled Fall 2006 (c):	510

GRADUATE INFORMATION

ESTIMATED STUDENT EXPENSES (FALL 2006)
[Expenses are for the 2006-2007 nine-month academic year and are based on an average credit load of: Graduate: 9]

	In-State	Out-of-State
Tuition and Fees:	$3,807	$10,255
Campus and Room and Board:	$6,183	$6,183
Books and Supplies:	$924	$924
Other Expenses:	$1,009	$1,009
Total Estimated Expenses:	**$11,923**	**$18,371**

Note: Additional fees of $10 and $40 per credit hour for any course offered by the College of Engineering.

NEW APPLICANTS/NEWLY ENROLLED STUDENTS
[Numbers are for the graduate engineering college for the Fall 2006 term]
Number of Applicants (a):	496
Of those, Number Offered Admission (b):	140
Of those, Number Enrolled Fall 2006 (c):	65

University of Nevada, Las Vegas

INSTITUTION INFORMATION
4505 Maryland Parkway
Las Vegas, NV 89154
Phone: (702) 895-3011
Fax: (702) 895-3850
Web: http://www.unlv.edu

GENERAL INFORMATION
[All Students - Fall 2006]
Undergraduate Enrollment	22,077
Graduate Enrollment	5,260
Professional Enrollment	786
Total Enrollment	**28,123**

ENGINEERING COLLEGE INFORMATION

HEAD OF ENGINEERING
Eric Sandgren
Dean
College of Engineering
University of Nevada, Las Vegas
4505 Maryland Parkway

Las Vegas, NV 89154
Phone: (702) 895-3699
Fax: (702) 895-4059
Email: eric.sandgren@unlv.edu

TYPES OF ENGINEERING DEGREES
Bachelor's: B.A., B.S.
Master's: M.S. with thesis, M.S. without thesis, but with project or report
Doctoral: Ph.D.

UNDERGRADUATE INFORMATION

ESTIMATED STUDENT EXPENSES (FALL 2006)
[Expenses are for the 2006-2007 nine-month academic year and are based on an average credit load of: Undergraduate: 15]

	In-State	Out-of-State
Tuition and Fees:	$3,480	$12,947
Campus and Room and Board:	$9,800	$9,800
Books and Supplies:	$850	$850
Other Expenses:	$450	$450
Total Estimated Expenses:	**$14,580**	**$24,047**

GRADUATE INFORMATION

ADMISSION INQUIRIES
Paul W Ferguson
Dean
University of Nevada, Las Vegas
Box 451017
Las Vegas , NV 89154-1017
Phone: (702) 895-3681
Fax: (702) 895-4180

ESTIMATED STUDENT EXPENSES (FALL 2006)
[Expenses are for the 2006-2007 nine-month academic year and are based on an average credit load of: Graduate: 15]

	In-State	Out-of-State
Tuition and Fees:	$4,636	$13,103
Campus and Room and Board:	$9,800	$9,800
Books and Supplies:	$850	$850
Other Expenses:	$450	$450
Total Estimated Expenses:	**$15,736**	**$24,203**

University of Nevada, Reno

INSTITUTION INFORMATION
College of Engineering
MS/256
Reno, NV 89557-0256
Phone: (775) 784-6925
Fax: (775) 784-4466
Web: http://engr.unr.edu

GENERAL INFORMATION
[All Students - Fall 2006]

Undergraduate Enrollment	12,499
Graduate Enrollment	3,312
Professional Enrollment	850
Total Enrollment	**16,661**

ENGINEERING COLLEGE INFORMATION

HEAD OF ENGINEERING
Ted E Batchman
Dean
Engineering\Engineering Dean's Office
University of Nevada, Reno
College of Engineering
MS/256
Reno, NV 89557-0256
Phone: (775) 784-6925
Fax: (775) 784-4466
Email: batch_t@unr.edu

TYPES OF ENGINEERING DEGREES
Bachelor's: B.S.
Master's: M.S. with thesis, M.S. without thesis, but with project or report
Doctoral: Ph.D.

UNDERGRADUATE INFORMATION

ADMISSION INQUIRIES
Bill Cathey
Vice Provost, Instruction and Undergraduate Programs

University of Nevada, Reno
Clark Administration, MS/005
Reno, NV 89557-0005
Phone: (775) 784-1740
Fax: (775) 784-6220
Email: billca@unr.edu

ESTIMATED STUDENT EXPENSES (FALL 2006)
[Expenses are for the 2006-2007 nine-month academic year and are based on an average credit load of: Undergraduate: 15]

	In-State	Out-of-State
Tuition and Fees:	$3,677	$13,600
Campus and Room and Board:	$7,599	$7,599
Books and Supplies:	$1,400	$1,400
Other Expenses:	$3,200	$3,200
Total Estimated Expenses:	**$15,876**	**$25,799**

GRADUATE INFORMATION

ADMISSION INQUIRIES
Marsha Read
Associate Vice President for Research and Graduate School
University of Nevada, Reno
Graduate School, MS/326
Reno , NV 89557-0326
Phone: (775) 784-6869
Fax: (775) 784-6064
Email: read@scs.unr.edu

ESTIMATED STUDENT EXPENSES (FALL 2006)
[Expenses are for the 2006-2007 nine-month academic year and are based on an average credit load of: Graduate: 9]

	In-State	Out-of-State
Tuition and Fees:	$3,100	$13,000
Campus and Room and Board:	$7,599	$7,599
Books and Supplies:	$1,400	$1,400
Other Expenses:	$3,200	$3,200
Total Estimated Expenses:	**$15,299**	**$25,199**

NEW APPLICANTS/NEWLY ENROLLED STUDENTS
[Numbers are for the graduate engineering college for the Fall 2006 term]

Number of Applicants (a):	291
Of those, Number Offered Admission (b):	199
Of those, Number Enrolled Fall 2006 (c):	109

University of New Hampshire

INSTITUTION INFORMATION
Thompson Hall
Main Street
Durham, NH 03824
Phone: (603) 868-0500
Web: http://www.unh.edu

GENERAL INFORMATION
[All Students - Fall 2006]

Undergraduate Enrollment	11,113
Graduate Enrollment	2,434
Professional Enrollment	2,439
Total Enrollment	**15,986**

ENGINEERING COLLEGE INFORMATION

HEAD OF ENGINEERING
Joseph Klewicki
Dean
College of Engineering & Physical Sciences
University of New Hampshire
Kingsbury Hall
College Road
Durham, NH 03824
Phone: (603) 862-1781

TYPES OF ENGINEERING DEGREES
Bachelor's: B.S.
Master's: M.S. with thesis, M.S. without thesis, but with project or report
Doctoral: Ph.D.

UNDERGRADUATE INFORMATION

ADMISSION INQUIRIES
Mark Rubinstein
Vice Provost for Enrollment Management

University of New Hampshire
Thompson Hall, Main Street
Durham, NH 03824
Phone: (603) 868-0500
Email: mark.rubinstein@unh.edu

ESTIMATED STUDENT EXPENSES (FALL 2006)
[Expenses are for the 2006-2007 nine-month academic year and are based on an average credit load of: Undergraduate: N/A]

	In-State	Out-of-State
Tuition and Fees:	$10,934	$23,384
Campus and Room and Board:	$7,584	$7,584
Books and Supplies:	$1,500	$1,500
Other Expenses:		
Total Estimated Expenses:	**$20,018**	**$32,468**

Note: Estimate course load is given as semester credit hours. Engineering and computer science students pay a differential tuition of $533 which is included in the numbers reported above

NEW APPLICANTS/NEWLY ENROLLED STUDENTS
[Numbers are for the undergraduate engineering college for the Fall 2006 term]

Number of Applicants (a):	1,767
Of those, Number Offered Admission (b):	1,273
Of those, Number Enrolled Fall 2006 (c):	433

GRADUATE INFORMATION

ADMISSION INQUIRIES
Harry J. Richards
Interim Dean
University of New Hampshire
Thompson Hall
Durham , NH 03824
Phone: (603) 868-0500
Fax: (603) 862-0275
Email: harry.richards@unh.edu

ESTIMATED STUDENT EXPENSES (FALL 2006)
[Expenses are for the 2006-2007 nine-month academic year and are based on an average credit load of: Graduate: N/A]

	In-State	Out-of-State
Tuition and Fees:	$10,416	$22,866
Campus and Room and Board:	$7,584	$7,584
Books and Supplies:	$1,500	$1,500
Other Expenses:		
Total Estimated Expenses:	**$19,500**	**$31,950**

Note: Estimate course load is given as semester credit hours. Engineering and computer science students pay a differential tuition of $533 which is included in the numbers reported above

NEW APPLICANTS/NEWLY ENROLLED STUDENTS
[Numbers are for the graduate engineering college for the Fall 2006 term]

Number of Applicants (a):	232
Of those, Number Offered Admission (b):	167
Of those, Number Enrolled Fall 2006 (c):	72

University of New Haven

INSTITUTION INFORMATION
329 Buckman Hall
300 Boston Post Road
West Haven, CT 06516
Phone: (203) 932-7168
Fax: (203) 932-7394
Web: http://www.newhaven.edu

GENERAL INFORMATION
[All Students - Fall 2006]

Undergraduate Enrollment	2,877
Graduate Enrollment	1,772
Professional Enrollment	0
Total Enrollment	**4,649**

ENGINEERING COLLEGE INFORMATION

HEAD OF ENGINEERING
Barry J Farbrother
Dean
Tagliatela College of Engineering
University of New Haven
300 Boston Post Road
West Haven, CT 06516
Phone: (203) 932-7167

2006 PROFILES OF ENGINEERING COLLEGES

Fax: (203) 932-7394
Email: bfarbrother@newhaven.edu

ENGINEERING COLLEGE INQUIRIES
Jane C Sangeloty
Director
University of New Haven
Bayer Hall
West Haven, CT 06516
Phone: (203) 932-7312
Fax: (203) 931-6093
Email: jsangeloty@newhaven.edu

TYPES OF ENGINEERING DEGREES
Bachelor's: B.S.
Master's: M.S. with thesis
Doctoral:

UNDERGRADUATE INFORMATION

ADMISSION INQUIRIES
Ali Golbazi
Chair
University of New Haven
Buckman Hall, 300 Orange Avenue
West Haven, CT 06516
Phone: (203) 932-7162
Email: agolbazi@newhaven.edu

ADMISSION INQUIRIES
Michael J Saliby
Undergraduate Program Coordinator
University of New Haven
Buckman Hall, 300 Boston Post Road
West Haven, CT 06516
Phone: (203) 932-7169
Fax: (203) 931-6077
Email: msaliby@newhaven.edu

ADMISSION INQUIRIES
David Harding
Department Chair, UG Coordinator Chemical Engr
University of New Haven
Buckman Hall, 300 Boston Post Road
West Haven, CT 06516
Phone: (203) 932-7438
Fax: (203) 931-6077
Email: dharding@newhaven.edu

ADMISSION INQUIRIES
Gregory Broderick
Undergraduate Program Coordinator
University of New Haven
Buckman Hall, 300 Boston Post Road
West Haven, CT 06516
Phone: (203) 932-7156
Fax: (203) 931-7158
Email: gbroderick@newhaven.edu

ADMISSION INQUIRIES
John Sarris
Department Chair
University of New Haven
300 Boston Post Road
West Haven, CT 06516
Phone: (203) 932-7146
Fax: (203) 931-6087
Email: jsarris@newhaven.edu

ADMISSION INQUIRIES
Samuel Daniels
Undergraduate Program Coordinator
University of New Haven
Buckman Hall, 300 Boston Post Road
West Haven, CT 06516
Phone: (203) 932-7405
Fax: (203) 931-6087
Email: sdaniels@newhaven.edu

ADMISSION INQUIRIES
Alice E Fischer
Undergraduate Program Coordinator
University of New Haven
Buckman Hall, 300 Boston Post Road
West Haven, CT 06516
Phone: (203) 932-7069
Fax: (203) 931-6091

ADMISSION INQUIRIES
David Eggert
Undergraduate Program Coordinator

University of New Haven
Buckman Hall, 300 Boston Post Road
West Haven, CT 06516
Phone: (203) 932-7097
Fax: (203) 931-6091
Email: deggert@newhaven.edu

ADMISSION INQUIRIES
Bijan Karimi
Undergraduate Program Coordinator
University of New Haven
Buckman Hall, 300 Boston Post Road
West Haven, CT 06516
Phone: (203) 932-7164
Fax: (203) 931-6091

ESTIMATED STUDENT EXPENSES (FALL 2006)
[Expenses are for the 2006-2007 nine-month academic year and are based on an average credit load of: Undergraduate: 1217]

	All Students
Tuition and fees:	$24,645
Campus and Room and Board:	$9,986
Books and Supplies:	$750
Other Expenses:	$1,500
Total Estimated Expenses:	**$36,881**

NEW APPLICANTS/NEWLY ENROLLED STUDENTS
[Numbers are for the undergraduate engineering college for the Fall 2006 term]

Number of Applicants (a):	481
Of those, Number Offered Admission (b):	305
Of those, Number Enrolled Fall 2006 (c):	92

GRADUATE INFORMATION

ADMISSION INQUIRIES
Agamemnon D Koutsospyros
Graduate Program Coordinator
University of New Haven
Buckman Hall, 300 Boston Post Road
West Haven , CT 06516
Phone: (203) 932-7398
Fax: (203) 931-7158
Email: akoutsospyros@newhaven.edu

ADMISSION INQUIRIES
Tahany Fergany
Graduate Program Coordinator
University of New Haven
Buckman Hall, 300 Boston Post Road
West Haven , CT 06516
Phone: (203) 932-7259
Fax: (203) 931-6091
Email: tfergany@newhaven.edu

ADMISSION INQUIRIES
Konstantine C Lambrakis
Graduate Program Coordinator
University of New Haven
Buckman Hall, 300 Boston Post Road
West Haven , CT 06516
Phone: (203) 932-7408
Fax: (203) 931-6087
Email: klambrakis@newhaven.edu

ADMISSION INQUIRIES
Alexis N Sommers
Graduate Program Coordinator
University of New Haven
Buckman Hall, 300 Boston Post Road
West Haven , CT 06516
Phone: (203) 932-7251
Fax: (203) 932-7394
Email: asommers@newhaven.edu

ADMISSION INQUIRIES
Pauline M Schwartz
Graduate Program Coordinator
University of New Haven
Buckman Hall, 300 Boston Post Road
West Haven , CT 06516
Phone: (203) 932-7170
Fax: (203) 931-6077

ADMISSION INQUIRIES
Bouzid Aliane
Graduate Program Coordinator
University of New Haven
Buckman Hall, 300 Boston Post Road
West Haven , CT 06516

Phone: (203) 932-7160
Fax: (203) 931-6091

ESTIMATED STUDENT EXPENSES (FALL 2006)
[Expenses are for the 2006-2007 nine-month academic year and are based on an average credit load of: Graduate: 9]

	All Students
Tuition and fees:	$16,185
Campus and Room and Board:	
Books and Supplies:	$900
Other Expenses:	
Total Estimated Expenses:	**$17,085**

NEW APPLICANTS/NEWLY ENROLLED STUDENTS
[Numbers are for the graduate engineering college for the Fall 2006 term]

Number of Applicants (a):	1,069
Of those, Number Offered Admission (b):	917
Of those, Number Enrolled Fall 2006 (c):	126

New Jersey Institute of Technology

INSTITUTION INFORMATION
University Heights
Newark, NJ 07102-1982
Phone: (973) 596-3000
Web: http://www.njit.edu

ENGINEERING COLLEGE INFORMATION

HEAD OF ENGINEERING
John R. Schuring
Dean
Newark College of Engineering
New Jersey Institute of Technology
University Heights
Newark, NJ 07102
Phone: (973) 596-5534
Email: john.schuring@njit.edu

TYPES OF ENGINEERING DEGREES
Bachelor's: B.S.
Master's: M.S. with thesis, M.S. without thesis, but with project or report
Doctoral: Ph.D.

UNDERGRADUATE INFORMATION

ADMISSION INQUIRIES
Kathryn Kelly
Director of Undergraduate Admissions
New Jersey Institute of Technology
University Heights
Newark, NJ 07102-1982
Phone: (973) 596-3301
Fax: (973) 596-3461
Email: kathryn.kelly@njit.edu

ESTIMATED STUDENT EXPENSES (FALL 2006)
[Expenses are for the 2006-2007 nine-month academic year and are based on an average credit load of: Undergraduate: N/A]

	In-State	Out-of-State
Tuition and Fees:	$10,506	$17,290
Campus and Room and Board:	$8,980	$8,980
Books and Supplies:	$1,400	$1,400
Other Expenses:	$3,500	$3,500
Total Estimated Expenses:	**$24,386**	**$31,170**

NEW APPLICANTS/NEWLY ENROLLED STUDENTS
[Numbers are for the undergraduate engineering college for the Fall 2006 term]

Number of Applicants (a):	1,407
Of those, Number Offered Admission (b):	729
Of those, Number Enrolled Fall 2006 (c):	400

GRADUATE INFORMATION

ADMISSION INQUIRIES
Stephen Eck
Director
New Jersey Institute of Technology
University Heights
Newark , NJ 07102-1982
Phone: (973) 596-3306
Fax: (973) 596-3461
Email: stephen.m.eck@njit.edu

ESTIMATED STUDENT EXPENSES (FALL 2006)
[Expenses are for the 2006-2007 nine-month academic year and are based on an average credit load of: Graduate: N/A]

	In-State	Out-of-State
Tutition and Fees:	$13,310	$18,314
Campus and Room and Board:	$8,980	$8,980
Books and Supplies:	$1,400	$1,400
Other Expenses:	$3,500	$3,500
Total Estimated Expenses:	**$27,190**	**$32,194**

NEW APPLICANTS/NEWLY ENROLLED STUDENTS
[Numbers are for the graduate engineering college for the Fall 2006 term]

Number of Applicants (a):	2,196
Of those, Number Offered Admission (b):	934
Of those, Number Enrolled Fall 2006 (c):	851

The College of New Jersey

INSTITUTION INFORMATION
P.O. Box 7718
Ewing, NJ 08628
Phone: (609) 771-1855
Fax: (609) 637-5148
Web: http://www.tcnj.edu

GENERAL INFORMATION
[All Students - Fall 2006]

Undergraduate Enrollment	6,091
Graduate Enrollment	798
Professional Enrollment	0
Total Enrollment	**6,889**

ENGINEERING COLLEGE INFORMATION

HEAD OF ENGINEERING
George N. Facas
Professor and Dean
School of Engineering
The College of New Jersey
P.O. Box 7718
Ewing, NJ 08628-0718
Phone: (609) 771-2529
Fax: (609) 637-5148
Email: facas@tcnj.edu

ENGINEERING COLLEGE INQUIRIES
George N. Facas
Professor and Dean
The College of New Jersey
P.O. Box 7718
Ewing, NJ 08628-0718
Phone: (609) 771-2529
Fax: (609) 637-5148
Email: facas@tcnj.edu

TYPES OF ENGINEERING DEGREES
Bachelor's: B.A., B.S.
Master's:
Doctoral:

UNDERGRADUATE INFORMATION

ESTIMATED STUDENT EXPENSES (FALL 2006)
[Expenses are for the 2006-2007 nine-month academic year and are based on an average credit load of: Undergraduate: N/A]

	In-State	Out-of-State
Tutition and Fees:	$10,776	$17,322
Campus and Room and Board:	$8,843	$8,843
Books and Supplies:	$1,200	$1,200
Other Expenses:		
Total Estimated Expenses:	**$20,819**	**$27,365**

NEW APPLICANTS/NEWLY ENROLLED STUDENTS
[Numbers are for the undergraduate engineering college for the Fall 2006 term]

Number of Applicants (a):	672
Of those, Number Offered Admission (b):	394
Of those, Number Enrolled Fall 2006 (c):	108

GRADUATE INFORMATION

ESTIMATED STUDENT EXPENSES (FALL 2006)
[Expenses are for the 2006-2007 nine-month academic year and are based on an average credit load of: Graduate: N/A]

	In-State	Out-of-State
Tuition and Fees:	$11,349	$15,977
Campus and Room and Board:	$8,843	$8,843
Books and Supplies:	$1,000	$1,000
Other Expenses:		
Total Estimated Expenses:	**$21,192**	**$25,820**

The University of New Mexico

INSTITUTION INFORMATION
The University of New Mexico
Albuquerque, NM 87131
Phone: (505) 277-0111
Web: http://www.unm.edu/

GENERAL INFORMATION
[All Students - Fall 2006]

Undergraduate Enrollment	18,199
Graduate Enrollment	4,366
Professional Enrollment	3,252
Total Enrollment	**25,817**

ENGINEERING COLLEGE INFORMATION

HEAD OF ENGINEERING
Joseph L Cecchi
Dean, School of Engineering
Dean's Office
The University of New Mexico
MSC 01 1140
1 University of New Mexico
Albuquerque, NM 87131
Phone: (505) 277-5522
Fax: (505) 277-1422
Email: cecchi@unm.edu

ENGINEERING COLLEGE INQUIRIES
Charles B Fleddermann
Associate Dean for Academic Affairs
The University of New Mexico
MSC 01 1140
Albuquerque, NM 87131
Phone: (505) 277-5521
Fax: (505) 277-1422
Email: cbf@unm.edu

ENGINEERING COLLEGE INQUIRIES
Kevin J Malloy
Associate Dean for Research
The University of New Mexico
MSC01 1140
Albuquerque, NM 87131
Phone: (505) 277-5521
Fax: (505) 277-1422
Email: malloy@chtm.unm.edu

ENGINEERING COLLEGE INQUIRIES
Steven A Peralta
Director, Engineering Student Services
The University of New Mexico
MSC01 1150
Albuquerque, NM 87131
Phone: (505) 277-1417
Fax: (505) 277-9676
Email: speralta@unm.edu

TYPES OF ENGINEERING DEGREES
Bachelor's: B.S.
Master's: M.S. with thesis, M.S. without thesis, but with project or report
Doctoral: Ph.D.

UNDERGRADUATE INFORMATION

ADMISSION INQUIRIES
Steven A Peralta
Director, Engineering Student Services
The University of New Mexico
MSC01 1150
Albuquerque, NM 87131
Phone: (505) 277-1417
Fax: (505) 277-9676
Email: speralta@unm.edu

ESTIMATED STUDENT EXPENSES (FALL 2006)
[Expenses are for the 2006-2007 nine-month academic year

---

and are based on an average credit load of: Undergraduate: 12]

	In-State	Out-of-State
Tutition and Fees:	$4,336	$14,177
Campus and Room and Board:	$6,318	$6,318
Books and Supplies:	$856	$856
Other Expenses:	$3,192	$3,192
Total Estimated Expenses:	**$14,702**	**$24,543**

NEW APPLICANTS/NEWLY ENROLLED STUDENTS
[Numbers are for the undergraduate engineering college for the Fall 2006 term]

Number of Applicants (a):	217
Of those, Number Offered Admission (b):	203
Of those, Number Enrolled Fall 2006 (c):	189

GRADUATE INFORMATION

ESTIMATED STUDENT EXPENSES (FALL 2006)
[Expenses are for the 2006-2007 nine-month academic year and are based on an average credit load of: Graduate: 12]

	In-State	Out-of-State
Tutition and Fees:	$5,125	$14,574
Campus and Room and Board:	$7,614	$7,614
Books and Supplies:	$964	$964
Other Expenses:	$4,266	$4,266
Total Estimated Expenses:	**$17,969**	**$27,418**

NEW APPLICANTS/NEWLY ENROLLED STUDENTS
[Numbers are for the graduate engineering college for the Fall 2006 term]

Number of Applicants (a):	435
Of those, Number Offered Admission (b):	225
Of those, Number Enrolled Fall 2006 (c):	112

New Mexico State University

INSTITUTION INFORMATION
College of Engineering
Box 30001, MSC 3449
Las Cruces, NM 88003-8001
Phone: (505) 646-7234
Fax: (505) 646-3549
Web: http://engr.nmsu.edu/

GENERAL INFORMATION
[All Students - Fall 2006]

Undergraduate Enrollment	13,196
Graduate Enrollment	3,187
Professional Enrollment	0
Total Enrollment	**16,383**

ENGINEERING COLLEGE INFORMATION

HEAD OF ENGINEERING
Steven P. Castillo
Dean of Engineering
College of Engineering
New Mexico State University
PO Box 30001, MSC 3449
Las Cruces, NM 88003-8001
Phone: (505) 646-2914
Fax: (505) 646-3549
Email: engrdean@nmsu.edu

TYPES OF ENGINEERING DEGREES
Bachelor's: B.S.
Master's: M.S. with thesis, M.S. without thesis, but with project or report
Doctoral: Ph.D.

UNDERGRADUATE INFORMATION

ESTIMATED STUDENT EXPENSES (FALL 2006)
[Expenses are for the 2006-2007 nine-month academic year and are based on an average credit load of: Undergraduate: 14]

	In-State	Out-of-State
Tutition and Fees:	$4,230	$13,804
Campus and Room and Board:	$5,800	$5,800
Books and Supplies:	$1,550	$1,550
Other Expenses:	$500	$500
Total Estimated Expenses:	**$12,080**	**$21,654**

NEW APPLICANTS/NEWLY ENROLLED STUDENTS
[Numbers are for the undergraduate engineering college for the Fall 2006 term]

Number of Applicants (a): 391
Of those, Number Offered Admission (b): 350
Of those, Number Enrolled Fall 2006 (c): 304

GRADUATE INFORMATION

ADMISSION INQUIRIES
Linda Lacey
Dean
New Mexico State University
Box 30001, MSC 3G
Las Cruces , NM 88003-8001
Phone: (505) 646-5746
Fax: (505) 646-7721
Email: lacey@nmsu.edu

ESTIMATED STUDENT EXPENSES (FALL 2006)
[Expenses are for the 2006-2007 nine-month academic year and are based on an average credit load of: Graduate: 9]

	In-State	Out-of-State
Tuition and Fees:	$4,543	$14,173
Campus and Room and Board:	$5,800	$5,800
Books and Supplies:	$1,550	$1,550
Other Expenses:	$500	$500
Total Estimated Expenses:	**$12,393**	**$22,023**

NEW APPLICANTS/NEWLY ENROLLED STUDENTS
[Numbers are for the graduate engineering college for the Fall 2006 term]
Number of Applicants (a): 395
Of those, Number Offered Admission (b): 249
Of those, Number Enrolled Fall 2006 (c): 107

University of New Orleans

INSTITUTION INFORMATION
2000 Lakeshore Drive
New Orleans, LA 70148
Phone: (504) 280-6000
Fax: (504) 280-7393
Web: http://www.uno.edu

GENERAL INFORMATION
[All Students - Fall 2006]
Undergraduate Enrollment 9,156
Graduate Enrollment 5,044
Professional Enrollment 308
Total Enrollment **14,508**

ENGINEERING COLLEGE INFORMATION

HEAD OF ENGINEERING
Russell E Trahan Jr.
Dean
College of Engineering
University of New Orleans
2000 Lakeshore Drive
College of Engineering Room 910
New Orleans, LA 70148
Phone: (504) 280-6328
Fax: (504) 280-7413
Email: rtrahan@uno.edu

ENGINEERING COLLEGE INQUIRIES
Russell E Trahan Jr.
Dean
University of New Orleans
2000 Lakeshore Drive, College of Engineering Room 910
New Orleans, LA 70148
Phone: (504) 280-6328
Fax: (504) 280-7413
Email: rtrahan@uno.edu

ENGINEERING COLLEGE INQUIRIES
Raphael J Kuchler
Coordinator, Community Relations & Economic Development
University of New Orleans
2000 Lakeshore Drive
New Orleans, LA 70148
Phone: (504) 280-5418
Fax: (504) 280-7413
Email: rkuchler@uno.edu

ENGINEERING COLLEGE INQUIRIES
Lucien J Wainie
Director of Academic Services

University of New Orleans
2000 Lakeshore Drive
New Orleans, LA 70148
Phone: (504) 280-6825
Fax: (504) 280-7413
Email: lwainie@uno.edu

TYPES OF ENGINEERING DEGREES
Bachelor's: B.S.
Master's: M.S. with thesis, M.S. without thesis, but with project or report
Doctoral: Ph.D.

UNDERGRADUATE INFORMATION

ADMISSION INQUIRIES
Nelly Benko-Hakim
Clerk Chief II/Undergraduate Advisor
University of New Orleans
2000 Lakeshore Drive, Room 929
New Orleans, LA 70148
Phone: (504) 280-6824

Fax: (504) 280-7413
Email: mbenkoh@uno.edu

ESTIMATED STUDENT EXPENSES (FALL 2006)
[Expenses are for the 2006-2007 nine-month academic year and are based on an average credit load of: Undergraduate: 137]

	In-State	Out-of-State
Tuition and Fees:	$3,292	$10,336
Campus and Room and Board:	$4,734	$4,734
Books and Supplies:	$1,150	$1,150
Other Expenses:	$2,416	$2,416
Total Estimated Expenses:	**$11,592**	**$18,636**

NEW APPLICANTS/NEWLY ENROLLED STUDENTS
[Numbers are for the undergraduate engineering college for the Fall 2006 term]
Number of Applicants (a): 426
Of those, Number Offered Admission (b): 344
Of those, Number Enrolled Fall 2006 (c): 218

GRADUATE INFORMATION

ADMISSION INQUIRIES
Paul M Chirlian
Associate Dean/Director - Engineering PhD Program
University of New Orleans
2000 Lakeshore Drive
New Orleans , LA 70148
Phone: (504) 280-5504
Fax: (504) 280-7413
Email: pchirlia@uno.edu

ADMISSION INQUIRIES
William S Vorus
Professor and Jerome Goldman Endowed Chair
University of New Orleans
2000 Lakeshore Drive
New Orleans , LA 70148
Phone: (504) 280-7180
Fax: (504) 280-5542
Email: wvorus@uno.edu

ADMISSION INQUIRIES
Michael D Folse
Associate Professor/Graduate Advisor
University of New Orleans
2000 Lakeshore Drive
New Orleans , LA 70148
Phone: (504) 280-7268
Fax: (504) 280-5586
Email: mfolse@uno.edu

ADMISSION INQUIRIES
Enrique La Motta
Professor/Graduate Advisor
University of New Orleans
2000 Lakeshore Drive
New Orleans , LA 70148
Phone: (504) 280-6668
Fax: (504) 280-5586
Email: elamotta@uno.edu

ADMISSION INQUIRIES
Rasheed M Azzam
Distinguished Professor/Graduate Advisor
University of New Orleans
2000 Lakeshore Drive

New Orleans , LA 70148
Phone: (504) 280-6181
Fax: (504) 280-3950
Email: razzam@uno.edu

ADMISSION INQUIRIES
Martin J Guillot
Associate Professor/Graduate Advisor
University of New Orleans
2000 Lakeshore Drive
New Orleans , LA 70148
Phone: (504) 280-6184
Fax: (504) 280-5539
Email: mjguillo@uno.edu

ESTIMATED STUDENT EXPENSES (FALL 2006)
[Expenses are for the 2006-2007 nine-month academic year and are based on an average credit load of: Graduate: 183]

	In-State	Out-of-State
Tuition and Fees:	$3,292	$10,336
Campus and Room and Board:	$4,734	$4,734
Books and Supplies:	$1,150	$1,150
Other Expenses:	$2,416	$2,416
Total Estimated Expenses:	**$11,592**	**$18,636**

NEW APPLICANTS/NEWLY ENROLLED STUDENTS
[Numbers are for the graduate engineering college for the Fall 2006 term]
Number of Applicants (a): 79
Of those, Number Offered Admission (b): 52
Of those, Number Enrolled Fall 2006 (c): 28

New York Institute of Technology

INSTITUTION INFORMATION
Northern Boulevard
Old Westbury, NY 11568-8000
Phone: (516) 686-7516
Web: http://www.nyit.edu/

GENERAL INFORMATION
[All Students - Fall 2006]
Undergraduate Enrollment 5,450
Graduate Enrollment 2,220
Professional Enrollment 1,187
Total Enrollment **8,857**

ENGINEERING COLLEGE INFORMATION

HEAD OF ENGINEERING
Heskia Heskiaoff
Dean
Engineering and Computing Sciences
New York Institute of Technology
Northern Blvd.
Old Westbury, NY 11568-8000
Phone: (516) 686-7931
Fax: (516) 686-7933
Email: heskiaoff@nyit.edu

TYPES OF ENGINEERING DEGREES
Bachelor's: B.S.
Master's: M.S. without thesis, but with project or report
Doctoral:

UNDERGRADUATE INFORMATION

ADMISSION INQUIRIES
Jacquelyn Nealon
Dean of Student Enrollment
New York Institute of Technology
Northern Boulevard
Old Westbury, NY 11568-8000
Phone: (516) 686-7520
Email: jnealon@nyit.edu

ESTIMATED STUDENT EXPENSES (FALL 2006)
[Expenses are for the 2006-2007 nine-month academic year and are based on an average credit load of: Undergraduate: N/A]

	All Students
Tuition and fees:	$19,818
Campus and Room and Board:	$4,000
Books and Supplies:	$800
Other Expenses:	
Total Estimated Expenses:	**$24,618**

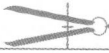

NEW APPLICANTS/NEWLY ENROLLED STUDENTS

[Numbers are for the undergraduate engineering college for the Fall 2006 term]

Number of Applicants (a):	1,165
Of those, Number Offered Admission (b):	789
Of those, Number Enrolled Fall 2006 (c):	296

GRADUATE INFORMATION

ESTIMATED STUDENT EXPENSES (FALL 2006)

[Expenses are for the 2006-2007 nine-month academic year and are based on an average credit load of: Graduate: N/A]

	All Students
Tuition and fees:	$700
Campus and Room and Board:	
Books and Supplies:	
Other Expenses:	
Total Estimated Expenses:	**$700**

NEW APPLICANTS/NEWLY ENROLLED STUDENTS

[Numbers are for the graduate engineering college for the Fall 2006 term]

Number of Applicants (a):	2,261
Of those, Number Offered Admission (b):	1,651
Of those, Number Enrolled Fall 2006 (c):	342

City College of the City University of New York

INSTITUTION INFORMATION

Convent Avenue at 138th Street
Room T142
New York, NY 10031
Phone: (212) 265-0543
Fax: (212) 265-5768
Web: http://www.engr.ccny.cuny.edu

GENERAL INFORMATION

[All Students - Fall 2006]

Undergraduate Enrollment	10,314
Graduate Enrollment	2,930
Professional Enrollment	13,244
Total Enrollment	**26,488**

ENGINEERING COLLEGE INFORMATION

HEAD OF ENGINEERING

Joseph Barba
Dean
Grove School of Engineering
City College of the City University of New York
Convent Avenue and West 138th Street
Steinman Hall, Room 142
New York, NY 10031
Phone: (212) 650-6939
Fax: (212) 650-5768
Email: JBarba@ccny.cuny.edu

TYPES OF ENGINEERING DEGREES

Bachelor's: B.Eng.
Master's: M.S. with thesis, M.S. without thesis, but with project or report, M.Eng.
Doctoral: Ph.D.

UNDERGRADUATE INFORMATION

ADMISSION INQUIRIES

Joseph Fantozzi
Director, Admissions
City College of the City University of New York
Administration Building, Room 100A
New York, NY 10031
Phone: (212) 650-7865
Fax: (212) 650-6417
Email: admissions@ccny.cuny.edu

ADMISSION INQUIRIES

Ardie Walser
Associate Professor & Associate Dean for Academic Affairs
City College of the City University of New York
Convent Avenue at 138th Street, Room T209
New York, NY 10031
Phone: (212) 650-8020
Fax: (212) 650-8090
Email: walser@ccny.cuny.edu

ESTIMATED STUDENT EXPENSES (FALL 2006)

[Expenses are for the 2006-2007 nine-month academic year and are based on an average credit load of: Undergraduate: 12]

	In-State	Out-of-State
Tuition and Fees:	$4,166	$6,103
Campus and Room and Board:	$11,800	$11,800
Books and Supplies:	$800	$800
Other Expenses:	$2,300	$2,300
Total Estimated Expenses:	**$19,066**	**$21,003**

NEW APPLICANTS/NEWLY ENROLLED STUDENTS

[Numbers are for the undergraduate engineering college for the Fall 2006 term]

Number of Applicants (a):	2,126
Of those, Number Offered Admission (b):	1,186
Of those, Number Enrolled Fall 2006 (c):	0

Note: This information is not available

GRADUATE INFORMATION

ESTIMATED STUDENT EXPENSES (FALL 2006)

[Expenses are for the 2006-2007 nine-month academic year and are based on an average credit load of: Graduate: 12]

	In-State	Out-of-State
Tuition and Fees:	$7,691	$13,511
Campus and Room and Board:	$11,800	$11,800
Books and Supplies:	$900	$900
Other Expenses:	$2,300	$2,300
Total Estimated Expenses:	**$22,691**	**$28,511**

NEW APPLICANTS/NEWLY ENROLLED STUDENTS

[Numbers are for the graduate engineering college for the Fall 2006 term]

Number of Applicants (a):	428
Of those, Number Offered Admission (b):	281
Of those, Number Enrolled Fall 2006 (c):	187

The State University of New York at Binghamton

INSTITUTION INFORMATION

4400 Vestal Parkway East
P.O. Box 6000
Binghamton, NY 13902-6000
Phone: (607) 777-2000
Fax: (607) 777-4000
Web: http://www.binghamton.edu

GENERAL INFORMATION

[All Students - Fall 2006]

Undergraduate Enrollment	11,405
Graduate Enrollment	2,820
Professional Enrollment	0
Total Enrollment	**14,225**

ENGINEERING COLLEGE INFORMATION

HEAD OF ENGINEERING

Charles R Westgate
Dean
The Watson School of Engineering and Applied Science
The State University of New York at Binghamton
4400 Vestal Parkway East
P.O. Box 6000
Binghamton, NY 13902-6000
Phone: (607) 777-2871
Fax: (607) 777-4822
Email: westgate@binghamton.edu

ENGINEERING COLLEGE INQUIRIES

Lorna Wells
Director of Student Services
The State University of New York at Binghamton
Vestal Parkway East, P.O. Box 6000
Binghamton, NY 13902-6000
Phone: (607) 777-6203
Fax: (607) 777-4822
Email: lornawel@binghamton.edu

TYPES OF ENGINEERING DEGREES

Bachelor's: B.S.
Master's: M.S. with thesis, M.S. without thesis, but with project or report, M.Eng.
Doctoral: Ph.D.

UNDERGRADUATE INFORMATION

ADMISSION INQUIRIES

Robert Piurowski
Undergraduate Engineering Admission Inquiries Contact
The State University of New York at Binghamton
4400 Vestal Parkway East, P.O. Box 6000
Binghamton, NY 13902-6000
Phone: (607) 777-2171
Fax: (607) 777-4445
Email: rpiurows@binghamton.edu

ESTIMATED STUDENT EXPENSES (FALL 2006)

[Expenses are for the 2006-2007 nine-month academic year and are based on an average credit load of: Undergraduate: 16]

	In-State	Out-of-State
Tuition and Fees:	$5,910	$12,170
Campus and Room and Board:	$8,588	$8,588
Books and Supplies:	$800	$800
Other Expenses:	$1,200	$1,200
Total Estimated Expenses:	**$16,498**	**$22,758**

NEW APPLICANTS/NEWLY ENROLLED STUDENTS

[Numbers are for the undergraduate engineering college for the Fall 2006 term]

Number of Applicants (a):	2,297
Of those, Number Offered Admission (b):	1,471
Of those, Number Enrolled Fall 2006 (c):	390

GRADUATE INFORMATION

ADMISSION INQUIRIES

Cheryl Foster
Assistant Dean
The State University of New York at Binghamton
Vestal Parkway East, P.O. Box 6000
Binghamton, NY 13902-6000
Phone: (607) 777-2072
Fax: (607) 777-2501
Email: cfoster@binghamton.edu

ADMISSION INQUIRIES

David Laber
Coordinator of Graduate Programs
The State University of New York at Binghamton
4400 Vestal Parkway East, P.O. Box 6000
Binghamton, NY 13902-6000
Phone: (607) 777-2873
Fax: (607) 777-4822
Email: dlaber@binghamton.edu

ESTIMATED STUDENT EXPENSES (FALL 2006)

[Expenses are for the 2006-2007 nine-month academic year and are based on an average credit load of: Graduate: 12]

	In-State	Out-of-State
Tuition and Fees:	$7,919	$11,939
Campus and Room and Board:	$10,352	$10,352
Books and Supplies:	$800	$800
Other Expenses:	$2,000	$2,000
Total Estimated Expenses:	**$21,071**	**$25,091**

NEW APPLICANTS/NEWLY ENROLLED STUDENTS

[Numbers are for the graduate engineering college for the Fall 2006 term]

Number of Applicants (a):	653
Of those, Number Offered Admission (b):	432
Of those, Number Enrolled Fall 2006 (c):	185

State University of New York at Buffalo

INSTITUTION INFORMATION

School of Engineering & Applied Sciences
412 Bonner Hall
Buffalo, NY 14260-1900
Phone: (716) 645-2771
Fax: (716) 645-2495
Web: http://www.eng.buffalo.edu/

GENERAL INFORMATION

[All Students - Fall 2006]

Undergraduate Enrollment	18,506
Graduate Enrollment	7,304
Professional Enrollment	2,013
Total Enrollment	**27,823**

ENGINEERING COLLEGE INFORMATION

HEAD OF ENGINEERING
Harvey G Stenger
Dean
Engineering
State University of New York at Buffalo
School of Engineering & Applied Sciences
412 Bonner Hall
Buffalo, NY 14260-1900
Phone: (716) 716-6456
Fax: (716) 716-2495
Email: hstenger@buffalo.edu

ENGINEERING COLLEGE INQUIRIES
John E. Van Benschoten
Associate Dean for Undergraduate Education & Professor
State University of New York at Buffalo
School of Engineering & Applied Sciences, 410 Bonner Hall
Buffalo, NY 14260-1900
Phone: (716) 645-2771
Fax: (716) 645-2495
Email: jev@buffalo.edu

TYPES OF ENGINEERING DEGREES
Bachelor's: B.A., B.S.
Master's: M.S. with thesis, M.S. without thesis, but with project or report, M.Eng.
Doctoral: Ph.D.

UNDERGRADUATE INFORMATION

ADMISSION INQUIRIES
John E. Van Benschoten
Associate Dean for Undergraduate Education & Professor
State University of New York at Buffalo
School of Engineering & Applied Sciences, 410 Bonner Hall
Buffalo, NY 14260-1900
Phone: (716) 645-2771
Fax: (716) 645-2495
Email: jev@buffalo.edu

ESTIMATED STUDENT EXPENSES (FALL 2006)
[Expenses are for the 2006-2007 nine-month academic year and are based on an average credit load of: Undergraduate: 12]

	In-State	Out-of-State
Tuition and Fees:	$6,129	$12,389
Campus and Room and Board:	$7,526	$7,526
Books and Supplies:	$893	$893
Other Expenses:	$1,975	$1,975
Total Estimated Expenses:	**$16,523**	**$22,783**

Note: Tuition is for 12 credit hours, however, full-time status for Teaching Assistants and Graduate Assistants is 9 credit hours. Fees are not covered by Tuition Scholarships.

NEW APPLICANTS/NEWLY ENROLLED STUDENTS
[Numbers are for the undergraduate engineering college for the Fall 2006 term]

Number of Applicants (a):	2,915
Of those, Number Offered Admission (b):	1,843
Of those, Number Enrolled Fall 2006 (c):	714

GRADUATE INFORMATION

ADMISSION INQUIRIES
Rajan Batta
Professor & Associate Dean for Graduate Education
State University of New York at Buffalo
School of Engineering & Applied Sciences, 412 Bonner Hall
Buffalo, NY 14260-1900
Phone: (716) 645-2771
Fax: (716) 645-2495
Email: batta@buffalo.edu

ESTIMATED STUDENT EXPENSES (FALL 2006)
[Expenses are for the 2006-2007 nine-month academic year and are based on an average credit load of: Graduate: 12]

	In-State	Out-of-State
Tuition and Fees:	$8,219	$12,239
Campus and Room and Board:	$9,581	$9,581
Books and Supplies:	$1,534	$1,534
Other Expenses:	$3,051	$3,051
Total Estimated Expenses:	**$22,385**	**$26,405**

Note: Tuition is for 12 credit hours, however, full-time status for Teaching Assistants and Graduate Assistants is 9 credit hours. Fees are not covered by Tuition Scholarships.

NEW APPLICANTS/NEWLY ENROLLED STUDENTS
[Numbers are for the graduate engineering college for the Fall 2006 term]

Number of Applicants (a):	3,629
Of those, Number Offered Admission (b):	1,221
Of those, Number Enrolled Fall 2006 (c):	379

SUNY College of Environmental Science and Forestry

INSTITUTION INFORMATION
206 Bray Hall
1 Forestry Drive
Syracuse, NY 13210
Phone: (315) 470-6500
Fax: (315) 470-6779
Web: http://www.esf.edu/

GENERAL INFORMATION
[All Students - Fall 2006]

Undergraduate Enrollment	1,544
Graduate Enrollment	0
Professional Enrollment	0
Total Enrollment	**1,544**

ENGINEERING COLLEGE INFORMATION

HEAD OF ENGINEERING
William P Tully
Director
Division of Engineering
SUNY College of Environmental Science and Forestry
One Forestry Drive
309 Bray Hall
Syracuse, NY 13210
Phone: (315) 470-6510
Fax: (315) 470-6779
Email: wptully@esf.edu

ENGINEERING COLLEGE INQUIRIES
William P Tully
Director
SUNY College of Environmental Science and Forestry
One Forestry Drive, 309 Bray Hall
Syracuse, NY 13210
Phone: (315) 470-6510
Fax: (315) 470-6779
Email: wptully@esf.edu

TYPES OF ENGINEERING DEGREES
Bachelor's: B.S.
Master's: M.S. with thesis, M.S. without thesis, but with project or report
Doctoral: Ph.D.

UNDERGRADUATE INFORMATION

ADMISSION INQUIRIES
Susan H Sanford
Director
SUNY College of Environmental Science and Forestry
107 Bray Hall, 1 Forestry Drive
Syracuse, NY 13210
Phone: (315) 470-6600
Fax: (315) 470-6933
Email: susan.sanford@esf.edu

ESTIMATED STUDENT EXPENSES (FALL 2006)
[Expenses are for the 2006-2007 nine-month academic year and are based on an average credit load of: Undergraduate: 12]

	In-State	Out-of-State
Tuition and Fees:	$5,069	$11,329
Campus and Room and Board:	$10,600	$10,600
Books and Supplies:	$1,200	$1,200
Other Expenses:	$1,050	$1,050
Total Estimated Expenses:	**$17,919**	**$24,179**

NEW APPLICANTS/NEWLY ENROLLED STUDENTS
[Numbers are for the undergraduate engineering college for the Fall 2006 term]

Number of Applicants (a):	140
Of those, Number Offered Admission (b):	85
Of those, Number Enrolled Fall 2006 (c):	41

GRADUATE INFORMATION

ADMISSION INQUIRIES
Dudley J Raynal
Dean of Graduate Studies
SUNY College of Environmental Science and Forestry
One Forestry Drive, 227 Bray Hall
Syracuse, NY 13210
Phone: (315) 470-6599
Fax: (315) 470-6779
Email: esfgrad@esf.edu

ESTIMATED STUDENT EXPENSES (FALL 2006)
[Expenses are for the 2006-2007 nine-month academic year and are based on an average credit load of: Graduate: 12]

	In-State	Out-of-State
Tuition and Fees:	$7,569	$11,589
Campus and Room and Board:	$10,600	$10,600
Books and Supplies:	$1,200	$1,200
Other Expenses:	$1,050	$1,050
Total Estimated Expenses:	**$20,419**	**$24,439**

NEW APPLICANTS/NEWLY ENROLLED STUDENTS
[Numbers are for the graduate engineering college for the Fall 2006 term]

Number of Applicants (a):	54
Of those, Number Offered Admission (b):	33
Of those, Number Enrolled Fall 2006 (c):	14

Stony Brook University

INSTITUTION INFORMATION
College of Engineering and Applied Sciences
Engineering Building, Room 100
Stony Brook, NY 11794-2200
Phone: (631) 632-8380
Fax: (631) 632-8205
Web: http://www.ceas.sunysb.edu

GENERAL INFORMATION
[All Students - Fall 2006]

Undergraduate Enrollment	14,851
Graduate Enrollment	7,081
Professional Enrollment	595
Total Enrollment	**22,527**

ENGINEERING COLLEGE INFORMATION

HEAD OF ENGINEERING
Yacov Shamash
Dean
College of Engineering and Applied Sciences
Stony Brook University
College of Engineering and Applied Sciences
100 Engineering Building
Stony Brook, NY 11794-2200
Phone: (631) 632-8380
Fax: (631) 632-8205
Email: yshamash@ccmail.sunysb.edu

TYPES OF ENGINEERING DEGREES
Bachelor's: B.S., B.E.
Master's: M.S. with thesis
Doctoral: Ph.D.

UNDERGRADUATE INFORMATION

ADMISSION INQUIRIES
Judith Berhannan
Director, Admissions and Enrollment Services
Stony Brook University
118 Administration Building
Stony Brook, NY 11794-1901
Phone: (631) 632-8765
Fax: (631) 632-9898
Email: glamens@ccmail.sunysb.edu

ESTIMATED STUDENT EXPENSES (FALL 2006)
[Expenses are for the 2006-2007 nine-month academic year and are based on an average credit load of: Undergraduate: 16]

	In-State	Out-of-State
Tuition and Fees:	$5,574	$11,834
Campus and Room and Board:	$8,424	$8,424
Books and Supplies:	$900	$900
Other Expenses:	$1,792	$1,792
Total Estimated Expenses:	**$16,690**	**$22,950**

Note: Other Expenses includes Transportation and Personal

Expenses. Graduate expenses also includes a $9,486 allowance for Room and Board.

NEW APPLICANTS/NEWLY ENROLLED STUDENTS
[Numbers are for the undergraduate engineering college for the Fall 2006 term]

Number of Applicants (a):	2,612
Of those, Number Offered Admission (b):	1,478
Of those, Number Enrolled Fall 2006 (c):	476

GRADUATE INFORMATION

ESTIMATED STUDENT EXPENSES (FALL 2006)
[Expenses are for the 2006-2007 nine-month academic year and are based on an average credit load of: Graduate: 8]

	In-State	Out-of-State
Tuition and Fees:	$7,604	$11,624
Campus and Room and Board:		
Books and Supplies:	$900	$900
Other Expenses:	$13,328	$13,328
Total Estimated Expenses:	**$21,832**	**$25,852**

Note: Other Expenses includes Transportation and Personal Expenses. Graduate expenses also includes a $9,486 allowance for Room and Board.

NEW APPLICANTS/NEWLY ENROLLED STUDENTS
[Numbers are for the graduate engineering college for the Fall 2006 term]

Number of Applicants (a):	2,317
Of those, Number Offered Admission (b):	902
Of those, Number Enrolled Fall 2006 (c):	279

North Carolina A & T State University

INSTITUTION INFORMATION
651 McNair Hall
1601 E. Market Street
Greensboro, NC 27411
Phone: (336) 334-7589
Fax: (336) 334-7540
Web: http://www.ncat.edu

GENERAL INFORMATION
[All Students - Fall 2006]

Undergraduate Enrollment	9,687
Graduate Enrollment	1,411
Professional Enrollment	0
Total Enrollment	**11,098**

ENGINEERING COLLEGE INFORMATION

HEAD OF ENGINEERING
Joseph Monroe
Dean
College of Engineering
North Carolina A & T State University
651 McNair Hall
1601 E. Market Street
Greensboro, NC 27411
Phone: (336) 334-7589
Fax: (336) 334-7540
Email: monroe@ncat.edu

ENGINEERING COLLEGE INQUIRIES
Gay N Davis
Adjunct Assistant Professor
North Carolina A & T State University
651 McNair Hall, 1601 E. Market Street
Greensboro, NC 27411
Phone: (336) 334-7589
Fax: (336) 334-7540

TYPES OF ENGINEERING DEGREES
Bachelor's: B.S.
Master's: M.S. with thesis, M.S. without thesis, but with project or report
Doctoral: Ph.D.

UNDERGRADUATE INFORMATION

ESTIMATED STUDENT EXPENSES (FALL 2006)
[Expenses are for the 2006-2007 nine-month academic year and are based on an average credit load of: Undergraduate: N/A]

	In-State	Out-of-State
Tuition and Fees:	$3,872	$13,314
Campus and Room and Board:	$6,686	$6,686

Books and Supplies:
Other Expenses:

Total Estimated Expenses:	**$10,558**	**$20,000**

NEW APPLICANTS/NEWLY ENROLLED STUDENTS
[Numbers are for the undergraduate engineering college for the Fall 2006 term]

Number of Applicants (a):	842
Of those, Number Offered Admission (b):	637
Of those, Number Enrolled Fall 2006 (c):	468

GRADUATE INFORMATION

ESTIMATED STUDENT EXPENSES (FALL 2006)
[Expenses are for the 2006-2007 nine-month academic year and are based on an average credit load of: Graduate: N/A]

	In-State	Out-of-State
Tuition and Fees:	$3,944	$13,529
Campus and Room and Board:	$6,686	$6,686
Books and Supplies:		
Other Expenses:		
Total Estimated Expenses:	**$10,630**	**$20,215**

NEW APPLICANTS/NEWLY ENROLLED STUDENTS
[Numbers are for the graduate engineering college for the Fall 2006 term]

Number of Applicants (a):	136
Of those, Number Offered Admission (b):	84
Of those, Number Enrolled Fall 2006 (c):	84

North Carolina State University

INSTITUTION INFORMATION
Holladay Hall
Box 7001
Raleigh, NC 27695-7001
Phone: (919) 515-2191
Fax: (919) 831-3545
Web: http://www.ncsu.edu

GENERAL INFORMATION
[All Students - Fall 2006]

Undergraduate Enrollment	21,438
Graduate Enrollment	6,481
Professional Enrollment	3,211
Total Enrollment	**31,130**

ENGINEERING COLLEGE INFORMATION

HEAD OF ENGINEERING
Louis Martin-Vega
Dean
Deans Office, College of Engineering
North Carolina State University
113 Page Hall
Box 7901
Raleigh, NC 27695-7901
Phone: (919) 515-2311
Fax: (919) 515-7951
Email: louis_martin-vega@ncsu.edu

ENGINEERING COLLEGE INQUIRIES
John S Strenkowski
Associate Dean
North Carolina State University
113 Page Hall, Box 7901
Raleigh, NC 27695-7901
Phone: (919) 515-3939
Fax: (919) 515-7951
Email: jsstren@ncsu.edu

TYPES OF ENGINEERING DEGREES
Bachelor's: B.S.
Master's: M.S. with thesis, M.S. without thesis, but with project or report
Doctoral: Ph.D.

UNDERGRADUATE INFORMATION

ADMISSION INQUIRIES
Richard F Keltie
Assoc. Dean
North Carolina State University
120C Page Hall, Box 7904
Raleigh, NC 27695-7904
Phone: (919) 515-3693

Fax: (919) 515-8702
Email: keltie@eos.ncsu.edu

ESTIMATED STUDENT EXPENSES (FALL 2006)
[Expenses are for the 2006-2007 nine-month academic year and are based on an average credit load of: Undergraduate: 16]

	In-State	Out-of-State
Tuition and Fees:	$4,783	$16,981
Campus and Room and Board:	$7,040	$7,040
Books and Supplies:	$900	$900
Other Expenses:	$1,730	$2,230
Total Estimated Expenses:	**$14,453**	**$27,151**

NEW APPLICANTS/NEWLY ENROLLED STUDENTS
[Numbers are for the undergraduate engineering college for the Fall 2006 term]

Number of Applicants (a):	3,870
Of those, Number Offered Admission (b):	2,576
Of those, Number Enrolled Fall 2006 (c):	1,397

GRADUATE INFORMATION

ADMISSION INQUIRIES
John S Strenkowski
Associate Dean
North Carolina State University
113 Page Hall, Box 7901
Raleigh, NC 27695-7901
Phone: (919) 515-3939
Fax: (919) 515-7951
Email: jsstren@ncsu.edu

ESTIMATED STUDENT EXPENSES (FALL 2006)
[Expenses are for the 2006-2007 nine-month academic year and are based on an average credit load of: Graduate: 9]

	In-State	Out-of-State
Tuition and Fees:	$5,302	$17,350
Campus and Room and Board:	$8,600	$8,600
Books and Supplies:	$900	$900
Other Expenses:	$3,500	$3,500
Total Estimated Expenses:	**$18,302**	**$30,350**

NEW APPLICANTS/NEWLY ENROLLED STUDENTS
[Numbers are for the graduate engineering college for the Fall 2006 term]

Number of Applicants (a):	3,500
Of those, Number Offered Admission (b):	813
Of those, Number Enrolled Fall 2006 (c):	582

University of North Carolina, Charlotte

INSTITUTION INFORMATION
9201 University City Boulevard
Charlotte, NC 28223-0001
Phone: (704) 687-2000
Web: http://www.uncc.edu/

GENERAL INFORMATION
[All Students - Fall 2006]

Undergraduate Enrollment	17,032
Graduate Enrollment	4,487
Professional Enrollment	0
Total Enrollment	**21,519**

ENGINEERING COLLEGE INFORMATION

HEAD OF ENGINEERING
Robert E. Johnson
Professor & Dean
The William States Lee College of Engineering
University of North Carolina, Charlotte
9201 University City Boulevard
310 Duke Centennial Hall
Charlotte, NC 28223-0001
Phone: (704) 687-8242
Fax: (704) 687-8267
Email: robejohn@uncc.edu

TYPES OF ENGINEERING DEGREES
Bachelor's: B.S.
Master's: M.S. with thesis, M.S. without thesis, but with project or report
Doctoral: Ph.D.

UNDERGRADUATE INFORMATION

ESTIMATED STUDENT EXPENSES (FALL 2006)
[Expenses are for the 2006-2007 nine-month academic year and are based on an average credit load of: Undergraduate: 15]

	In-State	Out-of-State
Tutition and Fees:	$3,899	$14,311
Campus and Room and Board:	$6,500	$6,500
Books and Supplies:	$1,200	$1,200
Other Expenses:	$1,520	$1,520
Total Estimated Expenses:	**$13,119**	**$23,531**

NEW APPLICANTS/NEWLY ENROLLED STUDENTS
[Numbers are for the undergraduate engineering college for the Fall 2006 term]

Number of Applicants (a):	1,005
Of those, Number Offered Admission (b):	771
Of those, Number Enrolled Fall 2006 (c):	309

GRADUATE INFORMATION

ESTIMATED STUDENT EXPENSES (FALL 2006)
[Expenses are for the 2006-2007 nine-month academic year and are based on an average credit load of: Graduate: 9]

	In-State	Out-of-State
Tutition and Fees:	$4,274	$14,480
Campus and Room and Board:	$6,500	$6,500
Books and Supplies:	$1,200	$1,200
Other Expenses:	$1,520	$1,520
Total Estimated Expenses:	**$13,494**	**$23,700**

NEW APPLICANTS/NEWLY ENROLLED STUDENTS
[Numbers are for the graduate engineering college for the Fall 2006 term]

Number of Applicants (a):	417
Of those, Number Offered Admission (b):	278
Of those, Number Enrolled Fall 2006 (c):	98

University of North Dakota

INSTITUTION INFORMATION
Upson II Room 165
243 Centennial Dr - STOP 8155
Grand Forks, ND 58202--815
Phone: (701) 777-3412
Fax: (701) 777-4838
Web: http://www.engineering.und.edu

GENERAL INFORMATION
[All Students - Fall 2006]

Undergraduate Enrollment	12,813
Graduate Enrollment	1,974
Professional Enrollment	480
Total Enrollment	**15,267**

ENGINEERING COLLEGE INFORMATION

HEAD OF ENGINEERING
John L Watson
Dean
School of Engineering and Mines
University of North Dakota
Upson II, Room 165,
243 Centennial Dr. – STOP 8155
Grand Forks, ND 58202-8155
Phone: (701) 777-3412
Fax: (701) 777-4838
Email: johnwatson@mail.und.edu

TYPES OF ENGINEERING DEGREES
Bachelor's: B.S.
Master's: M.S. with thesis, M.S. without thesis, but with project or report
Doctoral: Ph.D.

UNDERGRADUATE INFORMATION

ADMISSION INQUIRIES
Heidi Kippenhan
Director of Admissions
University of North Dakota
Box 8357, Campus Drive
Grand Forks, ND 58202
Phone: (701) 777-3821
Fax: (701) 777-2696
Email: heidi.kippenhan@mail.und.nodak.edu

ESTIMATED STUDENT EXPENSES (FALL 2006)
[Expenses are for the 2006-2007 nine-month academic year and are based on an average credit load of: Undergraduate: 15]

	In-State	Out-of-State
Tutition and Fees:	$5,792	$13,786
Campus and Room and Board:	$6,000	$6,000
Books and Supplies:	$800	$800
Other Expenses:	$3,000	$3,000
Total Estimated Expenses:	**$15,592**	**$23,586**

NEW APPLICANTS/NEWLY ENROLLED STUDENTS
[Numbers are for the undergraduate engineering college for the Fall 2006 term]

Number of Applicants (a):	531
Of those, Number Offered Admission (b):	399
Of those, Number Enrolled Fall 2006 (c):	226

GRADUATE INFORMATION

ADMISSION INQUIRIES
Joseph N Benoit
Dean
University of North Dakota
Box 8178, Campus Drive
Grand Forks, ND 58202
Phone: (701) 777-2786
Fax: (701) 777-3619
Email: J_benoit@mail.und.edu

ESTIMATED STUDENT EXPENSES (FALL 2006)
[Expenses are for the 2006-2007 nine-month academic year and are based on an average credit load of: Graduate: 12]

	In-State	Out-of-State
Tutition and Fees:	$6,154	$14,752
Campus and Room and Board:	$6,000	$6,000
Books and Supplies:	$800	$800
Other Expenses:	$3,000	$3,000
Total Estimated Expenses:	**$15,954**	**$24,552**

North Dakota State University

INSTITUTION INFORMATION
Box 5285, NDSU Station
Fargo, ND 58105-5285
Phone: (701) 231-7494
Web: http://www.ndsu.nodak.edu/ndsu/cea

ENGINEERING COLLEGE INFORMATION

HEAD OF ENGINEERING
Gary R Smith
Dean
College of Engineering and Architecture
North Dakota State University
CEA Administration 208
Fargo, ND 58105-5285
Phone: (701) 231-7525
Fax: (701) 231-8957
Email: Gary.Smith@ndsu.edu

TYPES OF ENGINEERING DEGREES
Bachelor's: B.S.
Master's: M.S. with thesis
Doctoral: Ph.D.

UNDERGRADUATE INFORMATION

ESTIMATED STUDENT EXPENSES (FALL 2006)
[Expenses are for the 2006-2007 nine-month academic year and are based on an average credit load of: Undergraduate: 12]

	In-State	Out-of-State
Tutition and Fees:	$3,854	$7,840
Campus and Room and Board:	$5,477	$5,477
Books and Supplies:	$700	$700
Other Expenses:		
Total Estimated Expenses:	**$10,031**	**$14,017**

NEW APPLICANTS/NEWLY ENROLLED STUDENTS
[Numbers are for the undergraduate engineering college for the Fall 2006 term]

Number of Applicants (a):	1,078
Of those, Number Offered Admission (b):	1,034
Of those, Number Enrolled Fall 2006 (c):	690

GRADUATE INFORMATION

ESTIMATED STUDENT EXPENSES (FALL 2006)
[Expenses are for the 2006-2007 nine-month academic year and are based on an average credit load of: Graduate: 9]

	In-State	Out-of-State
Tutition and Fees:	$3,268	$8,302
Campus and Room and Board:	$5,477	$5,477
Books and Supplies:	$700	$700
Other Expenses:		
Total Estimated Expenses:	**$9,445**	**$14,479**

NEW APPLICANTS/NEWLY ENROLLED STUDENTS
[Numbers are for the graduate engineering college for the Fall 2006 term]

Number of Applicants (a):	235
Of those, Number Offered Admission (b):	83
Of those, Number Enrolled Fall 2006 (c):	19

University of North Florida

INSTITUTION INFORMATION
4567 St. Johns Bluff Road South
Jacksonville, FL 32224
Phone: (904) 620-1000
Web: http://www.unf.edu

GENERAL INFORMATION
[All Students - Fall 2006]

Undergraduate Enrollment	14,479
Graduate Enrollment	1,612
Professional Enrollment	0
Total Enrollment	**16,091**

ENGINEERING COLLEGE INFORMATION

HEAD OF ENGINEERING
Stephan J Nix
Director
School of Engineering
University of North Florida
4567 St. Johns Bluff Road South
Jacksonville, FL 32224
Phone: (904) 620-1390
Fax: (904) 620-1391
Email: snix@unf.edu

HEAD OF ENGINEERING
Neal S Coulter
Dean and Professor
College of Computing, Engineering, and Construction
University of North Florida
4567 St. Johns Bluff Road South
Jacksonville, FL 32224
Phone: (904) 620-1356
Fax: (904) 620-2385
Email: ncoulter@unf.edu

ENGINEERING COLLEGE INQUIRIES
Jean Fryman
Outreach and Recruiting Coordinator
University of North Florida
4567 St. Johns Bluff Road South
Jacksonville, FL 32224
Phone: (904) 620-1869
Fax: (904) 620-1391

TYPES OF ENGINEERING DEGREES
Bachelor's: B.S.
Master's:
Doctoral:

UNDERGRADUATE INFORMATION

ADMISSION INQUIRIES
Richard V Conte
Instructor/Advisor
University of North Florida
4567 St. Johns Bluff Road South
Jacksonville, FL 32224
Phone: (904) 620-1680
Fax: (904) 620-2975
Email: rconte@unf.edu

ESTIMATED STUDENT EXPENSES (FALL 2006)
[Expenses are for the 2006-2007 nine-month academic year

and are based on an average credit load of: Undergraduate: 14]

	All Students
Tuition and fees:	$3,268
Campus and Room and Board:	$6,640
Books and Supplies:	$800
Other Expenses:	$3,458
Total Estimated Expenses:	**$14,166**

Note: "Other expenses" include transportation and miscellaneous expenses.

NEW APPLICANTS/NEWLY ENROLLED STUDENTS

[Numbers are for the undergraduate engineering college for the Fall 2006 term]

Number of Applicants (a):	415
Of those, Number Offered Admission (b):	305
Of those, Number Enrolled Fall 2006 (c):	158

University of North Texas

INSTITUTION INFORMATION

College of Engineering
P.O. Box 310440
Denton, TX 76203
Phone: (940) 565-4201
Fax: (940) 369-8570
Web: http://www.eng.unt.edu

GENERAL INFORMATION

[All Students - Fall 2006]

Undergraduate Enrollment	26,598
Graduate Enrollment	6,845
Professional Enrollment	0
Total Enrollment	**33,443**

ENGINEERING COLLEGE INFORMATION

HEAD OF ENGINEERING

Oscar N Garcia
Founding Dean
College of Engineering
University of North Texas
P.O. Box 310440
Denton, TX 76203
Phone: (940) 565-4300
Fax: (940) 369-8570
Email: ogarcia@unt.edu

ENGINEERING COLLEGE INQUIRIES

Reza A Mirshams
Associate Dean for Academic Affairs/Professor
University of North Texas
Department of Engineering Technology, UNT Research Park, 3940 N. Elm St., Suite F115
Denton, TX 76207
Phone: (940) 565-2022
Fax: (940) 565-2666
Email: mirshams@unt.edu

TYPES OF ENGINEERING DEGREES

Bachelor's: B.A., B.S.
Master's: M.S. with thesis, M.S. without thesis, but with project or report
Doctoral: Ph.D.

UNDERGRADUATE INFORMATION

ESTIMATED STUDENT EXPENSES (FALL 2006)

[Expenses are for the 2006-2007 nine-month academic year and are based on an average credit load of: Undergraduate: 15]

	In-State	Out-of-State
Tuition and Fees:	$4,723	$11,347
Campus and Room and Board:	$6,108	$6,108
Books and Supplies:	$1,500	$1,500
Other Expenses:	$500	$500
Total Estimated Expenses:	**$12,831**	**$19,455**

NEW APPLICANTS/NEWLY ENROLLED STUDENTS

[Numbers are for the undergraduate engineering college for the Fall 2006 term]

Number of Applicants (a):	1,265
Of those, Number Offered Admission (b):	947
Of those, Number Enrolled Fall 2006 (c):	624

GRADUATE INFORMATION

ESTIMATED STUDENT EXPENSES (FALL 2006)

[Expenses are for the 2006-2007 nine-month academic year

---

and are based on an average credit load of: Graduate: 15]

	In-State	Out-of-State
Tuition and Fees:	$3,635	$8,603
Campus and Room and Board:		
Books and Supplies:	$2,000	$2,000
Other Expenses:	$500	$500
Total Estimated Expenses:	**$6,135**	**$11,103**

Northeastern University

INSTITUTION INFORMATION

College of Engineering
230 Snell Engineering Center
Boston, MA 02115-5000
Phone: (617) 373-2152
Fax: (617) 373-8504
Web: http://www.coe.neu.edu

GENERAL INFORMATION

[All Students - Fall 2006]

Undergraduate Enrollment	18,056
Graduate Enrollment	4,780
Professional Enrollment	1,381
Total Enrollment	**24,217**

ENGINEERING COLLEGE INFORMATION

HEAD OF ENGINEERING

Mohamad Metghalchi
Interim Dean
Engineering
Northeastern University
230 Snell Engineering Center
Northeastern University
Boston, MA 02115
Phone: (617) 373-2152
Fax: (617) 373-8504
Email: asoyster@coe.neu.edu

TYPES OF ENGINEERING DEGREES

Bachelor's: B.S.
Master's: M.S. with thesis, M.S. without thesis, but with project or report
Doctoral: Ph.D.

UNDERGRADUATE INFORMATION

ADMISSION INQUIRIES

Ronne Patrick Turner
Dean of Admissions
Northeastern University
150 Richards Hall
Boston, MA 02115
Phone: (617) 373-2200
Fax: (617) 373-8780
Email: r.patrick@neu.edu

ADMISSION INQUIRIES

David Navick
Associate Dean, Undergraduate Engineering Enrollment
Northeastern University
230 Snell Engineering Center
Boston, MA 02115-5000
Phone: (617) 373-2152
Fax: (617) 373-8504
Email: dnavick@coe.neu.edu

ESTIMATED STUDENT EXPENSES (FALL 2006)

[Expenses are for the 2006-2007 nine-month academic year and are based on an average credit load of: Undergraduate: 17]

	All Students
Tuition and fees:	$29,910
Campus and Room and Board:	$10,580
Books and Supplies:	$1,200
Other Expenses:	$1,350
Total Estimated Expenses:	**$43,040**

Note: Room & Board costs vary by residence hall and meal plan. Books, supplies, and other expenses are estimates.

NEW APPLICANTS/NEWLY ENROLLED STUDENTS

[Numbers are for the undergraduate engineering college for the Fall 2006 term]

Number of Applicants (a):	2,663
Of those, Number Offered Admission (b):	1,698
Of those, Number Enrolled Fall 2006 (c):	445

GRADUATE INFORMATION

ADMISSION INQUIRIES

Stephen L. Gibson
Associate Director
Northeastern University
130 Snell Engineering Center
Boston, MA 02115
Phone: (617) 373-2711
Fax: (617) 373-2501
Email: sgibson@coe.neu.edu

ESTIMATED STUDENT EXPENSES (FALL 2006)

[Expenses are for the 2006-2007 nine-month academic year and are based on an average credit load of: Graduate: 12]

	All Students
Tuition and fees:	$16,360
Campus and Room and Board:	$10,000
Books and Supplies:	$1,200
Other Expenses:	$1,800
Total Estimated Expenses:	**$29,360**

Note: Room & Board costs vary by residence hall and meal plan. Books, supplies, and other expenses are estimates.

NEW APPLICANTS/NEWLY ENROLLED STUDENTS

[Numbers are for the graduate engineering college for the Fall 2006 term]

Number of Applicants (a):	1,492
Of those, Number Offered Admission (b):	900
Of those, Number Enrolled Fall 2006 (c):	282

Northern Arizona University

INSTITUTION INFORMATION

S. San Francisco St.
Flagstaff, AZ 86011
Phone: (928) 523-9011
Fax: (928) 523-2300
Web: http://www.nau.edu

GENERAL INFORMATION

[All Students - Fall 2006]

Undergraduate Enrollment	14,526
Graduate Enrollment	6,036
Professional Enrollment	0
Total Enrollment	**20,562**

ENGINEERING COLLEGE INFORMATION

HEAD OF ENGINEERING

Laura Huenneke
Dean of the College
College Engineering and Natural Sciences
Northern Arizona University
P.O. Box 5621
Flagstaff, AZ 86011-5621
Phone: (928) 523-2701
Fax: (928) 523-0516
Email: laura.huenneke@nau.edu

TYPES OF ENGINEERING DEGREES

Bachelor's: B.S.
Master's: M.Eng.
Doctoral:

UNDERGRADUATE INFORMATION

ESTIMATED STUDENT EXPENSES (FALL 2006)

[Expenses are for the 2006-2007 nine-month academic year and are based on an average credit load of: Undergraduate: 16]

	In-State	Out-of-State
Tuition and Fees:	$4,546	$13,486
Campus and Room and Board:	$6,260	$6,260
Books and Supplies:	$828	$828
Other Expenses:	$3,700	$4,224
Total Estimated Expenses:	**$15,334**	**$24,798**

GRADUATE INFORMATION

ADMISSION INQUIRIES

F. Ernesto Penado
Campus Director of the M. Eng. Program
Northern Arizona University
P.O. Box 15600
Flagstaff, AZ 86011-1560
Phone: (928) 523-9453

Fax: (928) 523-2300
Email: Ernesto.Penado@nau.edu

ESTIMATED STUDENT EXPENSES (FALL 2006)
[Expenses are for the 2006-2007 nine-month academic year and are based on an average credit load of: Graduate: 9]

	In-State	Out-of-State
Tuition and Fees:	$4,898	$10,438
Campus and Room and Board:	$7,094	$7,094
Books and Supplies:	$828	$828
Other Expenses:	$4,132	$4,656
Total Estimated Expenses:	**$16,952**	**$23,016**

NEW APPLICANTS/NEWLY ENROLLED STUDENTS
[Numbers are for the graduate engineering college for the Fall 2006 term]

Number of Applicants (a):	15
Of those, Number Offered Admission (b):	12
Of those, Number Enrolled Fall 2006 (c):	3

Northern Illinois University

INSTITUTION INFORMATION
College of Eng. & Eng. Technology
EB Room 321
DeKalb, IL 60115
Phone: (815) 753-2256
Fax: (815) 753-1310
Web: http://www.ceet.niu.edu

GENERAL INFORMATION
[All Students - Fall 2006]

Undergraduate Enrollment	18,816
Graduate Enrollment	6,182
Professional Enrollment	315
Total Enrollment	**25,313**

ENGINEERING COLLEGE INFORMATION

HEAD OF ENGINEERING
Promod Vohra
Dean
College of Engineering and Engineering Technology
Northern Illinois University
Engineering Building
Room 321
DeKalb, IL 60115
Phone: (815) 753-1269
Fax: (815) 753-1310
Email: vohra@ceet.niu.edu

TYPES OF ENGINEERING DEGREES
Bachelor's: B.S.
Master's: M.S. with thesis, M.S. without thesis, but with project or report
Doctoral:

UNDERGRADUATE INFORMATION

ESTIMATED STUDENT EXPENSES (FALL 2006)
[Expenses are for the 2006-2007 nine-month academic year and are based on an average credit load of: Undergraduate: 15]

	In-State	Out-of-State
Tuition and Fees:	$7,781	$13,421
Campus and Room and Board:	$7,488	$7,488
Books and Supplies:	$1,200	$1,200
Other Expenses:	$2,704	$2,704
Total Estimated Expenses:	**$19,173**	**$24,813**

Note: Room and Board: costs for housing varies depending on meal plan chosen, residence hall type, and room type ($4890-$8410)
Other Expenses: for undergrads includes medical insurance, transportation and personal. For graduate includes health insurance only.
A Technology Fee of $200 has been added for all students.

NEW APPLICANTS/NEWLY ENROLLED STUDENTS
[Numbers are for the undergraduate engineering college for the Fall 2006 term]

Number of Applicants (a):	753
Of those, Number Offered Admission (b):	534
Of those, Number Enrolled Fall 2006 (c):	182

GRADUATE INFORMATION

ESTIMATED STUDENT EXPENSES (FALL 2006)
[Expenses are for the 2006-2007 nine-month academic year and are based on an average credit load of: Graduate: 12]

	In-State	Out-of-State
Tuition and Fees:	$7,196	$12,092
Campus and Room and Board:	$7,488	$7,488
Books and Supplies:	$1,200	$1,200
Other Expenses:	$2,704	$2,704
Total Estimated Expenses:	**$18,588**	**$23,484**

Note: Room and Board: costs for housing varies depending on meal plan chosen, residence hall type, and room type ($4890-$8410)
Other Expenses: for undergrads includes medical insurance, transportation and personal. For graduate includes health insurance only.
A Technology Fee of $200 has been added for all students.

NEW APPLICANTS/NEWLY ENROLLED STUDENTS
[Numbers are for the graduate engineering college for the Fall 2006 term]

Number of Applicants (a):	345
Of those, Number Offered Admission (b):	118
Of those, Number Enrolled Fall 2006 (c):	55

Northwestern University

INSTITUTION INFORMATION
McCormick School of Engineering & Applied Science
2145 Sheridan Road
Evanston, IL 60208-3102
Phone: (847) 491-7379
Fax: (847) 491-5341
Web: http://www.northwestern.edu

GENERAL INFORMATION
[All Students - Fall 2006]

Undergraduate Enrollment	8,454
Graduate Enrollment	7,749
Professional Enrollment	1,483
Total Enrollment	**17,686**

ENGINEERING COLLEGE INFORMATION

HEAD OF ENGINEERING
Julio M. Ottino
Dean
Office of the Dean
Northwestern University
McCormick School of Engineering & Applied Science
2145 Sheridan Road
Evanston, IL 60208-3100
Phone: (847) 491-5220
Fax: (847) 491-8539
Email: jm-ottino@northwestern.edu

TYPES OF ENGINEERING DEGREES
Bachelor's: B.S.
Master's: M.S. with thesis, M.S. without thesis, but with project or report
Doctoral: Ph.D.

UNDERGRADUATE INFORMATION

ADMISSION INQUIRIES
Carol Lunkenheimer
Dean, Undergraduate Admissions
Northwestern University
1801 Hinman Avenue
Evanston, IL 60208
Phone: (847) 491-7271
Email: clunk@northwestern.edu

ESTIMATED STUDENT EXPENSES (FALL 2006)
[Expenses are for the 2006-2007 nine-month academic year and are based on an average credit load of: Undergraduate: 4]

	All Students
Tuition and fees:	$33,408
Campus and Room and Board:	$10,266
Books and Supplies:	$1,488
Other Expenses:	$500
Total Estimated Expenses:	**$45,662**

NEW APPLICANTS/NEWLY ENROLLED STUDENTS
[Numbers are for the undergraduate engineering college for the Fall 2006 term]

Number of Applicants (a):	2,970
Of those, Number Offered Admission (b):	1,288
Of those, Number Enrolled Fall 2006 (c):	363

GRADUATE INFORMATION

ADMISSION INQUIRIES
Bruce A Lindvall
Assistant Dean for Graduate Studies
Northwestern University
McCormick School of Engineering & Applied Science,
2145 Sheridan Road
Evanston , IL 60208-3103
Phone: (847) 491-4547
Fax: (847) 491-5341
Email: b-lindvall@northwestern.edu

ADMISSION INQUIRIES
Joseph T Walsh
Senior Associate Dean
Northwestern University
McCormick School of Engineering & Applied Science,
2145 Sheridan Road
Evanston , IL 60208-3103
Phone: (847) 491-3553
Fax: (847) 491-5341
Email: graduate-engineering@northwestern.edu

ESTIMATED STUDENT EXPENSES (FALL 2006)
[Expenses are for the 2006-2007 nine-month academic year and are based on an average credit load of: Graduate: 4]

	All Students
Tuition and fees:	$33,408
Campus and Room and Board:	$14,848
Books and Supplies:	$1,823
Other Expenses:	$1,724
Total Estimated Expenses:	**$51,803**

NEW APPLICANTS/NEWLY ENROLLED STUDENTS
[Numbers are for the graduate engineering college for the Fall 2006 term]

Number of Applicants (a):	2,567
Of those, Number Offered Admission (b):	708
Of those, Number Enrolled Fall 2006 (c):	358

Norwich University

INSTITUTION INFORMATION
The David Crawford School of Engineering
158 Harmon Drive
Northfield, VT 05663-1099
Phone: (802) 485-2000
Fax: (802) 485-2580
Web: http://www.norwich.edu

GENERAL INFORMATION
[All Students - Fall 2006]

Undergraduate Enrollment	1,970
Graduate Enrollment	1,250
Professional Enrollment	0
Total Enrollment	**3,220**

ENGINEERING COLLEGE INFORMATION

HEAD OF ENGINEERING
Eugene Sevi
Interim Dean of Engineering
The David Crawford School of Engineering
Norwich University
158 Harmon Drive
Northfield, VT 05663-1099
Phone: (802) 485-2000
Fax: (802) 485-2580
Email: sevi@norwich.edu

TYPES OF ENGINEERING DEGREES
Bachelor's: B.S.
Master's: M.Eng.
Doctoral:

UNDERGRADUATE INFORMATION

ESTIMATED STUDENT EXPENSES (FALL 2006)
[Expenses are for the 2006-2007 nine-month academic year and are based on an average credit load of: Undergraduate: 17]

	All Students
Tuition and fees:	$21,696
Campus and Room and Board:	$7,964

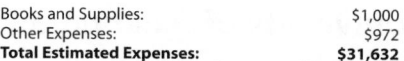

Books and Supplies: $1,000
Other Expenses: $972
Total Estimated Expenses: **$31,632**

NEW APPLICANTS/NEWLY ENROLLED STUDENTS
[Numbers are for the undergraduate engineering college for the Fall 2006 term]
Number of Applicants (a): 299
Of those, Number Offered Admission (b): 181
Of those, Number Enrolled Fall 2006 (c): 71

GRADUATE INFORMATION

ESTIMATED STUDENT EXPENSES (FALL 2006)
[Expenses are for the 2006-2007 nine-month academic year and are based on an average credit load of: Graduate: 6]

	All Students
Tutition and fees:	$12,150
Campus and Room and Board:	
Books and Supplies:	
Other Expenses:	
Total Estimated Expenses:	**$12,150**

University of Notre Dame

INSTITUTION INFORMATION
257 Fitzpatrick Hall
College of Engineering
Notre Dame, IN 46556
Phone: (574) 631-5531
Fax: (574) 631-8007
Web: http://www.nd.edu/~engineer

GENERAL INFORMATION
[All Students - Fall 2006]

Undergraduate Enrollment	8,427
Graduate Enrollment	1,898
Professional Enrollment	1,305
Total Enrollment	**11,630**

ENGINEERING COLLEGE INFORMATION

HEAD OF ENGINEERING
James L Merz
Dean
College of Engineering
University of Notre Dame
257 Fitzpatrick Hall of Engineering
Notre Dame, IN 46556
Phone: (574) 631-5534
Fax: (574) 631-8007
Email: jmerz@nd.edu

ENGINEERING COLLEGE INQUIRIES
Catherine F Pieronek
Director of Academic Affairs
University of Notre Dame
257 Fitzpatrick Hall
Notre Dame, IN 46556
Phone: (574) 631-4385
Fax: (574) 631-8007
Email: pieronek.1@nd.edu

TYPES OF ENGINEERING DEGREES
Bachelor's: B.S.
Master's: M.S. with thesis, M.S. without thesis, but with project or report
Doctoral: Ph.D.

UNDERGRADUATE INFORMATION

ADMISSION INQUIRIES
Daniel J Saracino
Assistant Provost, Enrollment
University of Notre Dame
220 Main
Notre Dame, IN 46556
Phone: (574) 631-7505
Fax: (574) 631-8865
Email: Daniel.J.Saracino.3@nd.edu

ESTIMATED STUDENT EXPENSES (FALL 2006)
[Expenses are for the 2006-2007 nine-month academic year and are based on an average credit load of: Undergraduate: 16]

	All Students
Tutition and fees:	$33,410
Campus and Room and Board:	$8,730
Books and Supplies:	$850

Other Expenses: $1,400
Total Estimated Expenses: **$44,390**

NEW APPLICANTS/NEWLY ENROLLED STUDENTS
[Numbers are for the undergraduate engineering college for the Fall 2006 term]
Number of Applicants (a): 12,800
Of those, Number Offered Admission (b): 3,484
Of those, Number Enrolled Fall 2006 (c): 2,061
Note: The number of engineering intents admitted was 552.

GRADUATE INFORMATION

ESTIMATED STUDENT EXPENSES (FALL 2006)
[Expenses are for the 2006-2007 nine-month academic year and are based on an average credit load of: Graduate: 9]

	All Students
Tutition and fees:	$32,800
Campus and Room and Board:	$7,250
Books and Supplies:	$1,255
Other Expenses:	$5,595
Total Estimated Expenses:	**$46,900**

NEW APPLICANTS/NEWLY ENROLLED STUDENTS
[Numbers are for the graduate engineering college for the Fall 2006 term]
Number of Applicants (a): 864
Of those, Number Offered Admission (b): 161
Of those, Number Enrolled Fall 2006 (c): 79

Oakland University

INSTITUTION INFORMATION
SECS
248 Dodge Hall of Engineering
Rochester, MI 48309
Phone: (248) 370-2212
Fax: (248) 370-4261
Web: http://www.oakland.edu

GENERAL INFORMATION
[All Students - Fall 2006]

Undergraduate Enrollment	13,701
Graduate Enrollment	4,036
Professional Enrollment	0
Total Enrollment	**17,737**

ENGINEERING COLLEGE INFORMATION

HEAD OF ENGINEERING
Pieter Frick
Professor and Dean
School of Engineering & Computer Science
Oakland University
248 Dodge Hall of Engineering
Rochester, MI 48309-4478
Phone: (248) 370-2217
Fax: (248) 370-4261
Email: frick@oakland.edu

TYPES OF ENGINEERING DEGREES
Bachelor's: B.S.
Master's: M.S. with thesis, M.S. without thesis, but with project or report
Doctoral: Ph.D.

UNDERGRADUATE INFORMATION

ESTIMATED STUDENT EXPENSES (FALL 2006)
[Expenses are for the 2006-2007 nine-month academic year and are based on an average credit load of: Undergraduate: 24]

	In-State	Out-of-State
Tutition and Fees:	$6,443	$12,306
Campus and Room and Board:	$6,385	$6,385
Books and Supplies:	$1,035	$1,035
Other Expenses:	$1,500	$1,500
Total Estimated Expenses:	**$15,363**	**$21,226**

GRADUATE INFORMATION

ESTIMATED STUDENT EXPENSES (FALL 2006)
[Expenses are for the 2006-2007 nine-month academic year and are based on an average credit load of: Graduate: 16]

	In-State	Out-of-State
Tutition and Fees:	$6,128	$10,660
Campus and Room and Board:	$6,385	$6,385
Books and Supplies:	$1,035	$1,035

Other Expenses: $1,500 $1,500
Total Estimated Expenses: **$15,048** **$19,580**

NEW APPLICANTS/NEWLY ENROLLED STUDENTS
[Numbers are for the graduate engineering college for the Fall 2006 term]
Number of Applicants (a): 226
Of those, Number Offered Admission (b): 203
Of those, Number Enrolled Fall 2006 (c): 0

Ohio Northern University

INSTITUTION INFORMATION
College of Engineering
525 S. Main St.
Ada, OH 45810
Phone: (419) 772-2371
Fax: (419) 772-2404
Web: http://www.onu.edu

GENERAL INFORMATION
[All Students - Fall 2006]

Undergraduate Enrollment	3,320
Graduate Enrollment	320
Professional Enrollment	0
Total Enrollment	**3,640**

ENGINEERING COLLEGE INFORMATION

HEAD OF ENGINEERING
Dr. Eric T. Baumgartner
Dean, Professor Mech Engineer
College of Engineering
Ohio Northern University
525 S. Main St.
Ada, OH 45810
Phone: (419) 772-2371
Fax: (419) 772-2404
Email: e-baumgartner@onu.edu

TYPES OF ENGINEERING DEGREES
Bachelor's: B.S.
Master's:
Doctoral:

UNDERGRADUATE INFORMATION

ESTIMATED STUDENT EXPENSES (FALL 2006)
[Expenses are for the 2006-2007 nine-month academic year and are based on an average credit load of: Undergraduate: 12]

	All Students
Tutition and fees:	$30,180
Campus and Room and Board:	$7,080
Books and Supplies:	$1,200
Other Expenses:	$1,800
Total Estimated Expenses:	**$40,260**

Note: Undergraduate Tuition includes a $70.00 per quarter technology fee. Graduate tuition (in Law) includes a $105 per semester technology fee.

NEW APPLICANTS/NEWLY ENROLLED STUDENTS
[Numbers are for the undergraduate engineering college for the Fall 2006 term]
Number of Applicants (a): 481
Of those, Number Offered Admission (b): 419
Of those, Number Enrolled Fall 2006 (c): 159
Note: ACT Composite is 25.8

GRADUATE INFORMATION

ESTIMATED STUDENT EXPENSES (FALL 2006)
[Expenses are for the 2006-2007 nine-month academic year and are based on an average credit load of: Graduate: 12]

	All Students
Tutition and fees:	$25,050
Campus and Room and Board:	$8,865
Books and Supplies:	$1,200
Other Expenses:	$3,150
Total Estimated Expenses:	**$38,265**

Note: Undergraduate Tuition includes a $70.00 per quarter technology fee. Graduate tuition (in Law) includes a $105 per semester technology fee.

The Ohio State University

INSTITUTION INFORMATION
Bricker Hall
190 N. Oval Mall
Columbus, OH 43210
Phone: (614) 292-2424
Fax: (614) 292-1231
Web: http://www.osu.edu

GENERAL INFORMATION
[All Students - Fall 2006]

Undergraduate Enrollment	45,417
Graduate Enrollment	10,418
Professional Enrollment	3,256
Total Enrollment	**59,091**

ENGINEERING COLLEGE INFORMATION

HEAD OF ENGINEERING
William A. Baeslack
Dean
College of Engineering
The Ohio State University
2070 Neil Avenue
142 Hitchcock Hall
Columbus, OH 43210
Phone: (614) 292-2836
Fax: (614) 292-9615
Email: Baeslack.1@osu.edu

TYPES OF ENGINEERING DEGREES
Bachelor's: B.S.
Master's: M.S. with thesis, M.S. without thesis, but with project or report
Doctoral: Ph.D.

UNDERGRADUATE INFORMATION

ESTIMATED STUDENT EXPENSES (FALL 2006)
[Expenses are for the 2006-2007 nine-month academic year and are based on an average credit load of: Undergraduate: 12]

	In-State	Out-of-State
Tuition and Fees:	$8,631	$20,526
Campus and Room and Board:	$7,704	$7,704
Books and Supplies:	$1,254	$1,254
Other Expenses:	$3,789	$3,789
Total Estimated Expenses:	**$21,378**	**$33,273**

NEW APPLICANTS/NEWLY ENROLLED STUDENTS
[Numbers are for the undergraduate engineering college for the Fall 2006 term]

Number of Applicants (a):	2,534
Of those, Number Offered Admission (b):	1,965
Of those, Number Enrolled Fall 2006 (c):	1,010

GRADUATE INFORMATION

ESTIMATED STUDENT EXPENSES (FALL 2006)
[Expenses are for the 2006-2007 nine-month academic year and are based on an average credit load of: Graduate: 10]

	In-State	Out-of-State
Tuition and Fees:	$9,426	$22,779
Campus and Room and Board:	$7,200	$7,200
Books and Supplies:	$1,254	$1,254
Other Expenses:	$6,360	$6,360
Total Estimated Expenses:	**$24,240**	**$37,593**

NEW APPLICANTS/NEWLY ENROLLED STUDENTS
[Numbers are for the graduate engineering college for the Fall 2006 term]

Number of Applicants (a):	2,255
Of those, Number Offered Admission (b):	631
Of those, Number Enrolled Fall 2006 (c):	255

Ohio University

INSTITUTION INFORMATION
150 Stocker Center
Athens, OH 45701
Phone: (740) 593-1474
Fax: (740) 593-0659
Web: http://www.ohio.edu/engineering/index.cfm

GENERAL INFORMATION
[All Students - Fall 2006]

Undergraduate Enrollment	16,468

Graduate Enrollment	3,061
Professional Enrollment	433
Total Enrollment	**19,962**

ENGINEERING COLLEGE INFORMATION

HEAD OF ENGINEERING
R. Dennis Irwin
Dean
Russ College of Engineering and Technology
Ohio University
150 Stocker Center
Athens, OH 45701
Phone: (740) 593-1474
Fax: (740) 593-0659
Email: irwind@ohio.edu

ENGINEERING COLLEGE INQUIRIES
Kendree J Sampson
Associate Dean
Ohio University
Stocker Engineering Center, 0157
Athens, OH 45701
Phone: (740) 593-1503
Fax: (740) 593-0659
Email: sampson@ohio.edu

TYPES OF ENGINEERING DEGREES
Bachelor's: B.S.
Master's: M.S. with thesis, M.S. without thesis, but with project or report
Doctoral: Ph.D.

UNDERGRADUATE INFORMATION

ADMISSION INQUIRIES
T. David Garcia
Director
Ohio University
120 Chubb Hall
Athens, OH 45701
Phone: (740) 593-4120
Fax: (740) 593-0659
Email: lewis@ohio.edu

ESTIMATED STUDENT EXPENSES (FALL 2006)
[Expenses are for the 2006-2007 nine-month academic year and are based on an average credit load of: Undergraduate: N/A]

	In-State	Out-of-State
Tuition and Fees:	$9,042	$18,006
Campus and Room and Board:	$7,839	$7,839
Books and Supplies:	$870	$870
Other Expenses:	$1,035	$1,035
Total Estimated Expenses:	**$18,786**	**$27,750**
Note: $1035 is for medical insurance

NEW APPLICANTS/NEWLY ENROLLED STUDENTS
[Numbers are for the undergraduate engineering college for the Fall 2006 term]

Number of Applicants (a):	643
Of those, Number Offered Admission (b):	521
Of those, Number Enrolled Fall 2006 (c):	280

Note: These data do not include 76 students admitted into Pre-Engineering. Pre-Engineering students meet the Ohio U. general admission requirements, however, do not meet the College's selective admission requirements; and must complete five courses (see undergraduate catalog) with C or better average prior to transferring into the College of Engineering.

GRADUATE INFORMATION

ESTIMATED STUDENT EXPENSES (FALL 2006)
[Expenses are for the 2006-2007 nine-month academic year and are based on an average credit load of: Graduate: N/A]

	In-State	Out-of-State
Tuition and Fees:	$9,618	$17,610
Campus and Room and Board:	$7,839	$7,839
Books and Supplies:	$870	$870
Other Expenses:	$1,035	$1,035
Total Estimated Expenses:	**$19,362**	**$27,354**
Note: $1035 is for medical insurance

NEW APPLICANTS/NEWLY ENROLLED STUDENTS
[Numbers are for the graduate engineering college for the Fall 2006 term]

Number of Applicants (a):	438
Of those, Number Offered Admission (b):	229
Of those, Number Enrolled Fall 2006 (c):	97

University of Oklahoma

INSTITUTION INFORMATION
202 West Boyd Street
Carson Engineering Center, Suite 107
Norman, OK 73019
Phone: (405) 325-2621
Fax: (405) 325-7508
Web: http://www.coe.ou.edu

GENERAL INFORMATION
[All Students - Fall 2006]

Undergraduate Enrollment	19,618
Graduate Enrollment	5,903
Professional Enrollment	499
Total Enrollment	**26,020**

ENGINEERING COLLEGE INFORMATION

HEAD OF ENGINEERING
Thomas L. Landers
Dean
College of Engineering
University of Oklahoma
202 West Boyd Street
Carson Engineering Center, Suite 107
Norman, OK 73019
Phone: (405) 325-2621
Fax: (405) 325-7508
Email: landers@ou.edu

TYPES OF ENGINEERING DEGREES
Bachelor's: B.S.
Master's: M.S. with thesis, M.S. without thesis, but with project or report
Doctoral: Ph.D.

UNDERGRADUATE INFORMATION

ADMISSION INQUIRIES
Patricia Lynch
Director, Admissions
University of Oklahoma
1000 Asp Avenue, Buchanan Hall, Room 127
Norman, OK 73019
Phone: (405) 325-2252
Fax: (405) 325-7124
Email: plynch@ou.edu

ESTIMATED STUDENT EXPENSES (FALL 2006)
[Expenses are for the 2006-2007 nine-month academic year and are based on an average credit load of: Undergraduate: 15]

	In-State	Out-of-State
Tuition and Fees:	$5,710	$13,999
Campus and Room and Board:	$6,863	$6,863
Books and Supplies:	$1,099	$1,099
Other Expenses:	$4,419	$4,419
Total Estimated Expenses:	**$18,091**	**$26,380**
Note: There are per credit hour fees, not included above, that range from $5-$25/credit hour depending on the college of the course.

Above expenses significantly higher for international students. Graduate Room and Board living off campus.

All Engineering students are required to purchase a laptop.

NEW APPLICANTS/NEWLY ENROLLED STUDENTS
[Numbers are for the undergraduate engineering college for the Fall 2006 term]

Number of Applicants (a):	1,332
Of those, Number Offered Admission (b):	1,060
Of those, Number Enrolled Fall 2006 (c):	547

GRADUATE INFORMATION

ADMISSION INQUIRIES
T.H. Lee Williams
Vice President, Research/Dean, Graduate College
University of Oklahoma
731 Elm Avenue, Robertson Hall, Room 100
Norman, OK 73019
Phone: (405) 325-3811
Fax: (405) 325-6029
Email: lwilliams@ou.edu

ESTIMATED STUDENT EXPENSES (FALL 2006)
[Expenses are for the 2006-2007 nine-month academic year

and are based on an average credit load of: Graduate: 12]

	In-State	Out-of-State
Tuition and Fees:	$5,389	$13,557
Campus and Room and Board:	$8,584	$8,584
Books and Supplies:	$1,099	$1,099
Other Expenses:	$4,419	$4,419
Total Estimated Expenses:	**$19,491**	**$27,659**

Note: There are per credit hour fees, not included above, that range from $5-$25/credit hour depending on the college of the course.

Above expenses significantly higher for international students. Graduate Room and Board living off campus.

All Engineering students are required to purchase a laptop.

NEW APPLICANTS/NEWLY ENROLLED STUDENTS
[Numbers are for the graduate engineering college for the Fall 2006 term]
Number of Applicants (a): 475
Of those, Number Offered Admission (b): 234
Of those, Number Enrolled Fall 2006 (c): 113

Oklahoma Christian University

INSTITUTION INFORMATION
PO Box 11000
Oklahoma City, OK 73136-1100
Phone: (405) 425-5000
Fax: (405) 425-5069
Web: http://www.oc.edu

GENERAL INFORMATION
[All Students - Fall 2006]
Undergraduate Enrollment 1,876
Graduate Enrollment 244
Professional Enrollment 0
Total Enrollment **2,120**

ENGINEERING COLLEGE INFORMATION

HEAD OF ENGINEERING
Robert Mitchell
Associate Dean for Engineering
School of Engineering
Oklahoma Christian University
PO Box 11000
Oklahoma City, OK 73136-1100
Phone: (405) 425-5425
Fax: (405) 425-5446
Email: robert.mitchell@oc.edu

ENGINEERING COLLEGE INQUIRIES
MaryAnn Brown
Administrative Assistant
Oklahoma Christian University
PO Box 11000
Oklahoma City, OK 73136-1100
Phone: (405) 425-5400
Fax: (405) 425-5446
Email: maryann.brown@oc.edu

TYPES OF ENGINEERING DEGREES
Bachelor's: B.S.
Master's:
Doctoral:

UNDERGRADUATE INFORMATION

ADMISSION INQUIRIES
Brent Williams
Engineering Admissions Specialist
Oklahoma Christian University
PO Box 11000
Oklahoma City, OK 73136-1100
Phone: (405) 425-5081
Fax: (405) 425-5069
Email: brent.williams@oc.edu

ESTIMATED STUDENT EXPENSES (FALL 2006)
[Expenses are for the 2006-2007 nine-month academic year and are based on an average credit load of: Undergraduate: 16]

	All Students
Tuition and fees:	$14,966
Campus and Room and Board:	$5,510
Books and Supplies:	$1,000

Other Expenses:
Total Estimated Expenses: **$21,476**

NEW APPLICANTS/NEWLY ENROLLED STUDENTS
[Numbers are for the undergraduate engineering college for the Fall 2006 term]
Number of Applicants (a): 182
Of those, Number Offered Admission (b): 182
Of those, Number Enrolled Fall 2006 (c): 78

Oklahoma State University

INSTITUTION INFORMATION
Dean, College of Engineering, Arch & Technology
201 Advanced Technology Research Center
Stillwater, OK 74078
Phone: (405) 744-5140
Fax: (405) 744-7545
Web: http://ceat.okstate.edu

GENERAL INFORMATION
[All Students - Fall 2006]
Undergraduate Enrollment 18,737
Graduate Enrollment 4,262
Professional Enrollment 308
Total Enrollment **23,307**

ENGINEERING COLLEGE INFORMATION

HEAD OF ENGINEERING
Karl N Reid
Dean
College of Engineering, Architecture, and Technology
Oklahoma State University
201 Advanced Technology Research Center
Stillwater, OK 74078
Phone: (405) 744-5140
Fax: (405) 744-7545
Email: kreid@okstate.edu

TYPES OF ENGINEERING DEGREES
Bachelor's: B.S.
Master's: M.S. with thesis, M.S. without thesis, but with project or report
Doctoral: Ph.D.

UNDERGRADUATE INFORMATION

ESTIMATED STUDENT EXPENSES (FALL 2006)
[Expenses are for the 2006-2007 nine-month academic year and are based on an average credit load of: Undergraduate: 15]

	In-State	Out-of-State
Tuition and Fees:	$5,530	$14,100
Campus and Room and Board:	$5,848	$5,848
Books and Supplies:	$880	$880
Other Expenses:	$3,810	$3,810
Total Estimated Expenses:	**$16,068**	**$24,638**

NEW APPLICANTS/NEWLY ENROLLED STUDENTS
[Numbers are for the undergraduate engineering college for the Fall 2006 term]
Number of Applicants (a): 841
Of those, Number Offered Admission (b): 731
Of those, Number Enrolled Fall 2006 (c): 464

GRADUATE INFORMATION

ADMISSION INQUIRIES
Gordon Emsley
Dean
Oklahoma State University
202 Whitehurst
Stillwater, OK 74078
Phone: (405) 744-6368
Fax: (405) 744-0355

ESTIMATED STUDENT EXPENSES (FALL 2006)
[Expenses are for the 2006-2007 nine-month academic year and are based on an average credit load of: Graduate: 9]

	In-State	Out-of-State
Tuition and Fees:	$6,840	$10,062
Campus and Room and Board:	$5,848	$5,848
Books and Supplies:	$1,250	$1,250
Other Expenses:	$3,810	$3,810
Total Estimated Expenses:	**$17,748**	**$20,970**

NEW APPLICANTS/NEWLY ENROLLED STUDENTS
[Numbers are for the graduate engineering college for the Fall 2006 term]
Number of Applicants (a): 999
Of those, Number Offered Admission (b): 455
Of those, Number Enrolled Fall 2006 (c): 150

Old Dominion University

INSTITUTION INFORMATION
Frank Batten College of Engineering and Technology
Dean's Office
Kaufman Hall Rm 102
Norfolk, VA 23529
Phone: (757) 683-3787
Fax: (757) 683-4898
Web: http://www.eng.odu.edu

GENERAL INFORMATION
[All Students - Fall 2006]
Undergraduate Enrollment 14,209
Graduate Enrollment 6,593
Professional Enrollment 0
Total Enrollment **20,802**

ENGINEERING COLLEGE INFORMATION

HEAD OF ENGINEERING
Oktay Baysal
Dean
Frank Batten College of Engineering and Technology
Old Dominion University
Frank Batten College of Engineering and Technology
Kaufman Hall Room 102
Norfolk, VA 23529
Phone: (757) 683-3789
Fax: (757) 683-4898
Email: obaysal@odu.edu

ENGINEERING COLLEGE INQUIRIES
Berndt H Bohm
Assistant Dean
Old Dominion University
Kaufman Hall Rm 102
Norfolk, VA 23529
Phone: (757) 683-4245
Fax: (757) 683-4898
Email: bbohm@odu.edu

TYPES OF ENGINEERING DEGREES
Bachelor's: B.S.
Master's: M.S. with thesis
Doctoral: Ph.D.

UNDERGRADUATE INFORMATION

ADMISSION INQUIRIES
Admission Office
Old Dominion University
108 Alfred B. Rollins, Jr. Hall
Norfolk, VA 23529
Phone: (757) 683-3685
Fax: (757) 683-3255

ESTIMATED STUDENT EXPENSES (FALL 2006)
[Expenses are for the 2006-2007 nine-month academic year and are based on an average credit load of: Undergraduate: 15]

	In-State	Out-of-State
Tuition and Fees:	$3,049	$8,329
Campus and Room and Board:	$6,640	$6,640
Books and Supplies:	$600	$600
Other Expenses:	$1,000	$1,000
Total Estimated Expenses:	**$11,289**	**$16,569**

NEW APPLICANTS/NEWLY ENROLLED STUDENTS
[Numbers are for the undergraduate engineering college for the Fall 2006 term]
Number of Applicants (a): 899
Of those, Number Offered Admission (b): 600
Of those, Number Enrolled Fall 2006 (c): 330
Note: Data not available

GRADUATE INFORMATION
Old Dominion University
108 Alfred B. Rollins, Jr. Hall
Norfolk, VA 23529
Phone: (757) 683-3685

Fax: (757) 683-3255
Email: gradadmit@odu.edu

ESTIMATED STUDENT EXPENSES (FALL 2006)
[Expenses are for the 2006-2007 nine-month academic year and are based on an average credit load of: Graduate: 12]

	In-State	Out-of-State
Tuition and Fees:	$3,514	$8,674
Campus and Room and Board:	$7,700	$7,700
Books and Supplies:	$600	$600
Other Expenses:	$1,000	$1,000
Total Estimated Expenses:	**$12,814**	**$17,974**

NEW APPLICANTS/NEWLY ENROLLED STUDENTS
[Numbers are for the graduate engineering college for the Fall 2006 term]

Number of Applicants (a):	505
Of those, Number Offered Admission (b):	221
Of those, Number Enrolled Fall 2006 (c):	179

OGI School of Science & Engineering at OHSU

INSTITUTION INFORMATION
20000 NW Walker Rd.
Beaverton, OR 97006-8921
Phone: (503) 748-1121
Fax: (503) 748-7056
Web: http://www.ogi.edu/

GENERAL INFORMATION
[All Students - Fall 2006]

Undergraduate Enrollment	0
Graduate Enrollment	293
Professional Enrollment	0
Total Enrollment	**293**

ENGINEERING COLLEGE INFORMATION

HEAD OF ENGINEERING
Edward W Thompson
Dean
Dean
OGI School of Science & Engineering at OHSU
20000 NW Walker Road
Beaverton, OR 97006
Phone: (503) 748-1358
Fax: (503) 748-7056
Email: thompsed@ohsu.edu

HEAD OF ENGINEERING
James J Huntzicker
Associate Dean
Management in Science and Technology and Center for Professional Development
OGI School of Science & Engineering at OHSU
20000 NW Walker Rd.
Beaverton, OR 97006
Phone: (503) 748-1028
Fax: (503) 748-1686
Email: huntzicj@ohsu.edu

TYPES OF ENGINEERING DEGREES
Bachelor's:
Master's: M.S. with thesis, M.S. without thesis, but with project or report
Doctoral: Ph.D.

GRADUATE INFORMATION

ADMISSION INQUIRIES
Amy Johnson
Graduate Education Manager
OGI School of Science & Engineering at OHSU
20000 NW Walker Rd.
Beaverton , OR 97006-8921
Phone: (503) 748-1028
Fax: (503) 748-1285
Email: johnsamy@ohsu.edu

ESTIMATED STUDENT EXPENSES (FALL 2006)
[Expenses are for the 2006-2007 nine-month academic year and are based on an average credit load of: Graduate: 9]

	All Students
Tuition and fees:	$23,060
Campus and Room and Board:	$6,000
Books and Supplies:	$1,200
Other Expenses:	

Total Estimated Expenses: $30,260
Note: All expenses are for four (4) academic quarters.

NEW APPLICANTS/NEWLY ENROLLED STUDENTS
[Numbers are for the graduate engineering college for the Fall 2006 term]

Number of Applicants (a):	125
Of those, Number Offered Admission (b):	58
Of those, Number Enrolled Fall 2006 (c):	27

Oregon Institute of Technology

INSTITUTION INFORMATION
3201 Campus Drive
Klamath Falls, OR 97601-8801
Phone: (541) 885-1000
Fax: (541) 885-1853
Web: http://www.oit.edu

GENERAL INFORMATION
[All Students - Fall 2006]

Undergraduate Enrollment	3,145
Graduate Enrollment	12
Professional Enrollment	0
Total Enrollment	**3,157**

ENGINEERING COLLEGE INFORMATION

HEAD OF ENGINEERING
Gary J Naseth
Associate Provost
Academic Affairs
Oregon Institute of Technology
3201 Campus Drive
Snell Hall 213
Klamath Falls, OR 97601-8801
Phone: (541) 885-1584
Fax: (541) 885-1853
Email: gary.naseth@oit.edu

ENGINEERING COLLEGE INQUIRIES
Sean W St. Clair
Assistant Professor
Oregon Institute of Technology
3201 Campus Drive, Owens Hall 107
Klamath Falls, OR 97601-8801
Phone: (541) 885-1602
Fax: (541) 885-1654
Email: sean.stclair@oit.edu

TYPES OF ENGINEERING DEGREES
Bachelor's: B.S.
Master's:
Doctoral:

UNDERGRADUATE INFORMATION

ESTIMATED STUDENT EXPENSES (FALL 2006)
[Expenses are for the 2006-2007 nine-month academic year and are based on an average credit load of: Undergraduate: 14]

	In-State	Out-of-State
Tuition and Fees:	$5,618	$13,356
Campus and Room and Board:	$7,552	$7,552
Books and Supplies:	$1,200	$1,200
Other Expenses:	$2,300	$2,300
Total Estimated Expenses:	**$16,670**	**$24,408**

NEW APPLICANTS/NEWLY ENROLLED STUDENTS
[Numbers are for the undergraduate engineering college for the Fall 2006 term]

Number of Applicants (a):	59
Of those, Number Offered Admission (b):	54
Of those, Number Enrolled Fall 2006 (c):	27

Oregon State University

INSTITUTION INFORMATION
101 Covell Hall
College of Engineering
Corvallis, OR 97331
Phone: (541) 737-3101
Fax: (541) 737-1805
Web: http://www.oregonstate.edu

GENERAL INFORMATION
[All Students - Fall 2006]

Undergraduate Enrollment	15,829
Graduate Enrollment	3,001
Professional Enrollment	532
Total Enrollment	**19,362**

ENGINEERING COLLEGE INFORMATION

HEAD OF ENGINEERING
Ronald L Adams
Dean of Engineering
College of Engineering
Oregon State University
101 Covell Hall
Corvallis, OR 97331-2409
Phone: (541) 737-7722
Fax: (541) 737-1805
Email: Ronald.Lynn.Adams@oregonstate.edu

TYPES OF ENGINEERING DEGREES
Bachelor's: B.S.
Master's: M.S. with thesis, M.S. without thesis, but with project or report, M.Eng.
Doctoral: Ph.D.

UNDERGRADUATE INFORMATION

ESTIMATED STUDENT EXPENSES (FALL 2006)
[Expenses are for the 2006-2007 nine-month academic year and are based on an average credit load of: Undergraduate: 15]

	In-State	Out-of-State
Tuition and Fees:	$6,933	$18,849
Campus and Room and Board:	$7,344	$7,344
Books and Supplies:	$1,443	$1,443
Other Expenses:	$2,328	$2,328
Total Estimated Expenses:	**$18,048**	**$29,964**

NEW APPLICANTS/NEWLY ENROLLED STUDENTS
[Numbers are for the undergraduate engineering college for the Fall 2006 term]

Number of Applicants (a):	1,975
Of those, Number Offered Admission (b):	1,569
Of those, Number Enrolled Fall 2006 (c):	964

GRADUATE INFORMATION

ESTIMATED STUDENT EXPENSES (FALL 2006)
[Expenses are for the 2006-2007 nine-month academic year and are based on an average credit load of: Graduate: 15]

	In-State	Out-of-State
Tuition and Fees:	$11,469	$16,989
Campus and Room and Board:	$7,344	$7,344
Books and Supplies:	$1,443	$1,443
Other Expenses:	$2,328	$2,328
Total Estimated Expenses:	**$22,584**	**$28,104**

NEW APPLICANTS/NEWLY ENROLLED STUDENTS
[Numbers are for the graduate engineering college for the Fall 2006 term]

Number of Applicants (a):	1,111
Of those, Number Offered Admission (b):	511
Of those, Number Enrolled Fall 2006 (c):	206

University of Ottawa, Faculty of Engineering

INSTITUTION INFORMATION
161 Louis Pasteur
Ottawa, ON K1N 6N5
Phone: (613) 562-5800
Fax: (613) 562-5517
Web: http://www.eng.uottawa.ca

GENERAL INFORMATION
[All Students - Fall 2006]

Undergraduate Enrollment	28,324
Graduate Enrollment	4,143
Professional Enrollment	0
Total Enrollment	**32,467**

ENGINEERING COLLEGE INFORMATION

HEAD OF ENGINEERING
Claude Laguë
Dean and Professor

Faculty of Engineering
University of Ottawa
161 Louis Pasteur
Ottawa, ON K1N 6N5
Phone: (613) 562-5800
Fax: (613) 562-5174
Email: claude.lague@uottawa.ca

ENGINEERING COLLEGE INQUIRIES
Line Roy
Assistant to the Dean, HR
University of Ottawa
161 Louis Pasteur
Ottawa, ON K1N 6N5
Phone: (613) 562-5800
Fax: (613) 562-5174
Email: lroy@uottawa.ca

TYPES OF ENGINEERING DEGREES
Bachelor's: B.S.
Master's: M.S. with thesis, M.Eng.
Doctoral: Ph.D.

UNDERGRADUATE INFORMATION

ADMISSION INQUIRIES
Isabelle Mayrand
Academic Administrator
University of Ottawa, Faculty of Engineering
800 King Edward Avenue
Ottawa, ON K1N 6N5
Phone: (613) 562-5800
Fax: (613) 562-5187
Email: isabelle.mayrand@uottawa.ca

ESTIMATED STUDENT EXPENSES (FALL 2006)
[Expenses are for the 2006-2007 nine-month academic year and are based on an average credit load of: Undergraduate: 3000]

	All Students
Tutition and fees:	$5,923
Campus and Room and Board:	$6,352
Books and Supplies:	$1,000
Other Expenses:	$948
Total Estimated Expenses:	**$14,223**

NEW APPLICANTS/NEWLY ENROLLED STUDENTS
[Numbers are for the undergraduate engineering college for the Fall 2006 term]

Number of Applicants (a):	3,570
Of those, Number Offered Admission (b):	1,760
Of those, Number Enrolled Fall 2006 (c):	410

GRADUATE INFORMATION

ADMISSION INQUIRIES
Murat Saatcioglu
Vice-Dean, Research and Development
University of Ottawa, Faculty of Engineering
161 Louis Pasteur
Ottawa , ON K1N 6N5
Phone: (613) 562-5800
Fax: (613) 562-5129
Email: muratsaatcioglu@uottawa.ca

ESTIMATED STUDENT EXPENSES (FALL 2006)
[Expenses are for the 2006-2007 nine-month academic year and are based on an average credit load of: Graduate: 2500]

	All Students
Tutition and fees:	$4,485
Campus and Room and Board:	$6,352
Books and Supplies:	$1,000
Other Expenses:	$948
Total Estimated Expenses:	**$12,785**

NEW APPLICANTS/NEWLY ENROLLED STUDENTS
[Numbers are for the graduate engineering college for the Fall 2006 term]

Number of Applicants (a):	878
Of those, Number Offered Admission (b):	364
Of those, Number Enrolled Fall 2006 (c):	150

University of the Pacific

INSTITUTION INFORMATION
3601 Pacific Avenue
School of Engineering & Computer Science
Stockton, CA 95211
Phone: (209) 946-2151

Fax: (209) 946-3086
Web: http://www.pacific.edu

GENERAL INFORMATION
[All Students - Fall 2006]

Undergraduate Enrollment	3,535
Graduate Enrollment	584
Professional Enrollment	2,132
Total Enrollment	**6,251**

ENGINEERING COLLEGE INFORMATION

HEAD OF ENGINEERING
Ravi Jain
Dean
School of Engineering & Computer Science
University of the Pacific
3601 Pacific Avenue
Baun Hall 3rd Floor
Stockton, CA 95211
Phone: (209) 946-3066
Fax: (209) 946-3086
Email: rjain@pacific.edu

ENGINEERING COLLEGE INQUIRIES
Gary R. Martin
Professor and Assistant Dean
University of the Pacific
3601 Pacific Avenue, Baun Hall 105
Stockton, CA 95211
Phone: (209) 946-3064
Fax: (209) 946-2682
Email: gmartin@pacific.edu

ENGINEERING COLLEGE INQUIRIES
Calvin Chen
Coordinator of Cooperative Education & Asst. Professor
University of the Pacific
3601 Pacific Avenue, Baun Hall
Stockton, CA 95211
Phone: (209) 946-3062
Fax: (209) 946-2682
Email: cchen1@pacific.edu

TYPES OF ENGINEERING DEGREES
Bachelor's: B.S.
Master's:
Doctoral:

UNDERGRADUATE INFORMATION

ESTIMATED STUDENT EXPENSES (FALL 2006)
[Expenses are for the 2006-2007 nine-month academic year and are based on an average credit load of: Undergraduate: 16]

	All Students
Tutition and fees:	$26,920
Campus and Room and Board:	$8,700
Books and Supplies:	$1,250
Other Expenses:	$430
Total Estimated Expenses:	**$37,300**

NEW APPLICANTS/NEWLY ENROLLED STUDENTS
[Numbers are for the undergraduate engineering college for the Fall 2006 term]

Number of Applicants (a):	480
Of those, Number Offered Admission (b):	402
Of those, Number Enrolled Fall 2006 (c):	101

GRADUATE INFORMATION

ESTIMATED STUDENT EXPENSES (FALL 2006)
[Expenses are for the 2006-2007 nine-month academic year and are based on an average credit load of: Graduate: N/A]

	All Students
Tutition and fees:	$26,920
Campus and Room and Board:	
Books and Supplies:	
Other Expenses:	
Total Estimated Expenses:	**$26,920**

University of Pennsylvania

INSTITUTION INFORMATION
School of Engineering and Applied Science
220 South 33rd Street
Philadelphia, PA 19104

Phone: (215) 898-7246
Fax: (215) 573-5577
Web: http://www.seas.upenn.edu

GENERAL INFORMATION
[All Students - Fall 2006]

Undergraduate Enrollment	11,922
Graduate Enrollment	11,821
Professional Enrollment	0
Total Enrollment	**23,743**

ENGINEERING COLLEGE INFORMATION

HEAD OF ENGINEERING
Eduardo D Glandt
Dean
School of Engineering and Applied Science
University of Pennsylvania
Office of the Dean
220 S. 33rd Street, 107 Towne Bldg.
Philadelphia, PA 19104
Phone: (215) 898-7244
Fax: (215) 573-2018
Email: eglandt@seas.upenn.edu

ENGINEERING COLLEGE INQUIRIES
Joseph S Sun
Director of Academic Affairs
University of Pennsylvania
School of Engineering and Applied Science, 220 South 33rd Street, 111 Towne
Philadelphia, PA 19104
Phone: (215) 898-7246
Fax: (215) 573-5577
Email: sunj@seas.upenn.edu

TYPES OF ENGINEERING DEGREES
Bachelor's: B.A., B.S.
Master's: M.S. with thesis, M.S. without thesis, but with project or report
Doctoral: Ph.D.

UNDERGRADUATE INFORMATION

ADMISSION INQUIRIES
Ellen M. Eckert
Associate Director for Admissions and Advising
University of Pennsylvania
School of Engineering and Applied Science, 220 S. 33rd Street, 111 Towne Bldg.
Philadelphia, PA 19104
Phone: (215) 898-4813
Fax: (215) 573-5577
Email: eckertel@seas.upenn.edu

ESTIMATED STUDENT EXPENSES (FALL 2006)
[Expenses are for the 2006-2007 nine-month academic year and are based on an average credit load of: Undergraduate: 4]

	All Students
Tutition and fees:	$34,156
Campus and Room and Board:	$9,804
Books and Supplies:	$900
Other Expenses:	$1,720
Total Estimated Expenses:	**$46,580**

NEW APPLICANTS/NEWLY ENROLLED STUDENTS
[Numbers are for the undergraduate engineering college for the Fall 2006 term]

Number of Applicants (a):	2,840
Of those, Number Offered Admission (b):	765
Of those, Number Enrolled Fall 2006 (c):	408

GRADUATE INFORMATION

ADMISSION INQUIRIES
Joseph S Sun
Director of Academic Affairs
University of Pennsylvania
School of Engineering and Applied Science, 220 South 33rd Street, 111 Towne
Philadelphia , PA 19104
Phone: (215) 898-7246
Fax: (215) 573-5577
Email: sunj@seas.upenn.edu

ESTIMATED STUDENT EXPENSES (FALL 2006)
[Expenses are for the 2006-2007 nine-month academic year and are based on an average credit load of: Graduate: 4]

	All Students
Tutition and fees:	$35,180

Campus and Room and Board:	$14,400
Books and Supplies:	$1,882
Other Expenses:	$4,830
Total Estimated Expenses:	**$56,292**

NEW APPLICANTS/NEWLY ENROLLED STUDENTS
[Numbers are for the graduate engineering college for the Fall 2006 term]

Number of Applicants (a):	2,555
Of those, Number Offered Admission (b):	826
Of those, Number Enrolled Fall 2006 (c):	334

Penn State Erie, The Behrend College

INSTITUTION INFORMATION
School of Engineering
5101 Jordan Road
Erie, PA 16563-1701
Phone: (814) 898-6153
Fax: (814) 898-6125
Web: http://behrend.psu.edu/engineering

GENERAL INFORMATION
[All Students - Fall 2006]

Undergraduate Enrollment	3,675
Graduate Enrollment	164
Professional Enrollment	0
Total Enrollment	**3,839**

ENGINEERING COLLEGE INFORMATION

HEAD OF ENGINEERING
Ralph M Ford
Director
School of Engineering
Penn State Erie, The Behrend College
5101 Jordan Road
Erie, PA 16563-1701
Phone: (814) 898-6153
Fax: (814) 898-6125
Email: rmf7@psu.edu

ENGINEERING COLLEGE INQUIRIES
Sherry C Johnson
Staff Assistant
Penn State Erie, The Behrend College
5101 Jordan Road
Erie, PA 16563-1701
Phone: (814) 898-6316
Fax: (814) 898-6125
Email: sdc4@psu.edu

TYPES OF ENGINEERING DEGREES
Bachelor's: B.S.
Master's:
Doctoral:

UNDERGRADUATE INFORMATION

ADMISSION INQUIRIES
Mary-Ellen Madigan
Director, Admissions and Financial Aid
Penn State Erie, The Behrend College
Glenhill Farmhouse, 4701 College Drive
Erie, PA 16563-1701
Phone: (814) 898-6100
Fax: (814) 898-6044
Email: mea1@psu.edu

ESTIMATED STUDENT EXPENSES (FALL 2006)
[Expenses are for the 2006-2007 nine-month academic year and are based on an average credit load of: Undergraduate: N/A]

	In-State	Out-of-State
Tuition and Fees:	$10,446	$15,994
Campus and Room and Board:	$6,850	$6,850
Books and Supplies:	$1,100	$1,100
Other Expenses:		
Total Estimated Expenses:	**$18,396**	**$23,944**

NEW APPLICANTS/NEWLY ENROLLED STUDENTS
[Numbers are for the undergraduate engineering college for the Fall 2006 term]

Number of Applicants (a):	620
Of those, Number Offered Admission (b):	527
Of those, Number Enrolled Fall 2006 (c):	300

GRADUATE INFORMATION

ESTIMATED STUDENT EXPENSES (FALL 2006)
[Expenses are for the 2006-2007 nine-month academic year and are based on an average credit load of: Graduate: N/A]

	In-State	Out-of-State
Tuition and Fees:	$13,972	$19,488
Campus and Room and Board:		
Books and Supplies:		
Other Expenses:		
Total Estimated Expenses:	**$13,972**	**$19,488**

The Pennsylvania State University

INSTITUTION INFORMATION
College of Engineering
101 Hammond Building
University Park, PA 16802
Phone: (814) 865-7537
Fax: (814) 863-0497
Web: http://www.engr.psu.edu

GENERAL INFORMATION
[All Students - Fall 2006]

Undergraduate Enrollment	66,173
Graduate Enrollment	9,793
Professional Enrollment	1,186
Total Enrollment	**77,152**

ENGINEERING COLLEGE INFORMATION

HEAD OF ENGINEERING
David N Wormley
Dean of Engineering
College of Engineering
The Pennsylvania State University
101 Hammond Building
University Park, PA 16802
Phone: (814) 865-7538
Fax: (814) 865-8767
Email: dnwdo@engr.psu.edu

TYPES OF ENGINEERING DEGREES
Bachelor's: B.A., B.S.
Master's: M.S. with thesis
Doctoral: Ph.D.

UNDERGRADUATE INFORMATION

ESTIMATED STUDENT EXPENSES (FALL 2006)
[Expenses are for the 2006-2007 nine-month academic year and are based on an average credit load of: Undergraduate: 12]

	In-State	Out-of-State
Tuition and Fees:	$12,851	$24,021
Campus and Room and Board:	$7,400	$7,400
Books and Supplies:	$1,360	$1,360
Other Expenses:		
Total Estimated Expenses:	**$21,611**	**$32,781**

NEW APPLICANTS/NEWLY ENROLLED STUDENTS
[Numbers are for the undergraduate engineering college for the Fall 2006 term]

Number of Applicants (a):	3,769
Of those, Number Offered Admission (b):	2,184
Of those, Number Enrolled Fall 2006 (c):	1,179

GRADUATE INFORMATION

ADMISSION INQUIRIES
Cynthia Nicosia
Director of Graduate Admissions and Programs
The Pennsylvania State University
114 Kern Graduate Building
University Park , PA 16802
Phone: (814) 865-2519
Email: cey1@psu.edu

ESTIMATED STUDENT EXPENSES (FALL 2006)
[Expenses are for the 2006-2007 nine-month academic year and are based on an average credit load of: Graduate: 9]

	In-State	Out-of-State
Tuition and Fees:	$14,490	$25,418
Campus and Room and Board:	$8,575	$8,575
Books and Supplies:	$1,500	$1,500
Other Expenses:		
Total Estimated Expenses:	**$24,565**	**$35,493**

NEW APPLICANTS/NEWLY ENROLLED STUDENTS
[Numbers are for the graduate engineering college for the Fall 2006 term]

Number of Applicants (a):	3,699
Of those, Number Offered Admission (b):	1,288
Of those, Number Enrolled Fall 2006 (c):	426

Philadelphia University

INSTITUTION INFORMATION
Philadelphia, PA 19144
Phone: (215) 595-1275
Fax: (215) 595-2651
Web: www.philau.edu/

GENERAL INFORMATION
[All Students - Fall 2006]

Undergraduate Enrollment	2,748
Graduate Enrollment	509
Professional Enrollment	0
Total Enrollment	**3,257**

ENGINEERING COLLEGE INFORMATION

HEAD OF ENGINEERING
David Brookstein
Dean and Professor of Engineering
School of Engineering & Textiles
Philadelphia University
School House Lane and Henry Avenue
Philadelphia, PA 19144
Phone: (215) 951-2751
Fax: (215) 951-2751
Email: brooksteind@philau.edu

TYPES OF ENGINEERING DEGREES
Bachelor's: B.S.
Master's: M.S. with thesis
Doctoral: Ph.D.

UNDERGRADUATE INFORMATION

ESTIMATED STUDENT EXPENSES (FALL 2006)
[Expenses are for the 2006-2007 nine-month academic year and are based on an average credit load of: Undergraduate: 15]

	All Students
Tuition and fees:	$23,818
Campus and Room and Board:	$8,212
Books and Supplies:	$1,200
Other Expenses:	$1,284
Total Estimated Expenses:	**$34,514**

NEW APPLICANTS/NEWLY ENROLLED STUDENTS
[Numbers are for the undergraduate engineering college for the Fall 2006 term]

Number of Applicants (a):	135
Of those, Number Offered Admission (b):	70
Of those, Number Enrolled Fall 2006 (c):	15

GRADUATE INFORMATION

ESTIMATED STUDENT EXPENSES (FALL 2006)
[Expenses are for the 2006-2007 nine-month academic year and are based on an average credit load of: Graduate: N/A]

	All Students
Tuition and fees:	$12,564
Campus and Room and Board:	
Books and Supplies:	
Other Expenses:	
Total Estimated Expenses:	**$12,564**

University of Pittsburgh

INSTITUTION INFORMATION
4200 Fifth Avenue
Pittsburgh, PA 15260
Phone: (412) 624-4200
Fax: (412) 624-7539
Web: http://www.pitt.edu/

GENERAL INFORMATION
[All Students - Fall 2006]

Undergraduate Enrollment	23,960
Graduate Enrollment	7,754
Professional Enrollment	1,860
Total Enrollment	**33,574**

ENGINEERING COLLEGE INFORMATION

HEAD OF ENGINEERING
Gerald D Holder
Dean of Engineering
School of Engineering
University of Pittsburgh
253 Benedum Hall
Pittsburgh, PA 15261
Phone: (412) 624-9809
Fax: (412) 624-0412
Email: holder@engr.pitt.edu

TYPES OF ENGINEERING DEGREES
Bachelor's: B.S.
Master's: M.S. with thesis, M.S. without thesis, but with project or report
Doctoral: Ph.D.

UNDERGRADUATE INFORMATION

ADMISSION INQUIRIES
Cheryl Paul
Coordinator of Recruitment
University of Pittsburgh
B80 Benedum Hall
Pittsburgh, PA 15261
Phone: (412) 624-9825
Fax: (412) 624-2827
Email: cpaul@engr.pitt.edu

ESTIMATED STUDENT EXPENSES (FALL 2006)
[Expenses are for the 2006-2007 nine-month academic year and are based on an average credit load of: Undergraduate: 12]

	In-State	Out-of-State
Tuition and Fees:	$12,896	$23,374
Campus and Room and Board:	$11,230	$11,230
Books and Supplies:	$880	$880
Other Expenses:	$1,090	$1,090
Total Estimated Expenses:	**$26,096**	**$36,574**

NEW APPLICANTS/NEWLY ENROLLED STUDENTS
[Numbers are for the undergraduate engineering college for the Fall 2006 term]

Number of Applicants (a):	1,872
Of those, Number Offered Admission (b):	1,299
Of those, Number Enrolled Fall 2006 (c):	403

GRADUATE INFORMATION

ADMISSION INQUIRIES
Rama Bazaz
Associate Director
University of Pittsburgh
Office of Administration, 253 Benedum Hall
Pittsburgh , PA 15261
Phone: (412) 624-9800
Fax: (412) 624-9808
Email: admin@engr.pitt.edu

ESTIMATED STUDENT EXPENSES (FALL 2006)
[Expenses are for the 2006-2007 nine-month academic year and are based on an average credit load of: Graduate: 9]

	In-State	Out-of-State
Tuition and Fees:	$16,688	$30,228
Campus and Room and Board:	$11,230	$11,230
Books and Supplies:	$880	$880
Other Expenses:	$1,090	$1,090
Total Estimated Expenses:	**$29,888**	**$43,428**

NEW APPLICANTS/NEWLY ENROLLED STUDENTS
[Numbers are for the graduate engineering college for the Fall 2006 term]

Number of Applicants (a):	1,273
Of those, Number Offered Admission (b):	439
Of those, Number Enrolled Fall 2006 (c):	148

Polytechnic University

INSTITUTION INFORMATION
Six MetroTech Center
Brooklyn, NY 11201
Phone: (718) 260-3600
Fax: (718) 260-3136
Web: http://www.poly.edu

GENERAL INFORMATION
[All Students - Fall 2006]

Undergraduate Enrollment	1,480
Graduate Enrollment	1,439
Professional Enrollment	0
Total Enrollment	**2,919**

ENGINEERING COLLEGE INFORMATION

HEAD OF ENGINEERING
F.H. (Bud) Griffis
Dept. Head, Civil Engineering
Civil Engineering
Polytechnic University
Six MetroTech Center
Brooklyn, NY 11201
Phone: (718) 260-3713
Fax: (718) 260-3063
Email: griffis@poly.edu

TYPES OF ENGINEERING DEGREES
Bachelor's: B.S.
Master's: M.S. with thesis, M.S. without thesis, but with project or report
Doctoral: Ph.D.

UNDERGRADUATE INFORMATION

ESTIMATED STUDENT EXPENSES (FALL 2006)
[Expenses are for the 2006-2007 nine-month academic year and are based on an average credit load of: Undergraduate: 16]

	All Students
Tuition and fees:	$29,789
Campus and Room and Board:	$8,500
Books and Supplies:	$1,000
Other Expenses:	$2,964
Total Estimated Expenses:	**$42,253**

NEW APPLICANTS/NEWLY ENROLLED STUDENTS
[Numbers are for the undergraduate engineering college for the Fall 2006 term]

Number of Applicants (a):	1,085
Of those, Number Offered Admission (b):	793
Of those, Number Enrolled Fall 2006 (c):	282

GRADUATE INFORMATION

ESTIMATED STUDENT EXPENSES (FALL 2006)
[Expenses are for the 2006-2007 nine-month academic year and are based on an average credit load of: Graduate: 9]

	All Students
Tuition and fees:	$18,808
Campus and Room and Board:	$8,500
Books and Supplies:	$1,000
Other Expenses:	$2,200
Total Estimated Expenses:	**$30,508**

NEW APPLICANTS/NEWLY ENROLLED STUDENTS
[Numbers are for the graduate engineering college for the Fall 2006 term]

Number of Applicants (a):	2,133
Of those, Number Offered Admission (b):	1,670
Of those, Number Enrolled Fall 2006 (c):	387

Polytechnic University of Puerto Rico

INSTITUTION INFORMATION
College of Engineering
377 Ponce de Leon Avenue
San Juan, PR 00919
Phone: (787) 754-8000
Fax: (787) 281-8342
Web: http://www.pupr.edu

GENERAL INFORMATION
[All Students - Fall 2006]

Undergraduate Enrollment	5,081
Graduate Enrollment	685
Professional Enrollment	0
Total Enrollment	**5,766**

ENGINEERING COLLEGE INFORMATION

HEAD OF ENGINEERING
Cuauhtémoc Godoy
Dean
College of Engineering and Geomatic Sciences
Polytechnic University of Puerto Rico

P.O. Box 192017
San Juan, PR 00919-2017
Phone: (787) 754-8000
Fax: (787) 281-8342
Email: cgodoy@pupr.edu

TYPES OF ENGINEERING DEGREES
Bachelor's: B.S.
Master's: M.S. with thesis, M.S. without thesis, but with project or report
Doctoral:

University of Portland

INSTITUTION INFORMATION
5000 N. Willamette Blvd.
Portland, OR 97203
Phone: (800) 227-4568
Fax: (503) 943-7399
Web: http://www.up.edu

GENERAL INFORMATION
[All Students - Fall 2006]

Undergraduate Enrollment	2,849
Graduate Enrollment	473
Professional Enrollment	0
Total Enrollment	**3,322**

ENGINEERING COLLEGE INFORMATION

HEAD OF ENGINEERING
Zia A Yamayee
Dean, School of Engineering
School of Engineering
University of Portland
5000 North Willamette Blvd.
Portland, OR 97203
Phone: (503) 943-7314
Fax: (503) 943-7316
Email: yamayee@up.edu

ENGINEERING COLLEGE INQUIRIES
Kitty Harmon
Engineering Program Counselor
University of Portland
5000 N. Willamette Blvd.
Portland, OR 97203
Phone: (503) 943-7180
Fax: (503) 943-7316
Email: harmonk@up.edu

TYPES OF ENGINEERING DEGREES
Bachelor's: B.S.
Master's: M.Eng.
Doctoral:

UNDERGRADUATE INFORMATION

ADMISSION INQUIRIES
Kitty Harmon
Engineering Program Counselor
University of Portland
5000 N. Willamette Blvd.
Portland, OR 97203
Phone: (503) 943-7180
Fax: (503) 943-7316
Email: harmonk@up.edu

ESTIMATED STUDENT EXPENSES (FALL 2006)
[Expenses are for the 2006-2007 nine-month academic year and are based on an average credit load of: Undergraduate: 16]

	All Students
Tuition and fees:	$26,000
Campus and Room and Board:	$4,000
Books and Supplies:	$1,500
Other Expenses:	$500
Total Estimated Expenses:	**$32,000**

NEW APPLICANTS/NEWLY ENROLLED STUDENTS
[Numbers are for the undergraduate engineering college for the Fall 2006 term]

Number of Applicants (a):	657
Of those, Number Offered Admission (b):	444
Of those, Number Enrolled Fall 2006 (c):	82

GRADUATE INFORMATION

ADMISSION INQUIRIES
Khalid H Khan
Associate Dean
University of Portland
5000 N. Willamette Blvd.
Portland , OR 97203
Phone: (503) 943-7276
Fax: (503) 943-7316
Email: khan@up.edu

ESTIMATED STUDENT EXPENSES (FALL 2006)
[Expenses are for the 2006-2007 nine-month academic year and are based on an average credit load of: Graduate: 9]

	All Students
Tuition and fees:	$13,104
Campus and Room and Board:	$4,000
Books and Supplies:	$1,500
Other Expenses:	$500
Total Estimated Expenses:	**$19,104**

Portland State University

INSTITUTION INFORMATION
P.O. Box 751
Portland, OR 97207
Phone: (503) 725-3000
Fax: (503) 725-4882
Web: http://www.pdx.edu/

GENERAL INFORMATION
[All Students - Fall 2006]

Undergraduate Enrollment	16,563
Graduate Enrollment	5,361
Professional Enrollment	0
Total Enrollment	**21,924**

ENGINEERING COLLEGE INFORMATION

HEAD OF ENGINEERING
Robert D Dryden
Dean of Engineering
Maseeh College of Engineering and Computer Science
Portland State University
P.O. Box 751
Portland, OR 97207
Phone: (503) 725-8398
Fax: (503) 725-4298
Email: drydenr@pdx.edu

TYPES OF ENGINEERING DEGREES
Bachelor's: B.S.
Master's: M.S. with thesis, M.S. without thesis, but with project or report
Doctoral: Ph.D.

UNDERGRADUATE INFORMATION

ESTIMATED STUDENT EXPENSES (FALL 2006)
[Expenses are for the 2006-2007 nine-month academic year and are based on an average credit load of: Undergraduate: 15]

	In-State	Out-of-State
Tuition and Fees:	$5,600	$17,435
Campus and Room and Board:	$8,940	$8,940
Books and Supplies:	$1,800	$1,800
Other Expenses:	$2,415	$2,415
Total Estimated Expenses:	**$18,755**	**$30,590**

NEW APPLICANTS/NEWLY ENROLLED STUDENTS
[Numbers are for the undergraduate engineering college for the Fall 2006 term]

Number of Applicants (a):	297
Of those, Number Offered Admission (b):	278
Of those, Number Enrolled Fall 2006 (c):	137

GRADUATE INFORMATION

ESTIMATED STUDENT EXPENSES (FALL 2006)
[Expenses are for the 2006-2007 nine-month academic year and are based on an average credit load of: Graduate: 9]

	In-State	Out-of-State
Tuition and Fees:	$7,652	$12,242
Campus and Room and Board:	$8,940	$8,940
Books and Supplies:	$1,800	$1,800

Other Expenses:	$2,415	$2,415
Total Estimated Expenses:	**$20,807**	**$25,397**

NEW APPLICANTS/NEWLY ENROLLED STUDENTS
[Numbers are for the graduate engineering college for the Fall 2006 term]

Number of Applicants (a):	567
Of those, Number Offered Admission (b):	427
Of those, Number Enrolled Fall 2006 (c):	210

Prairie View A&M University

INSTITUTION INFORMATION
Office of the President
P.O. Box 519 - M/S 1001
Prairie View, TX 77446
Phone: (936) 261-2111
Fax: (936) 261-3928
Web: http://www.pvamu.edu

GENERAL INFORMATION
[All Students - Fall 2006]

Undergraduate Enrollment	5,758
Graduate Enrollment	2,204
Professional Enrollment	0
Total Enrollment	**7,962**

ENGINEERING COLLEGE INFORMATION

HEAD OF ENGINEERING
Milton R. Bryant
Distinguised Professor and Dean
College of Engineering
Prairie View A&M University
P.O. Box 519 M/S 2501
College of Engineering
Prairie View, TX 77446
Phone: (936) 261-9900
Fax: (936) 261-9946
Email: mrbryant@pvamu.edu

ENGINEERING COLLEGE INQUIRIES
Betti P Blackshear
Assistant Dean
Prairie View A&M University
P.O. Box 519 MS 2503
Prairie View, TX 77446
Phone: (936) 261-9900
Fax: (936) 261-9946
Email: Bpblackshear@pvamu.edu

ENGINEERING COLLEGE INQUIRIES
Kendall T Harris
Professor and Associate Dean
Prairie View A&M University
P.O. 519 M/S 2500, Prairie View A&M University
Prairie View, TX 77446
Phone: (936) 261-9956
Fax: (936) 857-4246
Email: ktharris@pvamu.edu

TYPES OF ENGINEERING DEGREES
Bachelor's: B.S.
Master's: M.S. with thesis, M.S. without thesis, but with project or report
Doctoral: Ph.D.

UNDERGRADUATE INFORMATION

ESTIMATED STUDENT EXPENSES (FALL 2006)
[Expenses are for the 2006-2007 nine-month academic year and are based on an average credit load of: Undergraduate: 15]

	In-State	Out-of-State
Tuition and Fees:	$5,533	$13,783
Campus and Room and Board:	$6,158	$6,158
Books and Supplies:	$800	$800
Other Expenses:	$80	$80
Total Estimated Expenses:	**$12,571**	**$20,821**

Note: Applicants are for chemical, civil, computer, electrical and mechanical engineering and computer science.

NEW APPLICANTS/NEWLY ENROLLED STUDENTS
[Numbers are for the undergraduate engineering college for the Fall 2006 term]

Number of Applicants (a):	390

Of those, Number Offered Admission (b):	135
Of those, Number Enrolled Fall 2006 (c):	102

GRADUATE INFORMATION

ADMISSION INQUIRIES
John O. Attia
Professor and Head
Prairie View A&M University
College of Engineering, P.O. Box 519 MS 2520
Prairie View , TX 77446
Phone: (936) 261-9916
Fax: (936) 261-9930
Email: joattia@pvamu.edu

ADMISSION INQUIRIES
Barbara A Thompson
Administrative Assistant
Prairie View A&M University
College of Engineering, P.O. Box 519 M/S 2500
Prairie View , TX 77446
Phone: (936) 261-9896
Fax: (936) 857-4246
Email: bathompson@pvamu.edu

ESTIMATED STUDENT EXPENSES (FALL 2006)
[Expenses are for the 2006-2007 nine-month academic year and are based on an average credit load of: Graduate: 9]

	In-State	Out-of-State
Tuition and Fees:	$4,063	$9,049
Campus and Room and Board:	$6,320	$6,320
Books and Supplies:	$400	$400
Other Expenses:	$80	$80
Total Estimated Expenses:	**$10,863**	**$15,849**

Note: Applicanats are for chemical, civil, computer, electrical and mechanical engineering and computer science.

NEW APPLICANTS/NEWLY ENROLLED STUDENTS
[Numbers are for the graduate engineering college for the Fall 2006 term]

Number of Applicants (a):	49
Of those, Number Offered Admission (b):	45
Of those, Number Enrolled Fall 2006 (c):	33

Princeton University

INSTITUTION INFORMATION
Engineering Quadrangle
Olden Street
Princeton, NJ 08544-5263
Phone: (609) 258-2260
Fax: (609) 258-6744
Web: http://www.princeton.edu

GENERAL INFORMATION
[All Students - Fall 2006]

Undergraduate Enrollment	4,760
Graduate Enrollment	2,010
Professional Enrollment	0
Total Enrollment	**6,770**

ENGINEERING COLLEGE INFORMATION

HEAD OF ENGINEERING
Harold Vincent Poor
Dean
School of Engineering and Applied Science
Princeton University
C 226 Engineering Quadrangle
Princeton, NJ 08544-5263
Phone: (609) 258-2260
Fax: (609) 258-7305
Email: poor@princeton.edu

ENGINEERING COLLEGE INQUIRIES
Peter Bogucki
Associate Dean for Undergraduate Affairs
Princeton University
C207 Engineering Quadrangle, Olden Street
Princeton, NJ 08544-5263
Phone: (609) 258-4554
Fax: (609) 258-3996
Email: bogucki@princeton.edu

TYPES OF ENGINEERING DEGREES
Bachelor's: B.S.
Master's: M.A. without thesis, but with project or report, M.S. with thesis, M.Eng.
Doctoral: Ph.D.

UNDERGRADUATE INFORMATION

ADMISSION INQUIRIES
Janet L Rapelye
Dean of Admission
Princeton University
204A West College
Princeton, NJ 08544-5263
Phone: (609) 258-6150
Fax: (609) 258-6743
Email: jrapelye@princeton.edu

ESTIMATED STUDENT EXPENSES (FALL 2006)
[Expenses are for the 2006-2007 nine-month academic year and are based on an average credit load of: Undergraduate: N/A]

	All Students
Tutition and fees:	$33,000
Campus and Room and Board:	$9,200
Books and Supplies:	$3,300
Other Expenses:	
Total Estimated Expenses:	**$45,500**

NEW APPLICANTS/NEWLY ENROLLED STUDENTS
[Numbers are for the undergraduate engineering college for the Fall 2006 term]

Number of Applicants (a):	2,708
Of those, Number Offered Admission (b):	346
Of those, Number Enrolled Fall 2006 (c):	231

Note: Princeton does not require ACT test scores.

GRADUATE INFORMATION

ADMISSION INQUIRIES
Stephen Friedfeld
Associate Dean for Graduate Affairs
Princeton University
ACE-24, Engineering Quadrangle, Olden Street
Princeton , NJ 08544-5263
Phone: (609) 258-6740
Fax: (609) 258-6744
Email: sjf@princeton.edu

ESTIMATED STUDENT EXPENSES (FALL 2006)
[Expenses are for the 2006-2007 nine-month academic year and are based on an average credit load of: Graduate: N/A]

	All Students
Tutition and fees:	$34,000
Campus and Room and Board:	$10,400
Books and Supplies:	$3,400
Other Expenses:	
Total Estimated Expenses:	**$47,800**

NEW APPLICANTS/NEWLY ENROLLED STUDENTS
[Numbers are for the graduate engineering college for the Fall 2006 term]

Number of Applicants (a):	1,676
Of those, Number Offered Admission (b):	296
Of those, Number Enrolled Fall 2006 (c):	121

University of Puerto Rico, Mayaguez Campus

INSTITUTION INFORMATION
P.O. Box 9040
Mayaguez, PR 00681
Phone: (787) 265-3824
Fax: (787) 833-6965
Web: http://ing.uprm.edu/

GENERAL INFORMATION
[All Students - Fall 2006]

Undergraduate Enrollment	11,096
Graduate Enrollment	1,054
Professional Enrollment	230
Total Enrollment	**12,380**

ENGINEERING COLLEGE INFORMATION

HEAD OF ENGINEERING
Ramon E Vasquez-Espinosa
Dean of Engineering
College of Engineering
University of Puerto Rico, Mayaguez Campus
Dean of Engineering
PO Box 9040
Mayaguez, PR 00681-9040
Phone: (787) 265-3822

Fax: (787) 833-1190
Email: reve@ece.uprm.edu

TYPES OF ENGINEERING DEGREES
Bachelor's: B.S.
Master's: M.S. with thesis, M.S. without thesis, but with project or report, M.Eng.
Doctoral: Ph.D.

UNDERGRADUATE INFORMATION

ESTIMATED STUDENT EXPENSES (FALL 2006)
[Expenses are for the 2006-2007 nine-month academic year and are based on an average credit load of: Undergraduate: 17]

	All Students
Tutition and fees:	$1,707
Campus and Room and Board:	$6,620
Books and Supplies:	$1,320
Other Expenses:	$1,320
Total Estimated Expenses:	**$10,967**

NEW APPLICANTS/NEWLY ENROLLED STUDENTS
[Numbers are for the undergraduate engineering college for the Fall 2006 term]

Number of Applicants (a):	1,340
Of those, Number Offered Admission (b):	831
Of those, Number Enrolled Fall 2006 (c):	770

GRADUATE INFORMATION

ADMISSION INQUIRIES
Sonia M Bartolomei-Suarez
Associate Dean
University of Puerto Rico, Mayaguez Campus
Assoc. Dean of Academic Affairs, PO Box 9040
Mayaguez , PR 00681-9040
Phone: (787) 265-3823
Fax: (787) 833-6965
Email: sonia@ece.uprm.edu

ESTIMATED STUDENT EXPENSES (FALL 2006)
[Expenses are for the 2006-2007 nine-month academic year and are based on an average credit load of: Graduate: 9]

	All Students
Tutition and fees:	$2,147
Campus and Room and Board:	$7,870
Books and Supplies:	$2,200
Other Expenses:	$1,585
Total Estimated Expenses:	**$13,802**

Purdue University, Calumet

INSTITUTION INFORMATION
2200 169th Street
Hammond, IN 46323
Phone: (219) 989-2468
Fax: (219) 989-3139
Web: http://www.calumet.purdue.edu

ENGINEERING COLLEGE INFORMATION

HEAD OF ENGINEERING
Catherine M Murphy
Interim Dean, School of Engineering, Mathematics and Science
School of Engineering, Mathematics and Science
Purdue University, Calumet
2200 169th Street
Gyte Bldg., Room 181
Hammond, IN 46323
Phone: (219) 989-2468
Fax: (219) 989-3139
Email: murphycm@calumet.purdue.edu

TYPES OF ENGINEERING DEGREES
Bachelor's: B.S.
Master's: M.S. with thesis, M.S. without thesis, but with project or report
Doctoral:

GRADUATE INFORMATION

ADMISSION INQUIRIES
Toma I Hentea
Graduate Coordinator
Purdue University, Calumet

2200 169th Street, Potter Building
Hammond , IN 46323
Phone: (219) 989-2481
Fax: (219) 989-2898
Email: hentea@calumet.purdue.edu

Purdue University

INSTITUTION INFORMATION
College of Engineering, Room 101 ENAD
400 Centennial Mall Drive
West Lafayette, IN 47907-2016
Phone: (765) 494-5346
Fax: (765) 494-9321
Web: http://www.purdue.edu

GENERAL INFORMATION
[All Students - Fall 2006]

Undergraduate Enrollment	31,290
Graduate Enrollment	7,023
Professional Enrollment	915
Total Enrollment	**39,228**

ENGINEERING COLLEGE INFORMATION

HEAD OF ENGINEERING
Leah H. Jamieson
John A Edwardson Dean of Engineering; Ransburg Distinguished Professor of Electrical and Computer Engineering
College of Engineering
Purdue University
Engineering Administration Bldg, Rm 101
400 Centennial Mall Drive
West Lafayette, IN 47907-2016
Phone: (765) 494-5346
Fax: (765) 494-9321
Email: lhj@purdue.edu

ENGINEERING COLLEGE INQUIRIES
Klod Kokini
Assoc. Dean of Academic Affairs; Professor of Mechanical Engineering
Purdue University
Engineering Administration Bldg, Rm 101, 400 Centennial Mall Drive
West Lafayette, IN 47907-2016
Phone: (765) 494-5349
Fax: (765) 494-9321
Email: kokini@purdue.edu

ENGINEERING COLLEGE INQUIRIES
David C Robledo
Data Manager
Purdue University
ENAD, Rm 106, 400 Centennial Mall Drive
West Lafayette, IN 47907-2016
Phone: (765) 496-1044
Fax: (765) 496-1466
Email: drobledo@purdue.edu

ENGINEERING COLLEGE INQUIRIES
Jay P Gore
Assoc. Dean Research & Entreprenuership; Riley Professor of Mechanical Engineering; Dir. of Energy Ctr; Dir. of Hydrogen Ctr
Purdue University
AA Potter Engineering Center, 500 Central Drive
West Lafayette, IN 47907-2022
Phone: (765) 494-2122
Fax: (765) 496-8298
Email: gore@purdue.edu

ENGINEERING COLLEGE INQUIRIES
Vincent F Bralts
Assoc. Dean Resource Planning & Management, Professor of Agricultural & Biological Engineering;Interim Head Nuclear Engineering
Purdue University
Engineering Administration Bldg, Rm 101, 400 Centennial Mall Drive
West Lafayette, IN 47907-2016
Phone: (765) 494-5345
Fax: (765) 494-9321
Email: bralts@purdue.edu

ENGINEERING COLLEGE INQUIRIES
Michael Fosmire
Head of Engineering & Technology Library Division;

Professor of Library Sciences
Purdue University
Purdue University Libraries ENGR, 504 State Street
West Lafayette, IN 47907-2058
Phone: (765) 494-2859
Email: fosmire@purdue.edu

ENGINEERING COLLEGE INQUIRIES
Christopher J Martin
Director Financial Affairs College of Engineering
Purdue University
400 Centennial Mall Drive
West Lafayette, IN 47907-2016
Phone: (765) 494-5334
Fax: (765) 496-1466
Email: cjmartin@purdue.edu

ENGINEERING COLLEGE INQUIRIES
Michael H Stitsworth
Director of Advancement/Major Gifts
Purdue University
Room 101 ENAD, 400 Centennial Mall Drive
West Lafayette, IN 47907-2016
Phone: (765) 494-0164
Fax: (765) 494-9321
Email: mhs@purdue.edu

ENGINEERING COLLEGE INQUIRIES
Edgar Martinez
Asst. Dean of Engineering for Reasearch and Entrepreneurship; Chief Operating Officer for Nanotechnology Centers
Purdue University
A. A. Potter Engineering Bldg. Rm 322, 500 Central Drive
West Lafayette, IN 47907-2022
Phone: (765) 494-9546
Fax: (765) 496-8298
Email: martinez@purdue.edu

ENGINEERING COLLEGE INQUIRIES
Rwitti Roy
Director of Marketing and Communications
Purdue University
VisTech 1 Building, Suite B120, 1435 Win Hentschel Blvd
West Lafayette, IN 47906-4153
Phone: (765) 494-6801
Fax: (765) 496-6060
Email: rroy@purdue.edu

ENGINEERING COLLEGE INQUIRIES
Amy Noah
Director of Development
Purdue University
Engineering Advancement - Room G292, 550 Stadium Mall Drive
West Lafayette, IN 47907-2051
Phone: (765) 494-6490
Fax: (765) 496-6745
Email: arnoah@purdue.edu

ENGINEERING COLLEGE INQUIRIES
Sharon Whitlock
Administrative Director for College of Engineering
Purdue University
Room 101 ENAD, 400 Centennial Mall Drive
West Lafayette, IN 47907-2016
Phone: (765) 494-5345
Fax: (765) 494-9321
Email: whitlock@purdue.edu

ENGINEERING COLLEGE INQUIRIES
Charles Rutledge
Vice President for Research/Professor of Pharmacy
Purdue University
Vice President for Research Office, 610 Purdue Mall
West Lafayette, IN 47907-2040
Phone: (765) 494-6209
Email: chipr@purdue.edu

ENGINEERING COLLEGE INQUIRIES
Virginia Gleghorn
Director Minority Engineering Programs
Purdue University
College of Engineering, ENAD 222, 400 Centennial Mall Drive
West Lafayette, IN 47907-2016
Phone: (765) 494-3974
Fax: (765) 496-7399
Email: vboothgl@purdue.edu

ENGINEERING COLLEGE INQUIRIES
Beth Holloway
Director, Women in Engineering Program
Purdue University
Women in Engineering Office - CIVL G167, 550 Stadium Mall Drive
West Lafayette, IN 47907-2051
Phone: (765) 494-3889
Fax: (765) 496-1349
Email: holloway@purdue.edu

ENGINEERING COLLEGE INQUIRIES
David Carmichael
Interim Director Engineering Computer Network
Purdue University
Engineering Computing Network, 501 Northwestern Avenue
West Lafayette, IN 47907-2044
Phone: (765) 494-3546
Email: carmicha@purdue.edu

ENGINEERING COLLEGE INQUIRIES
Robert Stwalley, III
Director of the Office of Professional Practice
Purdue University
Professional Practice, 550 Stadium Mall Drive
West Lafayette, IN 47907-2051
Phone: (765) 494-7430
Email: rms3@purdue.edu

ENGINEERING COLLEGE INQUIRIES
David T Bowker
Director of Undergraduate Engineering Recruitment
Purdue University
Student Services Annex - One, 512 Third Street
West Lafayette, IN 47907-2080
Phone: (765) 494-3980
Email: dbowker@purdue.edu

ENGINEERING COLLEGE INQUIRIES
Arvind Varma
Department Head, Chemical Engineering; R. Gmes Slayer Distinguished Professor
Purdue University
Chemical Engineering, Forney Hall - 480 Stadium Mall
West Lafayette, IN 47907-2100
Phone: (765) 494-4075
Fax: (765) 494-0805
Email: avarma@purdue.edu

TYPES OF ENGINEERING DEGREES
Bachelor's: B.S.
Master's: M.S. with thesis, M.S. without thesis, but with project or report
Doctoral: Ph.D.

UNDERGRADUATE INFORMATION

ESTIMATED STUDENT EXPENSES (FALL 2006)
[Expenses are for the 2006-2007 nine-month academic year and are based on an average credit load of: Undergraduate: 16]

	In-State	Out-of-State
Tuition and Fees:	$7,300	$21,470
Campus and Room and Board:	$7,140	$7,140
Books and Supplies:	$990	$990
Other Expenses:	$2,070	$2,070
Total Estimated Expenses:	**$17,500**	**$31,670**

NEW APPLICANTS/NEWLY ENROLLED STUDENTS
[Numbers are for the undergraduate engineering college for the Fall 2006 term]

Number of Applicants (a):	6,757
Of those, Number Offered Admission (b):	5,854
Of those, Number Enrolled Fall 2006 (c):	1,744

GRADUATE INFORMATION

ADMISSION INQUIRIES
Heidi Diefes-Dux
Associate Professor Engineering Education
Purdue University
Engineering Administration Building, 400 Centennial Mall Drive
West Lafayette, IN 47907-2016
Phone: (765) 494-3887
Fax: (765) 494-5819
Email: hdiefes@purdue.edu

ADMISSION INQUIRIES
Dirk Maier
Dir. Post-harvest Education & Research Ctr; Assoc. Head and Professor Agricultural & Biological Engineering
Purdue University
Agricultural & Biological Engineering, 225 S. University St.
West Lafayette, IN 47907-2093
Phone: (765) 494-1175
Fax: (765) 496-1356
Email: maier@purdue.edu

ADMISSION INQUIRIES
Anastasios Lyrintziz
Professor of Aeronautical & Astronautical Engineering; Graduate Committee Chair
Purdue University
Aeronautical & Astronautical Engineering, 315 N. Grant St
West Lafayette, IN 47907-2023
Phone: (765) 494-5142
Fax: (765) 494-9321
Email: lyrintzi@purdue.edu

ADMISSION INQUIRIES
Chan Choi
Professor of Mechanical Engineering
Purdue University
Mechanical Engineering Building, 585 Purdue Mall
West Lafayette, IN 47907-2088
Phone: (765) 494-6789
Email: choi@purdue.edu

ADMISSION INQUIRIES
Charles Krousgrill
Professor of Mechanical Engineering; Academic Director Continuing Engineering Education
Purdue University
Mechanical Engineering Building, 585 Purdue Mall
West Lafayette, IN 47907-2088
Phone: (765) 494-5738
Email: krousgri@purdue.edu

ADMISSION INQUIRIES
Darcy Bullock
Professor of Civil Engineering
Purdue University
Civil Engineering Bldg, 550 Stadium Mall Drive
West Lafayette, IN 47907-2051
Phone: (765) 494-2226
Fax: (765) 496-7996
Email: darcy@purdue.edu

ADMISSION INQUIRIES
David Johnson
Associate Professor Materials Engineering
Purdue University
Materials Engineering, 501 Northwestern
West Lafayette, IN 47907-2044
Phone: (765) 494-7009
Email: davidjoh@purdue.edu

ADMISSION INQUIRIES
Kendall Thomson
Associate Professor of Chemical Engineering
Purdue University
Forney Hall of Chemical Engineering, 480 Stadium Mall Drive
West Lafayette, IN 47907-2100
Phone: (765) 496-6706
Email: thomsonk@purdue.edu

ADMISSION INQUIRIES
Michael Harris
Professor of Chemical Engineering; Interim Associate Dean of
Purdue University
Engineering Administration Building, Room 101, 400 Centennial Mall Drive
West Lafayette, IN 47907-2016
Phone: (765) 494-0963
Fax: (765) 494-1180
Email: mtharris@purdue.edu

ADMISSION INQUIRIES
Michael Melloch
Professor of Electrical & Computer Engineering
Purdue University
Electrical & Computer Engineering, 465 Northwestern Avenue
West Lafayette, IN 47907-2035
Phone: (765) 494-2035
Email: michael.r.melloch.1@purdue.edu

ADMISSION INQUIRIES
Osman Basaran
Reilly Professor of Fluid Mchanics
Purdue University
Chemical Engineering, 480 Stadium Mall
West Lafayette , IN 47907-2100
Phone: (765) 494-4031
Email: obasaran@purdue.edu

ADMISSION INQUIRIES
Susan K Fisher
Director of Graduate Programs
Purdue University
Graduate Education & Interdisciplinary Programs, Rm 374
- Potter Bldg - 500 Central Drive
West Lafayette , IN 47907-2022
Phone: (765) 494-0539
Fax: (765) 496-1180
Email: fishersk@purdue.edu

ADMISSION INQUIRIES
Andrew Brightman
Assistant School Head
Purdue University
Weldon School of Biomedical Engineering, 206
Intramural Drive
West Lafayette , IN 47907-2032
Phone: (765) 496-3537
Email: aob@purdue.edu

ESTIMATED STUDENT EXPENSES (FALL 2006)
[Expenses are for the 2006-2007 nine-month academic year and are based on an average credit load of: Graduate: 12]

	In-State	Out-of-State
Tuition and Fees:	$7,300	$21,470
Campus and Room and Board:	$7,140	$7,140
Books and Supplies:	$990	$990
Other Expenses:	$2,070	$2,070
Total Estimated Expenses:	**$17,500**	**$31,670**

NEW APPLICANTS/NEWLY ENROLLED STUDENTS
[Numbers are for the graduate engineering college for the Fall 2006 term]

Number of Applicants (a):	4,405
Of those, Number Offered Admission (b):	1,340
Of those, Number Enrolled Fall 2006 (c):	548

Rensselaer Polytechnic Institute

INSTITUTION INFORMATION
110 Eighth Street
Troy, NY 12180
Phone: (518) 276-6000
Fax: (518) 276-6003
Web: http://www.rpi.edu

GENERAL INFORMATION
[All Students - Fall 2006]

Undergraduate Enrollment	5,148
Graduate Enrollment	1,228
Professional Enrollment	92
Total Enrollment	**6,468**

ENGINEERING COLLEGE INFORMATION

HEAD OF ENGINEERING
Alan W Cramb
Dean of Engineering
School of Engineering
Rensselaer Polytechnic Institute
110 Eighth Street
Troy, NY 12180
Phone: (518) 276-6298
Fax: (518) 276-8788
Email: cramb@rpi.edu

TYPES OF ENGINEERING DEGREES
Bachelor's: B.S.
Master's: M.S. with thesis, M.Eng.
Doctoral: Ph.D., D.Eng

UNDERGRADUATE INFORMATION

ADMISSION INQUIRIES
James Nondorf
Vice President for Enrollment
Rensselaer Polytechnic Institute

110 Eighth Street
Troy, NY 12180
Phone: (518) 276-6143
Fax: (518) 276-6613
Email: nondoj@rpi.edu

ESTIMATED STUDENT EXPENSES (FALL 2006)
[Expenses are for the 2006-2007 nine-month academic year and are based on an average credit load of: Undergraduate: 16]

	All Students
Tuition and fees:	$32,600
Campus and Room and Board:	$9,915
Books and Supplies:	$1,770
Other Expenses:	$896
Total Estimated Expenses:	**$45,181**

Note: Laptop required and not folded into expense categories

NEW APPLICANTS/NEWLY ENROLLED STUDENTS
[Numbers are for the undergraduate engineering college for the Fall 2006 term]

Number of Applicants (a):	3,839
Of those, Number Offered Admission (b):	2,751
Of those, Number Enrolled Fall 2006 (c):	780

Note: 63% of entering undergraduate students ranked in the top 10% of their high school class

GRADUATE INFORMATION

ADMISSION INQUIRIES
James Nondorf
Vice President for Enrollment
Rensselaer Polytechnic Institute
110 Eighth Street
Troy , NY 12180
Phone: (518) 276-6143
Fax: (518) 276-6613
Email: nondoj@rpi.edu

ESTIMATED STUDENT EXPENSES (FALL 2006)
[Expenses are for the 2006-2007 nine-month academic year and are based on an average credit load of: Graduate: 12]

	All Students
Tuition and fees:	$32,600
Campus and Room and Board:	$9,000
Books and Supplies:	$1,722
Other Expenses:	
Total Estimated Expenses:	**$43,322**

Note: Laptop required and not folded into expense categories

NEW APPLICANTS/NEWLY ENROLLED STUDENTS
[Numbers are for the graduate engineering college for the Fall 2006 term]

Number of Applicants (a):	2,020
Of those, Number Offered Admission (b):	672
Of those, Number Enrolled Fall 2006 (c):	311

University of Rhode Island

INSTITUTION INFORMATION
President's Office
Green Hall
Kingston, RI 02881
Phone: (401) 874-2444
Fax: (401) 874-7149
Web: http://www.uri.edu

GENERAL INFORMATION
[All Students - Fall 2006]

Undergraduate Enrollment	11,875
Graduate Enrollment	2,631
Professional Enrollment	0
Total Enrollment	**14,506**

ENGINEERING COLLEGE INFORMATION

HEAD OF ENGINEERING
Bahram Nassersharif
Dean
College of Engineering
University of Rhode Island
College of Engineering
102 Bliss Hall
Kingston, RI 02881
Phone: (401) 874-2186

Fax: (401) 782-1066
Email: bn@egr.uri.edu

ENGINEERING COLLEGE INQUIRIES
Raymond M Wright
Associate Dean
University of Rhode Island
College of Engineering, 102 Biliss Hall
Kingston, RI 02881
Phone: (401) 874-5985
Fax: (401) 782-1066
Email: wrightr@egr.uri.edu

TYPES OF ENGINEERING DEGREES
Bachelor's: B.S.
Master's: M.S. with thesis, M.S. without thesis, but with project or report
Doctoral: Ph.D.

UNDERGRADUATE INFORMATION

ESTIMATED STUDENT EXPENSES (FALL 2006)
[Expenses are for the 2006-2007 nine-month academic year and are based on an average credit load of: Undergraduate: 16]

	In-State	Out-of-State
Tuition and Fees:	$8,452	$22,158
Campus and Room and Board:	$8,466	$8,466
Books and Supplies:	$1,500	$1,000
Other Expenses:	$1,079	$1,079
Total Estimated Expenses:	**$19,497**	**$32,703**

Note: Accident/Sickness insurance may be waived.

NEW APPLICANTS/NEWLY ENROLLED STUDENTS
[Numbers are for the undergraduate engineering college for the Fall 2006 term]

Number of Applicants (a):	1,020
Of those, Number Offered Admission (b):	769
Of those, Number Enrolled Fall 2006 (c):	242

GRADUATE INFORMATION

ESTIMATED STUDENT EXPENSES (FALL 2006)
[Expenses are for the 2006-2007 nine-month academic year and are based on an average credit load of: Graduate: 9]

	In-State	Out-of-State
Tuition and Fees:	$7,858	$19,114
Campus and Room and Board:	$8,466	$8,466
Books and Supplies:	$1,500	$1,000
Other Expenses:	$1,079	$1,079
Total Estimated Expenses:	**$18,903**	**$29,659**

Note: Accident/Sickness insurance may be waived.

NEW APPLICANTS/NEWLY ENROLLED STUDENTS
[Numbers are for the graduate engineering college for the Fall 2006 term]

Number of Applicants (a):	174
Of those, Number Offered Admission (b):	61
Of those, Number Enrolled Fall 2006 (c):	50

William Marsh Rice University

INSTITUTION INFORMATION
P.O. Box 1892
Houston, TX 77251-1892
Phone: (713) 348-8000
Fax: (713) 348-5300
Web: http://www.rice.edu

GENERAL INFORMATION
[All Students - Fall 2006]

Undergraduate Enrollment	2,995
Graduate Enrollment	2,013
Professional Enrollment	111
Total Enrollment	**5,119**

ENGINEERING COLLEGE INFORMATION

HEAD OF ENGINEERING
Sallie Keller-McNulty
Dean of Engineering
George R. Brown School of Engineering
William Marsh Rice University
Brown School of Engineering, MS-364
P.O. Box 1892
Houston, TX 77251-1892

Phone: (713) 348-4009
Fax: (713) 348-5300
Email: deng@rice.edu

TYPES OF ENGINEERING DEGREES
Bachelor's: B.A., B.S.
Master's: M.A. with thesis, M.A. without thesis, but with project or report, M.S. with thesis, M.S. without thesis, but with project or report
Doctoral: Ph.D.

UNDERGRADUATE INFORMATION

ADMISSION INQUIRIES
Julie M Browning
Dean for Undergradraduate Enrollment
William Marsh Rice University
P.O. Box 1892,
Houston, TX 77251-1892
Phone: (713) 348-2575
Fax: (713) 348-7423
Email: jmb@rice.edu

ADMISSION INQUIRIES
James B Sinclair
Associate Dean of Engineering
William Marsh Rice University
School of Engineering, MS-364, P.O. Box 1892
Houston, TX 77251-1892
Phone: (713) 348-6324
Fax: (713) 348-5300
Email: bs@rice.edu

ESTIMATED STUDENT EXPENSES (FALL 2006)
[Expenses are for the 2006-2007 nine-month academic year and are based on an average credit load of: Undergraduate: 16]

	All Students
Tuition and fees:	$26,974
Campus and Room and Board:	$9,590
Books and Supplies:	$800
Other Expenses:	$3,086
Total Estimated Expenses:	**$40,450**

NEW APPLICANTS/NEWLY ENROLLED STUDENTS
[Numbers are for the undergraduate engineering college for the Fall 2006 term]

Number of Applicants (a):	2,071
Of those, Number Offered Admission (b):	611
Of those, Number Enrolled Fall 2006 (c):	200

GRADUATE INFORMATION

ADMISSION INQUIRIES
Elaine Carrasco
Bioengineering Department Coordinator
William Marsh Rice University
P.O. Box 1892,
Houston, TX 77251-1892
Phone: (713) 348-2871
Fax: (713) 348-5300
Email: carrase@rice.edu

ADMISSION INQUIRIES
Cindy Wilkes
Accounting Asst I
William Marsh Rice University
P.O. Box 1892,
Houston, TX 77251-1892
Phone: (713) 348-2706
Fax: (713) 348-5300
Email: Cindy.Wilkes@rice.edu

ADMISSION INQUIRIES
Margaret Poon
Department Coordinator
William Marsh Rice University
P.O. Box 1892,
Houston, TX 77251-1892
Phone: (713) 348-8000
Fax: (713) 348-5300
Email: poon@rice.edu

ADMISSION INQUIRIES
Daria Lawrence
Department & Graduate Coordinator
William Marsh Rice University
P.O. Box 1892,
Houston, TX 77251-1892
Phone: (713) 348-4657

Fax: (713) 348-5300
Email: daria@rice.edu

ADMISSION INQUIRIES
BJ Smith
Department Coordinator
William Marsh Rice University
P.O. Box 1892,
Houston, TX 77251-1892
Phone: (713) 348-8213
Fax: (713) 348-5300
Email: bjsmith@rice.edu

ADMISSION INQUIRIES
Betrose Sparks
ECE Affiliates and CMC Administrator
William Marsh Rice University
P.O. Box 1892,
Houston, TX 77251-1892
Phone: (713) 348-6232
Fax: (713) 348-5300
Email: bsparks@rice.edu

ADMISSION INQUIRIES
Emily Hall
Department Coordinator
William Marsh Rice University
P.O. Box 1892,
Houston, TX 77251-1892
Phone: (713) 348-4656
Fax: (713) 348-5300
Email: ejphall@rice.edu

ADMISSION INQUIRIES
Judith Farhat
Department Graduate Coordinator
William Marsh Rice University
P.O. Box 1892,
Houston, TX 77251-1892
Phone: (713) 348-3582
Fax: (713) 348-5300
Email: farhat@rice.edu

ESTIMATED STUDENT EXPENSES (FALL 2006)
[Expenses are for the 2006-2007 nine-month academic year and are based on an average credit load of: Graduate: 12]

	All Students
Tuition and fees:	$23,938
Campus and Room and Board:	$9,590
Books and Supplies:	$800
Other Expenses:	$3,086
Total Estimated Expenses:	**$37,414**

NEW APPLICANTS/NEWLY ENROLLED STUDENTS
[Numbers are for the graduate engineering college for the Fall 2006 term]

Number of Applicants (a):	1,545
Of those, Number Offered Admission (b):	236
Of those, Number Enrolled Fall 2006 (c):	121

Robert Morris University

INSTITUTION INFORMATION
6001 University Blvd.
Moon Township, PA 15108
Phone: (412) 262-8616
Fax: (412) 397-2472
Web: www.rmu.edu/sems

GENERAL INFORMATION
[All Students - Fall 2006]

Undergraduate Enrollment	4,000
Graduate Enrollment	1,000
Professional Enrollment	0
Total Enrollment	**5,000**

ENGINEERING COLLEGE INFORMATION

HEAD OF ENGINEERING
Winston F. Erevelles
Dean
School of Engineering, Mathematics, and Science
Robert Morris University
206 John Jay Center
6001 University Blvd.
Moon Township, PA 15108
Phone: (412) 262-8616
Fax: (412) 269-3851
Email: erevelles@rmu.edu

ENGINEERING COLLEGE INQUIRIES
Winston F. Erevelles
Dean
Robert Morris University
206 John Jay Center, 6001 University Blvd.
Moon Township, PA 15108
Phone: (412) 262-8616
Fax: (412) 269-3851
Email: erevelles@rmu.edu

TYPES OF ENGINEERING DEGREES
Bachelor's:
Master's:
Doctoral:

UNDERGRADUATE INFORMATION

ESTIMATED STUDENT EXPENSES (FALL 2006)
[Expenses are for the 2006-2007 nine-month academic year and are based on an average credit load of: Undergraduate: 15]

	All Students
Tuition and fees:	$17,920
Campus and Room and Board:	$7,100
Books and Supplies:	$1,250
Other Expenses:	$300
Total Estimated Expenses:	**$26,570**

GRADUATE INFORMATION

ESTIMATED STUDENT EXPENSES (FALL 2006)
[Expenses are for the 2006-2007 nine-month academic year and are based on an average credit load of: Graduate: 12]

	All Students
Tuition and fees:	$14,640
Campus and Room and Board:	
Books and Supplies:	$1,000
Other Expenses:	$300
Total Estimated Expenses:	**$15,940**

University of Rochester

INSTITUTION INFORMATION
University of Rochester
Rochester, NY 14627
Phone: (585) 275-2121
Web: http://www.rochester.edu/

GENERAL INFORMATION
[All Students - Fall 2006]

Undergraduate Enrollment	4,683
Graduate Enrollment	3,898
Professional Enrollment	404
Total Enrollment	**8,985**

ENGINEERING COLLEGE INFORMATION

HEAD OF ENGINEERING
Kevin J Parker
Dean
School of Engineering and Applied Sciences
University of Rochester
Lattimore Hall 309
RC Box 270076
Rochester, NY 14627-0076
Phone: (158) 527-5415
Fax: (158) 546-4735
Email: parker@seas.rochester.edu

ENGINEERING COLLEGE INQUIRIES
Elayne M Stewart
Administrative Assistant for Undergraduate Programs
University of Rochester
Box 270076
Rochester, NY 14627-0076
Phone: (585) 275-3954
Fax: (585) 461-4735
Email: stewart@seas.rochester.edu

ENGINEERING COLLEGE INQUIRIES
Rosemary Boyd Parker
Administrator
University of Rochester
Lattimore Hall 309, RC Box 270076
Rochester, NY 14627-0076
Phone: (158) 527-5415
Fax: (158) 546-4735
Email: rosemary.b.parker@rochester.edu

TYPES OF ENGINEERING DEGREES

Bachelor's: B.A., B.S.
Master's: M.S. with thesis, M.S. without thesis, but with project or report
Doctoral: Ph.D.

UNDERGRADUATE INFORMATION

ADMISSION INQUIRIES

Elayne M Stewart
Administrative Assistant for Undergraduate Programs
University of Rochester
Box 270076
Rochester, NY 14627-0076
Phone: (585) 275-3954
Fax: (585) 461-4735
Email: stewart@seas.rochester.edu

ADMISSION INQUIRIES

Jonathan Burdick
Dean of Admissions and Financial Aid
University of Rochester
RC Box 270250
Rochester, NY 14627-0250
Phone: (585) 275-6805
Fax: (585) 461-4595
Email: deanafa@rochester.edu

ADMISSION INQUIRIES

Lisa G Norwood
Assistant Dean
University of Rochester
Box 270076
Rochester, NY 14627-0076
Phone: (585) 461-4155
Fax: (585) 461-4735
Email: lnrw@seas.rochester.edu

ESTIMATED STUDENT EXPENSES (FALL 2006)

[Expenses are for the 2006-2007 nine-month academic year and are based on an average credit load of: Undergraduate: 32]

	All Students
Tuition and fees:	$32,650
Campus and Room and Board:	$10,552
Books and Supplies:	$750
Other Expenses:	$3,600
Total Estimated Expenses:	**$47,552**

Note: Other expenses: travel; health, activity, and lab fees; and personal expenses.

NEW APPLICANTS/NEWLY ENROLLED STUDENTS

[Numbers are for the undergraduate engineering college for the Fall 2006 term]

Number of Applicants (a):	1,445
Of those, Number Offered Admission (b):	809
Of those, Number Enrolled Fall 2006 (c):	172

GRADUATE INFORMATION

ADMISSION INQUIRIES

Susan B Amon
Assistant to the Dean for Graduate Studies
University of Rochester
Box 270401
Rochester , NY 14627-0401
Phone: (585) 275-4153
Fax: (585) 273-2943
Email: gradstudies@mail.rochester.edu

ESTIMATED STUDENT EXPENSES (FALL 2006)

[Expenses are for the 2006-2007 nine-month academic year and are based on an average credit load of: Graduate: 32]

	All Students
Tuition and fees:	$32,650
Campus and Room and Board:	$12,500
Books and Supplies:	$950
Other Expenses:	$2,600
Total Estimated Expenses:	**$48,700**

Note: Other expenses: travel; health, activity, and lab fees; and personal expenses.

NEW APPLICANTS/NEWLY ENROLLED STUDENTS

[Numbers are for the graduate engineering college for the Fall 2006 term]

Number of Applicants (a):	1,339
Of those, Number Offered Admission (b):	263
Of those, Number Enrolled Fall 2006 (c):	136

Rochester Institute of Technology

INSTITUTION INFORMATION

One Lomb Memorial Drive
Rochester, NY 14623-5603
Phone: (585) 475-2411
Web: http://www.rit.edu

GENERAL INFORMATION

[All Students - Fall 2006]

Undergraduate Enrollment	13,140
Graduate Enrollment	2,417
Professional Enrollment	0
Total Enrollment	**15,557**

ENGINEERING COLLEGE INFORMATION

HEAD OF ENGINEERING

Harvey J Palmer
Dean
Dean's Office, Kate Gleason College of Engineering
Rochester Institute of Technology
77 Lomb Memorial Drive
Rochester, NY 14623-5603
Phone: (585) 475-2146
Fax: (585) 475-6879
Email: hjpeen@rit.edu

TYPES OF ENGINEERING DEGREES

Bachelor's: B.S.
Master's: M.S. with thesis, M.S. without thesis, but with project or report, M.Eng.
Doctoral: Ph.D.

UNDERGRADUATE INFORMATION

ESTIMATED STUDENT EXPENSES (FALL 2006)

[Expenses are for the 2006-2007 nine-month academic year and are based on an average credit load of: Undergraduate: 16]

	All Students
Tuition and fees:	$25,011
Campus and Room and Board:	$8,748
Books and Supplies:	$900
Other Expenses:	$1,025
Total Estimated Expenses:	**$35,684**

Note: Graduate tuition also charged at $755 per credit hour.

NEW APPLICANTS/NEWLY ENROLLED STUDENTS

[Numbers are for the undergraduate engineering college for the Fall 2006 term]

Number of Applicants (a):	3,094
Of those, Number Offered Admission (b):	1,859
Of those, Number Enrolled Fall 2006 (c):	590

Note: Does not include Software Engineering or Computer Science. They are housed in different RIT colleges outside of the College of Engineering.

GRADUATE INFORMATION

ADMISSION INQUIRIES

Mustafa A Abushagur
Director, Microsystems Engineering Ph.D. Program
Rochester Institute of Technology
77 Lomb Memorial Drive
Rochester , NY 14623-5603
Phone: (585) 475-2145
Fax: (585) 475-6879
Email: maaeen@rit.edu

ESTIMATED STUDENT EXPENSES (FALL 2006)

[Expenses are for the 2006-2007 nine-month academic year and are based on an average credit load of: Graduate: 12]

	All Students
Tuition and fees:	$27,096
Campus and Room and Board:	
Books and Supplies:	
Other Expenses:	
Total Estimated Expenses:	**$27,096**

Note: Graduate tuition also charged at $755 per credit hour.

NEW APPLICANTS/NEWLY ENROLLED STUDENTS

[Numbers are for the graduate engineering college for the Fall 2006 term]

Number of Applicants (a):	619
Of those, Number Offered Admission (b):	374
Of those, Number Enrolled Fall 2006 (c):	123

Roger Williams University

INSTITUTION INFORMATION

One Old Ferry Road
Bristol, RI 02809
Phone: (401) 254-3314
Fax: (401) 254-3562
Web: http://www.rwu.edu

GENERAL INFORMATION

[All Students - Fall 2006]

Undergraduate Enrollment	3,775
Graduate Enrollment	815
Professional Enrollment	0
Total Enrollment	**4,590**

ENGINEERING COLLEGE INFORMATION

HEAD OF ENGINEERING

Robert A Potter, Jr.
Dean, School of Engineering, Computing, and Construction Management
SECCM
Roger Williams University
One Old Ferry Road
Bristol, RI 02809
Phone: (401) 254-3314
Fax: (401) 254-3562
Email: bobpotter@rwu.edu

TYPES OF ENGINEERING DEGREES

Bachelor's: B.S.
Master's:
Doctoral:

UNDERGRADUATE INFORMATION

ESTIMATED STUDENT EXPENSES (FALL 2006)

[Expenses are for the 2006-2007 nine-month academic year and are based on an average credit load of: Undergraduate: 16]

	All Students
Tuition and fees:	$24,550
Campus and Room and Board:	$10,400
Books and Supplies:	$1,400
Other Expenses:	$1,510
Total Estimated Expenses:	**$37,860**

NEW APPLICANTS/NEWLY ENROLLED STUDENTS

[Numbers are for the undergraduate engineering college for the Fall 2006 term]

Number of Applicants (a):	462
Of those, Number Offered Admission (b):	0
Of those, Number Enrolled Fall 2006 (c):	112

Note: This figure represents all three programs for the School: CS, CM and Engineering. For Engineering, applicant total was 265 for 51 seats.

Rose-Hulman Institute of Technology

INSTITUTION INFORMATION

5500 Wabash Avenue
Terre Haute, IN 47803
Phone: (812) 877-1511
Fax: (812) 877-8001
Web: http://www.rose-hulman.edu

ENGINEERING COLLEGE INFORMATION

HEAD OF ENGINEERING

Arthur B Western
Vice President for Academic Affairs and Dean of Faculty
Academic Affairs
Rose-Hulman Institute of Technology
5500 Wabash Avenue
Terre Haute, IN 47803
Phone: (812) 877-8337
Fax: (812) 877-1035
Email: arthur.western@rose-hulman.edu

ENGINEERING COLLEGE INQUIRIES

Arthur B Western
Vice President for Academic Affairs and Dean of Faculty
Rose-Hulman Institute of Technology
5500 Wabash Avenue
Terre Haute, IN 47803

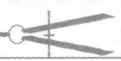

Phone: (812) 877-8337
Fax: (812) 877-1035
Email: arthur.western@rose-hulman.edu

TYPES OF ENGINEERING DEGREES
Bachelor's: B.S.
Master's: M.S. with thesis, M.S. without thesis, but with project or report, M.Eng.
Doctoral:

UNDERGRADUATE INFORMATION

ADMISSION INQUIRIES
James A Goecker
Dean of Admissions and Financial Aid
Rose-Hulman Institute of Technology
5500 Wabash Avenue, CM-1
Terre Haute, IN 47803
Phone: (812) 877-8213
Fax: (812) 877-8941
Email: james.goecker@rose-hulman.edu

ESTIMATED STUDENT EXPENSES (FALL 2006)
[Expenses are for the 2006-2007 nine-month academic year and are based on an average credit load of: Undergraduate: 16]

	All Students
Tuition and fees:	$28,530
Campus and Room and Board:	$7,869
Books and Supplies:	$1,500
Other Expenses:	$1,500
Total Estimated Expenses:	**$39,399**

Note: Additional other expenses: $3,200 is one-time-only laptop fee.

NEW APPLICANTS/NEWLY ENROLLED STUDENTS
[Numbers are for the undergraduate engineering college for the Fall 2006 term]

Number of Applicants (a):	3,059
Of those, Number Offered Admission (b):	2,205
Of those, Number Enrolled Fall 2006 (c):	525

GRADUATE INFORMATION

ADMISSION INQUIRIES
Daniel Moore
Associate Dean of the Faculty
Rose-Hulman Institute of Technology
5500 Wabash Avenue, CM-26
Terre Haute, IN 47803
Phone: (812) 877-8110
Fax: (812) 877-8061
Email: daniel.moore@rose-hulman.edu

ESTIMATED STUDENT EXPENSES (FALL 2006)
[Expenses are for the 2006-2007 nine-month academic year and are based on an average credit load of: Graduate: 8]

	All Students
Tuition and fees:	$28,530
Campus and Room and Board:	$7,869
Books and Supplies:	$1,500
Other Expenses:	
Total Estimated Expenses:	**$37,899**

Note: Additional other expenses: $3,200 is one-time-only laptop fee.

NEW APPLICANTS/NEWLY ENROLLED STUDENTS
[Numbers are for the graduate engineering college for the Fall 2006 term]

Number of Applicants (a):	66
Of those, Number Offered Admission (b):	47
Of those, Number Enrolled Fall 2006 (c):	35

Rowan University

INSTITUTION INFORMATION
201 Mullica Hill Road
Glassboro, NJ 08028
Phone: (856) 256-5300
Fax: (856) 256-5350
Web: http://www.rowan.edu/engineering

GENERAL INFORMATION
[All Students - Fall 2006]

Undergraduate Enrollment	8,430
Graduate Enrollment	1,148
Professional Enrollment	0
Total Enrollment	**9,578**

ENGINEERING COLLEGE INFORMATION

HEAD OF ENGINEERING
Dianne Dorland
Dean
College of Engineering
Rowan University
201 Mullica Hill Road
Glassboro,, NJ 08028
Phone: (856) 256-5300
Fax: (856) 256-5350
Email: dorland@rowan.edu

ENGINEERING COLLEGE INQUIRIES
Dianne Dorland
Dean
Rowan University
201 Mullica Hill Road
Glassboro,, NJ 08028
Phone: (856) 256-5300
Fax: (856) 256-5350
Email: dorland@rowan.edu

TYPES OF ENGINEERING DEGREES
Bachelor's: B.S.
Master's: M.S. with thesis, M.S. without thesis, but with project or report
Doctoral:

UNDERGRADUATE INFORMATION

ADMISSION INQUIRIES
Steven H Chin
Associate Dean
Rowan University
201 Mullica Hill Road
Glassboro, NJ 08028
Phone: (856) 256-5301
Fax: (856) 256-5350
Email: chin@rowan.edu

ESTIMATED STUDENT EXPENSES (FALL 2006)
[Expenses are for the 2006-2007 nine-month academic year and are based on an average credit load of: Undergraduate: 16]

	In-State	Out-of-State
Tuition and Fees:	$9,330	$16,128
Campus and Room and Board:	$8,742	$8,742
Books and Supplies:	$1,000	$1,000
Other Expenses:	$1,800	$1,800
Total Estimated Expenses:	**$20,872**	**$27,670**

NEW APPLICANTS/NEWLY ENROLLED STUDENTS
[Numbers are for the undergraduate engineering college for the Fall 2006 term]

Number of Applicants (a):	585
Of those, Number Offered Admission (b):	339
Of those, Number Enrolled Fall 2006 (c):	108

GRADUATE INFORMATION

ESTIMATED STUDENT EXPENSES (FALL 2006)
[Expenses are for the 2006-2007 nine-month academic year and are based on an average credit load of: Graduate: 11]

	In-State	Out-of-State
Tuition and Fees:	$11,769	$11,769
Campus and Room and Board:	$8,742	$8,742
Books and Supplies:	$1,000	$1,000
Other Expenses:	$1,800	$1,800
Total Estimated Expenses:	**$23,311**	**$23,311**

NEW APPLICANTS/NEWLY ENROLLED STUDENTS
[Numbers are for the graduate engineering college for the Fall 2006 term]

Number of Applicants (a):	20
Of those, Number Offered Admission (b):	20
Of those, Number Enrolled Fall 2006 (c):	20

Saginaw Valley State University

INSTITUTION INFORMATION
7400 Bay Road
University Center, MI 48710
Phone: (989) 964-4144
Fax: (989) 964-2717
Web: http://www.svsu.edu

GENERAL INFORMATION
[All Students - Fall 2006]

Undergraduate Enrollment	7,933
Graduate Enrollment	1,610
Professional Enrollment	0
Total Enrollment	**9,543**

ENGINEERING COLLEGE INFORMATION

HEAD OF ENGINEERING
Ronald R Williams
Dean, Science Engineering & Technology
Saginaw Valley State University
Zahnow 231
7400 Bay Road
University Center, MI 48710
Phone: (989) 964-4144
Fax: (989) 964-2717
Email: ron.williams@svsu.edu

TYPES OF ENGINEERING DEGREES
Bachelor's: B.S.
Master's:
Doctoral:

UNDERGRADUATE INFORMATION

ADMISSION INQUIRIES
James P Dwyer
Assistant Vice President & Director Undergraduate Admissions
Saginaw Valley State University
7400 Bay Road, Wickes Hall 185
University Center, MI 48710
Phone: (989) 964-4209
Fax: (989) 790-0180
Email: jdwyer@svsu.edu

ESTIMATED STUDENT EXPENSES (FALL 2006)
[Expenses are for the 2006-2007 nine-month academic year and are based on an average credit load of: Undergraduate: 15]

	All Students
Tuition and fees:	$5,543
Campus and Room and Board:	$6,380
Books and Supplies:	$900
Other Expenses:	$910
Total Estimated Expenses:	**$13,733**

NEW APPLICANTS/NEWLY ENROLLED STUDENTS
[Numbers are for the undergraduate engineering college for the Fall 2006 term]

Number of Applicants (a):	220
Of those, Number Offered Admission (b):	196
Of those, Number Enrolled Fall 2006 (c):	90

GRADUATE INFORMATION

ESTIMATED STUDENT EXPENSES (FALL 2006)
[Expenses are for the 2006-2007 nine-month academic year and are based on an average credit load of: Graduate: 12]

	All Students
Tuition and fees:	$7,555
Campus and Room and Board:	$6,380
Books and Supplies:	$900
Other Expenses:	$910
Total Estimated Expenses:	**$15,745**

Saint Cloud State University

INSTITUTION INFORMATION
Wick Science Building # 145
720 Fourth Avenue South
St. Cloud, MN 56301
Phone: (320) 308-2192
Fax: (320) 308-4262
Web: http://www.stcloudstate.edu

ENGINEERING COLLEGE INFORMATION

HEAD OF ENGINEERING
David K DeGroote
Dean of Science and Engineering
College of Science and Engineering
Saint Cloud State University
145, Mathematics & Science Center
720 Fourth Avenue South

St. Cloud, MN 56301-4498
Phone: (320) 308-2192
Fax: (320) 308-4262
Email: cose@stcloudstate.edu

TYPES OF ENGINEERING DEGREES
Bachelor's: B.S.
Master's: M.S. with thesis, M.S. without thesis, but with project or report
Doctoral:

UNDERGRADUATE INFORMATION

ESTIMATED STUDENT EXPENSES (FALL 2006)
[Expenses are for the 2006-2007 nine-month academic year and are based on an average credit load of: Undergraduate: 15]

	In-State	Out-of-State
Tuition and Fees:	$5,722	$11,630
Campus and Room and Board:	$5,250	$5,250
Books and Supplies:	$1,000	$1,000
Other Expenses:	$2,546	$2,546
Total Estimated Expenses:	**$14,518**	**$20,426**

NEW APPLICANTS/NEWLY ENROLLED STUDENTS
[Numbers are for the undergraduate engineering college for the Fall 2006 term]

Number of Applicants (a):	84
Of those, Number Offered Admission (b):	0
Of those, Number Enrolled Fall 2006 (c):	0

Note: N.A.

GRADUATE INFORMATION

ESTIMATED STUDENT EXPENSES (FALL 2006)
[Expenses are for the 2006-2007 nine-month academic year and are based on an average credit load of: Graduate: 10]

	In-State	Out-of-State
Tuition and Fees:	$5,528	$7,716
Campus and Room and Board:	$5,250	$5,250
Books and Supplies:		
Other Expenses:		
Total Estimated Expenses:	**$10,778**	**$12,966**

Saint Louis University - Parks College

INSTITUTION INFORMATION
3450 Lindell Boulevard
St. Louis, MO 63103
Phone: (314) 977-8203
Fax: (314) 977-8403
Web: http://parks.slu.edu

GENERAL INFORMATION
[All Students - Fall 2006]

Undergraduate Enrollment	7,420
Graduate Enrollment	2,100
Professional Enrollment	2,300
Total Enrollment	**11,820**

ENGINEERING COLLEGE INFORMATION

HEAD OF ENGINEERING
Manoj Patankar
Interim Dean
Deans Office
Saint Louis University - Parks College
3450 Lindell Blvd
St. Louis, MO 63103
Phone: (314) 977-8203
Fax: (314) 977-8403
Email: patankar@slu.edu

TYPES OF ENGINEERING DEGREES
Bachelor's: B.S.
Master's: M.S. with thesis, M.S. without thesis, but with project or report
Doctoral: Ph.D.

UNDERGRADUATE INFORMATION

ESTIMATED STUDENT EXPENSES (FALL 2006)
[Expenses are for the 2006-2007 nine-month academic year and are based on an average credit load of: Undergraduate: 14]

	All Students
Tuition and fees:	$26,250

Campus and Room and Board:	$8,000
Books and Supplies:	$1,040
Other Expenses:	$1,030
Total Estimated Expenses:	**$36,320**

NEW APPLICANTS/NEWLY ENROLLED STUDENTS
[Numbers are for the undergraduate engineering college for the Fall 2006 term]

Number of Applicants (a):	1,033
Of those, Number Offered Admission (b):	691
Of those, Number Enrolled Fall 2006 (c):	117

GRADUATE INFORMATION

ESTIMATED STUDENT EXPENSES (FALL 2006)
[Expenses are for the 2006-2007 nine-month academic year and are based on an average credit load of: Graduate: 5]

	All Students
Tuition and fees:	$12,420
Campus and Room and Board:	$9,600
Books and Supplies:	$1,040
Other Expenses:	$10,264
Total Estimated Expenses:	**$33,324**

NEW APPLICANTS/NEWLY ENROLLED STUDENTS
[Numbers are for the graduate engineering college for the Fall 2006 term]

Number of Applicants (a):	15
Of those, Number Offered Admission (b):	11
Of those, Number Enrolled Fall 2006 (c):	2

University of San Diego

INSTITUTION INFORMATION
Department of Engineering
5998 Alcala Park
San Diego, CA 92110-2492
Phone: (619) 260-4627
Fax: (619) 260-2303
Web: http://www.sandiego.edu/engineering

GENERAL INFORMATION
[All Students - Fall 2006]

Undergraduate Enrollment	4,962
Graduate Enrollment	1,376
Professional Enrollment	1,145
Total Enrollment	**7,483**

ENGINEERING COLLEGE INFORMATION

ENGINEERING COLLEGE INQUIRIES
Kathleen A. Kramer
Director of Engineering Programs
University of San Diego
University of San Diego, 5998 Alcala Park
San Diego, CA 92110-2492
Phone: (619) 260-4627
Fax: (619) 260-2303
Email: kramer@sandiego.edu

ENGINEERING COLLEGE INQUIRIES
Andrew T Allen
Interim Dean
University of San Diego
, 5998 Alcala Park
San Deigo, CA 92110-2492
Phone: (619) 260-4886
Fax: (619) 260-2303
Email: sbadean@sandiego.edu

TYPES OF ENGINEERING DEGREES
Bachelor's: B.A., B.S.
Master's:
Doctoral:

UNDERGRADUATE INFORMATION

ADMISSION INQUIRIES
Stephen Pultz
Director
University of San Diego
5998 Alcala Park
San Diego, CA 92110-2492
Phone: (619) 260-4627
Fax: (619) 260-6836
Email: pultzs@sandiego.edu

ESTIMATED STUDENT EXPENSES (FALL 2006)
[Expenses are for the 2006-2007 nine-month academic year and are based on an average credit load of: Undergraduate: 17]

	All Students
Tuition and fees:	$15,240
Campus and Room and Board:	$9,500
Books and Supplies:	
Other Expenses:	$80
Total Estimated Expenses:	**$24,820**

NEW APPLICANTS/NEWLY ENROLLED STUDENTS
[Numbers are for the undergraduate engineering college for the Fall 2006 term]

Number of Applicants (a):	60
Of those, Number Offered Admission (b):	60
Of those, Number Enrolled Fall 2006 (c):	56

Note: Students are not directly admitted to the Department of Engineering -- only to the University.

San Diego State University

INSTITUTION INFORMATION
5500 Campanile Drive
San Diego, CA 92182
Phone: (619) 594-5200
Web: http://www.sdsu.edu

GENERAL INFORMATION
[All Students - Fall 2006]

Undergraduate Enrollment	28,527
Graduate Enrollment	5,778
Professional Enrollment	0
Total Enrollment	**34,305**

ENGINEERING COLLEGE INFORMATION

HEAD OF ENGINEERING
David T Hayhurst
Dean of College of Engineering
College of Engineering
San Diego State University
5500 Campanile Drive
San Diego, CA 92182-1326
Phone: (619) 594-7005
Fax: (619) 594-6005
Email: hayhurst@engineering.sdsu.edu

ENGINEERING COLLEGE INQUIRIES
Larry Hinkle
Director of Engineering Student Services
San Diego State University
5500 Campanile Drive
San Diego, CA 92182
Phone: (619) 594-5807
Fax: (619) 594-3138
Email: lhinkle@mail.sdsu.edu

TYPES OF ENGINEERING DEGREES
Bachelor's: B.S.
Master's: M.S. with thesis, M.S. without thesis, but with project or report, M.Eng.
Doctoral: Ph.D.

UNDERGRADUATE INFORMATION

ADMISSION INQUIRIES
Bruce Westermo
Assistant Dean
San Diego State University
5500 Campanile Drive
San Diego, CA 92182
Phone: (619) 594-7007
Fax: (619) 594-3138
Email: westermo@engineering.sdsu.edu

ESTIMATED STUDENT EXPENSES (FALL 2006)
[Expenses are for the 2006-2007 nine-month academic year and are based on an average credit load of: Undergraduate: 13]

	In-State	Out-of-State
Tuition and Fees:	$3,160	$7,567
Campus and Room and Board:	$9,352	$9,352
Books and Supplies:	$1,283	$1,283
Other Expenses:	$2,496	$2,496
Total Estimated Expenses:	**$16,291**	**$20,698**

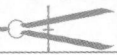

NEW APPLICANTS/NEWLY ENROLLED STUDENTS
[Numbers are for the undergraduate engineering college for the Fall 2006 term]

Number of Applicants (a):	3,225
Of those, Number Offered Admission (b):	1,850
Of those, Number Enrolled Fall 2006 (c):	505

GRADUATE INFORMATION

ADMISSION INQUIRIES
Lal Tummala
Professor and Chair of Electrical and Computer Engineering
San Diego State University
5500 Campanile Drive
San Diego , CA 92182-1309
Phone: (619) 594-7045
Fax: (619) 594-2654
Email: tummala@engineering.sdsu.edu

ADMISSION INQUIRIES
Khaled Morsi
Assistant Professor
San Diego State University
5500 Campanile Drive
San Diego , CA 92182
Phone: (619) 594-2903
Fax: (619) 594-3599
Email: kmorsi@mail.sdsu.edu

ADMISSION INQUIRIES
Julio Valdes
Assistant Professor
San Diego State University
5500 Campanile Drive
San Diego , CA 92182-1324
Phone: (619) 594-7070
Fax: (619) 594-8078
Email: jvaldes@engineering.sdsu.edu

ADMISSION INQUIRIES
Satchi Venkataraman
Assistant Professor
San Diego State University
5500 Campanile Drive
San Diego , CA 92182
Phone: (619) 594-6660
Fax: (619) 594-0933
Email: satchi@engineering.sdsu.edu

ADMISSION INQUIRIES
Gordon K Lee
Associate Dean and Director, Joint Doctoral Program
San Diego State University
5500 Campanile Drive
San Diego , CA 92182-1326
Phone: (619) 594-7006
Fax: (619) 594-6005
Email: glee@kahuna.sdsu.edu

ESTIMATED STUDENT EXPENSES (FALL 2006)
[Expenses are for the 2006-2007 nine-month academic year and are based on an average credit load of: Graduate: 9]

	In-State	Out-of-State
Tutition and Fees:	$3,742	$6,793
Campus and Room and Board:	$9,352	$9,352
Books and Supplies:	$1,283	$1,283
Other Expenses:	$2,496	$2,496
Total Estimated Expenses:	**$16,873**	**$19,924**

NEW APPLICANTS/NEWLY ENROLLED STUDENTS
[Numbers are for the graduate engineering college for the Fall 2006 term]

Number of Applicants (a):	504
Of those, Number Offered Admission (b):	283
Of those, Number Enrolled Fall 2006 (c):	121

San Jose State University

INSTITUTION INFORMATION
One Washington Square
San Jose, CA 95192
Phone: (408) 924-1000
Fax: (408) 924-3818
Web: http://www.sjsu.edu

GENERAL INFORMATION
[All Students - Fall 2006]

Undergraduate Enrollment	18,598
Graduate Enrollment	4,877
Professional Enrollment	612
Total Enrollment	**24,087**

ENGINEERING COLLEGE INFORMATION

HEAD OF ENGINEERING
Belle Wei
Dean of Engineering
College of Engineering
San Jose State University
One Washington Square
San Jose, CA 95192
Phone: (408) 924-3800
Fax: (408) 924-3818
Email: bwei@email.sjsu.edu

TYPES OF ENGINEERING DEGREES
Bachelor's: B.S.
Master's: M.S. with thesis, M.S. without thesis, but with project or report
Doctoral:

UNDERGRADUATE INFORMATION

ESTIMATED STUDENT EXPENSES (FALL 2006)
[Expenses are for the 2006-2007 nine-month academic year and are based on an average credit load of: Undergraduate: 12]

	In-State	Out-of-State
Tutition and Fees:	$3,296	
Campus and Room and Board:	$11,690	
Books and Supplies:	$1,300	
Other Expenses:	$2,664	
Total Estimated Expenses:	$18,950	

Note: Non-residents must add $339 per unit to registration fees.

NEW APPLICANTS/NEWLY ENROLLED STUDENTS
[Numbers are for the undergraduate engineering college for the Fall 2006 term]

Number of Applicants (a):	3,446
Of those, Number Offered Admission (b):	2,037
Of those, Number Enrolled Fall 2006 (c):	706

GRADUATE INFORMATION

ESTIMATED STUDENT EXPENSES (FALL 2006)
[Expenses are for the 2006-2007 nine-month academic year and are based on an average credit load of: Graduate: 9]

	In-State	Out-of-State
Tutition and Fees:	$3,878	
Campus and Room and Board:	$11,690	
Books and Supplies:	$1,300	
Other Expenses:	$2,664	
Total Estimated Expenses:	**$19,532**	

Note: Non-residents must add $339 per unit to registration fees.

NEW APPLICANTS/NEWLY ENROLLED STUDENTS
[Numbers are for the graduate engineering college for the Fall 2006 term]

Number of Applicants (a):	750
Of those, Number Offered Admission (b):	582
Of those, Number Enrolled Fall 2006 (c):	338

Santa Clara University

INSTITUTION INFORMATION
School of Engineering
500 El Camino Real
Santa Clara, CA 95053
Phone: (408) 554-4600
Fax: (408) 554-5474
Web: http://www.scu.edu

GENERAL INFORMATION
[All Students - Fall 2006]

Undergraduate Enrollment	5,243
Graduate Enrollment	2,392
Professional Enrollment	947
Total Enrollment	**8,582**

ENGINEERING COLLEGE INFORMATION

HEAD OF ENGINEERING
Jim Koch
Interim Dean of Engineering

Santa Clara University
School of Engineering
500 El Camino Real
Santa Clara, CA 95053
Phone: (408) 554-4600
Fax: (408) 554-5474
Email: jkoch@scu.edu

TYPES OF ENGINEERING DEGREES
Bachelor's: B.S.
Master's: M.S. with thesis, M.S. without thesis, but with project or report, M.Eng.
Doctoral: Ph.D.

UNDERGRADUATE INFORMATION

ESTIMATED STUDENT EXPENSES (FALL 2006)
[Expenses are for the 2006-2007 nine-month academic year and are based on an average credit load of: Undergraduate: 17]

	All Students
Tutition and fees:	$30,900
Campus and Room and Board:	$10,380
Books and Supplies:	$1,242
Other Expenses:	$2,925
Total Estimated Expenses:	**$45,447**

NEW APPLICANTS/NEWLY ENROLLED STUDENTS
[Numbers are for the undergraduate engineering college for the Fall 2006 term]

Number of Applicants (a):	804
Of those, Number Offered Admission (b):	628
Of those, Number Enrolled Fall 2006 (c):	154

GRADUATE INFORMATION

ADMISSION INQUIRIES
LeAnn Marchewka
Assistant Director
Santa Clara University
School of Engineering, 500 El Camino Real
Santa Clara , CA 95053
Phone: (408) 554-4765
Fax: (408) 554-5474
Email: LMarchewka@scu.edu

ADMISSION INQUIRIES
Wan Qiu Chen
Director
Santa Clara University
School of Engineering, 500 El Camino Real
Santa Clara , CA 95053
Phone: (408) 551-7839
Fax: (408) 554-5474
Email: wqchen@scu.edu

ADMISSION INQUIRIES
Diana L McDonald
Asst. Director
Santa Clara University
School of Engineering, 500 El Camino Real
Santa Clara , CA 95053
Phone: (408) 554-1857
Fax: (408) 554-5474

ESTIMATED STUDENT EXPENSES (FALL 2006)
[Expenses are for the 2006-2007 nine-month academic year and are based on an average credit load of: Graduate: N/A]

	All Students
Tutition and fees:	$15,078
Campus and Room and Board:	
Books and Supplies:	
Other Expenses:	
Total Estimated Expenses:	**$15,078**

NEW APPLICANTS/NEWLY ENROLLED STUDENTS
[Numbers are for the graduate engineering college for the Fall 2006 term]

Number of Applicants (a):	384
Of those, Number Offered Admission (b):	254
Of those, Number Enrolled Fall 2006 (c):	152

Seattle University

INSTITUTION INFORMATION
901 12th Avenue
P.O. Box 222000
Seattle, WA 98122
Phone: (206) 296-6000

Fax: (206) 296-2071
Web: http://www.seattleu.edu

GENERAL INFORMATION
[All Students - Fall 2006]
Undergraduate Enrollment	4,160
Graduate Enrollment	3,066
Professional Enrollment	0
Total Enrollment	**7,226**

ENGINEERING COLLEGE INFORMATION

HEAD OF ENGINEERING
George M Simmons
Dean
College of Science and Engineering
Seattle University
901 12th Avenue
P.O. Box 222000
Seattle, WA 98122-1090
Phone: (206) 296-5500
Fax: (206) 296-2179
Email: gsimmons@seattleu.edu

ENGINEERING COLLEGE INQUIRIES
George M Simmons
Dean
Seattle University
901 12th Avenue, P.O. Box 222000
Seattle, WA 98122-1090
Phone: (206) 296-5500
Fax: (206) 296-2179
Email: gsimmons@seattleu.edu

ENGINEERING COLLEGE INQUIRIES
Patricia Daniels
Associate Dean
Seattle University
901 12th Avenue, P.O. Box 222000
Seattle, WA 98122-1090
Phone: (206) 296-5504
Fax: (206) 296-2179
Email: daniels@seattleu.edu

TYPES OF ENGINEERING DEGREES
Bachelor's: B.A., B.S.
Master's: M.S. without thesis, but with project or report
Doctoral:

UNDERGRADUATE INFORMATION

ADMISSION INQUIRIES
Mara Rempe
Associate Dean
Seattle University
900 12th Avenue, P.O. Box 222000
Seattle, WA 98122-1090
Phone: (206) 296-5582
Fax: (206) 296-2179
Email: mrempe@seattle.edu

ESTIMATED STUDENT EXPENSES (FALL 2006)
[Expenses are for the 2006-2007 nine-month academic year and are based on an average credit load of: Undergraduate: 15]
	All Students
Tutition and fees:	$24,615
Campus and Room and Board:	$7,503
Books and Supplies:	$1,260
Other Expenses:	$3,504
Total Estimated Expenses:	**$36,882**

NEW APPLICANTS/NEWLY ENROLLED STUDENTS
[Numbers are for the undergraduate engineering college for the Fall 2006 term]
Number of Applicants (a):	392
Of those, Number Offered Admission (b):	221
Of those, Number Enrolled Fall 2006 (c):	55

GRADUATE INFORMATION

ADMISSION INQUIRIES
Michael Smith
Senior Administrative Assistant
Seattle University
901 12th Avenue, P.O. Box 222000
Seattle , WA 98122-1090
Phone: (206) 296-5510
Fax: (206) 296-2179

ESTIMATED STUDENT EXPENSES (FALL 2006)
[Expenses are for the 2006-2007 academic year and are based on an average credit load of: Graduate: 9]
	All Students
Tutition and fees:	$8,604
Campus and Room and Board:	$7,503
Books and Supplies:	$774
Other Expenses:	$3,628
Total Estimated Expenses:	**$20,509**

Seattle Pacific University

INSTITUTION INFORMATION
3307 Third Avenue West, Suite 307
Engineering Programs
Seattle, WA 98119
Phone: (206) 281-2140
Fax: (206) 378-5400
Web: http://www.spu.edu/

GENERAL INFORMATION
[All Students - Fall 2006]
Undergraduate Enrollment	2,979
Graduate Enrollment	794
Professional Enrollment	57
Total Enrollment	**3,830**

ENGINEERING COLLEGE INFORMATION

TYPES OF ENGINEERING DEGREES
Bachelor's: B.S.
Master's:
Doctoral:

UNDERGRADUATE INFORMATION

ESTIMATED STUDENT EXPENSES (FALL 2006)
[Expenses are for the 2006-2007 nine-month academic year and are based on an average credit load of: Undergraduate: 18]
	All Students
Tutition and fees:	$23,055
Campus and Room and Board:	$8,000
Books and Supplies:	
Other Expenses:	$340
Total Estimated Expenses:	**$31,395**

Smith College

INSTITUTION INFORMATION
51 College Lane
Northampton, MA 01063
Phone: (413) 548-2700
Web: http://www.smith.edu/

GENERAL INFORMATION
[All Students - Fall 2006]
Undergraduate Enrollment	2,750
Graduate Enrollment	300
Professional Enrollment	0
Total Enrollment	**3,050**

ENGINEERING COLLEGE INFORMATION

HEAD OF ENGINEERING
Linda E. Jones
Director and Chair
Picker Engineering Program
Smith College
51 College Lane
Northampton, MA 01063
Phone: (413) 585-7000
Email: ljones@smith.edu

ENGINEERING COLLEGE INQUIRIES
Dawn Scaparotti
Assistant to the Director
Smith College
51 College Lane
Northampton, MA 01063
Phone: (413) 585-4200
Fax: (413) 585-7001
Email: dscaparo@email.smith.edu

TYPES OF ENGINEERING DEGREES
Bachelor's: B.S.
Master's:
Doctoral:

UNDERGRADUATE INFORMATION

ESTIMATED STUDENT EXPENSES (FALL 2006)
[Expenses are for the 2006-2007 nine-month academic year and are based on an average credit load of: Undergraduate: 16]
	All Students
Tutition and fees:	$32,320
Campus and Room and Board:	$10,880
Books and Supplies:	
Other Expenses:	$238
Total Estimated Expenses:	**$43,438**

NEW APPLICANTS/NEWLY ENROLLED STUDENTS
[Numbers are for the undergraduate engineering college for the Fall 2006 term]
Number of Applicants (a):	151
Of those, Number Offered Admission (b):	78
Of those, Number Enrolled Fall 2006 (c):	33

Note: Students apply to Smith College directly and indicate their interest in Engineering

University of South Alabama

INSTITUTION INFORMATION
307 University Boulevard
EGCB 108
Mobile, AL 36688
Phone: (251) 460-6140
Fax: (251) 460-6343
Web: http://www.southalabama.edu

GENERAL INFORMATION
[All Students - Fall 2006]
Undergraduate Enrollment	10,078
Graduate Enrollment	2,736
Professional Enrollment	489
Total Enrollment	**13,303**

ENGINEERING COLLEGE INFORMATION

HEAD OF ENGINEERING
John W Steadman
Dean
College of Engineering
University of South Alabama
307 University Boulevard
EGCB 108
Mobile, AL 36688
Phone: (251) 460-6140
Fax: (251) 460-6343
Email: jsteadman@usouthal.edu

TYPES OF ENGINEERING DEGREES
Bachelor's: B.S.
Master's: M.S. with thesis, M.S. without thesis, but with project or report
Doctoral:

UNDERGRADUATE INFORMATION

ESTIMATED STUDENT EXPENSES (FALL 2006)
[Expenses are for the 2006-2007 nine-month academic year and are based on an average credit load of: Undergraduate: 15]
	In-State	Out-of-State
Tutition and Fees:	$4,502	$8,312
Campus and Room and Board:	$4,750	$4,750
Books and Supplies:	$1,000	$1,000
Other Expenses:		
Total Estimated Expenses:	**$10,252**	**$14,062**

Note: Other Expenses = $11.00 per credit hour fee for all undergraduate engineering courses. |

NEW APPLICANTS/NEWLY ENROLLED STUDENTS
[Numbers are for the undergraduate engineering college for the Fall 2006 term]
Number of Applicants (a):	241
Of those, Number Offered Admission (b):	222
Of those, Number Enrolled Fall 2006 (c):	127

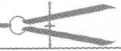

GRADUATE INFORMATION

ESTIMATED STUDENT EXPENSES (FALL 2006)
[Expenses are for the 2006-2007 nine-month academic year and are based on an average credit load of: Graduate: 15]

	In-State	Out-of-State
Tuition and Fees:	$4,700	$8,708
Campus and Room and Board:	$4,750	$4,750
Books and Supplies:	$1,000	$1,000
Other Expenses:		
Total Estimated Expenses:	**$10,450**	**$14,458**

Note: Other Expenses = $11.00 per credit hour fee for all undergraduate engineering courses.

NEW APPLICANTS/NEWLY ENROLLED STUDENTS
[Numbers are for the graduate engineering college for the Fall 2006 term]

Number of Applicants (a):	1,864
Of those, Number Offered Admission (b):	1,024
Of those, Number Enrolled Fall 2006 (c):	584

University of South Carolina

INSTITUTION INFORMATION
College of Engineering and Information Technology
Swearingen Engineering Center
Columbia, SC 29208
Phone: (803) 777-4177
Fax: (803) 777-0027
Web: http://www.engr.sc.edu/

GENERAL INFORMATION
[All Students - Fall 2006]

Undergraduate Enrollment	18,648
Graduate Enrollment	7,302
Professional Enrollment	1,440
Total Enrollment	**27,390**

ENGINEERING COLLEGE INFORMATION

HEAD OF ENGINEERING
Michael D Amiridis
Dean
College of Engineering & Information Technology
University of South Carolina
Swearingen Engineering Center
301 Main St.
Columbia, SC 29208
Phone: (803) 777-7356
Fax: (803) 777-9597
Email: amiridis@engr.sc.edu

ENGINEERING COLLEGE INQUIRIES
Ruth E Heacock
Budget Director
University of South Carolina
College of Engineering and Information Technology,
Swearingen Engineering Center
Columbia, SC 29208
Phone: (803) 777-6060
Fax: (803) 777-6769
Email: heacock@engr.sc.edu

ENGINEERING COLLEGE INQUIRIES
John W Weidner
Interim Associate Dean of Research
University of South Carolina
College of Engineering and Information Technology,
Swearingen Engineering Center
Columbia, SC 29208
Phone: (803) 777-3207
Fax: (803) 777-9597
Email: weidner@engr.sc.edu

TYPES OF ENGINEERING DEGREES
Bachelor's: B.S.
Master's: M.S. with thesis, M.Eng.
Doctoral: Ph.D.

UNDERGRADUATE INFORMATION

ADMISSION INQUIRIES
Mike Perkins
Director of Student Services
University of South Carolina
Swearingen Engineering Center
Columbia, SC 29208

Phone: (803) 777-2535
Fax: (803) 777-0027
Email: perkins@engr.sc.edu

ESTIMATED STUDENT EXPENSES (FALL 2006)
[Expenses are for the 2006-2007 nine-month academic year and are based on an average credit load of: Undergraduate: N/A]

	In-State	Out-of-State
Tuition and Fees:	$7,408	$19,836
Campus and Room and Board:	$6,520	$6,520
Books and Supplies:	$1,300	$1,300
Other Expenses:	$900	$900
Total Estimated Expenses:	**$16,128**	**$28,556**

NEW APPLICANTS/NEWLY ENROLLED STUDENTS
[Numbers are for the undergraduate engineering college for the Fall 2006 term]

Number of Applicants (a):	1,194
Of those, Number Offered Admission (b):	799
Of those, Number Enrolled Fall 2006 (c):	320

GRADUATE INFORMATION

ESTIMATED STUDENT EXPENSES (FALL 2006)
[Expenses are for the 2006-2007 nine-month academic year and are based on an average credit load of: Graduate: N/A]

	In-State	Out-of-State
Tuition and Fees:	$8,288	$17,916
Campus and Room and Board:	$8,145	$8,145
Books and Supplies:	$1,600	$1,600
Other Expenses:	$1,600	$1,600
Total Estimated Expenses:	**$19,633**	**$29,261**

NEW APPLICANTS/NEWLY ENROLLED STUDENTS
[Numbers are for the graduate engineering college for the Fall 2006 term]

Number of Applicants (a):	498
Of those, Number Offered Admission (b):	214
Of those, Number Enrolled Fall 2006 (c):	91

South Dakota School of Mines and Technology

INSTITUTION INFORMATION
501 East St. Joseph Street
Rapid City, SD 57701
Phone: (605) 394-2256
Fax: (605) 394-2490
Web: http://www.sdsmt.edu

GENERAL INFORMATION
[All Students - Fall 2006]

Undergraduate Enrollment	1,870
Graduate Enrollment	254
Professional Enrollment	0
Total Enrollment	**2,124**

ENGINEERING COLLEGE INFORMATION

HEAD OF ENGINEERING
Karen L. Whitehead
Vice President
Academic Affairs
South Dakota School of Mines and Technology
501 East Saint Joseph Street
Rapid City, SD 57701
Phone: (605) 394-2256
Fax: (605) 394-2490
Email: karen.whitehead@sdsmt.edu

HEAD OF ENGINEERING
Duane L Abata
Dean of the College of Engineering
College of Engineering
South Dakota School of Mines and Technology
501 East St. Joseph Street
Rapid City, SD 57701
Phone: (605) 394-5265
Fax: (605) 394-5266
Email: duane.abata@sdsmt.edu

ENGINEERING COLLEGE INQUIRIES
Duane L Abata
Dean of the College of Engineering
South Dakota School of Mines and Technology
501 East St. Joseph Street
Rapid City, SD 57701

Phone: (605) 394-5265
Fax: (605) 394-5266
Email: duane.abata@sdsmt.edu

TYPES OF ENGINEERING DEGREES
Bachelor's: B.S.
Master's: M.S. with thesis, M.S. without thesis, but with project or report
Doctoral: Ph.D.

UNDERGRADUATE INFORMATION

ADMISSION INQUIRIES
Julie A Smoragiewicz
Vice President for University & Public Relations
South Dakota School of Mines and Technology
501 East St. Joseph Street
Rapid City, SD 57701
Phone: (605) 394-5146
Fax: (605) 394-6177

ADMISSION INQUIRIES
Duane L Abata
Dean of the College of Engineering
South Dakota School of Mines and Technology
501 East St. Joseph Street
Rapid City, SD 57701
Phone: (605) 394-5265
Fax: (605) 394-5266
Email: duane.abata@sdsmt.edu

ESTIMATED STUDENT EXPENSES (FALL 2006)
[Expenses are for the 2006-2007 nine-month academic year and are based on an average credit load of: Undergraduate: 15]

	In-State	Out-of-State
Tuition and Fees:	$5,330	$6,520
Campus and Room and Board:	$4,410	$4,410
Books and Supplies:	$1,000	$1,000
Other Expenses:	$1,875	$1,875
Total Estimated Expenses:	**$12,615**	**$13,805**

NEW APPLICANTS/NEWLY ENROLLED STUDENTS
[Numbers are for the undergraduate engineering college for the Fall 2006 term]

Number of Applicants (a):	546
Of those, Number Offered Admission (b):	423
Of those, Number Enrolled Fall 2006 (c):	200

GRADUATE INFORMATION

ADMISSION INQUIRIES
Alvis L Lisenbee
Professor
South Dakota School of Mines and Technology
501 East St. Joseph Street
Rapid City , SD 57701
Phone: (605) 394-2430
Fax: (605) 394-6703
Email: alvis.lisenbee@sdsmt.edu

ADMISSION INQUIRIES
Umesh A Korde
Associate Professor
South Dakota School of Mines and Technology
501 East St. Joseph Street
Rapid City , SD 57701
Phone: (605) 394-2256
Fax: (605) 394-2490
Email: umesh.korde@sdsmt.edu

ESTIMATED STUDENT EXPENSES (FALL 2006)
[Expenses are for the 2006-2007 nine-month academic year and are based on an average credit load of: Graduate: 9]

	In-State	Out-of-State
Tuition and Fees:	$4,040	$8,220
Campus and Room and Board:	$5,650	$5,650
Books and Supplies:	$930	$930
Other Expenses:	$1,875	$1,875
Total Estimated Expenses:	**$12,495**	**$16,675**

NEW APPLICANTS/NEWLY ENROLLED STUDENTS
[Numbers are for the graduate engineering college for the Fall 2006 term]

Number of Applicants (a):	115
Of those, Number Offered Admission (b):	113
Of those, Number Enrolled Fall 2006 (c):	63

South Dakota State University

INSTITUTION INFORMATION
CEH 201 Box 2219
Brookings, SD 57007
Phone: (605) 688-4161
Fax: (605) 688-5878
Web: http://www3.sdstate.edu

GENERAL INFORMATION
[All Students - Fall 2006]

Undergraduate Enrollment	9,852
Graduate Enrollment	1,281
Professional Enrollment	244
Total Enrollment	**11,377**

ENGINEERING COLLEGE INFORMATION

HEAD OF ENGINEERING
Lewis F Brown
Dean of Engineering
College of Engineering
South Dakota State University
CEH 201 Box 2219
Brookings, SD 57007
Phone: (605) 688-4161
Fax: (605) 688-5878
Email: lewis.brown@sdstate.edu

ENGINEERING COLLEGE INQUIRIES
Lewis F Brown
Dean of Engineering
South Dakota State University
CEH 201 Box 2219
Brookings, SD 57007
Phone: (605) 688-4161
Fax: (605) 688-5878
Email: lewis.brown@sdstate.edu

TYPES OF ENGINEERING DEGREES
Bachelor's: B.S.
Master's: M.S. with thesis, M.S. without thesis, but with project or report
Doctoral: Ph.D.

UNDERGRADUATE INFORMATION

ADMISSION INQUIRIES
Steven M Hietpas
Coordinator & Professor
South Dakota State University
CEH 201 Box 2219
Brookings, SD 57007
Phone: (605) 688-4161
Fax: (605) 688-5878

ADMISSION INQUIRIES
Alireza Salehnia
Coordinator
South Dakota State University
AD 133 Box 2201
Brookings, SD 57007
Phone: (605) 688-5717
Fax: (605) 688-4532
Email: ALI_SALEHNIA@sdstate.edu

ADMISSION INQUIRIES
Oren Quist
Department Head
South Dakota State University
CEH 314 Box 2201
Brookings, SD 57007
Phone: (605) 688-5428
Fax: (605) 688-5878
Email: OREN.QUIST@sdstate.edu

ADMISSION INQUIRIES
Donell P Froehlich
Department Head
South Dakota State University
CEH 216A Box 2219
Brookings, SD 57007
Phone: (605) 688-5426
Fax: (605) 688-5878
Email: don.froehlich@sdstate.edu

ADMISSION INQUIRIES
Teresa J Hall
Department Head
South Dakota State University
SOL 116B Box 2223
Brookings, SD 57007
Phone: (605) 688-6417
Fax: (605) 688-5041
Email: teresa.hall@sdstate.edu

ADMISSION INQUIRIES
Tracy Welsh
Dir. of High School Relations & Admissions
South Dakota State University
AD 200 Box 2201
Brookings, SD 57007
Phone: (605) 688-4121
Fax: (605) 688-6384
Email: TRACY.WELSH@SDSTATE.EDU

ADMISSION INQUIRIES
Richard A Reid
Assistant Dean & Acting CE Dept. Head
South Dakota State University
CEH 201 Box 2219
Brookings, SD 57007
Phone: (605) 688-4161
Fax: (605) 688-5878
Email: richard.reid@sdstate.edu

ESTIMATED STUDENT EXPENSES (FALL 2006)
[Expenses are for the 2006-2007 nine-month academic year and are based on an average credit load of: Undergraduate: 16]

	In-State	Out-of-State
Tuition and Fees:	$5,751	$7,031
Campus and Room and Board:	$4,240	$4,240
Books and Supplies:	$750	$750
Other Expenses:	$600	$600
Total Estimated Expenses:	**$11,341**	**$12,621**

NEW APPLICANTS/NEWLY ENROLLED STUDENTS
[Numbers are for the undergraduate engineering college for the Fall 2006 term]

Number of Applicants (a):	426
Of those, Number Offered Admission (b):	411
Of those, Number Enrolled Fall 2006 (c):	254

GRADUATE INFORMATION
South Dakota State University
CEH 201 Box 2219
Brookings , SD 57007
Phone: (605) 688-4161
Fax: (605) 688-5878

ADMISSION INQUIRIES
Alex Moutsoglou
Professor
South Dakota State University
CEH 218 Box 2219
Brookings , SD 57007
Phone: (605) 688-6323
Fax: (605) 688-5878
Email: ALEX.MOUTSOGLOU@SDSTATE.EDU

ADMISSION INQUIRIES
Oren Quist
Department Head
South Dakota State University
CEH 314 Box 2201
Brookings , SD 57007
Phone: (605) 688-5428
Fax: (605) 688-5878
Email: OREN.QUIST@sdstate.edu

ADMISSION INQUIRIES
Kevin D Kephart
Dean of Graduate School
South Dakota State University
AD 130 Box 2201
Brookings , SD 57007
Phone: (605) 688-4181
Fax: (605) 688-6167
Email: Kevin.Kephart@SDSTATE.EDU

ADMISSION INQUIRIES
David Galipeau
Professor of Electrical Engineering
South Dakota State University
HH 213 Box 2220
Brookings , SD 57007

Phone: (605) 688-4618
Fax: (605) 688-5880
Email: david.galipeau@sdstate.edu

ADMISSION INQUIRIES
Delvin E DeBoer
Director
South Dakota State University
CEH 112 Box 2219
Brookings , SD 57007
Phone: (605) 688-6252
Fax: (605) 688-5878

ESTIMATED STUDENT EXPENSES (FALL 2006)
[Expenses are for the 2006-2007 nine-month academic year and are based on an average credit load of: Graduate: 9]

	In-State	Out-of-State
Tuition and Fees:	$4,320	$8,550
Campus and Room and Board:	$4,240	$4,240
Books and Supplies:	$750	$750
Other Expenses:	$600	$600
Total Estimated Expenses:	**$9,910**	**$14,140**

NEW APPLICANTS/NEWLY ENROLLED STUDENTS
[Numbers are for the graduate engineering college for the Fall 2006 term]

Number of Applicants (a):	320
Of those, Number Offered Admission (b):	113
Of those, Number Enrolled Fall 2006 (c):	32

University of South Florida

INSTITUTION INFORMATION
4202 E Fowler Ave.
ENB - 0118
Tampa, FL 33620
Phone: (813) 974-3782
Fax: (813) 974-5094
Web: http://usf.edu

GENERAL INFORMATION
[All Students - Fall 2006]

Undergraduate Enrollment	34,077
Graduate Enrollment	7,515
Professional Enrollment	1,906
Total Enrollment	**43,498**

ENGINEERING COLLEGE INFORMATION

HEAD OF ENGINEERING
Sunil Saigal
Dean for the College of Engineering
Engineering Dean
University of South Florida
4202 East Fowler Ave.,
ENB 118
Tampa, FL 33620
Phone: (813) 974-3787
Fax: (813) 974-5094
Email: saigal@eng.usf.edu

TYPES OF ENGINEERING DEGREES
Bachelor's: B.S.
Master's: M.S. with thesis, M.S. without thesis, but with project or report
Doctoral: Ph.D.

UNDERGRADUATE INFORMATION

ESTIMATED STUDENT EXPENSES (FALL 2006)
[Expenses are for the 2006-2007 nine-month academic year and are based on an average credit load of: Undergraduate: 9]

	In-State	Out-of-State
Tuition and Fees:	$3,342	$16,041
Campus and Room and Board:	$7,150	$7,150
Books and Supplies:	$925	$925
Other Expenses:	$3,990	$3,990
Total Estimated Expenses:	**$15,407**	**$28,106**
Note: Per academic year

NEW APPLICANTS/NEWLY ENROLLED STUDENTS
[Numbers are for the undergraduate engineering college for the Fall 2006 term]

Number of Applicants (a):	762
Of those, Number Offered Admission (b):	710
Of those, Number Enrolled Fall 2006 (c):	682

GRADUATE INFORMATION

ESTIMATED STUDENT EXPENSES (FALL 2006)
[Expenses are for the 2006-2007 nine-month academic year and are based on an average credit load of: Graduate: 12]

	In-State	Out-of-State
Tutition and Fees:	$6,048	$21,529
Campus and Room and Board:	$8,300	$8,300
Books and Supplies:	$925	$925
Other Expenses:	$3,990	$3,990
Total Estimated Expenses:	**$19,263**	**$34,744**

Note: Per academic year

NEW APPLICANTS/NEWLY ENROLLED STUDENTS
[Numbers are for the graduate engineering college for the Fall 2006 term]

Number of Applicants (a):	558
Of those, Number Offered Admission (b):	373
Of those, Number Enrolled Fall 2006 (c):	167

Southeast Missouri State University

INSTITUTION INFORMATION
Department of Physics and Engineering Physics
MS 6600
Cape Girardeau, MO 63701
Phone: (573) 651-2167
Fax: (573) 651-2392
Web: http://www.semo.edu

GENERAL INFORMATION
[All Students - Fall 2006]

Undergraduate Enrollment	8,977
Graduate Enrollment	1,500
Professional Enrollment	10,477
Total Enrollment	**20,954**

ENGINEERING COLLEGE INFORMATION

HEAD OF ENGINEERING
Chris McGowan
Dean
College of Science & Mathematics
Southeast Missouri State University
MS6000
Cape Girardeau, MO 63701
Phone: (573) 651-2163
Fax: (573) 651-2223
Email: cwmcgowan@semo.edu

TYPES OF ENGINEERING DEGREES
Bachelor's: B.S.
Master's:
Doctoral:

UNDERGRADUATE INFORMATION

ESTIMATED STUDENT EXPENSES (FALL 2006)
[Expenses are for the 2006-2007 nine-month academic year and are based on an average credit load of: Undergraduate: 15]

	All Students
Tutition and fees:	$6,000
Campus and Room and Board:	$6,000
Books and Supplies:	$200
Other Expenses:	
Total Estimated Expenses:	**$12,200**

University of Southern California

INSTITUTION INFORMATION
USC Viterbi School of Engineering
University Park
Los Angeles, CA 90089
Phone: (213) 740-2311
Fax: (213) 740-8493
Web: http://www.usc.edu

GENERAL INFORMATION
[All Students - Fall 2006]

Undergraduate Enrollment	16,500
Graduate Enrollment	16,500
Professional Enrollment	33,000
Total Enrollment	**66,000**

ENGINEERING COLLEGE INFORMATION

HEAD OF ENGINEERING
Yannis C Yortsos
Dean of Engineering
Andrew and Erna Viterbi School of Engineering
University of Southern California
Olin Hall of Engineering, Rm. 200
Los Angeles, CA 90089-1450
Phone: (213) 740-0617
Fax: (213) 740-8493
Email: engrdean@usc.edu

ENGINEERING COLLEGE INQUIRIES
Margery Berti
Associate Dean, Doctoral Programs
University of Southern California
Olin Hall of Engineering, Rm. 332
Los Angeles, CA 90089-1454
Phone: (213) 740-6241
Fax: (213) 821-2367
Email: berti@usc.edu

TYPES OF ENGINEERING DEGREES
Bachelor's: B.S.
Master's: M.S. with thesis, M.S. without thesis, but with project or report, M.Eng.
Doctoral: Ph.D.

UNDERGRADUATE INFORMATION

ADMISSION INQUIRIES
Louise A Yates
Associate Dean, Admissions and Student Affairs
University of Southern California
Ronald Tutor Hall, Rm. 110
Los Angeles, CA 90089-2900
Phone: (213) 740-4530
Fax: (213) 740-8690
Email: yates@usc.edu

ESTIMATED STUDENT EXPENSES (FALL 2006)
[Expenses are for the 2006-2007 nine-month academic year and are based on an average credit load of: Undergraduate: 16]

	All Students
Tuition and fees:	$33,892
Campus and Room and Board:	$10,144
Books and Supplies:	$750
Other Expenses:	$2,320
Total Estimated Expenses:	**$47,106**

NEW APPLICANTS/NEWLY ENROLLED STUDENTS
[Numbers are for the undergraduate engineering college for the Fall 2006 term]

Number of Applicants (a):	4,079
Of those, Number Offered Admission (b):	1,578
Of those, Number Enrolled Fall 2006 (c):	398

GRADUATE INFORMATION

ADMISSION INQUIRIES
Louise A Yates
Associate Dean, Admissions and Student Affairs
University of Southern California
Ronald Tutor Hall, Rm. 110
Los Angeles , CA 90089-2900
Phone: (213) 740-4530
Fax: (213) 740-8690
Email: yates@usc.edu

ESTIMATED STUDENT EXPENSES (FALL 2006)
[Expenses are for the 2006-2007 nine-month academic year and are based on an average credit load of: Graduate: 9]

	All Students
Tutition and fees:	$21,510
Campus and Room and Board:	$12,300
Books and Supplies:	$975
Other Expenses:	$1,835
Total Estimated Expenses:	**$36,620**

NEW APPLICANTS/NEWLY ENROLLED STUDENTS
[Numbers are for the graduate engineering college for the Fall 2006 term]

Number of Applicants (a):	5,706
Of those, Number Offered Admission (b):	2,784
Of those, Number Enrolled Fall 2006 (c):	1,252

Southern Illinois University Carbondale

INSTITUTION INFORMATION
Office of the Dean, MC 6603
College of Engineering
Carbondale, IL 62901
Phone: (618) 453-4321
Fax: (618) 453-4235
Web: http://www.engr.siu.edu

GENERAL INFORMATION
[All Students - Fall 2006]

Undergraduate Enrollment	16,294
Graduate Enrollment	3,999
Professional Enrollment	710
Total Enrollment	**21,003**

ENGINEERING COLLEGE INFORMATION

HEAD OF ENGINEERING
William P. Osborne
Dean
College of Engineering
Southern Illinois University Carbondale
Office of the Dean
Southern Illinois University Carbondale
Carbondale, IL 62901
Phone: (618) 453-4321
Fax: (618) 453-4235
Email: wosborne@siu.edu

ENGINEERING COLLEGE INQUIRIES
John W. Nicklow
Interim Associate Dean
Southern Illinois University Carbondale
College of Engineering, Southern Illinois University Carbondale
Carbondale, IL 62901-6603
Phone: (618) 453-4321
Fax: (618) 453-4235
Email: nicklow@engr.siu.edu

TYPES OF ENGINEERING DEGREES
Bachelor's: B.S.
Master's: M.S. with thesis, M.S. without thesis, but with project or report
Doctoral: Ph.D.

UNDERGRADUATE INFORMATION

ADMISSION INQUIRIES
Bruce Chrisman
Recruitment and Retention Coordinator
Southern Illinois University Carbondale
Office of the Dean, College of Engineering
Carbondale, IL 62901
Phone: (618) 453-7712
Fax: (618) 453-4235
Email: chrisman@engr.siu.edu

ADMISSION INQUIRIES
James L. Carl
Assistant Director
Southern Illinois University Carbondale
Carbondale, IL 62901
Phone: (618) 453-4381
Fax: (618) 453-3250
Email: jcarl@siu.edu

ESTIMATED STUDENT EXPENSES (FALL 2006)
[Expenses are for the 2006-2007 nine-month academic year and are based on an average credit load of: Undergraduate: 15]

	In-State	Out-of-State
Tuition and Fees:	$7,795	$16,507
Campus and Room and Board:	$6,138	$6,138
Books and Supplies:	$900	$900
Other Expenses:	$2,417	$2,417
Total Estimated Expenses:	**$17,250**	**$25,962**

Note: Undergraduate students who entered SIUC beginning Fall 2004 or later are guaranteed the same tuition rate for four continuous academic years.

Graduate students with assistantships are considered full-time with 6-credit enrollment, whereas students without assitantships are considered full time with 9-credit enrollment. Costs shown here for graduate students are based on 9-credit enrollment without assistantship.

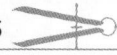

NEW APPLICANTS/NEWLY ENROLLED STUDENTS

[Numbers are for the undergraduate engineering college for the Fall 2006 term]

Number of Applicants (a):	505
Of those, Number Offered Admission (b):	447
Of those, Number Enrolled Fall 2006 (c):	190

GRADUATE INFORMATION

ADMISSION INQUIRIES

John W. Nicklow
Interim Associate Dean
Southern Illinois University Carbondale
College of Engineering, Southern Illinois University Carbondale
Carbondale , IL 62901-6603
Phone: (618) 453-4321
Fax: (618) 453-4235
Email: nicklow@engr.siu.edu

ESTIMATED STUDENT EXPENSES (FALL 2006)

[Expenses are for the 2006-2007 nine-month academic year and are based on an average credit load of: Graduate: 9]

	In-State	Out-of-State
Tuition and Fees:	$6,056	$12,617
Campus and Room and Board:	$8,106	$8,106
Books and Supplies:	$900	$900
Other Expenses:	$2,418	$2,418
Total Estimated Expenses:	**$17,480**	**$24,041**

Note: Undergraduate students who entered SIUC beginning Fall 2004 or later are guaranteed the same tuition rate for four continuous academic years.

Graduate students with assistantships are considered full-time with 6-credit enrollment, whereas students without assitantships are considered full time with 9-credit enrollment. Costs shown here for graduate students are based on 9-credit enrollment without assistantship.

NEW APPLICANTS/NEWLY ENROLLED STUDENTS

[Numbers are for the graduate engineering college for the Fall 2006 term]

Number of Applicants (a):	602
Of those, Number Offered Admission (b):	275
Of those, Number Enrolled Fall 2006 (c):	93

Southern Illinois University Edwardsville

INSTITUTION INFORMATION

School of Engineering
Campus Box 1804
Edwardsville, IL 62026-1804
Phone: (618) 650-2541
Fax: (618) 650-3374
Web: http://www.siue.edu

GENERAL INFORMATION

[All Students - Fall 2006]

Undergraduate Enrollment	10,960
Graduate Enrollment	2,127
Professional Enrollment	362
Total Enrollment	**13,449**

ENGINEERING COLLEGE INFORMATION

HEAD OF ENGINEERING

Hasan Sevim
Dean
School of Engineering
Southern Illinois University at Edwardsville
Campus Box 1804
Edwardsville, IL 62026-1804
Phone: (618) 650-2861
Fax: (618) 650-3374
Email: hsevim@siue.edu

ENGINEERING COLLEGE INQUIRIES

Jacob Van Roekel
Associate Dean
Southern Illinois University at Edwardsville
SIUE Box 1804
Edwardsville, IL 62026-1804
Phone: (618) 650-2534
Fax: (618) 650-3374
Email: jvanroe@siue.edu

TYPES OF ENGINEERING DEGREES

Bachelor's: B.A., B.S.
Master's: M.S. with thesis, M.S. without thesis, but with project or report
Doctoral:

UNDERGRADUATE INFORMATION

ESTIMATED STUDENT EXPENSES (FALL 2006)

[Expenses are for the 2006-2007 nine-month academic year and are based on an average credit load of: Undergraduate: 15]

	In-State	Out-of-State
Tuition and Fees:	$5,938	$13,076
Campus and Room and Board:	$6,470	$6,470
Books and Supplies:	$750	$750
Other Expenses:	$3,500	$3,500
Total Estimated Expenses:	**$16,658**	**$23,796**

GRADUATE INFORMATION

ADMISSION INQUIRIES

Jodi Olson
Contact Person for Graduate Records
Southern Illinois University at Edwardsville
Campus Box 1047
Edwardsville , IL 62026-1047
Phone: (618) 650-3167
Fax: (618) 650-3332
Email: joolson@siue.edu

ESTIMATED STUDENT EXPENSES (FALL 2006)

[Expenses are for the 2006-2007 nine-month academic year and are based on an average credit load of: Graduate: 12]

	In-State	Out-of-State
Tuition and Fees:	$6,280	$14,380
Campus and Room and Board:	$6,470	$6,470
Books and Supplies:	$1,350	$1,350
Other Expenses:	$3,750	$3,750
Total Estimated Expenses:	**$17,850**	**$25,950**

NEW APPLICANTS/NEWLY ENROLLED STUDENTS

[Numbers are for the graduate engineering college for the Fall 2006 term]

Number of Applicants (a):	569
Of those, Number Offered Admission (b):	201
Of those, Number Enrolled Fall 2006 (c):	79

University of Southern Maine

INSTITUTION INFORMATION

37 College Avenue
149 John Mitchell Center
Gorham, ME 04038
Phone: (207) 780-5287
Fax: (207) 780-5129
Web: http://usm.maine.edu

ENGINEERING COLLEGE INFORMATION

HEAD OF ENGINEERING

John R Wright
Dean
Schools of Applied Science, Engineering and Technology
University of Southern Maine
37 College Avenue
106 John Mitchell Center
Gorham, ME 04038
Phone: (207) 780-5585
Fax: (207) 780-5129
Email: jwright@usm.maine.edu

TYPES OF ENGINEERING DEGREES

Bachelor's: B.S.
Master's:
Doctoral:

Southern Methodist University

INSTITUTION INFORMATION

Hillcrest between Daniel & Mockingbird
Dallas, TX 75275

Phone: (214) 768-2000
Web: http://www.smu.edu

ENGINEERING COLLEGE INFORMATION

HEAD OF ENGINEERING

Geoffrey C Orsak
Dean and Professor
Electrical Engineering
Southern Methodist University
P.O. Box 750350
Dallas, TX 75275-0335
Phone: (214) 768-1259
Fax: (214) 768-3573
Email: gorsak@seas.smu.edu

ENGINEERING COLLEGE INQUIRIES

Andy Winstel
Financial and Information Officer
Southern Methodist University
Hillcrest between Daniel & Mockingbird
Dallas, TX 75275
Phone: (214) 768-3141
Email: andy@engr.smu.edu

TYPES OF ENGINEERING DEGREES

Bachelor's: B.A., B.S.
Master's: M.S. with thesis, M.S. without thesis, but with project or report
Doctoral: Ph.D., D.Eng

UNDERGRADUATE INFORMATION

ESTIMATED STUDENT EXPENSES (FALL 2006)

[Expenses are for the 2006-2007 nine-month academic year and are based on an average credit load of: Undergraduate: N/A]

	All Students
Tuition and fees:	$29,450
Campus and Room and Board:	
Books and Supplies:	$1,200
Other Expenses:	
Total Estimated Expenses:	**$30,650**

Note: Undergraduate tuition and fees are based on 12-18 term credit hours. Graduate is full-time w/o assistantship.

NEW APPLICANTS/NEWLY ENROLLED STUDENTS

[Numbers are for the undergraduate engineering college for the Fall 2006 term]

Number of Applicants (a):	582
Of those, Number Offered Admission (b):	403
Of those, Number Enrolled Fall 2006 (c):	143

GRADUATE INFORMATION

ADMISSION INQUIRIES

James L Dees
Sr. Director of Graduate Student Enrollment
Southern Methodist University
P.O. Box 750335
Dallas , TX 75275-0335
Phone: (214) 768-1456
Fax: (214) 768-3778
Email: jdees@engr.smu.edu

ADMISSION INQUIRIES

Marc P Valerin
Associate Director of Graduate Admissions
Southern Methodist University
PO Box 750335
Dallas , TX 75275-0335
Phone: (214) 768-1259
Fax: (214) 768-3778
Email: valerin@seas.smu.edu

ESTIMATED STUDENT EXPENSES (FALL 2006)

[Expenses are for the 2006-2007 nine-month academic year and are based on an average credit load of: Graduate: N/A]

	All Students
Tuition and fees:	$16,704
Campus and Room and Board:	
Books and Supplies:	
Other Expenses:	
Total Estimated Expenses:	**$16,704**

Note: Undergraduate tuition and fees are based on 12-18 term credit hours. Graduate is full-time w/o assistantship.

NEW APPLICANTS/NEWLY ENROLLED STUDENTS

[Numbers are for the graduate engineering college for the Fall 2006 term]

Number of Applicants (a):	667

Of those, Number Offered Admission (b): 336
Of those, Number Enrolled Fall 2006 (c): 200

Southern University and A&M College

INSTITUTION INFORMATION
J.S. Clark Administration Bldg.
P.O. Box 9374
Baton Rouge, LA 70813
Phone: (225) 771-4680
Fax: (225) 771-5522
Web: http://www.subr.edu

GENERAL INFORMATION
[All Students - Fall 2006]
Undergraduate Enrollment 8,500
Graduate Enrollment 1,200
Professional Enrollment 0
Total Enrollment **9,700**

ENGINEERING COLLEGE INFORMATION

HEAD OF ENGINEERING
Habib P Mohamadian
Dean
Engineering
Southern University and A&M College
P.B.S. Pinchback Hall
P.O. Box 9969
Baton Rouge, LA 70813
Phone: (225) 771-5292
Fax: (225) 771-5721
Email: mohamad@engr.subr.edu

ENGINEERING COLLEGE INQUIRIES
Charles L Burris
Associate Dean
Southern University and A&M College
P.B. S. Pinchback Engr Building, P.O. Box 9969
Baton Rouge, LA 70813
Phone: (225) 771-5292
Fax: (225) 771-5721
Email: cburris@engr.subr.edu

TYPES OF ENGINEERING DEGREES
Bachelor's: B.S.
Master's: M.S. with thesis, M.S. without thesis, but with project or report
Doctoral:

UNDERGRADUATE INFORMATION

ESTIMATED STUDENT EXPENSES (FALL 2006)
[Expenses are for the 2006-2007 nine-month academic year and are based on an average credit load of: Undergraduate: N/A]

	In-State	Out-of-State
Tuition and Fees:	$3,602	$5,792
Campus and Room and Board:	$4,000	$4,000
Books and Supplies:		
Other Expenses:		
Total Estimated Expenses:	**$7,602**	**$9,792**

Note: Fees and Expenses are subject to change without prior notice.

GRADUATE INFORMATION

ESTIMATED STUDENT EXPENSES (FALL 2006)
[Expenses are for the 2006-2007 nine-month academic year and are based on an average credit load of: Graduate: N/A]

	In-State	Out-of-State
Tuition and Fees:	$3,610	$5,166
Campus and Room and Board:	$4,000	$4,000
Books and Supplies:		
Other Expenses:		
Total Estimated Expenses:	**$7,610**	**$9,166**

Note: Fees and Expenses are subject to change without prior notice.

Stanford University

INSTITUTION INFORMATION
Terman School of Engineering
380 Panama Mall
Stanford, CA 94305
Phone: (650) 723-1575
Fax: (650) 725-7426
Web: http://www.stanford.edu

GENERAL INFORMATION
[All Students - Fall 2006]
Undergraduate Enrollment 6,422
Graduate Enrollment 10,285
Professional Enrollment 1,040
Total Enrollment **17,747**

ENGINEERING COLLEGE INFORMATION

HEAD OF ENGINEERING
James D Plummer
Dean - School of Engineering / Professor
School of Engineering
Stanford University
Dean's Office, Terman Engr. Center
380 Panama Mall
Stanford, CA 94305-4027
Phone: (650) 723-3938
Fax: (650) 725-8545
Email: plummer@ee.stanford.edu

TYPES OF ENGINEERING DEGREES
Bachelor's: B.S.
Master's: M.S. without thesis, but with project or report
Doctoral: Ph.D.

UNDERGRADUATE INFORMATION

ESTIMATED STUDENT EXPENSES (FALL 2006)
[Expenses are for the 2006-2007 nine-month academic year and are based on an average credit load of: Undergraduate: 17]

	All Students
Tuition and fees:	$32,994
Campus and Room and Board:	$10,367
Books and Supplies:	$1,290
Other Expenses:	$1,935
Total Estimated Expenses:	**$46,586**

Note: Graduate student expenses for School of Engineering only

NEW APPLICANTS/NEWLY ENROLLED STUDENTS
[Numbers are for the undergraduate engineering college for the Fall 2006 term]
Number of Applicants (a): 22,334
Of those, Number Offered Admission (b): 2,444
Of those, Number Enrolled Fall 2006 (c): 1,648

GRADUATE INFORMATION

ESTIMATED STUDENT EXPENSES (FALL 2006)
[Expenses are for the 2006-2007 nine-month academic year and are based on an average credit load of: Graduate: 10]

	All Students
Tuition and fees:	$35,184
Campus and Room and Board:	$15,550
Books and Supplies:	$1,590
Other Expenses:	$2,733
Total Estimated Expenses:	**$55,057**

Note: Graduate student expenses for School of Engineering only

NEW APPLICANTS/NEWLY ENROLLED STUDENTS
[Numbers are for the graduate engineering college for the Fall 2006 term]
Number of Applicants (a): 5,539
Of those, Number Offered Admission (b): 1,727
Of those, Number Enrolled Fall 2006 (c): 860

Stevens Institute of Technology

INSTITUTION INFORMATION
Castle Point on Hudson
Charles V. Schaefer, Jr. School of Eng.
Hoboken, NJ 07030
Phone: (201) 216-5263
Fax: (201) 216-8909
Web: http://www.stevens.edu

ENGINEERING COLLEGE INFORMATION

HEAD OF ENGINEERING
George Korfiatis

Dean of Engineering
Charles V. Schaefer, Jr. School of Engineering
Stevens Institute of Technology
Castle Point on Hudson
Hoboken, NJ 07030
Phone: (201) 216-5263
Fax: (201) 216-8909
Email: gkorfiat@stevens.edu

ENGINEERING COLLEGE INQUIRIES
Marta Quigley
Administrative Assistant to the Dean
Stevens Institute of Technology
Castle Point on Hudson, Charles V. Schaefer, Jr. School of Eng.
Hoboken, NJ 07030
Phone: (201) 216-5263
Fax: (201) 216-8909

TYPES OF ENGINEERING DEGREES
Bachelor's: B.E.
Master's: M.S. with thesis, M.S. without thesis, but with project or report, M.Eng.
Doctoral: Ph.D.

UNDERGRADUATE INFORMATION

ADMISSION INQUIRIES
Daniel Gallagher
Dean of University Admissions
Stevens Institute of Technology
Castle Point on Hudson, Charles V. Schaefer, Jr. School of Eng.
Hoboken, NJ 07030
Phone: (201) 216-5197
Fax: (201) 216-8348

ESTIMATED STUDENT EXPENSES (FALL 2006)
[Expenses are for the 2006-2007 nine-month academic year and are based on an average credit load of: Undergraduate: 15]

	All Students
Tuition and fees:	$31,750
Campus and Room and Board:	$10,000
Books and Supplies:	$900
Other Expenses:	$750
Total Estimated Expenses:	**$43,400**

Note: Graduate cost is listed as per credit.

NEW APPLICANTS/NEWLY ENROLLED STUDENTS
[Numbers are for the undergraduate engineering college for the Fall 2006 term]
Number of Applicants (a): 1,645
Of those, Number Offered Admission (b): 937
Of those, Number Enrolled Fall 2006 (c): 390

GRADUATE INFORMATION

ADMISSION INQUIRIES
Eden Downs
Director of Admissions and Information Systems
Stevens Institute of Technology
Castle Point on Hudson
Hoboken , NJ 07030
Phone: (201) 216-8353
Fax: (201) 216-8044
Email: edowns@stevens.edu

ESTIMATED STUDENT EXPENSES (FALL 2006)
[Expenses are for the 2006-2007 nine-month academic year and are based on an average credit load of: Graduate: 5]

	All Students
Tuition and fees:	$965
Campus and Room and Board:	$10,000
Books and Supplies:	$900
Other Expenses:	
Total Estimated Expenses:	**$11,865**

Note: Graduate cost is listed as per credit.

NEW APPLICANTS/NEWLY ENROLLED STUDENTS
[Numbers are for the graduate engineering college for the Fall 2006 term]
Number of Applicants (a): 1,008
Of those, Number Offered Admission (b): 661
Of those, Number Enrolled Fall 2006 (c): 192

Swarthmore College

INSTITUTION INFORMATION
500 College Avenue

Hicks Bldg. Room 203
Swarthmore, PA 19081-1390
Phone: (610) 328-8071
Fax: (610) 328-8082
Web: http://www.engin.swarthmore.edu

GENERAL INFORMATION

[All Students - Fall 2006]
Undergraduate Enrollment ... 1,479
Graduate Enrollment ... 0
Professional Enrollment ... 0
Total Enrollment ... **1,479**

ENGINEERING COLLEGE INFORMATION

HEAD OF ENGINEERING

Erik Cheever
Professor and Chair
Engineering
Swarthmore College
500 College Avenue
Dept. of Engineering
Swarthmore, PA 19081
Phone: (610) 328-8076
Fax: (610) 328-8082
Email: erik_cheever@swarthmore.edu

TYPES OF ENGINEERING DEGREES

Bachelor's: B.S.
Master's:
Doctoral:

UNDERGRADUATE INFORMATION

ESTIMATED STUDENT EXPENSES (FALL 2006)

[Expenses are for the 2006-2007 nine-month academic year and are based on an average credit load of: Undergraduate: 3]

	All Students
Tuition and fees:	$32,912
Campus and Room and Board:	$10,300
Books and Supplies:	
Other Expenses:	$320
Total Estimated Expenses:	**$43,532**

Note: Expenses for textbooks and supplies not calculated.

NEW APPLICANTS/NEWLY ENROLLED STUDENTS

[Numbers are for the undergraduate engineering college for the Fall 2006 term]
Number of Applicants (a): ... 480
Of those, Number Offered Admission (b): ... 141
Of those, Number Enrolled Fall 2006 (c): ... 39

Syracuse University

INSTITUTION INFORMATION

223 Link Hall
Syracuse, NY 13244
Phone: (315) 443-3604
Fax: (315) 443-4936
Web: http://www.ecs.syr.edu/admissions_grad_index.asp

GENERAL INFORMATION

[All Students - Fall 2006]
Undergraduate Enrollment ... 12,387
Graduate Enrollment ... 3,795
Professional Enrollment ... 759
Total Enrollment ... **16,941**

ENGINEERING COLLEGE INFORMATION

HEAD OF ENGINEERING

Shiu-Kai Chin
Interim Dean
College of Engineering and Computer Science, Deans' Office
Syracuse University
223 Link Hall
Syracuse, NY 13244
Phone: (315) 443-4341
Fax: (315) 443-4936
Email: efspina@syr.edu

ENGINEERING COLLEGE INQUIRIES

Sue Karlik
Assist to Sr Associate Dean of Acad & Stud Affairs
Syracuse University
223 Link Hall
Syracuse, NY 13244

Phone: (315) 443-3604
Fax: (315) 443-4936
Email: skarlik@syr.edu

TYPES OF ENGINEERING DEGREES

Bachelor's: B.S.
Master's: M.S. with thesis, M.S. without thesis, but with project or report
Doctoral: Ph.D.

UNDERGRADUATE INFORMATION

ESTIMATED STUDENT EXPENSES (FALL 2006)

[Expenses are for the 2006-2007 nine-month academic year and are based on an average credit load of: Undergraduate: 17]

	All Students
Tuition and fees:	$29,965
Campus and Room and Board:	$11,340
Books and Supplies:	$1,234
Other Expenses:	$1,642
Total Estimated Expenses:	**$44,181**

Note: Misc. Exp. include fees, estimate on personal expenses and medical insurance.

NEW APPLICANTS/NEWLY ENROLLED STUDENTS

[Numbers are for the undergraduate engineering college for the Fall 2006 term]
Number of Applicants (a): ... 1,946
Of those, Number Offered Admission (b): ... 1,507
Of those, Number Enrolled Fall 2006 (c): ... 373

GRADUATE INFORMATION

ESTIMATED STUDENT EXPENSES (FALL 2006)

[Expenses are for the 2006-2007 nine-month academic year and are based on an average credit load of: Graduate: 18]

	All Students
Tuition and fees:	$17,850
Campus and Room and Board:	$11,340
Books and Supplies:	$1,160
Other Expenses:	$3,590
Total Estimated Expenses:	**$33,940**

Note: Misc. Exp. include fees, estimate on personal expenses and medical insurance.

NEW APPLICANTS/NEWLY ENROLLED STUDENTS

[Numbers are for the graduate engineering college for the Fall 2006 term]
Number of Applicants (a): ... 1,672
Of those, Number Offered Admission (b): ... 862
Of those, Number Enrolled Fall 2006 (c): ... 266

Temple University

INSTITUTION INFORMATION

1947 12th Street N
College of Engineering
Philadelphia, PA 19122
Phone: (215) 204-7800
Fax: (215) 204-6936
Web: http://www.eng.temple.edu

GENERAL INFORMATION

[All Students - Fall 2006]
Undergraduate Enrollment ... 24,197
Graduate Enrollment ... 4,870
Professional Enrollment ... 3,093
Total Enrollment ... **32,160**

ENGINEERING COLLEGE INFORMATION

HEAD OF ENGINEERING

Keya Sadeghipour
Dean
College of Engineering
Temple University
College of Engineering/ Temple U
1947 North 12th St.
Philadelphia, PA 19122
Phone: (215) 204-7800
Fax: (215) 204-6936
Email: keya.sadeghipour@temple.edu

ENGINEERING COLLEGE INQUIRIES

Don Heller
Assistant Dean
Temple University
1947 12th Street N, College of Engineering

Philadelphia, PA 19122
Phone: (215) 204-5285
Fax: (215) 204-6936

TYPES OF ENGINEERING DEGREES

Bachelor's: B.S.
Master's: M.S. with thesis, M.S. without thesis, but with project or report
Doctoral: Ph.D.

UNDERGRADUATE INFORMATION

ADMISSION INQUIRIES

Steven Ridenour
Director of Undergraduate Studies
Temple University
1947 12th Street N, College of Engineering
Philadelphia, PA 19122
Phone: (215) 204-7800
Fax: (215) 204-6936
Email: steven.ridenour@temple.edu

ESTIMATED STUDENT EXPENSES (FALL 2006)

[Expenses are for the 2006-2007 nine-month academic year and are based on an average credit load of: Undergraduate: 16]

	In-State	Out-of-State
Tuition and Fees:	$10,180	$18,224
Campus and Room and Board:	$8,230	$8,230
Books and Supplies:	$1,200	$1,200
Other Expenses:	$750	$750
Total Estimated Expenses:	**$20,360**	**$28,404**

Note: Above expenses are for the academic year, that is two semesters.

NEW APPLICANTS/NEWLY ENROLLED STUDENTS

[Numbers are for the undergraduate engineering college for the Fall 2006 term]
Number of Applicants (a): ... 935
Of those, Number Offered Admission (b): ... 590
Of those, Number Enrolled Fall 2006 (c): ... 220

GRADUATE INFORMATION

ESTIMATED STUDENT EXPENSES (FALL 2006)

[Expenses are for the 2006-2007 nine-month academic year and are based on an average credit load of: Graduate: 6]

	In-State	Out-of-State
Tuition and Fees:	$511	$746
Campus and Room and Board:	$8,230	$8,230
Books and Supplies:	$1,300	$1,300
Other Expenses:	$750	$750
Total Estimated Expenses:	**$10,791**	**$11,026**

Note: Above expenses are for the academic year, that is two semesters.

NEW APPLICANTS/NEWLY ENROLLED STUDENTS

[Numbers are for the graduate engineering college for the Fall 2006 term]
Number of Applicants (a): ... 125
Of those, Number Offered Admission (b): ... 83
Of those, Number Enrolled Fall 2006 (c): ... 31

Tennessee State University

INSTITUTION INFORMATION

3500 John A. Meritt Blvd.
Nashville, TN 37209-1561
Phone: (615) 963-5331
Fax: (615) 963-5315
Web: http://www.tnstate.edu

GENERAL INFORMATION

[All Students - Fall 2006]
Undergraduate Enrollment ... 7,112
Graduate Enrollment ... 1,926
Professional Enrollment ... 9,038
Total Enrollment ... **18,076**

ENGINEERING COLLEGE INFORMATION

HEAD OF ENGINEERING

Decatur B Rogers
Professor and Dean
College of Engineering, Technology and Computer Science
Tennessee State University
College of Engineering, Technology and Computer

Science
3500 John A. Merritt Blvd.
Nashville, TN 37209
Phone: (615) 963-5401
Fax: (615) 963-5397
Email: drogers@tnstate.edu

TYPES OF ENGINEERING DEGREES
Bachelor's: B.S.
Master's: M.S. with thesis, M.Eng.
Doctoral: Ph.D.

UNDERGRADUATE INFORMATION

ADMISSION INQUIRIES
John Cade
Dean of Admissions and Records
Tennessee State University
3500 John A. Merritt Blvd.
Nashville, TN 37209
Phone: (615) 963-5107
Fax: (615) 963-5108
Email: jcade@tnstate.edu

ESTIMATED STUDENT EXPENSES (FALL 2006)
[Expenses are for the 2006-2007 nine-month academic year and are based on an average credit load of: Undergraduate: 16]

	In-State	Out-of-State
Tuition and Fees:	$4,564	$14,258
Campus and Room and Board:	$5,000	$5,000
Books and Supplies:	$1,500	$1,500
Other Expenses:	$1,800	$1,800
Total Estimated Expenses:	**$12,864**	**$22,558**

Note: On campus apartments cost $2,080.00 per student per semester

NEW APPLICANTS/NEWLY ENROLLED STUDENTS
[Numbers are for the undergraduate engineering college for the Fall 2006 term]

Number of Applicants (a):	723
Of those, Number Offered Admission (b):	407
Of those, Number Enrolled Fall 2006 (c):	184

GRADUATE INFORMATION

ADMISSION INQUIRIES
Mohan J Malkani
Professor and Associate Dean/Director-Engr. Research Inst. & Center Neural Engr.
Tennessee State University
College of Engineering, Technology and Computer Science, 3500 John A. Merritt Blvd.
Nashville , TN 37209
Phone: (615) 963-5400
Fax: (615) 963-5397
Email: mmalkani@tnstate.edu

ESTIMATED STUDENT EXPENSES (FALL 2006)
[Expenses are for the 2006-2007 nine-month academic year and are based on an average credit load of: Graduate: 9]

	In-State	Out-of-State
Tuition and Fees:	$5,874	$15,568
Campus and Room and Board:	$5,000	$5,000
Books and Supplies:	$1,500	$1,500
Other Expenses:	$1,800	$1,800
Total Estimated Expenses:	**$14,174**	**$23,868**

Note: On campus apartments cost $2,080.00 per student per semester

NEW APPLICANTS/NEWLY ENROLLED STUDENTS
[Numbers are for the graduate engineering college for the Fall 2006 term]

Number of Applicants (a):	40
Of those, Number Offered Admission (b):	25
Of those, Number Enrolled Fall 2006 (c):	16

Tennessee Technological University

INSTITUTION INFORMATION
Box 5005
1010 N. Peachtree Avenue, Clement Hall 201
Cookeville, TN 38505
Phone: (931) 372-3172
Fax: (931) 372-6172
Web: http://www.tntech.edu/

GENERAL INFORMATION
[All Students - Fall 2006]

Undergraduate Enrollment	7,569
Graduate Enrollment	2,164
Professional Enrollment	0
Total Enrollment	**9,733**

ENGINEERING COLLEGE INFORMATION

HEAD OF ENGINEERING
Glen E Johnson
Dean
College of Engineering
Tennessee Technological University
Box 5005
Cookeville, TN 38505
Phone: (931) 372-3172
Fax: (931) 372-6172
Email: gjohnson@tntech.edu

TYPES OF ENGINEERING DEGREES
Bachelor's: B.S.
Master's: M.S. with thesis, M.S. without thesis, but with project or report
Doctoral: Ph.D.

UNDERGRADUATE INFORMATION

ESTIMATED STUDENT EXPENSES (FALL 2006)
[Expenses are for the 2006-2007 nine-month academic year and are based on an average credit load of: Undergraduate: N/A]

	In-State	Out-of-State
Tuition and Fees:	$4,660	$14,620
Campus and Room and Board:	$6,450	$6,450
Books and Supplies:	$1,300	$1,300
Other Expenses:	$2,790	$2,930
Total Estimated Expenses:	**$15,200**	**$25,300**

NEW APPLICANTS/NEWLY ENROLLED STUDENTS
[Numbers are for the undergraduate engineering college for the Fall 2006 term]

Number of Applicants (a):	1,056
Of those, Number Offered Admission (b):	854
Of those, Number Enrolled Fall 2006 (c):	480

GRADUATE INFORMATION

ADMISSION INQUIRIES
Subramaniam Deivanayagam
Assoc. Dean of Engrg. for Grad. Studies & Research
Tennessee Technological University
Box 5005
Cookeville , TN 38505
Phone: (931) 372-3834
Fax: (931) 372-6172
Email: deivy@tntech.edu

ESTIMATED STUDENT EXPENSES (FALL 2006)
[Expenses are for the 2006-2007 nine-month academic year and are based on an average credit load of: Graduate: N/A]

	In-State	Out-of-State
Tuition and Fees:	$5,660	$13,440
Campus and Room and Board:	$6,450	$6,450
Books and Supplies:	$1,000	$1,000
Other Expenses:	$2,790	$2,930
Total Estimated Expenses:	**$15,900**	**$23,820**

NEW APPLICANTS/NEWLY ENROLLED STUDENTS
[Numbers are for the graduate engineering college for the Fall 2006 term]

Number of Applicants (a):	273
Of those, Number Offered Admission (b):	105
Of those, Number Enrolled Fall 2006 (c):	24

University of Tennessee, Chattanooga

INSTITUTION INFORMATION
College of Engineering & Computer Science
615 McCallie Avenue Dept 2452
Chattanooga, TN 37403-2598
Phone: (423) 425-2256
Web: http://www.utc.edu/Academic/Engineering/

GENERAL INFORMATION
[All Students - Fall 2006]

Undergraduate Enrollment	7,544
Graduate Enrollment	1,379
Professional Enrollment	0
Total Enrollment	**8,923**

ENGINEERING COLLEGE INFORMATION

HEAD OF ENGINEERING
J Ronald Bailey
Dean and Guerry Professor
College of Engineering and Computer Science
University of Tennessee, Chattanooga
450C EMCS Bldg. Dept 2452
615 McCallie Avenue
Chattanooga, TN 37403-2598
Phone: (423) 425-5536
Fax: (423) 425-5311
Email: Ronald-Bailey@utc.edu

TYPES OF ENGINEERING DEGREES
Bachelor's: B.S.,BSE, BSEE, BSME
Master's: M.S. with thesis, M.S. without thesis, but with project or report
Doctoral: Ph.D.

UNDERGRADUATE INFORMATION

ESTIMATED STUDENT EXPENSES (FALL 2006)
[Expenses are for the 2006-2007 nine-month academic year and are based on an average credit load of: Undergraduate: 12]

	In-State	Out-of-State
Tuition and Fees:	$4,688	$14,084
Campus and Room and Board:	$7,384	$7,384
Books and Supplies:	$950	$950
Other Expenses:	$3,032	$3,032
Total Estimated Expenses:	**$16,054**	**$25,450**

GRADUATE INFORMATION

ESTIMATED STUDENT EXPENSES (FALL 2006)
[Expenses are for the 2006-2007 nine-month academic year and are based on an average credit load of: Graduate: 9]

	In-State	Out-of-State
Tuition and Fees:	$5,434	$14,830
Campus and Room and Board:	$7,384	$7,384
Books and Supplies:	$950	$950
Other Expenses:	$3,032	$3,032
Total Estimated Expenses:	**$16,800**	**$26,196**

NEW APPLICANTS/NEWLY ENROLLED STUDENTS
[Numbers are for the graduate engineering college for the Fall 2006 term]

Number of Applicants (a):	78
Of those, Number Offered Admission (b):	46
Of those, Number Enrolled Fall 2006 (c):	26

University of Tennessee, Knoxville

INSTITUTION INFORMATION
College of Engineering
124 Perkins Hall
Knoxville, TN 37996-2000
Phone: (865) 974-5321
Fax: (865) 974-8890
Web: http://www.engr.utk.edu

GENERAL INFORMATION
[All Students - Fall 2006]

Undergraduate Enrollment	20,435
Graduate Enrollment	5,138
Professional Enrollment	725
Total Enrollment	**26,298**

ENGINEERING COLLEGE INFORMATION

HEAD OF ENGINEERING
Way Kuo
Dean
College of Engineering
University of Tennessee, Knoxville
124 Perkins Hall
Knoxville, TN 37996-2000
Phone: (865) 974-5321
Fax: (865) 974-8890
Email: way@utk.edu

TYPES OF ENGINEERING DEGREES

Bachelor's: B.S.
Master's: M.S. with thesis, M.S. without thesis, but with project or report
Doctoral: Ph.D.

UNDERGRADUATE INFORMATION

ADMISSION INQUIRIES

Masood Parang
Associate Dean for Student Affairs
University of Tennessee, Knoxville
College of Engineering, 101 Perkins Hall
Knoxville, TN 37996-2011
Phone: (865) 974-2454
Fax: (865) 974-9879
Email: mparang@utk.edu

ADMISSION INQUIRIES

Anne Mayhew
Vice Chancellor & Dean
University of Tennessee, Knoxville
533 Andy Holt Tower
Knoxville, TN 37996-0152
Phone: (865) 974-2445
Fax: (865) 974-4811
Email: amayhew@utk.edu

ADMISSION INQUIRIES

Nancy McGlasson
Assistant Dean of Enrollment Services and Director of Undergraduate Admissions
University of Tennessee, Knoxville
320 Student Services Building
Knoxville, TN 37996-0210
Phone: (865) 974-2184
Fax: (865) 974-1182
Email: nmcglass@utk.edu

ESTIMATED STUDENT EXPENSES (FALL 2006)

[Expenses are for the 2006-2007 nine-month academic year and are based on an average credit load of: Undergraduate: 15]

	In-State	Out-of-State
Tuition and Fees:	$5,622	$17,188
Campus and Room and Board:	$6,054	$6,054
Books and Supplies:	$1,250	$1,250
Other Expenses:	$4,866	$4,866
Total Estimated Expenses:	**$17,792**	**$29,358**

NEW APPLICANTS/NEWLY ENROLLED STUDENTS

[Numbers are for the undergraduate engineering college for the Fall 2006 term]

Number of Applicants (a):	1,124
Of those, Number Offered Admission (b):	957
Of those, Number Enrolled Fall 2006 (c):	461

GRADUATE INFORMATION

ADMISSION INQUIRIES

Masood Parang
Associate Dean for Student Affairs
University of Tennessee, Knoxville
College of Engineering, 101 Perkins Hall
Knoxville , TN 37996-2011
Phone: (865) 974-2454
Fax: (865) 974-9879
Email: mparang@utk.edu

ADMISSION INQUIRIES

Mohanan M.K.
Director Graduate & International Admissions
University of Tennessee, Knoxville
201 Student Services Building
Knoxville , TN 37996-0210
Phone: (865) 974-3251
Fax: (865) 974-6541

ESTIMATED STUDENT EXPENSES (FALL 2006)

[Expenses are for the 2006-2007 nine-month academic year and are based on an average credit load of: Graduate: 9]

	In-State	Out-of-State
Tuition and Fees:	$6,366	$17,932
Campus and Room and Board:	$8,464	$8,464
Books and Supplies:	$1,470	$1,470
Other Expenses:	$5,226	$5,226
Total Estimated Expenses:	**$21,526**	**$33,092**

NEW APPLICANTS/NEWLY ENROLLED STUDENTS

[Numbers are for the graduate engineering college for the

Fall 2006 term]

Number of Applicants (a):	1,019
Of those, Number Offered Admission (b):	485
Of those, Number Enrolled Fall 2006 (c):	142

University of Tennessee, Martin

INSTITUTION INFORMATION

Hall Moody Administration Building, Room 325
Martin, TN 38238
Phone: (731) 881-7500
Fax: (731) 881-7019
Web: http://www.utm.edu

GENERAL INFORMATION

[All Students - Fall 2006]

Undergraduate Enrollment	6,320
Graduate Enrollment	573
Professional Enrollment	0
Total Enrollment	**6,893**

ENGINEERING COLLEGE INFORMATION

HEAD OF ENGINEERING

Douglas Sterrett
Dean
College of Engineering and Natural Sciences
University of Tennessee, Martin
EPS Building, Room 113
Martin, TN 38238
Phone: (731) 881-7385
Fax: (731) 881-7375
Email: dsterret@utm.edu

ENGINEERING COLLEGE INQUIRIES

Laurinda S Lamb
Administrative Assistant II
University of Tennessee, Martin
EPS Bldg., Room 101
Martin, TN 38238
Phone: (731) 881-7571
Fax: (731) 881-7375
Email: lslamb@utm.edu

TYPES OF ENGINEERING DEGREES

Bachelor's: B.S.
Master's:
Doctoral:

UNDERGRADUATE INFORMATION

ESTIMATED STUDENT EXPENSES (FALL 2006)

[Expenses are for the 2006-2007 nine-month academic year and are based on an average credit load of: Undergraduate: 12]

	In-State	Out-of-State
Tuition and Fees:	$4,665	$14,137
Campus and Room and Board:	$4,310	$4,310
Books and Supplies:	$1,200	$1,200
Other Expenses:	$3,120	$3,120
Total Estimated Expenses:	**$13,295**	**$22,767**

NEW APPLICANTS/NEWLY ENROLLED STUDENTS

[Numbers are for the undergraduate engineering college for the Fall 2006 term]

Number of Applicants (a):	171
Of those, Number Offered Admission (b):	119
Of those, Number Enrolled Fall 2006 (c):	82

GRADUATE INFORMATION

ESTIMATED STUDENT EXPENSES (FALL 2006)

[Expenses are for the 2006-2007 nine-month academic year and are based on an average credit load of: Graduate: 9]

	In-State	Out-of-State
Tuition and Fees:	$5,400	$14,870
Campus and Room and Board:	$4,310	$4,310
Books and Supplies:	$1,200	$1,200
Other Expenses:	$3,120	$3,120
Total Estimated Expenses:	**$14,030**	**$23,500**

Texas A&M University

INSTITUTION INFORMATION

College of Engineering

TAMU 3470
College Station, TX 77843-3470
Phone: (979) 458-7471
Fax: (979) 458-7484
Web: http://engineering.tamu.edu/index.html

GENERAL INFORMATION

[All Students - Fall 2006]

Undergraduate Enrollment	36,580
Graduate Enrollment	8,291
Professional Enrollment	509
Total Enrollment	**45,380**

ENGINEERING COLLEGE INFORMATION

HEAD OF ENGINEERING

G. Kemble Bennett, Jr.
Dean of Engineering
College of Engineering
Texas A&M University
Dean of Engineering
TAMU 3126
College Station, TX 77843-3126
Phone: (979) 845-1321
Fax: (979) 845-8986
Email: engineeringadmin@tamu.edu

ENGINEERING COLLEGE INQUIRIES

Jo W Howze
Associate Dean
Texas A&M University
TAMU 3127
College Station, TX 77843-3127
Phone: (979) 862-4367
Fax: (979) 847-8654
Email: j-howze@tamu.edu

TYPES OF ENGINEERING DEGREES

Bachelor's: B.S.
Master's: M.S. with thesis, M.S. without thesis, but with project or report, M.Eng.,M.E.
Doctoral: Ph.D., D.Eng

UNDERGRADUATE INFORMATION

ADMISSION INQUIRIES

Jo W Howze
Associate Dean
Texas A&M University
TAMU 3127
College Station, TX 77843-3127
Phone: (979) 862-4367
Fax: (979) 847-8654
Email: j-howze@tamu.edu

ESTIMATED STUDENT EXPENSES (FALL 2006)

[Expenses are for the 2006-2007 nine-month academic year and are based on an average credit load of: Undergraduate: 15]

	In-State	Out-of-State
Tuition and Fees:	$6,966	$15,216
Campus and Room and Board:	$7,660	$7,660
Books and Supplies:	$1,280	$1,280
Other Expenses:	$2,552	$2,552
Total Estimated Expenses:	**$18,458**	**$26,708**

Note: Tuition & Fees: Based on 15 SCH flat rate for Undergraduate and 9 SCH for Graduate. Other Expenses are personal expenses and transportation.

NEW APPLICANTS/NEWLY ENROLLED STUDENTS

[Numbers are for the undergraduate engineering college for the Fall 2006 term]

Number of Applicants (a):	4,327
Of those, Number Offered Admission (b):	3,439
Of those, Number Enrolled Fall 2006 (c):	1,968

GRADUATE INFORMATION

ADMISSION INQUIRIES

N.K. Anand
Professor, Assistant Dean, & Interim Head
Texas A&M University
TAMU 3127
College Station , TX 77843-3127
Phone: (979) 862-8869
Fax: (979) 847-8654
Email: nkanand@tamu.edu

ESTIMATED STUDENT EXPENSES (FALL 2006)

[Expenses are for the 2006-2007 nine-month academic year and are based on an average credit load of: Graduate: 9]

	In-State	Out-of-State
Tuition and Fees:	$5,409	$10,359
Campus and Room and Board:	$9,306	$9,306
Books and Supplies:	$1,280	$1,280
Other Expenses:	$2,552	$2,552
Total Estimated Expenses:	**$18,547**	**$23,497**

Note: Tuition & Fees: Based on 15 SCH flat rate for Undergraduate ,and 9 SCH for Graduate. Other Expenses are personal expenses and transportation.

NEW APPLICANTS/NEWLY ENROLLED STUDENTS
[Numbers are for the graduate engineering college for the Fall 2006 term]

Number of Applicants (a):	4,458
Of those, Number Offered Admission (b):	1,689
Of those, Number Enrolled Fall 2006 (c):	653

Texas A&M University - Kingsville

INSTITUTION INFORMATION
700 University Blvd.
Kingsville, TX 78363
Phone: (361) 593-2011
Web: http://www.tamuk.edu

GENERAL INFORMATION
[All Students - Fall 2006]

Undergraduate Enrollment	5,208
Graduate Enrollment	1,495
Professional Enrollment	0
Total Enrollment	**6,703**

ENGINEERING COLLEGE INFORMATION

HEAD OF ENGINEERING
William A. Heenan
Dean
Frank H. Dotterweich College of Engineering
Texas A&M University - Kingsville
700 University Blvd., MSC-188
Kingsville, TX 78363
Phone: (361) 593-2001
Fax: (361) 593-2106
Email: w-heenan@tamuk.edu

ENGINEERING COLLEGE INQUIRIES
John L Chisholm
Assistant Dean & Associate Professor
Texas A&M University - Kingsville
700 University Blvd.
Kingsville, TX 78363
Phone: (361) 593-2001
Fax: (361) 593-2106
Email: chisholm@tamuk.edu

TYPES OF ENGINEERING DEGREES
Bachelor's: B.S.
Master's: M.S. with thesis, M.S. without thesis, but with project or report
Doctoral: Ph.D.

UNDERGRADUATE INFORMATION

ADMISSION INQUIRIES
Sheryl L. Custer
Executive Assistant to the Dean
Texas A&M University - Kingsville
700 University Blvd., MSC-188
Kingsville, TX 78363
Phone: (361) 593-2799
Fax: (361) 593-2106
Email: s-custer@tamuk.edu

ESTIMATED STUDENT EXPENSES (FALL 2006)
[Expenses are for the 2006-2007 nine-month academic year and are based on an average credit load of: Undergraduate: 16]

	In-State	Out-of-State
Tuition and Fees:	$4,580	$13,412
Campus and Room and Board:	$4,682	$4,672
Books and Supplies:	$1,027	$1,027
Other Expenses:	$2,286	$2,286
Total Estimated Expenses:	**$12,575**	**$21,397**

GRADUATE INFORMATION

ADMISSION INQUIRIES
Alberto Olivares
Dean
Texas A&M University - Kingsville
700 University Blvd., MSC-118
Kingsville , TX 78363
Phone: (361) 593-2808
Fax: (361) 593-2859
Email: kaao000@tamuk.edu

ESTIMATED STUDENT EXPENSES (FALL 2006)
[Expenses are for the 2006-2007 nine-month academic year and are based on an average credit load of: Graduate: 9]

	In-State	Out-of-State
Tuition and Fees:	$2,294	$7,962
Campus and Room and Board:	$4,672	$4,672
Books and Supplies:	$1,027	$2,286
Other Expenses:	$2,286	$2,286
Total Estimated Expenses:	**$10,279**	**$17,206**

Texas Christian University

INSTITUTION INFORMATION
Department of Engineering
TCU Box 298640
Fort Worth, TX 76129
Phone: (817) 257-7677
Fax: (817) 257-7704
Web: http://www.tcu.edu

GENERAL INFORMATION
[All Students - Fall 2006]

Undergraduate Enrollment	7,267
Graduate Enrollment	1,598
Professional Enrollment	0
Total Enrollment	**8,865**

ENGINEERING COLLEGE INFORMATION

HEAD OF ENGINEERING
Walton E. Williamson
Department Chair
Tucker Technology Center 203
Texas Christian University
TCU Box 298640
2840 West Bowie
Fort Worth, TX 76129
Phone: (817) 257-7677
Fax: (817) 257-7704
Email: w.e.williamson@tcu.edu

ENGINEERING COLLEGE INQUIRIES
Walton E. Williamson
Department Chair
Texas Christian University
TCU Box 298640, 2840 West Bowie
Fort Worth, TX 76129
Phone: (817) 257-7677
Fax: (817) 257-7704
Email: w.e.williamson@tcu.edu

TYPES OF ENGINEERING DEGREES
Bachelor's: B.S.
Master's:
Doctoral:

UNDERGRADUATE INFORMATION

ESTIMATED STUDENT EXPENSES (FALL 2006)
[Expenses are for the 2006-2007 nine-month academic year and are based on an average credit load of: Undergraduate: 15]

	All Students
Tuition and fees:	$22,980
Campus and Room and Board:	$7,120
Books and Supplies:	$810
Other Expenses:	$48
Total Estimated Expenses:	**$30,958**

Note: Average

NEW APPLICANTS/NEWLY ENROLLED STUDENTS
[Numbers are for the undergraduate engineering college for the Fall 2006 term]

Number of Applicants (a):	463
Of those, Number Offered Admission (b):	292

Of those, Number Enrolled Fall 2006 (c):	58

Note: Arts & Science premajors are not included

Texas Tech University

INSTITUTION INFORMATION
Box 45005
Lubbock, TX 79409-5005
Phone: (806) 742-2011
Fax: (806) 742-0980
Web: http://www.ttu.edu

GENERAL INFORMATION
[All Students - Fall 2006]

Undergraduate Enrollment	22,851
Graduate Enrollment	4,443
Professional Enrollment	702
Total Enrollment	**27,996**

ENGINEERING COLLEGE INFORMATION

HEAD OF ENGINEERING
Pamela Eibeck
Academic Dean, College of Engineering
Office of the Dean
Texas Tech University
College of Engineering
PO Box 43103
Lubbock, TX 79409-3103
Phone: (806) 742-3451
Fax: (806) 742-3493
Email: pamela.eibeck@ttu.edu

TYPES OF ENGINEERING DEGREES
Bachelor's: B.A., B.S.
Master's: M.S. with thesis, M.S. without thesis, but with project or report
Doctoral: Ph.D.

UNDERGRADUATE INFORMATION

ADMISSION INQUIRIES
Jeffrey C Woldstad
Associate Dean of Undergraduate Studies, Professor
Texas Tech University
College of Engineering, Box 43103
Lubbock, TX 79409-3103
Phone: (806) 742-3451
Fax: (806) 742-3493
Email: jeff.woldstad@ttu.edu

ESTIMATED STUDENT EXPENSES (FALL 2006)
[Expenses are for the 2006-2007 nine-month academic year and are based on an average credit load of: Undergraduate: 30]

	In-State	Out-of-State
Tuition and Fees:	$6,459	$14,709
Campus and Room and Board:	$7,288	$7,288
Books and Supplies:	$900	$900
Other Expenses:	$1,800	$1,800
Total Estimated Expenses:	**$16,447**	**$24,697**

NEW APPLICANTS/NEWLY ENROLLED STUDENTS
[Numbers are for the undergraduate engineering college for the Fall 2006 term]

Number of Applicants (a):	2,192
Of those, Number Offered Admission (b):	1,640
Of those, Number Enrolled Fall 2006 (c):	565

GRADUATE INFORMATION

ESTIMATED STUDENT EXPENSES (FALL 2006)
[Expenses are for the 2006-2007 nine-month academic year and are based on an average credit load of: Graduate: 24]

	In-State	Out-of-State
Tuition and Fees:	$6,576	$13,176
Campus and Room and Board:	$7,288	$7,288
Books and Supplies:	$900	$900
Other Expenses:	$1,800	$1,800
Total Estimated Expenses:	**$16,564**	**$23,164**

NEW APPLICANTS/NEWLY ENROLLED STUDENTS
[Numbers are for the graduate engineering college for the Fall 2006 term]

Number of Applicants (a):	1,176
Of those, Number Offered Admission (b):	405
Of those, Number Enrolled Fall 2006 (c):	182

The University of Texas at Arlington

INSTITUTION INFORMATION
P.O. Box 19088
701 S. Nedderman Dr.
Arlington, TX 76019
Phone: (817) 272-2101
Web: http://www.uta.edu

GENERAL INFORMATION
[All Students - Fall 2006]

Undergraduate Enrollment	19,355
Graduate Enrollment	5,641
Professional Enrollment	0
Total Enrollment	**24,996**

ENGINEERING COLLEGE INFORMATION

HEAD OF ENGINEERING
Bill D Carroll
Dean of Engineering
The University of Texas at Arlington
Box 19019
634 Nedderman Hall
Arlington, TX 76019
Phone: (817) 272-5725
Fax: (817) 272-5110
Email: carroll@uta.edu

TYPES OF ENGINEERING DEGREES
Bachelor's: B.S.
Master's: M.S. with thesis, M.S. without thesis, but with project or report
Doctoral: Ph.D.

UNDERGRADUATE INFORMATION

ADMISSION INQUIRIES
Dale Wasson
Associate Vice President for Student Enrollment
The University of Texas at Arlington
Box 19113, Davis Hall
Arlington, TX 76019
Phone: (817) 272-5401
Fax: (817) 272-5455
Email: wasson@uta.edu

ESTIMATED STUDENT EXPENSES (FALL 2006)
[Expenses are for the 2006-2007 nine-month academic year and are based on an average credit load of: Undergraduate: 12]

	In-State	Out-of-State
Tuition and Fees:	$6,150	$12,835
Campus and Room and Board:	$5,533	$5,533
Books and Supplies:	$824	$824
Other Expenses:	$3,604	$3,604
Total Estimated Expenses:	**$16,111**	**$22,796**

GRADUATE INFORMATION

ADMISSION INQUIRIES
Philip Cohen
Dean, Graduate School
The University of Texas at Arlington
Box 19167, 333 Davis Hall
Arlington , TX 76019
Phone: (817) 272-3186
Fax: (817) 272-2627
Email: cohen@uta.edu

ESTIMATED STUDENT EXPENSES (FALL 2006)
[Expenses are for the 2006-2007 nine-month academic year and are based on an average credit load of: Graduate: 9]

	In-State	Out-of-State
Tuition and Fees:	$5,988	$11,023
Campus and Room and Board:	$5,533	$5,533
Books and Supplies:	$824	$824
Other Expenses:	$3,604	$3,604
Total Estimated Expenses:	**$15,949**	**$20,984**

The University of Texas at Austin

INSTITUTION INFORMATION
1 University Station G3400

Austin, TX 78712-0565
Phone: (512) 471-3434
Fax: (512) 471-8102
Web: http://www.utexas.edu/

GENERAL INFORMATION
[All Students - Fall 2006]

Undergraduate Enrollment	37,037
Graduate Enrollment	11,353
Professional Enrollment	1,307
Total Enrollment	**49,697**

ENGINEERING COLLEGE INFORMATION

HEAD OF ENGINEERING
Ben G Streetman
Dean
Office of the Dean of Engineering
The University of Texas at Austin
1 University Station C2100
ECJ 10.310
Austin, TX 78712-0284
Phone: (512) 471-1166
Fax: (512) 475-7072
Email: bstreet@mail.utexas.edu

TYPES OF ENGINEERING DEGREES
Bachelor's: B.S.
Master's: M.A. with thesis, M.S. with thesis, M.S. without thesis, but with project or report
Doctoral: Ph.D.

UNDERGRADUATE INFORMATION

ADMISSION INQUIRIES
Bruce Walker
Vice Provost & Director of Admissions
The University of Texas at Austin
P.O. Box 8058
Austin, TX 78713-8058
Phone: (512) 475-7399
Fax: (512) 475-7478
Email: bruce.walker@mail.utexas.edu

ESTIMATED STUDENT EXPENSES (FALL 2006)
[Expenses are for the 2006-2007 nine-month academic year and are based on an average credit load of: Undergraduate: 15]

	In-State	Out-of-State
Tuition and Fees:	$8,432	$22,062
Campus and Room and Board:	$8,176	$8,176
Books and Supplies:	$800	$800
Other Expenses:	$3,150	$3,150
Total Estimated Expenses:	**$20,558**	**$34,188**

Note: A normal undergraduate course load in the College of Engineering is 15 to 18 hours a semester. Fewer than 14 hours requires written approval.

NEW APPLICANTS/NEWLY ENROLLED STUDENTS
[Numbers are for the undergraduate engineering college for the Fall 2006 term]

Number of Applicants (a):	5,862
Of those, Number Offered Admission (b):	1,469
Of those, Number Enrolled Fall 2006 (c):	1,318

GRADUATE INFORMATION

ADMISSION INQUIRIES
Pat Ellison
Associate Director of Admissions and Asst. Dean of Graduate Studies
The University of Texas at Austin
P.O. Box 7608
Austin , TX 78713-7608
Phone: (512) 475-7390
Fax: (512) 475-7395
Email: pat.ellison@mail.utexas.edu

ESTIMATED STUDENT EXPENSES (FALL 2006)
[Expenses are for the 2006-2007 nine-month academic year and are based on an average credit load of: Graduate: 9]

	In-State	Out-of-State
Tuition and Fees:	$7,100	$13,574
Campus and Room and Board:	$7,700	$7,700
Books and Supplies:	$900	$900
Other Expenses:	$3,650	$3,650
Total Estimated Expenses:	**$19,350**	**$25,824**

Note: A normal undergraduate course load in the College of Engineering is 15 to 18 hours a semester. Fewer than 14 hours requires written approval.

NEW APPLICANTS/NEWLY ENROLLED STUDENTS
[Numbers are for the graduate engineering college for the Fall 2006 term]

Number of Applicants (a):	4,340
Of those, Number Offered Admission (b):	1,290
Of those, Number Enrolled Fall 2006 (c):	534

The University of Texas at Dallas

INSTITUTION INFORMATION
P.O. Box 830688
2601 N.Floyd Road
Richardson, TX 75083-0688
Phone: (972) 883-2111
Fax: (972) 883-2813
Web: http://www.utdallas.edu

GENERAL INFORMATION
[All Students - Fall 2006]

Undergraduate Enrollment	9,375
Graduate Enrollment	5,148
Professional Enrollment	0
Total Enrollment	**14,523**

ENGINEERING COLLEGE INFORMATION

HEAD OF ENGINEERING
Robert Helms
Dean/Lars Magnus Ericsson Professor
Erik Jonsson School of Engineering and Computer Science
The University of Texas at Dallas
P.O. Box 830688, M/S-EC32
2601 N. Floyd Road
Richardson, TX 75083-0688
Phone: (972) 883-2974
Fax: (972) 883-2813
Email: robert.helms@utdallas.edu

TYPES OF ENGINEERING DEGREES
Bachelor's: B.S.
Master's: M.S. with thesis, M.S. without thesis, but with project or report
Doctoral: Ph.D.

UNDERGRADUATE INFORMATION

ADMISSION INQUIRIES
Barry Samsula
Assistant Dean for Student Enrollment
The University of Texas at Dallas
P.O. Box 830688, M/S-EC34, 2601 N. Floyd Road
Richardson, TX 75083-0688
Phone: (972) 883-4464
Fax: (972) 883-6845
Email: bsamsula@utdallas.edu

ESTIMATED STUDENT EXPENSES (FALL 2006)
[Expenses are for the 2006-2007 nine-month academic year and are based on an average credit load of: Undergraduate: 13]

	In-State	Out-of-State
Tuition and Fees:	$6,700	$13,300
Campus and Room and Board:	$6,540	$6,540
Books and Supplies:	$1,200	$1,200
Other Expenses:	$3,994	$3,994
Total Estimated Expenses:	**$18,434**	**$25,034**

NEW APPLICANTS/NEWLY ENROLLED STUDENTS
[Numbers are for the undergraduate engineering college for the Fall 2006 term]

Number of Applicants (a):	863
Of those, Number Offered Admission (b):	649
Of those, Number Enrolled Fall 2006 (c):	303

GRADUATE INFORMATION

ADMISSION INQUIRIES
Barry Samsula
Assistant Dean for Student Enrollment
The University of Texas at Dallas
P.O. Box 830688, M/S-EC34, 2601 N. Floyd Road
Richardson , TX 75083-0688
Phone: (972) 883-4464
Fax: (972) 883-6845
Email: bsamsula@utdallas.edu

ESTIMATED STUDENT EXPENSES (FALL 2006)

[Expenses are for the 2006-2007 nine-month academic year and are based on an average credit load of: Graduate: 7]

	In-State	Out-of-State
Tuition and Fees:	$6,000	$10,950
Campus and Room and Board:	$6,540	$6,540
Books and Supplies:	$1,200	$1,200
Other Expenses:	$3,994	$3,994
Total Estimated Expenses:	**$17,734**	**$22,684**

NEW APPLICANTS/NEWLY ENROLLED STUDENTS

[Numbers are for the graduate engineering college for the Fall 2006 term]

Number of Applicants (a):	1,560
Of those, Number Offered Admission (b):	821
Of those, Number Enrolled Fall 2006 (c):	356

University of Texas at El Paso

INSTITUTION INFORMATION

University of Texas at El Paso
500 W. University Ave.
El Paso, TX 79968
Phone: (915) 747-5000
Web: http://www.utep.edu

GENERAL INFORMATION

[All Students - Fall 2006]

Undergraduate Enrollment	16,561
Graduate Enrollment	2,521
Professional Enrollment	760
Total Enrollment	**19,842**

ENGINEERING COLLEGE INFORMATION

HEAD OF ENGINEERING

Stephen W Stafford
Interim Dean
College of Engineering
University of Texas at El Paso
500 West University Avenue
El Paso, TX 79968-0517
Phone: (915) 747-5460
Fax: (915) 747-5616
Email: stafford@utep.edu

TYPES OF ENGINEERING DEGREES

Bachelor's: B.S.
Master's: M.S. with thesis
Doctoral: Ph.D.

UNDERGRADUATE INFORMATION

ESTIMATED STUDENT EXPENSES (FALL 2006)

[Expenses are for the 2006-2007 nine-month academic year and are based on an average credit load of: Undergraduate: 12]

	In-State	Out-of-State
Tuition and Fees:	$4,120	$10,794
Campus and Room and Board:	$7,118	$7,118
Books and Supplies:	$672	$672
Other Expenses:	$1,376	$1,376
Total Estimated Expenses:	**$13,286**	**$19,960**

NEW APPLICANTS/NEWLY ENROLLED STUDENTS

[Numbers are for the undergraduate engineering college for the Fall 2006 term]

Number of Applicants (a):	615
Of those, Number Offered Admission (b):	609
Of those, Number Enrolled Fall 2006 (c):	330

GRADUATE INFORMATION

ESTIMATED STUDENT EXPENSES (FALL 2006)

[Expenses are for the 2006-2007 nine-month academic year and are based on an average credit load of: Graduate: 9]

	In-State	Out-of-State
Tuition and Fees:	$3,673	$8,711
Campus and Room and Board:	$7,118	$7,118
Books and Supplies:	$672	$672
Other Expenses:	$1,376	$1,376
Total Estimated Expenses:	**$12,839**	**$17,877**

NEW APPLICANTS/NEWLY ENROLLED STUDENTS

[Numbers are for the graduate engineering college for the Fall 2006 term]

Number of Applicants (a):	376

Of those, Number Offered Admission (b):	247
Of those, Number Enrolled Fall 2006 (c):	101

The University of Texas-Pan American

INSTITUTION INFORMATION

1201 W. University Drive
College of Science & Engineering
Edinburg, TX 78541
Phone: (956) 381-2404
Fax: (956) 381-2428
Web: http://www.panam.edu/

GENERAL INFORMATION

[All Students - Fall 2006]

Undergraduate Enrollment	17,048
Graduate Enrollment	5,380
Professional Enrollment	0
Total Enrollment	**22,428**

ENGINEERING COLLEGE INFORMATION

HEAD OF ENGINEERING

Edwin W. LeMaster
Dean
College of Science and Engineering
The University of Texas-Pan American
1201 West University Drive
ENGR 1.294
Edinburg, TX 78541-2999
Phone: (956) 381-2405
Fax: (956) 381-2428
Email: elemaster@panam.edu

ENGINEERING COLLEGE INQUIRIES

Miguel A Gonzalez
Interim Associate Dean / Director of School of Engineering
The University of Texas-Pan American
1201 W. University Drive, ENGR 1.294
Edinburg, TX 78541
Phone: (956) 381-2673
Fax: (956) 381-2428
Email: gonzalezma@panam.edu

TYPES OF ENGINEERING DEGREES

Bachelor's: B.S.
Master's: M.S. with thesis, M.S. without thesis, but with project or report
Doctoral:

UNDERGRADUATE INFORMATION

ADMISSION INQUIRIES

Miguel A Gonzalez
Interim Associate Dean / Director of School of Engineering
The University of Texas-Pan American
1201 W. University Drive, ENGR 1.294
Edinburg, TX 78541
Phone: (956) 381-2673
Fax: (956) 381-2428
Email: gonzalezma@panam.edu

ESTIMATED STUDENT EXPENSES (FALL 2006)

[Expenses are for the 2006-2007 nine-month academic year and are based on an average credit load of: Undergraduate: 12]

	In-State	Out-of-State
Tuition and Fees:	$3,336	$10,504
Campus and Room and Board:	$5,102	$5,102
Books and Supplies:	$1,000	$1,000
Other Expenses:	$3,632	$3,632
Total Estimated Expenses:	**$13,070**	**$20,238**

GRADUATE INFORMATION

ADMISSION INQUIRIES

Miguel A Gonzalez
Interim Associate Dean / Director of School of Engineering
The University of Texas-Pan American
1201 W. University Drive, ENGR 1.294
Edinburg , TX 78541
Phone: (956) 381-2673
Fax: (956) 381-2428
Email: gonzalezma@panam.edu

ESTIMATED STUDENT EXPENSES (FALL 2006)

[Expenses are for the 2006-2007 nine-month academic year and are based on an average credit load of: Graduate: 9]

	In-State	Out-of-State
Tuition and Fees:	$3,342	$7,725
Campus and Room and Board:	$5,102	$5,040
Books and Supplies:	$1,000	$620
Other Expenses:	$1,806	$3,544
Total Estimated Expenses:	**$11,250**	**$16,929**

University of Texas at San Antonio

INSTITUTION INFORMATION

College of Engineering
One UTSA Circle
San Antonio, TX 78249
Phone: (210) 458-4490
Fax: (210) 458-5515
Web: http://www.utsa.edu

GENERAL INFORMATION

[All Students - Fall 2006]

Undergraduate Enrollment	24,210
Graduate Enrollment	4,323
Professional Enrollment	0
Total Enrollment	**28,533**

ENGINEERING COLLEGE INFORMATION

HEAD OF ENGINEERING

C. Mauli Agrawal
Dean of Engineering
College of Engineering
University of Texas at San Antonio
One UTSA Circle
San Antonio, TX 78249-0665
Phone: (210) 458-5526
Fax: (210) 458-5515
Email: mauli.agrawal@utsa.edu

ENGINEERING COLLEGE INQUIRIES

Sheila Slife
Administrative Associate
University of Texas at San Antonio
One UTSA Circle
San Antonio, TX 78249-0665
Phone: (210) 458-7377
Fax: (210) 458-5515
Email: sheila.slife@utsa.edu

TYPES OF ENGINEERING DEGREES

Bachelor's: B.S.
Master's: M.S. with thesis, M.S. without thesis, but with project or report
Doctoral: Ph.D.

UNDERGRADUATE INFORMATION

NEW APPLICANTS/NEWLY ENROLLED STUDENTS

[Numbers are for the undergraduate engineering college for the Fall 2006 term]

Number of Applicants (a):	1,044
Of those, Number Offered Admission (b):	954
Of those, Number Enrolled Fall 2006 (c):	457

GRADUATE INFORMATION

ADMISSION INQUIRIES

Priscilla Garcia
Program Coordinator
University of Texas at San Antonio
One UTSA Circle
San Antonio ,TX 78249-0665
Phone: (210) 458-4492
Fax: (210) 458-5515
Email: priscilla.garcia@utsa.edu

NEW APPLICANTS/NEWLY ENROLLED STUDENTS

[Numbers are for the graduate engineering college for the Fall 2006 term]

Number of Applicants (a):	245
Of those, Number Offered Admission (b):	207
Of those, Number Enrolled Fall 2006 (c):	81

The University of Texas at Tyler

INSTITUTION INFORMATION
3900 University Blvd.
Tyler, TX 75799
Phone: (903) 566-7200
Fax: (903) 566-7068
Web: http://www.uttyler.edu

GENERAL INFORMATION
[All Students - Fall 2006]

Undergraduate Enrollment	4,766
Graduate Enrollment	1,182
Professional Enrollment	0
Total Enrollment	**5,948**

ENGINEERING COLLEGE INFORMATION

HEAD OF ENGINEERING
James K. Nelson, Jr
Dean of the College of Engineering and Computer Science
College of Engineering and Computer Science
The University of Texas at Tyler
3900 University Blvd.
RBS 2004
Tyler, TX 75799
Phone: (903) 566-7267
Fax: (903) 566-7148
Email: jknelson@uttyler.edu

ENGINEERING COLLEGE INQUIRIES
Jennifer H Scott
Engineering Recruiter/Advisor
The University of Texas at Tyler
RBS2003, 3900 University Blvd
Tyler, TX 75799
Phone: (903) 565-5716
Fax: (903) 566-7148
Email: jscott@uttyler.edu

TYPES OF ENGINEERING DEGREES
Bachelor's: B.S.
Master's: M.S. with thesis, M.S. without thesis, but with project or report, M.Eng.
Doctoral:

UNDERGRADUATE INFORMATION

ADMISSION INQUIRIES
Sarah Bowdin
Assistant Director of Admissions
The University of Texas at Tyler
3900 University Blvd.
Tyler, TX 75799
Phone: (903) 566-7202
Fax: (903) 566-7068
Email: admissions@uttyler.edu

ESTIMATED STUDENT EXPENSES (FALL 2006)
[Expenses are for the 2006-2007 nine-month academic year and are based on an average credit load of: Undergraduate: 15]

	In-State	Out-of-State
Tuition and Fees:	$4,942	$13,192
Campus and Room and Board:	$7,010	$7,010
Books and Supplies:	$750	$750
Other Expenses:	$1,886	$1,886
Total Estimated Expenses:	**$14,588**	**$22,838**

NEW APPLICANTS/NEWLY ENROLLED STUDENTS
[Numbers are for the undergraduate engineering college for the Fall 2006 term]

Number of Applicants (a):	431
Of those, Number Offered Admission (b):	268
Of those, Number Enrolled Fall 2006 (c):	141

GRADUATE INFORMATION

ADMISSION INQUIRIES
Ron W Welch
Professor and Chair, Civil and Environmental Engineering
The University of Texas at Tyler
RBS 1005, 3900 University Blvd.
Tyler, TX 75799
Phone: (903) 566-7002
Fax: (903) 566-7337
Email: rwelch@uttyler.edu

ADMISSION INQUIRIES
Jeffrey R Shenefelt
Assistant Professor, Mechanical Engineering
The University of Texas at Tyler
RBS 1037, 3900 University Blvd.
Tyler, TX 75799
Phone: (903) 566-7245
Fax: (903) 566-7337
Email: jshenefelt@uttyler.edu

ADMISSION INQUIRIES
Ralph D Hippenstiel
Professor and Chair, Electrical Engineering
The University of Texas at Tyler
RBS 1039, 3900 University Blvd.
Tyler, TX 75799
Phone: (903) 566-7108
Fax: (903) 566-7148
Email: rdhippen@uttyler.edu

ESTIMATED STUDENT EXPENSES (FALL 2006)
[Expenses are for the 2006-2007 nine-month academic year and are based on an average credit load of: Graduate: 10]

	In-State	Out-of-State
Tuition and Fees:	$3,762	$9,262
Campus and Room and Board:	$7,010	$7,010
Books and Supplies:	$750	$750
Other Expenses:	$2,025	$2,025
Total Estimated Expenses:	**$13,547**	**$19,047**

NEW APPLICANTS/NEWLY ENROLLED STUDENTS
[Numbers are for the graduate engineering college for the Fall 2006 term]

Number of Applicants (a):	90
Of those, Number Offered Admission (b):	20
Of those, Number Enrolled Fall 2006 (c):	9

The University of Toledo

INSTITUTION INFORMATION
2801 West Bancroft Street
Toledo, OH 43606-3390
Phone: (419) 530-4636
Web: http://www.utoledo.edu

GENERAL INFORMATION
[All Students - Fall 2006]

Undergraduate Enrollment	16,067
Graduate Enrollment	2,775
Professional Enrollment	1,873
Total Enrollment	**20,715**

ENGINEERING COLLEGE INFORMATION

HEAD OF ENGINEERING
Nagi G Naganathan
Dean / Professor
College of Engineering
The University of Toledo
5012 Nitschke Hall
Toledo, OH 43606-3390
Phone: (419) 530-8000
Fax: (419) 530-8006
Email: nagi.naganathan@utoledo.edu

ENGINEERING COLLEGE INQUIRIES
Brian W Randolph
Assoc Dean of Undergraduate Studies/ Professor
The University of Toledo
3006 Nitschke Hall
Toledo, OH 43606-3390
Phone: (419) 530-8121
Fax: (419) 530-8046
Email: brandolp@eng.utoledo.edu

ENGINEERING COLLEGE INQUIRIES
Bruce E Poling
Director of Assessment/Prof
The University of Toledo
5025 Nitschke Hall
Toledo, OH 43606-3390
Phone: (419) 530-8255
Fax: (419) 530-8006
Email: bpoling@eng.utoledo.edu

ENGINEERING COLLEGE INQUIRIES
Christine M. Smallman
Manager of College Relations and the MIME Senior Design Clinic

The University of Toledo
5012 Nitschke Hall
Toledo, OH 43606-3390
Phone: (419) 530-8121
Fax: (419) 530-8006
Email: csmallma@eng.utoledo.edu

TYPES OF ENGINEERING DEGREES
Bachelor's: B.S.
Master's: M.S. with thesis, M.S. without thesis, but with project or report
Doctoral: Ph.D.

UNDERGRADUATE INFORMATION

ADMISSION INQUIRIES
Brian W Randolph
Assoc Dean of Undergraduate Studies/ Professor
The University of Toledo
3006 Nitschke Hall
Toledo, OH 43606-3390
Phone: (419) 530-8121
Fax: (419) 530-8046
Email: brandolp@eng.utoledo.edu

ADMISSION INQUIRIES
Bruce E Poling
Director of Assessment/Prof
The University of Toledo
5025 Nitschke Hall
Toledo, OH 43606-3390
Phone: (419) 530-8255
Fax: (419) 530-8006
Email: bpoling@eng.utoledo.edu

ESTIMATED STUDENT EXPENSES (FALL 2006)
[Expenses are for the 2006-2007 nine-month academic year and are based on an average credit load of: Undergraduate: 16]

	In-State	Out-of-State
Tuition and Fees:	$8,178	$16,989
Campus and Room and Board:	$8,140	$8,140
Books and Supplies:	$900	$900
Other Expenses:		
Total Estimated Expenses:	**$17,218**	**$26,029**

NEW APPLICANTS/NEWLY ENROLLED STUDENTS
[Numbers are for the undergraduate engineering college for the Fall 2006 term]

Number of Applicants (a):	1,097
Of those, Number Offered Admission (b):	846
Of those, Number Enrolled Fall 2006 (c):	352

GRADUATE INFORMATION

ADMISSION INQUIRIES
Mohamed Samir Hefzy
Professor/Interim Associate Dean of Graduate Studies/Graduate Director of Mechanical, Industrial and Manufacturing Engineering
The University of Toledo
2801 West Bancroft Street
Toledo, OH 43606-3390
Phone: (419) 530-6086
Fax: (419) 530-7392
Email: mhefzy@eng.utoledo.edu

ESTIMATED STUDENT EXPENSES (FALL 2006)
[Expenses are for the 2006-2007 nine-month academic year and are based on an average credit load of: Graduate: 9]

	In-State	Out-of-State
Tuition and Fees:	$8,105	$14,714
Campus and Room and Board:	$8,140	$8,140
Books and Supplies:	$900	$900
Other Expenses:		
Total Estimated Expenses:	**$17,145**	**$23,754**

NEW APPLICANTS/NEWLY ENROLLED STUDENTS
[Numbers are for the graduate engineering college for the Fall 2006 term]

Number of Applicants (a):	336
Of those, Number Offered Admission (b):	220
Of those, Number Enrolled Fall 2006 (c):	81

Tri-State University

INSTITUTION INFORMATION
1 University Avenue
Angola, IN 46703-1764

Phone: (260) 665-4100
Fax: (260) 665-4578
Web: http://www.tristate.edu

GENERAL INFORMATION

[All Students - Fall 2006]
Undergraduate Enrollment 1,460
Graduate Enrollment 7
Professional Enrollment 0
Total Enrollment **1,467**

ENGINEERING COLLEGE INFORMATION

HEAD OF ENGINEERING

Roger J Hawks
Dean of Allen School of Engineering and Technology
Tri-State University
1 University Avenue
Angola, IN 46703-1764
Phone: (260) 665-4228
Fax: (260) 665-4188
Email: hawksr@tristate.edu

TYPES OF ENGINEERING DEGREES

Bachelor's: B.S.
Master's: M.S. with thesis, M.Eng.
Doctoral:

UNDERGRADUATE INFORMATION

ADMISSION INQUIRIES

Scott Goplin
Dean of Admission
Tri-State University
1 University Avenue
Angola, IN 46703-1764
Phone: (260) 665-4365
Fax: (260) 665-4578
Email: goplins@tristate.edu

ESTIMATED STUDENT EXPENSES (FALL 2006)

[Expenses are for the 2006-2007 nine-month academic year and are based on an average credit load of: Undergraduate: 16]

	All Students
Tuition and fees:	$21,210
Campus and Room and Board:	$6,240
Books and Supplies:	
Other Expenses:	
Total Estimated Expenses:	**$27,450**

NEW APPLICANTS/NEWLY ENROLLED STUDENTS

[Numbers are for the undergraduate engineering college for the Fall 2006 term]
Number of Applicants (a): 454
Of those, Number Offered Admission (b): 395
Of those, Number Enrolled Fall 2006 (c): 146

GRADUATE INFORMATION

ADMISSION INQUIRIES

Scott Goplin
Dean of Admission
Tri-State University
1 University Avenue
Angola , IN 46703-1764
Phone: (260) 665-4365
Fax: (260) 665-4578
Email: goplins@tristate.edu

ESTIMATED STUDENT EXPENSES (FALL 2006)

[Expenses are for the 2006-2007 nine-month academic year and are based on an average credit load of: Graduate: 9]

	All Students
Tuition and fees:	$11,934
Campus and Room and Board:	
Books and Supplies:	
Other Expenses:	
Total Estimated Expenses:	**$11,934**

NEW APPLICANTS/NEWLY ENROLLED STUDENTS

[Numbers are for the graduate engineering college for the Fall 2006 term]
Number of Applicants (a): 3
Of those, Number Offered Admission (b): 2
Of those, Number Enrolled Fall 2006 (c): 2

Trinity College

INSTITUTION INFORMATION

Department of Engineering, MCEC 307
300 Summit Street
Hartford, CT 06106
Phone: (860) 297-2517
Fax: (860) 297-3531
Web: http://www.trincoll.edu/Academics/Study/Engineering

GENERAL INFORMATION

[All Students - Fall 2006]
Undergraduate Enrollment 2,191
Graduate Enrollment 176
Professional Enrollment 0
Total Enrollment **2,367**

ENGINEERING COLLEGE INFORMATION

ENGINEERING COLLEGE INQUIRIES

Christine L Orde
Administrative Assistant
Trinity College
MCEC 307, 300 Summit Street
Hartford, CT 06106
Phone: (860) 297-2517
Fax: (860) 297-3531
Email: christine.orde@trincoll.edu

ENGINEERING COLLEGE INQUIRIES

Taikang Ning
Assoc Professor & Department Chair
Trinity College
MCEC 307, 300 Summit Street
Hartford, CT 06106
Phone: (860) 297-2219
Fax: (860) 297-3531
Email: taikang.ning@trincoll.edu

TYPES OF ENGINEERING DEGREES

Bachelor's: B.A., B.S.
Master's:
Doctoral:

UNDERGRADUATE INFORMATION

ESTIMATED STUDENT EXPENSES (FALL 2006)

[Expenses are for the 2006-2007 nine-month academic year and are based on an average credit load of: Undergraduate: 5]

	All Students
Tuition and fees:	$35,130
Campus and Room and Board:	$8,970
Books and Supplies:	$900
Other Expenses:	$900
Total Estimated Expenses:	**$45,900**

Tufts University

INSTITUTION INFORMATION

105 Anderson Hall
200 College Avenue
Medford, MA 02155
Phone: (617) 627-3237
Fax: (617) 627-3819
Web: http://www.tufts.edu

GENERAL INFORMATION

[All Students - Fall 2006]
Undergraduate Enrollment 4,994
Graduate Enrollment 2,977
Professional Enrollment 1,666
Total Enrollment **9,637**

ENGINEERING COLLEGE INFORMATION

HEAD OF ENGINEERING

Linda M Abriola
Dean of Engineering
School of Engineering
Tufts University
105 Anderson Hall
200 College Ave.
Medford, MA 02155
Phone: (617) 627-3237
Fax: (617) 627-3819

Email: linda.abriola@tufts.edu

TYPES OF ENGINEERING DEGREES

Bachelor's: B.S.
Master's: M.S. with thesis, M.S. without thesis, but with project or report,M.E.
Doctoral: Ph.D.

UNDERGRADUATE INFORMATION

ADMISSION INQUIRIES

Lee Coffin
Dean of Undergraduate Admissions
Tufts University
Bendetson Hall
Medford, MA 02155
Phone: (617) 627-3170
Email: lee.coffin@tufts.edu

ESTIMATED STUDENT EXPENSES (FALL 2006)

[Expenses are for the 2006-2007 nine-month academic year and are based on an average credit load of: Undergraduate: 5]

	All Students
Tuition and fees:	$34,730
Campus and Room and Board:	$9,770
Books and Supplies:	$2,000
Other Expenses:	$1,535
Total Estimated Expenses:	**$48,035**

NEW APPLICANTS/NEWLY ENROLLED STUDENTS

[Numbers are for the undergraduate engineering college for the Fall 2006 term]
Number of Applicants (a): 1,789
Of those, Number Offered Admission (b): 615
Of those, Number Enrolled Fall 2006 (c): 182

GRADUATE INFORMATION

ESTIMATED STUDENT EXPENSES (FALL 2006)

[Expenses are for the 2006-2007 nine-month academic year and are based on an average credit load of: Graduate: 3]

	All Students
Tuition and fees:	$33,672
Campus and Room and Board:	$16,268
Books and Supplies:	$800
Other Expenses:	$2,779
Total Estimated Expenses:	**$53,519**

NEW APPLICANTS/NEWLY ENROLLED STUDENTS

[Numbers are for the graduate engineering college for the Fall 2006 term]
Number of Applicants (a): 536
Of those, Number Offered Admission (b): 261
Of those, Number Enrolled Fall 2006 (c): 147

Tulane University

INSTITUTION INFORMATION

6823 St. Charles Avenue
New Orleans, LA 70118
Phone: (504) 865-5000
Web: http://www.tulane.edu

GENERAL INFORMATION

[All Students - Fall 2006]
Undergraduate Enrollment 6,533
Graduate Enrollment 2,305
Professional Enrollment 1,768
Total Enrollment **10,606**

ENGINEERING COLLEGE INFORMATION

HEAD OF ENGINEERING

Nicholas J Altiero
Dean
School of Science and Engineering
Tulane University
Office of the Dean
201 Lindy Boggs Center
New Orleans, LA 70118
Phone: (504) 865-5764
Fax: (504) 862-8747
Email: altiero@tulane.edu

ENGINEERING COLLEGE INQUIRIES

Sandra P Parker
Assistant Dean for Finance and Personnel
Tulane University

Office of the Dean, 201 Lindy Boggs Center
New Orleans, LA 70118
Phone: (504) 865-5764
Fax: (504) 862-8747
Email: sparker3@tulane.edu

TYPES OF ENGINEERING DEGREES
Bachelor's: B.S.
Master's: M.S. with thesis, M.S. without thesis, but with project or report
Doctoral: Ph.D.

UNDERGRADUATE INFORMATION

ADMISSION INQUIRIES
David W Seaver
Interim Director
Tulane University
6823 St. Charles Ave.
New Orleans, LA 70118
Phone: (504) 865-5731
Fax: (504) 862-8715
Email: dseaver@tulane.edu

ESTIMATED STUDENT EXPENSES (FALL 2006)
[Expenses are for the 2006-2007 nine-month academic year and are based on an average credit load of: Undergraduate: 16]

	All Students
Tuition and fees:	$34,896
Campus and Room and Board:	$8,680
Books and Supplies:	$800
Other Expenses:	$800
Total Estimated Expenses:	**$45,176**

NEW APPLICANTS/NEWLY ENROLLED STUDENTS
[Numbers are for the undergraduate engineering college for the Fall 2006 term]
Number of Applicants (a):	2,422
Of those, Number Offered Admission (b):	975
Of those, Number Enrolled Fall 2006 (c):	62

Note: Application is made to Newcomb-Tulane College.

GRADUATE INFORMATION

ADMISSION INQUIRIES
Christi J Longlois
Senior Program Coordinator
Tulane University
201 Lindy Boggs Center
New Orleans , LA 70118
Phone: (504) 865-5764
Fax: (504) 862-8747
Email: clongloi@tulane.edu

ESTIMATED STUDENT EXPENSES (FALL 2006)
[Expenses are for the 2006-2007 nine-month academic year and are based on an average credit load of: Graduate: 9]
	All Students
Tuition and fees:	$34,896
Campus and Room and Board:	$12,000
Books and Supplies:	$1,000
Other Expenses:	$1,000
Total Estimated Expenses:	**$48,896**

NEW APPLICANTS/NEWLY ENROLLED STUDENTS
[Numbers are for the graduate engineering college for the Fall 2006 term]
Number of Applicants (a):	44
Of those, Number Offered Admission (b):	25
Of those, Number Enrolled Fall 2006 (c):	18

University of Tulsa

INSTITUTION INFORMATION
600 South College Avenue
Tulsa, OK 74104
Phone: (918) 631-2478
Fax: (918) 631-2286
Web: http://www.utulsa.edu/

GENERAL INFORMATION
[All Students - Fall 2006]
Undergraduate Enrollment	2,882
Graduate Enrollment	667
Professional Enrollment	576
Total Enrollment	**4,125**

ENGINEERING COLLEGE INFORMATION

HEAD OF ENGINEERING
Steven J. Bellovich
Dean
College of Engineering and Natural Sciences
University of Tulsa
600 South College Avenue
Keplinger Hall M201
Tulsa, OK 74104-3189
Phone: (918) 631-2478
Fax: (918) 631-2286
Email: steven-bellovich@utulsa.edu

ENGINEERING COLLEGE INQUIRIES
Richard L Reeder
Associate Dean for Academic Affairs
University of Tulsa
600 South College Avenue, KEP M205
Tulsa, OK 74104
Phone: (918) 631-3159
Fax: (918) 631-2286

TYPES OF ENGINEERING DEGREES
Bachelor's: B.A., B.S.
Master's: M.S. with thesis, M.Eng.
Doctoral: Ph.D.

UNDERGRADUATE INFORMATION

ADMISSION INQUIRIES
John C. Corso
Dean of Admission
University of Tulsa
600 South College Avenue
Tulsa, OK 74104
Phone: (918) 631-2633
Fax: (918) 631-5003
Email: john-corso@utulsa.edu

ESTIMATED STUDENT EXPENSES (FALL 2006)
[Expenses are for the 2006-2007 nine-month academic year and are based on an average credit load of: Undergraduate: 18]
	All Students
Tuition and fees:	$21,163
Campus and Room and Board:	$7,052
Books and Supplies:	$1,400
Other Expenses:	$2,500
Total Estimated Expenses:	**$32,115**

Note: Other/Personal expenses will vary according to individual life styles.

NEW APPLICANTS/NEWLY ENROLLED STUDENTS
[Numbers are for the undergraduate engineering college for the Fall 2006 term]
Number of Applicants (a):	1,024
Of those, Number Offered Admission (b):	844
Of those, Number Enrolled Fall 2006 (c):	264

GRADUATE INFORMATION

ESTIMATED STUDENT EXPENSES (FALL 2006)
[Expenses are for the 2006-2007 nine-month academic year and are based on an average credit load of: Graduate: 9]
	All Students
Tuition and fees:	$14,468
Campus and Room and Board:	$7,452
Books and Supplies:	$1,000
Other Expenses:	$1,200
Total Estimated Expenses:	**$24,120**

Note: Other/Personal expenses will vary according to individual life styles.

NEW APPLICANTS/NEWLY ENROLLED STUDENTS
[Numbers are for the graduate engineering college for the Fall 2006 term]
Number of Applicants (a):	327
Of those, Number Offered Admission (b):	182
Of those, Number Enrolled Fall 2006 (c):	62

Tuskegee University

INSTITUTION INFORMATION
Tuskegee, AL 36088
Phone: (334) 727-8632
Fax: (334) 727-8499
Web: http://www.tuskegee.edu

GENERAL INFORMATION
[All Students - Fall 2006]
Undergraduate Enrollment	2,420
Graduate Enrollment	186
Professional Enrollment	236
Total Enrollment	**2,842**

ENGINEERING COLLEGE INFORMATION

HEAD OF ENGINEERING
Legand L. Burge
Dean
College of Engineering, Architecture & Physical Sciences
Tuskegee University
200 Luther Foster Hall
Engineering Building
Tuskegee, AL 36088
Phone: (334) 727-8355
Fax: (334) 727-8090
Email: lburge@tuskegee.edu

TYPES OF ENGINEERING DEGREES
Bachelor's: B.S.
Master's: M.S. with thesis
Doctoral: Ph.D.

UNDERGRADUATE INFORMATION

ESTIMATED STUDENT EXPENSES (FALL 2006)
[Expenses are for the 2006-2007 nine-month academic year and are based on an average credit load of: Undergraduate: 15]
	All Students
Tuition and fees:	$13,330
Campus and Room and Board:	$6,460
Books and Supplies:	$949
Other Expenses:	$3,517
Total Estimated Expenses:	**$24,256**

Note: Expenses are annual student expenses.

NEW APPLICANTS/NEWLY ENROLLED STUDENTS
[Numbers are for the undergraduate engineering college for the Fall 2006 term]
Number of Applicants (a):	259
Of those, Number Offered Admission (b):	158
Of those, Number Enrolled Fall 2006 (c):	81

GRADUATE INFORMATION

ESTIMATED STUDENT EXPENSES (FALL 2006)
[Expenses are for the 2006-2007 nine-month academic year and are based on an average credit load of: Graduate: 12]
	All Students
Tuition and fees:	$13,330
Campus and Room and Board:	$6,460
Books and Supplies:	$949
Other Expenses:	$3,517
Total Estimated Expenses:	**$24,256**

Note: Expenses are annual student expenses.

NEW APPLICANTS/NEWLY ENROLLED STUDENTS
[Numbers are for the graduate engineering college for the Fall 2006 term]
Number of Applicants (a):	59
Of those, Number Offered Admission (b):	39
Of those, Number Enrolled Fall 2006 (c):	18

Union College

INSTITUTION INFORMATION
807 Union Street
Schenectady, NY 12308
Phone: (518) 388-6000
Web: http://www.union.edu

GENERAL INFORMATION
[All Students - Fall 2006]
Undergraduate Enrollment	2,212
Graduate Enrollment	0
Professional Enrollment	0
Total Enrollment	**2,212**

ENGINEERING COLLEGE INFORMATION

HEAD OF ENGINEERING
Cherrice A Traver
Dean of Engineering and Computer Science
Union College

Steinmetz Hall, 200
Schenectady, NY 12308
Phone: (518) 388-6326
Fax: (518) 388-6789
Email: traverc@union.edu

TYPES OF ENGINEERING DEGREES
Bachelor's: B.S.
Master's:
Doctoral:

UNDERGRADUATE INFORMATION

ADMISSION INQUIRIES
Dianne Crozier
Director
Union College
Grant Hall, 807 Union Street
Schenectady, NY 12308
Phone: (518) 388-6112
Fax: (518) 388-6986

NEW APPLICANTS/NEWLY ENROLLED STUDENTS
[Numbers are for the undergraduate engineering college for the Fall 2006 term]
Number of Applicants (a): 4,373
Of those, Number Offered Admission (b): 1,862
Of those, Number Enrolled Fall 2006 (c): 560
Note: Based on all enrolled freshmen not just engineering division.

U.S. Air Force Academy

INSTITUTION INFORMATION
2354 Fairchild Drive, Suite 6L-155
USAF Academy, CO 80840-6240
Phone: (719) 333-2531
Fax: (719) 333-2944
Web: http://www.usafa.af.mil

ENGINEERING COLLEGE INFORMATION

HEAD OF ENGINEERING
Col Alan R Klayton
Engineering Division Head, Department Head of Electrical and Computer Engineering
Department of Electrical and Computer Engineering
U.S. Air Force Academy
2354 Fairchild Dr, Suite 2F6
USAF Academy, CO 80840
Phone: (719) 333-3190
Fax: (719) 333-3756
Email: Alan.Klayton@usafa.af.mil

ENGINEERING COLLEGE INQUIRIES
Major Charles M Gaona
Executive Officer, Engineering
U.S. Air Force Academy
2354 Fairchild Dr, Ste 2F6
USAF Academy, CO 80840-6200
Phone: (719) 333-3842
Fax: (719) 333-3756
Email: charles.gaona@usafa.af.mil

TYPES OF ENGINEERING DEGREES
Bachelor's: B.S.
Master's:
Doctoral:

UNDERGRADUATE INFORMATION

ADMISSION INQUIRIES
Col William D Carpenter
Director of Admissions
U.S. Air Force Academy
2304 Cadet Dr, Suite 200
USAF Academy, CO 80840
Phone: (719) 333-3070
Fax: (719) 333-3647
Email: William.Carpenter@usafa.af.mil

NEW APPLICANTS/NEWLY ENROLLED STUDENTS
[Numbers are for the undergraduate engineering college for the Fall 2006 term]
Number of Applicants (a): 9,255
Of those, Number Offered Admission (b): 1,720
Of those, Number Enrolled Fall 2006 (c): 1,334

U.S. Coast Guard Academy

INSTITUTION INFORMATION
27 Mohegan Avenue
New London, CT 06320-8101
Phone: (860) 444-8444
Fax: (860) 444-8546
Web: http://www.uscg.mil/hq/uscga/default.htm

GENERAL INFORMATION
[All Students - Fall 2006]
Undergraduate Enrollment 1,050
Graduate Enrollment 0
Professional Enrollment 0
Total Enrollment **1,050**

ENGINEERING COLLEGE INFORMATION

HEAD OF ENGINEERING
Richard J Hartnett
Department Head
Department of Engineering
U.S. Coast Guard Academy
27 Mohegan Ave.
New London, CT 06320-8101
Phone: (860) 444-0444
Fax: (860) 444-8546
Email: rhartnett@exmail.uscga.edu

TYPES OF ENGINEERING DEGREES
Bachelor's: B.S.
Master's:
Doctoral:

UNDERGRADUATE INFORMATION

ADMISSION INQUIRIES
Susan D Bibeau
Director of Admissions
U.S. Coast Guard Academy
31 Mohegan Avenue
New London, CT 06320-8103
Phone: (860) 444-8674
Fax: (860) 444-8546
Email: sbibeau@exmail.uscga.edu

U.S. Merchant Marine Academy

INSTITUTION INFORMATION
300 Steamboat Road
Kings Point, NY 11024-1699
Phone: (516) 773-5000
Fax: (516) 773-5390
Web: http://www.usmma.edu

GENERAL INFORMATION
[All Students - Fall 2006]
Undergraduate Enrollment 961
Graduate Enrollment 12
Professional Enrollment 0
Total Enrollment **973**

ENGINEERING COLLEGE INFORMATION

HEAD OF ENGINEERING
Jose Femenia
Professor/Department Head
Department of Engineering
U.S. Merchant Marine Academy
300 Steamboat Rd
Kings Point, NY 11024
Phone: (516) 773-5743
Fax: (516) 773-5479
Email: femeniaj@usmma.edu

TYPES OF ENGINEERING DEGREES
Bachelor's: B.S.
Master's: M.S. without thesis, but with project or report
Doctoral:

UNDERGRADUATE INFORMATION

ESTIMATED STUDENT EXPENSES (FALL 2006)
[Expenses are for the 2006-2007 nine-month academic year

and are based on an average credit load of: Undergraduate: 17]

	All Students
Tuition and fees:	$2,575
Campus and Room and Board:	
Books and Supplies:	$650
Other Expenses:	$2,960
Total Estimated Expenses:	**$6,185**

NEW APPLICANTS/NEWLY ENROLLED STUDENTS
[Numbers are for the undergraduate engineering college for the Fall 2006 term]
Number of Applicants (a): 1,594
Of those, Number Offered Admission (b): 439
Of those, Number Enrolled Fall 2006 (c): 270
Note: For the entire student body.

GRADUATE INFORMATION

NEW APPLICANTS/NEWLY ENROLLED STUDENTS
[Numbers are for the graduate engineering college for the Fall 2006 term]
Number of Applicants (a): 16
Of those, Number Offered Admission (b): 14
Of those, Number Enrolled Fall 2006 (c): 12

United States Military Academy

INSTITUTION INFORMATION
Institutional Research & Analysis Branch
Building 2101-5th floor
West Point, NY 10996-2101
Phone: (845) 938-4328
Fax: (845) 938-7380
Web: http://www.usma.edu

GENERAL INFORMATION
[All Students - Fall 2006]
Undergraduate Enrollment 4,404
Graduate Enrollment 0
Professional Enrollment 0
Total Enrollment **4,404**

ENGINEERING COLLEGE INFORMATION

HEAD OF ENGINEERING
Andre H Sayles
Professor & Head of Department of Electrical Engineering & Computer Science
USMA\Dean\EECS
United States Military Academy
MADN-EECS
Building 601, Rm. 1100
West Point, NY 10996-1905
Phone: (845) 938-2803
Fax: (845) 938-5956
Email: da7549@exmail.usma.edu

TYPES OF ENGINEERING DEGREES
Bachelor's: B.S.
Master's:
Doctoral:

UNDERGRADUATE INFORMATION

ADMISSION INQUIRIES
Michael L Jones
Director of Admissions
United States Military Academy
MAAR, Building 606
West Point, NY 10996-1905
Phone: (845) 938-2803
Fax: (845) -93-8121
Email: 8dad@exmail.usma.edu

ESTIMATED STUDENT EXPENSES (FALL 2006)
[Expenses are for the 2006-2007 nine-month academic year and are based on an average credit load of: Undergraduate: 0]

	All Students
Tuition and fees:	$0
Campus and Room and Board:	
Books and Supplies:	
Other Expenses:	
Total Estimated Expenses:	**$0**

NEW APPLICANTS/NEWLY ENROLLED STUDENTS
[Numbers are for the undergraduate engineering college for the Fall 2006 term]
Number of Applicants (a):	10,226
Of those, Number Offered Admission (b):	1,588
Of those, Number Enrolled Fall 2006 (c):	1,309

U.S. Naval Academy

INSTITUTION INFORMATION
121 Blake Road
Annapolis, MD 21402
Phone: (410) 293-1000
Web: http://www.usna.edu

GENERAL INFORMATION
[All Students - Fall 2006]
Undergraduate Enrollment	4,474
Graduate Enrollment	0
Professional Enrollment	0
Total Enrollment	**4,474**

ENGINEERING COLLEGE INFORMATION

HEAD OF ENGINEERING
Richard W White
Director (Captain, USN)
Division of Engineeing and Weapons
U.S. Naval Academy
Rickover Hall (R307), Mail Stop 11A
Annapolis, MD 21402
Phone: (410) 293-6311
Fax: (410) 293-2591
Email: rau@gwmail.usna.edu

TYPES OF ENGINEERING DEGREES
Bachelor's: B.S.
Master's:
Doctoral:

UNDERGRADUATE INFORMATION

NEW APPLICANTS/NEWLY ENROLLED STUDENTS
[Numbers are for the undergraduate engineering college for the Fall 2006 term]
Number of Applicants (a):	10,747
Of those, Number Offered Admission (b):	1,510
Of those, Number Enrolled Fall 2006 (c):	1,228

University of Utah

INSTITUTION INFORMATION
University of Utah
201 S. President's Circle
Salt Lake City, UT 84112
Phone: (801) 581-7200
Web: http://www.utah.edu

GENERAL INFORMATION
[All Students - Fall 2006]
Undergraduate Enrollment	22,155
Graduate Enrollment	6,464
Professional Enrollment	0
Total Enrollment	**28,619**

ENGINEERING COLLEGE INFORMATION

HEAD OF ENGINEERING
Richard B Brown
Dean
College of Engineering
University of Utah
1495 E. 100 S. Room 214 Kenn B
Salt Lake City, UT 84112-1114
Phone: (801) 581-6912
Fax: (801) 581-8692
Email: brown@utah.edu

TYPES OF ENGINEERING DEGREES
Bachelor's: B.S.
Master's: M.S. with thesis, M.S. without thesis, but with project or report, M.Eng.
Doctoral: Ph.D.

UNDERGRADUATE INFORMATION

ESTIMATED STUDENT EXPENSES (FALL 2006)
[Expenses are for the 2006-2007 nine-month academic year and are based on an average credit load of: Undergraduate: N/A]
	In-State	Out-of-State
Tuition and Fees:	$3,928	$12,226
Campus and Room and Board:	$8,900	$8,900
Books and Supplies:	$1,100	$1,100
Other Expenses:		
Total Estimated Expenses:	**$13,928**	**$22,226**

Note: Tuition & Fees is based on two 12 credit hour semesters for undergraduates and two 9 credit hour semesters for graduates.
Tuition for Juniors and Seniors is slightly higher.

GRADUATE INFORMATION

ESTIMATED STUDENT EXPENSES (FALL 2006)
[Expenses are for the 2006-2007 nine-month academic year and are based on an average credit load of: Graduate: N/A]
	In-State	Out-of-State
Tuition and Fees:	$3,817	$11,937
Campus and Room and Board:	$8,900	$8,900
Books and Supplies:	$1,100	$1,100
Other Expenses:		
Total Estimated Expenses:	**$13,817**	**$21,937**

Note: Tuition & Fees is based on two 12 credit hour semesters for undergraduates and two 9 credit hour semesters for graduates.
Tuition for Juniors and Seniors is slightly higher.

NEW APPLICANTS/NEWLY ENROLLED STUDENTS
[Numbers are for the graduate engineering college for the Fall 2006 term]
Number of Applicants (a):	1,456
Of those, Number Offered Admission (b):	512
Of those, Number Enrolled Fall 2006 (c):	207

Utah State University

INSTITUTION INFORMATION
College of Engineering
4100 Old Main Hill
Logan, UT 84322
Phone: (435) 797-2775
Fax: (435) 797-2769
Web: http://www.engineering.usu.edu/

GENERAL INFORMATION
[All Students - Fall 2006]
Undergraduate Enrollment	14,351
Graduate Enrollment	1,659
Professional Enrollment	16,010
Total Enrollment	**32,020**

ENGINEERING COLLEGE INFORMATION

HEAD OF ENGINEERING
Scott Hinton
Dean
Engineering Dean
Utah State University
UMC 4100
Logan, UT 84322
Phone: (435) 797-2776
Fax: (435) 797-2769
Email: hinton@engineering.usu.edu

TYPES OF ENGINEERING DEGREES
Bachelor's: B.S.
Master's: M.S. with thesis, M.S. without thesis, but with project or report, M.Eng.
Doctoral: Ph.D.

UNDERGRADUATE INFORMATION

ADMISSION INQUIRIES
David Roos
Director
Utah State University
Admissions Office, UMC 1600
Logan, UT 84322
Phone: (435) 797-8246
Fax: (435) 797-4077
Email: www.usu.edu

ESTIMATED STUDENT EXPENSES (FALL 2006)
[Expenses are for the 2006-2007 nine-month academic year and are based on an average credit load of: Undergraduate: 12]
	In-State	Out-of-State
Tuition and Fees:	$3,578	$10,702
Campus and Room and Board:	$4,800	$4,800
Books and Supplies:	$1,000	$1,000
Other Expenses:		
Total Estimated Expenses:	**$9,378**	**$16,502**

GRADUATE INFORMATION

ADMISSION INQUIRIES
James P Shaver
Dean
Utah State University
School of Graduate Studies, UMC 0900
Logan , UT 84322
Phone: (435) 797-8246
Fax: (435) 797-1192
Email: jamess@grad.usu.edu

ESTIMATED STUDENT EXPENSES (FALL 2006)
[Expenses are for the 2006-2007 nine-month academic year and are based on an average credit load of: Graduate: 9]
	In-State	Out-of-State
Tuition and Fees:	$3,452	$10,848
Campus and Room and Board:	$4,800	$4,800
Books and Supplies:	$1,000	$1,000
Other Expenses:		
Total Estimated Expenses:	**$9,252**	**$16,648**

NEW APPLICANTS/NEWLY ENROLLED STUDENTS
[Numbers are for the graduate engineering college for the Fall 2006 term]
Number of Applicants (a):	310
Of those, Number Offered Admission (b):	225
Of those, Number Enrolled Fall 2006 (c):	93

Valparaiso University

INSTITUTION INFORMATION
Kretzmann Hall
1700 Chapel Drive
Valparaiso, IN 46383
Phone: (219) 464-5000
Fax: (219) 464-5381
Web: http://www.valpo.edu

GENERAL INFORMATION
[All Students - Fall 2006]
Undergraduate Enrollment	2,963
Graduate Enrollment	385
Professional Enrollment	3,871
Total Enrollment	**7,219**

ENGINEERING COLLEGE INFORMATION

HEAD OF ENGINEERING
Kraig J Olejniczak
Dean of Engineering
College of Engineering
Valparaiso University
1900 Chapel Drive
Gellersen Center
Valparaiso, IN 46383
Phone: (219) 464-5121
Fax: (219) 464-5065
Email: Kraig.Olejniczak@valpo.edu

TYPES OF ENGINEERING DEGREES
Bachelor's: B.S.
Master's:
Doctoral:

UNDERGRADUATE INFORMATION

ESTIMATED STUDENT EXPENSES (FALL 2006)
[Expenses are for the 2006-2007 nine-month academic year and are based on an average credit load of: Undergraduate: 16]
	All Students
Tuition and fees:	$24,690
Campus and Room and Board:	$6,640
Books and Supplies:	$1,000
Other Expenses:	$1,370
Total Estimated Expenses:	**$33,700**

Note: Tuitions are for two semesters but do not include summer sessions.

NEW APPLICANTS/NEWLY ENROLLED STUDENTS
[Numbers are for the undergraduate engineering college for the Fall 2006 term]

Number of Applicants (a):	476
Of those, Number Offered Admission (b):	352
Of those, Number Enrolled Fall 2006 (c):	91

Vanderbilt University

INSTITUTION INFORMATION
5332 Science & Engineering Bldg.
VU Station B #351826
Nashville, TN 37235-1826
Phone: (615) 322-2762
Fax: (615) 343-8006
Web: http://www.vuse.vanderbilt.edu

GENERAL INFORMATION
[All Students - Fall 2006]

Undergraduate Enrollment	6,378
Graduate Enrollment	2,122
Professional Enrollment	3,107
Total Enrollment	**11,607**

ENGINEERING COLLEGE INFORMATION

HEAD OF ENGINEERING
Kenneth F Galloway
Dean and Professor of Electrical Engineering
School of Engineering
Vanderbilt University
5332 Science & Engineering Bldg.
VU Station B #351826
Nashville, TN 37235-1826
Phone: (615) 322-0720
Fax: (615) 343-8006
Email: kenneth.f.galloway@vanderbilt.edu

ENGINEERING COLLEGE INQUIRIES
K. Arthur Overholser
Senior Associate Dean
Vanderbilt University
5332 Science & Engineering Bldg., VU Station B #351826
Nashville, TN 37235-1826
Phone: (615) 343-3773
Fax: (615) 343-8006
Email: knowles.a.overholser@vanderbilt.edu

TYPES OF ENGINEERING DEGREES
Bachelor's: B.S., B.E,
Master's: M.S. with thesis, M.S. without thesis, but with project or report, M.Eng.
Doctoral: Ph.D.

UNDERGRADUATE INFORMATION

ADMISSION INQUIRIES
John Gaines
Director Undergraduate Admissions
Vanderbilt University
2305 West End Avenue
Nashville, TN 37203
Phone: (615) 343-3470
Fax: (615) 343-8326
Email: john.gaines@vanderbilt.edu

ADMISSION INQUIRIES
K. Arthur Overholser
Senior Associate Dean
Vanderbilt University
5332 Science & Engineering Bldg., VU Station B #351826
Nashville, TN 37235-1826
Phone: (615) 343-3773
Fax: (615) 343-8006
Email: knowles.a.overholser@vanderbilt.edu

ESTIMATED STUDENT EXPENSES (FALL 2006)
[Expenses are for the 2006-2007 nine-month academic year and are based on an average credit load of: Undergraduate: 15]

	All Students
Tuition and fees:	$32,620
Campus and Room and Board:	$10,890
Books and Supplies:	$1,104
Other Expenses:	$5,538
Total Estimated Expenses:	**$50,152**

NEW APPLICANTS/NEWLY ENROLLED STUDENTS
[Numbers are for the undergraduate engineering college for the Fall 2006 term]

Number of Applicants (a):	1,846
Of those, Number Offered Admission (b):	894
Of those, Number Enrolled Fall 2006 (c):	313

GRADUATE INFORMATION

ADMISSION INQUIRIES
George Cook
Associate Dean for Research & Graduate Studies
Vanderbilt University
5332 Science & Engineering Bldg., VU Station B #351826
Nashville , TN 37235-1826
Phone: (615) 322-2762
Fax: (615) 343-8006
Email: george.cook@vanderbilt.edu

ESTIMATED STUDENT EXPENSES (FALL 2006)
[Expenses are for the 2006-2007 nine-month academic year and are based on an average credit load of: Graduate: 9]

	All Students
Tuition and fees:	$24,462
Campus and Room and Board:	$11,800
Books and Supplies:	$1,500
Other Expenses:	$6,500
Total Estimated Expenses:	**$44,262**

NEW APPLICANTS/NEWLY ENROLLED STUDENTS
[Numbers are for the graduate engineering college for the Fall 2006 term]

Number of Applicants (a):	1,206
Of those, Number Offered Admission (b):	181
Of those, Number Enrolled Fall 2006 (c):	106

University of Vermont

INSTITUTION INFORMATION
College of Engineering and Mathematical Sciences
109 Votey Building
Burlington, VT 05405
Phone: (802) 656-3390
Fax: (802) 656-8802
Web: http://www.cems@uvm.edu

GENERAL INFORMATION
[All Students - Fall 2006]

Undergraduate Enrollment	9,040
Graduate Enrollment	1,351
Professional Enrollment	1,479
Total Enrollment	**11,870**

ENGINEERING COLLEGE INFORMATION

HEAD OF ENGINEERING
Domenico Grasso
Dean
Dean's Office
University of Vermont
College of Engineering and Mathematical Sciences
109 Votey Building
Burlington, VT 05405
Phone: (802) 656-3390
Fax: (802) 656-8802
Email: dgrasso@cems.uvm.edu

HEAD OF ENGINEERING
Jeffrey Marshall
Director
School of Engineering
University of Vermont
College of Engineering and Mathematical Sciences
301 Votey Building
Burlington, VT 05405
Phone: (802) 656-3826
Fax: (802) 656-3358
Email: soe@cems.uvm.edu

TYPES OF ENGINEERING DEGREES
Bachelor's: B.S.
Master's: M.S. with thesis, M.S. without thesis, but with project or report
Doctoral: Ph.D.

UNDERGRADUATE INFORMATION

ADMISSION INQUIRIES
Donald M Honeman

Director
University of Vermont
194 South Prospect Street
Burlington, VT 05405
Phone: (802) 656-3370
Fax: (802) 656-8611
Email: admissions@uvm.edu

ESTIMATED STUDENT EXPENSES (FALL 2006)
[Expenses are for the 2006-2007 nine-month academic year and are based on an average credit load of: Undergraduate: 15]

	In-State	Out-of-State
Tuition and Fees:	$11,324	$26,308
Campus and Room and Board:	$7,642	$7,642
Books and Supplies:	$900	$900
Other Expenses:	$1,125	$1,125
Total Estimated Expenses:	**$20,991**	**$35,975**

Note: Undergraduates may take 12 to 18 credits per semester for listed tuition and fees. Graduate students pay per credit hour: $410 in-state, $1034 out-of-state. Graduate data listed is for 12 credits per semester.

NEW APPLICANTS/NEWLY ENROLLED STUDENTS
[Numbers are for the undergraduate engineering college for the Fall 2006 term]

Number of Applicants (a):	1,359
Of those, Number Offered Admission (b):	938
Of those, Number Enrolled Fall 2006 (c):	148

GRADUATE INFORMATION

ADMISSION INQUIRIES
Ralph M Swenson
Graduate Admissions
University of Vermont
335 Waterman
Burlington , VT 05405
Phone: (802) 656-3160
Fax: (802) 656-0519

ESTIMATED STUDENT EXPENSES (FALL 2006)
[Expenses are for the 2006-2007 nine-month academic year and are based on an average credit load of: Graduate: 9]

	In-State	Out-of-State
Tuition and Fees:	$12,482	$27,468
Campus and Room and Board:	$7,642	$7,642
Books and Supplies:	$900	$900
Other Expenses:	$1,125	$1,125
Total Estimated Expenses:	**$22,149**	**$37,135**

Note: Undergraduates may take 12 to 18 credits per semester for listed tuition and fees. Graduate students pay per credit hour: $410 in-state, $1034 out-of-state. Graduate data listed is for 12 credits per semester.

NEW APPLICANTS/NEWLY ENROLLED STUDENTS
[Numbers are for the graduate engineering college for the Fall 2006 term]

Number of Applicants (a):	188
Of those, Number Offered Admission (b):	80
Of those, Number Enrolled Fall 2006 (c):	20

Villanova University

INSTITUTION INFORMATION
800 Lancaster Avenue
Villanova, PA 19085
Phone: (610) 519-6000
Fax: (610) 519-5859
Web: http://www.villanova.edu

GENERAL INFORMATION
[All Students - Fall 2006]

Undergraduate Enrollment	7,072
Graduate Enrollment	2,285
Professional Enrollment	917
Total Enrollment	**10,274**

ENGINEERING COLLEGE INFORMATION

HEAD OF ENGINEERING
Gary Gabriele
Dean
College of Engineering
Villanova University
800 Lancaster Avenue
310 CEER
Villanova, PA 19085
Phone: (610) 519-5860

Fax: (610) 519-4941
Email: marjorie.mcmanus@villanova.edu

TYPES OF ENGINEERING DEGREES
Bachelor's: B.S.
Master's: M.S. with thesis
Doctoral: Ph.D.

UNDERGRADUATE INFORMATION

ADMISSION INQUIRIES
Stephen Merritt
Dean of Enrollment Management
Villanova University
800 Lancaster Ave., 1st Floor
Villanova, PA 19085
Phone: (610) 519-4940
Fax: (610) 519-6450
Email: stephen.merritt@villanova.edu

ESTIMATED STUDENT EXPENSES (FALL 2006)
[Expenses are for the 2006-2007 nine-month academic year and are based on an average credit load of: Undergraduate: 18]

	All Students
Tuition and fees:	$33,580
Campus and Room and Board:	$9,820
Books and Supplies:	$1,000
Other Expenses:	
Total Estimated Expenses:	**$44,400**

NEW APPLICANTS/NEWLY ENROLLED STUDENTS
[Numbers are for the undergraduate engineering college for the Fall 2006 term]

Number of Applicants (a):	1,345
Of those, Number Offered Admission (b):	941
Of those, Number Enrolled Fall 2006 (c):	261

GRADUATE INFORMATION

ESTIMATED STUDENT EXPENSES (FALL 2006)
[Expenses are for the 2006-2007 nine-month academic year and are based on an average credit load of: Graduate: 9]

	All Students
Tuition and fees:	$14,130
Campus and Room and Board:	
Books and Supplies:	$500
Other Expenses:	
Total Estimated Expenses:	**$14,630**

NEW APPLICANTS/NEWLY ENROLLED STUDENTS
[Numbers are for the graduate engineering college for the Fall 2006 term]

Number of Applicants (a):	221
Of those, Number Offered Admission (b):	104
Of those, Number Enrolled Fall 2006 (c):	74

University of Virginia

INSTITUTION INFORMATION
Thornton Hall
Charlottesville, VA 22904
Phone: (434) 924-3155
Fax: (434) 982-2257
Web: http://www.virginia.edu

GENERAL INFORMATION
[All Students - Fall 2006]

Undergraduate Enrollment	13,353
Graduate Enrollment	4,791
Professional Enrollment	1,699
Total Enrollment	**19,843**

ENGINEERING COLLEGE INFORMATION

HEAD OF ENGINEERING
James H Aylor
Dean
School of Engineering and Applied Science
University of Virginia
Thornton Hall, 351 McCormick Rd
PO Box 400246
Charlottesville, VA 22904
Phone: (434) 924-3593
Fax: (434) 924-3555
Email: jha@virginia.edu

TYPES OF ENGINEERING DEGREES
Bachelor's: B.S.
Master's: M.S. with thesis, M.Eng.
Doctoral: Ph.D.

UNDERGRADUATE INFORMATION

ESTIMATED STUDENT EXPENSES (FALL 2006)
[Expenses are for the 2006-2007 nine-month academic year and are based on an average credit load of: Undergraduate: 15]

	In-State	Out-of-State
Tuition and Fees:	$7,845	$25,945
Campus and Room and Board:	$6,970	$6,970
Books and Supplies:	$1,000	$1,000
Other Expenses:	$1,974	$1,754
Total Estimated Expenses:	**$17,789**	**$35,669**

NEW APPLICANTS/NEWLY ENROLLED STUDENTS
[Numbers are for the undergraduate engineering college for the Fall 2006 term]

Number of Applicants (a):	2,123
Of those, Number Offered Admission (b):	1,192
Of those, Number Enrolled Fall 2006 (c):	544

GRADUATE INFORMATION

ADMISSION INQUIRIES
Kathryn C Thornton
Associate Dean for Graduate Programs
University of Virginia
Thornton Hall
Charlottesville , VA 22904
Phone: (434) 982-2074
Fax: (434) 982-3044

ESTIMATED STUDENT EXPENSES (FALL 2006)
[Expenses are for the 2006-2007 nine-month academic year and are based on an average credit load of: Graduate: 12]

	In-State	Out-of-State
Tuition and Fees:	$10,550	$20,550
Campus and Room and Board:		
Books and Supplies:	$2,104	$2,104
Other Expenses:	$13,744	$13,744
Total Estimated Expenses:	**$26,398**	**$36,398**

NEW APPLICANTS/NEWLY ENROLLED STUDENTS
[Numbers are for the graduate engineering college for the Fall 2006 term]

Number of Applicants (a):	1,631
Of those, Number Offered Admission (b):	339
Of those, Number Enrolled Fall 2006 (c):	160

Virginia Commonwealth University

INSTITUTION INFORMATION
910 W. Franklin St.
PO Box 842512
Richmond, VA 23284
Phone: (804) 828-1200
Fax: (804) 828-7532
Web: http://www.vcu.edu

GENERAL INFORMATION
[All Students - Fall 2006]

Undergraduate Enrollment	21,000
Graduate Enrollment	7,500
Professional Enrollment	1,600
Total Enrollment	**30,100**

ENGINEERING COLLEGE INFORMATION

HEAD OF ENGINEERING
Russell D Jamison
Dean
School of Engineering
Virginia Commonwealth University
601 West Main Street, Room 331A
P.O. Box 843068
Richmond, VA 23284-3068
Phone: (804) 828-3925
Fax: (804) 828-9866
Email: rjamison@vcu.edu

ENGINEERING COLLEGE INQUIRIES
Rodney D Hall
Director of Recruitment

Virginia Commonwealth University
601 West Main Street, P.O. Box 843068
Richmond, VA 23284-3068
Phone: (804) 827-7028
Fax: (804) 828-3846
Email: rdhall@vcu.edu

TYPES OF ENGINEERING DEGREES
Bachelor's: B.S.
Master's: M.S. with thesis, M.S. without thesis, but with project or report
Doctoral: Ph.D.

UNDERGRADUATE INFORMATION

ADMISSION INQUIRIES
Rodney D Hall
Director of Recruitment
Virginia Commonwealth University
601 West Main Street, P.O. Box 843068
Richmond, VA 23284-3068
Phone: (804) 827-7028
Fax: (804) 828-3846
Email: rdhall@vcu.edu

ESTIMATED STUDENT EXPENSES (FALL 2006)
[Expenses are for the 2006-2007 nine-month academic year and are based on an average credit load of: Undergraduate: 17]

	In-State	Out-of-State
Tuition and Fees:	$5,976	$17,440
Campus and Room and Board:	$8,540	$8,540
Books and Supplies:	$2,500	$2,500
Other Expenses:	$2,500	$2,500
Total Estimated Expenses:	**$19,516**	**$30,980**

NEW APPLICANTS/NEWLY ENROLLED STUDENTS
[Numbers are for the undergraduate engineering college for the Fall 2006 term]

Number of Applicants (a):	1,025
Of those, Number Offered Admission (b):	640
Of those, Number Enrolled Fall 2006 (c):	225

GRADUATE INFORMATION

ADMISSION INQUIRIES
L. Thomas Overby
Assistant Dean for Graduate Affairs
Virginia Commonwealth University
PO Box 843068, 601 W. Main Street
Richmond , VA 23284
Phone: (804) 827-7033
Fax: (804) 828-9866
Email: ltoverby@vcu.edu

ESTIMATED STUDENT EXPENSES (FALL 2006)
[Expenses are for the 2006-2007 nine-month academic year and are based on an average credit load of: Graduate: 12]

	In-State	Out-of-State
Tuition and Fees:	$7,750	$17,406
Campus and Room and Board:	$8,540	$8,540
Books and Supplies:	$2,500	$2,500
Other Expenses:	$2,500	$2,500
Total Estimated Expenses:	**$21,290**	**$30,946**

NEW APPLICANTS/NEWLY ENROLLED STUDENTS
[Numbers are for the graduate engineering college for the Fall 2006 term]

Number of Applicants (a):	169
Of those, Number Offered Admission (b):	102
Of those, Number Enrolled Fall 2006 (c):	42

Virginia Military Institute

INSTITUTION INFORMATION
Mechanical Engineering Department
Nichols Engineering Hall, Room 709
Lexington, VA 24450
Phone: (540) 464-7308
Fax: (540) 464-7663
Web: http://www.vmi.edu

ENGINEERING COLLEGE INFORMATION

HEAD OF ENGINEERING
Timothy M Hodges
Coordinator of Engineering
Division of Engineering
Virginia Military Institute

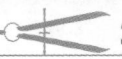

ME Dept - VMI
708 Nichols Engineering Building
Lexington, VA 24450
Phone: (540) 464-7123
Fax: (540) 464-7663
Email: hodgestm@vmi.edu

TYPES OF ENGINEERING DEGREES
Bachelor's: B.S.
Master's:
Doctoral:

UNDERGRADUATE INFORMATION

ADMISSION INQUIRIES
Vernon L Beitzel
Director of Admissions
Virginia Military Institute
319 Letcher Avenue
Lexington, VA 24450
Phone: (540) 464-7211
Fax: (540) 464-7746
Email: beitzelvl@vmi.edu

ESTIMATED STUDENT EXPENSES (FALL 2006)
[Expenses are for the 2006-2007 nine-month academic year and are based on an average credit load of: Undergraduate: N/A]

	In-State	Out-of-State
Tuition and Fees:	$4,776	$19,585
Campus and Room and Board:	$5,930	$5,930
Books and Supplies:		
Other Expenses:	$4,697	$4,697
Total Estimated Expenses:	**$15,403**	**$30,212**

Virginia Polytechnic Institute and State University

INSTITUTION INFORMATION
College of Engineering
333 Norris Hall
Blacksburg, VA 24061-0217
Phone: (540) 231-6641
Fax: (540) 231-3031
Web: http://www.eng.vt.edu

GENERAL INFORMATION
[All Students - Fall 2006]
Undergraduate Enrollment	21,996
Graduate Enrollment	6,111
Professional Enrollment	362
Total Enrollment	**28,469**

ENGINEERING COLLEGE INFORMATION

HEAD OF ENGINEERING
Richard C Benson
Dean
Virginia Polytechnic Institute and State University
College of Engineering
333 Norris Hall
Blacksburg, VA 24061-0217
Phone: (540) 231-6641
Fax: (540) 231-3031
Email: benson@vt.edu

TYPES OF ENGINEERING DEGREES
Bachelor's: B.S.
Master's: M.S. with thesis, M.S. without thesis, but with project or report
Doctoral: Ph.D.

UNDERGRADUATE INFORMATION

ESTIMATED STUDENT EXPENSES (FALL 2006)
[Expenses are for the 2006-2007 nine-month academic year and are based on an average credit load of: Undergraduate: 16]

	In-State	Out-of-State
Tuition and Fees:	$3,487	$9,525
Campus and Room and Board:	$7,020	$7,020
Books and Supplies:	$1,068	$1,068
Other Expenses:	$1,497	$1,497
Total Estimated Expenses:	**$13,072**	**$19,110**

NEW APPLICANTS/NEWLY ENROLLED STUDENTS
[Numbers are for the undergraduate engineering college for the Fall 2006 term]

Number of Applicants (a):	4,400
Of those, Number Offered Admission (b):	3,309
Of those, Number Enrolled Fall 2006 (c):	1,193

GRADUATE INFORMATION

ESTIMATED STUDENT EXPENSES (FALL 2006)
[Expenses are for the 2006-2007 nine-month academic year and are based on an average credit load of: Graduate: 12]

	In-State	Out-of-State
Tuition and Fees:	$4,270	$7,029
Campus and Room and Board:	$8,173	$8,173
Books and Supplies:	$1,067	$1,067
Other Expenses:	$3,263	$3,263
Total Estimated Expenses:	**$16,773**	**$19,532**

NEW APPLICANTS/NEWLY ENROLLED STUDENTS
[Numbers are for the graduate engineering college for the Fall 2006 term]

Number of Applicants (a):	3,172
Of those, Number Offered Admission (b):	883
Of those, Number Enrolled Fall 2006 (c):	510

Walla Walla College

INSTITUTION INFORMATION
204 S. College Avenue
College Place, WA 99324
Phone: (509) 527-2765
Fax: (509) 527-2867
Web: http://www.wwc.edu

GENERAL INFORMATION
[All Students - Fall 2006]
Undergraduate Enrollment	1,635
Graduate Enrollment	241
Professional Enrollment	0
Total Enrollment	**1,876**

ENGINEERING COLLEGE INFORMATION

HEAD OF ENGINEERING
Larry Aamodt
Dean
Walla Walla College/E.F. Cross School of Engineering
Walla Walla College
204 S. College Avenue
College Place, WA 99324
Phone: (509) 527-2765
Fax: (509) 527-2867
Email: aamola@wwc.edu

TYPES OF ENGINEERING DEGREES
Bachelor's: B.S.E.
Master's:
Doctoral:

UNDERGRADUATE INFORMATION

ESTIMATED STUDENT EXPENSES (FALL 2006)
[Expenses are for the 2006-2007 nine-month academic year and are based on an average credit load of: Undergraduate: 15]

	All Students
Tuition and fees:	$19,725
Campus and Room and Board:	$3,993
Books and Supplies:	$924
Other Expenses:	$192
Total Estimated Expenses:	**$24,834**

NEW APPLICANTS/NEWLY ENROLLED STUDENTS
[Numbers are for the undergraduate engineering college for the Fall 2006 term]

Number of Applicants (a):	133
Of those, Number Offered Admission (b):	81
Of those, Number Enrolled Fall 2006 (c):	79

University of Washington

INSTITUTION INFORMATION
College of Engineering
371 Loew Hall, Box 352180
Seattle, WA 98195
Phone: (206) 543-0340
Fax: (206) 685-0666
Web: http://www.engr.washington.edu

GENERAL INFORMATION
[All Students - Fall 2006]
Undergraduate Enrollment	27,836
Graduate Enrollment	9,886
Professional Enrollment	1,802
Total Enrollment	**39,524**

ENGINEERING COLLEGE INFORMATION

HEAD OF ENGINEERING
Matthew O'Donnell
Dean
College of Engineering
University of Washington
369 Loew Hall
Box 352180
Seattle, WA 98195-2180
Phone: (206) 543-0340
Fax: (206) 685-0666
Email: odonnel@engr.washington.edu

ENGINEERING COLLEGE INQUIRIES
Eve Riskin
Professor and Associate Dean / Dir. of ADVANCE & Ctr. for Institutional Change
University of Washington
356 Loew Hall, Box 352180
Seattle, WA 98195-2180
Phone: (206) 543-8590
Fax: (206) 685-0666
Email: riskin@u.washington.edu

TYPES OF ENGINEERING DEGREES
Bachelor's: B.S., B.S.E.
Master's: M.S. with thesis, M.S. without thesis, but with project or report, M. of Aerospace Engineering
Doctoral: Ph.D.

UNDERGRADUATE INFORMATION

ADMISSION INQUIRIES
Frank Ashby
Director, Introductory Academic Courses
University of Washington
College of Engineering, 362 Loew Hall, Box 352180
Seattle, WA 98195-2180
Phone: (206) 616-0996
Fax: (206) 616-8554
Email: ashby@engr.washington.edu

ADMISSION INQUIRIES
Carmen Sidbury
Assistant Dean
University of Washington
College of Engineering, 358 Loew Hall, Box 352180
Seattle, WA 98195-2180
Phone: (206) 543-6129
Fax: (206) 616-8554
Email: sidbury@engr.washington.edu

ADMISSION INQUIRIES
Dave Drischell
Academic Counselor
University of Washington
301 Loew Hall, Box 352180
Seattle, WA 98195-2180
Phone: (206) 543-1770
Fax: (206) 616-8554
Email: engradv@engr.washington.edu

ADMISSION INQUIRIES
Scott Winter
Associate Director
University of Washington
College of Engineering, 301 Loew Hall, Box 352180
Seattle, WA 98195-2180
Phone: (206) 685-4074
Fax: (206) 616-8554
Email: swinter@u.washington.edu

ESTIMATED STUDENT EXPENSES (FALL 2006)
[Expenses are for the 2006-2007 nine-month academic year and are based on an average credit load of: Undergraduate: 12]

	In-State	Out-of-State
Tuition and Fees:	$5,985	$21,283
Campus and Room and Board:	$8,001	$8,001
Books and Supplies:	$945	$945
Other Expenses:	$2,661	$2,661
Total Estimated Expenses:	**$17,592**	**$32,890**

NEW APPLICANTS/NEWLY ENROLLED STUDENTS
[Numbers are for the undergraduate engineering college for the Fall 2006 term]

Number of Applicants (a):	741
Of those, Number Offered Admission (b):	570
Of those, Number Enrolled Fall 2006 (c):	536

Note: The majority of the engineering depts. do not admit students directly from high school. Computer Sci. & Engr., Electrical Engr., and Industrial Engr. admit up to 10% of their annual admits directly from high school through their "Early Decision" process. Up to 25% of the students admitted to Bioengineering each year are considered for "Direct Admission" from high school. Early Decision and Direct Admission are for autumn quarter only.

GRADUATE INFORMATION

ADMISSION INQUIRIES
Eve Riskin
Professor and Associate Dean / Dir. of ADVANCE & Ctr. for Institutional Change
University of Washington
356 Loew Hall, Box 352180
Seattle , WA 98195-2180
Phone: (206) 543-8590
Fax: (206) 685-0666
Email: riskin@u.washington.edu

ADMISSION INQUIRIES
Joan W Abe
Director
University of Washington
301 Loew Hall, Box 352191
Seattle , WA 98195-2191
Phone: (206) 543-5929
Fax: (206) 543-8798
Email: jabe@u.washington.edu

ESTIMATED STUDENT EXPENSES (FALL 2006)
[Expenses are for the 2006-2007 nine-month academic year and are based on an average credit load of: Graduate: 10]

	In-State	Out-of-State
Tuition and Fees:	$8,818	$20,641
Campus and Room and Board:	$11,271	$11,271
Books and Supplies:	$1,104	$1,104
Other Expenses:	$3,651	$3,651
Total Estimated Expenses:	**$24,844**	**$36,667**

NEW APPLICANTS/NEWLY ENROLLED STUDENTS
[Numbers are for the graduate engineering college for the Fall 2006 term]

Number of Applicants (a):	2,686
Of those, Number Offered Admission (b):	921
Of those, Number Enrolled Fall 2006 (c):	399

Washington State University

INSTITUTION INFORMATION
Dana 146
PO Box 642714
Pullman, WA 99164-2714
Phone: (509) 335-5593
Fax: (509) 335-9608
Web: http://www.cea.wsu.edu

GENERAL INFORMATION
[All Students - Fall 2006]

Undergraduate Enrollment	19,554
Graduate Enrollment	3,320
Professional Enrollment	781
Total Enrollment	**23,655**

ENGINEERING COLLEGE INFORMATION

HEAD OF ENGINEERING
Candis S Claiborn
Dean and Professor
Office of the Dean
Washington State University
Dana 146
Box 642714
Pullman, WA 99164-2714
Phone: (509) 335-5593
Fax: (509) 335-9608
Email: claiborn@wsu.edu

TYPES OF ENGINEERING DEGREES
Bachelor's: B.A., B.S.
Master's: M.S. with thesis, M.S. without thesis, but with project or report,Master of Engineering and Technology Management
Doctoral: Ph.D.

UNDERGRADUATE INFORMATION

ADMISSION INQUIRIES
Robert Olsen
Associate Dean & Professor
Washington State University
Dana 146, PO Box 642714
Pullman, WA 99164-2714
Phone: (509) 335-4653
Fax: (509) 335-9608
Email: bgolsen@wsu.edu

ESTIMATED STUDENT EXPENSES (FALL 2006)
[Expenses are for the 2006-2007 nine-month academic year and are based on an average credit load of: Undergraduate: N/A]

	In-State	Out-of-State
Tuition and Fees:	$6,448	$16,088
Campus and Room and Board:	$7,326	$7,326
Books and Supplies:	$912	$912
Other Expenses:	$3,542	$3,542
Total Estimated Expenses:	**$18,228**	**$27,868**

NEW APPLICANTS/NEWLY ENROLLED STUDENTS
[Numbers are for the undergraduate engineering college for the Fall 2006 term]

Number of Applicants (a):	1,194
Of those, Number Offered Admission (b):	959
Of those, Number Enrolled Fall 2006 (c):	370

Note: WSU does not admit directly to a college or major. New students can only express an interest upon admission.

GRADUATE INFORMATION

ADMISSION INQUIRIES
Grant Norton
Associate Dean & Professor
Washington State University
Dana 146, PO Box 642714
Pullman , WA 99164-2714
Phone: (509) 335-8730
Fax: (509) 335-9608
Email: mg_norton@wsu.edu

ESTIMATED STUDENT EXPENSES (FALL 2006)
[Expenses are for the 2006-2007 nine-month academic year and are based on an average credit load of: Graduate: N/A]

	In-State	Out-of-State
Tuition and Fees:	$7,576	$17,714
Campus and Room and Board:	$8,780	$8,780
Books and Supplies:	$1,080	$1,080
Other Expenses:	$3,542	$3,542
Total Estimated Expenses:	**$20,978**	**$31,116**

NEW APPLICANTS/NEWLY ENROLLED STUDENTS
[Numbers are for the graduate engineering college for the Fall 2006 term]

Number of Applicants (a):	867
Of those, Number Offered Admission (b):	223
Of those, Number Enrolled Fall 2006 (c):	112

Washington University

INSTITUTION INFORMATION
1 Brookings Drive
Campus Box 1163
St. Louis, MO 63130
Phone: (314) 935-5000
Fax: (314) 935-5363
Web: http://www.wustl.edu

GENERAL INFORMATION
[All Students - Fall 2006]

Undergraduate Enrollment	7,469
Graduate Enrollment	6,067
Professional Enrollment	0
Total Enrollment	**13,536**

ENGINEERING COLLEGE INFORMATION

HEAD OF ENGINEERING
Mary J Sansalone

Dean
School of Engineering and Applied Science
Washington University
Campus Box 1163
One Brookings Drive
St. Louis, MO 63130
Phone: (314) 935-5363
Fax: (314) 935-6949
Email: sansalone@wustl.edu

TYPES OF ENGINEERING DEGREES
Bachelor's: B.S.
Master's: M.S. with thesis, M.S. without thesis, but with project or report
Doctoral: Sc.D.

UNDERGRADUATE INFORMATION

ADMISSION INQUIRIES
William P Darby
Senior Associate Dean for Academic Affairs
Washington University
1 Brookings Drive, Campus Box 1220
St. Louis, MO 63130
Phone: (314) 935-8147
Fax: (314) 935-5449
Email: darby@wustl.edu

ESTIMATED STUDENT EXPENSES (FALL 2006)
[Expenses are for the 2006-2007 nine-month academic year and are based on an average credit load of: Undergraduate: 15]

	All Students
Tuition and fees:	$33,788
Campus and Room and Board:	$10,452
Books and Supplies:	$1,100
Other Expenses:	$2,558
Total Estimated Expenses:	**$47,898**

NEW APPLICANTS/NEWLY ENROLLED STUDENTS
[Numbers are for the undergraduate engineering college for the Fall 2006 term]

Number of Applicants (a):	3,460
Of those, Number Offered Admission (b):	1,009
Of those, Number Enrolled Fall 2006 (c):	280

GRADUATE INFORMATION

ADMISSION INQUIRIES
Beth Schnettler
Director of Graduate Admissions
Washington University
1 Brookings Drive, Campus Box 1220
St. Louis , MO 63130
Phone: (314) 935-7974
Fax: (314) 935-5449
Email: BETHSCHNETTLER@WUSTL.EDU

ESTIMATED STUDENT EXPENSES (FALL 2006)
[Expenses are for the 2006-2007 nine-month academic year and are based on an average credit load of: Graduate: 12]

	All Students
Tuition and fees:	$33,468
Campus and Room and Board:	$12,000
Books and Supplies:	$1,588
Other Expenses:	$2,741
Total Estimated Expenses:	**$49,797**

NEW APPLICANTS/NEWLY ENROLLED STUDENTS
[Numbers are for the graduate engineering college for the Fall 2006 term]

Number of Applicants (a):	1,604
Of those, Number Offered Admission (b):	409
Of those, Number Enrolled Fall 2006 (c):	169

University of Waterloo

INSTITUTION INFORMATION
200 University Avenue West
Waterloo, ON N2L 3G1
Phone: (519) 888-4567
Web: http://www.uwaterloo.ca

GENERAL INFORMATION
[All Students - Fall 2006]

Undergraduate Enrollment	23,729
Graduate Enrollment	3,013
Professional Enrollment	0
Total Enrollment	**26,742**

ENGINEERING COLLEGE INFORMATION

HEAD OF ENGINEERING
Adel Sedra
Dean of Engineering
Faculty of Engineering
University of Waterloo
200 University Avenue West
CPH 4301
Waterloo, ON N2L 3G1
Phone: (519) 888-4567
Fax: (519) 746-1457
Email: sedra@engmail.uwaterloo.ca

TYPES OF ENGINEERING DEGREES
Bachelor's: BASc
Master's: M.Eng.,MASc with thesis, MMSc, MBET
Doctoral: Ph.D.

UNDERGRADUATE INFORMATION

ADMISSION INQUIRIES
Kim Boucher
Associate Director, Admissions
University of Waterloo
200 University Avenue
Waterloo, ON N2L 3G1
Phone: (519) 888-4894
Email: admissions@mail.eng.uwaterloo.ca

ESTIMATED STUDENT EXPENSES (FALL 2006)
[Expenses are for the 2006-2007 nine-month academic year and are based on an average credit load of: Undergraduate: N/A]

	Canadian Citizen	Non-Canadian
Tuition and Fees:	$9,450	$26,022
Campus and Room and Board:	$7,978	$7,978
Books and Supplies:	$1,416	$1,416
Other Expenses:		
Total Estimated Expenses:	**$18,844**	**$35,416**

Note: NOTES: All funds are in Canadian dollars. Room&Board (undergraduate and graduate) and graduate Books&Supplies represent the median value of a cost range estimated by the institution.

* Nanotechnology Engineering fees are higher.

GRADUATE INFORMATION
University of Waterloo
200 University Avenue
Waterloo , ON N2L 3G1
Phone: (519) 888-4567
Email: gsoffice@uwaterloo.ca

ESTIMATED STUDENT EXPENSES (FALL 2006)
[Expenses are for the 2006-2007 nine-month academic year and are based on an average credit load of: Graduate: N/A]

	Canadian Citizen	Non-Canadian
Tuition and Fees:	$4,230	$10,400
Campus and Room and Board:	$6,800	$6,800
Books and Supplies:	$450	$450
Other Expenses:	$3,000	$3,000
Total Estimated Expenses:	**$14,480**	**$20,650**

Note: NOTES: All funds are in Canadian dollars. Room&Board (undergraduate and graduate) and graduate Books&Supplies represent the median value of a cost range estimated by the institution.

* Nanotechnology Engineering fees are higher.

Wayne State University

INSTITUTION INFORMATION
5050 Anthony Wayne Drive
1100 Engineering Building
Detroit, MI 48202
Phone: (313) 577-3040
Fax: (313) 577-5300
Web: http://www.eng.wayne.edu

GENERAL INFORMATION
[All Students - Fall 2006]

Undergraduate Enrollment	20,892
Graduate Enrollment	9,078
Professional Enrollment	3,012
Total Enrollment	**32,982**

ENGINEERING COLLEGE INFORMATION

HEAD OF ENGINEERING
Ralph H Kummler
Professor and Dean
College of Engineering
Wayne State University
5050 Anthony Wayne Drive
1168 Engineering
Detroit, MI 48202
Phone: (313) 577-3817
Fax: (313) 577-5300
Email: rkummler@eng.wayne.edu

ENGINEERING COLLEGE INQUIRIES
Gerald Thompkins
Associate Dean for Student Affairs
Wayne State University
5050 Anthony Wayne Drive, 1170 Engineering
Detroit, MI 48202
Phone: (313) 577-3817
Fax: (313) 577-5300
Email: associatedean@eng.wayne.edu

ENGINEERING COLLEGE INQUIRIES
Michele J Grimm
Associate Dean-Academic Aff
Wayne State University
5050 Anthony Wayne Drive, 1172 Engineering
Detroit, MI 48202
Phone: (313) 577-3040
Fax: (313) 577-5300
Email: mgrimm@wayne.edu

TYPES OF ENGINEERING DEGREES
Bachelor's: B.S.
Master's: M.S. with thesis, M.S. without thesis, but with project or report
Doctoral: Ph.D.

UNDERGRADUATE INFORMATION

ADMISSION INQUIRIES
Darin Ellis
Associate Professor
Wayne State University
4815 Fourth Street, 2145 MEB Building
Detroit, MI 48202
Phone: (313) 577-3817
Fax: (313) 578-5908
Email: dellis@eng.wayne.edu

ADMISSION INQUIRIES
Syed Mahmud
Associate Professor
Wayne State University
5050 Anthony Wayne Drive, 3138 Engineering Building
Detroit, MI 48202
Phone: (313) 577-3817
Fax: (313) 578-5845
Email: smahmud@ece.eng.wayne.edu

ADMISSION INQUIRIES
Jerry Ku
Associate Professor and Co-Director of Alternative Energy Technologies Program
Wayne State University
5050 Anthony Wayne Drive, 2117 Engineering
Detroit, MI 48202
Phone: (313) 577-3817
Fax: (313) 577-8789
Email: jku@eng.wayne.edu

ESTIMATED STUDENT EXPENSES (FALL 2006)
[Expenses are for the 2006-2007 nine-month academic year and are based on an average credit load of: Undergraduate: 14]

	In-State	Out-of-State
Tuition and Fees:	$7,332	$15,928
Campus and Room and Board:	$7,014	$7,014
Books and Supplies:	$835	$835
Other Expenses:	$3,669	$3,669
Total Estimated Expenses:	**$18,850**	**$27,446**

Note: Provided figures are for a 9-month budget (Fall and Winter semesters). Tuition rates are for 28 credits for under-graduates (upper division), 16 credits for graduate students, over an academic year.

NEW APPLICANTS/NEWLY ENROLLED STUDENTS
[Numbers are for the undergraduate engineering college for the Fall 2006 term]

Number of Applicants (a):	808
Of those, Number Offered Admission (b):	505
Of those, Number Enrolled Fall 2006 (c):	176

Note: Information not available.

GRADUATE INFORMATION

ADMISSION INQUIRIES
Leslie Monplaisir
Associate Professor and Director of EMMP
Wayne State University
4815 Fourth Street, 2163 MEB
Detroit , MI 48202
Phone: (313) 577-3817
Fax: (313) 577-8833
Email: ad5365@wayne.edu

ADMISSION INQUIRIES
Yinlun Huang
Professor
Wayne State University
5050 Anthony Wayne Drive, 1129 Engineering Building
Detroit , MI 48202
Phone: (313) 577-3817
Fax: (313) 577-3810
Email: yhuang@eng.wayne.edu

ADMISSION INQUIRIES
Simon Ng
Professor & Co-Director of Alternative Energy Program
Wayne State University
5050 Anthony Wayne Drive, 1123 Engineering Building
Detroit , MI 48202
Phone: (313) 577-3817
Fax: (313) 577-3810
Email: sng@wayne.edu

ADMISSION INQUIRIES
Jerry Ku
Associate Professor and Co-Director of Alternative Energy Technologies Program
Wayne State University
5050 Anthony Wayne Drive, 2117 Engineering
Detroit , MI 48202
Phone: (313) 577-3817
Fax: (313) 577-8789
Email: jku@eng.wayne.edu

ADMISSION INQUIRIES
Rangaramanujam M Kannan
Associate Professor
Wayne State University
5050 Anthony Wayne Drive, 1121 Engineering Building
Detroit , MI 48202
Phone: (313) 577-3817
Fax: (313) 577-3810
Email: rkannan@eng.wayne.edu

ADMISSION INQUIRIES
Ratna Babu Chinnam
Associate Professor
Wayne State University
4815 Fourth Street, 2161 MEB
Detroit , MI 48202
Phone: (313) 577-3817
Fax: (313) 577-8833
Email: r_chinnam@eng.wayne.edu

ADMISSION INQUIRIES
Pepe Siy
Professor
Wayne State University
5050 Anthony Wayne Drive, 3125 Engineering Building
Detroit , MI 48202
Phone: (313) 577-3817
Fax: (313) 578-5851
Email: psiy@eng.wayne.edu

ADMISSION INQUIRIES
John M Cavanaugh
Associate Professor
Wayne State University
818 W. Hancock, 2206 Bioengineering
Detroit , MI 48201
Phone: (313) 577-3817
Fax: (313) 577-8333

ADMISSION INQUIRIES
Hwai-Chung Wu
Associate Professor
Wayne State University

5050 Anthony Wayne Drive, 2162 Engineering
Detroit , MI 48202
Phone: (313) 577-3817
Fax: (313) 578-3881
Email: hcwu@eng.wayne.edu

ADMISSION INQUIRIES
King Hay Yang
Professor and Director of the Bioengineering Center
Wayne State University
818 W. Hancock, 2208 Bioengineering
Detroit , MI 48202
Phone: (313) 577-3817
Fax: (313) 578-5701
Email: yang@eng.wayne.edu

ESTIMATED STUDENT EXPENSES (FALL 2006)
[Expenses are for the 2006-2007 nine-month academic year and are based on an average credit load of: Graduate: 8]

	In-State	Out-of-State
Tuition and Fees:	$7,282	$14,188
Campus and Room and Board:	$7,014	$7,014
Books and Supplies:	$835	$835
Other Expenses:	$3,669	$3,669
Total Estimated Expenses:	**$18,800**	**$25,706**

Note: Provided figures are for a 9-month budget (Fall and Winter semesters). Tuition rates are for 28 credits for undergraduates (upper division), 16 credits for graduate students, over an academic year.

NEW APPLICANTS/NEWLY ENROLLED STUDENTS
[Numbers are for the graduate engineering college for the Fall 2006 term]

Number of Applicants (a):	1,130
Of those, Number Offered Admission (b):	765
Of those, Number Enrolled Fall 2006 (c):	222

Wentworth Institute of Technology

INSTITUTION INFORMATION
550 Huntington Avenue
Boston, MA 02115
Phone: (617) 989-4590
Fax: (617) 989-4591
Web: http://www.wit.edu

GENERAL INFORMATION
[All Students - Fall 2006]

Undergraduate Enrollment	3,613
Graduate Enrollment	0
Professional Enrollment	0
Total Enrollment	**3,613**

ENGINEERING COLLEGE INFORMATION

HEAD OF ENGINEERING
Kuei-wu Tsai
Vice President of Academic Affairs & Provost
Office of the Provost
Wentworth Institute of Technology
550 Huntington Avenue
Boston, MA 02115
Phone: (617) 989-4485
Fax: (617) 989-4262
Email: tsaik@wit.edu

TYPES OF ENGINEERING DEGREES
Bachelor's: B.S.
Master's:
Doctoral:

UNDERGRADUATE INFORMATION

ADMISSION INQUIRIES
Maureen Dischino
Director of Admissions
Wentworth Institute of Technology
550 Huntington Avenue
Boston, MA 02115
Phone: (617) 989-4009
Fax: (617) 989-4010
Email: dischinom@wit.edu

ESTIMATED STUDENT EXPENSES (FALL 2006)
[Expenses are for the 2006-2007 nine-month academic year and are based on an average credit load of: Undergraduate: 16]

	All Students
Tutition and fees:	$19,300
Campus and Room and Board:	$9,300
Books and Supplies:	$1,000
Other Expenses:	$900
Total Estimated Expenses:	**$30,500**

NEW APPLICANTS/NEWLY ENROLLED STUDENTS
[Numbers are for the undergraduate engineering college for the Fall 2006 term]

Number of Applicants (a):	101
Of those, Number Offered Admission (b):	87
Of those, Number Enrolled Fall 2006 (c):	39

West Virginia University Institute of Technology

INSTITUTION INFORMATION
405 Fayette Pike
Montgomery, WV 25136
Phone: (304) 442-3161
Fax: (304) 442-1006
Web: http://www.wvutech.edu

GENERAL INFORMATION
[All Students - Fall 2006]

Undergraduate Enrollment	1,850
Graduate Enrollment	6
Professional Enrollment	397
Total Enrollment	**2,253**

ENGINEERING COLLEGE INFORMATION

TYPES OF ENGINEERING DEGREES
Bachelor's: B.S.
Master's: M.S. with thesis, M.S. without thesis, but with project or report
Doctoral:

UNDERGRADUATE INFORMATION

ESTIMATED STUDENT EXPENSES (FALL 2006)
[Expenses are for the 2006-2007 nine-month academic year and are based on an average credit load of: Undergraduate: N/A]

	In-State	Out-of-State
Tutition and Fees:	$5,342	$11,740
Campus and Room and Board:	$6,664	$6,664
Books and Supplies:	$1,400	$1,400
Other Expenses:		
Total Estimated Expenses:	**$13,406**	**$19,804**

GRADUATE INFORMATION

ESTIMATED STUDENT EXPENSES (FALL 2006)
[Expenses are for the 2006-2007 nine-month academic year and are based on an average credit load of: Graduate: N/A]

	In-State	Out-of-State
Tutition and Fees:	$5,628	$12,630
Campus and Room and Board:	$6,664	$6,664
Books and Supplies:	$1,400	$1,400
Other Expenses:		
Total Estimated Expenses:	**$13,692**	**$20,694**

West Virginia University

INSTITUTION INFORMATION
College of Engineering and Mineral Resources
P. O. Box 6101
Morgantown, WV 26506
Phone: (304) 293-4821
Fax: (304) 293-5024
Web: http://www.cemr.wvu.edu

GENERAL INFORMATION
[All Students - Fall 2006]

Undergraduate Enrollment	20,590
Graduate Enrollment	5,105
Professional Enrollment	1,420
Total Enrollment	**27,115**

ENGINEERING COLLEGE INFORMATION

HEAD OF ENGINEERING
Eugene V. Cilento
Dean and Professor

College of Engineering and Mineral Resources
West Virginia University
College of Engineering and Mineral Resources
P.O. Box 6070
Morgantown, WV 26506
Phone: (304) 293-4821
Fax: (304) 293-2037
Email: gene.cilento@mail.wvu.edu

ENGINEERING COLLEGE INQUIRIES
Eugene V. Cilento
Dean and Professor
West Virginia University
College of Engineering and Mineral Resources, P.O. Box 6070
Morgantown, WV 26506
Phone: (304) 293-4821
Fax: (304) 293-2037
Email: gene.cilento@mail.wvu.edu

TYPES OF ENGINEERING DEGREES
Bachelor's: B.S.
Master's: M.S. with thesis, M.S. without thesis, but with project or report
Doctoral: Ph.D.

UNDERGRADUATE INFORMATION

ADMISSION INQUIRIES
Yvonne Tait
Student Records Assistant
West Virginia University
College of Engineering and Mineral Resources, P. O. Box 6101
Morgantown, WV 26506
Phone: (304) 293-4821
Fax: (304) 293-5024
Email: yvonne.tait@mail.wvu.edu

ESTIMATED STUDENT EXPENSES (FALL 2006)
[Expenses are for the 2006-2007 nine-month academic year and are based on an average credit load of: Undergraduate: 18]

	In-State	Out-of-State
Tutition and Fees:	$5,194	$14,956
Campus and Room and Board:	$6,630	$6,630
Books and Supplies:	$900	$900
Other Expenses:	$2,442	$2,442
Total Estimated Expenses:	**$15,166**	**$24,928**

NEW APPLICANTS/NEWLY ENROLLED STUDENTS
[Numbers are for the undergraduate engineering college for the Fall 2006 term]

Number of Applicants (a):	1,486
Of those, Number Offered Admission (b):	1,325
Of those, Number Enrolled Fall 2006 (c):	629

GRADUATE INFORMATION

ADMISSION INQUIRIES
Linda D. Cox
Graduate Student Assistant
West Virginia University
College of Engineering and Mineral Resources, P.O. Box 6101
Morgantown , WV 26506
Phone: (304) 293-4821
Fax: (304) 293-5024
Email: linda.cox@mail.wvu.edu

ESTIMATED STUDENT EXPENSES (FALL 2006)
[Expenses are for the 2006-2007 nine-month academic year and are based on an average credit load of: Graduate: 9]

	In-State	Out-of-State
Tutition and Fees:	$5,644	$15,394
Campus and Room and Board:	$8,600	$8,600
Books and Supplies:	$900	$900
Other Expenses:	$2,756	$2,756
Total Estimated Expenses:	**$17,900**	**$27,650**

NEW APPLICANTS/NEWLY ENROLLED STUDENTS
[Numbers are for the graduate engineering college for the Fall 2006 term]

Number of Applicants (a):	1,028
Of those, Number Offered Admission (b):	440
Of those, Number Enrolled Fall 2006 (c):	202

Western Kentucky University

INSTITUTION INFORMATION
1906 College Heights Blvd.
Bowling Green, KY 42101
Phone: (270) 745-0111
Fax: (270) 745-5856
Web: http://www.wku.edu

GENERAL INFORMATION
[All Students - Fall 2006]
Undergraduate Enrollment 15,976
Graduate Enrollment 2,667
Professional Enrollment 0
Total Enrollment **18,643**

ENGINEERING COLLEGE INFORMATION

HEAD OF ENGINEERING
John C Reis
Head
Engineering
Western Kentucky University
1906 College Heights Blvd.
EBS 2101
Bowling Green, KY 42101-1082
Phone: (270) 745-2461
Fax: (270) 745-5856
Email: john.reis@wku.edu

TYPES OF ENGINEERING DEGREES
Bachelor's: B.A.
Master's:
Doctoral:

UNDERGRADUATE INFORMATION

ESTIMATED STUDENT EXPENSES (FALL 2006)
[Expenses are for the 2006-2007 nine-month academic year and are based on an average credit load of: Undergraduate: 15]

	In-State	Out-of-State
Tuition and Fees:	$5,952	$14,400
Campus and Room and Board:	$5,266	$5,266
Books and Supplies:	$800	$800
Other Expenses:	$1,700	$1,700
Total Estimated Expenses:	**$13,718**	**$22,166**

GRADUATE INFORMATION

ESTIMATED STUDENT EXPENSES (FALL 2006)
[Expenses are for the 2006-2007 nine-month academic year and are based on an average credit load of: Graduate: 9]

	In-State	Out-of-State
Tuition and Fees:	$6,520	$7,140
Campus and Room and Board:	$5,266	$5,266
Books and Supplies:	$800	$800
Other Expenses:	$1,700	$1,700
Total Estimated Expenses:	**$14,286**	**$14,906**

Western Michigan University

INSTITUTION INFORMATION
Engineering and Applied Sciences
1903 W. Michigan Avenue
Kalamazoo, MI 49008-5314
Phone: (269) 276-3253
Fax: (269) 276-3257
Web: http://www.wmich.edu/engineer

GENERAL INFORMATION
[All Students - Fall 2006]
Undergraduate Enrollment 19,261
Graduate Enrollment 4,544
Professional Enrollment 0
Total Enrollment **23,805**

ENGINEERING COLLEGE INFORMATION

HEAD OF ENGINEERING
Timothy J. Greene
Dean
College of Engineering and Applied Sciences
Western Michigan University
1903 W Michigan
Kalamazoo, MI 49008-5314
Phone: (269) 276-3253
Fax: (269) 276-3257
Email: tim.greene@wmich.edu

TYPES OF ENGINEERING DEGREES
Bachelor's: B.S.
Master's: M.S. with thesis, M.S. without thesis, but with project or report
Doctoral: Ph.D.

UNDERGRADUATE INFORMATION

ADMISSION INQUIRIES
Sandra F Blanchard
Director of Undergraduate Advising
Western Michigan University
1903 W. Michigan
Kalamazoo, MI 49008-5317
Phone: (269) 276-3270
Fax: (269) 276-3259
Email: sandra.blanchard@wmich.edu

ESTIMATED STUDENT EXPENSES (FALL 2006)
[Expenses are for the 2006-2007 nine-month academic year and are based on an average credit load of: Undergraduate: 16]

	In-State	Out-of-State
Tuition and Fees:	$6,866	$16,806
Campus and Room and Board:	$6,877	$6,877
Books and Supplies:	$906	$906
Other Expenses:	$3,008	$3,524
Total Estimated Expenses:	**$17,657**	**$28,113**

NEW APPLICANTS/NEWLY ENROLLED STUDENTS
[Numbers are for the undergraduate engineering college for the Fall 2006 term]
Number of Applicants (a): 1,281
Of those, Number Offered Admission (b): 1,100
Of those, Number Enrolled Fall 2006 (c): 419

GRADUATE INFORMATION

ADMISSION INQUIRIES
Osama Abudayyeh
Associate Dean for Research and Graduate Programs
Western Michigan University
1903 W. Michigan
Kalamazoo , MI 49008-5314
Phone: (269) 276-3253
Fax: (269) 276-3257
Email: osama.abudayyeh@wmich.edu

ESTIMATED STUDENT EXPENSES (FALL 2006)
[Expenses are for the 2006-2007 nine-month academic year and are based on an average credit load of: Graduate: 12]

	In-State	Out-of-State
Tuition and Fees:	$8,466	$18,214
Campus and Room and Board:	$6,877	$6,877
Books and Supplies:	$1,482	$1,482
Other Expenses:	$3,008	$3,524
Total Estimated Expenses:	**$19,833**	**$30,097**

NEW APPLICANTS/NEWLY ENROLLED STUDENTS
[Numbers are for the graduate engineering college for the Fall 2006 term]
Number of Applicants (a): 455
Of those, Number Offered Admission (b): 269
Of those, Number Enrolled Fall 2006 (c): 95

Western New England College

INSTITUTION INFORMATION
1215 Wilbraham Road
Springfield, MA 01119
Phone: (413) 782-3111
Fax: (413) 796-2116
Web: http://www.wnec.edu

GENERAL INFORMATION
[All Students - Fall 2006]
Undergraduate Enrollment 2,813
Graduate Enrollment 246
Professional Enrollment 595
Total Enrollment **3,654**

ENGINEERING COLLEGE INFORMATION

HEAD OF ENGINEERING
Carl E Rathmann
Dean
School of Engineering
Western New England College
1215 Wilbraham Road
Springfield, MA 01119
Phone: (413) ,41-3782
Fax: (413) ,41-2116
Email: crathmann@wnec.edu

TYPES OF ENGINEERING DEGREES
Bachelor's: B.S.
Master's: M.S. with thesis, M.S. without thesis, but with project or report
Doctoral:

UNDERGRADUATE INFORMATION

ADMISSION INQUIRIES
Charles R Pollock
Vice President of Enrollment Management
Western New England College
1215 Wilbraham Road
Springfield, MA 01119
Phone: (413) 782-1321
Fax: (413) 782-1777
Email: cpollock@wnec.edu

ESTIMATED STUDENT EXPENSES (FALL 2006)
[Expenses are for the 2006-2007 nine-month academic year and are based on an average credit load of: Undergraduate: 16]

	In-State	Out-of-State
Tuition and Fees:	$25,662	
Campus and Room and Board:	$9,526	
Books and Supplies:	$950	
Other Expenses:	$1,640	
Total Estimated Expenses:	**$37,778**	

NEW APPLICANTS/NEWLY ENROLLED STUDENTS
[Numbers are for the undergraduate engineering college for the Fall 2006 term]
Number of Applicants (a): 544
Of those, Number Offered Admission (b): 376
Of those, Number Enrolled Fall 2006 (c): 97

GRADUATE INFORMATION

ADMISSION INQUIRIES
Douglas Kenyon
Asst. VP for Grad. Studies & Cont. Ed.
Western New England College
1215 Wilbraham Road
Springfield , MA 01119
Phone: (413) 782-1573
Fax: (413) 782-1779
Email: dkenyon@wnec.edu

Wichita State University

INSTITUTION INFORMATION
Campus Box 44
1845 Fairmount
Wichita, KS 67260-0044
Phone: (316) 978-3400
Fax: (316) 978-3853
Web: http://www.wichita.edu

GENERAL INFORMATION
[All Students - Fall 2006]
Undergraduate Enrollment 11,203
Graduate Enrollment 3,095
Professional Enrollment 0
Total Enrollment **14,298**

ENGINEERING COLLEGE INFORMATION

HEAD OF ENGINEERING
Zulma R Toro-Ramos
Dean
College of Engineering
Wichita State University
Campus Box 44
Wichita State University
Wichita, KS 67260-0044

Phone: (316) 978-3400
Fax: (316) 978-3853
Email: zulma.toro-ramos@wichita.edu

ENGINEERING COLLEGE INQUIRIES
Janet E Wentz
Academic Records Manager
Wichita State University
Campus Box 44
Wichita, KS 67260-0044
Phone: (316) 978-6305
Fax: (316) 978-3853
Email: janet.wentz@wichita.edu

TYPES OF ENGINEERING DEGREES
Bachelor's: B.S.
Master's: M.S. with thesis, M.S. without thesis, but with project or report
Doctoral: Ph.D.

UNDERGRADUATE INFORMATION

ADMISSION INQUIRIES
Brenda Gile-Laflin
Assistant Dean
Wichita State University
Campus Box 44
Wichita, KS 67260-0044
Phone: (316) 978-6301
Fax: (316) 978-3853
Email: brenda.gile-laflin@wichita.edu

ESTIMATED STUDENT EXPENSES (FALL 2006)
[Expenses are for the 2006-2007 nine-month academic year and are based on an average credit load of: Undergraduate: 15]

	In-State	Out-of-State
Tuition and Fees:	$4,681	$12,135
Campus and Room and Board:	$5,465	$5,465
Books and Supplies:	$800	$800
Other Expenses:	$700	$700
Total Estimated Expenses:	**$11,646**	**$19,100**

Note: The tuition/fees fiugres are based on 30 credit hours per year for undergraduates and 18 credit hours per year for graduates. In addition to university tuition/fees, there is an engineering equipment fee of $14 per credit hour for engineering courses.

NEW APPLICANTS/NEWLY ENROLLED STUDENTS
[Numbers are for the undergraduate engineering college for the Fall 2006 term]

Number of Applicants (a):	606
Of those, Number Offered Admission (b):	488
Of those, Number Enrolled Fall 2006 (c):	288

GRADUATE INFORMATION

ADMISSION INQUIRIES
Janet E Wentz
Academic Records Manager
Wichita State University
Campus Box 44
Wichita , KS 67260-0044
Phone: (316) 978-6305
Fax: (316) 978-3853
Email: janet.wentz@wichita.edu

ESTIMATED STUDENT EXPENSES (FALL 2006)
[Expenses are for the 2006-2007 nine-month academic year and are based on an average credit load of: Graduate: 9]

	In-State	Out-of-State
Tuition and Fees:	$3,991	$9,723
Campus and Room and Board:	$5,465	$5,465
Books and Supplies:	$800	$800
Other Expenses:	$700	$700
Total Estimated Expenses:	**$10,956**	**$16,688**

Note: The tuition/fees fiugres are based on 30 credit hours per year for undergraduates and 18 credit hours per year for graduates. In addition to university tuition/fees, there is an engineering equipment fee of $14 per credit hour for engineering courses.

NEW APPLICANTS/NEWLY ENROLLED STUDENTS
[Numbers are for the graduate engineering college for the Fall 2006 term]

Number of Applicants (a):	621
Of those, Number Offered Admission (b):	344
Of those, Number Enrolled Fall 2006 (c):	175

Widener University

INSTITUTION INFORMATION
School of Engineering
One University Place
Chester, PA 19013
Phone: (610) 499-4037
Fax: (610) 499-4059
Web: http://www.widener.edu

GENERAL INFORMATION
[All Students - Fall 2006]

Undergraduate Enrollment	3,094
Graduate Enrollment	1,768
Professional Enrollment	1,615
Total Enrollment	**6,477**

ENGINEERING COLLEGE INFORMATION

HEAD OF ENGINEERING
Fred A Akl
Dean and Professor
School of Engineering
Widener University
One University Place
Chester, PA 19013-5792
Phone: (610) 499-4037
Fax: (610) 499-4059
Email: faakl@widener.edu

ENGINEERING COLLEGE INQUIRIES
Ronald L Mersky
Associate Professor
Widener University
One University Place
Chester, PA 19013-5792
Phone: (610) 499-1146
Fax: (610) 499-4059
Email: rlmersky@widener.edu

TYPES OF ENGINEERING DEGREES
Bachelor's: B.S.
Master's: M.Eng.
Doctoral:

UNDERGRADUATE INFORMATION

ESTIMATED STUDENT EXPENSES (FALL 2006)
[Expenses are for the 2006-2007 nine-month academic year and are based on an average credit load of: Undergraduate: 15]

	All Students
Tuition and fees:	$27,000
Campus and Room and Board:	$9,640
Books and Supplies:	$980
Other Expenses:	
Total Estimated Expenses:	**$37,620**

Note: Graduate tuition is given per credit.

NEW APPLICANTS/NEWLY ENROLLED STUDENTS
[Numbers are for the undergraduate engineering college for the Fall 2006 term]

Number of Applicants (a):	436
Of those, Number Offered Admission (b):	348
Of those, Number Enrolled Fall 2006 (c):	102

GRADUATE INFORMATION

ESTIMATED STUDENT EXPENSES (FALL 2006)
[Expenses are for the 2006-2007 nine-month academic year and are based on an average credit load of: Graduate: 12]

	All Students
Tuition and fees:	$750
Campus and Room and Board:	
Books and Supplies:	$610
Other Expenses:	$100
Total Estimated Expenses:	**$1,460**

Note: Graduate tuition is given per credit.

NEW APPLICANTS/NEWLY ENROLLED STUDENTS
[Numbers are for the graduate engineering college for the Fall 2006 term]

Number of Applicants (a):	145
Of those, Number Offered Admission (b):	50
Of those, Number Enrolled Fall 2006 (c):	40

Winona State University

INSTITUTION INFORMATION
175 W. Mark St.
P.O. Box 5838
Winona, MN 55987
Phone: (507) 457-5000
Fax: (507) 457-5054
Web: http://www.winona.edu/engineering

GENERAL INFORMATION
[All Students - Fall 2006]

Undergraduate Enrollment	7,613
Graduate Enrollment	573
Professional Enrollment	0
Total Enrollment	**8,186**

ENGINEERING COLLEGE INFORMATION

HEAD OF ENGINEERING
Jeffrey Anderson
Interim Dean
College of Science and Engineering
Winona State University
175 W. Mark St.
Pasteur Hall 101
Winona, MN 55987
Phone: (507) 457-5585
Fax: (507) 457-5681
Email: janderson@winona.edu

ENGINEERING COLLEGE INQUIRIES
Carol O'Laughlin
Office Manager
Winona State University
175 W. Mark St., Stark Hall 203
Winona, MN 55987
Phone: (507) 457-5685
Fax: (507) 457-5681
Email: colaughlin@winona.edu

TYPES OF ENGINEERING DEGREES
Bachelor's: B.S.
Master's:
Doctoral:

UNDERGRADUATE INFORMATION

ESTIMATED STUDENT EXPENSES (FALL 2006)
[Expenses are for the 2006-2007 nine-month academic year and are based on an average credit load of: Undergraduate: 15]

	In-State	Out-of-State
Tuition and Fees:	$6,100	$10,400
Campus and Room and Board:	$5,800	$5,800
Books and Supplies:	$800	$800
Other Expenses:	$1,000	$1,000
Total Estimated Expenses:	**$13,700**	**$18,000**

NEW APPLICANTS/NEWLY ENROLLED STUDENTS
[Numbers are for the undergraduate engineering college for the Fall 2006 term]

Number of Applicants (a):	123
Of those, Number Offered Admission (b):	110
Of those, Number Enrolled Fall 2006 (c):	45

GRADUATE INFORMATION

ESTIMATED STUDENT EXPENSES (FALL 2006)
[Expenses are for the 2006-2007 nine-month academic year and are based on an average credit load of: Graduate: 9]

	In-State	Out-of-State
Tuition and Fees:	$5,392	$7,883
Campus and Room and Board:	$5,800	$5,800
Books and Supplies:	$800	$800
Other Expenses:		
Total Estimated Expenses:	**$11,992**	**$14,483**

University of Wisconsin, Stout

INSTITUTION INFORMATION
Menomonie, WI 54751
Phone: (715) 232-1686
Fax: (715) 232-1330
Web: http://www.uwstout.edu

GENERAL INFORMATION

[All Students - Fall 2006]

Undergraduate Enrollment	7,500
Graduate Enrollment	600
Professional Enrollment	0
Total Enrollment	**8,100**

ENGINEERING COLLEGE INFORMATION

HEAD OF ENGINEERING

Robert Meyer
Dean
College of Technology, Engineering and Management
University of Wisconsin, Stout
280 Jarvis Hall - TW
Menomonie, WI 54751
Phone: (715) 232-1243
Fax: (715) 232-1274
Email: meyerb@uwstout.edu

ENGINEERING COLLEGE INQUIRIES

Peter Heimdahl
Associate Dean
University of Wisconsin, Stout
280 Jarvis Hall TW
Menomonie, WI 54751
Phone: (715) 232-1133
Fax: (715) 232-1274
Email: heimdahlp@uwstout.edu

TYPES OF ENGINEERING DEGREES

Bachelor's: B.S.
Master's: M.S. with thesis, M.S. without thesis, but with project or report
Doctoral:

UNDERGRADUATE INFORMATION

ADMISSION INQUIRIES

Richard Rothaupt
Chair - Engineering and Technology
University of Wisconsin, Stout
308 Fryklund Hall, Engineering and Technology Department
Menomonie, WI 54751
Phone: (715) 232-5021
Fax: (715) 232-1330
Email: rothauptr@uwstout.edu

ESTIMATED STUDENT EXPENSES (FALL 2006)

[Expenses are for the 2006-2007 nine-month academic year and are based on an average credit load of: Undergraduate: 15]

	In-State	Out-of-State
Tuition and Fees:	$232	$487
Campus and Room and Board:	$4,884	$4,884
Books and Supplies:		
Other Expenses:		
Total Estimated Expenses:	**$5,116**	**$5,371**

NEW APPLICANTS/NEWLY ENROLLED STUDENTS

[Numbers are for the undergraduate engineering college for the Fall 2006 term]

Number of Applicants (a):	0
Of those, Number Offered Admission (b):	48
Of those, Number Enrolled Fall 2006 (c):	42

Note: Students may be admitted to the college but must have a Math ACT of 22 to gain direct admission to the Manufacturing Engineering program from high school.

GRADUATE INFORMATION

ADMISSION INQUIRIES

Peter Heimdahl
Associate Dean
University of Wisconsin, Stout
280 Jarvis Hall TW
Menomonie , WI 54751
Phone: (715) 232-1133
Fax: (715) 232-1274
Email: heimdahlp@uwstout.edu

ESTIMATED STUDENT EXPENSES (FALL 2006)

[Expenses are for the 2006-2007 nine-month academic year and are based on an average credit load of: Graduate: N/A]

	In-State	Out-of-State
Tuition and Fees:	$317	$543
Campus and Room and Board:		
Books and Supplies:		

Other Expenses:		
Total Estimated Expenses:	**$317**	**$543**

NEW APPLICANTS/NEWLY ENROLLED STUDENTS

[Numbers are for the graduate engineering college for the Fall 2006 term]

Number of Applicants (a):	12
Of those, Number Offered Admission (b):	8
Of those, Number Enrolled Fall 2006 (c):	7

University of Wisconsin, Madison

INSTITUTION INFORMATION

500 Lincoln Drive
Madison, WI 53706
Phone: (608) 262-9946
Fax: (608) 262-8333
Web: http://www.wisc.edu

GENERAL INFORMATION

[All Students - Fall 2006]

Undergraduate Enrollment	28,462
Graduate Enrollment	8,832
Professional Enrollment	4,172
Total Enrollment	**41,466**

ENGINEERING COLLEGE INFORMATION

HEAD OF ENGINEERING

Paul S Peercy
Dean
College of Engineering
University of Wisconsin, Madison
Room 2610 Engineering Hall
1415 Engineering Drive
Madison, WI 53706
Phone: (608) 262-3482
Fax: (608) 262-6400
Email: peercy@engr.wisc.edu

TYPES OF ENGINEERING DEGREES

Bachelor's: B.S.
Master's: M.S. with thesis, M.S. without thesis, but with project or report
Doctoral: Ph.D.

UNDERGRADUATE INFORMATION

ESTIMATED STUDENT EXPENSES (FALL 2006)

[Expenses are for the 2006-2007 nine-month academic year and are based on an average credit load of: Undergraduate: 15]

	In-State	Out-of-State
Tuition and Fees:	$6,730	$20,730
Campus and Room and Board:	$6,920	$6,920
Books and Supplies:	$890	$890
Other Expenses:	$2,740	$2,740
Total Estimated Expenses:	**$17,280**	**$31,280**

NEW APPLICANTS/NEWLY ENROLLED STUDENTS

[Numbers are for the undergraduate engineering college for the Fall 2006 term]

Number of Applicants (a):	2,914
Of those, Number Offered Admission (b):	1,889
Of those, Number Enrolled Fall 2006 (c):	856

GRADUATE INFORMATION

ESTIMATED STUDENT EXPENSES (FALL 2006)

[Expenses are for the 2006-2007 nine-month academic year and are based on an average credit load of: Graduate: 8]

	In-State	Out-of-State
Tuition and Fees:	$9,184	$24,454
Campus and Room and Board:	$7,420	$7,420
Books and Supplies:	$890	$890
Other Expenses:	$4,830	$4,830
Total Estimated Expenses:	**$22,324**	**$37,594**

NEW APPLICANTS/NEWLY ENROLLED STUDENTS

[Numbers are for the graduate engineering college for the Fall 2006 term]

Number of Applicants (a):	2,362
Of those, Number Offered Admission (b):	601
Of those, Number Enrolled Fall 2006 (c):	399

University of Wisconsin, Milwaukee

INSTITUTION INFORMATION

College of Engineering and Applied Science
P. O. Box 784
Milwaukee, WI 53201
Phone: (414) 229-4667
Fax: (414) 229-6958
Web: http://www.uwm.edu

GENERAL INFORMATION

[All Students - Fall 2006]

Undergraduate Enrollment	23,640
Graduate Enrollment	4,716
Professional Enrollment	0
Total Enrollment	**28,356**

ENGINEERING COLLEGE INFORMATION

HEAD OF ENGINEERING

Al Ghorbanpoor
Interim Dean and Professor
Civil Engineering
University of Wisconsin, Milwaukee
P. O. Box 784
Milwaukee, WI 53201-0784
Phone: (414) 229-4126
Fax: (414) 229-6958
Email: algh@uwm.edu

ENGINEERING COLLEGE INQUIRIES

Ronald A Perez
Associate Dean & Associate Professor
University of Wisconsin, Milwaukee
College of Engineering and Applied Science, P. O. Box 784
Milwaukee, WI 53201
Phone: (414) 229-4126
Fax: (414) 229-6958
Email: perez@uwm.edu

TYPES OF ENGINEERING DEGREES

Bachelor's: B.S.
Master's: M.S. with thesis, M.S. without thesis, but with project or report
Doctoral: Ph.D.

UNDERGRADUATE INFORMATION

ADMISSION INQUIRIES

Todd R Johnson
Director of Student Services
University of Wisconsin, Milwaukee
College of Engineering & Applied Science, P.O. Box 784
Milwaukee, WI 53201-0784
Phone: (414) 229-2460
Fax: (414) 229-6958
Email: johnsont@uwm.edu

ESTIMATED STUDENT EXPENSES (FALL 2006)

[Expenses are for the 2006-2007 nine-month academic year and are based on an average credit load of: Undergraduate: 15]

	In-State	Out-of-State
Tuition and Fees:	$6,630	$16,232
Campus and Room and Board:	$6,950	$6,950
Books and Supplies:	$950	$950
Other Expenses:	$1,600	$1,600
Total Estimated Expenses:	**$16,130**	**$25,732**

NEW APPLICANTS/NEWLY ENROLLED STUDENTS

[Numbers are for the undergraduate engineering college for the Fall 2006 term]

Number of Applicants (a):	811
Of those, Number Offered Admission (b):	679
Of those, Number Enrolled Fall 2006 (c):	272

GRADUATE INFORMATION

ADMISSION INQUIRIES

Betty A Warras
Graduate Programs Coordinator
University of Wisconsin, Milwaukee
College of Engineering and Applied Science, P. O. Box 784
Milwaukee , WI 53201
Phone: (414) 229-6169
Fax: (414) 229-6958
Email: bwarras@uwm.edu

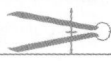

ESTIMATED STUDENT EXPENSES (FALL 2006)

[Expenses are for the 2006-2007 nine-month academic year and are based on an average credit load of: Graduate: 12]

	In-State	Out-of-State
Tuition and Fees:	$8,926	$23,292
Campus and Room and Board:	$6,950	$6,950
Books and Supplies:	$950	$950
Other Expenses:	$1,600	$1,600
Total Estimated Expenses:	**$18,426**	**$32,792**

NEW APPLICANTS/NEWLY ENROLLED STUDENTS

[Numbers are for the graduate engineering college for the Fall 2006 term]

Number of Applicants (a):	234
Of those, Number Offered Admission (b):	100
Of those, Number Enrolled Fall 2006 (c):	45

University of Wisconsin, Platteville

INSTITUTION INFORMATION

1 University Plaza
Platteville, WI 53818-3099
Phone: (608) 342-1234
Fax: (608) 342-1270
Web: http://www.uwplatt.edu

GENERAL INFORMATION

[All Students - Fall 2006]

Undergraduate Enrollment	6,344
Graduate Enrollment	701
Professional Enrollment	0
Total Enrollment	**7,045**

ENGINEERING COLLEGE INFORMATION

HEAD OF ENGINEERING

Richard D Shultz
Dean
College of Engineering, Mathematics, and Science
University of Wisconsin, Platteville
1 University Plaza
Platteville, WI 53818-3099
Phone: (608) 342-1561
Fax: (608) 342-1566
Email: shultz@uwplatt.edu

ENGINEERING COLLEGE INQUIRIES

Lisa A Riedle
Associate Dean
University of Wisconsin, Platteville
1 University Plaza
Platteville, WI 53818-3099
Phone: (608) 342-1686
Fax: (608) 342-1566
Email: riedle@uwplatt.edu

TYPES OF ENGINEERING DEGREES

Bachelor's: B.S.
Master's:
Doctoral:

UNDERGRADUATE INFORMATION

ADMISSION INQUIRIES

Angela Udelhofen
Dean of Admissions & Enrollment Mgmt.
University of Wisconsin, Platteville
1 University Plaza
Platteville, WI 53818-3099
Phone: (608) 342-1125
Fax: (608) 342-1122
Email: rulea@uwplatt.edu

ESTIMATED STUDENT EXPENSES (FALL 2006)

[Expenses are for the 2006-2007 nine-month academic year and are based on an average credit load of: Undergraduate: N/A]

	In-State	Out-of-State
Tuition and Fees:	$5,450	$12,925
Campus and Room and Board:	$4,880	$4,880
Books and Supplies:		
Other Expenses:		
Total Estimated Expenses:	**$10,330**	**$17,805**

Note: UW-Platteville students do not purchase their textbooks.

NEW APPLICANTS/NEWLY ENROLLED STUDENTS

[Numbers are for the undergraduate engineering college for the Fall 2006 term]

Number of Applicants (a):	1,204
Of those, Number Offered Admission (b):	1,119
Of those, Number Enrolled Fall 2006 (c):	545

GRADUATE INFORMATION

ESTIMATED STUDENT EXPENSES (FALL 2006)

[Expenses are for the 2006-2007 nine-month academic year and are based on an average credit load of: Graduate: N/A]

	In-State	Out-of-State
Tuition and Fees:	$6,570	$17,182
Campus and Room and Board:	$4,880	$4,880
Books and Supplies:		
Other Expenses:		
Total Estimated Expenses:	**$11,450**	**$22,062**

Note: UW-Platteville students do not purchase their textbooks.

Worcester Polytechnic Institute

INSTITUTION INFORMATION

100 Institute Road
Worcester, MA 01609
Phone: (508) 831-5000
Fax: (508) 831-5774
Web: http://www.wpi.edu

GENERAL INFORMATION

[All Students - Fall 2006]

Undergraduate Enrollment	2,860
Graduate Enrollment	1,042
Professional Enrollment	0
Total Enrollment	**3,902**

ENGINEERING COLLEGE INFORMATION

HEAD OF ENGINEERING

Carol Simpson
Provost and Senior Vice President
Academic Affairs
Worcester Polytechnic Institute
100 Institute Road
Worcester, MA 01609
Phone: (508) 831-5222
Fax: (508) 831-5774
Email: csimpson@wpi.edu

TYPES OF ENGINEERING DEGREES

Bachelor's: B.A., B.S.
Master's: M.S. with thesis, M.S. without thesis, but with project or report
Doctoral: Ph.D.

UNDERGRADUATE INFORMATION

ADMISSION INQUIRIES

Monica M Blondin
Director of Financial Aid
Worcester Polytechnic Institute
100 Institute Road
Worcester, MA 01609
Phone: (508) 831-5469
Fax: (508) 831-5039
Email: mmlucey@wpi.edu

ADMISSION INQUIRIES

Kristin R Tichenor
Associate Vice President, Enrollment Management
Worcester Polytechnic Institute
100 Institute Road
Worcester, MA 01609
Phone: (508) 831-6720
Fax: (508) 831-6067
Email: tichenor@wpi.edu

ADMISSION INQUIRIES

Edward J Connor
Director of Admisions
Worcester Polytechnic Institute
100 Institute Road
Worcester, MA 01609
Phone: (508) 831-5286
Fax: (508) 831-5875
Email: econnor@wpi.edu

ESTIMATED STUDENT EXPENSES (FALL 2006)

[Expenses are for the 2006-2007 nine-month academic year and are based on an average credit load of: Undergraduate: 9]

	All Students
Tuition and fees:	$33,318
Campus and Room and Board:	$9,960
Books and Supplies:	$2,200
Other Expenses:	
Total Estimated Expenses:	**$45,478**

Note: Undergraduate Credit Load: 9 credit hours per term with 4 terms per year.

NEW APPLICANTS/NEWLY ENROLLED STUDENTS

[Numbers are for the undergraduate engineering college for the Fall 2006 term]

Number of Applicants (a):	4,931
Of those, Number Offered Admission (b):	3,282
Of those, Number Enrolled Fall 2006 (c):	776

GRADUATE INFORMATION

ADMISSION INQUIRIES

Arlene R Lowenstein
Dean, Special Academic Programs
Worcester Polytechnic Institute
100 Institute Road
Worcester , MA 01609
Phone: (508) 831-5301
Fax: (508) 831-5717
Email: arlowe@wpi.edu

ESTIMATED STUDENT EXPENSES (FALL 2006)

[Expenses are for the 2006-2007 nine-month academic year and are based on an average credit load of: Graduate: 10]

	All Students
Tuition and fees:	$19,980
Campus and Room and Board:	$9,460
Books and Supplies:	$735
Other Expenses:	$9,049
Total Estimated Expenses:	**$39,224**

Graduate Credit Load: 10 credit hours per semester if student is a TA or RA.

Graduate Full-Time Tuition: Based on TA/RA load of 20 credits per year at $997 per credit plus $40 required fee.

NEW APPLICANTS/NEWLY ENROLLED STUDENTS

[Numbers are for the graduate engineering college for the Fall 2006 term]

Number of Applicants (a):	944
Of those, Number Offered Admission (b):	606
Of those, Number Enrolled Fall 2006 (c):	209

Wright State University

INSTITUTION INFORMATION

3640 Colonel Glenn Highway
Dayton, OH 45435
Phone: (937) 775-3232
Fax: (937) 775-3235
Web: http://www.wright.edu

GENERAL INFORMATION

[All Students - Fall 2006]

Undergraduate Enrollment	12,934
Graduate Enrollment	3,419
Professional Enrollment	517
Total Enrollment	**16,870**

ENGINEERING COLLEGE INFORMATION

HEAD OF ENGINEERING

Bor Z Jang
Dean
College of Engineering and Computer Science
Wright State University
3640 Colonel Glenn Highway
405 Russ Engineering Center
Dayton, OH 45435
Phone: (937) 775-5007
Fax: (937) 775-5009
Email: bor.jang@wright.edu

ENGINEERING COLLEGE INQUIRIES

Richard K Rathbun
Assistant Dean
Wright State University

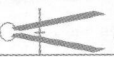
3640 Colonel Glenn Highway, 405 Russ Engineering Center
Dayton, OH 45435
Phone: (937) 775-5001
Fax: (937) 775-5009
Email: dick.rathbun@wright.edu

TYPES OF ENGINEERING DEGREES
Bachelor's: B.S.
Master's: M.S. with thesis, M.S. without thesis, but with project or report
Doctoral: Ph.D.

UNDERGRADUATE INFORMATION

ADMISSION INQUIRIES
Cathy Davis
Director
Wright State University
3640 Colonel Glenn Highway, E148 Student Union
Dayton, OH 45435
Phone: (937) 775-5700
Fax: (937) 775-5795
Email: cathy.davis@wright.edu

ESTIMATED STUDENT EXPENSES (FALL 2006)
[Expenses are for the 2006-2007 nine-month academic year and are based on an average credit load of: Undergraduate: 12]

	In-State	Out-of-State
Tuition and Fees:	$7,278	$14,004
Campus and Room and Board:	$9,876	$9,876
Books and Supplies:	$1,476	$1,476
Other Expenses:	$2,490	$2,490
Total Estimated Expenses:	**$21,120**	**$27,846**

NEW APPLICANTS/NEWLY ENROLLED STUDENTS
[Numbers are for the undergraduate engineering college for the Fall 2006 term]

Number of Applicants (a):	672
Of those, Number Offered Admission (b):	531
Of those, Number Enrolled Fall 2006 (c):	291

GRADUATE INFORMATION

ADMISSION INQUIRIES
Gerald C Malicki
Director
Wright State University
3640 Colonel Glenn Highway, E344 Student Union
Dayton , OH 45435
Phone: (937) 775-2976
Fax: (937) 775-3781
Email: wsugrad@wright.edu

ESTIMATED STUDENT EXPENSES (FALL 2006)
[Expenses are for the 2006-2007 nine-month academic year and are based on an average credit load of: Graduate: 8]

	In-State	Out-of-State
Tuition and Fees:	$9,720	$16,446
Campus and Room and Board:	$9,876	$9,876
Books and Supplies:	$1,476	$1,476
Other Expenses:	$2,490	$2,490
Total Estimated Expenses:	**$23,562**	**$30,288**

NEW APPLICANTS/NEWLY ENROLLED STUDENTS
[Numbers are for the graduate engineering college for the Fall 2006 term]

Number of Applicants (a):	973
Of those, Number Offered Admission (b):	587
Of those, Number Enrolled Fall 2006 (c):	187

University of Wyoming

INSTITUTION INFORMATION
College of Engineering Dept 3295
1000 E. University Ave.
Laramie, WY 82071
Phone: (307) 766-4253
Fax: (307) 766-4444
Web: http://www.uwyo.edu

GENERAL INFORMATION
[All Students - Fall 2006]

Undergraduate Enrollment	9,468
Graduate Enrollment	3,284
Professional Enrollment	451
Total Enrollment	**13,203**

ENGINEERING COLLEGE INFORMATION

HEAD OF ENGINEERING
Ovid A Plumb
Dean
College of Engineering Dean's Office
University of Wyoming
Dept 3295
1000 E. University Ave.
Laramie, WY 82071
Phone: (307) 766-4253
Fax: (307) 766-4444
Email: gplumb@uwyo.edu

ENGINEERING COLLEGE INQUIRIES
Richard J Schmidt
Associate Dean
University of Wyoming
Dept 3295, 1000 E. University Ave.
Laramie, WY 82071
Phone: (307) 766-4253
Fax: (307) 766-4444
Email: schmidt@uwyo.edu

TYPES OF ENGINEERING DEGREES
Bachelor's: B.S.
Master's: M.S. with thesis, M.S. without thesis, but with project or report
Doctoral: Ph.D.

UNDERGRADUATE INFORMATION

ESTIMATED STUDENT EXPENSES (FALL 2006)
[Expenses are for the 2006-2007 nine-month academic year and are based on an average credit load of: Undergraduate: 16]

	In-State	Out-of-State
Tuition and Fees:	$3,515	$10,055
Campus and Room and Board:	$6,861	$6,861
Books and Supplies:	$1,200	$1,200
Other Expenses:	$3,089	$3,089
Total Estimated Expenses:	**$14,665**	**$21,205**

Note: Tuition is charged on a per credit hour basis. Table is based on 15 credit hours per semester.
Other expenses include estimated travel and personal expenses

NEW APPLICANTS/NEWLY ENROLLED STUDENTS
[Numbers are for the undergraduate engineering college for the Fall 2006 term]

Number of Applicants (a):	667
Of those, Number Offered Admission (b):	656
Of those, Number Enrolled Fall 2006 (c):	351

GRADUATE INFORMATION

ADMISSION INQUIRIES
Richard J Schmidt
Associate Dean
University of Wyoming
Dept 3295, 1000 E. University Ave.
Laramie , WY 82071
Phone: (307) 766-4253
Fax: (307) 766-4444
Email: schmidt@uwyo.edu

ESTIMATED STUDENT EXPENSES (FALL 2006)
[Expenses are for the 2006-2007 nine-month academic year and are based on an average credit load of: Graduate: 9]

	In-State	Out-of-State
Tuition and Fees:	$4,193	$10,727
Campus and Room and Board:	$8,932	$8,932
Books and Supplies:	$1,200	$1,200
Other Expenses:	$3,090	$3,091
Total Estimated Expenses:	**$17,415**	**$23,950**

Note: Tuition is charged on a per credit hour basis. Table is based on 15 credit hours per semester.
Other expenses include estimated travel and personal expenses

Yale University/Faculty of Engineering

INSTITUTION INFORMATION
P.O. Box 208267
New Haven, CT 06520
Phone: (203) 432-4200

Fax: (203) 432-2797
Web: http://www.eng.yale.edu/

GENERAL INFORMATION
[All Students - Fall 2006]

Undergraduate Enrollment	5,333
Graduate Enrollment	2,580
Professional Enrollment	3,503
Total Enrollment	**11,416**

ENGINEERING COLLEGE INFORMATION

HEAD OF ENGINEERING
Paul A Fleury
Dean, Faculty of Engineering; Frederick W Beinecke Prof Engineering & Applied Physics; Prof., Physics
Faculty of Engineering, Office of the Dean
Yale University/Faculty of Engineering
P.O. Box 208267
New Haven, CT 06520-8267
Phone: (203) 432-4220
Fax: (203) 432-0358
Email: paul.fleury@yale.edu

ENGINEERING COLLEGE INQUIRIES
Roman B Kuc
Director of Undergraduate Affairs, Faculty of Engineering; Professor, Electrical Engineering
Yale University/Faculty of Engineering
P.O. Box 208267
New Haven, CT 06520-8267
Phone: (203) 432-0159
Fax: (203) 432-2797
Email: roman.kuc@yale.edu

TYPES OF ENGINEERING DEGREES
Bachelor's: B.A., B.S.
Master's: M.S. without thesis, but with project or report
Doctoral: Ph.D.

UNDERGRADUATE INFORMATION

ADMISSION INQUIRIES
Jeremiah J Quinlan
Assistant Director, Undergraduate Admissions; Acting Director, Student Outreach
Yale University/Faculty of Engineering
P.O. Box 208234
New Haven, CT 06520-8234
Phone: (203) 432-9316
Fax: (203) 432-9392
Email: jeremiah.quinlan@yale.edu

ESTIMATED STUDENT EXPENSES (FALL 2006)
[Expenses are for the 2006-2007 nine-month academic year and are based on an average credit load of: Undergraduate: 5]

	All Students
Tuition and fees:	$33,030
Campus and Room and Board:	$10,020
Books and Supplies:	$800
Other Expenses:	$2,000
Total Estimated Expenses:	**$45,850**

GRADUATE INFORMATION

ADMISSION INQUIRIES
Cara L Gibilisco
Student Services Officer, Graduate Program in Engineering
Yale University/Faculty of Engineering
P.O. Box 208267
New Haven , CT 06520-8267
Phone: (203) 432-4252
Fax: (203) 432-7736
Email: cara.gibilisco@yale.edu

ESTIMATED STUDENT EXPENSES (FALL 2006)
[Expenses are for the 2006-2007 nine-month academic year and are based on an average credit load of: Graduate: 4]

	All Students
Tuition and fees:	$29,300
Campus and Room and Board:	$16,850
Books and Supplies:	
Other Expenses:	
Total Estimated Expenses:	**$46,150**

NEW APPLICANTS/NEWLY ENROLLED STUDENTS
[Numbers are for the graduate engineering college for the Fall 2006 term]

Number of Applicants (a):   661
Of those, Number Offered Admission (b):   116
Of those, Number Enrolled Fall 2006 (c):   59

York College of Pennsylvania

INSTITUTION INFORMATION
Country Club Rd
York, PA 17405
Phone: (717) 846-7788
Web: http://www.ycp.edu

GENERAL INFORMATION
[All Students - Fall 2006]

Undergraduate Enrollment	4,849
Graduate Enrollment	116
Professional Enrollment	0
Total Enrollment	**4,965**

ENGINEERING COLLEGE INFORMATION

HEAD OF ENGINEERING
Timothy J Garrison
Associate Professor
Department of Physical Sciences
York College of Pennsylvania
Country Club Road
York, PA 17405
Phone: (717) 815-1710
Fax: (717) 849-1621
Email: garrison@ycp.edu

TYPES OF ENGINEERING DEGREES
Bachelor's: B.S.
Master's:
Doctoral:

UNDERGRADUATE INFORMATION

ADMISSION INQUIRIES
Nancy Spataro
Director of Admissions
York College of Pennsylvania
Country Club Rd
York, PA 17405
Phone: (717) 815-1368
Email: nspataro@ycp.edu

ESTIMATED STUDENT EXPENSES (FALL 2006)
[Expenses are for the 2006-2007 nine-month academic year and are based on an average credit load of: Undergraduate: 36]

	All Students
Tuition and fees:	$11,660
Campus and Room and Board:	$6,950
Books and Supplies:	$800
Other Expenses:	$1,500
Total Estimated Expenses:	**$20,910**

NEW APPLICANTS/NEWLY ENROLLED STUDENTS
[Numbers are for the undergraduate engineering college for the Fall 2006 term]

Number of Applicants (a):	210
Of those, Number Offered Admission (b):	129
Of those, Number Enrolled Fall 2006 (c):	62

2006 Profiles of Engineering Technology Colleges

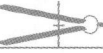

The University of Akron

INSTITUTION INFORMATION
Akron, OH 44325
Phone: (330) 972-7111
Web: http://www.uakron.edu

GENERAL INFORMATION
[All Students - Fall 2006]

Undergraduate Enrollment	19,673
Graduate Enrollment	3,327
Professional Enrollment	539
Total Enrollment	**23,539**

ENGINEERING TECHNOLOGY COLLEGE INFORMATION

TYPES OF ENGINEERING TECHNOLOGY DEGREES
2-year: Associate
Bachelor's: B.S.
Graduate:

ESTIMATED STUDENT EXPENSES (FALL 2006)
[Expenses are for the 2006-2007 nine-month academic year and are based on an average credit load of: Undergraduate: 15]

	In-State	Out-of-State
Tuition and fees:	$8,382	$17,631
Campus and Room and Board:	$7,640	$7,640
Books and Supplies:	$900	$900
Other Expenses:	$3,150	$3,150
Total Estimated Expenses:	**$20,072**	**$29,321**

Alabama A&M University

INSTITUTION INFORMATION
P.O. Box 818
Normal, AL 35762
Phone: (256) 372-5581
Fax: (256) 372-5586
Web: http://www.aamu.edu

GENERAL INFORMATION
[All Students - Fall 2006]

Undergraduate Enrollment	5,047
Graduate Enrollment	1,135
Professional Enrollment	0
Total Enrollment	**6,182**

ENGINEERING TECHNOLOGY COLLEGE INFORMATION

TYPES OF ENGINEERING TECHNOLOGY DEGREES
2-year:
Bachelor's: B.S.
Graduate:

ESTIMATED STUDENT EXPENSES (FALL 2006)
[Expenses are for the 2006-2007 nine-month academic year and are based on an average credit load of: Undergraduate: 16]

	In-State	Out-of-State
Tuition and fees:	$4,420	$8,320
Campus and Room and Board:	$4,470	$4,770
Books and Supplies:	$900	$900
Other Expenses:	$2,500	$2,900
Total Estimated Expenses:	**$12,290**	**$16,890**

Alfred State College

INSTITUTION INFORMATION
School of Management and Engineering Technology
Alfred, NY 14802
Phone: (607) 587-4611
Fax: (607) 587-4613
Web: http://www.alfredstate.edu

GENERAL INFORMATION
[All Students - Fall 2006]

Undergraduate Enrollment	3,201
Graduate Enrollment	0
Professional Enrollment	0
Total Enrollment	**3,201**

ENGINEERING TECHNOLOGY COLLEGE INFORMATION

HEAD OF ENGINEERING TECHNOLOGY
Austin C Cheney
Dean
Alfred State College
Rm 420, EJ Brown Hall, Alfred State College
Alfred, NY 14802
Phone: (607) 587-4692
Fax: (607) 587-4613
Email: cheneyac@alfredstate.edu

TYPES OF ENGINEERING TECHNOLOGY DEGREES
2-year: Associate
Bachelor's: B.S., B.Tech.
Graduate:

ESTIMATED STUDENT EXPENSES (FALL 2006)
[Expenses are for the 2006-2007 nine-month academic year and are based on an average credit load of: Undergraduate: 16]

	In-State	Out-of-State
Tuition and fees:	$4,375	$7,235
Campus and Room and Board:	$8,040	$8,040
Books and Supplies:	$3,600	$3,600
Other Expenses:	$1,056	$1,056
Total Estimated Expenses:	**$17,071**	**$19,931**

Note: Books and Supplies includes required laptop computer.

NEW APPLICANTS/NEWLY ENROLLED STUDENTS
[Numbers are for the undergraduate engineering technology college for the Fall 2006 term]

Number of Applicants (a):	1,171
Of those, Number Offered Admission (b):	775
Of those, Number Enrolled Fall 2006 (c):	296

Arizona State University, Polytechnic

INSTITUTION INFORMATION
College of Science and Technology
7001 East Williams Field Road
Mesa, AZ 85212
Phone: (480) 727-1874
Fax: (480) 727-1089
Web: http://technology.poly.asu.edu/

GENERAL INFORMATION
[All Students - Fall 2006]

Undergraduate Enrollment	5,589
Graduate Enrollment	956
Professional Enrollment	0
Total Enrollment	**6,545**

ENGINEERING TECHNOLOGY COLLEGE INFORMATION

HEAD OF ENGINEERING TECHNOLOGY
Timothy E Lindquist
Interim Dean and Professor
Arizona State University, Polytechnic
7001 East Williams Field Road
Mesa, AZ 85212
Phone: (480) 727-2783
Fax: (480) 727-1089
Email: timothy.lindquist@asu.edu

TYPES OF ENGINEERING TECHNOLOGY DEGREES
2-year:
Bachelor's: B.A., B.S., B.S.E.
Graduate: M.S.

ESTIMATED STUDENT EXPENSES (FALL 2006)
[Expenses are for the 2006-2007 nine-month academic year and are based on an average credit load of: Undergraduate: 12]

	In-State	Out-of-State
Tuition and fees:	$4,498	$15,848
Campus and Room and Board:	$6,900	$6,900
Books and Supplies:	$950	$950
Other Expenses:	$2,500	$2,500
Total Estimated Expenses:	**$14,848**	**$26,198**

NEW APPLICANTS/NEWLY ENROLLED STUDENTS
[Numbers are for the undergraduate engineering technology college for the Fall 2006 term]

Number of Applicants (a):	307
Of those, Number Offered Admission (b):	227
Of those, Number Enrolled Fall 2006 (c):	97

University of Arkansas at Little Rock

INSTITUTION INFORMATION
Donaghey College of Information Science & Systems Engineering
2801 S. University Ave
Little Rock 72204
Phone: (501) 569-3333
Fax: (501) 569-8002
Web: technologize.ualr.edu

GENERAL INFORMATION
[All Students - Fall 2006]

Undergraduate Enrollment	9,400
Graduate Enrollment	2,155
Professional Enrollment	500
Total Enrollment	**12,055**

ENGINEERING TECHNOLOGY COLLEGE INFORMATION

HEAD OF ENGINEERING TECHNOLOGY
Swaminadham Midturi
Chair, Professor
University of Arkansas at Little Rock
ETAS Building Room 227, 2801 South University Avenue
Little Rock, AR 72204
Phone: (501) 683-7015
Fax: (501) 569-8206

TYPES OF ENGINEERING TECHNOLOGY DEGREES
2-year: Associate
Bachelor's: B.S.
Graduate:

ESTIMATED STUDENT EXPENSES (FALL 2006)
[Expenses are for the 2006-2007 nine-month academic year and are based on an average credit load of: Undergraduate: 16]

	In-State	Out-of-State
Tuition and fees:	$4,736	$12,432
Campus and Room and Board:	$4,500	$4,500
Books and Supplies:	$1,000	$1,000
Other Expenses:	$3,000	$3,000
Total Estimated Expenses:	**$13,236**	**$20,932**

NEW APPLICANTS/NEWLY ENROLLED STUDENTS
[Numbers are for the undergraduate engineering technology college for the Fall 2006 term]

Number of Applicants (a):	10
Of those, Number Offered Admission (b):	10
Of those, Number Enrolled Fall 2006 (c):	10

Bradley University

INSTITUTION INFORMATION
Jobst Hall 124
Peoria, IL 61625
Phone: (309) 677-2720
Fax: (309) 677-3670
Web: http://www.bradley.edu

GENERAL INFORMATION
[All Students - Fall 2006]

Undergraduate Enrollment	5,314
Graduate Enrollment	800
Professional Enrollment	0
Total Enrollment	**6,114**

ENGINEERING TECHNOLOGY COLLEGE INFORMATION

HEAD OF ENGINEERING TECHNOLOGY
Richard T Johnson
Dean, College of Engineering & Technology
Bradley University
Peoria, IL 61625
Phone: (309) 677-2721
Fax: (309) 677-3670
Email: rtj@bradley.edu

ENGINEERING TECHNOLOGY COLLEGE INQUIRIES
Sharon L McBride
Undergraduate Student Advisor
Bradley University
125 Jobst Hall
Peoria, IL 61625
Phone: (309) 677-2975
Fax: (309) 677-3670
Email: mcbride@bradley.edu

TYPES OF ENGINEERING TECHNOLOGY DEGREES
2-year:
Bachelor's: B.S.
Graduate:

ESTIMATED STUDENT EXPENSES (FALL 2006)
[Expenses are for the 2006-2007 nine-month academic year and are based on an average credit load of: Undergraduate: 16]

	All Students
Tutition and fees:	$19,900
Campus and Room and Board:	$6,750
Books and Supplies:	$1,200
Other Expenses:	$150
Total Estimated Expenses:	**$28,000**

Note: Undergraduate tuition and fees is for 12-16 semester hours
Graduate tuition is based on 9 semester hours at $565/credit hour

Room & board is for a double room.

NEW APPLICANTS/NEWLY ENROLLED STUDENTS
[Numbers are for the undergraduate engineering technology college for the Fall 2006 term]

Number of Applicants (a):	48
Of those, Number Offered Admission (b):	25
Of those, Number Enrolled Fall 2006 (c):	9

Brigham Young University

INSTITUTION INFORMATION
Fulton College of Engineering and Technology
School of Technology
265 CTB
Provo, UT 84602
Phone: (801) 422-6300
Fax: (801) 422-0490
Web: www.et.byu.edu

GENERAL INFORMATION
[All Students - Fall 2006]

Undergraduate Enrollment	30,964
Graduate Enrollment	3,678
Professional Enrollment	0
Total Enrollment	**34,642**

ENGINEERING TECHNOLOGY COLLEGE INFORMATION

HEAD OF ENGINEERING TECHNOLOGY
Val D Hawks
Director
Brigham Young University
265 CTB
Provo, UT 84602
Phone: (801) 422-6300
Fax: (801) 422-0490
Email: erekson@byu.edu

TYPES OF ENGINEERING TECHNOLOGY DEGREES
2-year:
Bachelor's: B.S.
Graduate: M.S.

ESTIMATED STUDENT EXPENSES (FALL 2006)
[Expenses are for the 2006-2007 nine-month academic year and are based on an average credit load of: Undergraduate: 14516]

	Other Group 1	Other Group 2
Tutition and fees:	$3,620	$7,240
Campus and Room and Board:	$5,816	$5,816
Books and Supplies:	$1,380	$1,380
Other Expenses:	$3,700	$3,700
Total Estimated Expenses:	**$14,516**	**$18,136**

Note: Other 1: LDS Students; Other 2: Non-LDS Students

NEW APPLICANTS/NEWLY ENROLLED STUDENTS
[Numbers are for the undergraduate engineering technology college for the Fall 2006 term]

Number of Applicants (a):	7
Of those, Number Offered Admission (b):	5
Of those, Number Enrolled Fall 2006 (c):	4

Buffalo State College

INSTITUTION INFORMATION
Technology Department, UH 315
1300 Elmwood Avenue
Buffalo, NY 14222
Phone: (716) 878-6017
Fax: (716) 878-3033
Web: www.buffalostate.edu/depts/technology

GENERAL INFORMATION
[All Students - Fall 2006]

Undergraduate Enrollment	9,314
Graduate Enrollment	1,906
Professional Enrollment	11,220
Total Enrollment	**22,440**

ENGINEERING TECHNOLOGY COLLEGE INFORMATION

HEAD OF ENGINEERING TECHNOLOGY
Peter S Pawlik
Chairman
Buffalo State College
1300 Elmwood Avenue, Upton Hall 315
Buffalo, NY 14222
Phone: (716) 878-6017
Fax: (716) 878-3033
Email: pawlikps@buffalostate.edu

TYPES OF ENGINEERING TECHNOLOGY DEGREES
2-year:
Bachelor's: B.S.,BTECH
Graduate:

ESTIMATED STUDENT EXPENSES (FALL 2006)
[Expenses are for the 2006-2007 nine-month academic year and are based on an average credit load of: Undergraduate: 15]

	In-State	Out-of-State
Tutition and fees:	$5,275	$11,545
Campus and Room and Board:	$7,500	$7,500
Books and Supplies:	$900	$900
Other Expenses:	$2,100	$2,100
Total Estimated Expenses:	**$15,775**	**$22,045**

NEW APPLICANTS/NEWLY ENROLLED STUDENTS
[Numbers are for the undergraduate engineering technology college for the Fall 2006 term]

Number of Applicants (a):	148
Of those, Number Offered Admission (b):	67
Of those, Number Enrolled Fall 2006 (c):	23

California State Polytechnic University, Pomona

INSTITUTION INFORMATION
College of Engineering

3801 West Temple Ave
Pomona, CA 91768
Phone: (909) 869-2492
Web: http://www.csupomona.edu

GENERAL INFORMATION
[All Students - Fall 2006]

Undergraduate Enrollment	18,625
Graduate Enrollment	1,313
Professional Enrollment	572
Total Enrollment	**20,510**

ENGINEERING TECHNOLOGY COLLEGE INFORMATION

TYPES OF ENGINEERING TECHNOLOGY DEGREES
2-year:
Bachelor's: B.S.
Graduate:

ESTIMATED STUDENT EXPENSES (FALL 2006)
[Expenses are for the 2006-2007 nine-month academic year and are based on an average credit load of: Undergraduate: 16]

	In-State	Out-of-State
Tutition and fees:	$3,036	
Campus and Room and Board:	$7,973	
Books and Supplies:	$1,600	
Other Expenses:	$2,550	
Total Estimated Expenses:	**$15,159**	

Note: Figures are for full-time students, academic year

California State University, Long Beach

INSTITUTION INFORMATION
College of Engineering
1250 Bellflower Blvd.
Long Beach, CA 90840
Phone: (562) 985-8032

GENERAL INFORMATION
[All Students - Fall 2006]

Undergraduate Enrollment	29,578
Graduate Enrollment	5,998
Professional Enrollment	0
Total Enrollment	**35,576**

ENGINEERING TECHNOLOGY COLLEGE INFORMATION

TYPES OF ENGINEERING TECHNOLOGY DEGREES
2-year:
Bachelor's: B.S.
Graduate:

ESTIMATED STUDENT EXPENSES (FALL 2006)
[Expenses are for the 2006-2007 nine-month academic year and are based on an average credit load of: Undergraduate: N/A]

	In-State	Out-of-State
Tutition and fees:	$2,864	$11,000
Campus and Room and Board:		
Books and Supplies:		
Other Expenses:		
Total Estimated Expenses:	**$2,864**	**$11,000**

Capitol College

INSTITUTION INFORMATION
11301 Springfield Road
Laurel, MD 20708
Phone: (800) 950-1992
Fax: (301) 953-1442
Web: http://www.capitol-college.edu

ENGINEERING TECHNOLOGY COLLEGE INFORMATION

TYPES OF ENGINEERING TECHNOLOGY DEGREES
2-year: Associate
Bachelor's: B.S.
Graduate:

Central Connecticut State University

INSTITUTION INFORMATION
P.O.Box 4010 1615 Stanley Street
New Britain, CT 06050
Phone: (860) 832-1815
Fax: (860) 832-1811
Web: http://www.technology.ccsu.edu

GENERAL INFORMATION
[All Students - Fall 2006]
Undergraduate Enrollment	10,000
Graduate Enrollment	2,000
Professional Enrollment	0
Total Enrollment	**12,000**

ENGINEERING TECHNOLOGY COLLEGE INFORMATION

ENGINEERING TECHNOLOGY COLLEGE INQUIRIES
Peter F Baumann
Associate Professor
Central Connecticut State University
P.O.Box 4010 1615 Stanley Street
New Britain, CT 06050
Phone: (860) 832-1815
Fax: (860) 832-1811

ENGINEERING TECHNOLOGY COLLEGE INQUIRIES
Swamy Basim
Assistant Professor
Central Connecticut State University
P.O.Box 4010 1615 Stanley Street
New Britain, CT 06050
Phone: (860) 832-1815
Fax: (860) 832-1811

ENGINEERING TECHNOLOGY COLLEGE INQUIRIES
Zbigniew Prusak
Professor
Central Connecticut State University
P.O.Box 4010 1615 Stanley Street
New Britain, CT 06050
Phone: (860) 832-1815
Fax: (860) 832-1811

TYPES OF ENGINEERING TECHNOLOGY DEGREES
2-year:
Bachelor's: B.S.
Graduate:

University of Central Florida

INSTITUTION INFORMATION
Department of Engineering Technology
4000 Central Florida Blvd.
Orlando, FL 32816
Phone: (407) 823-4740
Web: http://www.ent.ucf.edu

GENERAL INFORMATION
[All Students - Fall 2006]
Undergraduate Enrollment	39,964
Graduate Enrollment	5,950
Professional Enrollment	1,312
Total Enrollment	**47,226**

ENGINEERING TECHNOLOGY COLLEGE INFORMATION

HEAD OF ENGINEERING TECHNOLOGY
Neal Gallagher
Dean, Professor of Electrical Engineering
University of Central Florida
4000 Central Florida Blvd., P.O. Box 162993
Orlando, FL 32816-2993
Phone: (407) 823-2156
Fax: (407) 823-5483
Email: nealg@mail.ucf.edu

TYPES OF ENGINEERING TECHNOLOGY DEGREES
2-year:
Bachelor's: B.S.
Graduate:

ESTIMATED STUDENT EXPENSES (FALL 2006)
[Expenses are for the 2006-2007 nine-month academic year and are based on an average credit load of: Undergraduate: 15]

	In-State	Out-of-State
Tuition and fees:	$3,492	$17,017
Campus and Room and Board:	$8,528	$8,528
Books and Supplies:	$888	$888
Other Expenses:	$4,000	$4,000
Total Estimated Expenses:	**$16,908**	**$30,433**

Note: Full time Fall/Spring

NEW APPLICANTS/NEWLY ENROLLED STUDENTS
[Numbers are for the undergraduate engineering technology college for the Fall 2006 term]
Number of Applicants (a):	165
Of those, Number Offered Admission (b):	87
Of those, Number Enrolled Fall 2006 (c):	58

University of Cincinnati

INSTITUTION INFORMATION
Nancy L. Zimpher
625 University Pavilion
Cincinnati, OH 45221-0063
Phone: (513) 556-2201
Fax: (513) 556-3010
Web: http://www.uc.edu/

GENERAL INFORMATION
[All Students - Fall 2006]
Undergraduate Enrollment	1,828
Graduate Enrollment	7,402
Professional Enrollment	1,751
Total Enrollment	**10,981**

ENGINEERING TECHNOLOGY COLLEGE INFORMATION

TYPES OF ENGINEERING TECHNOLOGY DEGREES
2-year:
Bachelor's: B.S.
Graduate:

ESTIMATED STUDENT EXPENSES (FALL 2006)
[Expenses are for the 2006-2007 nine-month academic year and are based on an average credit load of: Undergraduate: N/A]

	In-State	Out-of-State
Tuition and fees:	$9,380	$23,900
Campus and Room and Board:	$8,286	$8,286
Books and Supplies:	$1,185	$1,185
Other Expenses:	$4,150	$4,150
Total Estimated Expenses:	**$23,001**	**$37,521**

Colorado State University, Pueblo

INSTITUTION INFORMATION
2200 Bonforte Blvd
Pueblo, CO 81001
Phone: (719) 549-2884
Fax: (719) 549-2519
Web: www.colostate-pueblo.edu

GENERAL INFORMATION
[All Students - Fall 2006]
Undergraduate Enrollment	3,645
Graduate Enrollment	138
Professional Enrollment	0
Total Enrollment	**3,783**

ENGINEERING TECHNOLOGY COLLEGE INFORMATION

TYPES OF ENGINEERING TECHNOLOGY DEGREES
2-year:
Bachelor's: B.S.
Graduate:

ESTIMATED STUDENT EXPENSES (FALL 2006)
[Expenses are for the 2006-2007 nine-month academic year and are based on an average credit load of: Undergraduate: 9984]

	In-State	Out-of-State
Tuition and fees:	$2,974	$13,543
Campus and Room and Board:	$5,810	$5,810
Books and Supplies:	$1,000	$1,000
Other Expenses:	$200	$200
Total Estimated Expenses:	**$9,984**	**$20,553**

NEW APPLICANTS/NEWLY ENROLLED STUDENTS
[Numbers are for the undergraduate engineering technology college for the Fall 2006 term]
Number of Applicants (a):	97
Of those, Number Offered Admission (b):	84
Of those, Number Enrolled Fall 2006 (c):	34

University of Dayton

INSTITUTION INFORMATION
University of Dayton
300 College Park Avenue
Dayton, OH 45469--024
Phone: (937) 229-4216
Fax: (937) 229-4975

GENERAL INFORMATION
[All Students - Fall 2006]
Undergraduate Enrollment	7,473
Graduate Enrollment	3,030
Professional Enrollment	0
Total Enrollment	**10,503**

ENGINEERING TECHNOLOGY COLLEGE INFORMATION

TYPES OF ENGINEERING TECHNOLOGY DEGREES
2-year:
Bachelor's: B.S.
Graduate:

ESTIMATED STUDENT EXPENSES (FALL 2006)
[Expenses are for the 2006-2007 nine-month academic year and are based on an average credit load of: Undergraduate: 16]

	All Students
Tuition and fees:	$24,985
Campus and Room and Board:	$7,410
Books and Supplies:	$850
Other Expenses:	$1,300
Total Estimated Expenses:	**$34,545**

NEW APPLICANTS/NEWLY ENROLLED STUDENTS
[Numbers are for the undergraduate engineering technology college for the Fall 2006 term]
Number of Applicants (a):	1,221
Of those, Number Offered Admission (b):	1,046
Of those, Number Enrolled Fall 2006 (c):	313

DeVry University, Addison/DuPage

INSTITUTION INFORMATION
1221 North Swift Road
Addison, IL 60101
Phone: (630) 953-1300
Web: http://www.devry.edu

GENERAL INFORMATION
[All Students - Fall 2006]
Undergraduate Enrollment	1,440
Graduate Enrollment	0
Professional Enrollment	0
Total Enrollment	**1,440**

ENGINEERING TECHNOLOGY COLLEGE INFORMATION

TYPES OF ENGINEERING TECHNOLOGY DEGREES
2-year:
Bachelor's: B.S.
Graduate:

ESTIMATED STUDENT EXPENSES (FALL 2006)
[Expenses are for the 2006-2007 nine-month academic year and are based on an average credit load of: Undergraduate: N/A]

	All Students
Tutition and fees:	$12,650
Campus and Room and Board:	$8,708
Books and Supplies:	$1,300
Other Expenses:	$3,710
Total Estimated Expenses:	**$26,368**

Excelsior College

INSTITUTION INFORMATION
School of Business and Technology
7 Columbia Circle
albany, NY 12203
Phone: (518) 464-8500
Fax: (518) 464-8777
Web: www.excelsior.edu

GENERAL INFORMATION
[All Students - Fall 2006]

Undergraduate Enrollment	27,481
Graduate Enrollment	767
Professional Enrollment	0
Total Enrollment	**28,248**

ENGINEERING TECHNOLOGY COLLEGE INFORMATION

TYPES OF ENGINEERING TECHNOLOGY DEGREES
2-year:
Bachelor's: B.S.
Graduate:

NEW APPLICANTS/NEWLY ENROLLED STUDENTS
[Numbers are for the undergraduate engineering technology college for the Fall 2006 term]

Number of Applicants (a):	200
Of those, Number Offered Admission (b):	200
Of those, Number Enrolled Fall 2006 (c):	200

Ferris State University

INSTITUTION INFORMATION
College of Technology
1009 Campus Drive
JOH 200
Big Rapids, MI 49307
Phone: (231) 591-2890
Fax: (231) 591-2946
Web: www.ferris.edu

GENERAL INFORMATION
[All Students - Fall 2006]

Undergraduate Enrollment	11,409
Graduate Enrollment	518
Professional Enrollment	648
Total Enrollment	**12,575**

ENGINEERING TECHNOLOGY COLLEGE INFORMATION

HEAD OF ENGINEERING TECHNOLOGY
Thomas E. Oldfield
Dean
Ferris State University
1009 E. Campus Dr., Johnson 200
Big Rapids, MI 49307
Phone: (231) 591-2898
Fax: (231) 591-2946
Email: hoisingr@ferris.edu

TYPES OF ENGINEERING TECHNOLOGY DEGREES
2-year: Associate
Bachelor's: B.S.
Graduate:

ESTIMATED STUDENT EXPENSES (FALL 2006)
[Expenses are for the 2006-2007 nine-month academic year and are based on an average credit load of: Undergraduate: 15]

	In-State	Out-of-State
Tutition and fees:	$7,342	$14,782
Campus and Room and Board:	$7,220	$7,220
Books and Supplies:	$1,000	$1,000
Other Expenses:	$2,078	$2,078
Total Estimated Expenses:	**$17,640**	**$25,080**

University of Hartford

INSTITUTION INFORMATION
College of Engineering, Technology, and Architecture
200 Bloomfield Avenue
West Hartford, CT 06117
Phone: (860) 768-4112
Fax: (860) 768-5073
Web: www.hartford.edu

GENERAL INFORMATION
[All Students - Fall 2006]

Undergraduate Enrollment	5,572
Graduate Enrollment	1,708
Professional Enrollment	23
Total Enrollment	**7,303**

ENGINEERING TECHNOLOGY COLLEGE INFORMATION

HEAD OF ENGINEERING TECHNOLOGY
Lou Manzione
Dean
University of Hartford
200 Bloomfield Avenue
West Hartford, CT 06117
Phone: (860) 768-4844
Fax: (860) 768-5073
Email: manzione@hartford.edu

TYPES OF ENGINEERING TECHNOLOGY DEGREES
2-year: Associate
Bachelor's: B.S.
Graduate:

ESTIMATED STUDENT EXPENSES (FALL 2006)
[Expenses are for the 2006-2007 nine-month academic year and are based on an average credit load of: Undergraduate: 16]

	All Students
Tutition and fees:	$25,766
Campus and Room and Board:	$10,382
Books and Supplies:	$600
Other Expenses:	
Total Estimated Expenses:	**$36,748**

NEW APPLICANTS/NEWLY ENROLLED STUDENTS
[Numbers are for the undergraduate engineering technology college for the Fall 2006 term]

Number of Applicants (a):	588
Of those, Number Offered Admission (b):	474
Of those, Number Enrolled Fall 2006 (c):	145

University of Houston, College of Technology

INSTITUTION INFORMATION
College of Technology
Department of Engineering Technology
304 Technology Building
Houston, TX 77204
Phone: (713) 743-4040
Fax: (713) 743-4032
Web: http://www.tech.uh.edu/Departments/Engineering_Technology/

GENERAL INFORMATION
[All Students - Fall 2006]

Undergraduate Enrollment	26,243
Graduate Enrollment	5,053
Professional Enrollment	3,038
Total Enrollment	**34,334**

ENGINEERING TECHNOLOGY COLLEGE INFORMATION

HEAD OF ENGINEERING TECHNOLOGY
Enrique Barbieri
Professor and Chair
University of Houston
College of Technology, 304 Technology Building
Houston, TX 77204
Phone: (713) 743-4073
Fax: (713) 743-4032
Email: ebarbieri@uh.edu

TYPES OF ENGINEERING TECHNOLOGY DEGREES
2-year:
Bachelor's: B.S., Master's
Graduate: M.S.

ESTIMATED STUDENT EXPENSES (FALL 2006)
[Expenses are for the 2006-2007 nine-month academic year and are based on an average credit load of: Undergraduate: 12]

	In-State	Out-of-State
Tutition and fees:	$5,648	$12,248
Campus and Room and Board:	$4,037	$4,037
Books and Supplies:	$1,050	$1,050
Other Expenses:		
Total Estimated Expenses:	**$10,735**	**$17,335**

Note: Room and board is average of academic year costs across several on-campus housing options.

NEW APPLICANTS/NEWLY ENROLLED STUDENTS
[Numbers are for the undergraduate engineering technology college for the Fall 2006 term]

Number of Applicants (a):	187
Of those, Number Offered Admission (b):	103
Of those, Number Enrolled Fall 2006 (c):	67

Indiana University Purdue University at Indianapolis

INSTITUTION INFORMATION
799 W. Michigan Street
Room 215
Indianapolis, IN 46202
Phone: (317) 274-2533
Fax: (317) 274-4567
Web: http://www.engr.iupui.edu

GENERAL INFORMATION
[All Students - Fall 2006]

Undergraduate Enrollment	19,642
Graduate Enrollment	4,193
Professional Enrollment	4,858
Total Enrollment	**28,693**

ENGINEERING TECHNOLOGY COLLEGE INFORMATION

HEAD OF ENGINEERING TECHNOLOGY
H. Oner Yurtseven
Dean
Indiana University Purdue University at Indianapolis
799 West Michigan St., ET 219
Indianapolis, IN 46202
Phone: (317) 274-0802
Fax: (317) 274-4567
Email: hoyurt7@iupui.edu

TYPES OF ENGINEERING TECHNOLOGY DEGREES
2-year: Associate
Bachelor's: B.S.
Graduate:

Indiana University-Purdue University Fort Wayne

INSTITUTION INFORMATION
College of Engineering, Technology, and Computer

Science
2101 East Coliseum Blvd.
Fort Wayne, IN 46805
Phone: (260) 481-6839
Fax: (260) 481-5734
Web: http://www.etcs.ipfw.edu/

GENERAL INFORMATION
[All Students - Fall 2006]

Undergraduate Enrollment	10,890
Graduate Enrollment	782
Professional Enrollment	0
Total Enrollment	**11,672**

ENGINEERING TECHNOLOGY COLLEGE INFORMATION

HEAD OF ENGINEERING TECHNOLOGY
Gerard Voland
Dean
Indiana University-Purdue University Fort Wayne
2101 E. Coliseum Blvd.
Fort Wayne, IN 46805-1499
Phone: (260) 481-6839
Fax: (260) 481-5734
Email: volandg@ipfw.edu

TYPES OF ENGINEERING TECHNOLOGY DEGREES
2-year: Associate
Bachelor's: B.S.
Graduate: M.S.

ESTIMATED STUDENT EXPENSES (FALL 2006)
[Expenses are for the 2006-2007 nine-month academic year and are based on an average credit load of: Undergraduate: 15]

	In-State	Out-of-State
Tuition and fees:	$201	$461
Campus and Room and Board:	$4,940	
Books and Supplies:	$1,096	$1,096
Other Expenses:		
Total Estimated Expenses:	**$6,237**	**$1,557**

Note: Student Housing: $394-$630 per month.

Kansas State University

INSTITUTION INFORMATION
College of Engineering
1046 Rathbone Hall
Manhattan, KS 66506-5201
Phone: (785) 532-5590
Fax: (785) 532-7810
Web: http://www.engg.ksu.edu/

GENERAL INFORMATION
[All Students - Fall 2006]

Undergraduate Enrollment	18,762
Graduate Enrollment	3,946
Professional Enrollment	433
Total Enrollment	**23,141**

ENGINEERING TECHNOLOGY COLLEGE INFORMATION

HEAD OF ENGINEERING TECHNOLOGY
John E DeLeon
Professor, Head of Engineering Technology
Kansas State University
100C Technology Center, 2310 Centennial Road
Salina, KS 67401
Phone: (785) 826-2677
Fax: (785) 826-2941
Email: jd17@salina.k-state.edu

HEAD OF ENGINEERING TECHNOLOGY
Dennis K Kuhlman
Dean
Kansas State University
202C College Center, 2310 Centennial Road
Salina, KS 67401
Phone: (785) 826-2601
Fax: (785) 826-2998
Email: dkuhlman@salina.k-state.edu

TYPES OF ENGINEERING TECHNOLOGY DEGREES
2-year: Associate
Bachelor's: B.S.
Graduate:

ESTIMATED STUDENT EXPENSES (FALL 2006)
[Expenses are for the 2006-2007 nine-month academic year and are based on an average credit load of: Undergraduate: N/A]

	In-State	Out-of-State
Tuition and fees:	$5,608	$14,694
Campus and Room and Board:	$5,912	$5,912
Books and Supplies:	$900	$900
Other Expenses:		
Total Estimated Expenses:	**$12,420**	**$21,506**

Lake Superior State University

INSTITUTION INFORMATION
School of Engineering & Technology
650 W. Easterday Avenue
Sault Ste. Marie, MI 49783
Phone: (906) 635-2207
Fax: (906) 635-6663
Web: http://engineering.lssu.edu

ENGINEERING TECHNOLOGY COLLEGE INFORMATION

HEAD OF ENGINEERING TECHNOLOGY
Morrie Walworth
Dean
Lake Superior State University
650 W. Easterday Ave
Sault Ste. Marie, MI 49783
Phone: (906) 635-2206
Fax: (906) 635-6663
Email: mwalworth@lssu.edu

ENGINEERING TECHNOLOGY COLLEGE INQUIRIES
Jeanne M Shibley
Special Assistant to the Provost
Lake Superior State University
650 West Easterday Ave
Sault Ste. Marie, MI 49783
Phone: (906) 635-2597
Fax: (906) 635-6663
Email: jmshibly@lssu.edu

TYPES OF ENGINEERING TECHNOLOGY DEGREES
2-year: Associate
Bachelor's: B.S.
Graduate:

ESTIMATED STUDENT EXPENSES (FALL 2006)
[Expenses are for the 2006-2007 nine-month academic year and are based on an average credit load of: Undergraduate: 17]

	In-State	Out-of-State
Tuition and fees:	$6,558	$13,116
Campus and Room and Board:	$6,859	$6,859
Books and Supplies:	$1,500	$1,500
Other Expenses:	$1,500	$1,500
Total Estimated Expenses:	**$16,417**	**$22,975**

Note: In-state tuition rates apply in US dollars to Ontario, Canada residents. Midwest Consortium Agreement State residents: tuition $9840 per year. Room & Board for Grads assumes living in private room or townhouse.

NEW APPLICANTS/NEWLY ENROLLED STUDENTS
[Numbers are for the undergraduate engineering technology college for the Fall 2006 term]

Number of Applicants (a):	32
Of those, Number Offered Admission (b):	32
Of those, Number Enrolled Fall 2006 (c):	10

Lawrence Technological University

INSTITUTION INFORMATION
21000 West Ten Mile Road

Southfield, MI 48075
Phone: (800) 225-5588
Fax: (248) 204-3727
Web: http://www.ltu.edu

GENERAL INFORMATION
[All Students - Fall 2006]

Undergraduate Enrollment	2,681
Graduate Enrollment	1,368
Professional Enrollment	0
Total Enrollment	**4,049**

ENGINEERING TECHNOLOGY COLLEGE INFORMATION

TYPES OF ENGINEERING TECHNOLOGY DEGREES
2-year: Associate
Bachelor's: B.S.
Graduate:

ESTIMATED STUDENT EXPENSES (FALL 2006)
[Expenses are for the 2006-2007 nine-month academic year and are based on an average credit load of: Undergraduate: 15]

	All Students
Tuition and fees:	$19,373
Campus and Room and Board:	$7,266
Books and Supplies:	$1,196
Other Expenses:	$3,498
Total Estimated Expenses:	**$31,333**

Note: 1.) Room and Board cost shown is for a 2 bedroom 4 person apartment and includes a meal plan.
2.) Apartments are furnished with kitchens, bathrooms and laundry rooms.
3.) Graduate students do not reside on campus.

NEW APPLICANTS/NEWLY ENROLLED STUDENTS
[Numbers are for the undergraduate engineering technology college for the Fall 2006 term]

Number of Applicants (a):	109
Of those, Number Offered Admission (b):	81
Of those, Number Enrolled Fall 2006 (c):	37

LeTourneau University

INSTITUTION INFORMATION
School of Engineering and Engineering Technology
P. O. Box 7001
2100 S Mobberly
Longview, TX 75607-7001
Phone: (903) 233-3000
Fax: (903) 233-3105
Web: http://www.letu.edu

GENERAL INFORMATION
[All Students - Fall 2006]

Undergraduate Enrollment	3,643
Graduate Enrollment	340
Professional Enrollment	0
Total Enrollment	**3,983**

ENGINEERING TECHNOLOGY COLLEGE INFORMATION

HEAD OF ENGINEERING TECHNOLOGY
Thomas Hellmuth, Ph.D.,P.E.
Dean
LeTourneau University
P. O. Box 7001
Longview, TX 75607-7001
Phone: (903) 233-3900
Fax: (903) 233-3901
Email: TomHellmuth@letu.edu

TYPES OF ENGINEERING TECHNOLOGY DEGREES
2-year: Associate
Bachelor's: B.S.
Graduate:

ESTIMATED STUDENT EXPENSES (FALL 2006)
[Expenses are for the 2006-2007 nine-month academic year and are based on an average credit load of: Undergraduate: 16]

	All Students
Tuition and fees:	$16,920
Campus and Room and Board:	$6,590
Books and Supplies:	$1,240

Other Expenses: $1,000
Total Estimated Expenses: **$25,750**

Louisiana Tech University

INSTITUTION INFORMATION
College of Engineering and Science
P.O. Box 10348
600 West Arizona
Ruston, LA 71272
Phone: (318) 257-4647
Fax: (318) 257-2562
Web: http://www.latech.edu

GENERAL INFORMATION
[All Students - Fall 2006]
Undergraduate Enrollment 9,016
Graduate Enrollment 2,216
Professional Enrollment 0
Total Enrollment **11,232**

ENGINEERING TECHNOLOGY COLLEGE INFORMATION

HEAD OF ENGINEERING TECHNOLOGY
Stan Napper
Dean, College of Engineering and Science; Professor, Biomedical Engineering
Louisiana Tech University
P.O. Box 10348, 600 West Arizona
Ruston, LA 71272
Phone: (318) 257-4647
Fax: (318) 257-2562
Email: san@coes.latech.edu

ENGINEERING TECHNOLOGY COLLEGE INQUIRIES
James D Nelson
Associate Dean for Undergraduate Studies; Professor, Civil Engineering
Louisiana Tech University
P.O. Box 10348, 600 West Arizona
Ruston, LA 71272
Phone: (318) 257-2842
Fax: (318) 257-2562
Email: jdn@coes.latech.edu

TYPES OF ENGINEERING TECHNOLOGY DEGREES
2-year:
Bachelor's: B.S.
Graduate:

ESTIMATED STUDENT EXPENSES (FALL 2006)
[Expenses are for the 2006-2007 nine-month academic year and are based on an average credit load of: Undergraduate: N/A]

	In-State	Out-of-State
Tuition and fees:	$4,634	$9,539
Campus and Room and Board:	$4,390	$4,390
Books and Supplies:	$2,400	$2,400
Other Expenses:		
Total Estimated Expenses:	**$11,424**	**$16,329**

NEW APPLICANTS/NEWLY ENROLLED STUDENTS
[Numbers are for the undergraduate engineering technology college for the Fall 2006 term]
Number of Applicants (a): 27
Of those, Number Offered Admission (b): 24
Of those, Number Enrolled Fall 2006 (c): 17

University of Maine

INSTITUTION INFORMATION
College of Engineering
210 AMC Building
Orono, ME 04469-5769
Phone: (207) 581-2216
Fax: (207) 581-2220
Web: http://www.engineering.umaine.edu

GENERAL INFORMATION
[All Students - Fall 2006]
Undergraduate Enrollment 9,527
Graduate Enrollment 2,270

Professional Enrollment 0
Total Enrollment **11,797**

ENGINEERING TECHNOLOGY COLLEGE INFORMATION

HEAD OF ENGINEERING TECHNOLOGY
S David Dvorak
Director, School of Engineering Technology
University of Maine
119 Boardman Hall
Orono, ME 04469-5711
Phone: (207) 581-2340
Fax: (207) 581-2113
Email: David.Dvorak@umit.maine.edu

TYPES OF ENGINEERING TECHNOLOGY DEGREES
2-year:
Bachelor's: B.S.
Graduate:

NEW APPLICANTS/NEWLY ENROLLED STUDENTS
[Numbers are for the undergraduate engineering technology college for the Fall 2006 term]
Number of Applicants (a): 101
Of those, Number Offered Admission (b): 113
Of those, Number Enrolled Fall 2006 (c): 65

University of Massachusetts Lowell

INSTITUTION INFORMATION
Engineering Technology
One University Avenue
Lowell, MA 01854
Phone: (978) 934-2593
Fax: (978) 934-3007
Web: www.uml.edu

GENERAL INFORMATION
[All Students - Fall 2006]
Undergraduate Enrollment 8,649
Graduate Enrollment 2,559
Professional Enrollment 0
Total Enrollment **11,208**

ENGINEERING TECHNOLOGY COLLEGE INFORMATION

TYPES OF ENGINEERING TECHNOLOGY DEGREES
2-year: Associate
Bachelor's: B.S.
Graduate:

ESTIMATED STUDENT EXPENSES (FALL 2006)
[Expenses are for the 2006-2007 nine-month academic year and are based on an average credit load of: Undergraduate: 12]

	In-State	Out-of-State
Tuition and fees:	$8,444	$19,714
Campus and Room and Board:	$6,520	$6,520
Books and Supplies:	$725	$725
Other Expenses:	$900	$900
Total Estimated Expenses:	**$16,589**	**$27,859**

NEW APPLICANTS/NEWLY ENROLLED STUDENTS
[Numbers are for the undergraduate engineering technology college for the Fall 2006 term]
Number of Applicants (a): 8
Of those, Number Offered Admission (b): 8
Of those, Number Enrolled Fall 2006 (c): 8

McNeese State University

INSTITUTION INFORMATION
Department of Engineering Technology
P.O. Box 91780
Lake Charles, LA 70609
Phone: (337) 475-5854
Fax: (337) 475-5292
Web: dortego@mcneese.edu

GENERAL INFORMATION
[All Students - Fall 2006]
Undergraduate Enrollment 7,336
Graduate Enrollment 1,007
Professional Enrollment 0
Total Enrollment **8,343**

ENGINEERING TECHNOLOGY COLLEGE INFORMATION

HEAD OF ENGINEERING TECHNOLOGY
Nikos Kiritsis
Associate Professor, Dean
McNeese State University
P.O. Box 91860
Lake Charles, LA 70609
Phone: (337) 475-5857
Fax: (337) 475-5237
Email: nikosk@mcneese.edu

TYPES OF ENGINEERING TECHNOLOGY DEGREES
2-year: Associate
Bachelor's: B.S.
Graduate:

ESTIMATED STUDENT EXPENSES (FALL 2006)
[Expenses are for the 2006-2007 nine-month academic year and are based on an average credit load of: Undergraduate: 12]

	In-State	Out-of-State
Tuition and fees:	$3,200	
Campus and Room and Board:	$5,506	
Books and Supplies:	$700	
Other Expenses:	$200	
Total Estimated Expenses:	**$9,606**	

The University of Memphis

INSTITUTION INFORMATION
203 Engineering Technology Bldg
Memphis, TN 38152
Phone: (901) 678-2225
Fax: (901) 678-5145
Web: http://www.memphis.edu

GENERAL INFORMATION
[All Students - Fall 2006]
Undergraduate Enrollment 15,984
Graduate Enrollment 4,169
Professional Enrollment 409
Total Enrollment **20,562**

ENGINEERING TECHNOLOGY COLLEGE INFORMATION

TYPES OF ENGINEERING TECHNOLOGY DEGREES
2-year:
Bachelor's: B.S.
Graduate: M.S.

ESTIMATED STUDENT EXPENSES (FALL 2006)
[Expenses are for the 2006-2007 nine-month academic year and are based on an average credit load of: Undergraduate: 14]

	In-State	Out-of-State
Tuition and fees:	$5,256	$15,722
Campus and Room and Board:	$6,500	$6,500
Books and Supplies:	$1,200	$1,200
Other Expenses:	$1,000	$1,000
Total Estimated Expenses:	**$13,956**	**$24,422**

NEW APPLICANTS/NEWLY ENROLLED STUDENTS
[Numbers are for the undergraduate engineering technology college for the Fall 2006 term]
Number of Applicants (a): 38
Of those, Number Offered Admission (b): 30
Of those, Number Enrolled Fall 2006 (c): 16

Metropolitan State College of Denver

INSTITUTION INFORMATION
Engineering Technology Department
Campus Box 29, South Classroom 213
P. O. Box 173362
Denver, CO 80217-3362
Phone: (303) 556-2503
Fax: (303) 556-2972

GENERAL INFORMATION
[All Students - Fall 2006]
Undergraduate Enrollment	21,151
Graduate Enrollment	0
Professional Enrollment	0
Total Enrollment	**21,151**

ENGINEERING TECHNOLOGY COLLEGE INFORMATION

HEAD OF ENGINEERING TECHNOLOGY
Parris C Neal
Chair, Professor of Electrical Engineering Technology
Metropolitan State College of Denver
Campus Box 29, P. O. Box 173362
Denver, CO 80217-3362
Phone: (303) 556-2503
Fax: (303) 556-2972
Email: pneal1@mscd.edu

ENGINEERING TECHNOLOGY COLLEGE INQUIRIES
Zsuzsa Balogh
CET Coordinator, Assistant Professor
Metropolitan State College of Denver
Campus Box 61, P. O. Box 173362
Denver, CO 80217-3362
Phone: (303) 556-3277
Fax: (303) 556-2972
Email: balogh@mscd.edu

ENGINEERING TECHNOLOGY COLLEGE INQUIRIES
Linda Succo
Administrative Assistant III
Metropolitan State College of Denver
Campus Box 29, P.O. Box 173362
Denver, CO 80217-3362
Phone: (303) 556-2503
Fax: (303) 556-2972
Email: succo@mscd.edu

ENGINEERING TECHNOLOGY COLLEGE INQUIRIES
Joesph P Clark
EET Coordinator, Assistant Professor
Metropolitan State College of Denver
Campus Box 29, P. O. Box 173362
Denver, CO 80217-3362
Phone: (303) 352-2503
Fax: (303) 556-2972

ENGINEERING TECHNOLOGY COLLEGE INQUIRIES
Parris C Neal
Chair, Professor of Electrical Engineering Technology
Metropolitan State College of Denver
Campus Box 29, P. O. Box 173362
Denver, CO 80217-3362
Phone: (303) 556-2503
Fax: (303) 556-2972
Email: pneal1@mscd.edu

ENGINEERING TECHNOLOGY COLLEGE INQUIRIES
Mingli He
MET Coordinator, Associate Professor
Metropolitan State College of Denver
Campus Box 29, P. O. Box 173362
Denver, CO 80217-3362
Phone: (303) 556-2976
Fax: (303) 556-2972
Email: he@mscd.edu

TYPES OF ENGINEERING TECHNOLOGY DEGREES
2-year:
Bachelor's: B.S.
Graduate:

ESTIMATED STUDENT EXPENSES (FALL 2006)
[Expenses are for the 2006-2007 nine-month academic year and are based on an average credit load of: Undergraduate: 15]

	In-State	Out-of-State
Tuition and fees:	$4,175	$11,590
Campus and Room and Board:	$7,641	$7,641
Books and Supplies:	$1,698	$1,698
Other Expenses:	$1,836	$1,836
Total Estimated Expenses:	**$15,350**	**$22,765**

Note: The In-State tuition and fees includes a reduction ($2,580) by the College Opportunity Fund is the process by which Colorado provides state financial support to eligible students for higher education. It was created by an Act of the Colorado State Legislature and signed into law by Governor Owens in May 2004.

You only have to apply once, and you will receive the stipend every term that you take eligible undergraduate courses, and have not met your 145 credit hour life time limit. The stipend is $86 per credit hour.
Apply for your stipend at CollegeInColorado.org

NEW APPLICANTS/NEWLY ENROLLED STUDENTS
[Numbers are for the undergraduate engineering technology college for the Fall 2006 term]
Number of Applicants (a):	137
Of those, Number Offered Admission (b):	120
Of those, Number Enrolled Fall 2006 (c):	51

Miami University

INSTITUTION INFORMATION
School of Engineering & Applied Science
Department of Engineering Technology
1601 Univiversity Blvd
Hamilton, OH 45011
Phone: (513) 785-3132
Fax: (513) 785-3183

GENERAL INFORMATION
[All Students - Fall 2006]
Undergraduate Enrollment	18,746
Graduate Enrollment	1,380
Professional Enrollment	0
Total Enrollment	**20,126**

ENGINEERING TECHNOLOGY COLLEGE INFORMATION

HEAD OF ENGINEERING TECHNOLOGY
Ayo Abatan
Chair and Professor
Miami University
School of Engineering & Applied Science, 532 Mosler Hall
Hamilton, OH 45011
Phone: (513) 785-3230
Fax: (513) 785-3145

TYPES OF ENGINEERING TECHNOLOGY DEGREES
2-year: Associate
Bachelor's: B.S.
Graduate:

ESTIMATED STUDENT EXPENSES (FALL 2006)
[Expenses are for the 2006-2007 nine-month academic year and are based on an average credit load of: Undergraduate: 16]

	In-State	Out-of-State
Tuition and fees:	$11,863	$31,103
Campus and Room and Board:	$8,140	$8,140
Books and Supplies:	$1,140	$1,140
Other Expenses:	$4,836	$4,836
Total Estimated Expenses:	**$25,979**	**$45,219**

NEW APPLICANTS/NEWLY ENROLLED STUDENTS
[Numbers are for the undergraduate engineering technology college for the Fall 2006 term]
Number of Applicants (a):	40
Of those, Number Offered Admission (b):	40
Of those, Number Enrolled Fall 2006 (c):	24

Michigan Technological University

INSTITUTION INFORMATION
School of Technology
1400 Townsend Dr
Houghton, MI 49931-1295
Phone: (906) 487-2259
Fax: (906) 487-2583
Web: www.tech.mtu.edu

GENERAL INFORMATION
[All Students - Fall 2006]
Undergraduate Enrollment	5,634
Graduate Enrollment	916
Professional Enrollment	0
Total Enrollment	**6,550**

ENGINEERING TECHNOLOGY COLLEGE INFORMATION

HEAD OF ENGINEERING TECHNOLOGY
Scott J Amos
Dean, School of Technology
Michigan Technological University
1400 Townsend Drive
Houghton, MI 49931-1295
Phone: (906) 487-2259
Fax: (906) 487-2583

TYPES OF ENGINEERING TECHNOLOGY DEGREES
2-year:
Bachelor's: B.S.
Graduate:

ESTIMATED STUDENT EXPENSES (FALL 2006)
[Expenses are for the 2006-2007 nine-month academic year and are based on an average credit load of: Undergraduate: 15]

	In-State	Out-of-State
Tuition and fees:	$8,910	$20,679
Campus and Room and Board:	$6,840	$6,840
Books and Supplies:	$1,000	$1,000
Other Expenses:	$1,763	$2,213
Total Estimated Expenses:	**$18,513**	**$30,732**

Note: Graduate Tuition & Fees are based on 12 credit hours.

NEW APPLICANTS/NEWLY ENROLLED STUDENTS
[Numbers are for the undergraduate engineering technology college for the Fall 2006 term]
Number of Applicants (a):	237
Of those, Number Offered Admission (b):	176
Of those, Number Enrolled Fall 2006 (c):	81

Milwaukee School of Engineering

INSTITUTION INFORMATION
1025 North Broadway
Milwaukee, WI 53202-3109
Phone: (800) 332-6763
Fax: (414) 277-7475
Web: http://www.msoe.edu

GENERAL INFORMATION
[All Students - Fall 2006]
Undergraduate Enrollment	2,203
Graduate Enrollment	224
Professional Enrollment	0
Total Enrollment	**2,427**

ENGINEERING TECHNOLOGY COLLEGE INFORMATION

TYPES OF ENGINEERING TECHNOLOGY DEGREES
2-year:
Bachelor's: B.S.
Graduate:

ESTIMATED STUDENT EXPENSES (FALL 2006)
[Expenses are for the 2006-2007 nine-month academic year and are based on an average credit load of: Undergraduate: 15]

	All Students
Tutition and fees:	$24,960
Campus and Room and Board:	$6,189
Books and Supplies:	$1,500
Other Expenses:	$5,140
Total Estimated Expenses:	**$37,789**

NEW APPLICANTS/NEWLY ENROLLED STUDENTS
[Numbers are for the undergraduate engineering technology college for the Fall 2006 term]

Number of Applicants (a):	41
Of those, Number Offered Admission (b):	38
Of those, Number Enrolled Fall 2006 (c):	18

Minnesota State University, Mankato

INSTITUTION INFORMATION
131 Trafton Science Center North
Mankato, MN 56001
Phone: (507) 389-5998
Fax: (507) 389-1095
Web: http://www.mnsu.edu

GENERAL INFORMATION
[All Students - Fall 2006]

Undergraduate Enrollment	12,684
Graduate Enrollment	1,651
Professional Enrollment	0
Total Enrollment	**14,335**

ENGINEERING TECHNOLOGY COLLEGE INFORMATION

TYPES OF ENGINEERING TECHNOLOGY DEGREES
2-year:
Bachelor's: B.S.
Graduate: M.S.

ESTIMATED STUDENT EXPENSES (FALL 2006)
[Expenses are for the 2006-2007 nine-month academic year and are based on an average credit load of: Undergraduate: 15]

	In-State	Out-of-State
Tutition and fees:	$5,840	$11,668
Campus and Room and Board:	$5,083	$5,083
Books and Supplies:	$920	$920
Other Expenses:	$2,600	$3,000
Total Estimated Expenses:	**$14,443**	**$20,671**

Montana State University

INSTITUTION INFORMATION
College of Engineering
212 Roberts Hall
PO Box 173820
Bozeman, MT 59717-3820
Phone: (406) 994-2272
Fax: (406) 994-6665
Web: http://www.montana.edu

GENERAL INFORMATION
[All Students - Fall 2006]

Undergraduate Enrollment	10,508
Graduate Enrollment	1,506
Professional Enrollment	324
Total Enrollment	**12,338**

ENGINEERING TECHNOLOGY COLLEGE INFORMATION

HEAD OF ENGINEERING TECHNOLOGY
Robert J Marley
Dean of Engineering
Montana State University
212 Roberts Hall, P.O. Box 173820
Bozeman, MT 59717-3820
Phone: (406) 994-2272
Fax: (406) 994-6665
Email: marley@coe.montana.edu

TYPES OF ENGINEERING TECHNOLOGY DEGREES
2-year:
Bachelor's: B.S.
Graduate: Master

ESTIMATED STUDENT EXPENSES (FALL 2006)
[Expenses are for the 2006-2007 nine-month academic year and are based on an average credit load of: Undergraduate: 12]

	In-State	Out-of-State
Tutition and fees:	$5,730	$15,580
Campus and Room and Board:	$6,450	$6,450
Books and Supplies:	$1,000	$1,000
Other Expenses:	$2,670	$2,670
Total Estimated Expenses:	**$15,850**	**$25,700**

Note: Tuition & Fees: Does not include a $702 per semester supplemental health insurance fee required of students who do not have proof of insurance coverage.
Room & Board: Food and housing costs will vary depending on a student's living arrangements and lifestyle. Room and board figures are an average of costs incurred by students living on campus in a residence hall and off campus in a shared apartment.

NEW APPLICANTS/NEWLY ENROLLED STUDENTS
[Numbers are for the undergraduate engineering technology college for the Fall 2006 term]

Number of Applicants (a):	93
Of those, Number Offered Admission (b):	72
Of those, Number Enrolled Fall 2006 (c):	43

University of Nebraska, Lincoln

INSTITUTION INFORMATION
114 Othmer Hall
P.O. Box 880642
NE 68588
Phone: (402) 472-3181
Fax: (402) 472-7792
Web: www.nuengr.unl.edu

GENERAL INFORMATION
[All Students - Fall 2006]

Undergraduate Enrollment	17,371
Graduate Enrollment	4,257
Professional Enrollment	478
Total Enrollment	**22,106**

ENGINEERING TECHNOLOGY COLLEGE INFORMATION

HEAD OF ENGINEERING TECHNOLOGY
Ray Moore
Associate Dean of Engineering - Omaha Campus
University of Nebraska, Lincoln
100C Peter Kewitt Institute
Omaha, NE 68182-0178
Phone: (402) 554-2460
Fax: (402) 554-3850
Email: rmoore5@unl.edu

TYPES OF ENGINEERING TECHNOLOGY DEGREES
2-year: Associate
Bachelor's: B.S., ATC
Graduate:

ESTIMATED STUDENT EXPENSES (FALL 2006)
[Expenses are for the 2006-2007 nine-month academic year and are based on an average credit load of: Undergraduate: 15]

	In-State	Out-of-State
Tutition and fees:	$4,800	$14,250
Campus and Room and Board:	$6,183	$6,183
Books and Supplies:	$924	$924
Other Expenses:	$1,167	$1,167
Total Estimated Expenses:	**$13,074**	**$22,524**

Note: Additional fees of $10 and $40 per credit hour for any course offered by the College of Engineering.

New Jersey Institute of Technology

INSTITUTION INFORMATION
University Heights
Newark, NJ 07102-1982
Phone: (973) 596-3000
Web: http://www.njit.edu

ENGINEERING TECHNOLOGY COLLEGE INFORMATION

HEAD OF ENGINEERING TECHNOLOGY
John R. Schuring
Dean
New Jersey Institute of Technology
University Heights
Newark, NJ 07102
Phone: (973) 596-5534
Email: john.schuring@njit.edu

TYPES OF ENGINEERING TECHNOLOGY DEGREES
2-year:
Bachelor's:
Graduate:

ESTIMATED STUDENT EXPENSES (FALL 2006)
[Expenses are for the 2006-2007 nine-month academic year and are based on an average credit load of: Undergraduate: N/A]

	In-State	Out-of-State
Tutition and fees:	$10,506	$17,290
Campus and Room and Board:	$8,980	$8,980
Books and Supplies:	$1,400	$1,400
Other Expenses:	$3,500	$3,500
Total Estimated Expenses:	**$24,386**	**$31,170**

NEW APPLICANTS/NEWLY ENROLLED STUDENTS
[Numbers are for the undergraduate engineering technology college for the Fall 2006 term]

Number of Applicants (a):	39
Of those, Number Offered Admission (b):	20
Of those, Number Enrolled Fall 2006 (c):	16

New Mexico State University

INSTITUTION INFORMATION
Engineering Technology
Box 30001, MSC 3566
Las Cruces 88003-8001
Phone: (505) 646-2236
Fax: (505) 646-6107
Web: http://www.et.nmsu.edu

GENERAL INFORMATION
[All Students - Fall 2006]

Undergraduate Enrollment	13,196
Graduate Enrollment	3,187
Professional Enrollment	0
Total Enrollment	**16,383**

ENGINEERING TECHNOLOGY COLLEGE INFORMATION

ENGINEERING TECHNOLOGY COLLEGE INQUIRIES
Sonya L Cooper
Academic Department Head
New Mexico State University
Engineering Technology, Box 30001, MSC 3566
Las Cruces, NM 88003-8001
Phone: (505) 646-2236
Fax: (505) 646-6107
Email: socooper@nmsu.edu

TYPES OF ENGINEERING TECHNOLOGY DEGREES
2-year: Associate
Bachelor's: B.S.
Graduate:

ESTIMATED STUDENT EXPENSES (FALL 2006)
[Expenses are for the 2006-2007 nine-month academic year and are based on an average credit load of: Undergraduate: 14]

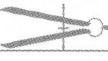

	In-State	Out-of-State
Tuition and fees:	$4,230	$13,804
Campus and Room and Board:	$5,800	$5,800
Books and Supplies:	$1,550	$1,550
Other Expenses:	$500	$500
Total Estimated Expenses:	**$12,080**	**$21,654**

NEW APPLICANTS/NEWLY ENROLLED STUDENTS
[Numbers are for the undergraduate engineering technology college for the Fall 2006 term]

Number of Applicants (a):	39
Of those, Number Offered Admission (b):	35
Of those, Number Enrolled Fall 2006 (c):	29

University of North Carolina, Charlotte

INSTITUTION INFORMATION
Department of Engineering Technology
The William States Lee College of Engineering
Charlotte, NC 28223-0001
Phone: (704) 687-2097
Fax: (704) 687-6653
Web: http://www.et.uncc.edu/

GENERAL INFORMATION
[All Students - Fall 2006]

Undergraduate Enrollment	17,032
Graduate Enrollment	4,487
Professional Enrollment	0
Total Enrollment	**21,519**

ENGINEERING TECHNOLOGY COLLEGE INFORMATION

ENGINEERING TECHNOLOGY COLLEGE INQUIRIES
Tara L Cavalline
Lecturer
University of North Carolina, Charlotte
9201 University City Boulevard
Charlotte, NC 28223-0001
Phone: (704) 687-6584
Fax: (704) 687-6653

TYPES OF ENGINEERING TECHNOLOGY DEGREES
2-year:
Bachelor's: B.S.
Graduate:

ESTIMATED STUDENT EXPENSES (FALL 2006)
[Expenses are for the 2006-2007 nine-month academic year and are based on an average credit load of: Undergraduate: 15]

	In-State	Out-of-State
Tuition and fees:	$3,899	$14,311
Campus and Room and Board:	$6,500	$6,500
Books and Supplies:	$1,200	$1,200
Other Expenses:	$1,520	$1,520
Total Estimated Expenses:	**$13,119**	**$23,531**

NEW APPLICANTS/NEWLY ENROLLED STUDENTS
[Numbers are for the undergraduate engineering technology college for the Fall 2006 term]

Number of Applicants (a):	153
Of those, Number Offered Admission (b):	109
Of those, Number Enrolled Fall 2006 (c):	82

University of North Texas

INSTITUTION INFORMATION
UNT Research Park, 3940 N. Elm Street
Denton 76207
Phone: (940) 565-2022
Fax: (940) 565-2666

GENERAL INFORMATION
[All Students - Fall 2006]

Undergraduate Enrollment	26,598
Graduate Enrollment	6,845
Professional Enrollment	0
Total Enrollment	**33,443**

ENGINEERING TECHNOLOGY COLLEGE INFORMATION

TYPES OF ENGINEERING TECHNOLOGY DEGREES
2-year:
Bachelor's: B.S.
Graduate: M.S.

ESTIMATED STUDENT EXPENSES (FALL 2006)
[Expenses are for the 2006-2007 nine-month academic year and are based on an average credit load of: Undergraduate: 15]

	In-State	Out-of-State
Tuition and fees:	$4,723	$11,347
Campus and Room and Board:	$6,108	$6,108
Books and Supplies:	$1,500	$1,500
Other Expenses:	$500	$500
Total Estimated Expenses:	**$12,831**	**$19,455**

Northeastern University

INSTITUTION INFORMATION
School of Engineering Technology
120 Snell Engineering Center
Boston, MA 02115
Phone: (617) 373-7777
Fax: (617) 373-2501
Web: http:www.coe.neu.edu/set

GENERAL INFORMATION
[All Students - Fall 2006]

Undergraduate Enrollment	18,056
Graduate Enrollment	4,780
Professional Enrollment	1,381
Total Enrollment	**24,217**

ENGINEERING TECHNOLOGY COLLEGE INFORMATION

TYPES OF ENGINEERING TECHNOLOGY DEGREES
2-year: Associate
Bachelor's: B.S.
Graduate:

ESTIMATED STUDENT EXPENSES (FALL 2006)
[Expenses are for the 2006-2007 nine-month academic year and are based on an average credit load of: Undergraduate: 17]

	All Students
Tuition and fees:	$29,910
Campus and Room and Board:	$10,580
Books and Supplies:	$1,200
Other Expenses:	$1,350
Total Estimated Expenses:	**$43,040**

Note: Room & Board costs vary by residence hall and meal plan. Books, supplies, and other expenses are estimates.

Northern Illinois University

INSTITUTION INFORMATION
College of Engineering & Engineering Technology
Still Gym 203
DeKalb, IL 60115
Phone: (815) 753-0531

GENERAL INFORMATION
[All Students - Fall 2006]

Undergraduate Enrollment	18,816
Graduate Enrollment	6,182
Professional Enrollment	315
Total Enrollment	**25,313**

ENGINEERING TECHNOLOGY COLLEGE INFORMATION

TYPES OF ENGINEERING TECHNOLOGY DEGREES
2-year:
Bachelor's: B.S.
Graduate:

ESTIMATED STUDENT EXPENSES (FALL 2006)
[Expenses are for the 2006-2007 nine-month academic year and are based on an average credit load of: Undergraduate: 15]

	In-State	Out-of-State
Tuition and fees:	$7,781	$13,421
Campus and Room and Board:	$7,488	$7,488
Books and Supplies:	$1,200	$1,200
Other Expenses:	$2,704	$2,704
Total Estimated Expenses:	**$19,173**	**$24,813**

Note: Room and Board: costs for housing varies depending on meal plan chosen, residence hall type, and room type ($4890-$8410)
Other Expenses: for undergrads includes medical insurance, transportation and personal. For graduate includes health insurance only.
A Technology Fee of $200 has been added for all students.

NEW APPLICANTS/NEWLY ENROLLED STUDENTS
[Numbers are for the undergraduate engineering technology college for the Fall 2006 term]

Number of Applicants (a):	71
Of those, Number Offered Admission (b):	38
Of those, Number Enrolled Fall 2006 (c):	18

Oklahoma State University

INSTITUTION INFORMATION
Division of Engineering Technology
294 Cordell South
Oklahoma State University
Stillwater, OK 74078
Phone: (405) 477-5638
Fax: (405) 744-7399
Web: http://www.tech.okstate.edu

GENERAL INFORMATION
[All Students - Fall 2006]

Undergraduate Enrollment	18,737
Graduate Enrollment	4,262
Professional Enrollment	308
Total Enrollment	**23,307**

ENGINEERING TECHNOLOGY COLLEGE INFORMATION

TYPES OF ENGINEERING TECHNOLOGY DEGREES
2-year:
Bachelor's: B.S.
Graduate:

ESTIMATED STUDENT EXPENSES (FALL 2006)
[Expenses are for the 2006-2007 nine-month academic year and are based on an average credit load of: Undergraduate: 15]

	In-State	Out-of-State
Tuition and fees:	$5,530	$14,100
Campus and Room and Board:	$5,848	$5,848
Books and Supplies:	$880	$880
Other Expenses:	$3,810	$3,810
Total Estimated Expenses:	**$16,068**	**$24,638**

NEW APPLICANTS/NEWLY ENROLLED STUDENTS
[Numbers are for the undergraduate engineering technology college for the Fall 2006 term]

Number of Applicants (a):	346
Of those, Number Offered Admission (b):	260
Of those, Number Enrolled Fall 2006 (c):	99

Old Dominion University

INSTITUTION INFORMATION
Frank Batten College of Engineering and Technology
Dean's Office
214 Kaufman Hall
Norfolk, VA 23529
Phone: (757) 683-3775
Fax: (757) 683-5655
Web: www.et.odu.edu

GENERAL INFORMATION

[All Students - Fall 2006]
Undergraduate Enrollment	14,209
Graduate Enrollment	6,593
Professional Enrollment	0
Total Enrollment	**20,802**

ENGINEERING TECHNOLOGY COLLEGE INFORMATION

HEAD OF ENGINEERING TECHNOLOGY

Gary R Crossman
Chair
Old Dominion University
214 Kaufman Hall
Norfolk, VA 23529
Phone: (757) 683-3765
Fax: (757) 683-5655

TYPES OF ENGINEERING TECHNOLOGY DEGREES

2-year:
Bachelor's: B.S.
Graduate:

ESTIMATED STUDENT EXPENSES (FALL 2006)

[Expenses are for the 2006-2007 nine-month academic year and are based on an average credit load of: Undergraduate: 15]

	In-State	Out-of-State
Tuition and fees:	$3,049	$8,329
Campus and Room and Board:	$6,640	$6,640
Books and Supplies:	$600	$600
Other Expenses:	$1,000	$1,000
Total Estimated Expenses:	**$11,289**	**$16,569**

NEW APPLICANTS/NEWLY ENROLLED STUDENTS

[Numbers are for the undergraduate engineering technology college for the Fall 2006 term]
Number of Applicants (a):	404
Of those, Number Offered Admission (b):	311
Of those, Number Enrolled Fall 2006 (c):	188

Oregon Institute of Technology

INSTITUTION INFORMATION

School of Engineering, Technology, and Management
3201 Campus Drive
Klamath Falls, OR 97601-8801
Phone: (541) 885-1000
Fax: (541) 885-1853
Web: http://www.oit.edu

GENERAL INFORMATION

[All Students - Fall 2006]
Undergraduate Enrollment	3,145
Graduate Enrollment	12
Professional Enrollment	0
Total Enrollment	**3,157**

ENGINEERING TECHNOLOGY COLLEGE INFORMATION

HEAD OF ENGINEERING TECHNOLOGY

Gary J Naseth
Associate Provost
Oregon Institute of Technology
3201 Campus Drive, Snell Hall 213
Klamath Falls, OR 97601-8801
Phone: (541) 885-1584
Fax: (541) 885-1853
Email: gary.naseth@oit.edu

ENGINEERING TECHNOLOGY COLLEGE INQUIRIES

Sean W St. Clair
Assistant Professor
Oregon Institute of Technology
3201 Campus Drive, Owens Hall 107
Klamath Falls, OR 97601-8801
Phone: (541) 885-1602
Fax: (541) 885-1654
Email: sean.stclair@oit.edu

TYPES OF ENGINEERING TECHNOLOGY DEGREES

2-year: Associate
Bachelor's: B.S.
Graduate:

ESTIMATED STUDENT EXPENSES (FALL 2006)

[Expenses are for the 2006-2007 nine-month academic year and are based on an average credit load of: Undergraduate: 14]

	In-State	Out-of-State
Tuition and fees:	$5,618	$13,356
Campus and Room and Board:	$7,552	$7,552
Books and Supplies:	$1,200	$1,200
Other Expenses:	$2,300	$2,300
Total Estimated Expenses:	**$16,670**	**$24,408**

NEW APPLICANTS/NEWLY ENROLLED STUDENTS

[Numbers are for the undergraduate engineering technology college for the Fall 2006 term]
Number of Applicants (a):	206
Of those, Number Offered Admission (b):	179
Of those, Number Enrolled Fall 2006 (c):	91

Penn State Erie, The Behrend College

INSTITUTION INFORMATION

School of Engineering
5101 Jordan Road
Erie, PA 16563-1701
Phone: (814) 898-6153
Fax: (814) 898-6125
Web: http://behrend.psu.edu

GENERAL INFORMATION

[All Students - Fall 2006]
Undergraduate Enrollment	3,675
Graduate Enrollment	164
Professional Enrollment	0
Total Enrollment	**3,839**

ENGINEERING TECHNOLOGY COLLEGE INFORMATION

HEAD OF ENGINEERING TECHNOLOGY

Ralph M Ford
Director
Penn State Erie, The Behrend College
5101 Jordan Road
Erie, PA 16563-1701
Phone: (814) 898-6153
Fax: (814) 898-6125
Email: rmf7@psu.edu

TYPES OF ENGINEERING TECHNOLOGY DEGREES

2-year: Associate
Bachelor's: B.S.
Graduate:

ESTIMATED STUDENT EXPENSES (FALL 2006)

[Expenses are for the 2006-2007 nine-month academic year and are based on an average credit load of: Undergraduate: N/A]

	In-State	Out-of-State
Tuition and fees:	$10,446	$15,994
Campus and Room and Board:	$6,850	$6,850
Books and Supplies:	$1,100	$1,100
Other Expenses:		
Total Estimated Expenses:	**$18,396**	**$23,944**

NEW APPLICANTS/NEWLY ENROLLED STUDENTS

[Numbers are for the undergraduate engineering technology college for the Fall 2006 term]
Number of Applicants (a):	77
Of those, Number Offered Admission (b):	73
Of those, Number Enrolled Fall 2006 (c):	56

Pittsburg State University

INSTITUTION INFORMATION

Department of Engineering Technology
1701 South Broadway

Pittsburg, KS 66762
Phone: (620) 235-4350
Fax: (620) 235-4004
Web: www.pittstate.edu/etech

GENERAL INFORMATION

[All Students - Fall 2006]
Undergraduate Enrollment	5,747
Graduate Enrollment	1,112
Professional Enrollment	0
Total Enrollment	**6,859**

ENGINEERING TECHNOLOGY COLLEGE INFORMATION

TYPES OF ENGINEERING TECHNOLOGY DEGREES

2-year:
Bachelor's: B.S.,B.S.E.T.
Graduate: M.S. M.E.T.

ESTIMATED STUDENT EXPENSES (FALL 2006)

[Expenses are for the 2006-2007 nine-month academic year and are based on an average credit load of: Undergraduate: 16]

	In-State	Out-of-State
Tuition and fees:	$3,800	$11,120
Campus and Room and Board:	$4,850	$4,850
Books and Supplies:	$1,000	$1,000
Other Expenses:		
Total Estimated Expenses:	**$9,650**	**$16,970**

NEW APPLICANTS/NEWLY ENROLLED STUDENTS

[Numbers are for the undergraduate engineering technology college for the Fall 2006 term]
Number of Applicants (a):	108
Of those, Number Offered Admission (b):	108
Of those, Number Enrolled Fall 2006 (c):	88

Prairie View A&M University

INSTITUTION INFORMATION

Department of Engineering Technology
P.O. Box 519 MS 2530
College of Engineering
Prairie View, TX 77446
Phone: (936) 261-9846
Fax: (936) 857-2097
Web: www.pvamu.edu

GENERAL INFORMATION

[All Students - Fall 2006]
Undergraduate Enrollment	5,758
Graduate Enrollment	2,204
Professional Enrollment	0
Total Enrollment	**7,962**

ENGINEERING TECHNOLOGY COLLEGE INFORMATION

TYPES OF ENGINEERING TECHNOLOGY DEGREES

2-year:
Bachelor's: B.S.
Graduate:

ESTIMATED STUDENT EXPENSES (FALL 2006)

[Expenses are for the 2006-2007 nine-month academic year and are based on an average credit load of: Undergraduate: 15]

	In-State	Out-of-State
Tuition and fees:	$5,533	$13,783
Campus and Room and Board:	$6,158	$6,158
Books and Supplies:	$800	$800
Other Expenses:	$80	$80
Total Estimated Expenses:	**$12,571**	**$20,821**

NEW APPLICANTS/NEWLY ENROLLED STUDENTS

[Numbers are for the undergraduate engineering technology college for the Fall 2006 term]
Number of Applicants (a):	75
Of those, Number Offered Admission (b):	24
Of those, Number Enrolled Fall 2006 (c):	23

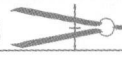

Purdue University College of Technology

INSTITUTION INFORMATION
College of Technology
Purdue University College of Technology
401 N Grant St, Knoy Hall
West Lafayette, IN 47907
Phone: (765) 494-4935
Fax: (765) 496-1924
Web: http://www.tech.purdue.edu

GENERAL INFORMATION
[All Students - Fall 2006]

Undergraduate Enrollment	30,875
Graduate Enrollment	6,932
Professional Enrollment	905
Total Enrollment	**38,712**

ENGINEERING TECHNOLOGY COLLEGE INFORMATION

HEAD OF ENGINEERING TECHNOLOGY
Dennis R. Depew
Dean
Purdue University - Main Campus
401 N. Grant Street
West Lafayette, IN 47907-2021
Phone: (765) 494-2552
Fax: (765) 494-0486
Email: bec@purdue.edu

TYPES OF ENGINEERING TECHNOLOGY DEGREES
2-year: Associate
Bachelor's: B.S.
Graduate: M.S.

ESTIMATED STUDENT EXPENSES (FALL 2006)
[Expenses are for the 2006-2007 nine-month academic year and are based on an average credit load of: Undergraduate: 17]

	In-State	Out-of-State
Tuition and fees:	$6,458	$19,824
Campus and Room and Board:	$6,830	$6,830
Books and Supplies:	$980	$980
Other Expenses:	$1,800	$1,890
Total Estimated Expenses:	**$16,068**	**$29,524**

NEW APPLICANTS/NEWLY ENROLLED STUDENTS
[Numbers are for the undergraduate engineering technology college for the Fall 2006 term]

Number of Applicants (a):	363
Of those, Number Offered Admission (b):	335
Of those, Number Enrolled Fall 2006 (c):	192

Rochester Institute of Technology

INSTITUTION INFORMATION
Undergraduate Admissions Office
60 Lomb Memorial Dr.
Rochester, NY 14623-5604
Phone: (585) 475-6631
Web: www.rit.edu/admissions

GENERAL INFORMATION
[All Students - Fall 2006]

Undergraduate Enrollment	13,140
Graduate Enrollment	2,417
Professional Enrollment	0
Total Enrollment	**15,557**

ENGINEERING TECHNOLOGY COLLEGE INFORMATION

HEAD OF ENGINEERING TECHNOLOGY
Carol Richardson
Interim Dean, College of Applied Science and Technology
Rochester Institute of Technology
15 Lomb Memorial Drive
Rochester, NY 14623-5603
Phone: (585) 475-5955
Fax: (585) 475-7080

TYPES OF ENGINEERING TECHNOLOGY DEGREES
2-year: Associate
Bachelor's: B.S.
Graduate: M.S.

ESTIMATED STUDENT EXPENSES (FALL 2006)
[Expenses are for the 2006-2007 nine-month academic year and are based on an average credit load of: Undergraduate: 16]

	All Students
Tuition and fees:	$25,011
Campus and Room and Board:	$8,748
Books and Supplies:	$900
Other Expenses:	$1,025
Total Estimated Expenses:	**$35,684**

NEW APPLICANTS/NEWLY ENROLLED STUDENTS
[Numbers are for the undergraduate engineering technology college for the Fall 2006 term]

Number of Applicants (a):	1,190
Of those, Number Offered Admission (b):	911
Of those, Number Enrolled Fall 2006 (c):	309

Saint Louis University - Parks College

INSTITUTION INFORMATION
3450 Lindell Boulevard
St. Louis, MO 63103
Phone: (314) 977-8207
Fax: (314) 977-8403
Web: parks.slu.edu

GENERAL INFORMATION
[All Students - Fall 2006]

Undergraduate Enrollment	7,420
Graduate Enrollment	2,100
Professional Enrollment	2,300
Total Enrollment	**11,820**

ENGINEERING TECHNOLOGY COLLEGE INFORMATION

HEAD OF ENGINEERING TECHNOLOGY
Manoj Patankar
Interim Dean
Saint Louis University - Parks College
3450 Lindell Blvd
St. Louis, MO 63103
Phone: (314) 977-8203
Fax: (314) 977-8403
Email: patankar@slu.edu

TYPES OF ENGINEERING TECHNOLOGY DEGREES
2-year:
Bachelor's: B.S.
Graduate:

ESTIMATED STUDENT EXPENSES (FALL 2006)
[Expenses are for the 2006-2007 nine-month academic year and are based on an average credit load of: Undergraduate: 14]

	All Students
Tuition and fees:	$26,250
Campus and Room and Board:	$8,000
Books and Supplies:	$1,040
Other Expenses:	$1,030
Total Estimated Expenses:	**$36,320**

NEW APPLICANTS/NEWLY ENROLLED STUDENTS
[Numbers are for the undergraduate engineering technology college for the Fall 2006 term]

Number of Applicants (a):	120
Of those, Number Offered Admission (b):	70
Of those, Number Enrolled Fall 2006 (c):	9

South Dakota State University

INSTITUTION INFORMATION
Engineering Technology & Management
SOH 116 Box 2223
Brookings, SD 57007

Phone: (605) 688-6417
Fax: (605) 688-5041
Web: http://www3.sdstate.edu/Academics/CollegeOf Engineering/redirect/EngineeringTechnology Management/Index.cfm

GENERAL INFORMATION
[All Students - Fall 2006]

Undergraduate Enrollment	9,852
Graduate Enrollment	1,281
Professional Enrollment	244
Total Enrollment	**11,377**

ENGINEERING TECHNOLOGY COLLEGE INFORMATION

ENGINEERING TECHNOLOGY COLLEGE INQUIRIES
Lewis F Brown
Dean of Engineering
South Dakota State University
CEH 201 Box 2219
Brookings, SD 57007
Phone: (605) 688-4161
Fax: (605) 688-5878
Email: lewis.brown@sdstate.edu

TYPES OF ENGINEERING TECHNOLOGY DEGREES
2-year:
Bachelor's: B.S.
Graduate:

ESTIMATED STUDENT EXPENSES (FALL 2006)
[Expenses are for the 2006-2007 nine-month academic year and are based on an average credit load of: Undergraduate: 16]

	In-State	Out-of-State
Tuition and fees:	$5,751	$7,031
Campus and Room and Board:	$4,240	$4,240
Books and Supplies:	$750	$750
Other Expenses:	$600	$600
Total Estimated Expenses:	**$11,341**	**$12,621**

NEW APPLICANTS/NEWLY ENROLLED STUDENTS
[Numbers are for the undergraduate engineering technology college for the Fall 2006 term]

Number of Applicants (a):	45
Of those, Number Offered Admission (b):	41
Of those, Number Enrolled Fall 2006 (c):	37

Southern Illinois University Carbondale

INSTITUTION INFORMATION
College of Engineering
Department of Technology
Carbondale, IL 62901
Phone: (161) 853-6339
Fax: (161) 845-4235
Web: www.engr.siu.edu

GENERAL INFORMATION
[All Students - Fall 2006]

Undergraduate Enrollment	16,294
Graduate Enrollment	3,999
Professional Enrollment	710
Total Enrollment	**21,003**

ENGINEERING TECHNOLOGY COLLEGE INFORMATION

HEAD OF ENGINEERING TECHNOLOGY
William P. Osborne
Dean
Southern Illinois University Carbondale
Office of the Dean, Southern Illinois University Carbondale
Carbondale, IL 62901
Phone: (618) 453-4321
Fax: (618) 453-4235
Email: wosborne@siu.edu

TYPES OF ENGINEERING TECHNOLOGY DEGREES
2-year:
Bachelor's: B.S.
Graduate:

ESTIMATED STUDENT EXPENSES (FALL 2006)
[Expenses are for the 2006-2007 nine-month academic year and are based on an average credit load of: Undergraduate: 15]

	In-State	Out-of-State
Tuition and fees:	$7,795	$16,507
Campus and Room and Board:	$6,138	$6,138
Books and Supplies:	$900	$900
Other Expenses:	$2,417	$2,417
Total Estimated Expenses:	**$17,250**	**$25,962**

Note: Undergraduate students who entered SIUC beginning Fall 2004 or later are guaranteed the same tuition rate for four continuous academic years.

NEW APPLICANTS/NEWLY ENROLLED STUDENTS
[Numbers are for the undergraduate engineering technology college for the Fall 2006 term]

Number of Applicants (a):	29
Of those, Number Offered Admission (b):	28
Of those, Number Enrolled Fall 2006 (c):	6

Southern Polytechnic State University

INSTITUTION INFORMATION
School of Engineering Technology and Management
1100 South Marietta Pkwy
Marietta, GA 30060-2896
Phone: (678) 915-7234
Fax: (678) 915-7134
Web: http://www.spsu.edu/home/academics/engineering.html

GENERAL INFORMATION
[All Students - Fall 2006]

Undergraduate Enrollment	3,701
Graduate Enrollment	503
Professional Enrollment	0
Total Enrollment	**4,204**

ENGINEERING TECHNOLOGY COLLEGE INFORMATION

HEAD OF ENGINEERING TECHNOLOGY
David Caudill
Interim Dean
Southern Polytechnic State University
1100 South Marietta Pkwy
Marietta, GA 30060-2896
Phone: (678) 915-7234
Fax: (678) 915-7134
Email: dcaudill@spsu.edu

HEAD OF ENGINEERING TECHNOLOGY
Wilson C Barnes
Dean
Southern Polytechnic State University
1100 South Marietta Pkwy
Marietta, GA 30060-2896
Phone: (678) 915-5481
Fax: (678) 915-3945
Email: wbarnes@spsu.edu

TYPES OF ENGINEERING TECHNOLOGY DEGREES
2-year:
Bachelor's: B.S.
Graduate: M.S.

ESTIMATED STUDENT EXPENSES (FALL 2006)
[Expenses are for the 2006-2007 nine-month academic year and are based on an average credit load of: Undergraduate: 12]

	In-State	Out-of-State
Tuition and fees:	$3,374	$11,788
Campus and Room and Board:	$5,610	$5,610
Books and Supplies:	$1,500	$1,500
Other Expenses:	$3,900	$3,900
Total Estimated Expenses:	**$14,384**	**$22,798**

NEW APPLICANTS/NEWLY ENROLLED STUDENTS
[Numbers are for the undergraduate engineering technology college for the Fall 2006 term]

Number of Applicants (a):	482
Of those, Number Offered Admission (b):	319
Of those, Number Enrolled Fall 2006 (c):	196

Southern University and A&M College

INSTITUTION INFORMATION
Electronics Engineering Technology
P.B.S. Pinchback Engr Building
Southern University and A&M College
Baton Rouge, LA 70813
Phone: (225) 771-4052
Fax: (225) 771-9828
Web: http://www.engr.subr.edu/eet/

GENERAL INFORMATION
[All Students - Fall 2006]

Undergraduate Enrollment	8,500
Graduate Enrollment	1,200
Professional Enrollment	0
Total Enrollment	**9,700**

ENGINEERING TECHNOLOGY COLLEGE INFORMATION

ENGINEERING TECHNOLOGY COLLEGE INQUIRIES
Charles L Burris
Associate Dean
Southern University and A&M College
P.B. S. Pinchback Engr Building, P.O. Box 9969
Baton Rouge, LA 70813
Phone: (225) 771-5292
Fax: (225) 771-5721
Email: cburris@engr.subr.edu

TYPES OF ENGINEERING TECHNOLOGY DEGREES
2-year:
Bachelor's: B.S.
Graduate:

ESTIMATED STUDENT EXPENSES (FALL 2006)
[Expenses are for the 2006-2007 nine-month academic year and are based on an average credit load of: Undergraduate: N/A]

	In-State	Out-of-State
Tuition and fees:	$3,602	$5,792
Campus and Room and Board:	$4,000	$4,000
Books and Supplies:		
Other Expenses:		
Total Estimated Expenses:	**$7,602**	**$9,792**

Note: Fees and Expenses are subject to change without prior notice.

Temple University

INSTITUTION INFORMATION
1947 12th Street N
College of Engineering
Philadelphia, PA 19122
Phone: (215) 204-7800
Fax: (215) 204-6936
Web: http://www.eng.temple.edu

GENERAL INFORMATION
[All Students - Fall 2006]

Undergraduate Enrollment	24,197
Graduate Enrollment	4,870
Professional Enrollment	3,093
Total Enrollment	**32,160**

ENGINEERING TECHNOLOGY COLLEGE INFORMATION

TYPES OF ENGINEERING TECHNOLOGY DEGREES
2-year:
Bachelor's: B.S.
Graduate:

ESTIMATED STUDENT EXPENSES (FALL 2006)
[Expenses are for the 2006-2007 nine-month academic year and are based on an average credit load of: Undergraduate: 16]

	In-State	Out-of-State
Tuition and fees:	$10,180	$18,224
Campus and Room and Board:	$8,230	$8,230
Books and Supplies:	$1,200	$1,200
Other Expenses:	$750	$750
Total Estimated Expenses:	**$20,360**	**$28,404**

Note: Above expenses are for the academic year, that is two semesters.

NEW APPLICANTS/NEWLY ENROLLED STUDENTS
[Numbers are for the undergraduate engineering technology college for the Fall 2006 term]

Number of Applicants (a):	90
Of those, Number Offered Admission (b):	43
Of those, Number Enrolled Fall 2006 (c):	16

University of Tennessee, Chattanooga

INSTITUTION INFORMATION
College of Engineering & Computer Science
615 McCallie Avenue Dept 2452
Chattanooga, TN 37403-2598
Phone: (423) 425-2256
Web: http://www.utc.edu/Academic/Engineering/

GENERAL INFORMATION
[All Students - Fall 2006]

Undergraduate Enrollment	7,544
Graduate Enrollment	1,379
Professional Enrollment	0
Total Enrollment	**8,923**

ENGINEERING TECHNOLOGY COLLEGE INFORMATION

TYPES OF ENGINEERING TECHNOLOGY DEGREES
2-year:
Bachelor's:
Graduate:

ESTIMATED STUDENT EXPENSES (FALL 2006)
[Expenses are for the 2006-2007 nine-month academic year and are based on an average credit load of: Undergraduate: 12]

	In-State	Out-of-State
Tuition and fees:	$4,688	$14,084
Campus and Room and Board:	$7,384	$7,384
Books and Supplies:	$950	$950
Other Expenses:	$3,032	$3,032
Total Estimated Expenses:	**$16,054**	**$25,450**

Texas A&M University

INSTITUTION INFORMATION
College of Engineering
TAMU 3470
College Station, TX 77843-3470
Phone: (979) 845-4951
Fax: (979) 847-9396
Web: http://etidweb.tamu.edu

GENERAL INFORMATION
[All Students - Fall 2006]

Undergraduate Enrollment	36,580
Graduate Enrollment	8,291
Professional Enrollment	509
Total Enrollment	**45,380**

ENGINEERING TECHNOLOGY COLLEGE INFORMATION

HEAD OF ENGINEERING TECHNOLOGY
G. Kemble Bennett, Jr.
Dean of Engineering
Texas A&M University
Dean of Engineering, TAMU 3126
College Station, TX 77843-3126
Phone: (979) 845-1321
Fax: (979) 845-8986
Email: engineeringadmin@tamu.edu

TYPES OF ENGINEERING TECHNOLOGY DEGREES
2-year:
Bachelor's: B.S.
Graduate:

ESTIMATED STUDENT EXPENSES (FALL 2006)
[Expenses are for the 2006-2007 nine-month academic year

and are based on an average credit load of: Undergraduate: 15]

	In-State	Out-of-State
Tutition and fees:	$6,966	$15,216
Campus and Room and Board:	$7,660	$7,660
Books and Supplies:	$1,280	$1,280
Other Expenses:	$2,552	$2,552
Total Estimated Expenses:	**$18,458**	**$26,708**

Note: Tuition & Fees: Based on 15 SCH flat rate for Undergraduate and 9 SCH for Graduate. Other Expenses are personal expenses and transportation.

NEW APPLICANTS/NEWLY ENROLLED STUDENTS
[Numbers are for the undergraduate engineering technology college for the Fall 2006 term]

Number of Applicants (a):	73
Of those, Number Offered Admission (b):	52
Of those, Number Enrolled Fall 2006 (c):	32

Texas Tech University

INSTITUTION INFORMATION
Box 43107
Lubbock, TX 79409-5005
Phone: (806) 742-3538
Fax: (806) 742-1699
Web: http://www.ttu.edu

GENERAL INFORMATION
[All Students - Fall 2006]

Undergraduate Enrollment	22,851
Graduate Enrollment	4,443
Professional Enrollment	702
Total Enrollment	**27,996**

ENGINEERING TECHNOLOGY COLLEGE INFORMATION

TYPES OF ENGINEERING TECHNOLOGY DEGREES
2-year:
Bachelor's: B.S.
Graduate:

ESTIMATED STUDENT EXPENSES (FALL 2006)
[Expenses are for the 2006-2007 nine-month academic year and are based on an average credit load of: Undergraduate: 30]

	In-State	Out-of-State
Tutition and fees:	$6,459	$14,709
Campus and Room and Board:	$7,288	$7,288
Books and Supplies:	$900	$900
Other Expenses:	$1,800	$1,800
Total Estimated Expenses:	**$16,447**	**$24,697**

NEW APPLICANTS/NEWLY ENROLLED STUDENTS
[Numbers are for the undergraduate engineering technology college for the Fall 2006 term]

Number of Applicants (a):	106
Of those, Number Offered Admission (b):	67
Of those, Number Enrolled Fall 2006 (c):	28

The University of Toledo

INSTITUTION INFORMATION
2801 West Bancroft Street
Toledo, OH 43606-3390
Phone: (419) 530-4636
Web: http://www.utoledo.edu

GENERAL INFORMATION
[All Students - Fall 2006]

Undergraduate Enrollment	16,067
Graduate Enrollment	2,775
Professional Enrollment	1,873
Total Enrollment	**20,715**

ENGINEERING TECHNOLOGY COLLEGE INFORMATION

HEAD OF ENGINEERING TECHNOLOGY
Nagi G Naganathan
Dean / Professor
The University of Toledo
5012 Nitschke Hall

Toledo, OH 43606-3390
Phone: (419) 530-8000
Fax: (419) 530-8006
Email: nagi.naganathan@utoledo.edu

HEAD OF ENGINEERING TECHNOLOGY
Daniel Solarek
Chair of Engineering Technology / Professor
The University of Toledo
1111 Engineering Technology Center
Toledo, OH 43606-3390
Phone: (419) 530-8121
Fax: (419) 530-3068
Email: dsolarek@toledolink.com

ENGINEERING TECHNOLOGY COLLEGE INQUIRIES
Brian W Randolph
Assoc Dean of Undergraduate Studies/ Professor
The University of Toledo
3006 Nitschke Hall
Toledo, OH 43606-3390
Phone: (419) 530-8121
Fax: (419) 530-8046
Email: brandolp@eng.utoledo.edu

ENGINEERING TECHNOLOGY COLLEGE INQUIRIES
Bruce E Poling
Director of Assessment/Prof
The University of Toledo
5025 Nitschke Hall
Toledo, OH 43606-3390
Phone: (419) 530-8255
Fax: (419) 530-8006
Email: bpoling@eng.utoledo.edu

ENGINEERING TECHNOLOGY COLLEGE INQUIRIES
Daniel Solarek
Chair of Engineering Technology / Professor
The University of Toledo
1111 Engineering Technology Center
Toledo, OH 43606-3390
Phone: (419) 530-8121
Fax: (419) 530-3068
Email: dsolarek@toledolink.com

ENGINEERING TECHNOLOGY COLLEGE INQUIRIES
Myrna Swanberg
Academic Program Coordinator
The University of Toledo
2801 West Bancroft Street
Toledo, OH 43606-3390
Phone: (419) 530-8121
Fax: (419) 530-3068

TYPES OF ENGINEERING TECHNOLOGY DEGREES
2-year:
Bachelor's: B.S.
Graduate:

ESTIMATED STUDENT EXPENSES (FALL 2006)
[Expenses are for the 2006-2007 nine-month academic year and are based on an average credit load of: Undergraduate: 16]

	In-State	Out-of-State
Tutition and fees:	$8,178	$16,989
Campus and Room and Board:	$8,140	$8,140
Books and Supplies:	$900	$900
Other Expenses:		
Total Estimated Expenses:	**$17,218**	**$26,029**

NEW APPLICANTS/NEWLY ENROLLED STUDENTS
[Numbers are for the undergraduate engineering technology college for the Fall 2006 term]

Number of Applicants (a):	392
Of those, Number Offered Admission (b):	225
Of those, Number Enrolled Fall 2006 (c):	113

Tri-State University

INSTITUTION INFORMATION
1 University Avenue
Angola, IN 46703-1764
Phone: (260) 665-4100
Fax: (260) 665-4578
Web: http://www.tristate.edu

GENERAL INFORMATION
[All Students - Fall 2006]

Undergraduate Enrollment	1,460
Graduate Enrollment	7
Professional Enrollment	0
Total Enrollment	**1,467**

ENGINEERING TECHNOLOGY COLLEGE INFORMATION

HEAD OF ENGINEERING TECHNOLOGY
Roger J Hawks
Dean of Allen School of Engineering and Technology
Tri-State University
1 University Avenue
Angola, IN 46703-1764
Phone: (260) 665-4228
Fax: (260) 665-4188
Email: hawksr@tristate.edu

TYPES OF ENGINEERING TECHNOLOGY DEGREES
2-year: Associate
Bachelor's: B.S.
Graduate: M.S.

ESTIMATED STUDENT EXPENSES (FALL 2006)
[Expenses are for the 2006-2007 nine-month academic year and are based on an average credit load of: Undergraduate: 16]

	All Students
Tutition and fees:	$21,210
Campus and Room and Board:	$6,240
Books and Supplies:	
Other Expenses:	
Total Estimated Expenses:	**$27,450**

NEW APPLICANTS/NEWLY ENROLLED STUDENTS
[Numbers are for the undergraduate engineering technology college for the Fall 2006 term]

Number of Applicants (a):	29
Of those, Number Offered Admission (b):	24
Of those, Number Enrolled Fall 2006 (c):	11

Wayne State University

INSTITUTION INFORMATION
Division of Engineering Technology
4855 Fourth Street
Detroit, MI 48201
Phone: (131) 357-7080
Fax: (131) 357-1781
Web: http://www.eng.wayne.edu

GENERAL INFORMATION
[All Students - Fall 2006]

Undergraduate Enrollment	20,892
Graduate Enrollment	9,078
Professional Enrollment	3,012
Total Enrollment	**32,982**

ENGINEERING TECHNOLOGY COLLEGE INFORMATION

HEAD OF ENGINEERING TECHNOLOGY
Chih-Ping Yeh
Associate Professor and Division Chair
Wayne State University
4855 Fourth Street, 1154 Engineering Technology
Detroit, MI 48202
Phone: (313) 577-3817
Fax: (313) 577-1781
Email: yeh@eng.wayne.edu

ENGINEERING TECHNOLOGY COLLEGE INQUIRIES
Chih-Ping Yeh
Associate Professor and Division Chair
Wayne State University
4855 Fourth Street, 1154 Engineering Technology
Detroit, MI 48202
Phone: (313) 577-3817
Fax: (313) 577-1781
Email: yeh@eng.wayne.edu

TYPES OF ENGINEERING TECHNOLOGY DEGREES
2-year:
Bachelor's: B.S.
Graduate: M.S.

ESTIMATED STUDENT EXPENSES (FALL 2006)
[Expenses are for the 2006-2007 nine-month academic year and are based on an average credit load of: Undergraduate: 14]

	In-State	Out-of-State
Tutition and fees:	$7,332	$15,928
Campus and Room and Board:	$7,014	$7,014
Books and Supplies:	$835	$835
Other Expenses:	$3,669	$3,669
Total Estimated Expenses:	**$18,850**	**$27,446**

Note: Provided figures are for a 9-month budget (Fall and Winter semesters). Tuition rates are for 28 credits for undergraduates (upper division), 16 credits for graduate students, over an academic year.

Weber State University

INSTITUTION INFORMATION
College of Applied Science & Technology
1801 University Circle
Ogden, UT 84408-1001
Phone: (801) 626-6304
Fax: (801) 626-6987

GENERAL INFORMATION
[All Students - Fall 2006]

Undergraduate Enrollment	18,303
Graduate Enrollment	454
Professional Enrollment	4
Total Enrollment	**18,761**

ENGINEERING TECHNOLOGY COLLEGE INFORMATION

HEAD OF ENGINEERING TECHNOLOGY
Warren R Hill
Dean and Professor
Weber State University
1801 University Circle
Ogden, UT 84408-1801
Phone: (801) 626-6304
Fax: (801) 626-6987
Email: whill@weber.edu

TYPES OF ENGINEERING TECHNOLOGY DEGREES
2-year: Associate
Bachelor's: B.S.
Graduate:

ESTIMATED STUDENT EXPENSES (FALL 2006)
[Expenses are for the 2006-2007 nine-month academic year and are based on an average credit load of: Undergraduate: 12]

	In-State	Out-of-State
Tutition and fees:	$3,434	$10,417
Campus and Room and Board:	$4,600	$4,600
Books and Supplies:	$800	$800
Other Expenses:	$250	$250
Total Estimated Expenses:	**$9,084**	**$16,067**

Wentworth Institute of Technology

INSTITUTION INFORMATION
550 Huntington Avenue
Boston, MA 02115
Phone: (617) 989-4590
Fax: (617) 989-4591
Web: http://www.wit.edu

GENERAL INFORMATION
[All Students - Fall 2006]

Undergraduate Enrollment	3,613
Graduate Enrollment	0
Professional Enrollment	0
Total Enrollment	**3,613**

ENGINEERING TECHNOLOGY COLLEGE INFORMATION

TYPES OF ENGINEERING TECHNOLOGY DEGREES
2-year: Associate
Bachelor's: B.S.
Graduate:

ESTIMATED STUDENT EXPENSES (FALL 2006)
[Expenses are for the 2006-2007 nine-month academic year and are based on an average credit load of: Undergraduate: 16]

	All Students
Tutition and fees:	$19,300
Campus and Room and Board:	$9,300
Books and Supplies:	$1,000
Other Expenses:	$900
Total Estimated Expenses:	**$30,500**

NEW APPLICANTS/NEWLY ENROLLED STUDENTS
[Numbers are for the undergraduate engineering technology college for the Fall 2006 term]

Number of Applicants (a):	1,358
Of those, Number Offered Admission (b):	1,073
Of those, Number Enrolled Fall 2006 (c):	428

West Virginia Institute of Technology, ET&IT

INSTITUTION INFORMATION
405 Fayette Pike
Montgomery, WV 25136
Phone: (304) 442-3000
Fax: (304) 442-3245
Web: http://ctc.wvutech.edu/

GENERAL INFORMATION
[All Students - Fall 2006]

Undergraduate Enrollment	600
Graduate Enrollment	0
Professional Enrollment	0
Total Enrollment	**600**

ENGINEERING TECHNOLOGY COLLEGE INFORMATION

HEAD OF ENGINEERING TECHNOLOGY
Thomas G. Minnich
Division Director
West Virginia Institute of Technology, ET&IT
Montgomery, WV 25136
Phone: (304) 442-3000
Fax: (304) 442-3245
Email: thomas.minnich@mail.wvu.edu

TYPES OF ENGINEERING TECHNOLOGY DEGREES
2-year:
Bachelor's:
Graduate:

ESTIMATED STUDENT EXPENSES (FALL 2006)
[Expenses are for the 2006-2007 nine-month academic year and are based on an average credit load of: Undergraduate: 16]

	In-State	Out-of-State
Tutition and fees:	$3,316	$10,932
Campus and Room and Board:	$6,664	$6,664
Books and Supplies:	$1,339	$1,339
Other Expenses:		
Total Estimated Expenses:	**$11,319**	**$18,935**

Western Michigan University

INSTITUTION INFORMATION
Engineering and Applied Sciences
1903 W. Michigan Avenue
Kalamazoo, MI 49008-5314
Phone: (269) 276-3253
Fax: (269) 276-3257
Web: http://www.wmich.edu/engineer

GENERAL INFORMATION
[All Students - Fall 2006]

Undergraduate Enrollment	19,261
Graduate Enrollment	4,544
Professional Enrollment	0
Total Enrollment	**23,805**

ENGINEERING TECHNOLOGY COLLEGE INFORMATION

TYPES OF ENGINEERING TECHNOLOGY DEGREES
2-year:
Bachelor's: B.S.
Graduate:

ESTIMATED STUDENT EXPENSES (FALL 2006)
[Expenses are for the 2006-2007 nine-month academic year and are based on an average credit load of: Undergraduate: 16]

	In-State	Out-of-State
Tutition and fees:	$6,866	$16,806
Campus and Room and Board:	$6,877	$6,877
Books and Supplies:	$906	$906
Other Expenses:	$3,008	$3,524
Total Estimated Expenses:	**$17,657**	**$28,113**

NEW APPLICANTS/NEWLY ENROLLED STUDENTS
[Numbers are for the undergraduate engineering technology college for the Fall 2006 term]

Number of Applicants (a):	90
Of those, Number Offered Admission (b):	60
Of those, Number Enrolled Fall 2006 (c):	26

2006 Indexes of Engineering and Engineering Technology Colleges and Programs

ALPHABETICAL INDEX OF PARTICIPATING ENGINEERING INSTITUTIONS

A

Air Force Institute of Technology (G)
The University of Akron (UG,G)
Alabama A&M University (UG)
University of Alabama at Birmingham (UG,G)
The University of Alabama in Huntsville (UG,G)
The University of Alabama (UG,G)
University of Alaska, Anchorage (UG)
University of Alaska Fairbanks (UG,G)
University of Alberta (UG,G)
Alfred University, NY State College of Ceramics (UG,G)
The University of Arizona (UG,G)
Arizona State University (UG,G)
University of Arkansas (UG,G)
Arkansas State University (UG)
Arkansas Tech University (UG)
University of Arkansas at Little Rock (UG)
Auburn University (UG,G)

B

Baker College (UG,G)
Baylor University (UG,G)
Boise State University (UG,G)
Boston University (UG,G)
Bradley University (UG,G)
University of Bridgeport (UG,G)
Brigham Young University (UG,G)
Brown University (UG,G)
Bucknell University (UG,G)

C

University of Calgary (UG,G)
California Institute of Technology (UG,G)
California Maritime Academy (UG)
California Polytechnic State University (UG,G)
California State Polytechnic University, Pomona (UG)
California State University, East Bay (UG,G)
California State University, Chico (UG)
California State University, Fresno (UG,G)
California State University, Fullerton (UG,G)
California State University, Long Beach (UG,G)
California State University, Los Angeles (UG,G)
California State University, Northridge (UG,G)
California State University, Sacramento (UG,G)
University of California, Berkeley (UG,G)
University of California, Davis (UG,G)
University of California, Irvine (UG,G)
University of California, Los Angeles (UG,G)
University of California, Riverside (UG,G)
University of California, San Diego (UG,G)
University of California, Santa Barbara (UG,G)
University of California-Santa Cruz (UG,G)
Calvin College (UG)
Capitol College (UG,G)
Carnegie Mellon University (UG,G)
Carroll College (UG)
Case Western Reserve University (UG,G)
The Catholic University of America (UG,G)
Cedarville University (UG)
University of Central Florida (UG,G)
Christian Brothers University (UG)
Christopher Newport University (UG)
University of Cincinnati (UG,G)
The Citadel (UG)
Clarkson University (UG,G)
Clemson University (UG,G)
Cleveland State University (UG,G)
Colorado School of Mines (UG,G)
Colorado State University (UG,G)
Colorado State University, Pueblo (UG,G)
Colorado Technical University (UG)
University of Colorado at Boulder (UG,G)
University of Colorado at Colorado Springs (UG,G)
University of Colorado at Denver and Health Sciences Center (UG,G)
Columbia University (UG,G)
Concordia University, Faculty of Engr. and Comp. Sci. (UG,G)
University of Connecticut (UG,G)
The Cooper Union (UG)
Cornell University (UG,G)

D

Dartmouth College (UG,G)
University of Dayton (UG,G)
University of Delaware (UG,G)
University of Denver (UG,G)
University of Detroit Mercy (UG,G)
University of the District of Columbia (UG)
Drexel University (UG,G)
Duke University Pratt School of Engineering (UG,G)

E

Ecole Polytechnique de Montreal (UG,G)
Ecole de Technologie Superieure (UG,G)
Embry Riddle Aeronautical Univ., Daytona Beach (UG,G)
Embry Riddle Aeronautical University, Prescott (UG)
University of Evansville (UG)

F

Fairfield University (UG)
Fairleigh Dickinson University (UG,G)
Ferris State University (UG)
University of Florida (UG,G)
Florida Atlantic University (UG,G)
Florida Institute of Technology (UG,G)
Florida International University (UG,G)
FAMU-FSU College of Engineering (UG,G)

G

Gannon University (UG,G)
George Mason University (UG,G)
The George Washington University (UG,G)
University of Georgia (UG,G)
Georgia Institute of Technology (UG,G)
Georgia Southern University (UG,G)
Gonzaga University (UG)
Grand Valley State University (UG,G)
Grove City College (UG)

H

University of Hartford (UG,G)
Harvard University (UG,G)
Harvey Mudd College (UG)
University of Hawaii at Manoa (UG,G)
Henry Cogswell College (UG)
Hofstra University (UG)

ALPHABETICAL INDEX OF PARTICIPATING ENGINEERING INSTITUTIONS

University of Houston, Cullen School of Engineering (UG,G)
Howard University (UG,G)
Humboldt State University (UG)

I

University of Idaho (UG,G)
Idaho State University (UG,G)
Illinois Institute of Technology (UG,G)
University of Illinois at Chicago (UG,G)
University of Illinois at Urbana-Champaign (UG,G)
Indiana Institute of Technology (UG)
Indiana University Purdue University at Indianapolis (UG,G)
Indiana University-Purdue University Fort Wayne (UG)
The University of Iowa (UG,G)
Iowa State University (UG,G)

J

John Brown University (UG)
The Johns Hopkins University (UG,G)

K

University of Kansas (UG,G)
Kansas State University (UG,G)
University of Kentucky (UG,G)
Kettering University formerly GMI (UG,G)

L

Lafayette College (UG)
Lake Superior State University (UG)
Lamar University (UG,G)
Lawrence Technological University (UG,G)
Lehigh University (UG,G)
LeTourneau University (UG)
Louisiana State University (UG,G)
Louisiana Tech University (UG,G)
University of Louisiana at Lafayette (UG,G)
University of Louisville (UG,G)
Loyola College in Maryland (UG,G)
Loyola Marymount University (UG,G)

M

University of Maine (UG,G)
Maine Maritime Academy (UG)
Manhattan College (UG,G)
Marietta College (UG)
Marquette University (UG,G)
University of Maryland, Baltimore County (UG,G)
University of Maryland, College Park (UG,G)
Massachusetts Institute of Technology (UG,G)
Massachusetts Maritime Academy (UG)
University of Massachusetts Amherst (UG,G)
University of Massachusetts Dartmouth (UG,G)
University of Massachusetts Lowell (UG,G)
McGill University, Faculty of Engineering (UG,G)
McNeese State University (UG,G)
The University of Memphis (UG,G)
Mercer University (UG,G)
Merrimack College (UG)
Messiah College (UG)
University of Miami (UG,G)
Miami University (UG,G)
University of Michigan (UG,G)
Michigan State University (UG,G)
Michigan Technological University (UG,G)
University of Michigan, Dearborn (UG,G)
Milwaukee School of Engineering (UG,G)
Minnesota State University, Mankato (UG,G)
University of Minnesota, Duluth (UG)
University of Minnesota -Twin Cities (UG,G)
The University of Mississippi (UG,G)
Mississippi State University (UG,G)
University of Missouri-Columbia (UG,G)
University of Missouri - Kansas City (UG,G)
University of Missouri - Rolla (UG,G)
Monmouth University (UG,G)
Montana State University (UG,G)
Montana Tech of the University of Montana (UG,G)
Morgan State University (UG,G)

N

Naval Postgraduate School (G)
University of Nebraska, Lincoln (UG,G)
University of Nevada, Las Vegas (UG,G)
University of Nevada, Reno (UG,G)
University of New Hampshire (UG,G)
University of New Haven (UG,G)
New Jersey Institute of Technology (UG,G)
The College of New Jersey (UG,G)
The University of New Mexico (UG,G)
New Mexico Institute of Mining & Technology (UG,G)
New Mexico State University (UG,G)
University of New Orleans (UG,G)
New York Institute of Technology (UG,G)
State University of New York Maritime College (UG)
City College of the City University of New York (UG,G)
The State University of New York at Binghamton (UG,G)
State University of New York at Buffalo (UG,G)
City University of New York, College of Staten Island (UG)
SUNY College of Environmental Science and Forestry (UG,G)
SUNY, New Paltz (UG)
Stony Brook University (UG,G)
North Carolina A & T State University (UG,G)
North Carolina State University (UG,G)
University of North Carolina at Chapel Hill (G)
University of North Carolina, Charlotte (UG,G)
University of North Dakota (UG,G)
North Dakota State University (UG,G)
University of North Florida (UG)
University of North Texas (UG,G)
Northeastern University (UG,G)
Northern Arizona University (UG,G)
Northern Illinois University (UG,G)
Northwestern University (UG,G)
Norwich University (UG)
University of Notre Dame (UG,G)

Alphabetical Index of Participating Engineering Institutions

O

Oakland University (UG,G)
Ohio Northern University (UG)
The Ohio State University (UG,G)
Ohio University (UG,G)
University of Oklahoma (UG,G)
Oklahoma Christian University (UG)
Oklahoma State University (UG,G)
Old Dominion University (UG,G)
Oral Roberts University (UG)
OGI School of Science & Engineering at OHSU (G)
Oregon Institute of Technology (UG)
Oregon State University (UG,G)
University of Ottawa, Faculty of Engineering (UG,G)

P

University of the Pacific (UG)
University of Pennsylvania (UG,G)
Pennsylvania State University Harrisburg (UG)
Penn State Erie, The Behrend College (UG)
The Pennsylvania State University (UG,G)
Philadelphia University (UG)
University of Pittsburgh (UG,G)
Polytechnic University (UG,G)
Polytechnic University of Puerto Rico (UG,G)
University of Portland (UG)
Portland State University (UG,G)
Prairie View A&M University (UG,G)
Princeton University (UG,G)
University of Puerto Rico, Mayaguez Campus (UG,G)
Purdue University, Calumet (UG,G)
Purdue University (UG,G)

R

Rensselaer Polytechnic Institute (UG,G)
University of Rhode Island (UG,G)
William Marsh Rice University (UG,G)
Robert Morris University (UG)
University of Rochester (UG,G)
Rochester Institute of Technology (UG,G)
Roger Williams University (UG)
Rose-Hulman Institute of Technology (UG,G)

Rowan University (UG,G)
Rutgers, The State University of New Jersey (UG,G)

S

Saginaw Valley State University (UG)
Saint Ambrose University (UG)
Saint Cloud State University (UG,G)
Saint Louis University - Parks College (UG,G)
Saint Martin's College (UG,G)
Saint Mary's University (UG,G)
University of Saint Thomas (UG,G)
University of San Diego (UG)
San Diego State University (UG,G)
San Francisco State University (UG,G)
San Jose State University (UG,G)
Santa Clara University (UG,G)
Seattle University (UG)
Seattle Pacific University (UG)
Smith College (UG)
University of South Alabama (UG,G)
University of South Carolina (UG,G)
South Dakota School of Mines and Technology (UG,G)
South Dakota State University (UG,G)
University of South Florida (UG,G)
Southeast Missouri State University (UG)
University of Southern California (UG,G)
Southern Illinois University Carbondale (UG,G)
Southern Illinois University Edwardsville (UG,G)
University of Southern Maine (UG)
Southern Methodist University (UG,G)
Southern University and A&M College (UG)
Stanford University (UG,G)
Stevens Institute of Technology (UG,G)
Swarthmore College (UG)
Syracuse University (UG,G)

T

Temple University (UG,G)
Tennessee State University (UG,G)
Tennessee Technological University (UG,G)
University of Tennessee, Chattanooga (UG,G)
University of Tennessee, Knoxville (UG,G)

University of Tennessee, Martin (UG)
Texas A&M University (UG,G)
Texas A&M University, Galveston (UG)
Texas A&M University - Kingsville (UG,G)
Texas Christian University (UG)
Texas Tech University (UG,G)
The University of Texas at Arlington (UG,G)
The University of Texas at Austin (UG,G)
The University of Texas at Dallas (UG,G)
University of Texas at El Paso (UG,G)
The University of Texas-Pan American (UG)
University of Texas at San Antonio (UG,G)
The University of Texas at Tyler (UG,G)
The University of Toledo (UG,G)
Tri-State University (UG,G)
Trinity University (UG)
Trinity College (UG)
Tufts University (UG,G)
Tulane University (UG,G)
University of Tulsa (UG,G)
Tuskegee University (UG,G)

U

Union College (UG)
U.S. Air Force Academy (UG)
U.S. Coast Guard Academy (UG)
U.S.Merchant Marine Academy (UG,G)
United States Military Academy (UG)
U.S. Naval Academy (UG)
University of Utah (UG,G)
Utah State University (UG,G)

V

Valparaiso University (UG)
Vanderbilt University (UG,G)
University of Vermont (UG,G)
Villanova University (UG,G)
University of Virginia (UG,G)
Virginia Commonwealth University (UG,G)
Virginia Military Institute (UG)
Virginia Polytechnic Institute and State University (UG,G)

W

Walla Walla College (UG)
University of Washington (UG,G)
Washington State University (UG,G)
Washington University (UG,G)
University of Waterloo (UG,G)
Wayne State University (UG,G)
Webb Institute (UG)
Wentworth Institute of Technology (UG)
West Virginia University Institute of Technology (UG)
West Virginia University (UG,G)
Western Kentucky University (UG)
Western Michigan University (UG,G)
Western New England College (UG)
Wichita State University (UG,G)
Widener University (UG,G)
Wilkes University (UG,G)
Winona State University (UG)
University of Wisconsin, Stout (UG,G)
University of Wisconsin, Madison (UG,G)
University of Wisconsin, Milwaukee (UG,G)
University of Wisconsin, Platteville (UG)
Worcester Polytechnic Institute (UG,G)
Wright State University (UG,G)
University of Wyoming (UG,G)

Y

Yale University/Faculty of Engineering (UG,G)
York College of Pennsylvania (UG)
Youngstown State University (UG,G)

GEOGRAPHICAL INDEX OF PARTICIPATING ENGINEERING INSTITUTIONS

UNITED STATES

Alabama

Alabama A&M University (UG)
University of Alabama at Birmingham (UG,G)
The University of Alabama in Huntsville (UG,G)
The University of Alabama (UG,G)
Auburn University (UG,G)
University of South Alabama (UG,G)
Tuskegee University (UG,G)

Alaska

University of Alaska, Anchorage (UG)
University of Alaska Fairbanks (UG,G)

Arizona

The University of Arizona (UG,G)
Arizona State University (UG,G)
Embry Riddle Aeronautical University, Prescott (UG)
Northern Arizona University (UG,G)

Arkansas

University of Arkansas (UG,G)
Arkansas State University (UG)
Arkansas Tech University (UG)
University of Arkansas at Little Rock (UG)
John Brown University (UG)

California

California Institute of Technology (UG,G)
California Maritime Academy (UG)
California Polytechnic State University (UG,G)
California State Polytechnic University, Pomona (UG)
California State University, East Bay (UG,G)
California State University, Chico (UG)
California State University, Fresno (UG,G)
California State University, Fullerton (UG,G)
California State University, Long Beach (UG,G)
California State University, Los Angeles (UG,G)
California State University, Northridge (UG,G)
California State University, Sacramento (UG,G)

University of California, Berkeley (UG,G)
University of California, Davis (UG,G)
University of California, Irvine (UG,G)
University of California, Los Angeles (UG,G)
University of California, Riverside (UG,G)
University of California, San Diego (UG,G)
University of California, Santa Barbara (UG,G)
University of California-Santa Cruz (UG,G)
Harvey Mudd College (UG)
Humboldt State University (UG)
Loyola Marymount University (UG,G)
Naval Postgraduate School (G)
University of the Pacific (UG)
University of San Diego (UG)
San Diego State University (UG,G)
San Francisco State University (UG,G)
San Jose State University (UG,G)
Santa Clara University (UG,G)
University of Southern California (UG,G)
Stanford University (UG,G)

Colorado

Colorado School of Mines (UG,G)
Colorado State University (UG,G)
Colorado State University, Pueblo (UG,G)
Colorado Technical University (UG)
University of Colorado at Boulder (UG,G)
University of Colorado at Colorado Springs (UG,G)
University of Colorado at Denver and Health Sciences Center (UG,G)
University of Denver (UG,G)
U.S. Air Force Academy (UG)

Connecticut

University of Bridgeport (UG,G)
University of Connecticut (UG,G)
Fairfield University (UG)
University of Hartford (UG,G)
University of New Haven (UG,G)
Trinity College (UG)
U.S. Coast Guard Academy (UG)
Yale University/Faculty of Engineering (UG,G)

Delaware

University of Delaware (UG,G)

District of Columbia

The Catholic University of America (UG,G)
University of the District of Columbia (UG)
The George Washington University (UG,G)
Howard University (UG,G)

Florida

University of Central Florida (UG,G)
Embry Riddle Aeronautical Univ., Daytona Beach (UG,G)
University of Florida (UG,G)
Florida Atlantic University (UG,G)
Florida Institute of Technology (UG,G)
Florida International University (UG,G)
FAMU-FSU College of Engineering (UG,G)
University of Miami (UG,G)
University of North Florida (UG)
University of South Florida (UG,G)

Georgia

University of Georgia (UG,G)
Georgia Institute of Technology (UG,G)
Mercer University (UG,G)

Hawaii

University of Hawaii at Manoa (UG,G)

Idaho

Boise State University (UG,G)
University of Idaho (UG,G)
Idaho State University (UG,G)

Illinois

Bradley University (UG,G)
Illinois Institute of Technology (UG,G)
University of Illinois at Chicago (UG,G)
University of Illinois at Urbana-Champaign (UG,G)
Northern Illinois University (UG,G)
Northwestern University (UG,G)

For more information, visit the ASEE web site at www.asee.org/colleges

GEOGRAPHICAL INDEX OF PARTICIPATING ENGINEERING INSTITUTIONS

Southern Illinois University Carbondale (UG,G)
Southern Illinois University Edwardsville (UG,G)

Indiana

University of Evansville (UG)
Indiana Institute of Technology (UG)
Indiana University Purdue University at Indianapolis (UG,G)
Indiana University-Purdue University Fort Wayne (UG)
University of Notre Dame (UG,G)
Purdue University, Calumet (UG,G)
Purdue University (UG,G)
Rose-Hulman Institute of Technology (UG,G)
Tri-State University (UG,G)
Valparaiso University (UG)

Iowa

The University of Iowa (UG,G)
Iowa State University (UG,G)
Saint Ambrose University (UG)

Kansas

University of Kansas (UG,G)
Kansas State University (UG,G)
Wichita State University (UG,G)

Kentucky

University of Kentucky (UG,G)
University of Louisville (UG,G)
Western Kentucky University (UG)

Louisiana

Louisiana State University (UG,G)
Louisiana Tech University (UG,G)
University of Louisiana at Lafayette (UG,G)
McNeese State University (UG,G)
University of New Orleans (UG,G)
Southern University and A&M College (UG)
Tulane University (UG,G)

Maine

University of Maine (UG,G)
Maine Maritime Academy (UG)
University of Southern Maine (UG)

Maryland

Capitol College (UG,G)
The Johns Hopkins University (UG,G)
Loyola College in Maryland (UG,G)
University of Maryland, Baltimore County (UG,G)
University of Maryland, College Park (UG,G)
Morgan State University (UG,G)
U.S. Naval Academy (UG)

Massachusetts

Boston University (UG,G)
Harvard University (UG,G)
Massachusetts Institute of Technology (UG,G)
Massachusetts Maritime Academy (UG)
University of Massachusetts Amherst (UG,G)
University of Massachusetts Dartmouth (UG,G)
University of Massachusetts Lowell (UG,G)
Merrimack College (UG)
Northeastern University (UG,G)
Smith College (UG)
Tufts University (UG,G)
Wentworth Institute of Technology (UG)
Western New England College (UG)
Worcester Polytechnic Institute (UG,G)

Michigan

Baker College (UG,G)
Calvin College (UG)
University of Detroit Mercy (UG,G)
Ferris State University (UG)
Grand Valley State University (UG,G)
Kettering University formerly GMI (UG,G)
Lake Superior State University (UG)
Lawrence Technological University (UG,G)
University of Michigan (UG,G)
Michigan State University (UG,G)
Michigan Technological University (UG,G)
University of Michigan, Dearborn (UG,G)
Oakland University (UG,G)
Saginaw Valley State University (UG)
Wayne State University (UG,G)
Western Michigan University (UG,G)

Minnesota

Minnesota State University, Mankato (UG,G)
University of Minnesota, Duluth (UG)
University of Minnesota -Twin Cities (UG,G)
Saint Cloud State University (UG,G)
University of Saint Thomas (UG,G)
Winona State University (UG)

Mississippi

The University of Mississippi (UG,G)
Mississippi State University (UG,G)

Missouri

University of Missouri-Columbia (UG,G)
University of Missouri - Kansas City (UG,G)
University of Missouri - Rolla (UG,G)
Saint Louis University - Parks College (UG,G)
Southeast Missouri State University (UG)
Washington University (UG,G)

Montana

Carroll College (UG)
Montana State University (UG,G)
Montana Tech of the University of Montana (UG,G)

Nebraska

University of Nebraska, Lincoln (UG,G)

Nevada

University of Nevada, Las Vegas (UG,G)
University of Nevada, Reno (UG,G)

Geographical Index of Participating Engineering Institutions

New Hampshire

Dartmouth College (UG,G)

University of New Hampshire (UG,G)

New Jersey

Fairleigh Dickinson University (UG,G)

Monmouth University (UG,G)

New Jersey Institute of Technology (UG,G)

The College of New Jersey (UG)

Princeton University (UG,G)

Rowan University (UG,G)

Rutgers, The State University of New Jersey (UG,G)

Stevens Institute of Technology (UG,G)

New Mexico

The University of New Mexico (UG,G)

New Mexico Institute of Mining & Technology (UG,G)

New Mexico State University (UG,G)

New York

Alfred University, NY State College of Ceramics (UG,G)

Clarkson University (UG,G)

Columbia University (UG,G)

The Cooper Union (UG)

Cornell University (UG,G)

Hofstra University (UG)

Manhattan College (UG,G)

New York Institute of Technology (UG,G)

State University of New York Maritime College (UG)

City College of the City University of New York (UG,G)

The State University of New York at Binghamton (UG,G)

State University of New York at Buffalo (UG,G)

City University of New York, College of Staten Island (UG)

SUNY College of Environmental Science and Forestry (UG,G)

SUNY, New Paltz (UG)

Stony Brook University (UG,G)

Polytechnic University (UG,G)

Rensselaer Polytechnic Institute (UG,G)

University of Rochester (UG,G)

Rochester Institute of Technology (UG,G)

Syracuse University (UG,G)

Union College (UG)

U.S. Merchant Marine Academy (UG,G)

United States Military Academy (UG)

Webb Institute (UG)

North Carolina

Duke University Pratt School of Engineering (UG,G)

North Carolina A & T State University (UG,G)

North Carolina State University (UG,G)

University of North Carolina at Chapel Hill (G)

University of North Carolina, Charlotte (UG,G)

North Dakota

University of North Dakota (UG,G)

North Dakota State University (UG,G)

Ohio

Air Force Institute of Technology (G)

The University of Akron (UG,G)

Case Western Reserve University (UG,G)

Cedarville University (UG,G)

University of Cincinnati (UG,G)

Cleveland State University (UG,G)

University of Dayton (UG,G)

Marietta College (UG)

Miami University (UG,G)

Ohio Northern University (UG)

The Ohio State University (UG,G)

Ohio University (UG,G)

The University of Toledo (UG,G)

Wright State University (UG,G)

Youngstown State University (UG,G)

Oklahoma

University of Oklahoma (UG,G)

Oklahoma Christian University (UG)

Oklahoma State University (UG,G)

Oral Roberts University (UG)

University of Tulsa (UG,G)

Oregon

OGI School of Science & Engineering at OHSU (G)

Oregon Institute of Technology (UG)

Oregon State University (UG,G)

University of Portland (UG)

Portland State University (UG,G)

Pennsylvania

Bucknell University (UG,G)

Carnegie Mellon University (UG,G)

Drexel University (UG,G)

Gannon University (UG,G)

Grove City College (UG)

Lafayette College (UG)

Lehigh University (UG,G)

Messiah College (UG)

University of Pennsylvania (UG,G)

Pennsylvania State University Harrisburg (UG)

Penn State Erie, The Behrend College (UG)

The Pennsylvania State University (UG,G)

Philadelphia University (UG)

University of Pittsburgh (UG,G)

Robert Morris University (UG)

Swarthmore College (UG)

Temple University (UG,G)

Villanova University (UG,G)

Widener University (UG,G)

Wilkes University (UG,G)

York College of Pennsylvania (UG)

Rhode Island

Brown University (UG,G)

University of Rhode Island (UG,G)

Roger Williams University (UG)

South Carolina

The Citadel (UG)

Clemson University (UG,G)

University of South Carolina (UG,G)

GEOGRAPHICAL INDEX OF PARTICIPATING ENGINEERING INSTITUTIONS

South Dakota

South Dakota School of Mines and Technology (UG,G)
South Dakota State University (UG,G)

Tennessee

Christian Brothers University (UG)
The University of Memphis (UG,G)
Tennessee State University (UG,G)
Tennessee Technological University (UG,G)
University of Tennessee, Chattanooga (UG,G)
University of Tennessee, Knoxville (UG,G)
University of Tennessee, Martin (UG)
Vanderbilt University (UG,G)

Texas

Baylor University (UG,G)
University of Houston, Cullen School of Engineering (UG,G)
Lamar University (UG,G)
LeTourneau University (UG)
University of North Texas (UG,G)
Prairie View A&M University (UG,G)
William Marsh Rice University (UG,G)
Saint Mary's University (UG,G)
Southern Methodist University (UG,G)
Texas A&M University (UG,G)
Texas A&M University, Galveston (UG)
Texas A&M University - Kingsville (UG,G)
Texas Christian University (UG)
Texas Tech University (UG,G)
The University of Texas at Arlington (UG,G)
The University of Texas at Austin (UG,G)
The University of Texas at Dallas (UG,G)
University of Texas at El Paso (UG,G)
The University of Texas-Pan American (UG)
University of Texas at San Antonio (UG,G)
The University of Texas at Tyler (UG,G)
Trinity University (UG)

Utah

Brigham Young University (UG,G)
University of Utah (UG,G)
Utah State University (UG,G)

Vermont

Norwich University (UG)
University of Vermont (UG,G)

Virginia

Christopher Newport University (UG)
George Mason University (UG,G)
Old Dominion University (UG,G)
University of Virginia (UG,G)
Virginia Commonwealth University (UG,G)
Virginia Military Institute (UG)
Virginia Polytechnic Institute and State University (UG,G)

Washington

Gonzaga University (UG)
Henry Cogswell College (UG)
Saint Martin's College (UG,G)
Seattle University (UG)
Seattle Pacific University (UG)
Walla Walla College (UG)
University of Washington (UG,G)
Washington State University (UG,G)

West Virginia

West Virginia University Institute of Technology (UG)
West Virginia University (UG,G)

Wisconsin

Marquette University (UG,G)
Milwaukee School of Engineering (UG,G)
University of Wisconsin, Stout (UG,G)
University of Wisconsin, Madison (UG,G)
University of Wisconsin, Milwaukee (UG,G)
University of Wisconsin, Platteville (UG)

Wyoming

University of Wyoming (UG,G)

PUERTO RICO

Puerto Rico

Polytechnic University of Puerto Rico (UG,G)
University of Puerto Rico, Mayaguez Campus (UG,G)

CANADA

Alberta

University of Alberta (UG,G)
University of Calgary (UG,G)

Ontario

University of Ottawa, Faculty of Engineering (UG,G)
University of Waterloo (UG,G)

Quebec

Concordia University, Faculty of Engr. and Comp. Sci. (UG,G)
Ecole Polytechnique de Montreal (UG,G)
Ecole de Technologie Superieure (UG,G)
McGill University, Faculty of Engineering (UG,G)

ALPHABETICAL INDEX OF PARTICIPATING UNDERGRADUATE DEGREE PROGRAMS

A

Acoustics and Music (B.S.E.)
University of Hartford

Aeronautical and Astronautical Engineering (B.S.)
University of Washington

Aeronautical Engineering (B.S.)
Clarkson University
Rensselaer Polytechnic Institute
U.S. Air Force Academy

Aeronautical Engineering (B.S.E.)
Western Michigan University

Aeronautical Engineering and Mechanical Engineering (B.S.)
University of California, Davis

Aeronautical Science and Engineering (B.S.)
University of California, Davis

Aeronautics and Astronautics Engineering (B.S.)
Purdue University

Aerospace Engineering (B.A.E.)
Auburn University

Aerospace Engineering (B.Ae.E.)
University of Minnesota-Twin Cities

Aerospace Engineering (B.S.)
The University of Alabama
The University of Arizona
Boston University
California Polytechnic State University
California State Polytechnic University, Pomona
California State University, Long Beach
University of California, Irvine
University of California, Los Angeles
University of California, San Diego
University of Cincinnati
Embry Riddle Aeronautical Univ., Daytona Beach
Embry Riddle Aeronautical University, Prescott
University of Florida
Florida Institute of Technology
Georgia Institute of Technology
Illinois Institute of Technology
University of Illinois at Urbana-Champaign
Iowa State University

University of Kansas
University of Maryland, College Park
University of Miami
Mississippi State University
University of Missouri - Rolla
State University of New York at Buffalo
North Carolina State University
University of Notre Dame
University of Oklahoma
Oklahoma State University
The Pennsylvania State University
Saint Louis University - Parks College
San Diego State University
San Jose State University
University of Southern California
Syracuse University
University of Tennessee, Knoxville
Texas A&M University
The University of Texas at Arlington
The University of Texas at Austin
U.S. Naval Academy
University of Virginia
Virginia Polytechnic Institute and State University
Washington University
West Virginia University
Wichita State University
Worcester Polytechnic Institute

Aerospace Engineering (B.S.A.E.)
University of Central Florida

Aerospace Engineering (B.S.E.)
Arizona State University
Case Western Reserve University
University of Michigan

Aerospace Engineering (S.B.)
Massachusetts Institute of Technology

Aerospace Engineering Sciences (B.S.)
University of Colorado at Boulder

Aerospace Engineering with Information Technology (S.B.)
Massachusetts Institute of Technology

Aerospace Science Engineering (B.S.)
Tuskegee University

Agricultural & Biosystems Engineering (B.S.)
The University of Arizona

Agricultural and Biological Engineering (B.S.)
The Pennsylvania State University
Purdue University

Agricultural and Biosystems Engineering (B.S.)
North Dakota State University
South Dakota State University

Agricultural Engineering (B.S.)
University of Florida
University of Idaho
University of Illinois at Urbana-Champaign
Iowa State University

Agricultural Engineering (B.S.A.E.)
University of Georgia
University of Nebraska, Lincoln

Applied and Computational Mathematics (B.S.)
California Institute of Technology

Applied and Engineering Sciences (B.S)
Wilkes University

Applied Computer Science (B.S.)
George Mason University

Applied Engineering Sciences (B.S.)
Michigan State University

Applied Geophysics (B.S.)
Michigan Technological University

Applied Mathematics & Statistics (B.S.)
Stony Brook University

Applied Mathematics & Statistics (B.S., B.A.)
The Johns Hopkins University

Applied Mathematics (A.B.)
Harvard University

Applied Mathematics (B.S.)
University of Colorado at Boulder
Columbia University
Northwestern University

Applied Mechanics (B.S.)
University of Southern California

Applied Physics (B.S.)
California Institute of Technology
Columbia University

(*) degree program awarded outside engineering

Applied Physics (B.S., B.A.)
Yale University/Faculty of Engineering

Applied Science & Technology (B.A.)
The George Washington University

Applied Science (B.S.)
Lehigh University

Applied Science in Biomedical Science (B.A.S.)
University of Pennsylvania

Applied Science in Computational Biology (B.A.S.)
University of Pennsylvania

Applied Science in Computer and Cog. Sci. (B.A.S.)
University of Pennsylvania

Applied Science in Computer Science (B.A.S.)
University of Pennsylvania

Applied Science in Engineering (B.S.)
Rutgers, The State University of New Jersey

Applied Science- Biomedical Engineering (B.S.)
Washington University

Applied Science- Chemical Engineering (B.S.)
Washington University

Applied Science- Computer Science (B.S.)
Washington University

Applied Science- Electrical Engineering (B.S.)
Washington University

Applied Science- Individualized (B.A.S.)
University of Pennsylvania

Applied Science- Systems Science (B.S.)
Washington University

Applied Sciences & Engineering (B.S.)
United States Military Academy

Appropriate Technology (B.S.)
Drexel University

Archaeology & Materials as recommended by the Department of Materials Science and Engineering (S.B.)
Massachusetts Institute of Technology

Architectural (B.S.)
Texas A&M University - Kingsville

Architectural Engineering (B.Arch.)
The Pennsylvania State University

Architectural Engineering (B.S.)
California Polytechnic State University
University of Colorado at Boulder
Drexel University
Illinois Institute of Technology
University of Kansas
Kansas State University
University of Miami
Milwaukee School of Engineering
University of Missouri - Rolla
North Carolina A & T State University
University of Oklahoma
Oklahoma State University
Tennessee State University
The University of Texas at Austin
University of Wyoming

Architectural Engineering (B.S.A.E.)
University of Nebraska, Lincoln

Architecture (B.S.)
Oklahoma State University

Astronautical and Aeronautical Engineering (B.S.)
The Ohio State University

Astronautical Engineering (B.S.)
Capitol College
U.S. Air Force Academy

Astronautics (B.S)
University of Southern California

Atmospheric, Oceanic and Space Science (B.S.)
University of Michigan

Automated Production Engineering (B.Eng.)
Ecole de Technologie Superieure

Aviation (B.S.)
The Ohio State University

B

B.Eng.
University of Guelph

Bachelor of Information Technology
University of Missouri - Kansas City

Bachelor of Science (B.S.)
Tufts University

Bachelor of Science in Engineering Physics (BSEP)
Tufts University

Bachelor of Science in Engineering Psychology (BS)
Tufts University

Bachelor of Science in Engineering Science (BSES)
Tufts University

Basic Engineering
Tennessee Technological University

Bio-Engineering (B.S.)
University of Louisville

Biochemical Engineering (B.S.)
University of California, Davis

Biochemistry (B.S.)
Lehigh University

Bioengineering (B.S.)
University of California, Berkeley
University of California, Los Angeles
University of California, San Diego
Clemson University
University of Hawaii at Manoa
University of Illinois at Chicago
University of Illinois at Urbana-Champaign
Lehigh University
University of Maryland, College Park
The State University of New York at Binghamton
Oregon State University
University of the Pacific
The Pennsylvania State University
University of Pittsburgh
The University of Toledo
Walla Walla College
University of Washington
Washington State University

Bioengineering (B.S.B)
William Marsh Rice University

Bioengineering (B.S.E.)
Arizona State University
University of Pennsylvania

(*) degree program awarded outside engineering

ALPHABETICAL INDEX OF PARTICIPATING UNDERGRADUATE DEGREE PROGRAMS

Bioengineering and Electrical & Computer Engineering (B.S.)
University of California, Berkeley

Bioengineering and Materials Science & Engineering (B.S.)
University of California, Berkeley

Bioengineering: Bioinformatics (B.S.)
University of California, San Diego

Bioengineering: Biotechnology (B.S.)
University of California, San Diego

Bioengineering: Premedical (B.S.)
University of California, San Diego

Bioinformatics & Computational Biology (B.S.)
State University of New York at Buffalo

Bioinformatics (B.INF.)
Baylor University

Bioinformatics (B.S.)
University of California-Santa Cruz
Gannon University

Biological & Food Process Engineering (B.S.)
Purdue University

Biological and Agricultural Engineering (B.S.)
Utah State University

Biological and Agricultural Engineering (B.S.)
Kansas State University
Texas A&M University

Biological Engineering
University of Maine

Biological Engineering (B.S.)
Cornell University
Louisiana State University
Mississippi State University
University of Missouri-Columbia
North Carolina A & T State University
North Carolina State University

Biological Engineering (B.S.B.E.)
University of Georgia

Biological Engineering (S.B.)
Massachusetts Institute of Technology

Biological Resources Engineering (B.S.)
University of Maryland, College Park

Biological Systems Engineering (B.S.)
University of California, Davis
University of Idaho
Texas A&M University
Virginia Polytechnic Institute and State University
Washington State University

Biological Systems Engineering (B.S.B.S.)
University of Nebraska, Lincoln

Biological Systems Engineering/Electrical and Computer Engineering (B.S.)
University of California, Davis

Biomedical Engineering- Electrical (B.S.)
University of Southern California

Biomedical (B.S.)
Marquette University
Syracuse University

Biomedical Engineering
Lawrence Technological University

Biomedical Engineering (B.A.)
The College of New Jersey

Biomedical Engineering (B.Bm.E.)
University of Minnesota -Twin Cities

Biomedical Engineering (B.E.)
The Catholic University of America
City College of the City University of New York
Stony Brook University
Stevens Institute of Technology
Vanderbilt University

Biomedical Engineering (B.S.)
The University of Akron
University of Alabama at Birmingham
Boston University
Brown University
Bucknell University
California Polytechnic State University
University of California, Davis
University of California, Irvine
University of California, Riverside
University of Cincinnati
Columbia University
Drexel University

Florida International University
The George Washington University
Georgia Institute of Technology
University of Houston, Cullen School of Engineering
Illinois Institute of Technology
Indiana Institute of Technology
The University of Memphis
University of Miami
Michigan Technological University
Milwaukee School of Engineering
University of Nebraska, Lincoln
New Jersey Institute of Technology
The College of New Jersey
North Carolina State University
Northwestern University
Oral Roberts University
Purdue University
Rensselaer Polytechnic Institute
University of Rhode Island
University of Rochester
Rose-Hulman Institute of Technology
Rutgers, The State University of New Jersey
Saint Louis University - Parks College
University of South Carolina
University of Southern California
University of Tennessee, Knoxville
Texas A&M University
The University of Texas at Austin
University of Utah
University of Virginia
Virginia Commonwealth University
Washington University
Western New England College
University of Wisconsin, Madison
Worcester Polytechnic Institute

Biomedical Engineering (B.S., B.A.)
The Johns Hopkins University
Yale University/Faculty of Engineering

Biomedical Engineering (B.S.B.E.)
Wright State University

(*) degree program awarded outside engineering

ALPHABETICAL INDEX OF PARTICIPATING UNDERGRADUATE DEGREE PROGRAMS

Biomedical Engineering (B.S.B.M.E.)
Indiana University Purdue University at Indianapolis

Biomedical Engineering (B.S.E.)
Case Western Reserve University
University of Connecticut
Duke University Pratt School of Engineering
University of Hartford
The University of Iowa
University of Michigan
Tulane University

Biomedical Engineering (BS)
Louisiana Tech University

Biomedical Engineering (BSBME)
Tufts University

Biomedical Engineering- Biochemical (B.S.)
University of Southern California

Biomedical Engineering- Mechanical (B.S.)
University of Southern California

Biomedical Engineering: Premedical (B.S.)
University of California, Irvine

Biomedical Materials Engineering Science (B.S.)
Alfred University, NY State College of Ceramics

Biomedical Mechanical Engineering (B.S.)
University of Ottawa, Faculty of Engineering

Biomedical Specialization (B.S.)
Mercer University

Biometric Systems (B.S.)
West Virginia University

BioResource & Agricultural Engineering (B.S.)
California Polytechnic State University

Bioresource Engineeering (B.S.)
Rutgers, The State University of New Jersey

Biosystems & Agricultural Engineering - Agricultural
Oklahoma State University

Biosystems and Agricultural Engineering (B.S.)
University of Kentucky

Biosystems Engineering (B.B.E.)
Auburn University

Biosystems Engineeering (B.S.)
The University of Arizona
Clemson University

Michigan State University
University of Tennessee, Knoxville

Biosystems Engineering- Biomechanical (B.S.)
Oklahoma State University

Biosystems Engineering- Bioprocessing and Biotechnology (B.S.)
Oklahoma State University

Biosystems Engineering- Environmental and Natural Resources (B.S.)
Oklahoma State University

Biosystme & Agricultural Engineering - Food Processing (BS)
Oklahoma State University

BS in Mechanical Engineering
Baker College

Building Engineering (B.Eng.)
Concordia University, Faculty of Engr. and Comp. Sci.

C

Ceramic and Materials Engineering (B.S.)
Clemson University

Ceramic Engineering (B.S.)
Clemson University
University of Missouri - Rolla
Rutgers, The State University of New Jersey

Ceramic Engineering Science (B.S.)
Alfred University, NY State College of Ceramics

Chemical Engineering (B.S)
Clarkson University

Chemical & Biochemical Engineering (B.S.)
Christian Brothers University
University of Maryland, Baltimore County

Chemical & Biomolecular Engineering (B.S.)
The University of Akron
Georgia Institute of Technology
The Johns Hopkins University

Chemical and Biological Engineering (B.S.)
University of Colorado at Boulder
Polytechnic University

Chemical and Biomolecular Engineering (B.S.E)
University of Pennsylvania

Chemical and Ocean Engineering (B.S.)
University of Rhode Island

Chemical Engineering
University of Dayton
University of Tulsa

Chemical Engineering (B.A.)
William Marsh Rice University

Chemical Engineering (B.Ch.E.)
Auburn University
University of Delaware
University of Minnesota -Twin Cities

Chemical Engineering (B.E.)
Cleveland State University
The Cooper Union
Ecole Polytechnique de Montreal
City College of the City University of New York
Stevens Institute of Technology
Vanderbilt University
Youngstown State University

Chemical Engineering (B.S.)
The University of Alabama
University of Alberta
The University of Arizona
University of Arkansas
Brigham Young University
Brown University
Bucknell University
California Institute of Technology
California State Polytechnic University, Pomona
California State University, Long Beach
University of California, Berkeley
University of California, Davis
University of California, Irvine
University of California, Los Angeles
University of California, Riverside
University of California, San Diego
University of California, Santa Barbara
Carnegie Mellon University
University of Cincinnati
Clemson University
Colorado School of Mines

(*) degree program awarded outside engineering

Colorado State University
University of Colorado at Boulder
Columbia University
Cornell University
Drexel University
University of Florida
Florida Institute of Technology
Florida International University
FAMU-FSU College of Engineering
University of Houston, Cullen School of Engineering
Howard University
University of Idaho
Illinois Institute of Technology
University of Illinois at Chicago
University of Illinois at Urbana-Champaign
Iowa State University
The Johns Hopkins University
University of Kansas
Kansas State University
University of Kentucky
Lafayette College
Lamar University
Lehigh University
Louisiana State University
University of Louisiana at Lafayette
University of Louisville
University of Maine
Manhattan College
University of Maryland, College Park
University of Massachusetts Amherst
University of Massachusetts Lowell
Michigan State University
Michigan Technological University
The University of Mississippi
Mississippi State University
University of Missouri-Columbia
University of Missouri - Rolla
Montana State University
University of Nevada, Reno
University of New Hampshire
University of New Haven

New Jersey Institute of Technology
The University of New Mexico
New Mexico Institute of Mining & Technology
New Mexico State University
State University of New York at Buffalo
North Carolina A & T State University
North Carolina State University
University of North Dakota
Northeastern University
Northwestern University
University of Notre Dame
The Ohio State University
Ohio University
University of Oklahoma
Oklahoma State University
Oregon State University
University of Ottawa, Faculty of Engineering
The Pennsylvania State University
University of Pittsburgh
Polytechnic University
Polytechnic University of Puerto Rico
Prairie View A&M University
Princeton University
University of Puerto Rico, Mayaguez Campus
Purdue University
Rensselaer Polytechnic Institute
University of Rhode Island
University of Rochester
Rose-Hulman Institute of Technology
Rowan University
Rutgers, The State University of New Jersey
San Jose State University
University of South Alabama
University of South Carolina
South Dakota School of Mines and Technology
University of South Florida
University of Southern California
Stanford University
Syracuse University
Tennessee Technological University
University of Tennessee, Knoxville

Texas A&M University
Texas A&M University - Kingsville
Texas Tech University
The University of Texas at Austin
The University of Toledo
Tri-State University
Tuskegee University
University of Utah
Villanova University
University of Virginia
Virginia Commonwealth University
Virginia Polytechnic Institute and State University
University of Washington
Washington State University
Washington University
Wayne State University
West Virginia University
Widener University
University of Wisconsin, Madison
Worcester Polytechnic Institute
University of Wyoming
Yale University/Faculty of Engineering

Chemical Engineering (B.S.CH)
University of Nebraska, Lincoln

Chemical Engineering (B.S.Ch.E)
William Marsh Rice University

Chemical Engineering (B.S.Ch.E.)
University of Minnesota, Duluth
West Virginia University Institute of Technology

Chemical Engineering (B.S.E)
University of Tennessee, Chattanooga

Chemical Engineering (B.S.E.)
The University of Alabama in Huntsville
Arizona State University
Case Western Reserve University
University of Connecticut
The University of Iowa
Miami University
University of Michigan
Tulane University
Western Michigan University

(*) degree program awarded outside engineering

Chemical Engineering (BASc)
University of Waterloo

Chemical Engineering (BS)
Louisiana Tech University

Chemical Engineering (BSc)
University of Calgary

Chemical Engineering (BSCHE)
Tufts University

Chemical Engineering (S.B.)
Massachusetts Institute of Technology

Chemical Engineering - Biomedical and Biochemical (BS)
Oklahoma State University

Chemical Engineering and Materials Science & Engineering (B.S.)
University of California, Berkeley

Chemical Engineering and Nuclear Engineering (B.S.)
University of California, Berkeley

Chemical Engineering B.Eng.
McGill University, Faculty of Engineering

Chemical Engineering Option (B.S.)
McNeese State University

Chemical Engineering, Environmental Option (B.S.)
University of Wyoming

Chemical Engineering, Petroleum Option (B.S.)
University of Wyoming

Chemical Engineering- Biochemical (B.S.)
University of Southern California

Chemical Engineering- Environmental (B.S.)
Oklahoma State University
University of Southern California

Chemical Engineering- Petroleum (B.S.)
University of Southern California

Chemical Engineering- Premedical (B.S.)
Oklahoma State University

Chemical Engineering/Computer Science
Texas Tech University

Chemical Engineering/Materials Science and Engineering (B.S.)
University of California, Davis

Chemical-Bioengineering (B.S.)
FAMU-FSU College of Engineering

Chemical-Biological Engineering (S.B.)
Massachusetts Institute of Technology

Chemical-Biomedical (B.S.)
FAMU-FSU College of Engineering

Chemical-Environmental (B.S.)
FAMU-FSU College of Engineering

Chemical-Materials (B.S.)
FAMU-FSU College of Engineering

Chemical/Biochemical Engineering (B.S.)
University of California, Davis

Chemistry (B.S.)
Colorado School of Mines
Lehigh University

CIS Math (B.S.)
University of Michigan, Dearborn

Civil Engineering (B.S.C.E.)
Temple University

Civil & Environmental Engineering (B.S.)
University of California, Berkeley
Christian Brothers University

Civil (B.S.)
Texas A&M University - Kingsville

Civil and Environmental Engineering (B.E.)
Vanderbilt University
Vanderbilt University

Civil and Environmental Engineering (B.S)
Princeton University

Civil and Environmental Engineering (B.S.)
Princeton University
University of South Carolina

Civil and Infrastructure Engineering (B.S.)
George Mason University

Civil Engineering
University of Dayton
Western Kentucky University
University of Wisconsin, Milwaukee

Civil Engineering & Applied Mechanics B.Eng.
McGill University, Faculty of Engineering

Civil Engineering (B.A.)
Carroll College
William Marsh Rice University

Civil Engineering (B.C.E.)
Auburn University
University of Delaware
University of Minnesota-Twin Cities

Civil Engineering (B.E.)
The Catholic University of America
Cleveland State University
The Cooper Union
University of Detroit Mercy
Ecole Polytechnique de Montreal
City College of the City University of New York
Stevens Institute of Technology
Youngstown State University

Civil Engineering (B.Eng.)
Concordia University, Faculty of Engr. and Comp. Sci.

Civil Engineering (B.S.)
The University of Akron
University of Alabama at Birmingham
The University of Alabama
University of Alaska, Anchorage
University of Alaska Fairbanks
University of Alberta
The University of Arizona
University of Arkansas
Boise State University
Bradley University
Brigham Young University
Brown University
Bucknell University
California Polytechnic State University
California State Polytechnic University, Pomona
California State University, Chico
California State University, Fresno
California State University, Fullerton
California State University, Long Beach
California State University, Los Angeles
California State University, Northridge
California State University, Sacramento
University of California, Davis
University of California, Irvine
University of California, Los Angeles

(*) degree program awarded outside engineering

ALPHABETICAL INDEX OF PARTICIPATING UNDERGRADUATE DEGREE PROGRAMS

Carnegie Mellon University
University of Cincinnati
The Citadel
Clarkson University
Clemson University
Colorado State University
University of Colorado at Boulder
University of Colorado at Denver and Health Sciences Center
Columbia University
Cornell University
University of the District of Columbia
Drexel University
Embry Riddle Aeronautical Univ., Daytona Beach
University of Evansville
University of Florida
Florida Atlantic University
Florida Institute of Technology
Florida International University
FAMU-FSU College of Engineering
The George Washington University
Georgia Institute of Technology
Gonzaga University
University of Hawaii at Manoa
University of Houston, Cullen School of Engineering
Howard University
University of Idaho
Idaho State University
Illinois Institute of Technology
University of Illinois at Chicago
University of Illinois at Urbana-Champaign
Iowa State University
The Johns Hopkins University
University of Kansas
Kansas State University
University of Kentucky
Lafayette College
Lamar University
Lawrence Technological University
Lehigh University
Louisiana State University
University of Louisiana at Lafayette

University of Louisville
University of Maine
Manhattan College
Marquette University
University of Maryland, College Park
University of Massachusetts Amherst
University of Massachusetts Dartmouth
University of Massachusetts Lowell
The University of Memphis
Merrimack College
University of Miami
Michigan State University
Michigan Technological University
Minnesota State University, Mankato
The University of Mississippi
Mississippi State University
University of Missouri-Columbia
University of Missouri - Kansas City
University of Missouri - Rolla
Montana State University
Morgan State University
University of Nevada, Las Vegas
University of Nevada, Reno
University of New Hampshire
University of New Haven
New Jersey Institute of Technology
The College of New Jersey
The University of New Mexico
New Mexico State University
University of New Orleans
State University of New York at Buffalo
North Carolina A & T State University
North Carolina State University
University of North Dakota
North Dakota State University
University of North Florida
Northeastern University
Northern Arizona University
Northwestern University
Norwich University
University of Notre Dame

The Ohio State University
Ohio University
University of Oklahoma
Oklahoma State University
Old Dominion University
Oregon Institute of Technology
Oregon State University
University of Ottawa, Faculty of Engineering
University of the Pacific
The Pennsylvania State University
University of Pittsburgh
Polytechnic University
Polytechnic University of Puerto Rico
University of Portland
Portland State University
Prairie View A&M University
University of Puerto Rico, Mayaguez Campus
Purdue University
Rensselaer Polytechnic Institute
University of Rhode Island
William Marsh Rice University
Rose-Hulman Institute of Technology
Rowan University
Rutgers, The State University of New Jersey
Saint Martin's College
San Diego State University
San Francisco State University
San Jose State University
Santa Clara University
Seattle University
University of South Alabama
South Dakota School of Mines and Technology
South Dakota State University
University of South Florida
University of Southern California
Southern Illinois University Carbondale
Southern Illinois University Edwardsville
Southern Methodist University
Southern University and A&M College
Stanford University
Syracuse University

(*) degree program awarded outside engineering

(*) degree program awarded outside engineering

ALPHABETICAL INDEX OF PARTICIPATING UNDERGRADUATE DEGREE PROGRAMS

Computer Engineering (B.S.)

University of Alaska, Anchorage
University of Alaska Fairbanks
University of Alberta
The University of Arizona
University of Arkansas
University of Bridgeport
Brigham Young University
Brown University
California Institute of Technology
California Polytechnic State University
California State Polytechnic University, Pomona
California State University, Chico
California State University, Fresno
California State University, Fullerton
California State University, Long Beach
California State University, Northridge
California State University, Sacramento
University of California, Davis
University of California, Irvine
University of California, Riverside
University of California, San Diego
University of California, San Diego
University of California, Santa Barbara
University of California-Santa Cruz
Capitol College
Cedarville University
University of Cincinnati
Clarkson University
Clemson University
Colorado Technical University
University of Colorado at Colorado Springs
Columbia University
University of Dayton
University of Denver
Drexel University
Embry Riddle Aeronautical Univ, Daytona Beach
Embry Riddle Aeronautical University, Prescott
University of Evansville
Fairfield University
Florida Atlantic University

Florida Institute of Technology
Florida International University
FAMU-FSU College of Engineering
George Mason University
The George Washington University
Georgia Institute of Technology
Gonzaga University
Hofstra University
University of Houston, Cullen School of Engineering
University of Idaho
Illinois Institute of Technology
University of Illinois at Chicago
University of Illinois at Urbana-Champaign
Indiana Institute of Technology
Iowa State University
The Johns Hopkins University
University of Kansas
Kansas State University
University of Kentucky
Kettering University formerly GMI
Lake Superior State University
Lawrence Technological University
Lehigh University
University of Maine
Manhattan College
Marquette University
University of Maryland, Baltimore County
University of Maryland, College Park
University of Massachusetts Dartmouth
University of Massachusetts Lowell
The University of Memphis
University of Miami
Michigan State University
Michigan Technological University
Milwaukee School of Engineering
Minnesota State University, Mankato
Mississippi State University
University of Missouri-Columbia
University of Missouri - Rolla
Montana State University
University of Nevada, Las Vegas

University of New Hampshire
University of New Haven
New Jersey Institute of Technology
The College of New Jersey
The University of New Mexico
The State University of New York at Binghamton
State University of New York at Buffalo
SUNY, New Paltz
North Carolina A & T State University
North Carolina State University
North Dakota State University
University of North Texas
Northeastern University
Northwestern University
Norwich University
University of Notre Dame
Oakland University
University of Oklahoma
Oklahoma Christian University
Old Dominion University
Oregon State University
University of Ottawa, Faculty of Engineering
Penn State Erie, The Behrend College
The Pennsylvania State University
University of Pittsburgh
Polytechnic University
Polytechnic University of Puerto Rico
Portland State University
Prairie View A&M University
University of Puerto Rico, Mayaguez Campus
Purdue University
Rensselaer Polytechnic Institute
University of Rhode Island
Rochester Institute of Technology
Rose-Hulman Institute of Technology
Saint Cloud State University
Saint Mary's University
San Diego State University
San Francisco State University
San Jose State University
Santa Clara University

(*) degree program awarded outside engineering

ALPHABETICAL INDEX OF PARTICIPATING UNDERGRADUATE DEGREE PROGRAMS

University of South Carolina
South Dakota School of Mines and Technology
University of South Florida
Southern Illinois University Edwardsville
Southern Methodist University
Syracuse University
Tennessee Technological University
University of Tennessee, Knoxville
Texas Tech University
Tri-State University
U.S. Air Force Academy
University of Utah
Utah State University
Valparaiso University
Villanova University
University of Virginia
Virginia Commonwealth University
Virginia Polytechnic Institute and State University
University of Washington
Washington State University
Washington University
West Virginia University
Wichita State University
University of Wisconsin, Madison
University of Wyoming

Computer Engineering (B.S.C.E.)
Wright State University

Computer Engineering (B.S.C.P.)
University of Nebraska, Lincoln

Computer Engineering (B.S.C.P.E.)
University of Central Florida

Computer Engineering (B.S.Cmp.E.)
Indiana University-Purdue University Fort Wayne

Computer Engineering (B.S.Comp.E.)
Indiana University Purdue University at Indianapolis

Computer Engineering (B.S.Cp.E.)
University of North Carolina, Charlotte
Ohio Northern University

Computer Engineering (B.S.E.)
The University of Alabama in Huntsville
Case Western Reserve University

University of Connecticut
Miami University
University of Michigan
University of Michigan, Dearborn
Tulane University
Western Michigan University

Computer Engineering (B.S.E.E.)
West Virginia University Institute of Technology

Computer Engineering (BASc)
University of Waterloo

Computer Engineering (BSc)
University of Calgary

Computer Engineering (BSCPE)
Tufts University

Computer Engineering (CEE) (B.S.)
University of Florida

Computer Engineering (CEN) (B.S.)
University of Florida

Computer Engineering and Computer Science (B.S.)
University of Louisville
University of Southern California

Computer Engineering and Electrical Engineering (B.S.)
University of California, Davis

Computer Engineering BSE
Purdue University, Calumet

Computer Engineering Option (B.S.)
The University of Alabama

Computer Engineering(B.S.)
The University of Akron

Computer Information Systems (B.S.)
Illinois Institute of Technology (*)
University of the Pacific
University of South Carolina

Computer Information Systems (B.S.C.I.S.)
The University of Texas at Tyler

Computer Science
California Institute of Technology
University of Tulsa
Wentworth Institute of Technology (*)
University of Wisconsin, Milwaukee

Computer Science & Engineering (B.S.)
University of California, Berkeley
Lehigh University
The University of Toledo

Computer Science & Engineering (B.S.E.)
University of Connecticut

Computer Science (A.B.)
Dartmouth College (*)
Harvard University

Computer Science (A.B., B.S.)
Duke University Pratt School of Engineering (*)

Computer Science (B. S.)
University of Louisiana at Lafayette (*)

Computer Science (B.A. & B.S.)
University of Delaware (*)

Computer Science (B.A.)
University of Arkansas (*)
Boston University (*)
University of California, Berkeley (*)
Clemson University
Drexel University
The George Washington University
The University of Iowa (*)
Loyola College in Maryland (*)
University of Nevada, Las Vegas
New Jersey Institute of Technology (*)
State University of New York at Buffalo
University of North Texas
William Marsh Rice University
Seattle University
Southern Illinois University Edwardsville
Southern Methodist University
Swarthmore College (*)
University of Vermont (*)
Washington State University
Wayne State University (*)

Computer Science (B.A., B.S.)
University of California, San Diego
University of California-Santa Cruz

Computer Science (B.Comp.Sc.)
Concordia University, Faculty of Engr. and Comp. Sci. (*)

(*) degree program awarded outside engineering

Computer Science (B.S)
Clarkson University (*)
Florida International University
U.S. Air Force Academy

Computer Science (B.S. and B.A.)
University of Rochester (*)

Computer Science (B.S.)
The University of Alabama
The University of Arizona (*)
Arizona State University
University of Arkansas
Arkansas Tech University (*)
University of Arkansas at Little Rock
Auburn University
Boise State University
University of Bridgeport
Brigham Young University (*)
California Institute of Technology
California Polytechnic State University
California State University, Fresno
California State University, Fullerton
California State University, Long Beach
California State University, Los Angeles
California State University, Northridge
California State University, Sacramento
University of California, Irvine (*)
University of California, Los Angeles
University of California, Riverside
University of California, Santa Barbara
Carnegie Mellon University (*)
Case Western Reserve University
The Catholic University of America
Cedarville University
University of Central Florida
University of Cincinnati
Clemson University
University of Colorado at Boulder
University of Colorado at Colorado Springs
Columbia University
University of Connecticut
Cornell University

University of the District of Columbia
Drexel University
Embry Riddle Aeronautical Univ., Daytona Beach
Embry Riddle Aeronautical University, Prescott (*)
University of Evansville
University of Florida
University of Florida (*)
Florida Atlantic University
Florida Institute of Technology
Gannon University
George Mason University
The George Washington University
Georgia Institute of Technology (*)
Gonzaga University
Grove City College (*)
University of Houston, Cullen School of Engineering (*)
University of Idaho
Idaho State University
Illinois Institute of Technology (*)
University of Illinois at Chicago
University of Illinois at Urbana-Champaign
Indiana University-Purdue University Fort Wayne (*)
The University of Iowa (*)
University of Kansas
Kansas State University
University of Kentucky
Lamar University (*)
Lehigh University
LeTourneau University (*)
Louisiana State University (*)
Loyola College in Maryland (*)
Manhattan College (*)
Marquette University (*)
University of Maryland, Baltimore County
University of Maryland, College Park (*)
University of Massachusetts Amherst (*)
University of Massachusetts Dartmouth
University of Massachusetts Lowell (*)
The University of Memphis (*)
University of Michigan (*)
Michigan State University

Michigan Technological University (*)
University of Minnesota, Duluth
The University of Mississippi
Mississippi State University
University of Missouri-Columbia
University of Missouri - Kansas City
Montana State University
University of Nevada, Las Vegas
University of Nevada, Reno
University of New Hampshire
University of New Haven
New Jersey Institute of Technology (*)
The University of New Mexico
New York Institute of Technology
City College of the City University of New York
The State University of New York at Binghamton
State University of New York at Buffalo
Stony Brook University
North Carolina A & T State University
North Carolina State University
University of North Texas
Northern Arizona University
Northwestern University
Norwich University (*)
University of Notre Dame
Oakland University
Ohio Northern University
Ohio University
University of Oklahoma
Oklahoma Christian University
Oregon State University
University of Ottawa, Faculty of Engineering
University of the Pacific
Pennsylvania State University Harrisburg
The Pennsylvania State University
University of Pittsburgh (*)
Polytechnic University
Polytechnic University of Puerto Rico
University of Portland
Portland State University
Prairie View A&M University

(*) degree program awarded outside engineering

Princeton University
Purdue University (*)
Rensselaer Polytechnic Institute (*)
Rochester Institute of Technology (*)
Roger Williams University
Rose-Hulman Institute of Technology
Rutgers, The State University of New Jersey (*)
Saint Cloud State University (*)
Seattle University
University of South Carolina
South Dakota School of Mines and Technology
South Dakota State University
University of South Florida
University of Southern California
Southern Illinois University Carbondale (*)
Southern Illinois University Edwardsville
Southern Methodist University
Stanford University
Stevens Institute of Technology (*)
Syracuse University
Tennessee State University
Tennessee Technological University (*)
University of Tennessee, Knoxville (*)
Texas A&M University
Texas A&M University - Kingsville
Texas Tech University
The University of Texas at Arlington
University of Texas at El Paso
University of Texas at San Antonio (*)
Union College
University of Utah
Vanderbilt University
University of Vermont
University of Virginia
Virginia Commonwealth University
Virginia Polytechnic Institute and State University
University of Washington
Washington State University
Washington University
Wayne State University (*)
West Virginia University

West Virginia University (*)
Western Michigan University
Wichita State University (*)
University of Wisconsin, Madison (*)
University of Wisconsin, Platteville
Worcester Polytechnic Institute (*)
University of Wyoming

Computer Science (B.S.) (B.A.)
University of Nebraska, Lincoln (*)
Valparaiso University (*)

Computer Science (B.S.) (B.S./M.S.)
University of Alaska Fairbanks (*)

Computer Science (B.S., B.A.)
The Johns Hopkins University

Computer Science (B.S.C.)
Tulane University

Computer Science (B.S.C.S
West Virginia University Institute of Technology

Computer Science (B.S.C.S.)
Alabama A&M University
Baylor University
William Marsh Rice University
The University of Texas at Dallas
The University of Texas at Tyler
Wright State University

Computer Science (B.S.Comp.Sc.)
University of Minnesota -Twin Cities

Computer Science (B.S.E.)
Miami University
University of Michigan
University of Pennsylvania

Computer Science (BS)
Louisiana Tech University

Computer Science (BSCS)
University of Detroit Mercy
Tufts University

Computer Science (FSU) (B.S.)
FAMU-FSU College of Engineering (*)

Computer Science (Mathematics) (B.S.)
Santa Clara University (*)

Computer Science -outside Engineering (B.S.)
University of California, Davis (*)

Computer Science and Business (B.S.)
Lehigh University

Computer Science and Engineering (B.S.)
Bucknell University
University of California, Irvine
University of California, Irvine (*)
University of California, Los Angeles
University of Colorado at Denver and Health Sciences Center
The Ohio State University
The University of Texas at Arlington

Computer Science and Engineering (B.S.E.)
University of Pennsylvania

Computer Science and Engineering (S.B.)
Massachusetts Institute of Technology

Computer Science and Engineering - inside Engineering (B.S.)
University of California, Davis

Computer Science BS
Purdue University, Calumet (*)

Computer Science with Specialization in Bioinformatics (B.S.)
University of California, San Diego

Computer Science:Computer Game Design (B.S.)
University of California-Santa Cruz

Computer Sciences (B.S.)
Tri-State University (*)

Computer Specialization (B.S.)
Mercer University

Computer Systems Engineering (B.S.)
Boston University
University of Massachusetts Amherst

Computer Systems Engineering (B.S.E.)
Arizona State University

Computer Systems Science (B.S.)
Michigan Technological University (*)

Construction
University of Southern California

Construction (B.S.)
Southern Illinois University Edwardsville

Construction Concentration (B.E.)
The Catholic University of America

(*) degree program awarded outside engineering

(*) degree program awarded outside engineering

(*) degree program awarded outside engineering

Electrical Engineering (B.S.) Computer Engineering (B.S.)
Colorado State University

Electrical Engineering (B.S.), Computer Engineering (B.S.)
University of South Alabama
Southern Illinois University Carbondale

Electrical Engineering (B.S., B.A.)
The Johns Hopkins University
Yale University/Faculty of Engineering

Electrical Engineering (B.S.,B.A.)
University of San Diego

Electrical Engineering (B.S.E.
Western Michigan University

Electrical Engineering (B.S.E.)
The University of Alabama in Huntsville
Arizona State University
Case Western Reserve University
University of Connecticut
Duke University Pratt School of Engineering
The University of Iowa

(*) degree program awarded outside engineering

ALPHABETICAL INDEX OF PARTICIPATING UNDERGRADUATE DEGREE PROGRAMS

Miami University
University of Michigan
University of Michigan, Dearborn
University of Pennsylvania
Tulane University

Electrical Engineering (B.S.E.); Computer Science (B.S.)
Loyola Marymount University

Electrical Engineering (B.S.E.E.)
Alabama A&M University
University of Central Florida
University of Hartford
Indiana University Purdue University at Indianapolis
Indiana University-Purdue University Fort Wayne
Minnesota State University, Mankato
University of Nebraska, Lincoln
University of North Carolina, Charlotte
Ohio Northern University
William Marsh Rice University
Saginaw Valley State University
University of Saint Thomas
The University of Texas at Dallas
The University of Texas at Tyler
West Virginia University Institute of Technology
Wright State University

Electrical Engineering (B.S.EE)
University of Tennessee, Chattanooga

Electrical Engineering (BASc)
University of Waterloo

Electrical Engineering (BS)
Louisiana Tech University

Electrical Engineering (BSc)
University of Calgary

Electrical Engineering (BSEE)
Tufts University

Electrical Engineering and Computer Engineering (B.S.)
University of California, Davis

Electrical Engineering and Computer Science (S.B.)
Massachusetts Institute of Technology

Electrical Engineering and Mechanical Engineering (B.S.)
University of California, Davis

Electrical Engineering BSE
Purdue University, Calumet

Electrical Engineering Option (B.S.)
McNeese State University

Electrical Engineering, Bioengineering Option (B.S.)
University of Wyoming

Electrical Engineering, Computer Engineering (B.S.)
Louisiana State University

Electrical Engineering- Computer (B.S.)
Oklahoma State University
University of Southern California

Electrical Engineering/Computer Science (B.S.)
Texas Tech University

Electrical Engineering/Materials Science (B.S.)
University of California, Davis

Electrical Engineering/Optical Science and Engineering (B.S.)
University of California, Davis

Electrical Engineerng (B.S.)
University of Southern Maine

Electrical Engrineering (B.S.)
San Jose State University

Electrical Science and Engineering (S.B.)
Massachusetts Institute of Technology

Electrical Sciences Engineering (B.S.)
Brown University

Electrical Specialization (B.S.)
Mercer University

Electrical/Computer Engineering (B.S.)
Howard University

Electrical/Electronic Engineering (B.S.)
California State University, Chico

Electromechanical Engineering
Wentworth Institute of Technology

Electronics Engineering (B.S.EL.)
University of Nebraska, Lincoln

Energy Resources Engineering (B.S.)
Stanford University

Engineering & Management Systems (B.S.)
Columbia University

Engineering (A.B.)
Lafayette College

Engineering (A.B., B.E.)
Dartmouth College

Engineering (B.A.)
The University of Arizona
Texas Tech University
Trinity College

Engineering (B.E.)
The University of Mississippi

Engineering (B.E.) with a concentration in Biomedical

Engineering (B.E.)
Stevens Institute of Technology

Engineering (B.S.)
Arkansas State University
California State University, Long Beach
University of California, Irvine
Calvin College
Colorado School of Mines
The Cooper Union
Harvey Mudd College
LeTourneau University
Michigan Technological University
Milwaukee School of Engineering
North Carolina State University
Northwestern University
University of Oklahoma
Philadelphia University
Roger Williams University
Santa Clara University
Smith College
Stanford University
Swarthmore College
Texas Christian University
Trinity College

Engineering (B.S.) Bioengineering Concentration
Santa Clara University

Engineering (B.S.) with concentrations in Mechanical, Electrical, and Computer Engineering
Oral Roberts University

Engineering (B.S.)-Electrical Concentration
John Brown University

(*) degree program awarded outside engineering

(*) degree program awarded outside engineering

(*) degree program awarded outside engineering

Florida Institute of Technology
University of Oklahoma
Southern Methodist University

Environmental Specialization (B.S.)
Mercer University

Environmental Systems Engineering (B.S.)
The Pennsylvania State University

EuroTechnology (B.S.E., B.A.)
University of Connecticut

F

Facilities Engineering (B.S.)
Massachusetts Maritime Academy

Facility Engineering (B.S.)
State University of New York Maritime College

Fiber Engineering (B.F.E.)
Auburn University

Financial Engineering (B.S.)
Columbia University

Fire Protection Engineering (B.S.)
University of Maryland, College Park

Food, Agricultural, and Biological Engrg. (B.S.)
The Ohio State University

Forest Engineering (B.S.)
SUNY College of Environmental Science and Forestry

G

General Engineering
Boston University
Carnegie Mellon University
Clemson University
Colorado State University, Pueblo
University of Denver
Kansas State University
Montana State University

General Engineering (B.A.)
The Johns Hopkins University

General Engineering (B.E.)
The Cooper Union

General Engineering (B.S.)
California Polytechnic State University
University of Illinois at Urbana-Champaign
Montana Tech of the University of Montana
University of New Haven
San Jose State University
U.S. Air Force Academy

General Engineering (B.S.E.)
Miami University

General Engineering (B.S.G.E.)
Gonzaga University

General; Applied Science Option (B.S.)
University of Maryland, College Park

General; Engineering Option (B.S.)
University of Maryland, College Park

Geography (B.A.)
The Johns Hopkins University

Geological Engineering (B.E.)
Ecole Polytechnique de Montreal

Geological Engineering (B.Geo.E.)
University of Minnesota -Twin Cities

Geological Engineering (B.S.)
University of Alaska Fairbanks
The University of Arizona
Colorado School of Mines
Michigan Technological University
University of Missouri - Rolla
Montana Tech of the University of Montana
New Mexico State University
University of North Dakota
South Dakota School of Mines and Technology
University of Wisconsin, Madison

Geological Engineering (BASc)
University of Waterloo

Geological Engr. (B.S.)
The University of Mississippi

Geological Sciences (B.S.)
Cornell University

Geological Sciences-Atmospheric Science Option (B.S.)
Cornell University

Geological Sciences-Geoscience Option (B.S.)
Cornell University

Geological Sciences-Science of Earth Systems Option (B.S.)
Cornell University

Geology (B.S.)
Michigan Technological University

Geomatics (B.S.)
University of Florida
North Carolina A & T State University
Oregon Institute of Technology

Geomatics Engineering (B.S.)
California State University, Fresno
The Ohio State University

Geomatics Engineering (BSc)
University of Calgary

Geomechanics (B.S.)
University of Rochester

Geophysical Engineering (B.S.)
Colorado School of Mines
Montana Tech of the University of Montana

Geoscience Engineering (B.S.)
New Jersey Institute of Technology

Geosystems Engineering and Hydrogeology (B.S.)
The University of Texas at Austin

Glass Engineering Science (B.S.)
Alfred University, NY State College of Ceramics

I

Independent Major (B.S.)
Cornell University

Industrial Engineering (B.S.)
Columbia University

Industrial & Systems Engineering (B.E.)
Youngstown State University

Industrial & Systems Engineering (B.S.)
Northern Illinois University
San Jose State University

Industrial & Systems Engineering (B.S.I.S.E.)
Wright State University

(*) degree program awarded outside engineering

Industrial and Management Engineering (B.S.)
Rensselaer Polytechnic Institute

Industrial and Manufacturing Engineering (B.S.)
Indiana Institute of Technology

Industrial and Operations Engineering (B.S.E.)
University of Michigan

Industrial and Systems Engineering (B.I.S.E.)
Auburn University

Industrial and Systems Engineering (B.S.)
University of Florida
Florida International University
The State University of New York at Binghamton
The Ohio State University
Philadelphia University
University of Southern California
Virginia Polytechnic Institute and State University

Industrial and Systems Engineering (B.S.,B.A.)
University of San Diego

Industrial and Systems Engineering (B.S.E.)
The University of Alabama in Huntsville
University of Michigan, Dearborn

Industrial and Systems Engineering- Information Systems
University of Southern California

Industrial and Systems Engr. (B.S.)
Ohio University

Industrial Concentration (B.S.E.)
University of Tennessee, Chattanooga

Industrial Engineering
California State University, East Bay
University of Wisconsin, Milwaukee

Industrial Engineering & Operations Research (B.S.)
University of California, Berkeley

Industrial Engineering (B.A.)
Drexel University

Industrial Engineering (B.E.)
Cleveland State University
Ecole Polytechnique de Montreal

Industrial Engineering (B.Eng.)
Concordia University, Faculty of Engr. and Comp. Sci.

Industrial Engineering (B.S.)
The University of Alabama
The University of Arizona
University of Arkansas
Bradley University
California Polytechnic State University
California State Polytechnic University, Pomona
California State University, Fresno
Clemson University
Colorado State University, Pueblo
FAMU-FSU College of Engineering
Georgia Institute of Technology
Hofstra University
University of Houston, Cullen School of Engineering
University of Illinois at Chicago
University of Illinois at Urbana-Champaign
Iowa State University
Kansas State University
Kettering University formerly GMI
Lamar University
Lehigh University
Louisiana State University
University of Louisville
University of Massachusetts Amherst
University of Miami
Milwaukee School of Engineering
Mississippi State University
University of Missouri-Columbia
Montana State University
Morgan State University
University of New Haven
New Jersey Institute of Technology
New Mexico State University
State University of New York at Buffalo
North Carolina A &T State University
North Carolina State University
North Dakota State University
Northeastern University
Northwestern University
University of Oklahoma
Oregon State University
The Pennsylvania State University
University of Pittsburgh
Polytechnic University of Puerto Rico
University of Puerto Rico, Mayaguez Campus
Purdue University
University of Rhode Island
Rochester Institute of Technology
Rutgers, The State University of New Jersey
Saint Ambrose University
Saint Mary's University
South Dakota School of Mines and Technology
University of South Florida
Southern Illinois University Edwardsville
Tennessee Technological University
University of Tennessee, Knoxville
Texas A&M University
Texas Tech University
The University of Texas at Arlington
University of Texas at El Paso
The University of Toledo
University of Washington
Wayne State University
West Virginia University
Western New England College
Wichita State University
University of Wisconsin, Madison
University of Wisconsin, Platteville
Worcester Polytechnic Institute

Industrial Engineering (B.S.E.)
Arizona State University
The University of Iowa
Western Michigan University

Industrial Engineering (B.S.I.E.)
University of Central Florida
University of Minnesota, Duluth
University of Nebraska, Lincoln

Industrial Engineering (BS)
Louisiana Tech University

Industrial Engineering and Management (B.S.)
Oklahoma State University

Industrial Management (B.S.)
Mercer University

(*) degree program awarded outside engineering

ALPHABETICAL INDEX OF PARTICIPATING UNDERGRADUATE DEGREE PROGRAMS

Industrial Specialization (B.S.)
Mercer University

Industrial Technology (B.S.)
Iowa State University
Texas A&M University - Kingsville

Industrial/Manufacturing Engineering
Ecole de Technologie Superieure

Informatics (B.S.)
University of California, Irvine (*)

Information and Computer Science (B.S.)
University of California, Irvine (*)

Information and Systems Engineering (B.S.)
Lehigh University

Information Management (B.S.)
Washington University

Information Science, Systems and Technology (B.S.)
Cornell University

Information Systems (B.A. and B.S.)
University of Maryland, Baltimore County

Information Systems (B.S.)
University of California, Riverside
Florida Institute of Technology
Kansas State University
University of South Florida

Information Systems Engineering (B.S.)
University of Maine

Information Systems Management (B.S)
University of California-Santa Cruz

Information Technology (B.A)
Florida International University

Information Technology (B.S)
Florida International University

Information Technology (B.S.)
University of Central Florida
George Mason University
University of Miami
University of Missouri-Columbia
New York Institute of Technology
Oakland University

Information Technology Engineering (B.Eng.)
Ecole de Technologie Superieure

Interdepartmental Engineering (B.S.)
University of Rochester

Interdisciplinary
Boston University

Interdisciplinary (B.S.)
University of Nebraska, Lincoln

Interdisciplinary Engineering (B.S.)
University of Missouri - Rolla
Purdue University

Interdisciplinary Engineering (B.S.E.)
Indiana University Purdue University at Indianapolis

Interdisciplinary Engineering Studies (B.S., B.S.E.)
University of Washington

Interdisciplinary Engnr Studies
University of Florida

Intergrated Business & Engineering (B.S.)
Lehigh University

Internet Technology (B.S.)
University of Evansville

L

Land Surveying & Geomatics Engineering (B.S.)
Purdue University

M

Management and Engineering for Manufacturing (B.S.)
University of Connecticut

Management Engineering (BASC)
University of Waterloo

Management Information Systems (B.S.)
Gannon University
University of Wyoming

Management Science (B.S.)
Southern Methodist University

Management Science and Engineering (B.S.)
Stanford University

Manufacturing and Design Engineering (B.S.)
Northwestern University

Manufacturing and Robotics (B.E.)
The University of New Mexico

Manufacturing Engineering (B.E.)
University of Detroit Mercy

Manufacturing Engineering (B.S.)
Boston University
Bradley University
California Polytechnic State University
California State Polytechnic University, Pomona
University of California, Berkeley
Kettering University formerly GMI
North Dakota State University
Oregon State University
Saint Cloud State University
Southern Illinois University Edwardsville
The University of Texas-Pan American
Utah State University
Wichita State University
University of Wisconsin, Stout
Worcester Polytechnic Institute

Manufacturing Engineering (B.S.E.)
Miami University
University of Michigan, Dearborn
Western Michigan University

Manufacturing Engineering (BSc)
University of Calgary

Manufacturing Systems Engineering (B.S.)
California State University, Northridge
Kansas State University

Marine Engineering and Shipyard Management (B.S.)
U.S. Merchant Marine Academy

Marine Engineering (B.S.)
Massachusetts Maritime Academy
Texas A&M University, Galveston
U.S. Merchant Marine Academy

Marine Engineering Systems (B.S.)
U.S. Merchant Marine Academy

Marine Systems Engineering (B.S.)
Maine Maritime Academy
State University of New York Maritime College

Maritime Systems Engineering (B.S.)
Texas A&M University, Galveston

(*) degree program awarded outside engineering

ALPHABETICAL INDEX OF PARTICIPATING UNDERGRADUATE DEGREE PROGRAMS

Material Engineering (B.S.)
Iowa State University

Material Science & Engineering (B.S.)
Washington State University

Material Science and Engineering (B.S.)
University of Idaho
Illinois Institute of Technology

Materials Engineering
University of Wisconsin, Milwaukee

Materials Engineering (B.E.)
Auburn University
Ecole Polytechnique de Montreal

Materials Engineering (B.S.)
University of Alabama at Birmingham
University of Alberta
California Polytechnic State University
University of California, Los Angeles
University of Cincinnati
University of Kentucky
University of Maryland, College Park
New Mexico Institute of Mining & Technology
Purdue University
Rensselaer Polytechnic Institute
San Jose State University

Materials Engineering Science (B.S.)
Alfred University, NY State College of Ceramics

Materials Science & Engineering (B.S.)
Boise State University
University of California, Berkeley
Columbia University
Drexel University
Michigan Technological University
University of Utah

Materials Science & Engineering and Mechanical Engineering (B.S.)
University of California, Berkeley

Materials Science (B.A.)
William Marsh Rice University

Materials Science (B.S.)
University of Massachusetts Dartmouth
University of Wisconsin, Madison

Materials Science and Engineering (B.Mat.S.E.)
University of Minnesota –Twin Cities

Materials Science and Engineering (B.S.)
The University of Arizona
University of California, Davis
Carnegie Mellon University
Clemson University
Cornell University
University of Florida
University of Illinois at Urbana-Champaign
The Johns Hopkins University
Lehigh University
Michigan State University
University of Nevada, Reno
North Carolina State University
Northwestern University
The Ohio State University
The Pennsylvania State University
University of Pittsburgh
Stanford University
University of Tennessee, Knoxville
Virginia Polytechnic Institute and State University
University of Washington

Materials Science and Engineering (B.S.E.)
Arizona State University
Case Western Reserve University
University of Connecticut
University of Michigan
University of Pennsylvania

Materials Science and Engineering (B.S.M.S.)
William Marsh Rice University
Wright State University

Materials Science and Engineering (S.B.)
Massachusetts Institute of Technology

Materials Science and Engineering/Mechanical Engineering (B.S.)
University of California, Davis

Materials Science Engineering (B.S.)
Brown University
University of California, Irvine
Georgia Institute of Technology

Mathematical and Computer Science (B.S.)
Colorado School of Mines

Mechanical and Aerospace Engineering (B.S.)
Princeton University
Princeton University

Mechanical and Ocean Engineering (S.B.)
Massachusetts Institute of Technology

Mechanical Engineering (B.M.E.)
University of Minnesota –Twin Cities

Mechanical Engineering
University of Dayton
University of Tulsa
Western Kentucky University
University of Wisconsin, Milwaukee

Mechanical Engineering (B.A.)
William Marsh Rice University

Mechanical Engineering (B.E.)
The Catholic University of America
Cleveland State University
The Cooper Union
University of Detroit Mercy
Ecole Polytechnique de Montreal
City College of the City University of New York
Stony Brook University
Stevens Institute of Technology
Vanderbilt University
Youngstown State University

Mechanical Engineering (B.Eng.)
Concordia University, Faculty of Engr. and Comp. Sci.
Ecole de Technologie Superieure

Mechanical Engineering (B.M.E.)
Auburn University
University of Delaware

Mechanical Engineering (B.S.)
The University of Akron
University of Alabama at Birmingham
The University of Alabama
University of Alaska, Anchorage
University of Alaska Fairbanks
University of Alberta
Alfred University, NY State College of Ceramics

(*) degree program awarded outside engineering

ALPHABETICAL INDEX OF PARTICIPATING UNDERGRADUATE DEGREE PROGRAMS

The University of Arizona
University of Arkansas
Arkansas Tech University
Boise State University
Boston University
Bradley University
Brigham Young University
Brown University
Bucknell University
California Institute of Technology
California Maritime Academy
California Polytechnic State University
California State Polytechnic University, Pomona
California State University, Chico
California State University, Fresno
California State University, Fullerton
California State University, Long Beach
California State University, Los Angeles
California State University, Northridge
California State University, Sacramento
University of California, Berkeley
University of California, Davis
University of California, Irvine
University of California, Los Angeles
University of California, Riverside
University of California, San Diego
University of California, Santa Barbara
Carnegie Mellon University
Cedarville University
Christian Brothers University
University of Cincinnati
Clarkson University
Clemson University
Colorado State University
University of Colorado at Boulder
University of Colorado at Colorado Springs
University of Colorado at Denver and Health Sciences Center
Columbia University
Cornell University
University of Denver
University of the District of Columbia

Drexel University
Embry Riddle Aeronautical Univ., Daytona Beach
University of Evansville
Fairfield University
University of Florida
Florida Atlantic University
Florida Institute of Technology
Florida International University
FAMU-FSU College of Engineering
Gannon University
The George Washington University
Georgia Institute of Technology
Gonzaga University
Grove City College
University of Hawaii at Manoa
Henry Cogswell College
Hofstra University
University of Houston, Cullen School of Engineering
Howard University
University of Idaho
Idaho State University
Illinois Institute of Technology
University of Illinois at Chicago
University of Illinois at Urbana-Champaign
Indiana Institute of Technology
Iowa State University
The Johns Hopkins University
University of Kansas
Kansas State University
University of Kentucky
Kettering University formerly GMI
Lafayette College
Lake Superior State University
Lamar University
Lawrence Technological University
Lehigh University
Louisiana State University
University of Louisiana at Lafayette
University of Louisville
University of Maine
Manhattan College

Marquette University
University of Maryland, Baltimore County
University of Maryland, College Park
University of Massachusetts Amherst
University of Massachusetts Dartmouth
University of Massachusetts Lowell
The University of Memphis
University of Miami
Michigan State University
Michigan Technological University
Milwaukee School of Engineering
The University of Mississippi
Mississippi State University
University of Missouri-Columbia
University of Missouri - Kansas City
University of Missouri - Rolla
Montana State University
University of Nevada, Las Vegas
University of Nevada, Reno
University of New Hampshire
University of New Haven
New Jersey Institute of Technology
The College of New Jersey
The University of New Mexico
New Mexico Institute of Mining & Technology
New Mexico State University
University of New Orleans
New York Institute of Technology
The State University of New York at Binghamton
State University of New York at Buffalo
North Carolina A & T State University
North Carolina State University
University of North Dakota
North Dakota State University
University of North Florida
Northeastern University
Northern Arizona University
Northern Illinois University
Northwestern University
Norwich University
University of Notre Dame

(*) degree program awarded outside engineering

(*) degree program awarded outside engineering

(*) degree program awarded outside engineering

Oregon State University
The Pennsylvania State University
Purdue University
Rensselaer Polytechnic Institute
University of Tennessee, Knoxville
Texas A&M University
United States Military Academy
University of Wisconsin, Madison

Nuclear Engineering and Radiological Science (B.S.E.)
University of Michigan

Nuclear Engineering Science (B.S.)
University of Florida

Nuclear Science and Engineering (S.B.)
Massachusetts Institute of Technology

O

Ocean Engineering (B.S.)
Florida Atlantic University
Florida Institute of Technology
University of Rhode Island
Texas A&M University
U.S. Naval Academy
Virginia Polytechnic Institute and State University

Ocean Engineering (S.B.)
Massachusetts Institute of Technology

Oceanography (B.S.)
Florida Institute of Technology

Oil & Gas Engineering (BSc)
University of Calgary

Operations Research & Management Science (B.A.)
University of California, Berkeley

Operations Research (B.S.)
Columbia University

Operations Research and Engineering (B.S.)
Cornell University

Operations Research and Financial Engineering (B.S.)
Princeton University

Optical Engineering (B.S.)
The University of Arizona
Rose-Hulman Institute of Technology

Optical Engineering (B.S.E.)
The University of Alabama in Huntsville

Optical Science and Electrical Engineering (B.S.)
University of California, Davis

Optical Science and Engineering (B.S.)
University of California, Davis

Optical Science and Engineering/Biological Systems Engineering (B.S.)
University of California, Davis

Optical Sciences & Engineering (B.S.)
The University of Arizona

Optics (B.S.)
University of Rochester

P

Paper Engineering (B.S.), Paper Science (B.S.)
SUNY College of Environmental Science and Forestry

Paper Engineering (B.S.E.)
Western Michigan University

Paper Science & Engineering (B.S.)
North Carolina State University

Paper Science and Engineering (B.S.E.)
Miami University

Petroleum and Natural Gas Eng. (B.S.)
West Virginia University

Petroleum and Natural Gas Engineering (B.S.)
New Mexico Institute of Mining & Technology

Petroleum Engineering
University of Tulsa

Petroleum Engineering (B.S.)
University of Alaska Fairbanks
University of Alberta
Colorado School of Mines
University of Kansas
Louisiana State University
University of Louisiana at Lafayette
Marietta College
University of Missouri - Rolla
Montana Tech of the University of Montana
University of Oklahoma

Texas A&M University
Texas Tech University
The University of Texas at Austin
University of Wyoming

Physics (B.S.)
University of Massachusetts Dartmouth
South Dakota State University
Washington University

Physics Engineering (B.E.)
Ecole Polytechnique de Montreal

Plastics Engineering (B.S.)
University of Massachusetts Lowell

Polymer & Fiber Engineering (B.S.)
Georgia Institute of Technology

Polymer Science
University of Southern California

Polymer Science and Engineering (B.S.E.)
Case Western Reserve University

R

Radiation Health Physics (B.S.)
Oregon State University

Radiological Health Engineering (B.S.)
Texas A&M University

S

School of Engineering
Alfred University, NY State College of Ceramics

Scientific Applications
University of Tennessee, Chattanooga

Software Engineering & Computer Applications (B.S.)
Saint Mary's University

Software Engineering (B.E.)
Ecole Polytechnique de Montreal

Software Engineering (B.Eng.)
Concordia University, Faculty of Engr. and Comp. Sci.
Ecole de Technologie Superieure

Software Engineering (B.S.)
California Polytechnic State University
Capitol College

(*) degree program awarded outside engineering

ALPHABETICAL INDEX OF PARTICIPATING UNDERGRADUATE DEGREE PROGRAMS

Clarkson University
Drexel University
Embry Riddle Aeronautical Univ., Daytona Beach
Fairfield University
Florida Institute of Technology
Gannon University
Iowa State University
Michigan Technological University (*)
University of Michigan, Dearborn
Milwaukee School of Engineering
Mississippi State University
Montana Tech of the University of Montana (*)
University of Ottawa, Faculty of Engineering
Penn State Erie, The Behrend College
Rochester Institute of Technology
Rose-Hulman Institute of Technology
South Dakota State University
The University of Texas at Arlington
University of Wisconsin, Platteville

Software Engineering (B.S.S.E.)
Monmouth University
The University of Texas at Dallas

Software Engineering (B.S.W.E.)
Auburn University

Software Engineering (BSc)
University of Calgary

Software Engineering (BSE)
University of Waterloo

Software Engineering(B.S.)
San Jose State University

Software Systems
University of Tennessee, Chattanooga

Statistics (B.A.)
William Marsh Rice University

Structural Engineering (B.S.)
University of California, San Diego
Lehigh University

Structures
University of Southern California

Surveying and Topography (B.S.)
University of Puerto Rico, Mayaguez Campus

Surveying Engineering (B.S.)
Ferris State University
New Mexico State University

Systems & Computer Science (B.S.)
Howard University

Systems Analysis (B.S.E.)
Miami University

Systems and Control Engineering (B.S.E.)
Case Western Reserve University

Systems and Information Science (B.S.)
Syracuse University

Systems Design Engineering (BASc)
University of Waterloo

Systems Engineering (B.S.)
The University of Arizona
University of Arkansas at Little Rock
George Mason University
The George Washington University
Oakland University
United States Military Academy
U.S. Naval Academy
University of Virginia

Systems Science and Engineering (B.S.E.)
University of Pennsylvania

Systems Science and Mathematics (B.S.)
Washington University

T

Technical Communication (B.S.)
Mercer University
University of Washington

Technological Systems Management (B.S.)
Stony Brook University

Telecommunications Engineering (B.S.T.E.)
The University of Texas at Dallas

Textile Chemistry (B.T.C.)
Auburn University

Textile Engineering (B.S.)
North Carolina State University

Textile Engineering Technology (B.S.)
Philadelphia University

Textile Management and Technology (B.T.M.T.)
Auburn University

Textiles Engineering (B.S.)
Philadelphia University

W

Welding Engineering (B.S.)
The Ohio State University

Wireless Engineering (B.W.E.)
Auburn University
Auburn University

(*) degree program awarded outside engineering

ALPHABETICAL INDEX OF PARTICIPATING GRADUATE DEGREE PROGRAMS

A

Acoustics (M.S.)
The Pennsylvania State University

Acoustics (Ph.D.)
The Pennsylvania State University

Aeronautical Engineering (M.S.)
Air Force Institute of Technology

Aeronautical Engineering (M.S., M.E.)
Rensselaer Polytechnic Institute

Aeronautical Engineering (Ph.D.)
Air Force Institute of Technology

Aeronautical Engineering (Ph.D., D. E.)
Rensselaer Polytechnic Institute

Aeronautics and Astronautics (Eng.)
Massachusetts Institute of Technology

Aeronautics and Astronautics (M.S.)
Stanford University

Aeronautics and Astronautics (Ph.D.)
Massachusetts Institute of Technology
Purdue University
Stanford University
University of Washington

Aeronautics and Astronautics (S.M.)
Massachusetts Institute of Technology

Aeronautics and Astronautics (Sc.D.)
Massachusetts Institute of Technology

Aeronautics and Astronautics Engineering (M.S.)
Purdue University

Aeronautics and Astronautics- Transportation (S.M.)
Massachusetts Institute of Technology

Aeronautics Engineering (M.S.)
California Institute of Technology

Aeronautics Engineering (Ph.D.)
California Institute of Technology

Aerospac0e0 Engineering (Ph.D.)
University of Illinois at Urbana-Champaign

Aerospace and Mechanical Engineering (Ph.D.)
University of Notre Dame

Aerospace and Mechanical Engineering(Ph.D.)
University of Notre Dame

Aerospace Engineering (D.E.)
Washington University

Aerospace Engineering (M.E.)
State University of New York at Buffalo
Old Dominion University
The University of Texas at Arlington

Aerospace Engineering (M.Eng.)
Concordia University, Faculty of Engr. and Comp. Sci.
Ecole de Technologie Superieure

Aerospace Engineering (M.S.)
The University of Alabama
The University of Arizona
Boston University
California Polytechnic State University
California State University, Long Beach
University of California, Los Angeles
University of California, San Diego
Case Western Reserve University
University of Cincinnati
University of Dayton
Embry Riddle Aeronautical Univ., Daytona Beach
Florida Institute of Technology
Georgia Institute of Technology
University of Houston, Cullen School of Engineering
University of Illinois at Urbana-Champaign
University of Maryland, College Park
Mississippi State University
University of Missouri - Rolla
University of Nevada, Las Vegas
State University of New York at Buffalo
North Carolina State University
University of Notre Dame
University of Oklahoma
Old Dominion University
San Diego State University
San Jose State University
University of Southern California
Syracuse University
University of Tennessee, Knoxville
The University of Texas at Arlington
The University of Texas at Austin

Washington University
West Virginia University
Wichita State University

Aerospace Engineering (M.S., M.E.)
Auburn University
Cornell University
Ecole Polytechnique de Montreal
University of Florida
University of Kansas
The Pennsylvania State University
Texas A&M University
Virginia Polytechnic Institute and State University

Aerospace Engineering (M.S., M.Eng.)
Iowa State University

Aerospace Engineering (M.S., M.S.E.)
Arizona State University

Aerospace Engineering (M.S.A.E.)
University of Central Florida

Aerospace Engineering (M.S.E.)
The University of Alabama in Huntsville
University of Michigan

Aerospace Engineering (Ph.D.)
The University of Arizona
Arizona State University
Auburn University
Boston University
University of California, Los Angeles
University of California, San Diego
Case Western Reserve University
University of Cincinnati
Cornell University
University of Dayton
University of Florida
Florida Institute of Technology
Georgia Institute of Technology
University of Houston, Cullen School of Engineering
Iowa State University
University of Maryland, College Park
University of Michigan
Mississippi State University
University of Missouri - Rolla

(*) degree program awarded outside engineering

(*) degree program awarded outside engineering

Applied Physics (M.E.)
Harvard University

Applied Physics (M.S.)
Air Force Institute of Technology
California Institute of Technology
University of California, San Diego
Columbia University
Cornell University
The Johns Hopkins University
William Marsh Rice University

Applied Physics (Ph.D.)
Air Force Institute of Technology
California Institute of Technology
University of California, San Diego
Colorado School of Mines
Columbia University
Cornell University
Harvard University
William Marsh Rice University

Applied Physics (S.M.)
Harvard University

Applied Remote Sensing and Geoinformation Systems (M.E.)
University of Michigan

Applied Science (M.A.S.)
University of Delaware

Applied Science (M.S.)
University of Arkansas at Little Rock
University of California, Davis
Southern Methodist University

Applied Science (Ph.D.)
University of California, Davis
Southern Methodist University

Applied Science and Technology (M.S.)
University of California, Berkeley

Applied Science and Technology (Ph.D.)
University of California, Berkeley

Applied Statistics (M.S.)
Rochester Institute of Technology

Architectural Engineering (M.A.E.)
University of Nebraska, Lincoln

Architectural Engineering (M.Arch.)
Oklahoma State University

Architectural Engineering (M.S.)
Illinois Institute of Technology
Kansas State University
University of Miami
The University of Texas at Austin

Architectural Engineering (M.S., M.A.E., M.E.)
The Pennsylvania State University

Architectural Engineering (M.S., M.C.M.)
University of Kansas

Architectural Engineering (Ph.D.)
University of Nebraska, Lincoln
The Pennsylvania State University

Architecture (M.Arch.)
Oklahoma State University

Arctic Engineering (M.S.)
University of Alaska Fairbanks

Arctic Engineering (Ph.D.)
University of Alaska Fairbanks

Astronautical and Aeronautical Engineering (M.S.)
The Ohio State University

Astronautical and Aeronautical Engineering (Ph D.)
The Ohio State University

Astronautical Engineering (M.S.)
Air Force Institute of Technology

Astronautical Engineering (Ph.D.)
Air Force Institute of Technology

Astronautics (M.S.)
University of Southern California

Astronautics (Ph.D.)
University of Southern California

Astronautics and Aeronautics Engineering (M.S., M.A.E.)
University of Washington

Atmospheric and Space Science (M.S.)
University of Michigan

Atmospheric and Space Sciences (Ph.D.)
University of Michigan

Atmospheric Science (M.S.)
Colorado State University
University of Wyoming

Atmospheric Science (Ph.D.)
Colorado State University
University of Wyoming

Atmospheric, Environmental and Water Resources (Ph.D.)
South Dakota State University

Atmospheric, Oceanic and Space Science (Ph.D.)
University of Michigan

Automated Production Engineering (M.Eng.)
Ecole de Technologie Superieure

Automotive Engineering (M.E.)
University of Michigan

Automotive Engineering (M.S.)
Clemson University
Lawrence Technological University

Automotive Engineering (Ph.D.)
Clemson University

Automotive Systems Engineering (M.S.E)
University of Michigan, Dearborn

Aviation Systems (M.S.)
University of Tennessee, Knoxville

B

Bio Medical Engineering (Ph.D.)
University of Cincinnati

Bio-Engineering (M.Eng.; M.S.)
University of Louisville

Bio-Medical Engineering (Ph.D.)
University of South Florida

Biochemical Engineering (M.S.)
Drexel University

Biochemical Engineering (Ph.D.)
Drexel University

Bioengineering (M.B.E.)
William Marsh Rice University

Bioengineering (M.E.)
University of Utah

Bioengineering (M.S.)
Arizona State University
California Institute of Technology
Clemson University

(*) degree program awarded outside engineering

Georgia Institute of Technology
University of Illinois at Chicago
University of Illinois at Urbana-Champaign
University of Maryland, College Park
University of Notre Dame
University of Oklahoma
The Pennsylvania State University
University of Pittsburgh
William Marsh Rice University
San Diego State University
Stanford University
Syracuse University
Temple University
The University of Toledo
University of Utah

Bioengineering (M.S., M.Eng.)
University of California, San Diego

Bioengineering (M.S., M.S.E, M.M.E.)
University of Washington

Bioengineering (M.S.E)
University of Pennsylvania

Bioengineering (Ph.D.)
Arizona State University
California Institute of Technology
University of California, Berkeley
University of California, San Diego
Clemson University
Georgia Institute of Technology
University of Illinois at Chicago
University of Illinois at Urbana-Champaign
University of Oklahoma
University of Pennsylvania
The Pennsylvania State University
University of Pittsburgh
William Marsh Rice University
Stanford University
Syracuse University
The University of Toledo
University of Utah
University of Washington

Bioengineering (M.S.)
University of California, Berkeley

Bioinformatics (M.S.)
Boston University
University of California-Santa Cruz
University of Illinois at Chicago

Bioinformatics (Ph.D.)
Boston University
University of California, San Diego
University of California-Santa Cruz
University of Illinois at Chicago

Bioinformatics and Computational Biology (M.S.)
Iowa State University

Bioinformatics and Computational Biology (Ph.D.)
Iowa State University

Biological and Agricultural Engineering (M.S.)
University of California, Davis
Kansas State University
Louisiana State University
Utah State University

Biological and Agricultural Engineering (M.S., M.E.)
North Carolina State University
Texas A&M University

Biological and Agricultural Engineering (Ph.D.)
University of California, Davis
University of Georgia
Kansas State University
North Carolina State University
Texas A&M University
Utah State University

Biological and Ecological Engineering (M.S.)
Oregon State University

Biological and Ecological Engineering (Ph.D.)
Oregon State University

Biological and Environmental Engineering (M.S., M.E.)
Cornell University

Biological and Environmental Engineering (Ph.D.)
Cornell University

Biological Engineering (M.S.)
University of Arkansas

University of Georgia
Illinois Institute of Technology
Illinois Institute of Technology
University of Maine
Mississippi State University
University of Missouri-Columbia

Biological Engineering (Ph.D.)
University of Arkansas
Massachusetts Institute of Technology
Mississippi State University
University of Missouri-Columbia

Biological Engineering (S.M.)
Massachusetts Institute of Technology

Biological Engineering (Sc.D)
Massachusetts Institute of Technology

Biological Resources Engineering (M.S.)
University of Maryland, College Park

Biological Resources Engineering (Ph.D.)
University of Maryland, College Park

Biological Systems Engineering (M.S.)
University of California, Davis

Biological Systems Engineering (M.S., M.E.)
Virginia Polytechnic Institute and State University

Biological Systems Engineering (Ph.D.)
University of California, Davis
University of Nebraska, Lincoln
Virginia Polytechnic Institute and State University

Biomaterials (M.S)
University of Missouri - Rolla

Biomedical and Biotechnology Engineering (joint Ph.D.)
University of Massachusetts Dartmouth

Biomedical Engineering (M.S., M.E.)
Virginia Polytechnic Institute and State University

Biomedical Engineering (D.E.)
The Catholic University of America
Washington University

Biomedical Engineering (M.E.)
The Catholic University of America
Massachusetts Institute of Technology
Stevens Institute of Technology
Tennessee State University

(*) degree program awarded outside engineering

(*) degree program awarded outside engineering

(*) degree program awarded outside engineering

ALPHABETICAL INDEX OF PARTICIPATING GRADUATE DEGREE PROGRAMS

Chemical and Biochemical Engineering (M.S.)
University of California, Irvine
The University of Iowa
Rutgers, The State University of New Jersey

Chemical and Biochemical Engineering (Ph.D.)
University of California, Irvine
The University of Iowa
Rutgers, The State University of New Jersey

Chemical and Biological Engineering
South Dakota School of Mines and Technology

Chemical and Biomolecular Engineering (M.S.E.)
University of Pennsylvania

Chemical and Biomolecular Engineering (Ph.D.)
University of Pennsylvania

Chemical and Environmental Engineering (M.S.)
University of California, Riverside
Rowan University

Chemical and Environmental Engineering (Ph.D.)
University of California, Riverside

Chemical and Materials Science Engineering (Ph.D.)
University of Minnesota -Twin Cities

Chemical and Petroleum Engineering (Ph.D.)
University of Kansas

Chemical Engineeering (M.S., M.E.)
University of North Dakota

Chemical Engineering
University of Massachusetts Lowell
University of Tennessee, Chattanooga
University of Tulsa

Chemical Engineering M.Eng.
McGill University, Faculty of Engineering

Chemical Engineering (D.E.)
Washington University

Chemical Engineering (DRChe,Ph.D)
Lamar University

Chemical Engineering (M.Ch.E.)
University of Delaware
William Marsh Rice University

Chemical Engineering (M.E)
Stevens Institute of Technology

Chemical Engineering (M.E.)
Clarkson University
The Cooper Union
University of Idaho
City College of the City University of New York
State University of New York at Buffalo
Oklahoma State University
University of Ottawa, Faculty of Engineering
Tufts University
University of Utah
University of Virginia

Chemical Engineering (M.E, M.E.S.)
Lamar University

Chemical Engineering (M.Eng.)
Widener University

Chemical Engineering (M.Eng.; M.S.)
University of Louisville

Chemical Engineering (M.S.)
The University of Alabama
The University of Arizona
University of Arkansas
Brigham Young University
Bucknell University
California Institute of Technology
University of California, Berkeley
University of California, Davis
University of California, Los Angeles
University of California, San Diego
University of California, Santa Barbara
Carnegie Mellon University
Case Western Reserve University
University of Cincinnati
Clarkson University
Clemson University
Cleveland State University
Colorado State University
Columbia University
University of Dayton
Drexel University
Florida Institute of Technology
FAMU-FSU College of Engineering

Georgia Institute of Technology
Howard University
University of Idaho
Illinois Institute of Technology
University of Illinois at Chicago
University of Illinois at Urbana-Champaign
University of Kansas
Kansas State University
University of Kentucky
Louisiana State University
University of Maine
Manhattan College
University of Maryland, Baltimore County
University of Massachusetts Amherst
University of Michigan
Michigan State University
Michigan Technological University
The University of Mississippi
Mississippi State University
University of Missouri-Columbia
University of Missouri - Rolla
Montana State University
University of Nebraska, Lincoln
University of Nevada, Reno
University of New Hampshire
New Jersey Institute of Technology
The University of New Mexico
New Mexico State University
State University of New York at Buffalo
North Carolina A & T State University
Northeastern University
Northwestern University
University of Notre Dame
The Ohio State University
Ohio University
University of Oklahoma
Oklahoma State University
Oregon State University
University of Ottawa, Faculty of Engineering
The Pennsylvania State University
University of Pittsburgh

(*) degree program awarded outside engineering

ALPHABETICAL INDEX OF PARTICIPATING GRADUATE DEGREE PROGRAMS

(*) degree program awarded outside engineering

ALPHABETICAL INDEX OF PARTICIPATING GRADUATE DEGREE PROGRAMS

University of Nevada, Reno
New Jersey Institute of Technology
The University of New Mexico
New Mexico State University
State University of New York at Buffalo
North Carolina State University
Northeastern University
Northwestern University
University of Notre Dame
The Ohio State University
Ohio University
University of Oklahoma
Oklahoma State University
Oregon State University
University of Ottawa, Faculty of Engineering
The Pennsylvania State University
University of Pittsburgh
Polytechnic University
Princeton University
University of Puerto Rico, Mayaguez Campus
Purdue University
University of Rhode Island
William Marsh Rice University
University of Rochester
University of South Carolina
University of South Florida
University of Southern California
Stanford University
Stevens Institute of Technology
Syracuse University
University of Tennessee, Knoxville
Texas A&M University
Texas Tech University
The University of Texas at Austin
The University of Toledo
Tufts University
Tulane University
University of Utah
Vanderbilt University
University of Virginia
Virginia Polytechnic Institute and State University

University of Washington
Washington State University
University of Waterloo
Wayne State University
West Virginia University
University of Wisconsin, Madison
Worcester Polytechnic Institute
University of Wyoming

Chemical Engineering (Ph.D, D.E.)
Rensselaer Polytechnic Institute

Chemical Engineering (PhD)
University of California, Santa Barbara

Chemical Engineering (S.M.)
Massachusetts Institute of Technology

Chemical Engineering (Sc.D.)
Massachusetts Institute of Technology

Chemical Engineering and Applied Biomedical Engineering (D.E.)
Cleveland State University

Chemical Engineering Option (M.S.E.)
University of Louisiana at Lafayette

Chemical Engineering Practice (S.M.)
Massachusetts Institute of Technology

Chemical Engineering, Ph.D.
McGill University, Faculty of Engineering

Chemical Eningeering (Ph.D.)
Columbia University

Chemistry/Geochemistry (M.S.)
Colorado School of Mines

Civil & Environmental Engineering (M.S.)
The George Washington University

Civil & Environmental Engineering (M.S., M.Eng.)
University of California, Berkeley

Civil and Environmental Engineering (Civil) (M.S., M.S.E.)
Arizona State University

Civil and Environmental Engineering (Civil) (Ph.D.)
Arizona State University

Civil and Environmental Engineering (D.E.)
University of Detroit Mercy

Civil and Environmental Engineering (D.Sc.)
The George Washington University

Civil and Environmental Engineering (Env.) (M.S., M.S.E.)
Arizona State University

Civil and Environmental Engineering (Env.) (Ph.D.)
Arizona State University

Civil and Environmental Engineering (M.E.)
University of Detroit Mercy
Massachusetts Institute of Technology
The University of Texas at Arlington

Civil and Environmental Engineering (M.E., M.E.S.)
Lamar University

Civil and Environmental Engineering (M.S.)
California Polytechnic State University
University of California, Davis
Carnegie Mellon University
The University of Iowa
University of Maine
University of Maryland, Baltimore County
University of Massachusetts Dartmouth
University of Nevada, Reno
Northwestern University
Princeton University
Princeton University
University of Rhode Island
Rowan University
Rutgers, The State University of New Jersey
Stanford University
The University of Texas at Arlington
University of Wisconsin, Madison

Civil and Environmental Engineering (M.S., M.E.)
Cornell University
University of South Carolina
University of South Florida

Civil and Environmental Engineering (Ph.D)
Clarkson University

Civil and Environmental Engineering (Ph.D.)
University of California, Davis
Carnegie Mellon University
Cornell University
Cornell University
The University of Iowa
Lehigh University

(*) degree program awarded outside engineering

(*) degree program awarded outside engineering

(*) degree program awarded outside engineering

University of California, Irvine
University of California, Los Angeles
Case Western Reserve University
The Catholic University of America
University of Central Florida
University of Cincinnati
Clemson University
Colorado State University
University of Colorado at Boulder
University of Colorado at Denver and Health Sciences Center
Concordia University, Faculty of Engr. and Comp. Sci.
University of Connecticut
University of Delaware
Drexel University
Duke University Pratt School of Engineering
Ecole Polytechnique de Montreal
University of Florida
Florida Institute of Technology
Florida International University
FAMU-FSU College of Engineering
Georgia Institute of Technology
University of Hawaii at Manoa
University of Houston, Cullen School of Engineering
University of Idaho
Illinois Institute of Technology
University of Illinois at Chicago
University of Illinois at Urbana-Champaign
Iowa State University
The Johns Hopkins University
Kansas State University
University of Kentucky
Lehigh University
Louisiana State University
University of Louisville
Marquette University
University of Maryland, College Park
University of Massachusetts Amherst
University of Miami
University of Michigan
Michigan State University
Michigan Technological University

University of Minnesota -Twin Cities
The University of Mississippi
Mississippi State University
University of Missouri-Columbia
University of Missouri - Rolla
University of Nebraska, Lincoln
University of Nevada, Las Vegas
New Jersey Institute of Technology
The University of New Mexico
New Mexico State University
State University of New York at Buffalo
North Carolina State University
North Dakota State University
Northeastern University
University of Notre Dame
The Ohio State University
University of Oklahoma
Oklahoma State University
Old Dominion University
Oregon State University
University of Ottawa, Faculty of Engineering
The Pennsylvania State University
University of Pittsburgh
Polytechnic University
University of Puerto Rico, Mayaguez Campus
Purdue University
University of Rhode Island
William Marsh Rice University
University of South Florida
University of Southern California
Southern Methodist University
Stevens Institute of Technology
Syracuse University
University of Tennessee, Knoxville
Texas A&M University
Texas Tech University
The University of Texas at Arlington
The University of Texas at Austin
University of Texas at El Paso
The University of Toledo
Tufts University

Tulane University
University of Utah
Utah State University
Vanderbilt University
University of Vermont
University of Virginia
Virginia Polytechnic Institute and State University
University of Washington
Washington State University
University of Waterloo
Wayne State University
West Virginia University
University of Wyoming

Civil Engineering (Ph.D., D.E.)
University of Kansas
Rensselaer Polytechnic Institute

Civil Engineering and Engineering Mechanics (Ph.D.
Columbia University

Civil Engineering and Environmental Engineering (M.S.)
University of Cincinnati

Civil Engineering Management (M.E.)- Joint w/CE
Portland State University

Civil Engineering Management (M.E.)- Joint w/ETM
Portland State University

Civil Engineering Option (M.S.E.)
University of Louisiana at Lafayette

Civil Engineering, Water Resources (M.S.)
University of Wyoming

Civil Transportation Engineering (M.S.)
University of Arkansas

Civil, Mining & Petroleum Engineering (M.S.)
University of Alberta
University of Alberta
University of Alberta

Civil, Mining, & Petroleum Engineering (Ph.D.)
University of Alberta
University of Alberta
University of Alberta

Civil/Environmental Engineering (M.S., M.E.)
University of North Dakota

(*) degree program awarded outside engineering

CMD,CNTRL,COMM/SYS TECH
Air Force Institute of Technology

Coastal & Oceanographic Engineering (M.S., M.E.)
University of Florida

Coastal & Oceanographic Engineering (Ph.D.)
University of Florida

Colloids, Polymers, and Surfaces (M.S.)
Carnegie Mellon University

Communication Theory and Systems (Ph.D.)
University of California, San Diego

CommunicationTheory&Systems (M.S.)
University of California, San Diego

Computation and Neural Systems (M.S.)
California Institute of Technology

Computation and Neural Systems (Ph.D.)
California Institute of Technology

Computation for Design and Optimization (S.M.)
Massachusetts Institute of Technology

Computational Analysis & Modeling (PhD)
Louisiana Tech University

Computational and Applied Math (M.C.A.M.)
William Marsh Rice University

Computational and Applied Mathematics (M.A.)
William Marsh Rice University

Computational and Applied Mathematics (Ph.D.)
William Marsh Rice University

Computational and Engineering Mechanics (M.S.)
Lehigh University

Computational and Engineering Mechanics (Ph.D.)
Lehigh University

Computational and Mathematical Engineering (M.S)
Stanford University

Computational and Mathematical Engineering (Ph.D.)
Stanford University

Computational and Systems Biology (Ph.D)
Massachusetts Institute of Technology

Computational Biology & Bioinformatics
Northwestern University

Computational Engineering
University of Tennessee, Chattanooga

Computational Engineering (M.S.)
Mississippi State University

Computational Engineering (Ph.D.)
Mississippi State University
University of Tennessee, Chattanooga

Computational Hydroscience (Ph.D)
The University of Mississippi

Computational Science & Engineering (Ph.D.)
Michigan Technological University

Computational Science and Engineering (M.C.S.E.)
William Marsh Rice University

Computational Science and Engineering (M.S.)
North Carolina A & T State University

Computational Science and Engineering (Ph.D.)
William Marsh Rice University

Computational Science and Statistics
South Dakota State University

Computer & Information Science (M.S.)
University of New Haven

Computer & Systems Engineering (Ph.D.)
University of Houston, Cullen School of Engineering

Computer and Information Science (M.S)
University of Michigan, Dearborn

Computer and Information Science (M.S.)
The University of Mississippi

Computer and Information Science (M.S., M.C.S.)
University of Minnesota -Twin Cities

Computer and Information Science (M.S.E.)
University of Pennsylvania

Computer and Information Science (Ph.D.)
The University of Mississippi
University of Pennsylvania
Syracuse University

Computer and Information Sciences (M.S.)
University of South Alabama (*)

Computer and Information Sciences (Ph.D.)
University of Delaware (*)
University of Minnesota -Twin Cities

Computer and Information Systems Engineering
Tennessee State University

Computer and Information Systems Engineering(M.S.)
Tennessee State University

Computer and Information Technology (M.C.I.T.)
University of Pennsylvania

Computer and Software Engineering (M.Eng.)
Widener University

Computer and Systems Engineering (M.S.)
University of Houston, Cullen School of Engineering

Computer and Systems Engineering (M.S., M.E.)
Rensselaer Polytechnic Institute

Computer and Systems Engineering (Ph.D., D.E.)
Rensselaer Polytechnic Institute

Computer Communication and Networks (option)
Tennessee State University

Computer Engineering (D.E.)
Washington University

Computer Engineering (D.Sc.)
The George Washington University

Computer Engineering (Engineer Degree)
Santa Clara University

Computer Engineering (M.B.A)
University of Denver

Computer Engineering (M.E.)
University of Idaho
Old Dominion University
Polytechnic University of Puerto Rico
Stevens Institute of Technology
University of Virginia
University of Virginia

Computer Engineering (M.S. and M.Eng)
Boise State University

Computer Engineering (M.S.)
Air Force Institute of Technology
University of Arkansas
University of Bridgeport
California State University, Long Beach
California State University, Sacramento
University of California, San Diego
University of California-Santa Cruz
Case Western Reserve University
University of Cincinnati

(*) degree program awarded outside engineering

Clemson University
Columbia University
University of Denver
Drexel University
Florida Atlantic University
Florida Institute of Technology
Florida International University
George Mason University
The George Washington University
University of Idaho
Illinois Institute of Technology
Iowa State University
University of Kansas
University of Louisiana at Lafayette
University of Maine
Manhattan College
University of Maryland, Baltimore County
University of Massachusetts Dartmouth
University of Massachusetts Lowell
Mercer University
University of Minnesota - Twin Cities
Mississippi State University
University of Missouri-Columbia
University of Missouri - Rolla
University of Nevada, Reno
New Jersey Institute of Technology
The University of New Mexico
North Carolina State University
North Dakota State University
University of North Texas
Old Dominion University
Polytechnic University
Polytechnic University of Puerto Rico
University of Puerto Rico, Mayaguez Campus
Rochester Institute of Technology
San Jose State University
Santa Clara University
University of Southern California
Southern Methodist University
Syracuse University
University of Tennessee, Knoxville

University of Texas at El Paso
University of Texas at San Antonio
Villanova University
University of Virginia
University of Virginia
Washington State University
Washington University
Wayne State University

Computer engineering (M.S., M.E.)
Ecole Polytechnique de Montreal
University of Florida
University of South Florida
Virginia Polytechnic Institute and State University

Computer Engineering (M.S., MBA&E)
Lehigh University

Computer Engineering (M.S.C.E.)
The University of Texas at Dallas
Wright State University

Computer Engineering (M.S.Cp.E.)
University of Central Florida

Computer Engineering (M.S.E.)
The University of Alabama in Huntsville
University of Michigan, Dearborn
Western Michigan University

Computer Engineering (MSE)
Purdue University, Calumet

Computer Engineering (Ph.D.)
Air Force Institute of Technology
University of Alabama at Birmingham
The University of Alabama in Huntsville
University of Arkansas
Boston University
University of California, San Diego
University of California, San Diego
University of California-Santa Cruz
Case Western Reserve University
University of Central Florida
Clemson University
Drexel University
Ecole Polytechnique de Montreal
University of Florida

Florida Atlantic University
Florida Institute of Technology
Illinois Institute of Technology
Iowa State University
Lehigh University
Lehigh University
University of Louisiana at Lafayette
University of Maryland, Baltimore County
Mississippi State University
University of Missouri - Rolla
University of Nebraska, Lincoln
New Jersey Institute of Technology
The University of New Mexico
North Carolina State University
Northeastern University
Santa Clara University
University of Southern California
Southern Methodist University
Stevens Institute of Technology
Syracuse University
University of Tennessee, Knoxville
The University of Texas at Dallas
University of Texas at El Paso
University of Virginia
Virginia Polytechnic Institute and State University
Wayne State University
West Virginia University

Computer Engineering and Computer Science (M.Eng.; M.S.)
University of Louisville

Computer Engineering and Computer Science (Ph.D.)
University of Missouri-Columbia

Computer Graphics and Game Technology (M.S.E.)
University of Pennsylvania

Computer Information Science (M.S.C.I.S)
Gannon University

Computer Information Systems (M.S.)
Florida Institute of Technology

Computer Information Systems (M.S.C.I.S.)
Prairie View A&M University

(*) degree program awarded outside engineering

ALPHABETICAL INDEX OF PARTICIPATING GRADUATE DEGREE PROGRAMS

Computer Networking (M.S.)
North Carolina State University
North Carolina State University

Computer Science
University of Colorado at Denver and Health Sciences Center
Montana State University
South Dakota State University
University of Tennessee, Chattanooga
University of Tulsa
University of Wisconsin, Milwaukee

Computer Science (M.S.)
Rochester Institute of Technology (*)

Computer Science (Ph.D.)
Boston University (*)

Computer Science & Computer Engineering (Ph.D.)
University of Cincinnati

Computer Science & Engineering (M.S.)
University of California, Berkeley

Computer Science & Engineering (Ph.D.)
University of California, Berkeley
The University of Toledo

Computer Science (D.E.)
The Catholic University of America
Washington University

Computer Science (D.Sc.)
The George Washington University

Computer Science (M.)
Polytechnic University of Puerto Rico

Computer Science (M.A.)
Boston University (*)
Wayne State University (*)

Computer Science (M.Ap.Comp.Sc. & M.Comp.Sc.)
Concordia University, Faculty of Engr. and Comp. Sci. (*)

Computer Science (M.C.S.)
Howard University
The University of Iowa (*)
William Marsh Rice University

Computer Science (M.CS.)
University of Virginia

Computer Science (M.E.)
Harvard University
University of Utah

Computer Science (M.E.,M.E.S)
Lamar University (*)

Computer Science (M.S)
Florida International University
Saint Cloud State University (*)

Computer Science (M.S.)
The University of Alabama
The University of Arizona (*)
University of Arkansas
University of Arkansas at Little Rock
Baylor University
Boise State University
University of Bridgeport
Brigham Young University (*)
California Institute of Technology
California Polytechnic State University
California State University, Fresno
California State University, Fullerton
California State University, Long Beach
California State University, Los Angeles
California State University, Northridge
California State University, Sacramento
University of California, Davis
University of California, Los Angeles
University of California, Riverside
University of California, San Diego
University of California, Santa Barbara
University of California-Santa Cruz
Carnegie Mellon University (*)
The Catholic University of America
University of Central Florida
University of Cincinnati
Clarkson University (*)
Clemson University
Columbia University
University of Delaware (*)
University of Detroit Mercy
Drexel University
Duke University Pratt School of Engineering (*)
University of Florida (*)
Florida Atlantic University
Florida Institute of Technology
FAMU-FSU College of Engineering (*)
George Mason University
The George Washington University
Georgia Institute of Technology (*)
University of Houston, Cullen School of Engineering (*)
University of Idaho
Illinois Institute of Technology (*)
University of Illinois at Chicago
University of Illinois at Urbana-Champaign
Indiana University-Purdue University Fort Wayne (*)
The University of Iowa (*)
University of Kansas
Kansas State University
University of Kentucky
University of Louisiana at Lafayette (*)
Loyola College in Maryland (*)
Marquette University (*)
University of Maryland, Baltimore County
University of Maryland, College Park (*)
University of Massachusetts Amherst (*)
University of Massachusetts Dartmouth
The University of Memphis (*)
Miami University
Michigan State University
Michigan Technological University (*)
Mississippi State University
University of Missouri-Columbia
University of Missouri - Kansas City
Montana State University
University of Nebraska, Lincoln (*)
University of Nevada, Las Vegas
University of Nevada, Reno
University of New Hampshire
New Jersey Institute of Technology (*)
The University of New Mexico
New York Institute of Technology
City College of the City University of New York

(*) degree program awarded outside engineering

The State University of New York at Binghamton
Stony Brook University
North Carolina A & T State University
University of North Texas
Northwestern University
Ohio University
University of Oklahoma
Oregon State University
University of Ottawa, Faculty of Engineering
Polytechnic University
Polytechnic University of Puerto Rico
Portland State University
Princeton University
Purdue University (*)
Rensselaer Polytechnic Institute (*)
William Marsh Rice University
University of Rochester (*)
Rutgers, The State University of New Jersey (*)
South Dakota School of Mines and Technology
University of Southern California
Southern Illinois University Carbondale (*)
Southern Illinois University Edwardsville
Southern Methodist University
Stanford University
Stevens Institute of Technology (*)
Syracuse University
University of Tennessee, Knoxville (*)
Texas A&M University - Kingsville
Texas Tech University
The University of Texas at Arlington
University of Texas at El Paso
University of Texas at San Antonio (*)
Tufts University
Tulane University
University of Utah
Vanderbilt University
University of Vermont
University of Virginia
Virginia Commonwealth University
Virginia Polytechnic Institute and State University
Washington State University

Washington University
Wayne State University (*)
West Virginia University
Western Michigan University
Wichita State University (*)
University of Wisconsin, Madison (*)
Worcester Polytechnic Institute (*)
University of Wyoming

Computer Science (M.S., M.C.S.)
Arizona State University
Texas A&M University

Computer Science (M.S., M.E.)
University of Colorado at Boulder
Cornell University
North Carolina State University
University of South Florida

Computer Science (M.S., MBA&E)
Lehigh University

Computer Science (M.S.C.S.)
Prairie View A&M University
The University of Texas at Dallas
Wright State University

Computer Science (M.S.E.)
The Johns Hopkins University

Computer Science (MS)
University of Colorado at Colorado Springs

Computer Science (MSCS)
Louisiana Tech University

Computer Science (Ph.D)
Florida International University

Computer Science (Ph.D.)
Air Force Institute of Technology
The University of Alabama
The University of Arizona (*)
Arizona State University
University of Arkansas
Brigham Young University (*)
California Institute of Technology
University of California, Davis
University of California, Los Angeles
University of California, Riverside

University of California, San Diego
University of California, Santa Barbara
University of California-Santa Cruz
Carnegie Mellon University (*)
The Catholic University of America
University of Central Florida
University of Cincinnati
Clemson University
University of Colorado at Boulder
University of Colorado at Denver and Health Sciences Center
Columbia University
Concordia University, Faculty of Engr. and Comp. Sci. (*)
Cornell University
Drexel University
Duke University Pratt School of Engineering (*)
Florida Atlantic University
Florida Institute of Technology
FAMU-FSU College of Engineering (*)
George Mason University
Georgia Institute of Technology (*)
Harvard University
University of Houston, Cullen School of Engineering (*)
University of Idaho
Illinois Institute of Technology (*)
University of Illinois at Chicago
University of Illinois at Urbana-Champaign
The University of Iowa (*)
The Johns Hopkins University
University of Kansas
Kansas State University
University of Kentucky
Lehigh University
Louisiana State University (*)
University of Louisiana at Lafayette (*)
University of Maryland, Baltimore County
University of Maryland, College Park (*)
University of Massachusetts Amherst (*)
The University of Memphis (*)
Michigan State University
Michigan Technological University (*)
Mississippi State University

(*) degree program awarded outside engineering

Alphabetical Index of Participating Graduate Degree Programs

University of Missouri-Columbia
University of Nebraska, Lincoln (*)
University of Nevada, Las Vegas
University of New Hampshire
New Jersey Institute of Technology (*)
The University of New Mexico
City College of the City University of New York
The State University of New York at Binghamton
Stony Brook University
North Carolina State University
University of North Texas
Northwestern University
University of Oklahoma
Oregon State University
University of Ottawa, Faculty of Engineering
University of Pittsburgh (*)
Polytechnic University
Portland State University
Princeton University
Purdue University (*)
Rensselaer Polytechnic Institute (*)
William Marsh Rice University
University of Rochester (*)
Rutgers, The State University of New Jersey (*)
University of Southern California
Southern Methodist University
Stanford University
Stevens Institute of Technology (*)
University of Tennessee, Knoxville (*)
Texas A&M University
Texas Tech University
The University of Texas at Arlington
The University of Texas at Dallas
University of Texas at San Antonio (*)
Tufts University
Tulane University
University of Utah
Vanderbilt University
University of Vermont
University of Virginia
Virginia Polytechnic Institute and State University

Washington State University
Wayne State University (*)
West Virginia University
Western Michigan University
University of Wisconsin, Madison (*)
Worcester Polytechnic Institute (*)
University of Wyoming

Computer Science (S.M.)
Harvard University

Computer Science and Engineering (M.E.)
The University of Texas at Arlington

Computer Science and Engineering (M.S.)
University of Michigan
State University of New York at Buffalo
University of Notre Dame
Oakland University
The Ohio State University
OGI School of Science & Engineering at OHSU
The University of Texas at Arlington
University of Washington

Computer Science and Engineering (M.S., M.E.)
University of Connecticut
The Pennsylvania State University
University of South Carolina

Computer Science and Engineering (M.S.E.)
University of Michigan

Computer Science and Engineering (Ph.D.)
University of Connecticut
University of Louisville
University of Michigan
University of Nevada, Reno
State University of New York at Buffalo
University of Notre Dame
The Ohio State University
OGI School of Science & Engineering at OHSU
The Pennsylvania State University
University of South Carolina
University of South Florida
The University of Texas at Arlington
University of Washington
Wright State University

Computer Science and Engineering Ph.D.
University of Bridgeport
University of Bridgeport

Computer Science and Engineering(Ph.D.)
University of Notre Dame

Computer Science and Master of Chemical Engineering (M.S.)
Illinois Institute of Technology (*)

Computer Science and Software Engineering (M.S., M.E.)
Auburn University

Computer Science and Software Engineering (Ph.D.)
Auburn University

Computer Science and Software Engineering
B.S./M.S.,M.S., M.S.E.)
University of Alaska Fairbanks (*)

Computer Science for Software Engineering (M.S.)
Loyola College in Maryland (*)

Computer Science with Major in Software Engineering (M.S.C.S.)
The University of Texas at Dallas

Computer Science- Computer Networks (M.S.)
University of Southern California

Computer Science- Intelligent Systems (M.S.)
University of Southern California

Computer Science- Multimedia (M.S.)
University of Southern California

Computer Science- Software Engineering (M.S.)
University of Southern California

Computer Science-Game Development
University of Southern California

Computer Science: Systems Science (M.S.)
Louisiana State University (*)

Computer Sciences (M.S.)
University of Pittsburgh (*)

Computer Systems (M.S.)
Air Force Institute of Technology

Computer Systems Engineering (M.S.)
Boston University
Illinois Institute of Technology
Northeastern University

Computer-Aided Engineering (M.E.)
University of Southern California

(*) degree program awarded outside engineering

ALPHABETICAL INDEX OF PARTICIPATING GRADUATE DEGREE PROGRAMS

Computing and Information Science (M.S.)
Case Western Reserve University

Computing and Information Science (Ph.D.)
Case Western Reserve University

Computing and Information Science and Engineering (Ph.D.)
University of Puerto Rico, Mayaguez Campus

Concurrent Marine Design (M.E.)
University of Michigan

Construction Engineering (M.E.)
Washington University

Construction Engineering (M.Eng.)
Ecole de Technologie Superieure

Construction Engineering (M.S.)
University of Nebraska, Lincoln

Construction Engineering (Ph.D.)
University of Nebraska, Lincoln

Construction Engineering and Management (Dual M.Eng./M.Arch.)
University of Michigan

Construction Engineering and Management (Dual M.S.E./M.Arch.)
University of Michigan

Construction Engineering and Management (Dual M.S.E./M.B.A.)
University of Michigan

Construction Engineering and Management (Joint M.Eng./M.B.A.)
University of Michigan

Construction Engineering and Management (M.E.)
University of Michigan

Construction Engineering and Management (M.S.)
Illinois Institute of Technology

Construction Engineering and Management (M.S.E.)
University of Michigan

Construction Engineering Management (M.S.)
Lawrence Technological University

Construction Management (M.C.M.)
The University of New Mexico

Construction Management (M.E.)
The Catholic University of America

Stevens Institute of Technology
Washington University

Construction Management (M.S.)
Florida International University
University of Nevada, Las Vegas
Polytechnic University

Construction Mgmt. and Wood Products Engineering
SUNY College of Environmental Science and Forestry

Construction Mgmt. and Wood Products Engineering (M.S., M.P.S.)
SUNY College of Environmental Science and Forestry

Construction Project Management (M.S.)
Worcester Polytechnic Institute

Control and Dynamical Systems (M.S.)
California Institute of Technology

Control and Dynamical Systems (Ph.D.)
California Institute of Technology

Control Engineering (M.E.)
Washington University

Control Systems and Engineering (D.E.)
Washington University

Control Systems Engineering (M.S.)
Oklahoma State University

Controls and Signal Processing (option)
Tennessee State University

Cost Analysis (M.S.)
Air Force Institute of Technology

D

Decision Sciences and Engineering Systems (Ph.D.)
Rensselaer Polytechnic Institute

Degree of Electrical Engineer (Ph.D.)
University of Utah

Design and Manufacturing (MEng)
University of Waterloo

Digital Arts & Sciences (M.S.)
University of Florida

Division of Engineering
Brown University

Doctor of Philosophy (Chemical)
University of North Dakota

Doctor of Philosophy (Civil)
University of North Dakota

Doctor of Philosophy (Electrical)
University of North Dakota

Doctor of Philosophy (Mechanical)
University of North Dakota

Doctor of Philosophy in Biomedical Engineering
Saint Louis University - Parks College

Dual Degree (M.Eng/M.B.A.)
Widener University

E

E-Commerce (M.S.)
George Mason University

Earth & Environmental Engineering (M.S.)
Columbia University

Earth and Environmental Engineering (Ph.D)
Columbia University

Electr'l Eng. & Atmos.,Oceanic & Space Sci. (Ph.D.)
University of Michigan

Electric Power Engineering (M.S., M.E.)
Rensselaer Polytechnic Institute

Electric Power engineering (Ph.D., D.E.)
Rensselaer Polytechnic Institute

Electric Power Engineering Certificate and MEng
University of Waterloo

Electrical and Systems Engineering (Ph.D.)
University of Pennsylvania

Electrical Engineering (M.E.)
University of Hartford

Electrical Engineering (Ph.D.)
The State University of New York at Binghamton

Electrical & Computer Engineering (M.Eng.)
University of California, San Diego

Electrical & Computer Engineering (M.S.)
Baylor University
University of California, Berkeley
University of Massachusetts Amherst
Oregon State University
Youngstown State University

(*) degree program awarded outside engineering

(*) degree program awarded outside engineering

Electrical Engineering (M. E.)
Stevens Institute of Technology

Electrical Engineering (M.B.A)
University of Denver

Electrical Engineering (M.E.)
The Catholic University of America
Clarkson University
Clemson University
The Cooper Union
University of Detroit Mercy
University of Idaho
City College of the City University of New York
State University of New York at Buffalo
Oklahoma State University
Old Dominion University
University of Ottawa, Faculty of Engineering
Polytechnic University of Puerto Rico
Tennessee State University
The University of Texas at Arlington
University of Utah
University of Virginia

Electrical Engineering (M.E., M.E.S)
Lamar University

Electrical Engineering (M.E.E.)
William Marsh Rice University

Electrical Engineering (M.Eng.)
Ecole de Technologie Superieure

Electrical Engineering (M.Eng.; M.S.)
University of Louisville

Electrical Engineering (M.S. and M.Eng)
Boise State University

Electrical Engineering (M.S.)
Air Force Institute of Technology
The University of Akron
University of Alabama at Birmingham
The University of Alabama
University of Alberta
Alfred University, NY State College of Ceramics
University of Arkansas
Boston University
Bradley University

University of Bridgeport
Bucknell University
California Institute of Technology
California Polytechnic State University
California State University, Fresno
California State University, Long Beach
California State University, Los Angeles
California State University, Northridge
University of California, Los Angeles
University of California, Riverside
University of California-Santa Cruz
Case Western Reserve University
University of Cincinnati
Clarkson University
Clemson University
Colorado State University
University of Colorado at Denver and Health Sciences Center
Columbia University
University of Dayton
University of Denver
Drexel University
Fairleigh Dickinson University
Florida Atlantic University
Florida Institute of Technology
Florida International University
FAMU-FSU College of Engineering
George Mason University
The George Washington University
University of Hawaii at Manoa
University of Idaho
Illinois Institute of Technology
University of Illinois at Urbana-Champaign
Indiana University Purdue University at Indianapolis
Iowa State University
The Johns Hopkins University
University of Kansas
University of Kentucky
Louisiana State University
University of Maine
Manhattan College
University of Maryland, Baltimore County

University of Maryland, College Park
University of Massachusetts Dartmouth
University of Massachusetts Lowell
The University of Memphis
Mercer University
University of Michigan
Michigan State University
Michigan Technological University
Minnesota State University, Mankato
University of Minnesota -Twin Cities
The University of Mississippi
Mississippi State University
University of Missouri-Columbia
University of Missouri - Kansas City
University of Missouri - Rolla
Montana State University
Montana Tech of the University of Montana
University of Nebraska, Lincoln
University of Nevada, Las Vegas
University of Nevada, Reno
University of New Hampshire
University of New Haven
New Jersey Institute of Technology
The University of New Mexico
New Mexico Institute of Mining & Technology
New Mexico State University
The State University of New York at Binghamton
State University of New York at Buffalo
Stony Brook University
North Carolina A & T State University
North Carolina State University
North Dakota State University
University of North Texas
Northeastern University
Northern Illinois University
University of Notre Dame
Ohio University
University of Oklahoma
Oklahoma State University
Old Dominion University
University of Ottawa, Faculty of Engineering

(*) degree program awarded outside engineering

University of Pittsburgh
Polytechnic University
Polytechnic University of Puerto Rico
Princeton University
University of Puerto Rico, Mayaguez Campus
University of Rhode Island
University of Rochester
Rochester Institute of Technology
Rose-Hulman Institute of Technology
Rowan University
Saint Cloud State University
Saint Mary's University
San Diego State University
San Jose State University
Santa Clara University
University of South Alabama
South Dakota School of Mines and Technology
South Dakota State University
University of Southern California
Southern Illinois University Edwardsville
Southern Methodist University
Stanford University
Syracuse University
Tennessee Technological University
University of Tennessee, Knoxville
Texas A&M University - Kingsville
Texas Tech University
The University of Texas at Arlington
University of Texas at El Paso
University of Texas at San Antonio
The University of Toledo
Tufts University
Tulane University
University of Utah
Utah State University
University of Vermont
Villanova University
University of Virginia
Washington State University
Washington University
Wayne State University

West Virginia University
Wichita State University
University of Wisconsin, Madison
University of Wyoming

Electrical Engineering (M.S.), Software Engineering (M.S.)
Cleveland State University

Electrical Engineering (M.S., M.E.)
Auburn University
University of Colorado at Boulder
University of Connecticut
Cornell University
Ecole Polytechnique de Montreal
University of Florida
University of Houston, Cullen School of Engineering
University of North Dakota
The Pennsylvania State University
Rensselaer Polytechnic Institute
University of South Carolina
University of South Florida
Texas A&M University
Vanderbilt University
Virginia Polytechnic Institute and State University

Electrical Engineering (M.S., M.E., MBA&E)
Lehigh University

Electrical Engineering (M.S., M.E.E.)
University of Alaska Fairbanks

Electrical Engineering (M.S., M.S.E.)
Arizona State University

Electrical Engineering (M.S.E.)
The University of Alabama in Huntsville
University of Michigan
University of Michigan, Dearborn
University of Pennsylvania
Temple University
Western Michigan University
Wright State University

Electrical Engineering (M.S.E.); Computer Science (M.S.)
Loyola Marymount University

Electrical Engineering (M.S.E, M.S.E.E.)
University of Washington

Electrical Engineering (M.S.E.C.E.)
University of Delaware

Electrical Engineering (M.S.E.E)
Gannon University

Electrical Engineering (M.S.E.E.)
University of Central Florida
Prairie View A&M University
The University of Texas at Dallas

Electrical Engineering (M.S.E.E, M.S.E., M.E.)
University of North Carolina, Charlotte

Electrical Engineering (MS)
University of Colorado at Colorado Springs

Electrical Engineering (MSc(Engl))
University of Calgary

Electrical Engineering (MSE)
Purdue University, Calumet

Electrical Engineering (Ph.D.)
Air Force Institute of Technology
University of Alabama at Birmingham
The University of Alabama in Huntsville
The University of Alabama
University of Alaska Fairbanks
University of Alberta
Arizona State University
University of Arkansas
Auburn University
Boston University
California Institute of Technology
University of California, Los Angeles
University of California, Riverside
University of California-Santa Cruz
Case Western Reserve University
The Catholic University of America
University of Central Florida
University of Cincinnati
Clemson University
Colorado State University
University of Colorado at Boulder
Columbia University
University of Connecticut
Cornell University

(*) degree program awarded outside engineering

University of Dayton
Drexel University
Ecole Polytechnique de Montreal
University of Florida
Florida Atlantic University
Florida Institute of Technology
Florida International University
FAMU-FSU College of Engineering
University of Hawaii at Manoa
University of Houston, Cullen School of Engineering
University of Idaho
Illinois Institute of Technology
University of Illinois at Urbana-Champaign
Iowa State University
University of Kansas
Kansas State University
University of Kentucky
Lehigh University
Louisiana State University
University of Louisville
University of Maine
University of Maryland, Baltimore County
University of Maryland, College Park
University of Massachusetts Dartmouth
University of Michigan
Michigan State University
Michigan Technological University
University of Minnesota - Twin Cities
The University of Mississippi
Mississippi State University
University of Missouri-Columbia
University of Missouri - Rolla
University of Nebraska, Lincoln
University of Nevada, Reno
New Jersey Institute of Technology
The University of New Mexico
New Mexico State University
State University of New York at Buffalo
Stony Brook University
North Carolina A & T State University
North Carolina State University

University of North Carolina, Charlotte
Northeastern University
University of Notre Dame
Ohio University
University of Oklahoma
Oklahoma State University
Old Dominion University
University of Ottawa, Faculty of Engineering
The Pennsylvania State University
University of Pittsburgh
Polytechnic University
Prairie View A&M University
Princeton University
University of Rhode Island
University of Rochester
Santa Clara University
University of South Carolina
University of South Florida
University of Southern California
Southern Methodist University
Stanford University
Stevens Institute of Technology
Syracuse University
University of Tennessee, Knoxville
Texas A&M University
Texas Tech University
The University of Texas at Arlington
The University of Texas at Dallas
University of Texas at San Antonio
The University of Toledo
Tufts University
Tulane University
University of Utah
Utah State University
Vanderbilt University
University of Vermont
University of Virginia
Virginia Polytechnic Institute and State University
University of Washington
Washington State University
Wayne State University

West Virginia University
Wichita State University
University of Wisconsin, Madison
University of Wyoming

Electrical Engineering (Ph.D., D.E.)
Rensselaer Polytechnic Institute

Electrical Engineering and AOSS (M.S.)
University of Michigan

Electrical Engineering and Computer Science (M.E.)
Massachusetts Institute of Technology

Electrical Engineering and Computer Science (Ph.D.)
Massachusetts Institute of Technology

Electrical Engineering and Computer Science (S.M.)
Massachusetts Institute of Technology

Electrical Engineering and Computer Science (Sc.D.)
Massachusetts Institute of Technology

Electrical Engineering Systems (M.S.)
University of Michigan

Electrical Engineering Systems (M.S.E.)
University of Michigan

Electrical Engineering- Multimedia (M.S.)
University of Southern California

Electrical Engineering- Systems (Ph.D.)
University of Michigan

Electrical Engineering- VLSI Design (M.S.)
University of Southern California

Electrical Sciences and Computer Engineering (M.S.)
Brown University

Electrical Sciences and Computer Engineering (Ph.D.)
Brown University

Electricity Markets (M.S.)
Illinois Institute of Technology

Electro-Optics (M.S.)
Air Force Institute of Technology
University of Dayton

Electro-Optics (Ph.D.)
Air Force Institute of Technology
University of Dayton

Electronic Circuits & Systems (M.S.)
University of California, San Diego

(*) degree program awarded outside engineering

(*) degree program awarded outside engineering

(*) degree program awarded outside engineering

Engineering Management (M.S.)
Kansas State University

Engineering Management (D.E.)
Southern Methodist University

Engineering Management (D.Sc.)
The George Washington University

Engineering Management (M.E.)
Cornell University
University of Detroit Mercy
University of Ottawa, Faculty of Engineering
Portland State University
Stevens Institute of Technology
Washington University

Engineering Management (M.E.M)
Old Dominion University

Engineering Management (M.E.M.)
The George Washington University
Northwestern University

Engineering Management (M.Eng.)
University of Louisville
Widener University

Engineering Management (M.S.)
Air Force Institute of Technology
California State University, Northridge
The Catholic University of America
University of Dayton
Drexel University
Florida Institute of Technology
Florida International University
FAMU-FSU College of Engineering
The George Washington University
University of Kansas
Lawrence Technological University
Marquette University
University of Maryland, Baltimore County
University of Michigan, Dearborn
University of Missouri - Rolla
New Jersey Institute of Technology
New Mexico Institute of Mining & Technology
University of New Orleans
University of North Carolina, Charlotte
Northeastern University
Oakland University
Old Dominion University
Portland State University
Rose-Hulman Institute of Technology
Saint Martin's College
Saint Mary's University
University of South Florida
University of Southern California
Southern Methodist University
Syracuse University
The University of Texas at Arlington
The University of Texas at Austin
Wayne State University
Western Michigan University

Engineering Management (M.S.) -Offered by ECE, MME and College of Business
Saint Cloud State University

Engineering Management (M.S.E)
Gannon University

Engineering Management (MBA/M.S.)
California Polytechnic State University

Engineering Management (Ph.D.)
University of Missouri - Rolla
Old Dominion University
Stevens Institute of Technology

Engineering Management and Leadership (M.S.)
Santa Clara University

Engineering Management and Techology (M.S.)
University of Louisiana at Lafayette

Engineering Management Concentration (M.S.)
McNeese State University

Engineering Management Systems (M.S.)
Columbia University

Engineering Mechanics (M.E.)
Cornell University
Old Dominion University

Engineering Mechanics (M.S.)
The University of Arizona
Case Western Reserve University
University of Cincinnati
Clemson University
Cleveland State University
University of Dayton
Michigan Technological University
University of Nebraska, Lincoln
New Mexico Institute of Mining & Technology
The University of Texas at Austin
University of Wisconsin, Madison

Engineering Mechanics (M.S., Aero.)
Old Dominion University

Engineering Mechanics (M.S., M.E.)
University of Florida
The Pennsylvania State University
Virginia Polytechnic Institute and State University

Engineering Mechanics (M.S., M.Eng.)
Iowa State University

Engineering Mechanics (M.S., Mech.)
Old Dominion University

Engineering Mechanics (Ph.D.)
The University of Arizona
University of Cincinnati
Clemson University
University of Florida
Iowa State University
University of Nebraska, Lincoln
The University of Texas at Austin
Virginia Polytechnic Institute and State University
University of Wisconsin, Madison

Engineering Mechanics (Ph.D., Aero.)
Old Dominion University

Engineering Mechanics (Ph.D., Mech.)
Old Dominion University

Engineering Operations & Strategy
Wilkes University

Engineering Physics (M.E.)
Cornell University

Engineering Physics (M.EP.)
University of Virginia

Engineering Physics (M.S.)
University of California, San Diego
University of Maine

(*) degree program awarded outside engineering

(*) degree program awarded outside engineering

ALPHABETICAL INDEX OF PARTICIPATING GRADUATE DEGREE PROGRAMS

(*) degree program awarded outside engineering

Environmental Health and Safety (M.S.)
University of Miami

Environmental Health Engineering (Ph.D.)
University of Alabama at Birmingham

Environmental Health Physics
Clemson University

Environmental Planning & Management (M.S.)
The Johns Hopkins University

Environmental Quality Management (M.E.)
University of Southern California

Environmental Quality Science (M.S.)
University of Alaska Fairbanks

Environmental Resources and Forest Engineering
SUNY College of Environmental Science and Forestry

Environmental Resources and Forest Engineering (M.S., M.P.S.)
SUNY College of Environmental Science and Forestry

Environmental Resources Management (M.S.)
Florida Institute of Technology

Environmental Science & Engineering (Ph.D)
Clarkson University

Environmental Science & Engineering(M.S)
Clarkson University

Environmental Science (M.E.S.)
William Marsh Rice University

Environmental Science (M.S.)
Florida Institute of Technology
Iowa State University
University of Kansas
University of Oklahoma

Environmental Science (M.S.E.S.)
Southern Methodist University

Environmental Science (Ph.D)
Florida Institute of Technology

Environmental Science (Ph.D.)
University of Cincinnati
Iowa State University
University of Kansas
University of Oklahoma

Environmental Science and Engineering (M.S.)
California Institute of Technology

Colorado School of Mines
William Marsh Rice University

Environmental Science and Engineering (Ph.D.)
California Institute of Technology
Colorado School of Mines
University of North Carolina at Chapel Hill
University of Texas at El Paso

Environmental Science and Engineering and Biochemistry and Molecular Biology (M.S.)
OGI School of Science & Engineering at OHSU

Environmental Science and Engineering Biochemistry and Molecular Biology (Ph.D.)
OGI School of Science & Engineering at OHSU

Environmental Science in Civil Engineering (Ph.D.)
University of Illinois at Urbana-Champaign

Environmental Science in Civil Engineering (M.S.)
University of Illinois at Urbana-Champaign

Environmental Sciences and Engineering (M.S.)
Virginia Polytechnic Institute and State University

Environmental Sciences and Engineering (Ph.D.)
University of Texas at San Antonio
Virginia Polytechnic Institute and State University

Environmental Sciences and Resources (Ph.D.)
Portland State University

Environmental Studies (M.S.)
University of Massachusetts Lowell

Environmental Systems - Environmental Resources Engineering (M.S.)
Humboldt State University

Environmental Systems Management (M.S.)
Southern Methodist University

Environmental Technology (M.S.)
New York Institute of Technology

Environmental Toxicology (Ph.D.)
Michigan State University

Ergonomics and Human Factors (Ph.D.)
University of Miami

Executive Master's in Technology Management (M.S.E)
University of Pennsylvania

F

Facilities Management (M.S.)
Southern Methodist University

Financial Engineering (M.S.)
Columbia University
University of Michigan

Financial Engineering (M.S.E.)
University of Michigan

Fire Protection Engineering (M.S.)
Worcester Polytechnic Institute

Fire Protection Engineering (M.S., M.E.)
University of Maryland, College Park

Fire Protection Engineering (Ph.D.)
Worcester Polytechnic Institute

Fluid /Thermal/Chemical Processes (M.S.)
Brown University

Fluid and Thermal Engineering Sciences (M.S.)
Case Western Reserve University

Fluid and Thermal Engineering Sciences (Ph.D.)
Case Western Reserve University

Fluid/Thermal/Chemical Processes (Ph.D.)
Brown University

Food Processing Engineering (M.S.)
Illinois Institute of Technology

Food Safety and Technology (M.S.)
Illinois Institute of Technology

Food, Agricultural, and Biological Engrg (M.S.)
The Ohio State University

Food, Agricultural, and Biological Engrg. (Ph.D.)
The Ohio State University

G

Gas Engineering (M.S.)
Illinois Institute of Technology

General Engineering (M.S.)
Boston University
University of Illinois at Urbana-Champaign
Montana Tech of the University of Montana
Rowan University
San Jose State University

(*) degree program awarded outside engineering

ALPHABETICAL INDEX OF PARTICIPATING GRADUATE DEGREE PROGRAMS

General Engineering - Chem (M.S.ENGR)
Prairie View A&M University

General Engineering - Civil (M.S.ENGR)
Prairie View A&M University

General Engineering - Mechanical (M.S.ENGR)
Prairie View A&M University

Geo-Environmental Engineering (M.S.)
The Pennsylvania State University

Geo-Environmental Engineering (Ph.D.)
The Pennsylvania State University

Geodetic Science and Surveying (M.S.)
The Ohio State University

Geodetic Science and Surveying (Ph.D.)
The Ohio State University

Geoenvironmental Engineering (M.S.)
Illinois Institute of Technology

Geography and Environmental Engineering (M.S., M.S.E., M.A.)
The Johns Hopkins University

Geography and Environmental Engineering (Ph.D.)
The Johns Hopkins University

Geological Engineering (M.S.)
University of Alaska Fairbanks
Michigan Technological University
University of Missouri - Rolla
University of North Dakota
University of Oklahoma
University of Wisconsin, Madison

Geological Engineering (M.S., M.Geo.E.)
University of Minnesota -Twin Cities

Geological Engineering (Ph.D.)
Michigan Technological University
University of Minnesota -Twin Cities
University of Missouri - Rolla
University of Oklahoma
University of Wisconsin, Madison

Geological Sciences (M.S.)
University of Notre Dame

Geological Sciences (M.S., M.E.)
Cornell University

Geological Sciences (Ph.D.)
Cornell University

Geology (M.S.)
Michigan Technological University

Geology (Ph.D.)
Michigan Technological University

Geology and Geological Engineering (M.S.)
The University of Mississippi
South Dakota School of Mines and Technology

Geology and Geological Engineering (Ph.D.)
South Dakota School of Mines and Technology

Geology and Geological Enginggering (Ph.D.)
The University of Mississippi

Geology/Hydrology and Geological Engineering (Ph.D.)
Colorado School of Mines

Geology/Hydrology/Geological Engineering (M.S., M.E.)
Colorado School of Mines

Geomatics Engineering (MEng)
University of Calgary

Geomatics Engineering (MSc(Eng))
University of Calgary

Geomatics Engineering (Ph.D.)
University of Calgary

Geophysics (M.S.)
Michigan Technological University

Geophysics and Geophysical Engineering (Ph.D.)
Colorado School of Mines

Geophysics/Geophysical Engineering (M.S, M.E.)
Colorado School of Mines

Geoscience (M.S.) option Geological Engineering
Montana Tech of the University of Montana

Geoscience (M.S.)option Geophyscial Engineering
Montana Tech of the University of Montana

Geoscience and Remote Sensing (M.S.)
University of Michigan
University of Michigan

Geoscience and Remote Sensing (Ph.D.)
University of Michigan

Geoscience and Remote Sensing (Ph.D.) Joint-AOSS
University of Michigan

Geospatial Science & Engineering
South Dakota State University

Geotechnical Engineering (M.S.)
Illinois Institute of Technology

Geotechnical Engineering and Geoscience (M.S.)
University of Illinois at Chicago

Geotechnical Engineering and GeoSciences (Ph.D.)
University of Illinois at Chicago

Geotechnics (M.E)
University of Missouri - Rolla

Glass Science (M.S.)
Alfred University, NY State College of Ceramics

Glass Science (Ph.D.)
Alfred University, NY State College of Ceramics

Global Automotive and Manufacturing Engineering (M.E.)
University of Michigan

Global Engineering (M.S.)
Boston University

Global Manufacturing Leadership (M.S.)
FAMU-FSU College of Engineering

H

Hazardous and Waste Materials Management (M.S.)
Southern Methodist University

Hazardous Waste Engineering (M.E.)
The University of New Mexico

Health Care Administration (M.S.)
Oklahoma State University

Health Care Technologies Management (M.S.)
Marquette University

Health Physics (M.S.)
University of Cincinnati
Georgia Institute of Technology
Texas A&M University

Health Systems (M.S.)
Georgia Institute of Technology

Human Computer Interaction (M.S.)
Iowa State University

Human Computer Interaction (Ph.D.)
Iowa State University

Human Factors (M.S.)
Tufts University

(*) degree program awarded outside engineering

(*) degree program awarded outside engineering

University of Oklahoma
Oklahoma State University
Oregon State University
University of Pittsburgh
Polytechnic University
University of Puerto Rico, Mayaguez Campus
Purdue University
Saint Mary's University
University of Tennessee, Knoxville
Texas A&M University - Kingsville
Texas Tech University
University of Texas at El Paso
The University of Toledo
Wayne State University
West Virginia University
Wichita State University
University of Wisconsin, Madison

Industrial Engineering (M.S., M.E.)
Ecole Polytechnique de Montreal
North Carolina State University
The Pennsylvania State University
Rensselaer Polytechnic Institute
University of South Florida
Texas A&M University

Industrial Engineering (M.S., M.E., MBA&E)
Lehigh University

Industrial Engineering (M.S., M.S.E.)
Arizona State University

Industrial Engineering (M.S.,M.S.E., M.S.I.E.)
University of Washington

Industrial Engineering (M.S.E.)
Western Michigan University

Industrial Engineering (M.S.I.E.)
University of Miami
University of Minnesota -Twin Cities

Industrial Engineering (M.S.I.E.), (M.S.)
University of Central Florida

Industrial Engineering (Ph.D)
University of Tennessee, Knoxville

Industrial Engineering (Ph.D.)
Arizona State University

University of Arkansas
University of Central Florida
University of Cincinnati
Clemson University
Columbia University
Ecole Polytechnique de Montreal
Florida International University
FAMU-FSU College of Engineering
University of Houston, Cullen School of Engineering
University of Illinois at Urbana-Champaign
The University of Iowa
Iowa State University
Kansas State University
Lehigh University
University of Louisville
University of Miami
University of Minnesota -Twin Cities
Mississippi State University
University of Missouri-Columbia
New Jersey Institute of Technology
New Mexico State University
State University of New York at Buffalo
North Carolina A & T State University
North Carolina State University
Northeastern University
University of Oklahoma
Oregon State University
The Pennsylvania State University
University of Pittsburgh
Purdue University
University of South Florida
Texas A&M University
Texas Tech University
The University of Texas at Arlington
The University of Toledo
University of Washington
Wayne State University
West Virginia University
Western Michigan University
Wichita State University
University of Wisconsin, Madison

Industrial Engineering and Management (Ph.D.)
Oklahoma State University

Industrial Engineering and Management Sci.(Ph.D.)
Northwestern University

Industrial Engineering and Operations Research (M.S, M.Eng.)
University of California, Berkeley

Industrial Engineering and Operations Research (Ph.D., D.Eng.)
University of California, Berkeley

Industrial Engineering. (M.S.)
The University of Texas at Arlington

Industrial Hygiene (M.S.)
Air Force Institute of Technology
West Virginia University

Industrial Management (M.S.)
Mercer University

Industrial Management Engineering (M.S.)
South Dakota State University

Information and Computer Science (M.S.)
University of California, Irvine (*)

Information and Computer Science (Ph.D)
University of California, Irvine (*)

Information and Systems Engineering (M.S., M.E.)
Lehigh University

Information Assurance (M.S.)
Air Force Institute of Technology
Iowa State University

Information Engineering and Management (M.S.I.E.M.)
Southern Methodist University

Information Management (M.E.)
Washington University

Information Networking Institute (M.S.)
Carnegie Mellon University

Information Operations
Air Force Institute of Technology

Information Resource Management (M.S.)
Air Force Institute of Technology

Information Science (Ph.D.)
Cornell University

Information Security and Assurance (M.S.)
George Mason University

(*) degree program awarded outside engineering

ALPHABETICAL INDEX OF PARTICIPATING GRADUATE DEGREE PROGRAMS

Information Systems & Technology (M.S.)
University of Michigan, Dearborn

Information Systems (M.S.)
George Mason University
Illinois Institute of Technology (*)
University of Maryland, Baltimore County
Northeastern University

Information Systems (Ph.D.)
University of Maryland, Baltimore County

Information Systems and Technology (M.S.)
The Johns Hopkins University

Information Systems Engineering
Oakland University

Information Systems Engineering (M.S.)
Polytechnic University

Information Systems Security Engineering (M.Eng. & M.A.Sc.)
Concordia University, Faculty of Engr. and Comp. Sci.

Information Technology (M.I.T.)
Northwestern University

Information Technology (M.S.)
Ecole de Technologie Superieure
University of Kansas
University of Miami

Information Technology (Ph.D.)
George Mason University

Information, Network & Computer Security (M.S.)
New York Institute of Technology

Infrastructure & Environmental Systems (Ph.D)
University of North Carolina, Charlotte

Infrastructure Systems Engineering (M.S.I.S.E.)
University of Minnesota -Twin Cities

Integrated Engineering (Ph.D.)
Ohio University

Integrated Manufacturing Systems (M.E.)
North Carolina State University

Integrated Media Systems (M.S.)
University of Southern California

Integrated Microsystems (M.E.)
University of Michigan

Integrated Product Development (M.E.)
Stevens Institute of Technology

Integrated Textile and Apparel Science (M.S.)
Auburn University

Integrated Textile and Apparel Science (Ph.D.)
Auburn University

Intelligence System Robotics and Control (Ph.D.)
University of California, San Diego

Intelligence Systems, Robotics & Control (M.S.)
University of California, San Diego

Intelligent Transportation Systems (Cert. of Grad Studies)
University of Michigan

Intercollege Degree (M.S.)
The Pennsylvania State University

Intercollege Degree (Ph.D.)
The Pennsylvania State University

Interdisciplinary
Villanova University

Interdisciplinary Engineering (M.S.)
Purdue University

Interdisciplinary Engineering (Ph.D.)
Northeastern University
Texas A&M University

Interdisciplinary Ph.D. Civil Engineering
University of Missouri - Kansas City

Interdisciplinary Ph.D. Computer Science
University of Missouri - Kansas City

Interdisciplinary Ph.D. Electrical Engineering
University of Missouri - Kansas City

Interdisciplinary Ph.D. Mechanical Engineering
University of Missouri - Kansas City

Interengineering (M.S., M.S.E.)
University of Washington

International Logistics (M.S.)
Georgia Institute of Technology

Internet Engineering (M.S.)
New Jersey Institute of Technology

Irrigation Engineering (M.S.)
Utah State University

Irrigation Engineering (Ph.D.)
Utah State University

ISE (M.S.E.)/MBA (Dual degree)
University of Michigan, Dearborn

L

Limnology and Marine Science (M.S.)
University of Wisconsin, Madison

Limnology and Marine Science (Ph.D.)
University of Wisconsin, Madison

Logistics (M.E.)
Massachusetts Institute of Technology

Logistics (M.S.)
The University of Texas at Arlington

Logistics Management (M.S.)
Air Force Institute of Technology

M

M. Eng.
Northern Arizona University
Northern Arizona University
Northern Arizona University

M.Eng., M.Sc.
University of Guelph

M.S. Engineering (pending)
Indiana University-Purdue University Fort Wayne

M.S.: Electrical and Computer, Mechanical and Astro, Systems
Naval Postgraduate School

Macromolecular Science (M.S.)
Case Western Reserve University

Macromolecular Science (Ph.D.)
Case Western Reserve University

Macromolecular Science and Engineering (M.S.)
University of Michigan

Macromolecular Science and Engineering (M.S.E.)
University of Michigan

Macromolecular Science and Engineering (Ph.D.)
University of Michigan

Management of Technology (M.S.)
University of Miami

Management of Technology (M.S.MOT.)
University of Minnesota -Twin Cities

Management of Technology @ Distance (MMSc)
University of Waterloo

(*) degree program awarded outside engineering

ALPHABETICAL INDEX OF PARTICIPATING GRADUATE DEGREE PROGRAMS

(*) degree program awarded outside engineering

Master of Engineering in Computer Engineering (MEng.)
The State University of New York at Binghamton
Master of Engineering in Electrical Engineering (MEng.)
The State University of New York at Binghamton
Master of Engineering in Industrial and Systems Engineering (MEng.)
The State University of New York at Binghamton
Master of Engineering in Mechanical Engineering (MEng.)
The State University of New York at Binghamton
Master of Engineering Management (M.E.M.)
Wichita State University
Master of Information Technology (M.I.T.)
University of Texas at El Paso
Master of Science for Teachers
Illinois Institute of Technology (*)
Master of Science in Civil Engineering (M.S.C.E.)
The University of Texas at Tyler
Master of Science in Computer Science (M.S.C.S.)
The University of Texas at Tyler
Master of Science in Computer Science and Engineering
University of Evansville
Master of Science in Engineering Management (M.S.)
Tufts University
Master of Science in Engineering Technology
Tri-State University
Master's of Engineering Management (M.E.M.)
Dartmouth College
Master's of Science (CS)
Dartmouth College (*)
Masters in Biotechnology
Northwestern University
Masters of Engineering (M.S.)
University of Illinois at Chicago
Masters of Engineering Management
Duke University Pratt School of Engineering
Material Science & Engineering (M.S.)
Washington State University
Material Science (M.S., M.E.)
Vanderbilt University
Material Science (Ph.D.)
Vanderbilt University

Material Science and Engineering (M.S.)
Illinois Institute of Technology
Material Science and Engineering (Ph.D.)
Illinois Institute of Technology
The Pennsylvania State University
Materials Engineering (M.S.)
University of Maryland, College Park
Materials Engineering (Ph.D.)
University of Maryland, College Park
Materials Science and Engineering (M.S.E.)
The Johns Hopkins University
Materials and Metallurgical Engineering (Ph.D.)
University of Alabama at Birmingham
Materials and Nuclear Engineering (M.S.)
University of Nevada, Las Vegas
Materials Engineer (Eng.)
Massachusetts Institute of Technology
Materials Engineering (M.S.)
University of Alabama at Birmingham
California State University, Northridge
University of California, Santa Barbara
University of Cincinnati
University of Dayton
University of Houston, Cullen School of Engineering
University of Idaho
University of Illinois at Chicago
New Mexico Institute of Mining & Technology
The State University of New York at Binghamton
San Jose State University
Materials Engineering (M.S., M.E.)
Auburn University
Rensselaer Polytechnic Institute
Materials Engineering (M.S., M.S.E.)
Arizona State University
Materials Engineering (Ph.D.)
Auburn University
University of California, Santa Barbara
University of Dayton
University of Houston, Cullen School of Engineering
University of Illinois at Chicago
New Mexico Institute of Mining & Technology

The State University of New York at Binghamton
Purdue University
Stevens Institute of Technology
Materials Engineering (Ph.D., D.E.)
Rensselaer Polytechnic Institute
Materials Engineering and Science (M.S.)
South Dakota School of Mines and Technology
Materials Engineering and Science (Ph.D.)
South Dakota School of Mines and Technology
Virginia Polytechnic Institute and State University
Materials Engineering Science (M.S.)
Alfred University, NY State College of Ceramics
Materials Process Engineering (M.S.)
Worcester Polytechnic Institute
Materials Science & Engineering (M.S. and M.Eng)
Boise State University
Materials Science & Engineering (M.S.)
Drexel University
Michigan Technological University
University of Missouri - Rolla
Materials Science & Engineering (M.S., M.Eng.)
University of California, Berkeley
Materials Science & Engineering (Ph.D)
University of Missouri - Rolla
Materials Science & Engineering (Ph.D.)
Drexel University
University of Idaho
Michigan Technological University
Stony Brook University
Materials Science (D.E.)
Washington University
Materials Science (M.M.S.)
William Marsh Rice University
Materials Science (M.MSE.)
University of Virginia
Materials Science (M.S.)
Air Force Institute of Technology
The University of Alabama in Huntsville
California Institute of Technology
University of California, San Diego
University of Connecticut

(*) degree program awarded outside engineering

University of New Hampshire
Oregon State University
University of Rochester
University of Vermont
University of Virginia
University of Wisconsin, Madison

Materials Science (Ph.D.)
Air Force Institute of Technology
University of Alabama at Birmingham
The University of Alabama in Huntsville
California Institute of Technology
University of California, San Diego
University of Cincinnati
University of Connecticut
University of Denver
University of North Texas
Oregon State University
University of Rochester
University of Southern California
University of Vermont
University of Virginia
Washington State University
University of Wisconsin, Madison

Materials Science (Ph.D.) (Electrical)
Howard University

Materials Science (Ph.D.), (Mechanical)
Howard University

Atmospheric Science (Ph.D.)
Howard University

Materials Science and Engineering (M.E.)
Massachusetts Institute of Technology
The University of Texas at Arlington
University of Utah

Materials Science and Engineering (M.M.S.E.)
University of Delaware

Materials Science and Engineering (M.S.)
The University of Arizona
University of California, Davis
University of California, Irvine
University of California, Los Angeles
Carnegie Mellon University
Case Western Reserve University

Clemson University
Columbia University
University of Illinois at Urbana-Champaign
Iowa State University
University of Kentucky
University of Massachusetts Lowell
Stony Brook University
University of North Texas
Northwestern University
The Ohio State University
The Pennsylvania State University
University of Pittsburgh
Stanford University
University of Tennessee, Knoxville
The University of Texas at Arlington
The University of Texas at Austin
University of Utah
Wayne State University
Worcester Polytechnic Institute

Materials Science and Engineering (M.S., M.E.)
Cornell University
University of Florida
Texas A&M University
Virginia Polytechnic Institute and State University

Materials Science and Engineering (M.S., M.E., MBA&E)
Lehigh University

Materials Science and Engineering (M.S.,M.S.M.S.E)
University of Washington

Materials Science and Engineering (M.S.E.)
University of Michigan
University of Pennsylvania
Wright State University

Materials Science and Engineering (M.S.M.S.)
University of Central Florida

Materials Science and Engineering (M.S.Mat.S.E.)
University of Minnesota -Twin Cities

Materials Science and Engineering (Ph.D.)
The University of Arizona
University of California, Davis
University of California, Irvine
University of California, Los Angeles

Carnegie Mellon University
Case Western Reserve University
University of Central Florida
Clemson University
Columbia University
Cornell University
University of Delaware
University of Florida
Georgia Institute of Technology
University of Illinois at Urbana-Champaign
Iowa State University
The Johns Hopkins University
University of Kentucky
Lehigh University
Massachusetts Institute of Technology
University of Michigan
University of Minnesota -Twin Cities
North Carolina State University
Northwestern University
The Ohio State University
University of Pennsylvania
University of Pittsburgh
William Marsh Rice University
Rutgers, The State University of New Jersey
Stanford University
University of Tennessee, Knoxville
Texas A&M University
The University of Texas at Arlington
The University of Texas at Austin
University of Texas at El Paso
University of Utah
University of Washington
Wayne State University
Worcester Polytechnic Institute

Materials Science and Engineering (Ph.D., D.Eng.)
University of California, Berkeley

Materials Science and Engineering (S.M.)
Massachusetts Institute of Technology

Materials Science and Engineering (Sc.D.)
Massachusetts Institute of Technology

(*) degree program awarded outside engineering

ALPHABETICAL INDEX OF PARTICIPATING GRADUATE DEGREE PROGRAMS

Materials Science Engineering
Alfred University, NY State College of Ceramics

Materials Science Engineering (M.S. - M.S.E.N.)
The University of Texas at Dallas

Materials Science Engineering (M.S.)
Brown University
Florida International University
Georgia Institute of Technology
Purdue University

Materials Science Engineering (M.S., M.E.)
North Carolina State University

Materials Science Engineering (Ph.D)
The University of Texas at Dallas

Materials Science Engineering (Ph.D.)
Brown University

Materials Science/Materials Engr.
University of Southern California

Mathematical and Computer Science (M.S.)
Colorado School of Mines

Mathematical and Computer Science (Ph.D.)
Colorado School of Mines

Mathematics
Louisiana Tech University

Mathematics (Ph.D.)
Ecole Polytechnique de Montreal

Measurement and Control Engineering (M.S.)
Idaho State University

Mechanical and Aerospace Engineering (Ph.D.)
Princeton University

Mechanical Engineering (M.E.)
City College of the City University of New York

Mechanical & Aerospace Engineering (D.Sc.)
The George Washington University

Mechanical & Aerospace Engineering (M.S.)
The George Washington University

Mechanical & Manufacturing Engineering (MEng)
University of Calgary

Mechanical & Manufacturing Engineering (Ph.D.)
University of Calgary

Mechanical (M.E.) Materials Sci & Eng (M.E.)/ Atmos.Sci.(M.E.
Howard University

Mechanical and Aeronautical Engineering (M.S.)
University of California, Davis

Mechanical and Aeronautical Engineering (Ph.D.)
University of California, Davis

Mechanical and Aerospace Engineering (M.S.)
University of California, Irvine
Illinois Institute of Technology
University of Missouri-Columbia
Princeton University
Princeton University
Rutgers, The State University of New Jersey

Mechanical and Aerospace Engineering (Ph.D.)
University of California, Irvine
Illinois Institute of Technology
University of Missouri-Columbia
Princeton University
Rutgers, The State University of New Jersey
Syracuse University
University of Virginia

Mechanical and Aerospace Engr (M.E.)
University of Virginia

Mechanical and Aerospace Engr (M.S.)
University of Virginia

Mechanical Engineer (Eng.)
Massachusetts Institute of Technology

Mechanical Engineering
California State Polytechnic University, Pomona
University of Tennessee, Chattanooga
University of Tulsa

Mechanical Engineering (M.S. & ME)
Rochester Institute of Technology

Mechanical Engineering (Ph.D.)
Florida Atlantic University
University of Illinois at Chicago

Mechanical Engineering (D.A.)
University of Miami

Mechanical Engineering (D.E.)
The Catholic University of America
Cleveland State University
University of Detroit Mercy

University of Kansas
Washington University

Mechanical Engineering (DRME)
Lamar University

Mechanical Engineering (ENG.D.)
University of Massachusetts Lowell

Mechanical Engineering (Engineer Degree)
Santa Clara University

Mechanical Engineering (M.B.A.)
University of Denver

Mechanical Engineering (M.E.)
The Catholic University of America
Clarkson University
Clemson University
The Cooper Union
University of Detroit Mercy
University of Hartford
University of Idaho
State University of New York at Buffalo
Oklahoma State University
Old Dominion University
University of Ottawa, Faculty of Engineering
Portland State University
Stevens Institute of Technology
Tennessee State University
The University of Texas at Arlington
Tufts University
University of Utah
Worcester Polytechnic Institute

Mechanical Engineering (M.E., M.E.S)
Lamar University

Mechanical Engineering (M.E.M.)
University of Delaware

Mechanical Engineering (M.Eng. & M.A.Sc.)
Concordia University, Faculty of Engr. and Comp. Sci.

Mechanical Engineering (M.Eng.)
Ecole de Technologie Superieure
University of Notre Dame
Widener University

Mechanical Engineering (M.Eng.; M.S.)
University of Louisville

(*) degree program awarded outside engineering

ALPHABETICAL INDEX OF PARTICIPATING GRADUATE DEGREE PROGRAMS

Mechanical Engineering (M.M.E.)
William Marsh Rice University

Mechanical Engineering (M.S. and M.Eng)
Boise State University

Mechanical Engineering (M.S.)
The University of Akron
University of Alabama at Birmingham
The University of Alabama
University of Alaska Fairbanks
University of Alberta
Alfred University, NY State College of Ceramics
The University of Arizona
University of Arkansas
Baylor University
Boston University
Bradley University
University of Bridgeport
Brigham Young University
Bucknell University
California Institute of Technology
California Polytechnic State University
California State University, Fresno
California State University, Fullerton
California State University, Long Beach
California State University, Northridge
California State University, Sacramento
University of California, Los Angeles
University of California, Riverside
University of California, San Diego
University of California, Santa Barbara
Carnegie Mellon University
Case Western Reserve University
The Catholic University of America
University of Cincinnati
Clarkson University
Clemson University
Cleveland State University
Colorado State University
University of Colorado at Denver and Health Sciences Center
Columbia University
University of Dayton

University of Denver
Drexel University
Duke University Pratt School of Engineering
Florida Atlantic University
Florida Institute of Technology
Florida International University
FAMU-FSU College of Engineering
Georgia Institute of Technology
University of Hawaii at Manoa
University of Idaho
Idaho State University
University of Illinois at Chicago
University of Illinois at Urbana-Champaign
Indiana University Purdue University at Indianapolis
The University of Iowa
Iowa State University
University of Kansas
Kansas State University
University of Kentucky
Lawrence Technological University
Louisiana State University
University of Maine
Manhattan College
Marquette University
University of Maryland, Baltimore County
University of Maryland, College Park
University of Massachusetts Amherst
University of Massachusetts Dartmouth
University of Massachusetts Lowell
The University of Memphis
University of Miami
University of Michigan
Michigan State University
Michigan Technological University
Minnesota State University, Mankato
University of Minnesota - Twin Cities
The University of Mississippi
Mississippi State University
University of Missouri - Kansas City
University of Missouri - Rolla
Montana State University

University of Nebraska, Lincoln
University of Nevada, Las Vegas
University of Nevada, Reno
University of New Hampshire
University of New Haven
New Jersey Institute of Technology
The University of New Mexico
New Mexico State University
The State University of New York at Binghamton
State University of New York at Buffalo
Stony Brook University
North Carolina A & T State University
North Carolina State University
North Dakota State University
Northeastern University
Northern Illinois University
Northwestern University
University of Notre Dame
Oakland University
The Ohio State University
Ohio University
University of Oklahoma
Oklahoma State University
Old Dominion University
Oregon State University
University of Ottawa, Faculty of Engineering
University of Pittsburgh
Polytechnic University
Portland State University
University of Puerto Rico, Mayaguez Campus
Purdue University
University of Rochester
Rose-Hulman Institute of Technology
Rowan University
Saint Cloud State University
San Diego State University
San Jose State University
Santa Clara University
University of South Alabama
South Dakota School of Mines and Technology
South Dakota State University

(*) degree program awarded outside engineering

ALPHABETICAL INDEX OF PARTICIPATING GRADUATE DEGREE PROGRAMS

University of Southern California
Southern Illinois University Carbondale
Southern Illinois University Edwardsville
Southern Methodist University
Stanford University
Syracuse University
Tennessee Technological University
University of Tennessee, Knoxville
Texas A&M University - Kingsville
Texas Tech University
The University of Texas at Arlington
The University of Texas at Austin
University of Texas at El Paso
University of Texas at San Antonio
The University of Toledo
Tufts University
Tulane University
University of Utah
Utah State University
University of Vermont
Villanova University
Washington State University
Washington University
Wayne State University
West Virginia University
Wichita State University
University of Wisconsin, Madison
Worcester Polytechnic Institute
University of Wyoming
Youngstown State University

Mechanical Engineering (M.S., M.E.)
Auburn University
University of Colorado at Boulder
University of Connecticut
Cornell University
Ecole Polytechnique de Montreal
University of Florida
University of Houston, Cullen School of Engineering
University of North Dakota
The Pennsylvania State University
Rensselaer Polytechnic Institute

University of South Carolina
University of South Florida
Texas A&M University
Vanderbilt University
Virginia Polytechnic Institute and State University

Mechanical Engineering (M.S., M.Eng.)
University of California, Berkeley

Mechanical Engineering (M.S., M.Engr., MBA&E)
Lehigh University

Mechanical Engineering (M.S., M.S.E.)
Arizona State University

Mechanical Engineering (M.S.E.)
The University of Alabama in Huntsville
Indiana University Purdue University at Indianapolis
The Johns Hopkins University
University of Michigan
University of Michigan, Dearborn
Temple University
Western Michigan University
Wright State University

Mechanical Engineering (M.S.E.); Systems Engineering (M.S.)
Loyola Marymount University

Mechanical Engineering (M.S.E., M.S.M.E.)
University of Washington

Mechanical Engineering (M.S.M.E)
Gannon University
Indiana University Purdue University at Indianapolis

Mechanical Engineering (M.S.M.E.)
University of Central Florida
University of Delaware

Mechanical Engineering (MASc)
University of Waterloo

Mechanical Engineering (MEng)
University of Calgary
University of Waterloo

Mechanical Engineering (MS)
University of Colorado at Colorado Springs

Mechanical Engineering (MSc(Eng))
University of Calgary

Mechanical Engineering (MSE)
Purdue University, Calumet

Mechanical Engineering (Ph.D)
Columbia University

Mechanical Engineering (Ph.D.)
University of Alabama at Birmingham
The University of Alabama in Huntsville
The University of Alabama
University of Alaska Fairbanks
University of Alberta
The University of Arizona
Arizona State University
University of Arkansas
Auburn University
Boston University
Brigham Young University
University of Calgary
California Institute of Technology
University of California, Los Angeles
University of California, Riverside
University of California, San Diego
University of California, Santa Barbara
Carnegie Mellon University
Case Western Reserve University
The Catholic University of America
University of Central Florida
University of Cincinnati
Clarkson University
Clemson University
Colorado State University
University of Colorado at Boulder
Concordia University, Faculty of Engr. and Comp. Sci.
University of Connecticut
Cornell University
University of Dayton
University of Delaware
Drexel University
Duke University Pratt School of Engineering
Ecole Polytechnique de Montreal
University of Florida
Florida Institute of Technology
Florida International University
FAMU-FSU College of Engineering

(*) degree program awarded outside engineering

Georgia Institute of Technology
University of Hawaii at Manoa
University of Houston, Cullen School of Engineering
University of Idaho
University of Illinois at Urbana-Champaign
Indiana University Purdue University at Indianapolis
The University of Iowa
Iowa State University
The Johns Hopkins University
University of Kansas
Kansas State University
University of Kentucky
Lehigh University
Louisiana State University
University of Louisville
University of Maine
Marquette University
University of Maryland, Baltimore County
University of Maryland, College Park
Massachusetts Institute of Technology
University of Massachusetts Amherst
University of Miami
University of Michigan
Michigan State University
University of Minnesota -Twin Cities
The University of Mississippi
Mississippi State University
University of Missouri - Rolla
University of Nebraska, Lincoln
University of Nevada, Las Vegas
University of Nevada, Reno
New Jersey Institute of Technology
The University of New Mexico
New Mexico State University
The State University of New York at Binghamton
State University of New York at Buffalo
Stony Brook University
North Carolina A & T State University
North Carolina State University
University of North Carolina, Charlotte
North Dakota State University

Northeastern University
Northwestern University
Oakland University
The Ohio State University
University of Oklahoma
Oklahoma State University
Old Dominion University
Oregon State University
University of Ottawa, Faculty of Engineering
The Pennsylvania State University
University of Pittsburgh
Polytechnic University
Purdue University
William Marsh Rice University
University of Rochester
Santa Clara University
University of South Carolina
University of South Florida
University of Southern California
Southern Methodist University
Stanford University
Stevens Institute of Technology
University of Tennessee, Knoxville
Texas A&M University
Texas Tech University
The University of Texas at Arlington
The University of Texas at Austin
The University of Toledo
Tufts University
Tulane University
University of Utah
Utah State University
Vanderbilt University
University of Vermont
Virginia Polytechnic Institute and State University
University of Washington
Washington State University
University of Waterloo
Wayne State University
West Virginia University
Western Michigan University

Wichita State University
University of Wisconsin, Madison
Worcester Polytechnic Institute
University of Wyoming

Mechanical Engineering (Ph.D., D.E.)
Rensselaer Polytechnic Institute

Mechanical Engineering (Ph.D., D.Eng.)
University of California, Berkeley

Mechanical Engineering (S.M.)
Massachusetts Institute of Technology

Mechanical Engineering (Sc.D.)
Massachusetts Institute of Technology

Mechanical Engineering - Engineering Mechanics (Ph.D.)
Michigan Technological University

Mechanical Engineering and Applied Mechanics (M.S.)
University of Rhode Island

Mechanical Engineering and Applied Mechanics (M.S.E)
University of Pennsylvania

Mechanical Engineering and Applied Mechanics (Ph.D.)
University of Pennsylvania
University of Rhode Island

Mechanical Engineering and Materials Science (M.S.)
William Marsh Rice University

Mechanical Engineering M.Eng.
McGill University, Faculty of Engineering

Mechanical Engineering Option (M.S. E.)
University of Louisiana at Lafayette

Mechanical Engineering, Ph.D.
McGill University, Faculty of Engineering

Mechanical Engineering (M.S.)
California State University, Los Angeles

Mechanical Engr & Engr Science (MSME, MSE, ME)
University of North Carolina, Charlotte

Mechanics (M.S.)
Michigan State University
Rensselaer Polytechnic Institute
Rutgers, The State University of New Jersey

Mechanics (Ph.D.)
Michigan State University
Rensselaer Polytechnic Institute
Rutgers, The State University of New Jersey

(*) degree program awarded outside engineering

ALPHABETICAL INDEX OF PARTICIPATING GRADUATE DEGREE PROGRAMS

Mechanics of Solids and Structures (M.S.)
Brown University

Mechanics of Solids and Structures (Ph.D.)
Brown University

Mechatronics Engineering Systems(M.S.)
Lawrence Technological University

Mechnical Engineering (M.S.)
Mercer University

Medical Device and Diagnostic Engr. (M.S.)
University of Southern California

Medical Informatics (Ph.D.)
University of Wisconsin, Milwaukee

Medical Physics
Georgia Institute of Technology

Medical Physics (M.S.)
Columbia University

Medical Physics (Ph.D.)
University of Cincinnati

Metallurgical and Materials Engineering (M.S.)
University of Texas at El Paso

Metallurgical and Materials Science/Eng (Ph.D.)
Colorado School of Mines

Metallurgical and Materials Science/Engineering (M.S., M.E.)
Colorado School of Mines

Metallurgical Engineer (Eng.)
Massachusetts Institute of Technology

Metallurgical Engineering (M.S.)
The University of Alabama
University of Idaho
University of Missouri - Rolla
University of Nevada, Reno
University of Wisconsin, Madison

Metallurgical Engineering (M.S., M.E.)
University of Connecticut

Metallurgical Engineering (Ph.D.)
University of Cincinnati
University of Connecticut
University of Missouri - Rolla
University of Nevada, Reno
University of Wisconsin, Madison

Metallurgical Engineering/Materials Science, Joint (Ph.D.)
The University of Alabama

Metallurgical/mineral processing engineering
Montana Tech of the University of Montana

Metallurgy Engineering (M.S., M.E.)
Ecole Polytechnique de Montreal

Metallurgy Engineering (Ph.D.)
Ecole Polytechnique de Montreal

Meterology (M.S.)
Florida Institute of Technology

Micro Electronics-Photonics (M.S.)
University of Arkansas

Micro Electronics-Photonics (Ph.D.)
University of Arkansas

Microelectronic Eng (M.S.); Microelectronics Mfg Eng (M.E.)
Rochester Institute of Technology

Microelectronics and Photonics (M.E.)
Stevens Institute of Technology

Microsystems Engineering (MMSE)
Louisiana Tech University

Microsystems Engineering (Ph.D.)
Rochester Institute of Technology

Mineral Economics (Ph.D.)
The University of Arizona
Colorado School of Mines

Mineral Economics/Engineering Technology Management (M.S.)
Colorado School of Mines

Mineral Engineering (M.S.)
New Mexico Institute of Mining & Technology

Mineral Engineering (M.S., M.E.)
Ecole Polytechnique de Montreal

Mineral Engineering (Ph.D.)
Ecole Polytechnique de Montreal

Mineral Processing (M.S.)
The Pennsylvania State University

Mineral Processing (Ph.D.)
The Pennsylvania State University

Mining and Earth Systems Engineering (Ph.D.)
Colorado School of Mines

Mining and Earth Systems Engineering/Mining Engineering (M.S., M.E.)
Colorado School of Mines

Mining and Geological Engineering (Ph.D.)
University of Alaska Fairbanks

Mining and Minerals Engineering (M.S., M.E.)
Virginia Polytechnic Institute and State University

Mining and Minerals Engineering (Ph.D.)
Virginia Polytechnic Institute and State University

Mining Engineering
The University of Arizona

Mining Engineering (M.S.)
University of Alaska Fairbanks
Michigan Technological University
University of Missouri - Rolla
Montana Tech of the University of Montana
Southern Illinois University Carbondale
West Virginia University

Mining Engineering (M.S., M.E.)
The Pennsylvania State University

Mining Engineering (M.S., M.M.E.)
University of Kentucky

Mining Engineering (Ph.D.)
University of Kentucky
Michigan Technological University
University of Missouri - Rolla
The Pennsylvania State University
West Virginia University

Mining, Geological & Geophysical Engineering (M.S)
The University of Arizona

Mining, Metals & Materials Engineering M.Eng.
McGill University, Faculty of Engineering

Mining, Metals & Materials Engineering, Ph.D.
McGill University, Faculty of Engineering

Mining,Geological & Geophysical Engineering(Ph.D.)
The University of Arizona

Modeling and Simulation (M.E.)
Old Dominion University

Modeling and Simulation (M.S.)
Old Dominion University

(*) degree program awarded outside engineering

ALPHABETICAL INDEX OF PARTICIPATING GRADUATE DEGREE PROGRAMS

Modeling and Simulation (Ph.D.)
Old Dominion University

Molecular Bioscience and Bioengineering
University of Hawaii at Manoa

Molecular Sciences & Nanotechnology (MSNT)
Louisiana Tech University

MS in Electrical Engineering
Western New England College

MS in Engineering
Western New England College

MS in Engineering Management
Western New England College

N

Nanoscience and Nanoengineering (Ph.D.)
South Dakota School of Mines and Technology

Natural Gas Engineering & Management (M.S.)
University of Oklahoma

Natural Gas Engineering (M.S.)
Texas A&M University - Kingsville

Naval Arch. and Marine Engineering (Intermediate)
University of Michigan

Naval Arch. and Marine Engineering (Joint M.S.E./M.B.A.)
University of Michigan

Naval Arch. and Marine Engineering (M.S.)
University of Michigan

Naval Arch. and Marine Engineering (Ph.D.)
University of Michigan

Naval Architecture and Marine Engineering (M.S.)
University of Michigan

Naval Architecture and Marine Engineering (M.S.E.)
University of Michigan

Naval Architecture and Marine Engineering (S.M.)
Massachusetts Institute of Technology

Naval Engineer (Eng.)
Massachusetts Institute of Technology

Network Engineering (M.S.)
Illinois Institute of Technology

Networked Information Systems (M.E.)
Stevens Institute of Technology

Networked Systems
University of California, Irvine

Neuroscience (M.S.)
Syracuse University

Nuclear Engineering (Ph.D.)
University of Maryland, College Park

Nuclear (M.S., M.E.)
University of Maryland, College Park

Nuclear Eng. and Engineering Physics (M.S.)
University of Wisconsin, Madison

Nuclear Eng. and Engineering Physics (Ph.D.)
University of Wisconsin, Madison

Nuclear Engineer (Eng.)
Massachusetts Institute of Technology

Nuclear Engineering
The University of Arizona

Nuclear Engineering (D.E.)
Rensselaer Polytechnic Institute

Nuclear Engineering (M,S.)
University of Cincinnati

Nuclear Engineering (M.S.)
Air Force Institute of Technology
University of Cincinnati
Ecole Polytechnique de Montreal
Georgia Institute of Technology
University of Illinois at Urbana-Champaign
Kansas State University
University of Missouri-Columbia
University of Missouri - Rolla
The University of New Mexico
The Ohio State University
Oregon State University
Purdue University
University of Tennessee, Knoxville
University of Utah

Nuclear Engineering (M.S., M.E.)
North Carolina State University
The Pennsylvania State University
Rensselaer Polytechnic Institute
University of South Carolina
Texas A&M University

Nuclear Engineering (M.S., M.Eng.)
University of California, Berkeley

Nuclear Engineering (MEng)
University of Waterloo

Nuclear Engineering (Ph.D)
University of South Carolina

Nuclear Engineering (Ph.D.)
Air Force Institute of Technology
University of Cincinnati
Ecole Polytechnique de Montreal
Georgia Institute of Technology
University of Illinois at Urbana-Champaign
Kansas State University
University of Michigan
University of Missouri-Columbia
University of Missouri - Rolla
The University of New Mexico
North Carolina State University
The Ohio State University
Oregon State University
The Pennsylvania State University
Purdue University
University of Tennessee, Knoxville
Texas A&M University
University of Utah

Nuclear Engineering (Ph.D., D.Eng.)
University of California, Berkeley

Nuclear Engineering and Radiological Science (Ph.D.)
University of Michigan

Nuclear Engineering and Radiological Sciences (M.S.)
University of Michigan

Nuclear Engineering and Radiological Sciences (M.S.E.)
University of Michigan

Nuclear Engineering and Science (Ph.D.)
Rensselaer Polytechnic Institute

Nuclear Engineering Science (M.S., M.E.)
University of Florida

Nuclear Engineering Science (Ph.D.)
University of Florida

Nuclear Science & Engineering (M.S.)
Idaho State University

Nuclear Science (M.S.)
University of Michigan

(*) degree program awarded outside engineering

(*) degree program awarded outside engineering

Optical Science and Engineering (Ph.D.)
The University of Alabama in Huntsville

Optical Sciences (Ph.D.)
The University of New Mexico

Optics (M.S.)
University of Rochester

Optics (Ph.D.)
University of Rochester

P

Packaging of Electronic and Optical Devices (M.S.)
Southern Methodist University

Paper & Imaging Science & Engineering (M.S.)
Western Michigan University

Paper & Imaging Science & Engineering (Ph.D.)
Western Michigan University

Paper Science (M.S.)
Georgia Institute of Technology

Paper Science and Engineering (M.S.)
Miami University

Paper Science and Engineering (Ph.D.)
SUNY College of Environmental Science and Forestry

Paper Science and Resource Engineering (M.S., M.P.S.)
SUNY College of Environmental Science and Forestry

Paper Science Engineering (Ph.D.)
Georgia Institute of Technology

Petroleum and Natural Gas Engineering (M.S.)
West Virginia University

Petroleum and Natural Gas Engineering (M.S.)
The Pennsylvania State University

Petroleum and Natural Gas Engineering (Ph.D.)
The Pennsylvania State University
West Virginia University

Petroleum Engineering
University of Tulsa

Petroleum Engineering (M.S.M.E.)
Colorado School of Mines

Petroleum Engineering (M.S.)
University of Alaska Fairbanks
University of Kansas
Louisiana State University
University of Missouri - Rolla
Montana Tech of the University of Montana
New Mexico Institute of Mining & Technology
University of Oklahoma
University of Pittsburgh
University of Southern California
Texas Tech University
The University of Texas at Austin
University of Wyoming

Petroleum Engineering (M.S., M.E.)
University of Houston, Cullen School of Engineering
Texas A&M University

Petroleum Engineering (Ph.D)
Texas Tech University

Petroleum Engineering (Ph.D.)
University of Alaska Fairbanks
Colorado School of Mines
Louisiana State University
University of Missouri - Rolla
New Mexico Institute of Mining & Technology
University of Oklahoma
University of Southern California
Stanford University
Texas A&M University
The University of Texas at Austin
University of Wyoming

Petroleum Engineering Option (M.S.E.)
University of Louisiana at Lafayette

Ph.D.
University of Guelph

Ph.D. Program (CS)
Dartmouth College (*)

Pharmaceutical Engineering (M.E.)
University of Michigan

Pharmaceutical Engineering (M.S.)
New Jersey Institute of Technology

Pharmaceutical Manufacturing (M.E.&M.S))
Stevens Institute of Technology

Photonics (M.S.)
Boston University
University of California, San Diego
Lehigh University

Photonics (Ph.D.)
University of California, San Diego

Physics (M.S.)
Colorado School of Mines
University of Illinois at Urbana-Champaign
University of Massachusetts Dartmouth

Physics (Ph.D.)
University of Illinois at Urbana-Champaign

Physics Engineering (M.S.)
South Dakota State University

Physics Engineering (M.S., M.E.)
Ecole Polytechnique de Montreal

Physics Engineering (Ph.D.)
Ecole Polytechnique de Montreal

Physics/Engr. Physics
Louisiana Tech University

Plastics (M.S.)
University of Massachusetts Lowell

Plastics Engineering (ENG.D.)
University of Massachusetts Lowell

Plastics Engineering (M.E.)
University of Michigan

Plastics Engineering (M.S.)
University of Massachusetts Lowell

Polymer Engineering (M.S.)
University of Tennessee, Knoxville

Polymer Engineering (Ph.D.)
University of Tennessee, Knoxville

Polymer Engineering Specialization (M.S.E.)
The University of Akron

Polymer Science (M.S.)
University of Connecticut

Polymer Science (Ph.D.)
University of Connecticut

Polymer Science and Engineering (M.S., M.E., MBA&E)
Lehigh University

Polymer Science and Engineering (Ph.D.)
Lehigh University

(*) degree program awarded outside engineering

ALPHABETICAL INDEX OF PARTICIPATING GRADUATE DEGREE PROGRAMS

(*) degree program awarded outside engineering

Alphabetical Index of Participating Graduate Degree Programs

Space and Planetary Physics (Ph.D.)
University of Michigan

Space and Planetary Sciences (M.S.)
University of Arkansas

Space and Planetary Sciences (Ph.D)
University of Arkansas

Space Engineering (M.E.)
University of Michigan

Space Systems (M.S.)
Air Force Institute of Technology

Space Systems-Aero (M.E.)
University of Michigan

Space Systems-AOSS (M.E.)
University of Michigan

Spatial Information Science & Engineering (M.S.)
University of Maine

Spatial Information Science and Engineering (Ph.D.)
University of Maine

Special Graduate Committee (M.S.)
University of Wisconsin, Madison

Special Graduate Committee (Ph.D.)
University of Wisconsin, Madison

Statistical Science (M.S.)
George Mason University

Statistics (M.A.)
William Marsh Rice University

Statistics (M.S.)
Cornell University
Georgia Institute of Technology

Statistics (M.Stat.)
William Marsh Rice University

Statistics (Ph.D.)
Cornell University
William Marsh Rice University

Strategic Leadership
Air Force Institute of Technology

Structural Design (M.E.)
University of Southern California

Structural Engineering (M.E.)
University of Michigan
Washington University

Structural Engineering (M.S.)
University of California, San Diego
Illinois Institute of Technology
Lehigh University
Milwaukee School of Engineering

Structural Engineering (Ph.D.)
University of California, San Diego

Sustainable Agriculture (M.S.)
Iowa State University

Sustainable Agriculture (Ph.D.)
Iowa State University

System Engineering (M.S.)
Polytechnic University

Systems & Engineering Management (M.S.)
Texas Tech University

Systems & Engineering Management (Ph.D.)
Texas Tech University

Systems Analysis (M.S.)
Miami University

Systems and Control (M.S.)
Case Western Reserve University

Systems and Control Engineering (Ph.D.)
Case Western Reserve University

Systems and Entrepreneurial Engineering (M.S.)
University of Illinois at Urbana–Champaign

Systems and Entrepreneurial Engineering (Ph.D.)
University of Illinois at Urbana–Champaign

Systems and Industrial Engineering (Ph.D.)
The University of Arizona

Systems and Information Science (M.S.)
Syracuse University

Systems Architecture and Engineering (M.S.)
University of Southern California

Systems Design (Ph.D.)
University of New Hampshire

Systems Design Engineering (MASc)
University of Waterloo

Systems Design Engineering (MEng)
University of Waterloo

Systems Design Engineering (Ph.D.)
University of Waterloo

Systems Engineering (D.Sc.)
The George Washington University

Systems Engineering (M.E.)
Cornell University
Old Dominion University
Portland State University
Stevens Institute of Technology
University of Virginia

Systems Engineering (M.Eng.)
Iowa State University

Systems Engineering (M.S)
The University of Arizona

Systems Engineering (M.S.)
Air Force Institute of Technology
Florida Institute of Technology
George Mason University
The George Washington University
The Johns Hopkins University
University of Maryland, College Park
University of Massachusetts Lowell
University of Missouri - Rolla
Oakland University
Southern Methodist University
The University of Texas at Arlington
University of Virginia

Systems Engineering (M.S.) (M.E.)
Virginia Polytechnic Institute and State University

Systems Engineering (M.S.E.)
University of Pennsylvania

Systems Engineering (Ph.D.)
Air Force Institute of Technology
Boston University
Oakland University
Stevens Institute of Technology
University of Virginia

(*) degree program awarded outside engineering

(*) degree program awarded outside engineering

Transportation Engineering (M.S.)
Villanova University

Transportation Engineering (M.S., M.E.)
Rensselaer Polytechnic Institute

Transportation Engineering (Ph.D., D.E.)
Rensselaer Polytechnic Institute

Transportation Engineering and Planning (M.S.)
Illinois Institute of Technology

Transportation Management (M.S.)
Polytechnic University

Transportation Planning and Engineering (M.S.)
Polytechnic University

Transportation Technology and Policy (M.S.)
University of California, Davis

Transportation Technology and Policy (Ph.D.)
University of California, Davis

U

Urban Systems Engineering and Management (M.S.)
Polytechnic University

W

Water Resources (M.S.)
The University of Arizona
Villanova University

Water Resources Administration (Ph.D.)
The University of Arizona

Water Resources Science (M.S.)
University of Kansas

Welding Engineering (M.S.)
The Ohio State University

Welding Engineering (Ph.D.)
The Ohio State University

Wireless and Network (M.S.)
Lehigh University

Wireless Innovation (M.E.)
Polytechnic University

(*) degree program awarded outside engineering

ALPHABETICAL INDEX OF PARTICIPATING ENGINEERING TECHNOLOGY INSTITUTIONS

Geographical Index of Participating Engineering Technology Institutions

UNITED STATES

Alabama
Alabama A&M University

Arizona
Arizona State University, Polytechnic

Arkansas
University of Arkansas at Little Rock

California
California Maritime Academy
California State Polytechnic University, Pomona
California State University, Long Beach
California State University, Sacramento

Colorado
Colorado State University, Pueblo
Colorado Technical University
Metropolitan State College of Denver

Connecticut
Central Connecticut State University
University of Hartford

District of Columbia
University of the District of Columbia

Florida
University of Central Florida

Georgia
Southern Polytechnic State University

Illinois
Bradley University
DeVry University, Addison/DuPage
Northern Illinois University
Southern Illinois University Carbondale

Indiana
Indiana University Purdue University at Indianapolis
Indiana University-Purdue University Fort Wayne
Purdue University College of Technology
Tri-State University

Kansas
Kansas State University
Pittsburg State University

Louisiana
Louisiana Tech University
McNeese State University
Southern University and A&M College

Maine
University of Maine

Maryland
Capitol College

Massachusetts
University of Massachusetts Lowell
Northeastern University
Wentworth Institute of Technology

Michigan
Ferris State University
Lake Superior State University
Lawrence Technological University
Michigan Technological University
Wayne State University
Western Michigan University

Minnesota
Minnesota State University, Mankato

Missouri
Saint Louis University - Parks College

Montana
Montana State University

Nebraska
University of Nebraska, Lincoln

New Jersey
New Jersey Institute of Technology

New Mexico
New Mexico State University

New York
Alfred State College
Buffalo State College
Excelsior College
Rochester Institute of Technology

North Carolina
University of North Carolina, Charlotte
Western Carolina University

Ohio
The University of Akron
University of Cincinnati
University of Dayton
Miami University
The University of Toledo
Youngstown State University

GEOGRAPHICAL INDEX OF PARTICIPATING ENGINEERING TECHNOLOGY INSTITUTIONS

Oklahoma

Oklahoma State University

Oregon

Oregon Institute of Technology

Pennsylvania

Pennsylvania State University Harrisburg

Penn State Erie, The Behrend College

Temple University

South Dakota

South Dakota State University

Tennessee

The University of Memphis

University of Tennessee, Chattanooga

Texas

University of Houston, College of Technology

LeTourneau University

University of North Texas

Prairie View A&M University

Texas A&M University

Texas Tech University

Utah

Brigham Young University

Weber State University

Virginia

Old Dominion University

Washington

Eastern Washington University

West Virginia

West Virginia Institute of Technology, ET&IT

Wisconsin

Milwaukee School of Engineering

For more information, visit the ASEE web site at www.asee.org/colleges

ALPHABETICAL INDEX OF PARTICIPATING ENGINEERING TECHNOLOGY DEGREE PROGRAMS

Miami University
Northern Illinois University
Texas A&M University
Wentworth Institute of Technology

Engineering Technology (B.S.E.T.)
University of Central Florida
The University of Memphis
Pittsburg State University

Engineering Technology (Elec/Elect Eng Tech) (B.S.)
Wayne State University

Engineering Technology (Electro/Mech Eng Tech) (B.S.)
Wayne State University

Engineering Technology (M.E.T.)
Pittsburg State University

Engineering Technology (M.S.)
The University of Memphis
University of North Texas

Engineering Technology (Manuf Indus ET) (B.S.)
Wayne State University

Engineering Technology (Mech Eng Tech) (B.S.)
Wayne State University

Engineering Technology (Product Dev Tech) (B.S.)
Wayne State University

Engineering Technology - CET (B.S.)
Northeastern University

Engineering Technology - EET (B.S.)
Northeastern University

Engineering Technology - MET (B.S.)
Northeastern University

Engineering Technology General
Old Dominion University

Engineering Technology/Electrical (M.S.)
Southern Polytechnic State University

Engineering Technology/Electronics/Instrumentation /Process Plant Technology
McNeese State University

Environmental Engineering Technology (B.S.)
California State University, Long Beach

F

Facilities Engineering Technology (B.S.)
California Maritime Academy

Facility Management Technology (B.S.)
Ferris State University

Fire Protection and Safety Technology (B.S.)
Oklahoma State University

Fire Protection Technology (B.S.)
University of Nebraska, Lincoln

Fire Safety Technology (B.S.E.T.)
University of North Carolina, Charlotte

G

General (B.S)
California State Polytechnic University, Pomona

General Engineering
Lake Superior State University

H

Heavy Equipment Service Engineering Technology (B.S.)
Ferris State University

HVACR Engineering Technology (B.S.)
Ferris State University

I

Industrial Distribution Technology (B.S.)
Western Carolina University

Industrial Engineering Technology (B.S.)
University of Dayton
Indiana University-Purdue University Fort Wayne
University of Nebraska, Lincoln
Southern Polytechnic State University
Western Carolina University

Industrial Management (B.S.)
South Dakota State University

Industrial Technology
Lake Superior State University

Information & Communication Technology
New Mexico State University

Information Systems Technology (B.S.)
University of Central Florida

Interdisciplinary (Contract Major)
University of Hartford

Interior Design Technology
Indiana University Purdue University at Indianapolis

M

M.S. in Technology
Indiana University-Purdue University Fort Wayne

Manuf. Eng. Tech / Quality Assurance (B.S.)
California State University, Long Beach

Manufacturing and Mechanical Systems Integration
Rochester Institute of Technology

Manufacturing Engineering Technology
Rochester Institute of Technology

Manufacturing Engineering Technology (B.S.)
Arizona State University, Polytechnic
Bradley University
Brigham Young University
Central Connecticut State University
University of Dayton
Ferris State University
Lake Superior State University
Minnesota State University, Mankato
University of Nebraska, Lincoln
University of North Texas
Oregon Institute of Technology
South Dakota State University
Wayne State University
Weber State University
Western Carolina University
Western Michigan University

Manufacturing Engineering Technology (B.S.E.T.)
Pittsburg State University

Manufacturing Engineering Technology (BET)
New Jersey Institute of Technology

Manufacturing Engineering Technology (M.S.)
Brigham Young University

Manufacturing Engineering Technology (MfgET)
Purdue University College of Technology

Manufacturing Engineering Technology (B.S.)
California State University, Long Beach

Manufacturing Technology (B.T.)
Alfred State College

Marine Engineering Technology (B.S.)
California Maritime Academy

Master of Industrial Distribution (M.I.D.)
Texas A&M University

Autodesk

Join your students at the Autodesk Student Engineering & Design Community today.

Take advantage of this online community, which includes a Faculty Lounge area. Share course ideas, discuss best practices, and download free Autodesk software.

www.students.autodesk.com